Street by Street

LONDON

Extended Coverage of the Capital

6th edition April 2012
© AA Media Limited 2012

Original edition printed May 2001

Enabled by Ordnance Survey This product includes map data licensed from Ordnance Survey® with the permission of the Controller of Her Majesty's Stationery Office. © Crown copyright 2012. All rights reserved. Licence number: 100021153.

The copyright in all PAF is owned by Royal Mail Group plc.

RoadPilot Information on fixed speed camera locations provided by RoadPilot © 2011 RoadPilot® Driving Technology.

Published by AA Publishing (a trading name of AA Media Limited, whose registered office is Fanum House, Basing View, Basingstoke, Hampshire RG21 4EA. Registered number 06112600)

Produced by the Mapping Services Department of The Automobile Association. (A04695)

A CIP Catalogue record for this book is available from the British Library.

Printed by Oriental Press in Dubai

The contents of this atlas are believed to be correct at the time of the latest revision. However, the publishers cannot be held responsible or liable for any loss or damage occasioned to any person acting or refraining from action as a result of any use or reliance on any material in this atlas, nor for any errors, omissions or changes in such material. This does not affect your statutory rights. The publishers would welcome information to correct any errors or omissions and to keep this atlas up to date. Please write to Publishing, The Automobile Association, Fanum House (FH12), Basing View, Basingstoke, Hampshire, RG21 4EA. E-mail: streetbystreet@theaa.com

Ref: MX039v

Key to map pages	ii–iii
Key to map symbols	iv–1
Enlarged map pages	2–19
Main map pages	20–181
Index – towns & villages	182
Index – streets	184–261
Index – featured places	262–283
River bus map	283
Acknowledgements	283

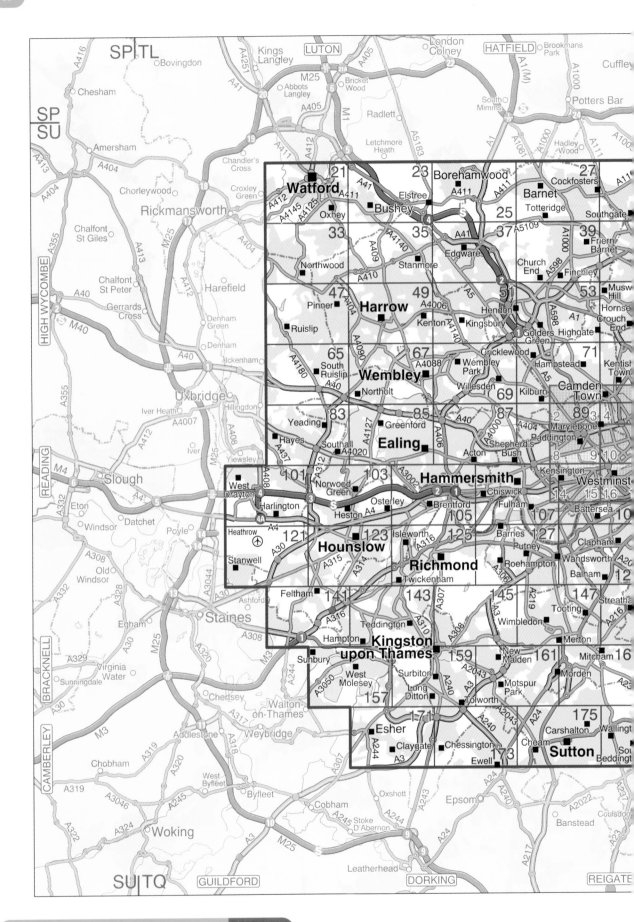

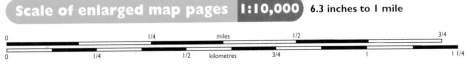

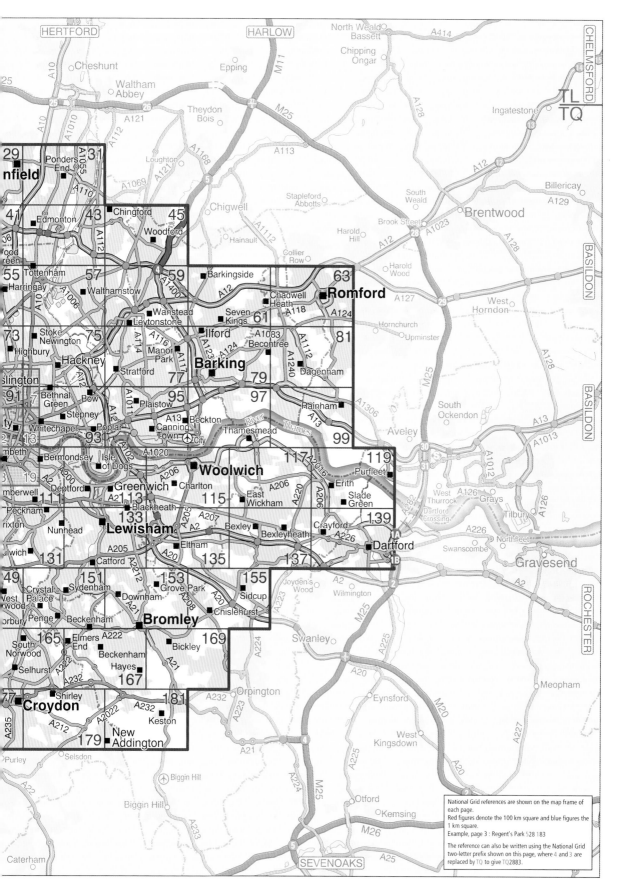

National Grid references are shown on the map frame of each page.
Red figures denote the 100 km square and blue figures the 1 km square.
Example: page 3 : Regent's Park 528 183

The reference can also be written using the National Grid two-letter prefix shown on this page, where 4 and 3 are replaced by TQ to give TQ2883.

4.2 inches to 1 mile **Scale of main map pages** 1:15,000

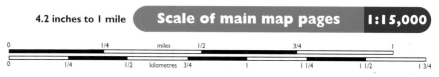

Junction 9	Motorway & junction		Railway & main railway station
Service	Motorway service area		Railway & minor railway station
	Primary road single/dual carriageway		Underground station
Service	Primary road service area		Docklands Light Railway (DLR) station
	A road single/dual carriageway		London Overground station
	B road single/dual carriageway		Light railway & station
	Other road single/dual carriageway	++++++++++++	Preserved private railway
	Minor/private road, access may be restricted	LC	Level crossing
← ←	One-way street	•—•—•—•—•	Tramway
	Pedestrian area	-------------	Ferry route
================	Track or footpath	....	Airport runway
	Road under construction	— · — · — · —	County, administrative boundary
⊏ = = = = ⊐	Road tunnel		Congestion Charging Zone *
30 **V**	Speed camera site (fixed location) with speed limit in mph or variable		Olympic Park Boundary
40 **V**	Selection of road with two or more fixed camera sites; speed limit in mph or variable		Low Emission Zone (LEZ) (visit **theaa.com** for further information)
50⏵◀50	Average speed (SPECS™) camera system with speed limit in mph	**93**	Page continuation 1:15,000
P	Parking	**7**	Page continuation to enlarged scale 1:10,000
P+	Park & Ride		River/canal, lake, pier
	Bus/coach station	465 ▲ Winter Hill	Peak (with height in metres)
			Aqueduct, lock, weir

* The AA central London congestion charging map is also available

Woodland		Golf course	
Park		Theme park	
Cemetery		Abbey, cathedral or priory	
Built-up area		Castle	
Industrial / business building		Historic house or building	
Leisure building		National Trust property	
Retail building		Museum or art gallery	
Other building		Roman antiquity	
City wall		Ancient site, battlefield or monument	
Hospital with 24-hour A&E department		Industrial interest	
Post Office, public library		Garden	
Tourist Information Centre, seasonal		Garden Centre Garden Centre Association Member	
Petrol station, 24 hour Major suppliers only		Garden Centre Wyevale Garden Centre	
Church/chapel		Arboretum	
Public toilets, with facilities for the less able		Farm or animal centre	
Public house AA recommended		Zoological or wildlife collection	
Restaurant AA inspected		Bird collection	
Hotel AA inspected		Nature reserve	
Theatre or performing arts centre		Aquarium	
Cinema		Visitor or heritage centre	
Camping AA inspected		Country park	
Caravan site AA inspected		Cave	
Camping & caravan site AA inspected		Windmill	
		Distillery, brewery or vineyard	

Wakehurst Place (NT) — National Trust property

Madeira Hotel — Hotel

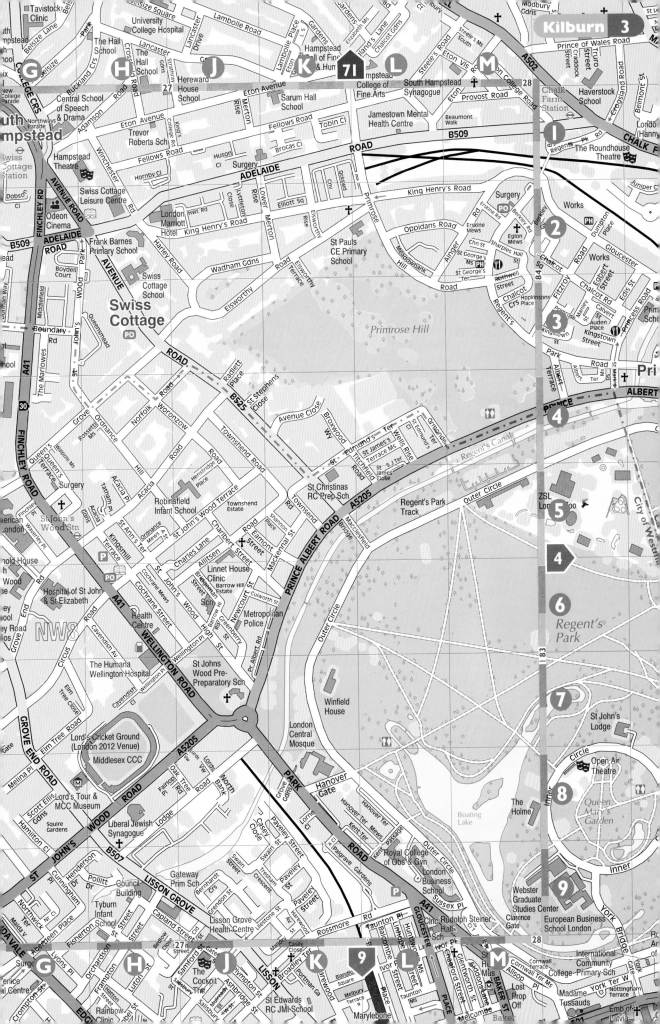

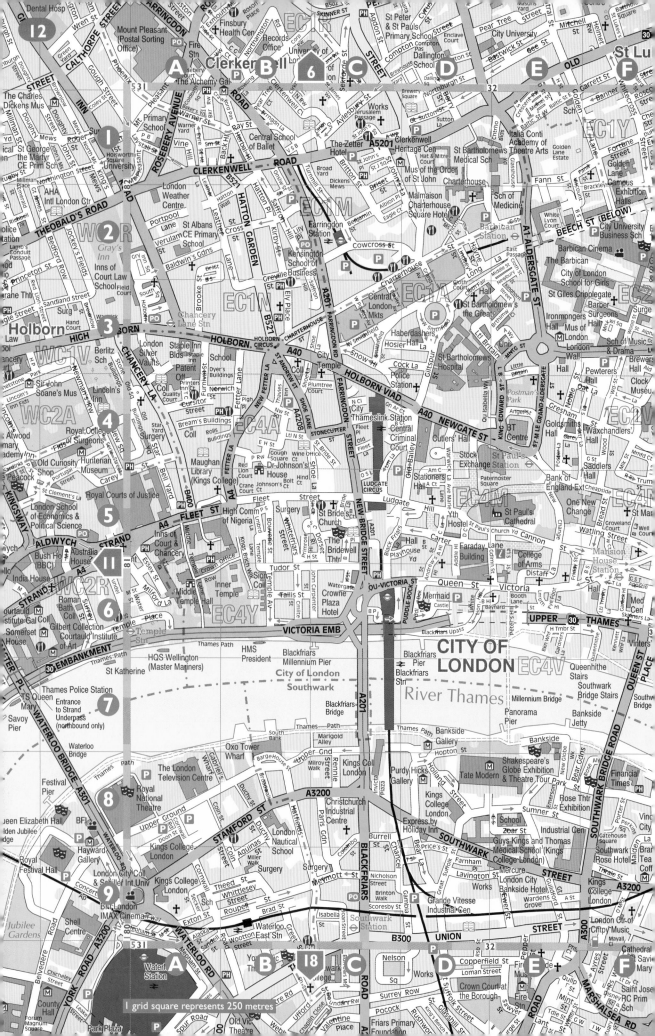

I grid square represents 250 metres

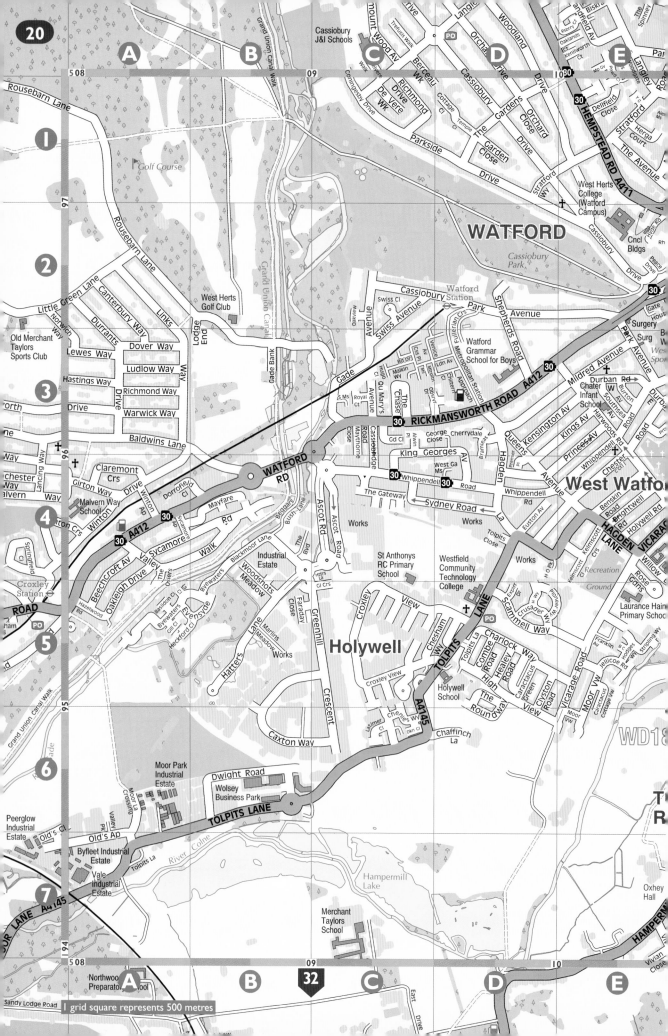

F **G** **H** **J**

16 17 18

The
Aldenham Road

Aldenham
Preparatory
School

Wards Lane

Slades
Farm

North Medburn
Farm

Butterfly Lane

1

WD

Elstree Golf &
Country Club

Golf Cours

2 OREH

The
Haberdashers
Askes School

Elstree Aerodrome

Aldenham Road

WATLING STREET

Tykes Water
Lake

3

Hogg Lane

Dagger Lane

Home
Farm

97

96

Hilfield Park Reservoir

P Aldenham
Country Park

Aldenham Road

24

ALLUM

Elstree Hill Nth

4

Allum
Ceme

Dagger Lane

Aldenham
Reservoir

Potters Msl
Surgery
Rmind

The Bartons

Lands
End

St Nicholas
St Nicholas School

Elstree

New Rd
Synagogue

ROMAN RD

Grd

5

A411

Fortune La

95

WATFORD ROAD

Schubert Rd

Rodgers Cl
Delius
Cl

West View
Garden

Summer
GV

M1

ELSTREE ROAD

A411

The
Wrrfrmt

Lismarrine
Industrial Park

Beethoven
Rd
Elgar
Close

ELSTREE HILL SOUTH

A5183

Sullivan Way

Coates Rd

A411 ELSTREE ROAD

La South

A409
Paynesfield Rd

**Caldecote
Hill**

Centennial Avenue

6

A41

BOURNE ROAD

ELSTREE HL S

Wg Frm Cl

Brockley Hill
Farm

Hertfordsh

M1

7

Junction 4

194

35

Royal National
Orthopaedic
Hospital

A5 BROCKLE

A41

F **G** **H** **J** **K**

16 17 18

Pagelford La
Capel Crs
Brigh

nd Lane

Nutt Gv

Bar

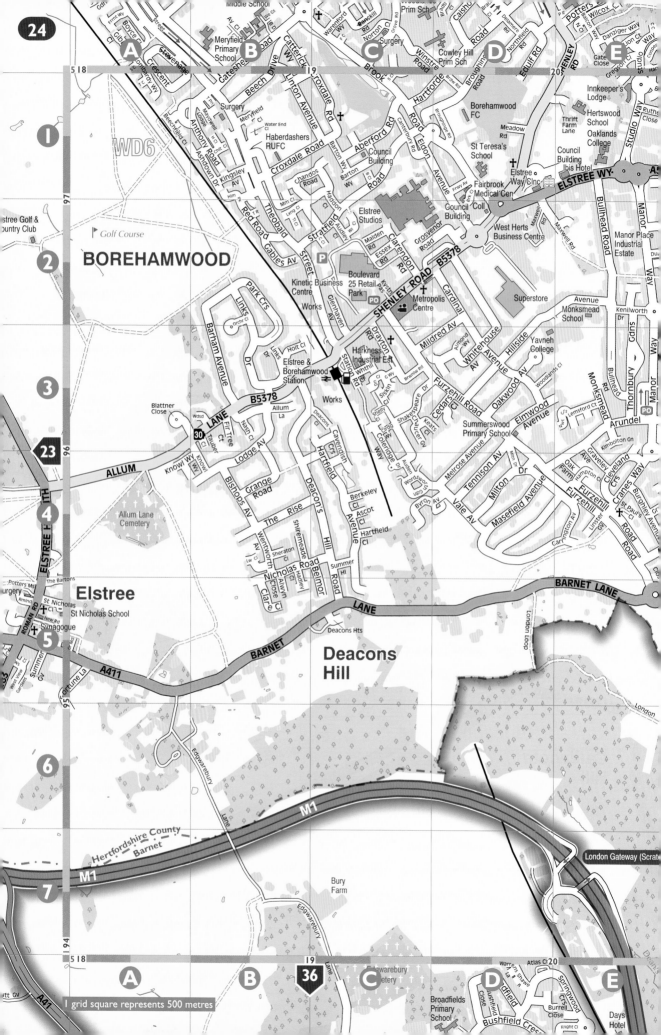

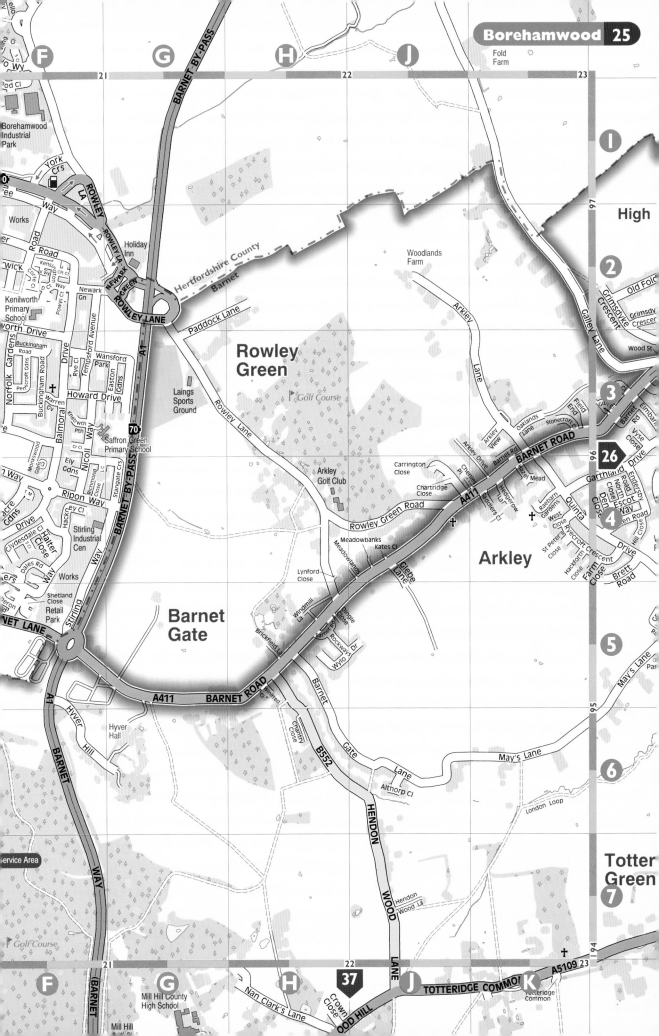

F   G   BARNET-BY-PASS   H   J

Fold Farm

21   22   23

1

High

Borehamwood Industrial Park

2

York Crs

Grimsdyke Crescent

Old Fold

ROWLEY LA

Grimsdy Cresce

Wood St

Calley Lane

Works

ROWLEY LA

Holiday Inn

Kenilworth Primary School

NEWARK GREEN

Hertfordshire County

Barnet

Woodlands Farm

97

Kensal Gn

Newark Gn

ROWLEY LANE

Paddock Lane

3

Field End

Barnet Rd

Embank

Howard Drive

A1

Rowley Green

Arkley Lane

Oaklands Lane

Stonecroft

Vise Drive

Wansford Park

Laings Sports Ground

Golf Course

Arkley View

Arkley Drive

Barnet Rd

BARNET ROAD

96   26

Garthland Road

Endsby Road

Ripon Way

Rowley Lane

Arkley Golf Club

Carrington Close

Chenies Pl

Hazel Mead

North Close

Den Close

Escot Way

4

Saffron Green Primary School

70

Chartridge Close

A411

Hedgerow

Rabarn Gardens West

Quinta

Hackworth Close

Farm Close

Brett Road

Stirling Industrial Cen

Rowley Green Road

St Peter's Close

Ryecroft Crescent

Arkley

Barnet Gate

Meadowbanks

Kates Cl

Glebe Lane

95

5

Shetland Close

Retail Park

Lynford Close

Windmill La

Dingle Close

Barnet Rd

Rockways Dr

May's Lane

Par

Stirling

Brickfield La

Wyld

BARNET LANE

A1

A411   BARNET ROAD

Barnet Gate Lane

Winifred

Chantry Close

May's Lane

6

HENDON WOOD LANE

Hyver Hill

Hyver Hall

B552

Althorp Cl

London Loop

BARNET WAY

Service Area

Totter Green

Hendon Wood La

7

Golf Course

F   BARNET   G   H   37   J   TOTTERIDGE COMMON   K

Mill Hill County High School

Nan Clark's Lane

Crown Close

WOOD HILL

Totteridge Common

A5109

21   22   23

94

Mill Hill

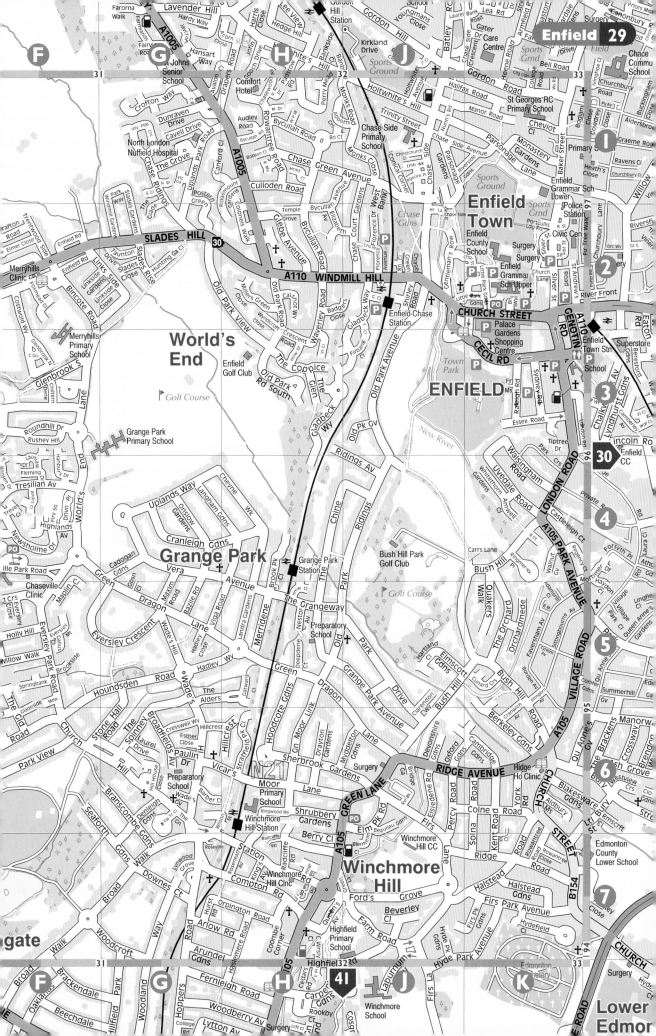

Carpenders Par

South Oxhey

Hatch End

Pinnerwood Park

Pinner Green

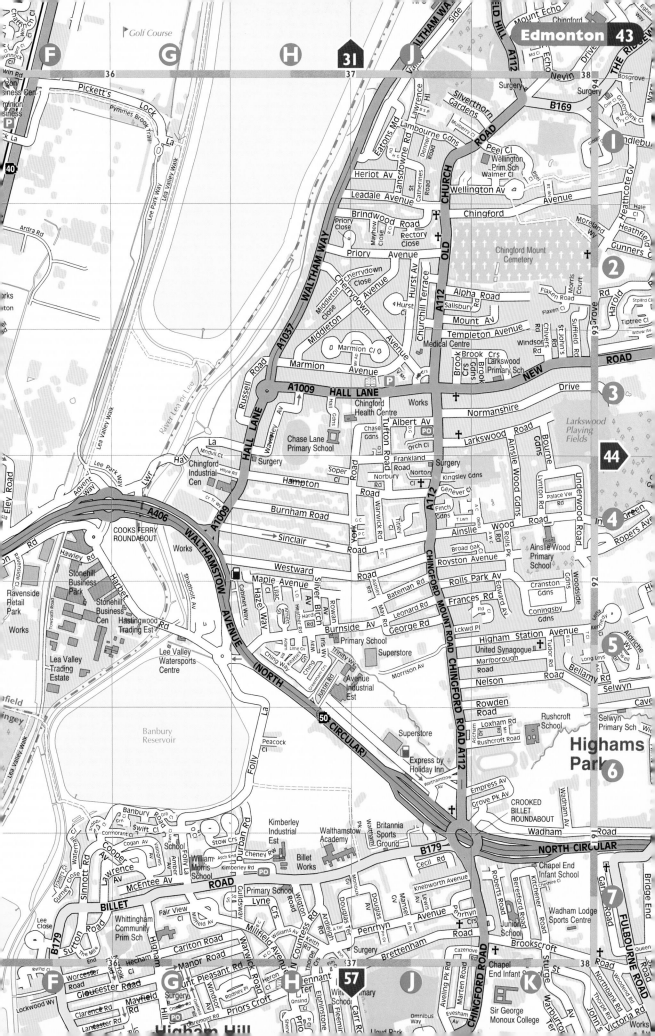

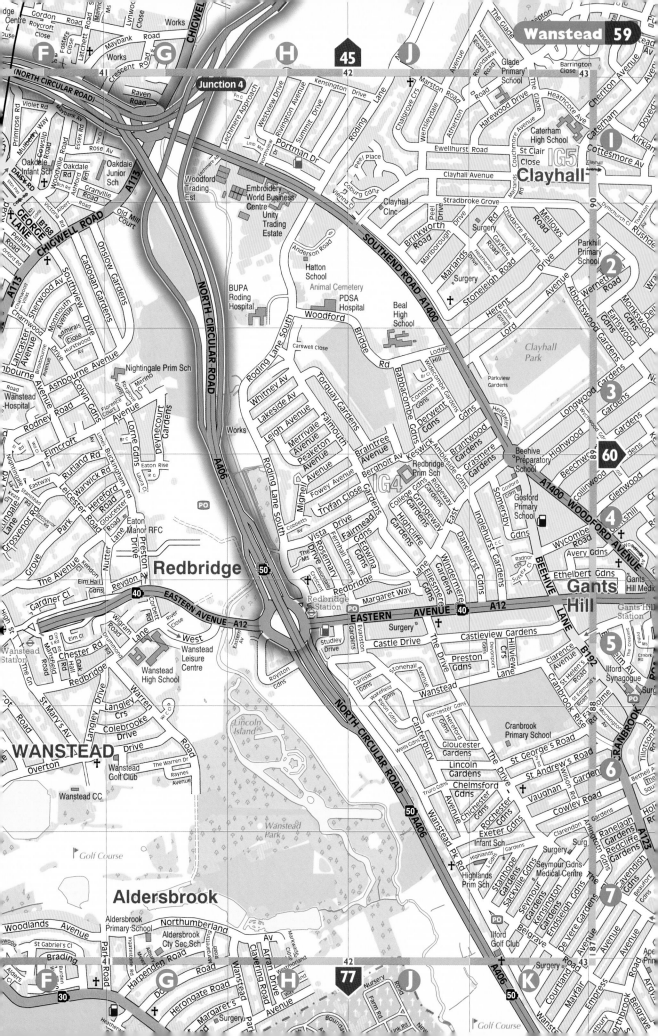

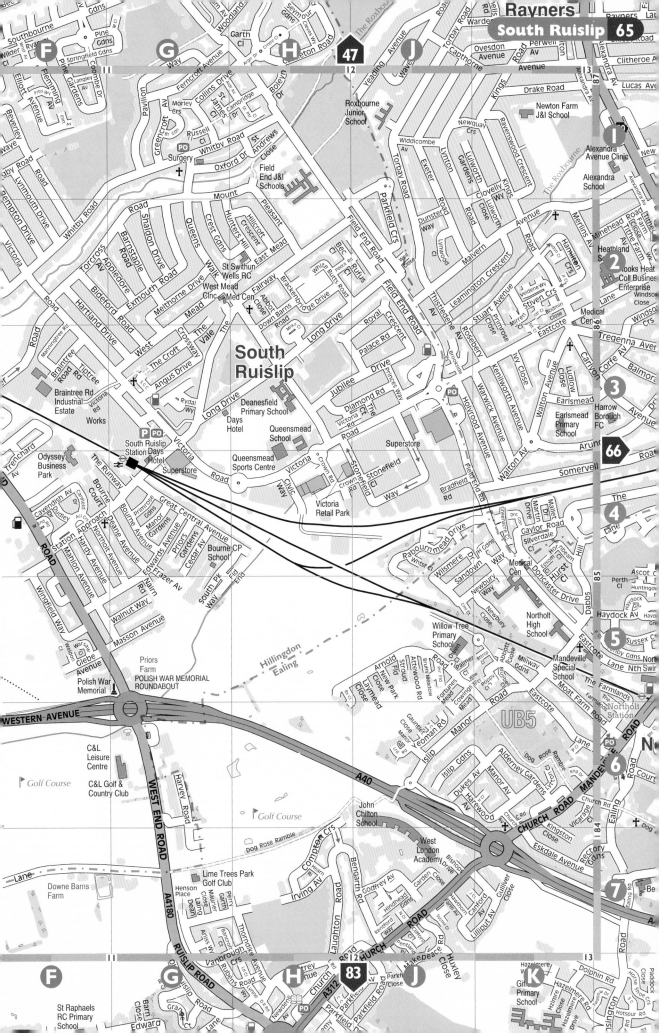

1 grid square represents 500 metres

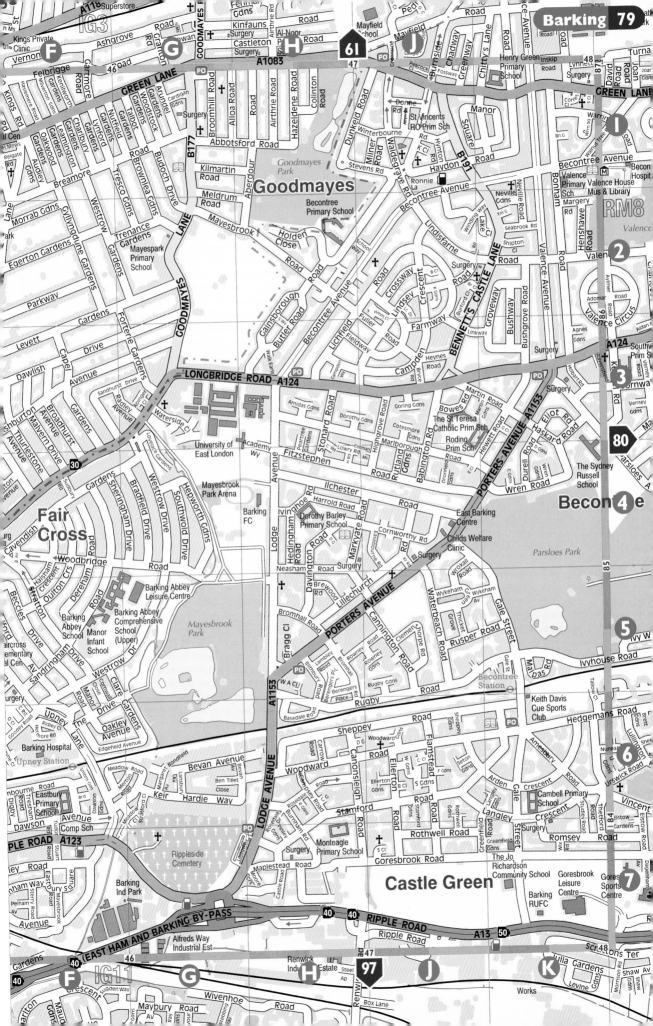

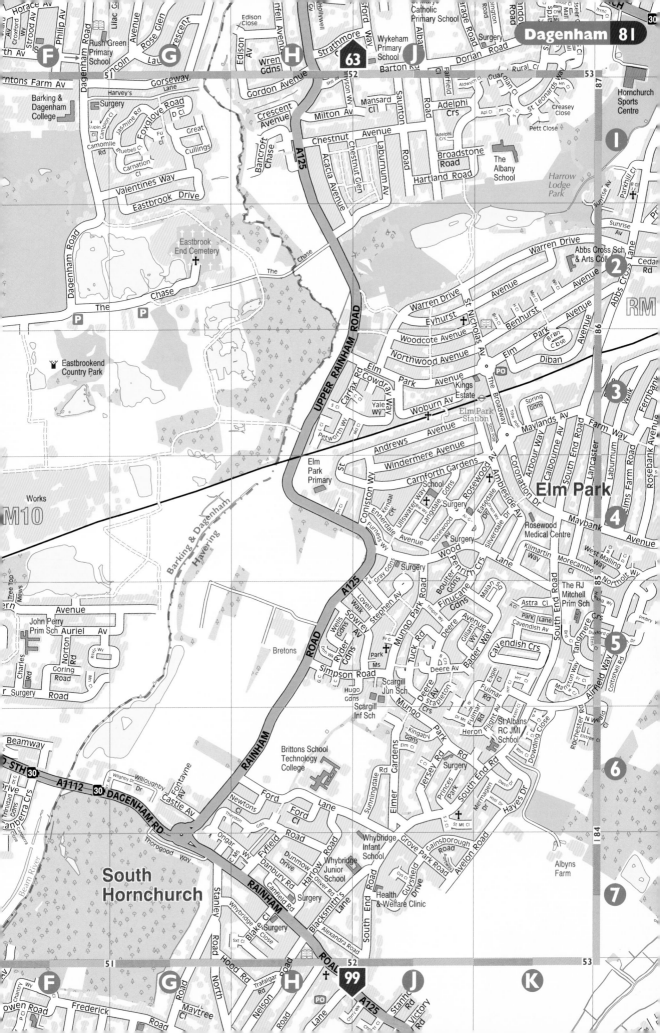

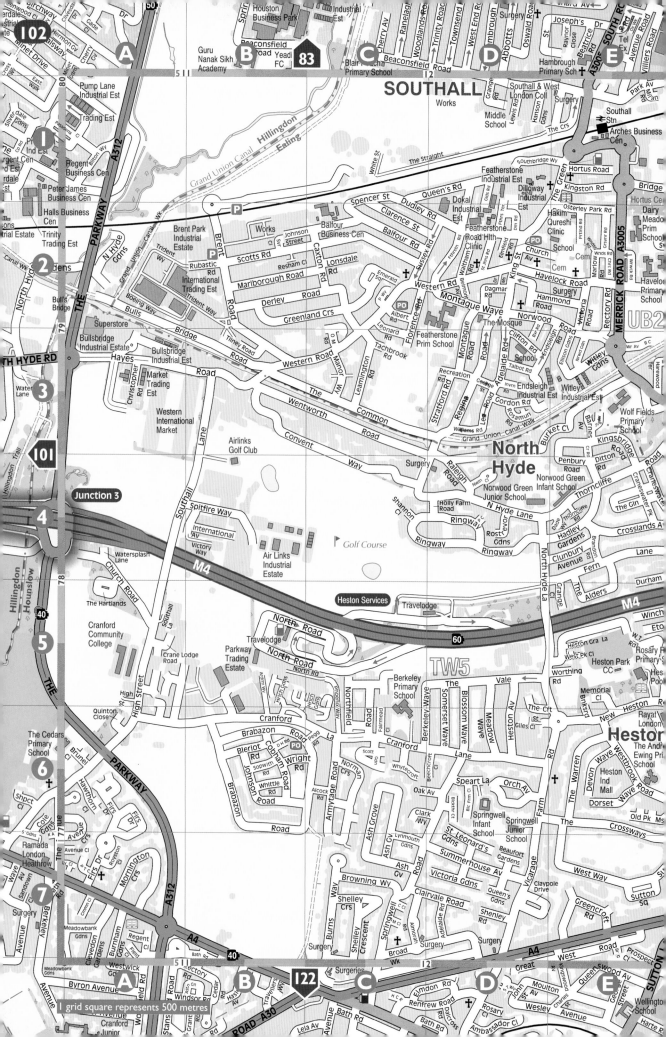

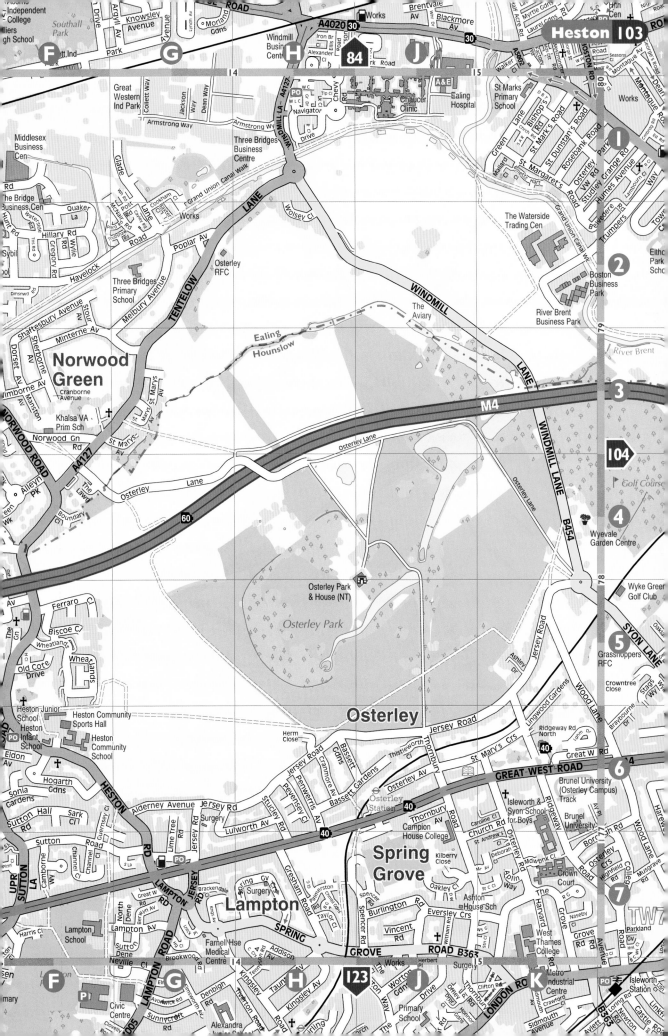

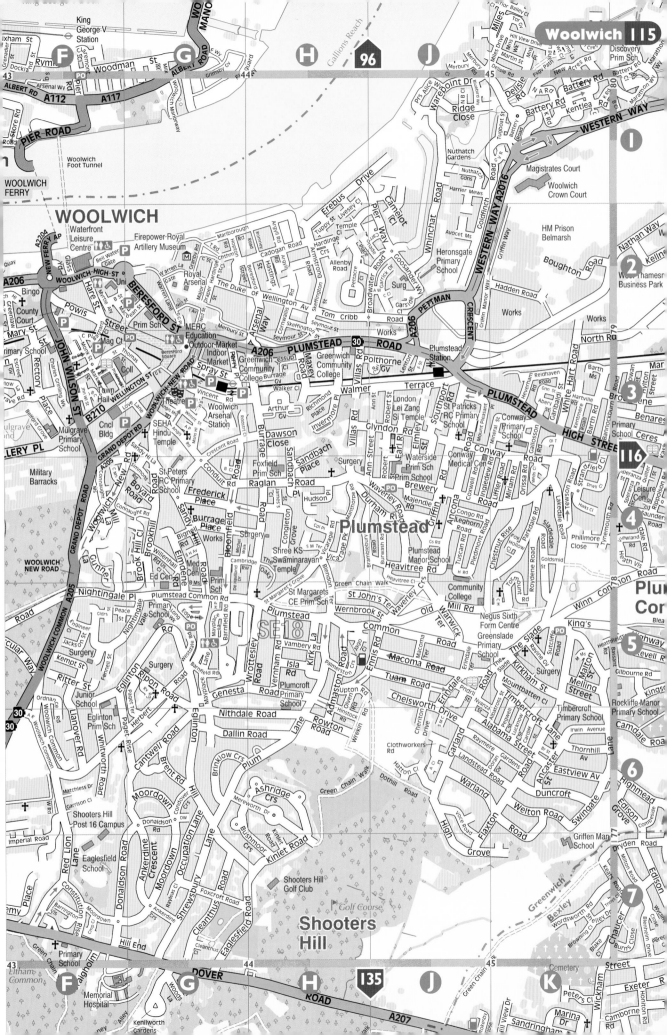

F G H J

Wennington
Marshes

Havering
Thurrock

54

A1306

A13

LONDON ROAD

I

Juliette Way
Juliette Wy
Juliette
Way

Kerry Avenue

et Ind
Park

Purfleet
Ind Park

Fanns Farm

1

Aveley
Marshes

NEW TANK HL RD

TANK
HILL RD

ARTERIAL ROAD PURFLEET

2

Purfleet
Industrial
Access Rd

Milehams
Industrial
Estate

79

Coldharbour La

Water Surgery

Marlow Av

Fanns Rise

Quarry Mes

Crusader Ct

Council
Building

TANK HILL RD

Thamley

Erith

Halfway

Water La

Tank

Lane

3

Marine
Court

Centurion
Way

Rapier Cl

Saladin

Close

Comet

Mulberry
Drive

Chieftan Drive

PO

Purfleet
Prim Sch

Beacon Hill
Industrial Est

River
Court

A1090

Caspian

Purfleet

Beacon
Indust

River

Crayford
Ness

HIGH ST

Church

The
Limes

Hollow

Hollow

Caspian
Wy

Works

Purfleet
Station

London Rd
Purfleet

Wngrv
TDr)

Bea

4

Thames

LONDON ROAD

Harrisons
Wharf

LC

78

80

5

Landau Way

Darent
Industrial
Park

Dayton Drive

Maypole
Crescent

Burnett

Road

Ness Road

Works

Dartford
Marshes

Long Rea

6

Wallhouse

Road

77

Darent Valley Path

Joyce Green Lane

Works

7

Crayford
Marshes

53 54 55

F G H **139** J K

Kent C

Bexl

Hyde Gv

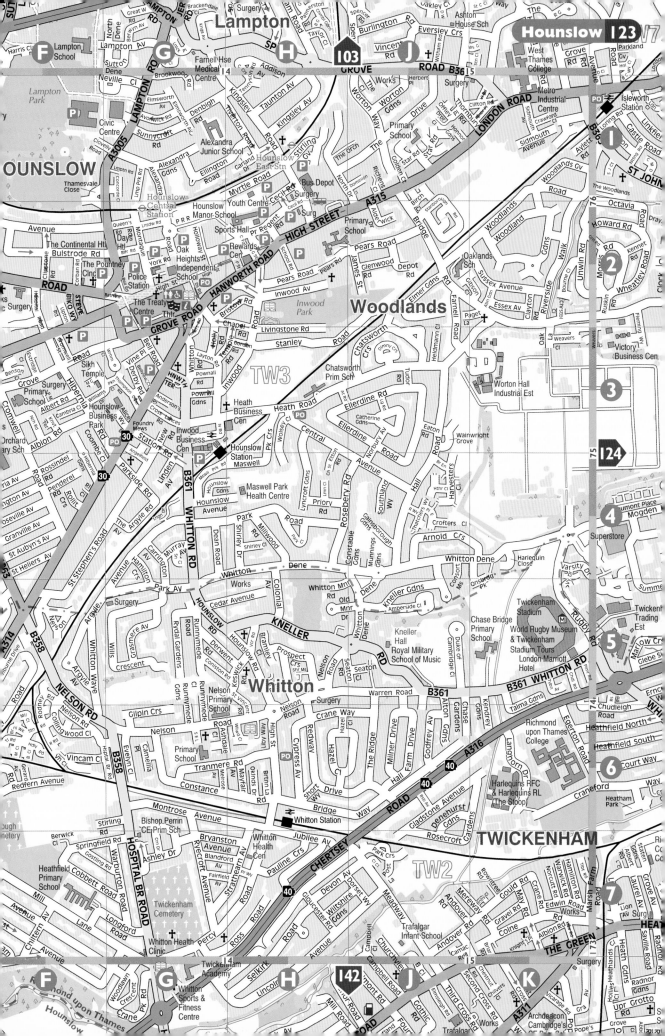

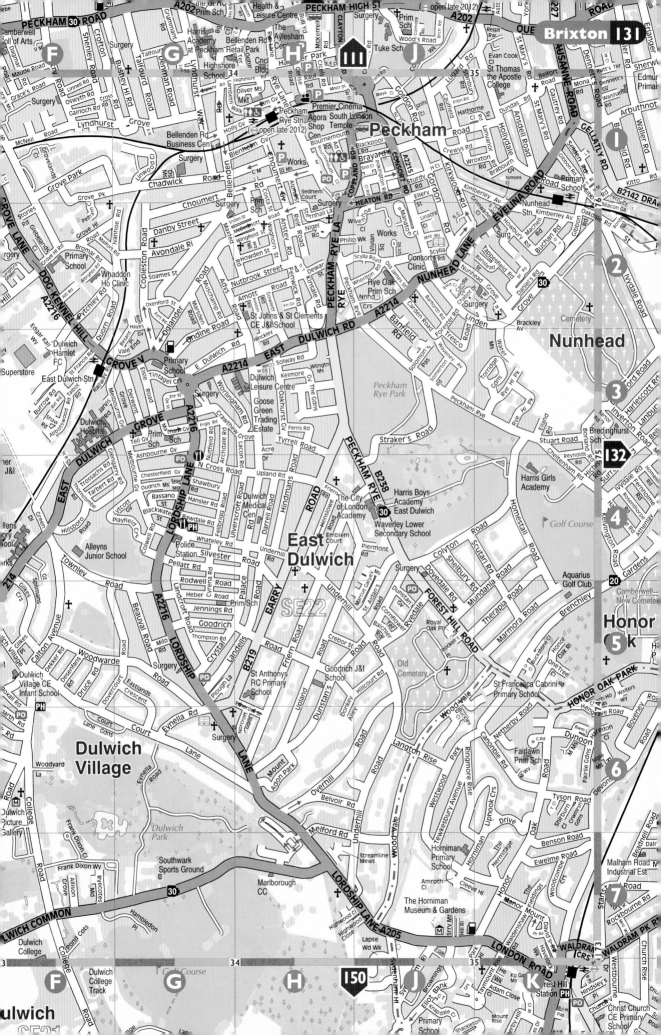

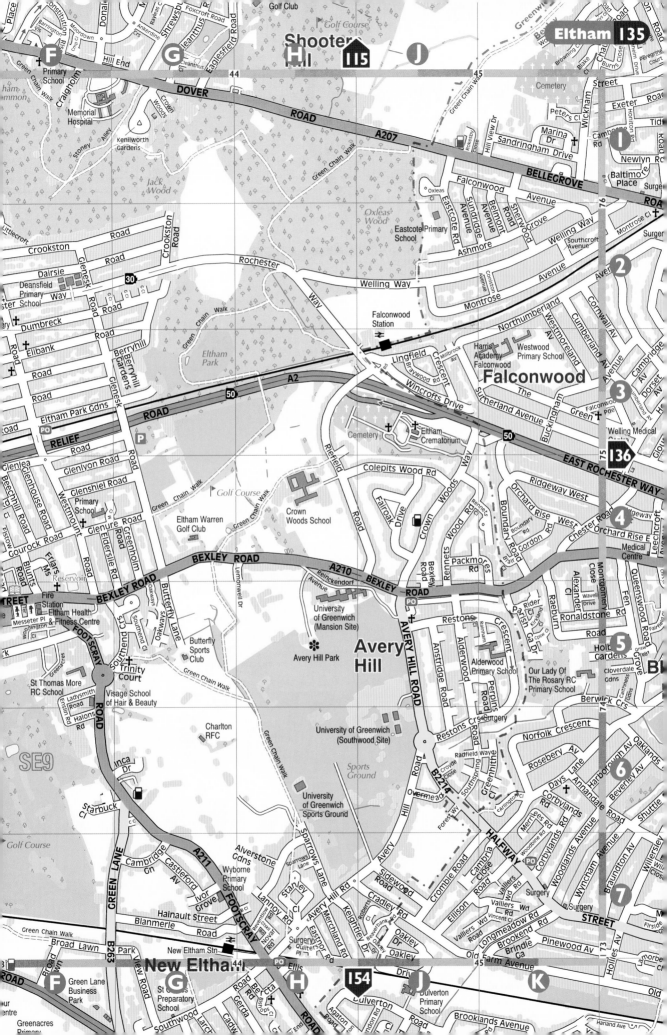

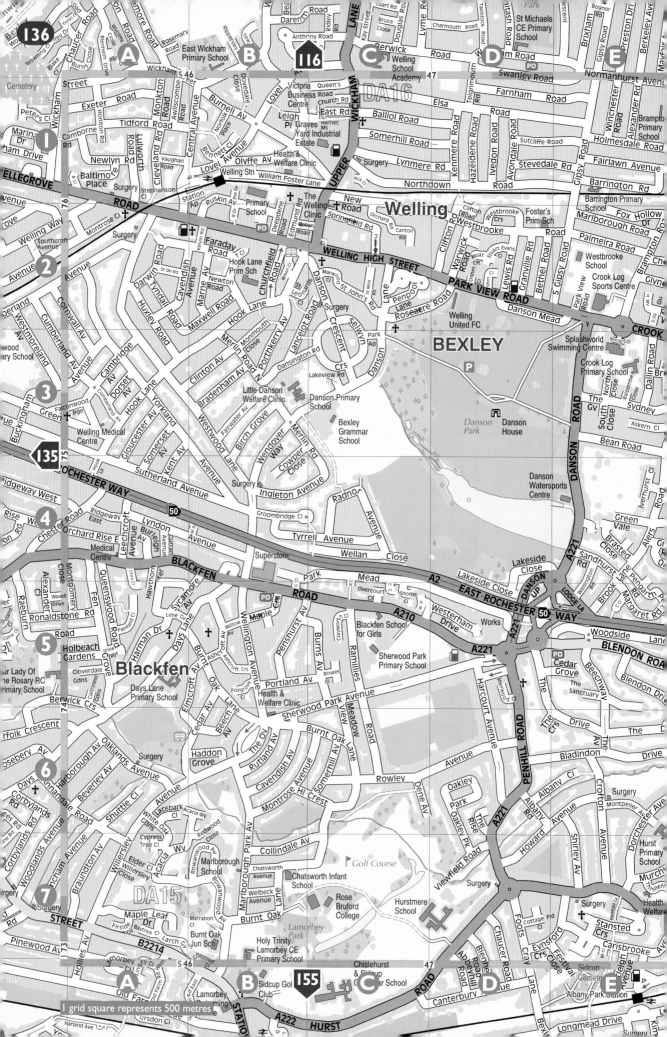

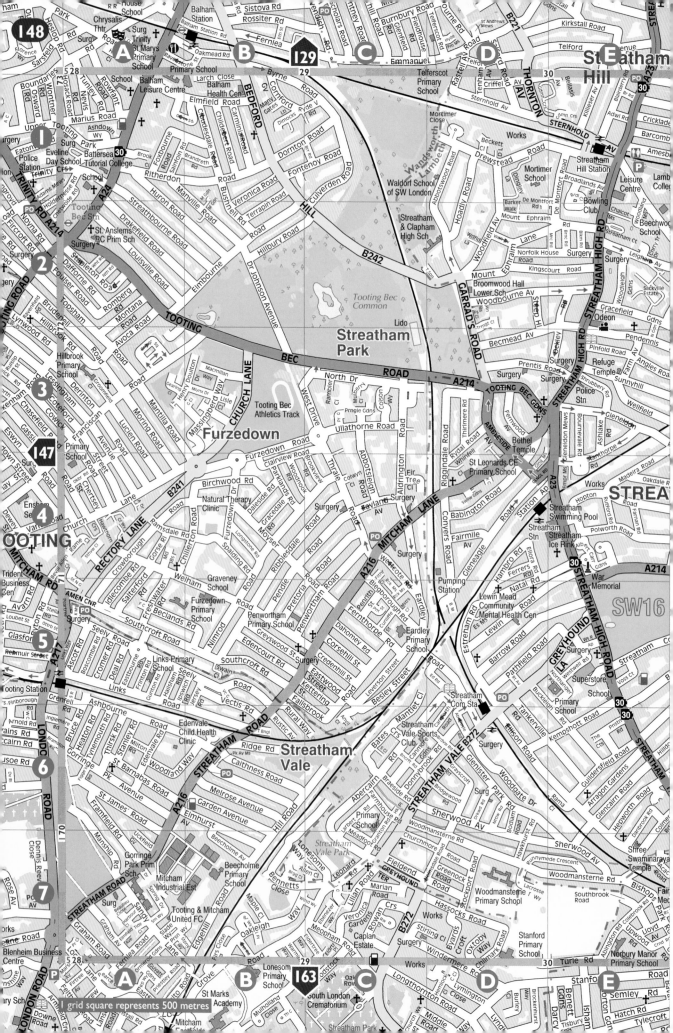

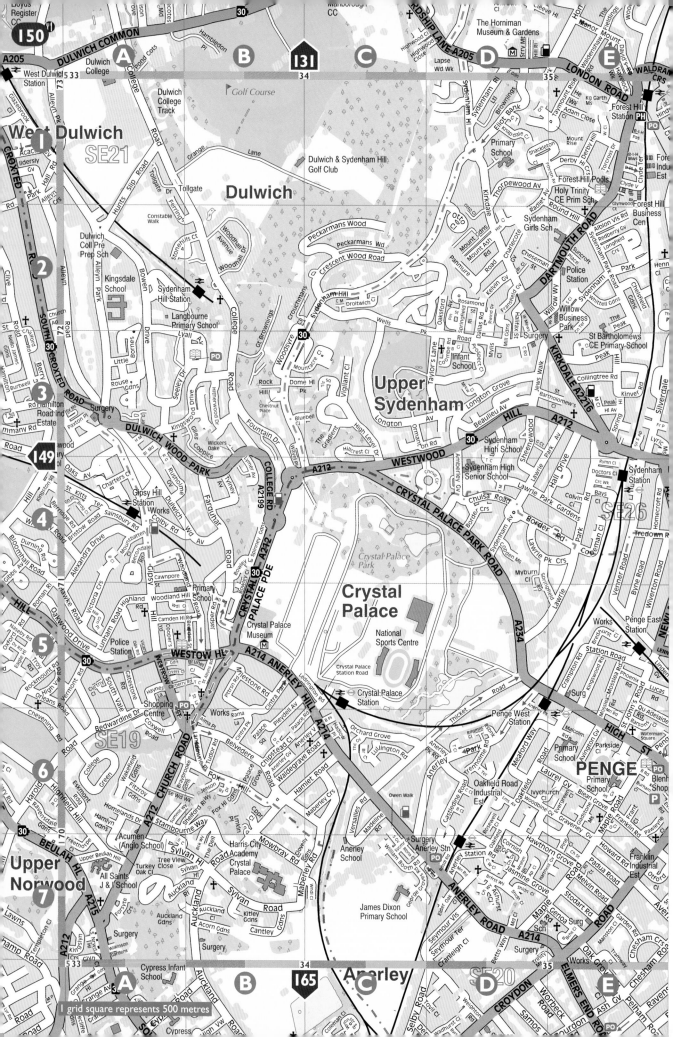

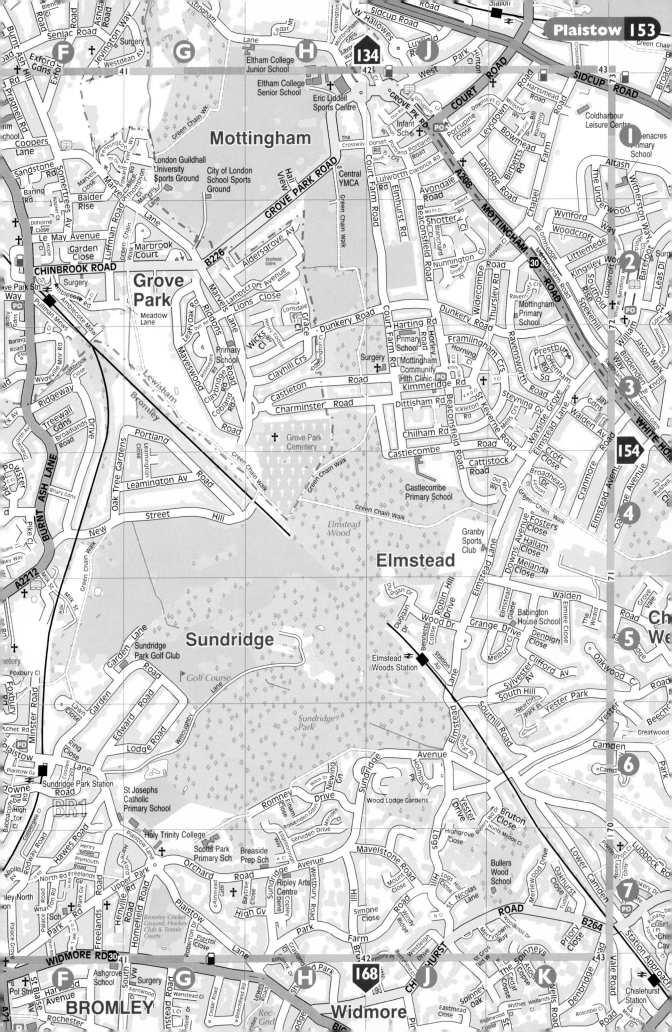

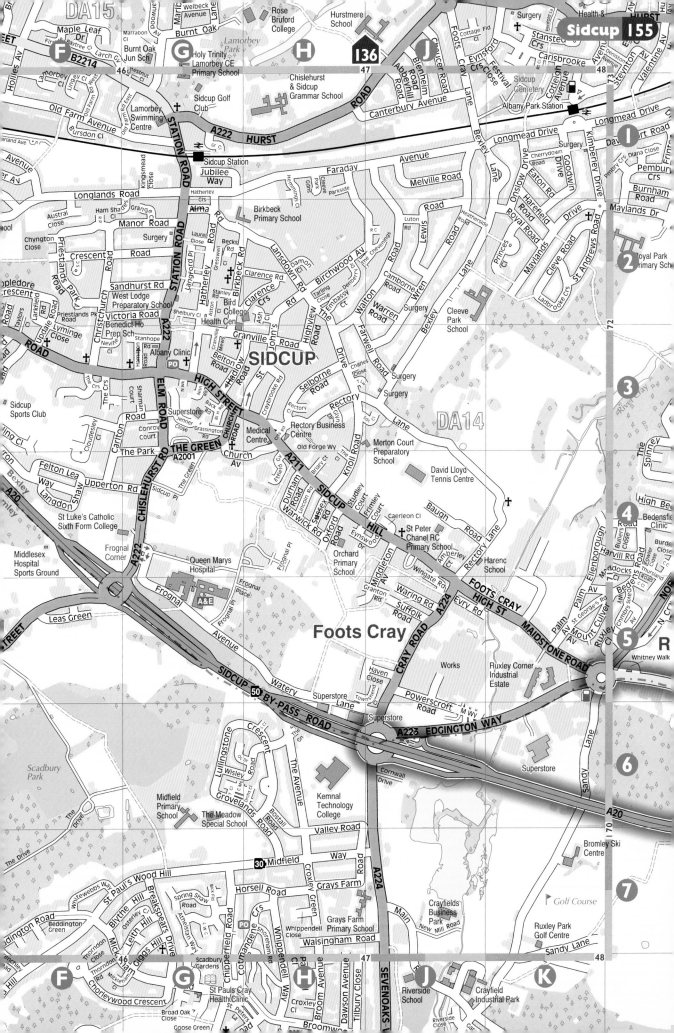

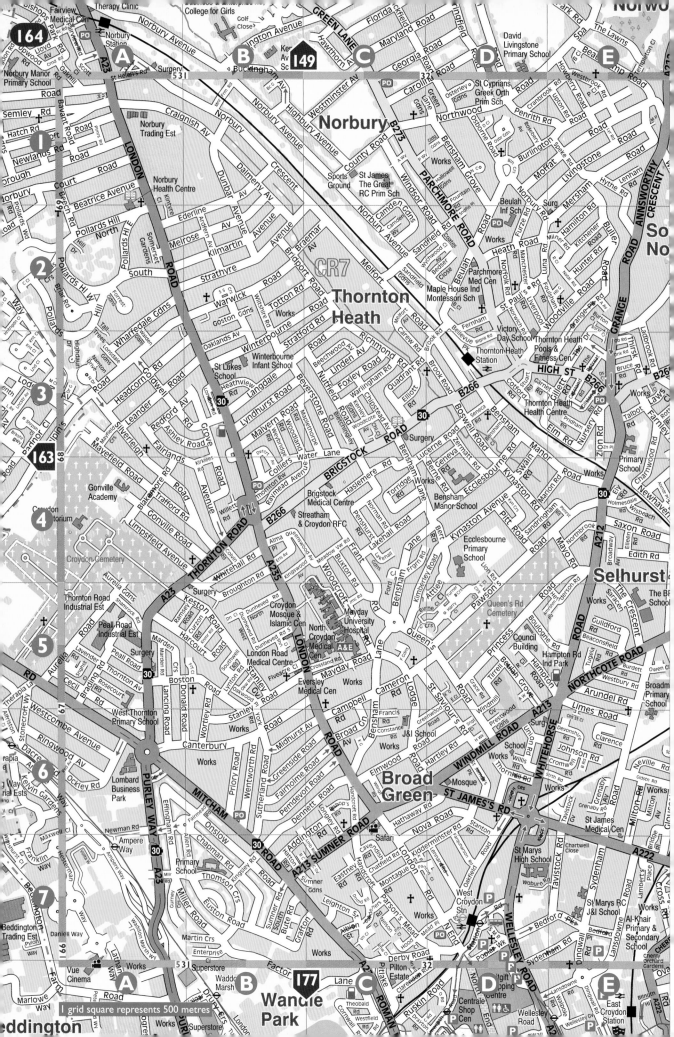

157

A B **157** C D E

66

513 14 15

River Mole

River Mole Business Park

Sandown Industrial Park

Works

Sherriff

Farm Road

Joseph Locke Wy

Mill Road

Douglas

Arran Way

Blair Avenue

Cranbrook Drive

Stanleigh Road

Woodlands

Woodend Road

The

Orchard Gate

Weston Green Road

Atma Road

School

Newlands Avenue

STATION ROAD

HAMPTON COURT

Weston Green

Weston Road

West

1

Lower Green

Golf Course

Works

Esher Station
Thames Ditton & Esher Golf Club

A307

PORTSMOUTH ROAD

Couchmo

Montgomery Avenue

Westmont Rd

Hillmor

KINGSTO

Lower Green

Thomas More Gdns

Wynfit Pl

(S.Gdns)

The Furlongs

Er Gn Dr

Th Glips

Surgery

Esher CE High School

Pelhams Walk

Sandown Park Racecourse

Sandown Grandstand & Exhibition Centre

Littleworth Common

Littleworth Close

Penates

Littleworth Road

Medina Av

Harefield

Heathside

Heathside

Greer

65

2

Wayneflete Tower Avenue

Electrical Trades Union College

Esher Pl Av

Latton Av

Esher Close

Telliford

Warren Cl

Odeon

Hillbrow Rd

Sandown Road

Ashburnham Park

New Road

Littleworth La

Littlemead

Riverside Dr

Pelhams

Winchester Cl

D'Abernon Cl

D'Abernon Close

Esher Gn

CHURCH ST

ESHER GN

HIGH ST

High St

PO

Sandown Road

Martineau Close

Littleworth Road

Littleworth Av

Manor Road

Oaken Lane

3

A244

LAMMAS LANE

Drake's

Hunting Cl

Clive Rd

Wolsey

Park Rd

H Pl

Civic Centre

ESHER

Willowmere

Sandown Av

KT10

Broomfields

Oaken Lane

64

Moore Place Golf Club

Golf Course

Pelhams Close

Esher Cl

Clive Rd

Belvedere Close

Broom Cl

Grantley Pl

Simmons Ga

Cranford Rd

Acorns Wy

Rosebriar

Park Av

Broomfields

Cavendish

4

Wend Gdns

Bloo House Sch

Clare Hl (No2)

Clare Hill

Fir Tree Cl

Charlotte Ct

Lynne Wk

Milbourne

Surgery

Shrewsbury Lodge School

Rythe

Loseberry Rd

Station Rd

Simmil Rd

The Avenue

Judge Walk

Meadow Rd

Oaken

Nightingale Av

Brisson

Howitts Cl

Park Close

West End Lane

PORTSMOUTH ROAD

Old Chestnut Av

Claremont Pk Rd

Pk Road

Home Farm

Drive

Milbourne La

Haymeads Dr

Orchard Way

Esher Church Prim Sch

Brendon Cl

Raleigh Dr

PH

Hare

Esher Church Prim Sch

Arbrook La

Aston Rd

Torrington

The Pde

PO

Athlone

Albany Crs

5

Neville

Sport Club

Courtlands Avenue

Hawkshill Way

The Mount

Hawkshill Cl

Clrmon End

Copsem Dr

Lakeside Dr

Orchard Way

High Garth

Milbrook

Brendon Dr

Arbrook Lane

Milbourne Lodge School

Claygate Station

Gordon Road

Foley

Claremont Av

Pd

Claremont

Claremont Fan Court School

Copsem Wy

Loseberry Farm

Beaconsfield

63

Claremont Park

Claremont Landscape Garden (NT)

COPSEM LANE

A244

Arbrook Common

Claremont Rd

Beaconsfield Cl

Qu Anne Dr

Vale

6

STONY HILL

A307

Albany Cl

Meadway

Arbrook Common

7

Blackhills

A244

Arbrook Farm

Birchwood

513 14 15

A B C D E

Black Pond

Esher Common

1 grid square represents 500 metres

Shirley

Upper Shirley

Addington Hills

Croham Hurst

UPPER SELSDON

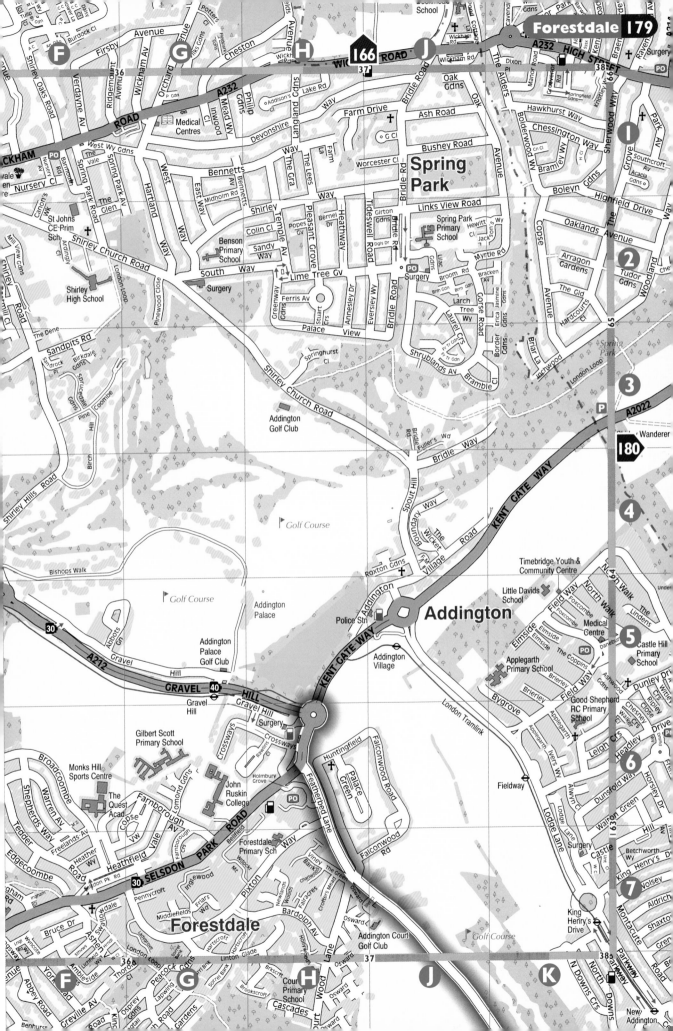

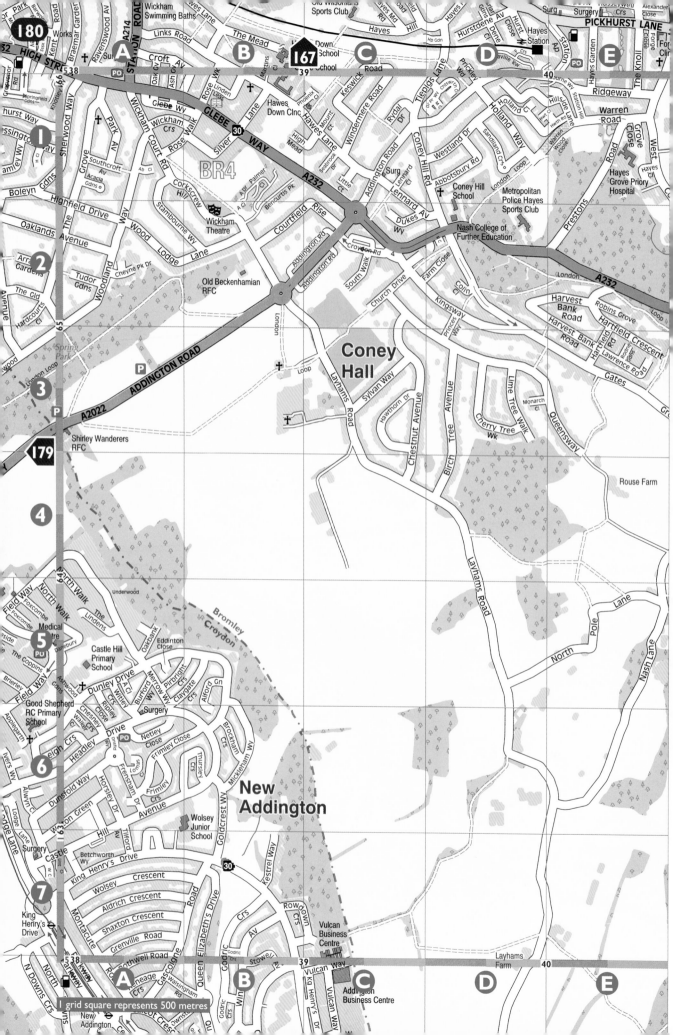

Abbey Wood.....116 C3
Acton.....86 E7
Acton Green.....106 A3
Addington.....179 J6
Addiscombe.....165 C6
Aldborough Hatch.....60 E3
Aldersbrook.....59 G7
Alperton.....68 A7
Anerley.....165 H1
Arkley.....25 K4
Ashford Common.....140 B5
Avery Hill.....135 H5
Balham.....128 E6
Bandonhill.....176 D4
Barking.....78 D6
Barkingside.....60 B2
Barnehurst.....138 A2
Barnes.....106 E7
Barnes Cray.....138 E3
Barnet.....26 D5
Barnet Gate.....25 C5
Barnsbury.....5 L1
Barwell.....171 J6
Battersea.....108 E6
Bayswater.....8 E1
Beckenham.....166 D1
Beckton.....95 K5
Becontree.....79 K4
Beddington.....176 E1
Beddington Corner.....163 F6
Bedford Park.....106 C2
Belgravia.....16 A5
Bell Green.....151 H2
Bellingham.....151 J3
Belmont.....174 E7
Belmont.....49 G1
Belvedere.....117 J4
Benhilton.....175 F2
Berrylands.....159 G5
Bethnal Green.....92 D2
Bexley.....136 D5
Bexleyheath.....137 G5
Bickley.....168 D1
Blackfen.....136 A5
Blackheath.....133 J1
Blackheath Park.....133 K3
Blackwall.....94 B6
Bloomsbury.....11 H2
Borehamwood.....24 C3
The Borough.....18 F2
Bow.....93 J1
Bow Common.....93 J4
Bowes Park.....40 E5
Bowmans.....138 C6
Brentford.....104 E5
Brentford End.....104 C5
Brimsdown.....31 G1
Brixton.....130 B3
Broad Green.....164 C6
Brockley.....132 C4
Bromley.....168 A1
Bromley.....93 K2
Bromley Common.....168 C5
Bromley Park.....152 C7
Brompton.....15 J4
Brondesbury.....70 C5
Brondesbury Park.....70 A5
Brook Green.....107 F2
Brunswick Park.....40 A2
Buckhurst Hill.....45 G2
Burnt Oak.....37 F6
Bushey.....22 C6
Bushey Heath.....22 E6
Bushey Mead.....161 G2
Bush Hill Park.....30 A5
Caldecote Hill.....23 F6
Camberwell.....111 G7
Camden Town.....4 B2
Canary Wharf.....93 J7
Canning Town.....95 F4
Cannon Hill.....161 G3
Canonbury.....6 E1
Canons Park.....36 A6
Carpenders Park.....33 K1
Carshalton.....175 J3
Carshalton Beeches.....175 J7
Carshalton on the Hill.....175 K6
Castle Green.....79 J7
Catford.....133 F7
Chadwell Heath.....61 K4
Charlton.....114 C4
Cheam.....174 C4
Chelsea.....15 H8
Chessington.....172 A5
Child's Hill.....70 C1
China Town.....11 H6
Chingford Hatch.....44 C3
Chipping Barnet.....26 C4
Chislehurst.....154 C6
Chislehurst West.....154 A5
Chiswick.....106 C3
Church End.....52 E1
Church End.....69 H6
City of London.....12 D6
Clapham.....129 G1
Clapham Park.....129 J5
Clapton Park.....75 H3
Claremont Park.....170 A6
Claygate.....171 J5
Clayhall.....59 K1
Clerkenwell.....6 A9
Cockfosters.....27 J4
Coldharbour.....118 D3
Cole Park.....124 B5
Colindale.....51 G2
College Park.....87 J2
Collier's Wood.....147 H6
Colney Hatch.....39 K5
Coney Hall.....180 C3
Coombe.....145 G6
Copse Hill.....145 J6
Cottenham Park.....145 K7
Cranbrook.....60 A6
Cranford.....101 K6
Cranley Gardens.....55 A3
Crayford.....138 D4
Creekmouth.....96 E4
Cricklewood.....70 B3
Crooked Billet.....145 K5
Crouch End.....54 C5
Croydon.....177 K2
Crystal Palace.....150 C4
Cubitt Town.....113 F3
Custom House.....95 J4
Dagenham.....80 D6
Dartford.....139 F6
Dartmouth Park.....72 A1
Deacons Hill.....24 C5
De Beauvoir Town.....7 J3
Deptford.....112 C5
Dollis Hill.....69 K2
Dormer's Wells.....84 B6
Downham.....152 B4

Ducks Island.....26 B6
Dudden Hill.....69 J4
Dulwich.....150 B1
Dulwich Village.....131 F6
Ealing.....85 J3
Earl's Court.....14 A6
Earlsfield.....128 B7
East Acton.....87 H6
East Barnet.....27 H6
East Bedfont.....120 E4
Eastbury.....32 D3
Eastcote.....47 F6
Eastcote Village.....47 F4
East Dulwich.....131 H4
East Finchley.....53 H2
East Ham.....95 J1
East Molesey.....157 H4
East Sheen.....126 A4
East Wickham.....116 B7
Eden Park.....166 C3
Edgware.....36 D3
Edmonton.....42 A3
Elmers End.....166 E4
Elm Park.....81 K4
Elmstead.....153 J4
Elstree.....24 A5
Eltham.....134 D5
Enfield.....29 J3
Enfield Highway.....30 E1
Enfield Town.....29 K2
Erith.....118 C4
Esher.....170 C3
Ewell.....173 J7
Fair Cross.....79 F4
Falconwood.....135 K3
Feltham.....141 F1
Felthamhill.....140 C5
Field Common.....156 E6
Finchley.....38 E7
Finsbury.....6 A7
Finsbury Park.....72 E1
Foots Cray.....155 H5
Forestdale.....179 G7
Forest Gate.....76 E4
Forest Hill.....132 A7
Fortis Green.....53 K3
Foxbury.....154 D4
Friday Hill.....44 B2
Friern Barnet.....39 J3
Fulham.....107 G6
Furzedown.....148 B3
Gants Hill.....59 K5
Gidea Park.....63 H1
Giggshill.....158 B6
Globe Town.....93 F2
Golders Green.....52 C5
Goodmayes.....79 H1
Gospel Oak.....72 A4
Grange Park.....29 G4
Greenford.....84 D3
Greenhill.....49 F4
Greenwich.....113 G4
Grove Park.....106 A7
Grove Park.....153 G2
Hackbridge.....176 B1
Hackney.....74 E5
Hackney Wick.....75 J5
Hadley.....26 D2
Haggerston.....7 M5
Hale End.....44 B5
Ham.....143 K2
Hammersmith.....106 E3
Hampstead.....71 H3
Hampstead Garden Suburb.....53 F4
Hampton.....142 B7
Hampton Hill.....142 C3
Hampton Wick.....143 H7
Hanwell.....84 D7
Hanworth.....141 H2
Harlesden.....87 G1
Harlington.....101 F5
Harmondsworth.....100 A5
Harringay.....55 G4
Harrow.....48 D5
Harrow on the Hill.....48 E7
Harrow Weald.....34 E6
Hatch End.....33 J6
Hatton.....121 H3
Hayes.....82 A4
Hayes.....168 A6
Hayes End.....82 B3
Hayes Town.....83 G7
Headstone.....48 B3
Heath Park.....63 K5
Hendon.....51 K4
Herne Hill.....130 D5
Heston.....102 E6
Higham Hill.....57 G1
Highams Park.....43 K6
High Barnet.....26 A2
Highbury.....73 H4
Highgate.....53 K6
Highwood Hill.....37 H1
Hinchley Wood.....171 F2
Hither Green.....133 H5
Holborn.....11 L3
Holders Hill.....38 B7
Holwell.....20 C5
Homerton.....75 F5
Honor Oak.....132 A5
Honor Oak Park.....132 B5
Hook.....172 A4
Hornsey.....54 E3
Hornsey Vale.....55 F4
Hounslow.....123 F1
Hounslow West.....122 C2
Hoxton.....7 J6
Hurst Park.....157 H1
The Hyde.....51 H4
Ilford.....78 B2
Isle of Dogs.....113 F3
Isleworth.....124 C2
Islington.....6 A3
Kennington.....109 K5
Kensal Green.....88 A1
Kensal Rise.....88 B1
Kensal Town.....88 C3
Kensington.....14 C4
Kentish Town.....72 C5
Kenton.....49 J4
Keston.....181 H3
Keston Mark.....181 J2
Kew.....105 G6
Kidbrooke.....134 B1
Kilburn.....70 C7
Kingsbury.....50 D5
Kingsland.....7 J1
Kingston upon Thames.....158 D2
Kingston Vale.....145 F4
Knightsbridge.....15 K1
Knight's Hill.....130 D7
Ladywell.....132 D3
Lambeth.....18 A3

Lampton.....103 G7
Lea Bridge.....75 F2
Lee.....133 J5
Lessness Heath.....117 J5
Lewisham.....133 F3
Leyton.....76 B2
Leytonstone.....58 D7
Limehouse.....93 G6
Lisson Grove.....9 M2
Little Heath.....61 J3
Little Ilford.....78 A4
Little Stanmore.....36 B7
Long Ditton.....158 C7
Longlands.....154 C2
Lower Clapton.....74 E3
Lower Edmonton.....42 A1
Lower Feltham.....140 C2
Lower Green.....170 B1
Lower Holloway.....73 F4
Lower Place.....86 E1
Lower Sydenham.....151 F3
Loxford.....78 C4
Maida Vale.....2 C7
Maitland Park.....71 K5
Manor Park.....77 J3
Marks Gate.....62 A1
Marylebone.....10 A3
Mayfair.....10 C7
Maypole.....138 B7
Merry Hill.....22 B7
Merton.....146 E7
Merton Park.....161 J1
Mile End.....93 G3
Mill Hill.....37 J4
Mill Meads.....94 B1
Millwall.....112 E2
Mitcham.....163 F2
Monken Hadley.....26 C1
Monks Orchard.....165 K6
Moor Park.....32 A3
Morden.....161 K3
Morden Park.....161 H5
Mortlake.....125 K1
Motspur Park.....160 D5
Mottingham.....153 C1
Muswell Hill.....54 A1
Nash.....181 F5
Neasden.....69 F3
New Addington.....180 B6
New Barnet.....27 F4
New Beckenham.....151 C5
Newbury Park.....60 D5
New Charlton.....114 C3
New Cross.....132 B1
New Cross Gate.....112 B7
New Eltham.....154 B1
Newington.....18 B4
New Malden.....160 C2
New Southgate.....40 C3
New Town.....139 J5
Noel Park.....55 H1
Norbiton.....159 G1
Norbury.....164 C1
North Acton.....86 E3
North Cheam.....174 B2
North End.....118 C7
North End.....53 G7
North Feltham.....122 A4
North Finchley.....39 G5
North Harrow.....47 K5
North Hyde.....102 D3
North Kensington.....88 B4
Northolt.....66 A6
North Sheen.....125 J1
Northumberland Heath.....117 K6
North Wembley.....49 H7
Northwood.....32 A7
Northwood Hills.....46 B1
North Woolwich.....114 D1
Norwood Green.....103 F3
Norwood New Town.....149 K5
Notting Hill.....8 C3
Nunhead.....131 K3
Oakleigh Park.....39 H1
Oakwood.....28 D5
Old Bexley.....137 H6
Old Ford.....75 C7
Old Malden.....160 A6
Old Oak Common.....87 H3
Olympic Park.....75 J6
Osidge.....40 C1
Osterley.....103 H6
Oxhey.....21 H5
Paddington.....9 G3
Palmers Green.....40 E2
Park Langley.....167 F5
Park Royal.....86 C2
Parsons Green.....127 K1
Peckham.....131 J1
Penge.....150 E6
Pentonville.....5 M5
Perivale.....67 J7
Petersham.....125 F7
Petts Wood.....169 J3
Pimlico.....16 E7
Pinner.....47 H3
Pinner Green.....47 G1
Pinnerwood Park.....33 C6
Plaistow.....94 D2
Plaistow.....152 E5
Plashet.....77 H5
Plumstead.....115 H4
Plumstead Common.....116 A5
Ponders End.....30 E4
Poplar.....93 J6
Preston.....49 K7
Primrose Hill.....4 B4
Purfleet.....119 K4
Putney.....127 G4
Putney Heath.....127 F6
Putney Vale.....145 J2
Queensbury.....50 A2
Queen's Park.....88 C1
Rainham.....99 K2
Rayners Lane.....47 K7
Raynes Park.....161 F2
Redbridge.....59 G4
Regent's Park.....4 D6
Richmond.....125 F4
Richmond Hill.....125 F5
Roehampton.....126 C4
Romford.....62 E4
The Rookery.....20 E6
Rosehill.....162 A7
Rotherhithe.....112 A2
Roundshaw.....177 F5
Rowley Green.....25 H3
Roxeth.....66 C1
Ruislip.....46 C5
Ruislip Common.....46 A3
Ruislip Gardens.....64 C2
Ruislip Manor.....64 E1
Rush Green.....63 F6

St Giles.....11 H4
St Helier.....162 B7
St James's.....11 G9
St Johns.....132 D1
St John's Wood.....2 F7
St Luke's.....6 F9
St Margarets.....124 D5
St Pancras.....5 K8
St George in the East.....92 D6
Sands End.....108 B7
Seething Wells.....158 C5
Selhurst.....164 E4
Seven Kings.....60 E7
Shacklewell.....74 C3
Shadwell.....92 E6
Shepherd's Bush.....87 K7
Shirley.....178 E1
Shooters Hill.....115 H7
Shoreditch.....7 H8
Shortlands.....167 H2
Sidcup.....155 H3
Silvertown.....114 B1
Sipson.....100 C4
Slade Green.....138 D1
Soho.....11 G5
Somers Town.....5 G6
Southall.....102 C1
South Beddington.....176 D5
Southborough.....168 E5
South Bromley.....94 B5
South Croydon.....177 H5
Southend.....152 A3
Southfields.....127 K7
Southgate.....28 E7
South Hackney.....74 E7
South Hampstead.....2 F1
South Harrow.....66 B2
South Hornchurch.....81 F7
South Kensington.....14 E6
South Lambeth.....109 K6
South Norwood.....164 E2
South Oxhey.....33 F2
South Ruislip.....65 H3
South Tottenham.....56 A4
South Wimbledon.....147 G4
South Woodford.....58 E1
Spitalfields.....92 C4
Spitalfields.....13 L2
Spring Grove.....103 J7
Spring Park.....179 J1
Stamford Hill.....56 B6
Stanmore.....35 H4
Stanwell.....120 A5
Stepney.....92 E4
Stockwell.....129 K2
Stoke Newington.....74 B1
Stoneleigh.....173 H4
Strand.....11 J6
Stratford.....76 A6
Stratford Marsh.....76 A7
Strawberry Hill.....142 D2
Streatham.....148 E4
Streatham Hill.....129 K7
Streatham Park.....148 C3
Streatham Vale.....148 B6
Stroud Green.....55 C5
Sudbury.....67 F4
Summerstown.....147 H1
Sunbury.....140 C7
Sunbury Common.....140 D6
Sundridge.....153 C5
Surbiton.....158 D7
Sutton.....175 G4
Swiss Cottage.....3 H3
Sydenham.....151 F4
Teddington.....142 D5
Temple Hill.....139 G3
Thames Ditton.....158 B6
Thamesmead.....97 G6
Thornton Heath.....164 C2
Tokyngton.....68 D5
Tolworth.....159 H7
Tooting.....147 K4
Tooting Graveney.....147 H4
Tottenham.....56 A1
Tottenham Hale.....56 B2
Totteridge.....26 D7
Totteridge Green.....26 A7
Tufnell Park.....72 C3
Tulse Hill.....130 C7
Twickenham.....123 K7
Underhill.....26 E5
Upper Clapton.....56 C7
Upper Edmonton.....42 C3
Upper Elmers End.....166 C4
Upper Holloway.....54 C7
Upper Norwood.....149 K7
Upper Shirley.....178 E3
Upper Sydenham.....150 C3
Upper Tooting.....147 J2
Upper Walthamstow.....58 A3
Upton.....77 F6
Upton Park.....77 G7
Vale of Health.....71 H2
Vauxhall.....17 K8
Waddon.....176 E1
Walham Green.....107 K7
Wallend.....78 A7
Wallington.....176 A4
Walthamstow.....57 H3
Walworth.....18 F8
Wandle Park.....177 C1
Wandsworth.....127 K3
Wanstead.....59 F6
Wapping.....92 D7
Watford.....20 D2
Watford Heath.....21 J6
Wealdstone.....49 G2
Welling.....136 C2
Welsh Harp.....51 F7
Wembley.....68 A3
Wembley Park.....68 C2
West Acton.....86 C5
West Barnes.....161 F4
West Bedfont.....120 C6
West Brompton.....14 A7
West Drayton.....100 A2
West Dulwich.....149 K1
West Ealing.....85 G7
West Ewell.....173 F5
West Green.....55 J2
West Hampstead.....70 E4
West Harrow.....48 C5
West Heath.....116 E5
West Heath.....71 F1
West Hendon.....51 J6
West Hill.....127 H6
West Kensington.....107 G4
West Kilburn.....88 C2
Westminster.....16 F4
West Molesey.....156 E3
West Norwood.....149 J3
Weston Green.....157 K7

West Ruislip.....46 A7
West Watford.....20 E4
West Wickham.....167 G2
Whetstone.....39 F1
Whitechapel.....92 C5
Whitechapel.....13 M6
Whitton.....123 H5
Widmore.....168 C3
Willesden.....69 J5
Willesden Green.....69 K6
Wimbledon.....146 C4
Winchmore Hill.....29 J7
Wood End.....82 C5
Wood End Green.....82 C4
Woodford.....45 F5
Woodford Bridge.....45 K6
Woodford Green.....44 E6
Woodford Wells.....45 F2
Wood Green.....41 G7
Woodlands.....123 J2
Woodside.....165 H5
Woodside Park.....38 E5
Woolwich.....115 F2
Worcester Park.....173 K1
World's End.....29 G3
The Wrythe.....175 J1
Yeading.....83 G3

USING THE STREET INDEX

Street names are listed alphabetically. Each street name is followed by its postal town or area locality, the Postcode District, the page number, and the reference to the square in which the name is found.

Standard index entries are shown as follows:

1 Av *WOOL/PLUM* SE18 .... **115** G2

Street names and selected addresses not shown on the map due to scale restrictions are shown in the index with an asterisk:

Abbeville Ms *CLAP* SW4 * **129** J4

Entries in red indicate streets located within the London Congestion Zone. Refer to the map pages for the location of the Zone boundary

GENERAL ABBREVIATIONS

ACC	ACCESS
ALY	ALLEY
AP	APPROACH
AR	ARCADE
ASS	ASSOCIATION
AV	AVENUE
BCH	BEACH
BLDS	BUILDINGS
BND	BEND
BNK	BANK
BR	BRIDGE
BRK	BROOK
BTM	BOTTOM
BUS	BUSINESS
BVD	BOULEVARD
BY	BYPASS
CATH	CATHEDRAL
CEM	CEMETERY
CEN	CENTRE
CFT	CROFT
CH	CHURCH
CHA	CHASE
CHYD	CHURCHYARD
CIR	CIRCLE
CIRC	CIRCUS
CL	CLOSE
CLFS	CLIFFS
CMP	CAMP
CNR	CORNER
CO	COUNTY
COLL	COLLEGE
COM	COMMON
COMM	COMMISSION
CON	CONVENT
COT	COTTAGE
COTS	COTTAGES
CP	CAPE
CPS	COPSE
CR	CREEK
CREM	CREMATORIUM
CRS	CRESCENT
CSWY	CAUSEWAY
CT	COURT
CTRL	CENTRAL
CTS	COURTS
CTYD	COURTYARD
CUTT	CUTTINGS
CV	COVE
CYN	CANYON
DEPT	DEPARTMENT
DL	DALE
DM	DAM
DR	DRIVE
DRO	DROVE
DRY	DRIVEWAY
DWGS	DWELLINGS
E	EAST
EMB	EMBANKMENT
EMBY	EMBASSY
ESP	ESPLANADE
EST	ESTATE
EX	EXCHANGE
EXPY	EXPRESSWAY
EXT	EXTENSION
F/O	FLYOVER
FC	FOOTBALL CLUB
FK	FORK
FLD	FIELD
FLDS	FIELDS
FLS	FALLS
FM	FARM
FT	FORT
FTS	FLATS
FWY	FREEWAY
FY	FERRY
GA	GATE
GAL	GALLERY
GDN	GARDEN
GDNS	GARDENS
GLD	GLADE
GLN	GLEN
GN	GREEN
GND	GROUND
GRA	GRANGE
GRG	GARAGE
GT	GREAT
GTWY	GATEWAY
GV	GROVE
HGR	HIGHER
HL	HILL
HLS	HILLS
HO	HOUSE
HOL	HOLLOW
HOSP	HOSPITAL
HRB	HARBOUR
HTH	HEATH
HTS	HEIGHTS
HVN	HAVEN
HWY	HIGHWAY
IMP	IMPERIAL
IN	INLET
IND EST	INDUSTRIAL ESTATE
INF	INFIRMARY
INFO	INFORMATION
INT	INTERCHANGE
IS	ISLAND
JCT	JUNCTION
JTY	JETTY
KG	KING
KNL	KNOLL
L	LAKE
LA	LANE
LDG	LODGE
LGT	LIGHT
LK	LOCK
LKS	LAKES
LNDG	LANDING
LTL	LITTLE
LWR	LOWER
MAG	MAGISTRATE
MAN	MANSIONS
MD	MEAD
MDW	MEADOWS
MEM	MEMORIAL
MI	MILL
MKT	MARKET
MKTS	MARKETS
ML	MALL
MNR	MANOR
MS	MEWS
MSN	MISSION
MT	MOUNT
MTN	MOUNTAIN
MTS	MOUNTAINS
MUS	MUSEUM
MWY	MOTORWAY
N	NORTH
NE	NORTH EAST
NW	NORTH WEST
O/P	OVERPASS
OFF	OFFICE
ORCH	ORCHARD
OV	OVAL
PAL	PALACE
PAS	PASSAGE
PAV	PAVILION
PDE	PARADE
PH	PUBLIC HOUSE
PK	PARK
PKWY	PARKWAY
PL	PLACE
PLN	PLAIN
PLNS	PLAINS
PLZ	PLAZA
POL	POLICE STATION
PR	PRINCE
PREC	PRECINCT
PREP	PREPARATORY
PRIM	PRIMARY
PROM	PROMENADE
PRS	PRINCESS
PRT	PORT
PT	POINT
PTH	PATH
PZ	PIAZZA
QD	QUADRANT
QU	QUEEN
QY	QUAY
R	RIVER
RBT	ROUNDABOUT
RD	ROAD
RDG	RIDGE
REP	REPUBLIC
RES	RESERVOIR
RFC	RUGBY FOOTBALL CLUB
RI	RISE
RP	RAMP
RW	ROW
S	SOUTH
SCH	SCHOOL
SE	SOUTH EAST
SER	SERVICE AREA
SH	SHORE
SHOP	SHOPPING
SKWY	SKYWAY
SMT	SUMMIT
SOC	SOCIETY
SP	SPUR
SPR	SPRING
SQ	SQUARE
ST	STREET
STN	STATION
STR	STREAM
STRD	STRAND
SW	SOUTH WEST
TDG	TRADING
TER	TERRACE
THWY	THROUGHWAY
TNL	TUNNEL
TOLL	TOLLWAY
TPK	TURNPIKE
TR	TRACK
TRL	TRAIL
TWR	TOWER
U/P	UNDERPASS
UNI	UNIVERSITY
UPR	UPPER
V	VALE
VA	VALLEY
VIAD	VIADUCT
VIL	VILLA
VIS	VISTA
VLG	VILLAGE
VLS	VILLAS
VW	VIEW
W	WEST
WD	WOOD
WHF	WHARF
WK	WALK
WKS	WALKS
WLS	WELLS
WY	WAY
YD	YARD
YHA	YOUTH HOSTEL

POSTCODE TOWNS AND AREA ABBREVIATIONS

ABYW	Abbey Wood
ACT	Acton
ALP/SUD	Alperton/Sudbury
ARCH	Archway
ASHF	Ashford (Surrey)
BAL	Balham
BANK	Bank
BAR	Barnet
BARB	Barbican
BARK	Barking
BARK/HLT	Barkingside/Hainault
BARN	Barnes
BAY/PAD	Bayswater/Paddington
BCTR	Becontree
BECK	Beckenham
BELMT	Belmont
BELV	Belvedere
BERM/RHTH	Bermondsey/Rotherhithe
BETH	Bethnal Green
BFN/LL	Blackfen/Longlands
BGVA	Belgravia
BKHH	Buckhurst Hill
BKHTH/KID	Blackheath/Kidbrooke
BLKFR	Blackfriars
BMLY	Bromley
BMSBY	Bloomsbury
BORE	Borehamwood
BOW	Bow
BROCKY	Brockley
BRXN/ST	Brixton north/Stockwell
BRXS/STRHM	Brixton south/Streatham Hill
BRYLDS	Berrylands
BTFD	Brentford
BTSEA	Battersea
BUSH	Bushey
BXLY	Bexley
BXLYHN	Bexleyheath north
BXLYHS	Bexleyheath south
CAMTN	Camden Town
CAN/RD	Canning Town/Royal Docks
CANST	Cannon Street station
CAR	Carshalton
CAT	Catford
CAVSQ/HST	Cavendish Square/Harley Street
CDALE/KGS	Colindale/Kingsbury
CEND/HSY/T	Crouch End/Hornsey/Turnpike Lane
CHARL	Charlton
CHCR	Charing Cross
CHDH	Chadwell Heath
CHEAM	Cheam
CHEL	Chelsea
CHIG	Chigwell
CHING	Chingford
CHSGTN	Chessington
CHST	Chislehurst
CHSWK	Chiswick
CITYW	City of London west
CLAP	Clapham
CLAY	Clayhall
CLKNW	Clerkenwell
CLPT	Clapton
CMBW	Camberwell
CONDST	Conduit Street
COVGDN	Covent Garden
CRICK	Cricklewood
CROY/NA	Croydon/New Addington
CRW	Collier Row
DAGE	Dagenham east
DAGW	Dagenham west
DART	Dartford
DEN/HRF	Denham/Harefield
DEPT	Deptford
DUL	Dulwich
E/WMO/HCT	East & West Molesey/Hampton Court
EA	Ealing
EBAR	East Barnet
EBED/NFELT	East Bedfont/North Feltham
ECT	Earl's Court
ED	Edmonton
EDGW	Edgware
EDUL	East Dulwich
EFNCH	East Finchley
EHAM	East Ham
ELTH/MOT	Eltham/Mottingham
EMB	Embankment
EMPK	Emerson Park
EN	Enfield
ENC/FH	Enfield Chase/Forty Hill
ERITH	Erith
ERITHM	Erith Marshes
ESH/CLAY	Esher/Claygate
EW	Ewell
FARR	Farringdon
FBAR/BDGN	Friern Barnet/Bounds Green
FELT	Feltham
FENCHST	Fenchurch Street
FITZ	Fitzrovia
FLST/FETLN	Fleet Street/Fetter Lane
FNCH	Finchley
FSBYE	Finsbury east
FSBYPK	Finsbury Park
FSBYW	Finsbury west
FSTGT	Forest Gate
FSTH	Forest Hill
FUL/PGN	Fulham/Parsons Green
GDMY/SEVK	Goodmayes/Seven Kings
GFD/PVL	Greenford/Perivale
GINN	Gray's Inn
GLDGN	Golders Green
GNTH/NBYPK	Gants Hill/Newbury Park
GNWCH	Greenwich
GPK	Gidea Park
GSTN	Garston
GTPST	Great Portland Street
GWRST	Gower Street
HACK	Hackney
HAMP	Hampstead
HAYES	Hayes
HBRY	Highbury
HCH	Hornchurch
HCIRC	Holborn Circus
HDN	Hendon
HDTCH	Houndsditch
HEST	Heston
HGDN/ICK	Hillingdon/Ickenham
HGT	Highgate
HHOL	High Holborn
HMSMTH	Hammersmith
HNHL	Herne Hill
HNWL	Hanwell
HOL/ALD	Holborn/Aldwych
HOLWY	Holloway
HOM	Homerton
HOR/WEW	Horton/West Ewell
HPTN	Hampton
HRW	Harrow
HSLW	Hounslow
HSLWW	Hounslow west
HTHAIR	Heathrow Airport
HYS/HAR	Hayes/Harlington
IL	Ilford
IS	Islington
ISLW	Isleworth
KCROSS	King's Cross
KENS	Kensington
KIL/WHAMP	Kilburn/West Hampstead
KTBR	Knightsbridge
KTN/HRWW/WS	Kenton/Harrow Weald/Wealdstone
KTTN	Kentish Town
KUT/HW	Kingston upon Thames/Hampton Wick
KUTN/CMB	Kingston upon Thames north/Coombe
LBTH	Lambeth
LEE/GVPK	Lee/Grove Park
LEW	Lewisham
LEY	Leyton
LINN	Lincoln's Inn
LOTH	Lothbury
LSQ/SEVD	Leicester Square/Seven Dials
LVPST	Liverpool Street
MANHO	Mansion House
MBLAR	Marble Arch
MHST	Marylebone High Street
MLHL	Mill Hill
MNPK	Manor Park
MON	Monument
MORT/ESHN	Mortlake/East Sheen
MRDN	Morden
MTCM	Mitcham
MUSWH	Muswell Hill
MV/WKIL	Maida Vale/West Kilburn
MYFR/PICC	Mayfair/Piccadilly
MYFR/PKLN	Mayfair/Park Lane
NFNCH/WDSPK	North Finchley/Woodside Park
NKENS	North Kensington
NOXST/BSQ	New Oxford Street/Bloomsbury Square
NRWD	Norwood
NTGHL	Notting Hill
NTHLT	Northolt
NTHWD	Northwood
NWCR	New Cross
NWDGN	Norwood Green
NWMAL	New Malden
OBST	Old Broad Street
OLYMPICPK	Olympic Park
ORP	Orpington
OXHEY	Oxhey
OXSTW	Oxford Street west
PECK	Peckham
PEND	Ponders End
PGE/AN	Penge/Anerley
PIM	Pimlico
PIN	Pinner
PLMGR	Palmers Green
PLSTW	Plaistow
POP/IOD	Poplar/Isle of Dogs
PUR	Purfleet
PUR/KEN	Purley/Kenley
PUT/ROE	Putney/Roehampton
RAIN	Rainham (Gt Lon)
RCH/KEW	Richmond/Kew
RCHPK/HAM	Richmond Park/Ham
RDART	Rural Dartford
REDBR	Redbridge
REGST	Regent Street
RKW/CH/CXG	Rickmansworth/Chorleywood/Croxley Green
ROM	Romford
ROMW/RG	Romford west/Rush Green
RSLP	Ruislip
RSQ	Russell Square
RYLN/HDSTN	Rayners Lane/Headstone
RYNPK	Raynes Park
SAND/SEL	Sanderstead/Selsdon
SCUP	Sidcup
SDTCH	Shoreditch
SEVS/STOTM	Seven Sisters/South Tottenham
SHB	Shepherd's Bush
SHPTN	Shepperton
SKENS	South Kensington
SNWD	South Norwood
SOCK/AV	South Ockendon/Aveley
SOHO/CST	Soho/Carnaby Street
SOHO/SHAV	Soho/Shaftesbury Avenue
SRTFD	Stratford
STAN	Stanmore
STBT	St Bart's
STHGT/OAK	Southgate/Oakwood
STHL	Southall
STHWK	Southwark
STJS	St James's
STJSPK	St James's Park
STJWD	St John's Wood
STKPK	Stockley Park
STLK	St Luke's
STMC/STPC	St Mary Cray/St Paul's Cray
STNW/STAM	Stoke Newington/Stamford Hill
STP	St Paul's
STPAN	St Pancras
STRHM/NOR	Streatham/Norbury
STWL/WRAY	Stanwell/Wraysbury
SUN	Sunbury
SURB	Surbiton
SUT	Sutton
SWFD	South Woodford
SYD	Sydenham
TEDD	Teddington
THDIT	Thames Ditton
THHTH	Thornton Heath
THMD	Thamesmead
TOOT	Tooting
TOTM	Tottenham
TPL/STR	Temple/Strand
TRDG/WHET	Totteridge/Whetstone
TWK	Twickenham
TWRH	Tower Hill
UED	Upper Edmonton
UX/CGN	Uxbridge/Colham Green
VX/NE	Vauxhall/Nine Elms
WALTH	Walthamstow
WALW	Walworth
WAN	Wanstead
WAND/EARL	Wandsworth/Earlsfield
WAP	Wapping
WAT	Watford
WATN	Watford north
WATW	Watford west
WBLY	Wembley
WBPTN	West Brompton
WCHMH	Winchmore Hill
WCHPL	Whitechapel
WDGN	Wood Green
WDR/YW	West Drayton/Yiewsley
WEA	West Ealing
WELL	Welling
WEST	Westminster
WESTW	Westminster west
WFD	Woodford
WHALL	Whitehall
WHTN	Whitton
WIM/MER	Wimbledon/Merton
WKENS	West Kensington
WLGTN	Wallington
WLSDN	Willesden
WNWD	West Norwood
WOOL/PLUM	Woolwich/Plumstead
WOT/HER	Walton-on-Thames/Hersham
WPK	Worcester Park
WWKM	West Wickham
YEAD	Yeading

1

1 Av WOOL/PLUM SE18.....115 G2

A

Aaron Hill Rd EHAM E6.....96 A4
Abberley Ms BTSEA SW11.....129 A4
Abbess Cl BRXS/STRHM SW2.....130 C7
Abbeville Ms CLAP SW4 *.....129 J4
Abbeville Rd CEND/HSY/T N8.....54 D3
  CLAP SW4.....129 H5
Abbey Av ALP/SUD HA0.....86 A1
Abbey Cl HYS/HAR UB3.....83 F3
  NTHLT UB5.....83 K2
  PIN HA5.....47 F2
  ROM RM1.....63 H5
Abbey Crs BELV DA17.....117 H3
Abbeydale Rd ALP/SUD HA0.....68 B7
Abbey Dr TOOT SW17.....148 A4
Abbeyfield Est
  BERM/RHTH SE16.....111 K3
Abbeyfield Rd
  BERM/RHTH SE16.....111 K3
Abbey Gdns CHST BR7.....154 D7
  HMSMTH W6.....107 H5
  STHWK SE1.....111 H3
  STJWD NW8.....2 E6
Abbey Gv ABYW SE2.....116 C3
Abbeyhill Rd BFN/LL DA15.....136 D7
Abbey La BECK BR3.....151 J6
  SRTFD E15.....94 A1
Abbey Ms ISLW TW7.....104 C7
  WALTH E17.....57 J4
Abbey Mt BELV DA17.....117 G4
Abbey Orchard St WEST SW1P.....17 H3
Abbey Pk BECK BR3.....151 J6
Abbey Pl DART DA1.....139 G4
Abbey Rd BARK IG11.....78 B7
  BELV DA17.....116 E3
  BXLYHN DA7.....137 F3
  CROY/NA CR0.....177 H2
  EN EN1.....30 A4
  GNTH/NBYPK IG2.....60 D4
  KIL/WHAMP NW6.....2 C3
  SRTFD E15.....76 C7
  WIM/MER SW19.....147 G6
  WLSDN NW10.....86 D1
Abbey St PLSTW E13.....94 E3
  STHWK SE1.....19 L3
Abbey Ter ABYW SE2.....116 D2
Abbey Vw MLHL NW7.....37 H2
Abbey Wk E/WMO/HCT KT8.....157 G2
Abbey Wood Rd ABYW SE2.....116 C3
Abbot Cl RSLP HA4.....65 H2
  WKENS W14.....107 H1
Abbotsbury Cl SRTFD E15.....94 A1
  WKENS W14.....107 J1
Abbotsbury Gdns PIN HA5.....47 G5
Abbotsbury Ms PECK SE15.....131 K2
Abbotsbury Rd MRDN SM4.....162 A3
  WKENS W14.....107 H1
  WWKM BR4.....180 D1
Abbots Cl STMC/STPC BR5.....169 H7
Abbots Dr RYLN/HDSTN HA2.....66 A1
Abbotsford Av
  SEVS/STOTM N15.....55 J3
Abbotsford Gdns WFD IG8.....44 E6
Abbotsford Rd
  GDMY/SEVK IG3.....79 G1
Abbots Gdns EFNCH N2.....53 H3
Abbots Gn CROY/NA CR0.....179 F5
Abbotshade Rd
  BERM/RHTH SE16 *.....93 F7
Abbotshall Av
  STHGT/OAK N14.....40 C2
Abbotshall Rd CAT SE6.....133 G1
Abbotsleigh Cl BELMT SM2.....175 F6
Abbotsleigh Rd
  STRHM/NOR SW16.....148 C3
Abbots Mnr PIM SW1V.....16 C7
Abbots Manor Est PIM SW1V.....16 C7
Abbotsmede Cl TWK TW1.....143 F1
Abbots Pk BRXS/STRHM SW2.....130 B7
Abbot's Pl KIL/WHAMP NW6.....2 C3
Abbots Rd EDGW HA8.....37 F6
  EHAM E6.....77 H7
Abbots Ter CEND/HSY/T N8.....54 E5
Abbotstone Rd
  PUT/ROE SW15.....127 F2
Abbot St HACK E8.....74 B5
Abbots Wk KENS W8 *.....14 C4
Abbots Wy BECK BR3.....166 B4
Abbotswell Rd BROCKY SE4.....132 C4
Abbotswood Cl BELV DA17.....117 F2
Abbotswood Gdns CLAY IG5.....59 K2
Abbotswood Rd EDUL SE22.....131 F3
  STRHM/NOR SW16.....148 D2
Abbotswood Wy
  HYS/HAR UB3.....83 F7
Abbott Av RYNPK SW20.....161 G1
Abbott Cl HPTN TW12.....141 J5
  NTHLT UB5.....65 K5
Abbott Rd POP/IOD E14 *.....94 A4
Abbotts Cl IS N1 *.....6 E1
  ROMW/RG RM7.....62 D2
  THMD SE28.....97 J6
Abbotts Crs CHING E4.....44 B3
  ENC/FH EN2.....29 H1
Abbotts Dr ALP/SUD HA0.....67 H1
Abbotts Md
  RCHPK/HAM TW10 *.....143 J3
Abbotts Park Rd LEY E10.....58 A6
Abbotts Rd BAR EN5.....27 F3
  CHEAM SM3.....174 C3
  MTCM CR4.....163 H3
  STHL UB1.....83 J7
Abbott's Wk BXLYHN DA7.....116 E7
Abchurch La MANHO EC4N.....13 H5
Abdale Rd SHB W12.....87 K7
Aberavon Rd BOW E3.....93 G2
Abercairn Rd
  STRHM/NOR SW16.....148 C6
Aberconway Rd MRDN SM4.....162 A2
Abercorn Cl MLHL NW7.....38 C6
  STJWD NW8.....2 E6
Abercorn Crs
  RYLN/HDSTN HA2.....48 A7
Abercorn Dell BUSH WD23.....34 C1
Abercorn Gdns CHDH RM6.....61 H5
  KTN/HRWW/WS HA3.....49 K6
Abercorn Gv RSLP HA4.....46 B3
Abercorn Ms
  RCHPK/HAM TW10.....125 G4
Abercorn Pl STJWD NW8.....2 E7
Abercorn Rd MLHL NW7.....38 C6
  STAN HA7.....35 J6
Abercorn Wk STJWD NW8.....2 E7

Abercorn Wy STHWK SE1.....111 H4
Abercrombie St BTSEA SW11.....128 D1
Aberdare Cl WWKM BR4.....180 A1
Aberdare Gdns
  KIL/WHAMP NW6.....2 B1
  MLHL NW7.....38 B6
Aberdare Rd PEND EN3.....30 E3
Aberdeen Cots STAN HA7 *.....35 J6
Aberdeen La HBRY N5.....73 H4
Aberdeen Pde UED N18 *.....42 D4
Aberdeen Pk HBRY N5.....73 H4
Aberdeen Pl BAY/PAD W2.....9 H1
Aberdeen Rd CROY/NA CR0.....177 J3
  HBRY N5.....73 J3
  KTN/HRWW/WS HA3.....49 H1
  UED N18.....42 C4
  WLSDN NW10.....69 H4
Aberdeen Ter BKHTH/KID SE3.....133 G1
Aberdour Rd GDMY/SEVK IG3.....79 H2
Aberdour St STHWK SE1.....19 J5
Aberfeldy St POP/IOD E14.....94 A5
Aberford Gdns
  WOOL/PLUM SE18.....114 D7
Aberford Rd BORE WD6.....24 C1
Aberfoyle Rd
  STRHM/NOR SW16.....148 D6
Abergeldie Rd LEE/GVPK SE12.....134 A5
Abernethy Rd LEW SE13.....133 H3
Abersham Rd HACK E8.....74 B4
Abery St WOOL/PLUM SE18.....115 K3
Abingdon Cl KUT/HW KT1.....159 H2
  KENS W8.....14 B4
  STRHM/NOR SW16.....148 E7
Abingdon Rd FNCH N3.....53 G1
  KENS W8.....14 B4
  STRHM/NOR SW16.....148 E7
Abingdon St WEST SW1P.....17 J2
Abingdon Vls KENS W8.....14 A4
Abinger Av BELMT SM2.....174 A7
  CROY/NA CR0.....180 A5
Abinger Cl BMLY BR1.....168 D2
  CROY/NA CR0.....180 A5
  GDMY/SEVK IG3.....79 G3
  WLGTN SM6.....176 E4
Abinger Ct
  KTN/HRWW/WS HA3.....35 J4
Abinger Dr NRWD SE19.....149 J6
Abinger Gdns ISLW TW7.....123 K2
Abinger Gv DEPT SE8.....112 C5
Abinger Ms MV/WKIL W9.....2 A9
Abinger Rd CHSWK W4.....106 C2
Ablett St BERM/RHTH SE16.....111 K4
Abney Park Ter
  STNW/STAM N16 *.....74 B1
Aboyne Dr RYNPK SW20.....160 D1
Aboyne Rd TOOT SW17.....147 G2
  WLSDN NW10.....69 G2
Abraham Cl OXHEY WD19.....33 F3
Abridge Wy BARK IG11.....97 H1
Abyssinia Cl BTSEA SW11.....128 D3
Abyssinia Rd BTSEA SW11 *.....128 D3
Acacia Av BTFD TW8.....104 C6
  HCH RM12.....81 H1
  HYS/HAR UB3.....82 D6
  RSLP HA4.....46 E7
  TOTM N17.....41 K6
  WBLY HA9.....68 A4
Acacia Cl DEPT SE8.....112 B3
  STAN HA7.....34 E5
  STMC/STPC BR5.....169 J4
Acacia Dr CHEAM SM3.....161 J6
Acacia Gdns STJWD NW8.....3 H5
  WWKM BR4.....180 A1
Acacia Gv DUL SE21.....149 K1
  NWMAL KT3.....160 B2
Acacia Pl STJWD NW8.....3 H5
Acacia Rd ACT W3.....86 C6
  BECK BR3.....166 C2
  DART DA1.....139 F7
  HPTN TW12.....142 A5
  MTCM CR4.....163 F1
  STJWD NW8.....3 H5
  STRHM/NOR SW16.....148 E7
  WALTH E17.....57 G5
  WAN E11.....76 C1
  WDGN N22.....41 G7
The Acacias EBAR EN4 *.....27 H4
Acacia Wy BFN/LL DA15.....136 A6
Academia Wy TOTM N17.....42 A5
Academy Fields Rd GPK RM2.....63 K3
Academy Gdns CROY/NA CR0.....165 G7
  NTHLT UB5.....83 H1
Academy Pl ISLW TW7.....103 K6
  WOOL/PLUM SE18.....114 E7
Academy Rd
  WOOL/PLUM SE18.....114 E6
Academy Wy BCTR RM8.....79 J3
Acanthus Dr STHWK SE1.....111 H4
Acanthus Rd BTSEA SW11.....129 F2
Accommodation Rd
  GLDGN NW11.....52 D6
Ace Pde CHSGTN KT9.....172 A2
Acer Av YEAD UB4.....83 J3
Acer Rd HACK E8 *.....7 M1
Acfold Rd FUL/PGN SW6.....108 A7
Achilles Cl STHWK SE1.....111 H4
Achilles Rd KIL/WHAMP NW6.....70 E4
Achilles St NWCR SE14.....112 B6
Acklam Rd NKENS W10.....88 D4
Acklington Dr
  CDALE/KGS NW9.....37 G7
Ackmar Rd FUL/PGN SW6.....107 K7
Ackroyd Dr BOW E3.....93 H4
Ackroyd Rd FSTH SE23.....132 A6
Acland Cl WOOL/PLUM SE18.....115 J6
Acland Crs CMBW SE5.....130 E3
Acland Rd CRICK NW2.....69 K5
Acock Gv NTHLT UB5.....66 B3
Acol Crs RSLP HA4.....65 F4
Acol Rd KIL/WHAMP NW6.....2 B1
Aconbury Rd BCTR RM8.....79 H1
Acorn Cl CHING E4.....43 K4
  CHST BR7.....154 C4
  HPTN TW12.....142 B5
  STAN HA7.....35 H6
Acorn Gdns ACT W3.....87 F4
  NRWD SE19.....150 B7
Acorn Gv HYS/HAR UB3.....101 J6
  RSLP HA4.....64 D3
Acorn Pde PECK SE15 *.....111 J6
Acorn Rd DART DA1.....138 C4
Acorns Rd ESH/CLAY KT10.....170 C4
Acorn Wy BECK BR3.....167 F4
  FSTH SE23.....151 F2
Acre Dr EDUL SE22.....131 H3
Acre La BRXS/STRHM SW2.....130 A3
  CAR SM5.....176 A3
Acre Rd DAGE RM10.....80 D6
  KUTN/CMB KT2.....144 A7
  WIM/MER SW19.....147 H5
Acre Wy NTHWD HA6.....32 D7
Acris St WAND/EARL SW18.....128 B4
Acton Cl ED N9.....42 C1
Acton Hill Ms ACT W3 *.....86 D7
Acton La CHSWK W4.....105 K2
  WLSDN NW10.....86 E2
Acton Ms HACK E8.....7 L3

Acton St FSBYW WC1X.....5 L8
Acuba Rd WAND/EARL SW18.....147 F1
Acworth Cl ED N9.....30 E6
Acworth Pl DART DA1 *.....139 F5
Ada Cl FBAR/BDGN N11.....39 K3
Ada Gdns POP/IOD E14.....94 B5
  SRTFD E15.....76 D7
Adair Cl SNWD SE25.....165 J2
Adair Rd NKENS W10.....88 C3
Adam Cl CAT SE6.....151 K1
  FSTH SE23.....150 E1
Adam Ct ECT SW5 *.....14 E5
Adam Rd CHING E4.....43 H5
Adams Cl BRYLDS KT5.....159 G5
  FNCH N3.....38 E6
  WBLY HA9.....68 C3
Adams Ct OBST EC2N.....13 H4
Adams Ms TOOT SW17.....147 J1
Adamson Rd CAN/RD E16.....94 E5
  HAMP NW3.....3 H1
Adamson Wy BECK BR3.....167 F4
Adams Rd BECK BR3.....166 B4
  TOTM N17.....55 H1
Adams Rw MYFR/PKLN W1K.....10 B7
Adam St CHCR WC2N.....11 K7
Adams Wk KUT/HW KT1.....159 F1
Adam Wy FUL/PGN SW6.....107 H6
Adare Wk STRHM/NOR SW16.....148 E1
Ada Rd ALP/SUD HA0 *.....67 J2
  CMBW SE5.....111 F6
Adastra Wy WLGTN SM6.....176 E5
Ada St HACK E8.....74 D7
Adderley Gdns ELTH/MOT SE9.....154 A3
Adderley Gv BTSEA SW11.....129 F4
Adderley Rd
  KTN/HRWW/WS HA3.....35 F1
Adderley St POP/IOD E14.....94 A5
Addey St DEPT SE8.....112 D6
Addington Dr
  NFNCH/WDSPK N12.....39 J5
Addington Gv SYD SE26.....151 G3
Addington Rd BOW E3.....94 C3
  CAN/RD E16.....94 C3
  CROY/NA CR0.....164 B7
  FSBYPK N4.....55 G6
  WWKM BR4.....180 A3
Addington Sq CMBW SE5.....110 D6
Addington St STHWK SE1.....17 M2
Addington Village Rd
  CROY/NA CR0.....179 H5
Addiscombe Av CROY/NA CR0.....165 H6
Addiscombe Cl
  KTN/HRWW/WS HA3.....49 J4
Addiscombe Court Rd
  CROY/NA CR0.....165 F7
Addiscombe Gv CROY/NA CR0.....177 J1
Addiscombe Rd CROY/NA CR0.....178 A1
  WATW WD18.....21 F3
Addison Av HSLW TW3.....103 H7
  NTGHL W11.....88 C7
  STHGT/OAK N14.....28 B5
Addison Bridge Pl
  WKENS W14.....107 J3
Addison Cl NTHWD HA6.....32 E7
  STMC/STPC BR5.....169 H5
Addison Crs WKENS W14.....107 H2
Addison Dr LEE/GVPK SE12.....134 A4
Addison Gdns BRYLDS KT5.....159 G3
  WKENS W14.....107 G2
Addison Pl NTGHL W11.....88 C7
Addison Rd HAYES BR2.....168 C4
  SNWD SE25.....165 H3
  TEDD TW11.....143 H5
  WALTH E17.....57 K4
  WAN E11.....58 E5
  WKENS W14.....107 H1
Addison's Cl CROY/NA CR0.....179 H1
Addison Ter CHSWK W4 *.....105 K3
Addle Hl BLKFR EC4V.....12 D6
Addle St CITYW EC2V *.....12 F4
Adecroft Wy E/WMO/HCT KT8.....157 J3
Adela Av NWMAL KT3.....160 E4
Adelaide Av BROCKY SE4.....132 D3
Adelaide Cl STAN HA7.....35 G3
Adelaide Ct NHWL W7 *.....104 A1
Adelaide Gdns CHDH RM6.....62 A4
Adelaide Gv SHB W12.....87 J7
Adelaide Rd CHST BR7.....154 B4
  HAMP NW3.....3 J1
  HEST TW5.....102 C6
  IL IG1.....78 B1
  LEY E10.....76 A2
  NWDGN UB2.....102 D3
  PUT/ROE SW15.....127 H3
  RCH/KEW TW9.....125 G4
  STJWD NW8.....3 G1
  SURB KT6.....159 F4
  TEDD TW11.....143 F5
  WEA W13.....104 B1
Adelaide St CHCR WC2N *.....11 J7
Adelaide Ter BTFD TW8 *.....104 E4
Adela St NKENS W10.....88 C3
Adelina Gv WCHPL E1.....92 E4
Adelina Ms BAL SW12.....129 J7
Adeline Pl RSQ WC1B.....11 J2
Adeliza Cl BARK IG11.....78 C6
Adelphi Crs HCH RM12.....81 J1
  YEAD UB4.....82 C2
Adelphi Ter CHCR WC2N *.....11 K7
Adelphi Wy YEAD UB4.....82 D2
Adeney Cl HMSMTH W6.....107 G5
Aden Gv STNW/STAM N16.....73 K3
Adenmore Rd CAT SE6.....132 D6
Aden Rd IL IG1.....60 B6
  EN EN1.....31 F3
Adhara Rd NTHWD HA6.....32 D4
Adie Rd HMSMTH W6.....107 F2
Adine Rd PLSTW E13.....94 E3
Adler St WCHPL E1.....92 C4
Adley St CLPT E5.....75 G3
Adlington Cl UED N18.....41 K4
Admaston Rd
  WOOL/PLUM SE18.....115 H6
Admiral Ms NKENS W10.....88 B3
Admiral Pl BERM/RHTH SE16.....93 G7
Admirals Cl SWFD E18.....59 F3
Admiral Seymour Rd
  ELTH/MOT SE9.....134 E3
Admiral's Ga GNWCH SE10.....112 E7
Admiral Sq WBPTN SW10 *.....108 B7
Admiral St DEPT SE8.....112 D7
Admiral's Wk HAMP NW3.....71 G1
Admirals Wy POP/IOD E14.....112 D1

Admiralty Cl DEPT SE8 *.....112 D7
Admiralty Rd TEDD TW11.....143 F5
Admiralty Wy TEDD TW11.....143 F5
Admiral Wk MV/WKIL W9.....8 B2
Adnams Wk RAIN RM13.....81 J4
Adolf St CAT SE6.....151 J3
Adolphus Rd FSBYPK N4.....73 H1
Adolphus St DEPT SE8.....112 C6
Adomar Rd BCTR RM8.....79 K2
Adpar St BAY/PAD W2.....9 G2
Adrian Cl BAR EN5.....26 A1
Adrian Ms WBPTN SW10.....14 D9
Adrienne Av STHL UB1.....83 K3
Advance Rd WNWD SE27.....149 J3
Advent Wy UED N18.....43 H4
Adys Lawn CRICK NW2.....69 K5
Adys Rd PECK SE15.....131 G2
Aerodrome Rd
  CDALE/KGS NW9.....51 H2
Aerodrome Wy HEST TW5.....102 B5
Aeroville CDALE/KGS NW9.....51 G5
Affleck St IS N1 *.....5 M6
Afghan Rd BTSEA SW11.....128 D1
Aftab Ter WCHPL E1 *.....92 D3
Agamemnon Rd
  KIL/WHAMP NW6.....70 D4
Agar Cl SURB KT6.....172 B1
Agar Gv CAMTN NW1.....5 H1
Agar Pl CAMTN NW1.....4 F2
Agar St CHCR WC2N.....11 J7
Agate Cl CAN/RD E16.....95 J7
Agate Rd HMSMTH W6.....107 F2
Agatha Cl WAP E1W.....92 D7
Agaton Rd ELTH/MOT SE9.....154 C1
Agave Rd CRICK NW2.....70 A3
Agdon St FSBYE EC1V.....6 C9
Agincourt Rd HAMP NW3.....71 K3
Agnes Av IL IG1.....78 A3
Agnes Cl EHAM E6.....96 A6
Agnesfield Cl
  NFNCH/WDSPK N12.....39 J5
Agnes Gdns BCTR RM8.....79 K3
Agnes Rd ACT W3.....106 C1
Agnes Riley Gdns CLAP SW4 *.....129 H6
Agnes St POP/IOD E14.....93 H5
Agnew Rd FSTH SE23.....132 B6
Agricola Pl EN EN1.....30 B4
Ailsa Av TWK TW1.....124 B4
Ailsa Rd TWK TW1.....124 C4
Ailsa St POP/IOD E14.....94 A4
Ainger Rd HAMP NW3.....3 M2
Ainsdale Crs PIN HA5.....48 A7
Ainsdale Dr STHWK SE1.....111 H4
Ainsdale Rd EA W5.....85 K3
  OXHEY WD19.....33 G2
Ainsley Av ROMW/RG RM7.....62 E5
Ainsley Cl ED N9.....30 A7
Ainsley St BETH E2.....92 D2
Ainslie Wood Crs CHING E4.....43 K4
Ainslie Wood Gdns CHING E4.....43 K3
Ainslie Wood Rd CHING E4.....43 J4
Ainsty St BERM/RHTH SE16.....111 K1
Ainsworth Cl CMBW SE5 *.....131 F1
  CRICK NW2.....69 J2
Ainsworth Rd CROY/NA CR0.....164 C7
  HOM E9.....74 E6
Ainsworth Wy STJWD NW8.....2 E3
Aintree Av EHAM E6.....77 J7
Aintree Cl UED N18.....42 E4
Aintree Crs BARK/HLT IG6.....60 C1
Aintree Rd GFD/PVL UB6.....85 H1
Aintree St FUL/PGN SW6.....107 H6
Airco Cl CDALE/KGS NW9.....50 E2
Airdrie Cl IS N1.....5 L2
  YEAD UB4.....83 J4
Airedale Av CHSWK W4.....106 C4
Airedale Av South
  CHSWK W4 *.....106 C4
Airedale Rd BAL SW12.....128 E6
  EA W5.....104 D2
Airfield Wy HCH RM12.....81 K5
Airlie Gdns IL IG1.....60 B7
  KENS W8.....8 A9
Air St REGST W1B.....10 E7
Airthrie Rd GDMY/SEVK IG3.....61 H7
Aisgill Av WKENS W14.....107 J4
Aisher Rd THMD SE28.....97 J6
Aislibie Rd LEE/GVPK SE12.....133 H3
Aiten Pl HMSMTH W6.....106 D3
Aitken Cl HACK E8.....74 C7
  MTCM CR4.....162 E6
Aitken Rd BAR EN5.....26 A5
  CAT SE6.....151 K1
Aitman Dr BTFD TW8 *.....105 H4
Ajax Av CDALE/KGS NW9.....51 G2
Ajax Rd KIL/WHAMP NW6.....70 D3
Akabusi Cl CROY/NA CR0.....165 H5
Akehurst St PUT/ROE SW15.....126 D5
Akenside Rd HAMP NW3.....71 H4
Akerman Rd BRXN/ST SW9.....110 C3
  SURB KT6.....158 D5
Alabama St WOOL/PLUM SE18.....115 J6
Alacross Rd EA W5.....104 D1
Alan Cl DART DA1.....139 F3
Alandale Dr PIN HA5.....33 F7
Alander Ms WALTH E17.....57 K3
Alan Dr BAR EN5.....26 C5
Alan Gdns ROMW/RG RM7.....62 C6
Alan Hocken Wy SRTFD E15.....94 C1
Alan Rd WIM/MER SW19.....146 C4
Alanthus Cl LEE/GVPK SE12.....133 J5
Alaska St STHWK SE1.....17 M1
Albacore Crs LEW SE13.....132 E5
Alba Gdns GLDGN NW11.....52 C5
Albany Cl BUSH WD23.....22 D5
  BXLY DA5.....136 D6
  ESH/CLAY KT10.....170 A7
  MORT/ESHN SW14.....125 J3
  SEVS/STOTM N15.....55 H3
Albany Cots HNWL W7 *.....10 E7
Albany Crs EDGW HA8.....36 C6
  ESH/CLAY KT10.....170 E5
Albany Ctyd MYFR/PICC W1J.....10 E7
Albany Ms BMLY BR1.....152 E5
  CMBW SE5.....110 D5
  IS N1.....6 B1
  KUTN/CMB KT2 *.....143 K5
  SUT SM1.....175 F4
Albany Pde BTFD TW8 *.....105 F5
Albany Park Av
  KUTN/CMB KT2.....143 K5
Albany Park Rd
  BTFD TW8.....104 E5
  BXLY DA5.....136 D6
  CHDH RM6.....62 B5
  CHST BR7.....154 B4
  CMBW SE5.....19 J9
  FSBYPK N4.....55 F7
  HCH RM12.....63 J7
  LEY E10.....57 J6

MNPK E12.....77 H3
NWMAL KT3.....160 A3
RCHPK/HAM TW10 *.....125 G4
UED N18.....42 D4
WALTH E17.....57 G5
WALW SE17.....110 E5
WEA W13.....85 H6
WIM/MER SW19.....147 F4
Albany Rw EFNCH N2 *.....53 F3
The Albany KUTN/CMB KT2.....143 K5
Alba Pl NTGHL W11.....88 D5
Albatross Cl EHAM E6.....95 K3
Albatross St
  WOOL/PLUM SE18.....115 K6
Albemarle Ap
  GNTH/NBYPK IG2.....60 B5
Albemarle Av WHTN TW2.....122 E1
Albemarle Gdns
  GNTH/NBYPK IG2.....60 B5
  NWMAL KT3.....160 A3
Albemarle Pk BECK BR3 *.....151 K7
  STAN HA7.....35 J4
Albemarle Rd BECK BR3.....151 K7
  EBAR EN4.....27 J6
Albemarle St CONDST W1S.....10 D7
Albemarle Wy FSBYE EC1V.....12 C1
Alberon Gdns GLDGN NW11.....52 D3
Alberta Av SUT SM1.....174 C3
Alberta Est WALW SE17.....18 D7
Alberta Rd EN EN1.....30 B5
  ERITH DA8.....117 K7
Alberta St WALW SE17.....18 D7
Albert Av CHING E4.....43 J5
  VX/NE SW8.....110 A6
Albert Basin Wy CAN/RD E16.....96 C6
Albert Br BTSEA SW11.....108 D6
Albert Bridge Ga BTSEA SW11.....108 E6
Albert Bridge Rd BTSEA SW11.....108 D5
Albert Carr Gdns
  STRHM/NOR SW16.....148 E4
Albert Cl HOM E9.....74 D7
  WDGN N22.....40 D7
Albert Cots WCHPL E1 *.....92 C4
Albert Crs CHING E4.....43 J5
Albert Dr WIM/MER SW19.....146 C1
Albert Emb STHWK SE1.....17 K7
Albert Gdns WCHPL E1.....93 F5
Albert Ga KTBR SW1X.....15 M1
Albert Gv RYNPK SW20.....146 B2
Albert Ms BROCKY SE4 *.....132 C3
  FSBYPK N4.....55 F7
  KENS W8.....14 E3
  POP/IOD E14 *.....93 G6
Albert Pl FNCH N3.....38 E7
  KENS W8.....14 D2
Albert Rd BCTR RM8.....62 B7
  BELV DA17.....117 G4
  BKHH IG9.....45 H1
  BXLY DA5.....137 H5
  CAN/RD E16.....95 J7
  EA W5.....85 H3
  EBAR EN4.....27 G3
  ELTH/MOT SE9.....153 J2
  FSBYPK N4.....55 F7
  HAYES BR2.....168 C3
  HDN NW4.....52 B3
  HPTN TW12.....142 C4
  HSLW TW3.....123 F3
  HYS/HAR UB3.....101 H2
  IL IG1.....78 C2
  KIL/WHAMP NW6.....88 D1
  KUT/HW KT1.....159 G1
  LEY E10.....76 A1
  MLHL NW7.....37 H4
  MTCM CR4.....162 E2
  NWDGN UB2.....102 C2
  NWMAL KT3.....160 C3
  PGE/AN SE20.....151 F6
  RCHPK/HAM TW10.....125 F4
  ROM RM1.....63 H5
  RYLN/HDSTN HA2.....48 C2
  SEVS/STOTM N15.....56 A5
  SNWD SE25.....165 J3
  SUT SM1.....175 H4
  SWFD E18.....59 F2
  TEDD TW11.....143 F5
  TWK TW1.....124 A7
  WALTH E17.....57 J4
  WDGN N22.....40 D7
Albert Rd North WAT WD17.....21 F2
Albert Rd South WAT WD17.....21 F2
Albert Sq SRTFD E15.....76 C4
  VX/NE SW8.....110 A6
Albert St CAMTN NW1.....4 D4
  NFNCH/WDSPK N12.....39 G4
Albert Ter CAMTN NW1.....4 A3
  EA W5 *.....85 H3
  WLSDN NW10 *.....69 F7
Albert Terrace Ms
  CAMTN NW1.....4 A3
Albert Wy PECK SE15.....111 J6
Albion Av MUSWH N10.....54 A3
  VX/NE SW8.....129 J1
Albion Cl BAY/PAD W2.....9 K6
  ROMW/RG RM7.....63 F5
Albion Dr HACK E8.....7 M2
Albion Est BERM/RHTH SE16 *.....111 K1
Albion Ga BAY/PAD W2.....9 K6
Albion Gv STNW/STAM N16.....74 A3
Albion Ms BAY/PAD W2.....9 K5
  HMSMTH W6.....106 E3
  IS N1.....6 A2
Albion Pl FARR EC1M.....12 C2
  HMSMTH W6.....106 E3
  SNWD SE25.....165 H2
Albion Riverside BTSEA SW11.....108 D6
Albion Rd BELMT SM2.....175 H5
  BXLYHS DA6.....137 G3
  HSLW TW3.....123 F3
  HYS/HAR UB3.....82 C5
  KUTN/CMB KT2.....144 E7
  STNW/STAM N16.....73 K4
  TOTM N17.....56 B2
  WALTH E17.....58 A2
  WHTN TW2.....123 K7
Albion Sq HACK E8.....7 L3
Albion St BAY/PAD W2.....9 K5
  BERM/RHTH SE16.....111 K1
  CROY/NA CR0.....164 C7
Albion Ter CHING E4 *.....31 K3
  HACK E8.....7 L3
Albion Villas Rd SYD SE26.....150 E2
Albion Wk IS N1.....5 K6
Albion Wy IS N1.....5 K6
  LEW SE13.....133 F3
  STBT EC1A *.....12 E2
  WBLY HA9.....68 C2
Albion Yd IS N1.....5 K6
Albrighton Rd EDUL SE22.....131 F2
Albury Av BELMT SM2.....174 A7
  BXLYHN DA7.....137 F1

ISLW TW7 104 A6
Albury Cl HOR/WEW KT19 172 D7
HPTN TW12 142 A5
Albury Dr PIN HA5 33 G7
Albury Ms MNPK E12 59 G7
Albury Rd CHSGTN KT9 172 A4
Albury St DEPT SE8 112 D5
Albyfield BMLY BR1 168 E2
Albyn Rd DEPT SE8 112 D7
Alcester Crs CLPT E5 74 D1
Alcester Rd WLGTN SM6 176 B3
Alcock Cl WLGTN SM6 176 D6
Alcock Rd HEST TW5 102 C6
Alconbury Rd CLPT E5 74 C1
Alcorn Cl CHEAM SM3 174 E1
Alcott Cl HNWL W7 85 F4
Alcuin Ct STAN HA7 35 J6
Aldborough Rd DAGE RM10 80 E5
Aldborough Rd North
GNTH/NBYPK IG2 61 F4
Aldborough Rd South
GDMY/SEVK IG3 60 E7
Aldbourne Rd SHB W12 87 H7
Aldbridge St WALW SE17 19 K7
Aldburgh Ms MHST W1U 10 B4
Aldbury Av WBLY HA9 68 D6
Aldbury Ms ED N9 29 K6
Aldebert Ter VX/NE SW8 110 A6
Aldeburgh Pl WFD IG8 44 E3
Aldeburgh St GNWCH SE10 113 K4
Alden Av SRTFD E15 94 D2
Aldenham Rd BORE WD6 23 F1
BUSH WD23 21 J4
OXHEY WD19 21 H5
Aldenham St CAMTN NW1 4 F6
Alden Md PIN HA5 * 34 A6
Aldensley Rd HMSMTH W6 106 E2
Alderbrook Rd BAL SW12 129 G5
Alderbury Rd BARN SW13 106 D5
Alder Cl PECK SE15 111 G5
Alder Gv CRICK NW2 69 J1
Alderholt Wy PECK SE15 * 111 F6
Alderman Av BARK IG11 97 G2
Aldermanbury CITYW EC2V * 12 F4
Aldermanbury Sq CITYW EC2V 12 F3
Alderman Cl DART DA1 138 B6
Alderman Judge Ml
KUT/HW KT1 * 159 F1
Alderman's Hl PLMGR N13 40 E3
Alderman's Wk LVPST EC2M 13 J3
Aldermary Rd BMLY BR1 152 E7
Aldermoor Rd CAT SE6 151 H2
Alderney Av HEST TW5 103 G6
Alderney Gdns NTHLT UB5 65 K6
Alderney Ms STHWK SE1 19 G3
Alderney Rd ERITH DA8 118 D6
WCHPL E1 93 F3
Alderney St PIM SW1V 16 C6
Alder Rd MORT/ESHN SW14 126 A2
SCUP DA14 154 E2
Alders Av WFD IG8 44 C5
Aldersbrook Av EN EN1 30 A1
Aldersbrook Dr
KUTN/CMB KT2 144 B5
Aldersbrook La MNPK E12 77 K2
Aldersbrook Rd MNPK E12 77 G1
Alders Cl EA W5 104 E2
EDGW HA8 36 E4
WAN E11 77 F1
Aldersey Gdns BARK IG11 78 D5
Aldersford Cl BROCKY SE4 132 A3
Aldersgate St CITYW EC2V 12 E4
Aldersgrove E/WMO/HCT KT8 157 J4
Aldersgrove Av
ELTH/MOT SE9 153 G2
Aldershot Rd
KIL/WHAMP NW6 70 D7
Aldershot Ter
WOOL/PLUM SE18 * 115 F6
Aldersmead Av CROY/NA CR0 166 A5
Aldersmead Rd BECK BR3 151 G6
Alderson Pl NWDGN UB2 84 C7
Alderson St NKENS W10 88 C3
Alders Rd EDGW HA8 36 E4
The Alders FELT TW13 141 J4
HEST TW5 102 E5
STRHM/NOR SW16 * 148 C3
WCHMH N21 29 G5
WWKM BR4 166 E7
Alderton Cl WLSDN NW10 69 F2
Alderton Crs HDN NW4 51 K4
Alderton Rd CROY/NA CR0 165 G6
HNHL SE24 130 D2
Alderton Wy HDN NW4 51 K4
Alderville Rd FUL/PGN SW6 127 J1
Alderwick Dr HSLW TW3 123 J2
Alderwood Rd ELTH/MOT SE9 135 J5
Aldford St MYFR/PKLN W1K 10 A8
Aldgate FENCHST EC3M 13 K5
Aldgate Barrs WCHPL E1 * 13 M4
Aldgate High St TWRH EC3N 13 L5
Aldine St SHB W12 107 F1
Aldingham Gdns HCH RM12 81 J6
Aldington Cl CHDH RM6 61 J6
Aldington Rd CHARL SE7 114 C2
Aldis Ms TOOT SW17 147 J4
Aldis St TOOT SW17 147 J4
Aldred Rd KIL/WHAMP NW6 70 E4
Aldren Rd TOOT SW17 147 G2
Aldrich Crs CROY/NA CR0 180 A7
Aldriche Wy CHING E4 44 A5
Aldrich Gdns CHEAM SM3 174 D2
Aldrich Ter WAND/EARL SW18 147 G1
Aldridge Av EDGW HA8 36 D6
RSLP HA4 65 G1
STAN HA7 36 A7
Aldridge Ri NWMAL KT3 160 B6
Aldridge Road Vls NTGHL W11 88 D4
Aldridge Wk STHGT/OAK N14 28 E6
Aldrington Rd
STRHM/NOR SW16 148 C4
Aldsworth Cl MV/WKIL W9 8 C1
Aldwick Cl ELTH/MOT SE9 154 D2
Aldwick Rd CROY/NA CR0 177 F3
Aldworth Gv LEW SE13 133 F5
Aldworth Rd SRTFD E15 76 C6
Aldwych HOL/ALD WC2B 11 L5
Aldwych Av BARK/HLT IG6 60 C3
Aldwych Cl HCH RM12 81 J1
Alers Rd BXLYHS DA6 136 E4
Alesia Cl WDGN N22 40 E6
Alestan Beck Rd CAN/RD E16 95 H5
Alexander Av WLSDN NW10 69 K6
Alexander Cl BFN/LL DA15 135 K4
EBAR EN4 27 H3
HAYES BR2 167 K7
NWDGN UB2 84 C7
WHTN TW2 142 E1
Alexander Evans Ms
FSTH SE23 151 F1
Alexander Ms BAY/PAD W2 8 C4
Alexander Pl SKENS SW7 15 J5
Alexander Rd ARCH N19 72 E2
BXLYHN DA7 136 E1
CHST BR7 154 B5
Alexander Sq CHEL SW3 15 J5
Alexander St BAY/PAD W2 8 B4
Alexander Ter ABYW SE2 * 116 C4
Alexandra DEPT SE8 112 C5
Alexandra Av BTSEA SW11 * 109 F7
RYLN/HDSTN HA2 47 K7
STHL UB1 83 K6
SUT SM1 174 E2
WDGN N22 40 D7
Alexandra Cl ASHF TW15 140 B6
RYLN/HDSTN HA2 66 A2
Alexandra Cots NWCR SE14 112 C7
Alexandra Crs BMLY BR1 152 D5
Alexandra Dr BRYLDS KT5 159 H6
NRWD SE19 150 A4
Alexandra Gdns CAR SM5 176 A7
HSLW TW3 123 G1
MUSWH N10 54 B3
Alexandra Ga SKENS SW7 15 G1
Alexandra Gv FSBYPK N4 55 H7
NFNCH/WDSPK N12 39 F4
Alexandra Ms EFNCH N2 53 K2
WAT WD17 20 E1
Alexandra Palace Wy
CEND/HSY/T N8 54 C3
Alexandra Pde
RYLN/HDSTN HA2 * 66 B3
Alexandra Park Rd
MUSWH N10 54 B1
Alexandra Pl CROY/NA CR0 165 F7
SNWD SE25 164 E4
STJWD NW8 2 F3
Alexandra Rd ASHF TW15 140 B6
BTFD TW8 104 E5
CEND/HSY/T N8 55 G2
CHDH RM6 61 K5
CHSWK W4 106 A1
CROY/NA CR0 165 F7
ED N9 * 30 D6
EHAM E6 96 A2
ERITH DA8 118 C5
HDN NW4 52 B3
HSLW TW3 123 G1
KUTN/CMB KT2 144 C6
LEY E10 76 A2
MORT/ESHN SW14 126 A2
MTCM CR4 147 J6
MUSWH N10 40 B7
PEND EN3 31 F3
PGE/AN SE20 151 F5
RAIN RM13 81 H7
RCH/KEW TW9 125 G1
ROM RM1 63 H5
SEVS/STOTM N15 55 K4
STJWD NW8 2 F3
SWFD E18 59 F2
THDIT KT7 158 A4
TWK TW1 124 D5
WALTH E17 57 H5
WAT WD17 20 E1
WIM/MER SW19 146 E4
Alexandra Sq MRDN SM4 161 K4
Alexandra St CAN/RD E16 94 E4
NWCR SE14 112 B6
Alexandria Rd WEA W13 85 G6
Alexis St BERM/RHTH SE16 111 H3
Alfearn Rd CLPT E5 74 E3
Alford Gn CROY/NA CR0 180 B5
Alford Pl IS N1 * 6 F6
Alford Rd ERITH DA8 117 K4
Alfoxton Av SEVS/STOTM N15 55 H3
Alfreda St BTSEA SW11 109 G7
Alfred Cl CHSWK W4 106 A3
Alfred Gdns STHL UB1 83 J6
Alfred Ms GWRST WC1E 11 G2
Alfred Pl GWRST WC1E 11 G2
Alfred Rd ACT W3 86 E7
BAY/PAD W2 8 B2
BELV DA17 117 G4
BKHH IG9 45 H1
FELT TW13 122 B7
KUT/HW KT1 159 F2
SNWD SE25 165 H4
SRTFD E15 76 D4
SUT SM1 175 G4
Alfred's Gdns BARK IG11 96 E1
Alfred St BOW E3 93 H2
Alfred's Way (East Ham &
Barking By-Pass) BARK IG11 96 D1
Alfred Vls WALTH E17 * 58 A3
Alfreton Cl WIM/MER SW19 146 B2
Alfriston BRYLDS KT5 159 G5
Alfriston Av CROY/NA CR0 163 K6
RYLN/HDSTN HA2 48 A5
Alfriston Cl BRYLDS KT5 159 G5
DART DA1 138 B5
Alfriston Rd BTSEA SW11 128 E4
Algar Cl STAN HA7 35 F4
Algar Rd ISLW TW7 124 B2
Algarve Rd WAND/EARL SW18 128 A7
Algernon Rd HDN NW4 51 J5
KIL/WHAMP NW6 2 A4
LEW SE13 132 E2
Algiers Rd LEW SE13 132 D3
Alguin Ct STAN HA7 * 35 J5
Alibon Gdns DAGE RM10 80 C4
Alibon Rd DAGE RM10 80 C4
Alice La BOW E3 75 H7
Alice St STHWK SE1 19 J4
Alice Thompson Cl
LEE/GVPK SE12 153 G1
Alice Walker Cl HNHL SE24 * 130 C3
Alice Wy HSLW TW3 123 G3
Alicia Av KTN/HRWW/WS HA3 49 H3
Alicia Cl KTN/HRWW/WS HA3 49 J3
Alicia Gdns
KTN/HRWW/WS HA3 49 H3
Alie St WCHPL E1 13 M5
Alington Crs CDALE/KGS NW9 50 E7
Alington Gv WLGTN SM6 176 D7
Alison Cl CROY/NA CR0 166 A7
EHAM E6 96 A5
PIN HA5 47 F5
Aliwal Ms BTSEA SW11 * 128 D3
Aliwal Rd BTSEA SW11 128 D3
Alkerden Rd CHSWK W4 106 B4
Alkham Rd STNW/STAM N16 74 B1
Allan Barclay Cl
SEVS/STOTM N15 56 B5
Allan Cl NWMAL KT3 160 A4
Allandale Av FNCH N3 52 C2
Allandale Rd EMPK RM11 63 H6
Allan Wy ACT W3 86 E4
Allard Crs BUSH WD23 34 C1
Allardyce St CLAP SW4 130 A3
Allbrook Cl TEDD TW11 142 E4
Allcot Cl EBED/NFELT TW14 121 J7
Allcroft Rd KTTN NW5 72 A5
Allder Wy SAND/SEL CR2 177 H6
Allenby Av SAND/SEL CR2 177 J7
Allenby Cl GFD/PVL UB6 84 A2
Allenby Rd FSTH SE23 151 G2
STHL UB1 84 A5
WOOL/PLUM SE18 115 H2
Allen Cl MTCM CR4 148 B7
SUN TW16 141 F7
Allendale Av STHL UB1 84 A5
Allendale Cl CMBW SE5 130 E1
SYD SE26 151 F4
Allendale Rd GFD/PVL UB6 67 H5
Allen Edwards Dr VX/NE SW8 109 K7
Allen Rd BECK BR3 166 A1
BOW E3 93 H1
CROY/NA CR0 164 A6
STNW/STAM N16 74 A3
SUN TW16 141 F7
Allensbury Pl CAMTN NW1 5 H2
Allens Rd PEND EN3 30 E4
Allen St KENS W8 14 B3
Allenswood Rd ELTH/MOT SE9 134 D2
Allerford Ct HRW HA1 48 B4
Allerford Rd CAT SE6 151 K3
Allerton Rd STNW/STAM N16 73 J1
Allerton St IS N1 7 H6
Allestree Rd FUL/PGN SW6 107 H6
Alleyn Crs DUL SE21 149 K1
Alleyndale Rd BCTR RM8 79 J1
Alleyn Pk DUL SE21 149 K1
NWDGN UB2 102 E4
Alleyn Rd DUL SE21 149 K2
Allfarthing La
WAND/EARL SW18 128 B5
Allgood Cl MRDN SM4 161 G5
Allgood St BETH E2 7 M6
Allhallows La CANST EC4R 13 G7
Allhallows Rd EHAM E6 95 J5
All Hallows Rd TOTM N17 42 A7
Alliance Cl ALP/SUD HA0 67 K3
HSLWW TW4 122 E4
Alliance Rd ACT W3 86 D3
PLSTW E13 95 G3
WOOL/PLUM SE18 116 B5
Allied Wy ACT W3 * 106 B1
Allingham Cl HNWL W7 85 F6
Allington Av TOTM N17 42 A5
Allington Cl GFD/PVL UB6 66 C6
WIM/MER SW19 146 B4
Allington Rd HDN NW4 51 K4
NKENS W10 88 C2
ORP BR6 169 K7
RYLN/HDSTN HA2 48 C4
Allington St BGVA SW1W 16 D4
WESTW SW1E 16 E4
Allison Cl GNWCH SE10 113 F7
Allison Gv DUL SE21 131 F7
Allison Rd ACT W3 86 E5
CEND/HSY/T N8 55 G4
Allitsen Rd STJWD NW8 3 J6
Allnutt Wy CLAP SW4 129 J4
Alloa Rd DEPT SE8 112 A4
GDMY/SEVK IG3 79 H1
Allonby Gdns WBLY HA9 49 J7
Alloway Rd BOW E3 93 G2
Allport Ms WCHPL E1 * 92 E4
All Saints' Cl ED N9 42 B1
All Saints Dr BKHTH/KID SE3 133 J1
All Saints Ms STAN HA7 34 E5
All Saints Pas
WAND/EARL SW18 * 127 K4
All Saints Rd SUT SM1 175 F2
WIM/MER SW19 147 G6
All Saints' Rd ACT W3 105 K2
NTGHL W11 88 D4
All Saints St IS N1 5 L5
Allsop Pl CAMTN NW1 9 M1
All Souls' Av WLSDN NW10 87 K1
All Souls' Pl REGST W1B 10 D3
Allum La BORE WD6 24 A4
Allum Wy TRDG/WHET N20 27 G7
Allwood Cl SYD SE26 151 F3
Alma Av CHING E4 44 A6
Almack Rd CLPT E5 74 E3
Alma Cl MUSWH N10 * 40 B7
Alma Ct RYLN/HDSTN HA2 * 66 D1
Alma Crs SUT SM1 174 C4
Alma Gv STHWK SE1 19 M6
Alma Pl NRWD SE19 150 B6
THHTH CR7 164 B4
WLSDN NW10 87 K2
Alma Rd BFN/LL DA15 155 G2
CAR SM5 175 J4
ESH/CLAY KT10 157 K7
MUSWH N10 40 A6
PEND EN3 31 G4
STHL UB1 83 J6
WAND/EARL SW18 128 B4
Alma Rw
KTN/HRWW/WS HA3 * 34 D7
Alma Sq STJWD NW8 2 F7
Alma St KTTN NW5 72 B5
SRTFD E15 76 B5
Alma Ter BOW E3 75 H7
KENS W8 14 B4
WAND/EARL SW18 128 C6
Almeida St IS N1 6 C3
Almeric Rd BTSEA SW11 128 E3
Almer Rd RYNPK SW20 145 J6
Almington St FSBYPK N4 * 54 E7
Almond Av CAR SM5 175 K1
EA W5 105 F2
WDR/YW UB7 100 D2
Almond Cl FELT TW13 121 K7
HAYES BR2 169 F6
HYS/HAR UB3 82 C6
PECK SE15 131 H1
RSLP HA4 64 D2
Almond Gv BTFD TW8 104 C6
Almond Rd BERM/RHTH SE16 111 J3
TOTM N17 42 C6
Almonds Av BKHH IG9 44 E1
Almond Wy BORE WD6 24 D3
HAYES BR2 169 F6
MTCM CR4 163 J4
RYLN/HDSTN HA2 48 B1
Almorah Rd HEST TW5 102 C7
IS N1 7 G2
Almshouse La CHSGTN KT9 171 J7
Alnwick Gv MRDN SM4 162 A3
Alnwick Rd CAN/RD E16 95 G5
LEE/GVPK SE12 134 A6
Alnwick Ter LEE/GVPK SE12 134 A6
Alperton La ALP/SUD HA0 85 K2
Alperton St NKENS W10 88 C3
Alphabet Gdns CAR SM5 162 C5
Alpha Cl CAMTN NW1 3 K9
Alpha Est HYS/HAR UB3 * 101 H1
Alpha Gv POP/IOD E14 112 D1
Alpha Pl CHEL SW3 15 K9
KIL/WHAMP NW6 2 B5
MRDN SM4 * 161 G6
Alpha Rd BRYLDS KT5 159 G5
CHING E4 43 J2
CROY/NA CR0 165 F7
NWCR SE14 112 C7
PEND EN3 31 G3
TEDD TW11 142 D4
UED N18 42 C5
Alpha St PECK SE15 131 H1
Alphea Cl WIM/MER SW19 147 J6
Alpine Av BRYLDS KT5 172 E1
Alpine Cl CROY/NA CR0 178 A2
Alpine Copse BMLY BR1 169 F1
Alpine Gv HOM E9 74 E6
Alpine Rd BERM/RHTH SE16 111 K3
LEY E10 75 K1
Alpine Vw CAR SM5 175 J4
Alpine Wk BUSH WD23 34 E1
Alpine Wy EHAM E6 96 A4
Alric Av NWMAL KT3 160 B2
WLSDN NW10 69 F6
Alroy Rd FSBYPK N4 55 G6
Alsace Rd WALW SE17 19 J7
Alscot Rd STHWK SE1 19 M4
Alscot Wy STHWK SE1 19 L5
Alsike Rd ERITHM DA18 116 E3
Alsom Av WPK KT4 173 H3
Alston Cl SURB KT6 158 C6
Alston Rd BAR EN5 26 C2
TOOT SW17 147 H3
UED N18 42 D4
Altair Cl TOTM N17 42 B5
Altair Wy NTHWD HA6 32 D4
Altash Wy ELTH/MOT SE9 153 K1
Altenburg Av WEA W13 104 C2
Altenburg Gdns BTSEA SW11 128 E3
Alt Gv WIM/MER SW19 146 D6
Altham Ct RYLN/HDSTN HA2 * 34 B7
Altham Gdns OXHEY WD19 33 H3
Altham Rd PIN HA5 33 J6
Althea St FUL/PGN SW6 128 A1
Althorne Gdns SWFD E18 58 D3
Althorne Wy DAGE RM10 80 C1
Althorp Cl BAR EN5 25 J6
Althorpe Rd HRW HA1 * 48 C4
Althorp Rd TOOT SW17 128 E7
Altmore Av EHAM E6 77 K6
Alton Av STAN HA7 35 F6
Alton Cl BXLY DA5 137 F7
ISLW TW7 124 A1
Alton Gdns BECK BR3 151 J6
WHTN TW2 123 J5
Alton Rd CROY/NA CR0 177 G2
PUT/ROE SW15 126 D7
RCH/KEW TW9 125 F3
TOTM N17 55 K2
Alton St POP/IOD E14 93 K4
Altyre Cl BECK BR3 166 C4
Altyre Rd CROY/NA CR0 177 K1
Altyre Wy BECK BR3 166 C4
Alvanley Gdns
KIL/WHAMP NW6 71 F4
Alva Wy OXHEY WD19 33 H1
Alverstone Av EBAR EN4 27 H6
WAND/EARL SW18 146 E1
Alverstone Gdns
ELTH/MOT SE9 135 G7
Alverstone Rd CRICK NW2 70 A6
MNPK E12 78 A3
NWMAL KT3 160 C3
WBLY HA9 50 B7
Alverston Gdns SNWD SE25 165 F4
Alverton St DEPT SE8 112 C4
Alveston Av
KTN/HRWW/WS HA3 49 H2
Alveston Sq SWFD E18 * 58 E1
Alvey St WALW SE17 19 J7
Alvia Gdns SUT SM1 175 G3
Alvington Crs HACK E8 74 B4
Alway Av HOR/WEW KT19 172 E4
Alwin Pl WATW WD18 20 C4
Alwold Crs LEE/GVPK SE12 134 B5
Alwyn Av CHSWK W4 106 A4
Alwyn Cl BORE WD6 24 B5
CROY/NA CR0 179 K6
Alwyne La IS N1 6 D1
Alwyne Pl IS N1 6 E1
Alwyne Rd HNWL W7 84 E6
IS N1 6 E1
WIM/MER SW19 146 D5
Alwyne Sq IS N1 73 J5
Alwyne Vls IS N1 6 D1
Alwyn Gdns ACT W3 86 D5
HDN NW4 51 J3
Alyn Bank CEND/HSY/T N8 * 54 D5
Alyth Gdns GLDGN NW11 52 D5
Amalgamated Dr BTFD TW8 104 B5
Amanda Ms ROMW/RG RM7 62 E4
Amar Ct WOOL/PLUM SE18 116 A3
Amardeep Ct
WOOL/PLUM SE18 116 A4
Amazon St WCHPL E1 92 D5
Ambassador Cl HSLW TW3 122 D1
Ambassador Gdns EHAM E6 95 K4
Ambassador Sq POP/IOD E14 112 E3
Amber Av WALTH E17 43 G7
Amberden Av FNCH N3 52 E2
Ambergate St WALW SE17 18 C7
Amber Gv CRICK NW2 52 B7
Amberley Cl PIN HA5 47 K2
Amberley Ct SCUP DA14 155 J4
Amberley Gdns
HOR/WEW KT19 173 H3
Amberley Gv CROY/NA CR0 165 G6
SYD SE26 150 D3
Amberley Rd ABYW SE2 116 E5
EN EN1 30 B6
LEY E10 57 J6
MV/WKIL W9 8 B2
PLMGR N13 41 F1
Amberley Wy HSLWW TW4 122 B4
MRDN SM4 161 J6
ROMW/RG RM7 62 D3
Amberside Cl ISLW TW7 123 J5
Amber St SRTFD E15 * 76 B5
Amberwood Cl WLGTN SM6 176 E4
Amberwood Ri NWMAL KT3 160 B5
Amblecote Cl LEE/GVPK SE12 153 F2
Amblecote Mdw
LEE/GVPK SE12 153 F2
Amblecote Mdws
LEE/GVPK SE12 * 153 F2
Amblecote Rd LEE/GVPK SE12 153 F2
Ambler Rd FSBYPK N4 73 H2
Ambleside BMLY BR1 152 B5
Ambleside Av BECK BR3 166 B4
HCH RM12 81 K4
STRHM/NOR SW16 148 D3
WOT/HER KT12 156 B7
Ambleside Cl HOM E9 74 E4
LEY E10 57 K6
SEVS/STOTM N15 56 B2
Ambleside Crs PEND EN3 31 F2
Ambleside Dr
EBED/NFELT TW14 121 J7
Ambleside Gdns BELMT SM2 175 G5
REDBR IG4 59 J3
WBLY HA9 49 K7
Ambleside Rd BXLYHN DA7 137 H1
WLSDN NW10 69 H6
Ambrey Wy WLGTN SM6 176 D7
Ambrook Rd BELV DA17 117 H2
Ambrosden Av WEST SW1P 16 F4
Ambrose Av GLDGN NW11 52 D5
Ambrose Cl DART DA1 138 C3
Ambrose St BERM/RHTH SE16 111 J3
Ambulance Rd WAN E11 58 B4
Amelia Cl ACT W3 86 D7
Amelia St WALW SE17 18 D7
Amen Cnr STP EC4M 12 D5
TOOT SW17 148 A5
Amen Ct STP EC4M 12 D5
Amenity Wy MRDN SM4 161 F6
America Sq TWRH EC3N 13 L6
America St STHWK SE1 12 E9
Amerland Rd PUT/ROE SW15 127 J5
Amersham Av UED N18 41 K5
Amersham Gv NWCR SE14 112 C6
Amersham Rd CROY/NA CR0 164 D5
NWCR SE14 112 C7
Amersham V NWCR SE14 112 C6
Amery Gdns WLSDN NW10 69 K7
Amery Rd HRW HA1 67 G1
Amesbury Av
BRXS/STRHM SW2 148 E1
Amesbury Cl WPK KT4 161 F7
Amesbury Dr CHING E4 31 K5
Amesbury Rd BMLY BR1 168 C2
DAGW RM9 79 K6
FELT TW13 141 H1
Ames Cots POP/IOD E14 * 93 G4
Amethyst Rd SRTFD E15 76 B3
Amherst Av WEA W13 85 J5
Amherst Gdns WEA W13 * 85 J5
Amherst Rd WEA W13 85 J5
Amhurst Gdns ISLW TW7 104 A7
Amhurst Pde
STNW/STAM N16 * 56 B6
Amhurst Pk STNW/STAM N16 56 A6
Amhurst Rd STNW/STAM N16 74 B3
Amhurst Ter STNW/STAM N16 74 C3
Amias Dr EDGW HA8 36 A3
Amidas Gdns BCTR RM8 79 H3
Amiel St WCHPL E1 92 E3
Amies St BTSEA SW11 128 E2
Amina Wy BERM/RHTH SE16 111 H2
Amis Av HOR/WEW KT19 172 C5
Amity Gv RYNPK SW20 146 A7
Amity Rd SRTFD E15 76 D6
Ammanford Gn
CDALE/KGS NW9 * 51 G5
Amner Rd BTSEA SW11 129 F5
Amor Rd HMSMTH W6 107 F2
Amott Rd PECK SE15 131 H2
Ampere Wy CROY/NA CR0 163 K6
Ampleforth Rd ABYW SE2 116 C1
Amport Pl MLHL NW7 38 C5
Ampthill Est CAMTN NW1 4 E6
Ampthill Sq CAMTN NW1 4 F6
Ampton St FSBYW WC1X 5 L8
Amroth Cl FSTH SE23 131 J7
Amroth Gn CDALE/KGS NW9 * 51 G5
Amsterdam Rd POP/IOD E14 113 F2
Amwell Cl ENC/FH EN2 29 K4
Amwell St CLKNW EC1R 6 A7
Amyand Cots TWK TW1 124 C5
Amyand Park Gdns TWK TW1 124 C6
Amyand Park Rd TWK TW1 124 B6
Amy Cl WLGTN SM6 176 E6
Amyruth Rd BROCKY SE4 132 D4
Amy Warne Cl EHAM E6 95 J4
Anatola Rd ARCH N19 72 B1
Ancaster Crs NWMAL KT3 160 D5
Ancaster Ms BECK BR3 166 A2
Ancaster Rd BECK BR3 166 A2
Ancaster St WOOL/PLUM SE18 115 K6
Anchorage Cl WIM/MER SW19 146 E4
Anchor Cl BARK IG11 97 H2
Anchor Dr RAIN RM13 99 K2
Anchor & Hope La CHARL SE7 114 A2
Anchor Rd MNPK E12 77 H1
Anchor St BERM/RHTH SE16 111 J3
Anchor Ter WCHPL E1 * 92 E3
Anchor Yd FSBYE EC1V * 6 F9
Ancill Cl HMSMTH W6 107 G5
Ancona Rd WLSDN NW10 87 J1
WOOL/PLUM SE18 115 J4
Andace Park Gdns
BMLY BR1 * 153 G7
Andalus Rd BRXN/ST SW9 129 K2
Ander Cl ALP/SUD HA0 67 K3
Anderson Cl ACT W3 87 F5
CHEAM SM3 161 K7
WCHMH N21 29 F4
Anderson Dr ASHF TW15 140 A3
Anderson Rd HOM E9 75 F5
WFD IG8 59 H2
Anderson's Pl HSLW TW3 123 G3
Anderson Sq IS N1 6 C4
Anderson St CHEL SW3 15 L7
Anderson Wy BELV DA17 117 J1
Andover Av CAN/RD E16 95 H5
Andover Cl EBED/NFELT TW14 121 J7
GFD/PVL UB6 84 B3
Andover Pl KIL/WHAMP NW6 2 C6
Andover Rd HOLWY N7 73 F1
ORP BR6 169 K7
WHTN TW2 123 J7
Andover Ter HMSMTH W6 * 106 E3
Andre St HACK E8 74 C4
Andrew Borde St
LSQ/SEVD WC2H * 11 H4
Andrew Cl DART DA1 138 A4
Andrewes Gdns EHAM E6 95 J5
Andrew Pl VX/NE SW8 109 J7
Andrews Cl BKHH IG9 45 G1
HRW HA1 48 D6
WPK KT4 174 B1
Andrews Rd BETH E2 74 D7
Andrew St POP/IOD E14 94 A5
Andrews Wk WALW SE17 110 C5
Andwell Cl ABYW SE2 116 C1
Anerley Gv NRWD SE19 150 B6
Anerley Hl NRWD SE19 150 B5
Anerley Pk PGE/AN SE20 150 D5
Anerley Park Rd PGE/AN SE20 150 D6
Anerley Rd PGE/AN SE20 150 C7
Anerley Station Rd
PGE/AN SE20 150 D7
Anerley V NRWD SE19 150 B6
Anfield Cl BAL SW12 129 H6
Angela Carter Cl
BRXN/ST SW9 130 B2
Angel Alley WCHPL E1 13 M3
Angel Cl HPTN TW12 142 C4
UED N18 42 B4
Angel Corner Pde UED N18 * 42 C4
Angelfield HSLW TW3 123 G3
Angel Hl SUT SM1 175 F2
Angel Hill Dr SUT SM1 175 F2
Angelica Dr EHAM E6 96 A4

Angelica Gdns CROY/NA CR0 166 A7
Angel La HYS/HAR UB3 82 B4
SRTFD E15 76 B5
Angell Park Gdns
BRXN/ST SW9 130 B2
Angell Rd BRXN/ST SW9 130 C2
Angell Town Est
BRXN/ST SW9 * 130 B1
Angel Ms IS N1 6 B6
PUT/ROE SW15 126 D6
WCHPL E1 92 D6
Angel Pas CANST EC4R 13 G7
Angel Rd HRW HA1 48 E5
THDIT KT7 158 B7
Angel Rd (North Circular)
UED N18 42 C4
Angel Sq FSBYE EC1V * 6 C6
Angel St STBT EC1A 12 E4
Angel Wk HMSMTH W6 107 F3
Angel Wy ROM RM1 63 G4
Angerstein La BKHTH/KID SE3 113 J6
Anglers La KTTN NW5 72 B5
Anglers Reach SURB KT6 * 158 E4
Anglesea Ms
WOOL/PLUM SE18 115 G3
Anglesea Rd KUT/HW KT1 158 E3
WOOL/PLUM SE18 115 G3
Anglesey Court Rd CAR SM5 176 A5
Anglesey Dr RAIN RM13 99 J3
Anglesey Gdns CAR SM5 176 A5
Anglesey Rd OXHEY WD19 33 G4
PEND EN3 30 D3
Anglesmede Crs PIN HA5 48 A2
Anglesmede Wy PIN HA5 47 K2
Angles Rd STRHM/NOR SW16 148 E3
Anglia Cl TOTM N17 42 D6
Anglian Cl WATN WD24 21 G1
Anglian Rd WAN E11 76 B2
Anglo Rd BOW E3 93 H1
Angus Cl CHSGTN KT9 172 C4
Angus Dr RSLP HA4 65 G3
Angus Gdns CDALE/KGS NW9 37 F7
Angus Rd PLSTW E13 95 G2
Angus St NWCR SE14 112 B6
Anhalt Rd BTSEA SW11 108 D6
Ankerdine Crs
WOOL/PLUM SE18 115 G7
Anlaby Rd TEDD TW11 142 E4
Anley Rd HMSMTH W6 107 G1
Anmersh Gv STAN HA7 35 K7
Annabel Cl POP/IOD E14 93 K5
Anna Cl HACK E8 7 M3
Annandale Gv HGDN/ICK UB10 64 A2
Annandale Rd BFN/LL DA15 135 K6
CHSWK W4 106 B3
CROY/NA CR0 178 C1
GNWCH SE10 113 J4
Anna Neagle Cl FSTGT E7 76 E3
Anne Boleyn's Wk
CHEAM SM3 174 B6
KUTN/CMB KT2 144 A4
Anne Case Ms NWMAL KT3 * 160 A2
Anne Compton Ms
LEE/GVPK SE12 133 J6
Anne of Cleves Rd DART DA1 139 G4
Annesley Av CDALE/KGS NW9 51 F2
Annesley Cl WLSDN NW10 69 G2
Annesley Dr CROY/NA CR0 179 H2
Annesley Rd BKHTH/KID SE3 114 A7
Annesmere Gdns
BKHTH/KID SE3 134 C2
Anne St PLSTW E13 94 E3
Annette Cl
KTN/HRWW/WS HA3 48 E1
Annette Rd HOLWY N7 73 F3
Annie Besant Cl BOW E3 * 75 H7
Anning St WCHPL E1 7 K9
Annington Rd EFNCH N2 53 K2
Annis Rd HOM E9 75 G5
Ann La WBPTN SW10 108 C6
Ann Moss Wy
BERM/RHTH SE16 111 K2
Ann's Cl KTBR SW1X 15 M2
Ann St WOOL/PLUM SE18 115 J3
Annsworthy Av THHTH CR7 164 E2
Annsworthy Crs SNWD SE25 164 E2
Ansar Gdns WALTH E17 57 G4
Ansdell Rd PECK SE15 131 K1
Ansdell St KENS W8 14 D3
Ansdell Ter KENS W8 14 D3
Ansell Gv CAR SM5 162 E7
Ansell Rd TOOT SW17 147 J2
Anselm Cl CROY/NA CR0 178 B2
Anselm Rd FUL/PGN SW6 107 K5
PIN HA5 33 K6
Ansford Rd BMLY BR1 152 A4
Ansleigh Pl NTGHL W11 88 B6
Anson Cl ROMW/RG RM7 62 D1
Anson Rd ARCH N19 72 C3
CRICK NW2 69 K4
Anson Wk NTHWD HA6 32 A3
Anstead Dr RAIN RM13 99 J1
Anstey Rd PECK SE15 131 H2
Anstice Cl CHSWK W4 106 B6
Anstridge Rd ELTH/MOT SE9 135 J5
Antelope Rd
WOOL/PLUM SE18 114 E2
Anthony Cl MLHL NW7 37 G3
OXHEY WD19 21 H7
Anthony Rd BORE WD6 24 A1
GFD/PVL UB6 84 E1
SNWD SE25 165 H5
WELL DA16 116 B7
Anthony's Cl WAP E1W 92 C7
Anthony St WCHPL E1 92 D5
Anthus Ms NTHWD HA6 32 B6
Antill Rd BOW E3 93 G2
SEVS/STOTM N15 56 C3
Antill Ter WCHPL E1 93 F5
Antlers Hl CHING E4 31 K4
Anton Crs SUT SM1 174 E2
Antoneys Cl PIN HA5 47 H1
Anton Pl WBLY HA9 68 D2
Anton St HACK E8 74 C4
Antrim Rd HAMP NW3 71 K5
Antrobus Cl SUT SM1 174 D4
Antrobus Rd CHSWK W4 105 K3
Anvil Cl STRHM/NOR SW16 148 C6
Anworth Cl WFD IG8 45 F5
Aostle Wy THHTH CR7 164 C1
Apeldoorn Dr WLGTN SM6 176 E7
Aperfield Rd ERITH DA8 118 C5
Apex Cl BECK BR3 151 K7
Apex Pde MLHL NW7 * 37 F3
Aplin Wy ISLW TW7 103 K7
Apollo Av BMLY BR1 153 F7
NTHWD HA6 32 E4
Apollo Cl HCH RM12 81 K1
Apollo Pl WAN E11 76 C2
WBPTN SW10 * 108 C6
Apollo Wy ERITH DA8 118 A3
THMD SE28 115 J2
Apothecary St BLKFR EC4V * 12 C5
Appach Rd BRXS/STRHM SW2 130 B4
Apple Blossom Ct
VX/NE SW8 * 109 J6
Appleby Cl CHING E4 44 A5
SEVS/STOTM N15 55 K4
STMC/STPC BR5 169 K6
UX/CGN UB8 82 A5
WHTN TW2 142 D1
Appleby Gdns
EBED/NFELT TW14 * 121 J7
Appleby Rd CAN/RD E16 94 E5
HACK E8 74 C6
Appleby St BETH E2 7 L5
Appledore Av BXLYHN DA7 117 K7
RSLP HA4 65 F2
Appledore Cl EDGW HA8 36 C7
HAYES BR2 167 J4
TOOT SW17 147 K1
Appledore Crs SCUP DA14 154 E2
Appledore Wy MLHL NW7 38 B6
Appleford Rd NKENS W10 88 C3
Apple Garth BTFD TW8 104 E3
Applegarth CROY/NA CR0 179 K6
ESH/CLAY KT10 171 F4
Applegarth Dr
GNTH/NBYPK IG2 61 F3
Applegarth Rd THMD SE28 97 H7
WKENS W14 * 107 G2
Apple Gv CHSGTN KT9 172 A3
EN EN1 30 A2
RYLN/HDSTN HA2 47 K7
Apple Ldg ALP/SUD HA0 * 67 J2
Apple Market KUT/HW KT1 158 E1
Apple Rd WAN E11 76 C2
Appleton Cl BXLYHN DA7 137 J1
Appleton Gdns NWMAL KT3 160 D5
Appleton Rd ELTH/MOT SE9 134 D2
Appletree Cl PGE/AN SE20 150 D7
Appletree Gdns EBAR EN4 27 J3
Apple Tree Yd STJS SW1Y 10 F8
Applewood Cl CRICK NW2 69 K2
TRDG/WHET N20 27 J7
Applewood Dr PLSTW E13 95 F3
Appold St ERITH DA8 118 C5
SDTCH EC2A 13 J2
Apprentice Gdns NTHLT UB5 83 K2
Apprentice Wy CLPT E5 74 D3
Approach La MLHL NW7 38 C4
Approach Rd ASHF TW15 140 A5
BETH E2 92 E1
E/WMO/HCT KT8 157 F4
EBAR EN4 27 G3
RYNPK SW20 161 F1
The Approach ACT W3 87 F5
EN EN1 30 D1
HDN NW4 52 B4
Aprey Gdns HDN NW4 52 A3
April Cl FELT TW13 140 E2
HNWL W7 84 E6
April Gln FSTH SE23 151 F2
April St HACK E8 74 B3
Apsley Cl HRW HA1 48 C4
Apsley Rd NWMAL KT3 159 K2
SNWD SE25 165 J3
Apsley Wy CRICK NW2 69 J1
MYFR/PICC W1J * 10 C9
Aquarius TWK TW1 * 124 C7
Aquarius Wy NTHWD HA6 32 E4
Aquila St STJWD NW8 3 H5
Aquinas St STHWK SE1 12 B9
Arabella Dr PUT/ROE SW15 126 B3
Arabin Rd BROCKY SE4 132 B3
Aragon Av EW KT17 173 K7
THDIT KT7 158 A4
Aragon Cl HAYES BR2 168 E7
SUN TW16 140 D6
Aragon Dr RSLP HA4 47 H7
Aragon Pl MRDN SM4 161 G6
Aragon Rd KUTN/CMB KT2 144 A4
MRDN SM4 161 G6
Arandora Crs CHDH RM6 61 H6
Arbery Rd BOW E3 93 G2
Arbor Cl BECK BR3 166 E1
Arborfield Cl
BRXS/STRHM SW2 130 A7
Arbor Rd CHING E4 44 B2
Arbour Rd PEND EN3 31 F3
Arbour Sq WCHPL E1 93 F5
Arbour Wy HCH RM12 81 K4
Arbroath Gn OXHEY WD19 32 E2
Arbroath Rd ELTH/MOT SE9 134 D2
Arbrook La ESH/CLAY KT10 170 D5
Arbuthnot La BXLY DA5 137 F5
Arbuthnot Rd NWCR SE14 132 A1
Arbutus St HACK E8 7 K3
Arcade Chambers
ELTH/MOT SE9 * 135 F5
Arcade Pde CHSGTN KT9 * 172 A3
The Arcade ELTH/MOT SE9 * 135 F5
LVPST EC2M * 13 J3
WALTH E17 * 57 J3
Arcadia Av FNCH N3 38 E7
Arcadia Cl CAR SM5 176 A3
Arcadian Av BXLY DA5 137 F5
Arcadian Cl BXLY DA5 137 F5
Arcadian Gdns WDGN N22 41 G6
Arcadian Pl WAND/EARL SW18 127 H6
Arcadian Rd BXLY DA5 137 F6
Arcadia St POP/IOD E14 93 J5
Archangel St
BERM/RHTH SE16 112 A1
Archbishop's Pl
BRXS/STRHM SW2 130 A5
Archdale Pl NWMAL KT3 159 J2
Archdale Rd EDUL SE22 131 G4
Archel Rd WKENS W14 107 J5
Archer Cl BAR EN5 26 D5
KUTN/CMB KT2 144 A6
Archer Ct FELT TW13 121 K7
Archer Ms HPTN TW12 142 C5
Archer Rd SNWD SE25 165 J3
Archers Dr PEND EN3 30 E1
Archer Sq NWCR SE14 112 B5
Archer St SOHO/SHAV W1D 11 G6
Archery Cl BAY/PAD W2 9 K5
KTN/HRWW/WS HA3 49 F2
Archery Rd ELTH/MOT SE9 134 E4
The Arches CHCR WC2N * 11 K8
RYLN/HDSTN HA2 66 B1
Archibald Rd HOLWY N7 72 D3
Archibald St BOW E3 93 J2
Archie Cl WDR/YW UB7 100 D1
Arch St STHWK SE1 18 E4
Archway Cl ARCH N19 * 72 C1
NKENS W10 88 B4
WIM/MER SW19 147 F3
WLGTN SM6 * 176 E2
Archway Rd ARCH N19 54 C7
HGT N6 53 K4
Archway St BARN SW13 126 B2
Arcola St HACK E8 74 B4
Arcon Dr NTHLT UB5 83 J3
Arctic St KTTN NW5 72 B4
Arcus Rd BMLY BR1 152 C5
Ardbeg Rd HNHL SE24 130 E5
Arden Cl BUSH WD23 23 F6
HRW HA1 66 D2
THMD SE28 97 K5
WHTN TW2 122 E6
Arden Court Gdns EFNCH N2 53 H5
Arden Crs DAGW RM9 79 K6
POP/IOD E14 112 D3
Arden Est IS N1 7 J6
Arden Mhor PIN HA5 47 F3
Arden Rd FNCH N3 52 C2
WEA W13 85 J6
Ardent Cl SNWD SE25 165 F2
Ardfern Av STRHM/NOR SW16 164 B2
Ardfillan Rd CAT SE6 133 G7
Ardgowan Rd CAT SE6 133 H6
Ardilaun Rd HBRY N5 73 J3
Ardingly Cl CROY/NA CR0 179 F2
Ardleigh Gdns CHEAM SM3 161 K7
Ardleigh Rd IS N1 74 A5
WALTH E17 43 H7
Ardleigh Ter WALTH E17 43 H7
Ardley Cl CAT SE6 151 G2
WLSDN NW10 69 G2
Ardlui Rd WNWD SE27 149 J1
Ardmay Gdns SURB KT6 * 159 F4
Ardmere Rd LEW SE13 133 G5
Ardoch Rd CAT SE6 152 B1
Ardra Rd ED N9 43 F2
Ardrossan Gdns WPK KT4 173 J2
Ardross Av NTHWD HA6 32 C4
Ardshiel Cl PUT/ROE SW15 127 G2
Ardwell Av BARK/HLT IG6 60 C4
Ardwell Rd BRXS/STRHM SW2 148 E1
Ardwick Rd CRICK NW2 70 E3
Arena Est FSBYPK N4 * 55 H5
Argall Av LEY E10 57 F6
Argall Wy LEY E10 57 F7
Argenta Wy WLSDN NW10 68 D6
Argent Ct SURB KT6 * 172 C1
SURB KT6 172 C2
Argon Ms FUL/PGN SW6 107 K6
Argon Rd UED N18 42 E4
Argosy La STWL/WRAY TW19 120 A6
Argus Wy NTHLT UB5 83 J2
Argyle Av HSLW TW3 123 F5
Argyle Cl WEA W13 85 G3
Argyle Cnr WEA W13 * 85 H6
Argyle Ct WATW WD18 * 20 D3
Argyle Pl HMSMTH W6 106 E3
Argyle Rd BAR EN5 26 A3
CAN/RD E16 95 F5
GFD/PVL UB6 85 F2
HSLW TW3 123 G4
IL IG1 78 A1
NFNCH/WDSPK N12 38 E4
RYLN/HDSTN HA2 48 B5
SRTFD E15 76 C3
TOTM N17 42 C7
UED N18 42 C3
WCHPL E1 93 F3
WEA W13 85 G5
Argyle Sq STPAN WC1H 5 K7
Argyle St KCROSS N1C 5 J7
STPAN WC1H 5 K8
Argyle Wk STPAN WC1H * 5 J8
Argyle Wy BERM/RHTH SE16 111 H4
Argyll Av STHL UB1 84 B7
Argyll Cl BRXN/ST SW9 130 A2
Argyll Gdns EDGW HA8 50 D1
Argyll Rd KENS W8 14 A2
WOOL/PLUM SE18 115 H2
Argyll St SOHO/SHAV W1D 10 E5
Arhchie St STHWK SE1 19 K2
Arica Rd BROCKY SE4 132 B3
Ariel Rd KIL/WHAMP NW6 70 E5
Ariel Wy HSLWW TW4 122 A2
SHB W12 88 A7
Aristotle Rd CLAP SW4 129 J2
Arkell Gv NRWD SE19 149 H6
Arkindale Rd CAT SE6 152 A2
Arkley Crs WALTH E17 57 H4
Arkley Dr BAR EN5 25 J3
Arkley La BAR EN5 25 J2
Arkley Rd WALTH E17 57 H4
Arkley Vw BAR EN5 25 K3
Arklow Rd NWCR SE14 112 C5
Arkwright Rd HAMP NW3 71 G4
Arlesford Rd BRXN/ST SW9 129 K2
Arlingford Rd
BRXS/STRHM SW2 130 B5
Arlington NFNCH/WDSPK N12 38 E2
Arlington Av IS N1 6 F4
Arlington Cl BFN/LL DA15 135 K6
LEW SE13 133 G4
SUT SM1 174 E1
TWK TW1 * 124 D5
Arlington Ct HYS/HAR UB3 101 G4
Arlington Dr CAR SM5 175 K1
RSLP HA4 46 B5
Arlington Gdns CHSWK W4 105 K4
IL IG1 59 K6
Arlington Pde
BRXS/STRHM SW2 * 130 A3
Arlington Rd CAMTN NW1 4 C3
RCHPK/HAM TW10 143 K1
STHGT/OAK N14 40 B1
SURB KT6 158 E5
TEDD TW11 143 F3
TWK TW1 124 D5
WEA W13 85 H5
WFD IG8 44 E7
Arlington Sq IS N1 6 F4
Arlington St MYFR/PICC W1J 10 E8
Arlington Wy CLKNW EC1R 6 B7
Arliss Wy NTHLT UB5 65 G7
Arlow Rd WCHMH N21 29 G7
Armadale Cl TOTM N17 56 D3
Armadale Rd
EBED/NFELT TW14 121 K4
FUL/PGN SW6 107 K6
Armada St DEPT SE8 112 D5
Armada Wy CAN/RD E16 96 B6
Armagh Rd BOW E3 75 H7
Armfield Cl E/WMO/HCT KT8 156 E4
Armfield Crs MTCM CR4 162 E1
Arminger Rd SHB W12 87 K7
Armistice Gdns SNWD SE25 165 H2
Armitage Rd GLDGN NW11 52 C7
GNWCH SE10 113 J3
Armour Cl HOLWY N7 73 F5
Armoury Rd DEPT SE8 132 E1
Armoury Wy
WAND/EARL SW18 127 K4
Armstead Wk DAGE RM10 80 C6
Armstrong Av WFD IG8 44 C5
Armstrong Cl BCTR RM8 61 K6
BMLY BR1 168 D2
BORE WD6 24 E2
EHAM E6 95 K5
RSLP HA4 46 E5
Armstrong Crs EBAR EN4 27 H2
Armstrong Rd ACT W3 87 H7
FELT TW13 141 J4
WLSDN NW10 69 G6
WOOL/PLUM SE18 115 H2
Armstrong Wy NWDGN UB2 103 G1
Armytage Rd HEST TW5 102 C6
Arnal Crs WAND/EARL SW18 127 H6
Arncliffe Cl FBAR/BDGN N11 40 A5
Arne St LSQ/SEVD WC2H 11 K5
Arnett Sq CHING E4 43 H5
Arne Wk LEW SE13 133 J3
Arneways Av CHDH RM6 61 K3
Arneway St WEST SW1P 17 H4
Arnewood Cl PUT/ROE SW15 126 D7
Arney's La MTCM CR4 163 F5
Arngask Rd CAT SE6 133 G6
Arnheim Pl POP/IOD E14 112 D2
Arnison Rd E/WMO/HCT KT8 157 J3
Arnold Circ BETH E2 7 L8
Arnold Cl KTN/HRWW/WS HA3 50 B6
Arnold Crs ISLW TW7 123 J4
Arnold Dr CHSGTN KT9 171 K5
Arnold Est STHWK SE1 19 M2
Arnold Gdns PLMGR N13 41 H4
Arnold Rd BOW E3 93 J2
DAGW RM9 80 B6
NTHLT UB5 65 J5
SEVS/STOTM N15 56 B2
TOOT SW17 147 K6
Arnold Ter STAN HA7 * 35 F4
Arnos Gv STHGT/OAK N14 40 D3
Arnos Rd FBAR/BDGN N11 40 C4
Arnott Cl CHSWK W4 106 A3
THMD SE28 97 J7
Arnould Av CMBW SE5 130 E3
Arnsberg Wy BXLYHN DA7 137 H3
Arnside Gdns WBLY HA9 49 K7
Arnside Rd BXLYHN DA7 117 H7
Arnside St WALW SE17 18 F9
Arnulf St CAT SE6 151 K3
Arnull's Rd STRHM/NOR SW16 149 H5
Arodene Rd
BRXS/STRHM SW2 130 A5
Arosa Rd TWK TW1 124 E5
Arragon Gdns
STRHM/NOR SW16 148 E6
WWKM BR4 179 K2
Arragon Rd EHAM E6 77 H7
TWK TW1 124 B6
WAND/EARL SW18 127 K7
Arran Cl ERITH DA8 118 A5
WLGTN SM6 176 C3
Arran Dr MNPK E12 59 H7
STAN HA7 35 J3
Arran Gn OXHEY WD19 * 33 H3
Arran Ms EA W5 86 B7
Arranmore Ct BUSH WD23 * 21 J3
Arran Rd CAT SE6 151 K1
Arran Wk IS N1 6 E1
Arran Wy ESH/CLAY KT10 170 B1
Arras Av MRDN SM4 162 B4
Arrol Rd BECK BR3 165 K2
Arrow Rd BOW E3 93 K2
Arsenal Rd ELTH/MOT SE9 134 E1
Arsenal Wy CAN/RD E16 115 F1
Artemis Pl WAND/EARL SW18 127 J6
Arterberry Rd RYNPK SW20 146 A6
Arterial Rd Purfleet
SOCK/AV RM15 119 K2
Artesian Cl ROM RM1 63 H5
WLSDN NW10 69 F6
Artesian Gv BAR EN5 27 G3
Artesian Houses
BAY/PAD W2 * 8 A5
Artesian Rd BAY/PAD W2 8 A5
Arthingworth St SRTFD E15 76 C7
Arthurdon Rd BROCKY SE4 132 D4
Arthur Gv WOOL/PLUM SE18 115 H3
Arthur Rd CHDH RM6 61 J6
ED N9 42 B1
EHAM E6 95 K1
HOLWY N7 73 F3
KUTN/CMB KT2 144 C6
NWMAL KT3 160 E4
WIM/MER SW19 146 E2
Arthur St BUSH WD23 21 H2
CANST EC4R 13 H7
ERITH DA8 118 C6
Artichoke Hl WAP E1W 92 D6
Artichoke Pl CMBW SE5 * 110 E7
Artillery Cl GNTH/NBYPK IG2 60 C5
Artillery La LVPST EC2M 13 K3
SHB W12 87 J5
Artillery Pas WCHPL E1 * 13 K3
Artillery Pl WOOL/PLUM SE18 114 E4
Artillery Rw WEST SW1P 17 G4
Artisan Cl EHAM E6 96 B6
Artizan St WCHPL E1 13 K4
Artwell Cl LEY E10 57 K5
Arundel Av MRDN SM4 161 J3
Arundel Cl BTSEA SW11 128 D4
BXLY DA5 137 G5
CROY/NA CR0 * 177 H2
HPTN TW12 142 B4
SRTFD E15 76 C3
Arundel Dr BORE WD6 24 E3
RYLN/HDSTN HA2 65 K3
WFD IG8 44 E6
Arundel Gdns EDGW HA8 37 F6
GDMY/SEVK IG3 79 G1
NTGHL W11 88 D6
WCHMH N21 29 G7
Arundel Gv IS N1 74 A4
Arundel Pl HOLWY N7 73 G5
Arundel Rd BELMT SM2 174 D6
CROY/NA CR0 164 E5
DART DA1 139 F3
EBAR EN4 27 J2
HSLWW TW4 122 B2
KUT/HW KT1 159 J1
Arundel Sq HOLWY N7 73 G5
Arundel St TPL/STR WC2R 11 M6
Arundel Ter BARN SW13 106 E5
Arungford Ms
BRXS/STRHM SW2 130 B4
Arvon Rd HBRY N5 73 G4
Asbaston Ter IL IG1 78 C4
Ascham Dr CHING E4 43 K6
Ascham End WALTH E17 43 G7
Ascham St KTTN NW5 72 C4
Aschurch Rd CROY/NA CR0 165 G6
Ascot Cl BORE WD6 24 C4
NTHLT UB5 66 A4
Ascot Gdns STHL UB1 83 K4
Ascot Ms WLGTN SM6 176 C7
Ascot Pde CLAP SW4 * 129 K3
Ascot Rd EBED/NFELT TW14 120 D7
EHAM E6 95 K2
SEVS/STOTM N15 55 K4
TOOT SW17 148 A5
UED N18 42 C3
WATW WD18 20 C4
Ascott Av EA W5 105 F1
Ascott Ct PIN HA5 * 46 E3
Ashanti Ms HACK E8 * 74 D5
Ashborurne Sq NTHWD HA6 32 C5
Ashbourne Av BXLYHN DA7 117 F6
GLDGN NW11 52 D4
RYLN/HDSTN HA2 * 66 D1
SWFD E18 59 F3
TRDG/WHET N20 39 K1
Ashbourne Cl EA W5 86 B4
NFNCH/WDSPK N12 39 F3
Ashbourne Gv CHSWK W4 106 B4
EDUL SE22 131 G4
MLHL NW7 37 F4
Ashbourne Pde EA W5 * 86 B3
GLDGN NW11 * 52 D3
Ashbourne Rd EA W5 86 B3
MTCM CR4 148 A5
Ashbourne Ter
WIM/MER SW19 146 E6
Ashbourne Wy GLDGN NW11 52 D4
Ashbridge Rd WAN E11 58 C6
Ashbridge St STJWD NW8 9 J1
Ashbrook EDGW HA8 * 36 B5
Ashbrook Rd ARCH N19 72 D1
DAGE RM10 80 D2
Ashburn Gdns SKENS SW7 14 E5
Ashburnham Av HRW HA1 49 F6
Ashburnham Cl EFNCH N2 53 H2
OXHEY WD19 * 32 E2
Ashburnham Dr OXHEY WD19 32 E2
Ashburnham Gdns HRW HA1 49 F5
Ashburnham Gv GNWCH SE10 112 E6
Ashburnham Pk
ESH/CLAY KT10 170 C3
Ashburnham Pl GNWCH SE10 112 E6
Ashburnham Retreat
GNWCH SE10 112 E6
Ashburnham Rd BELV DA17 117 K3
RCHPK/HAM TW10 143 H2
WBPTN SW10 * 108 B6
WLSDN NW10 88 A2
Ashburn Pl SKENS SW7 14 E5
Ashburton Av CROY/NA CR0 165 J7
GDMY/SEVK IG3 79 F3
Ashburton Cl CROY/NA CR0 165 H7
Ashburton Gdns
CROY/NA CR0 178 C1
Ashburton Rd CAN/RD E16 94 E5
CROY/NA CR0 178 C1
RSLP HA4 64 E1
Ashbury Gdns CHDH RM6 61 K4
Ashbury Pl WIM/MER SW19 147 G5
Ashbury Rd BTSEA SW11 128 E2
Ashby Av CHSGTN KT9 172 C5
Ashby Cl WWKM BR4 180 B2
Ashby Gv IS N1 6 F1
Ashby Ms BROCKY SE4 132 C2
Ashby Rd BROCKY SE4 132 C1
SEVS/STOTM N15 56 C4
Ashby St FSBYE EC1V 6 D8
Ashby Wk CROY/NA CR0 164 D5
Ashby Wy WDR/YW UB7 100 D6
Ashchurch Gv SHB W12 106 D1
Ashchurch Park Vls SHB W12 106 D2
Ashchurch Ter SHB W12 106 C2
Ash Cl CAR SM5 175 K1
EDGW HA8 36 E3
NWMAL KT3 160 A1
PGE/AN SE20 165 K1
SCUP DA14 155 H2
STAN HA7 35 G5
STMC/STPC BR5 169 J4
Ashcombe Av SURB KT6 158 E6
Ashcombe Gdns EDGW HA8 36 C3
Ashcombe Pk CRICK NW2 69 G2
Ashcombe Rd CAR SM5 176 A5
WIM/MER SW19 146 E4
Ashcombe Sq NWMAL KT3 159 K2
Ashcombe St FUL/PGN SW6 * 128 A1
Ash Ct HOR/WEW KT19 172 E3
Ashcroft PIN HA5 34 A5
Ashcroft Av BFN/LL DA15 136 B5
Ashcroft Crs BFN/LL DA15 136 B5
Ashcroft Rd BOW E3 93 G2
CHSGTN KT9 172 B2
Ashdale Cl WHTN TW2 123 G6
Ashdale Gv STAN HA7 35 F5
Ashdale Rd LEE/GVPK SE12 134 A7
Ashdene PIN HA5 47 G2
Ashdene Cl ASHF TW15 * 140 A6
Ashdon Cl WFD IG8 45 F5
Ashdon Rd BUSH WD23 21 H2
Ashdown WEA W13 * 85 H4
Ashdown Cl BECK BR3 166 E1
BXLY DA5 137 K6
Ashdown Crs KTTN NW5 * 72 A4
Ashdown Dr BORE WD6 24 B1
Ashdown Pl THDIT KT7 158 B5
Ashdown Rd KUT/HW KT1 159 F1
PEND EN3 30 E2
WLSDN NW10 69 G7
Ashdown Wy TOOT SW17 148 A1
Ashen EHAM E6 96 A5
Ashenden Rd CLPT E5 75 G4
Ashen Dr DART DA1 138 D5
Ashen Gv WIM/MER SW19 146 E2
Ashen V SAND/SEL CR2 179 F7
Asher Loftus Wy
FBAR/BDGN N11 39 K5
Asher Wy WAP E1W 92 C7
Ashfield Av BUSH WD23 22 B5
FELT TW13 122 A7
Ashfield Cl BECK BR3 151 J6
RCHPK/HAM TW10 125 F7
Ashfield Ct EA W5 * 86 A6
Ashfield La CHST BR7 154 C5
Ashfield Rd ACT W3 87 H7
FSBYPK N4 55 J5
STHGT/OAK N14 40 C2
Ashfield St WCHPL E1 92 D4
Ashfield Yd WCHPL E1 * 92 E4
Ashford Av CEND/HSY/T N8 54 E3
YEAD UB4 83 H5
Ashford Cl WALTH E17 57 H5
Ashford Crs PEND EN3 30 E1
Ashford Gn OXHEY WD19 33 H4
Ashford Ms TOTM N17 42 C7
Ashford Rd ASHF TW15 140 A6
CRICK NW2 70 B3
EHAM E6 77 K5
FELT TW13 140 B3
SWFD E18 59 F1
Ashford St IS N1 7 J7
Ash Gv ALP/SUD HA0 67 G3
CRICK NW2 70 B3
EA W5 105 F1
EBED/NFELT TW14 121 H7
EN EN1 30 A6
HACK E8 74 D7
HEST TW5 102 C7
HYS/HAR UB3 82 B6
MUSWH N10 54 B3

PGE/AN SE20 165 K1
PLMGR N13 41 J2
STHL UB1 84 A4
WWKM BR4 167 F7
Ashgrove Rd ASHF TW15 140 A4
BMLY BR1 152 B5
GDMY/SEVK IG3 61 F7
Ash Hill Cl BUSH WD23 22 B7
Ash Hill Dr PIN HA5 47 G2
Ashingdon Cl CHING E4 44 A3
Ashington Rd FUL/PGN SW6 * 127 J1
Ashlake Rd STRHM/NOR SW16 148 E3
Ashland Pl MHST W1U 10 A2
Ashlar Pl WOOL/PLUM SE18 115 G3
Ashleigh Gdns SUT SM1 175 F1
Ashleigh Rd
MORT/ESHN SW14 126 B2
PGE/AN SE20 165 J2
Ashley Av BARK/HLT IG6 60 B1
MRDN SM4 161 K4
Ashley Cl HDN NW4 52 A1
PIN HA5 47 F1
Ashley Crs BTSEA SW11 129 F2
WDGN N22 55 G1
Ashley Dr BORE WD6 24 E4
ISLW TW7 103 K5
WHTN TW2 123 G7
Ashley Gdns PLMGR N13 41 J3
RCHPK/HAM TW10 143 K2
WBLY HA9 68 A1
Ashley La CROY/NA CR0 177 H3
HDN NW4 52 A1
Ashley Pl WESTW SW1E 16 E4
Ashley Rd ARCH N19 54 E7
CHING E4 43 J4
FSTGT E7 77 G6
HPTN TW12 142 A7
PEND EN3 30 E1
RCH/KEW TW9 125 F2
THDIT KT7 158 A5
THHTH CR7 164 A3
TOTM N17 56 C2
WIM/MER SW19 147 F5
Ashleys Aly SEVS/STOTM N15 55 J3
Ashley Wk MLHL NW7 38 A6
Ashling Rd CROY/NA CR0 165 H7
Ashlin Rd SRTFD E15 76 B3
Ashlone Rd PUT/ROE SW15 127 G1
Ashlyn Cl BUSH WD23 21 J3
Ashlyns Wy CHSGTN KT9 171 K5
Ashmead STHGT/OAK N14 28 C4
Ashmead Ga BMLY BR1 153 G7
Ashmead Ms BROCKY SE4 132 D1
Ashmead Rd DEPT SE8 132 D1
EBED/NFELT TW14 121 K7
Ashmere Av BECK BR3 167 G1
Ashmere Cl CHEAM SM3 174 B4
Ashmere Gv
BRXS/STRHM SW2 129 K3
Ash Ms KTTN NW5 * 72 C4
Ashmill St STJWD NW8 9 J2
Ashmole St VX/NE SW8 110 A5
Ashmore Cl PECK SE15 111 G6
Ashmore Gv WELL DA16 135 J2
Ashmore Rd MV/WKIL W9 88 D2
Ashmount Rd
SEVS/STOTM N15 56 B4
Ashmount Ter EA W5 * 104 E3
Ashmour Gdns ROM RM1 63 F1
Ashneal Gdns HRW HA1 66 D2
Ashness Gdns GFD/PVL UB6 67 H5
Ashness Rd BTSEA SW11 128 E4
Ashridge Cl
KTN/HRWW/WS HA3 49 J5
Ashridge Crs
WOOL/PLUM SE18 115 H6
Ashridge Dr OXHEY WD19 33 G4
Ashridge Gdns PIN HA5 47 J3
PLMGR N13 40 E4
Ashridge Wy MRDN SM4 161 J3
SUN TW16 140 E5
Ash Rd CHEAM SM3 161 H7
CROY/NA CR0 179 J1
DART DA1 139 G7
SRTFD E15 76 C4
Ash Rw HAYES BR2 169 F5
Ashtead Rd STNW/STAM N16 56 C6
Ashton Cl SUT SM1 174 E3
Ashton Gdns CHDH RM6 62 A5
HSLWW TW4 122 E3
Ashton Rd SRTFD E15 76 B4
Ashton St POP/IOD E14 94 A6
Ashtree Av MTCM CR4 162 C1
Ash Tree Cl CROY/NA CR0 166 B5
SURB KT6 159 F7
Ash Tree Dell CDALE/KGS NW9 50 E4
Ash Tree Wy CROY/NA CR0 166 B4
Ashurst Cl DART DA1 138 C2
NTHWD HA6 32 C6
PGE/AN SE20 150 D7
Ashurst Dr GNTH/NBYPK IG2 60 B5
Ashurst Gdns
BRXS/STRHM SW2 * 130 B7
Ashurst Rd EBAR EN4 27 K4
NFNCH/WDSPK N12 39 J4
Ashurst Wk CROY/NA CR0 178 D1
Ashvale Rd TOOT SW17 147 K4
Ashville Rd WAN E11 76 B1
Ash Wk ALP/SUD HA0 67 J3
Ashwater Rd LEE/GVPK SE12 133 K7
Ashwell Cl EHAM E6 95 K5
Ashwin St HACK E8 74 B5
Ashwood Av RAIN RM13 99 K2
Ashwood Gdns CROY/NA CR0 179 K5
HYS/HAR UB3 101 J3
Ashwood Rd CHING E4 44 B2
Ashworth Cl CMBW SE5 130 E1
Ashworth Rd MV/WKIL W9 2 D7
Askern Cl BXLYHS DA6 136 E3
Aske St IS N1 7 J7
Askew Crs SHB W12 106 C1
Askew Rd NTHWD HA6 32 B3
SHB W12 106 C1
Askew Vls PLMGR N13 * 41 H2
Askham Rd SHB W12 87 J7
Askill Dr PUT/ROE SW15 127 H4
Askwith Rd RAIN RM13 99 F1
Asland Rd SRTFD E15 76 B7
Aslett St WAND/EARL SW18 128 A6
Asmara Rd CRICK NW2 70 C4
Asmuns Hl GLDGN NW11 52 E4
Asmuns Pl GLDGN NW11 52 D4
Asolando Dr WALW SE17 18 F7
Aspen Cl EA W5 105 G1
Aspen Copse BMLY BR1 168 E1
Aspen Ct HACK E8 * 74 C5
Aspen Dr ALP/SUD HA0 67 G2
Aspen Gdns ASHF TW15 140 A4
MTCM CR4 163 F4
Aspen Gn ERITHM DA18 117 G2
Aspen Gv PIN HA5 46 D2
Aspen La NTHLT UB5 83 J2
Aspenlea Rd HMSMTH W6 107 G5
Aspen Wy FELT TW13 141 F2
POP/IOD E14 94 A6
Aspern Gv HAMP NW3 71 J4
Aspinall Rd BROCKY SE4 132 A2
NWCR SE14 132 A2
Aspinden Rd
BERM/RHTH SE16 111 J3
Aspley Rd WAND/EARL SW18 128 A4
Asplins Rd TOTM N17 42 C7
Asplins Vls TOTM N17 * 42 C7
Asprey Ms BECK BR3 166 C4
Asquith Cl BCTR RM8 61 J7
Assam St WCHPL E1 92 C5
Assata Ms IS N1 73 H5
Assembly Pas WCHPL E1 92 E4
Assembly Wk CAR SM5 162 D6
Astall Cl KTN/HRWW/WS HA3 34 D7
Astbury Rd PECK SE15 111 K7
Astell St CHEL SW3 15 K7
Asteys Rw IS N1 6 C1
Astle St BTSEA SW11 129 F1
Astley Av CRICK NW2 70 A4
Aston Av KTN/HRWW/WS HA3 49 J6
Aston Cl BUSH WD23 22 C5
SCUP DA14 155 G2
WATN WD24 21 G1
Aston Gn HSLWW TW4 122 B1
Aston Pl STRHM/NOR SW16 149 H5
Aston Rd EA W5 85 K5
ESH/CLAY KT10 170 E4
RYNPK SW20 161 F1
Astons Rd NTHWD HA6 32 A2
Aston St POP/IOD E14 93 G5
Aston Ter BAL SW12 * 129 G5
Astonville St
WAND/EARL SW18 127 K7
Astor Av ROMW/RG RM7 62 D5
Astor Cl KUTN/CMB KT2 144 D5
Astoria Pde
STRHM/NOR SW16 * 148 E2
Astoria Wk BRXN/ST SW9 130 B2
Astra Cl HCH RM12 81 K5
Astrop Ms HMSMTH W6 107 F2
Astrop Ter HMSMTH W6 107 F2
Astwood Ms SKENS SW7 14 D5
Asylum Rd PECK SE15 111 J6
Atalanta St FUL/PGN SW6 107 G7
Atbara Rd TEDD TW11 143 H5
Atcham Rd HSLW TW3 123 H3
Atcost Rd BARK IG11 97 G4
Atheldene Rd
WAND/EARL SW18 128 A7
Athelney St CAT SE6 151 J2
Athelstane Gv BOW E3 93 H1
Athelstane Ms FSBYPK N4 55 G7
Athelstan Gdns
KIL/WHAMP NW6 * 70 C6
Athelstan Rd KUT/HW KT1 159 G3
Athelstan Wy STMC/STPC BR5 155 G7
Athelstone Rd
KTN/HRWW/WS HA3 48 D1
Athena Cl KUT/HW KT1 159 G2
RYLN/HDSTN HA2 66 D1
Athenaeum Pl MUSWH N10 54 B2
Athenaeum Rd
TRDG/WHET N20 27 G7
Athena Pl NTHWD HA6 32 D7
Athenlay Rd PECK SE15 132 A4
Athens Gdns MV/WKIL W9 * 8 A1
Atherden Rd CLPT E5 74 E3
Atherfold Rd BRXN/ST SW9 129 K2
Atherley Wy HSLWW TW4 122 E6
Atherstone Ms SKENS SW7 14 F5
Atherton Cl STWL/WRAY TW19 120 A5
Atherton Dr WIM/MER SW19 146 B3
Atherton Hts ALP/SUD HA0 67 J5
Atherton Ms FSTGT E7 76 D5
Atherton Pl RYLN/HDSTN HA2 48 C2
STHL UB1 84 A6
Atherton Rd BARN SW13 106 D6
CLAY IG5 59 J1
FSTGT E7 76 D4
Atherton St BTSEA SW11 128 D1
Athlone ESH/CLAY KT10 170 E5
Athlone Cl CLPT E5 74 D4
Athlone Ct WALTH E17 58 B2
Athlone Rd BRXS/STRHM SW2 130 A6
Athlone St KTTN NW5 72 A5
Athlon Rd ALP/SUD HA0 85 K1
Athol Cl PIN HA5 33 F7
Athole Gdns EN EN1 30 A4
Athol Gdns PIN HA5 33 F7
Atholl Rd GDMY/SEVK IG3 61 G6
Athol Rd ERITH DA8 117 K4
Athol Sq POP/IOD E14 94 A5
Atkins Dr WWKM BR4 180 B1
Atkinson Rd CAN/RD E16 95 G4
Atkins Rd BAL SW12 129 H6
LEY E10 57 K5
Atlanta Bvd ROM RM1 63 G5
Atlantic Rd BRXN/ST SW9 130 B3
Atlantis Av CAN/RD E16 96 C6
Atlantis Cl BARK IG11 97 H2
Atlas Crs EDGW HA8 36 D1
Atlas Gdns CHARL SE7 114 B3
Atlas Ms HACK E8 74 B5
Atlas Rd DART DA1 139 J2
FBAR/BDGN N11 40 A5
PLSTW E13 94 E1
WBLY HA9 68 E3
WLSDN NW10 87 G2
Atley Rd BOW E3 75 J7
Atlip Rd ALP/SUD HA0 68 A7
Atney Rd PUT/ROE SW15 127 H3
Atria Rd NTHWD HA6 32 E4
Attenborough Cl
OXHEY WD19 33 J2
Atterbury Rd FSBYPK N4 55 G5
Atterbury St WEST SW1P 17 H6
Attewood Av WLSDN NW10 69 G2
Attewood Rd NTHLT UB5 65 J5
Attfield Cl TRDG/WHET N20 39 H1
Attlee Cl THHTH CR7 164 D5
YEAD UB4 * 83 F2
Attlee Dr DART DA1 139 K4
Attlee Rd THMD SE28 97 H6
YEAD UB4 82 E2
Attlee Ter WALTH E17 57 K3
Attneave St FSBYW WC1X 6 A9
Atwell Pl THDIT KT7 158 B7
Atwell Rd PECK SE15 * 131 H1
Atwood Av RCH/KEW TW9 125 H1
Atwood Rd HMSMTH W6 106 E3
Aubert Pk HBRY N5 73 G3
Aubert Rd HBRY N5 73 H3
Aubrey Pl STJWD NW8 2 E6
Aubrey Rd CEND/HSY/T N8 * 54 E4
NTGHL W11 88 D7
WALTH E17 57 J2
Aubrey Wk KENS W8 88 D7
Auburn Cl NWCR SE14 112 B6
Aubyn Hl WNWD SE27 149 J3
Aubyn Sq PUT/ROE SW15 126 D3
Auckland Av RAIN RM13 99 H2
Auckland Cl NRWD SE19 150 B7
Auckland Gdns NRWD SE19 150 A7
Auckland Hl WNWD SE27 149 J3
Auckland Ri NRWD SE19 150 A7
Auckland Rd BTSEA SW11 128 D3
IL IG1 60 B7
KUT/HW KT1 159 G3
LEY E10 75 K2
NRWD SE19 150 B7
Auckland St LBTH SE11 17 L8
Aucuba Vls WELL DA16 * 136 C2
Audax CDALE/KGS NW9 51 H1
Auden Dr BORE WD6 24 C4
Auden Pl CAMTN NW1 4 A3
CHEAM SM3 * 174 A3
Audley Cl BORE WD6 24 C2
BTSEA SW11 129 F2
MUSWH N10 40 B6
Audley Ct PIN HA5 47 G1
WAN E11 58 D3
Audley Dr CAN/RD E16 95 F7
Audley Gdns GDMY/SEVK IG3 79 F1
Audley Pl BELMT SM2 175 F6
Audley Rd EA W5 86 B4
ENC/FH EN2 29 H1
HDN NW4 51 J5
RCHPK/HAM TW10 125 G4
Audley Sq MYFR/PKLN W1K * 10 B8
Audley St MYFR/PKLN W1K 10 B8
Audrey Cl BECK BR3 166 E5
Audrey Gdns ALP/SUD HA0 67 H1
Audrey Rd IL IG1 78 B2
Audrey St BETH E2 92 C1
Audric Cl KUTN/CMB KT2 144 C7
Augurs La PLSTW E13 95 F2
Augusta Cl E/WMO/HCT KT8 156 E2
Augusta Rd WHTN TW2 142 C1
Augustine Rd HMSMTH W6 107 G2
KTN/HRWW/WS HA3 34 B7
Augustus Cl BTFD TW8 104 E6
SHB W12 106 E1
STAN HA7 35 J2
Augustus Rd WIM/MER SW19 127 G7
Augustus St CAMTN NW1 4 D6
Aultone Wy CAR SM5 175 K2
SUT SM1 175 F1
Aulton Pl LBTH SE11 18 B8
Aurelia Gdns CROY/NA CR0 164 A4
Aurelia Rd CROY/NA CR0 163 K5
Auriel Av DAGE RM10 81 F5
Auriga Ms IS N1 73 K4
Auriol Cl WPK KT4 173 G2
Auriol Dr GFD/PVL UB6 66 D6
Auriol Park Rd WPK KT4 173 G2
Auriol Rd WKENS W14 107 H3
Austell Gdns MLHL NW7 37 G2
Austen Cl THMD SE28 97 H7
Austen Rd ERITH DA8 117 J6
RYLN/HDSTN HA2 66 B1
Austin Av HAYES BR2 168 D5
Austin Cl FSTH SE23 132 B6
TWK TW1 124 D4
Austin Friars OBST EC2N 13 H4
Austin Friars Sq OBST EC2N * 13 H4
Austin Rd BTSEA SW11 109 F7
HYS/HAR UB3 101 J1
Austins La HGDN/ICK UB10 64 A2
Austin St BETH E2 7 L8
Austral Cl BFN/LL DA15 155 F2
Australia Rd SHB W12 87 K6
Austral St LBTH SE11 18 C5
Austyn Gdns BRYLDS KT5 * 159 J7
Autumn Cl EN EN1 30 D1
WIM/MER SW19 147 G5
Autumn Dr BELMT SM2 175 F7
Autumn Gv BMLY BR1 153 F5
Autumn St BOW E3 75 J7
Avalon Cl ENC/FH EN2 29 G1
RYNPK SW20 161 H1
WEA W13 85 G4
Avalon Rd FUL/PGN SW6 108 A7
WEA W13 85 G3
Avarn Rd TOOT SW17 147 K5
Avebury Pk SURB KT6 * 158 E5
Avebury Rd WAN E11 58 B7
WIM/MER SW19 146 D7
Avebury St IS N1 7 G4
Aveley Cl ERITH DA8 118 C5
Aveley Rd ROM RM1 63 F3
Aveline St LBTH SE11 17 M7
Aveling Park Rd WALTH E17 57 J1
Avelon Rd RAIN RM13 81 J7
Ave Marie La STP EC4M 12 D5
Avenell Rd HBRY N5 73 H2
Avening Rd WAND/EARL SW18 127 K6
Avening Ter
WAND/EARL SW18 127 K5
Avenons Rd PLSTW E13 94 E4
Avenue Cl HEST TW5 102 A7
STHGT/OAK N14 28 C5
STJWD NW8 3 K4
WDR/YW UB7 100 A2
Avenue Crs ACT W3 105 J1
HEST TW5 102 A7
Avenue Elmers SURB KT6 159 F4
Avenue Gdns ACT W3 105 J1
HEST TW5 * 101 K6
MORT/ESHN SW14 126 B2
SNWD SE25 165 H2
TEDD TW11 143 F6
Avenue Ms MUSWH N10 54 B2
Avenue Pde SUN TW16 156 A2
WCHMH N21 * 29 K6
Avenue Park Rd WNWD SE27 149 H1
Avenue Ri BUSH WD23 22 A4
Avenue Rd ACT W3 105 J1
BTFD TW8 104 D4
BXLYHN DA7 137 F2
CHDH RM6 61 H6
ERITH DA8 117 K6
ERITH DA8 118 B5
FELT TW13 140 D2
FSTGT E7 77 F3
HAMP NW3 3 G1
HGT N6 54 C6
HPTN TW12 142 B7
ISLW TW7 103 K7
KUT/HW KT1 159 F2
NFNCH/WDSPK N12 39 G3
NWMAL KT3 160 B3
PGE/AN SE20 150 E7
PIN HA5 47 J2
RYNPK SW20 160 E1
SEVS/STOTM N15 55 K4
SNWD SE25 165 H1
STHGT/OAK N14 28 C5
STHL UB1 83 K7
STJWD NW8 3 H2
STRHM/NOR SW16 163 J1
TEDD TW11 143 G6
WFD IG8 45 G5
WLGTN SM6 176 C6
WLSDN NW10 87 H1
Avenue South BRYLDS KT5 159 G6
Avenue Ter NWMAL KT3 159 K2
OXHEY WD19 21 J5
The Avenue BAR EN5 26 C2
BECK BR3 151 K7
BELMT SM2 174 D7
BKHH IG9 45 G1
BMLY BR1 168 C2
BRYLDS KT5 159 G5
BUSH WD23 21 K3
BXLY DA5 136 E6
CAR SM5 176 A6
CEND/HSY/T N8 55 G2
CHING E4 44 B5
CHSWK W4 106 B2
CLAP SW4 129 F4
CROY/NA CR0 178 A2
ESH/CLAY KT10 170 E5
EW KT17 174 A6
FBAR/BDGN N11 40 B4
FNCH N3 52 E1
GNWCH SE10 113 G6
HEST TW5 101 K7
HPTN TW12 141 K5
HSLW TW3 123 G4
KIL/WHAMP NW6 70 C6
KTN/HRWW/WS HA3 35 F7
MUSWH N10 54 C1
NTHWD HA6 32 A5
PIN HA5 33 K5
PIN HA5 47 K5
RCH/KEW TW9 125 G1
ROM RM1 63 F3
STMC/STPC BR5 155 H6
SUN TW16 156 A1
TOTM N17 56 A1
TWK TW1 124 D4
WAN E11 59 F5
WAT WD17 20 E1
WBLY HA9 50 A7
WEA W13 85 H6
WPK KT4 173 H1
WWKM BR4 167 G6
Averil Gv STRHM/NOR SW16 149 H5
Averill St HMSMTH W6 107 G5
Avern Gdns E/WMO/HCT KT8 157 G3
Avern Rd E/WMO/HCT KT8 157 G3
Avery Farm Rw BGVA SW1W * 16 C6
Avery Gdns GNTH/NBYPK IG2 59 K4
Avery Hill Rd ELTH/MOT SE9 135 H7
Avery Rw MYFR/PKLN W1K 10 C6
Aviary Cl CAN/RD E16 94 D4
Aviation Dr CDALE/KGS NW9 51 J1
Aviemore Cl BECK BR3 166 C4
Aviemore Wy BECK BR3 166 B4
Avigdor Ms STNW/STAM N16 73 K1
Avignon Rd BROCKY SE4 132 A2
Avington Gv PGE/AN SE20 150 E6
Avington Wy PECK SE15 * 111 G6
Avion Crs CDALE/KGS NW9 51 J1
Avior Dr NTHWD HA6 32 D3
Avis Sq WCHPL E1 93 F5
Avoca Rd TOOT SW17 148 A3
Avocet Cl STHWK SE1 111 H4
Avocet Ms THMD SE28 115 J2
Avon Cl SUT SM1 175 G3
WPK KT4 173 J1
YEAD UB4 83 G3
Avon Ct PIN HA5 * 34 A6
Avondale Av CRICK NW2 69 G2
EBAR EN4 27 K7
ESH/CLAY KT10 171 G2
NFNCH/WDSPK N12 39 F4
WPK KT4 160 C7
Avondale Ct SWFD E18 45 F7
Avondale Crs PEND EN3 31 G2
REDBR IG4 59 H4
Avondale Dr HYS/HAR UB3 82 E7
Avondale Gdns HSLWW TW4 122 E4
Avondale Park Gdns
NTGHL W11 * 88 C6
Avondale Park Rd NTGHL W11 88 C6
Avondale Pavement
STHWK SE1 * 111 H4
Avondale Ri PECK SE15 131 G2
Avondale Rd BMLY BR1 152 C5
CAN/RD E16 94 C4
ELTH/MOT SE9 153 J1
FNCH N3 39 G7
KTN/HRWW/WS HA3 49 F2
MORT/ESHN SW14 126 A2
PLMGR N13 41 G1
SAND/SEL CR2 177 J5
SEVS/STOTM N15 55 H4
WALTH E17 57 J6
WELL DA16 136 D1
WIM/MER SW19 147 F4
Avondale Sq STHWK SE1 111 H4
Avonley Rd NWCR SE14 111 K6
Avonmore Gdns
WKENS W14 * 107 J3
Avonmore Pl WKENS W14 107 H3
Avonmore Rd WKENS W14 107 J3
Avonmouth Rd DART DA1 139 G4
Avonmouth St STHWK SE1 18 E3
Avon Rd BROCKY SE4 132 D2
GFD/PVL UB6 84 A3
SUN TW16 140 D6
WALTH E17 58 B2
Avon Wy SWFD E18 58 E3
Avonwick Rd HSLW TW3 123 G1
Avril Wy CHING E4 44 A4
Avro Wy WLGTN SM6 176 E6
Awberry Ct WATW WD18 * 20 B5
Awlfield Av TOTM N17 41 K7
Awliscombe Rd WELL DA16 136 A1
Axe St BARK IG11 78 C7
Axholme Av EDGW HA8 36 C7
Axis Ct GNWCH SE10 113 H5
Axminster Crs WELL DA16 116 D7
Axminster Rd HOLWY N7 72 E2
Axon Pl IL IG1 78 C1
Aybrook St MHST W1U 10 A3
Aycliff Ct KUT/HW KT1 * 159 H1
Aycliffe Cl BMLY BR1 168 E3
Aycliffe Rd SHB W12 87 H7
Aylands Cl WBLY HA9 68 A1
Aylesbury Cl FSTGT E7 76 D5
Aylesbury Est WALW SE17 19 H8
Aylesbury Rd HAYES BR2 167 K2
WALW SE17 19 H8
Aylesbury St CLKNW EC1R 12 C1
WLSDN NW10 69 F2
Aylesford Av BECK BR3 166 B4
Aylesford St PIM SW1V 17 G7
Aylesham Cl MLHL NW7 37 J6
Aylesham Rd ORP BR6 169 K6
Ayles Rd YEAD UB4 83 F2
Aylestone Av
KIL/WHAMP NW6 70 B6
Aylett Rd ISLW TW7 123 K1
SNWD SE25 165 J3
Ayley Cft EN EN1 30 C4
Ayliffe Cl KUT/HW KT1 159 H1
Aylmer Cl STAN HA7 35 G3
Aylmer Dr STAN HA7 35 G3
Aylmer Pde EFNCH N2 * 53 K4
Aylmer Rd BCTR RM8 80 A2
EFNCH N2 53 J4
SHB W12 106 B1
WAN E11 58 D6
Ayloffe Rd DAGW RM9 80 B5
Aylsham Dr HGDN/ICK UB10 64 A1
Aylton Est BERM/RHTH SE16 * 111 K1
Aylward Rd FSTH SE23 151 F1
RYNPK SW20 161 J1
Aylwards Ri STAN HA7 35 G3
Aylward St WCHPL E1 93 F5
Aynhoe Rd WKENS W14 107 G3
Aynho St WATW WD18 21 F4
Ayres Cl PLSTW E13 94 E2
Ayres Crs WLSDN NW10 69 F6
Ayres St STHWK SE1 18 F1
Ayrsome Rd STNW/STAM N16 74 A2
Ayrton Rd SKENS SW7 15 G3
Aysgarth Rd DUL SE21 130 E5
Aytoun Pl BRXN/ST SW9 130 A1
Aytoun Rd BRXN/ST SW9 130 A1
Azalea Cl HNWL W7 85 F7
IL IG1 78 B4
Azalea Ct WFD IG8 * 44 C6
Azalea Wk PIN HA5 47 F5
Azania Ms KTTN NW5 72 B4
Azenby Rd PECK SE15 131 G1
Azof St GNWCH SE10 113 H3

B

Baalbec Rd HBRY N5 73 H4
Babbacombe Cl CHSGTN KT9 171 K4
Babbacombe Gdns REDBR IG4 59 J3
Babbacombe Rd BMLY BR1 153 F7
Baber Bridge Pde
EBED/NFELT TW14 * 122 B5
Baber Dr EBED/NFELT TW14 122 B5
Babington Ri WBLY HA9 68 C5
Babington Rd BCTR RM8 79 J4
HCH RM12 63 K7
HDN NW4 51 K3
STRHM/NOR SW16 148 D4
Babmaes St STJS SW1Y 11 G8
Bache's St IS N1 7 H8
Back Church La WCHPL E1 92 C6
Back Hl CLKNW EC1R 12 B1
Back La BTFD TW8 104 E6
BXLY DA5 137 H6
CEND/HSY/T N8 54 E4
CHDH RM6 61 K6
EDGW HA8 36 E7
HAMP NW3 71 G3
RCHPK/HAM TW10 143 J2
Backley Gdns CROY/NA CR0 165 H5
Back Rd SCUP DA14 155 G3
TEDD TW11 142 E6
WALTH E17 58 A3
Bacon Gv STHWK SE1 19 L5
Bacon La CDALE/KGS NW9 50 D3
EDGW HA8 36 C7
Bacon's La HGT N6 54 A7
Bacon St BETH E2 7 M9
Bacton St BETH E2 92 E2
Baddow Cl DAGE RM10 80 C7
WFD IG8 45 H5
Baden Pl STHWK SE1 19 G1
Baden Powell Cl DAGW RM9 80 A7
SURB KT6 172 B1
Baden Rd CEND/HSY/T N8 54 D3
IL IG1 78 B4
Bader Wy PUT/ROE SW15 126 D5
RAIN RM13 81 J5
Badger Cl FELT TW13 141 F2
GNTH/NBYPK IG2 60 C5
HSLWW TW4 122 B2
Badgers Cl BORE WD6 * 24 B1
ENC/FH EN2 29 H2
HRW HA1 48 D5
HYS/HAR UB3 82 C7
Badgers Copse WPK KT4 173 H1
Badgers Ct WPK KT4 * 173 H1
Badgers Cft ELTH/MOT SE9 154 A2
TRDG/WHET N20 26 C6
Badgers Wk NWMAL KT3 160 B1
Badlis Rd WALTH E17 57 J1
Badlow Cl ERITH DA8 118 B6
Badminton Cl BORE WD6 24 C1
HRW HA1 * 48 E3
NTHLT UB5 66 A5
Badminton Ms CAN/RD E16 94 E7
Badminton Rd BAL SW12 129 F5
Badsworth Rd CMBW SE5 110 D6
Bafton Ga HAYES BR2 168 A7
Bagley Cl WDR/YW UB7 100 B1
Bagley House
WOOL/PLUM SE18 * 114 D6
Bagley's La FUL/PGN SW6 108 A7
Bagleys Spring CHDH RM6 62 A3
Bagshot Ct
WOOL/PLUM SE18 * 115 F7
Bagshot Rd EN EN1 30 B5
Bagshot St WALW SE17 19 K8
Baildon St DEPT SE8 112 C6
Bailey Cl FBAR/BDGN N11 40 D7
THMD SE28 96 E7
Bailey Cots POP/IOD E14 * 93 G4
Bailey Crs CHSGTN KT9 171 K6
Bailey House
WOOL/PLUM SE18 * 114 D6
Bailey Ms BRXS/STRHM SW2 130 B4
CHSWK W4 105 J5
Bailey Pl SYD SE26 150 E5
Baillie Cl RAIN RM13 99 K3
Bainbridge Cl
RCHPK/HAM TW10 144 A4
Bainbridge Rd DAGW RM9 80 B3
Bainbridge St
NOXST/BSQ WC1A 11 H4
Baines Cl SAND/SEL CR2 177 K4
Baird Av STHL UB1 84 B6
Baird Cl BUSH WD23 22 B5
CDALE/KGS NW9 50 E5
LEY E10 57 J7
Baird Gdns NRWD SE19 150 A3
Baird Memorial Cots
STHGT/OAK N14 * 40 D1
Baird Rd EN EN1 30 D2
Baird St STLK EC1Y 6 F9
Baizdon Rd BKHTH/KID SE3 133 H1
Baker Crs DART DA1 139 F6
Baker La MTCM CR4 163 F1
Baker Pl HOR/WEW KT19 172 E5
Baker Rd WLSDN NW10 69 G7
WOOL/PLUM SE18 114 D6

Bakers Av WALTH E17 ... 57 K5
Bakers Cl DART DA1 ... 139 G6
Bakers End RYNPK SW20 ... 161 H1
Bakers Gdns CAR SM5 ... 175 J4
Bakers Hl BAR EN5 ... 27 C5
  CLPT E5 ... 56 D7
Baker's Ms MHST W1U ... 10 A1
Bakers Rents BETH E2 ... 7 L1
Bakers Rw CLKNW EC1R ... 12 A1
Baker's Rw CLKNW EC1R * ... 12 A1
Baker St CAMTN NW1 ... 9 M1
  EN EN1 ... 29 K1
  MHST W1U ... 10 A5
Bakers Yd CLKNW EC1R * ... 12 A1
Bakery Cl BRXN/ST SW9 * ... 110 A6
Bakewell Wy NWMAL KT3 ... 160 B1
Balaams La STHGT/OAK N14 ... 40 D1
Balaam St PLSTW E13 ... 94 E2
Balaclava Rd STHWK SE1 ... 19 M6
  SURB KT6 ... 158 D6
Bala Gn CDALE/KGS NW9 * ... 51 G5
Balcaskie Rd ELTH/MOT SE9 ... 134 E4
Balchier Rd EDUL SE22 ... 131 J5
Balcombe St CAMTN NW1 ... 3 L9
Balcorne St HOM E9 ... 74 F6
Balder Ri LEE/GVPK SE12 ... 153 F1
Balderton St OXSTW W1C ... 10 B5
Baldock St BOW E3 ... 93 K1
Baldry Gdns
  STRHM/NOR SW16 ... 148 E5
Baldwin Crs CMBW SE5 ... 110 D7
Baldwin Gdns HSLW TW3 ... 103 H7
Baldwin Rd BTSEA SW11 ... 129 F5
Baldwin's Gdns FSBYW WC1X ... 12 A2
Baldwins La
  RKW/CH/CXG WD3 ... 20 A3
Baldwin St FSBYE EC1V ... 7 G9
Baldwin Ter IS N1 ... 6 E5
Baldwyn Gdns ACT W3 ... 86 E6
Bale Rd WCHPL E1 ... 93 G4
Bales Ter ED N9 * ... 42 B2
Balfern Gv CHSWK W4 ... 106 B4
Balfern St BTSEA SW11 ... 128 D1
Balfe St IS N1 ... 5 K6
Balfour Av WEA W13 ... 85 H7
Balfour Gv TRDG/WHET N20 ... 39 L2
Balfour Ms EN EN1 ... 29 K1
  MYFR/PKLN W1K ... 10 B8
Balfour Pl MYFR/PKLN W1K ... 10 B8
  PUT/ROE SW15 ... 126 E3
Balfour Rd ACT W3 ... 86 E4
  CAR SM5 ... 175 K6
  HAYES BR2 ... 168 C4
  HBRY N5 ... 73 J3
  HRW HA1 ... 48 D4
  HSLW TW3 ... 123 G2
  IL IG1 ... 78 B1
  NWDGN UB2 ... 102 C2
  SNWD SE25 ... 165 H3
  WEA W13 ... 104 C1
  WIM/MER SW19 ... 147 F6
Balfour St STHWK SE1 ... 19 G5
Balgores Crs GPK RM2 ... 63 K3
Balgores La GPK RM2 ... 63 K3
Balgores Sq GPK RM2 ... 63 K3
Balgowan Cl NWMAL KT3 ... 160 B3
Balgowan Rd BECK BR3 ... 166 B2
Balgowan St
  WOOL/PLUM SE18 ... 116 A3
Balham Gv BAL SW12 ... 129 F6
Balham High Rd BAL SW12 ... 129 G6
Balham Hl BAL SW12 ... 129 G6
Balham New Rd BAL SW12 ... 129 G6
Balham Park Rd BAL SW12 ... 128 E7
Balham Rd ED N9 ... 42 C1
Balham Station Rd BAL SW12 ... 129 F7
Balkan Wk WAP E1W * ... 92 D6
Balladier Wk POP/IOD E14 ... 93 K4
Ballamore Rd BMLY BR1 ... 152 E2
Ballance Rd HOM E9 ... 75 F5
Ballantine St
  WAND/EARL SW18 ... 128 B3
Ballantyne Cl ELTH/MOT SE9 ... 153 J3
Ballard Cl KUTN/CMB KT2 ... 145 F7
Ballards Cl DAGE RM10 ... 80 D7
Ballards Farm Rd
  SAND/SEL CR2 ... 178 C5
Ballards La FNCH N3 ... 39 F7
Ballards Ms EDGW HA8 ... 36 C5
Ballards Ri SAND/SEL CR2 ... 178 C5
Ballards Rd CRICK NW2 ... 69 J1
  DAGE RM10 ... 80 D7
Ballards Wy SAND/SEL CR2 ... 178 C5
Ballast Quay GNWCH SE10 ... 113 H3
Ballater Cl OXHEY WD19 ... 33 G3
Ballater Rd BRXS/STRHM SW2 ... 129 K3
  SAND/SEL CR2 ... 178 B4
Ballina St FSTH SE23 ... 132 A6
Ballingdon Rd BTSEA SW11 ... 129 F6
Ballinger Wy NTHLT UB5 ... 83 J3
Balliol Av CHING E4 ... 44 B3
Balliol Rd NKENS W10 ... 88 A5
  TOTM N17 ... 42 A7
  WELL DA16 ... 136 C1
Balloch Rd CAT SE6 ... 133 G7
Ballogie Av WLSDN NW10 ... 69 G3
Ballow Cl CMBW SE5 * ... 110 E6
Ball's Pond Pl IS N1 * ... 73 K5
Balls Pond Rd IS N1 ... 73 K5
Balmain Cl EA W5 ... 85 K7
Balmer Rd BOW E3 ... 93 H1
Balmes Rd IS N1 ... 7 H3
Balmoral Av BECK BR3 ... 166 B3
  FBAR/BDGN N11 ... 40 A5
Balmoral Cl PUT/ROE SW15 * ... 127 G5
Balmoral Crs
  E/WMO/HCT KT8 ... 157 F2
Balmoral Dr BORE WD6 ... 25 F3
  STHL UB1 ... 83 K4
  YEAD UB4 ... 82 C5
Balmoral Gdns BXLY DA5 ... 137 G6
  WEA W13 ... 104 B2
Balmoral Gv HOLWY N7 ... 73 F5
Balmoral Ms SHB W12 ... 106 C2
Balmoral Rd CRICK NW2 ... 69 K5
  FSTGT E7 ... 77 G3
  GPK RM2 ... 63 K3
  KUT/HW KT1 ... 159 G3
  LEY E10 ... 75 K1
  RYLN/HDSTN HA2 ... 66 A3
  WPK KT4 ... 173 K2
Balmore Crs EBAR EN4 ... 28 A4
Balmore St ARCH N19 ... 72 B1
Balmuir Gdns PUT/ROE SW15 ... 127 G3
Balnacraig Av WLSDN NW10 ... 69 G3
Baltic Cl WIM/MER SW19 ... 147 H6
Baltic Pl IS N1 ... 7 K3
Baltic St East FARR EC1Y ... 12 E1
Baltic St West FARR EC1M ... 12 E1
Baltimore Pl WELL DA16 ... 136 A1
Balvaird Pl PIM SW1V ... 17 H8

Balvernie Gv
  WAND/EARL SW18 ... 127 J6
Bamber Rd PECK SE15 ... 111 G7
Bamborough Gdns SHB W12 ... 107 F1
Bamford Av ALP/SUD HA0 ... 68 A7
Bamford Rd BMLY BR1 ... 152 B4
  BARK IG11 ... 78 B4
Bampfylde Cl WLGTN SM6 ... 176 C2
Bampton Dr MLHL NW7 ... 37 J6
Bampton Rd FSTH SE23 ... 151 F2
Banavie Gdns BECK BR3 ... 151 K6
Banbury Cl ENC/FH EN2 * ... 29 J1
Banbury Ct
  COVGDN WC2E * ... 11 J6
Banbury Rd HACK E8 ... 74 D6
  WALTH E17 ... 43 G7
Banbury St BTSEA SW11 * ... 128 D1
  WATW WD18 ... 20 E4
Banchory Rd BKHTH/KID SE3 ... 114 A6
Bancroft Av EFNCH N2 ... 53 J4
  BUSH WD23 ... 22 C7
Bancroft Gdns
  KTN/HRWW/WS HA3 ... 34 C7
Bancroft Rd
  KTN/HRWW/WS HA3 ... 48 C1
  WCHPL E1 ... 92 E3
Bandon Ri WLGTN SM6 ... 176 D4
Banfield Rd PECK SE15 ... 131 J2
Bangalore St PUT/ROE SW15 ... 127 F2
Bangor Ct NTHLT UB5 ... 66 B4
Banim St HMSMTH W6 ... 106 E2
Banister Rd NKENS W10 ... 88 B2
Bank Av MTCM CR4 ... 162 C1
Bank End STHWK SE1 ... 12 F8
Bank Bldgs CHING E4 * ... 44 B5
Bankfoot Rd BMLY BR1 ... 152 C2
Bank La KUTN/CMB KT2 ... 144 A6
  PUT/ROE SW15 ... 126 A4
Bank Ms SUT SM1 ... 175 G5
Banksia Rd UED N18 ... 42 E4
Bankside SAND/SEL CR2 ... 178 B5
  STHL UB1 ... 83 H7
  STHWK SE1 ... 12 E7
Bankside Av LEW SE13 ... 133 F2
  NTHLT UB5 ... 82 E1
Bankside Cl CAR SM5 ... 175 J4
  ISLW TW7 ... 124 A3
Bankside Dr THDIT KT7 ... 171 H1
Bankside Rd IL IG1 ... 78 C4
Banks La BXLYHS DA6 ... 137 G3
Banks Rd BORE WD6 ... 24 E1
Banks Wy MNPK E12 ... 78 A3
Banksyard HEST TW5 * ... 102 E5
The Bank HGT N6 * ... 54 B7
Bankton Rd BRXS/STRHM SW2 ... 130 B3
Bankwell Rd LEW SE13 ... 133 H3
Banner St STLK EC1Y ... 12 F1
Banning St GNWCH SE10 ... 113 H4
Bannister Cl BRXS/STRHM SW2 ... 130 B7
  GFD/PVL UB6 ... 66 D4
Bannockburn Rd
  WOOL/PLUM SE18 ... 115 K3
Bannow Cl HOR/WEW KT19 ... 173 G3
Banstead Ct SHB W12 * ... 87 H6
Banstead Gdns ED N9 ... 41 K2
Banstead Rd CAR SM5 ... 175 H6
Banstead St PECK SE15 ... 131 K2
Banstead Wy WLGTN SM6 ... 176 E4
Banstock Rd EDGW HA8 ... 36 D5
Banting Dr WCHMH N21 ... 29 F4
Banton Cl EN EN1 ... 30 D1
Bantry St CMBW SE5 ... 110 E6
Banwell Rd BXLY DA5 ... 136 E5
Banyard Rd BERM/RHTH SE16 ... 111 J2
Baptist Gdns KTTN NW5 ... 72 A5
Barandon Wk NTGHL W11 * ... 88 B6
Barbara Castle Cl
  FUL/PGN SW6 ... 107 J5
Barbara Hucklesbury Cl
  WDGN N22 ... 55 H1
Barbauld Rd STNW/STAM N16 ... 74 A2
Barber Cl WCHMH N21 ... 29 G6
Barbers Rd SRTFD E15 ... 93 K1
Barbican Rd GFD/PVL UB6 ... 84 B5
Barb Ms HMSMTH W6 ... 107 F2
Barbon Cl BMSBY WC1N ... 11 K2
Barbot Cl ED N9 ... 42 C2
Barchard St WAND/EARL SW18 ... 128 A4
Barchester Cl HNWL W7 ... 85 F7
Barchester Rd
  KTN/HRWW/WS HA3 ... 34 D7
Barchester St POP/IOD E14 ... 93 K4
Barclay Cl FUL/PGN SW6 ... 107 K6
  WATW WD18 ... 20 E5
Barclay Ov WFD IG8 ... 44 E3
Barclay Rd CROY/NA CR0 ... 177 K2
  FUL/PGN SW6 ... 107 K6
  PLSTW E13 ... 95 G3
  UED N18 ... 41 K5
  WALTH E17 ... 58 A4
Barcombe Av BRXS/STRHM SW2 ... 148 E1
Barden St WOOL/PLUM SE18 ... 115 K6
Bardfield Av CHDH RM6 ... 61 K2
Bardney Rd MRDN SM4 ... 162 A3
Bardolph Av CROY/NA CR0 ... 179 H7
Bardolph Rd HOLWY N7 ... 72 E3
  RCH/KEW TW9 ... 125 G2
Bard Rd NKENS W10 ... 88 B6
Bardsey Pl WCHPL E1 ... 92 E3
Bardsey Wk IS N1 * ... 73 J5
Bardsley Cl CROY/NA CR0 ... 178 B2
Bardsley La GNWCH SE10 ... 113 F5
Barfett St NKENS W10 ... 88 D3
Barfield Av TRDG/WHET N20 ... 39 K1
Barfield Rd BMLY BR1 ... 169 F2
  WAN E11 * ... 58 D7
Barford Cl HDN NW4 ... 51 J1
Barford St IS N1 ... 6 B4
Barforth Rd PECK SE15 ... 131 J2
Barfreston Wy PGE/AN SE20 ... 150 D7
Bargate Cl NWMAL KT3 ... 160 D6
  WOOL/PLUM SE18 ... 116 A4
Barge House Rd STHWK SE1 * ... 12 B8
Barge La BOW E3 ... 75 H7
Bargery Rd CAT SE6 ... 132 E7
Barge Wk KUT/HW KT1 ... 158 E1
Bargrove Cl PGE/AN SE20 ... 150 C6
Bargrove Crs CAT SE6 ... 151 H1
Barham Av BORE WD6 ... 24 B2
Barham Cl ALP/SUD HA0 ... 67 H5
  CHST BR7 ... 154 A4
  HAYES BR2 ... 168 C4
  ROMW/RG RM7 ... 62 D1
Barham Ct CHST BR7 ... 154 A4
  DART DA1 ... 139 K6
  RYNPK SW20 ... 145 J6
  SAND/SEL CR2 ... 177 J7
Baring Cl LEE/GVPK SE12 ... 152 E1

Baring Rd CROY/NA CR0 ... 165 H7
  EBAR EN4 ... 27 H2
  LEE/GVPK SE12 ... 153 F2
Baring St IS N1 ... 7 G4
Barker Rd NTHWD HA6 ... 32 D6
  NWMAL KT3 ... 159 J3
  RCH/KEW TW9 ... 125 J1
Barker Dr CAMTN NW1 ... 4 F2
Barker St WBPTN SW10 ... 14 E8
Barker Wk STRHM/NOR SW16 ... 148 D2
Barkham Rd TOTM N17 ... 41 K6
Barking Rd CAN/RD E16 ... 94 D4
  EHAM E6 ... 95 H1
  PLSTW E13 ... 95 F3
  POP/IOD E14 ... 94 C5
Bark Pl BAY/PAD W2 ... 8 C6
Barkston Gdns ECT SW5 ... 14 C6
Barkwood Cl ROMW/RG RM7 ... 62 E4
Barkworth Rd
  BERM/RHTH SE16 ... 111 J4
Barlborough St NWCR SE14 ... 112 A6
Barlby Gdns NKENS W10 ... 88 B3
Barlby Rd NKENS W10 ... 88 A4
Barley Cl ALP/SUD HA0 ... 67 K3
  BUSH WD23 ... 22 C5
Barleycorn Wy POP/IOD E14 ... 93 H6
Barley La GDMY/SEVK IG3 ... 61 G5
Barley Mow Pas CHSWK W4 ... 106 A4
  STBT EC1A ... 12 E3
Barlow Cl WLGTN SM6 ... 176 E5
Barlow Dr BKHTH/KID SE3 ... 114 D7
Barlow Pl MYFR/PICC W1J ... 10 D7
Barlow Rd ACT W3 ... 86 D7
  HPTN TW12 ... 142 A6
  KIL/WHAMP NW6 ... 70 D5
Barlow St WALW SE17 ... 19 H5
Barlow Wy RAIN RM13 ... 99 F5
Barlow Wy South RAIN RM13 ... 99 F5
Barmeston Rd CAT SE6 ... 151 K1
Barmor Cl RYLN/HDSTN HA2 ... 48 B1
Barmouth Av GFD/PVL UB6 ... 85 F1
Barmouth Rd CROY/NA CR0 ... 179 F1
  WAND/EARL SW18 ... 128 B5
Barnabas Rd HOM E9 ... 75 F4
Barnaby Cl RYLN/HDSTN HA2 ... 66 C1
Barnaby Pl SKENS SW7 ... 15 G5
Barnard Cl CHST BR7 ... 154 D7
  SUN TW16 ... 141 F6
  WLGTN SM6 ... 176 D6
  WOOL/PLUM SE18 ... 115 F3
Barnard Gdns NWMAL KT3 ... 160 D3
  YEAD UB4 ... 83 F3
Barnard Hl MUSWH N10 ... 54 B1
Barnardo Dr BARK/HLT IG6 ... 60 C3
Barnardo Gdns WCHPL E1 * ... 93 F5
Barnardo St WCHPL E1 ... 93 F5
Barnard Rd BTSEA SW11 ... 128 D3
  EN EN1 ... 30 D1
  MTCM CR4 ... 163 F2
Barnards Pl SAND/SEL CR2 ... 177 H7
Barnby Sq SRTFD E15 * ... 76 C7
Barnby St CAMTN NW1 ... 4 F6
  SRTFD E15 ... 76 C7
Barn Cl KTTN NW5 * ... 72 D4
  NTHLT UB5 ... 83 G1
Barn Crs STAN HA7 ... 35 J5
Barneby Cl WHTN TW2 ... 123 K7
Barnehurst Av BXLYHN DA7 ... 117 K7
Barnehurst Cl ERITH DA8 ... 117 K7
Barnehurst Rd BXLYHN DA7 ... 137 K1
Barnes Aly HPTN TW12 ... 157 H1
Barnes Av BARN SW13 ... 106 D6
  NWDGN UB2 ... 102 E3
Barnes Br CHSWK W4 ... 126 B1
Barnes Cl MNPK E12 ... 77 H3
Barnes Cray Rd DART DA1 ... 138 C3
Barnes End NWMAL KT3 ... 160 D4
Barnes High St BARN SW13 ... 126 C1
Barnes Rd IL IG1 ... 78 C4
  UED N18 ... 42 E3
Barnes St POP/IOD E14 ... 93 G5
Barnes Ter DEPT SE8 ... 112 C4
Barnet By-Pass BORE WD6 ... 25 G4
Barnet Dr HAYES BR2 ... 181 J1
Barnet Gate La BAR EN5 ... 25 H5
Barnet Gv BETH E2 ... 92 C2
Barnet Hl BAR EN5 ... 26 D3
Barnet La BORE WD6 ... 24 B5
  TRDG/WHET N20 ... 26 D7
Barnet Rd BAR EN5 ... 25 G5
Barnett Cl ERITH DA8 ... 138 C1
Barnetts Ct
  RYLN/HDSTN HA2 * ... 66 B2
Barnett St WCHPL E1 * ... 92 D5
Barnet Way (Barnet By-Pass)
  MLHL NW7 ... 25 F6
Barnet Wood Rd HAYES BR2 ... 181 H5
Barney Cl CHARL SE7 ... 114 B4
Barn Fld HAMP NW3 * ... 71 K4
Barnfield NWMAL KT3 ... 160 B5
Barnfield Av CROY/NA CR0 ... 165 J7
  KUTN/CMB KT2 ... 143 K3
  MTCM CR4 ... 163 H3
Barnfield Cl BECK BR3 ... 166 C5
Barnfield Gdns
  KUTN/CMB KT2 ... 144 A4
  WOOL/PLUM SE18 * ... 115 G5
Barnfield Pl POP/IOD E14 ... 112 D3
Barnfield Rd BELV DA17 ... 117 G5
  EA W5 ... 85 J3
  EDGW HA8 ... 36 E7
  SAND/SEL CR2 ... 178 A7
  WOOL/PLUM SE18 ... 115 G5
Barnfield Wood Cl BECK BR3 ... 167 G5
Barnfield Wood Rd BECK BR3 ... 167 G5
Barnham Dr THMD SE28 ... 97 F7
Barnham Rd GFD/PVL UB6 ... 84 C2
Barnham St STHWK SE1 ... 19 K1
Barn Hl WBLY HA9 ... 68 C1
Barnhill PIN HA5 ... 47 G4
Barn Hill WBLY HA9 ... 68 D1
Barnhill Av HAYES BR2 ... 167 K4
Barnhill La YEAD UB4 ... 83 F2
Barnhill Rd WBLY HA9 ... 68 E2
  YEAD UB4 ... 83 F3
Barnhurst Pth OXHEY WD19 ... 33 G3
Barningham Wy
  CDALE/KGS NW9 ... 50 E5
Barnlea Cl FELT TW13 ... 141 J1
Barnmead Gdns DAGW RM9 ... 80 A4
Barnmead Rd BECK BR3 ... 151 F7
  DAGW RM9 ... 80 A4
Barnock Cl DART DA1 ... 138 B6
Barn Ri WBLY HA9 ... 50 C7
Barnsbury Crs BRYLDS KT5 ... 159 K7
Barnsbury Est IS N1 * ... 5 M4
Barnsbury La BRYLDS KT5 ... 172 D1
Barnsbury Pk IS N1 ... 6 A1
Barnsbury Rd IS N1 ... 6 A4
Barnsbury Sq IS N1 ... 6 A1
Barnsbury St IS N1 ... 6 A1
Barnsbury Ter IS N1 ... 5 M1

Barnscroft RYNPK SW20 ... 160 E2
Barnsdale Av POP/IOD E14 ... 112 D3
Barnsdale Rd MV/WKIL W9 ... 88 D3
Barnsley St WCHPL E1 ... 92 D3
Barnstaple La LEW SE13 ... 133 F3
Barnstaple Rd RSLP HA4 ... 65 G2
Barnston Wk IS N1 * ... 6 E3
Barn Wy WBLY HA9 ... 50 C7
Barnwell Rd
  BRXS/STRHM SW2 ... 130 B4
  DART DA1 ... 139 J2
Barnwood Cl MV/WKIL W9 ... 8 C1
  RSLP HA4 ... 64 B3
Baron Cl FBAR/BDGN N11 ... 40 A4
Baroness Rd BETH E2 ... 7 M7
Baronet Gv TOTM N17 ... 42 C7
Baronet Rd TOTM N17 ... 42 C7
Baron Gdns BARK/HLT IG6 ... 60 C2
Baron Gv MTCM CR4 ... 162 D3
Baron Rd BCTR RM8 ... 61 K7
Barons Cl IS N1 * ... 6 A5
Barons Court Rd
  WKENS W14 * ... 107 H4
Baron's Court Rd WKENS W14 ... 107 H4
Baronsfield Rd TWK TW1 * ... 124 C5
Barons Ga EBAR EN4 ... 27 J5
Barons Keep WKENS W14 * ... 107 H4
Barons Md HRW HA1 ... 48 E3
Baronsmead Rd BARN SW13 ... 106 D7
Baronsmere Ct BAR EN5 * ... 26 C3
Baronsmere Rd EFNCH N2 ... 53 J3
The Barons TWK TW1 ... 124 C5
Baron St IS N1 ... 6 B6
Barons Wk CROY/NA CR0 ... 166 B5
Baron Wk CAN/RD E16 ... 94 D4
  MTCM CR4 ... 162 D3
Barque Ms DEPT SE8 ... 112 D5
Barrack Rd HSLWW TW4 ... 122 C3
Barra Hall Rd HYS/HAR UB3 ... 82 D6
Barras Av WDGN N22 ... 55 F1
Barratt Wy
  KTN/HRWW/WS HA3 ... 48 D2
Barrenger Rd MUSWH N10 ... 39 K7
Barrett Rd WALTH E17 ... 58 A3
Barrett's Green Rd
  WLSDN NW10 ... 86 E1
Barrett's Gv STNW/STAM N16 ... 74 A4
Barrett St MHST W1U ... 10 A4
Barrhill Rd BRXS/STRHM SW2 ... 148 E1
Barriedale NWCR SE14 ... 112 B7
Barrier Point Rd CAN/RD E16 ... 95 G7
Barringer Sq TOOT SW17 ... 148 A3
Barrington Cl CLAY IG5 ... 45 K7
  KTTN NW5 ... 72 A4
Barrington Rd BRXN/ST SW9 ... 130 C2
  BXLYHN DA7 ... 136 E1
  CEND/HSY/T N8 ... 54 D4
  CHEAM SM3 ... 161 K7
  MNPK E12 ... 78 A5
Barrington Vls
  WOOL/PLUM SE18 ... 115 F7
Barrington Wk NRWD SE19 * ... 150 A5
Barrow Av CAR SM5 ... 175 K6
Barrow Cl WCHMH N21 ... 41 H1
Barrowdene Cl PIN HA5 ... 47 J1
Barrowell Gn WCHMH N21 ... 41 H1
Barrowgate Rd CHSWK W4 ... 105 K4
Barrow Hedges Cl CAR SM5 ... 175 J7
Barrow Hedges Wy CAR SM5 ... 175 J7
Barrow Hl WPK KT4 ... 173 G1
Barrow Hill Cl WPK KT4 ... 173 G1
Barrow Hill Est STJWD NW8 * ... 3 J6
Barrow Hill Rd STJWD NW8 ... 3 J6
Barrow Point Av PIN HA5 ... 47 J1
Barrow Point La PIN HA5 ... 47 J1
Barrow Rd CROY/NA CR0 ... 177 G4
  STRHM/NOR SW16 ... 148 D4
Barrs Rd WLSDN NW10 ... 69 F5
Barry Av BXLYHN DA7 ... 117 F6
  SEVS/STOTM N15 ... 56 B5
Barry Pde EDUL SE22 ... 131 H3
Barry Rd EDUL SE22 ... 131 H5
  EHAM E6 ... 95 J5
  WLSDN NW10 ... 68 E6
Barset Rd PECK SE15 ... 131 K2
Barsons Cl PGE/AN SE20 ... 150 E6
Barston Rd WNWD SE27 ... 149 J1
Barstow Crs
  BRXS/STRHM SW2 ... 130 A7
Barter St NOXST/BSQ WC1A ... 11 K3
Barth Ms WOOL/PLUM SE18 ... 115 K3
Bartholomew Cl STBT EC1A ... 12 E3
  WAND/EARL SW18 ... 128 B3
Bartholomew La OBST EC2N ... 13 H4
Bartholomew Rd KTTN NW5 ... 72 C5
Bartholomew Sq FSBYE EC1V * ... 6 F9
Bartholomew St STHWK SE1 ... 19 G4
Bartholomew Vls KTTN NW5 ... 72 C5
Barth Rd WOOL/PLUM SE18 ... 115 K3
Bartle Av EHAM E6 ... 95 J1
Bartle Rd NTGHL W11 ... 88 B5
Bartlett Cl POP/IOD E14 ... 93 J5
Bartlett Ct FLST/FETLN EC4A * ... 12 B4
Bartlett St SAND/SEL CR2 ... 177 K4
Barton Av ROMW/RG RM7 ... 62 E7
Barton Cl BXLYHS DA6 ... 137 F4
  EHAM E6 ... 95 K5
  HDN NW4 ... 51 J4
  HOM E9 ... 74 E4
  PECK SE15 ... 131 J2
Barton Mdw BARK/HLT IG6 ... 60 B3
Barton Rd HCH RM12 ... 63 J7
  WKENS W14 ... 107 H4
The Bartons BORE WD6 ... 24 A5
Barton St WEST SW1P ... 17 J4
Barton Wy BORE WD6 ... 24 B1
Bartram Rd BROCKY SE4 ... 132 B4
Bartrip St HOM E9 ... 75 H5
Barts Cl BECK BR3 ... 166 D4
Barwell La CHSGTN KT9 * ... 171 J6
Barwell La CHSGTN KT9 ... 171 J6
Barwick Rd FSTGT E7 ... 77 F3
Barwood Av WWKM BR4 ... 166 E7
Bascome St BRXN/ST SW9 ... 130 C1
Bascombe Gv DART DA1 ... 138 B6
Basden Gv FELT TW13 ... 142 A1
Basedale Rd DAGW RM9 ... 79 H6
Baseing Cl EHAM E6 ... 96 B6
Basevi Wy DEPT SE8 ... 112 D5
Bashley Rd WLSDN NW10 ... 86 E4
Basil Av EHAM E6 ... 95 J2
Basildene Rd HSLWW TW4 ... 122 B2
Basildon Av CLAY IG5 ... 45 J7
Basildon Rd ABYW SE2 ... 116 B3
Basil Gdns CROY/NA CR0 ... 166 A7
  WNWD SE27 ... 149 J4
Basil St CHEL SW3 ... 15 L3
Basin Ap CAN/RD E16 ... 96 B6

  POP/IOD E14 ... 93 G5
Basing Cl THDIT KT7 ... 158 A6
Basing Ct PECK SE15 ... 111 G7
Basingdon Wy CMBW SE5 ... 130 E3
Basing Dr BXLY DA5 ... 137 G5
Basingfield Rd THDIT KT7 ... 158 A6
Basinghall Av CITYW EC2V ... 13 G3
Basinghall Gdns BELMT SM2 ... 175 F7
Basinghall St CITYW EC2V ... 13 G3
Basing Hl GLDGN NW11 ... 52 D7
  WBLY HA9 ... 68 B2
Basing Pl BETH E2 ... 7 K7
Basing St NTGHL W11 ... 88 D5
Basing Wy FNCH N3 ... 52 E2
  THDIT KT7 ... 158 A6
Basire St IS N1 ... 6 F3
Baskerville Gdns
  WLSDN NW10 ... 69 G3
Baskerville Rd
  WAND/EARL SW18 ... 128 D6
Basket Gdns ELTH/MOT SE9 ... 134 D4
Baslow Cl
  KTN/HRWW/WS HA3 ... 34 D7
Baslow Wk CLPT E5 ... 75 F3
Basnett Rd BTSEA SW11 * ... 129 F1
Bassano St EDUL SE22 ... 131 G4
Bassant Rd WOOL/PLUM SE18 ... 116 A5
Bassein Park Rd SHB W12 ... 106 C1
Bassett Cl BELMT SM2 ... 175 F7
Bassett Gdns ISLW TW7 ... 103 H6
Bassett Rd NKENS W10 ... 88 B5
Bassett St KTTN NW5 ... 72 A5
Bassett Wy GFD/PVL UB6 ... 84 B5
Bassingham Rd ALP/SUD HA0 ... 67 K5
  WAND/EARL SW18 ... 128 B6
Basswood Cl PECK SE15 ... 131 J2
Bastable Av BARK IG11 ... 97 F1
Bastion Rd ABYW SE2 ... 116 B4
Baston Manor Rd WWKM BR4 ... 181 F1
Baston Rd HAYES BR2 ... 181 F1
  HAYES BR2 ... 181 G3
Bastwick St FSBYE EC1V ... 6 E9
Basuto Rd FUL/PGN SW6 ... 107 K7
Batavia Ms NWCR SE14 ... 112 B6
Batavia Rd NWCR SE14 ... 112 B6
  SUN TW16 ... 141 F7
Batchelor St IS N1 ... 6 B4
Batchworth La NTHWD HA6 ... 32 A4
Bateman Cl BARK IG11 ... 78 C5
Bateman Ms CLAP SW4 ... 129 J5
Bateman Rd CHING E4 ... 43 J5
Bateman's Bldgs
  SOHO/SHAV W1D * ... 11 G5
Batemans Cnr CHSWK W4 * ... 106 A3
Bateman's Rw SDTCH EC2A * ... 7 K9
Bateman St SOHO/SHAV W1D ... 11 G5
Bates Crs CROY/NA CR0 ... 177 G4
  STRHM/NOR SW16 ... 148 C6
Bate St POP/IOD E14 ... 93 H6
Bathgate Rd WIM/MER SW19 ... 146 B2
Bath Gv BETH E2 ... 92 C1
Bath House Rd CROY/NA CR0 ... 163 K7
Bath Pas KUT/HW KT1 ... 158 E1
Bath Pl BAR EN5 ... 26 D2
  SDTCH EC2A * ... 7 J8
Bath Rd CHSWK W4 ... 106 B3
  DART DA1 ... 138 E6
  ED N9 ... 42 D1
  FSTGT E7 ... 77 H5
  HTHAIR TW6 ... 101 H4
  WDR/YW UB7 ... 100 A7
Baths Ap FUL/PGN SW6 ... 107 J6
Bath St FSBYE EC1V ... 6 F8
Bath Ter STHWK SE1 ... 18 F4
Bathurst Av WIM/MER SW19 ... 147 F7
Bathurst Gdns WLSDN NW10 ... 87 K1
Bathurst Ms BAY/PAD W2 ... 9 H6
Bathurst Rd IL IG1 ... 60 B7
Bathurst St BAY/PAD W2 ... 9 H6
Bathway WOOL/PLUM SE18 ... 115 F3
Batley Cl MTCM CR4 ... 162 E6
Batley Pl STNW/STAM N16 ... 74 B2
Batley Rd STNW/STAM N16 ... 74 B2
Batman Cl SHB W12 ... 87 K7
Batoum Gdns HMSMTH W6 ... 107 F2
Batson St SHB W12 ... 106 D1
Batsworth Rd MTCM CR4 ... 162 C3
Batten Cl EHAM E6 ... 95 K5
Batten St BTSEA SW11 ... 128 D2
Batten Cots POP/IOD E14 * ... 93 G4
Battenburg Wk NRWD SE19 * ... 150 A5
Battersby Rd CAT SE6 ... 152 B1
Battersea Br WBPTN SW10 ... 108 C6
Battersea Bridge Rd
  BTSEA SW11 ... 108 D6
Battersea Church Rd
  BTSEA SW11 ... 108 C7
Battersea High St
  BTSEA SW11 ... 128 C1
Battersea Park Rd
  BTSEA SW11 ... 109 G7
Battersea Ri BTSEA SW11 ... 128 D4
Battersea Sq BTSEA SW11 * ... 108 C6
Battery Rd THMD SE28 ... 115 K1
Battishill St IS N1 ... 6 C2
Battle Bridge La STHWK SE1 ... 13 J9
Battledean Rd HBRY N5 ... 73 H4
Battle Rd ERITH DA8 ... 117 K3
Batty St WCHPL E1 ... 92 C5
Baudwin Rd CAT SE6 ... 152 C1
Baugh Rd SCUP DA14 ... 155 J4
The Baulk WAND/EARL SW18 ... 127 K6
Bavant Rd STRHM/NOR SW16 ... 163 K1
Bavaria Rd ARCH N19 ... 72 E1
Bavent Rd CMBW SE5 ... 130 D1
Bawdale Rd EDUL SE22 ... 131 G4
Bawdsey Av GNTH/NBYPK IG2 ... 61 F3
Bawtree Rd NWCR SE14 ... 112 B6
Bawtry Rd TRDG/WHET N20 ... 39 K2
Baxendale TRDG/WHET N20 ... 39 G1
Baxendale St BETH E2 ... 92 C2
Baxter Cl NWDGN UB2 ... 103 G2
Baxter Rd CAN/RD E16 ... 95 G5
  IL IG1 ... 78 B4
  IS N1 ... 73 K5
  UED N18 ... 42 D3
Bay Ct EA W5 * ... 105 F2
Baycroft Cl PIN HA5 ... 47 G2
Bayfield Rd ELTH/MOT SE9 ... 134 C3
Bayford Ms HACK E8 * ... 74 E6
Bayford Rd WLSDN NW10 ... 88 B2
Bayford St HACK E8 ... 74 D6
Baygrove Ms KUT/HW KT1 * ... 143 J7
Bayham Pl CAMTN NW1 ... 4 E4
Bayham Rd CHSWK W4 ... 106 A2
  MRDN SM4 ... 162 A3
  WEA W13 ... 85 H6
Bayham St CAMTN NW1 ... 4 E3
Bayhurst Dr NTHWD HA6 ... 32 D5
Bayleaf Cl HPTN TW12 ... 142 D4
Bayley St FITZ W1T ... 11 G3
Baylis Ms TWK TW1 ... 124 C6

Baylis Rd *STHWK* SE1....18 A3
Bayliss Av *THMD* SE28....97 K6
Bayliss Cl *ENC/FH* EN2....28 E4
Bayly Rd *DART* DA1....139 K5
Bayne Cl *EHAM* E6....96 A5
Baynes Ms *HAMP* NW3....71 H5
Baynes St *CAMTN* NW1....4 F2
Baynham Cl *BXLY* DA5....137 G5
Bayonne Rd *HMSMTH* W6....107 H5
Bayshill Ri *NTHLT* UB5....66 B5
Bayston Rd *STNW/STAM* N16....74 B2
Bayswater Rd *BAY/PAD* W2....8 E7
Baythorne St *BOW* E3....93 H4
Baytree Cl *BFN/LL* DA15....136 A7
  BMLY BR1....153 J3
Baytree Ms *STHWK* SE1....19 G5
Baytree Rd *BRXS/STRHM* SW2....130 A3
Bazalgette Cl *NWMAL* KT3....159 K4
Bazalgette Gdns *NWMAL* KT3....160 K4
Bazely St *POP/IOD* E14....94 A6
Bazile Rd *WCHMH* N21....29 C5
Beacham Cl *CHARL* SE7....114 C5
Beachborough Rd *BMLY* BR1....152 A3
Beachcroft Rd *WAN* E11....76 C2
Beach Gv *FELT* TW13....142 A2
Beachy Rd *BOW* E3....75 J6
Beacon Ga *NWCR* SE14....132 A2
Beacon Hl *HOLWY* N7....72 E4
Beacon Pl *CROY/NA* CRO....176 B2
Beacon Rd *ERITH* DA8....118 E6
  HTHAIR TW6....120 B3
  LEW SE13....133 G5
Beaconsfield Cl
  BKHTH/KID SE3....113 K5
  CHSWK W4....105 K4
Beaconsfield Cots
  TRDG/WHET N20 *....38 E2
Beaconsfield Gdns
  ESH/CLAY KT10....170 D6
Beaconsfield Rd
  BKHTH/KID SE3....113 K5
  BMLY BR1....168 D3
  CAN/RD E16....94 D4
  CHSWK W4....106 A2
  CROY/NA CRO....164 E5
  ED N9....104 D1
  ELTH/MOT SE9....153 J3
  ESH/CLAY KT10....170 A3
  FBAR/BDGN N11....40 A3
  LEY E10....76 A2
  NWMAL KT3....160 A1
  SEVS/STOTM N15....56 A3
  STHL UB1....83 H7
  SURB KT6....159 G6
  TRDG/WHET N20....39 K2
  TWK TW1....124 C5
  WALTH E17....57 H5
  WALW SE17....19 H9
  WLSDN NW10....69 H5
  YEAD UB4....83 G7
Beaconsfield Terrace Rd
  WKENS W14....107 H2
Beaconsfield Wk
  FUL/PGN SW6....107 J7
Beacontree Av *WALTH* E17....44 B7
Beacontree Rd *WAN* E11....58 D6
Beadlow Cl *CAR* SM5....162 C5
Beadman Pl *WNWD* SE27 *....149 H3
Beadman St *WNWD* SE27....149 H3
Beadnell Rd *FSTH* SE23....132 A7
Beadon Rd *HAYES* BR2....167 K3
  HMSMTH W6....107 F3
Beaford Gv *RYNPK* SW20....161 J2
Beagle Cl *FELT* TW13....141 F3
Beak St *REGST* W1B....10 E6
Beal Cl *WELL* DA16....116 B7
Beale Cl *PLMGR* N13....41 H4
Beale Pl *BOW* E3....93 H1
Beale Rd *BOW* E3....75 H4
Beal Rd *IL* IG1....78 A1
Beam Av *DAGE* RM10....80 D7
Beames Rd *WLSDN* NW10....69 F7
Beaminster Gdns
  BARK/HLT IG6....60 B2
Beamish Dr *BUSH* WD23....22 C7
Beamish Rd *ED* N9....30 C7
Beamway *DAGE* RM10....81 F6
Beancare Ct *HOM* E9....75 H5
Bean Rd *BXLYHS* DA6....136 E3
Beanshaw *ELTH/MOT* SE9....154 A3
Beansland Gv *CHDH* RM6....62 A1
Bear Aly *FLST/FETLN* EC4A *....12 C4
Bear Cl *ROMW/RG* RM7....62 D5
Beardell Rd *NRWD* SE19....150 B5
Beardow Gv
  STHGT/OAK N14 *....28 C5
Beard Rd *KUTN/CMB* KT2....144 B4
Beardsfield *PLSTW* E13....76 E7
Beard's Hl *HPTN* TW12....142 A7
Beard's Hill Cl *HPTN* TW12....142 A7
Beardsley Wy *ACT* W3....106 A1
Beards Rd *ASHF* TW15....140 C5
Bearfield Rd *KUTN/CMB* KT2....144 A6
Bear Gdns *STHWK* SE1....12 E8
Bear La *STHWK* SE1....12 E8
Bear Rd *FELT* TW13....141 H3
Bearstead Ri *BROCKY* SE4....132 C4
Bearsted Ter *BECK* BR3 *....151 J2
Bear St *LSQ/SEVD* WC2H....11 H6
Beasant House *WATN* WD24 *....21 H1
Beatrice Av
  STRHM/NOR SW16....164 A3
  WBLY HA9....68 A4
Beatrice Cl *PIN* HA5....46 E3
  PLSTW E13....94 E3
Beatrice Pl *KENS* W8....14 C4
Beatrice Rd *ED* N9....30 E6
  FSBYPK N4....55 G6
  RCHPK/HAM TW10....125 G4
  STHL UB1....83 K7
  STHWK SE1....111 H3
  WALTH E17....57 H5
Beattie Cl *EBED/NFELT* TW14....121 J6
Beattock Ri *MUSWH* N10....54 B3
Beatty Rd *STAN* HA7....35 J5
  STNW/STAM N16....74 A3
Beatty St *CAMTN* NW1....4 E5
Beattyville Gdns *CLAY* IG5....60 A1
Beauchamp Cl *CHSWK* W4....105 K3
Beauchamp Pl *CHEL* SW3....15 K3
Beauchamp Rd *BTSEA* SW11....128 D3
  E/WMO/HCT KT8....157 J2
  FSTGT E7....77 F6
  NRWD SE19....149 J7
  SUT SM1....174 E4
  TWK TW1....124 B6
Beauchamp St *HCIRC* EC1N....12 A1
Beauchamp Ter *BARN* SW13....126 E2
Beauclerc Rd *HMSMTH* W6....106 E2
Beauclerk Cl *FELT* TW13....122 A7
Beaufort *EHAM* E6....96 A4

Beaufort Av
  KTN/HRWW/WS HA3....49 G3
Beaufort Cl *CHING* E4....43 K5
  EA W5....86 B4
  PUT/ROE SW15....127 F5
  ROMW/RG RM7....62 E3
Beaufort Ct
  RCHPK/HAM TW10....143 J3
Beaufort Dr *GLDGN* NW11....52 E3
Beaufort Gdns *CHEL* SW3....15 K3
  HDN NW4....52 A5
  HEST TW5....102 D7
  IL IG1....60 A7
  STRHM/NOR SW16....149 F6
Beaufort Rd *EA* W5....86 B4
  KUT/HW KT1....159 F3
  RCHPK/HAM TW10....143 J3
  RSLP HA4 *....64 B1
  TWK TW1....124 D6
Beaufort St *CHEL* SW3....15 G9
Beaufoy Rd *TOTM* N17....42 A6
Beaufoy Wk *LBTH* SE11....17 M6
Beaulieu Av *CAN/RD* E16....95 F7
  SYD SE26....150 D3
Beaulieu Cl *CDALE/KGS* NW9....51 G5
  CMBW SE5....130 E2
  HSLWW TW4....122 E4
  MTCM CR4....148 A7
  OXHEY WD19....21 G7
  TWK TW1....124 E5
Beaulieu Dr *PIN* HA5....47 J5
Beaulieu Gdns *WCHMH* N21....29 J6
Beaumaris Gn
  CDALE/KGS NW9 *....51 G5
Beaumont Av *ALP/SUD* HA0....67 J4
  RCH/KEW TW9....125 G2
  RYLN/HDSTN HA2....48 B5
  WKENS W14....107 J4
Beaumont Cl *EFNCH* N2....53 J3
  KUTN/CMB KT2....144 C6
Beaumont Ct *ALP/SUD* HA0 *....67 J4
Beaumont Crs *RAIN* RM13....81 J5
  WKENS W14....107 J4
Beaumont Dr *ASHF* TW15....140 B4
  WPK KT4....160 E7
Beaumont Gdns *HAMP* NW3....70 E1
  ISLW TW7....124 A4
Beaumont Gv *WCHPL* E1....93 F3
Beaumont Ms *MHST* W1U *....10 B2
  PIN HA5 *....47 J2
Beaumont Pl *FITZ* W1T....4 F9
  ISLW TW7....124 A4
Beaumont Ri *ARCH* N19....54 D7
Beaumont Rd *CHSWK* W4....105 K2
  LEY E10....57 K6
  NRWD SE19....149 J5
  PLSTW E13....95 F2
  STMC/STPC BR5....169 J5
  WIM/MER SW19....127 H6
Beaumont Sq *WCHPL* E1....93 F4
Beaumont St *CAVSQ/HST* W1G....10 B2
Beaumont Ter *LEW* SE13 *....133 H6
Beauvais Ter *NTHLT* UB5....83 H2
Beauval Rd *EDUL* SE22....131 G5
Beaverbank Rd
  ELTH/MOT SE9....135 J7
Beaver Cl *HPTN* TW12....142 B7
  MRDN SM4....161 F6
  PGE/AN SE20 *....150 C6
Beavers Crs *HSLWW* TW4....122 C3
Beavers La *HSLWW* TW4....122 B2
Beaverwood Rd *CHST* BR7....154 E4
Beavor La *HMSMTH* W6....106 D3
Bebbington Rd
  WOOL/PLUM SE18 *....115 K3
Beccles Dr *BARK* IG11....79 F5
Beccles St *POP/IOD* E14....93 H5
Bec Cl *RSLP* HA4....65 H2
Beck Cl *GNWCH* SE10....112 E7
  LEW SE13....112 E7
Beckenham Gdns *ED* N9....42 A2
Beckenham Gv *HAYES* BR2....167 G1
Beckenham Hill Rd
  BECK BR3....151 K5
Beckenham La *HAYES* BR2....167 H1
Beckenham Place Pk
  BECK BR3....151 K6
Beckenham Rd *BECK* BR3....166 E6
  PGE/AN SE20....151 F5
Becket Av *EHAM* E6....96 A2
Becket Cl *SNWD* SE25....165 H5
  WIM/MER SW19 *....147 F7
Becket Fold *HRW* HA1 *....49 F4
Becket Rd *UED* N18....30 E7
Becket St *STHWK* SE1....19 G3
Beckett Cl *BELV* DA17....117 F2
  STRHM/NOR SW16....148 D1
  WLSDN NW10....69 F4
Becketts Cl *BXLY* DA5....137 K7
  EBED/NFELT TW14....122 A5
Becketts Pl *KUT/HW* KT1....143 G5
Beckett Wk *BECK* BR3....151 G5
Beckford Dr *STMC/STPC* BR5....169 J6
Beckford Pl *WALW* SE17 *....18 F8
Beckford Rd *CROY/NA* CRO....165 G5
Beck La *BECK* BR3....166 A2
Becklow Rd *SHB* W12....106 C1
Beck River Pk *BECK* BR3....151 H1
Beck Rd *HACK* E8....74 D7
  MTCM CR4....148 B7
Becks Rd *SCUP* DA14....155 G2
Beckton Rd *CAN/RD* E16....94 D4
Beck Wy *BECK* BR3....166 C2
Beckway Rd
  STRHM/NOR SW16....163 J1
Beckway St *WALW* SE17 *....19 H6
Beckwith Rd *HNHL* SE24....130 E4
Beclands Rd *TOOT* SW17....148 A5
Becmead Av
  KTN/HRWW/WS HA3....49 H4
  STRHM/NOR SW16....148 D3
Becondale Rd *NRWD* SE19....150 A4
Becontree Av *BCTR* RM8....79 H3
Bective Rd *FSTGT* E7....76 E3
  PUT/ROE SW15....127 H3
Becton Pl *ERITH* DA8....117 J7
Bedale Rd *ENC/FH* EN2....29 J1
  ROMW/RG RM7....62 E1
Bedale St *STHWK* SE1....13 G9
Beddington Cross
  CROY/NA CRO....163 J7
Beddington Farm Rd
  CROY/NA CRO....163 K6
Beddington Gdns *WLGTN* SM6....176 D5
Beddington Gn
  STMC/STPC BR5....155 F7
Beddington La *CROY/NA* CRO....163 H5
Beddington Pth
  STMC/STPC BR5....155 F7
  GDMY/SEVK IG3....61 F6
  STMC/STPC BR5....154 E7

Beddington Ter
  CROY/NA CRO *....164 A6
Bede Cl *PIN* HA5....33 H7
Bede Rd *CHDH* RM6....61 J5
Bedevere Rd *ED* N9....42 C7
Bedfont Cl *EBED/NFELT* TW14....121 F5
  MTCM CR4....163 F1
Bedfont Green Cl
  EBED/NFELT TW14....121 F6
Bedfont La *EBED/NFELT* TW14....121 K7
Bedfont Rd
  EBED/NFELT TW14....121 F7
  STWL/WRAY TW19....120 C5
Bedford Av *BAR* EN5....26 D4
  RSQ WC1B....11 H3
  YEAD UB4....83 F5
Bedfordbury *CHCR* WC2N....11 J7
Bedford Cl *CHSWK* W4 *....106 B5
  MUSWH N10....54 B3
Bedford Cnr *CHSWK* W4 *....106 B3
Bedford Ct *CHCR* WC2N....11 J7
Bedford Gdns *KENS* W8....8 A3
Bedford Hl *BAL* SW12....148 B1
Bedford Ms *BAT* SE6....151 K1
  SEVS/STOTM N15....55 J5
Bedford Pk *CROY/NA* CRO....164 D7
Bedford Pl *CROY/NA* CRO....164 D7
  RSQ WC1B....11 J2
Bedford Rd *BFN/LL* DA15....154 C1
  CEND/HSY/T N8....54 D5
  CHSWK W4....106 A3
  CLAP SW4....129 K3
  DART DA1....139 K3
  ED N9....30 D6
  EFNCH N2....53 J2
  EHAM E6....78 A7
  HRW HA1....48 C5
  IL IG1....78 B2
  MLHL NW7....37 G1
  NTHWD HA6....32 B5
  RSLP HA4....64 D3
  SEVS/STOTM N15....55 J4
  SWFD E18....58 E1
  WALTH E17....57 J1
  WDGN N22....40 E7
  WEA W13....85 H6
  WHTN TW2....142 D2
  WPK KT4....174 D1
Bedford Rw *GINN* WC1R....11 M3
Bedford Sq *RSQ* WC1B....11 H3
Bedford St *COVGDN* WC2E....11 J6
Bedford Vls *KUT/HW* KT1....159 G1
Bedford Wy *STPAN* WC1H....11 J1
Bedgebury Gdns
  WIM/MER SW19....146 C1
Bedgebury Rd *ELTH/MOT* SE9....134 C3
Bedivere Rd *BMLY* BR1....152 E2
Bedlam Ms *LBTH* SE11....17 M5
Bedlow Cl *STJWD* NW8....9 H1
Bedlow Wy *CROY/NA* CRO....177 F3
Bedonwell Rd *BXLYHN* DA7....117 G2
Bedser Cl *LBTH* SE11....17 M9
  THHTH CR7....164 D2
Bedser Dr *GFD/PVL* UB6....66 D4
Bedster Gdns
  E/WMO/HCT KT8....157 G1
Bedwardine Rd *NRWD* SE19....150 A6
Bedwell Gdns *HYS/HAR* UB3....101 H3
Bedwell Rd *BELV* DA17....117 H4
  TOTM N17....42 A7
Beeby Rd *CAN/RD* E16....95 F4
Beech Av *ACT* W3....87 G7
  BFN/LL DA15....136 B6
  BKHH IG9....45 F1
  BTFD TW8....104 A6
  RSLP HA4....47 F7
  TRDG/WHET N20....27 J7
Beech Cl *ASHF* TW15....140 B4
  CAR SM5....175 K1
  DEPT SE8....112 C5
  ED N9....30 C5
  HCH RM12....81 K2
  PUT/ROE SW15....126 D6
  SUN TW16....156 C1
  WDR/YW UB7....100 D2
  WIM/MER SW19....146 A5
Beech Copse *BMLY* BR1....168 E1
  SAND/SEL CR2....178 A4
Beech Ct *ELTH/MOT* SE9 *....134 D5
Beechcroft *CHST* BR7....154 A6
Beechcroft Av *BXLYHN* DA7....118 A7
  GLDGN NW11....52 E6
  NWMAL KT3....144 E7
  RKW/CH/CXG WD3....20 A5
  RYLN/HDSTN HA2....48 A6
  STHL UB1....83 K7
Beechcroft Cl *HEST* TW5....102 D6
  STRHM/NOR SW16....149 F4
Beechcroft Gdns *WBLY* HA9....68 B2
  CHSGTN KT9....172 B5
  MORT/ESHN SW14 *....125 K2
  SWFD E18....59 F1
  TOOT SW17....147 K2
Beechdale *WCHMH* N21....41 F1
Beechdale Rd
  BRXS/STRHM SW2....130 A5
Beech Dell *HAYES* BR2....181 K3
  EFNCH N2....53 K2
Beechen Cliff Wy *ISLW* TW7....104 A7
Beechengrove *PIN* HA5....47 K2
Beechen Gv *WAT* WD17....21 H2
Beeches Av *CAR* SM5....175 J6
Beeches Rd *PGE/AN* SE20....150 E7
  CHEAM SM3....161 H7
  TOOT SW17....147 J2
The Beeches *HNWL* W7 *....104 A1
Beeches Wk *BELMT* SM2....175 H7
Beechfield Gdns
  ROMW/RG RM7....62 E6
Beechfield Rd *BMLY* BR1....168 B1
  CAT SE6....132 C7
  ERITH DA8....118 B6
  FSBYPK N4....55 J5
Beech Gdns *DAGE* RM10....80 D6
  EA W5....105 F1
Beech Gv *MTCM* CR4....163 J4
  NWMAL KT3....160 A2
Beech Hall Crs *CHING* E4....44 B6
Beech Hall Rd *CHING* E4....44 A6
Beech Hill *BAR* EN4....27 H1
Beech Hill Av *BAR* EN4....27 G1
Beech House Rd
  CROY/NA CRO....177 K2
Beech Lawns
  NFNCH/WDSPK N12 *....39 H4
Beechmont Cl *BMLY* BR1....152 C4
Beechmore Gdns *CHEAM* SM3....174 B1
Beechmore Rd *BTSEA* SW11....108 E7
Beechmount Av *HNWL* W7....84 D4

Beecholme Av *MTCM* CR4....148 B7
Beecholme Est *CLPT* E5 *....74 E2
Beech Rd *DART* DA1....139 G7
  EBED/NFELT TW14....121 H6
  FBAR/BDGN N11....40 E5
  STRHM/NOR SW16....163 K1
Beechrow *KUTN/CMB* KT2....144 A3
Beech St *ROMW/RG* RM7....62 E3
  BARB EC2Y....12 E2
Beech Tree Cl *IS* N1....6 A1
  STAN HA7....35 J4
Beech Tree Pl *SUT* SM1....175 F4
Beechvale Cl
  NFNCH/WDSPK N12....39 J4
  MLHL NW7....37 F4
Beech Wk *DART* DA1....138 D3
  MLHL NW7....37 F4
Beech Wy *WHTN* TW2....142 A2
  WLSDN NW10....69 F6
Beechwood Av *FNCH* N3....52 D2
  GFD/PVL UB6....84 B2
  HYS/HAR UB3....82 B6
  RCH/KEW TW9....105 H7
  RSLP HA4....64 D1
  RYLN/HDSTN HA2....66 B2
  SUN TW16....140 E5
  THHTH CR7....164 C3
Beechwood Cl *EFNCH* N2 *....53 K3
  MLHL NW7....37 G4
  SURB KT6....158 D6
Beechwood Crs *BXLYHN* DA7....136 E2
Beechwood Dr *HAYES* BR2....181 H3
  WFD IG8....44 D4
Beechwood Gdns *CLAY* IG5....59 K4
  RAIN RM13....99 K4
  RYLN/HDSTN HA2....66 B2
Beechwood Gv *ACT* W3....87 G6
Beechwood Ms *ED* N9....42 C1
Beechwood Pk *SWFD* E18....58 E2
Beechwood Ri *CHST* BR7....154 B3
Beechwood Rd
  CEND/HSY/T N8....54 D3
  HACK E8....74 B5
  SAND/SEL CR2....178 A7
Beechworth Cl *HAMP* NW3....70 E1
Beecroft La *BROCKY* SE4....132 B4
Beecroft Ms *BROCKY* SE4....132 B4
Beecroft Rd *BROCKY* SE4....132 B4
Beehive Cl *BORE* WD6....23 K5
  HACK E8....7 L1
Beehive La *REDBR* IG4....59 K4
Beehive Pl *BRXN/ST* SW9....130 B2
Beeleigh Rd *MRDN* SM4....162 A3
Beeston Cl *HACK* E8....74 C4
  OXHEY WD19....33 H3
Beeston Pl *BGVA* SW1W....16 D4
Beeston Rd *EBAR* EN4....27 H5
Beeston Wy
  EBED/NFELT TW14....122 B6
Beethoven Rd *BORE* WD6....23 J1
Beethoven St *NKENS* W10....88 C2
Beeton Cl *PIN* HA5....34 A6
Beeton Wy *WNWD* SE27....149 J3
Begbie Rd *BKHTH/KID* SE3....114 B7
Beggars Bush La *WATW* WD18....20 B4
Beggar's Roost La *SUT* SM1....174 E5
Begonia Cl *EHAM* E6....95 J4
Begonia Pl *HPTN* TW12....142 A5
Beira St *BAL* SW12....129 G6
Bekesbourne St
  POP/IOD E14 *....93 G5
Belcroft Cl *BMLY* BR1....152 D6
Beldham Gdns
  E/WMO/HCT KT8....157 G2
Belfairs Dr *CHDH* RM6....61 J6
Belfairs Gdn *OXHEY* WD19....33 H4
Belfairs Gn *OXHEY* WD19....33 H4
Belfast Rd *SNWD* SE25....165 J3
  STNW/STAM N16....74 B1
Belfield Rd *HOR/WEW* KT19....173 F7
Belford Gv *WOOL/PLUM* SE18....115 F3
Belfort Rd *PECK* SE15....131 K1
Belfry Cl *BERM/RHTH* SE16 *....111 J4
Belfry Rd *MNPK* E12....77 H2
Belgrade Rd *HPTN* TW12....142 B7
  STNW/STAM N16....74 A3
Belgrave Cl *ACT* W3....105 K1
  MLHL NW7....37 F4
  STHGT/OAK N14....28 C4
  STJWD NW8....2 D7
Belgrave Crs *SUN* TW16....141 F7
Belgrave Gdns *STAN* HA7....35 J4
  STHGT/OAK N14....28 D4
  STJWD NW8....2 B4
Belgrave Ms South
  KTBR SW1X....16 B3
Belgrave Ms West *KTBR* SW1X....16 A3
Belgrave Pl *KTBR* SW1X....16 B3
Belgrave Rd *BARN* SW13....106 C6
  HSLWW TW4....122 E2
  IL IG1....59 K7
  LEY E10....58 A7
  MTCM CR4....162 C2
  PIM SW1V....16 E6
  PLSTW E13....95 G3
  SNWD SE25....165 G3
  SUN TW16....141 F7
  WALTH E17....58 A3
  WAN E11....58 E7
Belgrave Sq *KTBR* SW1X....16 A3
Belgrave St *WCHPL* E1....93 F5
Belgrave Wk *MTCM* CR4....162 C2
Belgravia Cl *BAR* EN5....26 D2
Belgravia Gdns *BMLY* BR1....152 C5
Belgravia Ms *KUT/HW* KT1....158 E3
Belgravia St *KCROSS* N1C....5 J7
Belinda Rd *BRXN/ST* SW9....130 C2
Belitha Vls *IS* N1....5 M1
Bellamaine Cl *THMD* SE28....116 A1
Bellamy Cl *EDGW* HA8....36 E2
  POP/IOD E14....112 D1
  WKENS W14....107 J4
Bellamy Dr *STAN* HA7....35 H7
Bellamy Rd *CHING* E4....43 K5
  ENC/FH EN2....29 K1
Bellamy St *BAL* SW12....129 G6
Bel La *FELT* TW13....141 J2
Bellarmine Cl *THMD* SE28....116 A2
Bellasis Av *BRXS/STRHM* SW2....148 E1
Bell Av *WDR/YW* UB7....100 C3
Bellclose Rd *WDR/YW* UB7....100 B1
Bell Dr *WAND/EARL* SW18....127 J6
Bellefields Rd *BRXN/ST* SW9....130 A2
Bellegrove Cl *WELL* DA16....136 A1
Bellegrove Rd *WELL* DA16....135 K1
Bellenden Rd *PECK* SE15....131 G1
Belle Staines Pleasaunce
  CHING E4....43 J1
Belleville Rd *BTSEA* SW11....128 D4
Belle Vue *GFD/PVL* UB6....66 D1
Belle Vue La *BUSH* WD23....22 D7

Bellevue Pk *THHTH* CR7....164 D2
Bellevue Pl *WCHPL* E1 *....92 E3
Belle Vue Rd *HDN* NW4....58 B1
  WALTH E17....58 B1
Bellevue Rd *BARN* SW13....126 D1
  BXLYHS DA6....137 G4
  FBAR/BDGN N11....40 A3
  KUT/HW KT1....159 F2
  TOOT SW17....128 E6
  WEA W13....85 H3
Bellew St *TOOT* SW17....147 G2
Bellfield *CROY/NA* CRO....179 G7
Bellfield Av
  KTN/HRWW/WS HA3....34 D5
Bellfield Cl *BKHTH/KID* SE3....114 A6
Bell Gdns *LEY* E10 *....57 J7
Bellgate Ms *KTTN* NW5....72 B3
Bell Gn *SYD* SE26....151 H3
Bell Green La *SYD* SE26....151 H4
Bell House Rd *ROMW/RG* RM7....62 E7
Bellina Ms *KTTN* NW5....72 B3
Bellingham *CAT* SE6....151 J2
Bellingham Rd *CAT* SE6....152 A2
Bell Inn Yd *BANK* EC3V....13 H5
Bell La *CAN/RD* E16....94 D7
  HDN NW4....52 B3
  TWK TW1....124 B7
  WBLY HA9 *....67 K1
  WCHPL E1....13 L3
Bell Meadow *NRWD* SE19....150 A3
Bello Cl *HNHL* SE24....130 C7
Bellot St *GNWCH* SE10....113 H4
Bell Pde *HSLW* TW3 *....123 G3
  WWKM BR4 *....180 A1
Bellring Cl *BELV* DA17....117 H5
Bell Rd *E/WMO/HCT* KT8....157 J4
  HSLW TW3....123 G2
Bells Hl *BAR* EN5....26 B4
Bell St *BAY/PAD* W2....9 J2
  WOOL/PLUM SE18....114 D7
Belltrees Gv
  STRHM/NOR SW16....149 F4
Bellview Ct *HSLW* TW3....123 G3
Bell Water Ga
  WOOL/PLUM SE18....115 F2
Bell Wharf La *CANST* EC4R....12 F7
Bellwood Rd *PECK* SE15....132 A3
Bell Yd *LINN* WC2A....12 A5
Bell Yard Ms *STHWK* SE1....19 K2
Belmont Av *ALP/SUD* HA0....68 B7
  EBAR EN4....27 K4
  ED N9....30 C7
  NWDGN UB2....102 D3
  NWMAL KT3....160 D4
  PLMGR N13....40 E4
  TOTM N17....55 J2
  WELL DA16....135 K1
Belmont Cir
  KTN/HRWW/WS HA3 *....35 H7
Belmont Cl *CHING* E4....44 B4
  CLAP SW4....129 H2
  EBAR EN4....27 K3
  TRDG/WHET N20....27 F7
  WFD IG8....45 F3
Belmont Gv *CHSWK* W4....106 A3
  LEW SE13....133 G2
Belmont Hl *LEW* SE13....133 G2
Belmont La *CHST* BR7....154 C4
  STAN HA7....35 J6
Belmont Pde *CHST* BR7 *....154 B4
  GLDGN NW11 *....52 D4
Belmont Pk *LEW* SE13....133 H3
Belmont Park Cl *LEW* SE13....133 H3
Belmont Park Rd *LEY* E10....57 K5
Belmont Ri *BELMT* SM2....174 D6
Belmont Rd *BECK* BR3....166 B1
  BUSH WD23....21 J3
  CHST BR7....154 B4
  CLAP SW4....129 H2
  ERITH DA8....117 H6
  IL IG1....78 C2
  KTN/HRWW/WS HA3....49 F2
  SEVS/STOTM N15....55 J3
  SNWD SE25....165 J4
  WHTN TW2....142 D1
  WLGTN SM6....176 C4
Belmont St *CAMTN* NW1....4 B1
Belmont Ter *CHSWK* W4....106 A3
Belmor *BORE* WD6....24 C4
Belmore Av *YEAD* UB4....82 E5
Belmore La *HOLWY* N7....72 D4
Belmore St *VX/NE* SW8....109 J7
Beloe Cl *PUT/ROE* SW15....126 D3
Belsham St *HOM* E9....74 E5
Belsize Av *HAMP* NW3....71 H4
  PLMGR N13....41 F5
  WEA W13....104 C2
Belsize Court Gdns
  HAMP NW3 *....71 H4
Belsize Crs *HAMP* NW3....71 H4
Belsize Gdns *SUT* SM1....175 F3
Belsize Gv *HAMP* NW3....71 J5
Belsize La *HAMP* NW3....71 H5
Belsize Ms *HAMP* NW3 *....71 H5
Belsize Pk *HAMP* NW3....71 H5
Belsize Park Gdns *HAMP* NW3....71 H5
Belsize Park Ms *HAMP* NW3 *....71 H5
Belsize Pl *HAMP* NW3 *....71 H4
Belsize Rd *KIL/WHAMP* NW6....2 C3
  KTN/HRWW/WS HA3....34 D6
Belsize Sq *HAMP* NW3....71 H5
Belsize Ter *HAMP* NW3....71 H5
Belson Rd *WOOL/PLUM* SE18....114 D4
Beltane Dr *WIM/MER* SW19....146 B2
Belthorn Crs *BAL* SW12....129 H6
Belton Rd *FSTGT* E7....77 F6
  SCUP DA14....155 G3
  TOTM N17....56 A2
  WALTH E17....57 H5
  WLSDN NW10....69 J8
Belton Wy *BOW* E3....93 J4
Beltran Rd *FUL/PGN* SW6....128 A1
Beltwood Rd *BELV* DA17....117 K3
Belvedere Av *CLAY* IG5....60 B1
  WIM/MER SW19....146 C5
Belvedere Blds *STHWK* SE1....18 D2
Belvedere Cl *ESH/CLAY* KT10....170 B4
  TEDD TW11....142 E4
Belvedere Ct *BELV* DA17....117 G2
  OXHEY WD19....21 G6
Belvedere Dr *WIM/MER* SW19....146 C4
Belvedere Gdns
  E/WMO/HCT KT8....156 E4
  WIM/MER SW19....146 C4
Belvedere Ms *PECK* SE15....131 K2
Belvedere Pl
  BRXS/STRHM SW2....130 A3
Belvedere Rd *ABYW* SE2....97 K7
  BXLYHS DA7....137 G2
  BXLYHN DA7....137 G2
  HNWL W7....103 K2
  LEY E10....57 G7
  NRWD SE19....150 B5

STHWK SE1	17	L1
Belvedere Sq *WIM/MER* SW19	146	C4
Belvedere Strd		
CDALE/KGS NW9	51	H1
The Belvedere *WBPTN* SW10 *	108	A7
Belvedere Wy		
KTN/HRWW/WS HA3	50	A5
Belvoir Rd *EDUL* SE22	131	H4
Belvue Cl *NTHLT* UB5	66	A6
Belvue Rd *NTHLT* UB5	66	A6
Bembridge Cl		
KIL/WHAMP NW6	70	D6
Bembridge Gdns *RSLP* HA4	64	B7
Bemerton Est *IS* N1	5	L3
Bemerton St *IS* N1	5	L3
Bemish Rd *PUT/ROE* SW15	127	G2
Bempton Dr *RSLP* HA4	65	F1
Bemsted Rd *WALTH* E17	57	H2
Benares Rd *WOOL/PLUM* SE18	116	A3
Benbow Rd *HMSMTH* W6	106	E2
Benbow St *DEPT* SE8	112	D5
Benbury Cl *BMLY* BR1	152	A4
Bench Fld *SAND/SEL* CR2	178	B5
The Bench		
RCHPK/HAM TW10 *	143	J2
Bencroft Rd		
STRHM/NOR SW16	148	C6
Bencurtis Pk *WWKM* BR4	180	B2
Bendall Ms *CAMTN* NW1	9	K2
Bendemeer Rd		
PUT/ROE SW15	127	J6
Bendish Rd *EHAM* E6	77	J6
Bendmore Av *ABYW* SE2	116	B3
Bendon Va *WAND/EARL* SW18	128	A6
Bendysh Rd *BUSH* WD23	21	J3
Benedict Dr		
EBED/NFELT TW14	121	G6
Benedict Rd *BRXN/ST* SW9	130	A2
MTCM CR4	162	C1
Benedict Wy *EFNCH* N2 *	53	G2
Benedict Wharf *MTCM* CR4	162	D2
Benenden Gn *HAYES* BR2	167	K4
Benett Gdns		
STRHM/NOR SW16	163	K1
Benfleet Cl *SUT* SM1	175	G2
Benfleet Wy *FBAR/BDGN* N11	40	A1
Bengal Rd *IL* IG1	78	B3
Bengarth Dr		
KTN/HRWW/WS HA3	48	D1
Bengarth Rd *NTHLT* UB5	65	H1
Bengeworth Rd *CMBW* SE5	130	D2
HRW HA1	67	C1
Ben Hale Cl *STAN* HA7	35	C4
Benham Cl *CHSGTN* KT9	171	J4
Benham Gdns *HSLWW* TW4	122	K4
Benham Rd *HNWL* W7	84	D4
Benhill Av *SUT* SM1	175	F3
Benhill Rd *CMBW* SE5	110	E6
SUT SM1	175	H2
Benhill Wood Rd *SUT* SM1	175	H2
Benhilton Gdns *SUT* SM1	175	F2
Benhurst La		
STRHM/NOR SW16	149	G4
Benin St *LEW* SE13	133	G6
Benjafield Cl *UED* N18	42	D3
HACK E8	74	C7
Benjamin Ms *BAL* SW12	129	H6
Benjamin St *FARR* EC1M	12	C2
Ben Jonson Rd *WCHPL* E1	93	F4
Benledi St *POP/IOD* E14	94	B5
Bennelong Cl *SHB* W12	87	K6
Bennerley Rd *BTSEA* SW11	128	D4
Bennet Cl *KUT/HW* KT1	143	J7
Bennet's HI *BLKFR* EC4V	12	D6
Bennett Cl *HSLWW* TW4	122	H4
NTHWD HA6	32	D6
WELL DA16	136	B1
Bennett Gv *LEW* SE13	112	E7
Bennett Pk *BKHTH/KID* SE3	133	J2
Bennett Rd *BRXN/ST* SW9	130	B1
CHDH RM6	62	A5
PLSTW E13	95	G3
STNW/STAM N16	74	A3
Bennetts Av *CROY/NA* CR0	179	G1
GFD/PVL UB6	66	E2
Bennett's Castle La *BCTR* RM8	79	J3
Bennetts Cl *MTCM* CR4	148	B7
TOTM N17	42	C5
Bennetts Copse *CHST* BR7	153	J5
Bennetts Fld *BUSH* WD23	21	H4
Bennett St *CHSWK* W4	106	B5
WHALL SW1A	10	E8
Bennetts Wy *CROY/NA* CR0	179	G1
Bennett's Yd *WEST* SW1P	17	H4
Benningholme Rd *EDGW* HA8	37	G5
Bennington Rd *TOTM* N17	42	A7
WFD IG8 *	44	C6
Benn St *HOM* E9	75	G5
Bensbury Cl *PUT/ROE* SW15	126	E6
Bensham Cl *THHTH* CR7	164	D3
Bensham Gv *THHTH* CR7	164	D1
Bensham La *CROY/NA* CR0	164	C6
THHTH CR7	164	C6
Bensham Manor Rd		
THHTH CR7	164	D3
Benskin Rd *WATW* WD18	20	E4
Bensley Cl *FBAR/BDGN* N11	39	K4
Ben Smith Wy		
BERM/RHTH SE16	111	H2
Benson Av *PLSTW* E13	95	G1
Benson Cl *HSLW* TW3	123	F3
Benson Quay *WAP* E1W	92	E6
Benson Rd *CROY/NA* CR0	177	G2
FSTH SE23	131	K7
Benthal Rd *STNW/STAM* N16	74	C1
Bentham Rd *HOM* E9	75	F5
THMD SE28	97	H6
Ben Tillet Cl *BARK* IG11	79	G6
CAN/RD E16	95	K7
Bentinck Ms *MHST* W1U	10	B4
Bentinck St *MHST* W1U	10	B4
Bentley Cl *WIM/MER* SW19	146	E2
Bentley Dr *CRICK* NW2	70	D2
GNTH/NBYPK IG2	60	C5
Bentley Ms *EN* EN1	29	K5
Bentley Rd *IS* N1	74	A5
Bentley Wy *BAR* EN5	27	G3
STAN HA7	35	G4
WFD IG8	44	E2
Benton Rd *IL* IG1	60	C7
OXHEY WD19	33	H3
Benton's La *WNWD* SE27	149	J3
Benton's Ri *WNWD* SE27	149	K4
Bentry Cl *BCTR* RM8	80	A1
Bentry Rd *BCTR* RM8	80	A1
Bentworth Rd *SHB* W12	87	K5
Benwell Ct *SUN* TW16	140	E7
Benwell Rd *HOLWY* N7	73	G4
Benwick Cl *BERM/RHTH* SE16	111	J3
Benwood Ct *SUT* SM1	175	G2
Benworth St *BOW* E3	93	H2

Benyon Rd *IS* N1	7	H3
Benyon Whf *IS* N1	7	K3
Berberis Wk *WDR/YW* UB7	100	B3
Berber Pde *WOOL/PLUM* SE18	114	D7
Berber Rd *BTSEA* SW11	128	E4
Bercta Rd *ELTH/MOT* SE9	154	E1
Berengers Pl *DAGW* RM9	79	H5
Berenger Wk *WBPTN* SW10 *	108	C6
Berens Rd *WLSDN* NW10	88	B2
Beresford Av *ALP/SUD* HA0	68	C7
BRYLDS KT5	159	J7
HNWL W7	84	D4
TRDG/WHET N20	39	K1
TWK TW1	124	D5
Beresford Dr *BMLY* BR1	168	C2
WFD IG8	45	G3
Beresford Gdns *CHDH* RM6	62	A4
EN EN1	30	A3
HSLWW TW4	122	E4
Beresford Rd *BELMT* SM2	174	C6
CEND/HSY/T N8	55	G4
EFNCH N2	53	J2
HBRY N5	73	K4
HRW HA1	48	D4
KUTN/CMB KT2	144	B7
NWMAL KT3	159	K3
STHL UB1	83	H6
WALTH E17	43	K7
Beresford Sq		
WOOL/PLUM SE18	115	G3
Beresford St		
WOOL/PLUM SE18	115	G2
Beresford Ter *HBRY* N5	73	J4
Berestede Rd *HMSMTH* W6	106	C4
Bere St *WAP* E1W	93	F6
Berger Cl *STMC/STPC* BR5	169	J5
Berger Rd *HOM* E9	75	F5
Berghem Ms *WKENS* W14	107	G2
Bergholt Av *REDBR* IG4	59	J4
Bergholt Crs *STNW/STAM* N16	56	A6
Bergholt Ms *CAMTN* NW1	4	F3
Bering Sq *POP/IOD* E14	112	D4
Bering Wk *CAN/RD* E16	95	H5
Berisford Ms		
WAND/EARL SW18	128	B5
Berkeley Av *BXLYHN* DA7	116	E2
CLAY IG5	60	A1
GFD/PVL UB6	66	E5
HSLWW TW4	101	K7
Berkeley Cl *BORE* WD6	24	C4
KUTN/CMB KT2	144	A6
RSLP HA4	64	D2
STMC/STPC BR5	169	K6
Berkeley Ct		
RKW/CH/CXG WD3 *	20	A3
WLGTN SM6	176	C2
Berkeley Crs *DART* DA1	139	J7
EBAR EN4	27	H4
Berkeley Dr *E/WMO/HCT* KT8	156	E2
Berkeley Gdns *ESH/CLAY* KT10	171	G4
KENS W8	8	B9
WCHMH N21	29	K6
Berkeley Ms *MBLAR* W1H	9	K4
SUN TW16	156	B2
Berkeley Pl *WIM/MER* SW19	146	B5
Berkeley Rd *BARN* SW13	106	D7
CDALE/KGS NW9	50	C3
CEND/HSY/T N8	54	D4
HGDN/ICK UB10	64	A6
MNPK E12	77	J4
SEVS/STOTM N15	55	K5
The Berkeleys *SNWD* SE25 *	165	H3
Berkeley Waye *HEST* TW5	102	C6
Berkhampstead Rd		
BELV DA17	117	H4
Berkhamsted Av *WBLY* HA9	68	B5
Berkley Cl *WHTN* TW2 *	142	E2
Berkley Gv *CAMTN* NW1	4	A2
Berkley Rd *CAMTN* NW1	3	M2
Berkshire Gdns *PLMGR* N13	41	G5
UED N18	42	D4
Berkshire Rd *HOM* E9	75	H5
Berkshire Wy *MTCM* CR4	163	K3
Bermans Wy *WLSDN* NW10	69	G3
Bermondsey Sq *STHWK* SE1 *	19	K3
Bermondsey St *STHWK* SE1	19	J1
Bermondsey Wall East		
BERM/RHTH SE16	111	H1
Bermondsey Wall West		
STHWK SE1	111	H1
Bernal Cl *THMD* SE28	97	K6
Bernard Ashley Dr *CHARL* SE7	114	A4
Bernard Av *WEA* W13	104	C2
Bernard Cassidy St		
CAN/RD E16	94	D4
Bernard Gdns		
WIM/MER SW19	146	D4
Bernard Rd *ROMW/RG* RM7	62	E6
SEVS/STOTM N15	56	B4
WLGTN SM6	176	B3
Bernard St *BMSBY* WC1N	11	J1
Bernays Cl *STAN* HA7	35	J5
Bernay's Gv *BRXN/ST* SW9	130	A3
Bernel Dr *CROY/NA* CR0	179	H2
Berne Rd *THHTH* CR7	164	D4
Berners Dr *WEA* W13	85	G6
Berners Ms *FITZ* W1T	10	F3
Berners Pl *FITZ* W1T	10	F4
Berners Rd *IS* N1	6	C3
WDGN N22	41	G7
Berners St *FITZ* W1T	10	F3
Berner Ter *WCHPL* E1 *	92	C5
Berney Rd *CROY/NA* CR0	164	E6
Bernhardt Crs *STJWD* NW8	3	J9
Bernhart Cl *EDGW* HA8	36	E6
Bernwell Rd *CHING* E4	44	C2
Berridge Gn *EDGW* HA8	36	C6
Berridge Ms *KIL/WHAMP* NW6	70	E4
Berridge Rd *NRWD* SE19	149	K4
Berriman Rd *HOLWY* N7	73	F2
Berriton Rd *RYLN/HDSTN* HA2	47	K7
Berrybank Cl *CHING* E4	44	A1
Berry Cl *DAGE* RM10	80	C4
WCHMH N21	29	G7
Berry Cots *POP/IOD* E14 *	93	G5
Berrydale Rd *HYS/HAR* UB4	83	J3
Berryfield Cl *BMLY* BR1	153	F7
WALTH E17	57	K3
Berryfield Rd *WALW* SE17	18	D7
Berryhill *ELTH/MOT* SE9	135	G3
Berry HI *STAN* HA7	35	K3
Berryhill Gdns *ELTH/MOT* SE9	135	G3
Berrylands *BRYLDS* KT5	159	H5
RYNPK SW20	161	F2
Berrylands Rd *BRYLDS* KT5	159	G5
Berry La *DUL* SE21	149	K3
Berryman Cl *BCTR* RM8 *	79	J2
Berryman's La *SYD* SE26	151	F3
Berrymead Gdns *ACT* W3	86	D7
Berrymede Rd *CHSWK* W4	106	A2

Berry Pl *FSBYE* EC1V	6	D8
Berry St *FSBYE* EC1V	12	D1
Berry Wy *W5	105	F2
Bertal Rd *TOOT* SW17	147	H3
Berthons Gdns *WALTH* E17 *	58	A4
Berthon St *DEPT* SE8	112	D6
Bertie Rd *SYD* SE26	151	F5
WLSDN NW10	69	J5
Bertram Rd *EN* EN1	30	C3
HDN NW4	51	J5
KUTN/CMB KT2	144	C6
Bertram St *KTTN* NW5	72	B2
Bertrand St *LEW* SE13	132	E2
Bertrand Wy *THMD* SE28	97	H6
Bert Rd *THHTH* CR7	164	D4
Bert Wy *EN* EN1	30	B3
Berwick Av *YEAD* UB4	83	H5
Berwick Cl *STAN* HA7	35	F5
WHTN TW2	123	F7
Berwick Crs *BFN/LL* DA15	135	K5
Berwick Rd *CAN/RD* E16	95	F5
WDGN N22	41	H7
WELL DA16	116	C7
Berwick St *SOHO/CST* W1F	10	F5
Berwyn Av *HSLW* TW3	103	G7
Berwyn Rd *HNHL* SE24	130	C7
RCHPK/HAM TW10	125	J3
Beryl Av *EHAM* E6	95	J4
Beryl Rd *HMSMTH* W6	107	G4
Berystede *KUTN/CMB* KT2	144	D6
Besant Cl *CRICK* NW2 *	70	C2
Besant Pl *EDUL* SE22	131	G2
Besant Rd *CRICK* NW2	70	C3
Besant Wy *WLSDN* NW10	68	E4
Besley St *STRHM/NOR* SW16	148	C5
Bessant Dr *RCH/KEW* TW9	105	J7
Bessborough Gdns *PIM* SW1V *	17	H7
Bessborough Pl *PIM* SW1V	17	G7
PUT/ROE SW15	126	D7
Bessborough St *PIM* SW1V	17	G7
Bessemer Pl *GNWCH* SE10	113	J2
Bessemer Rd *CMBW* SE5	130	D1
Bessie Lansbury Cl *EHAM* E6	96	A5
Bessingby Rd *RSLP* HA4	64	E1
Besson St *NWCR* SE14	111	K7
Bessy St *BETH* E2 *	92	E2
Bestwood St *DEPT* SE8	112	A3
Beswick Ms *KIL/WHAMP* NW6 *	71	F5
Betam Rd *HYS/HAR* UB3	101	G1
Betchworth Cl *SUT* SM1	175	H4
Betchworth Rd		
GDMY/SEVK IG3	78	E1
Betchworth Wy *CROY/NA* CR0	180	A7
Betham Rd *GFD/PVL* UB6	84	D2
Bethany Waye		
EBED/NFELT TW14	121	H6
Bethecar Rd *HRW* HA1	48	E4
Bethel Cl *HDN* NW4	52	B4
Bethell Av *CAN/RD* E16	94	D3
IL IG1	60	A6
Bethel Rd *WELL* DA16	136	D2
Bethersden Cl *BECK* BR3	151	H6
Bethnal Green Rd *BETH* E2	7	M9
Bethune Av *FBAR/BDGN* N11	39	J3
Bethune Rd *STNW/STAM* N16	55	K6
WLSDN NW10	87	F3
Bethwin Rd *CMBW* SE5	110	C6
Betjeman Cl *RYLN/HDSTN* HA2	48	A3
Betony Cl *CROY/NA* CR0	166	A7
Betoyne Av *CHING* E4	44	C3
Betsham Rd *ERITH* DA8	118	C6
Betstyle Rd *FBAR/BDGN* N11	40	A3
Betterton Rd *RAIN* RM13	99	G1
Betterton St *LSQ/SEVD* WC2H	11	J5
Bettons Pk *SRTFD* E15	76	C7
Bettridge Rd *FUL/PGN* SW6	127	J1
Betts Cl *BECK* BR3	166	B1
Betts Ms *WALTH* E17	57	H5
Betts Rd *CAN/RD* E16	95	F5
Betts St *WAP* E1W	92	D6
Betts Wy *PGE/AN* SE20	165	J1
Betts St *WAP* E1W	92	D6
Beulah Av *THHTH* CR7 *	164	D1
Beulah Cl *EDGW* HA8	36	D2
Beulah Crs *THHTH* CR7	164	D1
Beulah Gv *CROY/NA* CR0	164	D5
Beulah HI *NRWD* SE19	149	H5
Beulah Rd *SUT* SM1	174	E3
THHTH CR7	164	D2
WALTH E17	57	K4
WIM/MER SW19	146	D6
Beult Rd *DART* DA1	138	D2
Bevan Av *BARK* IG11	79	G6
Bevan Ct *CROY/NA* CR0	177	G4
Bevan House *WATN* WD24	21	H1
Bevan Rd *ABYW* SE2	116	C4
EBAR EN4	27	K3
Bevan St *IS* N1	6	F4
Bev Callender Cl *VX/NE* SW8	129	G2
Bevenden St *IS* N1 *	7	G8
Beveridge Rd *WLSDN* NW10	69	G6
Beverley Av *BFN/LL* DA15	136	A6
HSLWW TW4	122	E3
RYNPK SW20	145	H7
Beverley Cl *BARN* SW13	126	C1
BTSEA SW11	128	C3
CHSGTN KT9	171	J3
WCHMH N21	29	J7
Beverley Ct *BROCKY* SE4	132	C2
WFD IG8 *	45	F1
Beverley Crs *WFD* IG8	45	F1
Beverley Dr *EDGW* HA8	50	B2
Beverley Gdns *BARN* SW13	126	C2
GLDGN NW11	52	C6
STAN HA7	35	G7
WBLY HA9	50	B7
WPK KT4	160	D7
Beverley La *KUTN/CMB* KT2	145	G6
WIM/MER SW19	161	J1
Beverley Ms *CHING* E4 *	44	B5
Beverley Pth *BARN* SW13	126	C1
Beverley Rd *BARN* SW13	126	C2
BXLYHN DA7	137	K1
CHING E4	44	B5
CHSWK W4	106	C4
DAGW RM9	80	A3
EHAM E6	95	H2
HAYES BR2	181	H1
KUT/HW KT1	143	J7
MTCM CR4	163	J3
NWDGN UB2	102	D3
NWMAL KT3	160	D3
PGE/AN SE20	165	J1
RSLP HA4	65	F1
SUN TW16	140	D7
WPK KT4	174	A1
Beverley Wy *RYNPK* SW20	145	H7
Beverley Way (Kingston		
By-Pass) *NWMAL* KT3	160	C1
Beversbrook Rd *ARCH* N19	72	D2
Beverstone Rd		
BRXS/STRHM SW2	130	A4
THHTH CR7	164	B3
Bevill Allen Cl *TOOT* SW17	147	K5

Bevill Cl *SNWD* SE25	165	H2
Bevin Cl *BERM/RHTH* SE16	93	G7
Bevington Rd *BECK* BR3	166	E1
NKENS W10	88	C4
Bevington St		
BERM/RHTH SE16	111	H1
Bevin Rd *YEAD* UB4	82	E2
Bevin Sq *TOOT* SW17	147	K2
Bevin Wy *FSBYW* WC1X	6	A6
Bevis Marks *HDTCH* EC3A	13	K4
Bewcastle Gdns *ENC/FH* EN2	28	E3
Bewdley St *IS* N1	6	A1
Bewick Ms *PECK* SE15	111	J6
Bewick St *VX/NE* SW8	129	G1
Bewley St *WCHPL* E1	92	D6
WIM/MER SW19	147	G5
Bewlys Rd *WNWD* SE27	149	H4
Bexhill Cl *FELT* TW13	141	J1
Bexhill Rd *BROCKY* SE4	132	C5
FBAR/BDGN N11	40	D4
MORT/ESHN SW14	125	K2
Bexley Gdns *CHDH* RM6	61	H4
ED N9	41	K2
Bexley High St *BXLY* DA5	137	H6
Bexley La *DART* DA1	138	B4
SCUP DA14	155	J3
Bexley Rd *ELTH/MOT* SE9	135	G5
ERITH DA8	117	K6
Beynon Rd *CAR* SM5	175	K4
Bianca Rd *PECK* SE15	111	G5
Bibsworth Rd *FNCH* N3	52	D1
Bibury Cl *PECK* SE15	111	F5
Bicester Rd *RCH/KEW* TW9	125	H2
Bickenhall St *MHST* W1U	9	M1
Bickersteth Rd *TOOT* SW17	147	K5
Bickerton Rd *ARCH* N19	72	C1
Bickles Yd *STHWK* SE1 *	19	K2
Bickley Crs *BMLY* BR1	168	E2
Bickley Park Rd *BMLY* BR1	168	E2
Bickley Rd *BMLY* BR1	168	C1
LEY E10	57	K6
Bickley St *TOOT* SW17	147	J4
Bicknell Rd *CMBW* SE5	130	D2
Bicknor Rd *ORP* BR6	169	K6
Bidborough Cl *HAYES* BR2	167	J4
Bidborough St *STPAN* WC1H	5	J8
Biddenden Wy *ELTH/MOT* SE9	154	A3
Bidder St *CAN/RD* E16	94	C4
Biddestone Rd *HOLWY* N7	73	F3
Biddulph Rd *MV/WKIL* W9	2	D8
SAND/SEL CR2	177	J7
Bideford Av *GFD/PVL* UB6	85	H2
Bideford Cl *EDGW* HA8	36	C7
FELT TW13	141	K2
Bideford Gdns *EN* EN1	30	A6
Bideford Rd *BMLY* BR1	152	D2
RSLP HA4	65	F2
WELL DA16	116	C6
Bidwell Gdns *FBAR/BDGN* N11	40	C6
Bidwell St *PECK* SE15	111	J7
Biggerstaff Rd *SRTFD* E15	76	A7
Biggerstaff St *FSBYPK* N4	73	G1
Biggin Av *MTCM* CR4	147	K7
Biggin HI *NRWD* SE19	149	H7
Biggin Wy *NRWD* SE19	149	H6
Bigginwood Rd		
STRHM/NOR SW16	149	H6
Bigg's Rw *PUT/ROE* SW15	127	G2
Biggs Sq *HOM* E9	75	H5
Big HI *CLPT* E5	56	D7
Bigland St *WCHPL* E1	92	D5
Bignell Rd *WOOL/PLUM* SE18	115	G4
Bignold Rd *FSTGT* E7	76	E3
Bigwood Rd *GLDGN* NW11	53	F5
Billet Rd *CHDH* RM6	61	H1
WALTH E17	43	F7
Billets Hart Cl *HNWL* W7	103	K1
Bill Hamling Cl *ELTH/MOT* SE9	153	K1
Billingford Cl *BROCKY* SE4	132	A3
Billing Pl *WBPTN* SW10 *	108	A6
Billing Rd *WBPTN* SW10	108	A6
Billings Cl *DAGW* RM9	79	J6
Billing St *WBPTN* SW10	108	A6
Billington Hl *CROY/NA* CR0	177	K1
Billington Rd *NWCR* SE14	112	A6
Billiter Sq *FENCHST* EC3M	13	K5
Billiter St *FENCHST* EC3M	13	K5
Bill Nicholson Wy *TOTM* N17	42	B6
Billockby Cl *CHSGTN* KT9	172	B5
Billson St *POP/IOD* E14	113	F3
Bilton Rd *ERITH* DA8	118	D6
GFD/PVL UB6	85	H1
Bilton Wy *HYS/HAR* UB3	102	A1
Bina Gdns *ECT* SW5	14	E6
Bincote Rd *ENC/FH* EN2	29	F2
Binden Rd *SHB* W12	106	C2
Binfield Rd *CLAP* SW4	109	K7
SAND/SEL CR2	178	B4
Bingfield St *IS* N1	5	K3
Bingham Cl *IS* N1 *	6	D1
Bingham Pl *MHST* W1U	10	A1
Bingham Rd *CROY/NA* CR0	165	J7
Bingham St *IS* N1	73	K5
Bingley Rd *CAN/RD* E16	95	G5
GFD/PVL UB6	84	C3
SUN TW16	140	E6
Binney St *MYFR/PKLN* W1K	10	B6
Binns Rd *CHSWK* W4	106	B4
Binsey Wk *ABYW* SE2	116	D1
Binstead Cl *YEAD* UB4	83	J4
Binyon Crs *STAN* HA7	35	F4
Birbetts Rd *ELTH/MOT* SE9	153	K1
Birchanger Rd *SNWD* SE25	165	H4
Birch Av *PLMGR* N13	41	H2
Birch Cl *BKHH* IG9	45	H2
BTFD TW8	104	C6
CAN/RD E16	94	C4
HSLW TW3	123	J1
ROMW/RG RM7	62	E3
TEDD TW11	143	G4
Birchdale Gdns *CHDH* RM6	61	K6
Birchdale Rd *FSTGT* E7	77	G4
Birchdene Dr *THMD* SE28	97	G7
Birchen Cl *CDALE/KGS* NW9	69	F1
Birchend Cl *SAND/SEL* CR2	177	K5
Birchen Gv *CDALE/KGS* NW9	69	F1
The Birches *BUSH* WD23	22	C4
CHARL SE7	114	A5
CMBW SE5	131	F1
HSLWW TW4 *	122	E6
Birchfield St *POP/IOD* E14	93	J6
Birch Gv *ACT* W3	86	C7
LEE/GVPK SE12	133	J6
WAN E11	76	C2
WELL DA16	136	B3
Birch HI *CROY/NA* CR0	179	F4
Birchington Rd *BXLYHN* DA7	117	J7

Birchington Rd *BRYLDS* KT5	159	G6
CEND/HSY/T N8	54	D5
KIL/WHAMP NW6	2	D1
Birchin La *BANK* EC3V	13	H5
Birchlands Av *BAL* SW12	128	E6
Birchmead Av *PIN* HA5	47	G3
Birchmere Wk *HBRY* N5	73	J2
Birchmore Wk *HBRY* N5	73	J2
Birch Rd *FELT* TW13	141	H4
ROMW/RG RM7	62	D2
Birch Rw *HAYES* BR2	169	H4
Birch Tree Av *WWKM* BR4	180	D4
Birch Tree Wy *CROY/NA* CR0	178	D1
Birch Wk *MTCM* CR4	148	B7
Birchway *HYS/HAR* UB3	82	E7
Birchwood Av *BECK* BR3	166	C3
MUSWH N10	54	A2
SCUP DA14	155	H2
WLGTN SM6	176	A2
Birchwood Ct *EDGW* HA8	50	E1
Birchwood Dr *HAMP* NW3	71	F2
Birchwood Gv *HPTN* TW12	142	A5
Birchwood La *ESH/CLAY* KT10	170	D7
Birchwood Rd		
STMC/STPC BR5	169	J3
TOOT SW17	148	B4
Birdbrook Cl *DAGE* RM10	80	E6
Birdbrook Rd *BKHTH/KID* SE3	134	B2
Birdcage Wk *STJSPK* SW1H	17	F2
WESTW SW1E	16	F2
Birdham Cl *BMLY* BR1	168	D4
Birdhurst Av *SAND/SEL* CR2	177	K3
Birdhurst Gdns *SAND/SEL* CR2	177	K3
Birdhurst Ri *SAND/SEL* CR2	178	A4
Birdhurst Rd		
WAND/EARL SW18	128	B3
WIM/MER SW19	147	J5
Bird In Bush Rd *PECK* SE15	111	H6
Bird-In-Hand La *BMLY* BR1	168	C1
Bird-In-Hand Ms *FSTH* SE23	150	E1
Bird-In-Hand Pas *FSTH* SE23	150	E1
Birdsfield La *BOW* E3	75	H7
Bird St *MHST* W1U	10	B5
Bird Wk *WHTN* TW2	122	E7
Birdwood Av *DART* DA1	139	J1
LEW SE13	133	G5
Birdwood Cl *TEDD* TW11	142	E3
Birkbeck Av *ACT* W3	86	E6
GFD/PVL UB6	66	C7
Birkbeck Gv *ACT* W3	106	A1
Birkbeck HI *DUL* SE21	149	H1
Birkbeck Ms *ACT* W3 *	87	F6
HACK E8	74	B4
Birkbeck Pl *DUL* SE21	130	C7
Birkbeck Rd *ACT* W3	87	F7
BECK BR3	165	K1
CEND/HSY/T N8	54	E3
EA W5	104	D3
GNTH/NBYPK IG2	60	D4
HACK E8	74	B4
MLHL NW7	37	H4
NFNCH/WDSPK N12	39	G4
ROMW/RG RM7	63	F7
SCUP DA14	155	G2
TOTM N17	42	B7
WIM/MER SW19	147	F5
Birkbeck St *BETH* E2	92	D2
Birkbeck Wy *GFD/PVL* UB6	66	C7
Birkdale Av *PIN* HA5	48	A3
Birkdale Cl		
BERM/RHTH SE16 *	111	J4
ORP BR6	169	J6
THMD SE28	97	J5
Birkdale Gdns *CROY/NA* CR0	179	F3
OXHEY WD19	33	H2
Birkdale Rd *ABYW* SE2	116	B3
EA W5	86	A3
Birkenhead Av		
KUTN/CMB KT2	159	G1
Birkenhead St *KCROSS* N1C	5	K7
Birkhall Rd *CAT* SE6	133	G7
Birkwood Cl *BAL* SW12	129	J6
Birley Rd *TRDG/WHET* N20	39	G1
Birley St *BTSEA* SW11	129	F1
Birling Rd *ERITH* DA8	118	A6
Birnam Rd *FSBYPK* N4	73	F1
Birnbeck Rd *GLDGN* NW11	52	D4
Birse Crs *WLSDN* NW10	69	G3
Birstal Gn *OXHEY* WD19	33	H3
Birstall Rd *SEVS/STOTM* N15	56	A4
Biscay Rd *HMSMTH* W6	107	G4
Biscoe Cl *HEST* TW5	103	F5
Biscoe Wy *LEW* SE13	133	G3
Bisenden Rd *CROY/NA* CR0	178	A1
Bisham Cl *CAR* SM5	162	E6
Bisham Gdns *HGT* N6	54	A7
Bishop Fox Wy		
E/WMO/HCT KT8	156	E3
Bishop Ken Rd		
KTN/HRWW/WS HA3	49	F1
Bishop King's Rd *WKENS* W14	107	H3
Bishop Ramsey Cl *RSLP* HA4	46	D6
Bishop Rd *STHGT/OAK* N14	28	B6
Bishops Av *BMLY* BR1	168	B4
BORE WD6	24	B4
CHDH RM6	61	J4
NTHWD HA6	32	C3
PLSTW E13	77	F7
Bishop's Av *FUL/PGN* SW6	127	G1
The Bishops Av *EFNCH* N2	53	H5
Bishop's Bridge Rd		
BAY/PAD W2	8	D2
Bishops Cl *BAR* EN5	26	B5
CHSWK W4	105	K4
ELTH/MOT SE9	154	C1
EN EN1	30	D1
RCHPK/HAM TW10	143	K2
SUT SM1	174	E2
Bishop's Cl *ARCH* N19	72	C2
WALTH E17	57	K3
Bishop's Ct *STP* EC4M	12	C4
Bishops Dr *EBED/NFELT* TW14	121	G5
NTHLT UB5	65	J1
Bishopsford Rd *MRDN* SM4	162	B6
Bishopsgate *LVPST* EC2M	13	J3
Bishopsgate Ar *LVPST* EC2M	13	J3
Bishops Gn *BMLY* BR1 *	153	G7
Bishops Gv *EFNCH* N2	53	H5
HPTN TW12	141	K3
Bishop's Hall *KUT/HW* KT1	158	E1
Bishops Md *CMBW* SE5 *	110	D6
Bishop's Park Rd		
STRHM/NOR SW16	148	E7
Bishop's Park Rd		
FUL/PGN SW6	127	G1
Bishops Pl *SUT* SM1	175	G4
Bishops Rd *FUL/PGN* SW6	107	J7
HGT N6	54	A5
Bishop's Rd *CROY/NA* CR0	164	C6
HNWL W7	103	K1
HYS/HAR UB3	82	A5

Bishop's Ter LBTH SE11 18 B5
Bishopsthorpe Rd SYD SE26 151 F3
Bishop St IS N1 6 E3
Bishops Wk CHST BR7 154 C7
CROY/NA CR0 179 F4
Bishop's Wy BETH E2 92 E1
Bishopswood Rd HGT N6 53 K6
Bishop Wilfred Wood Cl
PECK SE15 131 H1
Bisley Cl WPK KT4 161 F7
Bispham Rd WLSDN NW10 86 B2
Bisson Rd SRTFD E15 94 A1
Bistern Av WALTH E17 58 B2
Bittacy Cl MLHL NW7 38 B5
Bittacy Hl MLHL NW7 38 B5
Bittacy Park Av MLHL NW7 38 B4
Bittacy Ri MLHL NW7 38 B5
Bittacy Rd MLHL NW7 38 B5
Bittern Cl YEAD UB4 83 H4
Bittern Pl WDGN N22 * 55 F1
Bittern St STHWK SE1 18 E1
Bittoms Ct KUT/HW KT1 * 158 E2
The Bittoms KUT/HW KT1 158 E2
Bixley Cl NWDGN UB2 102 E3
Blackall St SDTCH EC2A 7 J9
Blackberry Farm Cl HEST TW5 102 D6
Blackberry Fld
STMC/STPC BR5 155 G7
Blackbird Hl WBLY HA9 68 E1
Blackbird Yd BETH E2 7 M7
Blackborne Rd DAGE RM10 80 C5
Black Boy La
SEVS/STOTM N15 55 J4
Blackbrook La HAYES BR2 169 F4
Blackburne's Ms
MYFR/PKLN W1K 10 A6
Blackburn Rd
KIL/WHAMP NW6 71 F5
Blackbush Av CHDH RM6 61 K4
Blackbush Cl BELMT SM2 175 F6
Blackdown Cl EFNCH N2 53 G1
Blackdown Ter
WOOL/PLUM SE18 * 114 E7
Blackenham Rd TOOT SW17 147 K3
Blackett St PUT/ROE SW15 127 G2
Blackfen Pde BFN/LL DA15 * 136 B5
Blackfen Rd BFN/LL DA15 136 A4
Blackford Cl SAND/SEL CR2 177 H7
Blackford Rd OXHEY WD19 33 H4
Blackfriars Br STHWK SE1 12 C7
Black Friars La BLKFR EC4V 12 C5
Blackfriars Pas BLKFR EC4V 12 C6
Blackfriars Rd STHWK SE1 12 C8
Blackfriars U/P BLKFR EC4V 12 C6
Blackheath Av GNWCH SE10 113 G6
Blackheath Gv
BKHTH/KID SE3 133 J1
Blackheath Hl GNWCH SE10 113 F7
Blackheath Pk
BKHTH/KID SE3 133 J2
Blackheath Ri LEW SE13 133 F1
Blackheath Rd GNWCH SE10 112 E7
Blackheath V BKHTH/KID SE3 133 H1
Black Horse Ct STHWK SE1 * 19 H4
Blackhorse La CROY/NA CR0 165 H6
WALTH E17 57 F2
Black Horse Pde PIN HA5 * 47 F4
Blackhorse Rd DEPT SE8 112 B5
Black Horse Rd SCUP DA14 155 G3
Blackhorse Rd WALTH E17 57 F3
Blacklands Dr YEAD UB4 82 A3
Blacklands Rd CAT SE6 152 A3
Blacklands Ter CHEL SW3 15 L6
Black Lion Ga BAY/PAD W2 8 D7
Black Lion La HMSMTH W6 106 D3
Blackmans Cl DART DA1 139 F7
Blackmans Yd WCHPL E1 * 7 M9
Blackmoor La WATW WD18 20 B4
Blackmore Av STHL UB1 84 D7
Blackmore Dr WLSDN NW10 68 D6
Blackmore's Gv TEDD TW11 143 G5
Blackness Cots HAYES BR2 * 181 H7
Blackness La HAYES BR2 181 H7
Blackpool Gdns YEAD UB4 82 C3
Blackpool Rd PECK SE15 131 J1
Black Prince Rd LBTH SE11 17 L6
Black Rod Cl HYS/HAR UB3 101 J2
Blackburn Wy HSLWW TW4 122 D4
Blackshaw Rd TOOT SW17 147 H4
Blacksmith Cl CHDH RM6 61 J5
Blacksmith's La RAIN RM13 81 H7
Black's Rd HMSMTH W6 107 F4
Blackstock Rd FSBYPK N4 73 H1
Blackstone Est HACK E8 74 C6
Blackstone Rd CRICK NW2 70 A4
Black Swan Yd STHWK SE1 19 J1
Blackthorn Av WDR/YW UB7 100 D3
Blackthorn Ct HEST TW5 102 D6
Blackthorne Av CROY/NA CR0 165 K7
Blackthorne Dr CHING E4 44 B3
Blackthorn Gv BXLYHN DA7 137 F2
Blackthorn Rd IL IG1 78 D4
Blackthorn St BOW E3 93 J3
Blacktree Ms BRXN/ST SW9 * 130 B2
Blackwall La GNWCH SE10 113 H4
Blackwall Tnl POP/IOD E14 94 B7
Blackwall Tunnel Ap
POP/IOD E14 94 A6
Blackwall Tunnel Northern Ap
BOW E3 75 J7
BOW E3 94 A2
Blackwall Wy POP/IOD E14 94 A6
Blackwater Cl FSTGT E7 76 D3
RAIN RM13 99 F4
Blackwater St EDUL SE22 131 G4
Blackwell Cl CLPT E5 75 G3
KTN/HRWW/WS HA3 34 D6
WCHMH N21 28 E4
Blackwell Dr OXHEY WD19 21 G5
Blackwell Gdns EDGW HA8 36 C3
Blackwood St WALW SE17 19 G7
Blade Ms PUT/ROE SW15 127 J3
Bladindon Dr BXLY DA5 136 E6
Bladon Gdns
RYLN/HDSTN HA2 48 B5
Blagden's La STHGT/OAK N14 40 D1
Blagdon Rd CAT SE6 132 E5
NWMAL KT3 160 C3
Blagdon Wk TEDD TW11 143 J5
Blagrove Rd NKENS W10 88 C4
Blair Av CDALE/KGS NW9 51 G6
ESH/CLAY KT10 170 C1
Blair Cl BFN/LL DA15 135 K4
HYS/HAR UB3 101 K3
IS N1 73 J5
Blairderry Rd
BRXS/STRHM SW2 148 E1
Blairhead Dr OXHEY WD19 33 F2
Blair St POP/IOD E14 94 A5
Blake Av BARK IG11 78 E7
Blake Cl CAR SM5 162 D7
NKENS W10 88 A4
RAIN RM13 81 H7
WELL DA16 115 K7
YEAD UB4 82 B1
Blakeden Dr ESH/CLAY KT10 171 F6
Blake Gdns DART DA1 139 J3
FUL/PGN SW6 107 K7
Blakehall Rd CAR SM5 175 K5
Blake Hall Rd WAN E11 58 E7
Blake Ms RCH/KEW TW9 105 H7
Blakemore Gdns BARN SW13 106 E5
Blakemore Rd
STRHM/NOR SW16 148 E2
THHTH CR7 164 A4
Blakemore Wy BELV DA17 117 F2
Blakeney Av BECK BR3 151 H7
Blakeney Cl CAMTN NW1 5 G2
HACK E8 74 C4
TRDG/WHET N20 27 G7
Blakeney Rd BECK BR3 151 H7
Blaker Ct CHARL SE7 * 114 B6
Blake Rd CAN/RD E16 94 D3
CROY/NA CR0 178 A1
FBAR/BDGN N11 40 C6
MTCM CR4 162 D2
Blaker Rd SRTFD E15 76 A7
Blakes Av NWMAL KT3 160 C4
Blakes Cl WLSDN NW10 69 J5
Blake's Gn WWKM BR4 167 F6
Blakes La NWMAL KT3 160 C4
Blakesley Av EA W5 85 J5
Blakes Rd PECK SE15 * 111 F6
Blake's Rd PECK SE15 111 F6
Blakes Ter NWMAL KT3 160 D4
Blakesware Gdns ED N9 29 K6
Blakewood Cl FELT TW13 141 G3
Blanchard Cl ELTH/MOT SE9 153 J2
Blanchard Dr WATW WD18 20 C3
Blanchard Wy HACK E8 * 74 C5
Blanch Cl PECK SE15 111 K6
Blanchedowne CMBW SE5 130 E3
Blanche St CAN/RD E16 94 D3
Blanchland Rd MRDN SM4 162 A4
Blandfield Rd BAL SW12 129 F5
Blandford Av BECK BR3 166 B1
WHTN TW2 123 G7
Blandford Cl CROY/NA CR0 176 E2
EFNCH N2 53 G4
ROMW/RG RM7 62 D3
Blandford Rd BECK BR3 166 A1
CHSWK W4 106 B2
EA W5 104 E1
NWDGN UB2 103 F3
TEDD TW11 142 D4
Blandford Sq CAMTN NW1 9 K1
Blandford St MHST W1U 9 M4
Blandford Waye YEAD UB4 83 G5
Bland St ELTH/MOT SE9 134 C3
Blaney Crs EHAM E6 96 B2
Blanmerle Rd ELTH/MOT SE9 135 G7
Blann Cl ELTH/MOT SE9 134 C5
Blantyre St WBPTN SW10 108 C6
Blantyre Wk WBPTN SW10 * 108 C6
Blashford St LEW SE13 133 G6
Blattner Cl BORE WD6 24 A3
Blawith Rd HRW HA1 48 E3
Blaydon Cl RSLP HA4 46 C6
TOTM N17 * 42 D6
Blaydon Wk TOTM N17 42 D6
Bleak Hill La
WOOL/PLUM SE18 116 A5
Blean Gv PGE/AN SE20 150 E6
Bleasdale Av GFD/PVL UB6 85 G1
Blechynden Gdns NKENS W10 88 B6
Blechynden St NKENS W10 * 88 B6
Bledlow Cl THMD SE28 97 J6
Bledlow Ri GFD/PVL UB6 84 C1
Bleeding Heart Yd
HCIRC EC1N * 12 B3
Blegborough Rd
STRHM/NOR SW16 148 C5
Blendon Dr BXLY DA5 136 E5
Blendon Rd BXLY DA5 136 E5
Blendon Ter
WOOL/PLUM SE18 115 H4
Blendworth Wy PECK SE15 111 F6
Blenheim CDALE/KGS NW9 * 51 H1
Blenheim Av GNTH/NBYPK IG2 60 A5
Blenheim Cl DART DA1 139 F5
GFD/PVL UB6 * 84 D1
LEE/GVPK SE12 134 A7
OXHEY WD19 21 G6
ROMW/RG RM7 62 E3
RYNPK SW20 161 F2
WCHMH N21 29 J7
WLGTN SM6 176 C6
Blenheim Ct BFN/LL DA15 154 D2
WFD IG8 45 F6
Blenheim Crs NTGHL W11 88 C5
RSLP HA4 64 B1
SAND/SEL CR2 177 J6
Blenheim Dr WELL DA16 116 A7
Blenheim Gdns
BRXS/STRHM SW2 130 A5
CRICK NW2 70 A4
KUTN/CMB KT2 144 D6
WBLY HA9 68 A2
WLGTN SM6 176 C5
Blenheim Gv PECK SE15 131 G1
Blenheim Park Rd
SAND/SEL CR2 177 J7
Blenheim Pas STJWD NW8 * 2 E5
Blenheim Pl TEDD TW11 143 F4
Blenheim Ri
SEVS/STOTM N15 * 56 B3
Blenheim Rd BAR EN5 26 B2
BFN/LL DA15 136 D7
BMLY BR1 168 D3
CHSWK W4 106 B2
DART DA1 139 F5
EHAM E6 95 H2
NTHLT UB5 66 B5
PGE/AN SE20 150 E6
RYLN/HDSTN HA2 48 B5
RYNPK SW20 161 F2
STJWD NW8 2 F5
SUT SM1 174 E2
WALTH E17 57 F2
WAN E11 76 C3
Blenheim St CONDST W1S 10 C5
Blenheim Ter STJWD NW8 2 E5
Blenheim Wy ISLW TW7 104 B7
Blenheim Ct ARCH N19 72 E1
Blenkarne Rd BTSEA SW11 128 E5
Bleriot Rd HEST TW5 102 B6
Blessbury Rd EDGW HA8 36 E7
Blessington Rd LEW SE13 133 G3
Blessing Wy BARK IG11 97 J1
Bletchingley Cl THHTH CR7 164 C3
Bletchley St IS N1 6 F6
Bletchmore Cl HYS/HAR UB3 101 G4
Bletsoe Wk IS N1 6 F5
Blincoe Cl WIM/MER SW19 146 B1
Blissett St GNWCH SE10 113 F7
Bliss Ms NKENS W10 88 C2
Blisworth Cl YEAD UB4 83 J3
Blithbury Rd DAGW RM9 79 H5
Blithdale Rd ABYW SE2 116 B3
Blithfield St KENS W8 14 C4
Blockley Rd ALP/SUD HA0 67 H1
Bloemfontein Av SHB W12 87 K7
Bloemfontein Rd SHB W12 87 K6
Blomfield Rd MV/WKIL W9 8 D2
Blomfield St LVPST EC2M 13 H3
Blomfield Vls BAY/PAD W2 8 D3
Blomville Rd BCTR RM8 80 A1
Blondell Cl WDR/YW UB7 100 A5
Blondel St BTSEA SW11 129 F1
Blondin Av EA W5 104 D3
Blondin St BOW E3 93 J1
Bloomfield Crs
GNTH/NBYPK IG2 60 B5
Bloomfield Pl
MYFR/PKLN W1K 10 D6
Bloomfield Rd HAYES BR2 168 C4
HGT N6 54 A5
KUT/HW KT1 159 F3
WOOL/PLUM SE18 115 G4
Bloomfield Ter BGVA SW1W 16 B7
Bloom Gv WNWD SE27 149 H2
Bloomhall Rd NRWD SE19 149 K4
Bloom Park Rd FUL/PGN SW6 107 J6
Bloomsbury Cl EA W5 86 B6
Bloomsbury Ct
NOXST/BSQ WC1A 11 K3
Bloomsbury Sq
NOXST/BSQ WC1A 11 K3
Bloomsbury St GWRST WC1E 11 H2
Bloomsbury Wy
NOXST/BSQ WC1A 11 J3
Blore Cl VX/NE SW8 109 J7
Blossom Cl DAGW RM9 80 B7
EA W5 105 F1
SAND/SEL CR2 178 B4
Blossom St WCHPL E1 13 K1
Blossom Wy WDR/YW UB7 100 D3
Blossom Waye HEST TW5 102 D5
Blount St POP/IOD E14 93 G5
Bloxam Gdns ELTH/MOT SE9 134 D4
Bloxhall Rd LEY E10 57 H7
Bloxham Crs HPTN TW12 141 K7
Bloxworth Cl WLGTN SM6 176 C2
Blucher Rd CMBW SE5 110 D6
Blue Anchor La
BERM/RHTH SE16 111 H3
Blue Anchor Yd WCHPL E1 92 C6
Blue Ball Yd WHALL SW1A 10 E9
Bluebell Av MNPK E12 77 H4
Bluebell Cl HOM E9 74 E7
NTHLT UB5 65 K5
ROMW/RG RM7 81 G1
SYD SE26 150 B3
WLGTN SM6 163 G7
Bluebell Wy IL IG1 78 B5
Blueberry Cl WFD IG8 44 E5
Bluebird La DAGE RM10 80 C6
Bluebird Wy THMD SE28 115 J1
Bluefield Cl HPTN TW12 142 A4
Bluegates EW KT17 173 J6
Bluehouse Rd CHING E4 44 C2
Blue Lion Pl STHWK SE1 19 J3
Blue Riband Est
CROY/NA CR0 * 177 H1
Blundell Cl HACK E8 74 C3
Blundell Rd EDGW HA8 37 F7
Blundell St HOLWY N7 5 K1
Blunden Cl BCTR RM8 61 J7
Blunt Rd SAND/SEL CR2 177 K4
Blunts Av WDR/YW UB7 100 D6
Blunts Rd ELTH/MOT SE9 135 F4
Blurton Rd CLPT E5 75 F3
Blyth Cl TWK TW1 124 A5
Blythe Cl CAT SE6 132 C6
Blythe Hl CAT SE6 132 C6
STMC/STPC BR5 155 F7
Blythe Hill La CAT SE6 132 C6
Blythe Hill Pl FSTH SE23 * 132 B6
Blythe Ms WKENS W14 * 107 G2
Blythe Rd WKENS W14 107 G2
Blythe St BETH E2 * 92 D2
Blytheswood Pl
STRHM/NOR SW16 149 F3
Blythe V CAT SE6 132 C7
Blyth Rd BMLY BR1 152 D7
HYS/HAR UB3 101 H1
THMD SE28 97 J6
WALTH E17 57 H6
Blyth's Whf POP/IOD E14 * 93 G6
Blythswood Rd
GDMY/SEVK IG3 61 G7
Blythwood Rd FSBYPK N4 54 E6
PIN HA5 33 H7
Boadicea St IS N1 5 L4
Boakes Cl CDALE/KGS NW9 50 E3
Boardman Av CHING E4 31 K4
Boardman Cl BAR EN5 26 C4
Boardwalk Pl POP/IOD E14 94 A7
Boathouse Wk PECK SE15 111 G6
RCH/KEW TW9 104 E7
Boat Lifter Wy
BERM/RHTH SE16 112 B3
Boat Quay CAN/RD E16 95 G6
Bob Anker Cl PLSTW E13 94 E2
Bobbin Cl CLAP SW4 129 H2
Bob Dunn Wy DART DA1 139 K3
Bob Marley Wy HNHL SE24 130 B3
Bockhampton Rd
KUTN/CMB KT2 144 B6
Bocking St HACK E8 74 D7
Boddicott Cl WIM/MER SW19 146 C1
Boddington Gdns ACT W3 105 H1
Bodiam Cl EN EN1 29 K1
Bodiam Rd STRHM/NOR SW16 148 D7
Bodiam Wy WLSDN NW10 86 B2
Bodicea Ms HSLWW TW4 122 E5
Bodley Cl NWMAL KT3 160 B4
Bodley Rd NWMAL KT3 160 B5
Bodmin Cl RYLN/HDSTN HA2 65 K2
Bodmin Gv MRDN SM4 162 A3
Bodmin St WAND/EARL SW18 127 K7
Bodnant Gdns RYNPK SW20 160 D2
Bodney Rd CLPT E5 74 D4
Boeing Wy NWDGN UB2 102 A2
Bofors House CHARL SE7 * 114 D6
Bognor Gdns OXHEY WD19 33 G4
Bognor Rd WELL DA16 116 E7
Bohemia Pl HACK E8 74 E5
Bohn Rd WCHPL E1 93 G4
Bohun Gv EBAR EN4 27 J5
Boileau Rd BARN SW13 106 D6
EA W5 86 B5
Bolden St DEPT SE8 132 E1
Boldero Pl STJWD NW8 * 9 J1
Bolderwood Wy WWKM BR4 179 K1
Boldmere Rd PIN HA5 47 G6
Boleyn Cl WALTH E17 57 J3
Boleyn Dr E/WMO/HCT KT8 156 E2
RSLP HA4 65 H1
Boleyn Gdns DAGE RM10 80 E6
WWKM BR4 179 K1
Boleyn Rd EHAM E6 95 H1
FSTGT E7 76 E6
STNW/STAM N16 74 A4
Boleyn Wy BAR EN5 27 G2
Bolina Rd BERM/RHTH SE16 111 K4
Bolingbroke Gv BTSEA SW11 128 D4
Bolingbroke Rd WKENS W14 107 G2
Bolingbroke Wk
BTSEA SW11 * 108 C6
Bolingbroke Wy
HYS/HAR UB3 82 B7
Bollo Bridge Rd ACT W3 105 J2
Bollo La ACT W3 105 J2
Bolney Ga SKENS SW7 15 J2
Bolney St VX/NE SW8 110 A6
Bolsover St GTPST W1W 10 D1
Bolstead Rd MTCM CR4 148 B7
Bolster Gv WDGN N22 * 40 D7
Bolt Ct FLST/FETLN EC4A 12 B5
Boltmore Cl HDN NW4 52 B2
Bolton Cl CHSGTN KT9 171 K5
Bolton Crs LBTH SE11 110 B5
Bolton Dr MRDN SM4 162 B6
Bolton Gdns BMLY BR1 152 D5
ECT SW5 14 D7
TEDD TW11 143 G5
WLSDN NW10 88 B1
Bolton Gardens Ms
WBPTN SW10 14 D7
Bolton Pl IS N1 6 C2
Bolton Rd CHSGTN KT9 171 K5
CHSWK W4 105 K6
HRW HA1 48 C3
SRTFD E15 76 D5
STJWD NW8 2 D4
UED N18 42 B4
WLSDN NW10 69 G7
Bolton's La HYS/HAR UB3 101 F6
Boltons Pl ECT SW5 14 E7
The Boltons ALP/SUD HA0 67 F3
WBPTN SW10 14 E7
WFD IG8 * 44 E3
Bolton St MYFR/PICC W1J 10 D8
Bombay St BERM/RHTH SE16 111 J3
Bomer Cl WDR/YW UB7 100 D6
Bomore Rd NTGHL W11 88 B6
Bonaparte Ms PIM SW1V 17 G7
Bonar Pl CHST BR7 153 J6
Bonar Rd PECK SE15 111 H6
Bonchester Cl CHST BR7 154 A6
Bonchurch Cl BELMT SM2 175 F6
Bonchurch Rd NKENS W10 88 C4
WEA W13 85 H7
Bondfield Av YEAD UB4 82 E2
Bond Gdns WLGTN SM6 176 C3
Bond Rd MTCM CR4 162 E1
SURB KT6 172 B1
Bond St EA W5 85 K6
SRTFD E15 76 C4
Bondway VX/NE SW8 17 K9
Boneta Rd WOOL/PLUM SE18 114 E2
Bonfield Rd LEW SE13 133 F3
Bonham Gdns BCTR RM8 79 K1
Bonham Rd BCTR RM8 79 K1
BRXS/STRHM SW2 130 A4
Bonheur Rd CHSWK W4 106 A1
Bonhill St SDTCH EC2A 13 H1
Boniface Gdns
KTN/HRWW/WS HA3 34 B6
Boniface Wk
KTN/HRWW/WS HA3 34 B6
Bonita Ms PECK SE15 132 A2
Bonner Hill Rd KUT/HW KT1 159 G2
Bonner Rd BETH E2 92 E1
Bonnersfield Cl HRW HA1 49 G5
Bonnersfield La HRW HA1 49 F5
Bonner St BETH E2 * 92 E1
Bonneville Gdns CLAP SW4 129 H5
Bonnington Sq VX/NE SW8 17 L9
Bonny St CAMTN NW1 4 E2
Bonser Rd TWK TW1 143 F1
Bonsor St CMBW SE5 111 F6
Bonville Gdns HDN NW4 51 J3
Bonville Rd BMLY BR1 152 D4
Booker Cl POP/IOD E14 93 H4
Booker Rd UED N18 42 C4
Boones Rd LEW SE13 133 H3
Boone St LEW SE13 133 H3
Boord St GNWCH SE10 113 H2
Boothby Rd ARCH N19 72 D1
Booth Cl HOM E9 74 D7
THMD SE28 97 H7
Booth La BLKFR EC4V 12 E6
Booth Rd CDALE/KGS NW9 37 F7
CROY/NA CR0 * 177 H1
Boot Pde EDGW HA8 * 36 C5
Boot St FSBYE EC1V 7 J8
Bordars Rd HNWL W7 84 E4
Bordars Wk HNWL W7 84 E4
Borden Av EN EN1 29 K5
Border Crs SYD SE26 150 D4
Border Gdns CROY/NA CR0 179 K3
Border Ga MTCM CR4 147 J7
Border Rd SYD SE26 150 D4
Bordesley Rd MRDN SM4 162 A3
Bordon Wk PUT/ROE SW15 126 D6
Boreas Wk IS N1 6 D6
Boreham Av CAN/RD E16 94 E5
Boreham Cl WAN E11 58 A7
Boreham Rd WDGN N22 41 J7
Borgard House CHARL SE7 * 114 D6
Borgard Rd WOOL/PLUM SE18 114 E3
Borland Rd PECK SE15 131 K3
TEDD TW11 143 H5
Borneo St PUT/ROE SW15 127 F2
Borough High St STHWK SE1 18 F2
Borough Hl CROY/NA CR0 177 H2
Borough Rd ISLW TW7 103 K7
KUTN/CMB KT2 144 C7
MTCM CR4 162 D1
STHWK SE1 18 C3
Borough Sq STHWK SE1 18 E2
Borrett Cl WALW SE17 18 E8
Borrodaile Rd
WAND/EARL SW18 128 A5
Borrowdale Av
KTN/HRWW/WS HA3 49 G1
Borrowdale Cl EFNCH N2 53 G1
REDBR IG4 59 J3
Borthwick Ms WAN E11 * 76 C3
Borthwick Rd
CDALE/KGS NW9 51 H5
SRTFD E15 76 C3
Borthwick St DEPT SE8 112 D4
Borwick Av WALTH E17 57 H2
Bosbury Rd CAT SE6 152 A2
Boscastle Rd KTTN NW5 72 B2
Boscobel Cl BMLY BR1 168 E1
Boscobel Pl BGVA SW1W 16 B5
Boscobel St BAY/PAD W2 9 H2
Boscombe Av LEY E10 58 B6
Boscombe Cl CLPT E5 75 G4
Boscombe Rd SHB W12 106 D1
TOOT SW17 148 A5
WIM/MER SW19 146 E7
WPK KT4 161 F7
Bose Cl FNCH N3 38 C7
Boss St STHWK SE1 19 L1
Bostall Heath ABYW SE2 * 116 D4
Bostall Hl ABYW SE2 116 C4
Bostall La ABYW SE2 116 C4
Bostall Manorway ABYW SE2 116 C3
Bostall Park Av BXLYHN DA7 117 F6
Bostall Rd STMC/STPC BR5 155 H6
Boston Gdns BTFD TW8 104 B3
CHSWK W4 106 B5
Boston Gv RSLP HA4 46 A5
Boston Manor Rd BTFD TW8 104 B3
Boston Pde HNWL W7 * 104 B3
Boston Park Rd BTFD TW8 * 104 D5
Boston Pl CAMTN NW1 9 L1
Boston Rd CROY/NA CR0 164 A5
EDGW HA8 36 E6
EHAM E6 95 J2
HNWL W7 84 E7
WALTH E17 57 J5
Bostonthorpe Rd HNWL W7 * 103 K1
Boston V HNWL W7 104 B3
Boswell Ct BMSBY WC1N 11 K2
Boswell Rd THHTH CR7 164 D3
Boswell St BMSBY WC1N 11 K2
Bosworth Cl WALTH E17 43 H7
Bosworth Rd BAR EN5 26 E2
DAGE RM10 80 C3
FBAR/BDGN N11 40 D5
NKENS W10 88 C3
Botany Bay La CHST BR7 169 H1
Botany Cl EBAR EN4 27 J3
Botany Ter PUR RM19 * 119 K4
Boteley Cl CHING E4 44 B1
Botham Cl EDGW HA8 36 E6
Botha Rd PLSTW E13 95 F4
Bothwell Cl CAN/RD E16 94 E4
Bothwell St HMSMTH W6 107 G5
Botolph Aly MON EC3R 13 J7
Botolph La MON EC3R 13 J7
Botsford Rd RYNPK SW20 161 H1
Bottonscroft Cl THHTH CR7 164 D2
Bott's Ms BAY/PAD W2 8 B5
Botwell Common Rd
HYS/HAR UB3 82 B6
Botwell Crs HYS/HAR UB3 82 C5
Botwell La HYS/HAR UB3 101 J1
Boucher Cl TEDD TW11 143 F4
Boughton Av HAYES BR2 167 J6
Boughton Rd THMD SE28 115 K2
Boulcott St WCHPL E1 93 F5
Boulevard WATW WD18 * 20 B4
Boulevard Dr CDALE/KGS NW9 51 H1
The Boulevard FUL/PGN SW6 128 B1
WATW WD18 20 B4
Boulogne Rd CROY/NA CR0 164 D5
Boulter Cl BMLY BR1 169 F2
Boulter Gdns RAIN RM13 81 J5
Boulton Rd BCTR RM8 80 A1
Boultwood Rd EHAM E6 95 K5
Bounces La ED N9 42 D1
Bounces Rd ED N9 42 D1
Boundaries Rd BAL SW12 147 K1
FELT TW13 122 B7
Boundary Av WALTH E17 57 H6
Boundary Business Ct
MTCM CR4 162 C2
Boundary Cl GDMY/SEVK IG3 78 E3
KUT/HW KT1 159 H2
NWDGN UB2 103 F4
Boundary La CMBW SE5 110 D5
PLSTW E13 95 H2
Boundary Ms STJWD NW8 * 2 F3
Boundary Pass WCHPL E1 7 L9
Boundary Rd BARK IG11 96 C1
BFN/LL DA15 135 K4
CAR SM5 176 A7
ED N9 30 E5
EFNCH N2 39 H7
PIN HA5 47 H5
PLSTW E13 95 G1
ROM RM1 63 J5
STJWD NW8 2 E4
WALTH E17 57 H6
WBLY HA9 68 A2
WDGN N22 55 H2
WIM/MER SW19 147 H5
WLGTN SM6 176 B5
Boundary Rw STHWK SE1 18 C1
Boundary St BETH E2 7 L8
ERITH DA8 118 C6
Boundary Wy CROY/NA CR0 179 J4
Boundfield Rd CAT SE6 152 C2
Bounds Green Rd
FBAR/BDGN N11 40 D5
Bourchier St SOHO/SHAV W1D 11 G6
Bourdon Pl MYFR/PKLN W1K 10 D6
Bourdon Rd PGE/AN SE20 165 K1
Bourdon St MYFR/PKLN W1K 10 C7
Bourke Cl CLAP SW4 129 K5
WLSDN NW10 69 G5
Bourlet Cl GTPST W1W 10 E3
Bourn Av EBAR EN4 27 H4
SEVS/STOTM N15 55 K3
Bournbrook Rd
BKHTH/KID SE3 134 C2
Bourne Av HYS/HAR UB3 101 F2
RSLP HA4 65 G4
STHGT/OAK N14 40 E1
Bourne Cl ISLW TW7 123 K2
THDIT KT7 171 F1
Bourne Ct RSLP HA4 65 F4
Bourne Dr MTCM CR4 162 C1
Bourne End Rd NTHWD HA6 32 C3
Bourne Est HCIRC EC1N * 12 A2
Bourne Gdns CHING E4 43 K3
Bournehall BUSH WD23 * 22 A5
Bournehall Av BUSH WD23 22 A4
Bournehall La BUSH WD23 22 A5
Bournehall Rd BUSH WD23 22 A5
Bourne Hl PLMGR N13 40 E1
Bourne Hill Cl PLMGR N13 * 41 F1
Bournemead BUSH WD23 22 A5
Bourne Md BXLY DA5 137 K4
Bournemead Av NTHLT UB5 82 E1
Bournemead Cl NTHLT UB5 82 E2
Bournemouth Cl PECK SE15 131 H1
Bournemouth Rd PECK SE15 131 H1
WIM/MER SW19 146 E7
Bourne Pde BXLY DA5 * 137 J6
Bourne Rd BUSH WD23 22 A4
BXLY DA5 137 J5
CEND/HSY/T N8 54 E5
HAYES BR2 168 C3
WAN E11 76 D2
Bourneside Crs
STHGT/OAK N14 28 D7
Bourneside Gdns CAT SE6 152 A4

Bourne St BGVA SW1W....16 A6
CROY/NA CR0....177 H1
Bourne Ter BAY/PAD W2....8 C2
The Bourne STHGT/OAK N14....28 D3
Bourne Vw HAYES BR2....167 K7
Bournevale Rd STRHM/NOR SW16....148 E3
Bourne Vw GFD/PVL UB6....67 F3
Bourne Wy HAYES BR2....180 E1
HOR/WEW KT19....172 E3
SUT SM1....174 D4
Bournewood Rd WOOL/PLUM SE18....116 B6
Bournville Rd CAT SE6....132 D6
Bournwell Cl BARn EN4....27 K1
Bourton Cl HYS/HAR UB3....82 E7
Bousfield Rd NWCR SE14....132 A1
Boutflower Rd BTSEA SW11....128 D3
Boutique Hall ISLW SE1 *....133 F3
Bouverie Gdns KTN/HRWW/WS HA3....49 K5
Bouverie Ms STNW/STAM N16....74 A1
Bouverie Pl BAY/PAD W2....9 J3
Bouverie Rd HRW HA1....48 C5
STNW/STAM N16....74 A1
Bouverie St EMBC EC4Y....12 B5
Boveney Rd FSTH SE23....132 E6
Bovill Rd FSTH SE23....132 A6
Bovingdon Av WBLY HA9....68 C5
Bovingdon La CDALE/KGS NW9....37 G7
Bovingdon Rd FUL/PGN SW6....108 A7
Bovington Cl ARCH N19....72 C1
Bow Arrow La DART DA1....139 K5
Bowater Cl BRXS/STRHM SW2....129 K5
CDALE/KGS NW9....51 F4
Bowater Gdns SUN TW16....141 G7
Bowater Pl BKHTH/KID SE3....114 A6
Bowater Rd WBLY HA9....68 D2
WOOL/PLUM SE18....114 C2
Bow Bridge Est BOW E3....93 K2
Bow Churchyard STP EC4M *....12 F4
Bow Common La BOW E3....93 H3
Bowden Cl EBED/NFELT TW14....121 H7
Bowden St LBTH SE11....18 B7
Bowditch DEPT SE8....112 C4
Bowdon Rd WALTH E17....57 J7
Bowen Dr DUL SE21....150 A2
Bowen Rd HRW HA1....48 C6
Bowen St POP/IOD E14....93 K5
Bowens CROY/NA CR0 *....179 H7
Bower Av GNWCH SE10....113 H7
Bower Cl NTHLT UB5....83 G1
Bowerdean St FUL/PGN SW6....108 A7
Bowerman Av NWCR SE14....112 B5
Bower St WCHPL E1 *....93 F5
Bowes Cl BFN/LL DA15....136 C5
Bowes Rd ACT W3....87 G6
BCTR RM8....79 J3
FBAR/BDGN N11....40 B4
Bowfell Rd HMSMTH W6....107 F5
Bowford Av BXLYHN DA7....117 F7
Bowhill Cl BRXN/ST SW9....110 B6
Bowie Cl CLAP SW4....129 J6
WFD IG8....45 G5
Bowland Rd CLAP SW4....129 J3
Bowland Yd KTBR SW1X *....15 M2
Bow La NFNCH/WDSPK N12....39 G6
STP EC4M....12 F5
Bowl Ct WCHPL E1....13 K1
Bowley Cl NRWD SE19....150 B5
Bowley La NRWD SE19....150 B4
Bowley St POP/IOD E14....93 H6
Bowling Green Cl PUT/ROE SW15....126 E6
Bowling Green La CLKNW EC1R....12 B1
Bowling Green Pl STHWK SE1 *....19 G1
Bowling Green Rw WOOL/PLUM SE18 *....114 E3
Bowling Green St LBTH SE11....18 B9
Bowling Green Wk IS N1....7 J7
Bow Locks BOW E3 *....94 A3
Bowls Cl STAN HA7....35 H4
Bowman Av CAN/RD E16....94 E5
Bowman Ms WAND/EARL SW18....127 J7
Bowmans Cl WEA W13....85 H7
Bowmans Lea FSTH SE23....131 K6
Bowman's Meadow WLGTN SM6....176 B2
Bowmans Ms WCHPL E1....92 C5
Bowman's Ms HOLWY N7....72 E2
Bowman's Pl HOLWY N7....72 E2
Bowmans Rd DART DA1....138 C6
Bowmead ELTH/MOT SE9....153 K1
Bowmore Wk CAMTN NW1 *....5 H2
Bowness Cl HACK E8 *....74 B5
Bowness Crs PUT/ROE SW15....145 F4
Bowness Dr HSLWW TW4....122 D3
Bowness Rd BXLYHN DA7....137 H1
CAT SE6....132 E6
Bowness Wy HCH RM12....81 J4
Bowood Rd CLAP SW4....129 K4
PEND EN3....31 F1
Bowring Gn OXHEY WD19....33 G4
Bow Rd BOW E3....93 J2
Bowrons Av ALP/SUD HA0....67 K6
Bowsley Ct FELT TW13....140 E1
Bow St COVGDN WC2E....11 K5
SRTFD E15....76 C4
Bowyer Cl EHAM E6....95 K4
Bowyer Pl CMBW SE5....110 E6
Bowyers Ct TWK TW1....124 C3
Bowyer St CMBW SE5....110 D6
Boxall Rd DUL SE21....131 F5
Boxelder Cl EDGW HA8....36 E4
Boxgrove Rd ABYW SE2....116 C1
Box La BARK IG11....97 H1
Boxley Rd MRDN SM4....162 B3
Boxley St CAN/RD E16....95 F7
Boxmoor Rd KTN/HRWW/WS HA3....49 H3
Boxoll Rd DAGW RM9....80 B2
Boxtree La KTN/HRWW/WS HA3....34 C7
Boxtree Rd KTN/HRWW/WS HA3....34 D6
Boxworth Cl WDR/YW UB7....100 C1
Boxworth Cl NFNCH/WDSPK N12....39 H4
Boxworth Gv IS N1....5 M3
Boyard Rd WOOL/PLUM SE18....115 G4
Boyce Wy PLSTW E13....94 E3
Boycroft Av CDALE/KGS NW9....50 E5
Boyd Av STHL UB1....83 K7
Boyd Cl KUTN/CMB KT2....144 C6
Boydell Ct STJWD NW8....3 G2
Boyd Rd WIM/MER SW19....147 H5
Boyd St WCHPL E1....92 C5
Boyfield St STHWK SE1....18 D2

Boyland Rd BMLY BR1....152 D4
Boyle Av STAN HA7....35 G5
Boyle Farm Rd THDIT KT7....158 B5
Boyne Av HDN NW4....52 B3
Boyne Rd DAGE RM10....80 C2
LEW SE13....133 F2
Boyne Terrace Ms NTGHL W11 *....88 D6
Boyton Cl CEND/HSY/T N8....54 E2
WCHPL E1....93 F3
Boyton Rd CEND/HSY/T N8....54 E2
Brabant Rd WDGN N22....55 F1
Brabazon Av WLGTN SM6....176 E6
Brabazon Rd HEST TW5....102 B6
NTHLT UB5....84 A1
Brabazon St POP/IOD E14....93 K5
Brabourne Cl NRWD SE19....150 A4
Brabourne Crs BXLYHN DA7....117 G5
Brabourne Ri BECK BR3....167 G4
Brabourn Gv PECK SE15....131 K1
Bracewell Av GFD/PVL UB6....67 G4
Bracewell Rd NKENS W10....88 A4
Bracewood Gdns CROY/NA CR0....178 B2
Bracey Ms FSBYPK N4 *....72 E1
Bracey St FSBYPK N4....72 E1
Bracken Av BAL SW12....129 F5
CROY/NA CR0....179 J2
Brackenbridge Dr RSLP HA4....65 H2
Brackenbury Gdns HMSMTH W6....106 E2
Brackenbury Rd EFNCH N2....53 G2
HMSMTH W6....106 E2
Bracken Cl EHAM E6....95 K4
SUN TW16 *....140 D5
WHTN TW2....123 F6
Brackendale WCHMH N21....41 F1
Brackendale Cl HSLW TW3....103 G7
Bracken End ISLW TW7....123 J4
Bracken Gdns BARN SW13....126 D1
Brackenhill RSLP HA4....65 J3
Bracken Hill Cl BMLY BR1....152 D7
Bracken Hill La BMLY BR1....152 D7
Bracken Ms ROMW/RG RM7....62 C5
The Brackens EN EN1....30 A6
The Bracken CHING E4....31 K2
Brackenwood SUN TW16....140 E7
Brackley Av PECK SE15....131 J2
Brackley Cl WLGTN SM6....176 E6
Brackley Rd BECK BR3....151 H1
CHSWK W4....106 B3
Brackley Sq WFD IG8....45 H6
Brackley St BARB EC2Y....12 F2
Brackley Ter CHSWK W4....106 B4
Bracklyn St IS N1....7 G3
Bracknell Cl WDGN N22....41 G7
Bracknell Gdns HAMP NW3....71 F4
Bracknell Wy HAMP NW3....71 F3
Bracondale ESH/CLAY KT10....170 C4
Bracondale Rd ABYW SE2....116 B3
Bradbourne Rd BXLY DA5....137 H6
Bradbourne St FUL/PGN SW6....127 K1
Bradbury Cl NWDGN UB2....102 E3
Bradbury St STNW/STAM N16....74 A4
Braddock Cl ISLW TW7....124 A2
Braddon Ct BAR EN5 *....26 C2
Braddon Rd RCH/KEW TW9....125 G2
Braddyll St GNWCH SE10....113 H4
Bradenham Av WELL DA16....136 B3
Bradenham Cl WALW SE17....19 G9
Bradenham Rd KTN/HRWW/WS HA3....49 H3
YEAD UB4....82 C2
Braden St MV/WKIL W9 *....8 C1
Bradfield Dr BARK IG11....79 G4
Bradfield Rd CAN/RD E16....113 K1
RSLP HA4....65 J4
Bradford Cl HAYES BR2....168 E7
SYD SE26....150 D3
TOTM N17....42 B5
Bradford Dr HOR/WEW KT19....173 H5
Bradford Rd ACT W3....106 B1
IL IG1....60 D7
Bradgate Cl BKHH IG9....45 H3
Bradgate Rd CAT SE6....132 E5
Brading Crs WAN E11....77 G1
Brading Rd BRXS/STRHM SW2....130 A6
CROY/NA CR0....164 A5
Brading Ter SHB W12....106 D2
Bradiston Rd MV/WKIL W9....88 D2
Bradley Cl HOLWY N7....5 K1
Bradley Gdns WEA W13....85 H5
Bradley Rd NRWD SE19....149 J5
WDGN N22....55 J1
Bradley's Cl IS N1....6 A1
Bradley Stone Rd EHAM E6....95 K5
Bradman Rw EDGW HA8 *....36 E6
Bradmead VX/NE SW8 *....109 G7
Bradmore Park Rd HMSMTH W6....106 E2
Bradshaw Cl WIM/MER SW19....146 E5
Bradshaw Cots POP/IOD E14 *....93 G5
Bradshaws Cl SNWD SE25....165 H2
Bradstock Rd EW KT17....173 K4
HOM E9....75 F5
Brad St STHWK SE1....12 B9
Bradwell Av DAGE RM10....80 C1
Bradwell Cl HCH RM12....81 H4
SWFD E18....58 D3
Bradwell Ms UED N18....42 C3
Bradwell St WCHPL E1....93 F2
Brady Dr BMLY BR1....169 F2
Bradymead EHAM E6....96 A5
Brady St WCHPL E1....92 D3
Braemar Av ALP/SUD HA0....67 K3
BXLYHN DA7....137 K3
THHTH CR7....164 B2
WDGN N22....40 E7
WIM/MER SW19....146 E1
WLSDN NW10....69 F2
Braemar Gdns BFN/LL DA15....154 D2
CDALE/KGS NW9....37 F7
WWKM BR4....180 A1
Braemar Rd BTFD TW8....104 E5
PLSTW E13....94 D3
SEVS/STOTM N15....56 A4
WPK KT4....173 K2
Braeside BECK BR3....151 J4
Braeside Av RYNPK SW20....160 E1
Braeside Cl PIN HA5....34 A5
Braeside Crs BXLYHN DA7....137 K3
Braeside Rd STRHM/NOR SW16....148 C6
Braes St IS N1....6 D2
Braesyde Cl BELV DA17....117 G3
Brafferton Rd CROY/NA CR0....177 J3
Braganza St WALW SE17....18 C8
Bragg Cl BCTR RM8....79 H5
Bragg Rd TEDD TW11....142 F5
Braham St WCHPL E1....13 M5
Braid Av ACT W3....87 G5
Braid Cl FELT TW13....141 K1
Braidwood Rd CAT SE6....133 G1
Braidwood St STHWK SE1....13 J9

Brailsford Cl WIM/MER SW19....147 J6
Brailsford Rd BRXS/STRHM SW2....130 B5
Brainton Av EBED/NFELT TW14....122 A6
Braintree Av REDBR IG4....59 J4
Braintree Rd DAGE RM10....80 C2
RSLP HA4....65 F3
Braintree St BETH E2 *....92 E2
Braithwaite Av ROMW/RG RM7....62 C6
Braithwaite Gdns STAN HA7....35 J7
Braithwaite Rd PEND EN3....31 H2
Bramall Cl SRTFD E15....76 D4
Bramber Ct EA W5....105 F3
Bramber Rd NFNCH/WDSPK N12....39 J4
WKENS W14....107 J5
Bramble Acres Cl BELMT SM2....174 E6
Bramble Banks CAR SM5....176 A7
Bramble Cl BECK BR3....167 F4
CROY/NA CR0....179 J3
SEVS/STOTM N15....56 C3
STAN HA7....35 K6
THHTH CR7....149 K7
Bramble Cft ERITH DA8....117 K3
Brambledown Cl WWKM BR4....167 H5
Brambledown Rd CAR SM5....176 A6
SAND/SEL CR2....178 A6
Bramble Gdns SHB W12....87 H6
Bramble La HPTN TW12....141 K5
Brambles Cl ISLW TW7....104 C6
The Brambles SUT SM1 *....175 H1
WDR/YW UB7 *....100 A4
WIM/MER SW19 *....146 D4
Bramblewood Cl CAR SM5....162 D7
Brambling Cl BUSH WD23....21 J3
The Bramblings CHING E4....44 B3
Bramcote Av MTCM CR4....162 E3
Bramcote Gv BERM/RHTH SE16....111 K4
Bramcote Rd PUT/ROE SW15....126 E3
Bramdean Crs LEE/GVPK SE12....133 K7
Bramdean Gdns LEE/GVPK SE12....133 K7
Bramerton Rd BECK BR3....166 C2
Bramerton St CHEL SW3....15 J9
Bramfield Rd BTSEA SW11....128 D5
Bramford Rd WAND/EARL SW18....128 B3
Bramham Gdns CHSGTN KT9 *....171 K4
ECT SW5....14 C7
Bramhope La CHARL SE7....114 A5
Bramlands Cl BTSEA SW11....128 D2
Bramleas WATW WD18....20 D4
Bramley Cl HYS/HAR UB3....82 E6
MLHL NW7....37 G2
ORP BR6....169 G7
PIN HA5....46 D2
SAND/SEL CR2....177 H4
STHGT/OAK N14....28 B4
WALTH E17....57 G1
WFD IG8....45 G6
WHTN TW2....123 H5
Bramley Crs GNTH/NBYPK IG2....60 A5
VX/NE SW8....109 J6
Bramley Gdns OXHEY WD19....33 G5
Bramley Hi SAND/SEL CR2....177 J3
Bramley Hyrst SAND/SEL CR2 *....177 J4
Bramley Ldg ALP/SUD HA0....67 K3
Bramley Pde STHGT/OAK N14....28 C3
Bramley Pl DART DA1....138 D3
Bramley Rd BELMT SM2....174 B7
EA W5....104 D2
NKENS W10....88 B5
STHGT/OAK N14....28 B4
SUT SM1....175 H4
Bramley Wy HSLWW TW4....122 E4
WWKM BR4....179 K1
Brampton Cl CLPT E5....74 D1
Brampton Gv HDN NW4....51 K3
KTN/HRWW/WS HA3....49 G3
WBLY HA9....50 C7
Brampton La HDN NW4....52 A3
Brampton Park Rd WDGN N22....55 G2
Brampton Rd BXLYHN DA7....136 E2
CDALE/KGS NW9....50 C3
CROY/NA CR0....165 G6
EHAM E6....95 H3
OXHEY WD19....32 E2
SEVS/STOTM N15....55 J4
Bramshaw Gdns OXHEY WD19....33 H4
Bramshaw Ri NWMAL KT3....160 B5
Bramshaw Rd HOM E9....75 F5
Bramshill Gdns KTTN NW5....72 B2
Bramshill Rd WLSDN NW10....87 G1
Bramshot Av CHARL SE7....114 A5
Bramshot Wy OXHEY WD19....32 E1
Bramston Rd MTCM CR4....147 K6
WLSDN NW10....87 J1
Bramwell Cl SUN TW16....156 C1
Bramwell Ms IS N1....5 M1
Brancaster Dr MLHL NW7....37 J6
Brancaster Rd GNTH/NBYPK IG2....60 D5
STRHM/NOR SW16....148 E2
Brancepeth Gdns BKHH IG9....44 E1
Branch Hl HAMP NW3....71 G2
Branch Pl IS N1....7 H3
Branch Rd POP/IOD E14....93 G6
Branch St CMBW SE5....111 F6
Brancker Rd KTN/HRWW/WS HA3....49 K2
Brand Cl FSBYPK N4....55 H7
Brandlehow Rd PUT/ROE SW15....127 J3
Brandon Est WALW SE17....18 E9
Brandon Ms BARB EC2Y *....13 G1
Brandon Rd DART DA1....139 K6
HOLWY N7....5 J1
NWDGN UB2....102 E4
SUT SM1....175 F3
WALTH E17....58 A3
Brandon St WALW SE17....18 F6
Brandram Ms LEW SE13 *....133 H3
Brandram Rd LEW SE13....133 H3
Brandreth Ct HRW HA1 *....49 F5
Brandreth Rd EHAM E6....95 K5
TOOT SW17....148 B1
The Brandries WLGTN SM6....176 D2
Brand St GNWCH SE10....113 F6
Brandville Gdns BARK/HLT IG6....60 B3
Brandville Rd WDR/YW UB7....100 B1
Brandy Wy BELMT SM2....174 E6
Brangbourne Rd BMLY BR1....152 A4
Brangton Rd LBTH SE11....17 M8
Brangwyn Crs WIM/MER SW19....147 H7

Branksea St FUL/PGN SW6....107 H6
Branksome Av UED N18....42 B5
Branksome Cl TEDD TW11....142 D3
Branksome Rd BRXS/STRHM SW2....129 K4
WIM/MER SW19....146 E7
Branksome Wy KTN/HRWW/WS HA3....50 B7
NWMAL KT3....159 K1
Bransby Rd CHSGTN KT9....172 A6
Branscombe Gdns WCHMH N21....29 G6
Branscombe St LEW SE13....132 E2
Bransdale Cl KIL/WHAMP NW6....2 B3
Bransgrove Rd EDGW HA8....36 B7
Branston Crs STMC/STPC BR5....169 J7
Branstone Rd RCH/KEW TW9....105 G7
Brants Wk HNWL W7....84 E3
Brantwood Av ERITH DA8....117 K6
ISLW TW7....124 B3
Brantwood Cl WALTH E17 *....57 K2
Brantwood Gdns ENC/FH EN2....28 E3
REDBR IG4....59 J4
Brantwood Rd BXLYHN DA7....137 J1
HNHL SE24....130 D4
SAND/SEL CR2....177 J7
TOTM N17....42 C5
Brasenose Dr BARN SW13....107 F5
Brasher Cl GFD/PVL UB6....66 C4
Brassey Rd KIL/WHAMP NW6....70 D5
Brassey Sq BTSEA SW11....129 F2
Brassie Av ACT W3....87 G5
Brasted Cl BXLYHS DA6....136 E4
SYD SE26....150 E3
Brasted Rd ERITH DA8....118 B6
Brathway Rd WAND/EARL SW18....127 K6
Braund Av GFD/PVL UB6....84 B3
Braundton Av BFN/LL DA15....136 A7
Braunston Dr YEAD UB4....83 J3
Bravington Pl MV/WKIL W9....88 D3
Bravington Rd MV/WKIL W9....88 D2
Bravingtons Wk IS N1....5 K6
Braxfield Rd BROCKY SE4....132 B3
Braxted Pk STRHM/NOR SW16....149 F5
Brayard's Rd PECK SE15....131 J1
Braybourne Dr ISLW TW7....104 A6
Braybrooke Gdns NRWD SE19....150 A6
Braybrook St SHB W12....87 H4
Brayburne Av VX/NE SW8....129 H1
Braycourt Av WOT/HER KT12....156 B6
Bray Crs BERM/RHTH SE16....112 A1
Braydon Rd STNW/STAM N16....56 C7
Bray Dr CAN/RD E16....94 D6
Brayfield Ter IS N1....6 A2
Brayford Sq WCHPL E1 *....92 E5
Bray Pl CHEL SW3....15 K6
Bray Rd MLHL NW7....38 B5
Brayton Gdns ENC/FH EN2....28 E3
Braywood Rd ELTH/MOT SE9....135 J3
Brazier Crs NTHLT UB5....83 K3
Brazil Cl CROY/NA CR0....163 K6
Breach La DAGW RM9....98 C2
Bread St STP EC4M....12 F5
Breakspears Dr STMC/STPC BR5....155 G7
Breakspears Ms BROCKY SE4....132 D1
Breakspears Rd BROCKY SE4....132 C1
Bream Cl TOTM N17....56 D3
Bream Gdns EHAM E6....96 A2
Breamore Cl PUT/ROE SW15....126 D7
Breamore Rd GDMY/SEVK IG3....79 F1
Bream's Blds LINN WC2A....12 A4
Bream St BOW E3....75 J6
Breamwater Gdns RCHPK/HAM TW10....143 H2
Brearley Cl EDGW HA8....36 E6
IS N1....6 B6
Breasley Cl PUT/ROE SW15....126 E3
Breasy Pl HDN NW4 *....51 K3
Brechin Pl SKENS SW7....14 F7
Brecknock Rd ARCH N19....72 C3
Brecknock Road Est ARCH N19 *....72 D4
Brecon Cl MTCM CR4....163 K3
WPK KT4....174 A1
Brecon Gn CDALE/KGS NW9 *....51 G5
Brecon Ms KTTN NW5....72 D5
Brecon Rd HMSMTH W6....107 H5
PEND EN3....30 E3
Brede Cl EHAM E6....96 A2
Bredgar Rd ARCH N19....72 B1
Bredhurst Cl PGE/AN SE20....150 E5
Bredon Rd CROY/NA CR0....165 G6
Breer St FUL/PGN SW6....128 A2
Breezers Hi WAP E1W *....92 C6
Bremans Rw WAND/EARL SW18....147 G1
Brember Rd RYLN/HDSTN HA2....66 C1
Bremer Ms WALTH E17....57 K3
Bremner Rd SKENS SW7....14 E3
Brenchley Cl CHST BR7....154 A7
HAYES BR2....167 J4
Brenchley Gdns EDUL SE22....131 H5
Brenchley Rd STMC/STPC BR5....154 E7
Brenda Rd TOOT SW17....147 K1
Brende Gdns E/WMO/HCT KT8....157 G3
Brendon Av WLSDN NW10....69 G3
Brendon Cl ERITH DA8....118 B7
ESH/CLAY KT10....170 C5
HYS/HAR UB3....101 F4
Brendon Dr ESH/CLAY KT10....170 C5
Brendon Gdns RYLN/HDSTN HA2....66 B3
GNTH/NBYPK IG2....60 D5
Brendon Gv EFNCH N2....53 G1
Brendon Rd BCTR RM8....62 B7
ELTH/MOT SE9....154 D1
Brendon St MBLAR W1H....9 K4
Brendon Vls WCHMH N21 *....29 J7
Brendon Wy EN EN1....30 A6
Brenley Cl MTCM CR4....163 F2
Brenley Gdns ELTH/MOT SE9....134 C3
Brent Cl BXLY DA5....137 F7
Brentcot Cl WEA W13....85 H4
Brent Crs WLSDN NW10....86 B1
Brent Cross F/O HDN NW4....52 A3
Brentfield WLSDN NW10....68 D6
Brentfield Gdns CRICK NW2 *....52 B1
Brentfield Rd DART DA1....139 K5
WLSDN NW10....69 F6
Brent Gn HDN NW4....52 A4
Brentham Wy EA W5....85 K3
Brenthouse Rd HACK E8....74 D6
Brenthurst Rd WLSDN NW10....69 H5
Brentlands Dr DART DA1....139 K5
Brent La DART DA1....139 J6
Brent Lea BTFD TW8....104 D6
Brentmead Cl HNWL W7....84 E6

Brentmead Gdns WLSDN NW10....86 B1
Brenton St POP/IOD E14....93 G5
Brent Park Rd CDALE/KGS NW9....51 J3
HDN NW4....51 K6
Brent Pl BAR EN5....26 D4
Brent River Park Wk HNWL W7....84 D4
Brent Rd BTFD TW8....104 D5
CAN/RD E16....94 E5
NWDGN UB2....102 B2
SAND/SEL CR2....178 D7
WOOL/PLUM SE18....115 G6
Brentside BTFD TW8....104 D5
Brentside Cl WEA W13....85 F5
Brent St HDN NW4....52 A3
Brent Ter CRICK NW2....70 A1
The Brent DART DA1....139 K6
Brentvale Av ALP/SUD HA0....68 D4
STHL UB1....84 D7
Brent View Rd CDALE/KGS NW9....51 J5
Brent Wy BTFD TW8....104 E6
FNCH N3....38 E5
WBLY HA9....68 D4
Brentwick Gdns BTFD TW8....105 F3
Brentwood Cl ELTH/MOT SE9....135 H1
Brentwood Rd ROM RM1....63 H5
Brereton Rd TOTM N17....42 B6
Bressay Dr MLHL NW7....37 J6
Bressenden Pl WESTW SW1E....16 D3
Bressey Gv SWFD E18....58 D1
Brett Cl NTHLT UB5....83 H1
STNW/STAM N16....74 A1
Brett Crs WLSDN NW10....69 H1
Brettell St WALW SE17....19 H8
Brettenham Av WALTH E17....43 J7
Brettenham Rd UED N18....42 C3
WALTH E17....57 J1
Brett Gdns DAGW RM9....80 A6
Brett Pas HACK E8....74 D4
Brett Rd BAR EN5....26 A4
HACK E8....74 D4
Brett Vls ACT W3 *....87 F5
Brewer St REGST W1B....10 F6
Brewery Cl ALP/SUD HA0....67 G4
Brewery Rd HAYES BR2....168 D7
WOOL/PLUM SE18....115 J4
Brewery Sq FSBYE EC1V *....12 D1
STHWK SE1....13 L9
Brewhouse La WAP E1W *....92 D7
Brewhouse Rd WOOL/PLUM SE18....114 E3
Brewhouse St PUT/ROE SW15....127 H3
Brewhouse Wk BERM/RHTH SE16....93 G7
Brewhouse Yd FSBYE EC1V *....6 C9
Brewood Rd BCTR RM8....79 H5
Brewster Gdns NKENS W10....88 A4
Brewster Rd LEY E10....57 K7
Brian Cl HCH RM12....81 K3
Brian Rd CHDH RM6....61 J4
Briants Cl PIN HA5....33 J7
Briant St NWCR SE14....112 A7
Briar Av STRHM/NOR SW16....149 F6
Briar Bank CAR SM5....176 A7
Briarbank Rd WEA W13....85 G5
Briar Cl BKHH IG9....45 H1
EFNCH N2....52 E1
HPTN TW12....141 K4
ISLW TW7....124 A4
PLMGR N13....41 J2
Briar Crs NTHLT UB5....66 B5
Briardale Gdns HAMP NW3....70 E2
Briarfield Av EFNCH N2....53 F2
Briarfield Cl BXLYHN DA7....137 H1
Briar Gdns HAYES BR2....181 J1
Briar La CAR SM5....176 A7
CROY/NA CR0....179 K3
Briar Rd CRICK NW2....70 A3
KTN/HRWW/WS HA3....49 J4
STRHM/NOR SW16....163 K2
WHTN TW2....123 K7
Briar Wk EDGW HA8....36 E6
NKENS W10 *....88 C3
PUT/ROE SW15....126 E3
Briar Wy WDR/YW UB7....100 D1
Briarwood Cl CDALE/KGS NW9 *....50 E5
FELT TW13....140 C2
Briar Wood Cl HAYES BR2....181 J1
Briarwood Ct WPK KT4 *....160 D1
Briarwood Dr NTHWD HA6....46 E1
Briarwood Rd CLAP SW4....129 J4
EW KT17....173 J5
Briary Cl EDGW HA8....50 D1
SCUP DA14....155 H4
Briary Gdns BMLY BR1....153 G4
Briary La ED N9....42 A2
Brickbarn Cl WBPTN SW10 *....108 B6
Brick Ct EMB EC4Y *....12 A5
Brickett Cl RSLP HA4....46 A4
Brickfield Cl BTFD TW8....104 D6
HOM E9....74 E5
Brickfield Cots WOOL/PLUM SE18....116 A5
Brickfield La BAR EN5....25 H5
HYS/HAR UB3....101 G5
Brickfield Rd BOW E3....93 K3
THHTH CR7....149 H7
WIM/MER SW19....147 F3
Brickfields RYLN/HDSTN HA2....66 D1
Brickfields Wy WDR/YW UB7....100 C2
Brickfield Vls CAR SM5 *....175 J2
Brick Kiln Cl OXHEY WD19....33 J2
Brick La BETH E2....7 M8
EN EN1....30 D1
NTHLT UB5....83 K2
PEND EN3....30 E1
STAN HA7....36 A6
WCHPL E1....13 M1
Brick St MYFR/PICC W1J....10 D8
Brickwall La RSLP HA4....46 C7
Brickwood Cl SYD SE26....150 D2
Brickwood Rd CROY/NA CR0....178 A1
Brideale Cl PECK SE15....111 G5
Bride La EMB EC4Y....12 C5
Bridel Ms FSBYE EC1V *....6 C6
Bride St HOLWY N7....73 F5
Bridewain St STHWK SE1....19 L3
Bridewell Pl BLKFR EC4V *....12 D5
WAP E1W....92 D7
Bridford Ms GTPST W1W....10 D2
Bridge Ap CAMTN NW1....4 A1
Bridge Av HMSMTH W6....107 F4
HNWL W7....84 D4
Bridge Cl EN EN1....30 D1
NKENS W10....88 B5
ROMW/RG RM7....63 G3
Bridge Dr PLMGR N13....41 F3

Bridge End WALTH E17 ....44 A7
Bridge End Cl KUTN/CMB KT2 ...144 C7
Bridgefield Rd SUT SM1 ...174 E5
Bridge Gdns ASHF TW15 ...140 A6
  E/WMO/HCT KT8 ...157 J3
  STNW/STAM N16 ...73 K3
Bridge Ga WCHMH N21 ...29 J6
Bridge House Quay
  POP/IOD E14 ...94 A7
Bridgelands Rd BECK BR3 ...151 H6
Bridgeland Cl BECK BR3 ...151 H6
Bridge La BTSEA SW11 ...108 D7
  HDN NW4 ...52 B3
Bridgeman Rd IS N1 ...5 M2
Bridgeman St STJWD NW8 ...3 J6
Bridge Mdw NWCR SE14 ...112 A5
Bridgen Rd BXLY DA5 ...137 F6
Bridge Pde
  STRHM/NOR SW16 * ...148 E4
  WCHMH N21 * ...29 J4
Bridge Pl CROY/NA CRO ...164 E7
  PIM SW1V ...16 D5
  WAT WD17 ...21 H4
Bridgepoint Pl HGT N6 ...54 B7
Bridge Rd BECK BR3 ...151 H6
  BXLYHN DA7 ...137 F2
  CHSGTN KT9 ...172 A4
  E/WMO/HCT KT8 ...157 K3
  ED N9 ...42 C2
  EHAM E6 ...77 K6
  ERITH DA8 ...118 C7
  HSLW TW3 ...123 J2
  LEY E10 ...58 B5
  NWDGN UB2 ...102 E1
  RAIN RM13 ...99 J3
  SRTFD E15 ...76 B7
  SUT SM1 ...175 F5
  TWK TW1 ...124 C5
  WALTH E17 ...57 H6
  WBLY HA9 ...68 C2
  WDGN N22 ...40 E7
  WLGTN SM6 ...176 B4
  WLSDN NW10 ...69 G5
Bridge Rw CROY/NA CRO * ...164 E7
Bridges Ct BTSEA SW11 ...128 C2
Bridges La CROY/NA CRO ...176 E3
Bridges Rd STAN HA7 ...35 F4
Bridges Road Ms
  WIM/MER SW19 ...147 F5
Bridge St CHSWK W4 ...106 A3
  PIN HA5 ...47 H2
  TWK TW1 ...124 E5
  WHALL SW1A ...17 J2
Bridge Ter LEW SE13 * ...133 G3
  SRTFD E15 * ...76 B6
The Bridge EA W5 * ...86 B7
  KTN/HRWW/WS HA3 ...49 F2
Bridgetown Cl NRWD SE19 ...150 A4
Bridgeview HMSMTH W6 ...107 H4
Bridge Vis WIM/MER SW19 * ...146 E4
Bridgewater Cl
  STMC/STPC BR5 ...169 K1
Bridgewater Rd ALP/SUD HA0 ...67 J7
Bridgewater Sq BARB EC2Y * ...12 E2
Bridgewater St BARB EC2Y ...12 E2
Bridgewater Wy BUSH WD23 ...22 B5
  BARK IG11 ...79 F6
Bridgeway ALP/SUD HA0 ...68 A2
  WHTN TW2 ...123 H6
Bridgeway St CAMTN NW1 ...4 F7
Bridge Wharf Rd ISLW TW7 ...124 C2
Bridgewood Cl PGE/AN SE20 ...150 D6
Bridgewood Rd
  STRHM/NOR SW16 ...148 D6
  WPK KT4 ...173 J3
Bridgford St
  WAND/EARL SW18 ...147 G2
Bridgman Rd CHSWK W4 ...105 K2
Bridgwater Rd RSLP HA4 ...64 D5
Bridle Cl HOR/WEW KT19 ...172 E3
  KUT/HW KT1 ...158 F3
Bridle La SOHO/CST W1F ...10 F6
  TWK TW1 ...124 C5
  WAT WD19 ...21 H1
The Bridle Pth WFD IG8 ...44 C6
Bridlepath Wy
  EBED/NFELT TW14 ...121 H6
Bridle Rd CROY/NA CRO ...179 J3
  ESH/CLAY KT10 ...171 H5
  PIN HA5 ...47 G5
Bridle Wy CROY/NA CRO ...179 J4
The Bridle Wy WLGTN SM6 ...176 C7
Bridlington Rd ED N9 ...30 D6
  OXHEY WD19 ...33 H2
Bridport Av ROMW/RG RM7 ...62 D5
Bridport Pl IS N1 ...7 J1
Bridport Rd GFD/PVL UB6 ...66 C1
  THHTH CR7 ...164 B2
  UED N18 ...42 A4
Bridstow Pl BAY/PAD W2 ...8 A5
Brief St BRXN/ST SW9 ...110 A1
Brierley CROY/NA CRO ...179 K5
Brierley Av ED N9 ...30 E7
Brierley Cl SNWD SE25 ...165 H3
Brierley Rd BAL SW12 ...148 C1
  WAN E11 ...76 B3
Brierly Gdns BETH E2 * ...92 E1
Brigade Cl RYLN/HDSTN HA2 ...66 D1
Brigade St BKHTH/KID SE3 ...133 J1
Briggeford Cl CLPT E5 ...74 C1
Briggs Cl MTCM CR4 ...148 B7
Bright Cl BELV DA17 ...116 E3
Brightfield Rd LEE/GVPK SE12 ...133 H4
Brightling Rd BROCKY SE4 ...132 C5
Brightlingsea Pl POP/IOD E14 ...93 H6
Brightman Rd
  WAND/EARL SW18 ...128 C2
Brighton Av WALTH E17 ...57 H4
Brighton Dr NTHLT UB5 ...66 A5
Brighton Rd BELMT SM2 ...175 G6
  EFNCH N2 ...53 G1
  EHAM E6 ...96 A3
  SAND/SEL CR2 ...177 J7
  STNW/STAM N16 ...74 A4
  SURB KT6 ...158 D5
Brighton Ter BRXN/ST SW9 ...130 A3
Brights Av RAIN RM13 ...99 K3
Brightside Rd LEW SE13 ...133 G5
Bright St POP/IOD E14 ...93 K5
Brightwell Cl CROY/NA CRO ...164 B7
Brightwell Crs TOOT SW17 ...147 K4
Brightwell Rd WATW WD18 ...20 E4
Brigstock Rd BELV DA17 ...117 J3
  THHTH CR7 ...164 C4
Brill Pl CAMTN NW1 ...5 H4

Brim Hl EFNCH N2 ...53 G3
Brimpsfield Cl ABYW SE2 ...116 C2
Brindle Ga BFN/LL DA15 ...135 K2
Brindley Cl ALP/SUD HA0 ...67 J7
  BXLYHN DA7 ...137 H2
Brindley St BROCKY SE4 ...112 C4
Brindley Wy BMLY BR1 ...152 E4
  STHL UB1 ...84 B6
Brinkburn Cl ABYW SE2 ...116 B3
  EDGW HA8 ...50 D7
Brinkburn Gdns EDGW HA8 ...50 C2
Brinkley Rd WPK KT4 ...173 K1
Brinklow Crs
  WOOL/PLUM SE18 ...115 G6
Brinkworth Cl CLAY IG5 ...59 J2
Brinkworth Wy HOM E9 ...75 H5
Brinsdale Rd HDN NW4 ...52 B2
Brinsley Rd
  KTN/HRWW/WS HA3 ...48 D3
Brinsley St WCHPL E1 * ...92 D5
Brinsworth Cl WHTN TW2 ...142 D1
Brinton Wk STHWK SE1 ...12 C9
Brion Pl POP/IOD E14 ...94 A4
Brisbane Av WIM/MER SW19 ...147 F7
Brisbane Rd IL IG1 ...60 C6
  LEY E10 ...75 K1
Brisbane St CMBW SE5 ...110 E6
Briscoe Cl WAN E11 ...76 D1
Briscoe Rd WIM/MER SW19 ...147 H5
  ELTH/MOT SE9 ...134 C2
Briset St FARR EC1M ...12 C2
Briset Wy HOLWY N7 ...73 F1
Bristol Cl HSLWW TW4 ...123 F6
  STWL/WRAY TW19 ...120 B5
  WLGTN SM6 ...176 E7
Bristol Gdns MV/WKIL W9 ...8 D1
Bristol Ms MV/WKIL W9 ...8 D1
Bristol Park Rd WALTH E17 * ...57 G3
Bristol Rd FSTGT E7 ...77 G5
  GFD/PVL UB6 ...66 B2
  MRDN SM4 ...162 B4
Briston Gv CEND/HSY/T N8 ...54 E5
Briston Ms MLHL NW7 ...37 H6
Bristowe Cl BRXS/STRHM SW2 ...130 B5
Bristow Rd BXLYHN DA7 ...117 F7
  CROY/NA CRO ...176 B3
  HSLW TW3 ...123 H3
  NRWD SE19 ...150 A4
Britannia Cl CLAP SW4 ...129 J3
  ERITH DA8 ...118 C5
  NTHLT UB5 ...83 H3
Britannia Ga CAN/RD E16 ...94 E7
Britannia La WHTN TW2 ...123 H6
Britannia Rd BRYLDS KT5 ...159 G6
  FUL/PGN SW6 ...108 A6
  IL IG1 ...78 B2
  NFNCH/WDSPK N12 ...39 G2
  POP/IOD E14 ...112 D3
Britannia Rw IS N1 ...6 E1
Britannia St FSBYW WC1X ...5 L7
Britannia Wk IS N1 ...7 G6
Britannia Wy FUL/PGN SW6 ...108 A6
  STWL/WRAY TW19 ...120 A6
  WLSDN NW10 ...86 D3
British Gv BOW E3 ...93 H2
British Gv CHSWK W4 * ...106 C4
British Grove Pas
  CHSWK W4 * ...106 C4
British Legion Rd CHING E4 ...44 D1
British St BOW E3 ...93 H2
Brittage Rd WLSDN NW10 ...69 G6
Brittain Rd BCTR RM8 ...80 A2
Britten Cl BORE WD6 ...23 K5
  GLDGN NW11 ...53 F7
Britten Dr STHL UB1 ...84 A5
Britten St CHEL SW3 ...15 J5
Brittidge Rd WLSDN NW10 ...69 G6
Britton Cl CAT SE6 ...133 G6
Britton St FARR EC1M ...12 C1
Brixham Crs RSLP HA4 ...46 E7
Brixham Gdns
  GDMY/SEVK IG3 ...78 E4
Brixham Rd WELL DA16 ...116 E7
Brixham St CAN/RD E16 ...95 K7
Brixton Hl BRXS/STRHM SW2 ...130 A5
Brixton Hill Pl
  BRXS/STRHM SW2 ...129 K6
Brixton Rd BRXN/ST SW9 ...130 B3
  LBTH SE11 ...110 B5
Brixton Station Rd
  BRXN/ST SW9 ...130 B2
Brixton Water La
  BRXS/STRHM SW2 ...130 A4
Broadbent Cl HGT N6 ...54 B7
Broadbent St
  MYFR/PKLN W1K * ...10 C6
Broadberry Ct UED N18 ...42 D4
Broad Bridge Cl
  BKHTH/KID SE3 ...113 K6
Broad Common Est
  STNW/STAM N16 * ...56 C7
Broadcombe SAND/SEL CR2 ...179 F6
Broad Ct COVGDN WC2E * ...11 L5
Broadcroft Av STAN HA7 ...49 K1
Broadcroft Rd
  STMC/STPC BR5 ...169 J6
Broadeaves Cl SAND/SEL CR2 ...178 A4
Broadfield Cl CAMTN NW1 ...5 J2
Broadfield Ct BUSH WD23 ...34 E1
Broadfield Pde EDGW HA8 ...36 D2
Broadfield Rd CAT SE6 ...133 H7
Broadfields E/WMO/HCT KT8 ...157 J3
  RYLN/HDSTN HA2 ...48 B1
Broadfields Av EDGW HA8 ...36 D2
  WCHMH N21 ...29 G6
Broadfields Hts EDGW HA8 ...36 D3
Broadfield Sq EN EN1 ...30 D2
Broadfield Wy WLSDN NW10 ...69 H4
Broadford Ln CHING E4 ...45 G2
Broadgates Rd
  WAND/EARL SW18 ...128 C7
Broad Green Av CROY/NA CRO ...164 C6
Broadhead Strd
  CDALE/KGS NW9 ...51 H1
Broadheath Dr CHST BR7 ...153 K4
Broadhinton Rd CLAP SW4 ...129 G2
Broadhurst EDGW HA8 ...36 D3
Broadhurst Av GDMY/SEVK IG3 ...79 F3
Broadhurst Cl
  KIL/WHAMP NW6 ...71 G5
Broadhurst Gdns
  KIL/WHAMP NW6 ...71 F5
  RSLP HA4 ...65 G1
Broadhurst Cl
  RCHPK/HAM TW10 ...125 G4
Broadlands FELT TW13 ...141 K2
Broadlands Av HGT N6 ...30 D2
  STRHM/NOR SW16 ...148 E1
Broadlands Cl HGT N6 ...54 M1

PEND EN3 ...30 D2
  STRHM/NOR SW16 ...148 E1
Broadlands Rd BMLY BR1 ...153 F5
  HGT N6 ...53 K6
Broadlands Wy NWMAL KT3 ...160 C5
Broad La HPTN TW12 ...141 K6
  SEVS/STOTM N15 ...56 B4
Broad Lawn ELTH/MOT SE9 ...135 F7
Broadlawns Ct
  KTN/HRWW/WS HA3 ...35 F1
Broadley St STJWD NW8 ...9 J1
Broadley Ter CAMTN NW1 ...9 K1
Broadmead CAT SE6 ...151 J2
Broadmead Av WPK KT4 ...160 D6
Broadmead Cl HPTN TW12 ...142 A5
  PIN HA5 * ...33 J6
Broadmead Rd WFD IG8 ...44 E5
  YEAD UB4 ...83 J3
Broad Oak SUN TW16 ...140 D7
  WFD IG8 ...45 F4
Broad Oak Cl CHING E4 ...43 J4
Broadoak Rd ERITH DA8 ...118 A6
Broad Oaks SURB KT6 ...159 J7
Broad Oaks Wy HAYES BR2 ...167 J4
Broadstone Pl MHST W1U ...10 A3
Broadstone Rd HCH RM12 ...81 J1
Broad St DAGE RM10 ...80 C6
  TEDD TW11 ...143 F5
Broad Street Pl LVPST EC2M ...13 H3
Broadview CDALE/KGS NW9 ...50 C5
Broadview Rd
  STRHM/NOR SW16 ...148 D6
Broad Wk WCHMH N21 ...41 F1
  BKHTH/KID SE3 ...134 B1
  HEST TW5 ...102 C7
  RCH/KEW TW9 ...105 G6
Broadwalk
  RYLN/HDSTN HA2 * ...48 B4
  SWFD E18 ...58 D2
Broadwalk La GLDGN NW11 ...52 D6
The Broad Wk BAY/PAD W2 ...8 D8
  KENS W8 ...14 E1
The Broadwalk NTHWD HA6 ...46 A1
Broadwall STHWK SE1 ...12 B8
Broadwater Rd THMD SE28 ...115 J2
  TOOT SW17 ...147 J3
  TOTM N17 ...56 A1
Broadway BARK IG11 ...78 C7
  BXLYHS DA6 ...137 F3
  GPK RM2 ...63 J2
  HNWL W7 ...84 E7
  RAIN RM13 ...99 J3
  SRTFD E15 ...76 B6
  STJSPK SW1H ...17 G3
  SURB KT6 ...159 J7
  WEA W13 ...85 H6
Broadway CROY/NA CRO ...164 E4
  TWK TW1 * ...124 C5
Broadway Cl WFD IG8 ...45 F5
Broadway Ct WIM/MER SW19 * ...146 E5
Broadway Gdns MTCM CR4 ...162 D3
Broadway Market HACK E8 ...74 D7
Broadway Market Ms
  HACK E8 * ...74 C7
Broadway Ms PLMGR N13 ...41 F4
  STNW/STAM N16 ...56 B6
  WCHMH N21 ...29 H7
Broadway Pde CHING E4 * ...44 A5
  HYS/HAR UB3 ...101 J1
  RYLN/HDSTN HA2 * ...48 B1
  WDR/YW UB7 ...100 B1
The Broadway ACT W3 * ...105 H1
  BCTR RM8 ...80 B1
  CDALE/KGS NW9 ...51 H5
  CEND/HSY/T N8 ...54 E4
  CHEAM SM3 ...174 C5
  EA W5 ...85 K6
  FBAR/BDGN N11 * ...39 K4
  HCH RM12 ...81 K3
  KTN/HRWW/WS HA3 ...48 E1
  MLHL NW7 ...37 G4
  PIN HA5 ...33 K6
  PLSTW E13 ...94 E1
  RYLN/HDSTN HA2 ...66 D1
  STAN HA7 ...35 J4
  SUT SM1 ...175 G5
  THDIT KT7 ...157 K7
  WAT WD17 ...21 G2
  WFD IG8 ...45 F5
  WIM/MER SW19 ...146 D5
Broadwell Pde
  KIL/WHAMP NW6 * ...71 G5
Broadwick St SOHO/CST W1F ...10 F6
Broadwood Av RSLP HA4 ...46 C5
Broadwood Ter WKENS W14 * ...107 J3
Broad Yd FARR EC1M ...12 C1
Brocas Cl HAMP NW3 ...3 K1
Brockdene Dr HAYES BR2 ...181 H3
Brockdish Av BARK IG11 ...79 F4
Brockenhurst
  E/WMO/HCT KT8 ...156 E4
Brockenhurst Av WPK KT4 ...160 B7
Brockenhurst Gdns IL IG1 ...78 C4
  MLHL NW7 ...37 G4
Brockenhurst Ms UED N18 ...42 C3
Brockenhurst Rd
  CROY/NA CRO ...165 J6
Brockenhurst Wy
  STRHM/NOR SW16 ...163 J1
Brockham Cl WIM/MER SW19 ...146 D4
Brockham Crs CROY/NA CRO ...180 B6
Brockham Dr
  BRXS/STRHM SW2 ...130 A6
  GNTH/NBYPK IG2 ...60 C5
Brockham St STHWK SE1 ...18 F3
Brockhurst Cl STAN HA7 ...35 F5
Brockill Crs BROCKY SE4 ...132 B3
Brocklebank Rd CHARL SE7 ...114 A3
  WAND/EARL SW18 ...128 B6
Brocklehurst St NWCR SE14 ...112 A6
Brocklesby Rd SNWD SE25 ...165 J3
Brocklesbury Cl WATN WD24 ...21 H2
Brockley Av STAN HA7 ...36 A3
Brockley Cl STAN HA7 ...36 A4
Brockley Cross BROCKY SE4 ...132 B2
Brockley Gdns BROCKY SE4 ...132 C1
Brockley Gv BROCKY SE4 ...132 C4
Brockley Hall Rd BROCKY SE4 ...132 B5
Brockley Hill STAN HA7 ...35 K1
Brockley Ms BROCKY SE4 ...132 B4
Brockley Pk FSTH SE23 ...132 B6
Brockley Ri FSTH SE23 ...132 B6
Brockley Rd BROCKY SE4 ...132 C1
Brockleyside STAN HA7 ...35 K3
Brockley Vw FSTH SE23 ...132 B6
Brockley Wy FSTH SE23 ...131 K5
Brockman Ri BMLY BR1 ...152 B3
Brock Pl BOW E3 ...93 K3
Brock Rd PLSTW E13 ...95 F4
Brocks Dr CHEAM SM3 ...174 B2
Brockshot Cl BTFD TW8 ...104 E4
Brock St PECK SE15 * ...131 K2
Brockton Cl ROM RM1 ...63 H4

Brockway Cl WAN E11 ...76 C1
Brockwell Av BECK BR3 ...166 E4
Brockwell Park Gdns
  HNHL SE24 ...130 C6
Brockwell Park Rw
  BRXS/STRHM SW2 ...130 B6
Brodewater Rd BORE WD6 ...24 D1
Brodia Rd STNW/STAM N16 ...73 M1
Brodie St STHWK SE1 ...19 M7
Brodie Rd CHING E4 ...31 K6
Brodlove La WAP E1W ...93 F6
Brodrick Gv ABYW SE2 ...116 C3
Brodrick Rd TOOT SW17 ...147 J1
Brograve Gdns BECK BR3 ...166 E1
Broken Whf BLKFR EC4V ...12 E6
Brokesley St BOW E3 ...93 H3
Broke Wk HACK E8 * ...74 C7
Bromar Rd CMBW SE5 ...131 F2
Bromborough Gn
  OXHEY WD19 ...33 G4
Bromefield STAN HA7 ...35 J7
Bromehead St WCHPL E1 ...92 E5
Brome House CHARL SE7 * ...114 D6
Bromell's Rd CLAP SW4 ...129 H3
Brome Rd ELTH/MOT SE9 ...134 E2
Bromefelde Rd CLAP SW4 ...129 J2
Bromfield St IS N1 ...6 B5
Bromhall Rd DAGW RM9 ...79 H5
Bromhedge ELTH/MOT SE9 ...153 K2
Bromholm Rd ABYW SE2 ...116 C2
Bromley BMLY BR1 ...152 C6
Bromley Common HAYES BR2 ...168 B2
Bromley Ct BMLY BR1 ...152 C5
Bromley Crs HAYES BR2 ...167 J2
  RSLP HA4 ...64 D3
Bromley Gdns HAYES BR2 ...167 J1
Bromley Gv HAYES BR2 ...167 G1
Bromley Hall Rd POP/IOD E14 ...94 A4
Bromley Hl BMLY BR1 ...152 B4
Bromley High St BOW E3 ...93 K2
Bromley La CHST BR7 ...154 C6
Bromley Pl FITZ W1T ...10 E1
Bromley Rd BECK BR3 ...151 J2
  CAT SE6 ...151 K2
  CHST BR7 ...154 B7
  HAYES BR2 ...167 H1
  LEY E10 ...57 K5
  TOTM N17 ...42 C7
  UED N18 ...41 K3
  WALTH E17 ...57 J2
Bromley St WCHPL E1 ...93 F4
Brompton Ar CHEL SW3 * ...15 L2
Brompton Cl HSLWW TW4 ...122 E4
Brompton Dr ERITH DA8 ...118 E6
Brompton Gv EFNCH N2 ...53 J3
Brompton Park Crs
  FUL/PGN SW6 ...108 A5
Brompton Pl CHEL SW3 ...15 J5
Brompton Rd CHEL SW3 ...15 J5
Brompton Sq CHEL SW3 ...15 J4
Brompton Ter
  WOOL/PLUM SE18 * ...115 F7
Bromwich Av HGT N6 ...72 A1
Bromyard Av ACT W3 ...87 G7
Bronde Cl ERITH DA8 ...118 D4
Brondesbury Ms
  KIL/WHAMP NW6 * ...2 A2
Brondesbury Pk
  KIL/WHAMP NW6 ...70 A6
Brondesbury Rd
  KIL/WHAMP NW6 ...88 D1
Brondesbury Vls
  KIL/WHAMP NW6 ...88 D1
Bronhill Ter TOTM N17 * ...42 C7
Bronsart Rd FUL/PGN SW6 ...107 H6
Bronson Rd RYNPK SW20 ...161 G1
Bronte Cl ERITH DA8 ...117 J6
  FSTGT E7 * ...76 E3
  GNTH/NBYPK IG2 ...60 A3
Bronte Gv DART DA1 ...139 J3
Bronti Cl WALW SE17 ...18 F7
Bronze Age Wy BELV DA17 ...117 K2
Bronze St DEPT SE8 ...112 D6
Brook Av DAGE RM10 ...80 D7
  EDGW HA8 ...36 D5
  WBLY HA9 ...68 B2
Brookbank Av HNWL W7 ...84 D4
Brookbank Rd LEW SE13 ...132 D2
Brook Cl ACT W3 ...86 C7
  BORE WD6 ...24 D2
  HOR/WEW KT19 ...173 G4
  RSLP HA4 ...46 C6
  RYNPK SW20 ...160 E2
  STWL/WRAY TW19 ...120 C6
  TOOT SW17 ...148 A1
Brook Crs CHING E4 ...43 J3
  ED N9 ...42 D3
Brookdale FBAR/BDGN N11 ...40 C3
Brookdale Rd BXLY DA5 ...137 F5
  CAT SE6 ...132 E6
  WALTH E17 ...57 J2
Brookdene Av OXHEY WD19 ...21 F7
Brookdene Dr NTHWD HA6 ...32 D6
Brookdene Rd
  WOOL/PLUM SE18 ...115 K3
Brook Dr HRW HA1 ...48 E3
  LBTH SE11 ...18 B4
  RSLP HA4 ...46 B4
Brooke Av RYLN/HDSTN HA2 ...66 C2
Brooke Cl BUSH WD23 ...22 C6
Brookehowse Rd CAT SE6 ...151 J1
Brookend Rd BFN/LL DA15 ...135 K7
Brooke Rd STNW/STAM N16 ...74 C2
  WALTH E17 ...58 A3
Brooke's Market
  HCIRC EC1N * ...12 A2
Brooke St HCIRC EC1N ...12 A3
Brooke Wy BUSH WD23 ...22 C6
Brookfield EA W5 ...85 J3
  MLHL NW7 ...37 K5
  SUT SM1 ...175 ...
  WALTH E17 ...58 A3
Brookfield Cl MLHL NW7 ...37 K5
Brookfield Crs
  KTN/HRWW/WS HA3 ...50 B4
  MLHL NW7 ...37 K5
Brookfield Gdns
  ESH/CLAY KT10 ...171 F5
Brookfield Pk KTTN NW5 ...72 B2
Brookfield Pth WFD IG8 ...44 D5
Brookfield Rd CHSWK W4 ...106 A1
  ED N9 ...42 C2
  HOM E9 ...75 G5
Brookfields PEND EN3 ...31 F3
Brookfields Av MTCM CR4 ...162 D4
Brook Gdns BARN SW13 ...126 C2
  CHING E4 ...43 K3
  KUTN/CMB KT2 ...144 E7
Brook Gn HMSMTH W6 ...107 F2
Brookhill Cl EBAR EN4 ...27 J4
Brook Hill Cl
  WOOL/PLUM SE18 ...115 G4
Brookhill Rd EBAR EN4 ...27 H4
  WOOL/PLUM SE18 ...115 G4

Brookhouse Gdns CHING E4 ...44 C3
Brooking Cl BCTR RM8 ...79 J2
Brooking Rd FSTGT E7 ...76 E4
Brookland Cl GLDGN NW11 ...52 E3
Brookland Garth
  GLDGN NW11 ...52 E3
Brookland Hi GLDGN NW11 ...52 E3
Brookland Ri GLDGN NW11 ...52 E3
Brooklands DART DA1 ...139 H7
Brooklands Ap ROM RM1 ...63 H5
Brooklands Cl BFN/LL DA15 ...154 D1
  WIM/MER SW19 ...63 F3
Brooklands Ct KIL/WHAMP NW6 * ...70 D6
  WCHMH N21 ...29 K4
Brooklands Dr GFD/PVL UB6 ...67 J7
Brooklands La
  ROMW/RG RM7 ...63 H5
Brooklands Pk BKHTH/KID SE3 ...133 K2
Brooklands Pl HPTN TW12 ...142 B4
Brooklands Rd
  ROMW/RG RM7 ...63 H5
  THDIT KT7 ...158 A7
The Brooklands ISLW TW7 * ...103 J7
Brook La BKHTH/KID SE3 ...134 A1
  BMLY BR1 ...152 E5
  BXLY DA5 ...136 E5
Brook La North BTFD TW8 ...104 E4
Brooklea Cl CDALE/KGS NW9 ...37 G7
Brooklyn Av SNWD SE25 ...165 J3
Brooklyn Cl CAR SM5 ...175 J1
Brooklyn Gv SNWD SE25 ...165 J3
Brooklyn Rd HAYES BR2 ...168 C4
  SNWD SE25 ...165 J3
Brooklyn Wy WDR/YW UB7 ...100 A2
Brookmead CROY/NA CRO ...163 H5
Brookmead Av HAYES BR2 ...168 C4
Brook Meadow
  NFNCH/WDSPK N12 ...39 F3
Brook Meadow Cl WFD IG8 ...44 C5
Brookmead Rd CROY/NA CRO ...163 H5
Brook Ms North BAY/PAD W2 ...8 F6
Brookmill Cl OXHEY WD19 * ...21 F6
Brookmill Rd DEPT SE8 ...112 D7
Brook Park Cl WCHMH N21 ...29 H5
Brook Pk BAR EN5 ...25 J4
Brook Rd CEND/HSY/T N8 ...54 E4
  CRICK NW2 ...69 J1
  GNTH/NBYPK IG2 ...60 C1
  GPK RM2 ...63 H1
  SURB KT6 ...172 A1
  THHTH CR7 ...164 C3
  TWK TW1 ...124 B5
  WDGN N22 ...55 F1
Brook Rd South BTFD TW8 ...104 E5
Brooks Av EHAM E6 ...95 K3
Brooksbank Cl HOM E9 * ...75 F5
Brooksby Ms IS N1 ...6 A1
Brooksby St IS N1 ...6 A1
Brooksby's Wk HOM E9 ...75 F4
Brookscroft CROY/NA CRO ...179 H7
Brookscroft Rd WALTH E17 ...43 K7
Brookshill
  KTN/HRWW/WS HA3 ...34 E5
Brookshill Av
  KTN/HRWW/WS HA3 ...34 D4
Brookshill Dr
  KTN/HRWW/WS HA3 ...34 D4
Brookside CAR SM5 ...176 A4
  EBAR EN4 ...27 J5
  WCHMH N21 ...29 F5
Brookside Cl BAR EN5 ...26 B5
  FELT TW13 ...140 E2
  KTN/HRWW/WS HA3 ...49 K4
  RSLP HA4 ...65 J3
Brookside Crs WPK KT4 ...160 D7
Brookside Rd ARCH N19 ...72 C1
  ED N9 ...42 D3
  GLDGN NW11 ...52 C5
  OXHEY WD19 ...21 F6
  YEAD UB4 ...83 G6
Brookside South EBAR EN4 ...27 J5
Brookside Wy CROY/NA CRO ...166 A5
Brooks La CHSWK W4 ...105 H5
Brook's Ms MYFR/PKLN W1K ...10 C6
Brook's Rd PLSTW E13 ...76 E7
Brook St BAY/PAD W2 ...9 H6
  BELV DA17 ...117 J4
  KUT/HW KT1 ...159 F1
  MYFR/PKLN W1K ...10 C6
  TOTM N17 ...56 B1
Brooksville Av
  KIL/WHAMP NW6 ...70 C7
Brookview Rd
  STRHM/NOR SW16 ...148 C4
Brookville Rd FUL/PGN SW6 ...107 J6
Brook Wk EDGW HA8 ...37 F5
  EFNCH N2 ...39 H7
Brook Water La HDN NW4 * ...52 B4
Brookway BKHTH/KID SE3 ...133 K2
  RAIN RM13 ...99 K4
Brookwood Av BARN SW13 ...126 C2
Brookwood Cl HAYES BR2 ...167 J3
Brookwood Rd HSLW TW3 ...123 G1
  WAND/EARL SW18 ...127 J7
Broom Cl ESH/CLAY KT10 ...170 B4
  HAYES BR2 ...168 D5
  TEDD TW11 ...143 H6
Broomcroft Av NTHLT UB5 ...83 G2
Broome Rd HPTN TW12 ...141 K7
Broome Wy CMBW SE5 ...110 E6
Broomfield SUN TW16 ...140 D7
  WALTH E17 ...57 H6
Broomfield Av PLMGR N13 ...41 F4
Broomfield Cots WEA W13 * ...85 H7
Broomfield La PLMGR N13 ...40 E3
Broomfield Pl WEA W13 ...85 H7
Broomfield Rd BECK BR3 ...166 B2
  BXLYHS DA6 ...137 H4
  CHDH RM6 ...61 K6
  PLMGR N13 ...40 E4
  RCH/KEW TW9 ...105 G7
  SURB KT6 ...159 G7
  TEDD TW11 ...143 J5
  WEA W13 ...85 H7
Broomfields ESH/CLAY KT10 ...170 C4
Broomfield St POP/IOD E14 ...93 J4
Broom Gdns CROY/NA CRO ...179 J2
Broomgrove Gdns EDGW HA8 ...36 C7
Broomgrove Rd
  BRXN/ST SW9 ...130 A1
Broomhall Rd SAND/SEL CR2 ...177 K7
Broomhill Ri BXLYHS DA6 ...137 H4
Broomhill Rd DART DA1 ...138 D5
  GDMY/SEVK IG3 ...79 G1
  WAND/EARL SW18 ...127 K4
  WFD IG8 ...44 E5

Broomhouse La FUL/PGN SW6..127 K1
Broomhouse Rd
  FUL/PGN SW6...............127 K1
Broomloan La SUT SM1......174 E1
Broom Lock TEDD TW11 *....143 J4
Broom Md BXLYHS DA6.......137 H5
Broom Pk TEDD TW11.........143 K6
  TEDD TW11...................143 H4
Broomsleigh St
  KIL/WHAMP NW6 *............70 E4
Broom Water TEDD TW11....143 J4
Broom Water West
  TEDD TW11...................143 J4
Broomwood Cl CROY/NA CR0..166 A4
Broomwood Rd BTSEA SW11..128 D5
Broseley Gv SYD SE26.........151 L4
Brosse Wy HAYES BR2..........181 J7
Broster Gdns SNWD SE25....165 G2
Brougham Rd ACT W3..........86 E6
  HACK E8.......................74 C7
Brougham St BTSEA SW11....128 E1
  VX/NE SW8...................109 K6
Broughinge Rd BORE WD6....24 D1
Broughton Av FNCH N3.........52 C2
  RCHPK/HAM TW10............143 J3
Broughton Dr BRXN/ST SW9..130 B3
Broughton Gdns HGT N6......54 C5
Broughton Rd FUL/PGN SW6..128 A1
  THHTH CR7...................164 D1
  WEA W13......................85 H6
Broughton Road Ap
  FUL/PGN SW6................128 A1
Broughton St VX/NE SW8.....129 A1
Brouncker Rd ACT W3.........105 K1
Browells La FELT TW13.........141 K1
Brown Cl WLGTN SM6...........176 D6
Brownfield St POP/IOD E14...93 K5
Browngraves Rd
  HYS/HAR UB3..................101 F6
Brown Hart Gdns
  MYFR/PKLN W1K...............10 B6
Brownhill Rd CAT SE6..........133 F6
Browning Av HNWL W7.........85 F5
  SUT SM1......................175 J3
  WPK KT4......................160 E2
Browning Cl HPTN TW12.......141 K3
  MV/WKIL W9 *....................8 A4
  WALTH E17....................58 A3
  WELL DA16...................115 K7
Browning Ms
  CAVSQ/HST W1G *.............10 B3
Browning Rd DART DA1.........139 J3
  MNPK E12.....................77 K5
  WAN E11......................58 D6
Browning St WALW SE17.......18 F7
Browning Wy HEST TW5.......102 C7
Brownlea Gdns
  GDMY/SEVK IG3................79 G1
Brownlow Cl EBAR EN4.........27 H4
Brownlow Ms BMSBY WC1N....5 M9
Brownlow Rd BORE WD6.......24 C3
  CROY/NA CR0.................178 A3
  FBAR/BDGN N11...............40 E3
  FNCH N3.......................38 F3
  FSTGT E7......................76 E3
  HACK E8........................7 M3
  WEA W13 *.....................85 G7
  WLSDN NW10...................69 F6
Brownlow St HHOL WC1V......11 M3
Brownspring Dr
  ELTH/MOT SE9................154 B2
Brown's Rd BRYLDS KT5.......159 G6
  WALTH E17....................57 J2
Brown St MBLAR W1H.............9 K4
Brownswell Rd EFNCH N2......53 H1
Brownswood Rd FSBYPK N4...73 J1
Broxash Rd BTSEA SW11......129 F5
Broxbourne Av SWFD E18....59 F3
Broxbourne House BOW E3 *...93 K3
Broxbourne Rd FSTGT E7.....76 E2
Broxholme Cl SNWD SE25....164 E3
Broxholm Rd WNWD SE27....149 G2
Broxted Rd CAT SE6..........151 H1
Broxwood Wy STJWD NW8.......3 K4
Bruce Castle Rd TOTM N17....42 A7
  WELL DA16...................116 C7
Bruce Dr SAND/SEL CR2......179 F7
Bruce Gdns TRDG/WHET N20..39 K2
Bruce Gv TOTM N17.............56 B1
Bruce Rd BAR EN5.............26 C2
  BOW E3........................93 K2
  KTN/HRWW/WS HA3............48 C1
  MTCM CR4....................148 A6
  SNWD SE25...................164 E3
  WLSDN NW10...................69 F6
Bruckner St NKENS W10........88 C2
Brudenell Rd TOOT SW17.....147 K2
Bruffs Meadow NTHLT UB5.....65 J5
Bruford Ct DEPT SE8...........112 D5
Bruges Pl CAMTN NW1 *........4 F2
Brumfield Rd
  HOR/WEW KT19...............172 E4
Brunel Cl HEST TW5...........102 A6
  NRWD SE19...................150 B1
  NTHLT UB5....................83 K2
  ROM RM1.......................63 G3
Brunel Ct WLSDN NW10........87 J2
Brunel Est BAY/PAD W2..........8 A3
Brunel House
  WOOL/PLUM SE18 *...........114 D6
Brunel Ms NKENS W10.........88 B2
Brunel Rd ACT W3...............87 G4
  BERM/RHTH SE16.............111 K1
  WALTH E17.....................57 G5
  WFD IG8........................45 K4
Brunel St CAN/RD E16..........94 D5
Brunel Wk WHTN TW2.........123 F6
Brunner Cl GLDGN NW11.......13 L5
Brunner Cl GLDGN NW11......53 F4
Brunner Rd EA W5...............85 K3
  WALTH E17.....................57 H1
Bruno Pl CDALE/KGS NW9......68 E1
Brunswick Av
  FBAR/BDGN N11................40 A2
Brunswick Cl BXLYHS DA6...136 E3
  PIN HA5.......................47 J3
  THDIT KT7....................158 A7
  WHTN TW2.....................142 D2
Brunswick Ct STHWK SE1 *....19 K2
Brunswick Crs
  FBAR/BDGN N11................40 A2
  KENS W8.........................8 B9
Brunswick Gv
  FBAR/BDGN N11................40 A2
  STRHM/NOR SW16.............148 D5
Brunswick Pk NWD SE25......150 E7
Brunswick Park Gdns
  FBAR/BDGN N11................40 A1

Brunswick Park Rd
  FBAR/BDGN N11................40 A2
Brunswick Pl CAMTN NW1......10 B1
  IS N1............................7 H8
  NRWD SE19...................150 C6
Brunswick Quay
  BERM/RHTH SE16.............112 A2
Brunswick Sq BMSBY WC1N....5 K9
  TOTM N17.....................42 B5
Brunswick St WALTH E17.......58 A4
Brunswick Vls CMBW SE5....111 F7
Brunswick Wy
  FBAR/BDGN N11................40 B3
Brunton Pl POP/IOD E14.......93 G5
Brushfield St WCHPL E1.........13 K2
Brushwood Cl POP/IOD E14....93 K4
Brussels Rd BTSEA SW11.....128 C5
Bruton Cl CHST BR7...........153 K6
Bruton La MYFR/PICC W1J.....10 D7
Bruton Pl MYFR/PICC W1J.....10 D7
Bruton Rd MRDN SM4.........162 B3
Bruton St MYFR/PICC W1J.....10 D7
Bruton Wy WEA W13............85 G4
Bryan Av WLSDN NW10..........69 K6
Bryan Cl SUN TW16...........140 E6
Bryan Rd BERM/RHTH SE16...112 C1
Bryanston Av WHTN TW2......123 F7
Bryanston Cl NWDGN UB2....102 E3
Bryanstone Rd
  CEND/HSY/T N8................54 D4
Bryanston Ms East
  MBLAR W1H......................9 L3
Bryanston Ms West
  MBLAR W1H......................9 L3
Bryanston Pl MBLAR W1H.......9 L3
Bryanston Sq MBLAR W1H.....9 L3
Bryanston St MBLAR W1H......9 L5
Bryant Cl BAR EN5..............26 D4
Bryant Rd NTHLT UB5..........83 G2
Bryant St SRTFD E15...........76 B6
Bryantwood Rd HOLWY N7....73 G4
Brycedale Crs STHGT/OAK N14..40 D3
Bryce Rd BCTR RM8.............79 J3
Bryden Cl SYD SE26...........151 L4
Brydges Pl CHCR WC2N........11 J7
Brydges Rd SRTFD E15.........76 B4
Brydon Wk IS N1.................5 K3
Bryett Rd HOLWY N7............72 E2
Brymay Cl BOW E3..............93 J1
Brynmaer Rd BTSEA SW11...108 E7
Bryn-Y-Mawr Rd EN EN1.......30 B3
Bryony Rd SHB W12.............87 J6
Bryony Wy SUN TW16.........140 E5
Buchanan Cl WCHMH N21.....29 F4
Buchanan Ct BORE WD6 *......24 E1
Buchanan Gdns WLSDN NW10..87 K1
Buchan Rd PECK SE15.........131 K2
Bucharest Rd
  WAND/EARL SW18.............128 B6
Buckden Cl LEE/GVPK SE12...133 J5
Buckfast Rd MRDN SM4......162 A3
Buckfast St BETH E2............92 C2
Buckhold Rd
  WAND/EARL SW18.............127 K5
Buckhurst Av CAR SM5........162 D7
Buckhurst St WCHPL E1........92 D3
Buckhurst Wy BKHH IG9.......45 K2
Buckingham Av
  E/WMO/HCT KT8..............157 G1
  EBED/NFELT TW14............122 A5
  GFD/PVL UB6...................67 G7
  THHTH CR7...................149 G2
  TRDG/WHET N20...............27 G6
  WELL DA16...................135 K3
Buckingham Cl EA W5...........85 J4
  EN EN1.........................30 A1
  HPTN TW12...................141 K4
  STMC/STPC BR5...............169 K6
Buckingham Dr CHST BR7....154 B4
Buckingham Gdns
  E/WMO/HCT KT8..............157 G1
  STAN HA7......................36 A6
  THHTH CR7...................164 B1
Buckingham Ga WESTW SW1E..16 E3
Buckingham La FSTH SE23...132 B6
Buckingham Ms IS N1...........74 A5
  WESTW SW1E...................16 E3
  WLSDN NW10...................87 H1
Buckingham Palace Rd
  BGVA SW1W....................16 C5
Buckingham Pde STAN HA7 *..35 J4
Buckingham Pl WESTW SW1E..16 E3
Buckingham Rd BORE WD6....25 F3
  EDGW HA8......................36 B6
  HPTN TW12...................141 K4
  HRW HA1.......................48 D4
  IL IG1..........................78 D1
  IS N1...........................74 A5
  KUT/HW KT1..................159 G3
  LEY E10.........................75 K2
  MTCM CR4....................163 K4
  RCHPK/HAM TW10............143 K1
  SRTFD E15......................76 D4
  SWFD E18......................44 D7
  WAN E11........................59 F3
  WDGN N22......................40 E7
  WLSDN NW10...................87 H1
Buckingham St CHCR WC2N...11 K7
Buckland Crs HAMP NW3........3 J1
Buckland Ri PIN HA5............47 G5
Buckland Rd CHSGTN KT9....172 B4
  LEY E10........................76 A1
Bucklands OXHEY WD19 *......33 H2
Buckland St IS N1..............7 H6
Bucklands Whf KUT/HW KT1 *..158 E1
Buckland Wk MRDN SM4......162 B3
Buckland Wy WPK KT4........161 F7
Buck La CDALE/KGS NW9.......51 F4
Buckleigh Av RYNPK SW20...161 J2
Buckleigh Rd
  STRHM/NOR SW16.............148 D5
Bucklersbury MANHO EC4N....13 G5
Bucklers' Wy CAR SM5........175 K3
Buckle St WCHPL E1............13 M4
Buckley Cl DART DA1..........138 C1
  FSTH SE23 *..................131 K6
Buckley Rd KIL/WHAMP NW6...70 D6
Buckmaster Rd BTSEA SW11..128 D3
Bucknall St NOXST/BSQ WC1A..11 J4
Bucknall Wy BECK BR3........166 E3
Bucknell Cl BRXS/STRHM SW2..130 A3
Buckner Rd BRXS/STRHM SW2..130 A3
Buckrell Rd CHING E4...........44 B1

Bucks Av OXHEY WD19..........21 J6
Buckstone Cl FSTH SE23.....131 K5
Buckstone Rd UED N18.........42 C5
Buck St CAMTN NW1 *...........4 D3
Buckters Rents
  BERM/RHTH SE16.............93 H7
Buckthorne Rd BROCKY SE4..132 B5
Budd Cl NFNCH/WDSPK N12...39 F3
Buddings Cir WBLY HA9........68 E2
Bude Cl WALTH E17.............57 H4
Budge La MTCM CR4...........162 E6
Budleigh Crs WELL DA16......116 D7
Budoch Dr GDMY/SEVK IG3....79 J1
Buer Rd FUL/PGN SW6.........127 H1
Bugsby's Wy GNWCH SE10....113 K3
Bulganak Rd THHTH CR7......164 D3
Bulinca St WEST SW1P *........17 J6
Bullace Rw CMBW SE5.........110 E7
Bullard Rd TEDD TW11........142 E5
Bullards Pl BETH E2............93 F2
Bullbanks Rd BELV DA17......117 K3
Bulleid Wy BGVA SW1W.........16 D6
Bullen St BTSEA SW11.........128 D1
Buller Cl PECK SE15...........111 H6
Buller Rd BARK IG11............78 E6
  THHTH CR7...................164 E2
  TOTM N17......................56 C1
  WDGN N22......................55 G1
  WLSDN NW10....................88 B2
Bullers Wood Dr CHST BR7...153 J7
Bullescroft Rd EDGW HA8......36 C2
Bullhead Rd BORE WD6........24 D2
Bullivant St POP/IOD E14......94 A6
Bull La CHST BR7..............154 D6
  DAGE RM10.....................80 D2
  UED N18.........................42 D4
Bull Rd SRTFD E15..............94 D1
Bullrush Cl CAR SM5..........175 J1
  CROY/NA CR0.................165 F5
Bull's Aly MORT/ESHN SW14..126 A2
Bull's Br NWDGN UB2..........102 A3
Bulls Bridge Rd NWDGN UB2..102 A3
Bullsbrook Rd YEAD UB4.......83 G7
Bull's Gdns CHEL SW3...........15 K5
Bull Yd PECK SE15.............111 H7
Bulmer Gdns
  KTN/HRWW/WS HA3............49 K6
Bulmer Ms NTGHL W11.........8 A8
Bulstrode Av HSLW TW3......122 E2
Bulstrode Gdns HSLW TW3...123 F2
Bulstrode Pl MHST W1U........10 B3
Bulstrode Rd HSLW TW3......123 F2
Bulstrode St MHST W1U.......10 B4
Bulwer Court Rd WAN E11.....58 B7
Bulwer Gdns BAR EN5..........27 F3
Bulwer Rd BAR EN5............27 F3
  UED N18........................42 A4
  WAN E11........................58 B7
Bulwer St SHB W12.............88 A7
Bunces La WFD IG8............44 D6
Bungalow Rd SNWD SE25....165 F3
The Bungalows
  RYLN/HDSTN HA2 *............65 K2
  STRHM/NOR SW16.............148 B6
Bunhill Rw STLK EC1Y...........7 G9
Bunhouse Pl BGVA SW1W......16 B7
Bunkers HI GLDGN NW11.......53 G6
Bunker's HI BELV DA17........117 H3
Bunning Wy HOLWY N7.........5 K1
Bunn's La MLHL NW7............37 G5
Bunsen St BOW E3 *.............93 G1
Buntingbridge Rd
  BARK/HLT IG6...................60 D4
Bunting Cl ED N9................31 F7
  MTCM CR4....................162 E4
Bunton St WOOL/PLUM SE18..115 F2
Bunyan Rd WALTH E17..........57 G2
Burbage Cl HYS/HAR UB3......82 B5
  STHWK SE1.....................19 G4
Burbage Rd HNHL SE24.......130 E5
Burberry Cl NWMAL KT3.......160 B1
Burbridge Wy TOTM N17......56 C2
Burcham St POP/IOD E14......93 K5
Burcharbro Rd ABYW SE2....116 E5
Burchell Ct BUSH WD23 *......22 C6
Burchell Rd LEY E10.............57 K7
  PECK SE15....................111 K7
Burcher Gale Gv PECK SE15..111 F6
Burcote Rd WAND/EARL SW18..128 C3
Burden Cl BTFD TW8............104 D4
Burdenshott Av
  RCHPK/HAM TW10............125 J3
Burden Wy WAN E11.............77 H1
Burder Cl IS N1..................74 A5
Burder Rd IS N1..................74 A5
Burdett Av RYNPK SW20......145 J7
Burdett Cl HNWL W7 *..........85 J7
Burdett Ms BAY/PAD W2........8 F3
  KIL/WHAMP NW6................2 B2
Burdett Rd BOW E3.............93 H3
  CROY/NA CR0.................164 E5
  POP/IOD E14...................93 H5
  RCH/KEW TW9.................125 G1
Burdetts Rd DAGW RM9........80 B7
Burdock Cl CROY/NA CR0.....166 A7
Burdock Rd TOTM N17..........56 C2
Burdon La BELMT SM2.........174 C6
Burdon Pk BELMT SM2........174 C7
Burfield Cl TOOT SW17.........147 G3
Burford Cl BARK/HLT IG6......60 C5
  BCTR RM8......................79 J2
Burford Gdns PLMGR N13......41 F2
Burford Rd BMLY BR1..........168 D3
  BTFD TW8.....................105 F4
  CAT SE6.......................151 H1
  EHAM E6........................95 J2
  SRTFD E15.....................76 B6
  SUT SM1......................174 E7
  WPK KT4......................160 D6
Burford Wk FUL/PGN SW6....108 A6
Burford Wy CROY/NA CR0....180 A5
Burgate Cl DART DA1..........138 C2
Burges Gv BARN SW13.........106 E6
Burges Rd EHAM E6............77 K6
Burgess Av CDALE/KGS NW9...51 F5
Burgess Cl FELT TW13.........141 J3
Burgess Hl CRICK NW2..........70 D3
Burgess Rd SRTFD E15........76 C3
  SUT SM1......................175 F3
Burgess St POP/IOD E14.......93 J4
Burge St STHWK SE1............19 H4
Burghill Rd SYD SE26.........151 F3
Burghley Av BORE WD6........24 E4
  NWMAL KT3...................145 F7
Burghley Hall Cl
  WIM/MER SW19................127 H7
Burghley Pl MTCM CR4.......162 E3
Burghley Rd CEND/HSY/T N8..55 G2
  KTTN NW5.......................72 B3
  WAN E11 *......................58 C7
  WIM/MER SW19................146 B3

Burgos Gv GNWCH SE10.......112 E7
Burgoyne Rd BRXN/ST SW9..130 A2
  FSBYPK N4.....................55 H5
  SNWD SE25...................165 G3
  SUN TW16....................140 D5
Burham Cl PGE/AN SE20.....150 E6
Burhill Gv PIN HA5..............47 J1
Burke Cl PUT/ROE SW15......126 B3
Burke St CAN/RD E16...........94 D4
Burket Cl NWDGN UB2.........102 D3
Burland Rd BTSEA SW11......128 E4
Burleigh Av BFN/LL DA15.....136 A4
  WLGTN SM6...................176 A2
Burleigh Ct ROMW/RG RM7....62 D3
Burleigh Gdns ASHF TW15...140 A4
  STHGT/OAK N14................28 C7
Burleigh Pde
  STHGT/OAK N14 *..............28 D7
Burleigh Pl PUT/ROE SW15..127 G4
Burleigh Rd CHEAM SM3.....161 H7
  EN EN1.........................30 A3
Burleigh St COVGDN WC2E....11 K6
Burleigh Wk CAT SE6..........133 F7
Burleigh Wy ENC/FH EN2.....29 K2
Burley Cl CHING E4..............43 J4
  STRHM/NOR SW16.............163 J1
Burley Rd CAN/RD E16..........95 G5
Burlington Ar RCH/KEW TW9..105 H7
  ROMW/RG RM7.................62 D5
Burlington Cl
  EBED/NFELT TW14............121 G6
  EHAM E6.......................95 J5
  MV/WKIL W9 *...................2 A9
  PIN HA5........................47 F2
Burlington Gdns ACT W3.......86 E7
  CHDH RM6......................62 A6
  CHSWK W4....................105 K4
  FUL/PGN SW6.................127 H1
Burlington La CHSWK W4.....105 K6
Burlington Ms ACT W3...........86 E7
Burlington Pde CRICK NW2 *...70 B3
Burlington Pl FUL/PGN SW6..127 H1
  WFD IG8.........................44 E2
Burlington Ri EBAR EN4........27 J7
Burlington Rd CHSWK W4 *..105 K4
  FUL/PGN SW6.................127 H1
  ISLW TW7.....................103 J7
  MUSWH N10....................54 A2
  NWMAL KT3...................160 C3
  THHTH CR7...................164 D1
  TOTM N17......................42 C7
Burma Rd STNW/STAM N16...73 K3
Burma Ter NRWD SE19 *.....150 A4
Burmester Rd TOOT SW17...147 G2
Burnaby Crs CHSWK W4......105 J5
Burnaby Gdns CHSWK W4....105 J5
Burnaby St WBPTN SW10....108 B6
Burnbrae Cl
  NFNCH/WDSPK N12...........39 F5
Burnbury Rd BAL SW12.......129 H7
Burn Cl GSTN WD25.............22 D3
Burncroft Av PEND EN3........30 E1
Burne Cl YEAD UB4 *.........83 H4
Burnell Av RCHPK/HAM TW10..143 J4
Burnell Gdns STAN HA7.......49 K1
Burnell Rd SUT SM1...........175 F3
Burnell Wk STHWK SE1 *......19 M7
Burnels Av EHAM E6............96 A2
Burness Cl HOLWY N7..........73 F5
Burne St CAMTN NW1...........9 J2
Burnet Cl HOM E9................74 E4
Burnett Rd ERITH DA8.........119 G5
Burney Av BRYLDS KT5.......159 G4
Burney St GNWCH SE10......113 F6
Burnfoot Av FUL/PGN SW6...107 H7
Burnham Av HGDN/ICK UB10..64 C7
Burnham Cl
  KTN/HRWW/WS HA3............49 G3
  MLHL NW7......................37 J6
  STHWK SE1....................19 M6
Burnham Crs DART DA1.......139 F3
  WAN E11........................59 G3
Burnham Dr WPK KT4.........174 A1
Burnham Gdns CROY/NA CR0..165 G6
  HSLWW TW4...................102 A1
  HYS/HAR UB3..................101 G2
Burnham Rd CHING E4..........43 H5
  DAGW RM9......................79 H6
  DART DA1.....................139 F3
  MRDN SM4....................162 A4
  ROMW/RG RM7.................62 E2
Burnham St BETH E2............92 E2
  KUTN/CMB KT2...............144 C7
Burnham Ter SYD SE26 *.....151 G4
Burnham Wy SYD SE26.......151 J4
  WEA W13......................104 C3
Burnhill Rd BECK BR3........166 D1
Burnley Cl OXHEY WD19......33 G4
Burnley Rd BRXN/ST SW9....130 A1
  WLSDN NW10...................69 H4
Burnsall St CHEL SW3..........15 K7
Burns Av BFN/LL DA15.......136 C5
  CHDH RM6......................61 J6
  EBED/NFELT TW14............121 K5
  STHL UB1......................84 A6
Burns Cl CAR SM5.............176 A7
  ERITH DA8.....................118 B7
  WALTH E17.....................58 A3
  WELL DA16...................116 A7
  WIM/MER SW19................147 H5
  YEAD UB4.......................82 E4
Burnside Av CHING E4...........43 H5
Burnside Cl BAR EN5...........26 E2
  BERM/RHTH SE16.............93 G7
  TWK TW1.....................124 B5
Burnside Crs ALP/SUD HA0...67 K7
Burnside Rd BCTR RM8........79 J1
  BTSEA SW11...................128 E1
  WEA W13......................104 C1
Burn's Rd WLSDN NW10........69 H6
Burns Wy HEST TW5..........102 C7
Burnt Ash Hi LEE/GVPK SE12..133 J5
Burnt Ash La BMLY BR1......152 E5
Burnt Ash Rd LEE/GVPK SE12..133 J4
Burnthwaite Rd
  FUL/PGN SW6.................107 J6
Burnt Oak Broadway
  EDGW HA8.....................36 D6
Burnt Oak Flds EDGW HA8....36 E7
Burnt Oak La BFN/LL DA15...136 B7
  BFN/LL DA15.................136 B7
Burntwood Cl
  WAND/EARL SW18 *............128 C3
Burntwood Grange Rd
  WAND/EARL SW18.............128 C2
Burntwood La TOOT SW17....147 H1
Burntwood Vw NRWD SE19 *..150 B4
Buross St WCHPL E1............92 D5
Burpham Cl YEAD UB4..........83 H4
Burrage Gv WOOL/PLUM SE18..115 H3

Burrage Pl WOOL/PLUM SE18..115 G4
Burrage Rd WOOL/PLUM SE18..115 H5
Burrard Rd CAN/RD E16.........94 E5
  KIL/WHAMP NW6................70 E4
Burr Cl BXLYHN DA7...........137 G2
  WAP E1W.......................92 C7
Burrell Cl CROY/NA CR0......166 A5
  EDGW HA8......................36 D1
Burrell Rw BECK BR3..........166 D1
Burrell St STHWK SE1...........12 D9
Burrells Wharf Sq
  POP/IOD E14..................112 E4
Burrell Wharf Rd POP/IOD E14..112 E4
Burritt Rd KUT/HW KT1.......159 H1
Burroughs Cots
  POP/IOD E14 *.................93 G4
Burroughs Gdns HDN NW4....51 K3
The Burroughs HDN NW4......51 K3
Burrow Rd EDUL SE22.........131 F3
Burrow Wk DUL SE21 *.........18 C1
Burrows Ms STHWK SE1........18 C1
Burrows Rd WLSDN NW10......88 B2
Burr Rd WAND/EARL SW18...127 K7
Bursar St STHWK SE1............13 J9
Bursdon Cl BFN/LL DA15....155 F1
Bursland Rd PEND EN3.........31 F1
Burslem St WCHPL E1...........92 D5
Burstock Rd PUT/ROE SW15..127 H3
Burston Rd PUT/ROE SW15..127 G4
Burstow Rd RYNPK SW20....146 C7
Burtenshaw Rd THDIT KT7...158 B6
Burtley Cl FSBYPK N4...........73 J6
Burton Av WATW WD18.........20 E3
Burton Bank IS N1 *..............7 J2
Burton Cl CHSGTN KT9.......171 K6
  THHTH CR7...................164 E2
Burton Gdns HEST TW5.......102 E7
Burton Gv WALW SE17..........19 G8
Burtonhole Cl MLHL NW7.....38 B3
Burtonhole La MLHL NW7.....38 B3
Burton La BRXN/ST SW9......130 B1
Burton Ms BGVA SW1W.........16 B6
Burton Pl STPAN WC1H..........5 H9
Burton Rd BRXN/ST SW9.....130 C1
  KIL/WHAMP NW6................70 D6
  KUTN/CMB KT2...............144 A6
  SWFD E18......................59 F2
Burtons Ct SRTFD E15 *........76 B6
Burton's Rd HPTN TW12......142 B3
Burt Rd CAN/RD E16............95 G7
Burwash La WNWD SE27.....149 K3
Burwash Rd
  WOOL/PLUM SE18.............115 J4
Burway Cl SAND/SEL CR2....178 A5
Burwell Av GFD/PVL UB6......66 E5
Burwell Cl WCHPL E1...........92 D5
Burwell Rd LEY E10.............75 G6
Burwood Av HAYES BR2......181 F1
  PIN HA5.........................47 F5
Burwood Cl SURB KT6........159 H7
Burwood Gdns RAIN RM13....99 H2
Burwood Pl BAY/PAD W2........9 K4
  EBAR EN4......................28 A1
Bury Av RSLP HA4...............46 A5
  YEAD UB4.......................82 C1
Bury Cl BERM/RHTH SE16....93 F7
Bury Ct HDTCH EC3A............13 K4
Bury Gv MRDN SM4...........162 A4
Bury Ms ROM RM1...............63 H5
Bury Rd DAGE RM10............80 E4
  WDGN N22.....................55 G1
Buryside Cl GNTH/NBYPK IG2..61 F4
Bury St ED N9....................30 B6
  HDTCH EC3A...................13 K5
  RSLP HA4.......................46 B5
  STJS SW1Y.....................10 E8
Bury St West ED N9.............30 A6
Bury Wk CHEL SW3..............15 J6
Busby Pl KTTN NW5.............72 D5
Busch Cl ISLW TW7............104 C7
Bushbaby Cl STHWK SE1.......19 J3
Bushberry Rd HOM E9...........75 G5
Bush Cl GNTH/NBYPK IG2.....60 D4
Bush Cots WAND/EARL SW18..127 K4
Bushell Cl BRXS/STRHM SW2..149 F1
Bushell Gn BUSH WD23........34 D1
Bushell Wy CHST BR7.........154 A4
Bush Elms Rd EMPK RM11....63 J6
Bushey Av STMC/STPC BR5..169 J6
  SWFD E18......................58 D2
Bushey Cl CHING E4.............44 A2
Bushey Grove Rd BUSH WD23..21 J1
Bushey Hall Dr BUSH WD23...21 J3
Bushey Hall Pk BUSH WD23...21 J3
Bushey Hall Rd BUSH WD23...21 J3
Bushey Hill Rd CMBW SE5...111 G7
Bushey La SUT SM1...........174 E2
Bushey Lees BFN/LL DA15 *..136 A5
Bushey Mill La BUSH WD23...21 K1
Bushey Rd CROY/NA CR0....179 J1
  HYS/HAR UB3..................101 H3
  PLSTW E13......................95 G1
  RYNPK SW20..................160 E2
  SEVS/STOTM N15..............56 A5
  SUT SM1......................174 E3
Bushey Wy BECK BR3.........167 G5
Bushfield Cl EDGW HA8........36 D1
Bushfield Crs EDGW HA8......36 D1
Bush Gv CDALE/KGS NW9.....50 E6
  STAN HA7......................35 K6
Bushgrove Rd BCTR RM8......79 J3
Bush Hill WCHMH N21..........29 J6
Bush Hill Pde ED N9 *...........29 K6
Bush Hill Rd
  KTN/HRWW/WS HA3............50 B5
  WCHMH N21....................29 K5
Bush House
  WOOL/PLUM SE18 *...........114 D6
Bush La CANST EC4R.............13 G6
Bushmead Cl
  SEVS/STOTM N15 *.............56 B3
Bushmoor Crs
  WOOL/PLUM SE18.............115 G6
Bushnell Rd TOOT SW17.....148 B1
Bush Rd BKHH IG9...............45 H3
  DEPT SE8.....................112 A3
  HACK E8........................74 D7
  RCH/KEW TW9.................105 G5
  WAN E11........................58 D6
Bushway BCTR RM8.............79 K3
Bushwood WAN E11.............58 D7
Bushwood Dr STHWK SE1.....19 M6
Bushwood Rd RCH/KEW TW9..105 H5
Bushy Park Gdns TEDD TW11..142 D4
Bushy Park Rd TEDD TW11...143 G4
Bushy Rd TEDD TW11.........142 E5
Butcher Rw WAP E1W...........93 F6
Butchers Rd CAN/RD E16......94 E5
Bute Av RCHPK/HAM TW10..144 A1
Bute Gdns HMSMTH W6......107 G3
  RCHPK/HAM TW10 *..........125 F7
  WLGTN SM6...................176 C4
Bute Gdns West WLGTN SM6..176 C4

Bute Ms GLDGN NW11 53 F4
Bute Rd BARK/HLT IG6 60 B4
CROY/NA CR0 164 B7
WLGTN SM6 176 C3
Bute St SKENS SW7 15 G5
Bute Wk IS N1 * 73 K5
Butler Av HRW HA1 48 D6
Butler Cl EDGW HA8 50 D1
Butler Rd BCTR RM8 79 H3
HRW HA1 48 C6
WLSDN NW10 69 H6
Butlers Cl HSLWW TW4 122 E3
Butlers & Colonial Whf
STHWK SE1 19 M1
Butlers Farm Cl
RCHPK/HAM TW10 143 K3
Butler St BETH E2 * 92 E2
Buttercup Cl NTHLT UB5 65 K5
Buttercup Sq
STWL/WRAY TW19 * 120 A7
Butterfield Cl
BERM/RHTH SE16 * 111 H1
TOTM N17 41 J5
TWK TW1 124 A5
Butterfield House
CHARL SE7 * 114 D6
Butterfield Ms
WOOL/PLUM SE18 115 G5
Butterfields WALTH E17 58 A4
Butterfield Sq EHAM E6 95 K5
Butterfly La BORE WD6 23 H2
ELTH/MOT SE9 135 G5
Butterfly Wk CMBW SE5 * 110 E7
Butter Hl CAR SM5 176 A2
Butteridges Cl DAGW RM9 80 B7
Buttermere Cl
EBED/NFELT TW14 121 J7
MRDN SM4 161 G5
SRTFD E15 76 B3
STHWK SE1 19 L6
Buttermere Dr
PUT/ROE SW15 127 H4
Buttermere Wk HACK E8 74 B5
Butterwick HMSMTH W6 107 F3
Butterworth Gdns WFD IG8 44 E5
Buttery Ms STHGT/OAK N14 40 E2
Buttesland St IS N1 7 H7
Buttfield Cl DAGE RM10 80 D5
Buttmarsh Cl
WOOL/PLUM SE18 115 G4
Buttsbury Rd IL IG1 78 C4
Butts Crs FELT TW13 142 A2
Buttsmead NTHWD HA6 32 A6
Butts Piece NTHLT UB5 83 F1
Butts Rd BMLY BR1 152 C4
The Butts BTFD TW8 104 E5
Buxhall Crs HOM E9 75 H5
Buxted Rd EDUL SE22 131 F3
HACK E8 7 L1
NFNCH/WDSPK N12 39 J4
Buxton Cl WFD IG8 45 H5
Buxton Crs CHEAM SM3 174 C3
Buxton Dr NWMAL KT3 160 A1
WAN E11 58 C3
Buxton Gdns ACT W3 86 D6
Buxton Ms CLAP SW4 129 J1
Buxton Pth OXHEY WD19 * 33 G2
Buxton Rd ARCH N19 54 D7
CRICK NW2 69 K5
EHAM E6 95 J2
ERITH DA8 118 A6
GNTH/NBYPK IG2 60 E5
MORT/ESHN SW14 126 B2
SRTFD E15 76 C4
THHTH CR7 164 C4
WALTH E17 57 G3
Buxton St WCHPL E1 13 M1
Byam St FUL/PGN SW6 128 B1
Byards Cft STRHM/NOR SW16 148 D7
Bychurch End TEDD TW11 * 143 F4
Bycroft Rd STHL UB1 84 A4
Bycroft St PGE/AN SE20 151 F6
Bycullah Av ENC/FH EN2 29 H2
Bycullah Rd ENC/FH EN2 29 H1
Byelands Cl BERM/RHTH SE16 93 F7
The Bye ACT W3 87 G5
Byewaters WATW WD18 20 A5
Bye Ways WHTN TW2 142 B2
The Byeways BRYLDS KT5 159 H4
The Bye Wy
KTN/HRWW/WS HA3 34 E7
The Byeway
MORT/ESHN SW14 125 K2
Byfeld Gdns BARN SW13 106 D7
Byfield Cl BERM/RHTH SE16 112 B1
Byfield Rd ISLW TW7 124 B2
Byford Cl SRTFD E15 76 C6
Bygrove CROY/NA CR0 179 K5
Bygrove Rd WIM/MER SW19 147 H5
Bygrove St POP/IOD E14 93 K5
Byland Cl ABYW SE2 116 C2
CAR SM5 162 B6
STHGT/OAK N14 29 F6
Byne Rd CAR SM5 175 J1
SYD SE26 150 E5
Bynes Rd SAND/SEL CR2 177 K6
Byng Pl GWRST WC1E 11 H1
Byng Rd BAR EN5 26 B2
Byng St POP/IOD E14 112 D1
Bynon Av BXLYHN DA7 137 F2
Byre Rd STHGT/OAK N14 28 A5
Byrne Cl CROY/NA CR0 164 C5
Byrne Rd BAL SW12 129 G7
Byron Av BORE WD6 24 C4
CDALE/KGS NW9 50 D3
HSLWW TW4 122 A1
MNPK E12 77 J5
NWMAL KT3 160 D4
SUT SM1 175 H3
SWFD E18 58 D2
Byron Av East SUT SM1 175 H3
Byron Cl HACK E8 74 C7
HPTN TW12 141 K3
PGE/AN SE20 * 165 J2
SYD SE26 * 151 G3
THMD SE28 97 J7
WOT/HER KT12 156 D7
Byron Ct ENC/FH EN2 29 H1
Byron Dr EFNCH N2 53 H5
ERITH DA8 117 J6
Byron Gdns SUT SM1 175 H3
Byron Hill Rd
RYLN/HDSTN HA2 48 D7
Byron Ms HAMP NW3 71 J4
MV/WKIL W9 2 B9
Byron Rd ALP/SUD HA0 67 J1
CRICK NW2 69 K1
EA W5 86 B7
HRW HA1 48 E5
KTN/HRWW/WS HA3 49 F1
LEY E10 57 K7
MLHL NW7 37 J4
WALTH E17 57 J2
Byron St POP/IOD E14 94 A5
Byron Ter ED N9 * 30 E6
Byron Wy NTHLT UB5 83 J2
WDR/YW UB7 100 C3
YEAD UB4 82 C3
Bysouth Cl SEVS/STOTM N15 55 K3
By The Wd OXHEY WD19 33 H1
Bythorn St BRXN/ST SW9 130 A2
Byton Rd TOOT SW17 147 K5
Byward Av EBED/NFELT TW14 122 B5
Byward St MON EC3R 13 K7
Bywater Pl BERM/RHTH SE16 93 G7
Bywater St CHEL SW3 15 L7
The Byway BELMT SM2 175 H7
HOR/WEW KT19 173 H3
Bywell Pl GTPST W1W * 10 E3
Bywood Av CROY/NA CR0 165 K5

C

Cabbell St CAMTN NW1 9 J3
Cabinet Wy CHING E4 43 H5
Cable Pl GNWCH SE10 113 F7
Cables Cl ERITH DA8 117 K2
Cable St WCHPL E1 92 C6
Cable Trade Pk CHARL SE7 * 113 K4
Cabot Sq POP/IOD E14 93 J7
Cabot Wy EHAM E6 77 H7
Cabul Rd BTSEA SW11 128 D1
Cactus Cl CMBW SE5 * 131 F1
Cadbury Cl ISLW TW7 104 B7
SUN TW16 140 C6
Cadbury Rd SUN TW16 140 C6
Cadbury Wy
BERM/RHTH SE16 19 M4
Caddington Cl EBAR EN4 27 J4
Caddington Rd CRICK NW2 70 C2
Caddis Cl STAN HA7 * 35 F6
Cadell Cl BETH E2 7 M6
Cade Rd GNWCH SE10 113 G7
Cader Rd WAND/EARL SW18 128 B5
Cadet Dr STHWK SE1 19 M7
Cadet Pl GNWCH SE10 113 H4
Cadiz Rd DAGE RM10 80 E6
Cadiz St WALW SE17 18 F8
Cadman Cl BRXN/ST SW9 110 C6
Cadmer Cl NWMAL KT3 160 B3
Cadmus Cl CLAP SW4 129 J3
Cadogan Cl HOM E9 * 75 H6
RYLN/HDSTN HA2 66 B3
TEDD TW11 142 E4
Cadogan Ct BELMT SM2 175 F5
Cadogan Gdns CHEL SW3 15 M5
FNCH N3 * 39 F7
SWFD E18 59 F2
WCHMH N21 29 G4
Cadogan Ga KTBR SW1X 15 M5
Cadogan La KTBR SW1X 16 A3
Cadogan Pl KTBR SW1X 15 M3
Cadogan Rd SURB KT6 158 E4
WOOL/PLUM SE18 115 H2
Cadogan Sq KTBR SW1X 15 L4
Cadogan St CHEL SW3 15 L6
KTBR SW1X 15 M5
Cadogan Ter HOM E9 75 H5
Cadoxton Av
SEVS/STOTM N15 56 B5
Cadwallon Rd ELTH/MOT SE9 154 B1
Caedmon Rd HOLWY N7 73 F3
Caerleon Cl ESH/CLAY KT10 171 H6
SCUP DA14 155 J4
Caernarvon Cl MTCM CR4 163 K2
Caesars Wk MTCM CR4 162 E4
Cahill St STLK EC1Y * 12 F1
Cahir St POP/IOD E14 112 E3
Cain's La EBED/NFELT TW14 121 G4
Caird St NKENS W10 88 C2
Cairn Av EA W5 85 K7
Cairndale Cl BMLY BR1 152 D6
Cairnfield Av CRICK NW2 69 G2
Cairngorm Cl TEDD TW11 143 G4
Cairns Av WFD IG8 45 J5
Cairns Cl DART DA1 139 G4
Cairns Rd BTSEA SW11 128 D4
Cairn Wy STAN HA7 35 F5
Cairo New Rd CROY/NA CR0 177 H1
Cairo Rd WALTH E17 * 57 J3
Caister Ms BAL SW12 129 G7
Caistor Park Rd SRTFD E15 76 D7
Caistor Rd BAL SW12 129 G6
Caithness Gdns BFN/LL DA15 136 A5
Caithness Rd MTCM CR4 148 B6
WKENS W14 107 G2
Calabria Rd HBRY N5 73 H5
Calais St CMBW SE5 110 C7
Calbourne Av HCH RM12 81 K4
Calbourne Rd BAL SW12 128 E6
Caldbeck Av WPK KT4 173 K1
Caldecote Gdns BUSH WD23 22 E5
Caldecote La BUSH WD23 23 F6
Caldecot Rd CMBW SE5 130 D1
Caldecott Wy CLPT E5 75 F2
Calder Av GFD/PVL UB6 85 F1
Calder Gdns EDGW HA8 50 C2
Calderon Rd WAN E11 76 A3
Calder Rd MRDN SM4 162 B4
Caldervale Rd CLAP SW4 129 J4
Calderwood St
WOOL/PLUM SE18 115 F3
Caldew St CMBW SE5 110 E6
Caldicote Gn
CDALE/KGS NW9 * 51 G5
Caldwell Rd OXHEY WD19 33 H3
Caldwell St BRXN/ST SW9 110 A6
Caldy Rd BELV DA17 117 J2
Caldy Wk IS N1 * 73 J5
Caledonian Cl
GDMY/SEVK IG3 * 61 H7
Caledonian Rd HOLWY N7 73 F4
IS N1 5 L5
Caledonian Sq CAMTN NW1 72 D5
Caledonian Wharf Rd
POP/IOD E14 113 G3
Caledonia Rd
STWL/WRAY TW19 120 B7
Caledonia St IS N1 5 K6
Caledon Rd EHAM E6 77 K7
WLGTN SM6 176 A3
Calendar Ms SURB KT6 158 E5
Cale St CHEL SW3 15 J7
Calidore Cl
BRXS/STRHM SW2 * 130 A5
California La BUSH WD23 22 D7
California Rd NWMAL KT3 159 K3
Callaby Ter IS N1 * 73 K5
Callaghan Cl LEW SE13 133 H3
Callaghan Cots WCHPL E1 * 92 E4
Callander Rd CAT SE6 151 K1
The Callanders BUSH WD23 * 22 E7
Callard Av PLMGR N13 41 H4
Callcott Rd KIL/WHAMP NW6 70 D6
Callcott St KENS W8 8 A8
Callendar Rd SKENS SW7 15 G3
Callingham Cl POP/IOD E14 93 H4
Callis Farm Cl
STWL/WRAY TW19 120 B5
Callisons Pl GNWCH SE10 113 H4
Callis Rd WALTH E17 57 H5
Callow St CHEL SW3 15 G9
Calmington Rd CMBW SE5 19 K8
Calmont Rd BMLY BR1 152 B5
Calonne Rd WIM/MER SW19 146 B3
Calshot Rd HTHAIR TW6 120 E1
Calshot St IS N1 5 L5
Calshot Wy ENC/FH EN2 29 H2
HTHAIR TW6 120 D1
Calthorpe Gdns EDGW HA8 36 B4
SUT SM1 175 G2
Calthorpe St FSBYW WC1X 5 M9
Calton Av DUL SE21 131 F5
Calton Rd BAR EN5 27 G5
Calverley Cl BECK BR3 151 K5
Calverley Crs DAGE RM10 80 C1
Calverley Gv ARCH N19 54 D7
Calverley Rd EW KT17 173 J5
Calvert Av WCHPL E1 7 K8
Calvert Cl BELV DA17 117 H3
Calverton Rd EHAM E6 78 A7
Calvert Rd BAR EN5 26 B1
GNWCH SE10 113 J4
Calvert St CAMTN NW1 4 A3
Calvin St WCHPL E1 13 L1
Calydon Rd CHARL SE7 114 A4
Calypso Crs PECK SE15 111 F6
Calypso Wy BERM/RHTH SE16 112 C2
Camac Rd WHTN TW2 123 J7
Camarthen Gn
CDALE/KGS NW9 * 51 G5
Cambalt Rd PUT/ROE SW15 127 G4
Camberley Av EN EN1 30 A3
RYNPK SW20 160 E1
Camberley Cl CHEAM SM3 174 B2
Camberley Rd HTHAIR TW6 120 D2
Cambert Wy BKHTH/KID SE3 134 A3
Camberwell Church St
CMBW SE5 110 E7
Camberwell Glebe CMBW SE5 110 E7
Camberwell Gn CMBW SE5 110 E7
Camberwell Gv CMBW SE5 110 E7
Camberwell New Rd
CMBW SE5 110 C6
Camberwell Rd CMBW SE5 110 D5
Camberwell Station Rd
CMBW SE5 110 D7
Cambeys Rd DAGE RM10 80 E4
Camborne Av WEA W13 104 C1
Camborne Cl HTHAIR TW6 120 D2
Camborne Crs HTHAIR TW6 120 D2
Camborne Ms
WAND/EARL SW18 127 K6
Camborne Rd BELMT SM2 174 E6
CROY/NA CR0 165 H6
RYNPK SW20 161 G4
SCUP DA14 155 J2
WAND/EARL SW18 127 K6
WELL DA16 135 K1
Camborne Wy HEST TW5 103 F7
HTHAIR TW6 120 D2
Cambourne Av ED N9 31 F6
Cambourne Ms NTGHL W11 88 C5
Cambray Rd BAL SW12 129 H7
Cambria Cl BFN/LL DA15 135 J7
HSLW TW3 123 F3
Cambria Ct EBED/NFELT TW14 122 A6
Cambria Gdns
STWL/WRAY TW19 120 B6
Cambrian Av GNTH/NBYPK IG2 60 E4
Cambrian Cl WNWD SE27 149 H2
Cambrian Gn CDALE/KGS NW9 51 G4
Cambrian Rd LEY E10 57 J6
RCHPK/HAM TW10 125 G5
Cambria Rd CMBW SE5 130 D2
Cambria St FUL/PGN SW6 108 A6
Cambridge Av GFD/PVL UB6 67 F4
KIL/WHAMP NW6 2 B5
NWMAL KT3 160 B1
WELL DA16 136 A3
Cambridge Barracks Rd
WOOL/PLUM SE18 114 E3
Cambridge Circ
SOHO/SHAV W1D 11 H5
Cambridge Cl EBAR EN4 28 A7
HSLWW TW4 122 D3
RYNPK SW20 145 K7
WALTH E17 57 H5
WDGN N22 * 41 G7
WDR/YW UB7 100 A5
WLSDN NW10 68 E2
Cambridge Crs BETH E2 92 D1
TEDD TW11 * 143 G4
Cambridge Dr LEE/GVPK SE12 133 K4
RSLP HA4 65 G1
Cambridge Gdns EN EN1 30 C1
KIL/WHAMP NW6 2 B5
KUT/HW KT1 159 H1
MUSWH N10 40 A7
NKENS W10 88 B5
TOTM N17 41 K6
WCHMH N21 29 K6
Cambridge Ga CAMTN NW1 4 C8
Cambridge Gate Ms
CAMTN NW1 4 D8
Cambridge Gn ELTH/MOT SE9 135 G7
Cambridge Gv HMSMTH W6 106 E3
PGE/AN SE20 * 150 D7
Cambridge Grove Rd
KUT/HW KT1 159 H1
Cambridge Heath Rd BETH E2 92 D2
Cambridge Pde EN EN1 * 30 C1
Cambridge Pk TWK TW1 124 D6
Cambridge Park Rd WAN E11 58 D6
Cambridge Pas HOM E9 74 E6
Cambridge Pl KENS W8 * 14 D2
Cambridge Rd ASHF TW15 140 A6
BARK IG11 78 C6
BARN SW13 126 C1
BMLY BR1 152 E6
BTSEA SW11 108 E7
CAR SM5 175 J5
E/WMO/HCT KT8 156 E3
GDMY/SEVK IG3 60 E7
HNWL W7 104 A1
HPTN TW12 141 K6
HSLWW TW4 122 D3
KIL/WHAMP NW6 2 B6
KUT/HW KT1 159 H1
MTCM CR4 163 H2
NWMAL KT3 160 A3
PGE/AN SE20 165 H2
RCH/KEW TW9 105 H6
RYLN/HDSTN HA2 48 A4
RYNPK SW20 145 K7
SCUP DA14 154 E3
STHL UB1 * 83 K7
TEDD TW11 143 G3
TWK TW1 124 E5
WAN E11 58 E5
WATW WD18 * 21 G3
WOT/HER KT12 156 A5
Cambridge Rd North
CHSWK W4 105 J4
Cambridge Rd South
CHSWK W4 105 J4
Cambridge Rw
WOOL/PLUM SE18 115 G4
Cambridge Sq BAY/PAD W2 9 J4
Cambridge St PIM SW1V 16 D7
Cambridge Ter CAMTN NW1 4 C8
ED N9 * 30 B6
Cambridge Terrace Ms
CAMTN NW1 * 4 D8
Cambridge Yd HNWL W7 * 104 A1
Cambus Cl YEAD UB4 83 J4
Cambus Rd CAN/RD E16 94 E4
Camdale Rd
WOOL/PLUM SE18 116 A6
Camden Av FELT TW13 141 G1
YEAD UB4 83 G6
Camden Cl CHST BR7 154 C7
Camden Gdns CAMTN NW1 4 D2
SUT SM1 175 F4
THHTH CR7 164 C2
Camden Gv CHST BR7 154 B5
Camden High St CAMTN NW1 4 D2
Camden Hill Rd NRWD SE19 150 A5
Camdenhurst St POP/IOD E14 93 G5
Camden Lock Pl CAMTN NW1 4 C2
Camden Ms CAMTN NW1 5 G1
Camden Park Rd CAMTN NW1 72 D5
CHST BR7 153 K6
Camden Pas IS N1 6 C5
Camden Rd BXLY DA5 137 G7
CAMTN NW1 4 E2
CAR SM5 175 K3
SUT SM1 175 F4
WALTH E17 57 H5
WAN E11 59 F5
Camden Rw BKHTH/KID SE3 133 H1
PIN HA5 * 47 G2
Camden Sq CAMTN NW1 5 G1
Camden St CAMTN NW1 4 D2
Camden Ter CAMTN NW1 72 D5
Camden Wk IS N1 6 C4
Camden Wy CHST BR7 153 K6
THHTH CR7 164 C2
Camelford Wk NTGHL W11 * 88 C5
Camel Gv KUTN/CMB KT2 143 K4
Camellia Pl WHTN TW2 123 G6
Camellia St VX/NE SW8 109 K6
Camelot Cl THMD SE28 115 J1
WIM/MER SW19 146 D3
Camel Rd CAN/RD E16 95 H7
Camera Pl WBPTN SW10 108 C5
Cameron Cl TRDG/WHET N20 39 J1
UED N18 42 D3
Cameron Crs EDGW HA8 36 D7
Cameron Dr DART DA1 139 J1
Cameron Pl
STRHM/NOR SW16 149 G1
Cameron Rd CAT SE6 * 151 H1
CROY/NA CR0 164 C5
GDMY/SEVK IG3 60 E7
HAYES BR2 167 K3
Cameron Sq MTCM CR4 147 J7
Cameron Ter
LEE/GVPK SE12 * 153 F2
Camerton Cl HACK E8 74 B5
Camilla Cl SUN TW16 * 140 D5
Camilla Rd BERM/RHTH SE16 111 J3
Camille Cl SNWD SE25 165 H2
Camlan Rd BMLY BR1 152 D3
Camlet St BETH E2 7 L9
Camlet Wy EBAR EN4 26 E1
Camley St CAMTN NW1 5 G3
Camm Gdns KUT/HW KT1 * 159 G1
THDIT KT7 157 K6
Camomile Av MTCM CR4 147 K7
Camomile St HDTCH EC3A 13 K4
OBST EC2N 13 J4
Camomile Rd ROMW/RG RM7 81 F1
Campana Rd FUL/PGN SW6 107 K7
Campbell Av BARK/HLT IG6 60 C3
Campbell Cl RSLP HA4 46 E5
STRHM/NOR SW16 * 148 D4
WHTN TW2 123 J7
WOOL/PLUM SE18 115 F7
Campbell Cots MTCM CR4 * 163 F1
Campbell Cft EDGW HA8 36 C4
Campbell Gordon Wy
CRICK NW2 69 K3
Campbell Rd BOW E3 93 J2
CROY/NA CR0 164 C6
EHAM E6 77 J7
HNWL W7 84 E6
SRTFD E15 76 C3
TOTM N17 42 B7
WALTH E17 57 H3
WHTN TW2 142 D1
Campbell Wk IS N1 * 5 K3
Campdale Rd HOLWY N7 72 D2
Campden Crs ALP/SUD HA0 67 H2
BCTR RM8 79 J3
Campden Gv KENS W8 14 B1
Campden Hl KENS W8 14 A1
Campden Hill Gdns KENS W8 8 A8
Campden Hill Pl NTGHL W11 * 88 D7
Campden Hill Rd KENS W8 14 A1
Campden Hill Sq KENS W8 88 D7
Campden House Cl KENS W8 14 A1
Campden House Ter
KENS W8 * 8 B9
Campden Rd SAND/SEL CR2 178 A4
Campden St KENS W8 8 A9
Campden Ter CHSWK W4 * 106 B4
Campden Wy BCTR RM8 79 H3
Campen Cl WIM/MER SW19 146 C1
Camperdown St WCHPL E1 13 M5
Campfield Rd ELTH/MOT SE9 134 C6
Campion Cl CROY/NA CR0 178 A3
EHAM E6 95 K6
KTN/HRWW/WS HA3 50 B5
ROMW/RG RM7 81 F1
Campion Ct ALP/SUD HA0 * 86 A1
Campion Gdns WFD IG8 44 E4
Campion Pl THMD SE28 97 H7
Campion Rd ISLW TW7 104 A7
LEY E10 57 K6
PUT/ROE SW15 127 F3
Campion Ter CRICK NW2 70 B2
Campion Wy EDGW HA8 36 E3
Camplin Rd
KTN/HRWW/WS HA3 50 A4
Camplin St NWCR SE14 112 A6
Camp Rd WIM/MER SW19 145 K4
Campsbourne Pde
CEND/HSY/T N8 * 54 E3
Campsbourne Rd
CEND/HSY/T N8 54 E2
The Campsbourne
CEND/HSY/T N8 54 E3
Campsey Gdns DAGW RM9 79 H6
Campsey Rd DAGW RM9 79 H6
Campshill Pl LEW SE13 133 F4
Campshill Rd LEW SE13 133 F4
Campus Rd WALTH E17 57 H5
Camp Vw WIM/MER SW19 145 K4
Cam Rd SRTFD E15 76 B7
Camrose Av EDGW HA8 50 B1
ERITH DA8 117 J5
FELT TW13 141 F3
STAN HA7 50 A1
Camrose Cl CROY/NA CR0 166 B6
MRDN SM4 161 K3
Camrose St WOOL/PLUM SE18 116 B4
Canada Av UED N18 41 J5
Canada Crs ACT W3 86 E4
Canada Park Pde EDGW HA8 * 36 D7
Canada Rd ACT W3 86 E4
ERITH DA8 118 E6
Canada Sq POP/IOD E14 93 K7
Canada St BERM/RHTH SE16 112 A1
Canada Wy SHB W12 87 K6
Canadian Av CAT SE6 132 E7
Canal Ap DEPT SE8 112 B4
Canal Bvd KTTN NW5 72 D5
Canal Cl NKENS W10 88 B3
WCHPL E1 93 G3
Canal Gv PECK SE15 111 H5
Canal Pth BETH E2 7 L4
Canal St CMBW SE5 110 E5
Canal Wk CROY/NA CR0 165 F5
IS N1 7 H3
WLSDN NW10 * 68 E6
Canal Wy NKENS W10 88 B3
Canal Whf GFD/PVL UB6 * 67 G7
Canal Yd NWDGN UB2 * 102 A3
Canberra Cl DAGE RM10 81 F6
HDN NW4 51 J2
Canberra Crs DAGE RM10 81 F6
Canberra Dr NTHLT UB5 83 G2
Canberra Rd HTHAIR TW6 120 D2
ABYW SE2 116 E5
CHARL SE7 114 B5
EHAM E6 77 K7
HTHAIR TW6 120 D2
WEA W13 85 G7
Canbury Av KUTN/CMB KT2 144 B7
Canbury Ms SYD SE26 150 C2
Canbury Park Rd
KUTN/CMB KT2 144 A7
Cancell Rd BRXN/ST SW9 110 B7
Candahar Rd BTSEA SW11 128 D1
Candle Gv PECK SE15 131 J2
Candlelight Ct SRTFD E15 76 D5
Candler Ms TWK TW1 124 B6
Candler St SEVS/STOTM N15 * 55 K5
Candover Cl WDR/YW UB7 100 A6
Candover Rd HCH RM12 63 K7
Candover St GTPST W1W * 10 E3
Candy St BOW E3 75 H7
Caney Ms CRICK NW2 70 B1
Canfield Dr RSLP HA4 65 F4
Canfield Gdns
KIL/WHAMP NW6 2 D1
Canfield Pl KIL/WHAMP NW6 71 G5
Canfield Rd RAIN RM13 81 H7
WFD IG8 45 J6
Canford Av NTHLT UB5 65 J7
Canford Cl ENC/FH EN2 29 G1
Canford Gdns NWMAL KT3 160 B5
Canford Pl TEDD TW11 143 J5
Canford Rd CLAP SW4 129 F3
Canham Rd CHSWK W4 106 B1
SNWD SE25 165 F2
Canmore Gdns
STRHM/NOR SW16 148 C6
Cann Hall Rd WAN E11 76 D3
Canning Crs WDGN N22 41 F7
Canning Cross CMBW SE5 131 F1
Canning Pas KENS W8 * 14 E3
Canning Pl KENS W8 14 E3
Canning Place Ms KENS W8 * 14 E3
Canning Rd CROY/NA CR0 178 B1
HBRY N5 73 H2
KTN/HRWW/WS HA3 48 E2
SRTFD E15 94 C1
WALTH E17 57 H2
Cannington Rd DAGW RM9 79 J5
Cannizaro Rd WIM/MER SW19 146 A5
Cannonbury Av PIN HA5 47 H5
Cannon Cl HPTN TW12 142 B5
RYNPK SW20 161 F2
Cannon Dr POP/IOD E14 93 J6
Cannon Hl KIL/WHAMP NW6 71 F4
STHGT/OAK N14 40 E2
Cannon Hill La RYNPK SW20 161 G4
Cannon La HAMP NW3 71 H2
PIN HA5 47 J6
Cannon Pl CHARL SE7 114 D4
HAMP NW3 71 G2
Cannon Rd BXLYHN DA7 117 F7
STHGT/OAK N14 40 E2
WATW WD18 21 G4
Cannon St BLKFR EC4V 12 E5
Cannon Street Rd WCHPL E1 92 D5
Cannon Wy E/WMO/HCT KT8 157 F3
Canon Av CHDH RM6 61 J4
Canon Beck Rd
BERM/RHTH SE16 111 K1
Canonbie Rd FSTH SE23 131 K6
Canonbury Crs IS N1 6 F1
Canonbury Gv IS N1 6 E1
Canonbury La IS N1 6 C1
Canonbury Pk North IS N1 73 J5
Canonbury Pk South IS N1 73 J5
Canonbury Rd IS N1 6 D1
Canonbury Sq IS N1 6 D1
Canonbury St IS N1 6 E1
Canonbury Vls IS N1 6 D2
Canon Mohan Cl
STHGT/OAK N14 28 A5
Canon Rd BMLY BR1 168 B2
Canon Rw WHALL SW1A 17 J2
Canons Cl EDGW HA8 36 B5
EFNCH N2 53 H6
Canons Cots EDGW HA8 * 36 B5
Canons Ct EDGW HA8 * 36 B5
Canons Dr EDGW HA8 36 B5
Canonsleigh Rd DAGW RM9 79 H6
Canon St IS N1 6 E4
Canon's Wk CROY/NA CR0 179 F2
Canopus Wy NTHWD HA6 32 E3
STWL/WRAY TW19 120 B6
Canrobert St BETH E2 92 D1
Cantelowes Rd CAMTN NW1 72 D5
Canterbury Av BFN/LL DA15 155 J1
IL IG1 59 J6
Canterbury Cl BECK BR3 151 K7
CMBW SE5 * 130 D1

DART DA1 .... 139 K6
EHAM E6 .... 95 K5
GFD/PVL UB6 .... 84 B4
NTHWD HA6 .... 32 D5
Canterbury Crs BRXN/ST SW9 .... 130 B2
Canterbury Gv WNWD SE27 .... 149 G2
Canterbury Pl WALW SE17 .... 18 E6
Canterbury Rd BORE WD6 .... 24 C1
CROY/NA CRO 164 A6
FELT TW13 .... 141 J1
HRW HA1 .... 48 B4
KIL/WHAMP NW6 .... 2 A6
LEY E10 .... 58 A6
MRDN SM4 .... 162 B5
RYLN/HDSTN HA2 .... 48 B4
WAT WD17 .... 21 F1
Canterbury Ter KIL/WHAMP NW6 .... 2 A5
Canterbury Wy RKW/CH/CXG WD3 .... 20 A2
Cantley Gdns GNTH/NBYPK IG2 .... 60 C5
NRWD SE19 .... 150 B6
Cantley Rd HNWL W7 .... 104 B2
Canton St POP/IOD E14 .... 93 J3
Cantrell Rd BOW E3 .... 93 J3
Cantwell Rd WOOL/PLUM SE18 .... 115 G6
Canvey St STHWK SE1 .... 12 C8
Cape Cl BARK IG11 .... 78 B6
Capel Av WLGTN SM6 .... 177 F4
Capel Cl HAYES BR2 .... 168 D7
TRDG/WHET N20 .... 39 G2
Capel Crs STAN HA7 .... 35 G7
Capel Gdns GDMY/SEVK IG3 .... 79 F3
PIN HA5 .... 47 K3
Capella Rd NTHWD HA6 .... 32 D4
Capel Rd EBAR EN4 .... 27 J5
FSTGT E7 .... 77 F3
OXHEY WD19 .... 21 H5
Capeners Cl KTBR SW1X 15 M2
Capener's Cl KTBR SW1X 16 A1
Capern Rd WAND/EARL SW18 .... 128 B7
Cape Rd TOTM N17 .... 56 C2
Cape Yd WAP E1W 92 C7
Capital Interchange Wy BTFD TW8 .... 105 H4
Capitol Wy CDALE/KGS NW9 .... 50 E2
Capland St STJWD NW8 .... 3 H9
Caple Pde WLSDN NW10 .... 87 H1
Caple Rd WLSDN NW10 .... 87 H1
Caprea Cl YEAD UB4 .... 83 H4
Capri Rd CROY/NA CRO 165 G6
Capstan Cl CHDH RM6 .... 61 J4
Capstan Dr RAIN RM13 .... 99 J4
Capstan Ride ENC/FH EN2 .... 29 G1
Capstan Sq POP/IOD E14 .... 113 F1
Capstan Wy BERM/RHTH SE16 .... 93 G7
Capstone Rd BMLY BR1 .... 152 D3
Capthorne Av RYLN/HDSTN HA2 .... 47 J7
Capuchin Cl STAN HA7 .... 35 H5
Capulet Ms CAN/RD E16 .... 94 E7
Capworth St LEY E10 .... 57 J7
Caractacus Cottage Vw WATW WD18 .... 20 E6
Caractacus Gn WATW WD18 .... 20 D6
Caradoc Cl BAY/PAD W2 .... 8 A4
Caradoc Evans Cl FBAR/BDGN N11 .... 40 B4
Caradoc St GNWCH SE10 .... 113 H4
Caradon Cl WAN E11 .... 58 C7
Caradon Wy SEVS/STOTM N15 .... 55 K3
Caravel Cl POP/IOD E14 .... 112 D2
Caravel Ms DEPT SE8 .... 112 D5
Caraway Cl PLSTW E13 .... 95 F4
Caraway Pl WLGTN SM6 .... 176 B2
Carberry Rd NRWD SE19 .... 150 A5
Carbery Av ACT W3 .... 105 G1
Carbis Rd POP/IOD E14 .... 93 H5
Carburton St GTPST W1W 10 D2
Cardale St POP/IOD E14 .... 113 G2
Carden Rd PECK SE15 .... 131 J2
Cardiff Rd HNWL W7 .... 104 B2
PEND EN3 .... 31 F4
Cardiff St WOOL/PLUM SE18 .... 115 K6
Cardigan Gdns GDMY/SEVK IG3 .... 79 G1
Cardigan Pl LEW SE13 .... 133 G3
Cardigan Rd BARN SW13 .... 126 D1
BOW E3 .... 93 H1
RCHPK/HAM TW10 .... 125 F5
WIM/MER SW19 .... 147 G5
Cardigan St LBTH SE11 .... 18 A7
Cardigan Wk IS N1 * 6 F1
Cardinal Av BORE WD6 .... 24 D2
KUTN/CMB KT2 .... 144 A4
MRDN SM4 .... 161 H5
Cardinal Bourne St STHWK SE1 * 19 H4
Cardinal Cl CHST BR7 .... 154 D7
EDGW HA8 .... 36 E6
MRDN SM4 .... 161 H5
WPK KT4 .... 173 J3
Cardinal Crs NWMAL KT3 .... 159 K1
Cardinal Dr WOT/HER KT12 .... 156 C7
RSLP HA4 .... 47 H7
Cardinal Hinsey Cl WLSDN NW10 .... 87 J1
Cardinal Pl PUT/ROE SW15 .... 127 G3
Cardinal Rd FELT TW13 .... 122 A7
RSLP HA4 .... 47 H7
Cardinals Wk SUN TW16 .... 140 C5
Cardinal's Wk HPTN TW12 .... 142 C6
Cardinals Wy ARCH N19 .... 54 D7
Cardinal Wy KTN/HRWW/WS HA3 .... 48 E2
Cardine Ms PECK SE15 .... 111 J6
Cardington Sq HSLWW TW4 .... 122 C3
Cardington St CAMTN NW1 .... 4 F7
Cardozo Rd HOLWY N7 .... 72 E4
Cardrew Av NFNCH/WDSPK N12 .... 39 H4
Cardross St HMSMTH W6 .... 106 E2
Cardwell Rd HOLWY N7 .... 72 E3
Cardwell Ter HOLWY N7 * 72 E3
Carew Cl HOLWY N7 .... 73 F1
Carew Rd ASHF TW15 .... 140 A5
MTCM CR4 .... 163 F1
NTHWD HA6 .... 32 C5
THHTH CR7 .... 164 C2
TOTM N17 .... 56 C1
WEA W13 .... 104 D1
WLGTN SM6 .... 176 C5
Carew St CMBW SE5 .... 130 D1
Carew Wy OXHEY WD19 .... 33 K2
Carey Gdns VX/NE SW8 * 129 J1
Carey La CITYW EC2V 12 E4
Carey Pl PIM SW1V 17 G6
Carey Rd DAGW RM9 .... 80 A3
Carey St LINN WC2A 11 M5
Carey Wy WBLY HA9 .... 68 D3

Carfax Pl CLAP SW4 .... 129 J3
Carfax Rd HCH RM12 .... 81 H3
HYS/HAR UB3 .... 101 K4
The Carfax SYD SE26 * 150 E2
Carfree Cl IS N1 .... 6 B1
Cargill Rd WAND/EARL SW18 .... 128 A7
Cargreen Rd SNWD SE25 .... 165 G3
Carholme Rd FSTH SE23 .... 132 B7
Carisbrooke Av BXLY DA5 .... 136 E7
Carisbrooke Cl HSLWW TW4 .... 122 A4
STAN HA7 .... 49 K1
Carisbrooke Ct NTHLT UB5 * 65 K7
Carisbrooke Gdns PECK SE15 .... 111 G6
Carisbrooke Rd HAYES BR2 .... 168 B3
MTCM CR4 .... 163 K3
WALTH E17 * 57 G3
Carker's La ARCH N19 .... 54 D6
KTTN NW5 .... 72 B4
Carleton Av WLGTN SM6 .... 176 D7
Carleton Cl ESH/CLAY KT10 .... 157 F3
Carleton Gdns ARCH N19 * 72 C4
Carleton Rd DART DA1 .... 139 K6
HOLWY N7 .... 72 D3
Carleton Vls KTTN NW5 * 72 C4
Carlile Cl BOW E3 .... 93 H1
Carlina Gdns WFD IG8 .... 45 F4
Carlingford Rd HAMP NW3 .... 71 H3
MRDN SM4 .... 161 G5
SEVS/STOTM N15 .... 55 H2
Carlisle Av ACT W3 .... 87 G5
TWRH EC3N 13 L5
Carlisle Cl KUTN/CMB KT2 .... 144 C1
PIN HA5 .... 47 J6
Carlisle Gdns IL IG1 .... 59 J5
KTN/HRWW/WS HA3 .... 49 K6
Carlisle La STHWK SE1 .... 17 M3
Carlisle Pl FBAR/BDGN N11 .... 40 B3
WEST SW1P 16 E4
Carlisle Rd CDALE/KGS NW9 .... 50 E2
DART DA1 .... 139 K5
FSBYPK N4 .... 55 G6
HPTN TW12 .... 142 B6
KIL/WHAMP NW6 .... 70 D1
LEY E10 .... 57 J7
ROM RM1 .... 63 H4
SUT SM1 .... 174 D5
Carlisle St SOHO/SHAV W1D 11 G5
Carlisle Wk HACK E8 .... 74 B5
Carlisle Wy TOOT SW17 .... 148 A4
Carlos Pl MYFR/PKLN W1K 10 B7
Carlow St CAMTN NW1 .... 4 E4
Carlton Av EBED/NFELT TW14 .... 122 A5
HYS/HAR UB3 .... 101 H3
KTN/HRWW/WS HA3 .... 49 H4
SAND/SEL CR2 .... 177 K6
STHGT/OAK N14 .... 28 D4
Carlton Av East WBLY HA9 .... 67 K1
Carlton Av West ALP/SUD HA0 .... 67 H2
Carlton Cl BORE WD6 .... 25 F3
CHSGTN KT9 .... 171 K5
EDGW HA8 .... 36 C4
HAMP NW3 .... 70 E1
Carlton Crs CHEAM SM3 .... 174 C3
Carlton Dene EW KT17 * 173 K4
Carlton Dr BARK/HLT IG6 .... 60 D2
PUT/ROE SW15 .... 127 G4
Carlton Gdns EA W5 .... 85 J5
STJS SW1Y 11 G9
Carlton Ga MV/WKIL W9 * 8 B2
Carlton Gn SCUP DA14 * 155 F3
Carlton Gv PECK SE15 .... 111 J7
Carlton HI STJWD NW8 .... 2 E5
Carlton House Ter STJS SW1Y 11 G9
Carlton Ms KIL/WHAMP NW6 * 70 E4
Carlton Pde WBLY HA9 * 50 A4
Carlton Park Av RYNPK SW20 .... 161 F1
Carlton Rd CHSWK W4 .... 106 A1
EA W5 .... 85 J6
ERITH DA8 .... 117 J6
FBAR/BDGN N11 .... 40 A4
FSBYPK N4 .... 55 G6
GPK RM2 .... 63 J4
MNPK E12 .... 77 H3
MORT/ESHN SW14 .... 125 K2
NWMAL KT3 .... 160 B1
SAND/SEL CR2 .... 177 K6
SCUP DA14 .... 155 F4
SUN TW16 .... 140 D6
WALTH E17 .... 43 G7
WAN E11 .... 58 D7
WELL DA16 .... 136 C2
WOT/HER KT12 .... 156 A6
Carlton Sq WCHPL E1 * 93 F3
Carlton St STJS SW1Y 11 G7
Carlton Ter SYD SE26 .... 150 E2
UED N18 .... 41 K3
WAN E11 .... 58 E4
Carlton Tower Pl KTBR SW1X 15 M3
Carlton V KIL/WHAMP NW6 .... 2 C4
Carlwell St TOOT SW17 .... 147 J4
Carlyle Av BMLY BR1 .... 168 C2
STHL UB1 .... 83 K6
Carlyle Cl E/WMO/HCT KT8 .... 157 G1
EFNCH N2 .... 53 G5
WLSDN NW10 .... 69 F7
Carlyle Ct WBPTN SW10 * 108 B7
Carlyle Gdns STHL UB1 .... 83 K6
Carlyle Pl PUT/ROE SW15 .... 127 G3
Carlyle Rd CROY/NA CRO 178 C1
EA W5 .... 104 D3
MNPK E12 .... 77 J3
THMD SE28 .... 97 H6
Carlyle Sq CHEL SW3 .... 15 H8
Carlyon Av RYLN/HDSTN HA2 .... 65 K3
Carlyon Cl ALP/SUD HA0 .... 68 A7
Carlyon Rd ALP/SUD HA0 .... 86 A1
YEAD UB4 .... 83 G4
Carlys Cl BECK BR3 .... 166 A1
Carmalt Gdns PUT/ROE SW15 .... 127 F3
Carmelite Rd KTN/HRWW/WS HA3 .... 34 C8
Carmelite St EMB EC4Y 12 B6
Carmel Wy RCH/KEW TW9 .... 125 H1
Carmen St POP/IOD E14 .... 93 K5
Carmichael Cl BTSEA SW11 .... 128 C2
RSLP HA4 .... 64 C3
Carmichael Ms WAND/EARL SW18 .... 128 C6
Carmichael Rd SNWD SE25 .... 165 H4
Carminia Rd TOOT SW17 .... 148 B1
Carnaby St SOHO/CST W1F 10 E5
Carnac St WNWD SE27 .... 149 K3
Carnanton Rd WALTH E17 .... 44 B7
Carnarvon Av EN EN1 .... 30 B1
Carnarvon Dr HYS/HAR UB3 .... 101 F2
Carnarvon Rd BAR EN5 .... 26 C2
LEY E10 .... 58 A5
SRTFD E15 .... 76 D5
SWFD E18 .... 44 D7
Carnation St ABYW SE2 .... 116 C4
Carnbrook Rd BKHTH/KID SE3 .... 134 C2

Carnecke Gdns ELTH/MOT SE9 .... 134 D4
Carnegie Cl SURB KT6 * 172 B1
Carnegie Pl WIM/MER SW19 .... 146 B2
Carnegie St IS N1 .... 5 L4
Carnet Cl DART DA1 .... 138 B6
Carnforth Cl HOR/WEW KT19 .... 172 D5
Carnforth Gdns HCH RM12 .... 81 J4
Carnforth Rd STRHM/NOR SW16 .... 148 D6
Carnoustie Cl THMD SE28 * 97 K5
Carnoustie Dr IS N1 .... 5 L3
Carnwath Rd FUL/PGN SW6 .... 127 K2
Carol Cl HDN NW4 .... 52 B3
Carolina Cl SRTFD E15 .... 76 C4
Carolina Rd THHTH CR7 .... 164 C1
Caroline Cl BAY/PAD W2 .... 8 D7
CROY/NA CRO 178 A3
ISLW TW7 .... 103 J6
MUSWH N10 .... 54 B1
STRHM/NOR SW16 .... 149 F2
WDR/YW UB7 .... 100 A1
Caroline Ct STAN HA7 * 35 G5
Caroline Gdns BETH E2 * 7 K7
PECK SE15 * 111 J6
Caroline Pl BAY/PAD W2 .... 8 D6
BTSEA SW11 .... 129 F1
HYS/HAR UB3 .... 101 H6
OXHEY WD19 .... 21 H3
Caroline Place Ms BAY/PAD W2 * 8 D7
Caroline Rd WIM/MER SW19 .... 146 D6
Caroline St WCHPL E1 .... 93 F5
Caroline Ter BGVA SW1W 16 A6
Caroline Wk HMSMTH W6 .... 107 H5
Carol St CAMTN NW1 .... 4 E3
Carpenders Av OXHEY WD19 .... 33 J2
Carpenter Cl EW KT17 .... 173 H7
Carpenter Gdns WCHMH N21 .... 41 H1
Carpenters Cl BAR EN5 .... 27 F5
Carpenters Pl CLAP SW4 * 129 J3
Carpenters Rd SRTFD E15 .... 75 K6
Carpenter St MYFR/PKLN W1K 10 C7
Carrara Ms HACK E8 * 74 C4
Carr Cl STAN HA7 .... 35 G5
Carre Ms CMBW SE5 * 110 C7
Carr Gv WOOL/PLUM SE18 .... 114 D3
Carriage Dr East CHEL SW3 .... 109 F5
Carriage Dr North BTSEA SW11 .... 108 E6
Carriage Dr South BTSEA SW11 .... 108 E7
Carriage Dr West BTSEA SW11 .... 108 E6
Carriage Ms IL IG1 .... 78 C1
Carrick Cl ISLW TW7 .... 124 B2
Carrick Gdns TOTM N17 .... 42 A6
Carrick Ms DEPT SE8 * 112 D5
Carrill Wy BELV DA17 .... 116 E3
Carrington Av BORE WD6 .... 24 D4
HSLW TW3 .... 123 G4
Carrington Cl BAR EN5 .... 25 J7
CROY/NA CRO 166 B6
Carrington Gdns FSTGT E7 * 76 E3
Carrington Pl ESH/CLAY KT10 * 170 B3
Carrington Rd DART DA1 .... 139 K5
RCHPK/HAM TW10 .... 125 H3
Carrington Sq KTN/HRWW/WS HA3 .... 34 C6
Carrington St MYFR/PICC W1J 10 C9
Carrol Cl KTTN NW5 .... 72 B3
Carroll Cl SRTFD E15 .... 76 D4
Carronade Pl THMD SE28 .... 115 H2
Carron Cl POP/IOD E14 .... 93 K5
Carroun Rd VX/NE SW8 .... 110 A6
Carroway La GFD/PVL UB6 .... 84 D2
Carrow Rd DAGW RM9 .... 79 H6
Carr Rd NTHLT UB5 .... 66 B5
WALTH E17 .... 57 J1
Carrs La WCHMH N21 .... 29 J4
Carr St POP/IOD E14 .... 93 G4
Carshalton Gv SUT SM1 .... 175 H3
Carshalton Park Rd CAR SM5 .... 175 K4
Carshalton Pl CAR SM5 .... 176 A4
Carshalton Rd MTCM CR4 .... 163 F4
SUT SM1 .... 175 G4
Carslake Rd PUT/ROE SW15 .... 127 F5
Carson Rd CAN/RD E16 .... 94 E4
DUL SE21 .... 149 J1
EBAR EN4 .... 27 K3
Carstairs Rd CAT SE6 .... 152 A2
Carston Cl LEE/GVPK SE12 .... 133 J4
Carswell Cl REDBR IG4 .... 59 H3
Carswell Rd CAT SE6 .... 133 F6
Carter Cl CDALE/KGS NW9 .... 51 F5
WLGTN SM6 .... 176 D6
Carteret St STJSPK SW1H 17 G2
Carteret Wy DEPT SE8 .... 112 B3
Carterhatch La EN EN1 .... 30 B1
Carter La BLKFR EC4V 12 D5
Carter Pl WALW SE17 .... 18 F8
Carter Rd PLSTW E13 .... 77 F7
WIM/MER SW19 .... 147 H5
Carters Cl KTTN NW5 * 72 D4
WPK KT4 .... 174 B1
Carters Hill Cl ELTH/MOT SE9 .... 134 B7
Carter St WALW SE17 .... 18 E8
Carters Yd WAND/EARL SW18 * 127 K4
Carter's Yd WAND/EARL SW18 * 127 K4
Carthew Rd HMSMTH W6 .... 106 E2
Carthew Vls HMSMTH W6 .... 106 E2
Carthusian St FARR EC1M 12 E1
Cartier Cir POP/IOD E14 .... 94 A7
Carting La TPL/STR WC2R 11 K7
Cartmel TOTM N17 .... 42 D6
Cartmel Ct NTHLT UB5 .... 65 J5
Cartmel Gdns MRDN SM4 .... 162 B4
Cartmel Rd BXLYHN DA7 .... 117 H7
Cartwright Gdns STPAN WC1H 5 H8
Cartwright St WCHPL E1 .... 13 M6
Cartwright Wy BARN SW13 .... 106 E6
Carver Cl CHSWK W4 .... 105 K2
Carver Rd HNHL SE24 .... 130 D5
Carville Crs BTFD TW8 .... 105 F3
Cary Rd WAN E11 .... 76 C3
Carysfort Rd CEND/HSY/T N8 .... 54 D4
STNW/STAM N16 .... 73 K2
Cascade Av MUSWH N10 .... 54 C3
Cascade Rd BKHH IG9 .... 45 H1
Casella Rd NWCR SE14 .... 112 A6
Casewick Rd WNWD SE27 .... 149 H4
Casey Cl STJWD NW8 .... 3 J8
Casino Av HNHL SE24 .... 130 D4
Caspian Cl PUR RM19 .... 119 K4
Caspian St CMBW SE5 .... 110 E6
Caspian Wk CAN/RD E16 .... 95 H5
Caspian Wy PUR RM19 .... 119 K4
Cassandra Cl NTHLT UB5 .... 66 D3
Casselden Rd WLSDN NW10 .... 69 F6

Cassidy Rd FUL/PGN SW6 .... 107 K6
Cassilda Rd ABYW SE2 .... 116 B3
Cassilis Rd POP/IOD E14 .... 112 D1
TWK TW1 .... 124 C5
Cassiobridge Ter RKW/CH/CXG WD3 * 20 B4
Cassiobury Av EBED/NFELT TW14 .... 121 J5
Cassiobury Dr WAT WD17 .... 20 J6
Cassiobury Park Av WATW WD18 .... 20 C2
Cassiobury Rd WALTH E17 .... 57 F4
Cassio Pl WATW WD18 .... 20 F4
Cassland Rd HOM E9 .... 75 F6
THHTH CR7 .... 164 E3
Casslee Rd CAT SE6 .... 132 C6
Casson St WCHPL E1 .... 92 C4
Castellain Av MV/WKIL W9 .... 2 C9
Castellan Av GPK RM2 .... 63 K3
Castellane Cl STAN HA7 .... 35 F6
Castello Av PUT/ROE SW15 .... 127 F4
Castelnau BARN SW13 .... 106 E5
Casterbridge Rd BKHTH/KID SE3 .... 133 K2
Casterton St HACK E8 .... 74 D5
Castilion Rd WOOL/PLUM SE18 .... 115 F3
Castle Av CHING E4 .... 44 B4
EW KT17 .... 173 J7
RAIN RM13 .... 81 G6
Castlebar HI WEA W13 .... 85 H4
Castlebar Ms EA W5 .... 85 H4
Castlebar Pk EA W5 .... 85 H4
Castlebar Rd WEA W13 .... 85 H5
Castle Baynard St BLKFR EC4V 12 D6
Castlebrook Cl LBTH SE11 .... 18 C5
Castlecombe Cl ACT W3 * 105 J1
BUSH WD23 .... 22 B5
HAYES BR2 .... 167 H2
SUN TW16 .... 140 C6
WIM/MER SW19 .... 146 B2
Castlecombe Dr WIM/MER SW19 .... 127 G6
Castlecombe Rd ELTH/MOT SE9 .... 153 J4
Castle Ct BANK EC3V * 13 H5
SYD SE26 .... 151 G3
Castle Dr REDBR IG4 .... 59 J5
Castleford Av ELTH/MOT SE9 .... 135 G7
Castleford Cl TOTM N17 .... 42 B5
Castlegate RCH/KEW TW9 .... 125 G2
Castlehaven Rd CAMTN NW1 .... 4 C2
Castle Hill Av CROY/NA CRO 179 K7
Castle Hill Pde WEA W13 * 85 H6
Castle La WESTW SW1E 16 E3
Castleleigh Ct ENC/FH EN2 * 29 K4
Castlemaine Av EW KT17 .... 173 K7
SAND/SEL CR2 .... 178 A4
Castle Ms CMBW SE5 * 110 D6
NFNCH/WDSPK N12 * 39 G4
TOOT SW17 .... 147 J3
Castle Pde EW KT17 * 173 J6
Castle Pl CAMTN NW1 .... 72 B5
CHSWK W4 * 106 A4
Castlereagh St MBLAR W1H 9 L4
Castle Rd CAMTN NW1 .... 72 B5
DAGW RM9 .... 79 H7
NFNCH/WDSPK N12 * 39 G4
NTHLT UB5 .... 66 B5
NWDGN UB2 * 102 E2
Castle Rw CHSWK W4 * 106 A4
KUT/HW KT1 .... 159 F1
Castleton Av BXLYHN DA7 .... 118 A7
WBLY HA9 .... 68 A3
Castleton Cl CROY/NA CRO 166 B5
Castleton Gdns WBLY HA9 .... 68 A2
Castleton Rd ELTH/MOT SE9 .... 153 H4
GDMY/SEVK IG3 .... 61 H7
MTCM CR4 .... 163 J3
RSLP HA4 .... 47 H7
WALTH E17 .... 58 B1
Castletown Rd WKENS W14 .... 107 H4
Castleview Cl FSBYPK N4 .... 55 J7
Castleview Gdns IL IG1 .... 59 J5
Castle Vls CRICK NW2 * 69 J5
Castle Wk SUN TW16 * 156 B2
Castle Wy FELT TW13 .... 141 G4
WIM/MER SW19 .... 146 B2
Castlewood Dr ELTH/MOT SE9 .... 134 E1
Castlewood Rd EBAR EN4 .... 27 H2
STNW/STAM N16 .... 56 C6
Castle Yd HGT N6 * 54 A6
RCH/KEW TW9 .... 124 E4
STHWK SE1 .... 12 D8
Castor La POP/IOD E14 .... 93 K6
Catalina Rd HTHAIR TW6 .... 120 C2
Catalpa Ct LEW SE13 * 133 G5
Caterham Av CLAY IG5 .... 60 A1
Caterham Rd LEW SE13 .... 133 F2
Catesby St WALW SE17 .... 19 H6
Catford Broadway CAT SE6 .... 132 E7
Catford HI CAT SE6 .... 132 C7
Catford Island CAT SE6 * 132 E6
Catford Rd CAT SE6 .... 132 D7
Cathall Rd WAN E11 .... 76 C2
Cathay St BERM/RHTH SE16 .... 111 J1
Cathcart Hl ARCH N19 .... 72 C2
Cathcart Rd WBPTN SW10 .... 14 D9
Cathcart St KTTN NW5 .... 72 B5
Cathedral Pl STP EC4M * 12 E4
Catherall Rd HBRY N5 .... 73 J2
Catherine Gv GNWCH SE10 .... 112 E7
Catherine Griffiths Ct CLKNW EC1R * 6 B9
Catherine Gv GNWCH SE10 .... 112 E7
Catherine Pl HRW HA1 .... 49 F4
WESTW SW1E 16 E3
Catherine Rd GPK RM2 .... 63 K2
SURB KT6 .... 158 E4
Catherines Cl WDR/YW UB7 * 100 A1
Catherine St HOL/ALD WC2B 11 L6
Catherine Vls RYNPK SW20 * 145 K6
Catherine Wheel Aly LVPST EC2M * 13 J2
Catherine Wheel Rd BTFD TW8 .... 104 E6
Catherine Wheel Yd WHALL SW1A * 10 E9
Cat HI EBAR EN4 .... 27 J3
Cathles Rd BAL SW12 .... 129 G5
Cathnor Rd SHB W12 .... 106 E1

Catling Cl FSTH SE23 .... 150 E2
Catlin's La PIN HA5 .... 47 F2
Catlin St BERM/RHTH SE16 .... 111 H4
Cator La BECK BR3 .... 166 C1
Cato Rd CLAP SW4 .... 129 J2
Cator Rd CAR SM5 .... 175 K4
SYD SE26 .... 151 F5
Cato St MBLAR W1H 9 L3
Catsey La BUSH WD23 .... 22 C6
Catsey Wd BUSH WD23 .... 22 C6
Catterick Cl FBAR/BDGN N11 .... 40 A5
Cattistock Rd ELTH/MOT SE9 .... 153 J4
Cattley Cl BAR EN5 .... 26 C3
Catton St RSQ WC1B 11 L3
Caudwell Ter WAND/EARL SW18 * 128 C5
Caulfield Rd CHSWK W4 .... 105 K4
EHAM E6 .... 77 K6
PECK SE15 .... 131 J1
Causeway EBED/NFELT TW14 .... 122 A3
The Causeway BELMT SM2 .... 175 G7
CAR SM5 .... 176 A2
CHSGTN KT9 .... 172 A3
EFNCH N2 .... 53 H3
ESH/CLAY KT10 .... 171 H3
TEDD TW11 .... 143 F5
WAND/EARL SW18 .... 128 A3
WIM/MER SW19 .... 146 A4
Causeyware Rd ED N9 .... 30 D6
Causton Cots POP/IOD E14 * 93 G5
Causton Rd HGT N6 * 54 B6
Causton Sq DAGE RM10 .... 80 C6
Causton St WEST SW1P 17 H6
Cautley Av CLAP SW4 .... 129 H4
Cavalier Cl CHDH RM6 .... 61 J3
Cavalier Gdns HYS/HAR UB3 .... 82 B5
Cavalry Crs HSLWW TW4 .... 122 C3
Cavalry Gdns PUT/ROE SW15 .... 127 H4
Cavan Pl PIN HA5 .... 33 K7
Cavaye Pl WBPTN SW10 * 14 F8
Cavell Crs DART DA1 .... 139 K3
Cavell Dr ENC/FH EN2 .... 29 G1
Cavell Rd TOTM N17 .... 41 K6
Cavell St WCHPL E1 .... 92 D4
Cavendish Av BFN/LL DA15 .... 136 A1
ERITH DA8 .... 117 K5
FNCH N3 .... 52 E2
HRW HA1 .... 66 D3
NWMAL KT3 .... 160 D4
RSLP HA4 .... 65 F4
STJWD NW8 .... 3 H6
WEA W13 .... 85 G4
WELL DA16 .... 136 A2
WFD IG8 .... 45 F7

Cavendish Cl KIL/WHAMP NW6 .... 70 D5
STJWD NW8 .... 3 H7
SUN TW16 .... 140 D5
UED N18 * 42 C4
YEAD UB4 .... 82 C4
Cavendish Ct RKW/CH/CXG WD3 * 20 B4
SUN TW16 .... 140 D5
Cavendish Crs BORE WD6 .... 24 C3
HCH RM12 .... 81 K5
Cavendish Dr EDGW HA8 .... 36 B5
ESH/CLAY KT10 .... 170 E4
WAN E11 .... 58 B7
Cavendish Gdns BARK IG11 .... 79 F4
CHDH RM6 .... 61 K4
CLAP SW4 .... 129 H5
IL IG1 .... 60 A7
Cavendish Ms SUT SM1 * 175 G1
Cavendish Ms North GTPST W1W * 10 D2
Cavendish Ms South GTPST W1W * 10 D3
Cavendish Pde CLAP SW4 * 129 H3
HSLWW TW4 * 122 D1
Cavendish Pl BAL SW12 .... 129 H7
BMLY BR1 .... 168 E3
CAVSQ/HST W1G 10 D4
CRICK NW2 .... 70 B5
Cavendish Rd BAL SW12 .... 129 H6
BAR EN5 .... 26 A2
BELMT SM2 .... 174 C6
CHING E4 .... 44 A5
CHSWK W4 * 105 K7
CLAP SW4 .... 129 G5
CROY/NA CRO 164 C7
FSBYPK N4 .... 55 H5
KIL/WHAMP NW6 .... 70 C6
NWMAL KT3 .... 160 C4
SUN TW16 .... 140 D5
UED N18 .... 42 C4
WIM/MER SW19 .... 147 J6
Cavendish Sq CAVSQ/HST W1G 10 D4
Cavendish St IS N1 .... 7 G6
Cavendish Ter BOW E3 * 93 H2
FELT TW13 .... 140 E1
Cavendish Wy WWKM BR4 .... 166 E1
Cavenham Gdns IL IG1 .... 78 D2
Caverleigh Wy WPK KT4 .... 160 D6
Caverley Gdns KTN/HRWW/WS HA3 .... 49 K6
Cave Rd PLSTW E13 .... 95 F1
RCHPK/HAM TW10 .... 143 J3
Caversham Av CHEAM SM3 .... 174 C1
PLMGR N13 .... 41 G2
Caversham Rd KTTN NW5 .... 72 C5
KUT/HW KT1 .... 159 G1
SEVS/STOTM N15 .... 55 J3
Caversham St CHEL SW3 .... 15 L9
Caverswall St SHB W12 .... 88 A5
Cawdor Crs HNWL W7 .... 104 B3
Cawnpore St NRWD SE19 .... 150 A4
Caxton Gv BOW E3 .... 93 J2
Caxton Ms BTFD TW8 * 104 E5
Caxton Rd NWDGN UB2 .... 102 C2
SHB W12 .... 107 H1
WDGN N22 .... 55 F1
WIM/MER SW19 .... 147 G4
The Caxtons BRXN/ST SW9 * 110 C6
Caxton St CAN/RD E16 .... 94 D5
Caxton St North CAN/RD E16 .... 94 D6
Caxton Wy ROM RM1 .... 63 G5
WATW WD18 .... 20 B6
Cayenne Ct STHWK SE1 .... 13 L9
Caygill Cl HAYES BR2 .... 167 J3
Cayley Rd NWDGN UB2 * 103 G2
Cayton Rd GFD/PVL UB6 .... 84 E1
Cayton St FSBYE EC1V 6 G8
Cazenove Rd STNW/STAM N16 .... 74 B1
WALTH E17 .... 43 J7
Cecil Av BARK IG11 .... 78 D6
EN EN1 .... 30 B3
WBLY HA9 .... 68 B4
Cecil Cl ASHF TW15 .... 140 A5
CHSGTN KT9 .... 171 K3
EA W5 * 85 K4

Cecil Ct BAR EN5 .... 26 B2
  LSQ/SEVD WC2H 11 H7
Cecile Pk CEND/HSY/T N8 .... 54 E5
Cecilia Cl EFNCH N2 .... 53 G2
Cecilia Rd HACK E8 .... 74 B4
Cecil Manning Cl
  GFD/PVL UB6 .... 67 G7
Cecil Pk PIN HA5 .... 47 J3
Cecil Pl MTCM CR4 .... 162 E4
Cecil Rd ACT W3 .... 86 E4
  ASHF TW15 .... 140 A6
  CDALE/KGS NW9 .... 51 F3
  CHDH RM6 .... 61 K6
  CROY/NA CRO 163 K5
  ENC/FH EN2 .... 29 K3
  HSLW TW3 .... 123 H2
  IL IG1 .... 78 B3
  KTN/HRWW/WS HA3 .... 48 C5
  MUSWH N10 .... 54 B1
  PLSTW E13 .... 76 E7
  STHGT/OAK N14 .... 28 B7
  SUT SM1 .... 174 D5
  WALTH E17 .... 43 J7
  WAN E11 .... 76 C1
  WIM/MER SW19 .... 147 F6
  WLSDN NW10 .... 69 G7
Cecil Wy HAYES BR2 .... 167 K7
Cedar Av BFN/LL DA15 .... 136 B6
  CHDH RM6 .... 62 A4
  EBAR EN4 .... 27 J6
  HYS/HAR UB3 .... 82 E5
  PEND EN3 .... 30 E1
  RSLP HA4 .... 65 G4
  WHTN TW2 .... 123 G5
Cedar Cl BKHH IG9 .... 45 H1
  BOW E3 .... 75 H7
  CAR SM5 .... 175 K5
  DUL SE21 .... 130 D7
  HAYES BR2 .... 181 J1
  IL IG1 .... 78 D4
  KUTN/CMB KT2 .... 145 F3
  ROMW/RG RM7 .... 62 E5
Cedar Copse BMLY BR1 .... 168 E1
Cedar Ct CHARL SE7 * 114 B6
  ELTH/MOT SE9 * 134 D5
  WIM/MER SW19 .... 146 B2
Cedar Crs HAYES BR2 .... 181 J2
Cedarcroft Rd CHSGTN KT9 .... 172 B3
Cedar Dr EFNCH N2 .... 53 J3
  GLDGN NW11 .... 52 E3
  PIN HA5 .... 34 A3
Cedar Gdns BELMT SM2 .... 175 C5
  EA W5 .... 104 E2
  STHL UB1 .... 84 A4
Cedar Gv BXLY DA5 .... 136 E5
Cedar Hts RCHPK/HAM TW10 .... 125 F3
Cedarhurst BMLY BR1 * 152 C6
Cedarhurst Dr ELTH/MOT SE9 .... 134 C4
Cedar Lawn Av BAR EN5 .... 26 C4
Cedarne Rd FUL/PGN SW6 .... 107 K6
Cedar Mt ELTH/MOT SE9 .... 134 C7
Cedar Park Gdns CHDH RM6 .... 61 K6
  WIM/MER SW19 .... 145 K4
Cedar Pl CHARL SE7 .... 114 B4
  STHGT/OAK N14 .... 28 A6
Cedar Rd BELMT SM2 .... 175 C5
  BMLY BR1 .... 168 B1
  CRICK NW2 .... 70 A3
  CROY/NA CRO 178 A1
  DART DA1 .... 139 G7
  E/WMO/HCT KT8 .... 157 K3
  EBED/NFELT TW14 .... 121 G7
  ERITH DA8 .... 118 D7
  HSLWW TW4 .... 122 B1
  OXHEY WD19 .... 21 G5
  ROMW/RG RM7 .... 62 E5
  TEDD TW11 .... 143 G4
  TOTM N17 .... 42 B7
Cedars Av MTCM CR4 .... 163 F4
  WALTH E17 .... 57 J4
Cedars Cl BORE WD6 .... 24 D3
  HDN NW4 .... 52 B2
  LEW SE13 .... 133 G2
Cedars Cots PUT/ROE SW15 * 126 D5
  EA W5 .... 42 A1
Cedars Ms CLAP SW4 .... 129 G3
Cedars Rd BARN SW13 .... 126 C1
  BECK BR3 .... 166 B1
  CHSWK W4 .... 105 K5
  CLAP SW4 .... 129 G2
  CROY/NA CRO 176 E2
  ED N9 .... 42 C1
  KUT/HW KT1 .... 143 J7
  MRDN SM4 .... 161 K3
  SRTFD E15 .... 76 C5
  WCHMH N21 .... 41 H1
The Cedars HOM E9 * 75 H5
  SRTFD E15 * 76 D7
  TEDD TW11 .... 143 F5
Cedar Ter RCH/KEW TW9 .... 125 F3
Cedar Tree Gv WNWD SE27 .... 149 H4
Cedarville Gdns
  STRHM/NOR SW16 .... 149 F6
Cedar Wk ESH/CLAY KT10 .... 171 F5
Cedar Wy KCROSS N1C 5 G2
Cedric Av ROM RM1 .... 63 G2
Cedric Rd ELTH/MOT SE9 .... 154 D2
Celadon Cl PEND EN3 .... 31 G2
Celandine Cl POP/IOD E14 .... 93 J4
Celandine Dr HACK E8 .... 7 L1
  THMD SE28 .... 97 H7
Celandine Gv STHGT/OAK N14 .... 28 C5
Celandine Wy SRTFD E15 .... 94 C2
Celbridge Ms BAY/PAD W2 .... 8 E4
Celestial Gdns LEW SE13 .... 133 G3
Celia Rd ARCH N19 .... 72 C3
Celtic Av HAYES BR2 .... 167 G2
Celtic St POP/IOD E14 .... 93 K4
Cemetery La CHARL SE7 .... 114 D5
Cemetery Rd ABYW SE2 .... 116 C5
  FSTGT E7 .... 76 D4
  TOTM N17 .... 42 A6
Cenacle Cl HAMP NW3 .... 70 E2
Centaur Ct BTFD TW8 * 105 F4
Centaur St STHWK SE1 .... 17 M3
Centenary Rd PEND EN3 .... 31 H3
Centenary Wk MNPK E12 .... 77 K3
  WAN E11 .... 58 C6
  WFD IG8 .... 44 C8
Centennial Av BORE WD6 .... 23 J4
Centennial Pk BORE WD6 * 24 A4
Central Av E/WMO/HCT KT8 .... 157 G3
  ED N9 .... 42 A2
  EFNCH N2 .... 53 H3
  EN EN1 .... 30 C1
  HDN NW4 .... 51 H5
  HYS/HAR UB3 .... 101 J3
  MNPK E12 .... 77 J4
  PIN HA5 .... 47 K5
  WAN E11 .... 76 B1
  WELL DA16 .... 136 B1
  WLGTN SM6 .... 176 E4

Central Blds EA W5 * 85 K6
Central Circ HDN NW4 .... 51 K4
Central Hall Blds ARCH N19 * 72 C1
Central HI NRWD SE19 .... 149 J4
Central Pde ACT W3 * 105 H1
  BFN/LL DA15 * 155 G2
  E/WMO/HCT KT8 * 156 B3
  GFD/PVL UB6 .... 85 G2
  HRW HA1 .... 49 F4
  PEND EN3 * 30 B1
  PGE/AN SE20 * 151 F6
  STRHM/NOR SW16 * 149 F6
  SURB KT6 * 159 F5
  WALTH E17 * 57 J3
Central Park Av DAGE RM10 .... 80 D2
Central Park Est
  HSLWW TW4 .... 122 C3
Central Park Rd EHAM E6 .... 95 H1
Central Pl SNWD SE25 * 165 H3
Central Rd ALP/SUD HA0 .... 67 G4
  DART DA1 .... 139 H4
  MRDN SM4 .... 162 A4
  WPK KT4 .... 173 J1
Central Sq E/WMO/HCT KT8 .... 156 E3
  GLDGN NW11 .... 52 E5
Central St FSBYE EC1V 6 E7
Central Ter BECK BR3 * 166 A2
Central Wy CAR SM5 .... 175 J6
  EBED/NFELT TW14 .... 122 A4
  NTHWD HA6 .... 32 C6
  THMD SE28 .... 97 G6
  WLSDN NW10 .... 86 E2
Centre Av ACT W3 .... 87 F7
Centre Common Rd CHST BR7 .... 154 C5
Centre Rd DAGE RM10 .... 98 D1
  WAN E11 .... 76 E1
Centre St BETH E2 .... 92 D1
Centre Wy ED N9 .... 42 E1
Centric Cl CAMTN NW1 * 4 C3
Centurion Sq
  WOOL/PLUM SE18 .... 114 D7
Centurian Wy ERITH DA18 .... 117 L1
Centurion Cl HOLWY N7 .... 5 L1
Centurion Ct WLGTN SM6 .... 176 B1
Centurion La BOW E3 .... 93 H1
Centurion Sq CHARL SE7 .... 114 D6
Centurion Wy PUR RM19 .... 119 J3
Century Cl HDN NW4 .... 52 B4
Century Ct WATW WD18 * 20 A6
Century Ms CLPT E5 * 74 E3
  HBRY N5 * 73 H2
Century Pk WAT WD17 * 21 G3
Century Rd WALTH E17 .... 57 G2
Cephas Av WCHPL E1 .... 92 E3
Cephas St WCHPL E1 .... 92 E3
Ceres Rd WOOL/PLUM SE18 .... 116 A3
Cerise Rd PECK SE15 .... 111 H7
Cerne Cl YEAD UB4 .... 83 G6
Cerne Rd MRDN SM4 .... 162 B5
Cerney Ms BAY/PAD W2 .... 9 K6
Cervantes Ct BAY/PAD W2 * 8 D5
  NTHWD HA6 .... 32 D4
Ceylon Rd WKENS W14 .... 107 G2
Chabot Dr PECK SE15 .... 131 J2
Chadacre Av CLAY IG5 .... 59 K2
Chadacre Rd HOR/WEW KT19 .... 173 K4
Chadbourn St POP/IOD E14 .... 93 K4
Chad Crs ED N9 .... 42 E2
Chadd Dr BMLY BR1 .... 168 D2
Chadville Gdns CHDH RM6 .... 61 K4
Chadway BCTR RM8 .... 79 J1
Chadwell Av CHDH RM6 .... 61 H6
Chadwell Heath La CHDH RM6 .... 61 G3
Chadwell La CEND/HSY/T N8 .... 55 F2
Chadwell St CLKNW EC1R 6 B7
Chadwick Av CHING E4 .... 44 B3
  WCHMH N21 .... 29 F4
  WIM/MER SW19 .... 146 E5
Chadwick Pl SURB KT6 * 158 D5
Chadwick Rd IL IG1 .... 78 B2
  PECK SE15 .... 131 G1
  WAN E11 .... 58 C6
  WLSDN NW10 .... 87 H1
Chadwick St WEST SW1P 17 H4
Chadwin Rd PLSTW E13 .... 95 F4
Chadworth Wy
  ESH/CLAY KT10 .... 170 D4
Chaffinch Av CROY/NA CRO 166 A5
Chaffinch Cl CROY/NA CRO 166 A4
  ED N9 .... 31 F7
  SURB KT6 .... 172 C2
Chaffinch La WATW WD18 .... 20 D6
Chaffinch Rd BECK BR3 .... 151 G7
Chafford Wy CHDH RM6 .... 61 J3
Chagford Rd CAMTN NW1 .... 9 L1
Chailey Av EN EN1 .... 30 B1
Chailey Cl HEST TW5 .... 102 C1
Chailey St CLPT E5 .... 74 E2
Chalbury Wk IS N1 .... 5 M5
Chalcombe Rd ABYW SE2 .... 116 C2
Chalcot Cl BELMT SM2 .... 174 E6
Chalcot Crs CAMTN NW1 .... 3 M3
Chalcot Gdns HAMP NW3 .... 71 K5
Chalcot Ms STRHM/NOR SW16 * 148 E2
Chalcot Rd CAMTN NW1 .... 4 A1
Chalcot Sq CAMTN NW1 .... 4 A1
Chalcott Gdns SURB KT6 * 158 D7
Chalcroft Rd LEW SE13 .... 133 H4
Chaldon Rd FUL/PGN SW6 .... 107 H6
Chale Rd BRXS/STRHM SW2 .... 129 K5
Chalet Cl BXLY DA5 .... 137 K5
Chalet Est MLHL NW7 .... 37 J3
Chalfont Av WBLY HA9 .... 68 C5
Chalfont Gn ED N9 .... 42 A2
Chalfont Ms
  WAND/EARL SW18 * 127 J7
  HYS/HAR UB3 .... 101 K1
  SNWD SE25 .... 165 G2
Chalfont Wk PIN HA5 .... 47 G1
Chalfont Wy WEA W13 .... 104 C2
Chalford Cl E/WMO/HCT KT8 .... 157 G3
Chalforde Gdns GPK RM2 .... 63 K2
Chalford Rd DUL SE21 .... 149 K5
Chalford Wk WFD IG8 .... 45 H7
Chalgrove Av MRDN SM4 .... 161 K4
Chalgrove Crs CLAY IG5 .... 59 J2
Chalgrove Gdns FNCH N3 .... 52 C2
Chalgrove Rd BELMT SM2 .... 175 H6
  HOM E9 .... 74 C5
  TOTM N17 .... 42 D7
Chalice Cl WLGTN SM6 .... 176 D5
Chalkenden Cl PGE/AN SE20 .... 150 D6
Chalk Farm Pde HAMP NW3 * 4 A1
Chalk Farm Rd CAMTN NW1 .... 4 A1
Chalk Hill OXHEY WD19 .... 21 J5
Chalk Hill Rd HMSMTH W6 .... 107 G3
Chalkhill Rd WBLY HA9 .... 68 C2
Chalklands WBLY HA9 .... 68 E3
Chalk La EBAR EN4 .... 27 K2

Chalkley Cl MTCM CR4 .... 162 E1
Chalkmill Dr EN EN1 .... 30 D2
Chalk Pit Rd SUT SM1 .... 175 G6
Chalk Rd PLSTW E13 .... 95 F4
Chalkstone Cl WELL DA16 .... 116 B7
Chalkwell Park Av EN EN1 .... 30 A3
Chalky La CHSGTN KT9 .... 171 K7
Challenge Cl WLSDN NW10 .... 69 G6
Challenge Rd ASHF TW15 .... 140 A3
Challice Wy BRXS/STRHM SW2 .... 130 A7
Challin St PGE/AN SE20 .... 150 E7
Challis Rd BTFD TW8 .... 104 E4
Challoner Crs WKENS W14 .... 107 J4
Challoners Cl E/WMO/HCT KT8 .... 157 J3
Challoner St WKENS W14 .... 107 J4
Chalmers Wk WALW SE17 * 110 C5
Chalmers Wy EBED/NFELT TW14 .... 122 A4
  TWK TW1 .... 124 C3
Chalsey Rd BROCKY SE4 .... 132 C3
Chalton Dr EFNCH N2 .... 53 G5
Chalton St CAMTN NW1 .... 5 G5
Chamberlain Cl IL IG1 .... 78 C2
  THMD SE28 .... 115 J2
Chamberlain Cots
  CMBW SE5 * 110 E7
Chamberlain Crs WWKM BR4 .... 166 E7
Chamberlain Gdns HSLW TW3 .... 103 H7
Chamberlain La PIN HA5 .... 46 E3
Chamberlain Pl WALTH E17 .... 57 G2
Chamberlain Rd EFNCH N2 .... 53 G1
  WEA W13 .... 104 B1
Chamberlain St HAMP NW3 * 3 A1
Chamberlain Wy PIN HA5 .... 47 F2
  SURB KT6 .... 159 F6
Chamberlayne Av WBLY HA9 .... 68 A2
Chamberlayne Rd
  WLSDN NW10 .... 70 A7
Chamberlens Garages
  HMSMTH W6 * 106 E3
Chambers Gdns EFNCH N2 .... 39 H7
Chambers La WLSDN NW10 .... 69 K6
Chambers Pl SAND/SEL CR2 * 177 K6
Chambers Rd HOLWY N7 .... 72 E3
Chambers St
  BERM/RHTH SE16 .... 111 H1
Chamber St WCHPL E1 .... 13 M6
Chambon Pl HMSMTH W6 .... 106 D3
Chambord St BETH E2 .... 7 M8
Champa Cl TOTM N17 .... 56 B1
Champion Crs SYD SE26 .... 151 G3
Champion Gv CMBW SE5 .... 130 E2
Champion HI CMBW SE5 .... 130 E2
Champion Pk CMBW SE5 .... 130 E2
Champion Rd SYD SE26 .... 151 G3
Champness Cl WNWD SE27 * 149 K3
Champness Rd BARK IG11 .... 79 F6
Champneys Cl BELMT SM2 .... 174 D6
Champneys OXHEY WD19 .... 33 J1
Chancellor Gv DUL SE21 .... 149 J1
Chancellor Pl CDALE/KGS NW9 .... 51 H1
Chancellors Rd HMSMTH W6 .... 107 F4
Chancellors St HMSMTH W6 .... 107 F4
Chancellor Whf HMSMTH W6 * 107 F5
Chancelot Rd ABYW SE2 .... 116 C3
Chancel St STHWK SE1 .... 12 C8
Chancery La BECK BR3 .... 166 E1
  LINN WC2A 11 M3
Chance St BETH E2 .... 7 L9
Chanctonbury Cl
  ELTH/MOT SE9 .... 154 B2
Chanctonbury Gdns
  BELMT SM2 .... 175 F6
Chanctonbury Wy
  NFNCH/WDSPK N12 .... 38 E3
Chandler Av CAN/RD E16 .... 94 E4
Chandler Cl HPTN TW12 .... 141 K7
Chandlers Av GNWCH SE10 .... 113 J2
Chandlers Cl E/WMO/HCT KT8 * 156 C2
  EBED/NFELT TW14 .... 121 J6
Chandlers Dr ERITH DA8 .... 118 A3
Chandlers Ms POP/IOD E14 .... 112 D1
Chandlers Wy ROM RM1 .... 63 G4
Chandler Wy PECK SE15 .... 111 G6
  DAGE RM10 .... 81 F5
  FSTGT E7 .... 77 F6
  WEA W13 .... 85 G5
  WIM/MER SW19 .... 146 E7
Chandos Av EA W5 .... 104 D3
  STHGT/OAK N14 .... 40 C2
  TRDG/WHET N20 .... 27 H2
  WALTH E17 * 57 J1
Chandos Cl BKHH IG9 .... 45 F1
Chandos Ct STAN HA7 .... 35 H5
Chandos Crs EDGW HA8 .... 36 B6
Chandos Pl CHCR WC2N 11 J7
Chandos Rd BORE WD6 .... 24 B1
  CRICK NW2 .... 70 A4
  EFNCH N2 .... 53 H1
  HRW HA1 .... 48 C4
  PIN HA5 .... 47 G6
  SRTFD E15 .... 76 B4
  TOTM N17 .... 42 A1
  WLSDN NW10 .... 87 G3
Chandos St CAVSQ/HST W1G 10 D3
Chandos Wy GLDGN NW11 .... 53 F7
Channel Cl HEST TW5 .... 103 F7
Channel Gate Rd NKENS W10 * 88 A4
  WLSDN NW10 .... 87 G2
Channel Islands Est IS N1 .... 73 K5
Channelsea Rd SRTFD E15 .... 76 B7
Chantress Cl DAGE RM10 .... 80 E7
Chantrey Rd BRXN/ST SW9 .... 130 A2
Chantry Cl ABYW SE2 .... 116 D2
  KTN/HRWW/WS HA3 .... 50 B4
  MLHL NW7 .... 25 H7
  MV/WKIL W9 .... 88 D3
  SUN TW16 .... 140 D7
Chantry Crs WLSDN NW10 .... 69 G4
Chantry La HAYES BR2 .... 168 C4
Chantry Pl
  KTN/HRWW/WS HA3 .... 34 B7
Chantry Rd CHSGTN KT9 .... 172 B4
  KTN/HRWW/WS HA3 .... 34 B7
Chantry Sq KENS W8 * 14 C4
Chantry St IS N1 .... 6 C4
Chantry Wy MTCM CR4 .... 162 C2
  RAIN RM13 .... 99 F1
Chant Sq SRTFD E15 .... 76 B6
Chant St SRTFD E15 .... 76 B6
Chapel Av DART DA1 .... 138 D4
  WLSDN NW10 .... 69 H4
Chapel Cl DART DA1 .... 138 B3
Chapel Farm Rd
  ELTH/MOT SE9 .... 153 K2
Chapel HI DART DA1 .... 138 B3
Chapel House St POP/IOD E14 .... 112 E4
Chapel La CHDH RM6 .... 61 K6
  PIN HA5 .... 47 H2

Chapel Market IS N1 .... 6 A5
Chapel Mill Rd KUT/HW KT1 .... 159 G2
Chapel Pl CAVSQ/HST W1G 10 C3
  IS N1 .... 6 B5
  TOTM N17 .... 42 B6
Chapel Rd BXLYHN DA7 .... 137 H3
  HSLW TW3 .... 123 G2
  IL IG1 .... 78 A2
  TWK TW1 .... 124 C6
  WEA W13 .... 85 H7
  WNWD SE27 .... 149 H3
Chapel Side BAY/PAD W2 .... 8 C6
Chapel St BAY/PAD W2 .... 9 J3
  ENC/FH EN2 .... 29 J2
  KTBR SW1X 16 B3
Chapel Vw SAND/SEL CR2 .... 178 E6
Chaplemount Rd WFD IG8 .... 45 K5
Chaplin Cl ALP/SUD HA0 .... 67 K5
  STHWK SE1 .... 18 B1
Chaplin Crs SUN TW16 .... 140 C5
Chaplin Rd ALP/SUD HA0 .... 67 J5
  CRICK NW2 .... 69 J5
  SRTFD E15 .... 94 C1
  TOTM N17 .... 56 B2
  WBLY HA9 .... 67 K4
Chapman Crs KTN/HRWW/WS HA3 .... 50 A4
Chapman Rd BELV DA17 .... 117 H4
  CROY/NA CRO 164 B7
  HOM E9 .... 75 H5
Chapmans Gn WDGN N22 .... 41 F1
Chapman Sq WIM/MER SW19 .... 146 B1
Chapman St WCHPL E1 .... 92 D6
Chapman Ter WDGN N22 * 41 H7
Chapter Cl CHSWK W4 .... 105 K2
Chapter Rd CRICK NW2 .... 69 J4
  WALW SE17 .... 18 D8
Chapter St WEST SW1P 17 G6
Chapter Wy HPTN TW12 .... 142 A3
  WIM/MER SW19 .... 147 H7
Chara Pl CHSWK W4 .... 106 A5
Charcroft Gdns PEND EN3 .... 31 F3
Chardin Rd CHSWK W4 * 106 B3
Chardmore Rd
  STNW/STAM N16 .... 56 C7
Chardwell Cl EHAM E6 .... 95 J5
Charecroft Wy WKENS W14 .... 107 G1
Charford Rd CAN/RD E16 .... 94 E4
Chargeable La PLSTW E13 .... 94 D3
Chargeable St CAN/RD E16 .... 94 D3
Chargrove Cl
  BERM/RHTH SE16 .... 112 A1
Charing Cross CHCR WC2N * 11 J8
Charing Cross Rd
  LSQ/SEVD WC2H 11 H6
Chariot Cl BOW E3 .... 75 J7
Charlbert St STJWD NW8 .... 3 J6
Charlbury Av STAN HA7 .... 35 K4
Charlbury Gdns
  GDMY/SEVK IG3 .... 79 F1
Charlbury Gv EA W5 .... 85 J5
Charldane Rd ELTH/MOT SE9 .... 154 D2
Charlecote Gv SYD SE26 .... 150 D2
Charlecote Rd BCTR RM8 .... 80 A2
Charlemont Rd EHAM E6 .... 95 K2
Charles Babbage Cl
  CHSGTN KT9 .... 171 J6
Charles Barry Cl CLAP SW4 .... 129 H2
Charles Cl SCUP DA14 .... 155 H3
Charles Cobb Gdns
  CROY/NA CRO 177 G4
Charles Coveney Rd
  CMBW SE5 .... 111 G7
Charles Dickens Ter
  PGE/AN SE20 * 150 E6
Charlesfield ELTH/MOT SE9 .... 153 G2
Charles Flemwell Ms
  CAN/RD E16 * 94 E7
Charles Grinling Wk
  WOOL/PLUM SE18 .... 115 F3
Charles Haller St
  BRXS/STRHM SW2 .... 130 B6
Charles II St STJS SW1Y 15 K8
Charles La STJWD NW8 .... 3 J6
Charles Pl CAMTN NW1 * 4 F8
Charles Rd CHDH RM6 .... 61 K6
  DAGE RM10 .... 81 F5
  FSTGT E7 .... 77 G6
  WEA W13 .... 85 G5
  WIM/MER SW19 .... 146 E7
Charles Sevright Dr
  MLHL NW7 .... 38 B4
Charles Sq IS N1 .... 7 H8
Charles Square Est IS N1 .... 7 H8
Charles St BARN SW13 .... 126 B2
  CAN/RD E16 .... 95 G7
  CROY/NA CRO 177 J2
  EN EN1 .... 30 B4
  HSLW TW3 .... 122 E1
  MYFR/PICC W1J 10 C8
Charleston Cl FELT TW13 .... 140 E2
Charleston St WALW SE17 .... 18 F6
Charles Whincup Rd
  CAN/RD E16 .... 95 F7
Charleville Circ SYD SE26 .... 150 C4
Charleville Rd WKENS W14 .... 107 H4
Charlieville Rd ERITH DA8 .... 117 K6
Charlmont Rd TOOT SW17 .... 147 J5
Charlock Wy WATW WD18 .... 20 D5
Charlotte Cl BXLYHS DA6 .... 137 F4
  OXHEY WD19 .... 21 G6
Charlotte Despard Av
  BTSEA SW11 .... 109 G7
Charlotte Ms ESH/CLAY KT10 * 170 B3
  FITZ W1T 10 F2
  NKENS W10 .... 88 B5
  WKENS W14 .... 107 H3
Charlotte Pde FSTH SE23 * 151 G1
Charlotte Park Av BMLY BR1 .... 168 D2
Charlotte Pl FITZ W1T 10 F2
  SDTCH EC2A 7 J8
  WLGTN SM6 .... 176 C5
Charlotte Rd BARN SW13 .... 126 C1
  DAGE RM10 .... 80 D5
  SDTCH EC2A 7 J8
  WLGTN SM6 .... 176 C5
Charlotte Rw CLAP SW4 .... 129 H2
Charlotte St FITZ W1T 10 F2
Charlotte Ter IS N1 .... 5 M4
Charlow Cl FUL/PGN SW6 .... 128 B1
Charlton Church La
  CHARL SE7 .... 114 B4
Charlton Crs BARK IG11 .... 97 F1
Charlton Dene CHARL SE7 .... 114 B6
Charlton King's Rd KTTN NW5 .... 72 D4
Charlton La CHARL SE7 .... 114 C4
Charlton Park La CHARL SE7 .... 114 C6
Charlton Park Rd CHARL SE7 .... 114 C5
Charlton Pl IS N1 .... 6 C5
Charlton Rd BKHTH/KID SE3 .... 114 A6
  CHARL SE7 .... 114 B5
  ED N9 .... 31 F7

  KTN/HRWW/WS HA3 .... 49 K3
  WBLY HA9 .... 50 B3
  WLSDN NW10 .... 69 G7
Charlton Wy BKHTH/KID SE3 .... 113 J6
  GNWCH SE10 .... 113 H7
Charlwood CROY/NA CRO 179 K7
Charlwood Cl
  KTN/HRWW/WS HA3 .... 34 E6
Charlwood Pl PIM SW1V 16 F6
Charlwood Rd PUT/ROE SW15 .... 127 G2
Charlwood St PIM SW1V 16 F6
  PIM SW1V 16 F6
Charlwood Ter
  PUT/ROE SW15 * 127 G3
Charmian Av STAN HA7 .... 49 K2
Charminster Av
  WIM/MER SW19 .... 147 K1
Charminster Rd
  ELTH/MOT SE9 .... 153 G7
  WPK KT4 .... 161 G7
Charmouth Rd WELL DA16 .... 116 D1
Charnock Rd CLPT E5 .... 74 D2
Charnwood Av
  WIM/MER SW19 .... 161 K1
Charnwood Cl NWMAL KT3 .... 160 B3
Charnwood Dr SWFD E18 .... 59 F2
Charnwood Gdns
  POP/IOD E14 .... 112 D3
Charnwood Pl
  TRDG/WHET N20 .... 39 G2
Charnwood Rd SNWD SE25 .... 164 E4
Charnwood St CLPT E5 * 74 C1
Charnwood Vls SWFD E18 .... 59 F2
Charrington Rd CROY/NA CRO * 177 H1
Charrington St CAMTN NW1 .... 5 G5
Charsley Rd CAT SE6 .... 151 K1
Chart Cl CROY/NA CRO 165 K5
  HAYES BR2 .... 167 J3
  MTCM CR4 .... 162 E3
Charter Av GNTH/NBYPK IG2 .... 60 D7
Charter Crs HSLWW TW4 .... 122 D3
Charter Dr BXLY DA5 .... 137 F6
Charterhouse Av
  ALP/SUD HA0 .... 67 J3
Charterhouse Blds
  FARR EC1M 12 E1
Charterhouse Ms FARR EC1M 12 E2
Charterhouse Sq FARR EC1M 12 E2
Charterhouse St HCIRC EC1N 12 B3
The Charterhouse
  FARR EC1M * 12 E1
Charteris Rd FSBYPK N4 .... 55 F7
  KIL/WHAMP NW6 .... 70 D7
  WFD IG8 .... 45 F5
Charter Pl WAT WD17 * 21 F3
Charter Rd KUT/HW KT1 .... 159 J2
The Charter Rd WFD IG8 .... 44 C5
Charters Cl NRWD SE19 .... 150 A4
Charter Sq KUT/HW KT1 .... 159 J1
Charter Wy FNCH N3 .... 52 D3
  STHGT/OAK N14 .... 40 B5
Chartfield Av PUT/ROE SW15 .... 126 E4
Chartfield Sq PUT/ROE SW15 .... 127 G4
Chartham Gv WNWD SE27 * 149 G2
Chartham Rd SNWD SE25 .... 165 J2
Chart Hills Cl THMD SE28 * 98 A5
Chartley Av CRICK NW2 .... 69 G2
  STAN HA7 .... 35 F5
Chartley Pde CRICK NW2 * 69 G2
Charton Cl BELV DA17 .... 117 G5
Chartridge OXHEY WD19 * 33 H1
Chartridge Cl BAR EN5 .... 25 J4
  BUSH WD23 .... 22 C5
Chart St IS N1 .... 7 H7
Chartwell Cl CROY/NA CRO 164 E7
  ELTH/MOT SE9 .... 154 D1
  GFD/PVL UB6 .... 66 D1
Chartwell Ct NTHWD HA6 * 32 D2
Chartwell Gdns CHEAM SM3 .... 174 C2
Chartwell Pl CHEAM SM3 .... 174 C3
  RYLN/HDSTN HA2 .... 66 D1
Chartwell Wy PGE/AN SE20 .... 150 D7
Charville La HGDN/ICK UB10 .... 82 A2
Charwood STRHM/NOR SW16 .... 149 G3
Chase Ct RYNPK SW20 .... 161 H1
Chase Court Gdns
  ENC/FH EN2 .... 29 J2
Chasefield Rd TOOT SW17 .... 147 K3
Chase Gdns CHING E4 .... 43 J3
  WHTN TW2 .... 123 J5
Chase Gn ENC/FH EN2 .... 29 J2
Chase Green Av ENC/FH EN2 .... 29 H1
Chase HI ENC/FH EN2 .... 29 J2
Chase La BARK/HLT IG6 .... 60 D4
Chaseley Ct CHSWK W4 * 105 J4
Chaseley St POP/IOD E14 .... 93 G5
Chasemore Gdns
  CROY/NA CRO 177 G4
Chase Ridings ENC/FH EN2 .... 29 G1
Chase Rd ACT W3 .... 87 F3
  STHGT/OAK N14 .... 28 D7
Chase Side STHGT/OAK N14 .... 28 A5
Chase Side Av ENC/FH EN2 .... 29 J1
  RYNPK SW20 .... 146 C7
Chase Side Pl ENC/FH EN2 .... 29 J1
The Chase BMLY BR1 .... 168 A2
  BXLYHN DA7 .... 137 J2
  CLAP SW4 .... 129 G2
  EDGW HA8 .... 77 H3
  FSTGT E7 .... 77 H3
  PIN HA5 .... 47 K3
  ROM RM1 .... 63 G2
  ROMW/RG RM7 .... 81 F1
  STAN HA7 .... 35 G5
  STRHM/NOR SW16 .... 149 F6
  SUN TW16 .... 141 F7
  WATW WD18 .... 20 E4
  WLGTN SM6 .... 176 E4
Chaseville Park Rd
  WCHMH N21 .... 28 E4
Chase Wy STHGT/OAK N14 .... 28 B7
Chasewood Av ENC/FH EN2 .... 29 H1
Chasewood Pk HRW HA1 * 66 E1
Chastilian Rd DART DA1 .... 138 D6
Chatfield Rd BTSEA SW11 .... 128 B2
  CROY/NA CRO 164 C7
Chatham Av HAYES BR2 .... 167 J6
Chatham Cl CHEAM SM3 .... 161 J6
  GLDGN NW11 .... 52 E5
Chatham Pl HOM E9 .... 74 E5
Chatham Rd BTSEA SW11 .... 128 E5
  KUT/HW KT1 .... 159 H1
  SWFD E18 .... 58 D1
  WALTH E17 .... 57 G2
Chatham St WALW SE17 .... 19 G5
  WOOL/PLUM SE18 .... 115 G2
Chatsfield Pl EA W5 .... 86 A3
Chatsworth Av BFN/LL DA15 .... 136 B7

BMLY BR1...153 F4
HDN NW4...52 A1
RYNPK SW20...146 C2
WBLY HA9...68 B4
Chatsworth Cl *BORE* WD6...24 C2
CHSWK W4 *...105 K5
HDN NW4...52 A1
WWKM BR4...180 D1
Chatsworth Dr *EN* EN1...30 C6
Chatsworth Est *CLPT* E5 *...75 F3
Chatsworth Gdns *ACT* W3...86 D6
NWMAL KT3...160 C4
RYLN/HDSTN HA2...48 B7
Chatsworth Pl *MTCM* CR4...162 E2
TEDD TW11...143 G3
Chatsworth Ri *EA* W5...86 A4
Chatsworth Rd *CHEAM* SM3...174 B3
CHSWK W4...105 K5
CLPT E5...74 E2
CRICK NW2...70 B5
CROY/NA CR0...177 K3
DART DA1...139 F3
EA W5...86 A3
SRTFD E15...76 D4
YEAD UB4...83 F5
Chatsworth Wy *WNWD* SE27...149 H2
Chattern Rd *ASHF* TW15...140 A3...
Chatterton Ms *FSBYPK* N4...73 H2
Chatterton Rd *FSBYPK* N4...73 H2
HAYES BR2...168 C4
Chatto Rd *BTSEA* SW11...128 E4
Chaucer Av *HSLWW* TW4...122 A1
RCH/KEW TW9...125 H1
YEAD UB4...82 A5
Chaucer Cl *FBAR/BDGN* N11...40 C4
Chaucer Dr *STHWK* SE1...19 M6
Chaucer Gdns *SUT* SM1...174 E2
Chaucer Gn *CROY/NA* CR0...165 J6
Chaucer Gv *BORE* WD6...24 C3
Chaucer Pk *DART* DA1...139 F3
Chaucer Rd *ACT* W3...86 E7
BFN/LL DA15...136 D7
FSTGT E7...76 E5
HNHL SE24...130 B4
SUT SM1...174 E3
WALTH E17...44 A7
WAN E11...58 E5
WELL DA16...116 A7
Chaucer Wy *DART* DA1...139 K3
WIM/MER SW19...147 H5
Chauncey Cl *ED* N9...42 C2
Chaundrye Cl *ELTH/MOT* SE9...134 E5
Chauntler Rd *CAN/RD* E16...95 F6
Cheam Common Rd *WPK* KT4...173 K1
Cheam Man *CHEAM* SM3 *...174 C5
Cheam Park Wy *CHEAM* SM3...174 B5
Cheam Rd *BELMT* SM2...174 B7
Cheam St *PECK* SE15 *...131 J2
Cheapside *CITYW* EC2V *...12 F5
EFNCH N2 *...53 K2
PLMGR N13...41 J3
WDGN N22 *...55 C2
Cheddar Cl *FBAR/BDGN* N11...39 K5
Cheddar Waye *YEAD* UB4...83 F5
Cheddington Rd *UED* N18...42 A3
Cheeseman Cl *HPTN* TW12...141 J5
Cheesemans Ter *WKENS* W14 *...107 J4
Cheethams Rd *MNPK* E12...77 J2
Chelford Rd *BMLY* BR1...152 B4
Chelmer Crs *BARK* IG11...97 H1
Chelmer Rd *HOM* E9...75 F4
Chelmsford Cl *BELMT* SM2...174 E7
EHAM E6...95 K5
HMSMTH W6...107 G5
Chelmsford Gdns *IL* IG1...59 J6
Chelmsford Rd
STHGT/OAK N14...28 C6
SWFD E18...44 D7
WALTH E17...57 J5
WAN E11...58 C7
Chelmsford Sq *WLSDN* NW10...70 A7
Chelsea Br *BGVA* SW1W...16 B9
Chelsea Bridge Ga *VX/NE* SW8...109 F5
Chelsea Bridge Rd
BGVA SW1W...16 A7
Chelsea Cl *EDGW* HA8...50 C1
HPTN TW12...142 C4
WLSDN NW10...69 F7
WPK KT4...160 D6
Chelsea Crs *CRICK* NW2 *...70 D5
WBPTN SW10 *...108 B7
Chelsea Emb *CHEL* SW3...16 A9
Chelsea Gdns *CHEAM* SM3...174 C3
WEA W13...85 F4
Chelsea Harbour Dr
WBPTN SW10...108 B7
Chelsea Manor Gdns
CHEL SW3...15 J9
Chelsea Manor St *CHEL* SW3...15 J9
Chelsea Ms *EMPK* RM11...63 K7
Chelsea Park Gdns *CHEL* SW3...15 G9
Chelsea Sq *CAR* SM5...175 K7
CHEL SW3...15 H8
Chelsea Village
FUL/PGN SW6 *...108 A6
Chelsfield Av *ED* N9...31 F6
Chelsfield Gdns *SYD* SE26...150 E2
Chelsham Rd *CLAP* SW4...129 J2
SAND/SEL CR2...177 K6
Chelston Rd *RSLP* HA4...64 E1
Chelsworth Dr
WOOL/PLUM SE18...115 J5
Cheltenham Av *TWK* TW1...124 B6
Cheltenham Cl *NTHLT* UB5...66 B5
NWMAL KT3...159 K2
Cheltenham Gdns *EHAM* E6...95 J1
Cheltenham Pl *ACT* W3...105 K1
KTN/HRWW/WS HA3...50 A3
Cheltenham Rd *LEY* E10...58 A4
PECK SE15...131 K3
Cheltenham Ter *CHEL* SW3...15 M7
Chelton Av *MLHL* NW7...38 A1
Chelverton Rd *PUT/ROE* SW15...127 H4
Chelwood Cl *CHING* E4...31 K5
NTHWD HA6...32 A4
Chelwood Gdns
RCH/KEW TW9...125 H1
Chenappa Cl *PLSTW* E13...94 E2
Chenduit Wy *STAN* HA7...35 F4
Cheney Rw *WALTH* E17...43 H7
Cheneys Rd *WAN* E11...76 C2
Cheney St *PIN* HA5...47 G3
Chenies Ms *GWRST* WC1E...11 G1
Chenies Pl *BAR* EN5...25 J4
CAMTN NW1...5 H1
The Chenies *ORP* BR6...169 K6
Chenies Wy *WATW* WD18...20 C6
Cheniston Gdns *KENS* W8...14 C3
Chepstow Cl *PUT/ROE* SW15...127 H4
Chepstow Cnr *BAY/PAD* W2 *...8 C5
Chepstow Crs *GDMY/SEVK* IG3...60 E5

NTGHL W11...8 A6
Chepstow Pl *STHL* UB1...83 K5
Chepstow Pl *BAY/PAD* W2...8 C5
Chepstow Ri *CROY/NA* CR0...178 A2
Chepstow Rd *BAY/PAD* W2...8 B4
CROY/NA CR0...178 A2
HNWL W7...104 B2
Chepstow Vls *NTGHL* W11...88 D3
Chequers Cl *CDALE/KGS* NW9...51 G2
Chequers La *DAGW* RM9...98 B3
Chequers Pde *PLMGR* N13 *...41 H4
The Chequers *PIN* HA5 *...47 H2
Chequer St *STLK* EC1Y...12 F1
Chequers Wy *PLMGR* N13...41 H4
Cherbury Cl *THMD* SE28...97 K5
Cherbury St *IS* N1...7 H4
Cherimoya Gdns
E/WMO/HCT KT8...157 G2
Cherington Rd *HNWL* W7 *...85 F7
Cheriton Av *CLAY* IG5...60 A1
HAYES BR2...167 J4
Cheriton Cl *EA* W5...85 J3
EBAR EN4...27 K2
Cheriton Dr *WOT/HER* KT12...156 B2
Cheriton Sq *TOOT* SW17...148 A1
Cherry Av *STHL* UB1...83 H7
Cherry Blossom Cl
PLMGR N13...41 H4
Cherry Cl *BRXS/STRHM* SW2 *...130 B4
CAR SM5...175 K1
CDALE/KGS NW9...51 H1
EA W5...104 D2
MRDN SM4...161 H3
RSLP HA4...64 D2
Cherry Crs *BTFD* TW8...104 C6
Cherry Ct *PIN* HA5...33 H7
Cherry Croft Gdns *PIN* HA5 *...33 K6
Cherrydale *WATW* WD18...20 D3
Cherrydown Av *CHING* E4...43 H2
Cherrydown Cl *CHING* E4...43 H2
Cherrydown Rd *SCUP* DA14...155 K1
Cherrydown Wk
ROMW/RG RM7...62 D1
Cherry Gdns *DAGW* RM9...80 B4
NTHLT UB5...66 B6
Cherry Garden St
BERM/RHTH SE16...111 J1
Cherry Garth *BTFD* TW8...104 E3
Cherry Gv *HYS/HAR* UB3...83 F7
UX/CGN UB8...82 A4
Cherry Hl *BAR* EN5...27 F5
KTN/HRWW/WS HA3...34 E5
Cherry Hill Gdns
CROY/NA CR0...177 F3
Cherry Hills *OXHEY* WD19...33 J4
Cherrylands Cl
CDALE/KGS NW9 *...68 E1
Cherry La *WDR/YW* UB7...100 C3
Cherry Orch *CHARL* SE7...114 B5
WDR/YW UB7...100 C3
Cherry Orchard Gdns
CROY/NA CR0...164 E7
E/WMO/HCT KT8...156 E2
Cherry Orchard Rd
CROY/NA CR0...164 E7
E/WMO/HCT KT8...157 G2
HAYES BR2...181 J1
Cherry Rd *ROMW/RG* RM7...63 F4
Cherry Tree Cl *ALP/SUD* HA0...67 G3
HOM E9...74 E7
RAIN RM13...99 J1
Cherry Tree Ct *CHARL* SE7...114 B5
Cherry Tree Dr
STRHM/NOR SW16...148 E2
Cherry Tree Hl *EFNCH* N2...53 J4
Cherry Tree La *RAIN* RM13...99 G2
Cherry Tree Rd *EFNCH* N2...53 K3
SRTFD E15...76 C4
Cherry Tree Wk *BECK* BR3...166 C3
STLK EC1Y...12 F1
WWKM BR4...180 E3
Cherry Tree Wy *PLSTW* E13...95 H3
STAN HA7...35 H5
Cherry Wk *HAYES* BR2...167 K7
RAIN RM13...99 H1
Cherry Wy *HOR/WEW* KT19...173 F5
Cherrywood Cl *BOW* E3...93 G2
KUTN/CMB KT2...144 C6
Cherrywood Dr
PUT/ROE SW15...127 G4
Cherrywood La *RYNPK* SW20...161 H1
Chertsey Dr *CHEAM* SM3...174 C1
Chertsey Rd *FELT* TW13...140 C3
IL IG1...78 D3
SUN TW16...140 C5
TWK TW1...124 B5
WAN E11...76 B1
WHTN TW2...123 H7
Chertsey St *TOOT* SW17...148 A4
Chervil Cl *FELT* TW13...140 E2
Chervil Ms *THMD* SE28...97 H7
Cherwell Ct *HOR/WEW* KT19...172 E5
Cherwell Wy *RSLP* HA4...46 A4
Cheryls Cl *FUL/PGN* SW6...108 A7
Cheseman St *SYD* SE26...150 D2
Chesfield Rd *KUTN/CMB* KT2...144 A6
Chesham Av *STMC/STPC* BR5...169 G5
Chesham Cl *KTBR* SW1X *...16 A3
ROMW/RG RM7...63 F3
Chesham Crs *PGE/AN* SE20...150 E7
Chesham Ms *KTBR* SW1X...16 A3
Chesham Pl *KTBR* SW1X...16 A3
PGE/AN SE20...165 K1
WIM/MER SW19...147 H5
Chesham St *KTBR* SW1X...16 A4
WLSDN NW10...69 F2
Chesham Ter *WEA* W13...104 C1
Chesham Wy *WATW* WD18...20 C5
Cheshire Cl *MTCM* CR4...163 K2
WALTH E17...43 K7
Cheshire Gdns *CHSGTN* KT9...171 K5
Cheshire Rd *WDGN* N22...41 F6
Cheshire St *BETH* E2...92 C3
Chesholm Rd
STNW/STAM N16...74 A2
Cheshunt Rd *BELV* DA17...117 H4
FSTGT E7...77 F5
Chesilton Rd *FUL/PGN* SW6...107 J7
Chesil Wy *YEAD* UB4...82 D2
Chesley Gdns *EHAM* E6...95 H1
Chesney Crs *CROY/NA* CR0...180 A6
Chesney St *BTSEA* SW11...109 F7
Chesnut Av North *WALTH* E17...58 A3
Chesnut Gv *TOTM* N17...56 B2
Chesnut Rd *TOTM* N17...56 B2
Chesnut Rw *FNCH* N3 *...38 E6
Chessell Cl *THHTH* CR7...164 C3
Chessholme Rd *ASHF* TW15...140 A5
Chessington Av *BXLYHN* DA7...117 F6
FNCH N3...52 C2

Chessington Cl
HOR/WEW KT19...172 E5
Chessington Ct *PIN* HA5...47 K3
Chessington Hall Gdns
CHSGTN KT9...171 K6
Chessington Hill Pk
CHSGTN KT9...172 C5
Chessington Pde
CHSGTN KT9 *...171 K4
Chessington Rd *CHSGTN* KT9...172 C5
HOR/WEW KT19...172 D5
Chessington Wy *WWKM* BR4...179 K1
Chesson Rd *WKENS* W14...107 J5
Chesswood Wy *PIN* HA5...47 H1
Chester Av *RCHPK/HAM* TW10...125 G5
WHTN TW2...122 E7
Chester Cl *ASHF* TW15...140 B4
BARN SW13...126 E2
KTBR SW1X...16 B2
SUT SM1...174 E1
Chester Cl North *CAMTN* NW1...4 D7
Chester Cl South *CAMTN* NW1...4 D8
Chester Crs *HACK* E8...74 B4
Chester Dr *RYLN/HDSTN* HA2...48 A5
Chesterfield Dr *DART* DA1...138 E4
ESH/CLAY KT10...171 G1
Chesterfield Gdns *FSBYPK* N4...55 H4
GNWCH SE10 *...113 G6
MYFR/PICC W1J *...10 C7
Chesterfield Gv *EDUL* SE22...131 G4
Chesterfield Hl
MYFR/PKLN W1K...10 C7
Chesterfield Ms *FSBYPK* N4...55 H4
Chesterfield Rd *BAR* EN5...26 B4
CHSWK W4...105 K5
FNCH N3...38 E5
HOR/WEW KT19...173 F6
LEY E10...58 A4
Chesterfield St
MYFR/PICC W1J...10 C7
Chesterfield Wy
HYS/HAR UB3...101 K1
PECK SE15...111 K6
Chesterford Gdns *HAMP* NW3...71 F3
Chesterford Rd *MNPK* E12...77 K4
Chester Gdns *MRDN* SM4...162 B4
PEND EN3...30 D5
WEA W13...85 H5
Chester Ga *CAMTN* NW1...4 C8
Chester Ms *KTBR* SW1X...16 C3
Chester Pl *CAMTN* NW1...4 C7
NTHWD HA6...32 D6
Chester Rd *ARCH* N19...72 B1
BFN/LL DA15...135 K6
BORE WD6...24 C2
CAMTN NW1...4 B8
CAN/RD E16...94 C3
ED N9...30 D7
FSTGT E7...77 H6
GDMY/SEVK IG3...61 F7
HSLWW TW4...122 A2
HTHAIR TW6...120 B3
NTHWD HA6...32 D6
TOTM N17...55 K1
WALTH E17...57 F4
WAN E11...59 F5
WATW WD18...20 E4
WIM/MER SW19...146 A5
Chester Rw *BGVA* SW1W...16 A6
Chester Sq *BGVA* SW1W...16 B5
Chester Square Ms
BGVA SW1W *...16 C4
The Chesters *NWMAL* KT3...145 F7
Chester St *BETH* E2...92 C3
KTBR SW1X...16 B3
Chester Ter *CAMTN* NW1...4 C7
Chesthunte Rd *TOTM* N17...41 J7
Chestnut Aly *FUL/PGN* SW6 *...107 J5
Chestnut Av *ALP/SUD* HA0...67 H4
BKHH IG9...45 H2
BTFD TW8...104 E3
CEND/HSY/T N8...54 E4
E/WMO/HCT KT8...158 A2
EDGW HA8...36 A5
ESH/CLAY KT10...157 J2
FSTGT E7...77 F3
HCH RM12...81 H1
HOR/WEW KT19...173 G3
HPTN TW12...142 A7
MNPK E12...77 J1
MORT/ESHN SW14...126 A2
NTHWD HA6...46 D1
TEDD TW11...143 F6
WWKM BR4...180 C4
Chestnut Av South
WALTH E17...58 A3
Chestnut Cl *BFN/LL* DA15...155 G1
BKHH IG9...45 H2
CAR SM5...162 E7
CAT SE6...152 A3
HYS/HAR UB3...82 C6
HYS/HAR UB3...101 H5
NWCR SE14...112 C7
STHGT/OAK N14...28 C4
STNW/STAM N16...73 K1
STRHM/NOR SW16...149 G3
SUN TW16...140 D5
Chestnut Cots
TRDG/WHET N20 *...26 C7
Chestnut Dr *BXLYHN* DA7...136 E2
KTN/HRWW/WS HA3...35 H6
PIN HA5...47 H5
WAN E11...58 E5
Chestnut Gln *HCH* RM12...81 H1
Chestnut Gv *ALP/SUD* HA0...67 H4
BAL SW12...129 F6
EA W5...104 E2
EBAR EN4...27 K4
ISLW TW7...124 B3
MTCM CR4...163 H4
NWMAL KT3...160 A2
SAND/SEL CR2...178 D6
Chestnut La *TRDG/WHET* N20...26 A7
Chestnut Ms *WFD* IG8 *...44 E5
Chestnut Pl *SYD* SE26...150 B3
Chestnut Ri *BUSH* WD23...22 D6
WOOL/PLUM SE18...115 K4
Chestnut Rd *ASHF* TW15...140 A4
DART DA1...139 G7
KUTN/CMB KT2...144 A6
RYNPK SW20...161 G1
WHTN TW2...142 E1
WNWD SE27...149 H2

Chilworth Gdns *SUT* SM1...175 G2
Chilworth Ms *BAY/PAD* W2...8 F5
Chilworth St *BAY/PAD* W2...8 F5
Chimes Av *PLMGR* N13...41 G3
China Hall Ms
BERM/RHTH SE16...111 K3
China Ms *BRXS/STRHM* SW2...130 A6
Chinbrook Crs *LEE/GVPK* SE12...153 F2
Chinbrook Rd *LEE/GVPK* SE12...153 F2
Chinchilla Dr *HSLWW* TW4...122 B1
The Chine *ALP/SUD* HA0...67 H4
MUSWH N10...54 B2
WCHMN N21...29 H5
Chingdale Rd *CHING* E4...44 C2
Chingford Av *CHING* E4...44 A2
Chingford La *WFD* IG8...44 C3
Chingford Mount Rd
CHING E4...43 J4
Chingford Rd *CHING* E4...43 J5
WALTH E17...57 K1
Chingley Cl *BMLY* BR1...152 C5
Chinnor Crs *GFD/PVL* UB6...84 C1
Chipka St *POP/IOD* E14...113 F1
Chipley St *NWCR* SE14...112 B5
Chippendale St *CLPT* E5...75 F2
Chippenham Cl *PIN* HA5 *...46 A3
Chippenham Gdns
KIL/WHAMP NW6...2 A1
Chippenham Ms *MV/WKIL* W9...8 A1
Chippenham Rd *MV/WKIL* W9...2 A9
Chipping Cl *BAR* EN5...26 C2
Chipstead Av *THHTH* CR7...164 C3
Chipstead Cl *BELMT* SM2...175 F7
NRWD SE19...150 B5
Chipstead Gdns *CRICK* NW2...69 K1
Chipstead Rd *ERITH* DA8...118 B6
HTHAIR TW6...120 C3
Chipstead Sq *FUL/PGN* SW6...107 K7
Chirk Cl *YEAD* UB4...83 J3
Chisenhale Rd *BOW* E3...93 G1
Chisholm Rd *CROY/NA* CR0...178 A1
RCHPK/HAM TW10...125 G5
Chislehurst Av
NFNCH/WDSPK N12...39 G6
Chislehurst High St *CHST* BR7...154 B5
Chislehurst Rd *BMLY* BR1...168 D1
RCHPK/HAM TW10...125 F5
SCUP DA14...155 J4
STMC/STPC BR5...169 K3
Chislet Cl *BECK* BR3...151 J6
Chisley Rd *SEVS/STOTM* N15...56 A5
Chiswell Sq *BKHTH/KID* SE3...134 A1
Chiswell St *CMBW* SE5...110 E6
STLK EC1Y...13 G2
Chiswick Br *CHSWK* W4...105 K1
Chiswick Cl *CROY/NA* CR0...177 F2
Chiswick Common Rd
CHSWK W4...106 A3
Chiswick High Rd *CHSWK* W4...105 H4
Chiswick House Grounds
CHSWK W4 *...106 A5
Chiswick La *CHSWK* W4...106 B4
Chiswick La South *CHSWK* W4...106 C5
Chiswick Ml *CHSWK* W4...106 C5
Chiswick Pk *CHSWK* W4 *...105 J3
Chiswick Pier *CHSWK* W4...106 C6
Chiswick Quay *CHSWK* W4...105 K3
Chiswick Rd *CHSWK* W4...105 K3
ED N9...42 C1
Chiswick Sq *CHSWK* W4 *...106 B5
Chiswick Staithe *CHSWK* W4...105 K5
Chiswick Village *CHSWK* W4...105 H5
Chiswick Whf *CHSWK* W4...106 C6
Chitterfield Ga *WDR/YW* UB7...100 D5
Chitty's La *BCTR* RM8...79 K1
Chitty St *FITZ* W1T...10 F2
Chivalry Rd *BTSEA* SW11...128 D4
Chivenor Gv *KUTN/CMB* KT2...143 K4
Chivers Rd *CHING* E4...43 K2
Choats Manor Wy *DAGW* RM9...98 B3
Choats Rd *BARK* IG11...98 A2
DAGW RM9...98 A2
Chobham Gdns *WIM/MER* SW19...146 B1
Chobham Rd *SRTFD* E15...76 B4
Cholmeley Cl *HGT* N6 *...54 B6
Cholmeley Crs *HGT* N6...54 B6
Cholmeley Pk *HGT* N6...54 B7
Cholmley Gdns
KIL/WHAMP NW6...70 E4
Cholmley Rd *THDIT* KT7...158 C5
Cholmley Ter *THDIT* KT7 *...158 C6
Cholmley Vls *THDIT* KT7 *...158 C6
Cholmondeley Av *WLSDN* NW10...87 J1
Chopwell Cl *SRTFD* E15...76 B6
Choumert Gv *PECK* SE15...131 H1
Choumert Ms *PECK* SE15...131 H1
Choumert Rd *PECK* SE15...131 G2
Chow Sq *HACK* E8 *...74 B4
HACK E8 *...74 B4
Chrislaine Cl *STWL/WRAY* TW19...120 A5
Chrisp St *POP/IOD* E14...93 K4
Christabel Cl *ISLW* TW7...123 K2
Christchurch Av *ALP/SUD* HA0...68 A5
ERITH DA8...118 A5
KIL/WHAMP NW6...70 B7
KTN/HRWW/WS HA3...49 F3
NFNCH/WDSPK N12...39 G5
RAIN RM13...99 H1
TEDD TW11...143 G4
Christchurch Cl *ENC/FH* EN2...29 H1
NFNCH/WDSPK N12 *...39 H6
WIM/MER SW19...147 H6
Christchurch Gdns
KTN/HRWW/WS HA3...49 G3
Christchurch Hl *HAMP* NW3...71 H2
Christ Church La *BAR* EN5...26 C1
Christchurch Ldg *EBAR* EN4 *...27 K3
Christchurch Pk *BELMT* SM2...175 G6
Christ Church Rd *BECK* BR3 *...166 D1
BRYLDS KT5...159 G6
CEND/HSY/T N8...54 E5
Christchurch Rd *BFN/LL* DA15...155 F3
BRXS/STRHM SW2...130 A7
DART DA1...139 G5
IL IG1...60 D7
MORT/ESHN SW14...125 J4
WIM/MER SW19...147 H6
Christchurch Sq *HOM* E9 *...74 E7
Christchurch St *CHEL* SW3...15 L9
Christchurch Ter *CHEL* SW3 *...15 L9
Christchurch Wy *GNWCH* SE10...113 H4
Christian Flds
STRHM/NOR SW16...149 G6
Christian St *WCHPL* E1...92 C5
Christie Dr *WATW* WD18...20 C3
Christie Gv *CROY/NA* CR0...165 H4
Christie Rd *HOM* E9...75 G5
Christina Sq *FSBYPK* N4...73 H1
Christina St *SDTCH* EC2A...7 J9
Christine Worsley Cl
WCHMN N21...29 H7
Christopher Av *HNWL* W7...104 B2

Christopher Cl
 BERM/RHTH SE16....112 A1
 BFN/LL DA15....136 A4
Christopher Gdns *DAGW* RM9...79 K4
Christopher Pl *CAMTN* NW1 *....5 H7
Christopher Rd *NWDGN* UB2...102 A3
Christophers Ms *NTGHL* W11 *...88 C7
Christy Ter *WFD* IG8....45 J6
Chryssell Rd *BRXN/ST* SW9....110 B6
Chubworthy St *NWCR* SE14....112 B5
Chudleigh Crs *GDMY/SEVK* IG3...78 E3
Chudleigh Gdns *SUT* SM1....175 G2
Chudleigh Rd *BROCKY* SE4....132 C4
 KIL/WHAMP NW6....70 A6
 WHTN TW2....123 K5
Chudleigh St *WCHPL* E1....93 F5
Chudleigh Wy *RSLP* HA4....46 E7
Chulsa Rd *SYD* SE26....150 D4
Chumleigh St *CMBW* SE5....19 J9
Chumleigh Wk *BRYLDS* KT5...159 G5
Church Ap *DUL* SE21....149 K2
Church Av *BECK* BR3....151 J7
 CAMTN NW1....4 B5
 CHING E4....44 B5
 MORT/ESHN SW14....126 A3
 NTHLT UB5....65 K6
 NWDGN UB2....102 D2
 PIN HA5....47 J5
 RSLP HA4....46 B7
 SCUP DA14....155 G4
Churchbury Cl *EN* EN1....30 A1
Churchbury La *EN* EN1....30 A2
Churchbury Rd
 ELTH/MOT SE9....134 C6
 EN EN1....30 A1
Church Cl *EDGW* HA8....36 E4
 HSLW TW3....122 E1
 HYS/HAR UB3....82 B4
 NTHWD HA6....32 D6
 TRDG/WHET N20....39 J2
 WDR/YW UB7....100 B3
Church Crs *FNCH* N3....38 D7
 HOM E9....75 F6
 MUSWH N10....54 B3
 TRDG/WHET N20....39 J2
Churchcroft Cl *BAL* SW12...129 F6
Churchdown *BMLY* BR1....152 C3
Church Dr *CDALE/KGS* NW9...51 F1
 RYLN/HDSTN HA2....48 A5
 WWKM BR4....180 C2
Church Elm La *DAGE* RM10...80 C5
Church End *HDN* NW4....51 K2
 WALTH E17....57 K3
Church Farm *EBAR* EN4 *...27 K4
Church Farm La *CHEAM* SM3...174 C5
Churchfield Av
 NFNCH/WDSPK N12....39 G5
Churchfield Cl *HYS/HAR* UB3...82 B4
 RYLN/HDSTN HA2....48 C3
Churchfield Rd *ACT* W3....86 E7
 HNWL W7....103 K1
 WEA W13....85 H7
 WELL DA16....136 B2
Churchfields *E/WMO/HCT* KT8...157 F2
 GNWCH SE10....113 F5
 SWFD E18....44 E7
Churchfields Av *FELT* TW13...141 K3
Churchfields Rd *BECK* BR3...166 A1
Churchfield Wy
 NFNCH/WDSPK N12....39 G5
Church Gdns *ALP/SUD* HA0...67 G3
 EA W5....104 E1
Church Garth *ARCH* N19 *...72 D1
Church Ga *FUL/PGN* SW6....127 H2
Church Gn *BRXN/ST* SW9 *...130 B1
 HYS/HAR UB3....82 D5
Church Gv *KUT/HW* KT1....143 J7
 LEW SE13....132 E3
Church Hill *CAR* SM5....175 K4
 DART DA1....138 B3
 HRW HA1....48 E7
 WALTH E17....57 J3
 WCHMH N21....29 F6
 WIM/MER SW19....146 D4
 WOOL/PLUM SE18....114 E2
Church Hill Rd *CHEAM* SM3...174 B3
 EBAR EN4....27 J5
 SURB KT6....159 F4
 WALTH E17....57 K3
Church Hollow *PUR* RM19...119 K4
Church Hyde
 WOOL/PLUM SE18....115 K5
Churchill Av
 KTN/HRWW/WS HA3....49 H5
Churchill Cl *EBED/NFELT* TW14...121 J7
Churchill Gdns *ACT* W3....86 C5
 PIM SW1V....16 E8
Churchill Gardens Rd
 PIM SW1V....16 D8
Churchill Ms *WFD* IG8....44 D5
Churchill Pl *POP/IOD* E14....93 K7
Churchill Rd *CAN/RD* E16....95 C5
 CRICK NW2....69 K5
 EDGW HA8....36 B5
 KTTN NW5....72 C3
 SAND/SEL CR2....177 J7
Churchill Ter *CHING* E4....43 J3
Churchill Wk *HOM* E9....74 E4
Churchill Wy *BMLY* BR1....167 K1
 SUN TW16....140 E7
Churchlands Wy *WPK* KT4...174 F1
Church La *CDALE/KGS* NW9...50 E7
 CEND/HSY/T N8....55 E3
 CHSGTN KT9....172 B5
 CHST BR7....154 C7
 DAGE RM10....80 D5
 EA W5....104 D1
 ED N9....42 C1
 EFNCH N2....53 H2
 ENC/FH EN2....29 K2
 HAYES BR2....168 D7
 KTN/HRWW/WS HA3....35 F7
 PIN HA5....47 J2
 PUR RM19 *....119 K4
 ROM RM1....63 G5
 TEDD TW11....143 K5
 THDIT KT7....158 A5
 TOOT SW17....147 K4
 TOTM N17....42 A7
 TWK TW1....124 B7
 WALTH E17....57 K3
 WAN E11....58 C2
 WIM/MER SW19....146 E7
 WLSDN NW10....69 J2
Churchley Rd *SYD* SE26....150 D3
Church Manor Wy *ABYW* SE2...116 B2
Church Manorway *ERITH* DA8...118 A2
Churchmead Cl *EBAR* EN4...27 J5
Church Meadow *SURB* KT6...171 J1
Church Md *CMBW* SE5 *...110 D6
Churchmead Rd
 WLSDN NW10....69 J5

Churchmore Rd
 STRHM/NOR SW16....148 C7
Church Mt *EFNCH* N2....53 H4
Church Paddock Ct
 WLGTN SM6....176 D2
Church Pas *BAR* EN5 *....26 D2
Church Pth *CHSWK* W4....105 K2
 MTCM CR4....162 D2
 NFNCH/WDSPK N12 *....39 G4
 RYNPK SW20....161 J1
 WAN E11....58 E4
 WIM/MER SW19....161 J1
Church Pl *EA* W5....104 E1
 MTCM CR4....162 D2
Church Rd *LEY* E10....75 K1
Church Ri *CHSGTN* KT9....172 B5
 FSTH SE23....132 A7
Church Rd *ACT* W3....105 K1
 BARK IG11....78 C5
 BARN SW13....126 D1
 BXLYHN DA7....137 G1
 CHEAM SM3....174 C5
 CROY/NA CR0....177 J3
 E/WMO/HCT KT8....157 J2
 ERITH DA8....117 K4
 ESH/CLAY KT10....171 F5
 FELT TW13....141 K4
 GNTH/NBYPK IG2....60 E5
 HAYES BR2....167 H2
 HAYES BR2....181 H6
 HDN NW4....51 K3
 HEST TW5....102 A4
 HGT N6....54 A5
 HNWL W7....84 E6
 HOR/WEW KT19....173 J7
 HYS/HAR UB3....82 D7
 IS N1....73 J5
 ISLW TW7....103 J7
 KUT/HW KT1....159 G1
 LEY E10....57 J7
 MNPK E12....77 J4
 MTCM CR4....162 D2
 NRWD SE19....150 A6
 NTHLT UB5....65 K6
 NTHWD HA6....32 D6
 NWDGN UB2....102 D2
 PEND EN3....30 E5
 RCHPK/HAM TW10....125 F4
 RCHPK/HAM TW10....144 A3
 SCUP DA14....155 G3
 STAN HA7....35 H4
 SURB KT6....158 D7
 TEDD TW11....142 E5
 TOTM N17....42 A7
 WALTH E17....57 G1
 WDR/YW UB7....100 A1
 WELL DA16....136 C1
 WIM/MER SW19....146 C3
 WIM/MER SW19....162 C1
 WLGTN SM6....176 C2
 WLSDN NW10....69 G5
 WPK KT4....160 B7
Church Rw *CHST* BR7....154 C7
 FUL/PGN SW6 *....108 A6
 HAMP NW3....71 G3
 WAND/EARL SW18....128 A4
Church Row Ms *CHST* BR7 *...154 C7
Church St *BAY/PAD* W2....9 A1
 CHSWK W4....106 B5
 CROY/NA CR0....177 J2
 DAGE RM10....80 D6
 ED N9....29 K6
 ENC/FH EN2....29 K2
 ESH/CLAY KT10....170 B3
 EW KT17....173 J7
 HPTN TW12....142 C7
 HSLW TW3....123 H4
 ISLW TW7....124 C2
 KUT/HW KT1....158 E1
 SRTFD E15....76 C7
 TWK TW1....124 B7
 WATW WD18 *....21 G3
Church Street Est
 STJWD NW8....9 H1
Church St North *SRTFD* E15...76 C7
Church Ter *BKHTH/KID* SE3...133 H2
 FUL/PGN SW6 *....128 A1
 HDN NW4....51 K2
 RCHPK/HAM TW10....124 E4
Church V *EFNCH* N2....53 K2
 FSTH SE23....150 E1
Church Vw *FSTH* SE23....151 F1
Church View Gv *SYD* SE26...151 F5
Churchview Rd *WHTN* TW2...123 J7
Church Wk *BTFD* TW8....104 D5
 BUSH WD23....22 A5
 CDALE/KGS NW9....69 F1
 CRICK NW2....70 D2
 HYS/HAR UB3....82 C5
 RYNPK SW20....161 K3
 STNW/STAM N16....73 K3
 STRHM/NOR SW16....163 H1
 THDIT KT7....158 A6
Churchway *CAMTN* NW1....5 H7
Church Wy *EBAR* EN4....27 K3
 TRDG/WHET N20....39 J2
Churchyard Rw *LBTH* SE11...18 B5
Churston Av *PLSTW* E13....77 F7
Churston Cl
 BRXS/STRHM SW2 *....130 A7
Churston Dr *MRDN* SM4....161 G4
Churston Gdns
 FBAR/BDGN N11....40 C5
Churton Pl *CHSWK* W4 *...105 J5
 PIM SW1V....16 F6
Churton St *PIM* SW1V....16 F6
Chyngton Cl *BFN/LL* DA15...155 F2
Cibber Rd *FSTH* SE23....151 F1
Cicada Rd *WAND/EARL* SW18...128 B5
Cicely Rd *PECK* SE15....111 H7
Cinderford Wy *BMLY* BR1...152 C3
Cinema Pde *EDGW* HA8 *....36 C5
Cinnamon Cl *CROY/NA* CR0...163 K6
 PECK SE15....111 G6
Cinnamon St *WAP* E1W....92 D7
Cintra Pk *NRWD* SE19....150 B6
Circle Gdns *WIM/MER* SW19...161 K1
The Circle *CRICK* NW2....69 G2
 MLHL NW7....37 F5
The Circuits *PIN* HA5....47 G3
Circular Rd *TOTM* N17....56 B2
Circular Wy *WOOL/PLUM* SE18...114 D6
Circus Ms *MBLAR* W1H *...8 L2
Circus Pl *LVPST* EC2M *....13 H2
Circus Rd *STJWD* NW8....3 G2
Circus St *GNWCH* SE10....113 F6
Cirencester St *BAY/PAD* W2...8 C2
Cissbury Ring North
 NFNCH/WDSPK N12....38 D4
Cissbury Ring South
 NFNCH/WDSPK N12....38 D4
Cissbury Rd *SEVS/STOTM* N15...55 K4
Citadel Pl *LBTH* SE11....17 L7

Citizen Rd *HOLWY* N7....73 G2
Citron Ter *PECK* SE15 *....131 J2
City Barracks *SHB* W12 *...88 A7
City Garden Rw *IS* N1....6 D6
City Rd *FSBYE* EC1V....6 C6
 STLK EC1Y....13 H1
City Wk *STHWK* SE1....19 J3
Civic Wy *BARK/HLT* IG6....60 C3
 RSLP HA4....65 H4
Clabon Ms *KTBR* SW1X....15 L4
Clack St *BERM/RHTH* SE16...111 K1
Clacton Rd *TOTM* N17 *....56 B1
 WALTH E17....57 G5
Claire Ct *NFNCH/WDSPK* N12...39 J2
Claire Gdns *STAN* HA7....35 J4
Claire Pl *POP/IOD* E14....112 D2
Clairvale Rd *HEST* TW5....102 C7
Clairview Rd
 STRHM/NOR SW16....148 B4
Clairville Gdns *HNWL* W7....84 E7
Clamp HI *STAN* HA7....34 C4
Clancarty Rd *FUL/PGN* SW6...127 K1
Clandon Cl *ACT* W3....105 J1
 EW KT17....173 H5
Clandon Gdns *FNCH* N3....52 E3
Clandon Rd *GDMY/SEVK* IG3...78 E1
Clandon St *DEPT* SE8....132 D1
Clandon Ms *RYNPK* SW20 *...161 G1
Clanricarde Gdns
 BAY/PAD W2....8 B7
Clapgate Rd *BUSH* WD23....22 B5
Clapham Common North Side
 CLAP SW4....129 F3
Clapham Common South Side
 CLAP SW4....129 G4
Clapham Common West Side
 BTSEA SW11....128 E3
Clapham Court Ter
 CLAP SW4 *....129 K4
Clapham Crs *CLAP* SW4....129 J3
Clapham High St *CLAP* SW4...129 J2
Clapham Manor St *CLAP* SW4...129 H2
Clapham Park Est *CLAP* SW4 *...129 J6
Clapham Park Rd *CLAP* SW4...129 H3
Clapham Park Ter
 BRXS/STRHM SW2 *....129 K4
Clapham Rd *BRXN/ST* SW9...129 K1
Claps Gate La *EHAM* E6....96 B3
Clapton Common *CLPT* E5...56 C6
Clapton Sq *CLPT* E5....74 E4
Clapton Ter *CLPT* E5....56 D6
Clapton Wy *CLPT* E5....74 C3
Clara Pl *WOOL/PLUM* SE18...115 F3
Clare Cl *BORE* WD6....24 B5
 EFNCH N2....53 G2
Clare Cnr *ELTH/MOT* SE9...135 G4
Clare Ct *NTHWD* HA6....32 C4
Claredale St *BETH* E2....92 C1
Clare Gdns *BARK* IG11....79 F5
 FSTGT E7....76 E3
 NTGHL W11 *....88 C5
Clare HI *ESH/CLAY* KT10....170 B4
Clare La *IS* N1....6 F2
Clare Lawn Av
 MORT/ESHN SW14....126 A4
Clare Ms *FUL/PGN* SW6....108 A6
Claremont Av
 KTN/HRWW/WS HA3....50 A4
 NWMAL KT3....160 E4
 SUN TW16....141 F7
Claremont Cl
 BRXS/STRHM SW2....130 A7
 CAN/RD E16....96 A7
 IS N1....6
Claremont Crs *DART* DA1....138 B3
 RKW/CH/CXG WD3....20 A4
Claremont Dr *ESH/CLAY* KT10...170 B4
Claremont End
 ESH/CLAY KT10....170 B5
Claremont Gdns
 GDMY/SEVK IG3....78 E1
 SURB KT6....159 F3
Claremont Gv *CHSWK* W4....106 B6
 WFD IG8....45 G5
Claremont House
 WATW WD18 *....20 B3
Claremont La *ESH/CLAY* KT10...170 B4
Claremont Pk *FNCH* N3....38 C7
Claremont Park Rd
 ESH/CLAY KT10....170 A5
Claremont Rd *BMLY* BR1....168 D3
 CRICK NW2....52 A4
 CROY/NA CR0....165 H7
 EMPK RM11....63 J5
 ESH/CLAY KT10....170 B6
 FSTGT E7....77 F4
 GLDGN NW11....70 B2
 HGT N6....54 B6
 KTN/HRWW/WS HA3....48 E1
 MV/WKIL W9....88 C1
 SURB KT6....159 F4
 TEDD TW11....143 F4
 WALTH E17....57 G2
 WAN E11....76 B2
 WEA W13....85 G4
Claremont Sq *IS* N1....6
Claremont St *GNWCH* SE10...112 E5
 UED N18....42 C5
Claremont Ter *THDIT* KT7 *...158 C6
Claremont Vls *CMBW* SE5 *...110 E6
 KUT/HW KT1 *....159 G1
Claremont Wy *CRICK* NW2...52 A7
Clarence Av *BMLY* BR1....168 D3
 CLAP SW4....129 J5
 IL IG1....59 K5
 NWMAL KT3....159 K1
Clarence Cl *BUSH* WD23....23 H6
 EBAR EN4....27 H4
Clarence Ct *MLHL* NW7 *....37 G4
Clarence Crs *CLAP* SW4....129 J5
 SCUP DA14....155 H2
Clarence Dr *ENC/FH* EN2...29 H1
Clarence Gdns *CAMTN* NW1...4 D8
Clarence Ga *CAMTN* NW1 *....3 M9
Clarence La *PUT/ROE* SW15...126 C5
Clarence Ms
 BERM/RHTH SE16....93 F7
 CLPT E5....74 E4
 TOOT SW17....147 G2
Clarence Pas *KCROSS* N1C *...5 J5
Clarence Pl *CLPT* E5....74 E4
Clarence Rd *BMLY* BR1....168 D3
 BXLYHS DA6....137 F3
 CAN/RD E16....94 C3
 CHSWK W4....105 H4
 CLPT E5....74 D3
 CROY/NA CR0....164 E6
 DEPT SE8....112 D5
 ELTH/MOT SE9....153 J1
 KIL/WHAMP NW6....70 D6
 MNPK E12....77 J3
 PEND EN3....30 E1
 RCH/KEW TW9....105 G7

 SCUP DA14....155 H2
 SEVS/STOTM N15....55 J4
 SUT SM1....175 F3
 TEDD TW11....143 F5
 WALTH E17....57 F1
 WDGN N22....40 E6
 WIM/MER SW19....147 F5
 WLGTN SM6....176 B4
Clarence St *KUT/HW* KT1....158 E1
 NWDGN UB2....102 C2
 RCH/KEW TW9....125 F3
Clarence Ter *CAMTN* NW1....3 M9
 HSLW TW3....123 G3
Clarence Vls *KUT/HW* KT1 *...159 G1
Clarence Wk *CLAP* SW4....129 K1
Clarence Wy *CAMTN* NW1....4 C1
Clarenden Crs *WHTN* TW2...142 D2
Clarendon Cross *NTGHL* W11...88 C6
Clarendon Dr *PUT/ROE* SW15...127 F3
Clarendon Gdns *HDN* NW4....51 J2
 IL IG1....59 K7
 MV/WKIL W9....8 F1
 WBLY HA9....67 K2
Clarendon Gn *BAY/PAD* W2 *...9 A6
Clarendon Gv *MTCM* CR4....162 E2
Clarendon Ms *BAY/PAD* W2...9 A6
 BORE WD6 *....24 C2
Clarendon Pl *BAY/PAD* W2...9 A6
Clarendon Ri *LEW* SE13....133 F2
Clarendon Rd *BORE* WD6....24 C2
 CEND/HSY/T N8....55 F2
 CROY/NA CR0....177 H1
 EA W5....86 A2
 HRW HA1....48 E5
 HYS/HAR UB3....101 J1
 NTGHL W11....88 C6
 SEVS/STOTM N15....55 H3
 SWFD E18....58 E2
 UED N18....42 C4
 WALTH E17....57 K5
 WAT WD17....21 F2
 WDGN N22....55 F1
 WIM/MER SW19....147 G6
 WLGTN SM6....176 C4
Clarendon St *PIM* SW1V....16 D7
Clarendon Ter *MV/WKIL* W9...2 F9
Clarendon Wy *WCHMH* N21...29 J6
Clarens St *CAT* SE6....151 H1
Clare Pde *GFD/PVL* UB6 *....66 D5
Clare Rd *GFD/PVL* UB6....66 D5
 HSLWW TW4....122 E2
 NWCR SE14....132 C1
 STWL/WRAY TW19....120 A6
 WAN E11....58 B3
 WLSDN NW10....69 J6
Clare St *BETH* E2....92 D1
Claret Gdns *SNWD* SE25....165 F3
Clareville Gv *SKENS* SW7...14 F6
Clareville St *SKENS* SW7....14 F6
Clare Wy *BXLYHN* DA7....117 F7
Clarges Ms *MYFR/PICC* W1J...10 C8
Clarges St *MYFR/PICC* W1J...10 D8
Claribel Rd *BRXN/ST* SW9...130 C1
Clarice Wy *WLGTN* SM6....176 E7
Claridge Rd *BCTR* RM8....61 K5
Clarissa Rd *CHDH* RM6....61 K5
Clarissa St *HACK* E8....7 L3
Clark Cl *ERITH* DA8....118 D7
Clarke Ms *ED* N9....42 D2
Clarke Cl *CROY/NA* CR0....164 D7
Clarke Path *STNW/STAM* N16...56 C7
Clarkers La *KTTN* NW5....72 B4
Clarkes Av *WPK* KT4....161 G7
Clark Gv *IL* IG1....78 E3
Clarks Md *BUSH* WD23....22 C6
Clarkson Rd *CAN/RD* E16....94 D5
Clarkson Rw *CAMTN* NW1....4 E6
Clarkson St *BETH* E2 *....92 D2
Clark's Rd *IL* IG1....78 D1
Clark St *WCHPL* E1....92 E5
Clark Wy *HEST* TW5....102 C6
Classon Cl *WDR/YW* UB7....100 B1
Claston Cl *DART* DA1....138 B3
Claude Monet Ct *EDUL* SE22 *...131 H4
Claude Rd *LEY* E10....76 A1
 PECK SE15....131 J1
 PLSTW E13....77 F7
Claude St *POP/IOD* E14....112 D3
Claudia Pl *WIM/MER* SW19...127 H1
Claudius Cl *STAN* HA7....35 K3
Claughton Rd *PLSTW* E13...95 G1
Clauson Av *NTHLT* UB5....66 C4
Clavell St *GNWCH* SE10....113 F5
Claverdale Rd
 BRXS/STRHM SW2....130 A6
Clavering Av *BARN* SW13....106 E5
Clavering Cl *TEDD* TW11....143 G3
Clavering Pl *BAL* SW12....129 F5
Clavering Rd *MNPK* E12....59 H1
Claverley Gv *FNCH* N3....38 E1
Claverley Vls *FNCH* N3....39 F6
Claverton St *PIM* SW1V....16 F8
Clave St *WAP* E1W....92 E7
Claxton Gv *HMSMTH* W6....107 G4
Claxton Pk *KTN/HRWW/WS* HA3...34 D7
Claybank Gv *LEW* SE13....132 E2
Claybridge Rd *LEE/GVPK* SE12...153 G3
Claybrook Cl *EFNCH* N2....53 H3
Claybrook Rd *HMSMTH* W6...107 G5
Claybury *BUSH* WD23....22 B6
Claybury Rd *WFD* IG8....45 J6
Clay Ct *KTN/HRWW/WS* HA3...49 K3
Claydon Dr *CROY/NA* CR0...176 E3
Claydown Ms
 WOOL/PLUM SE18....115 F4
Clayfarm Rd *ELTH/MOT* SE9...154 C1
Claygate Cl *HCH* RM12....81 J4
Claygate Crs *CROY/NA* CR0...180 A5
Claygate La *ESH/CLAY* KT10...171 G4
 THDIT KT7....158 B7
Claygate Lodge Cl
 ESH/CLAY KT10....170 E6
Claygate Rd *WEA* W13....104 C2
Clayhall Av *CLAY* IG5....59 J1
Clayhill Crs *ELTH/MOT* SE9...153 H3
Claylands Pl *VX/NE* SW8....110 B6
Claylands Rd *VX/NE* SW8....110 A5
Clay La *BUSH* WD23....22 D5
 STWL/WRAY TW19....120 C6
Claymore Cl *MRDN* SM4....161 K6
Claypole Dr *HEST* TW5....102 D7
Claypole Rd *SRTFD* E15 *....94 A1
Clayponds Av *BTFD* TW8....105 F3
Clayponds Gdns *EA* W5....104 E4
Clayponds La *BTFD* TW8....105 F4
Clay St *MHST* W1U....9 M3
Clayton Av *ALP/SUD* HA0....68 A4
Clayton Cl *EHAM* E6....95 K5
Clayton Crs *BTFD* TW8....104 E4
 IS N1....5 L4
Clayton Dr *DEPT* SE8....112 B4

Clayton Fld *CDALE/KGS* NW9...37 G7
Clayton Ms *GNWCH* SE10....113 G7
Clayton Rd *CHSGTN* KT9....171 J3
 HYS/HAR UB3....101 H1
 ISLW TW7....123 K2
 PECK SE15....111 H7
 ROMW/RG RM7....62 E7
Clayton St *LBTH* SE11....18 A9
Clayton Ter *YEAD* UB4....83 J4
Claytonville Ter *BELV* DA17 *...117 K1
Clay Wood Cl *ORP* BR6....169 K6
Clayworth Cl *BFN/LL* DA15...136 C5
Cleanthus Cl
 WOOL/PLUM SE18....115 G7
Cleanthus Rd
 WOOL/PLUM SE18....115 G7
Clearbrook Wy *WCHPL* E1 *...92 E5
Clearwater Pl *SURB* KT6....158 C6
Clearwater Ter *NTGHL* W11...107 G1
Cleave Av *HYS/HAR* UB3....101 H3
Cleaveland Rd *SURB* KT6....158 E4
Cleaverholme Cl *SNWD* SE25...165 J5
Cleaver Sq *LBTH* SE11....18 B7
Cleaver St *LBTH* SE11....18 A7
Cleeve Ct *EBED/NFELT* TW14...121 J7
Cleeve HI *FSTH* SE23....131 J7
Cleeve Park Gdns *SCUP* DA14...155 H3
Cleeve Wy *PUT/ROE* SW15...126 C5
 SUT SM1....162 A7
Clegg St *PLSTW* E13....94 E1
 WAP E1W....92 D7
Clematis Cots *SHB* W12 *....87 J6
Clematis Gdns *WFD* IG8....44 E4
Clematis St *SHB* W12....87 H6
Clem Attlee Ct *FUL/PGN* SW6 *...107 J5
Clem Attlee Pde
 FUL/PGN SW6 *....107 J5
Clemence Rd *DAGE* RM10....80 E7
Clemence St *POP/IOD* E14....93 H4
Clement Av *CLAP* SW4....129 J3
Clement Cl *CHSWK* W4....106 A3
 KIL/WHAMP NW6....70 A6
Clement Gdns *HYS/HAR* UB3...101 H3
Clementhorpe Rd *DAGW* RM9...79 J5
Clementina Rd *LEY* E10....57 H7
Clementine Cl *WEA* W13....104 C1
Clement Rd *BECK* BR3....166 A1
 WIM/MER SW19....146 C4
Clements Av *CAN/RD* E16....94 E6
Clements Cl
 NFNCH/WDSPK N12....39 F3
Clements La *IL* IG1....78 B2
Clement's La *MANHO* EC4N...13 H6
 IL IG1....78 B2
Clements Rd
 BERM/RHTH SE16 *....111 H2
 EHAM E6....77 K6
 IL IG1....78 B2
Clement's Rd
 BERM/RHTH SE16....111 H2
Clendon Wy
 WOOL/PLUM SE18....115 J3
Clennam St *STHWK* SE1 *....18 F1
Clensham Ct *SUT* SM1....174 E1
Clensham La *SUT* SM1....174 E1
Clenston Ms *MBLAR* W1H....9 L4
Cleopatra Cl *STAN* HA7....35 K2
Clephane Rd *IS* N1....73 J5
Clere Pl *SDTCH* EC2A....7 H9
Clere St *SDTCH* EC2A....7 H9
Clerkenwell Gn *CLKNW* EC1R...12 C5
Clerkenwell Gn *CLKNW* EC1R...12 C1
Clermont Rd *HOM* E9....74 E7
Clevedon Gdns *HEST* TW5....122 A1
 HYS/HAR UB3....101 G2
Clevedon Rd *KUT/HW* KT1....159 H1
 PGE/AN SE20....151 F7
 TWK TW1....124 E5
Cleveland Av *CHSWK* W4....106 C4
 HPTN TW12....141 K6
Cleveland Crs *BORE* WD6....24 E4
Cleveland Gdns *BARN* SW13...126 C1
 BAY/PAD W2....8 E5
 CRICK NW2....70 B1
 SEVS/STOTM N15....173 J4
 WPK KT4....173 G1
Cleveland Gv *WCHPL* E1....92 E3
Cleveland Ms *FITZ* W1T....10 E2
Cleveland Park Av *WALTH* E17...57 J3
Cleveland Park Crs
 WALTH E17....57 J3
Cleveland Pl *STJS* SW1Y....10 F8
Cleveland Ri *MRDN* SM4....161 G6
Cleveland Rd *BARN* SW13....126 C1
 CHSWK W4....105 K2
 ED N9....30 D6
 IL IG1....78 B2
 IS N1....73 K5
 ISLW TW7....124 B3
 NWMAL KT3....160 B3
 SWFD E18....58 E2
 WEA W13....85 G4
 WELL DA16....136 A1
 WPK KT4....173 G1
Cleveland Rw *WHALL* SW1A...10 F9
Cleveland Sq *BAY/PAD* W2...8 E5
Cleveland St *CAMTN* NW1....10 D1
Cleveland Ter *BAY/PAD* W2...8 E4
Cleveland Wy *WCHPL* E1....92 E3
Cleveley Crs *EA* W5....86 A1
Cleveleys Rd *CLPT* E5....74 D2
Cleverly Est *SHB* W12 *....87 J7
Cleve Rd *KIL/WHAMP* NW6...70 E6
 SCUP DA14....155 K2
Cleves Av *EW* KT17....173 K7
Cleves Rd *EHAM* E6....77 H7
 RCHPK/HAM TW10....143 J2
Cleves Wy *HPTN* TW12....141 K6
 RSLP HA4....47 H7
 SUN TW16....140 D5
Clewer Crs
 KTN/HRWW/WS HA3....34 D7
Clifden Ms *CLPT* E5....75 F3
Clifden Rd *BTFD* TW8....104 E5
 CLPT E5....74 E4
 TWK TW1....124 A7
Cliffe Rd *SAND/SEL* CR2....177 K4
Clifford Av *CHST* BR7....153 K4
 MORT/ESHN SW14....125 J2
 RCH/KEW TW9....125 J2
 WLGTN SM6....176 C3
Clifford Cl *NTHLT* UB5....65 J7
 PLSTW E13 *....95 F2
Clifford Dr *BRXN/ST* SW9....130 C3
Clifford Gdns *HYS/HAR* UB3...101 G3
 WLSDN NW10....87 K1
Clifford Rd *ALP/SUD* HA0....67 K7
 BAR EN5....27 F2
 CAN/RD E16....94 D3
 ED N9....30 E5

HSLWW TW4 122 C2
RCHPK/HAM TW10 143 K1
SNWD SE25 165 H3
WALTH E17 58 A1
Clifford Wy WLSDN NW10 69 H3
Cliff Rd CAMTN NW1 72 D5
Cliff Ter DEPT SE8 132 D2
Cliffview Rd LEW SE13 132 D2
Cliff Vls CAMTN NW1 72 D5
Cliff Wk CAN/RD E16 94 D4
Clifton Av FELT TW13 141 H6
FNCH N3 38 D7
KTN/HRWW/WS HA3 49 H1
SHB W12 106 C1
WALTH E17 57 F3
WBLY HA9 68 B5
Clifton Ct PECK SE15 * 151 K7
Clifton Crs PECK SE15 111 J6
Clifton Gdns CHSWK W4 106 A3
ENC/FH EN2 28 E3
GLDGN NW11 52 D5
MV/WKIL W9 8 E1
SEVS/STOTM N15 56 B5
Clifton Gv HACK E8 74 C5
Clifton HI STJWD NW8 2 D1
Clifton Ms SNWD SE25 165 H3
Clifton Pde FELT TW13 * 141 G3
Clifton Park Av RYNPK SW20 161 F1
Clifton Pl BAY/PAD W2 9 H6
BERM/RHTH SE16 111 K3
KUTN/CMB KT2 * 144 C7
Clifton Ri NWCR SE14 112 B6
Clifton Rd CAN/RD E16 94 C5
CEND/HSY/T N8 54 D5
EMPK RM11 81 J5
FNCH N3 39 G7
FSTGT E7 77 H5
GFD/PVL UB6 84 C3
GNTH/NBYPK IG2 60 D5
HTHAIR TW6 120 C2
IS N1 73 J5
ISLW TW7 123 K1
KTN/HRWW/WS HA3 50 B3
KUTN/CMB KT2 144 B7
MV/WKIL W9 2 E7
NWDGN UB2 102 D3
SCUP DA14 154 E3
SNWD SE25 165 H3
TEDD TW11 142 E3
WATW WD18 21 F4
WDGN N22 40 C7
WELL DA16 136 D2
WIM/MER SW19 146 B5
WLGTN SM6 176 B4
WLSDN NW10 87 J1
Clifton St SDTCH EC2A 13 J1
Clifton Ter FSBYPK N4 73 G1
Clifton Vls MV/WKIL W9 8 E1
Clifton Wy ALP/SUD HA0 68 A7
PECK SE15 111 K6
Cline Rd FBAR/BDGN N11 40 C5
Clink St STHWK SE1 13 G8
Clinton Av E/WMO/HCT KT8 157 H3
WELL DA16 136 B3
Clinton Rd BOW E3 93 G2
FSTGT E7 76 E3
SEVS/STOTM N15 55 K3
Clinton Ter DEPT SE8 * 112 D5
SUT SM1 175 G4
Clipper Cl BERM/RHTH SE16 112 A1
Clipper Wy LEW SE13 133 F3
Clippesby Cl CHSGTN KT9 * 172 B5
Clipstone Ms GTPST W1W 10 E2
Clipstone Rd HSLW TW3 123 F2
Clipstone St GTPST W1W 10 E2
Clissold Cl EFNCH N2 53 K2
Clissold Crs STNW/STAM N16 73 K3
Clissold Rd STNW/STAM N16 73 K3
Clitheroe Av RYLN/HDSTN HA2 48 A7
Clitheroe Gdns OXHEY WD19 33 H2
Clitheroe Rd BRXN/ST SW9 129 J1
Clitherow Av HNWL W7 104 B2
Clitherow Rd BTFD TW8 104 C4
Clitterhouse Crs CRICK NW2 52 A1
Clitterhouse Rd CRICK NW2 52 A1
Clive Av DART DA1 138 C5
UED N18 42 C5
Cliveden Cl NFNCH/WDSPK N12 39 G3
Cliveden Pl BGVA SW1W 16 A5
Cliveden Rd WIM/MER SW19 146 D7
Clivedon Ct WEA W13 85 H4
Clivedon Rd CHING E4 44 C4
Clive Rd BELV DA17 117 H3
DUL SE21 149 K2
EBED/NFELT TW14 121 K5
EN EN1 30 C3
ESH/CLAY KT10 170 B3
GPK RM2 63 K4
TWK TW1 143 F3
WIM/MER SW19 147 J5
Clivesdale Dr HYS/HAR UB3 82 E7
Clive Wy EN EN1 30 D3
Cloak La CANST EC4R * 12 F6
Clockhouse Av BARK IG11 78 C7
Clockhouse Cl WIM/MER SW19 146 A2
Clock House Pde PLMGR N13 * 41 G4
Clockhouse Pl PUT/ROE SW15 127 H4
Clock House Rd BECK BR3 166 B2
Clock Pde ENC/FH EN2 * 29 K4
Clocktower Ms HNWL W7 * 84 E7
Clock Tower Ms IS N1 * 6 C4
THMD SE28 97 H6
Clock Tower Pl HOLWY N7 72 E5
Clock Tower Rd ISLW TW7 124 A2
Clock View Crs HOLWY N7 72 E5
Cloister Cl RAIN RM13 99 K3
TEDD TW11 143 H4
Cloister Gdns EDGW HA8 36 E4
SNWD SE25 165 J5
Cloister Rd ACT W3 86 E4
CRICK NW2 70 D2
Cloisters Av HAYES BR2 168 E4
Clonard Wy PIN HA5 34 A5
Clonbrock Rd STNW/STAM N16 74 A3
Cloncurry St FUL/PGN SW6 127 G1
Clonmel Cl RYLN/HDSTN HA2 48 D7
Clonmel Rd TOTM N17 55 K2
FUL/PGN SW6 107 J5
TEDD TW11 142 D3
Clonmore St WAND/EARL SW18 127 J7
Clorane Gdns HAMP NW3 70 E2
The Close ALP/SUD HA0 67 H3
BECK BR3 166 B3
BUSH WD23 * 22 A5
BXLY DA5 137 H5

CAR SM5 175 J7
CHDH RM6 62 A5
CHEAM SM3 161 J6
CHING E4 44 A2
EBAR EN4 27 K5
GNTH/NBYPK IG2 60 E5
ISLW TW7 123 J1
MTCM CR4 162 E3
NWMAL KT3 159 K1
PIN HA5 47 G6
RCH/KEW TW9 125 J2
SCUP DA14 155 H6
SNWD SE25 165 H5
STHGT/OAK N14 40 D1
STMC/STPC BR5 169 K5
SURB KT6 159 F6
TRDG/WHET N20 38 D1
WBLY HA9 68 C2
Cloth Ct STBT EC1A 12 D3
Cloth Fair STBT EC1A 12 D3
Clothier St HDTCH EC3A 13 K4
Cloth St STBT EC1A 12 E2
Clothworkers Rd WOOL/PLUM SE18 115 J6
Cloudesdale Rd TOOT SW17 148 B1
Cloudesley Pl IS N1 6 A4
Cloudesley Rd BXLYHN DA7 117 G2
ERITH DA8 118 C7
IS N1 6 A3
Cloudesley Sq IS N1 6 B4
Cloudesley St IS N1 6 B4
Clouston Cl WLGTN SM6 176 E4
Clova Rd FSTGT E7 76 E4
Clove Crs POP/IOD E14 94 B6
Clovelly Av CDALE/KGS NW9 51 H3
HGDN/ICK UB10 64 A3
Clovelly Cl HGDN/ICK UB10 64 A3
PIN HA5 47 F2
Clovelly Gdns EN EN1 30 A6
NRWD SE19 150 B7
Clovelly Rd BXLYHN DA7 117 G5
CEND/HSY/T N8 54 D3
CHSWK W4 * 106 A1
EA W5 104 D1
HSLW TW3 123 F1
Clovelly Wy RYLN/HDSTN HA2 65 K2
WCHPL E1 92 E5
Clover Cl WAN E11 * 76 B1
Cloverdale Gdns BFN/LL DA15 136 A5
The Clover Fld BUSH WD23 21 K5
Clover Ms CHEL SW3 15 J9
Clover Wy WLGTN SM6 163 F7
Clove St PLSTW E13 94 E3
Clowders Rd CAT SE6 151 H2
Clowser Cl SUT SM1 175 G4
Cloysters Gn WAP E1W * 92 C7
Cloyster Wd EDGW HA8 35 K6
Club Gardens Rd HAYES BR2 167 K6
Club Rw BETH E2 7 L9
The Clumps ASHF TW15 140 B3
Clunbury Av NWDGN UB2 102 E4
Clunbury St IS N1 7 H6
Cluny Est STHWK SE1 19 J3
Cluny Ms ECT SW5 14 A6
Cluny Pl STHWK SE1 19 J3
Clutton St POP/IOD E14 93 K4
Clydach Rd EN EN1 30 B3
Clyde Circ SEVS/STOTM N15 56 A3
Clyde Ct CAMTN NW1 * 5 H5
Clyde Flats FUL/PGN SW6 * 107 J6
Clyde Pl LEY E10 57 K6
Clyde Rd CROY/NA CR0 178 B1
SEVS/STOTM N15 56 A3
STWL/WRAY TW19 120 A7
SUT SM1 174 E4
WDGN N22 40 D7
WLGTN SM6 176 C4
Clydesdale PEND EN3 31 F3
Clydesdale Av STAN HA7 49 K2
Clydesdale Cl BORE WD6 25 F4
ISLW TW7 124 A2
Clydesdale Gdns RCHPK/HAM TW10 125 J3
Clydesdale Pth BORE WD6 * 25 F4
Clydesdale Rd EMPK RM11 63 K6
NTGHL W11 88 D5
Clyde St DEPT SE8 112 C5
Clyde Ter FSTH SE23 150 E1
Clyde V FSTH SE23 150 E1
Clydon Cl ERITH DA8 118 B5
Clyfford Rd RSLP HA4 64 D3
Clymping Dene EBED/NFELT TW14 122 A6
Clyston Rd WATW WD18 20 D5
Clyston St VX/NE SW8 129 H1
Coach & Horses Yd CONDST W1S 10 D6
Coach House La HBRY N5 73 H3
WIM/MER SW19 146 B3
Coach House Ms FSTH SE23 131 K5
NWCR SE14 * 112 A7
Coach House Yd WAND/EARL SW18 128 A3
Coalecroft Rd PUT/ROE SW15 127 F3
Coates Av WAND/EARL SW18 128 D5
Coates Cl THHTH CR7 164 D2
Coates Hill Rd BMLY BR1 169 F1
Coates Rd BORE WD6 23 K6
Coate St BETH E2 92 C1
Cobalt Cl BECK BR3 166 A3
Cobb Cl BORE WD6 24 E4
Cobbett Rd ELTH/MOT SE9 134 D2
WHTN TW2 123 F7
Cobbetts Av REDBR IG4 59 H4
Cobbett St VX/NE SW8 110 A6
Cobble La IS N1 6 B1
Cobble Ms HBRY N5 73 J2
Cobbler's Wk TEDD TW11 142 E5
Cobblestone Pl CROY/NA CR0 164 D7
Cobbold Ms SHB W12 * 106 C1
Cobbold Rd SHB W12 106 C1
WAN E11 76 D2
WLSDN NW10 69 H5
Cobb's Rd HSLWW TW4 122 E3
Cobb St WCHPL E1 13 L4
Cobden Ms SYD SE26 150 D4
Cobden Rd SNWD SE25 165 H4
WAN E11 76 C2
Cobham Av NWMAL KT3 160 D4
Cobham Cl BFN/LL DA15 136 C5
BTSEA SW11 128 D5
EDGW HA8 50 D1
EN EN1 30 C2
HAYES BR2 168 D5
WLGTN SM6 176 E5
Cobham Ms CAMTN NW1 * 5 G1
Cobham Pl BXLYHS DA6 136 E4
Cobham Rd GDMY/SEVK IG3 78 E1
HEST TW5 102 B5
KUT/HW KT1 159 H1
WALTH E17 44 A1
WLGTN SM6 176 D5
Cobland Rd LEE/GVPK SE12 153 G3

Coborn Rd BOW E3 93 H2
Coborn St BOW E3 93 H2
Cobourg Rd CMBW SE5 19 L5
Cobourg St CAMTN NW1 4 F8
Coburg Cl WEST SW1P 16 E5
Coburg Crs BRXS/STRHM SW2 130 A7
Coburg Dwellings WCHPL E1 * 92 E6
Coburg Gdns CLAY IG5 59 H1
Coburg Rd WDGN N22 55 F1
Cochrane Ms STJWD NW8 3 G5
Cochrane Rd WIM/MER SW19 146 C6
Cochrane St STJWD NW8 3 G5
Cockcrow Hl SURB KT6 * 158 E7
Cockerell Rd WALTH E17 57 G6
Cockfosters Pde EBAR EN4 * 28 A3
Cockfosters Rd EBAR EN4 27 K2
Cock La STBT EC1A 12 C3
Cockpit Crt STJS SW1Y 11 H8
Cockspur Ct STJS SW1Y 11 H8
Cockspur St STJS SW1Y 11 H8
Coda Ct WCHPL E1 13 H1
Codicote Dr WAP E1W 92 C7
Codling Wy ALP/SUD HA0 67 K3
Codrington HI FSTH SE23 132 B6
Codrington Ms NTGHL W11 88 C5
Cody Cl KTN/HRWW/WS HA3 49 K2
WLGTN SM6 176 D6
Cody Rd CAN/RD E16 94 B3
Coe Av SNWD SE25 165 H5
Coe's Aly BAR EN5 26 C3
Coffey St DEPT SE8 112 D6
Cogan Av WALTH E17 43 G7
Coin St STHWK SE1 12 A8
Coity Rd KTTN NW5 72 A5
Cokers La DUL SE21 130 D7
Coke St WCHPL E1 92 C5
Colas Ms KIL/WHAMP NW6 2 B3
Colbeck Ms SKENS SW7 14 D6
Colbeck Rd HRW HA1 48 C6
Colberg Pl STNW/STAM N16 56 B6
Colborne Wy WPK KT4 174 A2
Colbrook Av HYS/HAR UB3 101 G2
Colbrook Cl HYS/HAR UB3 101 G2
Colburn Av PIN HA5 33 J5
Colburn Wy SUT SM1 175 H2
Colby Rd NRWD SE19 150 A4
Colchester Dr PIN HA5 47 H4
Colchester Rd EDGW HA8 36 E6
NTHWD HA6 46 E1
WALTH E17 57 J5
Coldbath Sq CLKNW EC1R 12 A1
Coldbath St LEW SE13 112 E7
Cold Blow Crs BXLY DA5 138 A7
Cold Blow La NWCR SE14 112 A6
Coldershaw Rd WEA W13 104 B1
Coldfall Av MUSWH N10 53 K1
Coldharbour POP/IOD E14 94 A7
Coldharbour Crest ELTH/MOT SE9 * 154 A2
Coldharbour La BRXN/ST SW9 130 B3
BUSH WD23 22 B5
HYS/HAR UB3 101 J1
RAIN RM13 99 J1
Coldharbour Pl CMBW SE5 130 D1
Coldharbour Rd CROY/NA CR0 177 G4
Coldharbour Wy CROY/NA CR0 177 G4
Coldstream Gdns WAND/EARL SW18 127 J5
Colebeck Ms IS N1 73 H5
Colebert Av WCHPL E1 92 E3
Colebrook Cl MLHL NW7 38 B6
Colebrooke Av WEA W13 85 H5
Colebrooke Dr WAN E11 59 F6
Colebrooke Pl IS N1 6 C4
Colebrooke Rw IS N1 5 J4
Colebrook Rd STRHM/NOR SW16 148 E7
Colebrook Wy FBAR/BDGN N11 40 B4
Coleby Pth CMBW SE5 * 110 E6
Cole Cl THMD SE28 97 H7
Coledale Dr STAN HA7 35 J7
Coleford Rd WAND/EARL SW18 128 B4
Cole Gdns HEST TW5 101 K6
Colegrave Rd SRTFD E15 76 B4
Colegrove Rd PECK SE15 111 G5
Coleherne Ms WBPTN SW10 14 D7
Coleherne Rd WBPTN SW10 14 C7
Colehill Gdns FUL/PGN SW6 * 107 H7
Colehill La FUL/PGN SW6 107 H7
Coleman Cl SNWD SE25 165 H1
Coleman Flds IS N1 6 F3
Coleman Rd BELV DA17 117 H2
CMBW SE5 111 F6
Colemans Heath ELTH/MOT SE9 154 A2
Coleman St CITYW EC2V 13 G4
Colenso Dr MLHL NW7 37 J6
Colenso Rd CLPT E5 74 E3
GNTH/NBYPK IG2 60 E7
Cole Park Gdns TWK TW1 124 B5
Cole Park Rd TWK TW1 124 B6
Colepits Wood Rd ELTH/MOT SE9 135 J4
Coleraine Rd BKHTH/KID SE3 113 J5
CEND/HSY/T N8 55 G2
Coleridge Av MNPK E12 77 J5
SUT SM1 175 J3
Coleridge Cl VX/NE SW8 129 G1
Coleridge Dr RSLP HA4 47 F5
Coleridge Gdns KIL/WHAMP NW6 2 B1
WBPTN SW10 108 B6
Coleridge Rd CEND/HSY/T N8 54 D5
CROY/NA CR0 165 K6
DART DA1 139 K3
FSBYPK N4 73 G1
NFNCH/WDSPK N12 39 G4
WALTH E17 57 H3
Coleridge Sq WEA W13 85 G5
Coleridge Wk GLDGN NW11 52 E3
Coleridge Wy BORE WD6 24 A1
WDR/YW UB7 100 B3
YEAD UB4 82 D5
Cole Rd TWK TW1 124 B5
Colesburg Rd BECK BR3 166 C2
Coles Crs RYLN/HDSTN HA2 66 B1
Coles Gn BUSH WD23 22 C7
Coles Green Rd CRICK NW2 51 J1
Coleshill Rd TEDD TW11 142 E5
Colestown St BTSEA SW11 128 D1
Cole St STHWK SE1 18 F2
Colet Cl PLMGR N13 41 H5
Colet Gdns WKENS W14 107 G3
Coley St FSBYW WC1X 11 M1

Colfe & Hatcliffe Glebe LEW SE13 * 132 E4
Colfe Rd FSTH SE23 132 B7
Colina Ms SEVS/STOTM N15 55 H4
Colina Rd CEND/HSY/T N8 55 H4
Colin Cl CDALE/KGS NW9 51 H3
CROY/NA CR0 179 H2
WWKM BR4 180 D2
Colin Crs CDALE/KGS NW9 51 H3
Colindale Av CDALE/KGS NW9 51 F2
Colindeep Gdns HDN NW4 51 J4
Colindeep La CDALE/KGS NW9 51 H3
Colinette Rd PUT/ROE SW15 127 F3
Colin Gdns CDALE/KGS NW9 51 H4
Colin Park Rd CDALE/KGS NW9 51 G2
Colinton Rd GDMY/SEVK IG3 79 H1
Coliston Rd WAND/EARL SW18 127 K6
Collamore Av WAND/EARL SW18 128 D3
Collapit Cl HRW HA1 48 B5
Collard Cl CAMTN NW1 4 C1
College Ap GNWCH SE10 113 F5
College Av KTN/HRWW/WS HA3 34 E7
College Cl KTN/HRWW/WS HA3 34 E7
UED N18 42 B4
WHTN TW2 123 J7
College Ct EA W5 * 86 A6
College Crs HAMP NW3 71 G5
College Cross IS N1 6 B1
College Dr RSLP HA4 46 E6
College East WCHPL E1 * 13 M3
College Gdns CHING E4 31 K6
NWMAL KT3 160 C4
REDBR IG4 59 J4
TOOT SW17 147 J1
UED N18 * 42 B4
College Gn NRWD SE19 150 A6
College Gv CAMTN NW1 5 G4
College HI CANST EC4R * 12 F6
College Hill Rd KTN/HRWW/WS HA3 34 E6
College Ms IS N1 6 B2
College Pde KIL/WHAMP NW6 * 70 C7
College Park Cl LEW SE13 133 F3
College Pl CAMTN NW1 4 F3
WALTH E17 58 C3
WBPTN SW10 108 B6
College Rd BMLY BR1 152 E7
CROY/NA CR0 177 K1
DUL SE21 131 F7
ENC/FH EN2 29 J2
HRW HA1 48 E5
ISLW TW7 104 A7
KTN/HRWW/WS HA3 34 A7
NRWD SE19 150 B4
TOTM N17 42 B5
WALTH E17 58 A4
WBLY HA9 49 K7
WCHMH N21 41 F1
WEA W13 85 H5
WIM/MER SW19 147 H5
WLSDN NW10 88 A1
College St CANST EC4R * 12 F6
College Ter FNCH N3 38 D7
College Vw ELTH/MOT SE9 134 C7
College Yd KIL/WHAMP NW6 * 70 C7
KTTN NW5 72 B3
Collent St HOM E9 74 E5
Colless Rd SEVS/STOTM N15 56 B4
Collett Rd BERM/RHTH SE16 111 H2
Collett Wy NWDGN UB2 103 H1
Collier Cl EHAM E6 96 B6
HOR/WEW KT19 172 C5
Collier Dr EDGW HA8 50 C1
Colliers Shaw HAYES BR2 181 J4
Collier St IS N1 5 L6
Colliers Water La THHTH CR7 164 B4
Collindale Av BFN/LL DA15 136 B7
CDALE/KGS NW9 51 G2
Collingbourne Rd SHB W12 87 K7
Collingham Gdns ECT SW5 14 C6
Collingham Pl ECT SW5 14 C6
Collingham Rd ECT SW5 14 D5
Collings Cl WDGN N22 41 F5
Collington St GNWCH SE10 113 H4
Collingtree Rd SYD SE26 150 E3
Collingwood Av BRYLDS KT5 159 K7
MUSWH N10 54 A2
Collingwood Cl PGE/AN SE20 150 D7
WHTN TW2 123 F6
Collingwood Rd MTCM CR4 162 D1
RAIN RM13 99 H1
SEVS/STOTM N15 56 A3
SUT SM1 174 E3
Collingwood St WCHPL E1 92 D3
Collins Av STAN HA7 50 A1
Collins Dr RSLP HA4 65 G1
Collinson St STHWK SE1 18 E2
Collinson Wk STHWK SE1 18 E2
Collins Rd HBRY N5 73 J3
Collins Sq BKHTH/KID SE3 133 J2
Collins St BKHTH/KID SE3 133 H1
Collinwood Av PEND EN3 30 E2
Collinwood Gdns GNTH/NBYPK IG2 59 K4
Collyer Av CROY/NA CR0 176 E3
Collyer Pl PECK SE15 111 H7
Collyer Rd CROY/NA CR0 176 E3
Colman Pde EN EN1 * 30 A2
Colman Rd CAN/RD E16 95 G4
Colmar Cl WCHPL E1 93 F3
Colmer Pl KTN/HRWW/WS HA3 34 E6
Colmer Rd STRHM/NOR SW16 148 E6
Colmore Ms PECK SE15 111 J7
Colmore Rd PEND EN3 30 E3
Colnbrook St LBTH SE11 18 C4
Colne Av OXHEY WD19 21 F5
WATW WD18 20 D4
Colne Ct HOR/WEW KT19 172 E3
Colne Ldg BUSH WD23 * 21 H3
Colne Rd CLPT E5 75 G3
WHTN TW2 123 K7
Colne St PLSTW E13 94 E2
Colney Hatch La FBAR/BDGN N11 39 K5
Colney Rd DART DA1 139 G3
Cologne Rd BTSEA SW11 128 C3
Colombo Rd IL IG1 60 C7
Colombo St STHWK SE1 12 C8
Colonels Wk ENC/FH EN2 29 H1
Colonial Av WHTN TW2 123 H5
Colonial Dr CHSWK W4 105 K3

Colonial Rd EBED/NFELT TW14 121 H6
Colonnade BMSBY WC1N 11 J1
The Colonnade DEPT SE8 * 112 C5
Colosseum Ter CAMTN NW1 * 4 D9
Colson Rd CROY/NA CR0 177 K1
Colson Wy STRHM/NOR SW16 148 C3
Colsterworth Rd SEVS/STOTM N15 56 B3
Colston Av CAR SM5 175 J3
Colston Rd FSTGT E7 77 H5
MORT/ESHN SW14 125 K5
Colthurst Crs FSBYPK N4 73 H1
Colthurst Dr ED N9 42 D2
Coltness Crs ABYW SE2 116 C4
Colton Gdns TOTM N17 55 J2
Colton Rd HRW HA1 48 E4
Colts Yd WAN E11 * 58 D7
Columbas Dr HAMP NW3 71 H1
Columbia Av EDGW HA8 36 D7
RSLP HA4 47 F7
WPK KT4 160 C6
Columbia Rd BETH E2 7 L7
PLSTW E13 94 D3
Columbia Whf PEND EN3 * 31 F4
Columbine Av EHAM E6 95 J4
SAND/SEL CR2 177 H6
Columbine Wy LEW SE13 133 F1
Columbus Gdns NTHWD HA6 32 E7
Colvestone Crs HACK E8 74 B4
Colville Est IS N1 7 H4
Colville Gdns NTGHL W11 88 D5
Colville Houses NTGHL W11 88 D5
Colville Ms NTGHL W11 88 D5
Colville Pl FITZ W1T * 10 E3
Colville Rd ACT W3 105 J3
ED N9 30 D7
NTGHL W11 88 D5
WALTH E17 57 G1
WAN E11 76 A2
Colville Sq NTGHL W11 * 88 D5
Colville Square Ms NTGHL W11 * 88 D5
Colville Ter NTGHL W11 88 D5
Colvin Cl SYD SE26 150 E4
Colvin Gdns CHING E4 44 A2
SWFD E18 59 F3
Colvin Rd EHAM E6 77 J6
THHTH CR7 164 B4
Colwall Gdns WFD IG8 44 E4
Colwell Rd EDUL SE22 131 G4
Colwick Cl HGT N6 54 D6
Colwith Rd HMSMTH W6 107 F5
Colwood Gdns WIM/MER SW19 147 H6
Colworth Gv WALW SE17 18 F6
Colworth Rd CROY/NA CR0 165 H7
WAN E11 58 C5
Colwyn Av GFD/PVL UB6 85 F1
Colwyn Cl STRHM/NOR SW16 148 C4
Colwyn Crs HSLW TW3 103 H7
Colwyn Gn CDALE/KGS NW9 * 51 G5
Colwyn Rd CRICK NW2 69 K2
Colyer Cl ELTH/MOT SE9 154 B1
IS N1 5 L3
Colyers Cl ERITH DA8 118 A7
Colyers La ERITH DA8 117 K7
Colyton Cl ALP/SUD HA0 67 J3
WELL DA16 116 E7
Colyton La STRHM/NOR SW16 149 G4
Colyton Rd EDUL SE22 131 J4
Colyton Wy UED N18 42 C4
Combe Av BKHTH/KID SE3 113 J6
Combedale Rd GNWCH SE10 113 K4
Combemartin Rd WAND/EARL SW18 127 H6
Comber Cl CRICK NW2 69 J1
Comber Gv CMBW SE5 110 D6
Combermere Rd BRXN/ST SW9 130 A2
MRDN SM4 162 A5
Combe Rd WATW WD18 20 D5
Comberton Rd CLPT E5 74 D1
Combeside WOOL/PLUM SE18 116 A6
Combes Rd DAGW RM9 80 B6
Combwell Crs ABYW SE2 116 B2
Comely Bank Rd WALTH E17 58 A4
Comeragh Ms WKENS W14 107 H4
Comeragh Rd WKENS W14 107 H4
Comerford Rd BROCKY SE4 132 B3
Comet Cl MNPK E12 77 H3
PUR RM19 119 K3
Comet Pl DEPT SE8 112 D6
Comet Rd STWL/WRAY TW19 120 A6
Comet St DEPT SE8 112 D6
Comfort St PECK SE15 111 F6
Commerce Rd BTFD TW8 104 D5
WDGN N22 41 F7
Commerce Wy CROY/NA CR0 177 F2
Commercial Rd POP/IOD E14 93 G5
UED N18 42 A4
Commercial St WCHPL E1 13 L1
Commercial Wy CMBW SE5 111 G7
WLSDN NW10 86 D1
Commerell Pl GNWCH SE10 113 J4
Commerell St GNWCH SE10 113 H4
Commodore Pde STRHM/NOR SW16 149 F6
Commodore St WCHPL E1 93 H4
Commondale PUT/ROE SW15 127 F1
Common La ESH/CLAY KT10 171 G6
Common Rd BARN SW13 126 D2
ESH/CLAY KT10 171 G5
STAN HA7 34 D2
Commonside HAYES BR2 181 G3
Commonside East MTCM CR4 163 H3
Commonside West MTCM CR4 163 F2
The Common EA W5 86 A7
NWDGN UB2 102 C3
SRTFD E15 76 D5
STAN HA7 35 F1
Commonwealth Av HYS/HAR UB3 82 B5
SHB W12 87 K6
Commonwealth Rd TOTM N17 42 C6
Commonwealth Wy ABYW SE2 116 C4
Community Cl HEST TW5 102 A7
Community La HOLWY N7 72 D4
Community Rd GFD/PVL UB6 84 C1
SRTFD E15 76 B5
Como Rd FSTH SE23 151 G1
Como St ROMW/RG RM7 63 F4
Compass Cl ASHF TW15 140 A6
EDGW HA8 36 B3
Compass HI RCHPK/HAM TW10 124 E5
Compayne Gdns KIL/WHAMP NW6 2 C1
Compton Av ALP/SUD HA0 67 H3
EHAM E6 95 H1
GPK RM2 63 K2
HGT N6 53 J6

IS N1 ... 73 H5
Compton Cl *CAMTN* NW1 ... 4 D8
EDGW HA8 ... 36 E6
ESH/CLAY KT10 ... 170 D5
CLDGN NW11 ... 30 B2
PECK SE15 ... 111 H6
WEA W13 ... 85 G5
Compton Crs *CHSGTN* KT9 ... 172 A5
CHSWK W4 ... 105 A5
NTHLT UB5 ... 65 H7
TOTM N17 ... 41 J6
Compton Pas *FSBYE* EC1V ... 6 D9
Compton Cl *ERITH* DA8 ... 118 C5
OXHEY WD19 ... 33 J3
STPAN NW1 ... 5 J9
Compton Ri *PIN* HA5 ... 47 J4
Compton Rd *CROY/NA* CR0 ... 165 J7
HYS/HAR UB3 ... 82 C6
IS N1 ... 73 H5
WCHMH N21 ... 29 H7
WIM/MER SW19 ... 146 D5
WLSDN NW10 ... 88 B2
Compton St *FSBYE* EC1V ... 6 C9
Compton Ter *IS* N1 ... 73 H5
WCHMH N21 * ... 29 G7
Comus Pl *WALW* SE17 ... 19 J6
Comyn Rd *BTSEA* SW11 ... 128 D3
Comyns Cl *CAN/RD* E16 ... 94 D4
Comyns Rd *DAGW* RM9 ... 80 C6
The Comyns WD23 ... 22 C7
Conant Ms *WCHPL* E1 ... 92 C6
Concanon Rd *CLAP* SW4 ... 130 A3
Concert Hall Ap *STHWK* SE1 ... 11 M9
Concord Cl *NTHLT* UB5 ... 83 H2
Concorde Cl *HSLW* TW3 ... 123 G1
Concorde Dr *EHAM* E6 ... 95 K4
Concorde Wy
BERM/RHTH SE16 ... 112 A3
PEND EN3 ... 30 E4
Concord Wy
BERM/RHTH SE16 * ... 112 A3
Condell Rd *VX/NE* SW8 ... 109 H7
Conder St *POP/IOD* E14 ... 93 C5
Condover Crs
WOOL/PLUM SE18 ... 115 G6
Condray Pl *BTSEA* SW11 ... 108 D6
Conduit Ct *COVGDN* WC2E * ... 11 J6
Conduit La *SAND/SEL* CR2 ... 178 C4
UED N18 ... 42 E4
Conduit Ms *BAY/PAD* W2 ... 9 G5
Conduit Pl *BAY/PAD* W2 ... 9 G5
Conduit Rd *WOOL/PLUM* SE18 ... 115 F4
Conduit Wy *WLSDN* NW10 ... 68 G6
Conewood St *HBRY* N5 ... 73 H2
Coney Burrows *CHING* E4 ... 44 C1
Coney Hall Pde *WWKM* BR4 * ... 180 C2
Coney Hill Rd *WWKM* BR4 ... 180 C1
Coney Wy *VX/NE* SW8 ... 110 A5
Conference Cl *CHING* E4 ... 44 A1
Conference Rd *ABYW* SE2 ... 116 D3
Congleton Gv
WOOL/PLUM SE18 ... 115 H4
Congo Dr *ED* N9 ... 42 E2
Congo Rd *WOOL/PLUM* SE18 ... 115 J4
Congress Rd *ABYW* SE2 ... 116 D3
Congreve Rd *ELTH/MOT* SE9 ... 134 E2
Congreve St *WALW* SE17 ... 19 J6
Conical Cnr *ENC/FH* EN2 ... 29 J1
Conifer Gdns *EN* EN1 ... 29 K5
STRHM/NOR SW16 ... 149 F2
SUT SM1 ... 175 F1
Conifers Cl *TEDD* TW11 ... 143 H6
Conifer Wy *ALP/SUD* HA0 ... 67 J2
HYS/HAR UB3 ... 82 E6
Coniger Rd *FUL/PGN* SW6 ... 127 K1
Coningham Ms *SHB* W12 ... 87 J7
Coningham Rd *SHB* W12 ... 106 E1
Coningsby Av
CDALE/KGS NW9 ... 51 G1
Coningsby Cots *EA* W5 * ... 104 E1
Coningsby Gdns *CHING* E4 ... 43 K5
Coningsby Rd *EA* W5 ... 104 D1
FSBYPK N4 ... 55 H6
SAND/SEL CR2 ... 177 J7
Conington Rd *LEW* SE13 ... 132 E1
Conisbee Ct *STHGT/OAK* N14 ... 28 C4
Conisborough Crs *CAT* SE6 ... 152 E2
Coniscliffe Cl *CHST* BR7 ... 154 A7
Coniscliffe Rd *PLMGR* N13 ... 41 J2
Coniston Av *BARK* IG11 ... 78 E6
GFD/PVL UB6 ... 85 K2
WELL DA16 ... 135 K2
Coniston Cl *BARN* SW13 ... 106 C6
BXLYHN DA7 ... 117 K3
CHSWK W4 ... 105 K7
DART DA1 ... 138 E7
ERITH DA8 ... 118 B6
MRDN SM4 ... 161 G5
Coniston Ct *BAY/PAD* W2 * ... 9 G4
Conistone Wy *HOLWY* N7 ... 5 K1
Coniston Gdns *BELMT* SM2 * ... 174 E6
CDALE/KGS NW9 ... 51 F4
ED N9 ... 30 E7
PIN HA5 ... 46 E3
REDBR IG4 ... 59 J3
WBLY HA9 ... 49 J7
Coniston Rd *BMLY* BR1 ... 152 C5
BXLYHN DA7 ... 117 K3
CROY/NA CR0 ... 165 H6
MUSWH N10 ... 54 B1
TOTM N17 ... 42 C5
WHTN TW2 ... 123 G5
Coniston Wk *HOM* E9 ... 74 E4
Coniston Wy *CHSGTN* KT9 ... 172 A2
HCH RM12 ... 81 J4
Conlan St *NKENS* W10 ... 88 C3
Conley Rd *WLSDN* NW10 ... 69 G5
Conley St *GNWCH* SE10 ... 113 H4
Connaught Av *EBAR* EN4 ... 27 K7
EN EN1 ... 30 A1
HSLWW TW4 ... 122 D4
MORT/ESHN SW14 ... 125 K2
Connaught Br *CAN/RD* E16 ... 95 H6
Connaught Cl *BAY/PAD* W2 ... 9 H5
EN EN1 ... 30 A1
LEY E10 ... 75 G1
SUT SM1 ... 175 H1
UX/CGN UB8 * ... 82 A4
Connaught Dr *GLDGN* NW11 ... 52 E3
Connaught Gdns *MRDN* SM4 ... 162 B4
MUSWH N10 ... 54 B3
PLMGR N13 ... 41 H3
Connaught La *IL* IG1 ... 78 C1
Connaught Ms
FUL/PGN SW6 * ... 107 H7
HAMP NW3 * ... 71 J4
WOOL/PLUM SE18 ... 115 F4
Connaught Rd *BAR* EN5 ... 26 B5
CAN/RD E16 ... 95 H7
FSBYPK N4 ... 55 G6
IL IG1 ... 78 D1

KTN/HRWW/WS HA3 ... 35 F7
NWMAL KT3 ... 160 B3
RCHPK/HAM TW10 * ... 125 G4
SUT SM1 ... 175 H1
TEDD TW11 ... 142 D4
WALTH E17 * ... 57 J4
WAN E11 ... 58 B7
WEA W13 ... 85 H6
WLSDN NW10 ... 87 G1
WOOL/PLUM SE18 ... 115 F4
Connaught Sq *BAY/PAD* W2 ... 9 K5
Connaught St *BAY/PAD* W2 ... 9 K5
Connaught Wy *PLMGR* N13 ... 41 H3
Connect La *BARK/HLT* IG6 ... 60 C1
Connell Crs *EA* W5 ... 86 B3
Connemara Cl *BORE* WD6 ... 24 E5
Connington Crs *CHING* E4 ... 44 B2
Connor Cl *WAN* E11 ... 58 C7
Connor Rd *DAGW* RM9 ... 80 B3
Connor St *HOM* E9 ... 75 F7
Conolly Rd *HNWL* W7 ... 84 E1
Conrad Dr *WPK* KT4 ... 161 F7
Conroy Ct *SCUP* DA14 ... 155 G3
Consfield Av *NWMAL* KT3 ... 160 D3
Consort Cl *FBAR/BDGN* N11 ... 39 K4
Consort Ms *ISLW* TW7 ... 123 J5
Consort Rd *PECK* SE15 ... 111 J7
Cons St *STHWK* SE1 * ... 18 B1
Constable Av *CAN/RD* E16 ... 95 F7
Constable Cl *FBAR/BDGN* N11 ... 40 B4
GLDGN NW11 ... 53 F5
YEAD UB4 ... 82 A1
Constable Crs
SEVS/STOTM N15 ... 56 C4
Constable Gdns *EDGW* HA8 ... 36 C7
ISLW TW7 ... 123 J4
Constable Ms *BCTR* RM8 ... 79 H4
Constable Wk *DUL* SE21 ... 150 A2
Constance Crs *HAYES* BR2 ... 167 J7
Constance Gv *DART* DA1 ... 139 G5
Constance Rd *CROY/NA* CR0 ... 164 C6
EN EN1 ... 30 A5
SUT SM1 ... 175 G3
WHTN TW2 ... 123 G6
Constance St *CAN/RD* E16 ... 95 J7
Constantine Rd *HAMP* NW3 ... 71 J4
Constitution HI
MYFR/PICC W1J ... 16 C1
Constitution Ri
WOOL/PLUM SE18 ... 115 F7
Consul Av *DAGW* RM9 ... 98 E3
Content St *WALW* SE17 ... 18 F6
Control Tower Rd
HTHAIR TW6 ... 120 D2
BECK BR3 ... 152 A6
Convent Gdns *EA* W5 ... 104 D3
NTGHL W11 ... 88 D5
Convent HI *NRWD* SE19 ... 149 J5
Convent Wy *NWDGN* UB2 ... 102 B3
Conway Cl *RAIN* RM13 ... 81 J6
STAN HA7 ... 35 G5
Conway Crs *CHDH* RM6 ... 61 J6
GFD/PVL UB6 ... 84 E1
Conway Dr *ASHF* TW15 ... 140 A5
BELMT SM2 ... 175 F5
HYS/HAR UB3 ... 101 G3
Conway Gdns *MTCM* CR4 ... 163 J3
WBLY HA9 ... 49 J6
Conway Gv *ACT* W3 ... 87 F4
Conway Ms *FITZ* W1T * ... 10 E2
Conway Rd *CRICK* NW2 ... 70 A1
FELT TW13 ... 141 H4
HSLWW TW4 ... 122 E6
RYNPK SW20 ... 146 A7
SEVS/STOTM N15 ... 55 H4
STHGT/OAK N14 ... 40 E2
WOOL/PLUM SE18 ... 115 J3
Conway St *FITZ* W1T ... 10 E1
Conybeare *HAMP* NW3 ... 3 K1
Conyers Rd
STRHM/NOR SW16 ... 148 D3
Conyer St *BOW* E3 * ... 93 G1
Cooden Cl *BMLY* BR1 ... 153 F6
Cookes Cl *WAN* E11 ... 76 D1
Cookes La *CHEAM* SM3 ... 174 C5
Cookham Cl *NWDGN* UB2 ... 103 G2
Cookham Dene Cl *CHST* BR7 ... 154 D1
Cookhill Rd *ABYW* SE2 ... 116 C1
Cooks Ferry Rbt *UED* N18 ... 43 G4
Cooks Md *BUSH* WD23 ... 22 B5
Cookson Gv *ERITH* DA8 ... 117 J6
Cooks Rd *SRTFD* E15 ... 93 K1
WALW SE17 ... 18 C9
Coolfin Rd *CAN/RD* E16 ... 94 E5
Coolgardie Av *CHING* E4 ... 44 B4
Coolgardie Rd *ASHF* TW15 ... 140 A4
Coolhurst Rd *HGT* N6 ... 54 D5
Cool Oak Br *CDALE/KGS* NW9 ... 51 H6
Cool Oak La *CDALE/KGS* NW9 ... 51 H6
Coomassie Rd *MV/WKIL* W9 ... 88 D3
Coombe Av *CROY/NA* CR0 ... 178 A3
Coombe Bank *KUTN/CMB* KT2 ... 145 J2
Coombe Cl *EDGW* HA8 ... 50 B1
HSLW TW3 ... 123 F3
Coombe Cnr *WCHMH* N21 ... 29 H7
Coombe Crs *HPTN* TW12 ... 141 J6
Coombe Dr *RSLP* HA4 ... 47 F7
Coombe End *KUTN/CMB* KT2 ... 145 F6
Coombefield Cl *NWMAL* KT3 ... 160 B4
Coombe Gdns *NWMAL* KT3 ... 160 D3
RYNPK SW20 ... 160 E1
Coombe Hill Gld
NWMAL KT3 ... 145 F7
Coombe Hill Rd
KUTN/CMB KT2 ... 145 G6
Coombe House Cha
NWMAL KT3 ... 145 F7
Coombehurst Cl *EBAR* EN4 ... 27 K1
Coombe La *CROY/NA* CR0 ... 178 C5
Coombe La West
KUTN/CMB KT2 ... 144 E7
Coombe Lea *BMLY* BR1 ... 168 D2
Coombe Ldg *CHARL* SE7 ... 114 B5
Coombe Neville
KUTN/CMB KT2 ... 144 E6
Coombe Pk *KUTN/CMB* KT2 ... 144 E4
Coombe Ridings
KUTN/CMB KT2 ... 144 E4
Coombe Ri *KUTN/CMB* KT2 ... 144 E7
Coombe Rd *BUSH* WD23 ... 22 C6
CHSWK W4 ... 106 B4
CROY/NA CR0 ... 177 K3
HPTN TW12 ... 141 K6
KUTN/CMB KT2 ... 144 E7
NWMAL KT3 ... 160 B2
SAND/SEL CR2 ... 178 A3
SYD SE26 ... 150 D3
WEA W13 ... 104 C1
WLSDN NW10 ... 69 F2

Coomber Wy *CROY/NA* CR0 ... 163 J6
Coombewood Dr *CHDH* RM6 ... 62 B5
Coombe Wood Rd
KUTN/CMB KT2 ... 144 E4
Coombs St *IS* N1 ... 6 C7
Coomer Ms *FUL/PGN* SW6 * ... 107 J5
Coomer Pl *FUL/PGN* SW6 ... 107 J5
Cooms Wk *EDGW* HA8 ... 36 D7
Cooperage Cl *TOTM* N17 ... 42 B5
Cooper Av *WALTH* E17 ... 43 F7
Cooper Cl *STHWK* SE1 ... 18 B2
Cooperdale Cl *WFD* IG8 ... 45 G6
Cooper Rd *CROY/NA* CR0 ... 177 G3
HDN NW4 ... 52 B5
WLSDN NW10 ... 69 H4
Coopersale Cl *WFD* IG8 ... 45 G6
Coopersale Rd *HOM* E9 ... 75 F4
Coopers Cl *DAGE* RM10 ... 80 D5
WCHPL E1 ... 92 E3
Coopers La *CAMTN* NW1 ... 5 H6
LEE/GVPK SE12 ... 153 F1
Cooper's La *LEY* E10 ... 57 K7
Coopers Ms *BECK* BR3 ... 166 D1
Cooper's Rd *STHWK* SE1 ... 19 M8
Cooper's Rw *TWRH* EC3N ... 13 L6
Cooper St *CAN/RD* E16 ... 94 D4
Coopers Yd *IS* N1 * ... 6 C2
Cooper's Yd *NRWD* SE19 ... 150 A5
Coote Rd *BCTR* RM8 ... 80 B2
BXLYHN DA7 ... 117 G2
Copeland Rd *PECK* SE15 ... 131 H1
WALTH E17 ... 57 K4
Copeman Cl *SYD* SE26 ... 150 E4
Copenhagen Gdns *CHEL* SW3 ... 15 J5
CHSWK W4 ... 106 A1
Copenhagen Pl *POP/IOD* E14 ... 93 H5
Copenhagen St *IS* N1 ... 5 K4
Cope Pl *KENS* W8 ... 14 A4
Copers Cope Rd *BECK* BR3 ... 151 H6
Cope St *BERM/RHTH* SE16 ... 112 A3
Copford Wk *IS* N1 * ... 6 E3
Copgate Pth
STRHM/NOR SW16 ... 149 F5
Copland Av *ALP/SUD* HA0 ... 67 K4
Copland Cl *ALP/SUD* HA0 ... 67 J4
Copland Ms *ALP/SUD* HA0 ... 68 A5
Copland Rd *ALP/SUD* HA0 ... 68 A5
Copleston Rd *PECK* SE15 ... 131 G2
Copley Cl *HNWL* W7 ... 85 F5
WALW SE17 ... 110 C5
Copley Dene *BMLY* BR1 ... 153 H7
Copley Pk *STRHM/NOR* SW16 ... 149 F5
Copley Rd *STAN* HA7 ... 35 J4
Copley St *WCHPL* E1 ... 93 F4
Coppard Gdns *CHSGTN* KT9 ... 171 J5
Coppelia Rd *BKHTH/KID* SE3 ... 133 J3
Coppen Rd *BCTR* RM8 ... 62 B7
Copperas St *DEPT* SE8 ... 112 E5
Copper Cl *NRWD* SE19 ... 150 B6
TOTM N17 ... 42 D6
Copperdale Rd *HYS/HAR* UB3 ... 101 K1
Copperfield Dr
SEVS/STOTM N15 ... 56 B3
Copperfield Rd *BOW* E3 ... 93 G3
THMD SE28 ... 97 J5
Copperfields *SUN* TW16 * ... 140 D5
Copperfield St *STHWK* SE1 ... 18 D1
Copperfield Wy *CHST* BR7 ... 154 C5
PIN HA5 ... 47 K3
Coppergate Cl *BMLY* BR1 ... 153 F7
Coppermead Cl *CRICK* NW2 ... 70 A2
Copper Mill Dr *ISLW* TW7 ... 124 A1
Copper Mill La *TOOT* SW17 ... 147 G3
Coppermill La *WALTH* E17 ... 56 E5
Copper Rw *STHWK* SE1 ... 13 L9
Coppetts Cl
NFNCH/WDSPK N12 ... 39 K6
Coppetts Rd *MUSWH* N10 ... 39 K5
Coppice Cl *BECK* BR3 ... 166 E3
RSLP HA4 ... 46 B4
RYNPK SW20 ... 161 F2
STAN HA7 ... 35 F5
Coppice Dr *PUT/ROE* SW15 ... 126 D5
The Coppice *BAR* EN5 * ... 26 E5
ENC/FH EN2 ... 29 H1
OXHEY WD19 ... 21 G5
Coppice Wk *TRDG/WHET* N20 ... 38 E2
Coppice Wy *SWFD* E18 ... 58 D3
Coppies Gv *FBAR/BDGN* N11 ... 40 A3
Copping Cl *CROY/NA* CR0 ... 178 A3
The Coppins *CROY/NA* CR0 ... 179 K5
KTN/HRWW/WS HA3 ... 34 E5
Coppock Cl *BTSEA* SW11 ... 128 D1
Coppsfield *E/WMO/HCT* KT8 ... 157 F2
Copse Av *WWKM* BR4 ... 179 K2
Copse Cl *CHARL* SE7 ... 114 A5
NTHWD HA6 ... 32 A7
WDR/YW UB7 ... 100 A2
Copse Gld *SURB* KT6 ... 158 E7
Copse HI *BELMT* SM2 ... 175 F6
RYNPK SW20 ... 145 J7
Copsem Dr *ESH/CLAY* KT10 ... 170 A5
Copsem La *ESH/CLAY* KT10 ... 170 B5
Copsem Wy *ESH/CLAY* KT10 ... 170 C5
The Copse *BUSH* WD23 ... 22 B7
CHING E4 * ... 44 E1
Copse Vw *SAND/SEL* CR2 ... 179 F6
Copsewood Cl *BFN/LL* DA15 ... 135 K5
Copse Wood Wy *NTHWD* HA6 ... 32 A7
Coptefield Dr *BELV* DA17 ... 116 E2
Copthall Av *LOTH* EC2R ... 13 H4
Copthall Dr *MLHL* NW7 ... 37 J6
Copthall Gdns *MLHL* NW7 ... 37 J6
TWK TW1 ... 124 A7
Copthorne Av *BAL* SW12 ... 129 J6
BARK/HLT IG6 ... 60 E1
HAYES BR2 ... 181 K1
Copthorne Ms *HYS/HAR* UB3 ... 101 H3
Coptic St *NOXST/BSQ* WC1A ... 11 J3
Copton Cl *BOW* E3 ... 93 J4
Copwood Cl
NFNCH/WDSPK N12 ... 39 H4
Coral Cl *CHDH* RM6 ... 61 J2
Coraline Cl *STHL* UB1 ... 83 K2
Coralline Wk *ABYW* SE2 ... 116 D1
Coral Rw *BTSEA* SW11 ... 128 B2
Coral St *STHWK* SE1 ... 18 A2
Coran Cl *ED* N9 ... 31 F6
Corban Rd *HSLW* TW3 ... 123 F2
Corbet Ct *BANK* EC3V ... 13 H5
Corbet Pl *WCHPL* E1 ... 13 L2
Corbett Gv *FBAR/BDGN* N11 ... 40 A3
Corbett Rd *WALTH* E17 ... 58 B1
WAN E11 ... 59 F5
Corbett's La *BERM/RHTH* SE16 ... 111 K3
Corbicum *WAN* E11 ... 58 C6
Corbiere Ct *WIM/MER* SW19 ... 146 B5
Corbin's La *RYLN/HDSTN* HA2 ... 66 C1
Corbridge Crs *BETH* E2 ... 92 D1

Corbridge Ms *ROM* RM1 ... 63 H4
Corby Crs *ENC/FH* EN2 ... 28 E3
Corbylands Rd *BFN/LL* DA15 ... 135 K6
Corbyn St *FSBYPK* N4 ... 54 E7
Corby Rd *WLSDN* NW10 ... 86 E1
Cordelia Gdns
STWL/WRAY TW19 ... 120 B6
Cordelia Rd *STWL/WRAY* TW19 ... 120 B6
Cordelia St *POP/IOD* E14 ... 93 K5
Cordingley Rd *RSLP* HA4 ... 46 B7
Cording St *POP/IOD* E14 ... 93 K4
Cordwell Rd *LEW* SE13 ... 133 G4
Corfe Av *RYLN/HDSTN* HA2 ... 66 A3
Corfe Cl *BORE* WD6 ... 25 F2
HSLWW TW4 ... 122 D7
YEAD UB4 ... 83 D5
Corfield Rd *WCHMH* N21 ... 29 F4
Corfield St *BETH* E2 ... 92 D3
Corfton Rd *EA* W5 ... 86 A5
Coriander Av *POP/IOD* E14 ... 94 B5
Cories Cl *BCTR* RM8 ... 79 K1
Corinium Cl *WBLY* HA9 ... 68 B3
Corinne Rd *ARCH* N19 ... 72 C3
Corinthian Manorway
ERITH DA8 ... 118 A3
Corinthian Rd *ERITH* DA8 ... 118 A3
Corkran Rd *SURB* KT6 ... 158 E6
Cork St Ms *CONDST* W1S ... 10 E7
Cork Sq *WAP* E1W ... 92 D7
Cork St *CONDST* W1S ... 10 D7
Cork Tree Wy *CHING* E4 ... 43 G4
Corlett St *CAMTN* NW1 ... 9 J2
Cormont Rd *CMBW* SE5 ... 110 C7
Cormorant Cl *WALTH* E17 ... 43 F7
Cormorant Rd *FSTGT* E7 ... 76 D4
Cornbury Rd *EDGW* HA8 ... 35 K6
Cornelia Dr *YEAD* UB4 ... 83 G4
Cornelia St *HOLWY* N7 ... 73 F5
Corner Fielde
BRXS/STRHM SW2 * ... 130 A7
Corner Gn *BKHTH/KID* SE3 ... 133 K1
Corner Md *CDALE/KGS* NW9 ... 37 H6
Cornerside *ASHF* TW15 ... 140 A6
The Corner *EA* W5 * ... 86 A7
Corney Reach Wy *CHSWK* W4 ... 106 B6
Corney Rd *CHSWK* W4 ... 106 B5
Cornfield Rd *BUSH* WD23 ... 22 B3
Cornflower La *CROY/NA* CR0 ... 166 A7
Cornflower Ter *EDUL* SE22 ... 131 J5
Cornford Cl *HAYES* BR2 ... 167 K4
Cornford Gv *BAL* SW12 ... 148 B1
Cornhill *BANK* EC3V ... 13 H5
Cornish Ct *ED* N9 ... 30 D6
Cornish Gv *PGE/AN* SE20 ... 150 D7
Cornmill La *LEW* SE13 ... 132 E2
Cornmow Dr *WLSDN* NW10 ... 69 H4
Cornshaw Rd *BCTR* RM8 ... 61 K7
Cornthwaite Rd *CLPT* E5 ... 74 E2
Cornwall Av *BETH* E2 ... 92 E2
ESH/CLAY KT10 ... 171 F6
FNCH N3 ... 38 E6
STHL UB1 ... 83 K4
WDGN N22 ... 40 D7
WELL DA16 ... 135 K2
Cornwall Cl *BARK* IG11 ... 79 F5
Cornwall Crs *NTGHL* W11 ... 88 C6
Cornwall Dr *STMC/STPC* BR5 ... 155 J6
Cornwall Gdns *SKENS* SW7 ... 14 C4
SNWD SE25 ... 165 G3
WLSDN NW10 ... 69 K5
Cornwall Gardens Wk
SKENS SW7 ... 14 C4
Cornwallis Av *CHSWK* W4 ... 106 D4
ED N9 ... 42 D1
Cornwallis Cl *ERITH* DA8 ... 118 C5
Cornwallis Gv *ED* N9 ... 42 D1
Cornwallis Rd *ARCH* N19 ... 72 E1
DAGW RM9 ... 80 A3
ED N9 ... 42 D1
WALTH E17 ... 57 F3
WOOL/PLUM SE18 ... 115 H4
Cornwallis Sq *ARCH* N19 ... 72 E1
FSBYPK N4 ... 73 G1
Cornwallis Wk *ELTH/MOT* SE9 ... 134 E2
Cornwall Ms South
SKENS SW7 ... 14 D4
Cornwall Ms West
SKENS SW7 ... 14 C4
Cornwall Rd *BELMT* SM2 ... 174 D6
CROY/NA CR0 ... 177 H1
DART DA1 ... 139 J2
FSBYPK N4 ... 55 G6
HRW HA1 ... 48 C5
PIN HA5 ... 33 K6
RSLP HA4 ... 64 D1
SEVS/STOTM N15 ... 55 K4
STHWK SE1 ... 12 A8
TWK TW1 ... 124 B6
UED N18 ... 42 C4
Cornwall St *WCHPL* E1 ... 92 D6
Cornwall Ter *CAMTN* NW1 ... 9 M1
Cornwall Terrace Ms
CAMTN NW1 ... 9 M1
Corn Wy *WAN* E11 ... 76 B2
Cornwood Cl *EFNCH* N2 ... 53 H4
Cornwood Dr *WCHPL* E1 ... 92 E5
Cornworthy Rd *BCTR* RM8 ... 79 J4
Corona Rd *LEE/GVPK* SE12 ... 133 K6
Coronation Cl *BARK/HLT* IG6 ... 60 C1
BXLY DA5 ... 136 E5
Coronation Dr *HCH* RM12 ... 81 K4
Coronation Rd *HYS/HAR* UB3 ... 101 J3
PLSTW E13 ... 95 G2
WLSDN NW10 ... 86 D3
Coronation Vls
WLSDN NW10 ... 86 D3
Coronet Pde *ALP/SUD* HA0 * ... 68 A5
Coronet St *IS* N1 ... 7 J8
Corporation Av *HSLWW* TW4 ... 122 D3
Corporation Rw *CLKNW* EC1R ... 6 A9
Corporation St *HOLWY* N7 ... 72 E4
SRTFD E15 ... 94 C1
Corrance Rd
BRXS/STRHM SW2 ... 129 K3
Corri Av *STHGT/OAK* N14 ... 40 D3
Corrib Dr *SUT* SM1 ... 175 J4
Corrigan Cl *HDN* NW4 ... 52 A2
Corringham Rd *GLDGN* NW11 ... 52 E6
WBLY HA9 ... 68 C1
Corringway *EA* W5 ... 86 B4
GLDGN NW11 ... 53 F6
Corris Gn *CDALE/KGS* NW9 * ... 51 G5
Corry Dr *BRXN/ST* SW9 ... 130 C3
Corsair Cl *STWL/WRAY* TW19 ... 120 A6
Corsair Rd *STWL/WRAY* TW19 ... 120 B6
Corscombe Cl *KUTN/CMB* KT2 ... 144 E4
Corsehill St *STRHM/NOR* SW16 ... 148 C5
Corsellis Sq *TWK* TW1 ... 124 C3
Corsham St *IS* N1 ... 7 H8

Corsica St *HBRY* N5 ... 73 H5
Cortayne Rd *FUL/PGN* SW6 * ... 127 J1
Cortina Dr *DAGW* RM9 ... 98 E2
Cortis Rd *PUT/ROE* SW15 ... 126 E5
Cortis Ter *PUT/ROE* SW15 ... 126 K4
Cortland Cl *DART* DA1 ... 138 B5
Corunna Rd *VX/NE* SW8 ... 109 H7
Corunna Ter *VX/NE* SW8 ... 109 H7
Corwell Gdns *UX/CGN* UB8 ... 82 A5
Corwell La *UX/CGN* UB8 ... 82 A5
Coryton Pth *MV/WKIL* W9 ... 88 D3
Cosbycote Av *HNHL* SE24 ... 130 D4
Cosdach Av *WLGTN* SM6 ... 176 D6
Cosgrove Cl *WCHMH* N21 ... 41 J1
YEAD UB4 ... 83 H3
Cosmo Pl *RSO* WC1B ... 11 K2
Cosmur Cl *SHB* W12 ... 106 C2
Cossall Wk *PECK* SE15 ... 111 J7
Cossar Ms *BRXS/STRHM* SW2 ... 130 B5
Cosser St *STHWK* SE1 ... 17 M3
Costa St *PECK* SE15 ... 131 H1
Costons Av *GFD/PVL* UB6 ... 84 D2
Costons La *GFD/PVL* UB6 ... 84 D2
Cosway St *CAMTN* NW1 ... 9 K2
Cotall St *POP/IOD* E14 ... 93 J5
Coteford Cl *PIN* HA5 ... 46 E4
Coteford St *TOOT* SW17 ... 147 K3
Cotelands *CROY/NA* CR0 ... 178 A2
Cotesbach Rd *CLPT* E5 ... 74 E2
Cotesmore Gdns *BCTR* RM8 ... 79 J3
Cotford Rd *THHTH* CR7 ... 164 D3
Cotham St *WALW* SE17 ... 18 F6
Cotherstone *HOR/WEW* KT19 ... 173 F7
Cotherstone Rd
BRXS/STRHM SW2 ... 130 A3
Cotleigh Av *BXLY* DA5 ... 155 K1
Cotleigh Rd *KIL/WHAMP* NW6 ... 2 A1
ROMW/RG RM7 ... 63 F5
Cotman Cl *GLDGN* NW11 ... 53 G5
Cotman Ms *BCTR* RM8 ... 79 H4
Cotmans Cl *HYS/HAR* UB3 ... 82 E7
Coton Rd *WELL* DA16 ... 136 B2
Cotswold Av *BUSH* WD23 ... 22 C5
Cotswold Cl *BXLYHN* DA7 ... 118 B7
ESH/CLAY KT10 ... 171 F1
KUTN/CMB KT2 ... 144 D5
Cotswold Gdns *CRICK* NW2 ... 70 B1
EHAM E6 ... 95 H2
GNTH/NBYPK IG2 ... 60 D6
Cotswold Ga *CRICK* NW2 ... 52 C7
Cotswold Gn *ENC/FH* EN2 ... 29 F3
Cotswold Ms *BTSEA* SW11 ... 108 C7
Cotswold Rd *HPTN* TW12 ... 142 A5
Cotswold St *WNWD* SE27 ... 149 H3
Cotswold Wy *ENC/FH* EN2 ... 29 F2
WPK KT4 ... 174 A1
Cottage Cl *RSLP* HA4 ... 46 B7
RYLN/HDSTN HA2 ... 66 D1
WAT WD17 ... 20 D7
Cottage Field Cl *SCUP* DA14 ... 136 D7
Cottage Gn *CMBW* SE5 ... 110 E6
Cottage Gv *BRXN/ST* SW9 ... 129 K2
SURB KT6 ... 158 E5
Cottage Pl *CHEL* SW3 ... 15 J3
Cottage Rd *HOLWY* N7 ... 73 F4
HOR/WEW KT19 ... 173 F6
The Cottages *HAMP* NW3 * ... 36 D6
Cottage St *POP/IOD* E14 ... 93 K6
Cottenham Dr
CDALE/KGS NW9 ... 51 H2
RYNPK SW20 ... 145 K6
Cottenham Park Rd
RYNPK SW20 ... 145 J7
Cottenham Pl *RYNPK* SW20 ... 145 K6
Cottenham Rd *WALTH* E17 ... 57 H3
Cotterill Rd *SURB* KT6 ... 172 B1
Cottesbrook St *NWCR* SE14 ... 112 B6
Cottesloe Ms *STHWK* SE1 ... 18 B3
Cottesmore Av *CLAY* IG5 ... 59 K1
Cottesmore Gdns *KENS* W8 ... 14 D3
Cottimore Av *WOT/HER* KT12 ... 156 A6
Cottimore Crs *WOT/HER* KT12 ... 156 A6
Cottimore La *WOT/HER* KT12 ... 156 A6
Cottimore Ter *WOT/HER* KT12 ... 156 A6
Cottingham Cha *RSLP* HA4 ... 64 E2
Cottingham Rd *PGE/AN* SE20 ... 151 F6
VX/NE SW8 ... 110 A6
Cottington Rd *FELT* TW13 ... 141 K2
Cottington St *LBTH* SE11 ... 18 B7
Cotton Av *ACT* W3 ... 87 F5
Cotton Cl *DAGW* RM9 ... 79 J6
WAN E11 ... 76 C1
Cotton Gardens Est
LBTH SE11 ... 18 C6
Cottongrass Cl *CROY/NA* CR0 ... 166 A7
Cottonham Cl
NFNCH/WDSPK N12 ... 39 H4
Cotton HI *BMLY* BR1 ... 152 B3
Cotton Rw *BTSEA* SW11 ... 128 B2
Cottons Ap *ROMW/RG* RM7 ... 63 F4
Cotton's Gdns *BETH* E2 ... 7 K7
Cotton St *POP/IOD* E14 ... 94 A6
Couchmore Av *CLAY* IG5 ... 59 K1
ESH/CLAY KT10 ... 170 E1
Coulgate St *BROCKY* SE4 ... 132 B2
Coulson Cl *BCTR* RM8 ... 61 J7
Coulson St *CHEL* SW3 ... 15 L7
Coulter Cl *YEAD* UB4 ... 83 J3
Coulter Rd *HMSMTH* W6 ... 106 E2
Councillor St *CMBW* SE5 ... 110 D6
Countess Rd *KTTN* NW5 ... 72 C4
Countisbury Av *EN* EN1 ... 30 B6
Country Wy *FELT* TW13 ... 141 G4
County Ga *BAR* EN5 ... 27 F5
ELTH/MOT SE9 ... 154 C2
County Gv *CMBW* SE5 ... 110 D7
County Pde *BTFD* TW8 * ... 104 E6
County Rd *EHAM* E6 ... 96 B4
THHTH CR7 ... 164 C1
County St *STHWK* SE1 ... 18 F4
Coupland Pl
WOOL/PLUM SE18 ... 115 H4
Courcy Rd *CEND/HSY/T* N8 ... 55 G2
Courier Rd *DAGW* RM9 ... 98 E3
Courland Gv *VX/NE* SW8 ... 109 J7
Courland Rd *VX/NE* SW8 ... 109 J7
Courland St *VX/NE* SW8 ... 109 J7
The Course *ELTH/MOT* SE9 ... 154 A2
Courtauld Rd *ARCH* N19 ... 54 D7
Courtaulds Cl *THMD* SE28 ... 97 G2
Court Av *BELV* DA17 ... 117 G4
Court Cl *KTN/HRWW/WS* HA3 ... 49 K3
STJWD NW8 ... 3 G2
WHTN TW2 ... 142 B2
WLGTN SM6 ... 176 D6
Court Close Av *WHTN* TW2 ... 142 B2
Court Crs *CHSGTN* KT9 ... 171 K5
Court Downs Rd *BECK* BR3 ... 166 E1
Court Dr *CROY/NA* CR0 ... 177 F3
STAN HA7 ... 36 A3

SUT SM1 ...175 J3
Courtenay Av BELMT SM2 ...174 E7
HGT N6 ...53 J6
KTN/HRWW/WS HA3 ...34 B6
Courtenay Dr BECK BR3 ...167 G4
Courtenay Ms WALTH E17 ...57 G4
Courtenay Pl WALTH E17 ...57 G4
Courtenay Rd PGE/AN SE20 ...151 J2
WALTH E17 ...57 F4
WAN E11 * ...76 D1
WBLY HA9 * ...67 K2
WPK KT4 ...174 A2
Courtenay Sq LBTH SE11 * ...18 A3
Courtenay St LBTH SE11 ...17 M7
Courten Ms STAN HA7 ...35 J6
Court Farm Av HOR/WEW KT19 ...173 H4
Court Farm Rd ELTH/MOT SE9 ...153 H1
NTHLT UB5 ...66 A6
Courtfield Av HRW HA1 * ...49 F4
Courtfield Crs HRW HA1 * ...49 F4
Courtfield Gdns ECT SW5 ...14 D6
RSLP HA4 ...64 D1
WEA W13 ...85 G5
Courtfield Ms ECT SW5 * ...14 D6
Courtfield Ri WWKM BR4 ...180 B2
Courtfield Rd SKENS SW7 ...14 D6
Court Gdns HOLWY N7 ...73 G5
Courthill Rd LEW SE13 ...133 F3
Courthope Rd GFD/PVL UB6 ...84 B4
HAMP NW3 ...71 K3
WIM/MER SW19 ...146 C5
Courthope Vls WIM/MER SW19 ...146 C6
Courthouse La STNW/STAM N16 ...74 B3
Court House Rd FNCH N3 ...39 F5
Courtland Av CHING E4 ...44 D1
IL IG1 ...97 K1
MLHL NW7 ...37 F2
STRHM/NOR SW16 ...149 F6
Courtland Gv THMD SE28 ...97 K6
Courtland Rd EHAM E6 ...77 J6
Courtlands CHST BR7 ...154 B6
RCHPK/HAM TW10 ...125 H4
Courtlands Av HAYES BR2 ...167 H7
HPTN TW12 ...141 K6
LEE/GVPK SE12 ...134 A4
RCH/KEW TW9 ...125 J1
Courtlands CI RSLP HA4 ...46 D6
Courtlands Dr HOR/WEW KT19 ...173 G5
Courtlands Rd BRYLDS KT5 ...159 H1
Court La DUL SE21 ...131 G6
Court Lane Gdns DUL SE21 ...131 H6
Courtleet Dr BXLYHN DA7 ...117 J7
Courtleigh Gdns GLDGN NW11 ...52 C3
Courtman Rd TOTM N17 ...41 J6
Court Md NTHLT UB5 ...83 K2
Courtmead CI HNHL SE24 ...130 D5
Courtnell St BAY/PAD W2 ...8 B4
Courtney CI NRWD SE19 ...150 A5
Courtney Crs CAR SM5 ...175 K6
Courtney PI CROY/NA CR0 ...177 G2
Courtney Rd CROY/NA CR0 ...177 G2
HOLWY N7 ...73 G4
HTHAIR TW6 ...120 D2
WBLY HA9 ...67 K2
WIM/MER SW19 ...147 J6
Courtney Wy HTHAIR TW6 ...120 D2
Courtrai Rd FSTH SE23 ...132 B5
Court Rd ELTH/MOT SE9 ...153 J1
NWDGN UB2 ...102 E3
SNWD SE25 ...165 G1
Courtside HGT N6 ...54 D5
SYD SE26 * ...150 E2
The Courts STRHM/NOR SW16 ...148 E6
Courtstreet BMLY BR1 ...167 K1
Court St WCHPL E1 ...92 D4
The Court MUSWH N10 * ...54 C3
RSLP HA4 ...65 J3
Court Vw HGT N6 * ...72 B1
Court Wy ACT W3 ...86 E4
BARK/HLT IG6 ...60 C2
CDALE/KGS NW9 ...51 G3
WHTN TW2 ...124 A6
The Courtway OXHEY WD19 ...33 J1
Court Yd ELTH/MOT SE9 ...134 D5
Courtyard Ms RAIN RM13 ...81 H7
STMC/STPC BR5 ...155 G6
The Courtyards WATW WD18 * ...20 B6
The Courtyard IS N1 ...5 M1
Cousin La CANST EC4R ...13 G6
Couthurst Rd BKHTH/KID SE3 ...114 A4
Coutts Av CHSGTN KT9 ...172 A4
Coutts Crs KTTN NW5 * ...72 A2
Couzins Wk DART DA1 ...139 J1
Coval Gdns MORT/ESHN SW14 ...125 J3
Coval La MORT/ESHN SW14 ...125 J3
Coval Rd MORT/ESHN SW14 ...125 K3
Coveless Wall EHAM E6 ...96 A5
Covent Gdn WC2E ...11 K6
Covent Garden Piazza COVGDN WC2E ...11 K6
Coventry CI EHAM E6 ...95 K5
KIL/WHAMP NW6 ...2 C1
Coventry Cross Est BOW E3 ...94 A3
Coventry Rd BETH E2 ...92 D2
IL IG1 ...60 B7
SNWD SE25 ...165 H3
WCHPL E1 ...92 D3
Coventry St SOHO/SHAV W1D ...11 H7
Coverack CI HNHL SE24 ...166 B6
STHGT/OAK N14 ...28 C5
Coverdale Gdns CROY/NA CR0 ...178 B2
Coverdale Rd CRICK NW2 ...70 B6
FBAR/BDGN N11 ...40 A5
SHB W12 ...87 K7
The Coverdales BARK IG11 ...96 D1
Coverley CI WCHPL E1 * ...92 C4
Coverton Rd TOOT SW17 ...147 J3
Coverts Rd ESH/CLAY KT10 ...171 F6
The Covert NRWD SE19 * ...150 B6
NTHWD HA6 ...32 A6
ORP BR6 ...169 K5
Covert Wy EBAR EN4 ...27 G1
Covey CI WIM/MER SW19 ...162 A1
Covey Rd WPK KT4 ...174 B1
Covington Gdns STRHM/NOR SW16 ...149 H6
Covington Wy STRHM/NOR SW16 ...149 G6
Cowbridge La BARK IG11 ...78 B6
Cowbridge Rd KTN/HRWW/WS HA3 ...50 B3
Cowcross St FARR EC1M ...12 C2
Cowden Rd CAT SE6 ...151 J3
Cowdenbeath Pth IS N1 ...5 L3
Cowden St CAT SE6 * ...151 J3
Cowdray Rd HGDN/ICK UB10 ...64 A7
Cowdray Wy HCH RM12 ...81 J3
Cowdrey CI EN EN1 ...30 A1
Cowdrey Ct DART DA1 ...138 E6

Cowdrey Rd WIM/MER SW19 ...147 F5
Cowen Av HRW HA1 ...66 D1
Cowgate Rd GFD/PVL UB6 ...84 D2
Cowick Rd TOOT SW17 ...147 K3
Cowings Md NTHLT UB5 ...65 J6
Cowland Av PEND EN3 ...30 E4
Cow La BUSH WD23 * ...22 A5
Cow Leaze EHAM E6 ...96 A5
Cowleaze Rd KUTN/CMB KT2 ...144 A7
Cowley CI SAND/SEL CR2 ...178 E7
Cowley Ct WAN E11 * ...76 C2
Cowley La WAN E11 * ...76 C2
Cowley PI HDN NW4 ...52 A4
Cowley Rd ACT W3 ...87 H7
BRXN/ST SW9 ...110 B7
IL IG1 ...59 K6
MORT/ESHN SW14 ...126 B2
WAN E11 ...59 F4
Cowley St WEST SW1P ...17 J3
Cowling CI NTCHL W11 ...88 C6
Cowper Av EHAM E6 ...77 J6
SUT SM1 ...175 H3
Cowper CI HAYES BR2 ...168 C3
WELL DA16 ...136 B4
Cowper Gdns STHGT/OAK N14 ...28 B5
WLGTN SM6 ...176 C5
Cowper Rd ACT W3 ...87 F7
BELV DA17 ...117 G3
HAYES BR2 ...168 C3
HNWL W7 ...85 F6
KUTN/CMB KT2 ...144 B5
RAIN RM13 ...99 J3
STHGT/OAK N14 ...28 B6
STNW/STAM N16 ...74 A3
UED N18 ...42 C4
WIM/MER SW19 ...147 G5
Cowper St STLK EC1Y ...7 H9
Cowper Ter NKENS W10 * ...88 B4
Cowslip Rd SWFD E18 ...59 F1
Cowthorpe Rd VX/NE SW8 ...109 J7
Coxe PI KTN/HRWW/WS HA3 ...49 K3
Cox La CHSGTN KT9 ...172 A3
Coxmount Rd CHARL SE7 ...114 C4
Coxson Wy STHWK SE1 ...19 L2
Coxwell Rd NRWD SE19 ...150 A6
Crab HI BECK BR3 ...152 B6
Crabtree Av ALP/SUD HA0 ...86 A1
CHDH RM6 ...61 K3
Crabtree CI BETH E2 ...7 L6
BUSH WD23 ...22 A4
Crabtree La FUL/PGN SW6 ...107 G6
Crabtree Manorway North BELV DA17 ...117 K1
Crabtree Manorway South BELV DA17 ...117 K1
Crabtree Wk CROY/NA CR0 ...165 H4
Craddock Rd EN EN1 ...30 B2
Craddock St KTTN NW5 * ...72 A5
Cradley Rd ELTH/MOT SE9 ...135 J7
Cragie Lea MUSWH N10 * ...54 B1
Craigdale Rd EMPK RM11 ...63 H5
Craigen Av CROY/NA CR0 ...165 J7
Craigerne Rd BKHTH/KID SE3 ...114 A6
Craig Gdns SWFD E18 ...58 D1
Craigholm WOOL/PLUM SE18 ...135 F1
Craigmuir Pk ALP/SUD HA0 ...68 A7
Craignair Rd BRXS/STRHM SW2 ...130 A6
Craignish Av STRHM/NOR SW16 ...164 A1
Craig Park Rd UED N18 ...42 D3
Craig Rd RCHPK/HAM TW10 ...143 J3
Craig's Ct WHALL SW1A ...11 J1
Craigton Rd ELTH/MOT SE9 ...134 E3
Craigweil CI STAN HA7 ...35 K4
Craigweil Dr STAN HA7 ...35 K4
Craigwell Av FELT TW13 ...140 E2
Crail Rw WALW SE17 ...19 H6
Crakers Md WATW WD18 * ...21 F2
Cramer St MHST W1U ...10 B3
Cramond CI HMSMTH W6 ...107 H5
Cramond Ct EBED/NFELT TW14 ...121 G7
Crampton Rd PGE/AN SE20 ...150 E5
Crampton St WALW SE17 ...18 E7
Cranberry CI NTHLT UB5 ...83 H1
Cranberry La CAN/RD E16 ...94 C3
Cranborne Av NWDGN UB2 ...103 F3
SURB KT6 ...172 C2
Cranborne Rd BARK IG11 ...78 D7
Cranborne Waye YEAD UB4 ...83 F5
Cranbourn Av WAN E11 ...59 F3
Cranbourne CI STRHM/NOR SW16 ...163 K2
Cranbourne Dr PIN HA5 ...47 H4
Cranbourne Gdns BARK/HLT IG6 ...60 C2
GLDGN NW11 ...52 C4
Cranbourne Rd MNPK E12 ...77 J4
MUSWH N10 ...54 B1
NTHWD HA6 ...46 D2
SRTFD E15 ...76 A3
Cranbourn St LSQ/SEVD WC2H ...11 H6
Cranbrook CI HAYES BR2 ...167 K5
Cranbrook Dr ESH/CLAY KT10 ...157 H7
GPK RM2 ...63 K3
WHTN TW2 ...123 G7
Cranbrook La FBAR/BDGN N11 ...40 B3
Cranbrook Pk WDGN N22 ...41 G7
Cranbrook Ri IL IG1 ...59 K5
Cranbrook Rd BARK/HLT IG6 ...60 C2
BXLYHN DA7 ...117 G3
CHSWK W4 ...106 B4
DEPT SE8 ...112 D7
EBAR EN4 ...27 H5
GNTH/NBYPK IG2 ...60 C7
HSLWW TW4 ...122 E3
IL IG1 ...78 A1
THHTH CR7 ...164 D1
WIM/MER SW19 ...146 C6
Cranbrook St BETH E2 ...93 F1
Cranbury Rd FUL/PGN SW6 ...128 A1
Crane Av ACT W3 ...86 E6
ISLW TW7 ...124 B4
Cranebank Ms TWK TW1 * ...124 C3
Cranebrook WHTN TW2 ...142 C1
Crane Ct DAGE RM10 ...80 D5
Crane Ct FLST/FETLN EC4A ...12 A5
MORT/ESHN SW14 * ...125 K3
Cranefield Dr WATN WD24 ...21 H1
Craneford Wy WHTN TW2 ...123 K6
Crane Gdns HYS/HAR UB3 ...101 J3
Crane Gv HOLWY N7 ...73 G5
Crane Md BERM/RHTH SE16 ...112 A3
Crane Park Rd WHTN TW2 ...142 B1
Crane Rd STWL/WRAY TW19 ...120 B6
WHTN TW2 ...123 K7
Cranesbill CI CDALE/KGS NW9 ...51 F2
STRHM/NOR SW16 ...163 J1

Cranes Dr BRYLDS KT5 ...159 F3
Cranes Pk BRYLDS KT5 ...159 F3
Cranes Park Av BRYLDS KT5 ...159 F3
Cranes Park Crs BRYLDS KT5 ...159 G3
Crane St PECK SE15 ...111 G7
Craneswater HYS/HAR UB3 ...101 J6
Craneswater Pk NWDGN UB2 ...102 E4
Crane Wy WHTN TW2 ...123 H6
Cranfield Dr CDALE/KGS NW9 ...37 G7
Cranfield Rd BROCKY SE4 ...132 C2
Cranfield Rd East CAR SM5 ...176 A7
Cranfield Rd West CAR SM5 * ...175 K7
Cranford Av PLMGR N13 ...40 E4
STWL/WRAY TW19 ...120 B6
Cranford CI RYNPK SW20 ...145 K6
STWL/WRAY TW19 ...120 B6
Cranford Cots WAP E1W * ...93 F6
Cranford Dr HYS/HAR UB3 ...101 J3
Cranford La HYS/HAR UB3 ...101 G5
Cranford Ms HAYES BR2 ...168 D4
Cranford Park Rd HYS/HAR UB3 ...101 J3
Cranford Ri ESH/CLAY KT10 ...170 C4
Cranford St WAP E1W ...93 F6
Cranford Wy CEND/HSY/T N8 ...55 F4
Cranham Rd EMPK RM11 ...63 K5
Cranhurst Rd CRICK NW2 ...70 A4
Cranleigh CI BXLY DA5 ...137 J5
PGE/AN SE20 ...165 J1
Cranleigh Gdns BARK IG11 ...78 D6
KTN/HRWW/WS HA3 ...50 A4
SAND/SEL CR2 ...178 B7
SNWD SE25 ...165 F2
STHL UB1 ...83 K5
SUT SM1 ...175 F1
WCHMH N21 ...29 G4
Cranleigh Ms BTSEA SW11 ...128 D1
Cranleigh Rd ESH/CLAY KT10 ...157 H7
FELT TW13 ...140 D3
SEVS/STOTM N15 ...55 J4
WIM/MER SW19 ...161 K2
Cranleigh St CAMTN NW1 ...4 F5
Cranley Dr GNTH/NBYPK IG2 ...60 C6
RSLP HA4 ...64 D1
Cranley Gdns MUSWH N10 ...54 B3
PLMGR N13 ...41 F2
SKENS SW7 ...14 F7
WLGTN SM6 ...176 C6
Cranley Ms SKENS SW7 ...14 F7
Cranley PI SKENS SW7 ...15 G6
Cranley Rd HDN NW4 * ...52 B1
PLSTW E13 ...95 F4
Cranley Ter HDN NW4 * ...52 B1
Cranmer Av WEA W13 ...104 C1
Cranmer CI MRDN SM4 ...161 G5
RSLP HA4 ...47 H7
STAN HA7 ...35 J6
Cranmer Ct HPTN TW12 ...142 B4
KUTN/CMB KT2 ...143 K3
Cranmer Farm CI MTCM CR4 ...162 E3
Cranmer Gdns DAGE RM10 ...80 E3
Cranmer Rd BRXN/ST SW9 ...110 B6
CROY/NA CR0 ...177 H2
EDGW HA8 ...36 D2
FSTGT E7 ...77 F3
HPTN TW12 ...142 B4
HYS/HAR UB3 ...82 B5
KUTN/CMB KT2 ...144 A4
MTCM CR4 ...162 E3
Cranmer Ter TOOT SW17 ...147 H4
Cranmore Av ISLW TW7 ...103 H6
Cranmore Rd BMLY BR1 ...152 C2
CHST BR7 ...153 K4
Cranmore Wy MUSWH N10 ...54 C3
Cranston CI HGDN/ICK UB10 ...64 B1
Cranston Est IS N1 ...7 G6
Cranston Gdns CHING E4 ...43 K5
Cranston Rd FSTH SE23 ...132 B7
Cranswick Rd BERM/RHTH SE16 ...111 J4
Crantock Rd CAT SE6 ...152 A1
Cranwell CI BOW E3 ...93 K3
Cranwich Av WCHMH N21 ...29 K6
Cranwich Rd STNW/STAM N16 ...56 A6
Cranwood St FSBYE EC1V ...7 H8
Cranworth Gdns BRXN/ST SW9 ...110 B7
Craster Rd BRXS/STRHM SW2 ...130 A6
Crathie Rd LEE/GVPK SE12 ...134 A5
Cravan Av FELT TW13 ...140 E1
Craven Av EA W5 ...85 J6
STHL UB1 ...83 K4
Craven CI STNW/STAM N16 * ...56 C6
YEAD UB4 ...82 E5
Craven Gdns BARK IG11 ...96 E1
BARK/HLT IG6 ...60 D1
WIM/MER SW19 ...147 F3
Craven Hill BAY/PAD W2 ...8 E6
Craven Hill Gdns BAY/PAD W2 ...8 D6
Craven Hill Ms BAY/PAD W2 ...8 E6
Craven Ms BTSEA SW11 ...129 F2
Craven Pk WLSDN NW10 ...69 G6
Craven Park Ms WLSDN NW10 ...69 G6
Craven Park Rd SEVS/STOTM N15 ...56 B5
WLSDN NW10 ...69 G6
Craven Pas CHCR WC2N ...11 J8
Craven Rd BAY/PAD W2 ...8 E5
CROY/NA CR0 ...165 J7
KUTN/CMB KT2 ...144 B1
WEA W13 ...85 J6
WLSDN NW10 ...69 G7
Craven St CHCR WC2N ...11 J8
Craven Ter BAY/PAD W2 ...8 E6
Craven Wk STNW/STAM N16 ...56 C6
Crawford Av ALP/SUD HA0 ...67 K4
Crawford CI ISLW TW7 ...123 K1
Crawford Gdns NTHLT UB5 ...83 K2
PLMGR N13 ...41 H2
Crawford Ms MBLAR W1H * ...9 L3
Crawford Pas CLKNW EC1R ...12 A1
Crawford PI MBLAR W1H ...9 K4
Crawford Rd CMBW SE5 ...130 D1
Crawford St MBLAR W1H ...9 M3
WLSDN NW10 ...69 F6
Crawley Rd EN EN1 ...30 A6
LEY E10 ...57 K7
WDGN N22 ...55 J1
Crawshay Ct BRXN/ST SW9 * ...110 B7
Crawthew Gv EDUL SE22 ...131 G3
Craybrooke Rd SCUP DA14 ...155 H3
Craybury End ELTH/MOT SE9 ...154 C1
Cray CI DART DA1 ...138 D3
Craydene Rd ERITH DA8 ...118 C7
Crayford High St DART DA1 ...138 B3
Crayford Rd DART DA1 ...138 C4
HOLWY N7 ...72 D3
Crayford Wy DART DA1 ...138 D2
Crayke HI CHSGTN KT9 ...172 A6

Crayleigh Ter SCUP DA14 * ...155 J5
Crayonne CI SUN TW16 ...140 C7
Cray Rd BELV DA17 ...117 H5
SCUP DA14 ...155 J5
Crealock Gv WFD IG8 ...44 D4
Crealock St WAND/EARL SW18 ...128 A5
Creasey CI EMPK RM11 ...81 K1
Crebor St EDUL SE22 ...131 H5
Credenhill St STRHM/NOR SW16 ...148 C5
Crediton HI KIL/WHAMP NW6 ...71 F4
Crediton Rd CAN/RD E16 ...94 E5
WLSDN NW10 ...70 D7
Crediton Wy ESH/CLAY KT10 ...171 G4
Credon Rd BERM/RHTH SE16 ...111 J4
PLSTW E13 ...95 G1
Creechurch La HDTCH EC3A ...13 K5
Creechurch PI HDTCH EC3A * ...13 L5
Creed La BLKFR EC4V ...12 D5
Creek Cots E/WMO/HCT KT8 * ...157 K3
Creek Rd BARK IG11 ...97 F2
DEPT SE8 ...112 D5
E/WMO/HCT KT8 ...157 K3
Creekside DEPT SE8 ...112 E6
RAIN RM13 ...99 H3
Creek Wy RAIN RM13 ...99 G5
Creeland Gv CAT SE6 ...132 C7
Crefeld CI HMSMTH W6 ...107 H5
Creffield Rd EA W5 ...86 C6
Creighton Av EFNCH N2 ...53 K1
EHAM E6 ...95 H1
Creighton CI SHB W12 ...87 K6
Creighton Rd EA W5 ...104 C2
KIL/WHAMP NW6 ...88 B1
TOTM N17 ...42 A6
Creigton Av EFNCH N2 ...53 J2
Cremer St BETH E2 ...7 L6
Cremorne Est WBPTN SW10 * ...108 C6
Cremorne Gdns HOR/WEW KT19 ...173 F7
Cremorne Rd WBPTN SW10 ...108 B6
Crescent TWRH EC3N ...13 L6
Crescent EH GNWCH SE10 ...113 F5
Crescent Av HCH RM12 ...81 H1
Crescent Dr STMC/STPC BR5 ...169 G5
Crescent Gdns RSLP HA4 ...47 F6
WIM/MER SW19 ...146 E2
Crescent Gv CLAP SW4 ...129 H3
MTCM CR4 ...162 D3
Crescent La CLAP SW4 ...129 J4
Crescent PI CHEL SW3 ...15 J5
Crescent Ri EBAR EN4 ...27 K4
FNCH N3 ...38 D7
WDGN N22 ...40 D7
Crescent Rd BECK BR3 ...166 E1
BFN/LL DA15 ...155 F2
BMLY BR1 ...152 E6
CEND/HSY/T N8 ...54 D6
DAGE RM10 ...80 D2
EBAR EN4 ...27 J4
ED N9 ...30 C7
EHAM E6 ...77 G7
ENC/FH EN2 ...29 H3
FBAR/BDGN N11 ...39 K3
FNCH N3 ...38 D7
KUTN/CMB KT2 ...144 C6
LEY E10 ...75 K1
PLSTW E13 ...76 E7
RYNPK SW20 ...146 B7
SEVS/STOTM N15 * ...55 H2
SWFD E18 ...59 G1
WDGN N22 ...40 C7
WOOL/PLUM SE18 ...115 G4
Crescent Rw FSBYE EC1Y ...12 E1
The Crescent ACT W3 ...87 G5
ALP/SUD HA0 ...67 H1
BAR EN5 ...26 E2
BARN SW13 ...126 C1
BECK BR3 ...151 J7
BXLY DA5 ...136 D6
CRICK NW2 ...69 K2
CROY/NA CR0 ...164 E5
E/WMO/HCT KT8 ...156 E3
FBAR/BDGN N11 ...39 K3
GNTH/NBYPK IG2 ...60 B4
HYS/HAR UB3 ...101 F6
NWMAL KT3 ...159 K1
RYLN/HDSTN HA2 ...48 C7
SCUP DA14 ...155 F3
STHL UB1 ...102 D2
SURB KT6 ...159 F4
SUT SM1 ...175 H4
WATW WD18 ...21 G3
WIM/MER SW19 ...146 E2
WWKM BR4 ...167 H5
Crescent Wy BROCKY SE4 ...132 D2
STRHM/NOR SW16 ...149 F6
Crescentway NFNCH/WDSPK N12 ...39 J5
Crescent Wood Rd SYD SE26 ...150 C2
Cresford Rd FUL/PGN SW6 ...108 A7
Crespigny Rd HDN NW4 ...51 K5
Cressage CI STHL UB1 ...84 A3
Cresset Rd HOM E9 ...74 E5
Cresset St CLAP SW4 ...129 J2
Cressfield CI KTTN NW5 ...72 A4
Cressida Rd ARCH N19 ...54 C7
Cressingham Gv SUT SM1 ...175 G3
Cressingham Rd EDGW HA8 ...37 F5
LEW SE13 ...133 F2
Cressington CI STNW/STAM N16 * ...74 A4
Cresswell Gdns ECT SW5 * ...14 E6
Cresswell Pk BKHTH/KID SE3 ...133 J2
Cresswell PI WBPTN SW10 ...14 E6
Cresswell Rd FELT TW13 ...141 J2
SNWD SE25 ...165 H3
TWK TW1 ...124 E5
Cresswell Wy WCHMH N21 ...29 G6
Cressy Ct HMSMTH W6 ...106 E2
WCHPL E1 ...92 E4
Cressy Houses WCHPL E1 * ...92 E4
Cressy PI WCHPL E1 ...92 E4
Cressy Rd HAMP NW3 ...71 K4
Cressys Cnr HSLW TW3 * ...123 G2
Crestbrook Av PLMGR N13 ...41 H2
Crestbrook PI PLMGR N13 ...41 H2
Crestfield St KCROSS N1C ...5 K7
Crest Gdns RSLP HA4 ...65 G2
Creston Wy WPK KT4 ...161 G7
Crest Rd CRICK NW2 ...69 H1
HAYES BR2 ...167 J7
SAND/SEL CR2 ...178 B7
The Crest BRYLDS KT5 ...159 H4
HDN NW4 ...52 A4
HOLWY N7 * ...72 D3
PLMGR N13 ...41 G3
Crest Vw PIN HA5 ...47 H3
Crest View Dr STMC/STPC BR5 ...169 G4

Crestway PUT/ROE SW15 ...126 D5
Crestwood Wy HSLWW TW4 ...122 E4
Creswell Dr BECK BR3 ...166 E4
Creswick Rd ACT W3 ...86 D6
Creswick Wk GLDGN NW11 ...52 E3
Creukhorne Rd WLSDN NW10 ...69 G6
Crewdson Rd BRXN/ST SW9 ...110 B6
Crewe PI WLSDN NW10 ...87 H2
Crews St POP/IOD E14 ...112 D3
Crewys Rd CRICK NW2 ...70 D1
PECK SE15 ...131 J1
Crichton Av WLGTN SM6 ...176 D4
Crichton Rd CAR SM5 ...175 K6
Crichton St VX/NE SW8 ...129 H1
Cricketers Arms Rd ENC/FH EN2 * ...29 J1
Cricketers CI CHSGTN KT9 ...171 K4
ERITH DA8 ...118 B4
STHGT/OAK N14 ...28 C6
Cricketers Ms BAL SW12 ...129 G6
WAND/EARL SW18 ...128 A4
Cricketers Wk SYD SE26 ...150 E4
Cricketfield Rd CLPT E5 ...74 D3
Cricket Gn MTCM CR4 ...162 E2
Cricket Ground Rd CHST BR7 ...154 B7
Cricket La BECK BR3 ...151 G5
HPTN TW12 ...142 C4
Cricket Rw EFNCH N2 * ...53 H2
Cricklade Av BRXS/STRHM SW2 ...148 E1
Cricklewood Broadway CRICK NW2 ...70 B3
Cricklewood La CRICK NW2 ...70 C3
Cridland St SRTFD E15 ...76 D7
Crieff Ct TEDD TW11 ...143 J6
Crieff Rd WAND/EARL SW18 ...128 B5
Criffel Av BRXS/STRHM SW2 ...148 D1
Crimscott St STHWK SE1 ...19 K4
Crimsworth Rd VX/NE SW8 ...109 J6
Crinan St IS N1 ...5 K5
Cringle St VX/NE SW8 ...109 H6
Cripplegate St BARB EC2Y * ...12 E2
Crispen Rd FELT TW13 ...141 J3
Crispian CI WLSDN NW10 ...69 G3
Crispin Crs CROY/NA CR0 ...176 D1
Crispin Ms GLDGN NW11 ...52 D4
Crispin Rd EDGW HA8 ...36 E5
Crispin St WCHPL E1 ...13 L3
Crisp Rd HMSMTH W6 ...107 F4
Cristowe Rd FUL/PGN SW6 * ...127 J1
Critchley Av DART DA1 ...139 G5
Criterion Ms ARCH N19 ...72 D1
HNHL SE24 ...130 C4
Crockerton Rd TOOT SW17 ...147 K1
Crockham Wy ELTH/MOT SE9 ...154 A4
Crocus CI CROY/NA CR0 ...166 A7
Crocus Fld BAR EN5 ...26 D5
Croft Av WWKM BR4 ...167 F7
Croft CI ABYW SE2 ...117 C4
CHST BR7 ...153 K4
HYS/HAR UB3 ...101 F6
MLHL NW7 ...37 G2
Croft Ct BORE WD6 ...25 F2
RSLP HA4 * ...65 H7
SUT SM1 ...175 H1
Croftdown Rd KTTN NW5 ...72 A2
Crofters CI ISLW TW7 ...123 J4
Crofters Ct DEPT SE8 * ...112 B3
Crofters Md CROY/NA CR0 ...179 H7
Crofters Rd NTHWD HA6 ...32 C3
Crofters Wy CAMTN NW1 ...5 G3
Croft Gdns HNWL W7 ...104 B1
RSLP HA4 ...46 C7
Croft Lodge CI WFD IG8 ...45 F5
Croft Ms NFNCH/WDSPK N12 ...39 G2
Crofton Av BXLY DA5 ...136 E6
CHSWK W4 ...105 K6
Crofton Gate Wy BROCKY SE4 ...132 B4
Crofton Gv CHING E4 ...44 B3
Crofton La STMC/STPC BR5 ...169 J7
Crofton Park Rd BROCKY SE4 ...132 C5
Crofton Rd CMBW SE5 ...111 F7
PLSTW E13 ...95 F3
Crofton Ter RCH/KEW TW9 ...125 G3
Crofton Wy BAR EN5 * ...27 F5
ENC/FH EN2 ...29 G1
Croft Rd BMLY BR1 ...153 F5
STRHM/NOR SW16 ...149 G6
SUT SM1 ...175 H4
WIM/MER SW19 ...147 G6
Crofts Rd HRW HA1 ...49 G5
Croft St DEPT SE8 ...112 B3
WCHPL E1 ...92 C6
The Croft ALP/SUD HA0 ...67 J4
BAR EN5 ...26 C3
CHING E4 ...44 C1
EA W5 ...86 A4
HEST TW5 ...102 B6
PIN HA5 ...47 K6
RSLP HA4 ...65 G3
WLSDN NW10 ...87 H1
Croft Wy BFN/LL DA15 ...154 E2
RCHPK/HAM TW10 ...143 F2
Crogsland Rd CAMTN NW1 ...4 A1
Croham CI SAND/SEL CR2 ...178 A6
Croham Manor Rd SAND/SEL CR2 ...178 A6
Croham Park Av SAND/SEL CR2 ...178 B4
Croham Mt SAND/SEL CR2 ...177 K4
Croham Valley Rd SAND/SEL CR2 ...178 C5
Croindene Rd STRHM/NOR SW16 ...148 E7
Cromartie Rd ARCH N19 ...54 D6
Cromarty Rd EDGW HA8 ...36 D1
Cromarty Vls BAY/PAD W2 * ...8 D4
Crombie CI REDBR IG4 ...59 K4
Crombie Ms BTSEA SW11 * ...128 D1
Crombie Rd BFN/LL DA15 ...135 J7
Cromer CI UX/CGN UB8 ...82 A5
Cromer Hyde MRDN SM4 * ...162 A4
Crome Rd WLSDN NW10 ...69 G5
Cromer Rd BAR EN5 ...27 G3
CHDH RM6 ...62 A5
HTHAIR TW6 ...120 D2
LEY E10 ...58 B6
ROMW/RG RM7 ...62 E5
SNWD SE25 ...165 J2
TOOT SW17 ...148 A5
TOTM N17 ...56 C2
Cromer Rd West HTHAIR TW6 ...120 D2
Cromer St STPAN WC1H ...5 K9
Cromer Ter HACK E8 ...74 C4
Cromer Villas Rd WAND/EARL SW18 ...127 J5
Cromford Rd PUT/ROE SW15 ...127 J4
Cromford Wy NWMAL KT3 ...145 J7
Cromlix CI CHST BR7 ...169 G1
Crompton St BAY/PAD W2 ...9 G1
Cromwell Av HAYES BR2 ...168 A2

HGT N6 .... 54 B7
HMSMTH W6 .... 106 E4
NWMAL KT3 .... 160 C4
Cromwell CI CHSWK W4 * 105 J4
EFNCH N2 ....
HAYES BR2 .... 168 A3
WOT/HER KT12 .... 156 A7
Cromwell Ct ALP/SUD HA0 .... 86 A1
PEND EN3 .... 31 H4
Cromwell Crs ECT SW5 .... 14 A5
Cromwell Gdns SKENS SW7 .... 15 H5
Cromwell Gv HMSMTH W6 .... 107 F2
Cromwell Ms SKENS SW7 * 15 H5
Cromwell Pde ALP/SUD HA0 * 86 A1
Cromwell PI ACT W3 .... 86 E7
HGT N6 * 54 B7
MORT/ESHN SW14 .... 125 K2
SKENS SW7 .... 15 H5
Cromwell Rd ALP/SUD HA0 .... 85 K1
BECK BR3 .... 166 B1
BRXN/ST SW9 .... 110 C7
CROY/NA CR0 .... 164 E6
ECT SW5 .... 14 B5
FELT TW13 .... 122 A7
FNCH N3 .... 53 C1
FSTGT E7 .... 77 G6
HSLW TW3 .... 123 F3
HYS/HAR UB3 .... 82 B5
KUTN/CMB KT2 .... 144 A7
MUSWH N10 .... 40 A1
SKENS SW7 .... 14 D5
TEDD TW11 .... 143 G5
WALTH E17 .... 58 A4
WIM/MER SW19 .... 146 E4
WPK KT4 .... 173 F2
Cromwell St HSLW TW3 .... 123 F3
Cromwell Ter HSLW TW3 * 123 F3
Crondace Rd FUL/PGN SW6 .... 107 K7
Crondall St IS N1 .... 7 H6
Cronin St PECK SE15 .... 111 G7
Crooked Billet Rbt CHING E4 .... 43 K6
Crooked Usage FNCH N3 .... 52 C2
Crooke Rd DEPT SE8 .... 112 B4
Crookham Rd FUL/PGN SW6 .... 107 J7
Crook Log BXLYHS DA6 .... 136 E2
Crookston Rd ELTH/MOT SE9 .... 135 F2
Croombs Rd CAN/RD E16 .... 95 G4
Croom's HI GNWCH SE10 .... 113 G6
Croom's Hill Gv GNWCH SE10 .... 113 F6
Cropley St IS N1 .... 7 G5
Croppath Rd DAGE RM10 .... 80 C3
Cropthorne Ct MV/WKIL W9 .... 2 F8
Crosby CI FELT TW13 .... 141 J3
Crosby Rd DAGE RM10 .... 98 D1
FSTGT E7 .... 76 E5
Crosby Rw STHWK SE1 .... 19 G2
Crosby Sq HDTCH EC3A 13 J3
Crosby Wk HACK E8 .... 74 B5
Crosier CI BKHTH/KID SE3 .... 114 D7
Crosier Rd HGDN/ICK UB10 .... 64 A3
Crosier Wy RSLP HA4 .... 64 C2
Crosland PI BTSEA SW11 .... 129 F2
Crossbrook Rd
BKHTH/KID SE3 .... 134 D1
Cross Deep TWK TW1 .... 143 F3
Cross Deep Gdns TWK TW1 .... 143 F3
Crossfield Est DEPT SE8 .... 112 D6
Crossfield Rd HAMP NW3 .... 71 H5
TOTM N17 .... 55 J2
Crossfield St DEPT SE8 .... 112 D6
Crossford St BRXN/ST SW9 .... 130 A1
Crossgate EDGW HA8 .... 36 C2
GFD/PVL UB6 .... 67 H5
MHST W1U 10 B3
Cross Lances Rd HSLW TW3 .... 123 G3
Crossland Rd THHTH CR7 .... 164 C5
Crosslands Av EA W5 .... 86 B7
NWDGN UB2 .... 102 A4
Crosslands Pde
NWDGN UB2 * 103 F4
Crosslands Rd
HOR/WEW KT19 .... 173 F5
Cross La BXLY DA5 .... 137 G6
CEND/HSY/T N8 .... 55 F5
MON EC3R 13 J7
Crosslet St WALW SE17 .... 19 H5
Crosslet Vw GNWCH SE10 .... 112 E7
Crossley St HOLWY N7 .... 73 G5
Crossmead ELTH/MOT SE9 .... 134 E7
OXHEY WD19 .... 21 F5
Crossmead Av GFD/PVL UB6 .... 84 A2
Crossness Rd BARK IG11 .... 97 F2
Cross Rd CHDH RM6 .... 61 J4
CMBW SE5 .... 131 F1
CROY/NA CR0 .... 164 E6
DART DA1 .... 139 F5
EN EN1 .... 30 A3
FBAR/BDGN N11 .... 40 B4
FELT TW13 .... 141 J3
HAYES BR2 .... 181 J1
HRW HA1 .... 48 D3
KTN/HRWW/WS HA3 .... 49 G1
KUTN/CMB KT2 .... 144 B6
OXHEY WD19 .... 21 J5
ROMW/RG RM7 .... 62 C2
RYLN/HDSTN HA2 .... 66 A2
SCUP DA14 .... 155 H3
SUT SM1 .... 175 H4
WDGN N22 .... 41 G5
WFD IG8 .... 45 G5
WIM/MER SW19 .... 146 E6
Cross St BARN SW13 .... 126 A1
ERITH DA8 .... 118 B5
HPTN TW12 .... 142 C4
IS N1 .... 6 D3
UED N18 .... 42 C4
WAT WD17 .... 21 C2
Crossthwaite Av HNHL SE24 .... 130 D6
Crosswall TWRH EC3N 13 L6
Crossway BCTR RM8 .... 79 J2
CDALE/KGS NW9 .... 51 H3
EN EN1 .... 30 A6
Cross Wy HYS/HAR UB3 .... 101 K1
Crossway NFNCH/WDSPK N12 .... 39 H5
NWMAL KT3 .... 161 F3
PIN HA5 .... 47 F1
RSLP HA4 .... 65 G3
STMC/STPC BR5 .... 169 J3
STNW/STAM N16 .... 74 A4
THMD SE28 .... 97 J5
WEA W13 .... 85 G3
Crossway Pde WDGN N22 * 41 H6
Crossways BELMT SM2 .... 175 H7
GPK RM2 .... 63 K2
SAND/SEL CR2 .... 179 G4
SUN TW16 .... 140 D7
Crossways Rd BECK BR3 .... 166 D3
MTCM CR4 .... 163 G2
Crossways Ter CLPT E5 * 74 E3
The Crossways BRYLDS KT5 * 159 H7
HEST TW5 .... 102 E6
WBLY HA9 .... 68 C1

The Cross Wy
KTN/HRWW/WS HA3 .... 48 E1
The Crossway ELTH/MOT SE9 .... 153 H1
WDGN N22 .... 41 H6
Croston St HACK E8 .... 74 C7
Crosts La WDGN N22 .... 41 G6
Crothall CI PLMGR N13 .... 41 F2
Crouch Av BARK IG11 .... 97 H1
Crouch CI BECK BR3 .... 151 J3
Crouch Cft ELTH/MOT SE9 .... 154 A3
Crouch End HI
CEND/HSY/T N8 .... 54 D6
Crouch Hall Rd
CEND/HSY/T N8 .... 54 D5
Crouch HI CEND/HSY/T N8 .... 54 E6
Crouchmans CI SYD SE26 .... 150 B3
Crouch Rd WLSDN NW10 .... 69 F6
Crowborough Pth
OXHEY WD19 .... 33 H3
Crowborough Rd TOOT SW17 .... 148 A4
Crowden Wy THMD SE28 .... 97 J6
Crowder CI
NFNCH/WDSPK N12 .... 39 G6
Crowder St WCHPL E1 .... 92 D6
Crowfoot CI HOM E9 .... 75 H4
THMD SE28 .... 96 E7
Crowhurst CI BRXN/ST SW9 .... 130 B1
Crowland Av HYS/HAR UB3 .... 101 H3
Crowland Gdns
STHGT/OAK N14 .... 28 E6
Crowland Rd
SEVS/STOTM N15 .... 56 B4
THHTH CR7 * 164 D3
Crowlands Av ROMW/RG RM7 .... 62 D5
Crowland Ter IS N1 .... 7 G1
Crowland Wk MRDN SM4 .... 162 A5
Crow La ROMW/RG RM7 .... 62 B6
Crowley Crs CROY/NA CR0 .... 177 G4
Crowline Wk IS N1 * 73 J5
Crowmarsh Gdns FSTH SE23 .... 131 K6
Crown Ar KUT/HW KT1 * 158 E1
Crownbourne Ct SUT SM1 * 175 F3
Crown CI BOW E3 .... 75 J7
HYS/HAR UB3 .... 101 J1
KIL/WHAMP NW6 .... 71 F5
MLHL NW7 .... 37 J1
WOT/HER KT12 .... 156 B6
Crown Ct HOL/ALD WC2B 11 K5
Crown DI NRWD SE19 .... 149 J5
Crowndale Rd CAMTN NW1 .... 4 F5
Crownfield Av
GNTH/NBYPK IG2 .... 60 E4
Crownfield Rd SRTFD E15 .... 76 B4
Crown HI CROY/NA CR0 .... 177 J1
Crown Green Ms WBLY HA9 .... 68 A1
Crownhill Rd WLSDN NW10 .... 69 H7
Crown La CHST BR7 .... 154 C7
HAYES BR2 .... 168 C4
MRDN SM4 .... 161 K2
STHGT/OAK N14 .... 28 C7
STRHM/NOR SW16 .... 149 G4
Crown Lane Gdns
STRHM/NOR SW16 * 149 G4
Crown Lane Sp HAYES BR2 * 168 C5
Crownmead Wy
ROMW/RG RM7 .... 62 D3
Crown Office Rw EMB EC4Y 12 A6
Crown Pde MRDN SM4 * 162 A3
STHGT/OAK N14 * 28 C7
Crown Pas STJS SW1Y 10 F9
Crown PI NKENS NW5 .... 72 B5
SDTCH EC2A 13 J1
Crown Rd BARK/HLT IG6 .... 60 D3
EN EN1 .... 30 C2
KUTN/CMB KT2 .... 144 E7
MRDN SM4 .... 161 K3
MUSWH N10 .... 40 A6
RSLP HA4 .... 65 H4
SUT SM1 .... 174 E3
TWK TW1 .... 124 C5
Crownstone Rd
BRXS/STRHM SW2 .... 130 B4
Crown St ACT W3 .... 86 D7
CMBW SE5 .... 110 D6
DAGE RM10 .... 80 D5
RYLN/HDSTN HA2 .... 48 D7
Crown Ter CRICK NW2 * 70 B3
RCH/KEW TW9 .... 125 G3
STHGT/OAK N14 * 28 C7
Crowntree CI ISLW TW7 .... 104 A5
Crown Vis ACT W3 * 105 K1
Crown Wk WBLY HA9 .... 68 B2
Crown Woods La
WOOL/PLUM SE18 .... 135 G1
Crown Woods Wy
ELTH/MOT SE9 .... 135 J4
Crown Yd HSLW TW3 * 123 H2
Crowshott Av STAN HA7 .... 35 J7
Crows Rd BARK IG11 .... 78 B5
BOW E3 .... 94 A5
Crowther Av BTFD TW8 .... 105 F4
Crowther CI FUL/PGN SW6 .... 107 J5
Crowther Rd SNWD SE25 .... 165 H3
Crowthorne CI
WAND/EARL SW18 .... 127 J6
Crowthorne Rd NKENS W10 .... 88 B5
Croxdale Rd BORE WD6 .... 24 B1
Croxden CI EDGW HA8 .... 50 C2
Croxden Wk MRDN SM4 .... 162 B5
Croxford Gdns WDGN N22 .... 41 H6
Croxford Wy ROMW/RG RM7 .... 63 F7
Croxley Gn STMC/STPC BR5 .... 155 J7
Croxley Rd MV/WKIL W9 .... 88 C2
Croxley Vw WATW WD18 .... 20 C5
Croxted CI DUL SE21 .... 130 D6
Croxted Ms HNHL SE24 .... 130 D5
Croxted Rd DUL SE21 .... 130 D6
Croyde Av GFD/PVL UB6 .... 84 C2
HYS/HAR UB3 .... 101 H3
Croyde CI BFN/LL DA15 .... 135 G6
The Croydon F/O
CROY/NA CR0 .... 177 H3
Croydon Gv CROY/NA CR0 .... 164 C7
Croydon Rd BECK BR3 .... 166 A4
CROY/NA CR0 .... 176 E3
HAYES BR2 .... 181 J2
MTCM CR4 .... 163 G4
PGE/AN SE20 .... 165 J1
PLSTW E13 .... 94 D3
WLGTN SM6 .... 176 C3
WWKM BR4 .... 180 C2
Croyland Rd ED N9 .... 30 C7
Croylands Dr SURB KT6 .... 159 F6
Crozier Ter HOM E9 .... 75 F4
Crucible CI CHDH RM6 .... 61 H5
Crucifix La STHWK SE1 .... 19 J1
Cruden St IS N1 .... 6 C4
Cruickshank St FSBYW WC1X 6 A7
Cruikshank Rd SRTFD E15 .... 76 C3
Crummock Gdns
CDALE/KGS NW9 .... 51 G4
Crumpsall St ABYW SE2 .... 116 D3

Crundale Av CDALE/KGS NW9 .... 50 C4
Crunden Rd SAND/SEL CR2 .... 177 K6
Crusader CI PUR RM19 .... 119 K3
Crusader Gdns CROY/NA CR0 .... 178 A2
Crusoe Ms STNW/STAM N16 .... 73 K1
Crusoe Rd ERITH DA8 .... 118 A4
MTCM CR4 .... 147 K6
Crutched Friars TWRH EC3N 13 K6
Crutchfield La WOT/HER KT12 .... 156 A7
Crutchley Rd CAT SE6 .... 152 C1
Crystal Palace NRWD SE19 * 150 C4
Crystal Palace Pde
NRWD SE19 .... 150 B5
Crystal Palace Park Rd
SYD SE26 .... 150 C4
Crystal Palace Rd EDUL SE22 .... 131 G5
Crystal Palace Station Rd
NRWD SE19 .... 150 C5
Crystal Ter NRWD SE19 .... 149 K5
Crystal Wy BCTR RM8 .... 61 J4
DAGE RM8 .... 49 F4
Cuba Dr PEND EN3 .... 30 E1
Cuba St POP/IOD E14 .... 112 D1
Cubitt Sq NWDGN UB2 * 84 C7
Cubitt St FSBYW WC1X 5 M8
Cubitt Ter CLAP SW4 .... 129 H2
Cuckoo Av HNWL W7 .... 84 E3
Cuckoo Dene HNWL W7 .... 84 D4
Cuckoo Hall La ED N9 .... 30 E6
Cuckoo HI PIN HA5 .... 47 G2
Cuckoo Hill Dr PIN HA5 .... 47 G2
Cuckoo Hill Rd PIN HA5 .... 47 H3
Cuckoo La HNWL W7 .... 84 E6
Cuda's CI HOR/WEW KT19 .... 173 H4
Cuddington Av WPK KT4 .... 173 H2
Cudham St CAT SE6 .... 132 E6
Cudworth St WCHPL E1 .... 92 D3
Culford Gdns CHEL SW3 .... 15 M6
Culford Gv IS N1 .... 74 A5
Culford Ms IS N1 .... 73 K5
Culford Rd IS N1 .... 7 J1
Culgaith Gdns ENC/FH EN2 .... 28 E3
Cullera CI NTHWD HA6 .... 32 D5
Culling Rd BERM/RHTH SE16 .... 111 K2
Cullington CI
KTN/HRWW/WS HA3 .... 49 G3
Cullingworth Rd
WLSDN NW10 .... 69 K4
Culloden CI BERM/RHTH SE16 .... 111 H4
CHARL SE7 .... 114 B5
Culloden Rd ENC/FH EN2 .... 29 H1
Culloden St POP/IOD E14 .... 94 A5
Cullum St FENCHST EC3M 13 J6
Culmington Pde WEA W13 * 85 J6
Culmington Rd SAND/SEL CR2 .... 177 J6
WEA W13 .... 85 J7
Culmore Rd PECK SE15 .... 111 J6
Culmstock Rd BTSEA SW11 .... 129 F4
Culpepper CI UED N18 .... 42 D4
Culross CI SEVS/STOTM N15 .... 55 J3
Culross St MYFR/PKLN W1K 10 A7
Culsac Rd SURB KT6 .... 172 A1
Culverden Rd BAL SW12 .... 148 C2
OXHEY WD19 .... 33 F2
Culver Gv STAN HA7 .... 49 J1
Culverhouse Gdns
STRHM/NOR SW16 .... 149 F3
Culverlands CI STAN HA7 .... 35 H3
Culverley Rd CAT SE6 .... 132 E7
Culvers Av CAR SM5 .... 175 K1
Culvers Retreat CAR SM5 .... 162 E7
Culverstone CI HAYES BR2 .... 167 J5
Culvers Wy CAR SM5 .... 175 K1
Culvert PI BTSEA SW11 .... 129 F1
Culvert Rd BTSEA SW11 .... 128 E1
SEVS/STOTM N15 .... 56 A4
Culworth St STJWD NW8 .... 3 J6
Cumberland Av WELL DA16 .... 135 K2
WLSDN NW10 .... 86 D2
Cumberland CI BARK E8 .... 74 B5
RYNPK SW20 .... 146 B6
TWK TW1 .... 124 C5
Cumberland Crs WKENS W14 .... 107 H3
Cumberland Dr BXLYHN DA7 .... 117 F6
CHSGTN KT9 .... 172 A2
DART DA1 .... 139 J4
ESH/CLAY KT10 .... 171 G1
Cumberland Gdns
FSBYW WC1X * 5 M7
HDN NW4 .... 52 B1
Cumberland Ga BAY/PAD W2 .... 9 L6
CAMTN NW1 * 4 C7
Cumberland House
KUTN/CMB KT2 .... 144 E7
Cumberland Market
CAMTN NW1 .... 4 D7
Cumberland Ms LBTH SE11 .... 18 B8
Cumberland Pk ACT W3 .... 86 E6
LEW SE13 .... 133 H3
Cumberland Pl CAMTN NW1 * 4 C7
CAT SE6 .... 133 J7
Cumberland Rd ACT W3 .... 86 E6
BARN SW13 .... 106 C7
ED N9 .... 30 E7
HAYES BR2 .... 167 H3
HNWL W7 .... 104 A1
HRW HA1 .... 48 B4
MNPK E12 .... 77 H3
PLSTW E13 .... 95 F4
RCH/KEW TW9 .... 105 H7
SNWD SE25 .... 165 J5
STAN HA7 .... 50 B2
WALTH E17 .... 57 G1
WDGN N22 .... 55 F1
Cumberland St PIM SW1V 16 D7
Cumberland Ter CAMTN NW1 * 4 C6
PGE/AN SE20 * 150 D6
Cumberland Terrace Ms
CAMTN NW1 * 4 C6
Cumberlow Av SNWD SE25 .... 165 H2
Cumbernauld Gdns SUN TW16 .... 140 D4
Cumberton Rd TOTM N17 .... 41 K7
Cumbrae Gdns SURB KT6 .... 171 K1
Cumbrian Av BXLYHN DA7 .... 138 B1
Cumbrian Gdns CRICK NW2 .... 70 B1
Cumming St IS N1 .... 5 M6
Cumnor CI BRXN/ST SW9 .... 130 A1
Cumnor Gdns EW KT17 .... 173 J5
Cumnor Rd BELMT SM2 .... 175 G5
Cunard Crs WCHMH N21 .... 29 K5
Cunard Rd WLSDN NW10 .... 87 F2
Cunard Wk CAN/RD E16 .... 95 G6
Cundy Rd CAN/RD E16 .... 95 G5
Cundy St BGVA SW1W 16 B6
Cunliffe Rd HOR/WEW KT19 .... 173 H4
Cunliffe St STRHM/NOR SW16 .... 148 C5
Cunningham CI CHDH RM6 .... 61 J4
WWKM BR4 .... 179 K1
Cunningham Pk HRW HA1 .... 48 D4
Cunningham PI STJWD NW8 .... 3 H1
Cunningham Rd
SEVS/STOTM N15 * 56 C3
Cunnington St CHSWK W4 .... 105 K2

Cupar Rd BTSEA SW11 .... 109 F7
Cupola CI BMLY BR1 .... 153 F4
Cureton St WEST SW1P 17 H7
Curlew CI THMD SE28 .... 97 K6
Curlew St STHWK SE1 .... 19 L1
Curlew Wy YEAD UB4 .... 83 H4
Curness St LEW SE13 .... 133 F3
Curnick's La WNWD SE27 .... 149 J3
Curran Av BFN/LL DA15 .... 136 A4
WLGTN SM6 .... 176 A2
Currey Rd NTHLT UB5 .... 66 C5
Curricle St ACT W3 .... 87 G7
Currie Hill CI WIM/MER SW19 .... 146 D3
Curry Ri MLHL NW7 .... 38 B5
Cursitor St FLST/FETLN EC4A 12 A4
Curtain PI SDTCH EC2A 7 K8
Curtain Rd FSBYE EC1V * 13 J1
SDTCH EC2A 13 J1
Curthwaite Gdns ENC/FH EN2 .... 28 E3
Curtis Dr ACT W3 .... 87 F5
Curtis Field Rd
STRHM/NOR SW16 .... 149 F3
Curtis La ALP/SUD HA0 .... 68 A5
Curtis Rd HOR/WEW KT19 .... 172 E6
HSLWW TW4 .... 122 E6
Curtis St STHWK SE1 .... 19 L5
Curtis Wy STHWK SE1 .... 19 L5
The Curve SHB W12 .... 87 J6
Curwen Av FSTGT E7 .... 77 F3
Curwen Rd SHB W12 .... 106 D1
Curzon Av PEND EN3 .... 31 F4
STAN HA7 .... 35 G7
Curzon Crs BARK IG11 .... 97 F2
WLSDN NW10 .... 69 G6
Curzon PI PIN HA5 .... 47 G4
Curzon Rd EA W5 .... 85 H3
MUSWH N10 .... 54 B1
THHTH CR7 .... 164 B5
Curzon St MYFR/PKLN W1K 10 B9
Custom House Reach
BERM/RHTH SE16 * 112 C2
Cutcombe Rd CMBW SE5 .... 130 D1
Cuthberga CI BARK IG11 .... 78 C6
Cuthbert Gdns SNWD SE25 .... 165 F2
Cuthbert Rd CROY/NA CR0 .... 177 H1
UED N18 .... 42 C4
WALTH E17 .... 58 A2
Cuthbert St BAY/PAD W2 .... 9 G1
Cutlers Gardens Ar
LVPST EC2M 13 K4
Cutler St HDTCH EC3A 13 K4
Cutter La GNWCH SE10 .... 113 H1
The Cut STHWK SE1 .... 18 B1
Cuxton CI BXLYHS DA6 .... 137 F4
Cyclamen CI HPTN TW12 .... 142 A5
Cyclamen Wy HOR/WEW KT19 .... 172 E5
Cygnet Av EBED/NFELT TW14 .... 122 B6
Cygnet CI NTHWD HA6 .... 32 A6
WLSDN NW10 .... 69 F4
The Cygnets FELT TW13 .... 141 J3
Cygnet St WCHPL E1 .... 7 M9
Cygnet Wy YEAD UB4 .... 83 H4
Cymbeline Ct HRW HA1 * 49 F5
Cynthia St IS N1 .... 5 M6
Cypress Av WHTN TW2 .... 123 H6
Cypress CI CLPT E5 .... 74 C1
Cypress Gdns BROCKY SE4 .... 132 B4
Cypress PI FITZ W1T 10 F1
Cypress Rd
KTN/HRWW/WS HA3 .... 48 D1
SNWD SE25 .... 165 F1
Cyprus Av FNCH N3 .... 52 C1
Cyprus CI FSBYPK N4 .... 55 G5
Cyprus Gdns FNCH N3 .... 52 C1
Cyprus PI BETH E2 .... 92 E1
EHAM E6 .... 96 A6
Cyprus Rd ED N9 .... 42 B1
FNCH N3 .... 52 D1
Cyprus St BETH E2 .... 92 E1
Cyrena Rd EDUL SE22 .... 131 G5
Cyril Rd BXLYHN DA7 .... 137 F1
Cyrus St FSBYE EC1V 6 D9
Czar St DEPT SE8 .... 112 D5

D

Dahomey Rd
STRHM/NOR SW16 .... 148 C5
Daimler Wy WLGTN SM6 .... 176 E6
Daines CI MNPK E12 .... 77 K2
Dainford CI BMLY BR1 .... 152 B4
Daintry CI
KTN/HRWW/WS HA3 .... 49 G3
Dairsie Rd ELTH/MOT SE9 .... 135 F2
Dairy CI BMLY BR1 * 153 F6
FUL/PGN SW6 .... 107 J7
THHTH CR7 .... 164 D1
WLSDN NW10 .... 69 J7
Dairy La WOOL/PLUM SE18 .... 114 D3
Dairyman CI CRICK NW2 .... 70 B2
Dairy Ms EFNCH N2 .... 53 J3
BRXN/ST SW9 .... 129 K3
Daisy CI CDALE/KGS NW9 .... 68 E1
CROY/NA CR0 .... 166 A7
Daisy La FUL/PGN SW6 .... 127 K2
Daisy Rd SWFD E18 .... 59 F1
Dakin PI WCHPL E1 .... 93 G4
Dakota CI WLGTN SM6 .... 177 H5
Dalberg Rd BRXS/STRHM SW2 .... 130 B4
Dalberg Wy ABYW SE2 .... 116 E2
Dalby Rd WAND/EARL SW18 .... 128 B3
Dalby St KTTN NW5 .... 72 B5
Dalcross Rd HSLWW TW4 .... 122 D1
Dale Av EDGW HA8 .... 36 B7
HSLWW TW4 .... 122 D2
Dalebury Rd TOOT SW17 .... 147 K1
Dale CI BAR EN5 .... 27 F5
BKHTH/KID SE3 .... 133 K2
DART DA1 .... 138 C5
Dale Dr YEAD UB4 .... 82 D3
Dale Gdns WFD IG8 .... 45 F3
Dale Green Rd FBAR/BDGN N11 .... 40 B2
Daleham Gdns HAMP NW3 .... 71 H4
Daleham Ms HAMP NW3 * 71 H5
Dalemain Ms CAN/RD E16 .... 94 E7
Dale Park Av CAR SM5 .... 175 K1
Dale Park Rd NRWD SE19 .... 149 J7
Dale Rd DART DA1 .... 138 C5
KTTN NW5 .... 72 A4
STHL UB1 .... 102 C3
SUN TW16 .... 140 D6
SUT SM1 .... 174 D3
WALW SE17 .... 110 C5
Dale Rw NTGHL W11 .... 88 C5
Daleside Rd HOR/WEW KT19 .... 173 F5
STRHM/NOR SW16 .... 148 B4
Dales Pth BORE WD6 * 25 F4
Dales Rd BORE WD6 .... 25 F4
Dale St CHSWK W4 .... 106 B4
The Dale HAYES BR2 .... 181 H5
Dale Vw BAR EN5 * 26 D2
ERITH DA8 .... 138 D1
Dale View Av CHING E4 .... 44 A1
Dale View Crs CHING E4 .... 44 A2
Dale View Gdns CHING E4 .... 44 B2
Daleview Rd
SEVS/STOTM N15 .... 73 K5
Dalewood Gdns WPK KT4 .... 173 K1
Dale Wood Rd ORP BR6 .... 169 K6
Daley St HOM E9 .... 75 F5
Daley Thompson Wy
VX/NE SW8 .... 129 G1
Dalgarno Gdns NKENS W10 .... 88 A4
Dalgarno Wy NKENS W10 .... 88 A3
Dalkeith Gv STAN HA7 .... 35 K4
Dalkeith Rd DUL SE21 .... 130 D7
IL IG1 .... 78 C2
Dallas Rd CHEAM SM3 .... 174 C5
EA W5 .... 86 B4
HDN NW4 .... 51 J6
SYD SE26 .... 150 D3
Dallas Ter HYS/HAR UB3 .... 101 J2
Dallega CI HYS/HAR UB3 .... 82 A6
Dallinger Rd LEE/GVPK SE12 .... 133 J5
Dalling Rd HMSMTH W6 .... 106 E3
Dallington Sq FSBYE EC1V * 6 D9
Dallington St FSBYE EC1V 6 D9
Dallin Rd BXLYHS DA6 .... 136 E4
WOOL/PLUM SE18 .... 115 G6
Dalmain Rd FSTH SE23 .... 132 A7
Dalmally Rd CROY/NA CR0 .... 165 G6
Dalmeny Av HOLWY N7 .... 72 D3
STRHM/NOR SW16 .... 164 B1
Dalmeny CI ALP/SUD HA0 .... 67 J3
Dalmeny Crs HSLW TW3 .... 123 J3
Dalmeny Rd ARCH N19 .... 72 B1
BAR EN5 .... 27 G5
CAR SM5 .... 176 A6
ERITH DA8 .... 117 J7
HOLWY N7 .... 72 D3
WPK KT4 .... 173 K2
Dalmeyer Rd WLSDN NW10 .... 69 H5
Dalmore Av ESH/CLAY KT10 .... 171 G5
Dalmore Rd DUL SE21 .... 149 J1
Dalrymple CI STHGT/OAK N14 .... 28 D5
Dalrymple Rd BROCKY SE4 .... 132 B3
Dalston Gdns STAN HA7 .... 50 B1
Dalston La HACK E8 .... 74 B5
Dalton Av MTCM CR4 .... 147 J1
Dalton CI YEAD UB4 .... 82 B3
Dalton St WNWD SE27 .... 149 H1
Dalton Wy WAT WD17 .... 21 H4
Dalwood St CMBW SE5 .... 111 F7
Dalyell Rd BRXN/ST SW9 .... 130 A2
Damask Crs CAN/RD E16 .... 94 C3
Damer Ter WBPTN SW10 * 108 B6
Dames Rd FSTGT E7 .... 76 E3
Dame St IS N1 .... 6 E5
Damien CI WCHPL E1 .... 155 H4
Damon CI SCUP DA14 .... 155 H2
Damsel Ct BERM/RHTH SE16 * 111 J1
Damson Dr HYS/HAR UB3 .... 82 E6
Damson Wy CAR SM5 .... 175 K7
Damsonwood Rd
NWDGN UB2 .... 103 F2
Danbrook Rd
STRHM/NOR SW16 .... 148 E7
Danbury CI CHDH RM6 .... 61 K2
Danbury Ms WLGTN SM6 .... 176 B3
Danbury Rd RAIN RM13 .... 81 H7
Danbury St IS N1 .... 6 D5
Danbury Wy WFD IG8 .... 45 G5
Danby St PECK SE15 .... 131 G2
Dancer Rd FUL/PGN SW6 .... 107 J7
RCH/KEW TW9 .... 125 H2
Dandelion CI ROMW/RG RM7 .... 63 F1
Dando Crs BKHTH/KID SE3 .... 134 A2
Dandridge CI GNWCH SE10 .... 113 J4
Danebury CROY/NA CR0 .... 179 K5
Danebury Av PUT/ROE SW15 .... 126 C5
Daneby Rd CAT SE6 .... 152 A2
Dane CI BXLY DA5 .... 137 H6
Danecourt Gdns
CROY/NA CR0 .... 178 B2
Danecroft Rd HNHL SE24 .... 130 D4
Danehurst Gdns REDBR IG4 .... 59 J4

Danehurst St FUL/PGN SW6......107 H7
Daneland EBAR EN4......27 K5
Danemead Gv NTHLT UB5......66 B4
Danemere St PUT/ROE SW15......127 G7
Dane Pl BOW E3......93 G1
Dane Rd ASHF TW15......140 K1
　IL IG1......78 C4
　STHL UB1......83 J8
　UED N18......42 E3
　WEA W13......85 H3
　WIM/MER SW19......147 G7
Danesbury Rd FELT TW13......122 A4
Danescombe LEE/GVPK SE12......133 K7
Danescourt Crs SUT SM1......175 G1
Danescroft HDN NW4......52 B4
Danescroft Av HDN NW4......52 B4
Danescroft Gdns HDN NW4......52 B4
Danesdale Rd HOM E9......75 G5
Danes Ga HRW HA1......48 E2
Danes Rd ROMW/RG RM7......62 E6
Dane St GINN WC1R......11 L3
Daneswood Av CAT SE6......152 A2
Danethorpe Rd ALP/SUD HA0......67 K5
Danetree Cl HOR/WEW KT19......172 E6
Danetree Rd HOR/WEW KT19......172 E6
Danette Gdns DAGE RM10......80 B1
Daneville Rd CMBW SE5......110 E7
Dangan Rd WAN E11......58 E5
Daniel Bolt Cl POP/IOD E14......93 K4
Daniel Cl HSLWW TW4......122 E6
　TOOT SW17......147 J5
　UED N18......42 E3
Daniel Gdns PECK SE15......111 G6
Daniell Wy CROY/NA CR0......163 K7
Daniel Pl HDN NW4......51 K5
Daniel Rd EA W5......86 B6
Daniel's Rd PECK SE15......131 K2
Dan Leno Wk FUL/PGN SW6 *......108 A7
Dansey Pl SOHO/SHAV W1D......11 G6
Dansington Rd WELL DA16......136 B3
Danson Crs WELL DA16......136 C2
Danson La WELL DA16......136 C3
Danson Md WELL DA16......136 D2
Danson Rd BXLYHS DA6......136 E5
Danson Rd BXLYHS DA6......136 D5
Dante Rd LBTH SE11......18 A5
Danube Cl ED N9......42 E2
Danube St CHEL SW3......15 K7
Danvers Rd CEND/HSY/T N8......54 C3
Danvers St CHEL SW3......108 C5
Daphne Gdns CHING E4......44 A2
Daphne St WAND/EARL SW18......128 B5
Daplyn St WCHPL E1......92 C4
D'Arblay St SOHO/CST W1F......10 F5
Darby Crs SUN TW16......156 B1
Darby Gdns SUN TW16......156 B1
Darcy Av WLGTN SM6......176 C3
Darcy Cl TRDG/WHET N20......39 H1
D'Arcy Dr KTN/HRWW/WS HA3......49 K4
D'Arcy Gdns DAGW RM9......80 B5
　KTN/HRWW/WS HA3......50 A3
D'Arcy Pl HAYES BR2......167 K3
Darcy Rd ISLW TW7......104 B7
　STRHM/NOR SW16......163 K1
D'Arcy Rd CHEAM SM3......174 B3
Darell Rd RCH/KEW TW9......125 H2
Darenth Rd STNW/STAM N16......56 B7
　WELL DA16......116 B7
Darent Valley Pth DART DA1......139 C3
Darfield Rd BROCKY SE4......132 C4
Darfield Wy NKENS W10......88 B6
Darfur St PUT/ROE SW15......127 G2
Dargate Cl NRWD SE19......150 B6
Darien Rd BTSEA SW11......128 C2
Darlands Dr BAR EN5......26 B4
Darlan Rd FUL/PGN SW6......107 J6
Darlaston Rd WIM/MER SW19......146 B6
Darley Cl CROY/NA CR0......166 A5
Darley Dr NWMAL KT3......160 A1
Darley Gdns MRDN SM4......162 A5
Darley Rd BTSEA SW11......128 E5
　ED N9......30 B7
Darling Rd BROCKY SE4......132 D2
Darling Rw WCHPL E1......92 D3
Darlington Rd WNWD SE27......149 H4
Darlton Cl DART DA1......138 C4
Darmaine Cl SAND/SEL CR2......177 J6
Darnaway Pl POP/IOD E14......94 A4
Darndale Cl WALTH E17......57 H1
　WFD IG8......44 E7
Darnley Rd HACK E8......74 D5
　HDN NW4 *......51 J5
Darnley Ter NTGHL W11......88 B6
Darrell Rd EDUL SE22......131 H4
Darren Cl FSBYPK N4......55 A6
Darris Cl YEAD UB4......83 J3
Darsley Dr VX/NE SW8......109 J7
Dartford Av ED N9......30 E5
Dartford Gdns CHDH RM6......61 H4
Dartford Rd BXLY DA5......137 K7
　DART DA1......138 D5
Dartmoor Wk POP/IOD E14 *......112 D3
Dartmouth Cl NTGHL W11......88 D5
Dartmouth Gv GNWCH SE10......113 F7
Dartmouth Hl GNWCH SE10......113 F7
Dartmouth Park Av
　KTTN NW5......72 B2
Dartmouth Park Hl KTTN NW5......72 B2
Dartmouth Park Rd
　KTTN NW5......72 B2
Dartmouth Pl CHSWK W4......106 B5
　FSTH SE23......150 E1
Dartmouth Rd CRICK NW2......70 B6
　HAYES BR2......167 K6
　HDN NW4......51 J5
　RSLP HA4......64 C2
　SYD SE26......150 D2
Dartmouth Rw GNWCH SE10......133 F1
Dartmouth St STJSPK SW1H......17 G2
Dartmouth Ter GNWCH SE10......113 G7
Dartnell Rd CROY/NA CR0......165 G6
Dartrey Wk WBPTN SW10......108 B6
Dart St NKENS W10......88 C2
Darville Rd STNW/STAM N16......74 B2
Darwell Cl EHAM E6......96 A1
Darwin Cl FBAR/BDGN N11......40 B2
Darwin Dr STHL UB1......84 B5
Darwin Gdns OXHEY WD19......33 G4
Darwin Rd EA W5......104 D4
　WDGN N22......41 H7
　WELL DA16......136 A2
Darwin St WALW SE17......19 H5
Daryngton Dr GFD/PVL UB6......84 D1
Dashwood Cl BXLYHS DA6......137 H5
Dashwood Rd
　CEND/HSY/T N8......55 F5
Dassett Rd WNWD SE27......149 H4
Datchelor Pl CMBW SE5 *......110 E7
Datchet Rd CAT SE6......151 H2
Date St WALW SE17......19 G8
Daubeney Gdns TOTM N17......41 J6
Daubeney Rd CLPT E5......75 G3
　TOTM N17......41 J6
Dault Rd WAND/EARL SW18......128 B5

Davema Cl CHST BR7......154 A7
Davenant Rd ARCH N19......72 D1
Davenant St WCHPL E1......92 C4
Davenham Av NTHWD HA6......32 D3
Davenport Cl TEDD TW11 *......143 G5
Davenport Rd CAT SE6......132 E5
　SCUP DA14......155 K1
Daventer Dr STAN HA7......35 F6
Daventry Av WALTH E17......57 J5
Daventry St CAMTN NW1......9 J1
Davern Cl GNWCH SE10......113 J3
Davey Cl HOLWY N7......73 F5
　PLMGR N13......41 F4
Davey Rd HOM E9......75 J4
Davey St PECK SE15......111 G5
David Av GFD/PVL UB6......84 D2
David Cl HYS/HAR UB3......101 G6
Davidge St STHWK SE1......18 C2
David Ms MHST W1U *......9 M1
David Rd BCTR RM8......80 A1
Davidson Gdns VX/NE SW8......109 K6
Davidson Rd CROY/NA CR0......165 F7
Davidson Wy ROMW/RG RM7......63 G5
David's Rd FSTH SE23......131 K7
David St SRTFD E15......76 B5
David Twigg Cl
　KUTN/CMB KT2......144 A7
Davies Cl CROY/NA CR0......165 G5
Davies La WAN E11......76 C1
Davies Ms MYFR/PKLN W1K......10 C6
Davies Wk ISLW TW7......103 J7
Davington Gdns BCTR RM8......79 H5
Davington Rd BCTR RM8......79 H5
Davinia Cl WFD IG8......45 K5
Davis Rd ACT W3......87 H7
　CHSGTN KT9......172 C3
Davis St PLSTW E13......95 F1
Davisville Rd SHB W12......106 D1
Dawes Av ISLW TW7......124 B4
Dawes La ESH/CLAY KT10......170 B3
Dawes Rd FUL/PGN SW6......107 H6
Dawes St WALW SE17......19 H7
Dawley Pde HYS/HAR UB3......82 A6
Dawley Rd HYS/HAR UB3......82 B6
Dawlish Av GFD/PVL UB6......85 H1
　PLMGR N13......40 E3
　WAND/EARL SW18......147 F1
Dawlish Dr GDMY/SEVK IG3......79 F3
　PIN HA5......47 J3
　RSLP HA4......64 E1
Dawlish Rd CRICK NW2......70 B5
　LEY E10......76 A1
　TOTM N17......56 C2
Dawnay Gdns
　WAND/EARL SW18......147 H1
Dawnay Rd WAND/EARL SW18......147 G1
Dawn Cl HSLWW TW4......122 D2
Dawn Crs SRTFD E15......76 B7
Daws La MLHL NW7......37 H4
Dawpool Rd CRICK NW2......69 H1
Dawson Av BARK IG11......79 F6
Dawson Cl HYS/HAR UB3......82 B4
　WOOL/PLUM SE18......115 H3
Dawson Dr RAIN RM13......81 K6
Dawson Gdns BARK IG11......79 F6
Dawson Pl BAY/PAD W2......8 A6
Dawson Rd CRICK NW2......70 A4
　KUT/HW KT1......159 G2
Dawson St BETH E2......7 M4
Dawson Ter ED N9......30 E7
Daybrook Rd WIM/MER SW19......162 A1
Daylesford Av PUT/ROE SW15......126 D3
Daymer Gdns PIN HA5......47 G3
Daysbrook Rd
　BRXS/STRHM SW2......130 A7
Days La BFN/LL DA15......135 K6
Dayton Dr ERITH DA8......119 G5
Dayton Gv PECK SE15......111 K7
Deacon Cl PUR/KEN CR8......176 E7
The Deacon Est CHING E4 *......43 H5
Deacon Ms IS N1......7 J1
Deacon Rd CRICK NW2......69 J5
　KUTN/CMB KT2......144 B7
Deacons Hts BORE WD6......24 C3
Deacons Hl OXHEY WD19......21 H1
Deacon's Hill Rd BORE WD6......24 B4
Deacons Ri EFNCH N2......53 H4
Deacons Ter IS N1 *......73 J5
Deacon Wy WALW SE17......18 E5
　WFD IG8......45 K6
Deakin Cl WATW WD18......20 C6
Deal Porters Wy
　BERM/RHTH SE16......111 K2
Deal Rd TOOT SW17......148 A5
Deals Gtwy LEW SE13......112 E7
Deal St WCHPL E1......92 C4
Dealtry Rd PUT/ROE SW15......127 F3
Deal Wk BRXN/ST SW9......110 B6
Dean Bradley St WEST SW1P......17 J4
Dean Cl BERM/RHTH SE16......93 F7
　HOM E9......74 E4
Dean Ct ALP/SUD HA0......67 H2
Deancross St WCHPL E1......92 E5
Dean Dr STAN HA7......50 A1
Deane Av RSLP HA4......65 F4
Deane Ct NTHWD HA6......32 C7
Deane Croft Rd PIN HA5......47 G5
Deanery Cl EFNCH N2......53 J3
Deanery Ms
　MYFR/PKLN W1K *......10 B8
Deanery Rd SRTFD E15......76 C5
Deanery St MYFR/PKLN W1K......10 B8
Deane Wy RSLP HA4......47 F5
Dean Farrar St STJSPK SW1H......17 H3
Deanfield Gdns
　CROY/NA CR0 *......177 K3
Dean Gdns WALTH E17......58 B3
Deanhill Ct
　MORT/ESHN SW14 *......125 J3
Deanhill Rd MORT/ESHN SW14...125 J3
Dean Rd CRICK NW2......70 A5
　CROY/NA CR0......177 K3
　HPTN TW12......142 A4
　HSLW TW3......123 G4
　THMD SE28......97 G6
Dean Ryle St WEST SW1P......17 J5
Deansbrook Cl EDGW HA8......36 E6
Deansbrook Rd EDGW HA8......36 E6
Dean's Blds WALW SE17......19 H6
Dean's Cl CHSWK W4......105 J5
　CROY/NA CR0......178 B2
　EDGW HA8......36 E5
Dean's Ct STP EC4M......12 D5
Deanscroft Av
　CDALE/KGS NW9......68 E1
Deans Dr PLMGR N13......41 H5
Dean's Dr EDGW HA8......37 F4
Deans Gate Cl FSTH SE23......151 F2
Dean's La EDGW HA8......36 E5

Dean's Ms CAVSQ/HST W1G *......10 D4
Deans Rd SUT SM1......175 F2
Dean's Rd HNWL W7......104 A1
Dean Stanley St WEST SW1P......17 J4
Dean St FSTGT E7......76 E4
　SOHO/SHAV W1D......11 G4
Deansway ED N9......42 A2
　EFNCH N2......53 H3
Deans Yd WEST SW1P......17 H3
Dean Trench St WEST SW1P......17 J4
Dearne Cl STAN HA7......35 G4
De'Arn Gdns MTCM CR4......162 D2
Dearsley Rd EN EN1......30 C2
Deason St SRTFD E15 *......76 A7
De Barowe Ms HBRY N5......73 H3
Debden Cl CDALE/KGS NW9......37 G7
　KUTN/CMB KT2......143 K4
　WFD IG8......45 H6
De Bohun Av STHGT/OAK N14...28 B5
Deborah Cl ISLW TW7......103 K7
Deborah Crs RSLP HA4......46 B6
Debrabant Cl ERITH DA8......118 A5
De Broome Rd FELT TW13......122 A7
Deburgh Rd WIM/MER SW19...147 G6
Decima St STHWK SE1......19 J3
Decimus Cl THHTH CR7......164 E3
Deck Cl BERM/RHTH SE16......93 F7
Decoy Av GLDGN NW11......52 C4
De Crespigny Pk CMBW SE5......130 E1
Deeley Rd VX/NE SW8......109 J7
Deena Cl ACT W3......86 A5
Deepdale WIM/MER SW19......146 B3
Deepdale Av HAYES BR2......167 J3
Deepdale Cl FBAR/BDGN N11...40 A5
Deepdene Av CROY/NA CR0...178 B2
Deepdene Ct WCHMH N21......29 H5
Deepdene Gdns
　BRXS/STRHM SW2......130 A6
Deepdene Rd HNHL SE24......130 D5
　WELL DA16......136 B2
Deepwell Cl ISLW TW7......104 B7
Deepwood La GFD/PVL UB6......84 D2
Deerbrook Rd HNHL SE24......130 C6
Deerdale Rd HNHL SE24......130 D3
Deere Av RAIN RM13......81 J5
Deerfield Cl CDALE/KGS NW9...51 H4
Deerhurst Cl FELT TW13......140 E3
Deerhurst Crs HPTN TW12......142 C4
Deerhurst Rd
　KIL/WHAMP NW6......70 E6
　STRHM/NOR SW16......149 F4
Deerings Dr PIN HA5......46 E4
Deerleap Gv CHING E4......31 K4
Dee Rd RCH/KEW TW9......125 G3
Deer Park Cl KUTN/CMB KT2...144 D6
Deer Park Gdns MTCM CR4 *...162 C3
Deer Park Rd WIM/MER SW19...162 A1
Deer Park Wy WWKM BR4......180 D1
Deeside Rd TOOT SW17......147 H2
Dee St POP/IOD E14......94 A5
Defence Cl THMD SE28......97 K7
Defiant Wy WLGTN SM6......176 E6
Defoe Av RCH/KEW TW9......105 H6
Defoe Cl TOOT SW17......147 J5
Defoe Pl TOOT SW17......147 J1
　STNW/STAM N16......74 A1
Defoe Rd BERM/RHTH SE16......112 C1
De Frene Rd SYD SE26......151 F3
De Gama Pl POP/IOD E14......112 D4
Degema Rd CHST BR7......154 B4
Dehar Crs CDALE/KGS NW9......51 H6
De Haviland Dr
　WOOL/PLUM SE18......115 G4
Dehavilland Cl NTHLT UB5......83 H1
De Havilland Ct IL IG1......60 D7
De Havilland Rd EDGW HA8......50 D1
　HEST TW5......102 B6
De Havilland Wy
　STWL/WRAY TW19......120 A5
Dekker Rd DUL SE21......131 F5
Delacourt Rd BKHTH/KID SE3...114 A6
Delafield Rd CHARL SE7......114 A4
Delaford Rd
　BERM/RHTH SE16......111 J4
Delaford St FUL/PGN SW6......107 H6
Delamare Crs CROY/NA CR0...165 K5
Delamere Gdns MLHL NW7......37 F6
Delamere Rd EA W5......86 A7
　RYNPK SW20......146 B1
　YEAD UB4......83 H6
Delamere St BAY/PAD W2......8 D3
Delamere Ter BAY/PAD W2......8 D3
Delancey Pas CAMTN NW1......4 D4
Delancey St CAMTN NW1......4 D4
De Laune St WALW SE17......18 C8
Delaware Rd MV/WKIL W9......2 C8
Delawyk Crs HNHL SE24......130 E5
Delcombe Av WPK KT4......161 F7
Delhi Rd EN EN1......30 B6
Delhi St IS N1......5 K4
Delia St WAND/EARL SW18......128 A6
Delisle Rd THMD SE28......96 E7
Delius Cl BORE WD6......23 J3
Delius Gv SRTFD E15......94 A1
Della Pth CLPT E5......74 C2
Dellbow Rd
　EBED/NFELT TW14......122 A4
Dell Cl SRTFD E15......76 B7
　WFD IG8......45 F2
　WLGTN SM6......176 C3
Dell Farm Rd RSLP HA4......46 A4
Dellfield Cl BECK BR3......152 A7
　WAT WD17......20 C1
Dell La EW KT17......173 J4
Dellors Cl BAR EN5......26 B4
Dellow Cl GNTH/NBYPK IG2......60 D6
Dellow St WCHPL E1......92 D6
Dell Rd EW KT17......173 J5
　WDR/YW UB7......100 C2
Dells Cl CHING E4......31 K6
　TEDD TW11......143 F5
Dell's Ms PIM SW1V *......16 E7
The Dell ABYW SE2......116 E4
　ALP/SUD HA0......67 H4
　BECK BR3 *......151 J6
　BTFD TW8......104 D5
　BXLY DA5......136 D7
　EBED/NFELT TW14......122 A6
　NRWD SE19......150 B7
　NTHWD HA6......32 C5
　PIN HA5......47 H2
　SYD SE26......150 E3
　WFD IG8......45 F2
Dell Wk NWMAL KT3......160 B1
Dell Wy WEA W13......85 J5

Dellwood Gdns CLAY IG5......60 A2
Delme Crs BKHTH/KID SE3......134 A1
Delmey Cl CROY/NA CR0......178 B2
Deloraine St DEPT SE8......112 D7
Delorme St HMSMTH W6......107 G5
Delta Cl WPK KT4......173 G2
Delta Est BETH E2 *......92 C2
Delta Gain OXHEY WD19......33 H1
Delta Gv NTHLT UB5......83 H2
Delta Rd WPK KT4......173 G2
Delta St BETH E2 *......92 C2
De Luci Rd ERITH DA8......117 K4
De Lucy St ABYW SE2......116 C3
Delvers Md DAGE RM10......80 E3
Delverton Rd WALW SE17......18 D7
Delvino Rd FUL/PGN SW6......107 K7
Demesne Rd WLGTN SM6......176 D3
Demeta Cl WBLY HA9......68 E2
De Montfort Pde
　STRHM/NOR SW16 *......148 E2
De Montfort Rd
　STRHM/NOR SW16......148 D1
De Morgan Rd FUL/PGN SW6...128 A2
Dempster Cl SURB KT6......158 D6
Dempster Rd
　WAND/EARL SW18......128 B4
Denbar Pde ROMW/RG RM7...62 D3
Denberry Dr SCUP DA14......155 H2
Denbigh Cl CHST BR7......153 K5
　NTGHL W11......88 D6
　STHL UB1......83 K5
　SUT SM1......174 D4
Denbigh Dr HYS/HAR UB3......101 F7
Denbigh Gdns
　RCHPK/HAM TW10......125 G4
Denbigh Pl PIM SW1V......16 E7
Denbigh Rd EHAM E6......95 H2
　HSLW TW3......123 G1
　NTGHL W11......88 D6
　STHL UB1......83 K5
　WEA W13......85 H6
Denbigh St PIM SW1V......16 E6
Denbigh Ter NTGHL W11......88 D6
Denbridge Rd BMLY BR1......168 E1
Den Cl BECK BR3......167 G3
Dendy St BAL SW12......129 F7
Dene Av BFN/LL DA15......136 C6
　HSLW TW3......122 E2
Dene Cl BROCKY SE4......132 B2
　HAYES BR2......167 J7
　LEY E10......75 K1
　WPK KT4......173 H1
Dene Gdns STAN HA7......35 J4
　THDIT KT7......171 G1
Denehurst Gdns ACT W3......86 D7
　HDN NW4......52 A5
　RCHPK/HAM TW10......125 H3
　WFD IG8......45 F3
　WHTN TW2......123 H6
Dene Rd DART DA1......139 J6
　NTHWD HA6......32 A5
　TRDG/WHET N20......27 K7
The Dene CROY/NA CR0......179 F3
　E/WMO/HCT KT8......156 E4
　WBLY HA9......68 A3
　WEA W13......85 H4
Denewood BAR EN5......27 G4
Denewood Rd HGT N6......53 J5
Dengie Ws IS N1 *......6 E3
Denham Cl WELL DA16......136 D2
Denham Crs MTCM CR4......162 E3
Denham Dr GNTH/NBYPK IG2...60 C5
Denham Rd
　EBED/NFELT TW14......122 A5
　TRDG/WHET N20......39 K1
Denham St GNWCH SE10......113 K4
Denham Wy BARK IG11......78 E7
Denholme Rd MV/WKIL W9......88 D2
Denholme Wk RAIN RM13......81 H5
Denison Cl EFNCH N2......53 G2
Denison Rd EA W5......85 J3
　FELT TW13......140 D3
　WIM/MER SW19......147 H5
Deniston Av BXLY DA5......136 E3
Denleigh Gdns THDIT KT7 *......157 K5
　WCHMH N21......29 G6
Denman Dr North
　GLDGN NW11 *......52 E4
Denman Dr South
　GLDGN NW11......52 E4
Denman Rd PECK SE15......111 G7
Denman St SOHO/SHAV W1D...10 F7
Denmark Av WIM/MER SW19...146 C6
Denmark Ct MRDN SM4......161 K4
Denmark Gdns CAR SM5......175 K2
Denmark Gv IS N1......6 A5
Denmark Hl HNHL SE24......130 D3
Denmark Hill Dr
　CDALE/KGS NW9......51 J2
Denmark Rd BMLY BR1......153 F7
　CAR SM5......175 K2
　CEND/HSY/T N8......55 F3
　CMBW SE5......110 D7
　KIL/WHAMP NW6......88 D1
　KUT/HW KT1......159 F2
　SNWD SE25......165 H4
　WEA W13......85 H6
　WHTN TW2......142 D2
　WIM/MER SW19......146 B5
Denmark St LSO/SEVD WC2H...11 H5
　PLSTW E13......95 F4
　TOTM N17......42 D7
　WAN E11......76 C2
　WAT WD17......21 G3
Denmark Ter EFNCH N2 *......53 K2
Denmead Rd CROY/NA CR0...164 C7
Denner Rd CHING E4......43 J1
Denne Ter HACK E8......7 M4
Dennett's Gv NWCR SE14......132 A1
Dennett's Rd NWCR SE14......111 K7
Denning Av CROY/NA CR0......177 G3
Denning Cl HPTN TW12......141 K4
　MV/WKIL W9......2 B8
Denning Ms BAL SW12......129 F5
Denning Rd HAMP NW3......71 H3
Dennington Park Rd
　KIL/WHAMP NW6......70 E5
The Denningtons WPK KT4......173 G1
Dennis Av WBLY HA9......68 B4
Dennis Gdns STAN HA7......35 J4
Dennis La STAN HA7......35 H3
Dennis Pde STHGT/OAK N14 *...28 D7
Dennis Park Crs RYNPK SW20...146 C1
Dennis Reeve Cl MTCM CR4...147 K7
Dennis Rd E/WMO/HCT KT8...157 H3
Dennis Wy CLAP SW4 *......129 J2
Denny Crs LBTH SE11......17 M7
Denny Gdns DAGW RM9......79 H6
Denny Rd ED N9......30 D7

Denny St LBTH SE11......18 B7
Den Rd HAYES BR2......167 G2
Densham Rd SRTFD E15......76 C7
Densole Cl BECK BR3 *......151 G7
Densworth Gv ED N9......42 E1
Denton Cl BAR EN5......26 A4
　CEND/HSY/T N8......55 F4
　DART DA1......138 B6
　TWK TW1......124 E5
　UED N18......42 A3
　WELL DA16......116 D6
Denton St WAND/EARL SW18...128 A5
Denton Wy CLPT E5......75 F2
Dents Rd BTSEA SW11......128 E5
Denvale Trade Pk MTCM CR4...162 C4
Denver Cl ORP BR6......169 K5
Denver Rd DART DA1......138 D6
　STNW/STAM N16......56 A6
Denyer St CHEL SW3......15 K5
Denzil Rd WLSDN NW10......69 H4
Deodar Rd PUT/ROE SW15......127 H3
Deodora Cl TRDG/WHET N20...39 J2
Depot Ap CRICK NW2......70 B3
Depot Rd HSLW TW3......123 J2
　SHB W12......88 A6
Depot St CMBW SE5......110 E5
Deptford Br DEPT SE8......112 D7
Deptford Broadway
　NWCR SE14......112 D7
Deptford Church St DEPT SE8...112 D5
Deptford High St DEPT SE8......112 D7
Deptford Market DEPT SE8 *...112 D6
Deptford Whf DEPT SE8......112 C3
De Quincey Ms CAN/RD E16 *...94 E7
De Quincey Rd TOTM N17......41 K7
Derby Av KTN/HRWW/WS HA3...34 D7
　NFNCH/WDSPK N12......39 G4
　ROMW/RG RM7......62 D5
Derby Ga WHALL SW1A......17 J2
Derby Hl FSTH SE23......150 E1
Derby Hill Crs FSTH SE23......150 E1
Derby Rd BRYLDS KT5......159 H7
　CROY/NA CR0......177 H1
　FSTGT E7......77 G6
　GFD/PVL UB6......66 B7
　HOM E9......75 F7
　HSLW TW3......123 G3
　MORT/ESHN SW14......125 J3
　PEND EN3......30 D4
　SUT SM1......174 D5
　SWFD E18......44 D7
　UED N18......44 D7
　WAT WD17......21 G3
　WIM/MER SW19......146 E6
Derbyshire St BETH E2......92 C2
Derby St MYFR/PICC W1J......10 B9
Dereham Pl SDTCH EC2A......7 K9
Dereham Rd BARK IG11......79 F5
Derek Av HOR/WEW KT19......172 C5
　WBLY HA9......68 D6
　WLGTN SM6......176 B3
Derek Cl HOR/WEW KT19......172 D4
Derek Walcott Cl HNHL SE24 *...130 C3
Deri Av RAIN RM13......99 K3
Dericote St HACK E8......74 C7
Deri Dene Cl
　STWL/WRAY TW19 *......120 B5
Derifall Cl EHAM E6......95 K4
Dering Pl CROY/NA CR0......177 J3
Dering Rd CROY/NA CR0......177 J3
Dering St OXSTW W1C......10 C5
Derinton Rd TOOT SW17......148 A3
Derley Rd NWDGN UB2......102 B2
Dermody Gdns LEW SE13......133 G4
Dermody Rd LEW SE13......133 G4
Deronda Rd HNHL SE24......130 C7
Deroy Cl CAR SM5......175 K6
Derrick Gdns CHARL SE7 *......114 B2
Derrick Rd BECK BR3......166 C3
Derry Rd CROY/NA CR0......176 E2
Derry St KENS W8......14 C2
Dersingham Av MNPK E12......77 K3
Dersingham Rd CRICK NW2......70 C2
Derwent Av CDALE/KGS NW9...51 J4
　EBAR EN4......27 K7
　MLHL NW7......37 F5
　PIN HA5......33 J5
　PUT/ROE SW15......145 G3
　UED N18......41 K4
Derwent Cl DART DA1......138 E7
　EBED/NFELT TW14......121 J7
　ESH/CLAY KT10......170 E4
Derwent Crs BXLYHN DA7......137 H1
　NFNCH/WDSPK N12......39 G2
　STAN HA7......49 J2
Derwent Dr STMC/STPC BR5...169 J6
　YEAD UB4......82 C4
Derwent Gdns REDBR IG4......59 J3
　WBLY HA9......49 J6
Derwent Gv EDUL SE22......131 G3
Derwent Ri CDALE/KGS NW9...51 G5
Derwent Rd EA W5......104 D2
　PGE/AN SE20......165 H1
　PLMGR N13......41 F3
　RYNPK SW20......161 F5
　STHL UB1......83 K5
　WHTN TW2......123 G5
Derwent St GNWCH SE10......113 H4
Derwentwater Rd ACT W3......86 E7
Derwent Wy HCH RM12......81 K4
Derwent Yd EA W5 *......104 D2
De Salis Rd HGDN/ICK UB10...82 A3
Desenfans Rd DUL SE21......131 F5
Desford Rd CAN/RD E16......94 C3
Desmond St NWCR SE14......112 B5
Desmond Tutu Dr FSTH SE23...151 H1
Despard Rd ARCH N19......54 C7
Desvignes Dr LEW SE13......133 G5
Detling Rd BMLY BR1......152 E4
　ERITH DA8......118 A6
Detmold Rd CLPT E5......74 D1
Devalls Cl EHAM E6......96 A6
Devana End CAR SM5......175 K2
Devas Rd RYNPK SW20......146 A1
Devas St BOW E3......93 K3
Devenay Rd SRTFD E15......76 D6
Devenish Rd ABYW SE2......116 B1
Deventer Crs EDUL SE22 *......131 F4
De Vere Cottages KENS W8 *...14 E3
De Vere Gdns IL IG1......59 K7
　KENS W8......14 E2
Deverell St STHWK SE1......19 G4
De Vere Ms KENS W8 *......14 E3
Devereux Ct TPL/STR WC2R *...11 M5
Devereux La BARN SW13......106 E6
Devereux Rd BTSEA SW11......128 E5
De Vere Wk WAT WD17......20 C1
Devey Cl KUTN/CMB KT2......145 H6
Devizes St IS N1 *......7 H4
Devon Av WHTN TW2......123 H7
Devon Cl BKHH IG9......45 F1

GFD/PVL UB6 .... 67 J7
TOTM N17 .... 56 B2
Devoncroft Gdns TWK TW1 .... 124 C5
Devon Gdns FSBYPK N4 .... 55 H5
Devonhurst Pl CHSWK W4 * 106 A4
Devonia Gdns UED N18 .... 41 J5
Devonia Rd IS N1 .... 6 D5
Devon Man
  KTN/HRWW/WS HA3 * 49 J4
Devonport Gdns IL IG1 .... 59 H5
Devonport Ms SHB W12 * 87 K7
Devonport Rd SHB W12 .... 87 K7
Devonport St WCHPL E1 .... 92 E5
Devon Ri EFNCH N2 .... 53 H3
Devon Rd BARK IG11 .... 78 E2
  BELMT SM2 .... 174 C7
Devons Est BOW E3 .... 93 K2
Devonshire Av BELMT SM2 .... 175 G6
  DART DA1 .... 138 C5
Devonshire Cl
  CAVSQ/HST W1G 10 C2
  SRTFD E15 .... 76 C3
Devonshire Ct FELT TW13 * 141 F1
Devonshire Crs MLHL NW7 .... 38 B6
Devonshire Dr GNWCH SE10 .... 112 E7
  SURB KT6 .... 158 E5
Devonshire Gdns CHSWK W4 .... 105 K6
  TOTM N17 .... 41 J5
  WCHMH N21 .... 29 J6
Devonshire Gv PECK SE15 .... 111 J5
Devonshire Hill La TOTM N17 .... 41 J5
Devonshire Ms CHSWK W4 .... 106 B4
Devonshire Ms South
  CAVSQ/HST W1G 10 C2
Devonshire Ms West
  CAVSQ/HST W1G 10 B1
Devonshire Pl
  CAVSQ/HST W1G 10 B1
  CRICK NW2 .... 70 E2
  KENS W8 * 14 C4
Devonshire Place Ms
  CAVSQ/HST W1G 10 B1
Devonshire Rd BELMT SM2 .... 175 G6
  BXLYHS DA6 .... 137 F3
  CAN/RD E16 .... 95 F5
  CAR SM5 .... 176 A3
  CHSWK W4 .... 106 B4
  CROY/NA CRO 164 E6
  EA W5 .... 104 D2
  ED N9 .... 30 E7
  ELTH/MOT SE9 .... 153 J1
  FELT TW13 .... 141 J2
  FSTH SE23 .... 132 A6
  GNTH/NBYPK IG2 .... 60 D6
  HRW HA1 .... 48 D5
  MLHL NW7 .... 38 B6
  PIN HA5 .... 47 C5
  PLMGR N13 .... 41 F3
  STHL UB1 .... 84 A4
  TOTM N17 .... 41 J5
  WALTH E17 .... 57 J5
  WIM/MER SW19 .... 147 J6
Devonshire Rw LVPST EC2M 13 H3
Devonshire Row Ms
  GTPST W1W 10 D1
  LVPST EC2M 13 K4
Devonshire Sq HAYES BR2 .... 168 J3
  LVPST EC2M 13 K4
Devonshire St
  CAVSQ/HST W1G 10 B2
  CHSWK W4 .... 106 B4
Devonshire Ter BAY/PAD W2 .... 8 F5
  EDUL SE22 * 131 H3
Devonshire Wy CROY/NA CRO 179 H1
  YEAD UB4 .... 83 F5
Devons Rd BOW E3 .... 93 J4
Devon St PECK SE15 .... 111 J5
Devon Wy CHSGTN KT9 .... 171 J3
  HOR/WEW KT19 .... 172 D4
Devon Waye HEST TW5 .... 102 E6
De Walden St
  CAVSQ/HST W1G 10 B3
Dewar St PECK SE15 .... 131 H2
Dewberry Gdns EHAM E6 .... 95 J4
Dewberry St POP/IOD E14 .... 94 A5
Dewey La BRXS/STRHM SW2 .... 130 B5
Dewey Rd DAGE RM10 .... 80 E5
  IS N1 .... 6 A1
Dewey St TOOT SW17 .... 147 K4
Dewhurst Rd HMSMTH W6 .... 107 G2
Dewsbury Cl PIN HA5 .... 47 J5
Dewsbury Gdns WPK KT4 .... 173 J2
Dewsbury Rd WLSDN NW10 .... 69 J4
Dexter Rd BAR EN5 .... 26 B5
Deynecourt Gdns WAN E11 .... 59 H3
D'Eynsford Rd CMBW SE5 .... 110 E7
  CMBW SE5 .... 110 E7
Diadem Ct SOHO/CST W1F * 11 G4
Diamedes Av
  STWL/WRAY TW19 .... 120 A6
Diameter Rd STMC/STPC BR5 .... 169 G6
Diamond Cl BCTR RM8 .... 61 J7
Diamond Rd RSLP HA4 .... 65 H3
  WLSDN NW10 .... 69 F6
Diamond Ter GNWCH SE10 .... 113 F6
Diana Cl DEPT SE8 .... 112 C5
  SWFD E18 .... 45 F2
Diana Gdns SURB KT6 .... 172 B1
Diana Rd WALTH E17 .... 57 H2
Dianne Wy EBAR EN4 .... 27 J3
Dianthus Cl ABYW SE2 * 116 C3
Diban Av HCH RM12 .... 81 K3
Dibden St IS N1 .... 6 D1
Dibden Cl SUT SM1 .... 174 E2
Dibdin Rd SUT SM1 .... 174 E2
Dicey Av CRICK NW2 .... 70 A4
Dickens Av DART DA1 .... 139 K3
  FNCH N3 .... 39 G7
Dickens Cl ERITH DA8 .... 117 J6
  HYS/HAR UB3 .... 101 H3
  RCHPK/HAM TW10 .... 144 A1
Dickens Dr CHST BR7 .... 154 C5
Dickens Est
  BERM/RHTH SE16 * 111 H2
Dickens La UED N18 .... 42 A4
Dickens Ms FARR EC1M 12 C1
Dickenson Cl ED N9 .... 30 C7
Dickenson Rd
  CEND/HSY/T N8 .... 54 E6
  FELT TW13 .... 141 H4
Dickenson's La SNWD SE25 .... 165 H5
Dickenson's Rd SNWD SE25 .... 165 H4
Dickens Rd EHAM E6 .... 95 H1
Dickens Sq STHWK SE1 .... 18 E4
Dickens St VX/NE SW8 .... 129 G1
Dickens Wy ROM RM1 .... 63 G3
Dickens Wood Cl NRWD SE19 .... 149 H6
Dickerage La NWMAL KT3 .... 159 K2
Dickerage Rd NWMAL KT3 .... 159 K1
Dickson Fold PIN HA5 .... 47 H3
Dickson House CHARL SE7 * 114 D6
Dickson Rd ELTH/MOT SE9 .... 134 D2

Dick Turpin Wy
  EBED/NFELT TW14 .... 121 J3
Didsbury Cl EHAM E6 .... 77 K7
Digby Crs FSBYPK N4 .... 73 J1
Digby Gdns DAGE RM10 .... 80 C7
Digby Pl CROY/NA CRO 178 B2
Digby Rd BARK IG11 .... 79 F6
  HOM E9 .... 75 F3
Digby St BETH E2 .... 93 F2
Diggon Rd WCHPL E1 .... 93 F4
Dighton Rd WAND/EARL SW18 .... 128 B4
Dignum St IS N1 * 6 A5
Digswell St HOLWY N7 .... 73 G5
Dilhorne Cl LEE/GVPK SE12 .... 153 F2
Dilke St CHEL SW3 .... 15 M9
Dillwyn Cl SYD SE26 .... 151 G3
Dilston Cl NTHLT UB5 .... 83 G2
Dilton Gdns PUT/ROE SW15 .... 126 D7
Dimes Pl HMSMTH W6 .... 106 E3
Dimmock Dr GFD/PVL UB6 .... 66 D4
Dimond Cl FSTGT E7 .... 76 E3
Dimsdale Dr CDALE/KGS NW9 .... 50 E7
  EN EN1 .... 30 C6
Dimsdale Wk PLSTW E13 .... 76 E7
Dimson Crs BOW E3 .... 93 J3
Dingle Cl BAR EN5 .... 25 H5
Dingle Gdns POP/IOD E14 * 93 J6
Dingley La STRHM/NOR SW16 .... 148 D1
Dingley Pl FSBYE EC1V 6 E8
Dingley Rd FSBYE EC1V 6 D8
Dingwall Av CROY/NA CRO 177 J1
Dingwall Gdns GLDGN NW11 .... 52 E5
Dingwall Rd CAR SM5 .... 175 K7
  CROY/NA CRO 177 K1
  WAND/EARL SW18 .... 128 B6
Dinmont St BETH E2 .... 92 D1
Dinsdale Gdns BAR EN5 .... 27 F4
  SNWD SE25 .... 165 F4
Dinsdale Rd BKHTH/KID SE3 .... 113 J5
Dinsmore Rd BAL SW12 .... 129 G6
Dinton Rd KUTN/CMB KT2 .... 144 B6
  WIM/MER SW19 .... 147 H5
Diploma Av EFNCH N2 .... 53 J3
Dirleton Rd SRTFD E15 .... 76 D7
Disbrowe Rd HMSMTH W6 .... 107 H5
Discovery Wk WAP E1W 92 D7
Disney Pl STHWK SE1 .... 18 F1
Disney St STHWK SE1 .... 18 F1
Disraeli Cl THMD SE28 .... 97 H7
  WEA W13 .... 85 K7
Disraeli Rd EA W5 .... 85 K7
  FSTGT E7 .... 76 E6
  PUT/ROE SW15 .... 127 H3
  WLSDN NW10 .... 86 E1
Diss St BETH E2 .... 7 L7
Distaff La BLKFR EC4V 12 E6
Distillery La HMSMTH W6 .... 107 F4
Distillery Rd HMSMTH W6 .... 107 F4
Distin St LBTH SE11 .... 18 A6
District Rd ALP/SUD HA0 .... 67 H4
Ditchburn St POP/IOD E14 .... 94 A6
Ditchfield Rd YEAD UB4 .... 83 J3
Dittisham Rd ELTH/MOT SE9 .... 153 J3
Ditton Cl THDIT KT7 .... 158 B6
Dittoncroft Cl CROY/NA CRO 178 A3
Ditton Grange Cl SURB KT6 .... 158 E7
Ditton Grange Dr SURB KT6 .... 158 E7
Ditton Hl SURB KT6 .... 158 D7
Ditton Hill Rd SURB KT6 .... 158 D7
Ditton Lawn THDIT KT7 .... 158 B7
Ditton Pl PGE/AN SE20 * 150 D7
Ditton Reach THDIT KT7 .... 158 C5
Ditton Rd BXLYHS DA6 .... 136 E4
  NWDGN UB2 .... 102 E4
  SURB KT6 .... 159 F7
Divisional Rd MNPK E12 .... 77 H2
Dixey Cots EFNCH N2 * 53 J1
Dixon Cl EHAM E6 .... 95 K5
Dixon Pl WWKM BR4 .... 166 E7
Dixon Rd NWCR SE14 .... 112 B7
  SNWD SE25 .... 165 F2
Dixon Wy WLSDN NW10 .... 69 G6
Dobbin Cl
  KTN/HRWW/WS HA3 .... 49 G1
Dobell Rd ELTH/MOT SE9 .... 134 E4
Dobree Av WLSDN NW10 .... 69 K6
Dobson Cl KIL/WHAMP NW6 .... 3 G2
Dockers Tanner Rd
  POP/IOD E14 .... 112 C2
Dockhead STHWK SE1 .... 19 M2
Dock Hill Av BERM/RHTH SE16 .... 112 A1
Dockland St CAN/RD E16 .... 96 A7
Dockley Rd BERM/RHTH SE16 .... 111 H2
Dock Rd BTFD TW8 .... 104 E6
  CAN/RD E16 .... 94 D6
Dockside Rd CAN/RD E16 .... 95 H6
Dock St WCHPL E1 .... 92 C6
Dockwell Cl
  EBED/NFELT TW14 .... 121 J1
Doctors Cl SYD SE26 .... 150 E4
Docwra's Blds IS N1 .... 74 A5
Dodbrooke Rd WNWD SE27 .... 149 G2
Doddington Gv WALW SE17 .... 18 C9
Doddington Pl WALW SE17 .... 18 C9
Dodsley Pl ED N9 .... 42 E2
Dodson St STHWK SE1 .... 18 B2
Dod St POP/IOD E14 .... 93 J5
Doebury Wk
  WOOL/PLUM SE18 .... 116 B5
Doel Cl WIM/MER SW19 .... 147 G6
Doggett Rd CAT SE6 .... 132 D6
Doggetts Ct EBAR EN4 .... 27 J4
Doghurst Av WDR/YW UB7 .... 100 A6
Doghurst Dr WDR/YW UB7 .... 100 B6
Dog Kennel Hl CMBW SE5 .... 131 J2
Dog La WLSDN NW10 .... 69 G3
Dog Rose Ramble NTHLT UB5 .... 65 H1
  YEAD UB4 .... 64 E7
Dog Rose Ramble & Hillingdon
  Trail YEAD UB4 .... 82 D1
Doherty Rd PLSTW E13 .... 94 E3
Dolben Ct DEPT SE8 * 112 C2
Dolben St STHWK SE1 * 12 D9
Dolby Rd FUL/PGN SW6 .... 127 J1
Dolland St LBTH SE11 .... 17 M8
Dollary Pde KUT/HW KT1 * 159 J2
Dollis Av FNCH N3 .... 38 D7
Dollis Crs RSLP HA4 .... 47 G7
Dollis Hill Av CRICK NW2 .... 69 K2
Dollis Hill Est CRICK NW2 .... 69 J2
Dollis Hill La CRICK NW2 .... 69 G3
Dollis Pk FNCH N3 .... 38 D7
Dollis Rd MLHL NW7 .... 38 C7
Dollis Valley Dr BAR EN5 .... 26 D4
Dollis Valley Green Wk
  FNCH N3 .... 52 C3
  TRDG/WHET N20 .... 39 F2
Dollis Valley Wy EBAR EN4 .... 27 H3
Dolman Cl FNCH N3 .... 53 G1
Dolman Rd CHSWK W4 .... 106 A4
Dolman St CLAP SW4 .... 130 A3
Dolphin Ap ROM RM1 .... 63 H3
Dolphin Cl BERM/RHTH SE16 .... 112 A1

SURB KT6 .... 158 E5
THMD SE28 .... 97 J5
Dolphin Ct SUN TW16 * 140 C7
Dolphin La POP/IOD E14 .... 93 K6
Dolphin Rd NTHLT UB5 .... 83 K1
  SUN TW16 .... 140 C7
Dolphin Rd North SUN TW16 .... 140 B7
Dolphin Rd South SUN TW16 .... 140 C7
Dolphin Rd West SUN TW16 .... 140 C7
Dolphin Sq CHSWK W4 * 106 A6
  PIM SW1V 16 F9
Dolphin St KUT/HW KT1 .... 159 F1
Dombey St BMSBY WC1N 11 L2
Dome Blds RCH/KEW TW9 * 124 E4
Dome Hill Pk SYD SE26 .... 150 B3
Domett Cl CMBW SE5 .... 130 E3
Domfe Pl CLPT E5 * 75 F3
Domingo St FSBYE EC1V 6 E9
Dominica Cl PLSTW E13 .... 95 H2
Dominion Cl HSLW TW3 .... 123 J1
Dominion Pde HRW HA1 * 49 F4
Dominion Rd CROY/NA CRO 165 G6
  NWDGN UB2 .... 102 D2
Dominion St LVPST EC2M 13 H2
Dominion Wy RAIN RM13 .... 99 J2
Domonic Dr ELTH/MOT SE9 .... 154 B3
Domville Cl TRDG/WHET N20 .... 39 H1
Donald Dr CHDH RM6 .... 61 J4
Donald Rd CROY/NA CRO 164 A5
  PLSTW E13 .... 77 F7
Donaldson Rd
  KIL/WHAMP NW6 .... 70 D7
  WOOL/PLUM SE18 .... 115 F7
Donald Woods Gdns
  BRYLDS KT5 .... 172 D1
Doncaster Crs HMSMTH W6 .... 106 E2
Doncaster Dr NTHLT UB5 .... 65 K4
Doncaster Gdns FSBYPK N4 * 55 J5
  NTHLT UB5 .... 65 K4
Doncaster Gn OXHEY WD19 .... 33 G4
Doncaster Rd ED N9 .... 30 D6
Donegal St IS N1 .... 5 M6
Doneraile St FUL/PGN SW6 .... 127 G1
Dongola Rd PLSTW E13 .... 95 F2
  TOTM N17 .... 56 A2
  WCHPL E1 .... 93 G4
Dongola Rd West PLSTW E13 .... 95 F2
Donington Av BARK/HLT IG6 .... 60 C4
Donkey Aly EDUL SE22 .... 131 H6
Donkey La EN EN1 .... 30 C1
Donnefield Av EDGW HA8 .... 36 A5
Donne Pl CHEL SW3 .... 15 K5
  MTCM CR4 .... 163 G3
Donne Rd BCTR RM8 .... 79 J1
Donnington Rd
  KTN/HRWW/WS HA3 .... 49 K4
  WLSDN NW10 .... 69 K7
  WPK KT4 .... 173 J1
Donnybrook Rd
  STRHM/NOR SW16 .... 148 C6
Donoghue Cots
  POP/IOD E14 * 93 G4
Donovan Av MUSWH N10 .... 54 B1
Donovan Pl WCHMH N21 .... 29 F4
Don Phelan Cl CMBW SE5 .... 110 E7
Doone Cl TEDD TW11 .... 143 G5
Doon St STHWK SE1 .... 12 A8
Doral Wy CAR SM5 .... 175 K4
Dorando Cl SHB W12 * 87 K6
Doran Gv WOOL/PLUM SE18 .... 115 K6
Dora Rd WIM/MER SW19 .... 146 E4
Dora St POP/IOD E14 .... 93 H5
Dorchester Av BXLY DA5 .... 136 E7
  PLMGR N13 .... 41 J3
  RYLN/HDSTN HA2 .... 48 C5
Dorchester Cl DART DA1 .... 139 J4
  ESH/CLAY KT10 .... 171 F1
  NTHLT UB5 .... 66 B4
  STMC/STPC BR5 .... 155 H6
Dorchester Ct CRICK NW2 .... 70 A2
  HNHL SE24 .... 130 D4
  RKW/CH/CXG WD3 * 20 A4
  STHGT/OAK N14 .... 28 B6
Dorchester Dr
  EBED/NFELT TW14 .... 121 H5
  HNHL SE24 .... 130 D4
Dorchester Gdns CHING E4 .... 43 J4
  GLDGN NW11 .... 52 E3
Dorchester Gv CHSWK W4 .... 106 B4
Dorchester Ms TWK TW1 .... 124 D5
Dorchester Pde
  STRHM/NOR SW16 * 148 E1
Dorchester Rd MRDN SM4 .... 162 A6
  NTHLT UB5 .... 66 B4
  WPK KT4 .... 161 F1
Dorchester Ter HDN NW4 * 52 B2
Dorchester Wy
  KTN/HRWW/WS HA3 .... 50 B4
Dorchester Waye YEAD UB4 .... 83 F5
Dorcis Av BXLYHN DA7 .... 137 F1
Dordrecht Rd ACT W3 .... 87 G7
Dore Av MNPK E12 .... 78 A4
Doreen Av CDALE/KGS NW9 .... 51 F7
Dore Gdns MRDN SM4 .... 162 A6
Dorell Cl STHL UB1 .... 83 K4
Dorian Rd HCH RM12 .... 63 J5
Doria Rd FUL/PGN SW6 .... 127 J1
Doric Wy CAMTN NW1 .... 5 G7
Dorie Ms NFNCH/WDSPK N12 .... 39 F3
Dorien Rd RYNPK SW20 .... 161 G1
Doris Ashby Cl GFD/PVL UB6 .... 67 G7
Doris Av ERITH DA8 .... 117 K7
Doris Rd ASHF TW15 .... 140 B5
  FSTGT E7 .... 76 E6
Dorking Cl DEPT SE8 .... 112 C5
  WPK KT4 .... 174 B1
Dorlcote Rd
  WAND/EARL SW18 .... 128 C6
Dorman Pl ED N9 * 42 C1
Dormans Cl NTHWD HA6 .... 32 B6
Dorman Wy STJWD NW8 .... 3 G1
Dormay St WAND/EARL SW18 .... 128 A4
Dormer Cl BAR EN5 .... 26 B4
  SRTFD E15 .... 76 D5
Dormer's Av STHL UB1 .... 84 A5
Dormers Ri STHL UB1 .... 84 B6
Dormer's Wells La STHL UB1 .... 84 A5
Dormywood RSLP HA4 .... 46 D4
Dornberg Cl BKHTH/KID SE3 .... 113 K6
Dornberg Rd
  BKHTH/KID SE3 * 114 A6
Dorncliffe Rd FUL/PGN SW6 .... 127 H1
Dorney NW3 .... 71 J6
Dorney Ri STMC/STPC BR5 .... 155 H6
Dorney Wy HSLWW TW4 .... 122 D4
Dornfell St KIL/WHAMP NW6 .... 70 D4
Dornton Rd BAL SW12 .... 148 B1
  SAND/SEL CR2 .... 178 A4
Dorothy Av ALP/SUD HA0 .... 68 A6
Dorothy Evans Cl
  BXLYHN DA7 .... 137 J3
Dorothy Gdns BCTR RM8 .... 79 H5
Dorothy Rd BTSEA SW11 .... 128 E2
Dorrington St HCIRC EC1N 12 A2
Dorrington Wy BECK BR3 .... 167 F4
Dorrit Ms UED N18 .... 42 B3

Dorrit St STHWK SE1 * 18 F1
Dorrit Wy CHST BR7 .... 154 C5
Dorrofield Cl
  RKW/CH/CXG WD3 .... 20 A4
Dors Cl CDALE/KGS NW9 .... 51 F7
Dorset Av NWDGN UB2 .... 103 F3
  ROM RM1 .... 63 F2
  WELL DA16 .... 136 A3
  YEAD UB4 .... 82 C2
Dorset Blds EMB EC4Y * 12 C5
Dorset Cl CAMTN NW1 .... 9 L2
  YEAD UB4 * 82 C2
Dorset Dr EDGW HA8 .... 36 B5
Dorset Gdns MTCM CR4 .... 164 A3
Dorset Ms FNCH N3 .... 38 E7
  KTBR SW1X 16 C3
Dorset Pl SRTFD E15 .... 76 B5
Dorset Ri EMB EC4Y 12 C5
Dorset Rd BECK BR3 .... 166 A2
  EA W5 .... 104 D2
  ELTH/MOT SE9 .... 153 J1
  FSTGT E7 .... 77 G6
  HRW HA1 .... 48 D5
  MTCM CR4 .... 162 D1
  SEVS/STOTM N15 .... 55 K3
  VX/NE SW8 .... 110 A6
  WDGN N22 .... 40 E7
  WIM/MER SW19 .... 146 E7
Dorset Sq CAMTN NW1 .... 9 L1
Dorset St MHST W1U 9 M3
Dorset Wy WHTN TW2 .... 123 J7
Dorset Waye HEST TW5 .... 102 E6
Dorton Cl PECK SE15 .... 111 F6
Douai Gv HPTN TW12 .... 142 C7
Doughty Ms BMSBY WC1N 11 L1
Doughty St BMSBY WC1N 5 L9
Douglas Av ALP/SUD HA0 .... 68 A6
  NWMAL KT3 .... 160 E3
  WALTH E17 .... 43 J7
Douglas Crs YEAD UB4 .... 83 G3
Douglas Dr CROY/NA CRO 179 J3
Douglas Est IS N1 * 73 J5
Douglas Ms CRICK NW2 .... 70 C2
Douglas Pth POP/IOD E14 .... 113 F6
Douglas Pl POP/IOD E14 * 94 A4
Douglas Rd CAN/RD E16 .... 94 E4
  ESH/CLAY KT10 .... 170 B1
  GDMY/SEVK IG3 .... 61 G6
  HSLW TW3 .... 123 G2
  IS N1 .... 6 E1
  KIL/WHAMP NW6 .... 70 D7
  KUT/HW KT1 .... 159 J1
  ROM RM1 .... 63 H5
  STWL/WRAY TW19 .... 120 A5
  SURB KT6 .... 172 B2
  WDGN N22 .... 41 G7
  WELL DA16 .... 116 C7
Douglas Rd North IS N1 .... 73 J5
Douglas Rd South IS N1 .... 73 J5
Douglas Sq WEST SW1P 17 G4
Douglas Ter WALTH E17 * 43 H7
Douglas Vls KUT/HW KT1 * 159 J1
Douglas Wy NWCR SE14 .... 112 C6
Doulton Ms KIL/WHAMP NW6 * 71 F5
Dounesforth Gdns
  WAND/EARL SW18 .... 128 A7
Douro Pl KENS W8 .... 14 D3
Douro St BOW E3 .... 93 J1
Douthwaite Sq WAP E1W * 92 C7
Dove Ap EHAM E6 .... 95 J4
Dove Cl MLHL NW7 .... 37 J6
  NTHLT UB5 .... 83 H3
  WLGTN SM6 .... 176 F7
Dovecot Cl PIN HA5 .... 47 G4
Dove Ct LOTH EC2R * 13 G5
Dovedale Av CLAY IG5 .... 60 A1
  KTN/HRWW/WS HA3 .... 49 J5
Dovedale Cl WELL DA16 .... 116 B7
Dovedale Ri MTCM CR4 .... 147 K6
Dovedale Rd EDUL SE22 .... 131 J4
Dove House Gdns CHING E4 .... 43 J1
Dovehouse Md BARK IG11 .... 96 D1
Dovehouse St CHEL SW3 .... 15 J8
Dove Ms ECT SW5 .... 14 E6
Dove Pk PIN HA5 .... 33 K6
Dove Pl ESH/CLAY KT10 .... 171 G7
Dover Cl CRICK NW2 .... 70 B1
  CRW RM5 .... 62 E1
Dovercourt Av THHTH CR7 .... 164 B3
Dovercourt Est IS N1 * 73 J5
Dovercourt Gdns STAN HA7 .... 36 A4
Dovercourt La SUT SM1 .... 175 G2
Dovercourt Rd DUL SE21 .... 131 F5
Doverfield Rd
  BRXS/STRHM SW2 .... 129 K6
Dover Gdns CAR SM5 .... 175 K2
Dover House Rd
  PUT/ROE SW15 .... 126 D3
Doveridge Gdns PLMGR N13 .... 41 H3
Dove Rd IS N1 .... 73 K5
Dove Rw BETH E2 .... 92 C1
Dover Park Dr PUT/ROE SW15 .... 126 E5
Dover Patrol BKHTH/KID SE3 .... 134 A1
Dover Rd ED N9 .... 42 E1
  MNPK E12 .... 77 G1
  NRWD SE19 .... 149 K5
  WOOL/PLUM SE18 .... 135 G4
Dover St CONDST W1S 10 D7
Dover Ter RCH/KEW TW9 * 125 J1
Dover Wy RKW/CH/CXG WD3 .... 20 A3
Doves Cl HAYES BR2 .... 181 J1
Doves Yd IS N1 .... 6 A1
Doveton Rd SAND/SEL CR2 .... 177 K4
Doveton St WCHPL E1 .... 92 E3
Dowanhill Rd CAT SE6 .... 133 G7
Dowd Cl FBAR/BDGN N11 .... 40 A1
Dowdeswell Cl
  PUT/ROE SW15 .... 126 B3
Dowding Pl STAN HA7 .... 35 G5
Dower Av WLGTN SM6 .... 176 B7
Dowgate HI CANST EC4R 13 G6
Dowland St NKENS W10 .... 88 C2
Dowlas St CMBW SE5 .... 111 F6
Dowman Cl WIM/MER SW19 * 147 F6
Downage HDN NW4 .... 52 A2
Downalong BUSH WD23 .... 22 D7
Downbank Av BXLYHN DA7 .... 118 A7
Down Barns Rd RSLP HA4 .... 65 H3

MTCM CR4 .... 162 E1
Downes Cl TWK TW1 .... 124 C5
Downes Ct WCHMH N21 .... 29 G7
Downfield WPK KT4 .... 160 C7
Downfield Cl MV/WKIL W9 .... 8 C2
Down Hall Rd KUT/HW KT1 .... 143 K7
Downham La BMLY BR1 .... 152 B4
Downham Rd IS N1 .... 7 H2
Downham Wy BMLY BR1 .... 152 C4
Downhills Av TOTM N17 .... 55 K2
Downhills Park Rd TOTM N17 .... 55 J3
Downhills Wy TOTM N17 .... 55 J1
Downhurst Av MLHL NW7 .... 37 F4
Downing Cl RYLN/HDSTN HA2 .... 48 C2
Downing Dr GFD/PVL UB6 .... 66 D7
Downing Rd DAGW RM9 .... 80 B7
Downings EHAM E6 .... 96 A5
Downing St WHALL SW1A 17 J1
Downland Cl TRDG/WHET N20 .... 27 G7
Downleys Cl ELTH/MOT SE9 .... 153 J1
Downman Rd ELTH/MOT SE9 .... 134 D2
Down Pl HMSMTH W6 .... 106 E3
Downs Av CHST BR7 .... 153 K4
  DART DA1 .... 139 K6
  PIN HA5 .... 65 K3
Downs Bridge Rd BECK BR3 .... 152 B7
Downs Court Pde HACK E8 * 74 D5
Downsell Rd SRTFD E15 .... 76 B3
Downshall Av GDMY/SEVK IG3 .... 60 E5
Downs HI BECK BR3 .... 152 B7
Downside BECK BR3 * 151 J7
  SUN TW16 .... 140 E7
  TWK TW1 .... 143 F2
Downside Cl WIM/MER SW19 .... 147 G5
Downside Crs HAMP NW3 .... 71 J4
  WEA W13 .... 85 G3
Downside Rd BELMT SM2 .... 175 H5
Downs La CLPT E5 .... 74 D3
Downs Park Rd HACK E8 .... 74 C4
Downs Rd BECK BR3 .... 166 E1
  CLPT E5 .... 74 C3
  EN EN1 .... 30 A3
  THHTH CR7 .... 149 J7
The Downs RYNPK SW20 .... 146 B6
Down St E/WMO/HCT KT8 .... 157 F4
  MYFR/PICC W1J 10 C9
Downs Vw ISLW TW7 .... 104 A7
Downsview Gdns NRWD SE19 .... 149 J6
The Downsway BELMT SM2 .... 175 G7
Downton Av
  BRXS/STRHM SW2 .... 149 F1
Downtown Rd
  BERM/RHTH SE16 .... 112 B1
Downway
  NFNCH/WDSPK N12 .... 39 J6
Dowrey St IS N1 * 6 A3
Dowsett Rd TOTM N17 .... 56 B2
Dowson Cl CMBW SE5 .... 130 E3
Doyce St STHWK SE1 * 18 E1
Doyle Cl ERITH DA8 .... 118 B7
Doyle Gdns WLSDN NW10 .... 69 K7
Doyle Rd SNWD SE25 .... 165 H3
D'Oyley St BGVA SW1W 16 B6
Doynton St ARCH N19 .... 72 B1
Draco St WALW SE17 .... 18 E9
Dragmore St CLAP SW4 .... 129 J5
Dragonfly Cl PLSTW E13 .... 95 F2
Dragon Rd LBTH SE11 .... 17 M6
  PECK SE15 .... 111 F6
Dragoon Rd DEPT SE8 .... 112 C4
Dragor Rd WLSDN NW10 .... 86 E2
Drake Cl BERM/RHTH SE16 .... 112 A1
Drake Crs THMD SE28 .... 97 J5
Drakefell Rd NWCR SE14 .... 132 A1
Drakefield Rd TOOT SW17 .... 148 A2
Drake Ms HAYES BR2 .... 168 B3
  HCH RM12 .... 81 J4
Drake Rd BROCKY SE4 .... 132 D2
  CHSGTN KT9 .... 172 C4
  CROY/NA CRO 164 A6
  MTCM CR4 .... 163 F5
  RYLN/HDSTN HA2 .... 65 K1
Drake's Cl ESH/CLAY KT10 .... 170 A3
Drakes Ctyd KIL/WHAMP NW6 .... 70 D6
Drake St FSBYW WC1X 11 L3
Drakewood Rd
  STRHM/NOR SW16 .... 148 D6
Draper Cl BELV DA17 .... 117 G3
  ISLW TW7 .... 123 J1
Draper Est STHWK SE1 .... 18 D5
Draper Pl IS N1 * 6 D3
Drapers Rd ENC/FH EN2 .... 29 H1
  SRTFD E15 .... 76 B3
  TOTM N17 .... 56 B2
Drapers Wy
  BERM/RHTH SE16 .... 111 H3
Draven Cl HAYES BR2 .... 167 J6
Drawell Cl WOOL/PLUM SE18 .... 115 K4
Drax Av RYNPK SW20 .... 145 J6
Draxmont WIM/MER SW19 .... 146 C5
Draycot Rd SURB KT6 .... 159 H7
  WAN E11 .... 59 F5
Draycott Av CHEL SW3 .... 15 K6
  KTN/HRWW/WS HA3 .... 49 J5
Draycott Cl CMBW SE5 .... 110 E6
  CRICK NW2 .... 70 B2
  KTN/HRWW/WS HA3 .... 49 J5
Draycott Pl CHEL SW3 .... 15 L6
Draycott Ter CHEL SW3 .... 15 L5
Drayford Cl MV/WKIL W9 .... 88 D3
Dray Gdns BRXS/STRHM SW2 .... 130 A4
Draymans Ms PECK SE15 .... 131 G1
Draymans Wy ISLW TW7 .... 124 A2
Drayson Ms KENS W8 .... 14 B2
Drayton Av ORP BR6 .... 169 G7
  WEA W13 .... 85 G6
Drayton Bridge Rd HNWL W7 .... 85 F6
  WEA W13 .... 85 F6
Drayton Cl HSLWW TW4 .... 122 E4
  IL IG1 .... 60 D7
Drayton Gdns WDR/YW UB7 * 100 A1
Drayton Green Rd WEA W13 .... 85 H6
Drayton Gdns WBPTN SW10 .... 14 F7
  WCHMH N21 .... 29 H6
  WDR/YW UB7 .... 100 A1
  WEA W13 .... 85 H6
Drayton Gn WEA W13 .... 85 G6
Drayton Green Rd WEA W13 .... 85 H6
Drayton Gv WEA W13 .... 85 G6
Drayton Park Ms HOLWY N7 * 73 F4
Drayton Rd BORE WD6 .... 24 C3
  CROY/NA CRO 177 H1
  TOTM N17 .... 56 A1
  WAN E11 .... 58 B7
  WEA W13 .... 85 H6

WLSDN NW10	69	H7
Drayton Waye		
KTN/HRWW/WS HA3	49	H5
Dreadnought Cl		
WIM/MER SW19	162	B1
Dreadnought St GNWCH SE10	113	H2
Drenon Sq HYS/HAR UB3	82	D6
Dresden Cl KIL/WHAMP NW6	71	H1
Dresden Rd ARCH N19	54	C7
Dressington Av BROCKY SE4	132	D5
Drew Av MLHL NW7	38	C5
Drewery Ct BKHTH/KID SE3 *	133	J1
Drew Gdns GFD/PVL UB6	67	F5
Drew Rd CAN/RD E16	95	J7
Drews Cots		
STRHM/NOR SW16 *	148	D1
Drewstead La		
STRHM/NOR SW16	148	D1
Drewstead Rd		
STRHM/NOR SW16	148	D1
Driffield Rd BOW E3	93	G1
The Drift HAYES BR2	181	H2
The Driftway MTCM CR4	148	A7
Drinkwater Rd		
RYLN/HDSTN HA2	66	B1
Drive Ct EDGW HA8 *	36	C4
The Drive ACT W3	86	E5
ASHF TW15	140	B6
BAR EN5	26	C2
BARK IG11	79	F6
BECK BR3	166	D1
BXLY DA5	136	D5
CHST BR7	155	F6
EBED/NFELT TW14	122	A6
EDGW HA8	36	C4
ERITH DA8	117	J6
ESH/CLAY KT10	157	H7
FBAR/BDGN N11	40	C5
FNCH N3	38	E5
GLDGN NW11	52	C6
HGT N6	53	K4
HOLWY N7	73	F5
HOR/WEW KT19	173	H5
HSLW TW3	123	J1
IL IG1	59	J5
KUTN/CMB KT2	144	E6
MRDN SM4	162	B4
NTHWD HA6	32	C7
RYLN/HDSTN HA2	48	A6
RYNPK SW20	146	A6
SCUP DA14	155	H2
SURB KT6	159	F6
SWFD E18	58	E2
THHTH CR7	164	E3
WALTH E17	57	K2
WBLY HA9	68	E1
WWKM BR4	167	G6
Dr Johnson Av TOOT SW17	148	B2
Droitwich Cl SYD SE26	150	C2
Dromey Gdns		
KTN/HRWW/WS HA3	35	F6
Dromore Rd PUT/ROE SW15	127	H5
Dronfield Gdns BCTR RM8	79	J4
Droop St NKENS W10	88	C3
Drovers Pl PECK SE15	111	J6
Drovers Rd SAND/SEL CR2	177	K4
Drovers Wy HOLWY N7	72	G5
Druce Rd DUL SE21	131	F5
Druid St STHWK SE1	19	K1
Druids Wy HAYES BR2	167	G3
Drumaline Rdg WPK KT4	173	C1
Drummond Av		
ROMW/RG RM7	63	F3
Drummond Cl ERITH DA8	118	D7
Drummond Crs CAMTN NW1	5	G7
Drummond Dr STAN HA7	35	F6
Drummond Ga PIM SW1V	17	H7
Drummond Rd		
BERM/RHTH SE16	111	J2
CROY/NA CR0	177	J1
ROMW/RG RM7	62	E3
WAN E11	59	F5
Drummonds Pl RCH/KEW TW9	125	F3
Drummond St CAMTN NW1	4	E9
Drury Crs CROY/NA CR0	177	G1
Drury La COVGDN WC2E	11	K5
Drury Rd HRW HA1	48	C6
Drury Wy WLSDN NW10	69	G4
Dryad St PUT/ROE SW15	127	G2
Dryburgh Gdns		
CDALE/KGS NW9	50	C2
Dryburgh Rd PUT/ROE SW15	126	E2
Dryden Av HNWL W7	85	F5
Dryden Cl CLAP SW4	129	J4
Dryden Rd EN EN1	30	A5
KTN/HRWW/WS HA3	35	F7
WELL DA16	116	A7
WIM/MER SW19	147	G5
Dryden St COVGDN WC2E	11	K5
Dryfield Cl WLSDN NW10	68	E5
Dryfield Rd EDGW HA8	36	E5
Dryhill Rd BELV DA17	117	G5
Drylands Rd CEND/HSY/T N8	54	E5
Drysdale Av CHING E4	31	K5
Drysdale Dwellings HACK E8 *	74	B4
Drysdale Pl IS N1	7	L4
Drysdale St IS N1	7	K8
Dublin Av HACK E8	74	C7
Du Burstow Ter HNWL W7	103	K1
Ducal St BETH E2	7	M8
Du Cane Cl SHB W12 *	88	A5
Du Cane Rd SHB W12	87	K5
Duchess Cl FBAR/BDGN N11	40	B4
SUT SM1	175	G3
Duchess Ms CAVSQ/HST W1G	10	D3
Duchess of Bedford's Wk		
KENS W8	107	J1
Duchess St REGST W1B	10	D3
Duchy St STHWK SE1	12	B8
Ducie St CLAP SW4	129	K3
Duckett Ms FSBYPK N4	55	H5
Duckett Rd FSBYPK N4	55	H5
Ducketts Rd DART DA1	138	C4
Duckett St WCHPL E1	93	F4
Ducking Stool Ct ROM RM1	63	G3
Duck La SOHO/CST W1F	11	G5
Duck Lees La PEND EN3	31	G3
Du Cros Dr STAN HA7	35	K5
Du Cros Rd ACT W3	87	G7
Dudden Hill La WLSDN NW10	69	H5
Dudden Hill Pde		
WLSDN NW10 *	69	H4
Duddington Cl ELTH/MOT SE9	153	H4
Dudley Av		
KTN/HRWW/WS HA3	49	J3
Dudley Dr MRDN SM4	161	H4
RSLP HA4	65	F4
Dudley Gdns		
RYLN/HDSTN HA2	48	D7
WEA W13	104	C1
Dudley Pl HYS/HAR UB3	101	G3

Dudley Rd EBED/NFELT TW14	121	G7
FNCH N3	53	F1
IL IG1	78	B3
KIL/WHAMP NW6	88	C1
KUT/HW KT1	159	G2
NWDGN UB2	102	C1
RCH/KEW TW9	125	G1
RYLN/HDSTN HA2	66	C1
WALTH E17	57	J1
WIM/MER SW19	146	E5
Dudley St BAY/PAD W2 *	9	G3
Dudlington Rd CLPT E5	74	E1
Dudmaston Ms CHEL SW3	15	H7
Dudrich Cl		
NFNCH/WDSPK N12	39	K5
Dudrich Ms EDUL SE22	131	G4
Dudsbury Rd DART DA1	138	E5
Dudset La HEST TW5	101	K2
Dufferin Av STLK EC1Y	13	G1
Dufferin St STLK EC1Y	12	F1
Duffield Cl HRW HA1	49	F4
Duffield Dr SEVS/STOTM N15	56	B3
Duff St POP/IOD E14	93	K5
Dufour's Pl SOHO/CST W1F	10	F5
Dugard Wy LBTH SE11	18	C5
Duggan Dr CHST BR7	153	J5
Dugolly Av WBLY HA9	68	D2
Duke Humphrey Rd		
BKHTH/KID SE3	113	H7
Duke of Cambridge Cl		
WHTN TW2	123	J5
Duke of Edinburgh Rd		
SUT SM1	175	H2
The Duke of Wellington Av		
WOOL/PLUM SE18	115	G2
Duke of Wellington Pl		
KTBR SW1X	16	B1
Duke of York Sq CHEL SW3	15	M7
Duke of York St STJS SW1Y	10	F8
Duke Rd BARK/HLT IG6	60	D3
CHSWK W4	106	A4
Dukes Av EDGW HA8	36	B5
FNCH N3	39	F7
HRW HA1	48	E3
HSLWW TW4	122	D3
MUSWH N10	54	C2
NTHLT UB5	65	J6
NWMAL KT3	160	B2
PIN HA5	47	K5
RCHPK/HAM TW10	143	J3
Duke's Av CHSWK W4	106	A4
Dukes Cl ASHF TW15	140	A3
HPTN TW12	141	K4
Dukes Ga CHSWK W4 *	105	K3
Dukes Green Av		
EBED/NFELT TW14	121	K4
Dukes La KENS W8	14	C1
Dukes Ms MUSWH N10	54	B2
Duke's Ms MHST W1U	10	B4
Dukes Orch BXLY DA5	137	K3
Duke's Pl HDTCH EC3A	13	L5
Dukes Point HGT N6 *	54	B7
Dukes Rd ACT W3	86	C3
EHAM E6	78	A7
Duke's Rd CAMTN NW1	5	H8
Dukesthorpe Rd SYD SE26	151	F3
Duke St MHST W1U	10	B4
RCH/KEW TW9	124	E3
SUT SM1	175	H3
WAT WD17	21	G2
Duke Street Hl STHWK SE1	13	H8
Duke Street St James's		
MYFR/PICC W1J	10	F8
Dukes Wy WBLY HA9	68	A4
WWKM BR4	180	C2
Duke's Yd MYFR/PKLN W1K	10	B6
Dulas St FSBYPK N4	55	F7
Dulford St NTGHL W11	88	C6
Dulka Rd BTSEA SW11	128	E4
Dulverton Rd ELTH/MOT SE9	154	C1
RSLP HA4	64	E1
Dulwich Common DUL SE21	130	E7
The Dulwich Oaks DUL SE21 *	150	B2
Dulwich Rd HNHL SE24	130	B4
Dulwich Village DUL SE21	130	E5
Dulwich Wood Av NRWD SE19	150	A4
Dulwich Wood Pk NRWD SE19	150	A3
Dumbarton Rd		
BRXS/STRHM SW2	129	K5
Dumbleton Cl KUT/HW KT1	144	D7
Dumbreck Rd ELTH/MOT SE9	135	F3
Dumfries Cl OXHEY WD19	32	C2
Dumont Rd STNW/STAM N16	74	A2
Dumpton Pl CAMTN NW1	4	B2
Dunbar Av BECK BR3	166	B3
DAGE RM10	80	C2
STRHM/NOR SW16	164	B1
Dunbar Cl YEAD UB4	82	E4
Dunbar Gdns DAGE RM10	80	C4
Dunbar Rd FSTGT E7	76	E5
NWMAL KT3	159	K3
WDGN N22	41	G7
Dunbar St WNWD SE27	149	J2
Dunblane Rd ELTH/MOT SE9	134	D2
Dunboyne Rd HAMP NW3	71	K4
Dunbridge St BETH E2	92	C3
Duncan Cl BAR EN5	27	G3
Duncan Gv ACT W3	87	G5
Duncannon St CHCR WC2N	11	J7
Duncan Rd HACK E8	74	D7
RCH/KEW TW9	125	F3
Duncan St IS N1	6	C5
Duncan Ter IS N1	6	C6
Duncan Wy BUSH WD23	21	K1
Dunch St WCHPL E1	92	D5
Duncombe Hl FSTH SE23	132	B6
Duncombe Rd ARCH N19	54	D7
Duncrievie Rd LEW SE13	133	G5
Duncroft WOOL/PLUM SE18	115	K6
Dundalk Rd BROCKY SE4	132	B2
Dundas Gdns		
E/WMO/HCT KT8	157	G2
Dundas Rd PECK SE15	131	K1
Dundee Rd PLSTW E13	95	F1
SNWD SE25	165	J4
Dundee St WAP E1W	92	D7
Dundee Wy PEND EN3	31	G2
Dundee Whf POP/IOD E14	93	H6
Dundela Gdns WPK KT4	173	K3
Dundonald Cl EHAM E6	95	J5
Dundonald Rd		
WIM/MER SW19	146	D6
WLSDN NW10	70	B7
Dunedin Rd IL IG1	60	C7
LEY E10	75	K2
RAIN RM13	99	H2
Dunedin Wy YEAD UB4	83	G3
Duneim St WCHPL E1	93	F5
Dunfield Rd CAT SE6	151	K4
Dunford Rd HOLWY N7	73	F1
Dungarvan Av		
PUT/ROE SW15	126	D3
Dunheved Cl THHTH CR7	164	B5

Dunheved Rd North		
THHTH CR7	164	B5
Dunheved Rd South		
THHTH CR7	164	B5
Dunheved Rd West		
THHTH CR7	164	B5
Dunholme Gn ED N9	42	B2
Dunholme La ED N9	42	B2
Dunholme Rd ED N9	42	B2
Dunkeld Rd BCTR RM8	79	H1
SNWD SE25	164	E3
Dunkery Rd ELTH/MOT SE9	153	H3
Dunkin Rd DART DA1	139	K3
Dunkirk St WNWD SE27 *	149	J3
Dunlace Rd CLPT E5	74	E4
Dunleary Cl HSLWW TW4	122	E6
Dunley Dr CROY/NA CR0	180	A5
Dunloe Av TOTM N17	55	K2
Dunloe St BETH E2	7	L6
Dunlop Pl BERM/RHTH SE16	19	M4
Dunmore Rd		
KIL/WHAMP NW6	70	C7
RYNPK SW20	146	A7
Dunmow Cl CHDH RM6	61	J4
FELT TW13 *	141	J3
Dunmow Dr RAIN RM13	81	H7
Dunmow Rd SRTFD E15	76	B3
Dunmow Wk IS N1 *	6	E3
Dunnage Crs		
BERM/RHTH SE16	112	B3
Dunningford Cl HCH RM12	81	H4
Dunn Md CDALE/KGS NW9	37	H6
Dunnock Cl BORE WD6	24	C3
ED N9	31	F7
Dunnock Rd EHAM E6	95	J5
Dunn St HACK E8	74	B4
Dunollie Pl KTTN NW5	72	C4
Dunollie Rd KTTN NW5	72	C4
Dunoon Gdns FSTH SE23	132	A6
Dunoon Rd FSTH SE23	131	K6
Dunraven Dr ENC/FH EN2	29	G1
Dunraven Rd SHB W12	87	J1
Dunraven St MYFR/PKLN W1K	9	M6
Dunsany Rd HMSMTH W6	107	G2
Dunsbury Cl BELMT SM2	175	F7
Dunsfold Wy PUT/ROE SW15	126	E6
Dunsford Wy PUT/ROE SW15	126	E6
YEAD UB4	83	H3
Dunsmore Cl BUSH WD23	22	D5
YEAD UB4	83	J4
Dunsmore Rd WOT/HER KT12	156	A6
Dunsmore Wy BUSH WD23	22	D5
Dunsmure Rd		
STNW/STAM N16	56	A7
Dunspring La CLAY IG5	60	B1
Dunstable Ms		
CAVSQ/HST W1G	10	B2
Dunstable Rd		
E/WMO/HCT KT8	156	E3
RCH/KEW TW9	125	F3
Dunstall Rd RYNPK SW20	145	K5
Dunstall Wy E/WMO/HCT KT8	157	G2
Dunstall Welling Est		
WELL DA16 *	136	C1
Dunstan Cl EFNCH N2 *	53	G2
Dunstan Gld		
STMC/STPC BR5 *	169	J5
Dunstan Houses WCHPL E1 *	92	E4
Dunstan Rd GLDGN NW11	52	D7
Dunstan's Gv EDUL SE22	131	J5
Dunstan's Rd EDUL SE22	131	H6
Dunster Av MRDN SM4	161	G7
Dunster Cl BAR EN5	26	B3
CRW RM5	62	E1
Dunster Ct BORE WD6	25	F2
MON EC3R	13	J6
Dunster Dr CDALE/KGS NW9	50	E7
Dunster Gdns		
KIL/WHAMP NW6	70	D6
Dunsterville Wy RYLN/HDSTN HA2 *	65	J2
Dunston Rd BTSEA SW11	129	F1
HACK E8	7	L4
Dunston St HACK E8	7	K3
Dunton Cl SURB KT6	159	F7
Dunton Rd LEY E10	57	K6
ROM RM1	63	G3
STHWK SE1	19	L6
Duntshill Rd		
WAND/EARL SW18	128	A7
Dunvegan Cl E/WMO/HCT KT8	157	G3
Dunvegan Rd ELTH/MOT SE9	134	E3
Dunwich Rd BXLYHN DA7	117	G1
Dunworth Ms NTGHL W11	88	D5
Duplex Ride KTBR SW1X	15	M2
Dupont Rd RYNPK SW20	161	G1
Duppas Av CROY/NA CR0	177	H3
Duppas Hill La CROY/NA CR0	177	H3
Duppas Hill Ter CROY/NA CR0	177	G2
Duppas Rd CROY/NA CR0	177	G2
Dupree Rd CHARL SE7	114	A4
Dura Den Cl BECK BR3	151	K6
Durand Gdns BRXN/ST SW9	110	A7
Durands Wy PEND EN3	31	J1
Durants Park Av PEND EN3	31	F3
Durants Rd PEND EN3	30	E3
Durban Gdns DAGE RM10	80	E6
Durban Rd BECK BR3	166	C1
GNTH/NBYPK IG2	60	E7
SRTFD E15	94	C2
TOTM N17	42	A5
WALTH E17	43	H7
WNWD SE27	149	J3
Durban Rd East WATW WD18	20	D3
Durban Rd West WATW WD18	20	D3
Durbin Rd CHSGTN KT9	172	A3
Durdans Rd STHL UB1	83	K5
Durell Gdns DAGW RM9	79	K4
Durell Rd DAGW RM9	79	K4
Durfey Pl CMBW SE5	110	E6
Durford Crs PUT/ROE SW15	126	E2
Durham Av HAYES BR2	167	J3
HEST TW5	102	E5
WFD IG8	45	H4
Durham Hi BMLY BR1	152	D3
Durham House St		
CHCR WC2N *	11	K7
Durham Pl CHEL SW3	15	L8
Durham Ri WOOL/PLUM SE18	115	H4
Durham Rd BORE WD6	24	C2
CAN/RD E16	94	C3
DAGE RM10	80	E4
EA W5	104	D3
EBED/NFELT TW14	122	B6
ED N9	42	C1
EFNCH N2	53	J2
HAYES BR2	167	J3
HOLWY N7	73	F1
HRW HA1	48	B4
MNPK E12	77	H3
RYNPK SW20	145	K7
SCUP DA14	155	H4

Durham Rw WCHPL E1	93	F4
Durham St LBTH SE11	17	L8
Durham Ter BAY/PAD W2	8	C4
PGE/AN SE20 *	150	D6
Durham Wharf Dr BTFD TW8	104	D6
Duriun Wy ERITH DA8	118	C6
Durley Av PIN HA5	47	J5
Durley Rd STNW/STAM N16	56	A6
Durlston Rd CLPT E5	74	C1
KUTN/CMB KT2	144	A5
Durnford St SEVS/STOTM N15	56	A4
Durning Rd NRWD SE19	149	K5
Durnsford Av WIM/MER SW19	146	E1
Durnsford Rd WDGN N22	40	D6
WIM/MER SW19	146	E2
Durrants Dr		
RKW/CH/CXG WD3	20	A2
Durrell Rd FUL/PGN SW6	107	H7
Durrington Av RYNPK SW20	146	A6
Durrington Park Rd		
RYNPK SW20	146	A7
Durrington Rd CLPT E5	75	G3
Dursley Cl BKHTH/KID SE3	134	B1
Dursley Gdns BKHTH/KID SE3	114	C7
Dursley Rd BKHTH/KID SE3	134	A1
Durward St WCHPL E1	92	D4
Durweston Ms MHST W1U *	9	M3
Durweston St MBLAR W1H	9	L3
Dutch Barn Cl		
STWL/WRAY TW19	120	A5
Dutch Gdns KUTN/CMB KT2	144	E6
Dutch Yd WAND/EARL SW18	127	K4
Duthie St POP/IOD E14	94	A6
Dutton St GNWCH SE10	113	F7
Duxberry Cl HAYES BR2	168	D4
Duxford Cl HCH RM12	81	K5
Dwight Rd WATW WD18	20	B6
Dye House La BOW E3	75	J7
Dyer's Blds FLST/FETLN EC4A	12	A3
Dyers Hall Rd WAN E11	76	B1
Dyer's La PUT/ROE SW15	126	E2
Dykes Wy HAYES BR2	167	J2
Dylan Cl BORE WD6 *	23	K6
Dylan Rd BELV DA17	117	H2
HNHL SE24	130	C3
Dylways CMBW SE5	130	E3
Dymchurch Cl CLAY IG5	60	A2
Dymock St FUL/PGN SW6	128	A2
Dymoke Rd ROM RM1	63	H6
Dyneley Rd LEE/GVPK SE12	153	G3
Dyne Rd KIL/WHAMP NW6	70	D6
Dynevor Rd		
RCHPK/HAM TW10	125	F4
STNW/STAM N16	74	A2
Dynham Rd KIL/WHAMP NW6	2	A1
Dyott St LSQ/SEVD WC2H	11	H4
RSO WC1B	11	H3
Dysart Av KUTN/CMB KT2	143	J4
Dysart St SDTCH EC2A	13	H1
Dyson Ct ALP/SUD HA0	67	K4
Dyson Rd SRTFD E15	76	D5
WAN E11	58	C5
Dyson's Rd UED N18	42	D5

E

Eade Rd FSBYPK N4	55	J6
Eagans Cl EFNCH N2 *	53	H2
Eagle Av CHDH RM6	62	A5
Eagle Cl BERM/RHTH SE16	111	J4
HCH RM12	81	K5
PEND EN3	30	E3
WLGTN SM6	176	E5
Eagle Ct FARR EC1M	12	C2
Eagle Dr CDALE/KGS NW9	51	G1
Eagle Hl NRWD SE19	149	K5
Eagle House Ms CLAP SW4	129	H4
Eagle La WAN E11	58	E3
Eagle Ms IS N1	74	A5
Eagle Pl SKENS SW7	14	F7
Eagle Rd ALP/SUD HA0	67	K6
HTHAIR TW6	121	J2
Eaglesfield Rd		
WOOL/PLUM SE18	115	G7
Eagle Ter WFD IG8	45	F6
Eagle Wharf Rd IS N1	6	F5
Eagling Cl BOW E3	93	J2
Ealdham Sq ELTH/MOT SE9	134	B3
Ealing Golf Course		
GFD/PVL UB6 *	85	G2
Ealing Gn EA W5	85	K7
Ealing Park Gdns EA W5	104	D3
Ealing Rd ALP/SUD HA0	86	A1
BOW E3	93	K2
EA W5	104	E3
NTHLT UB5	66	A5
Ealing Village EA W5	86	A5
Eamont St STJWD NW8	3	J3
Eardemont Cl DART DA1	138	C3
Eardley Crs ECT SW5	14	B7
Eardley Rd BELV DA17	117	H4
STRHM/NOR SW16	148	C5
Earl Cl FBAR/BDGN N11	40	B4
Earldom Rd PUT/ROE SW15	127	F3
Earle Gdns KUTN/CMB KT2	144	A6
Earlham Gv FSTGT E7	76	D4
WDGN N22	41	F6
Earlham St LSQ/SEVD WC2H	11	H5
Earl Ri WOOL/PLUM SE18	115	J3
Earl Rd MORT/ESHN SW14	125	K3
Earlsbury Gdns EDGW HA8	36	C3
Earl's Court Gdns ECT SW5	14	C6
Earl's Court Rd KENS W8	14	B5
Earl's Court Sq ECT SW5	14	C7
Earls Crs HRW HA1	48	E3
Earlsferry Wy IS N1	5	K2
Earlsfield Rd		
WAND/EARL SW18	128	B7
Earlshall Rd ELTH/MOT SE9	134	E3
Earlsmead RYLN/HDSTN HA2	65	K3
Earlsmead Rd		
SEVS/STOTM N15	56	B4
WLSDN NW10	88	A2
Earls Ms WAND/EARL SW18	128	B6
Earls Ter KENS W8	107	J2
Earlsthorpe Ms BAL SW12	129	F5
Earlsthorpe Rd SYD SE26	151	F3
Earlstoke Est FSBYE EC1V *	6	C7
Earlstoke St FSBYE EC1V	6	C7
Earlston Gv HOM E9	74	D7
Earl St SDTCH EC2A	13	J2
Earlswood Av THHTH CR7	164	B4
Earlswood Gdns CLAY IG5	60	A2
Earlswood St GNWCH SE10	113	H4

Earnshaw St		
NOXST/BSQ WC1A	11	H4
Easby St WKENS W14	107	H5
Easebourne Rd BCTR RM8	79	J4
Easedale Dr HCH RM12	81	J4
East Acton Ar ACT W3 *	87	H5
East Acton La ACT W3	87	G6
East Av EHAM E6	77	J6
HYS/HAR UB3	101	J1
STHL UB1	83	K6
WALTH E17	57	K3
WLGTN SM6	177	H3
East Bank STNW/STAM N16	56	A6
Eastbank Rd HPTN TW12	142	C4
East Barnet Rd BAR EN5	27	G3
East Boundary Rd MNPK E12	77	K2
Eastbourne Av ACT W3	87	F5
Eastbourne Gdns		
MORT/ESHN SW14	125	K2
Eastbourne Ms BAY/PAD W2 *	8	E4
Eastbourne Rd BTFD TW8	104	E4
CHSWK W4	105	K5
EHAM E6	96	A2
FELT TW13	141	H1
SEVS/STOTM N15	56	A5
SRTFD E15	76	C7
TOOT SW17	148	A5
Eastbourne Ter BAY/PAD W2	8	E4
Eastbournia Av ED N9	42	D2
Eastbrook Av ED N9	30	E6
Eastbrook Cl DAGE RM10	80	E3
Eastbrook Dr ROMW/RG RM7	81	G1
Eastbrook Rd BKHTH/KID SE3	114	A7
Eastbury Av BARK IG11	78	E7
NTHWD HA6	32	C4
Eastbury Ct OXHEY WD19 *	21	G6
Eastbury Gv CHSWK W4	106	B4
Eastbury Rd EHAM E6	96	A3
KUTN/CMB KT2	144	A6
NTHWD HA6	32	C5
OXHEY WD19	21	G6
ROMW/RG RM7	63	F3
STMC/STPC BR5	169	H6
Eastbury Sq BARK IG11	79	F7
Eastbury Ter WCHPL E1	93	F3
Eastcastle St GTPST W1W	10	E4
Eastcheap FENCHST EC3M	13	H6
East Churchfield Rd ACT W3	87	F7
Eastchurch Rd HTHAIR TW6	121	H1
East Cl EA W5	86	C3
EBAR EN4	28	A3
GFD/PVL UB6	84	C1
RAIN RM13	99	H3
Eastcombe Av CHARL SE7	114	A5
Eastcote Av E/WMO/HCT KT8	156	E4
GFD/PVL UB6	67	G4
RYLN/HDSTN HA2	66	B3
Eastcote La NTHLT UB5	65	K5
Eastcote La North NTHLT UB5	65	K5
Eastcote Rd PIN HA5	47	H4
RSLP HA4	46	C6
RYLN/HDSTN HA2	66	B1
WELL DA16	135	J1
Eastcote St BRXN/ST SW9	129	K1
Eastcote Vw PIN HA5	47	G3
Eastcott Cl KUTN/CMB KT2	144	E4
East Ct ALP/SUD HA0	67	J1
East Crs EN EN1	30	A4
FBAR/BDGN N11	39	K3
Eastcroft Rd HOR/WEW KT19	173	G6
East Cross Route HOM E9	75	H5
Eastdown Pk LEW SE13	133	G3
East Dr CAR SM5	175	J7
NTHWD HA6	32	C1
East Duck Lees La PEND EN3	31	G3
East Dulwich Gv EDUL SE22	131	F4
East Dulwich Rd EDUL SE22	131	G3
East End Rd FNCH N3	52	E1
East End Wy PIN HA5	47	J2
East Entrance DAGE RM10	98	D1
Eastern Av CHDH RM6	61	H3
GNTH/NBYPK IG2	60	C5
PIN HA5	47	H6
WAN E11	59	G5
Eastern Av East ROM RM1	63	F7
Eastern Av West CHDH RM6	62	A3
Eastern Gtwy CAN/RD E16	95	G6
Eastern Perimeter Rd		
HTHAIR TW6	121	H1
Eastern Rd BROCKY SE4	132	D3
EFNCH N2	53	K2
PLSTW E13	95	F1
ROM RM1	63	G4
WALTH E17	58	A4
WDGN N22	40	E7
Easternville Gdns		
GNTH/NBYPK IG2	60	C5
Eastern Wy THMD SE28	116	B1
East Ferry Rd POP/IOD E14	112	E3
Eastfield Gdns DAGE RM10	80	C3
Eastfield Rd CEND/HSY/T N8	54	E2
DAGE RM10	80	C3
WALTH E17	57	J3
Eastfields PIN HA5	47	G4
Eastfields Av		
WAND/EARL SW18	127	K3
Eastfields Rd ACT W3	86	E4
MTCM CR4	163	F1
Eastfield St POP/IOD E14	93	G4
East Gdns TOOT SW17	147	J5
Eastgate Cl THMD SE28	97	K5
Eastglade NTHWD HA6	32	C6
PIN HA5	47	K2
Eastham Cl BAR EN5	26	C4
East Ham Manor Wy		
EHAM E6	96	A5
East Harding St		
FLST/FETLN EC4A	12	B4
East Heath Rd HAMP NW3	71	H2
East Hl DART DA1	139	J6
WAND/EARL SW18	128	B4
WBLY HA9	68	C1
East Hill Dr DART DA1	139	J6
Eastholm GLDGN NW11	53	F3
East Holme ERITH DA8	118	A7
Eastholme HYS/HAR UB3	82	E7
East India Dock Rd		
POP/IOD E14	93	K5
East India Wy CROY/NA CR0	165	G7
Eastlake Rd CMBW SE5	130	C1
Eastlands Crs EDUL SE22	131	J3
East La ALP/SUD HA0	67	J2
BERM/RHTH SE16	111	H1
KUT/HW KT1	158	E2
Eastlea Ms CAN/RD E16	94	C3
Eastleigh Av		
RYLN/HDSTN HA2	66	B1
Eastleigh Cl BELMT SM2	175	F6
CRICK NW2	69	G2
Eastleigh Rd BXLYHN DA7	137	K1

WALTH E17 ... 57 H1
Eastleigh Wy
  EBED/NFELT TW14 ... 121 E1
Eastman Rd ACT W3 ... 106 A1
East Md RSLP HA4 ... 65 H2
Eastmead Av GFD/PVL UB6 ... 84 B2
Eastmead Cl BMLY BR1 ... 168 D3
Eastmearn Rd WNWD SE27 ... 149 H3
Eastmont Rd ESH/CLAY KT10 ... 171 F1
Eastmoor Pl CHARL SE7 ... 114 C2
Eastmoor St CHARL SE7 ... 114 C3
  WOOL/PLUM SE18 ... 114 C3
East Mount St WCHPL E1 * ... 92 D4
Eastney Rd CROY/NA CRO ... 164 C7
Eastney St GNWCH SE10 ... 113 G4
Eastnor Rd ELTH/MOT SE9 ... 135 H7
Easton Gdns BORE WD6 ... 25 G3
Easton St FSBYW WC1X ... 6 A9
East Park Cl CHDH RM6 ... 61 K4
East Parkside GNWCH SE10 ... 113 H1
East Pas STBT EC1A ... 12 B1
East Pl WNWD SE27 ... 149 J3
East Pole Cots
  STHGT/OAK N14 * ... 28 D3
East Poultry Av FARR EC1M ... 12 C5
East Rp HTHAIR TW6 ... 100 E5
East Rd CHDH RM6 ... 62 K4
  CHEL SW3 ... 16 A8
  EBAR EN4 ... 28 A7
  EBED/NFELT TW14 ... 121 D6
  EDGW HA8 ... 36 D7
  IS N1 ... 7 H7
  KUTN/CMB KT2 ... 144 B1
  ROMW/RG RM7 ... 63 F6
  SRTFD E15 ... 76 B2
  WDR/YW UB7 ... 100 C3
  WELL DA16 ... 136 C1
  WIM/MER SW19 ... 147 G5
East Rochester Wy
  BFN/LL DA15 ... 135 K4
  BFN/LL DA15 ... 136 D5
  DART DA1 ... 138 A6
East Rw NKENS W10 ... 88 C3
  WAN E11 ... 58 E5
Eastry Av HAYES BR2 ... 167 J5
Eastry Rd ERITH DA8 ... 117 H6
East Sheen Av
  MORT/ESHN SW14 ... 126 A4
East Side BUSH W12 * ... 107 F1
Eastside Rd GLDGN NW11 ... 52 D3
East Smithfield WAP E1W ... 13 M7
East St BARK IG11 ... 78 C6
  BMLY BR1 ... 167 K1
  BTFD TW8 ... 104 D6
  BXLYHN DA7 ... 137 H3
  WALW SE17 ... 18 F7
East Surrey Gv PECK SE15 ... 111 G6
East Tenter St WCHPL E1 ... 13 M5
East Ter BFN/LL DA15 * ... 135 K7
East Towers PIN HA5 ... 47 H5
East V ACT W3 ... 87 H7
East Vw BAR EN5 ... 26 D1
  CHING E4 ... 44 A4
Eastview Av
  WOOL/PLUM SE18 ... 115 K6
Eastville Av GLDGN NW11 ... 52 D4
East Wk EBAR EN4 ... 28 A7
  HYS/HAR UB3 ... 101 K1
East Wy CROY/NA CRO ... 179 F1
  HYS/HAR UB3 ... 82 E7
  RSLP HA4 ... 46 E7
Eastway BOW E3 ... 75 G2
  HAYES BR2 ... 167 K6
  MRDN SM4 ... 161 G4
  WAN E11 ... 59 F4
  WLGTN SM6 ... 176 C3
Eastway Crs
  RYLN/HDSTN HA2 ... 66 B1
Eastwell Cl BECK BR3 ... 151 G7
Eastwood Cl HOLWY N7 ... 73 G4
  SWFD E18 ... 58 E1
  TOTM N17 * ... 42 D6
Eastwood Dr RAIN RM13 ... 99 K5
Eastwood Rd GDMY/SEVK IG3 ... 61 G6
  MUSWH N10 ... 54 A1
  SWFD E18 ... 58 E1
  WDR/YW UB7 ... 100 D1
Eastwood St
  STRHM/NOR SW16 ... 148 C5
Eatington Rd LEY E10 ... 58 B4
Eaton Cl BGVA SW1W ... 16 E6
  STAN HA7 ... 35 H3
Eaton Ct EDGW HA8 ... 36 C3
  KUTN/CMB KT2 ... 144 C6
Eaton Dr BRXN/ST SW9 ... 130 C3
Eaton Gdns DAGW RM9 ... 80 A6
Eaton Ga BGVA SW1W ... 16 A5
  NTHWD HA6 ... 32 A5
Eaton La BGVA SW1W ... 16 D4
Eaton Ms North KTBR SW1X ... 16 B4
Eaton Ms South BGVA SW1W ... 16 B5
Eaton Ms West BGVA SW1W ... 16 B5
Eaton Park Rd PLMGR N13 ... 41 G1
Eaton Pl KTBR SW1X ... 16 A4
Eaton Ri EA W5 ... 85 J4
  WAN E11 ... 59 H5
Eaton Rd BELMT SM2 ... 175 H5
  EN EN1 ... 30 A2
  HDN NW4 ... 52 A4
  HSLW TW3 ... 123 J3
  SCUP DA14 ... 155 K3
Eaton Rw BGVA SW1W ... 16 C4
Eatons Md CHING E4 ... 43 J1
Eaton Sq BGVA SW1W ... 16 A5
Eaton Ter BGVA SW1W ... 16 A5
  BOW E3 ... 93 G2
Eaton Terrace Ms BGVA SW1W * ... 16 A5
Eatonville Rd TOOT SW17 ... 147 K1
Eatonville Vls TOOT SW17 ... 147 K1
Ebbisham Dr VX/NE SW8 ... 17 L9
Ebbisham Rd WPK KT4 ... 174 A1
Ebbsfleet Rd CRICK NW2 ... 70 C4
Ebdon Wy BKHTH/KID SE3 ... 134 A2
Ebenezer St IS N1 ... 7 G7
Ebenezer Wk
  STRHM/NOR SW16 ... 148 C7
Ebley Cl PECK SE15 ... 111 G6
Ebner St WAND/EARL SW18 ... 128 A4
Ebor St WCHPL E1 ... 7 L9
Ebrington Rd
  KTN/HRWW/WS HA3 ... 49 K5
Ebsworth St FSTH SE23 ... 132 A6
Eburne Rd HOLWY N7 ... 72 E2
Ebury Br BGVA SW1W ... 16 C7
Ebury Bridge Rd BGVA SW1W ... 16 B8
Ebury Ms BGVA SW1W ... 16 B5
Ebury Ms East BGVA SW1W ... 16 B5
Ebury Rd WAT WD17 ... 21 H2
Ebury Sq BGVA SW1W ... 16 B6
Ebury St BGVA SW1W ... 16 B6
Ecclesbourne Cl PLMGR N13 ... 41 G4

Ecclesbourne Gdns
  PLMGR N13 ... 41 G4
Ecclesbourne Rd IS N1 ... 6 F2
  THHTH CR7 ... 164 D4
Eccles Rd BTSEA SW11 ... 128 E3
Eccleston Br EBAR EN4 ... 27 J4
  ORP BR6 * ... 169 J7
Eccleston Crs CHDH RM6 ... 61 H6
Eccleston Ct WBLY HA9 ... 68 A4
Eccleston Ms WBLY HA9 ... 68 A4
Eccleston Pl WBLY HA9 ... 68 A4
Eccleston Ms KTBR SW1X ... 16 A4
Eccleston Pl BGVA SW1W ... 16 C4
Eccleston Rd WEA W13 ... 85 G6
Eccleston Sq PIM SW1V ... 16 D6
Eccleston Square Ms
  PIM SW1V ... 16 D6
Eccleston St BGVA SW1W ... 16 D6
Echo Hts CHING E4 * ... 31 K7
Eckford St IS N1 ... 6 A5
Eckstein Rd BTSEA SW11 ... 128 D3
Eclipse Rd PLSTW E13 ... 95 F4
Ector Rd CAT SE6 ... 152 C1
Edans Ct SHB W12 ... 106 C1
Edbrooke Rd MV/WKIL W9 ... 8 A2
Eddinton Cl CROY/NA CRO ... 180 A5
Eddiscombe Rd FUL/PGN SW6 ... 127 J1
Eddy Cl ROMW/RG RM7 ... 62 D5
Eddystone Rd BROCKY SE4 ... 132 B4
Ede Cl HSLW TW3 ... 122 E2
Edenbridge Cl
  BERM/RHTH SE16 * ... 111 J4
Edenbridge Rd EN EN1 ... 30 A5
  HOM E9 * ... 75 F6
Eden Cl ALP/SUD HA0 ... 67 K7
  HAMP NW3 ... 70 E1
Edencourt Rd
  STRHM/NOR SW16 ... 148 B5
Edendale Rd BXLYHN DA7 ... 118 A1
Edenfield Gdns WPK KT4 ... 173 H2
Eden Gv HOLWY N7 ... 73 F4
  WLSDN NW10 ... 88 D3
Edenham Wy NKENS W10 ... 88 D3
Edenhurst Av FUL/PGN SW6 ... 127 J2
Eden Pde BECK BR3 * ... 166 B3
Eden Park Av BECK BR3 ... 166 B3
Eden Rd BECK BR3 ... 166 B3
  CROY/NA CRO ... 177 K3
  WALTH E17 ... 57 K4
  WNWD SE27 ... 149 H4
Edensor Rd CHSWK W4 ... 106 B6
Eden St KUT/HW KT1 ... 158 E1
Edenvale Rd MTCM CR4 ... 148 A6
Edenvale St FUL/PGN SW6 ... 128 A1
Eden Wk KUT/HW KT1 * ... 159 F1
Eden Wy BECK BR3 ... 166 C4
  BOW E3 ... 75 H7
Ederline Av
  STRHM/NOR SW16 ... 164 A2
Edgar Kail Wy CMBW SE5 ... 131 F1
Edgarley Ter FUL/PGN SW6 ... 107 H7
Edgar Rd BOW E3 ... 93 K2
  HSLWW TW4 ... 122 E6
  WDR/YW UB7 ... 100 B2
Edgar Wallace Cl PECK SE15 ... 111 F6
Edgbaston Rd OXHEY WD19 ... 33 F2
Edgeborough Wy BMLY BR1 ... 153 H7
Edgecombe Cl KUTN/CMB KT2 ... 145 F7
Edgecoombe SAND/SEL CR2 ... 179 F7
Edgecote Cl ACT W3 ... 86 E7
Edgefield Av BARK IG11 ... 79 F6
Edge Hl WIM/MER SW19 ... 146 B6
  WOOL/PLUM SE18 ... 115 G5
Edge Hill Ct WIM/MER SW19 ... 146 B6
Edgehill Cl WOT/HER KT12 * ... 156 B7
Edgehill Gdns DAGE RM10 ... 80 C3
Edgehill Rd CHST BR7 ... 154 C2
  MTCM CR4 ... 148 B7
  WEA W13 ... 85 J5
Edgeley La CLAP SW4 ... 129 J2
Edgeley Rd CLAP SW4 ... 129 H2
Edge St WAND/EARL SW18 ... 128 A3
Edge Point Cl
  STRHM/NOR SW16 ... 149 H4
Edge St KENS W8 ... 8 B8
Edgewood Gn CROY/NA CRO ... 166 A7
Edgeworth Av HDN NW4 ... 51 J4
Edgeworth Cl HDN NW4 ... 51 J4
Edgeworth Crs HDN NW4 ... 51 J4
Edgeworth Rd EBAR EN4 ... 27 J3
  ELTH/MOT SE9 ... 134 B3
Edgington Rd
  STRHM/NOR SW16 ... 148 D5
Edgington Wy SCUP DA14 ... 155 K6
Edgwarebury Gdns
  EDGW HA8 ... 36 C4
Edgwarebury La EDGW HA8 ... 24 B7
Edgware Rd BAY/PAD W2 ... 9 G1
  CDALE/KGS NW9 ... 51 F2
  CRICK NW2 ... 70 A1
Edgware Road High St
  EDGW HA8 ... 36 C5
Edgware Road The Hyde
  CDALE/KGS NW9 ... 51 G3
**Edgware Way (Watford
  By-Pass)** EDGW HA8 ... 36 A1
Edinburgh Cl BETH E2 ... 92 E1
  PIN HA5 ... 47 J4
Edinburgh Ct KUT/HW KT1 * ... 159 F2
Edinburgh Ga KTBR SW1X ... 15 L1
Edinburgh Rd HNWL W7 ... 104 A1
  PLSTW E13 ... 95 F1
  SUT SM1 ... 175 G1
  UED N18 * ... 42 C4
  WALTH E17 ... 57 H4
Edington Rd ABYW SE2 ... 116 C2
  PEND EN3 ... 30 E1
Edison Av HCH RM12 ... 63 H7
Edison Cl HCH RM12 ... 63 H7
  WDR/YW UB7 ... 100 C1
Edison Dr STHL UB1 ... 84 B5
  WBLY HA9 ... 50 B7
Edison Gv WOOL/PLUM SE18 ... 116 A6
Edison Rd CEND/HSY/T N8 ... 54 D5
  HAYES BR2 ... 167 J1
  WELL DA16 ... 116 A7
Edis St CAMTN NW1 ... 4 A3
Edith Cavell Wy
  WOOL/PLUM SE18 ... 114 D7
Edith Gdns BRYLDS KT5 ... 159 J6
Edith Gv WBPTN SW10 ... 108 B5
Edithna St BRXN/ST SW9 ... 129 K2
Edith Nesbit Wk
  ELTH/MOT SE9 ... 134 D3
Edith Neville Cots
  CAMTN NW1 ... 5 G7
Edith Rd CHDH RM6 ... 61 K6
  EHAM E6 ... 77 H6
  FBAR/BDGN N11 ... 40 D6
  SNWD SE25 ... 165 E3
  SRTFD E15 ... 76 B4

WIM/MER SW19 ... 147 F5
  WKENS W14 ... 107 H3
Edith Rw FUL/PGN SW6 ... 108 A7
Edith Ter WBPTN SW10 * ... 108 B6
Edith Vls WKENS W14 ... 107 J3
Edith Yd WBPTN SW10 ... 108 C6
Edison Cl WALTH E17 ... 57 J4
Edmansons Cl TOTM N17 ... 56 B1
Edmund Gv FELT TW13 ... 141 K1
Edmund Halley Wy
  GNWCH SE10 ... 113 J1
Edmund Hurst Dr EHAM E6 ... 96 B4
Edmund Rd MTCM CR4 ... 162 D2
  RAIN RM13 ... 99 G2
  WELL DA16 ... 136 B2
Edmunds Cl YEAD UB4 ... 83 G4
Edmund St CMBW SE5 ... 110 E6
Edmunds Wk EFNCH N2 ... 53 J3
Edna Rd RYNPK SW20 ... 161 G1
Edna St BTSEA SW11 ... 108 D7
Edrick Rd EDGW HA8 ... 36 E5
Edrick Wk EDGW HA8 ... 36 E5
Edric Rd NWCR SE14 ... 112 A6
Edridge Cl BUSH WD23 ... 22 C4
Edridge Rd CROY/NA CRO ... 177 J2
Edulf Rd BORE WD6 ... 24 D1
Edward Av CHING E4 ... 43 K4
  MRDN SM4 ... 162 C4
  ED N9 ... 30 B6
  HPTN TW12 ... 142 C4
Edward Ct CAN/RD E16 ... 94 E4
  CROY/NA CRO ... 178 E1
  HEST TW5 ... 103 F6
Edward Gv EBAR EN4 ... 27 H4
Edward Mann Cl East
  WCHPL E1 ... 93 F5
Edward Mann Cl West
  WCHPL E1 * ... 93 F5
Edward Ms CAMTN NW1 ... 4 D7
Edward Pl DEPT SE8 ... 112 C5
Edward Rd BMLY BR1 ... 153 F5
  CHDH RM6 ... 62 A5
  CHST BR7 ... 154 B4
  CROY/NA CRO ... 165 F6
  EBAR EN4 ... 27 H4
  EBED/NFELT TW14 ... 121 G4
  HPTN TW12 ... 142 C4
  NTHLT UB5 ... 83 G1
  PGE/AN SE20 ... 151 F6
  RYLN/HDSTN HA2 ... 48 C2
  WALTH E17 ... 57 F3
Edwards Av RSLP HA4 ... 65 G4
Edwards Cl WPK KT4 ... 174 B1
Edward's La STNW/STAM N16 ... 73 K1
Edwards Ms IS N1 ... 6 B1
  MHST W1U ... 10 A5
Edwards Pl FBAR/BDGN N11 ... 40 D6
Edwards Sq IS N1 ... 5 L4
Edwards Rd BELV DA17 ... 117 H3
Edward St CAN/RD E16 ... 94 E3
  NWCR SE14 ... 112 B6
Edward's Wy BROCKY SE4 ... 132 C4
Edward Temme Av SRTFD E15 ... 76 D6
Edward Tyler Rd
  LEE/GVPK SE12 ... 153 F1
Edwina Gdns REDBR IG4 ... 59 J4
Edwin Av EHAM E6 ... 96 A1
Edwin Cl BXLYHN DA7 ... 117 G5
Edwin Pl CROY/NA CRO ... 164 E7
Edwin Rd EDGW HA8 ... 37 F5
  WHTN TW2 ... 123 K7
Edwin's Md HOM E9 ... 75 G3
Edwin St CAN/RD E16 ... 94 E4
  WCHPL E1 ... 92 E3
Edwin Ware Ct PIN HA5 * ... 47 G1
Edwyn Cl BAR EN5 ... 26 A5
Eel Brook Cl FUL/PGN SW6 * ... 108 A7
Effie Rd FUL/PGN SW6 ... 107 K6
Effingham Cl BELMT SM2 ... 175 F6
Effingham Rd
  CEND/HSY/T N8 ... 55 G4
  CROY/NA CRO ... 164 A6
  LEE/GVPK SE12 ... 133 H4
  SURB KT6 ... 158 C6
Effort St TOOT SW17 ... 147 J4
Effra Pde BRXS/STRHM SW2 ... 130 B4
Effra Rd BRXS/STRHM SW2 ... 130 B4
  WIM/MER SW19 ... 147 F5
Egan Wy HYS/HAR UB3 ... 82 C6
Egbert St CAMTN NW1 ... 4 A3
Egerton Cl DART DA1 ... 138 E2
  PIN HA5 ... 46 E3
Egerton Crs CHEL SW3 ... 15 K5
Egerton Dr GNWCH SE10 ... 112 E7
Egerton Gdns CHEL SW3 ... 15 J4
  GDMY/SEVK IG3 ... 79 F2
  HDN NW4 ... 51 K3
  WEA W13 ... 85 H5
  WLSDN NW10 * ... 70 A7
Egerton Gardens Ms
  CHEL SW3 ... 15 K4
Egerton Pl CHEL SW3 ... 15 K4
Egerton Rd ALP/SUD HA0 ... 68 B6
  NWMAL KT3 ... 160 C3
  SNWD SE25 ... 165 F2
  STNW/STAM N16 ... 56 B6
  WHTN TW2 ... 123 K6
Egerton Ter CHEL SW3 ... 15 K4
Egerton Wy HYS/HAR UB3 ... 100 E6
Egham Cl CHEAM SM3 ... 174 C1
Egham Crs CHEAM SM3 ... 174 B2
Egham Rd PLSTW E13 ... 95 F4
Eglantine Rd
  WAND/EARL SW18 ... 128 B4
Egleston Rd MRDN SM4 ... 162 A5
Eglinton Hl WOOL/PLUM SE18 ... 115 G5
Eglinton Rd
  WOOL/PLUM SE18 ... 115 G5
Egliston Ms PUT/ROE SW15 ... 127 F2
Egliston Rd PUT/ROE SW15 ... 127 F2
Eglon Ms CAMTN NW1 ... 3 M2
Egmont Av SURB KT6 ... 159 G6
Egmont Rd HOR/WEW KT19 ... 173 F4
Egmont Rd BELMT SM2 ... 175 G6
  NWMAL KT3 ... 160 C3
  SURB KT6 ... 159 G6
  WOT/HER KT12 ... 156 A6
Egmont St NWCR SE14 ... 112 A6
Egremont Rd WNWD SE27 ... 149 G2
Egret Wy YEAD UB4 ... 83 H5
Eider Cl LBTH SE15 ... 76 D4
Eighteenth Rd MTCM CR4 ... 163 K3
Eighth Av HYS/HAR UB3 ... 82 E7
  MNPK E12 ... 77 K3
Eileen Rd SNWD SE25 ... 164 E4
Eindhoven Cl CAR SM5 ... 163 F7
  WIM/MER SW19 ... 147 F3

Eisenhower Dr EHAM E6 ... 95 J4
Elaine Gv KTTN NW5 ... 72 A4
Elam Cl CMBW SE5 ... 130 C5
Elam St CMBW SE5 ... 130 C1
Eland Rd BTSEA SW11 ... 128 E2
  CROY/NA CRO ... 177 H2
Elba Pl WALW SE17 * ... 18 F5
Elberon Av CROY/NA CRO ... 163 H5
Elbe St FUL/PGN SW6 ... 128 B3
Elborough Rd SNWD SE25 ... 165 H4
Elborough St
  WAND/EARL SW18 ... 127 K7
Elbury Dr CAN/RD E16 ... 94 E5
Elcho St BTSEA SW11 ... 108 D6
Elcot Av PECK SE15 ... 111 J6
Elder Av CEND/HSY/T N8 ... 54 E4
Elderberry Rd EA W5 ... 105 F1
Elder Cl BFN/LL DA15 ... 136 A1
  TRDG/WHET N20 ... 39 F1
Elder Ct BUSH WD23 ... 34 E1
Elderfield Rd CLPT E5 ... 75 F3
Elderfield Wk WAN E11 ... 59 F4
Elderflower Wy SRTFD E15 ... 76 C6
Elder Oak Cl PGE/AN SE20 ... 150 D7
Elder Rd WNWD SE27 ... 149 J4
Elderslie Cl BECK BR3 ... 166 D5
Elderslie Rd ELTH/MOT SE9 ... 135 F4
Elder St WCHPL E1 ... 13 L2
Elderton Rd SYD SE26 ... 151 G3
Eldertree Pl MTCM CR4 ... 148 C7
Eldertree Wy MTCM CR4 ... 148 B7
Elder Wk IS N1 ... 6 D3
Eldon Av BORE WD6 ... 24 C1
  CROY/NA CRO ... 178 E1
  HEST TW5 ... 103 F6
Eldon Gv HAMP NW3 ... 71 H4
Eldon Pde WDGN N22 * ... 41 H7
Eldon Rd ED N9 ... 30 E7
  KENS W8 ... 14 D4
  WALTH E17 ... 57 H3
  WDGN N22 ... 41 H7
Eldon St LVPST EC2M ... 13 H3
Eldon Wy WLSDN NW10 ... 86 D1
Eldrick Ct EBED/NFELT TW14 ... 121 G7
Eldridge Cl EBED/NFELT TW14 ... 121 F7
Eleanora Ter SUT SM1 * ... 175 G4
Eleanor Cl BERM/RHTH SE16 ... 112 A1
  SEVS/STOTM N15 ... 56 B2
Eleanor Crs MLHL NW7 ... 38 B3
Eleanor Gdns BAR EN5 ... 26 A4
  DAGW RM9 ... 80 B2
Eleanor Gv BARN SW13 ... 126 B2
Eleanor Rd FBAR/BDGN N11 ... 40 E5
  HACK E8 ... 74 D5
  SRTFD E15 ... 76 D5
Eleanor St BOW E3 ... 93 J2
Electra Av HTHAIR TW6 ... 121 J2
Electric Av BRXN/ST SW9 ... 130 B3
Electric La BRXN/ST SW9 ... 130 B3
Electric Pde SURB KT6 ... 158 D5
Elephant & Castle STHWK SE1 ... 18 D5
Elephant La BERM/RHTH SE16 ... 111 K1
Elephant Rd WALW SE17 ... 18 E5
Elers Rd HYS/HAR UB3 ... 101 F3
  WEA W13 ... 104 D1
Eley Rd UED N18 ... 43 F4
Elfindale Rd HNHL SE24 ... 130 D4
Elfin Gv TEDD TW11 ... 143 F4
Elford Cl BKHTH/KID SE3 ... 134 B3
Elfort Rd HBRY N5 ... 73 G3
Elfrida Crs CAT SE6 ... 151 J3
Elfrida Rd WATW WD18 ... 21 G4
Elf Rw WAP E1W ... 92 E6
Elgar Av BRYLDS KT5 ... 159 J7
  EA W5 ... 105 F1
  STRHM/NOR SW16 ... 163 K2
  WLSDN NW10 ... 69 F5
Elgar Cl BKHH IG9 ... 45 H1
  BORE WD6 ... 112 D6
  DEPT SE8 ... 112 D6
  PLSTW E13 ... 95 G1
Elgar St BERM/RHTH SE16 ... 112 B1
Elgin Av ASHF TW15 ... 140 A5
  KTN/HRWW/WS HA3 ... 49 H1
  MV/WKIL W9 ... 8 C1
  SHB W12 ... 106 D1
Elgin Cl SHB W12 ... 106 E1
Elgin Crs HTHAIR TW6 ... 121 H1
  NTGHL W11 ... 88 C6
Elgin Est MV/WKIL W9 * ... 8 A1
Elgin Ms NTGHL W11 ... 88 C5
Elgin Ms North MV/WKIL W9 ... 2 D8
Elgin Ms South MV/WKIL W9 ... 2 D8
Elgin Rd CROY/NA CRO ... 178 B1
  GDMY/SEVK IG3 ... 60 E7
  SUT SM1 ... 175 G2
  WDGN N22 ... 54 C1
  WLGTN SM6 ... 176 C5
Elgood Av NTHWD HA6 ... 32 E5
Elgood Cl NTGHL W11 ... 88 C6
Elham Cl BMLY BR1 ... 153 H6
Elia Ms IS N1 ... 6 C6
Elias Pl VX/NE SW8 ... 110 B5
Elia St IS N1 ... 6 C5
Elibank Rd ELTH/MOT SE9 ... 135 F3
Elim St STHWK SE1 ... 19 J3
Elim Wy PLSTW E13 ... 94 D2
Eliot Bank FSTH SE23 ... 150 D1
Eliot Dr RYLN/HDSTN HA2 ... 66 B1
Eliot Gdns PUT/ROE SW15 ... 126 D3
Eliot Hl LEW SE13 ... 133 F1
Eliot Ms STJWD NW8 ... 2 E6
Eliot Pk LEW SE13 ... 133 F1
Eliot Rd DAGW RM9 ... 79 K3
Eliot V BKHTH/KID SE3 ... 133 G1
Elizabeth Wy
  STWL/WRAY TW19 ... 120 A6
Elizabeth Av ENC/FH EN2 ... 29 H2
  IL IG1 ... 78 D1
  IS N1 ... 6 F2
Elizabeth Barnes Ct
  FUL/PGN SW6 * ... 128 A1
Elizabeth Br BGVA SW1W ... 16 C6
Elizabeth Cl BAR EN5 ... 26 A3
  MV/WKIL W9 * ... 8 F1
  SUT SM1 ... 174 D3
Elizabeth Clyde Cl
  SEVS/STOTM N15 ... 56 A3
Elizabeth Cots RCH/KEW TW9 ... 105 G7
Elizabeth Fry Pl
  WOOL/PLUM SE18 ... 114 D7
Elizabeth Fry Rd HACK E8 ... 74 D6
Elizabeth Gdns ACT W3 ... 87 H7
  ISLW TW7 ... 124 B3
  STAN HA7 ... 35 J5
  SUN TW16 ... 156 B2
Elizabeth Ms HAMP NW3 ... 71 J5
Elizabeth Br BGVA SW1W ... 16 C6
Elizabeth Ride ED N9 ... 30 D6
Elizabeth Rd EHAM E6 ... 77 H7

RAIN RM13 ... 99 K3
  SEVS/STOTM N15 ... 56 A4
Elizabeth Sq
  BERM/RHTH SE16 ... 93 G6
Elizabeth St BGVA SW1W ... 16 B5
Elizabeth Wy FELT TW13 ... 141 G3
  NRWD SE19 ... 149 K6
Elkanette Ms
  TRDG/WHET N20 ... 39 G1
Elkington Rd PLSTW E13 ... 95 F3
The Elkins ROM RM1 ... 63 G1
Elkstone Rd NKENS W10 ... 88 D4
Ella Ms HAMP NW3 ... 71 K3
Ellanby Crs UED N18 ... 42 D4
Elland Cl BAR EN5 ... 27 H4
Elland Rd PECK SE15 ... 131 K3
Ella Rd CEND/HSY/T N8 ... 54 E6
Ellement Cl PIN HA5 ... 47 H4
Ellenborough Pl
  PUT/ROE SW15 ... 126 D3
Ellenborough Rd SCUP DA14 ... 155 K5
  WDGN N22 ... 41 J7
Ellenbridge Wy SAND/SEL CR2 ... 178 A7
Ellen Cl BMLY BR1 ... 168 C2
Ellen Ct ED N9 ... 42 E1
Ellen St WCHPL E1 ... 92 C5
Ellen Webb Dr
  KTN/HRWW/WS HA3 ... 48 E2
Elleray Rd TEDD TW11 ... 143 F5
Ellerby St FUL/PGN SW6 ... 107 G7
Ellerdale Cl HAMP NW3 ... 71 G4
Ellerdale Rd HAMP NW3 ... 71 G4
Ellerdale St LEW SE13 ... 132 E3
Ellerdine Rd HSLW TW3 ... 123 H3
Ellerker Gdns
  RCHPK/HAM TW10 ... 125 F5
Ellerman Av WHTN TW2 ... 122 E7
Ellerslie Rd SHB W12 ... 87 K7
Ellerton Gdns DAGW RM9 ... 79 J6
Ellerton Rd BARN SW13 ... 106 D7
  DAGW RM9 ... 79 J6
  RYNPK SW20 ... 145 J6
  SURB KT6 ... 172 B1
  WAND/EARL SW18 ... 128 C2
Ellery Rd NRWD SE19 ... 149 K6
Ellery St PECK SE15 ... 131 J1
Ellesborough Cl OXHEY WD19 ... 33 G4
Ellesmere Av BECK BR3 ... 166 E1
  MLHL NW7 ... 37 F2
Ellesmere Cl RSLP HA4 ... 46 A6
  WAN E11 ... 58 D4
Ellesmere Gdns REDBR IG4 ... 59 J4
Ellesmere Gv BAR EN5 ... 26 D4
Ellesmere Rd BOW E3 ... 93 G1
  GFD/PVL UB6 ... 84 C3
  TWK TW1 ... 124 D5
  WLSDN NW10 ... 69 J4
Ellesmere St POP/IOD E14 ... 93 K5
Ellingfort Rd HACK E8 ... 74 D6
Ellingham Rd CHSGTN KT9 ... 171 K5
  SHB W12 ... 106 D1
  SRTFD E15 ... 76 B3
Ellington Rd FELT TW13 ... 140 D3
  HSLW TW3 ... 123 G1
  MUSWH N10 ... 54 B3
Ellington St HOLWY N7 ... 73 G5
Elliot Cl SRTFD E15 ... 76 C6
  WBLY HA9 ... 68 B2
  WFD IG8 ... 45 J5
Elliot Rd HDN NW4 ... 51 K5
Elliott Av RSLP HA4 ... 65 F1
Elliott Rd BRXN/ST SW9 ... 110 C6
  CHSWK W4 ... 106 B3
  HAYES BR2 ... 168 C3
  STAN HA7 ... 35 G5
  THHTH CR7 ... 164 C3
Elliott's Pl IS N1 ... 6 C4
Elliott Sq HAMP NW3 ... 3 K2
Elliotts Rw LBTH SE11 ... 18 C5
Ellis Av RAIN RM13 ... 99 J4
Ellis Cl EDGW HA8 ... 37 G5
  ELTH/MOT SE9 ... 154 C1
  WLSDN NW10 ... 70 A5
Elliscombe Mt CHARL SE7 * ... 114 B5
Elliscombe Rd CHARL SE7 ... 114 B4
Ellisfield Dr PUT/ROE SW15 ... 126 C6
Ellison Gdns NWDGN UB2 ... 102 E3
Ellison Rd BARN SW13 ... 126 C1
  BFN/LL DA15 ... 135 J7
  STRHM/NOR SW16 ... 148 D6
  NWDGN UB2 ...
Ellis Rd MTCM CR4 ... 162 E5
  NWDGN UB2 ...
Ellis St KTBR SW1X ... 15 M5
Ellora Rd STRHM/NOR SW16 ... 148 D4
Ellsworth St BETH E2 * ... 92 D2
Elm Av EA W5 ... 86 A7
  OXHEY WD19 ... 21 J6
  RSLP HA4 ... 46 E7
Elmbank STHGT/OAK N14 ... 28 E6
Elmbank Av BAR EN5 ... 26 A3
Elmbank Dr BMLY BR1 ... 168 C1
Elm Bank Gdns BARN SW13 ... 126 B1
Elmbank Wy HNWL W7 ... 84 D4
Elmbourne Dr BELV DA17 ... 117 J3
Elmbourne Rd TOOT SW17 ... 148 B2
Elmbridge Av BRYLDS KT5 ... 159 K5
Elmbridge Cl RSLP HA4 ... 46 E5
Elmbridge Dr RSLP HA4 ... 46 B5
Elmbridge Wk HACK E8 * ... 74 C6
Elmbrook Cl SUN TW16 ... 141 F7
Elmbrook Gdns
  ELTH/MOT SE9 ... 134 D3
Elmbrook Rd SUT SM1 ... 174 D3
Elm Cl BKHH IG9 ... 45 H1
  BRYLDS KT5 ... 159 K6
  CAR SM5 ... 162 E7
  DART DA1 ... 139 F7
  HDN NW4 ... 52 B4
  HYS/HAR UB3 ... 82 C5
  RYLN/HDSTN HA2 ... 48 B5
  RYNPK SW20 ... 161 F3
  SAND/SEL CR2 ... 177 K5
  STWL/WRAY TW19 ... 120 A7
  WAN E11 ... 59 F5
  WHTN TW2 ... 142 C1
Elm Cots MTCM CR4 * ... 162 E1
Elm Ct EA W5 * ... 85 K5
  EBED/NFELT TW14 ... 121 J5
Elmcroft CEND/HSY/T N8 ... 55 F4
Elm Crs EA W5 ... 105 K1
  KUTN/CMB KT2 ... 144 A7
Elmcroft Av BFN/LL DA15 ... 136 A6
  ED N9 ... 30 D5
  GLDGN NW11 ... 52 D6
  WAN E11 ... 59 F4
Elmcroft Cl CHSGTN KT9 ... 172 A2
  EA W5 ... 85 K5
  EBED/NFELT TW14 ... 121 J5
Elmcroft Crs GLDGN NW11 ... 52 B6
  RYLN/HDSTN HA2 ... 48 A2
Elmcroft Dr CHSGTN KT9 ... 172 A3

Elmcroft Gdns
CDALE/KGS NW9 50 C4
Elmcroft St *CLPT* E5 74 E3
Elmdale Rd *PLMGR* N13 41 F4
Elmdene *BRYLDS* KT5 159 K7
Elmdene Cl *BECK* BR3 166 C4
Elmdene Rd
WOOL/PLUM SE18 115 G4
Elmdon Rd *HSLWW* TW4 122 C1
HTHAIR TW6 121 J2
Elm Dr *RYLN/HDSTN* HA2 48 B5
SUN TW16 156 B1
Elmer Cl *ENC/FH* EN2 29 F2
RAIN RM13 81 J6
Elmer Gdns *EDGW* HA8 36 D6
ISLW TW7 123 J2
RAIN RM13 81 J6
Elmer Rd *CAT* SE6 133 F6
Elmer's Dr *TEDD* TW11 143 H5
Elmers End Rd *BECK* BR3 165 K2
Elmerside Rd *BECK* BR3 166 B3
Elmers Rd *SNWD* SE25 165 H6
Elmfield Av *CEND/HSY/T* N8 54 E4
MTCM CR4 148 A7
TEDD TW11 143 F4
Elmfield Cl *HRW* HA1 66 E1
Elmfield Pk *BMLY* BR1 167 K2
Elmfield Rd *BMLY* BR1 167 K2
CHING E4 44 A1
EFNCH N2 53 H2
NWDGN UB2 102 D2
TOOT SW17 148 B1
WALTH E17 57 F5
Elmfield Wy *MV/WKIL* W9 8 A2
SAND/SEL CR2 178 B7
Elm Friars Wk *CAMTN* NW1 5 H2
Elm Gdns *EFNCH* N2 53 G2
ESH/CLAY KT10 171 F5
MTCM CR4 163 J3
Elmgate Av *FELT* TW13 141 F2
Elmgate Gdns *EDGW* HA8 36 E4
Elm Gn *ACT* W3 87 G5
Elmgreen Cl *SRTFD* E15 76 C7
Elm Gv *CEND/HSY/T* N8 54 E5
CRICK NW2 70 B3
ERITH DA8 118 A6
KUTN/CMB KT2 144 A7
PECK SE15 131 H1
RYLN/HDSTN HA2 48 A6
SUT SM1 175 F3
WIM/MER SW19 146 C6
Elmgrove Crs *HRW* HA1 49 F4
Elmgrove Gdns *HRW* HA1 49 G4
Elm Grove Pde *CAR* SM5 176 A2
Elm Grove Rd *BARN* SW13 126 D1
EA W5 105 F1
Elmgrove Rd *CROY/NA* CR0 165 J6
HRW HA1 49 F4
Elm Hall Gdns *WAN* E11 59 F5
Elm Hatch *PIN* HA5 33 K6
Elmhurst *BELV* DA17 117 F5
Elmhurst Av *EFNCH* N2 * 53 H2
MTCM CR4 148 A6
Elmhurst Cl *BUSH* WD23 21 J3
Elmhurst Crs *EFNCH* N2 53 H2
Elmhurst Dr *SWFD* E18 58 E1
Elmhurst Rd *ELTH/MOT* SE9 153 J1
FSTGT E7 77 F6
TOTM N17 56 A1
Elmhurst St *CLAP* SW4 129 J2
Elmington Cl *BXLY* DA5 137 J6
Elmington Est *CMBW* SE5 110 D6
Elmington Rd *CMBW* SE5 110 E7
Elmira St *LEW* SE13 132 E2
Elm La *CAT* SE6 151 H1
Elmlee Cl *CHST* BR7 153 K5
Elmley St *WOOL/PLUM* SE18 115 J3
Elmore Cl *ALP/SUD* HA0 86 A1
Elmore Rd *WAN* E11 76 A2
Elmore St *IS* N1 7 G1
Elm Pde *SCUP* DA14 * 155 G3
Elm Pk *BRXS/STRHM* SW2 130 A5
STAN HA7 35 H4
Elm Park Av *HCH* RM12 81 J3
SEVS/STOTM N15 56 B4
Elm Park Gdns *HDN* NW4 52 B4
WBPTN SW10 15 G8
Elm Park La *CHEL* SW3 15 G9
Elm Park Rd *CHEL* SW3 15 G9
FNCH N3 38 D6
LEY E10 57 G7
PIN HA5 47 H2
SNWD SE25 165 G2
WCHMH N21 29 J6
Elm Pl *SKENS* SW7 15 G7
Elm Rd *BAR* EN5 26 D3
BECK BR3 166 C1
CHSGTN KT9 172 A3
DART DA1 139 G7
EBED/NFELT TW14 121 G7
ERITH DA8 118 D7
ESH/CLAY KT10 171 F5
EW KT17 173 H5
FSTGT E7 76 D5
KUTN/CMB KT2 144 B6
MORT/ESHN SW14 125 K2
NWMAL KT3 160 A2
ROMW/RG RM7 62 D1
SCUP DA14 155 G3
THHTH CR7 164 D3
WALTH E17 58 A4
WBLY HA9 68 A4
WDGN N22 41 H7
WLGTN SM6 163 F7
Elm Rd West *CHEAM* SM3 161 J6
Elm Rw *HAMP* NW3 71 G2
Elms Av *HDN* NW4 52 A4
MUSWH N10 54 B2
Elms Cl *EMPK* RM11 63 K6
Elmscott Gdns *WCHMH* N21 29 J5
Elmscott Rd *BMLY* BR1 152 C4
Elms Ct *ALP/SUD* HA0 67 F3
Elms Crs *CLAP* SW4 129 H5
Elmsdale Rd *WALTH* E17 57 H3
Elmsdene Ms *NTHWD* HA6 32 A5
Elms Gdns *ALP/SUD* HA0 67 G3
DAGW RM9 80 B3
Elmshaw Rd *PUT/ROE* SW15 126 D4
Elmshurst Crs *EFNCH* N2 53 G3
Elmside *CROY/NA* CR0 179 K5
Elmside Rd *WBLY* HA9 68 C2
Elms La *ALP/SUD* HA0 67 G3
Elmsleigh Av
KTN/HRWW/WS HA3 49 H3
Elmsleigh Rd *WHTN* TW2 142 D1
Elmslie Cl *WFD* IG8 45 K5
Elms Ms *BAY/PAD* W2 9 G6
Elms Park Av *ALP/SUD* HA0 67 G3
Elms Rd *CLAP* SW4 129 H4
KTN/HRWW/WS HA3 34 E6
Elmstead Av *CHST* BR7 153 K4
WBLY HA9 50 A7
Elmstead Cl *HOR/WEW* KT19 173 G4
TRDG/WHET N20 38 E1
Elmstead Gdns *WPK* KT4 173 J2
Elmstead Gld *CHST* BR7 153 K5
Elmstead La *CHST* BR7 153 J6
Elmstead Rd *ERITH* DA8 118 B7
GDMY/SEVK IG3 78 E1
Elmsted Crs *WELL* DA16 116 D5
The Elms *BARN* SW13 126 C2
ESH/CLAY KT10 * 171 F6
NFNCH/WDSPK N12 * 39 J4
TOOT SW17 * 148 A2
WLGTN SM6 * 176 C3
Elmstone Rd *FUL/PGN* SW6 107 K7
Elm St *FSBYW* WC1X 11 M1
Elmsworth Av *HSLW* TW3 123 G1
Elm Ter *CRICK* NW2 70 E2
ELTH/MOT SE9 135 F5
KTN/HRWW/WS HA3 34 D6
Elmton Wy *CLPT* E5 74 C2
Elm Tree Av *ESH/CLAY* KT10 157 J6
Elm Tree Cl *NTHLT* UB5 83 K1
STJWD NW8 3 G7
Elm Tree Ct *CHARL* SE7 * 114 B5
Elm Tree Rd *STJWD* NW8 3 G7
Elmtree Rd *TEDD* TW11 142 E4
Elm Vis *HNWL* W7 * 84 E6
Elm Wk *GPK* RM2 63 J2
HAMP NW3 70 E1
ORP BR6 181 K2
RYNPK SW20 161 F3
Elm Wy *FBAR/BDGN* N11 40 A5
HOR/WEW KT19 173 F4
WLSDN NW10 69 G3
WPK KT4 174 A2
Elmwood Av *BORE* WD6 24 D3
FELT TW13 141 F2
KTN/HRWW/WS HA3 49 G4
PLMGR N13 40 E4
Elmwood Cl *EW* KT17 173 J6
WLGTN SM6 176 B1
Elmwood Crs *CDALE/KGS* NW9 50 E3
Elmwood Dr *BXLY* DA5 137 F6
EW KT17 173 J6
Elmwood Gdns *HNWL* W7 84 E5
Elmwood Rd *CHSWK* W4 105 K5
CROY/NA CR0 164 C6
HNHL SE24 130 E4
MTCM CR4 162 E2
Elmworth Gv *DUL* SE21 149 K1
Elnathan Ms *MV/WKIL* W9 8 D1
Elphinstone Rd *WALTH* E17 57 H1
Elphinstone St *HBRY* N5 73 H3
Elrick Cl *ERITH* DA8 118 B5
Elrington Rd *HACK* E8 74 C5
WFD IG8 44 E4
Elruge Cl *WDR/YW* UB7 100 A2
Elsa Cots *POP/IOD* E14 * 93 G4
Elsa Rd *WELL* DA16 136 D1
Elsa St *WCHPL* E1 * 93 G4
Elsdale St *HOM* E9 74 E5
Elsden Ms *BETH* E2 * 92 E1
Elsden Rd *TOTM* N17 42 B7
Elsenham Rd *MNPK* E12 77 K4
Elsenham St
WAND/EARL SW18 127 J7
Elsham Rd *WAN* E11 76 C2
WKENS W14 107 H1
Elsham Ter *WKENS* W14 * 107 H1
Elsiedene Rd *WCHMH* N21 29 J6
Elsie Lane Ct *BAY/PAD* W2 8 B3
Elsiemaud Rd *BROCKY* SE4 132 C4
Elsie Rd *EDUL* SE22 131 G3
Elsinore Av
STWL/WRAY TW19 * 120 B6
Elsinore Gdns *CRICK* NW2 * 70 C2
Elsinore Rd *FSTH* SE23 132 B7
Elsinore Wy *RCH/KEW* TW9 125 J2
Elsley Rd *BTSEA* SW11 128 E2
Elspeth Rd *ALP/SUD* HA0 68 A4
BTSEA SW11 128 E3
Elsrick Av *MRDN* SM4 161 K4
Elstan Wy *CROY/NA* CR0 166 B6
Elsted St *WALW* SE17 19 H6
Elstow Cl *ELTH/MOT* SE9 134 E4
RSLP HA4 47 H6
Elstow Gdns *DAGW* RM9 80 A7
Elstow Rd *DAGW* RM9 80 A6
Elstree Gdns *BELV* DA17 117 F3
ED N9 30 D7
IL IG1 78 C4
Elstree Ga *BORE* WD6 * 25 F1
Elstree Hl *BMLY* BR1 152 C6
Elstree Hl North *BORE* WD6 23 K4
Elstree Hl South *BORE* WD6 23 K6
Elstree Pk *BORE* WD6 * 25 F5
Elstree Rd *BORE* WD6 23 G5
BUSH WD23 22 D7
Elstree Wy *BORE* WD6 24 E1
Elswick Rd *LEW* SE13 132 E1
Elswick St *FUL/PGN* SW6 128 B1
Elsworth Cl *EBED/NFELT* TW14 121 H7
Elsworthy *THDIT* KT7 157 K5
Elsworthy Ri *HAMP* NW3 3 K2
Elsworthy Rd *HAMP* NW3 3 J3
Elsworthy Ter *HAMP* NW3 3 K2
Elsynge Rd *WAND/EARL* SW18 128 C4
Eltham Gn *ELTH/MOT* SE9 134 B4
Eltham High St *ELTH/MOT* SE9 134 E5
Eltham Hl *ELTH/MOT* SE9 134 C4
Eltham Palace Rd
ELTH/MOT SE9 134 B5
Eltham Park Gdns
ELTH/MOT SE9 135 F3
Eltham Rd *ELTH/MOT* SE9 134 B4
LEE/GVPK SE12 133 K4
Elthiron Rd *FUL/PGN* SW6 107 K7
Elthorne Av *HNWL* W7 104 A1
Elthorne Ct *FELT* TW13 122 B7
Elthorne Park Rd *HNWL* W7 104 A2
Elthorne Rd *ARCH* N19 72 D1
CDALE/KGS NW9 51 F6
Elthorne Wy *CDALE/KGS* NW9 51 F5
Elthruda Rd *LEW* SE13 133 G5
Eltisley Rd *IL* IG1 78 B3
Elton Av *ALP/SUD* HA0 67 H4
BAR EN5 26 D4
GFD/PVL UB6 67 F5
Elton Cl *KUT/HW* KT1 143 J6
Elton Pk *WAT* WD17 20 E1
Elton Pl *STNW/STAM* N16 74 A4
Elton Rd *KUTN/CMB* KT2 144 B7
Eltringham St
WAND/EARL SW18 128 B3
Elvaston Ms *SKENS* SW7 14 F4
Elvaston Pl *SKENS* SW7 14 E4
Elveden Pl *WLSDN* NW10 86 C1
Elveden Rd *WLSDN* NW10 86 C1
Elvedon Rd *FELT* TW13 140 D2
Elvendon Rd *FBAR/BDGN* N11 40 E5
Elver Gdns *BETH* E2 92 C2
Elverson Ms *DEPT* SE8 * 112 C6
Elverson Rd *DEPT* SE8 132 E1
Elverton St *WEST* SW1P 17 G5
Elvington Gn *HAYES* BR2 167 J4
Elvington La *CDALE/KGS* NW9 37 G7
Elvino Rd *SYD* SE26 151 F4
Elvis Rd *CRICK* NW2 70 A5
Elwill Wy *BECK* BR3 167 F3
Elwin St *BETH* E2 92 C2
Elwood Cl *BAR* EN5 27 G3
Elwood St *HBRY* N5 73 H2
Elwyn Gdns *LEE/GVPK* SE12 133 K6
Ely Cl *ERITH* DA8 138 C1
NWMAL KT3 160 C1
Ely Cots *VX/NE* SW8 * 110 A6
Ely Gdns *BORE* WD6 25 F4
DAGE RM10 80 E2
Elyne Rd *FSBYPK* N4 55 G5
Ely Pl *HCIRC* EC1N 12 B3
Ely Rd *CROY/NA* CR0 164 E4
HSLWW TW4 122 B2
HTHAIR TW6 121 J1
LEY E10 58 A5
Elysan Pl *SAND/SEL* CR2 177 J6
Elysian Av *STMC/STPC* BR5 169 K5
Elysium Pl *FUL/PGN* SW6 127 J1
Elysium St *FUL/PGN* SW6 127 J1
Elystan Cl *WLGTN* SM6 176 C7
Elystan Pl *CHEL* SW3 15 K7
Elystan St *CHEL* SW3 15 J6
Elystan Wk *IS* N1 6 A4
Emanuel Av *ACT* W3 86 E5
Embankment *PUT/ROE* SW15 127 G2
Embankment Gdns *CHEL* SW3 15 M9
Embankment Pl *CHCR* WC2N 11 K8
The Embankment *TWK* TW1 124 B7
Embassy Ct *SCUP* DA14 155 H2
WLGTN SM6 * 176 B5
Emba St *BERM/RHTH* SE16 111 H1
Ember Cl *STMC/STPC* BR5 169 H6
Embercourt Rd *THDIT* KT7 157 K5
Ember Farm Av
E/WMO/HCT KT8 157 J5
Ember Farm Wy
E/WMO/HCT KT8 157 J4
Ember Gdns *THDIT* KT7 157 K6
Ember La *ESH/CLAY* KT10 157 J6
Emblem Ct *EDUL* SE22 131 H4
Embleton Rd *LEW* SE13 132 E3
OXHEY WD19 32 E2
Embry Cl *STAN* HA7 35 G3
Embry Dr *STAN* HA7 35 G5
Embry Wy *STAN* HA7 35 G4
Emden Cl *WDR/YW* UB7 100 D1
Emden St *FUL/PGN* SW6 108 A7
Emerald Cl *CAN/RD* E16 95 J5
Emerald Gdns *BCTR* RM8 62 B7
Emerald Rd *WLSDN* NW10 69 F7
Emerald Sq *NWDGN* UB2 102 C2
Emerald St *BMSBY* WC1N 11 L2
Emerson Gdns
KTN/HRWW/WS HA3 50 B5
Emerson Rd *IL* IG1 60 A6
Emerson St *STHWK* SE1 12 E8
Emerton Cl *BXLYHS* DA6 137 F3
Emery Hill St *WEST* SW1P 16 F4
Emery St *STHWK* SE1 18 B3
Emes Rd *ERITH* DA8 117 K6
Emilia Cl *PEND* EN3 30 D4
Emily St *CAN/RD* E16 94 D5
Emlyn Rd *SHB* W12 106 B1
Emmanuel Rd *BAL* SW12 129 H7
NTHWD HA6 32 D6
Emma Rd *PLSTW* E13 94 D1
Emma St *BETH* E2 92 D1
Emma Ter *RYNPK* SW20 * 146 A6
Emmott Av *BARK/HLT* IG6 60 C4
Emmott Cl *GLDGN* NW11 53 G5
WCHPL E1 93 G3
Emperor's Ga *SKENS* SW7 14 E5
Empire Av *UED* N18 41 J5
Empire Ms *STRHM/NOR* SW16 148 E4
Empire Pde *UED* N18 * 41 K5
WBLY HA9 * 68 C2
Empire Rd *GFD/PVL* UB6 67 H7
Empire Sq *STHWK* SE1 19 G2
Empire Wy *WBLY* HA9 68 B3
Empire Wharf Rd
POP/IOD E14 113 G3
Empress Av *CHING* E4 43 K6
IL IG1 78 A1
MNPK E12 77 G1
WFD IG8 44 D6
Empress Dr *CHST* BR7 154 B5
Empress Pde *CHING* E4 * 43 J6
Empress Pl *FUL/PGN* SW6 14 A8
Empress St *WALW* SE17 18 F9
Empson St *BOW* E3 93 K3
Emsworth Cl *ED* N9 30 E7
Emsworth Rd *BARK/HLT* IG6 60 B1
Emsworth St
BRXS/STRHM SW2 149 F1
Emu Rd *VX/NE* SW8 129 G1
Ena Rd *STRHM/NOR* SW16 163 K2
Enbrook St *NKENS* W10 88 C2
Enclave Ct *FSBYE* EC1V 6 D9
Endale Cl *CAR* SM5 175 K1
Endeavour Wy *BARK* IG11 97 G1
CROY/NA CR0 163 J6
WIM/MER SW19 147 F3
Endell St *LSQ/SEVD* WC2H 11 J4
Enderby St *GNWCH* SE10 113 H4
Enderley Rd
KTN/HRWW/WS HA3 34 D7
Endersby Rd *BAR* EN5 26 A4
Endersleigh Gdns *HDN* NW4 51 J3
Endlebury Rd *CHING* E4 44 A1
Endlesham Rd *BAL* SW12 129 F6
Endsleigh Gdns *IL* IG1 59 K7
STPAN WC1H 5 G9
SURB KT6 158 D5
Endsleigh Pl *STPAN* WC1H 5 H9
Endsleigh Rd *NWDGN* UB2 102 D3
WEA W13 85 G7
Endsleigh St *STPAN* WC1H 5 H9
Endway *BRYLDS* KT5 159 H6
Endwell Rd *BROCKY* SE4 132 B1
Endymion Rd
BRXS/STRHM SW2 130 A5
FSBYPK N4 55 H6
Energen Cl *WLSDN* NW10 69 G5
Enfield Rd *ACT* W3 105 J1
BTFD TW8 104 E4
ENC/FH EN2 28 D3
HTHAIR TW6 121 H1
IS N1 7 K2
Enford St *CAMTN* NW1 9 L2
Engadine Cl *CROY/NA* CR0 178 B2
Engadine St
WAND/EARL SW18 127 J7
Engate St *LEW* SE13 133 F3
Engel Pk *MLHL* NW7 38 A5
Engineer Cl *WOOL/PLUM* SE18 115 F5
Engineers Wy *WBLY* HA9 68 C3
England's La *HAMP* NW3 71 K5
England Wy *NWMAL* KT3 159 J3
Englefield Cl *CROY/NA* CR0 164 D5
ENC/FH EN2 29 G1
Englefield Rd *IS* N1 7 H1
Engleheart Dr
EBED/NFELT TW14 121 J5
Engleheart Rd *CAT* SE6 132 E6
Englewood Rd *BAL* SW12 129 G5
English Grounds *STHWK* SE1 * 13 J9
English St *BOW* E3 93 H3
Enid St *BERM/RHTH* SE16 19 M3
Enmore Av *SNWD* SE25 165 H4
Enmore Gdns
MORT/ESHN SW14 126 A4
Enmore Rd *PUT/ROE* SW15 127 F3
SNWD SE25 165 H4
STHL UB1 84 A3
Ennerdale Av *HCH* RM12 81 J4
STAN HA7 49 J2
Ennerdale Cl
EBED/NFELT TW14 121 J7
SUT SM1 174 D3
Ennerdale Dr *CDALE/KGS* NW9 51 G4
Ennerdale Gdns *WBLY* HA9 49 J7
Ennerdale Rd *BXLYHN* DA7 117 H7
RCH/KEW TW9 125 G1
Ennersdale Rd *LEW* SE13 133 G4
Ennismore Av *CHSWK* W4 106 B3
GFD/PVL UB6 66 E5
Ennismore Gdns *SKENS* SW7 15 H3
THDIT KT7 157 K5
Ennismore Gardens Ms
SKENS SW7 15 H3
Ennismore Ms *SKENS* SW7 15 J2
Ennismore St *SKENS* SW7 15 J3
Ennis Rd *FSBYPK* N4 55 G7
WOOL/PLUM SE18 115 J5
Ensign Cl *HTHAIR* TW6 121 H1
STWL/WRAY TW19 120 A7
Ensign Dr *PLMGR* N13 41 J2
Ensign St *WCHPL* E1 92 C6
Ensign Wy *STWL/WRAY* TW19 120 A7
WLGTN SM6 176 E6
Enslin Rd *ELTH/MOT* SE9 135 F5
Ensor Ms *SKENS* SW7 15 G7
Enstone Rd *PEND* EN3 31 G2
Enterprise Cl *CROY/NA* CR0 164 B7
Enterprise Rw
SEVS/STOTM N15 56 B4
Enterprise Wy *TEDD* TW11 143 F4
WAND/EARL SW18 127 K3
WLSDN NW10 87 H2
Enterprize Wy *DEPT* SE8 * 112 C3
Envoy Av *HTHAIR* TW6 121 J2
Epcot Ms *WLSDN* NW10 * 88 B2
Epirus Ms *FUL/PGN* SW6 107 K6
Epirus Rd *FUL/PGN* SW6 107 J6
Epping Cl *POP/IOD* E14 112 D3
ROMW/RG RM7 62 D2
Epping Pl *IS* N1 73 G5
Epping Wy *CHING* E4 31 K5
Epple Rd *FUL/PGN* SW6 107 J7
Epsom Cl *BXLYHN* DA7 137 J2
NTHLT UB5 65 K4
Epsom Rd *CHEAM* SM3 * 161 J6
CROY/NA CR0 177 G3
GDMY/SEVK IG3 61 F5
LEY E10 58 A5
MRDN SM4 161 J5
Epstein Rd *THMD* SE28 97 H7
Epworth Rd *ISLW* TW7 104 C6
Epworth St *SDTCH* EC2A 13 H1
Equity Sq *BETH* E2 7 M8
Erasmus St *WEST* SW1P 17 H6
Erconwald St *SHB* W12 87 H5
Erebus Dr *THMD* SE28 115 H2
Eresby Dr *BECK* BR3 166 D7
Eresby Pl *KIL/WHAMP* NW6 2 A2
Erica Gdns *CROY/NA* CR0 179 K3
Erica St *SHB* W12 87 J6
Eric Clarke La *EHAM* E6 96 B3
Ericcson Cl *WAND/EARL* SW18 127 K4
Eric Est *BOW* E3 93 H3
Eric Rd *CHDH* RM6 61 K6
FSTGT E7 76 E3
WLSDN NW10 69 H5
Eric St *BOW* E3 93 H3
Eridge Rd *CHSWK* W4 106 A2
Erin Cl *BMLY* BR1 152 C6
FUL/PGN SW6 107 K6
Erindale *WOOL/PLUM* SE18 115 J5
Erindale Ter
WOOL/PLUM SE18 115 J5
Erin Ms *WDGN* N22 * 41 H7
Erith Ct *PUR* RM19 119 K3
Erith High St *ERITH* DA8 118 B4
Erith Rd *BELV* DA17 117 J4
BXLYHN DA7 137 J2
Erlanger Rd *NWCR* SE14 112 A7
Erlesmere Gdns *HNWL* W7 104 B2
Erlich Cots *WCHPL* E1 * 92 E4
Ermine Cl *HSLWW* TW4 122 B1
Ermine Rd *LEW* SE13 132 E2
SEVS/STOTM N15 56 B5
Ermine Side *EN* EN1 30 C4
Ermington Rd *ELTH/MOT* SE9 154 C1
Ernald Av *EHAM* E6 95 J1
Erncroft Wy *TWK* TW1 124 A5
Ernest Av *WNWD* SE27 149 H3
Ernest Cl *BECK* BR3 166 D4
Ernest Gdns *CHSWK* W4 105 J5
Ernest Gv *BECK* BR3 166 C4
Ernest Rd *KUT/HW* KT1 159 J1
Ernest St *WCHPL* E1 93 F3
Ernle Rd *RYNPK* SW20 145 K6
Ernshaw Pl *PUT/ROE* SW15 127 H4
Erpingham Rd
PUT/ROE SW15 127 F2
Erridge Rd *WIM/MER* SW19 161 K1
Errington Rd *MV/WKIL* W9 88 D3
Errol Gdns *NWMAL* KT3 160 D3
YEAD UB4 83 F3
Erroll Rd *ROM* RM1 63 H3
Errol St *STLK* EC1Y 12 F1
Erskine Cl *SUT* SM1 175 J2
Erskine Crs *TOTM* N17 56 D3
Erskine Hl *GLDGN* NW11 52 E3
Erskine Ms *HAMP* NW3 3 M2
Erskine Rd *HAMP* NW3 3 M2
SUT SM1 175 H3
WALTH E17 57 H3
Erwood Rd *CHARL* SE7 114 D4
Esam Wy *STRHM/NOR* SW16 149 G4
Escot Rd *SUN* TW16 140 C6
Escot Wy *BAR* EN5 26 A4
Escreet Gv *WOOL/PLUM* SE18 115 F3
Esher Av *CHEAM* SM3 174 B2
ROMW/RG RM7 62 E5
WOT/HER KT12 156 A7
Esher Cl *BXLY* DA5 137 F7
ESH/CLAY KT10 170 B4
Esher Crs *HTHAIR* TW6 121 J1
Esher Gn *ESH/CLAY* KT10 170 B3
Esher Green Dr
ESH/CLAY KT10 170 A2
Esher Ms *MTCM* CR4 163 F2
Esher Park Av *ESH/CLAY* KT10 170 C4
Esher Place Av *ESH/CLAY* KT10 170 A3
Esher Rd *E/WMO/HCT* KT8 157 J4
GDMY/SEVK IG3 78 E2
Eskdale Av *NTHLT* UB5 65 K7
Eskdale Cl *WBLY* HA9 67 K1
Eskdale Rd *BXLYHN* DA7 137 H1
Eskmont Rdg *NRWD* SE19 150 A6
Esk Rd *PLSTW* E13 95 F3
Esmar Crs *CDALE/KGS* NW9 51 J6
Esmeralda Rd *STHWK* SE1 111 H3
Esmond Cl *RAIN* RM13 * 81 K6
Esmond Gdns *CHSWK* W4 * 106 A3
Esmond Rd *CHSWK* W4 106 A2
KIL/WHAMP NW6 70 D7
Esmond St *PUT/ROE* SW15 127 H3
Esparto St *WAND/EARL* SW18 128 A6
Essenden Rd *BELV* DA17 117 H4
SAND/SEL CR2 178 A6
Essendine Rd *MV/WKIL* W9 2 B9
Essex Av *ISLW* TW7 123 K2
Essex Cl *MRDN* SM4 161 G6
ROMW/RG RM7 62 D3
RSLP HA4 47 H7
WALTH E17 57 G3
Essex Ct *BARN* SW13 126 C1
EMB EC4Y * 12 A5
Essex Gdns *FSBYPK* N4 55 H5
Essex Gv *NRWD* SE19 149 K5
Essex Pk *FNCH* N3 39 F5
Essex Park Ms *ACT* W3 87 G7
Essex Pl *CHSWK* W4 105 K3
Essex Place Sq *CHSWK* W4 * 106 A3
Essex Rd *ACT* W3 86 E6
BARK IG11 78 D6
BORE WD6 24 C2
CHDH RM6 61 J7
CHSWK W4 106 A3
DAGE RM10 80 E4
DART DA1 * 139 G5
ENC/FH EN2 29 K3
IS N1 6 D3
LEY E10 58 A5
MNPK E12 77 J4
ROMW/RG RM7 62 D3
SWFD E18 59 F1
WALTH E17 57 G5
WAT WD17 20 E1
WLSDN NW10 69 G6
Essex Rd South *WAN* E11 58 B6
Essex St *FSTGT* E7 76 E4
TPL/STR WC2R 12 A5
Essex Vls *KENS* W8 14 A2
Essex Whf *CLPT* E5 * 75 F1
Essian St *WCHPL* E1 93 G4
Essoldo Wy *EDGW* HA8 50 B2
Estate Wy *LEY* E10 57 H7
Estcourt Rd *FUL/PGN* SW6 107 J6
SNWD SE25 165 J5
WAT WD17 21 G2
Estella Av *NWMAL* KT3 160 E3
Estelle Rd *HAMP* NW3 71 K3
Esterbrooke St *WEST* SW1P 17 G6
Este Rd *BTSEA* SW11 128 D2
Esther Cl *WCHMH* N21 29 G6
Esther Rd *WAN* E11 58 C6
Estoria Cl *BRXS/STRHM* SW2 130 B6
Estreham Rd
STRHM/NOR SW16 148 D5
Estridge Cl *HSLW* TW3 123 F3
Estuary Cl *BARK* IG11 97 H2
Eswyn Rd *TOOT* SW17 147 K3
Etchingham Park Rd
FNCH N3 39 F6
Etchingham Rd *SRTFD* E15 76 A3
Eternit Wk *FUL/PGN* SW6 107 F7
Etfield Gv *SCUP* DA14 155 H4
Ethelbert Gdns *REDBR* IG4 59 K4
Ethelbert Rd *BMLY* BR1 167 K2
ERITH DA8 117 K6
RYNPK SW20 146 B7
Ethelbert St *BAL* SW12 129 G7
Ethelburga St *BTSEA* SW11 * 108 D7
Etheldene Av *MUSWH* N10 54 C3
Ethelden Rd *SHB* W12 87 K7
Ethelred Est *LBTH* SE11 18 A6
Ethel Rd *CAN/RD* E16 95 F6
Ethel St *WALW* SE17 * 18 F6
Etheridge Rd *CRICK* NW2 52 A6
Etherley Rd *SEVS/STOTM* N15 55 J4
Etherow St *EDUL* SE22 131 H5
Etherstone Rd
STRHM/NOR SW16 149 G3
Ethnard Rd *PECK* SE15 111 J5
Ethronvi Rd *BXLYHN* DA7 137 F2
Etloe Rd *LEY* E10 75 J1
Eton Av *ALP/SUD* HA0 67 J3
EBAR EN4 27 J5
HAMP NW3 3 H1
HEST TW5 102 E5
NFNCH/WDSPK N12 39 G6
NWMAL KT3 160 A4
Eton Cl *WAND/EARL* SW18 128 A6
Eton College Rd *HAMP* NW3 71 K5
Eton Garages *HAMP* NW3 71 J5
Eton Gv *CDALE/KGS* NW9 50 C2
LEW SE13 133 H2
Eton Pl *HAMP* NW3 * 4 A1
Eton Ri *HAMP* NW3 * 71 K5
Eton Rd *HAMP* NW3 3 M1
HYS/HAR UB3 101 J6
IL IG1 78 C3
Eton St *RCH/KEW* TW9 124 E4
Eton Vis *HAMP* NW3 71 K5
Eton Wy *DART* DA1 139 F3
Etta St *DEPT* SE8 112 B5
Etton Rd *HSLW* TW3 123 H4
Ettrick St *POP/IOD* E14 94 A5
Etwell Pl *BRYLDS* KT5 159 G5
Eucalyptus Ms
STRHM/NOR SW16 148 D5
Euesdon Cl *ED* N9 42 D2
Eugenia Rd *BERM/RHTH* SE16 111 K4
Eureka Rd *KUT/HW* KT1 159 H1
Europa Pl *FSBYE* EC1V 6 E8
Europe Rd *WOOL/PLUM* SE18 114 E2
Eustace Pl *WOOL/PLUM* SE18 114 E3
Eustace Rd *CHDH* RM6 61 K6
EHAM E6 95 J2
FUL/PGN SW6 107 K6
Euston Av *WATW* WD18 20 D4
Euston Centre *CAMTN* NW1 4 E9
Euston Rd *CAMTN* NW1 4 E9
CROY/NA CR0 164 B7
STPAN WC1H 5 J7
Euston Sq *CAMTN* NW1 5 G8
Euston St *CAMTN* NW1 4 F9
Evan Cook Cl *PECK* SE15 111 K7
Evandale Rd *BRXN/ST* SW9 130 B1
Evangelist Rd *KTTN* NW5 72 B3

Evans Cl HACK E8 ... 74 B5
Evansdale RAIN RM13 ... 99 H2
Evans Gv FELT TW13 ... 142 A1
Evans Rd CAT SE6 ... 152 C1
Evanston Av CHING E4 ... 44 A6
Evanston Gdns REDBR IG4 ... 59 J5
Eva Rd CHDH RM6 ... 61 K8
Evelina Rd PECK SE15 ... 131 K2
 PGE/AN SE20 ... 150 E6
Eveline Lowe Est
 BERM/RHTH SE16 ... 111 H2
Eveline Rd MTCM CR4 ... 147 H2
 RSLP HA4 ... 46 D6
Evelyn Av WHTN TW2 ... 123 C6
Evelyn Av CDALE/KGS NW9 ... 51 F3
Evelyn Crs SUN TW16 ... 140 D7
Evelyn Denington Rd
 EHAM E6 ... 95 J3
Evelyn Dr PIN HA5 ... 33 H6
Evelyn Est DEPT SE8 ... 112 B5
Evelyn Gdns RCH/KEW TW9 ... 125 F3
 SKENS SW7 ... 14 F8
Evelyn Gv EA W5 ... 86 B7
 STHL UB1 ... 83 K5
Evelyn Rd CAN/RD E16 ... 94 E7
 EBAR EN4 ... 27 K3
 RCHPK/HAM TW10 ... 125 F2
 RCH/KEW TW9 ... 143 J2
 WALTH E17 ... 58 A3
 WIM/MER SW19 ... 147 F4
Evelyn St DEPT SE8 ... 112 B5
 GNWCH SE10 ... 113 F5
Evelyn Ter RCH/KEW TW9 ... 123 F2
Evelyn Wk IS N1 ... 7 G6
Evelyn Wy SUN TW16 ... 140 D7
 WLGTN SM6 ... 176 D3
Evensyde WATW WD18 ... 20 A5
Evenwood Cl
 PUT/ROE SW15 * ... 127 H4
Everard Av HAYES BR2 ... 167 K7
Everard Wy WBLY HA9 ... 68 A2
Everatt Cl WAND/EARL SW18 * ... 127 J5
Everdon Rd BARN SW13 ... 106 D5
Everest Pl POP/IOD E14 ... 94 A4
 STWL/WRAY TW19 ... 120 A6
Everest Rd ELTH/MOT SE9 ... 134 D4
 STWL/WRAY TW19 ... 120 A6
Everett Cl BUSH WD23 ... 22 E7
 PIN HA5 ... 46 D2
The Everglades HSLW TW3 * ... 123 H4
Everglade Strd
 CDALE/KGS NW9 ... 37 H7
Evergreen Cl PGE/AN SE20 ... 150 E6
Evergreen Ct
 STWL/WRAY TW19 * ... 120 A6
Evergreen Sq HACK E8 ... 7 L1
Evergreen Wy HYS/HAR UB3 ... 82 D6
 STWL/WRAY TW19 ... 120 A6
Everilda St IS N1 ... 5 M4
Evering Rd STNW/STAM N16 ... 74 B2
Everington Rd MUSWH N10 ... 53 K1
Everington St HMSMTH W6 ... 107 G5
Everitt Rd WLSDN NW10 ... 87 F2
Everleigh St FSBYPK N4 ... 55 F7
Eve Rd ISLW TW7 ... 124 B3
 SRTFD E15 ... 94 C1
 TOTM N17 ... 56 A2
 WAN E11 ... 76 C3
Eversfield Gdns EDGW HA8 ... 36 B7
Eversfield Rd RCH/KEW TW9 ... 125 G1
Evershed Wk CHSWK W4 ... 105 K2
Evershot St CAMTN NW1 * ... 4 E5
Evershot Rd FSBYPK N4 ... 55 F7
Eversleigh Rd BAR EN5 ... 27 G4
 BTSEA SW11 ... 128 E2
 EHAM E6 ... 77 H7
 FNCH N3 ... 38 D6
Eversley Av BXLYHN DA7 ... 138 A5
 WBLY HA9 ... 68 C1
Eversley Cl WCHMH N21 ... 29 F5
Eversley Crs ISLW TW7 ... 103 J7
 RSLP HA4 ... 64 C1
 WCHMH N21 ... 29 F5
Eversley Cross BXLYHN DA7 ... 138 B5
Eversley Mt WCHMH N21 ... 29 F5
Eversley Pk WIM/MER SW19 ... 145 K4
Eversley Park Rd
 WCHMH N21 ... 29 F5
Eversley Rd BRYLDS KT5 ... 159 G3
 CHARL SE7 ... 114 A5
 NRWD SE19 ... 149 K6
Eversley Wy CROY/NA CRO ... 179 J2
Everthorpe Rd PECK SE15 ... 131 G2
Everton Blds CAMTN NW1 * ... 4 E8
Everton Dr STAN HA7 ... 50 A2
Everton Rd CROY/NA CRO ... 165 H7
Evesham Av WALTH E17 ... 57 J1
Evesham Cl BELMT SM2 ... 174 E6
 GFD/PVL UB6 ... 84 B3
Evesham Gn MRDN SM4 ... 162 A5
 MRDN SM4 ... 162 A5
 SRTFD E15 ... 76 D3
Evesham Rd FBAR/BDGN N11 ... 40 C3
Evesham Ter SURB KT6 * ... 158 E6
Evesham Wk BRXN/ST SW9 ... 130 B1
 CMBW SE5 ... 130 E1
Evesham Wy BTSEA SW11 ... 129 F2
 CLAY IG5 ... 60 A2
Evry Rd SCUP DA14 ... 155 J5
Ewald Rd FUL/PGN SW6 ... 127 J1
Ewanrigg Ter WFD IG8 ... 45 G4
Ewart Gv WDGN N22 ... 41 G7
Ewart Pl BOW E3 ... 93 H1
Ewart Rd FSTH SE23 ... 132 A6
Ewe Cl HOLWY N7 ... 72 E5
Ewell By-Pass EW KT17 ... 173 H5
Ewell Court Av
 HOR/WEW KT19 ... 173 G4
Ewellhurst Rd CLAY IG5 ... 59 J1
Ewell Park Gdns EW KT17 ... 173 J6
Ewell Park Wy EW KT17 ... 173 J5
Ewell Rd SURB KT6 ... 159 J7
 CHEAM SM3 ... 174 B5
 SURB KT6 ... 158 C6
Ewelme Rd FSTH SE23 ... 131 K7
Ewen Crs BRXS/STRHM SW2 ... 130 B6
Ewer St STHWK SE1 ... 12 E9
Ewhurst Av SAND/SEL CR2 ... 178 B7
Ewhurst Cl BELMT SM2 ... 174 A7
 WCHPL E1 ... 92 E4
Ewhurst Rd BROCKY SE4 ... 132 C5
Exbury Rd CAT SE6 ... 151 J1
Excel Cl LSQ/SEVD WC2H ... 11 H7
Excel Marina CAN/RD E16 ... 94 E6
Excelsior Cl KUT/HW KT1 ... 159 H1
Excel Waterfront CAN/RD E16 ... 95 F6
Exchange Ar LVPST EC2M ... 13 J2
Exchange Rd WATW WD18 ... 21 F3
Exchange Sq SDTCH EC2A * ... 13 J2
Exchange St ROMW/RG RM7 ... 63 G5
Exchange Wk PIN HA5 ... 47 J5
Exeter Cl EHAM E6 ... 95 K5

WATN WD24 ... 21 G1
Exeter Gdns IL IG1 ... 59 K7
Exeter Ms FUL/PGN SW6 ... 107 K6
Exeter Pde CRICK NW2 * ... 70 C5
Exeter Rd CAN/RD E16 ... 94 E5
 CRICK NW2 ... 70 C4
 CROY/NA CRO ... 165 F6
 DAGE RM10 ... 80 D5
 ED N9 ... 42 E1
 FELT TW13 ... 141 K2
 HTHAIR TW6 ... 121 H2
 PEND EN3 ... 31 F2
 RYLN/HDSTN HA2 ... 65 J1
 STHGT/OAK N14 ... 28 B7
 WALTH E17 ... 57 J4
 WELL DA16 ... 136 A1
Exeter St COVGDN WC2E ... 11 K6
Exeter Wy HTHAIR TW6 ... 121 H1
 NWCR SE14 ... 112 C6
Exford Gdns LEE/GVPK SE12 ... 134 A7
Exford Rd LEE/GVPK SE12 ... 153 F1
Exhibition Grounds
 WBLY HA9 * ... 68 D3
Exhibition Rd SKENS SW7 ... 15 H4
Exit Rd EFNCH N2 ... 53 H1
Exmoor St NKENS W10 ... 88 B3
Exmouth Market
 CLKNW EC1R ... 6 A9
Exmouth Ms CAMTN NW1 * ... 4 F8
Exmouth Pl HACK E8 ... 74 D7
Exmouth Rd RSLP HA4 ... 65 G2
 WALTH E17 ... 57 H4
 WELL DA16 ... 116 D7
 YEAD UB4 ... 82 C2
Exmouth St WCHPL E1 ... 92 E5
Exning Rd CAN/RD E16 ... 94 C3
Exon St WALW SE17 ... 19 J6
Explorer Av STWL/WRAY TW19 ... 120 B7
Explorer Dr WATW WD18 ... 20 D5
Express Dr GDMY/SEVK IG3 ... 61 H7
Exton Cl BCTR RM8 ... 79 J4
Exton Rd WLSDN NW10 ... 68 G6
Exton St STHWK SE1 ... 12 A9
Eyhurst Av HCH RM12 ... 81 J2
Eyhurst Cl CRICK NW2 ... 69 J1
Eylewood Rd WNWD SE27 ... 149 J4
Eynella Rd DUL SE21 ... 131 G6
Eynham Rd SHB W12 ... 88 A5
Eynsford Cl STMC/STPC BR5 ... 169 H6
Eynsford Crs SCUP DA14 ... 136 D7
Eynsford Rd GDMY/SEVK IG3 ... 78 E1
Eynsham Dr ABYW SE2 ... 116 C2
Eynswood Dr SCUP DA14 ... 155 H4
Eyot Gdns HMSMTH W6 ... 106 C4
Eyre Cl GPK RM2 ... 63 K3
Eyre Street HI CLKNW EC1R ... 12 A1
Eythorne Rd BRXN/ST SW9 ... 110 B7
Ezra St BETH E2 ... 7 M7

F

Faber Gdns HDN NW4 ... 51 J3
Fabian Rd FUL/PGN SW6 ... 107 J6
Fabian St EHAM E6 ... 95 K3
The Façade FSTH SE23 * ... 150 E1
Factory La CROY/NA CRO ... 177 G1
 TOTM N17 ... 56 B1
Factory Pl POP/IOD E14 ... 113 F4
Factory Rd CAN/RD E16 ... 95 J7
Factory Yd HNWL W7 ... 84 E7
Faggs Rd EBED/NFELT TW14 ... 121 J3
Fairacre ISLW TW7 * ... 103 J7
 NWMAL KT3 ... 160 B2
Fair Acres HAYES BR2 ... 167 K4
Fairacres CROY/NA CRO ... 179 H7
 PUT/ROE SW15 ... 126 C3
 RSLP HA4 ... 46 D6
Fairbank Est IS N1 * ... 7 G6
Fairbanks Rd TOTM N17 ... 56 C2
Fairbourne Rd CLAP SW4 ... 129 J5
 TOTM N17 ... 56 A2
Fairbridge Rd ARCH N19 ... 72 D1
Fairbrook Cl PLMGR N13 ... 41 G4
Fairby Rd LEE/GVPK SE12 ... 134 A4
Fairchild Cl BTSEA SW11 ... 128 C1
Fairchild Pl SDTCH EC2A * ... 13 K1
Fairchild St SDTCH EC2A ... 13 K1
Fair Cl BUSH WD23 ... 22 B6
Fairdale Gdns HYS/HAR UB3 ... 101 K1
 PUT/ROE SW15 ... 126 E3
Fairey CDALE/KGS NW9 * ... 51 H1
Fairey Av HYS/HAR UB3 ... 101 J2
Fairfax Av EW KT17 ... 173 K7
Fairfax Cl WOT/HER KT12 ... 156 A7
Fairfax Gdns BKHTH/KID SE3 ... 114 B7
Fairfax Ms CAN/RD E16 ... 95 F7
 CEND/HSY/T N8 * ... 55 H3
 PUT/ROE SW15 ... 127 F3
Fairfax Pl KIL/WHAMP NW6 ... 2 F1
 WKENS W14 ... 107 H2
Fairfax Rd CEND/HSY/T N8 ... 55 G3
 CHSWK W4 ... 106 B2
 DART DA1 ... 139 K5
 KIL/WHAMP NW6 ... 2 F1
 TEDD TW11 ... 143 G6
Fairfax Wy MUSWH N10 ... 40 A4
Fairfield Av EDGW HA8 ... 36 D5
 HDN NW4 ... 51 K5
 OXHEY WD19 ... 33 G2
 RSLP HA4 ... 46 A6
 WHTN TW2 ... 123 G7
Fairfield Cl BFN/LL DA15 ... 136 A5
 HCH RM12 ... 63 J7
 MTCM CR4 ... 147 J6
 NFNCH/WDSPK N12 ... 39 G3
 PEND EN3 ... 31 F5
Fairfield Cnr KUT/HW KT1 * ... 159 G1
Fairfield Ct RSLP HA4 ... 46 B7
Fairfield Crs EDGW HA8 ... 36 D5
Fairfield Dr GFD/PVL UB6 ... 67 J7
 RYLN/HDSTN HA2 ... 48 C2
 WAND/EARL SW18 ... 128 A4
Fairfield Gdns
 CEND/HSY/T N8 ... 54 E4
Fairfield Gv CHARL SE7 ... 114 C5
Fairfield North
 KUTN/CMB KT2 ... 159 F1
Fairfield Pth CROY/NA CRO ... 177 K2
Fairfield Pl KUT/HW KT1 ... 159 F2
Fairfield Rd BECK BR3 ... 166 D1
 BMLY BR1 ... 152 E6
 BOW E3 ... 93 J1
 BXLYHN DA7 ... 137 G1
 CEND/HSY/T N8 ... 54 E4
 CROY/NA CRO ... 177 K2

IL IG1 ... 78 B5
 KUT/HW KT1 ... 159 F1
 STHL UB1 ... 83 K5
 STMC/STPC BR5 ... 169 J5
 UED N18 ... 42 D3
 WALTH E17 ... 57 G1
 WFD IG8 ... 44 E5
Fairfields CAT SE6 ... 132 E6
Fairfields Cl CDALE/KGS NW9 ... 50 E4
Fairfields Crs CDALE/KGS NW9 ... 50 E3
Fairfield South KUT/HW KT1 ... 159 F2
Fairfield St WAND/EARL SW18 ... 128 A4
Fairfield Wy BAR EN5 ... 26 E4
 HOR/WEW KT19 ... 173 G4
Fairfield West KUT/HW KT1 ... 159 F1
Fairfoot Rd BOW E3 * ... 93 J3
Fairford Av BXLYHN DA7 ... 117 K7
 CROY/NA CRO ... 166 A4
Fairford Cl CROY/NA CRO ... 166 A4
Fairford Ct BELMT SM2 * ... 175 F6
Fairford Gdns WPK KT4 ... 173 H2
Fairgreen EBAR EN4 ... 27 K2
Fairgreen Ct EBAR EN4 * ... 27 K3
Fairgreen Rd THHTH CR7 ... 164 C4
Fairhaven Av CROY/NA CRO ... 166 A5
Fairhaven Crs OXHEY WD19 ... 32 E2
Fairhazel Gdns
 KIL/WHAMP NW6 ... 2 E1
Fairholme EBED/NFELT TW14 ... 121 G6
Fairholme Av GPK RM2 ... 63 J4
Fairholme Cl FNCH N3 ... 52 C3
Fairholme Crs PIN HA5 * ... 34 A5
 YEAD UB4 ... 82 D3
Fairholme Gdns FNCH N3 ... 52 C2
Fairholme Rd CROY/NA CRO ... 164 B6
 HRW HA1 ... 48 E4
 IL IG1 ... 59 K6
 SUT SM1 ... 174 D5
 WKENS W14 ... 107 H4
Fairholt Rd STNW/STAM N16 ... 55 J7
Fairholt St SKENS SW7 ... 15 K3
Fairlands Av BKHH IG9 ... 44 E1
 SUT SM1 ... 174 E1
 THHTH CR7 ... 164 A3
Fairlawn CHARL SE7 ... 114 B6
Fairlawn Av BXLYHN DA7 ... 136 E1
 CHSWK W4 ... 105 K3
 EFNCH N2 ... 53 J3
Fairlawn Cl ESH/CLAY KT10 ... 171 F5
 FELT TW13 ... 141 K3
 KUTN/CMB KT2 ... 144 E5
 STHGT/OAK N14 ... 28 D5
Fairlawn Ct CHARL SE7 * ... 114 B6
Fairlawn Dr WFD IG8 ... 44 E6
Fairlawn Gdns STHL UB1 ... 83 K6
Fairlawn Gv CHSWK W4 ... 105 K3
Fairlawn Pk SYD SE26 ... 151 G4
Fairlawn Rd WIM/MER SW19 ... 146 D6
Fairlawns PIN HA5 ... 47 J2
 TWK TW1 ... 124 D5
Fairlea Pl EA W5 ... 85 J4
Fairlie Gdns FSTH SE23 ... 131 K6
Fairlight Av CHING E4 ... 44 B1
 WFD IG8 ... 44 E5
 WLSDN NW10 ... 87 G1
Fairlight Cl CHING E4 ... 44 B1
 WPK KT4 ... 174 A3
Fairlight Rd TOOT SW17 ... 147 H3
Fairlop Cl HCH RM12 ... 81 K5
Fairlop Pl STJWD NW8 ... 3 H8
Fairlop Rd BARK/HLT IG6 ... 60 C1
 WAN E11 ... 58 B6
Fairmead BMLY BR1 ... 168 E3
 BRYLDS KT5 ... 159 J7
Fairmead Cl BMLY BR1 ... 168 E3
 HEST TW5 ... 102 C6
 NWMAL KT3 ... 160 A2
Fairmead Crs EDGW HA8 ... 36 E3
Fairmead Gdns REDBR IG4 ... 59 H4
Fairmead Rd ARCH N19 ... 72 E2
 CROY/NA CRO ... 164 A7
Fairmile Av STRHM/NOR SW16 ... 148 D4
Fairmont Av POP/IOD E14 ... 94 B6
Fairmont Cl BELV DA17 ... 117 G4
Fairmont Rd
 BRXS/STRHM SW2 ... 130 A5
Fairoak Cl STMC/STPC BR5 ... 169 G6
Fairoak Dr ELTH/MOT SE9 ... 135 J4
Fairoak Gdns ROM RM1 ... 63 H1
Fair Oak Pl BARK/HLT IG6 ... 60 C1
Fairseat Cl BUSH WD23 * ... 34 E1
Fairstead Wk IS N1 * ... 6 E1
Fair St HSLW TW3 ... 123 H2
 STHWK SE1 ... 19 K1
Fairthorn Rd CHARL SE7 ... 113 K4
Fairview ERITH DA8 ... 118 C6
Fairview Av ALP/SUD HA0 ... 67 K5
Fairview Cl SYD SE26 ... 151 G4
Fair View Pl WALTH E17 * ... 43 G7
Fairview Ct HDN NW4 * ... 52 B1
Fairview Crs
 RYLN/HDSTN HA2 ... 48 A7
Fairview Gdns WFD IG8 ... 45 F7
Fairview Pl BRXS/STRHM SW2 ... 130 A6
Fairview Rd SEVS/STOTM N15 ... 56 B5
 STRHM/NOR SW16 ... 149 F7
 SUT SM1 ... 175 H4
Fairview Ws CHING E4 * ... 43 J6
Fairview Wy EDGW HA8 ... 36 C3
Fairwater Av WELL DA16 ... 136 B3
Fairway BORE WD6 ... 24 D1
Fairway BXLYHS DA6 ... 137 F4
 RYNPK SW20 ... 161 F2
 STMC/STPC BR5 ... 169 J5
 WFD IG8 ... 45 G4
The Fairway ACT W3 ... 87 G5
 ALP/SUD HA0 ... 67 H1
 BAR EN5 * ... 27 F1
 E/WMO/HCT KT8 ... 157 F2
 HAYES BR2 ... 168 E4
 HNWL W7 * ... 84 E6
 MLHL NW7 ... 37 F2
 NTHLT UB5 ... 66 C5
 NTHWD HA6 ... 32 C3
 NWMAL KT3 ... 145 F7
 PLMGR N13 ... 41 J2
 RSLP HA4 ... 65 J3
 STHGT/OAK N14 ... 28 B5
Fairway Cl CROY/NA CRO ... 166 B4
 GLDGN NW11 ... 53 G6
 HOR/WEW KT19 ... 172 E3
 HSLWW TW4 ... 122 B4
Fairway Ct MLHL NW7 * ... 37 F2
Fairway Dr GFD/PVL UB6 ... 66 B6
 THMD SE28 ... 97 K5
Fairway Gdns BECK BR3 ... 167 G5
 IL IG1 ... 78 C4
Fairways ISLW TW7 * ... 103 J7
 STAN HA7 ... 50 A1
 TEDD TW11 ... 143 K6
 WALTH E17 * ... 58 A3
The Fairways ACT W3 * ... 87 G5

Fairweather Cl
 SEVS/STOTM N15 ... 56 A3
Fairweather Rd
 STNW/STAM N16 ... 56 C5
Fairwyn Rd SYD SE26 ... 151 G2
Faithfield BUSH WD23 * ... 21 G2
Fakenham Cl MLHL NW7 ... 37 J6
 NTHLT UB5 ... 66 A5
Fakruddin St WCHPL E1 ... 92 C3
Falaize Av IL IG1 ... 78 B3
Falcon Av BMLY BR1 ... 168 D2
Falconberg Ct
 SOHO/SHAV W1D * ... 11 G4
Falconberg Ms
 SOHO/SHAV W1D ... 11 G4
Falcon Cl CHSWK W4 ... 105 J5
 DART DA1 ... 139 J4
 NTHWD HA6 ... 32 C6
Falcon Ct IS N1 ... 6 D6
Falcon Crs PEND EN3 ... 31 F4
Falcon Dr STWL/WRAY TW19 ... 120 A5
Falconer Rd BUSH WD23 ... 22 A5
Falcon Gv BTSEA SW11 ... 128 D2
Falcon La BTSEA SW11 ... 128 D2
Falcon Rd BTSEA SW11 ... 128 D2
 HPTN TW12 ... 141 K6
 PEND EN3 ... 31 F4
Falcon St PLSTW E13 ... 94 E3
Falcon Ter BTSEA SW11 * ... 128 D2
Falcon Wy CDALE/KGS NW9 ... 51 G1
 KTN/HRWW/WS HA3 ... 50 A4
 POP/IOD E14 ... 112 E3
 WAN E11 ... 58 E3
Falconwood Av WELL DA16 ... 135 J1
Falconwood Pde WELL DA16 ... 135 K4
Falconwood Rd CROY/NA CRO ... 179 H7
Falcourt Cl SUT SM1 ... 175 F4
Falkirk Gdns OXHEY WD19 ... 33 H4
Falkirk St IS N1 ... 7 K6
Falkland Av FBAR/BDGN N11 ... 40 A3
 FNCH N3 ... 38 E6
Falkland Park Av SNWD SE25 ... 165 F1
Falkland Pl KTTN NW5 ... 72 C4
Falkland Rd BAR EN5 ... 26 C1
 CEND/HSY/T N8 ... 55 H3
 KTTN NW5 ... 72 C4
Falloden Wy GLDGN NW11 ... 52 E3
Fallow Cl BERM/RHTH SE16 * ... 111 H4
Fallow Court Av
 NFNCH/WDSPK N12 ... 39 G5
Fallowfield STAN HA7 ... 35 F3
Fallowfield Ct STAN HA7 ... 35 G2
Fallowfields Dr
 NFNCH/WDSPK N12 ... 39 J5
Fallows Cl EFNCH N2 ... 53 H1
Fallsbrook Rd
 STRHM/NOR SW16 ... 148 B5
Falman Cl ED N9 ... 30 C7
Falmer Rd EN EN1 ... 30 A3
 SEVS/STOTM N15 ... 55 J4
 WALTH E17 ... 57 K2
Falmouth Av CHING E4 ... 44 B4
Falmouth Cl LEE/GVPK SE12 * ... 133 J4
 WDGN N22 ... 41 F6
Falmouth Gdns REDBR IG4 ... 59 H3
Falmouth Rd STHWK SE1 ... 18 F4
Falmouth St SRTFD E15 ... 76 B4
Falstaff Cl DART DA1 ... 138 D6
Falstaff Ms HPTN TW12 ... 142 D4
Fambridge Cl SYD SE26 ... 151 H3
Fambridge Rd BCTR RM8 ... 62 C7
Fancourt Ms BMLY BR1 ... 169 F2
Fane St WKENS W14 ... 107 J5
Fanns Ri PUR RM19 ... 119 K3
Fann St FARR EC1M ... 12 E1
 STLK EC1Y ... 12 E1
Fanshawe Av BARK IG11 ... 78 C5
Fanshawe Crs DAGW RM9 ... 80 A4
Fanshawe Rd
 RCHPK/HAM TW10 ... 143 J3
Fanshaw St IS N1 ... 7 J7
Fantail Cl THMD SE28 ... 97 J5
Fanthorpe St PUT/ROE SW15 ... 127 F2
Faraday Av SCUP DA14 ... 155 H1
Faraday Cl HOLWY N7 ... 73 F5
 WATW WD18 ... 20 B5
Faraday Pl E/WMO/HCT KT8 * ... 157 F3
Faraday Rd ACT W3 ... 86 E6
 E/WMO/HCT KT8 ... 157 F3
 NKENS W10 ... 88 C4
 SRTFD E15 ... 76 B5
 STHL UB1 ... 84 B6
 WELL DA16 ... 136 B2
 WIM/MER SW19 ... 147 F5
Faraday Wy
 WOOL/PLUM SE18 ... 114 C2

The Farmlands NTHLT UB5 ... 65 K5
Farmland Wk CHST BR7 ... 154 A4
Farm La CROY/NA CRO ... 179 H1
 FUL/PGN SW6 ... 107 K5
 STHGT/OAK N14 ... 28 A5
Farmleigh STHGT/OAK N14 ... 28 C6
Farm Pl DART DA1 ... 138 D3
 KENS W8 ... 8 A8
Farm Rd BELMT SM2 ... 175 H6
 EDGW HA8 ... 36 E4
 ESH/CLAY KT10 ... 157 F7
 HSLWW TW4 ... 122 B4
 MNPK E12 ... 77 J1
 MRDN SM4 ... 162 A4
 NTHWD HA6 ... 32 A4
 WCHMH N21 ... 29 J7
 WLSDN NW10 ... 69 F6
Farmstead Rd CAT SE6 ... 151 K3
 KTN/HRWW/WS HA3 ... 34 D7
Farm St MYFR/PICC W1J ... 10 C7
The Farm WIM/MER SW19 * ... 127 J5
Farm V BXLY DA5 ... 137 J5
Farm Wk GLDGN NW11 ... 52 D4
Farmway BCTR RM8 ... 79 J3
Farm Wy BKHH IG9 ... 45 G3
 BUSH WD23 ... 22 B3
 HCH RM12 ... 81 K3
 NTHWD HA6 ... 32 C3
 WPK KT4 ... 174 A2
Farnaby Rd BMLY BR1 ... 152 C7
 ELTH/MOT SE9 ... 134 B3
Farnan Av WALTH E17 ... 57 J1
Farnan Rd STRHM/NOR SW16 ... 148 E4
Farnborough Av
 SAND/SEL CR2 ... 179 G6
 WALTH E17 ... 57 G2
Farnborough Cl WBLY HA9 ... 68 D1
Farnborough Crs HAYES BR2 ... 167 J3
 SAND/SEL CR2 ... 179 G6
Farnborough Wy PECK SE15 * ... 111 F6
Farncombe St
 BERM/RHTH SE16 ... 111 H1
Farndale Av PLMGR N13 ... 41 H2
Farndale Crs GFD/PVL UB6 ... 84 C2
Farnell Ms ECT SW5 ... 14 C7
Farnell Pl ACT W3 ... 86 D6
Farnell Rd ISLW TW7 ... 123 J2
Farnham Cl TRDG/WHET N20 ... 27 G6
Farnham Gdns RYNPK SW20 ... 160 E1
Farnham Pl STHWK SE1 ... 12 D9
Farnham Rd GDMY/SEVK IG3 ... 61 F5
 WELL DA16 ... 136 D1
Farnham Royal LBTH SE11 ... 17 M8
Farningham Rd TOTM N17 ... 42 D6
Farnley Rd SNWD SE25 ... 164 E3
Farnol Rd DART DA1 ... 139 K3
Faro Cl BMLY BR1 ... 169 F1
Faroe Rd WKENS W14 ... 107 G2
Farquhar Rd NRWD SE19 ... 150 B4
 WIM/MER SW19 ... 146 D2
Farquharson Rd
 CROY/NA CRO ... 164 D6
Farraline Rd WATW WD18 ... 21 F3
Farrance Rd CHDH RM6 ... 62 A5
Farrance St POP/IOD E14 ... 93 J5
Farrant Av WDGN N22 ... 55 G1
Farr Av BARK IG11 ... 97 G1
Farren Rd FSTH SE23 ... 151 G1
Farrer Ms CEND/HSY/T N8 ... 54 C3
Farrer Rd CEND/HSY/T N8 ... 54 C3
 KTN/HRWW/WS HA3 ... 50 A4
Farrier Cl BMLY BR1 ... 168 C2
Farrier Rd NTHLT UB5 ... 84 A1
Farrier St CAMTN NW1 ... 4 C1
Farriers Wy BORE WD6 ... 25 F5
Farrier Wk WBPTN SW10 ... 14 E9
Farringdon La CLKNW EC1R ... 12 B1
Farringdon Rd CLKNW EC1R ... 6 A7
 HCIRC EC1N ... 12 C3
Farringdon St
 FLST/FETLN EC4A ... 12 C3
Farrington Av BUSH WD23 ... 22 B3
Farrington Pl CHST BR7 ... 154 D6
Farrins Rents
 BERM/RHTH SE16 ... 93 G7
Farrow La NWCR SE14 ... 111 K6
Farrow Pl BERM/RHTH SE16 ... 112 B2
Farthingale Wk SRTFD E15 ... 76 B6
Farthing Av WATW WD18 ... 21 G4
Farthing Cl DART DA1 ... 139 K3
Farthing Flds WAP E1W * ... 92 D7
Farthings Cl CHING E4 ... 44 C2
 PIN HA5 ... 47 F5
The Farthings KUTN/CMB KT2 ... 144 C7
Farthing St HAYES BR2 ... 181 K6
Farwell Rd SCUP DA14 ... 155 H3
Farwig La BMLY BR1 ... 152 E7
Fashion St WCHPL E1 ... 13 L3
Fashoda Rd HAYES BR2 ... 168 C3
Fassett Rd HACK E8 ... 74 C5
 KUT/HW KT1 ... 159 F3
Fassett Sq HACK E8 ... 74 C5
Fauconberg Rd CHSWK W4 ... 105 K5
Faulkner Cl BCTR RM8 ... 61 K6
Faulkner St NWCR SE14 ... 111 K7
Fauna Cl CHDH RM6 ... 61 J5
 STAN HA7 ... 35 K2
Faunce St WALW SE17 ... 18 C8
Favart Rd FUL/PGN SW6 ... 107 K7
Faversham Av EN EN1 ... 29 K5
Faversham Rd BECK BR3 ... 166 C1
 CAT SE6 ... 132 C6
 MRDN SM4 ... 162 A5
Fawcett Cl BTSEA SW11 ... 128 C1
 STRHM/NOR SW16 ... 149 G3
Fawcett Est CLPT E5 * ... 56 C7
Fawcett Rd CROY/NA CRO ... 177 H2
 WLSDN NW10 ... 69 H6
Fawcett St WBPTN SW10 ... 14 E9
Fawcus Cl ESH/CLAY KT10 ... 170 E5
Fawe Park Rd PUT/ROE SW15 ... 127 J3
Fawe St POP/IOD E14 ... 93 K4
Fawley Rd KIL/WHAMP NW6 ... 71 F4
Fawnbrake Av HNHL SE24 ... 130 C4
Fawn Rd PLSTW E13 ... 95 G1
 CHING E4 ... 44 B1
Fawns Manor Cl
 EBED/NFELT TW14 ... 121 F7
Fawood Av WLSDN NW10 ... 69 F6
Faygate Crs BXLYHS DA6 ... 137 H4
Faygate Rd BRXS/STRHM SW2 ... 148 A1
Fayland Av STRHM/NOR SW16 ... 148 C4
Fearnley Crs HPTN TW12 ... 141 J4
Fearon St GNWCH SE10 ... 113 K4
Featherbed La SAND/SEL CR2 ... 179 G6
Feathers Pl GNWCH SE10 ... 113 G5
Featherstone Av
 FSTH SE23 ... 150 E1
Featherstone Gdns
 BORE WD6 ... 25 F3
Featherstone Rd MLHL NW7 ... 37 K5
 NWDGN UB2 ... 102 D2
Featherstone St STLK EC1Y ... 7 G9

Featherstone Ter NWDGN UB2 ...102 D2
Featley Rd BRXN/ST SW9 ...130 C2
Federal Rd GFD/PVL UB6 ...85 J1
Federation Rd ABYW SE2 ...116 C2
Fee Farm Rd ESH/CLAY KT10 ...171 F6
Feeny Cl WLSDN NW10 ...69 H3
Felbridge Av STAN HA7 ...35 G7
Felbridge Cl BELMT SM2 ...175 F7
 STRHM/NOR SW16 ...149 G4
Felday Rd LEW SE13 ...132 E5
Felden Cl PIN HA5 ...33 J6
Felden Rd FUL/PGN SW6 ...107 J7
Feldman Cl STNW/STAM N16 ...56 C7
Felgate Ms HMSMTH W6 ...106 E3
Felhampton Rd ELTH/MOT SE9 ...154 B2
Felix Av CEND/HSY/T N8 ...54 E5
Felix Rd BRXS/STRHM SW2 ...130 B4
Felix Rd WEA W13 ...85 G6
Felixstowe Rd ABYW SE2 ...116 C2
 ED N9 ...42 C2
 SEVS/STOTM N15 ...56 A5
 WLSDN NW10 ...87 K2
Felix St BETH E2 * ...92 D1
Fellbrigg Rd EDUL SE22 ...131 G4
Fellbrigg St WCHPL E1 ...92 D3
Fellbrook RCHPK/HAM TW10 ...143 H2
Fellmongers Yd CROY/NA CRO * ...177 J2
Fellowes Cl YEAD UB4 ...83 H3
Fellowes Rd CAR SM5 ...175 J2
Fellows Rd HAMP NW3 ...3 H1
Fell Pth BORE WD6 * ...25 F4
Fell Rd CROY/NA CRO ...177 J2
Felltram Wy CHARL SE7 ...113 K4
Felmersham Cl CLAP SW4 ...129 K3
Felmingham Rd PGE/AN SE20 ...165 K1
Felsberg Rd BRXS/STRHM SW2 ...129 K5
Fels Cl DAGE RM10 ...80 D2
Fels Farm Av DAGE RM10 ...80 D2
Felsham Ms PUT/ROE SW15 ...127 G2
Felsham Rd PUT/ROE SW15 ...127 F2
Felspar Cl WOOL/PLUM SE18 ...116 A4
Felstead Cl HOM E9 ...75 J5
 WAN E11 ...58 E5
Felstead Rd HOM E9 ...75 H5
Felsted Rd CAN/RD E16 ...95 H5
Feltham Av E/WMO/HCT KT8 ...157 K3
Felthambrook Wy FELT TW13 ...141 F2
Feltham Hill Rd ASHF TW15 ...140 A5
Feltham Rd MTCM CR4 ...162 E1
Felton Cl STMC/STPC BR5 ...169 G5
Felton Lea SCUP DA14 ...155 F4
Felton Rd BARK IG11 ...96 E1
 WEA W13 ...104 D1
Felton St IS N1 ...7 H4
Fenchurch Av FENCHST EC3M ...13 J5
Fenchurch Blds FENCHST EC3M ...13 J5
Fenchurch Pl FENCHST EC3M ...13 K6
Fenchurch St FENCHST EC3M ...13 J6
Fendall Rd HOR/WEW KT19 ...172 E4
Fendall St STHWK SE1 ...19 K3
Fendyke Rd BELV DA17 ...116 E3
Fenelon Pl WKENS W14 ...107 J3
Fen Gv BFN/LL DA15 ...136 A5
Fenham Rd PECK SE15 ...111 H6
Fenman Ct TOTM N17 ...42 E7
Fenman Gdns GDMY/SEVK IG3 ...61 H7
Fenn Cl BMLY BR1 ...152 E5
Fennel Cl CAN/RD E16 ...94 C3
 CROY/NA CRO ...
Fennells Md HOR/WEW KT19 ...173 H7
Fenner Cl BERM/RHTH SE16 ...111 J3
Fenner Sq BTSEA SW11 * ...128 C2
Fennings Rd CLAP SW4 ...129 J5
Fenn St HOM E9 ...75 F4
Fenstanton Av NFNCH/WDSPK N12 ...39 H4
Fen St CAN/RD E16 ...94 D6
Fentiman Rd VX/NE SW8 ...110 A5
Fentiman Wy RYLN/HDSTN HA2 ...66 B3
 CHST BR7 ...153 K4
 HACK E8 ...74 B5
Fenton's Av PLSTW E13 ...95 F1
Fenton St WCHPL E1 ...92 D5
Fenwick Gv PECK SE15 ...131 H2
Fenwick Pl BRXN/ST SW9 ...129 K2
 SAND/SEL CR2 ...177 H6
Fenwick Rd PECK SE15 ...131 H2
Ferdinand Dr PECK SE15 ...111 F6
Ferdinand Pl CAMTN NW1 ...4 A1
Ferdinand St CAMTN NW1 ...4 A1
Ferguson Av BRYLDS KT5 ...159 G4
Ferguson Cl BECK BR3 ...167 F2
Ferguson Dr ACT W3 ...87 F5
Ferguson's Cl POP/IOD E14 ...112 D3
Fergus Rd HBRY N5 ...73 H4
Ferme Park Rd CEND/HSY/T N8 ...54 E4
Fermor Rd FSTH SE23 ...132 B7
Fermoy Rd GFD/PVL UB6 ...84 B3
 MV/WKIL W9 ...88 D3
Fern Av MTCM CR4 ...163 J3
Fernbank Av ALP/SUD HA0 ...67 J5
 WOT/HER KT12 ...156 D6
Fernbank Ms BAL SW12 ...129 G5
Fernbrook Dr RYLN/HDSTN HA2 ...48 B6
Fernbrook Rd LEW SE13 ...133 H5
Ferncliff Rd HACK E8 ...74 C4
Fern Cl ERITH DA8 ...118 E7
 IS N1 ...7 J5
Fern Ct NWCR SE14 ...132 A1
Ferncroft Av HAMP NW3 ...70 E2
 NFNCH/WDSPK N12 ...39 J5
 RSLP HA4 ...65 G1
Ferndale BMLY BR1 ...168 B1
Ferndale Av HSLWW TW4 ...122 C2
 WALTH E17 ...58 B4
Ferndale Cl BXLYHN DA7 ...117 F7
Ferndale Rd CLAP SW4 ...129 K3
 CRW RM5 ...62 E1
 FSTGT E7 ...77 F1
 SEVS/STOTM N15 ...56 B5
 SNWD SE25 ...165 J4
 WAN E11 ...76 D1
Ferndale Ter HRW HA1 ...49 F3
Fern Dene WEA W13 ...85 H4
Ferndene Rd HNHL SE24 ...130 D3
Ferndene Wy ROMW/RG RM7 ...62 D5
Ferndown NTHWD HA6 ...46 E1
Ferndown Av ORP BR6 ...169 J7

Ferndown Cl BELMT SM2 ...175 H5
 PIN HA5 ...33 J6
Ferndown Rd ELTH/MOT SE9 ...134 C6
 OXHEY WD19 ...33 G2
Ferney Meade Wy ISLW TW7 ...124 B1
Ferney Rd EBAR EN4 ...28 A6
Fern Gv EBED/NFELT TW14 ...122 A6
Fernhall Dr REDBR IG4 ...59 H4
Fernham Rd THHTH CR7 ...164 D2
Fernhead Rd MV/WKIL W9 ...88 D2
Fernhill Ct WALTH E17 ...58 B1
Fernhill Gdns KUTN/CMB KT2 ...143 K4
Fernhill Rd CAN/RD E16 ...95 K7
Fernholme Rd PECK SE15 ...132 A4
Fernhurst Gdns EDGW HA8 ...36 C5
Fernhurst Rd ASHF TW15 ...140 A4
 CROY/NA CRO ...165 H6
 FUL/PGN SW6 ...107 H7
Fern La HEST TW5 ...102 E4
Fernlea Rd BAL SW12 ...129 G7
 MTCM CR4 ...163 F1
Fernleigh Cl CROY/NA CRO ...177 G3
 MV/WKIL W9 ...88 D2
Fernleigh Ct RYLN/HDSTN HA2 ...48 B1
 WBLY HA9 ...50 A1
Fernleigh Rd WCHMH N21 ...41 G1
Fernley Cl PIN HA5 ...46 E3
Fernsbury St FSBYW WC1X ...6
Fernshaw Cl WBPTN SW10 ...108 B5
Fernshaw Rd WBPTN SW10 ...108 B5
Fernside GLDGN NW11 ...70 E1
 THDIT KT7 ...158 A7
Fernside Av FELT TW13 ...141 F3
 MLHL NW7 ...37 F2
Fernside Rd BAL SW12 ...128 E7
Ferns Rd SRTFD E15 ...76 C5
Fern St BOW E3 ...93 J3
Fernthorpe Rd STRHM/NOR SW16 ...148 C5
Ferntower Rd HBRY N5 ...73 K4
Fernways IL IG1 ...78 B2
Fernwood Av ALP/SUD HA0 ...67 J5
 STRHM/NOR SW16 ...148 D3
Fernwood Crs TRDG/WHET N20 ...39 K2
Ferranti Cl WOOL/PLUM SE18 ...114 C2
Ferraro Cl HEST TW5 ...103 F5
Ferrers Av WDR/YW UB7 ...100 A1
 WLGTN SM6 ...176 D3
Ferrers Rd STRHM/NOR SW16 ...148 D4
Ferrestone Rd CEND/HSY/T N8 ...55 F3
Ferrey Ms BRXN/ST SW9 ...130 A1
Ferriby Cl IS N1 ...6 A1
Ferrier St WAND/EARL SW18 ...128 A3
Ferring Cl RYLN/HDSTN HA2 ...48 C7
Ferrings DUL SE21 ...150 A1
Ferris Av CROY/NA CRO ...179 J2
Ferris Rd EDUL SE22 ...131 H3
Ferron Rd CLPT E5 * ...74 D2
Ferro Rd RAIN RM13 ...99 J3
Ferryhills Cl OXHEY WD19 ...33 G2
Ferry La BARN SW13 ...106 C5
 BTFD TW8 ...105 F5
 RAIN RM13 ...99 G5
 TOTM N17 ...56 D3
Ferrymead Av GFD/PVL UB6 ...84 A1
Ferrymead Dr GFD/PVL UB6 ...84 A2
Ferrymead Gdns GFD/PVL UB6 ...84 C1
Ferrymoor RCHPK/HAM TW10 ...143 H2
Ferry Rd BARN SW13 ...106 D6
 E/WMO/HCT KT8 ...157 H3
 TEDD TW11 ...143 H4
 THDIT KT7 ...158 C5
 TWK TW1 ...124 C7
Ferry Sq BTFD TW8 ...105 F5
Ferry St POP/IOD E14 ...113 F4
Festing Rd PUT/ROE SW15 ...127 G2
Festival Cl BXLY DA5 ...136 E7
 ERITH DA8 ...118 C6
Festoon Wy CAN/RD E16 ...95 H6
Fetter La FLST/FETLN EC4A ...11 J4
Ffinch St DEPT SE8 ...112 D6
Fidgeon Cl BMLY BR1 ...169 F2
Fidler Pl BUSH WD23 ...22 B5
Field Cl BKHH IG9 ...45 G2
 BMLY BR1 ...168 B1
 CHING E4 ...43 K5
 CHSGTN KT9 ...171 J4
 CRICK NW2 ...69 J1
 E/WMO/HCT KT8 ...157 G4
 HSLWW TW4 ...102 A7
 HYS/HAR UB3 ...101 K1
 RSLP HA4 ...46 A7
Fieldcommon La WOT/HER KT12 ...156 D7
Field Cots EFNCH N2 * ...53 K2
 FUL/PGN SW6 * ...127 J1
Field Ct GINN WC1R ...11 M3
Field End BAR EN5 ...25 K3
 RSLP HA4 ...65 H5
Fieldend TEDD TW11 ...143 F5
Field End Cl OXHEY WD19 ...21 J6
Field End Rd PIN HA5 ...47 F4
 RSLP HA4 ...65 H2
Fieldend Rd STRHM/NOR SW16 ...148 C7
Fielders Cl EN EN1 ...30 A3
 RYLN/HDSTN HA2 ...48 C7
Fieldfare Rd THMD SE28 ...97 J6
Fieldgate St WCHPL E1 ...92 C4
Fieldhouse Cl SWFD E18 ...45 F7
Fieldhouse Rd BAL SW12 ...129 H7
Fielding Av WHTN TW2 ...142 H3
Fielding La HAYES BR2 ...168 B3
Fielding Rd CHSWK W4 ...106 A2
 WKENS W14 ...107 G2
The Fieldings FSTH SE23 ...131 K7
Fielding St WALW SE17 ...18 E9
Fielding Ter EA W5 * ...86 B6
Field La BTFD TW8 ...104 D6
 TEDD TW11 ...143 G4
Field Md CDALE/KGS NW9 ...37 G6
Fieldpark Gdns CROY/NA CRO ...166 B7
Field Pl NWMAL KT3 ...160 C5
Field Point FSTGT E7 ...76 E3
 HMSMTH W6 ...107 H4
 OXHEY WD19 ...21 J3
 TOTM N17 ...55 J2
Fieldsend Rd CHEAM SM3 ...174 C4
Fields Est HACK E8 * ...74 C6
Fieldside Cots TRDG/WHET N20 * ...26 D6
Fieldside Rd BMLY BR1 ...152 B4
Fields Park Crs CHDH RM6 ...61 K4
Field St FSBYW WC1X ...5 L7
Field Vw FELT TW13 ...140 A3
Fieldview WAND/EARL SW18 ...128 C7

Field View Cl ROMW/RG RM7 ...62 C2
Fieldview Cots STHGT/OAK N14 * ...40 C1
Fieldway STMC/STPC BR5 ...169 J5
 BCTR RM8 ...79 H3
Field Wy CROY/NA CRO ...179 K5
 GFD/PVL UB6 ...66 B2
 RSLP HA4 ...46 A7
 WLSDN NW10 ...68 E6
Fieldway Crs HBRY N5 ...73 G4
Fiennes Cl BCTR RM8 ...61 J7
Fiesta Dr RAIN RM13 ...98 E3
Fife Rd CAN/RD E16 ...94 E4
 KUT/HW KT1 ...159 F1
 MORT/ESHN SW14 ...125 K4
 WDGN N22 ...41 H6
Fife Ter IS N1 ...5 M5
Fifield Pth FSTH SE23 ...151 F2
Fifth Av HYS/HAR UB3 ...82 D7
 MNPK E12 ...77 K3
Fifth Wy WBLY HA9 ...68 D3
Fifth Cross Rd WHTN TW2 ...142 H5
Figge's Rd MTCM CR4 ...148 A6
Fig Tree Cl WLSDN NW10 ...69 G7
Filby Rd CHSGTN KT9 ...172 B5
Filey Av STNW/STAM N16 ...56 C7
Filey Cl BELMT SM2 ...175 G6
Filey Waye RSLP HA4 ...64 E1
Fillebrook Av EN EN1 ...30 A1
Fillebrook Rd WAN E11 ...58 B7
Filmer Chambers FUL/PGN SW6 * ...107 J7
Filmer Rd FUL/PGN SW6 ...107 J7
Filton Cl CDALE/KGS NW9 ...51 G1
Finborough Rd TOOT SW17 ...147 K6
 WBPTN SW10 ...14 D9
Finchale Rd ABYW SE2 ...116 B2
Fincham Cl HGDN/ICK UB10 ...64 A2
Finch Av WNWD SE27 ...149 K3
Finch Cl BAR EN5 ...26 E5
Finch Dr EBED/NFELT TW14 ...122 C6
Finch Gdns CHING E4 ...43 J4
Finchingfield Av WFD IG8 ...45 G6
Finch La BANK EC3V ...13 H5
 BUSH WD23 ...21 K1
Finchley Cl DART DA1 ...139 K5
Finchley La HDN NW4 ...52 B3
Finchley Pk NFNCH/WDSPK N12 ...39 G3
Finchley Pl STJWD NW8 ...3 G3
Finchley Rd GLDGN NW11 ...52 D2
 HAMP NW3 ...70 E3
 STJWD NW8 ...3 G3
Finchley Vls NFNCH/WDSPK N12 * ...39 H3
Finchley Wy FNCH N3 ...38 E5
Finch Ms PECK SE15 * ...111 F7
Finchs Ct POP/IOD E14 ...93 K6
Finden Rd FSTGT E7 ...77 G4
Findhorn Av YEAD UB4 ...83 F4
Findhorn St POP/IOD E14 ...94 A5
Findon Cl RYLN/HDSTN HA2 * ...66 B2
 WAND/EARL SW18 ...127 K5
Findon Gdns RAIN RM13 ...99 J4
Findon Rd ED N9 ...30 D7
 SHB W12 ...106 D1
Fingal St GNWCH SE10 ...113 J4
Finland Rd BROCKY SE4 ...132 B2
Finland St BERM/RHTH SE16 ...112 B2
Finlays Cl CHSGTN KT9 ...172 C4
Finlay St FUL/PGN SW6 ...107 G7
Finney La ISLW TW7 ...104 B7
Finnis St BETH E2 ...92 D2
Finnymore Rd DAGW RM9 ...80 A6
Finsbury Av LVPST EC2M * ...13 H3
Finsbury Circ LVPST EC2M ...13 H3
Finsbury Cots WDGN N22 ...40 E6
Finsbury Est CLKNW EC1R ...6
Finsbury Market SDTCH EC2A ...13 J1
Finsbury Pavement LVPST EC2M ...13 H2
Finsbury Park Av FSBYPK N4 ...55 J5
Finsbury Park Rd FSBYPK N4 ...73 H1
Finsbury Pavement LVPST EC2M ...13 H2
Finsbury Rd WDGN N22 ...41 F6
Finsbury Sq SDTCH EC2A ...13 H1
Finsbury St STLK EC1Y ...13 G2
Finsbury Wy BXLY DA5 ...137 G5
Finsen Rd CMBW SE5 ...130 D3
Finstock Rd NKENS W10 ...88 B5
Finucane Gdns RAIN RM13 ...81 J5
Finucane Ri BUSH WD23 ...34 C1
Finway Ct WATW WD18 * ...20 D4
Fiona Ct ENC/FH EN2 ...29 H1
Firbank Cl CAN/RD E16 ...95 H4
 ENC/FH EN2 ...29 J3
Firbank Dr OXHEY WD19 ...21 J6
Firbank Rd PECK SE15 ...131 J1
Fircroft Gdns HRW HA1 ...66 E2
Fircroft Rd CHSGTN KT9 ...172 B3
 TOOT SW17 ...147 K2
Firdene BRYLDS KT5 ...159 K7
Fir Dene ORP BR6 ...181 K2
Fire Bell Aly SURB KT6 ...159 F5
Firebell Ms SURB KT6 ...159 F5
Firecrest Dr HAMP NW3 ...71 F2
Firefly Cl WLGTN SM6 ...176 E6
Firefly Gdns EHAM E6 ...95 J3
Firemans Cots EFNCH N2 * ...53 K2
Firethorn Cl EDGW HA8 ...36 E3
Fir Gv NWMAL KT3 ...160 C5
Fir Grove Rd BRXN/ST SW9 * ...130 B1
Firhill Rd CAT SE6 ...151 J3
Firle Pl WAND/EARL SW18 ...128 B6
Firman Cl NWMAL KT3 ...160 B3
Firmin Rd DART DA1 ...139 F4
Fir Rd CHEAM SM3 ...161 J7
 FELT TW13 ...141 H4
Firs Av FBAR/BDGN N11 ...40 A5
 MORT/ESHN SW14 ...125 K3
 MUSWH N10 ...54 A2
Firsby Av CROY/NA CRO ...166 A7
Firsby Rd STNW/STAM N16 ...56 C7
Firs Cl ESH/CLAY KT10 ...170 E5
 FSTH SE23 ...132 A6
 MTCM CR4 ...163 G1
Firscroft PLMGR N13 ...41 J2
Firs La PLMGR N13 ...41 J4
Firside Gv BFN/LL DA15 ...136 A7
Firs La PLMGR N13 ...41 J4
Firs Park Av WCHMH N21 ...29 K7
Firs Park Gdns WCHMH N21 ...29 K7
First Av ACT W3 ...87 H7
 BXLYHN DA7 ...116 D6
 CHDH RM6 ...61 J4
 DAGE RM10 ...98 D1
 E/WMO/HCT KT8 ...156 E3
 EN EN1 ...30 B4
 HDN NW4 ...52 A3
 HOR/WEW KT19 ...173 G4
 HYS/HAR UB3 ...82 D7
 MNPK E12 ...77 J3
 MORT/ESHN SW14 ...126 B2

 NKENS W10 ...88 D3
 PLSTW E13 ...94 E2
 UED N18 ...42 E3
 WALTH E17 ...57 K4
 WBLY HA9 ...67 K1
First Cl E/WMO/HCT KT8 ...156 G5
First Cross Rd WHTN TW2 ...142 E1
First Dr WLSDN NW10 ...68 E6
The Firs BXLY DA5 ...138 A7
 EA W5 ...85 K4
 EBED/NFELT TW14 * ...121 K5
 EDGW HA8 * ...37 F3
 TRDG/WHET N20 ...27 H7
First St CHEL SW3 ...15 K5
Firstway RYNPK SW20 ...161 F1
First Wy WBLY HA9 ...68 D3
Firs Wk NTHWD HA6 ...32 B5
 WFD IG8 ...44 E4
Firswood Av HOR/WEW KT19 ...173 G4
Firth Gdns FUL/PGN SW6 ...107 H7
Firtree Av MTCM CR4 ...163 F1
Fir Tree Av WDR/YW UB7 ...100 D3
Fir Tree Cl EA W5 ...86 A5
 ESH/CLAY KT10 ...170 C4
 HOR/WEW KT19 ...173 H5
 ROM RM1 ...63 F2
 STRHM/NOR SW16 ...148 B4
Fir Tree Ct BORE WD6 ...24 B3
Fir Tree Gdns CROY/NA CRO ...179 J3
Fir Tree Gv CAR SM5 ...175 K6
Fir Tree Rd HSLWW TW4 ...122 D3
 LEY E10 ...58 A7
Fir Trees Cl BERM/RHTH SE16 ...93 G7
Fir Tree Wk EN EN1 ...30 A2
Fir Wk CHEAM SM3 ...174 B5
Fisher Cl CROY/NA CRO ...165 G7
 GFD/PVL UB6 ...84 A2
Fisherdene ESH/CLAY KT10 ...171 G6
Fisherman Cl RCHPK/HAM TW10 ...143 J3
Fishermans Dr BERM/RHTH SE16 ...112 A1
Fisher Rd KTN/HRWW/WS HA3 ...49 F1
Fishers Cl BUSH WD23 ...21 J3
 STRHM/NOR SW16 ...148 D2
Fishers Ct NWCR SE14 ...112 A7
Fisher's La CHSWK W4 ...106 A3
Fisher St CAN/RD E16 ...94 E4
 RSO WC1B ...11 L3
Fisher's Wy BELV DA17 ...98 E7
Fisherton St STJWD NW8 ...9 G1
Fishguard Wy CAN/RD E16 ...96 B7
Fishponds Rd HAYES BR2 ...181 H4
 TOOT SW17 ...147 J3
Fish Street Hl MON EC3R ...13 H7
Fisk Cl SUN TW16 ...140 D5
Fisons Rd CAN/RD E16 ...94 E7
Fitzalan Rd ESH/CLAY KT10 ...170 E6
 FNCH N3 ...52 C2
Fitzalan St LBTH SE11 ...17 M5
Fitzgeorge Av NWMAL KT3 ...145 F7
 WKENS W14 ...107 H3
Fitzgerald Av MORT/ESHN SW14 ...126 B2
Fitzgerald Rd MORT/ESHN SW14 ...126 A2
 THDIT KT7 ...158 B5
 WAN E11 ...58 E4
Fitzhardinge St MBLAR W1H ...10 A4
Fitzhugh Gv WAND/EARL SW18 ...128 C5
Fitzjames Av CROY/NA CRO ...178 C1
 WKENS W14 ...107 H3
Fitzjohn Av BAR EN5 ...26 C4
Fitzjohn's Av HAMP NW3 ...71 H4
Fitzmaurice Pl MYFR/PICC W1J * ...10 D8
Fitzneal St SHB W12 ...87 H5
Fitzroy Cl HGT N6 ...53 K7
Fitzroy Crs CHSWK W4 ...106 A6
Fitzroy Gdns NRWD SE19 ...150 A6
Fitzroy Ms FITZ W1T ...10 E1
Fitzroy Pk HGT N6 ...53 K7
Fitzroy Rd CAMTN NW1 ...4 A1
Fitzroy Sq FITZ W1T ...10 E1
Fitzroy St FITZ W1T ...10 E1
Fitzstephen Rd BCTR RM8 ...79 H4
Fitzwarren Gdns HGT N6 ...54 C7
Fitzwilliam Av RCH/KEW TW9 ...125 G1
Fitzwilliam Cl TRDG/WHET N20 ...27 K7
Fitzwilliam Ms CAN/RD E16 ...94 E7
Fitzwilliam Rd CLAP SW4 ...129 H2
Fitz Wygram Cl HPTN TW12 ...142 C4
Five Acre CDALE/KGS NW9 ...51 H1
Five Elms Rd DAGW RM9 ...80 B2
 HAYES BR2 ...181 J1
Five Fields Cl OXHEY WD19 ...33 K1
Fiveways Cnr ELTH/MOT SE9 ...154 A1
Five Ways Jct HDN NW4 ...37 J7
Fiveways Rd BRXN/ST SW9 ...130 B1
Fladbury Rd SEVS/STOTM N15 ...55 K5
Fladgate Rd WAN E11 ...58 C5
Flag Cl CROY/NA CRO ...166 A2
Flag Wk PIN HA5 ...46 E5
Flamband Rd HRW HA1 ...49 G5
Flamborough Rd RSLP HA4 ...64 C2
Flamborough St POP/IOD E14 ...93 G5
Flamborough Wk POP/IOD E14 ...93 G6
Flamingo Wk HCH RM12 ...81 J6
Flamstead Gdns DAGW RM9 ...79 J6
Flamstead Rd DAGW RM9 ...79 J6
Flamsteed Av WBLY HA9 ...68 D3
Flamsteed Rd CHARL SE7 ...114 D4
Flanchford Rd SHB W12 ...106 C2
Flanders Crs TOOT SW17 ...147 K6
Flanders Rd CHSWK W4 ...106 B3
 EHAM E6 ...95 K1
Flanders Wy HOM E9 ...75 F5
Flank St WCHPL E1 ...92 C6
Flask Wk HAMP NW3 ...71 H3
Flather Cl STRHM/NOR SW16 ...148 C5
Flavell Ms GNWCH SE10 ...113 H4
Flaxen Cl CHING E4 ...43 K2
Flaxen Rd CHING E4 ...43 K2
Flaxley Rd MRDN SM4 ...162 A5
Flaxman Ct STPAN WC1H ...5 H9
Flaxman Ter STPAN WC1H ...5 H9
Flaxton Rd WOOL/PLUM SE18 ...115 J7
Flecker Cl STAN HA7 ...35 F4
Fleece Dr ED N9 ...42 C3
Fleece Rd SURB KT6 ...158 D7
Fleece Wk HOLWY N7 * ...72 E5
Fleeming Cl WALTH E17 ...57 H1
Fleeming Rd WALTH E17 ...57 H1
Fleet Cl E/WMO/HCT KT8 ...156 E4
 RSLP HA4 ...46 A5
Fleet Pl FLST/FETLN EC4A ...12 C4
Fleet Rd HAMP NW3 ...71 J4
Fleetside E/WMO/HCT KT8 ...156 E4
Fleet Sq FSBYW WC1X ...5 L8

Fleet St EMB EC4Y ...12 A5
Fleet Street Hl WCHPL E1 * ...92 C3
Fleet Ter CAT SE6 * ...133 F2
Fleetwood Cl CAN/RD E16 ...95 H4
 CHSGTN KT9 ...171 K6
 CROY/NA CRO ...178 B3
Fleetwood Rd KUT/HW KT1 ...159 J2
 WLSDN NW10 ...69 J4
Fleetwood Sq KUT/HW KT1 ...159 J2
Fleetwood St STNW/STAM N16 ...74 A1
Fleming Cl MV/WKIL W9 ...8 A1
Fleming Ct CROY/NA CRO ...177 G4
Fleming Dr WCHMH N21 ...29 F4
Fleming Md MTCM CR4 ...147 J6
Fleming Rd STHL UB1 ...84 B4
 WALW SE17 ...18 D9
Fleming Wk CDALE/KGS NW9 * ...51 G1
Fleming Wy ISLW TW7 ...124 A1
 THMD SE28 ...97 K6
Flemming Av RSLP HA4 ...47 F7
Flempton Rd LEY E10 ...57 G7
Fletcher Cl EHAM E6 ...96 B6
Fletcher La LEY E10 ...58 A6
Fletcher Rd CHSWK W4 ...105 K2
Fletchers Cl HAYES BR2 ...168 A3
Fletcher St WCHPL E1 ...92 C6
Fletching Rd CHARL SE7 ...114 C5
 CLPT E5 ...74 E2
Fletton Rd FBAR/BDGN N11 ...40 E6
Fleur De Lis St WCHPL E1 ...13 K1
Fleur Gates WIM/MER SW19 ...127 G6
Flexmere Rd TOTM N17 ...41 K7
Flight Ap CDALE/KGS NW9 * ...37 H7
Flimwell Cl BMLY BR1 ...152 C4
Flint Cl SRTFD E15 ...76 D5
Flint Down Cl STMC/STPC BR5 * ...155 C7
 ELTH/MOT SE9 ...134 C2
Flinton St WALW SE17 ...19 K7
Flint St WALW SE17 ...19 H6
Flitcroft St LSO/SEVD WC2H ...11 H5
Floathaven Cl THMD SE28 ...97 G7
Flock Mill Pl WAND/EARL SW18 ...128 A7
Flockton St BERM/RHTH SE16 ...111 H1
Flodden Rd CMBW SE5 ...110 D7
Flood La TWK TW1 * ...124 B7
Flood St CHEL SW3 ...15 K8
Flood Wk CHEL SW3 ...15 K8
Flora Cl POP/IOD E14 ...93 K5
 STAN HA7 ...35 K2
Flora Gdns CHDH RM6 ...61 J3
 HMSMTH W6 ...106 E3
Floral Pl IS N1 ...73 K4
Floral St COVGDN WC2E ...11 K6
Flora St BELV DA17 ...117 G4
Florence Av ENC/FH EN2 ...29 J2
 MRDN SM4 ...162 B4
Florence Cl WOT/HER KT12 ...156 A6
Florence Ct WAN E11 ...59 F3
Florence Dr ENC/FH EN2 ...29 J2
Florence Elson Cl MNPK E12 ...78 A3
Florence Gdns CHSWK W4 ...105 K5
 ROM RM1 ...63 G1
Florence Rd ABYW SE2 ...116 D2
 BECK BR3 ...166 A1
 BMLY BR1 ...152 E7
 CHSWK W4 ...106 A2
 EA W5 ...86 A6
 EHAM E6 ...77 G7
 FELT TW13 ...122 A7
 FSBYPK N4 ...55 H7
 KUTN/CMB KT2 ...144 B6
 NWCR SE14 ...112 C7
 NWDGN UB2 ...102 C3
 PLSTW E13 ...94 E1
 SAND/SEL CR2 ...177 K7
 WIM/MER SW19 ...147 F5
 WDGN N22 ...156 K6
Florence St CAN/RD E16 ...94 D3
 HDN NW4 ...52 A2
 IS N1 ...6 C2
Florence Ter NWCR SE14 ...112 C7
Florence Vls HGT N6 * ...54 B6
Florence Wy BAL SW12 ...128 E7
Florey Sq WCHMH N21 ...29 F4
Florfield Rd HACK E8 * ...74 D5
Florian Av SUT SM1 ...175 H3
Florian Rd PUT/ROE SW15 ...127 H3
Florida Cl BUSH WD23 ...34 D1
Florida Rd THHTH CR7 ...149 H7
Florida St BETH E2 ...92 C2
Floris Pl CLAP SW4 ...129 H1
Floriston Av HGDN/ICK UB10 ...64 A6
Floriston Cl STAN HA7 ...35 H7
Floriston Gdns STAN HA7 ...35 H7
Floss St PUT/ROE SW15 ...127 F1
Flower & Dean Wk WCHPL E1 ...13 M3
Flower La MLHL NW7 ...37 H4
Flower Ms GLDGN NW11 ...52 C5
Flowerpot Cl SEVS/STOTM N15 ...56 B5
Flowers Av RSLP HA4 ...46 E5
Flowers Cl CRICK NW2 ...69 J2
Flowers Ms ARCH N19 * ...72 C1
Floyd Rd CHARL SE7 ...114 B4
Floyer Cl RCHPK/HAM TW10 ...125 G4
Fludyer St LEW SE13 ...133 H3
Foley Ms ESH/CLAY KT10 ...170 E6
Foley Rd ESH/CLAY KT10 ...170 E6
Foley St GTPST W1W ...10 E3
Foley Wd ESH/CLAY KT10 ...171 F6
Folgate St WCHPL E1 ...13 K2
Foliot St SHB W12 ...87 H5
Folkestone Rd EHAM E6 ...96 A1
 UED N18 ...42 B3
 WALTH E17 ...57 K3
Folkingham La CDALE/KGS NW9 ...37 F7
Folkington Cnr NFNCH/WDSPK N12 ...38 D4
Follett St POP/IOD E14 ...94 A5
Folly La WALTH E17 ...43 G7
Folly Wall POP/IOD E14 ...113 F1
Fontaine Rd STRHM/NOR SW16 ...149 G5
Fontarabia Rd BTSEA SW11 ...129 F4
Fontayne Av RAIN RM13 ...81 G6
 ROM RM1 ...63 G1
Fontenoy Rd BAL SW12 ...148 B2
Fonteyne Gdns WFD IG8 ...59 H1
Fonthill Ms FSBYPK N4 ...73 F1
Fonthill Rd FSBYPK N4 ...73 F1
Font Hills EFNCH N2 ...53 G1
Fontley Wy PUT/ROE SW15 ...126 D6
Fontwell Cl KTN/HRWW/WS HA3 ...34 E6
 NTHLT UB5 ...66 A5
Fontwell Dr HAYES BR2 ...169 F4

The Footpath
  PUT/ROE SW15 * ...126 D4
Foots Cray High St
  SCUP DA14 ...155 J5
Foots Cray La SCUP DA14 ...136 D7
Footscray Rd ELTH/MOT SE9 ...135 G7
Forbes Cl CRICK NW2 ...69 J2
  HCH RM12 ...63 K7
Forbes St WCHPL E1 ...92 C5
Forbes Wy RSLP HA4 ...65 F1
Forburg Rd STNW/STAM N16 ...56 C7
Ford Cl BUSH WD23 ...22 C3
  HRW HA1 ...48 D6
  RAIN RM13 ...81 H6
  THHTH CR7 ...164 C5
Forde Av BMLY BR1 ...168 B2
Fordel Rd CAT SE6 ...133 G7
Ford End WFD IG8 ...45 F5
Fordham Cl BARK KT4 ...160 E7
Fordham St WCHPL E1 ...92 C5
Fordhook Av EA W5 ...86 B6
Fordingley Rd MV/WKIL W9 ...88 D2
Fordington Rd HGT N6 ...53 K3
Ford La RAIN RM13 ...81 H6
Fordmill Rd CAT SE6 ...151 J2
Ford Rd BOW E3 ...93 G1
  DAGW RM9 ...80 B6
Ford's Gv WCHMH N21 ...29 J7
Fords Park Rd CAN/RD E16 ...94 E5
Ford Sq WCHPL E1 ...92 D4
Ford St BOW E3 ...75 J7
  CAN/RD E16 ...94 D5
Fordwych Rd CRICK NW2 ...70 C4
Fordyce Rd LEW SE13 ...133 F5
Fordyke Rd BCTR RM8 ...80 A1
Foreland Ct HDN NW4 ...38 C1
Foreland St WOOL/PLUM SE18 ...115 J3
Foreshore DEPT SE8 ...112 C4
Forest Ap WFD IG8 ...44 D6
Forest Cl CHST BR7 ...154 A7
  KIL/WHAMP NW6 ...70 C6
  WAN E11 ...58 B3
  WFD IG8 ...45 F3
Forest Ct WAN E11 ...58 D6
Forestdale STHGT/OAK N14 ...40 D3
Forest Dr HAYES BR2 ...181 J2
  MNPK E12 ...77 H2
  SUN TW16 ...140 B6
  WFD IG8 ...44 B6
Forest Dr East WAN E11 ...58 B6
Forest Dr West WAN E11 ...58 A6
Forest Edge BKHH IG9 ...45 G2
Forester Rd PECK SE15 ...131 J3
Foresters Cl WLGTN SM6 ...176 D6
Foresters Crs BXLYHN DA7 ...137 J3
Foresters Dr WALTH E17 ...58 B3
  WLGTN SM6 ...176 D6
Forest Gdns TOTM N17 ...56 B1
Forest Ga CDALE/KGS NW9 ...51 G3
Forest Gld CHING E4 ...44 C4
  WAN E11 ...58 C5
Forest Gv HACK E8 ...74 B5
Forest Hill Rd EDUL SE22 ...131 J5
Forestholme Cl FSTH SE23 ...150 E1
  SYD SE26 * ...
Forest La FSTGT E7 ...76 E4
Forest Mount Rd WFD IG8 ...44 B6
Fore St BARB EC2Y ...13 G3
  ED N9 ...42 C3
  PIN HA5 ...46 D3
  UED N18 ...42 C4
Forest Rdg BECK BR3 ...166 D2
  HAYES BR2 ...181 J3
Forest Ri WALTH E17 ...58 B3
Forest Rd CHEAM SM3 ...161 K7
  ED N9 ...30 D8
  ERITH DA8 ...118 D7
  FELT TW13 ...141 G1
  FSTGT E7 ...76 E3
  HACK E8 ...74 B5
  RCH/KEW TW9 ...105 H6
  ROMW/RG RM7 ...62 D2
  TOTM N17 ...57 J2
  WALTH E17 ...57 G2
  WAN E11 ...58 A6
  WAN E11 ...44 E2
Forest Side FSTGT E7 ...77 F3
  WPK KT4 ...160 C7
Forest St FSTGT E7 ...76 E4
The Forest WAN E11 ...58 C3
Forest Vw CHING E4 ...44 B6
Forest View Av LEY E10 ...58 B4
Forest View Rd MNPK E12 ...77 J3
  WALTH E17 ...44 A7
Forest Wy BFN/LL DA15 ...135 J6
  WFD IG8 ...45 F3
Forfar Rd BTSEA SW11 ...109 F7
  WDGN N22 ...41 H7
Forge Cl HAYES BR2 ...167 K7
  HYS/HAR UB3 ...101 G5
Forge Cots EA W5 * ...85 K7
Forge Dr ESH/CLAY KT10 ...171 G6
Forge La CHEAM SM3 ...174 C6
  FELT TW13 ...141 J4
  NTHWD HA6 ...32 C7
  RCHPK/HAM TW10 ...125 F7
Forge Ms CROY/NA CRO ...179 J4
Forge Pl CAMTN NW1 ...72 A5
Forman Pl STNW/STAM N16 ...74 B3
Formby Av
  KTN/HRWW/WS HA3 ...49 J2
Formosa St MV/WKIL W9 ...8 D1
Formunt Cl CAN/RD E16 ...94 D4
Forres Gdns GLDGN NW11 ...52 E5
Forrester Pth SYD SE26 ...150 E4
Forrest Gdns
  STRHM/NOR SW16 ...164 A2
Forris Av HYS/HAR UB3 ...82 D7
Forset St MBLAR W1H ...9 K4
Forstal Cl HAYES BR2 ...167 K2
Forster Cl CHING E4 ...44 B6
Forster Rd BECK BR3 ...166 B2
  BRXS/STRHM SW2 ...129 K6
  TOTM N17 ...56 B2
  WALTH E17 ...57 G5
Forsters Cl CHDH RM6 ...62 C5
Forston St IS N1 ...6 F5
Forsyte Crs NRWD SE19 * ...150 A7
Forsythia Cl IL IG1 ...78 B4
Forsyth Pl EN EN1 ...30 A4
Forterie Gdns GDMY/SEVK IG3 ...79 G2
Fortescue Av WHTN TW2 ...142 C2
Fortescue Rd EDGW HA8 ...37 F7
  WIM/MER SW19 ...147 H6
Fortess Gv KTTN NW5 ...72 B4
Fortess Rd KTTN NW5 ...72 B3
Fortess Wk KTTN NW5 ...72 B4
Forthbridge Rd BTSEA SW11 ...129 F3
Fortis Cl CAN/RD E16 ...95 G5
Fortis Gn EFNCH N2 ...53 K2
Fortis Green Av EFNCH N2 ...54 A2

Fortis Green Rd MUSWH N10 ...54 A2
Fortismere Av MUSWH N10 ...54 A2
Fortnam Rd ARCH N19 ...72 D1
Fortnums Acre STAN HA7 ...35 F5
Fort Rd NTHLT UB5 ...66 A6
  STHWK SE1 ...19 M6
Fortrose Cl POP/IOD E14 ...94 B5
Fortrose Gdns
  BRXS/STRHM SW2 ...129 K7
Fort St CAN/RD E16 ...95 F7
  WCHPL E1 ...13 K3
Fortuna Cl HOLWY N7 * ...73 F5
Fortune Av EDGW HA8 ...36 D7
Fortunegate Rd WLSDN NW10 ...69 G7
Fortune Green Rd
  KIL/WHAMP NW6 ...70 E4
Fortune La BORE WD6 ...23 K5
Fortune Pl STHWK SE1 ...19 M8
Fortunes Md NTHLT UB5 ...65 J5
Fortune St STLK EC1Y ...12 F1
Forty Acre La CAN/RD E16 ...94 E4
Forty Av WBLY HA9 ...68 B2
Forty Cl WBLY HA9 ...68 B1
Forty La WBLY HA9 ...68 D1
Forum Cl BOW E3 ...75 J7
Forum Magnum Sq
  STHWK SE1 ...17 L1
Forumside EDGW HA8 ...36 C5
The Forum E/WMO/HCT KT8 ...157 G3
Forval Cl MTCM CR4 ...162 E4
Forward Dr
  KTN/HRWW/WS HA3 ...49 F3
Fosbury Ms BAY/PAD W2 ...8 D7
Foscote Ms MV/WKIL W9 ...8 B1
Foscote Rd HDN NW4 ...51 K5
Foskett Rd FUL/PGN SW6 ...127 J1
Foss Av CROY/NA CRO ...177 G4
Fossdene Rd CHARL SE7 ...114 A4
Fossdyke Cl YEAD UB4 ...83 J4
Fosse Wy WEA W13 ...85 G4
Fossil Rd LEW SE13 ...132 D2
Fossington Rd BELV DA17 ...116 E3
Foss Rd TOOT SW17 ...147 H3
Fossway BCTR RM8 ...79 J1
Foster Ct ACT W3 ...87 G6
  CHSWK W4 ...106 A4
  PLSTW E13 ...94 E3
Fosters Cl CHST BR7 ...153 K4
  SWFD E18 ...45 F5
Fothergill Cl PLSTW E13 ...76 E7
Fothergill Dr WCHMH N21 ...28 E4
Fotheringham Rd EN EN1 ...30 B4
Foubert's Pl SOHO/CST W1F ...10 E5
Foulden Rd STNW/STAM N16 ...74 B3
Foulden Ter STNW/STAM N16 ...74 B3
Foulis Ter SKENS SW7 ...15 C6
Foulser Rd TOOT SW17 ...147 K2
Foulsham Rd THHTH CR7 ...164 D2
Foundation Pl
  ELTH/MOT SE9 * ...135 F4
Founder Cl EHAM E6 ...96 B5
Founders Cl NTHLT UB5 ...83 K2
Founders Gdns NRWD SE19 ...149 J6
Foundry Cl BERM/RHTH SE16 ...93 G7
Foundry Ms CAMTN NW1 ...4 F9
  HSLW TW3 ...123 G3
Foundry Pl
  WAND/EARL SW18 * ...128 A6
Fountain Cl UX/CGN UB8 ...82 A4
Fountain Dr CAR SM5 ...175 K6
  NRWD SE19 ...150 B3
Fountain Green Sq
  BERM/RHTH SE16 ...111 H1
Fountain Ms HAMP NW3 ...71 K5
Fountain Pl BRXN/ST SW9 ...110 B7
Fountain Rd THHTH CR7 ...164 D1
  TOOT SW17 ...147 H4
Fountains Av FELT TW13 ...141 K2
Fountains Cl FELT TW13 ...141 K1
Fountains Crs
  STHGT/OAK N14 ...28 E6
Fountayne Rd
  SEVS/STOTM N15 ...56 C3
  STNW/STAM N16 ...74 C1
Fount St VX/NE SW8 ...109 J6
Fourland Wk EDGW HA8 ...36 E5
Fournier St WCHPL E1 ...13 L2
Four Seasons Cl BOW E3 ...93 J1
Four Seasons Crs CHEAM SM3 ...174 D1
Fourth Av HYS/HAR UB3 ...82 D7
  MNPK E12 ...77 K3
  NKENS W10 ...88 C3
  ROMW/RG RM7 ...62 E7
Fourth Cross Rd WHTN TW2 ...142 D1
Fourth Wy WBLY HA9 ...68 E3
The Four Tubs BUSH WD23 ...22 D6
The Four Wents CHING E4 ...44 B1
Fowey Av REDBR IG4 ...59 H4
Fowey Cl WAP E1W ...92 D7
Fowler Cl BTSEA SW11 ...128 C2
Fowler Rd FSTGT E7 ...76 E3
  IS N1 ...6 D3
Fowler's Wk EA W5 ...85 K3
Fownes St BTSEA SW11 ...128 D2
Foxberry Rd BROCKY SE4 ...132 B3
Foxborough Gdns
  BROCKY SE4 ...132 D5
Foxbourne Rd TOOT SW17 ...148 A1
Foxbury Av CHST BR7 ...154 D5
Foxbury Cl BMLY BR1 ...153 F5
Foxbury Rd BMLY BR1 ...153 F5
Fox Cl BORE WD6 ...23 K5
  BUSH WD23 ...22 B4
  CAN/RD E16 ...94 E4
  WCHPL E1 ...92 E3
Foxcombe CROY/NA CRO ...179 K5
Foxcroft Rd
  WOOL/PLUM SE18 ...115 G7
Foxdell NTHWD HA6 ...32 B5
Foxdene Cl SWFD E18 ...59 F2
Foxearth Sp SAND/SEL CR2 ...178 E7
Foxes Dt BKHTH/KID SE3 ...133 K2
  HAYES BR2 ...167 G5
Foxfield Cl NTHWD HA6 ...32 D5
Foxglove Cl BFN/LL DA15 ...136 B5
  ED N9 ...30 E7
  STHL UB1 ...83 J6
  STWL/WRAY TW19 ...120 A7
Foxglove Gdns WAN E11 ...59 G3
Foxglove La CHSGTN KT9 ...172 C3
Foxglove Pth THMD SE28 ...115 K1
Foxglove Rd ROMW/RG RM7 ...81 G1
Foxglove St ACT W3 ...87 H6
Foxglove Wy WLGTN SM6 ...163 F6
Fox Gv WOT/HER KT12 ...156 A6
Foxgrove Av BECK BR3 ...151 K6
Foxgrove Pth OXHEY WD19 ...33 H4
Foxgrove Rd BECK BR3 ...151 K6

Foxham Rd ARCH N19 ...72 D2
Fox Hl HAYES BR2 ...181 G4
  NRWD SE19 ...150 B6
Fox Hill Gdns NRWD SE19 ...150 B6
Foxhole Rd ELTH/MOT SE9 ...134 D4
Fox Hollow Cl
  WOOL/PLUM SE18 ...115 K4
Fox Hollow Dr BXLYHN DA7 ...136 E2
Foxholt Gdns WLSDN NW10 ...68 E6
Foxhome Cl CHST BR7 ...154 A7
Fox House Rd BELV DA17 ...117 J3
Fox & Knot St FARR EC1M * ...12 D1
Foxlands Crs DAGE RM10 ...80 E4
Foxlands Rd DAGE RM10 ...80 E4
Fox La EA W5 ...86 A4
  HAYES BR2 ...181 F1
  PLMGR N13 ...41 F2
Foxlees ALP/SUD HA0 ...67 G5
Foxley Cl HACK E8 ...74 C4
Foxley Rd CMBW SE5 ...110 B6
  THHTH CR7 ...164 C3
Foxleys OXHEY WD19 ...33 J2
Foxmead Cl ENC/FH EN2 ...29 F2
Foxmore St BTSEA SW11 ...108 E7
Fox Rd CAN/RD E16 ...94 D4
Foxton Gv MTCM CR4 ...162 C1
Foxwarren ESH/CLAY KT10 ...171 F7
Foxwell St BROCKY SE4 ...132 B2
Foxwood Cl FELT TW13 ...141 F2
  MLHL NW7 ...37 G4
Foxwood Green Cl EN EN1 ...30 A5
Foxwood Rd BKHTH/KID SE3 ...133 J3
Foyle Rd BKHTH/KID SE3 ...113 J5
  TOTM N17 ...42 C7
Framfield Cl
  NFNCH/WDSPK N12 ...38 E3
Framfield Rd HBRY N5 ...73 H4
  HNWL W7 ...85 F5
  MTCM CR4 ...148 A6
Framlingham Crs
  ELTH/MOT SE9 ...153 J3
Frampton Cl BELMT SM2 ...174 E6
Frampton Park Rd HOM E9 ...74 E6
Frampton Rd HSLWW TW4 ...122 D4
Frampton St STJWD NW8 ...9 J1
Francemary Rd LEW SE13 ...132 D4
Frances Rd CHING E4 ...43 J5
Frances St WOOL/PLUM SE18 ...114 E3
Franche Court Rd TOOT SW17 ...147 G2
Francis Av BXLYHN DA7 ...137 H1
  FELT TW13 ...140 E2
  IL IG1 ...78 D1
Francis Barber Cl
  STRHM/NOR SW16 * ...149 F3
Francis Bentley Ms CLAP SW4 ...129 H2
Franciscan Rd TOOT SW17 ...148 A3
Francis Chichester Wy
  BTSEA SW11 * ...109 F7
Francis Cl HOR/WEW KT19 ...173 F3
Francis Cv WIM/MER SW19 ...146 D6
Francis Ms LEE/GVPK SE12 * ...133 J5
Francis Rd CROY/NA CRO ...164 C6
  DART DA1 ...139 G4
  EFNCH N2 * ...53 K3
  GFD/PVL UB6 ...85 J1
  HRW HA1 ...49 G4
  HSLWW TW4 ...122 C1
  LEY E10 ...76 A1
  PIN HA5 ...47 G4
  WATW WD18 ...21 F3
  WLGTN SM6 ...176 C5
Francis St SRTFD E15 ...76 C4
  WEST SW1P ...16 F5
Francis Ter ARCH N19 ...72 C2
Francis Wk IS N1 ...5 L1
Francklyn Gdns EDGW HA8 ...36 C2
Francombe Gdns ROM RM1 ...63 J5
Franconia Rd CLAP SW4 ...129 H4
Frank Burton Cl CHARL SE7 ...114 A4
Frank Dixon Cl DUL SE21 ...131 F6
Frank Dixon Wy DUL SE21 ...131 F7
Frankfurt Rd HNHL SE24 ...130 D4
Frankham St DEPT SE8 ...112 D5
Frankland Cl
  BERM/RHTH SE16 ...111 J3
  WFD IG8 ...45 G4
Frankland Rd CHING E4 ...43 J4
  SKENS SW7 ...15 G4
Franklin Av WATW WD18 ...20 E5
Franklin Cl KUT/HW KT1 ...159 H2
  LEW SE13 ...112 E7
  TRDG/WHET N20 ...27 G6
  WNWD SE27 ...149 H2
Franklin Crs MTCM CR4 ...163 H3
Franklin Pl GNWCH SE10 ...112 E7
Franklin Rd BXLYHN DA7 ...117 F7
  PGE/AN SE20 ...150 E6
  WAT WD17 ...21 F1
Franklins Ms
  RYLN/HDSTN HA2 ...66 C1
Franklin Sq WKENS W14 ...107 J4
Franklin's Rw CHEL SW3 ...15 M7
Franklin St BOW E3 ...93 K2
  SEVS/STOTM N15 ...56 A5
Franklin Wy CROY/NA CRO ...163 K6
Franklyn Rd WLSDN NW10 ...69 H6
  WOT/HER KT12 ...156 A5
Frank Ms STHWK SE1 ...111 J3
Franks Av NWMAL KT3 ...159 K3
Franks Wood Av
  STMC/STPC BR5 ...169 G4
Franlaw Crs PLMGR N13 ...41 J3
Franmil Rd HCH RM12 ...63 H5
Fransfield Gv SYD SE26 ...150 D2
Frant Cl PGE/AN SE20 ...150 E6
Frant Rd THHTH CR7 ...164 C4
Fraser Cl BXLY DA5 ...137 K7
  EHAM E6 ...95 J5
Fraser Rd ED N9 ...42 D2
  ERITH DA8 ...117 K4
  GFD/PVL UB6 ...67 J1
  WALTH E17 ...57 K4
Fraser St CHSWK W4 ...106 B4
Frating Crs WFD IG8 ...44 E5
Frays Av WDR/YW UB7 ...100 A2
Frays Cl WDR/YW UB7 ...100 A3
Frazer Av RSLP HA4 ...65 G4
Frazier Cl ROM RM1 ...63 H6
Frazier St STHWK SE1 ...18 A2
Frean St BERM/RHTH SE16 ...111 H2
Freda Corbett Cl PECK SE15 ...111 H6
Frederica Rd HOLWY N7 * ...5 L1
Frederica St HOLWY N7 ...5 L1
Frederick Crs BRXN/ST SW9 ...110 C6
  PEND EN3 ...30 E1
Frederick Gdns CROY/NA CRO ...164 C6
  SUT SM1 ...174 D4
Frederick Pl
  WOOL/PLUM SE18 ...115 G4

Frederick Rd RAIN RM13 ...99 F1
  SUT SM1 ...174 D4
  WALW SE17 ...18 D8
Frederick's Pl LOTH EC2R * ...13 G5
  NFNCH/WDSPK N12 ...39 G3
Frederick Sq
  BERM/RHTH SE16 ...93 G6
Frederick's Rw FSBYE EC1V ...6 C7
Frithville Gdns SHB W12 ...88 A7
Frederick's Rw FSBYE EC1V ...5 L8
Frederick Ter HACK E8 ...7 L3
Frederic Ms KTBR SW1X * ...16 A2
Fredora Av YEAD UB4 ...82 D4
Freeborne Gdns RAIN RM13 ...81 J5
Freedom Cl WALTH E17 ...57 F3
Freedom Rd TOTM N17 ...55 K1
Freedom St BTSEA SW11 ...128 E1
Freegrove Rd HOLWY N7 ...72 E4
Freeland Pk HDN NW4 ...52 C1
Freeland Rd EA W5 ...86 B6
Freelands Av SAND/SEL CR2 ...179 F7
Freelands Gv BMLY BR1 ...153 F7
Freelands Rd BMLY BR1 ...153 F7
Freeland Wy ERITH DA8 ...118 D7
Freeling St IS N1 * ...5 L2
Freeman Cl NTHLT UB5 ...65 J6
Freeman Dr E/WMO/HCT KT8 ...156 E3
Freeman Rd MRDN SM4 ...162 C4
Freemans La HYS/HAR UB3 ...82 C6
Freemantle Av PEND EN3 ...31 F4
Freemantle St WALW SE17 ...19 J7
Freeman Wk ELTH/MOT SE9 ...134 B4
Freemasons Rd CAN/RD E16 ...95 F4
Freemason's Rd
  CROY/NA CRO ...165 F7
Freethorpe Cl NRWD SE19 ...150 A7
Freight La KCROSS N1C ...5 A7
Freightmaster Est
  RAIN RM13 * ...118 D3
Freke Rd BTSEA SW11 ...129 F3
Fremantle Rd BARK/HLT IG6 ...60 B1
  BELV DA17 ...117 H3
Fremont St HOM E9 ...74 D7
French Pl SDTCH EC2A ...7 K8
French St SUN TW16 ...156 B1
Frendsbury Rd BROCKY SE4 ...132 B3
Frensham Cl STHL UB1 ...83 K3
Frensham Ct MTCM CR4 ...162 C3
Frensham Dr CROY/NA CRO ...180 A6
  PUT/ROE SW15 ...145 J1
Frensham Rd ELTH/MOT SE9 ...154 D1
Frensham St PECK SE15 ...111 H5
Frere St BTSEA SW11 ...128 D1
Freshfield Av HACK E8 ...7 L1
Freshfield Cl LEW SE13 ...133 G3
Freshfield Dr STHGT/OAK N14 ...28 B7
Freshfields CROY/NA CRO ...166 C6
Freshford St TOOT SW17 ...147 G2
Fresh Mill La STHL UB1 ...84 A3
Freshwater Cl TOOT SW17 ...148 A5
Freshwater Rd BCTR RM8 ...61 K7
  TOOT SW17 ...148 A5
Freshwell Av CHDH RM6 ...61 J3
Fresh Wharf Rd BARK IG11 ...78 B7
Freshwood Cl BECK BR3 ...151 K7
Freshwood Wy WLGTN SM6 ...176 C7
Freston Gdns EBAR EN4 ...28 A4
Freston Pk FNCH N3 ...52 D1
Freston Rd NKENS W10 ...88 B6
Freta Rd BXLYHS DA6 ...137 G4
Frewin Rd WAND/EARL SW18 ...128 C7
Friar Ms WNWD SE27 ...149 H2
Friar Rd YEAD UB4 ...83 H3
Friars Av PUT/ROE SW15 ...127 K6
  TRDG/WHET N20 ...39 J2
Friars Cl CHING E4 ...44 A2
  IL IG1 ...60 D7
  NTHLT UB5 ...83 G2
  STHWK SE1 ...12 C9
Friars Gdns ACT W3 ...87 F5
Friars Gate Cl WFD IG8 ...44 E3
Friars La RCH/KEW TW9 ...124 E4
Friars Md POP/IOD E14 ...113 F2
Friars Ms ELTH/MOT SE9 ...135 F4
Friars Place La ACT W3 ...87 F6
Friars Rd EHAM E6 ...77 H7
Friars Stile Rd
  RCHPK/HAM TW10 ...125 F5
Friars Wk ABYW SE2 ...116 E4
  STHGT/OAK N14 ...28 B7
Friars Wy ACT W3 ...87 F5
Friars Wood CROY/NA CRO ...179 G7
Friary Cl NFNCH/WDSPK N12 ...39 J4
Friary Park Ct ACT W3 * ...86 E5
Friary Rd ACT W3 ...86 E5
  NFNCH/WDSPK N12 ...39 H3
  PECK SE15 ...111 H6
Friary Est PECK SE15 * ...111 H6
Friary La WFD IG8 ...44 E3
Friary Pk
  NFNCH/WDSPK N12 * ...39 J3
Friary Wy NFNCH/WDSPK N12 ...39 K2
Friday Hl CHING E4 ...44 C2
Friday Hl East CHING E4 ...44 D2
Friday Hl West CHING E4 ...44 C2
Friday Rd ERITH DA8 ...118 A4
  MTCM CR4 ...147 K6
Friday St STP EC4M ...12 E6
Frideswide Pl KTTN NW5 * ...72 C4
Friendly Pl LEW SE13 ...112 E7
Friendly St DEPT SE8 ...112 D7
Friendly Street Ms DEPT SE8 ...132 D1
Friendship Wy SRTFD E15 * ...76 A7
Friends' Rd CROY/NA CRO ...177 K2
Friend St FSBYE EC1V ...6 C7
Friern Barnet La
  TRDG/WHET N20 ...39 H1
Friern Barnet Rd
  FBAR/BDGN N11 ...40 A4
Friern Mount Dr
  TRDG/WHET N20 ...27 G6
Friern Pk NFNCH/WDSPK N12 ...39 H4
Friern Rd EDUL SE22 ...131 H5
Friern Watch Av
  NFNCH/WDSPK N12 ...39 H3
Frigate Ms DEPT SE8 ...112 D5
Frimley Av WLGTN SM6 ...176 E4
Frimley Cl CROY/NA CRO ...180 A6
  WIM/MER SW19 ...146 C1
Frimley Ct SCUP DA14 ...155 J4
Frimley Crs CROY/NA CRO ...180 A6
Frimley Gdns MTCM CR4 ...162 D2
Frimley Rd CHSGTN KT9 ...171 K4
  GDMY/SEVK IG3 ...78 E2
Frimley Wy WCHPL E1 ...93 F3
Frinstead Rd ERITH DA8 ...118 A6
Frinton Cl OXHEY WD19 ...33 F1
Frinton Dr WFD IG8 ...44 B1
Frinton Ms GNTH/NBYPK IG2 ...60 A5
Frinton Rd CRICK NW2 ...69 J5
  SCUP DA14 ...155 J1
  SEVS/STOTM N15 ...56 A5
  TOOT SW17 ...148 A5
Friston St FUL/PGN SW6 ...128 A1
Friswell Pl BXLYHN DA7 ...137 H3

Fritham Cl NWMAL KT3 ...160 B5
Frith Ct MLHL NW7 ...38 C6
Frith La MLHL NW7 ...38 C6
Frith Manor Farm Cots
  MLHL NW7 * ...38 C4
Frith Rd CROY/NA CRO ...177 J1
  WAN E11 ...76 A3
Frith St SOHO/SHAV W1D ...11 H5
Frithville Gdns SHB W12 ...88 A7
Frithwood Av NTHWD HA6 ...32 D5
Frizlands La DAGE RM10 ...80 D2
Frobisher Cl BUSH WD23 ...22 A5
  PIN HA5 ...47 H6
Frobisher Crs BARB EC2Y * ...12 F2
  STWL/WRAY TW19 ...120 B6
Frobisher Gdns LEY E10 * ...57 K7
Frobisher Ms ENC/FH EN2 ...29 K3
Frobisher Rd CEND/HSY/T N8 ...55 G3
  EHAM E6 ...95 K5
  ERITH DA8 ...118 D6
Frog La RAIN RM13 ...99 F4
Frogley Rd EDUL SE22 ...131 G3
Frogmore WAND/EARL SW18 ...127 K4
Frogmore Av YEAD UB4 ...82 C3
Frogmore Cl CHEAM SM3 ...174 B2
Frogmore Est HBRY N5 * ...73 J3
Frogmore Gdns CHEAM SM3 ...174 C3
  YEAD UB4 ...82 C3
Frognal HAMP NW3 ...71 G4
Frognal Av HRW HA1 ...49 F3
  SCUP DA14 ...155 G5
Frognal Cl HAMP NW3 ...71 G4
Frognal Gdns HAMP NW3 ...71 G3
Frognal La HAMP NW3 ...71 F4
Frognal Man HAMP NW3 * ...71 G5
Frognal Pde HAMP NW3 * ...71 G4
Frognal Pl SCUP DA14 ...155 G5
Frognal Ri HAMP NW3 ...71 G3
Frognal Wy HAMP NW3 ...71 G3
Froissart Rd ELTH/MOT SE9 ...134 D4
Frome Rd SEVS/STOTM N15 ...55 H2
Frome St IS N1 ...6 E4
Fromondes Rd CHEAM SM3 ...174 C4
Fromows Cnr CHSWK W4 * ...105 K4
Frostic Wk WCHPL E1 ...13 M3
Froude St VX/NE SW8 ...129 G1
Fruen Rd EBED/NFELT TW14 ...121 J6
Fryatt Rd TOTM N17 ...41 K6
Fryday Grove Ms BAL SW12 ...129 H6
Fryent Cl KTN/HRWW/WS HA3 ...50 C5
Fryent Crs CDALE/KGS NW9 ...51 G5
Fryent Flds CDALE/KGS NW9 ...51 G5
Fryent Gv CDALE/KGS NW9 ...51 G5
Fryent Wy CDALE/KGS NW9 ...50 C4
Frying Pan Aly WCHPL E1 ...13 K3
Fryston Av CROY/NA CRO ...178 C1
Fuchsia Cl ROMW/RG RM7 ...81 G1
Fuchsia St ABYW SE2 ...116 C4
Fulbeck Dr CDALE/KGS NW9 ...37 G7
Fulbeck Wy RYLN/HDSTN HA2 ...48 C3
Fulbourne Rd WALTH E17 ...44 A7
Fulbourne St WCHPL E1 ...92 D4
Fulbrook Ms ARCH N19 ...72 C3
Fulbrook Rd ARCH N19 ...72 C3
Fulford Gv OXHEY WD19 ...33 F1
Fulford Rd HOR/WEW KT19 ...173 F6
Fulford St BERM/RHTH SE16 ...111 J1
Fulham Broadway
  FUL/PGN SW6 ...107 K6
Fulham High St FUL/PGN SW6 ...127 H3
Fulham Palace Rd
  FUL/PGN SW6 ...107 G6
Fulham Park Gdns
  FUL/PGN SW6 ...127 J1
Fulham Park Rd
  FUL/PGN SW6 ...127 J1
Fulham Rd FUL/PGN SW6 ...108 A6
  WBPTN SW10 ...14 F9
Fullbrooks Av WPK KT4 ...160 C7
Fuller Cl BETH E2 * ...92 C3
  BUSH WD23 ...22 D6
Fullerian Crs WATW WD18 ...20 D3
Fuller Rd BCTR RM8 ...79 J2
Fullers Av SURB KT6 ...172 B1
  WFD IG8 ...44 D6
Fuller's Rd SWFD E18 ...44 D7
Fuller St HDN NW4 ...52 A3
Fullers Wy North SURB KT6 ...172 B3
Fullers Wy South CHSGTN KT9 ...172 A3
Fuller's Wd CROY/NA CRO ...179 J4
Fullerton Rd CAR SM5 ...175 J7
  CROY/NA CRO ...165 G6
  WAND/EARL SW18 ...128 B4
Fullwoods Ms IS N1 ...7 H7
Fulmar Ct BRYLDS KT5 ...159 G5
Fulmar Rd HCH RM12 ...81 J6
Fulmead St FUL/PGN SW6 ...108 A7
Fulmer Cl HPTN TW12 ...141 J4
Fulmer Rd CAN/RD E16 ...95 H4
  WEA W13 ...104 C2
Fulready Rd LEY E10 ...58 B4
Fulstone Cl HSLWW TW4 ...122 E3
Fulthorp Rd BKHTH/KID SE3 ...133 J1
Fulton Ms BAY/PAD W2 ...8 E6
Fulton Rd WBLY HA9 ...68 C2
Fulwell Park Av WHTN TW2 ...142 C1
Fulwell Rd TEDD TW11 ...142 D3
Fulwich Rd DART DA1 ...139 J5
Fulwood Av ALP/SUD HA0 ...86 A5
Fulwood Gdns TWK TW1 ...124 A5
Fulwood Wk WIM/MER SW19 ...127 H7
Furber St HMSMTH W6 ...106 E2
Furham Fld PIN HA5 ...34 A5
Furley Rd PECK SE15 ...111 H6
Furlong Cl WLGTN SM6 ...163 F6
Furlong Rd HOLWY N7 ...73 G5
The Furlongs ESH/CLAY KT10 ...170 A3
Furmage St WAND/EARL SW18 ...128 A6
Furneaux Av WNWD SE27 ...149 H4
Furner Cl DART DA1 ...138 C2
Furness Rd FUL/PGN SW6 ...128 A1
  MRDN SM4 ...162 A5
  RYLN/HDSTN HA2 ...48 B6
  WLSDN NW10 ...87 J1
Furness Wy HCH RM12 ...81 J4
Furnival St FLST/FETLN EC4A ...12 A4
Furrow La HOM E9 ...74 E4
Fursby Av FNCH N3 ...38 E5
Further Acre CDALE/KGS NW9 ...51 H1
Furtherfield Cl CROY/NA CRO ...164 B5
Further Green Rd CAT SE6 ...133 H6
Furze Cl OXHEY WD19 ...33 G4
Furzedown Dr TOOT SW17 ...148 B4
Furzedown Rd TOOT SW17 ...148 B4
Furze Farm Cl CHDH RM6 ...62 A1
Furzefield CHST BR7 * ...154 A5
Furzefield Rd BKHTH/KID SE3 ...114 A5
Furzeground Wy STKPK UB11 ...82 A7

Furzeham Rd *WDR/YW* UB7 ....100 B1
Furzehill Pde *BORE* WD6 * 24 C3
Furzehill Rd *BORE* WD6 ....24 C3
Furze Rd *THHTH* CR7 ....164 D2
Furze St *BOW* E3 * 93 J4
Furzewood *SUN* TW16 ....140 E7
Fye Foot La *BLKFR* EC4V 12 E6
Fyfe Wy *BMLY* BR1 ....167 K3
Fyfield Cl *HAYES* BR2 ....167 G3
Fyfield Rd *BRXN/ST* SW9 ....130 B2
  EN EN1 ....30 A2
  RAIN RM13 ....81 H7
  WALTH E17 ....58 B2
  WFD IG8 ....45 G6
Fynes St *WEST* SW1P 17 G5

G

Gable Cl *DART* DA1 ....138 D4
  PIN HA5 ....34 A6
Gable Ct *SYD* SE26 ....150 D3
Gable Ms *HAYES* BR2 ....181 J1
Gables Av *BORE* WD6 ....24 B2
Gables Cl *CMBW* SE5 ....111 F7
  LEE/GVPK SE12 ....133 K7
The Gables *NRWD* SE19 * 150 A5
  WBLY HA9 ....68 B3
Gabriel Cl *FELT* TW13 ....141 J3
Gabrielle Cl *WBLY* HA9 ....68 B2
Gabriel St *FSTH* SE23 ....132 A6
Gabriel's Whf *STHWK* SE1 * 12 A8
Gad Cl *PLSTW* E13 ....95 F2
Gaddesden Av *WBLY* HA9 ....68 B5
Gade Av *WATW* WD18 ....20 A5
Gade Bank *RKW/CH/CXG* WD3 ...20 B7
Gade Cl *HYS/HAR* UB3 ....83 F7
  WATW WD18 ....20 C3
Gadesden Rd *HOR/WEW* KT19 ...172 E5
Gadsbury Cl *CDALE/KGS* NW9 ...51 H5
Gadwall Cl *CAN/RD* E16 ....95 F5
Gage Rd *CAN/RD* E16 ....94 C4
Gage St *BMSBY* WC1N 11 J1
Gainford St *IS* N1 ....6 A3
Gainsboro Gdns *GFD/PVL* UB6 ...66 E4
Gainsborough Av *DART* DA1 ......139 H4
  MNPK E12 ....78 A4
Gainsborough Cl *BECK* BR3 ....151 J6
  ESH/CLAY KT10 * 157 J7
Gainsborough Ct *SHB* W12 ....107 F1
Gainsborough Gdns
  EDGW HA8 ....50 B1
  GLDGN NW11 ....52 D6
  HAMP NW3 ....71 H2
  HSLW TW3 ....123 J4
Gainsborough Ms *DUL* SE21 .....130 D7
  SYD SE26 * 150 D2
Gainsborough Rd *BCTR* RM8 .....79 H3
  CHSWK W4 ....106 C4
  NFNCH/WDSPK N12 ....39 G4
  NWMAL KT3 ....160 A5
  RAIN RM13 ....81 J7
  RCH/KEW TW9 ....125 G1
  SRTFD E15 ....94 C2
  WAN E11 ....58 C6
  WFD IG8 ....45 J5
  YEAD UB4 ....82 A1
Gainsborough Sq *BXLYHS* DA6 ..136 E2
Gainsborough St *HOM* E9 ....75 H5
Gainsborough Ter
  BELMT SM2 * 174 D6
Gainsford Rd *WALTH* E17 ....57 H3
Gainsford St *STHWK* SE1 ....13 L9
Gairloch Rd *CMBW* SE5 ....131 F1
Gaisford St *KTTN* NW5 ....72 C5
Gaitskell Rd *ELTH/MOT* SE9 .....135 H7
Gaitskell Wy *STHWK* SE1 * 18 E1
Galahad Rd *BMLY* BR1 ....152 E2
  ED N9 ....42 C1
Galata Rd *BARN* SW13 ....106 D6
Galatea Sq *PECK* SE15 ....131 J2
Galbraith St *POP/IOD* E14 ....113 F2
Galdana Av *BAR* EN5 ....27 G2
Galeborough Av *WFD* IG8 ....44 B6
Gale Cl *HPTN* TW12 ....141 J5
  MTCM CR4 ....162 C2
Galena Rd *HMSMTH* W6 ....106 E3
Galesbury Rd
  WAND/EARL SW18 ....128 B5
Gales Gdns *BETH* E2 ....92 D2
Gale St *BOW* E3 ....93 J4
  DAGW RM9 ....79 K6
Gales Wy *WFD* IG8 ....45 J6
Galgate Cl *WIM/MER* SW19 ......127 G7
Gallants Farm Rd *EBAR* EN4 ......27 J4
Galleon Cl *BERM/RHTH* SE16 ....111 K1
  ERITH DA8 ....118 A3
Galleons Dr *BARK* IG11 ....97 G2
The Galleries *IS* N1 * 6 A3
Gallery Gdns *NTHLT* UB5 ....83 H1
Gallery Rd *DUL* SE21 ....131 F5
Galley La *BAR* EN5 ....25 K2
Galleywall Rd
  BERM/RHTH SE16 ....111 J3
Galliard Rd *ED* N9 ....30 C6
Gallia Rd *HBRY* N5 ....73 H4
Gallions Cl *BARK* IG11 ....97 G2
Gallions Rd *CAN/RD* E16 ....96 B6
  CHARL SE7 ....114 A3
Gallions View Rd *THMD* SE28 ...115 K1
Gallion Cl *CHARL* SE7 ....114 A3
The Gallops *ESH/CLAY* KT10 .....170 B2
The Gallop *BELMT* SM2 ....175 F7
  SAND/SEL CR2 ....178 D6
Gallosson Rd
  WOOL/PLUM SE18 ....115 K3
Galloway Dr *DART* DA1 ....138 B2
Galloway Pth *CROY/NA* CR0 .....177 K3
Galloway Rd *SHB* W12 ....87 J7
Gallus Cl *WCHMN* N21 ....29 F5
Gallus Sq *BKHTH/KID* SE3 ....134 A2
Galpin's Rd *THHTH* CR7 ....163 K3
Galsworthy Av *CHDH* RM6 ....61 H6
  POP/IOD E14 ....93 G4
Galsworthy Cl *THMD* SE28 ....97 H7
Galsworthy Crs
  BKHTH/KID SE3 ....114 B7
Galsworthy Rd *CRICK* NW2 ....70 C3
  KUTN/CMB KT2 ....144 D7
Galton St *NKENS* W10 ....88 C3
Galva Cl *EBAR* EN4 ....28 A3
Galveston Rd *PUT/ROE* SW15 ...127 J4
Galway Cl *BERM/RHTH* SE16 * ...111 J4
Galway St *FSBYE* EC1V 6 F8
Gambetta St *VX/NE* SW8 ....129 G7
Gambia St *STHWK* SE1 ....12 D9
Gamble Rd *TOOT* SW17 ....147 J4
Games Rd *EBAR* EN4 ....27 J2
Gamlen Rd *PUT/ROE* SW15 ......127 G3
Gamuel Cl *WALTH* E17 ....57 J5
Gander Green Crs *HPTN* TW12 ..142 A7

Gander Green La *CHEAM* SM3 ...174 C1
  SUT SM1 ....174 D5
Gandhi Cl *WALTH* E17 ....57 J5
Gandhi Ct *WATW* WD24 ....57 J5
Gandolfi St *CMBW* SE5 ....111 F5
Ganton St *REGST* W1B 10 E5
Ganton Wk *OXHEY* WD19 * 33 J3
Gantshill Crs *GNTH/NBYPK* IG2 ..60 A4
Gap Rd *WIM/MER* SW19 ....146 E4
Garage Rd *ACT* W3 ....86 C5
Garbrand Wk *EW* KT17 ....173 H7
Garbutt Pl *MHST* W1U * 10 B2
Garden Av *BXLYHN* DA7 ....137 G2
  MTCM CR4 ....148 B6
Garden City *EDGW* HA8 ....36 C5
  BAR EN5 ....26 A3
  CHING E4 ....43 J4
  HPTN TW12 ....141 K4
  LEE/GVPK SE12 ....153 F2
  NTHLT UB5 ....65 J7
  PUT/ROE SW15 ....126 E6
  RSLP HA4 ....64 C1
  WAT WD17 ....20 D1
  WLGTN SM6 ....176 B4
Garden Cl *CHSWK* W4 ....105 K2
  EMB EC4Y * 12 A6
  HPTN TW12 ....141 K4
Gardeners Rd *CROY/NA* CR0 ....164 C7
Garden Flats *HMSMTH* W6 * 107 H5
Gardenia Rd *BMLY* BR1 ....169 F2
  EN EN1 ....30 A5
Gardenia Wy *WFD* IG8 ....44 E5
Garden La *BMLY* BR1 ....153 F5
  BRXS/STRHM SW2 ....130 A7
Garden Lodge Ct *EFNCH* N2 * 53 H2
Garden Pl *HACK* E8 ....7 L3
Garden Rd *BMLY* BR1 ....153 F6
  PGE/AN SE20 ....150 E7
  RCH/KEW TW9 ....125 H2
  STJWD NW8 ....2 F7
  WOT/HER KT12 ....156 A5
Garden Rw *STHWK* SE1 ....18 C4
The Gardens *BARK* IG11 ....167 F1
  CEND/HSY/T N8 * 54 E3
  CLPT E5 * 56 B6
  EBED/NFELT TW14 ....121 G5
  EDUL SE22 ....131 H3
  ESH/CLAY KT10 ....170 A3
  HRW HA1 ....48 C5
  PIN HA5 * 47 K5
  WAT WD17 ....20 D1
Garden Rw *WCHPL* E1 ....93 H4
Garden Studios *BAY/PAD* W2 * 8 A3
Gardens Wy *MNPK* E12 ....77 J2
Garden Ter *PIM* SW1V 17 G7
Garden Vls *ESH/CLAY* KT10 * 171 F6
Garden Wk *BECK* BR3 ....151 H1
  SDTCH EC2A 7 J9
Garden Wy *WLSDN* NW10 ....68 G5
Gardiner Av *CRICK* NW2 ....70 A4
Gardiner Cl *BCTR* RM8 ....79 K3
  PEND EN3 ....31 F5
Gardiner House *CHARL* SE7 * ...114 D6
Gardner Cl *WAN* E11 ....59 F5
Gardner Pl *EBED/NFELT* TW14 ..122 A5
Gardner Rd *PLSTW* E13 ....95 F3
Gardners Cl *FBAR/BDGN* N11 ....40 A1
Gardners La *BLKFR* EC4V 12 E6
Gardnor Rd *HAMP* NW3 * 71 H3
Gard St *FSBYE* EC1V 6 E8
Garendon Gdns *MRDN* SM4 .....162 A6
Garendon Rd *MRDN* SM4 ....162 A6
Gareth Cl *WPK* KT4 ....174 B1
Gareth Gv *BMLY* BR1 ....152 E3
Gareth Gv *HSLW* TW5 ....123 H1
Garfield Ms *BTSEA* SW11 ....129 G2
Garfield Rd *BTSEA* SW11 ....129 F2
  PEND EN3 ....30 E3
  PLSTW E13 ....94 D3
  TWK TW1 ....124 B7
  WIM/MER SW19 ....147 G5
Garford St *POP/IOD* E14 ....93 J6
Gargany Wk *WOOL/PLUM* SE18 ...98 A4
Garibaldi St *WOOL/PLUM* SE18 ..115 K3
Garland Dr *HSLW* TW3 ....123 H1
Garland Rd *STAN* HA7 ....35 K7
  WOOL/PLUM SE18 ....115 J6
Garlick Hl *BLKFR* EC4V 12 F6
Garlies Rd *FSTH* SE23 ....151 G2
Garlinge Rd *CRICK* NW2 ....70 D5
Garman Cl *UED* N18 ....41 K4
Garman Rd *TOTM* N17 ....42 D6
Garnault Ms *CLKNW* EC1R * 6 B8
Garnault Pl *CLKNW* EC1R * 6 B8
Garner Cl *BCTR* RM8 ....61 K7
Garner Rd *WALTH* E17 ....44 A4
Garner St *BETH* E2 ....92 C1
Garnet Rd *THHTH* CR7 ....164 D3
  WLSDN NW10 ....69 G5
Garnet St *WAP* E1W 92 E6
Garnett Cl *ELTH/MOT* SE9 ....134 E2
Garnett Rd *HAMP* NW3 ....71 K4
Garnham St *STNW/STAM* N16 ....74 B1
Garnies Cl *PECK* SE15 ....111 F6
Garrad's Rd
  STRHM/NOR SW16 ....148 D2
Garrard Cl *BXLYHN* DA7 ....137 H2
  CHST BR7 ....154 B4
Garratt Wk *WLSDN* NW10 * 69 G5
Garratt La *TOOT* SW17 ....147 G2
  WAND/EARL SW18 ....128 A6
Garratt Rd *EDGW* HA8 ....36 C6
Garratts Rd *BUSH* WD23 ....22 C6
Garratt Ter *TOOT* SW17 ....147 J3
Garrett Cl *ACT* W3 ....87 F4
Garrett St *STLK* EC1Y 6 F9
Garrick Av *GLDGN* NW11 ....52 C5
Garrick Cl *EA* W5 ....86 A3
  RCH/KEW TW9 ....124 D4
  WAND/EARL SW18 ....128 B3
Garrick Crs *CROY/NA* CR0 ....178 A1
Garrick Dr *HDN* NW4 ....38 A2
  THMD SE28 ....115 J2
Garrick Gdns *WMO/HCT* KT8 ....157 F2
Garrick Pk *HDN* NW4 ....52 B1
Garrick Rd *CDALE/KGS* NW9 .....51 H5
  GFD/PVL UB6 ....84 B3
  RCH/KEW TW9 ....125 H1
Garrick St *COVGDN* WC2E * 11 J5
Garrick Wy *HDN* NW4 ....52 B3
Garrick Yd *CHCR* WC2N * 11 J6
Garrison Cl *HSLWW* TW4 ....122 E4
  WOOL/PLUM SE18 ....115 F6
Garrison La *CHSGTN* KT9 ....171 K6
Garrison Rd *BOW* E3 ....75 J7
Garsdale Ter *WKENS* W14 * 107 J4
Garside Cl *HPTN* TW12 ....142 B5
  THMD SE28 ....115 J2
Garsington Ms *BROCKY* SE4 .....132 C2
Garter Wy *BERM/RHTH* SE16 ...112 A1
Garth Cl *KUTN/CMB* KT2 ....144 B4

  MRDN SM4 ....161 G6
  RSLP HA4 ....47 H6
Garthland Dr *BAR* EN5 ....25 K4
Garth Ms *EA* W5 * 86 A3
Garthorne Rd *FSTH* SE23 ....132 A6
Garth Rd *CHSWK* W4 ....70 D1
  CRICK NW2 ....70 D1
  KUTN/CMB KT2 ....144 B4
  MRDN SM4 ....161 G7
Garthside *KUTN/CMB* KT2 ....144 A4
The Garth *HPTN* TW12 ....142 B5
  KTN/HRWW/WS HA3 ....50 B1
  NFNCH/WDSPK N12 * 39 J4
Gartlet Rd *WAT* WD17 ....21 F2
Gartmoor Gdns
  WIM/MER SW19 ....127 J6
Gartmore Rd *GDMY/SEVK* IG3 ...61 F6
Garton Pl *WAND/EARL* SW18 ...128 B5
Gartons Cl *PEND* EN3 ....30 E4
Gartons Wy *BTSEA* SW11 ....128 B2
Garvary Rd *CAN/RD* E16 ....95 F5
Garway Rd *BAY/PAD* W2 ....8 C5
Gascoigne Gdns *WFD* IG8 ....44 C6
Gascoigne Pl *BETH* E2 ....7 L7
Gascoigne Rd *BARK* IG11 ....78 C7
  CROY/NA CR0 ....180 A6
Gascony Av *KIL/WHAMP* NW6 ......2 A2
Gascoyne Dr *DART* DA1 ....138 C2
Gascoyne Rd *HOM* E9 ....75 F6
Gaselee St *POP/IOD* E14 ....94 A6
Gasholder Pl *LBTH* SE11 ....17 M8
Gaskarth Rd *BAL* SW12 ....129 G6
  EDGW HA8 ....36 E7
Gaskell Rd *HGT* N6 ....53 K5
Gaskell St *CLAP* SW4 ....129 K1
Gaskin St *IS* N1 ....6 C3
Gaspar Cl *ECT* SW5 ....14 D5
Gaspar Ms *ECT* SW5 ....14 D5
Gassiot Rd *TOOT* SW17 ....147 K3
Gassiot Wy *SUT* SM1 ....175 H2
Gastein Rd *HMSMTH* W6 ....107 G5
Gaston Bell Cl *RCH/KEW* TW9 ..125 G2
Gaston Rd *MTCM* CR4 ....163 F2
Gataker St *BERM/RHTH* SE16 ...111 J2
Gatcombe Ms *EA* W5 ....86 B6
Gatcombe Rd *ARCH* N19 ....72 D2
Gatcombe Wy *EBAR* EN4 ....27 K2
Gate Cots *EDGW* HA8 ....36 C1
Gate End *NTHWD* HA6 ....32 E6
Gateforth St *STJWD* NW8 ....9 J1
Gatehill Rd *NTHWD* HA6 ....32 D6
Gatehouse Cl *KUTN/CMB* KT2 ..144 E6
Gate House Pl *WATW* WD18 ....20 D4
Gatehouse Sq *STHWK* SE1 * 12 F8
Gateley Rd *BRXN/ST* SW9 ....130 A2
Gate Ms *SKENS* SW7 ....15 K2
Gates Green Rd *WWKM* BR4 .....180 A5
Gateshead Rd *BORE* WD6 ....24 B1
Gateside Rd *TOOT* SW17 ....147 K2
Gatestone Rd *NRWD* SE19 ....150 A5
Gate St *LINN* WC2A 11 L4
Gateway *WALW* SE17 ....18 F9
Gateway Ar *IS* N1 * 6 C5
Gateway Cl *NTHWD* HA6 ....32 A6
Gateway Gdns *EHAM* E6 ....95 J2
Gateway Ms *FBAR/BDGN* N11 ....40 C5
  HACK E8 * 74 B4
The Gateways
  RCH/KEW TW9 * 124 E3
The Gateway *WATW* WD18 ....20 E3
Gatfield Gv *FELT* TW13 ....142 A1
Gathorne Rd *WDGN* N22 ....55 J5
Gathorne St *BETH* E2 ....93 F1
Gatley Av *HOR/WEW* KT19 ....172 D4
Gatliff Rd *BGVA* SW1W 16 B8
Gatling Rd *ABYW* SE2 ....116 B4
Gatonby St *PECK* SE15 ....111 G7
Gatton Cl *BELMT* SM2 ....175 F7
Gatton Rd *TOOT* SW17 ....147 J3
Gatward Cl *WCHMN* N21 ....29 H5
Gatward Gn *ED* N9 ....42 A1
Gatwick Rd *WAND/EARL* SW18 ..127 J6
Gauden Cl *CLAP* SW4 ....129 J2
Gauden Rd *CLAP* SW4 ....129 J1
Gaumont Ap *WAT* WD17 ....21 F2
Gaumont Ter *SHB* W12 * 107 F1
Gauntlet Cl *NTHLT* UB5 ....65 J6
Gauntlett Ct *ALP/SUD* HA0 ....67 G4
Gauntlett Rd *SUT* SM1 ....175 H4
Gaunt St *STHWK* SE1 ....18 D3
Gautrey Rd *PECK* SE15 ....131 K1
Gavel St *WALW* SE17 ....19 H5
Gaverick Ms *POP/IOD* E14 ....112 D3
Gavestone Crs *LEE/GVPK* SE12 .134 A6
Gavestone Rd *LEE/GVPK* SE12 .134 A6
Gavina Cl *MRDN* SM4 ....162 D4
Gawain Wk *ED* N9 ....42 D2
Gawber St *BETH* E2 ....92 E2
Gawsworth Cl *SRTFD* E15 ....76 D4
Gawthorne Av *MLHL* NW7 ....38 C4
Gay Cl *CRICK* NW2 ....69 K4
Gaydon La *CDALE/KGS* NW9 ......37 G7
Gayfere Rd *CLAY* IG5 ....59 K2
  EW KT17 ....173 J4
Gayfere St *WEST* SW1P 17 J4
Gayford Rd *SHB* W12 ....106 C1
Gay Gdns *DAGE* RM10 ....80 E3
Gayhurst Rd *HACK* E8 ....74 C6
Gaylor Rd *NTHLT* UB5 ....65 J4
Gaynesford Rd *CAR* SM5 ....175 K6
  FSTH SE23 ....151 F1
Gaynes Hill Rd *WFD* IG8 ....45 J6
Gay Rd *SRTFD* E15 ....94 B1
Gaysham Av *GNTH/NBYPK* IG2 ..60 A4
Gayton Crs *HAMP* NW3 ....71 H3
Gayton Rd *HAMP* NW3 ....71 H3
  HRW HA1 ....49 F5
  WOOL/PLUM SE18 ....115 K4
Gayville Rd *BTSEA* SW11 ....128 E5
Gaywood Cl
  BRXS/STRHM SW2 ....130 A7
Gaywood Rd *WALTH* E17 ....57 J2
Gaywood St *STHWK* SE1 ....18 C4
Gaza St *WALW* SE17 ....18 C8
Geariesville Gdns
  BARK/HLT IG6 ....60 B3
Gearing Cl *TOOT* SW17 ....148 A3
Geary Rd *WLSDN* NW10 ....69 J4
Geary St *HOLWY* N7 ....73 F4
Geddes Pl *BXLYHS* DA6 ....137 H3
Geddes Rd *BUSH* WD23 * 22 C3
Gedeney Rd *TOTM* N17 ....41 J7
Gedling Pl *STHWK* SE1 ....19 L3
Geere Rd *SRTFD* E15 ....76 D7
Gees Ct *MHST* W1U 10 B5
Gee St *FSBYE* EC1V 6 E9
Geffrye Est *IS* N1 * 7 K6
Geffrye St *BETH* E2 ....7 L5
Geldart Rd *PECK* SE15 ....111 J6
Geldeston Rd *CLPT* E5 ....74 C1
Gellatly Rd *NWCR* SE14 ....131 K1
General Gordon Pl
  WOOL/PLUM SE18 ....115 G3

General Wolfe Rd
  GNWCH SE10 ....113 G7
Genesis Cl *STWL/WRAY* TW19 ..120 C7
Genesta Rd *WOOL/PLUM* SE18 .115 G5
Geneva Dr *BRXN/ST* SW9 ....130 B3
Geneva Gdns *CHDH* RM6 ....62 A4
Geneva Rd *KUT/HW* KT1 ....159 F3
  THHTH CR7 ....164 D4
Genever Cl *CHING* E4 ....43 J4
Genoa Av *PUT/ROE* SW15 ....127 F4
Genoa Rd *PGE/AN* SE20 ....150 E7
Genotin Rd *EN* EN1 ....29 K2
Gentleman's Rw *ENC/FH* EN2 .....29 J1
Geoffrey Cl *CMBW* SE5 ....130 D1
Geoffrey Gdns *EHAM* E6 ....95 J1
Geoffrey Rd *BROCKY* SE4 ....132 C2
George Beard Rd *DEPT* SE8 ......112 C3
George Cl *WATW* WD18 ....20 C3
George Crs *MUSWH* N10 ....40 A6
George Downing Est
  STNW/STAM N16 * 74 B1
George Gange Wy
  KTN/HRWW/WS HA3 ....48 E2
George Groves Rd
  PGE/AN SE20 ....150 C7
George La *HAYES* BR2 ....168 A7
  LEW SE13 ....133 F5
  SWFD E18 ....58 E1
George Lowe Ct *BAY/PAD* W2 * ...8 C2
George Mathers Rd
  LBTH SE11 ....18 C6
George Ms *BRXN/ST* SW9 ....130 D1
  CAMTN NW1 ....4 D8
George Pl *CHING* E4 ....43 J5
  KUTN/CMB KT2 ....144 B6
  NWMAL KT3 ....160 C3
George Rw *BERM/RHTH* SE16 ...111 H1
Georges Md *BORE* WD6 ....24 A5
George Rd *HOLWY* N7 ....73 F5
  HOLWY N7 * 73 F4
George's Rd *HOLWY* N7 ....73 F4
George St *BARK* IG11 ....78 C6
  CROY/NA CR0 ....177 J1
  HNWL W7 ....84 E7
  HSLW TW3 ....122 E1
  MBLAR W1H 9 L4
  NWDGN UB2 ....102 D3
  RCH/KEW TW9 ....124 E4
  ROM RM1 ....63 H5
  WATW WD18 ....21 G3
Georgetown Cl *NRWD* SE19 ......150 A4
Georgette Pl *GNWCH* SE10 ....113 F6
George V Av *PIN* HA5 ....48 A3
Georgeville Gdns
  BARK/HLT IG6 ....60 B3
George V Wy *GFD/PVL* UB6 ....67 G1
George Wyver Cl
  WIM/MER SW19 ....127 H6
George Yd *BANK* EC3V 13 H5
  MYFR/PKLN W1K 10 B6
Georgiana Cl *CAMTN* NW1 * 4 F3
  STAN HA7 ....35 G6
Georgian Ct *WBLY* HA9 ....68 C5
Georgian Wy *HRW* HA1 ....66 D1
Georgia Rd *NWMAL* KT3 ....159 K3
  THHTH CR7 ....149 H7
Georgina Gdns *BETH* E2 * 7 M7
Geraint Rd *BMLY* BR1 ....152 E2
Geraldine Rd *CHSWK* W4 ....105 H5
  WAND/EARL SW18 ....128 B4
Geraldine St *LBTH* SE11 ....18 C4
Gerald Rd *BCTR* RM8 ....80 B1
  BGVA SW1W 16 B5
  CAN/RD E16 ....94 D3
Gerald Av *HSLWW* TW4 ....123 F6
Gerard Gdns *RAIN* RM13 ....99 G2
Gerard Rd *BARN* SW13 ....106 C7
  HRW HA1 ....49 G5
Gerards Cl *BERM/RHTH* SE16 ...111 K5
Gerda Rd *ELTH/MOT* SE9 ....154 C1
Germander Wy *SRTFD* E15 ....94 C2
Gernon Rd *BOW* E3 ....93 G1
Geron Wy *CRICK* NW2 ....70 A1
Gerrard Av *HSLWW* TW4 ....123 F6
Gerrard Gdns *PIN* HA5 ....46 E4
Gerrard Pl *SOHO/SHAV* W1D * ...11 H6
Gerrard Rd *IS* N1 ....6 C5
Gerrards Cl *STHGT/OAK* N14 .....28 C4
Gerrard St *SOHO/SHAV* W1D 11 H6
Gerridge St *STHWK* SE1 ....18 B2
Gertrude Rd *BELV* DA17 ....117 H3
Gertrude St *WBPTN* SW10 ....108 B5
Gervase Cl *WBLY* HA9 ....68 E2
Gervase Rd *EDGW* HA8 ....36 E7
Gervase St *PECK* SE15 ....111 J6
Ghent St *CAT* SE6 ....151 J1
Ghent Wy *HACK* E8 ....74 B5
Giant Arches Rd *HNHL* SE24 .....130 D6
Giant Tree Hl *BUSH* WD23 ....34 D1
Gibbfield Cl *CHDH* RM6 ....62 A2
Gibbins Rd *SRTFD* E15 ....76 A6
Gibbon Rd *ACT* W3 ....87 G6
  KUTN/CMB KT2 ....144 A7
  PECK SE15 ....131 K1
Gibbons La *DART* DA1 ....139 G5
Gibbons Ms *GLDGN* NW11 ....52 D4
Gibbons Rd *WLSDN* NW10 ....69 F5
Gibbon Wk *PUT/ROE* SW15 * ...126 D3
Gibbs Av *NRWD* SE19 ....149 K5
Gibbs Cl *NRWD* SE19 ....149 K4
Gibbs Couch *OXHEY* WD19 ....33 H2
Gibbs Gn *EDGW* HA8 ....36 E3
  WKENS W14 * 107 J4
Gibbs Green Cl *WKENS* W14 .....107 J4
Gibbs Rd *UED* N18 ....42 E3
Gibbs Sq *NRWD* SE19 ....149 K4
Gibraltar Wk *BETH* E2 ....7 M8
Gibson Cl *CHSGTN* KT9 ....171 J4
  ISLW TW7 ....123 J2
  WCHMN N21 ....29 G5
  WCHPL E1 ....92 E3
Gibson Gdns
  STNW/STAM N16 * 74 B1
Gibson Rd *BCTR* RM8 ....61 J7
  LBTH SE11 ....17 M6
  SUT SM1 ....175 F4
Gibson's Hl *STRHM/NOR* SW16 .149 G6
Gibson Sq *IS* N1 ....6 B3
Gibson St *GNWCH* SE10 ....113 H4
Gidea Av *GPK* RM2 ....63 J2
Gidea Cl *GPK* RM2 ....63 J2
Gideon Cl *BELV* DA17 ....117 J3
Gideon Ms *EA* W5 * 104 E1
Gideon Rd *BTSEA* SW11 ....129 F2
Gilbach Rd *ARCH* N19 ....72 D2
Giffard Rd *UED* N18 ....42 A4
Giffin St *DEPT* SE8 ....112 D6
Gifford Gdns *HNWL* W7 ....84 D4
Gifford Rd *WLSDN* NW10 ....69 G6
Gifford St *IS* N1 ....5 L1
Gift La *SRTFD* E15 ....76 C7
Giggs Hill Gdns *THDIT* KT7 ....158 B7
Giggs Hill Rd *THDIT* KT7 ....158 A6

Gilbert Cl *WIM/MER* SW19 * 147 F7
  WOOL/PLUM SE18 ....114 E7
Gilbert Gv *EDGW* HA8 ....36 E7
Gilbert Pl *NOXST/BSQ* WC1A * ...11 J3
Gilbert Rd *BELV* DA17 ....117 H2
  BMLY BR1 ....152 E6
  LBTH SE11 ....18 B6
  PIN HA5 ....47 H3
  ROM RM1 ....63 H4
  WIM/MER SW19 ....147 G6
Gilbert St *HSLW* TW3 ....123 H2
  MYFR/PKLN W1K 10 B5
  SRTFD E15 ....76 C3
Gilbert White Cl *GFD/PVL* UB6 ...67 G7
Gilbey Rd *TOOT* SW17 ....147 J3
Gilbeys Yd *CAMTN* NW1 * 4 B2
Gilbourne Rd
  WOOL/PLUM SE18 ....116 A5
Gilda Av *PEND* EN3 ....31 G4
Gilda Crs *STNW/STAM* N16 ....56 C7
Gilda Rd *PIN* HA5 * 34 A6
Gildea Cl *PIN* HA5 ....34 A6
Gildea St *GTPST* W1W 10 D3
Gildersome St
  WOOL/PLUM SE18 ....115 F5
Gilders Rd *CHSGTN* KT9 ....172 B5
Giles Coppice *NRWD* SE19 ....150 B3
Giles Crs *DUL* SE21 ....131 F5
Gilkes Pl *DUL* SE21 ....131 F5
Gillam Wy *RAIN* RM13 ....81 J5
Gillards Ms *WALTH* E17 * 57 J3
Gillards Wy *WALTH* E17 ....57 J3
Gill Av *CAN/RD* E16 ....94 E5
Gill Cl *WATW* WD18 ....20 A5
Gillender St *BOW* E3 ....94 A3
Gillespie Rd *HBRY* N5 ....73 G2
Gillett Av *EHAM* E6 ....95 J1
Gillett Pl *HACK* E8 * 74 A4
Gillett Rd *THHTH* CR7 ....164 E3
Gillett St *STNW/STAM* N16 ....74 A4
Gillham Ter *TOTM* N17 ....42 C5
Gillian Park Rd *CHEAM* SM3 .....161 J7
Gillian St *LEW* SE13 ....132 E4
Gillian Ter *BRYLDS* KT5 * 159 G5
Gillies St *KTTN* NW5 ....72 A4
Gillingham Rd *CRICK* NW2 ....70 C2
Gillingham Rw *PIM* SW1V * 16 E6
Gillingham St *PIM* SW1V 16 D6
Gillison Wk
  BERM/RHTH SE16 * 111 H2
Gilman Dr *SRTFD* E15 ....76 C7
Gilpin Cl *BAY/PAD* W2 * 8 C2
  MTCM CR4 ....162 D1
Gilmore Rd *LEW* SE13 ....133 G3
Gilpin Av *MORT/ESHN* SW14 ....126 A3
Gilpin Cl *BAY/PAD* W2 * 8 C2
  MTCM CR4 ....162 D1
Gilpin Crs *UED* N18 ....42 B4
  WHTN TW2 ....123 G6
Gilpin Rd *CLPT* E5 ....75 G3
Gilpin Wy *HYS/HAR* UB3 ....101 G6
Gilroy Cl *RAIN* RM13 ....81 J5
Gilsland Rd *THHTH* CR7 ....164 E3
Gilson Pl *MUSWH* N10 ....39 K4
Gilstead Rd *FUL/PGN* SW6 ....128 A1
Gilston Rd *WBPTN* SW10 ....108 B5
Gilton Rd *CAT* SE6 ....152 C2
Giltspur St *STBT* EC1A 12 D4
Gilwell Cl *CHING* E4 ....31 K3
Gippeswyck Cl *PIN* HA5 ....33 H7
Gipsy Hl *NRWD* SE19 ....150 B4
Gipsy La *PUT/ROE* SW15 ....126 D2
Gipsy Rd *WELL* DA16 ....136 E1
  WNWD SE27 ....149 K3
Gipsy Road Gdns *WNWD* SE27 ..149 J3
Giralda Cl *CAN/RD* E16 ....95 H4
Giraud St *POP/IOD* E14 ....93 K5
Girdlers Rd *WKENS* W14 ....107 H2
Girdwood Rd
  WAND/EARL SW18 ....127 H6
Girling Wy *EBED/NFELT* TW14 ..121 K2
Gironde Rd *FUL/PGN* SW6 ....107 J6
Girton Av *CDALE/KGS* NW9 ....50 C1
Girton Cl *NTHLT* UB5 ....66 C5
Girton Gdns *CROY/NA* CR0 ....179 J2
Girton Rd *NTHLT* UB5 ....66 C5
  SYD SE26 ....151 F4
Girton Wy *RKW/CH/CXG* WD3 ....20 A4
Gisbourne Cl *WLGTN* SM6 ....176 D2
Gisburn Rd *CEND/HSY/T* N8 ....55 F3
Gissing Wk *IS* N1 ....6 B1
Gittens Cl *BMLY* BR1 ....152 D3
Glacier Wy *ALP/SUD* HA0 ....85 K1
Gladbeck Wy *ENC/FH* EN2 ....29 H3
Gladding Rd *MNPK* E12 ....77 H3
Glade Cl *SURB* KT6 * 171 K1
Glade Gdns *CROY/NA* CR0 ....166 B6
Glade La *NWDGN* UB2 ....103 G1
Gladeside *CROY/NA* CR0 ....166 A6
  WCHMN N21 ....29 F6
Gladesmore Rd
  SEVS/STOTM N15 ....56 B5
The Glade *BELMT* SM2 ....174 C7
  BMLY BR1 ....168 C1
  CHARL SE7 ....114 B6
  CLAY IG5 ....45 K7
  CROY/NA CR0 ....166 B6
  ENC/FH EN2 ....29 G2
  EW KT17 ....173 J5
  HACK E8 * 74 B5
  NFNCH/WDSPK N12 * 39 H3
  SHB W12 ....106 E1
  WCHMN N21 ....29 F6
  WFD IG8 ....45 F2
  WWKM BR4 ....179 K2
Gladiator St *FSTH* SE23 ....132 B5
Glading Ter *STNW/STAM* N16 .....74 B2
Gladioli Cl *HPTN* TW12 ....142 A5
Gladsdale Dr *PIN* HA5 ....46 E3
Gladsmuir Rd *ARCH* N19 ....54 C7
  BAR EN5 ....26 C1
Gladstone Av
  EBED/NFELT TW14 ....121 K5
  MNPK E12 ....77 J6
  WDGN N22 ....55 H1
  WHTN TW2 ....123 H6
Gladstone Ms
  KIL/WHAMP NW6 * 70 D6
  PGE/AN SE20 * 150 E6
  WDGN N22 ....55 H1
Gladstone Pde *CRICK* NW2 * 70 A2
Gladstone Park Gdns
  CRICK NW2 ....69 K2
Gladstone Pl *BAR* EN5 ....26 B3
  E/WMO/HCT KT8 * 157 K4
Gladstone Rd *CHSWK* W4 ....106 A2
  CROY/NA CR0 ....164 E6
  DART DA1 ....139 J5
  KUT/HW KT1 ....159 H2
  NWDGN UB2 ....102 D3
  SURB KT6 ....171 K1

WAT WD17 .... 21 G2
WIM/MER SW19 .... 146 E6
Gladstone St STHWK SE1 .... 18 C5
Gladstone Ter VX/NE SW8 * 109 G7
WNWD SE27 * 149 J3
Gladstone Wy
KTN/HRWW/WS HA3 .... 48 G2
Gladwell Rd BMLY BR1 .... 152 E3
CEND/HSY/T N8 .... 55 E2
Gladwyn Rd PUT/ROE SW15 .... 127 G2
Gladys Rd KIL/WHAMP NW6 .... 2 B1
Glaisher St DEPT SE8 .... 112 D5
Glamis Crs HYS/HAR UB3 .... 101 F2
Glamis Rd WAP E1W 92 E6
Glamis Wy NTHLT UB5 .... 66 C5
Glamorgan Cl MTCM CR4 .... 163 K2
Glamorgan Rd KUT/HW KT1 .... 143 J6
Glandford Wy CHDH RM6 .... 61 H4
Glanfield Rd BECK BR3 .... 166 C3
Glanleam Rd STAN HA7 .... 35 K3
Glanville Ms STAN HA7 .... 35 K3
Glanville Rd
BRXS/STRHM SW2 .... 129 K4
HAYES BR2 .... 168 A3
Glasbrook Av WHTN TW2 .... 122 E7
Glasbrook Rd ELTH/MOT SE9 .... 134 C6
Glaserton Rd
STNW/STAM N16 .... 56 A6
Glasford St TOOT SW17 .... 147 K5
Glasgow Rd PLSTW E13 .... 95 F1
UED N18 .... 42 D4
Glasgow Ter PIM SW1V 16 E8
Glaskin Ms HOM E9 .... 75 G5
Glasse Cl WEA W13 .... 85 G6
Glasshill St STHWK SE1 .... 18 C1
Glasshouse Flds WAP E1W 93 F6
Glasshouse St REGST W1B 10 C6
Glasshouse Wk LBTH SE11 .... 17 K7
Glasshouse Yd FARR EC1M 12 C1
Glasslyn Rd CEND/HSY/T N8 .... 54 D4
Glassmill La HAYES BR2 .... 167 J1
Glass St BETH E2 * 92 D3
Glass Yd WOOL/PLUM SE18 .... 115 F2
Glastonbury Av WFD IG8 .... 45 H6
Glastonbury Pl WCHPL E1 * 92 E5
Glastonbury Rd ED N9 .... 30 C7
MRDN SM4 .... 161 K5
Glastonbury St
KIL/WHAMP NW6 .... 70 D4
Glaston Ct EA W5 * 85 K7
Glaucus St BOW E3 .... 93 K4
Glazbury Rd WKENS W14 .... 107 H3
Glazebrook Rd DUL SE21 .... 149 K1
Glebe Av ENC/FH EN2 .... 29 H2
HGDN/ICK UB10 .... 64 A3
KTN/HRWW/WS HA3 .... 50 A2
MTCM CR4 .... 162 D1
RSLP HA4 .... 65 F5
WFD IG8 .... 44 E5
Glebe Cl CHSWK W4 * 106 B4
HGDN/ICK UB10 .... 64 A3
Glebe Ct BKHTH/KID SE3 * 133 H2
EA W5 .... 85 K7
STAN HA7 .... 35 J4
Glebe Crs HDN NW4 .... 52 A3
KTN/HRWW/WS HA3 .... 50 A2
Glebe Gdns NWMAL KT3 .... 160 B6
Glebe House Dr HAYES BR2 .... 168 A7
Glebelands DART DA1 .... 138 C3
E/WMO/HCT KT8 .... 157 G4
ESH/CLAY KT10 .... 171 F7
Glebelands Av
GNTH/NBYPK IG2 .... 60 D6
SWFD E18 .... 58 E1
Glebelands Cl CMBW SE5 .... 131 F2
NFNCH/WDSPK N12 .... 39 F1
Glebelands Rd
EBED/NFELT TW14 .... 121 K6
Glebe La BAR EN5 .... 25 J4
KTN/HRWW/WS HA3 .... 50 A3
Glebe Pth MTCM CR4 .... 162 E2
Glebe Pl CHEL SW3 .... 15 J9
Glebe Rd BARN SW13 .... 126 D1
BELMT SM2 .... 174 E7
BMLY BR1 .... 152 E7
CAR SM5 .... 175 K5
CEND/HSY/T N8 .... 55 F3
DAGE RM10 .... 80 D5
FNCH N3 .... 39 G7
HACK E8 * 7 L1
RAIN RM13 .... 99 K2
STAN HA7 .... 35 J4
WLSDN NW10 .... 69 J5
Glebe Side TWK TW1 .... 124 A5
Glebe Sq MTCM CR4 * 162 E2
Glebe St CHSWK W4 .... 106 A4
The Glebe BKHTH/KID SE3 * 133 H2
CHST BR7 .... 154 C7
STRHM/NOR SW16 * 148 D4
WDR/YW UB7 .... 100 C3
WPK KT4 .... 160 C7
Glebe Wy ERITH DA8 .... 118 B5
FELT TW13 .... 142 A4
Glebeway WFD IG8 .... 45 G4
Glebe Wy WWKM BR4 .... 180 A1
Gledhow Gdns ECT SW5 .... 14 B6
Gledstanes Rd WKENS W14 .... 107 H4
Gledwood Av YEAD UB4 .... 82 E4
Gledwood Crs YEAD UB4 .... 82 D4
Gledwood Dr YEAD UB4 .... 82 D4
Gledwood Gdns YEAD UB4 .... 82 E4
Gleed Av BUSH WD23 .... 34 D1
Glegg Pl PUT/ROE SW15 * 127 G3
Glenaffric Av POP/IOD E14 .... 113 F3
Glen Albyn Rd
WIM/MER SW19 .... 146 B1
Glenalla Rd RSLP HA4 .... 46 D6
Glenalmond Rd
KTN/HRWW/WS HA3 .... 50 A3
Glenalvon Wy
WOOL/PLUM SE18 .... 114 D3
Glena Mt SUT SM1 .... 175 G3
Glenarm Rd CLPT E5 .... 74 E3
Glenavon Cl ESH/CLAY KT10 .... 171 G6
Glenavon Rd SRTFD E15 .... 76 C6
Glenbarr Cl ELTH/MOT SE9 .... 135 G2
Glenbow Rd BMLY BR1 .... 152 C5
Glenbrook North ENC/FH EN2 .... 29 F3
Glenbrook Rd
KIL/WHAMP NW6 .... 70 D4
Glenbrook South ENC/FH EN2 .... 29 F3
Glenbuck Rd SURB KT6 .... 158 E5
Glenburnie Rd TOOT SW17 .... 147 K2
Glencairn Dr EA W5 .... 85 H3
Glencairn Cl CAN/RD E16 .... 95 H4
Glencairn Rd
STRHM/NOR SW16 .... 148 E6
Glencoe Av GNTH/NBYPK IG2 .... 60 D6
Glencoe Dr DAGE RM10 .... 80 C3
DAGE RM10 .... 80 C3
YEAD UB4 .... 83 H3
Glencorse Gn OXHEY WD19 * 33 H3

Glen Crs WFD IG8 .... 45 F5
Glendale Av CHDH RM6 .... 61 J6
WDGN N22 .... 41 G6
Glendale Cl ELTH/MOT SE9 .... 135 F2
Glendale Dr WIM/MER SW19 .... 146 D4
Glendale Gdns WBLY HA9 .... 49 K7
Glendale Ms BECK BR3 .... 151 K1
Glendale Rd ERITH DA8 .... 117 K3
Glendale Wy THMD SE28 .... 97 J7
Glendall St BRXN/ST SW9 .... 130 A2
Glendarvon St PUT/ROE SW15 .... 127 G2
Glendevon Cl EDGW HA8 .... 36 D2
Glendish Rd TOTM N17 .... 42 C7
Glendor Gdns MLHL NW7 .... 37 F3
Glendower Gdns
MORT/ESHN SW14 .... 126 A2
Glendower Pl SKENS SW7 .... 15 G5
Glendown Rd ABYW SE2 .... 116 B4
Glendun Rd ACT W3 .... 87 G6
Gleneagle Ms
STRHM/NOR SW16 .... 148 D4
Gleneagle Rd
STRHM/NOR SW16 .... 148 D4
Gleneagles STAN HA7 .... 35 H5
Gleneagles Cl
BERM/RHTH SE16 * 111 J4
ORP BR6 .... 169 J7
OXHEY WD19 * 33 H4
Gleneldon Ms
STRHM/NOR SW16 .... 148 E3
Gleneldon Rd
STRHM/NOR SW16 .... 148 E3
Glenelg Rd BRXS/STRHM SW2 .... 129 K4
Glenesk Rd ELTH/MOT SE9 .... 135 F2
Glenfarg Rd CAT SE6 .... 133 G7
Glenfield Crs RSLP HA4 .... 46 B6
Glenfield Rd BAL SW12 .... 129 H7
WEA W13 .... 104 C1
Glenfinlas Wy CMBW SE5 .... 110 C6
Glenforth St GNWCH SE10 .... 113 J5
Glengall Br POP/IOD E14 .... 112 E2
Glengall Gv POP/IOD E14 .... 112 E2
Glengall Pas KIL/WHAMP NW6 .... 2 B1
Glengall Rd BXLYHN DA7 .... 137 F2
EDGW HA8 .... 36 D2
KIL/WHAMP NW6 .... 70 D1
PECK SE15 .... 19 M9
WFD IG8 .... 44 E5
Glengall Ter PECK SE15 .... 19 M9
Glen Gdns CROY/NA CR0 .... 177 G2
Glengarnock Av POP/IOD E14 .... 113 F3
Glengarry Rd EDUL SE22 .... 131 F3
Glenham Dr GNTH/NBYPK IG2 .... 60 B4
Glenhaven Av BORE WD6 .... 24 C2
Glenhead Cl ELTH/MOT SE9 .... 135 G2
Glenhill Cl FNCH N3 .... 52 E1
Glenhouse Rd ELTH/MOT SE9 .... 135 F4
Glenhurst Av BXLY DA5 .... 137 G7
KTTN NW5 .... 72 A3
RSLP HA4 .... 46 A6
Glenhurst Ri NRWD SE19 .... 149 J6
Glenhurst Rd BTFD TW8 .... 104 D5
NFNCH/WDSPK N12 .... 39 H3
Glenilla Rd HAMP NW3 .... 71 J5
Glenister Park Rd
STRHM/NOR SW16 .... 148 D6
Glenister Rd GNWCH SE10 .... 113 J4
Glenlea Rd ELTH/MOT SE9 .... 135 F4
Glenloch Rd HAMP NW3 .... 71 J5
PEND EN3 .... 30 E1
Glenluge Rd BKHTH/KID SE3 .... 113 K5
Glenlyon Rd ELTH/MOT SE9 .... 135 F4
Glenmere Av MLHL NW7 .... 37 J6
Glenmere Rw LEE/GVPK SE12 .... 133 K5
Glen Ms WALTH E17 * 57 H4
Glenmill HPTN TW12 .... 141 K4
Glenmore Lawns WEA W13 * 85 G5
Glenmore Pde ALP/SUD HA0 * 68 A2
Glenmore Rd HAMP NW3 .... 71 J5
WELL DA16 .... 116 A7
Glenmore Wy BARK IG11 .... 97 G2
Glennie Rd WNWD SE27 .... 149 G2
Glenny Rd BARK IG11 .... 78 C5
Glenorchy Cl YEAD UB4 .... 83 J4
Glenparke Rd FSTGT E7 .... 77 F5
Glen Ri WFD IG8 .... 45 F5
Glen Rd CHSGTN KT9 .... 172 A3
PLSTW E13 .... 95 G3
WALTH E17 .... 57 H4
Glen Road End WLGTN SM6 .... 176 B7
Glenrosa St FUL/PGN SW6 .... 128 B1
Glenroy St SHB W12 .... 88 A3
Glensdale Rd BROCKY SE4 .... 132 C2
Glenshiel Rd ELTH/MOT SE9 .... 135 F4
Glentanner Wy TOOT SW17 .... 147 H2
Glentham Cots BARN SW13 * 106 D5
Glentham Gdns BARN SW13 .... 106 E4
Glentham Rd BARN SW13 .... 106 D5
The Glen BELMT SM2 * 175 G5
CROY/NA CR0 .... 179 F2
ENC/FH EN2 .... 29 H1
HAYES BR2 .... 182 B6
NTHWD HA6 .... 46 A2
NWDGN UB2 .... 102 E4
ORP BR6 .... 181 K2
PIN HA5 .... 47 H4
WBLY HA9 .... 67 K3
Glenthorne Av CROY/NA CR0 .... 165 K7
Glenthorne Cl CHEAM SM3 .... 161 K7
Glenthorne Gdns
BARK/HLT IG6 .... 60 A2
CHEAM SM3 .... 161 K7
Glenthorne Rd
FBAR/BDGN N11 .... 39 K4
HMSMTH W6 .... 106 E3
KUT/HW KT1 .... 159 G3
WALTH E17 .... 57 G4
Glenthorpe Rd MRDN SM4 .... 161 G4
Glenton Rd LEW SE13 .... 133 H3
Glentworth St CAMTN NW1 .... 9 M1
Glenure Rd ELTH/MOT SE9 .... 135 F4
Glenview ABYW SE2 .... 116 E5
Glen View Rd BMLY BR1 .... 168 C1
Glenville Gv DEPT SE8 .... 112 C6
Glenville Ms
WAND/EARL SW18 .... 128 A6
Glenville Rd KUTN/CMB KT2 .... 144 C7
Glenwood Av
CDALE/KGS NW9 .... 51 G7
RAIN RM13 .... 99 J3
Glenwood Cl HRW HA1 .... 49 F4
Glenwood Dr GPK RM2 .... 63 K3
Glenwood Gdns
GNTH/NBYPK IG2 .... 60 A4
Glenwood Gv
CDALE/KGS NW9 .... 50 E7
Glenwood Rd CAT SE6 .... 132 C7
EW KT17 .... 173 J5
HSLW TW3 .... 123 J2
MLHL NW7 .... 37 G2

SEVS/STOTM N15 .... 55 H4
Glenwood Rw NRWD SE19 * 150 B7
Glenwood Wy CROY/NA CR0 .... 166 A5
Glenworth Av POP/IOD E14 .... 113 G3
Gliddon Rd WKENS W14 .... 107 H3
Glimpsing Gn ERITH DA18 .... 117 F2
Globe Pond Rd
BERM/RHTH SE16 .... 93 G7
Globe Rd BETH E2 .... 92 E2
EMPK RM11 .... 63 J5
SRTFD E15 .... 76 D4
WCHPL E1 .... 92 E2
WFD IG8 .... 45 G5
Globe St STHWK SE1 .... 19 G2
Globe Ter BETH E2 * 92 E2
Glossop Rd SAND/SEL CR2 .... 177 K7
Gloster Rd NWMAL KT3 .... 160 B3
Gloucester Av BFN/LL DA15 .... 154 E1
CAMTN NW1 .... 4 C1
WELL DA16 .... 136 A4
Gloucester Circ GNWCH SE10 .... 113 F6
Gloucester Cl THDIT KT7 * 158 B7
WLSDN NW10 .... 69 F6
Gloucester Ct MTCM CR4 * 163 K4
RCH/KEW TW9 * 105 H6
TWRH EC3N * 13 K7
Gloucester Crs CAMTN NW1 .... 4 C3
Gloucester Dr FSBYPK N4 .... 73 H1
GLDGN NW11 .... 52 E3
Gloucester Gdns BAY/PAD W2 .... 8 A5
EBAR EN4 .... 28 A3
GLDGN NW11 .... 52 D6
IL IG1 .... 59 J6
SUT SM1 .... 175 F1
Gloucester Ga CAMTN NW1 * 4 C5
Gloucester Gate Ms
CAMTN NW1 * 4 C5
Gloucester Gv EDGW HA8 .... 37 F7
Gloucester Ms BAY/PAD W2 .... 8 C5
LEY E10 .... 57 J6
Gloucester Ms West
BAY/PAD W2 .... 8 B5
Gloucester Pde
BFN/LL DA15 * 136 B4
HYS/HAR UB3 * 101 F2
Gloucester Pl CAMTN NW1 .... 3 L9
MHST W1U 9 M3
Gloucester Place Ms
MHST W1U 9 M4
Gloucester Rd ACT W3 .... 105 K1
BAR EN5 .... 27 F4
BELV DA17 .... 117 G4
CROY/NA CR0 .... 164 E6
DART DA1 .... 138 E5
EA W5 .... 104 D1
FELT TW13 .... 122 D7
HPTN TW12 .... 142 B6
HRW HA1 .... 48 B4
HSLWW TW4 .... 122 D3
KUT/HW KT1 .... 159 H4
LEY E10 .... 57 J6
MNPK E12 .... 77 K2
RCH/KEW TW9 .... 105 H6
ROM RM1 .... 63 G5
SKENS SW7 .... 14 E5
TEDD TW11 .... 142 E4
TOTM N17 .... 55 K1
UED N18 .... 42 B4
WALTH E17 .... 57 F1
WAN E11 .... 59 F4
WHTN TW2 .... 123 J7
Gloucester Sq BAY/PAD W2 .... 9 H5
BETH E2 * 74 C7
Gloucester St PIM SW1V 16 E7
Gloucester Ter BAY/PAD W2 .... 8 C4
STHGT/OAK N14 * 28 D7
Gloucester Wk KENS W8 .... 14 B1
Gloucester Wy CLKNW EC1R 6 B8
Glover Cl ABYW SE2 .... 116 D3
Glover Dr UED N18 .... 42 E5
Glover Rd PIN HA5 .... 47 H5
Glycena Rd BTSEA SW11 .... 128 E2
Glyn Av EBAR EN4 .... 27 J3
Glyn Cl EW KT17 .... 173 J7
SNWD SE25 .... 165 F1
Glyn Ct STAN HA7 .... 35 H5
Glynde Ms CHEL SW3 .... 15 K4
Glynde Rd BXLYHN DA7 .... 136 E2
Glynde St BROCKY SE4 .... 132 C5
Glyndon Rd WOOL/PLUM SE18 .... 115 H4
Glyn Dr SCUP DA14 .... 155 H3
Glynfield Rd WLSDN NW10 .... 69 G6
Glynne Rd WDGN N22 .... 55 G1
Glyn Rd CLPT E5 .... 75 F3
PEND EN3 .... 30 E3
WPK KT4 .... 174 B1
Glyn St LBTH SE11 .... 17 L8
Glynwood Ct FSTH SE23 .... 150 E1
Goat Rd MTCM CR4 .... 163 F6
Goat Whf BTFD TW8 .... 105 F5
Godalming Av WLGTN SM6 .... 176 E4
Godalming Rd POP/IOD E14 .... 93 K4
Godbold Rd SRTFD E15 .... 94 C3
Goddard Dr BUSH WD23 .... 22 B3
Goddard Pl ARCH N19 .... 72 C2
Goddard Rd BECK BR3 .... 166 A3
Goddards Wy IL IG1 .... 60 D7
Godfrey Hl WOOL/PLUM SE18 .... 114 E3
Godfrey Rd WOOL/PLUM SE18 .... 114 E3
Godfrey St CHEL SW3 .... 15 K7
SRTFD E15 .... 94 A1
Godfrey Wy HSLWW TW4 .... 122 D6
Goding St LBTH SE11 .... 17 K8
Godley Rd WAND/EARL SW18 .... 128 C7
Godliman St BLKFR EC4V 12 D5
Godman Rd PECK SE15 .... 131 J1
Godolphin Cl PLMGR N13 .... 41 H5
Godolphin Pl ACT W3 .... 87 F6
Godolphin Rd SHB W12 .... 87 K7
Godric Crs CROY/NA CR0 .... 180 B7
Godson Rd CROY/NA CR0 .... 177 G2
Godson St IS N1 .... 6 A5
Godstone Rd SUT SM1 .... 175 G3
TWK TW1 .... 124 B5
Godstone Rd ABYW SE2 .... 116 E5
Godwin Cl HOR/WEW KT19 .... 172 E5
IS N1 .... 7 H5
Godwin Rd BMLY BR1 .... 168 B2
FSTGT E7 .... 77 F3
Goffers Rd BKHTH/KID SE3 .... 113 H7
Goffs Rd ASHF TW15 .... 140 B5
Goidel Cl WLGTN SM6 .... 176 D3
Golborne Gdns NKENS W10 * 88 C3
Golborne Ms NKENS W10 .... 88 C4
Golborne Rd NKENS W10 .... 88 C4
Golda Cl BAR EN5 .... 26 B5
Goldbeaters Gv EDGW HA8 .... 37 F6
Goldcliff Cl MRDN SM4 .... 161 K6
Golden Ct CAN/RD E16 .... 95 H4
THMD SE28 .... 97 J6
Goldcrest Ms EA W5 * 85 K4

Goldcrest Wy BUSH WD23 .... 22 C7
CROY/NA CR0 .... 180 B7
Golden Ct HSLW TW3 .... 123 J1
Golden Crs HYS/HAR UB3 .... 82 C7
Golden Cross Ms NTGHL W11 * 88 D5
Golden Hind Pl DEPT SE8 * 112 C3
Golden Jubilee Br STHWK SE1 .... 11 J8
Golden La STLK EC1Y 6 E9
Golden Lane Est STLK EC1Y 12 E1
Golden Mnr HNWL W7 .... 84 E6
Golden Pde WALTH E17 * 58 A2
Golden Plover Cl CAN/RD E16 .... 94 E5
Golden Sq SOHO/CST W1F 10 F6
Golden Yd HAMP NW3 * 71 G3
Golders Cl EDGW HA8 .... 36 D4
Golders Gdns GLDGN NW11 .... 52 C6
Golders Green Crs
GLDGN NW11 .... 52 D6
Golders Green Rd
GLDGN NW11 .... 52 C5
Golders Hl HAMP NW3 * 71 F1
Golderslea GLDGN NW11 * 52 D7
Golders Manor Dr
GLDGN NW11 .... 52 B5
Golders Park Cl GLDGN NW11 .... 52 E6
Golders Ri HDN NW4 .... 52 B4
Golders Wy GLDGN NW11 .... 52 D6
Goldfinch Rd THMD SE28 .... 115 J2
Goldfinch Wy BORE WD6 .... 24 C3
Goldhawk Ms SHB W12 .... 106 E1
Goldhawk Rd HMSMTH W6 .... 106 C3
SHB W12 .... 106 D2
Goldhaze Cl WFD IG8 .... 45 G6
Gold Hl EDGW HA8 .... 37 F5
Goldhurst Ter
KIL/WHAMP NW6 .... 2 D2
Golding St WCHPL E1 .... 92 C5
Goldington Crs CAMTN NW1 .... 4 C5
Goldington St CAMTN NW1 .... 5 G5
Gold La EDGW HA8 .... 37 F5
Goldman Cl BETH E2 .... 92 C3
Goldney Rd MV/WKIL W9 .... 8 A1
Goldrill Dr FBAR/BDGN N11 .... 40 A1
Goldsboro Rd VX/NE SW8 .... 109 J7
Goldsborough Crs CHING E4 .... 43 K1
Goldsdown Cl PEND EN3 .... 31 G1
Goldsdown Rd PEND EN3 .... 31 F1
Goldsmid St
WOOL/PLUM SE18 .... 115 K4
Goldsmith Av ACT W3 .... 87 F6
CDALE/KGS NW9 .... 51 G4
MNPK E12 .... 77 J5
ROMW/RG RM7 .... 62 C6
Goldsmith Cl
RYLN/HDSTN HA2 .... 48 A7
Goldsmith La CDALE/KGS NW9 .... 50 E3
Goldsmith Pl
KIL/WHAMP NW6 * 2 C1
Goldsmith Rd
FBAR/BDGN N11 .... 39 K4
LEY E10 .... 57 K7
PECK SE15 .... 111 H7
WALTH E17 .... 57 F1
Goldsmith's Cl ACT W3 * 87 F7
Goldsmith's Rw BETH E2 .... 92 C1
Goldsmith St CITYW EC2V 12 F4
Goldsworthy Gdns
BERM/RHTH SE16 .... 111 K3
Goldwell Rd THHTH CR7 .... 164 A3
Goldwing Cl CAN/RD E16 .... 94 E5
Golf Cl BUSH WD23 .... 21 H2
STAN HA7 .... 35 J6
THHTH CR7 .... 149 G7
Golf Club Dr KUTN/CMB KT2 .... 145 F6
Golfe Rd IL IG1 .... 78 D2
Golf Rd BMLY BR1 .... 169 F2
EA W5 * 86 B5
Golf Side WHTN TW2 .... 142 D2
Golf Side NWMAL KT3 .... 160 A2
Golfside Cl TRDG/WHET N20 .... 39 J2
Gollogly Ter CHARL SE7 .... 114 B4
Gomer Gdns TEDD TW11 .... 143 G5
Gomer Pl TEDD TW11 .... 143 G5
Gomm Rd BERM/RHTH SE16 .... 111 K2
Gomshall Av WLGTN SM6 .... 176 E4
Gondar Gdns CRICK NW2 .... 70 D4
Gonson St DEPT SE8 .... 112 E5
Gonston Cl WIM/MER SW19 .... 146 B1
Gonville Crs NTHLT UB5 .... 66 B5
Gonville Rd THHTH CR7 .... 164 A4
Gonville St FUL/PGN SW6 .... 127 H2
Goodall Rd WAN E11 .... 76 A2
Gooden Ct HRW HA1 .... 66 E2
Goodenough Rd
WIM/MER SW19 .... 146 D6
Goodey Rd BARK IG11 .... 79 F6
Goodge Pl FITZ W1T 10 E3
Goodge St FITZ W1T 10 F3
Goodhall Cl STAN HA7 .... 35 G5
Goodhall St WLSDN NW10 .... 87 G2
Goodhart Wy WWKM BR4 .... 167 H7
Goodhew Rd CROY/NA CR0 .... 165 H5
Gooding Cl NWMAL KT3 .... 159 K3
Goodinge Cl HOLWY N7 .... 72 E5
Goodinge Rd HOLWY N7 .... 72 E5
Goodison Cl BUSH WD23 .... 22 B3
Goodman Crs
BRXS/STRHM SW2 .... 148 D1
CROY/NA CR0 .... 164 C5
Goodman Rd LEY E10 .... 58 A6
Goodmans Ct ALP/SUD HA0 * 67 K3
Goodman's Yd TWRH EC3N 13 L6
Goodmayes Av
GDMY/SEVK IG3 .... 61 G7
Goodmayes La
GDMY/SEVK IG3 .... 79 G1
Goodmayes Rd
GDMY/SEVK IG3 .... 61 G7
Goodrich Rd EDUL SE22 .... 131 G5
Goodson Rd WLSDN NW10 .... 69 G6
Goods Wy KCROSS N1C5 .... 5 J5
Goodwin Cl MTCM CR4 .... 162 C2
Goodwin Dr SCUP DA14 .... 155 K1
Goodwin Gdns CROY/NA CR0 .... 177 H5
Goodwin Rd CROY/NA CR0 .... 177 H5
ED N9 .... 30 E7
SHB W12 .... 106 D1
Goodwins Ct CHCR WC2N 11 J6
Goodwin St FSBYPK N4 .... 73 G1
Goodwood Cl MRDN SM4 .... 161 K3
Goodwood Dr NTHLT UB5 .... 66 A5
Goodwood Pde BECK BR3 .... 166 B3
Goodwood Rd NWCR SE14 .... 112 B6
Goodwyn Av MLHL NW7 .... 37 G5
Goodwyn's Vd MUSWH N10 .... 40 A7
Goodyers Gdns HDN NW4 .... 52 B4
Goosander Wy THMD SE28 .... 115 J2
Gooseacre La
KTN/HRWW/WS HA3 .... 49 K4

Gooseley La EHAM E6 .... 96 A2
Goossens Cl SUT SM1 * 175 G4
Gophir La CANST EC4R * 13 G6
Gopsall St IS N1 .... 7 H4
Gordon Av CHING E4 .... 44 C5
HCH RM12 .... 81 H1
MORT/ESHN SW14 .... 126 B3
STAN HA7 .... 35 F5
TWK TW1 .... 124 C4
Gordonbrock Rd BROCKY SE4 .... 132 D4
Gordon Cl WALTH E17 .... 57 J5
Gordon Crs CROY/NA CR0 .... 165 F7
HYS/HAR UB3 .... 101 K3
Gordondale Rd
WIM/MER SW19 .... 146 E1
Gordon Gdns EDGW HA8 .... 50 D1
Gordon Gv CMBW SE5 .... 130 C1
Gordon House Rd KTTN NW5 .... 72 A3
Gordon Pl KENS W8 .... 14 B1
Gordon Rd BARK IG11 .... 78 E7
BECK BR3 .... 166 C2
BELV DA17 .... 117 K3
BFN/LL DA15 .... 135 K4
BRYLDS KT5 .... 159 H5
CAR SM5 .... 175 K5
CHDH RM6 .... 61 J5
CHSWK W4 .... 105 J5
DART DA1 .... 139 G6
EA W5 .... 85 J6
ED N9 .... 42 D1
ESH/CLAY KT10 .... 170 E6
FBAR/BDGN N11 .... 40 D5
FNCH N3 .... 38 D6
HYS/HAR UB3 .... 82 D5
IL IG1 .... 78 D2
KTN/HRWW/WS HA3 .... 48 E2
KIL/CMB KT2 .... 144 B7
NWDGN UB2 .... 102 D3
PECK SE15 .... 131 J1
RCH/KEW TW9 .... 125 G3
SRTFD E15 .... 76 A3
SWFD E18 .... 45 F7
WAN E11 .... 58 E5
Gordon Sq STPAN WC1H 5 G9
STPAN WC1H 5 G9
Gordon St PLSTW E13 .... 94 E2
STPAN WC1H 5 G9
Gordon Wy BAR EN5 .... 26 D3
BMLY BR1 .... 152 E7
Gorefield Pl KIL/WHAMP NW6 .... 2 A5
Gore Rd HOM E9 .... 74 E7
RYNPK SW20 .... 161 F1
Goresbrook Rd DAGW RM9 .... 79 J7
Gore St SKENS SW7 .... 14 F3
Gorham Pl NTGHL W11 .... 88 C6
Goring Gdns BCTR RM8 .... 79 J3
Goring Rd DAGE RM10 .... 81 F5
FBAR/BDGN N11 * 40 E5
Goring St HDTCH EC3A 13 K4
Goring Wy GFD/PVL UB6 .... 84 C1
Gorleston Rd
SEVS/STOTM N15 .... 55 K4
Gorleston St WKENS W14 .... 107 H3
Gorman Rd WOOL/PLUM SE18 .... 114 E3
Gorringe Park Av MTCM CR4 .... 148 A6
Gorse Cl CAN/RD E16 .... 94 E5
Gorse Ri TOOT SW17 .... 148 A4
Gorse Rd CROY/NA CR0 .... 179 J2
Gorseway ROMW/RG RM7 .... 63 G7
Gorst Rd BTSEA SW11 .... 128 E5
WLSDN NW10 .... 86 E3
Gosberton Rd BAL SW12 .... 128 E7
Gosbury Hl CHSGTN KT9 .... 172 A3
Gosfield Rd BCTR RM8 .... 62 C7
Gosfield St GTPST W1W 10 D2
Gosford Gdns REDBR IG4 .... 59 K4
Gosforth La OXHEY WD19 .... 32 E2
Gosforth Pth OXHEY WD19 .... 32 D2
Goshawk Gdns YEAD UB4 .... 82 C2
Goslett Yd SOHO/SHAV W1D 11 H4
Gosling Cl GFD/PVL UB6 .... 84 A2
Gosling Wy BRXN/ST SW9 .... 110 B7
Gospatrick Rd TOTM N17 .... 41 J6
Gosport Rd WALTH E17 .... 57 H4
Gosport Wy PECK SE15 .... 111 G6
Gossage Rd WOOL/PLUM SE18 .... 115 J4
Gosset St BETH E2 .... 92 C2
Gosshill Rd BMLY BR1 .... 169 F1
Gossington Cl CHST BR7 .... 154 B3
Gosterwood St DEPT SE8 .... 112 B5
Gostling Rd WHTN TW2 .... 123 F7
Goston Gdns THHTH CR7 .... 164 B2
Goswell Pl FSBYE EC1V 6 C8
Goswell Rd FSBYE EC1V 6 D7
Gothic Cl HYS/HAR UB3 .... 101 K3
Gothic Rd WHTN TW2 .... 142 D1
Gottfried Ms KTTN NW5 .... 72 C3
Goudhurst Rd BMLY BR1 .... 152 C4
Gough Rd EN EN1 .... 30 D1
SRTFD E15 .... 76 D3
Gough Sq FLST/FETLN EC4A 12 B4
Gough St FSBYW WC1X 5 M9
Goulding Gdns THHTH CR7 .... 164 C1
Gould Rd EBED/NFELT TW14 .... 121 H4
WHTN TW2 .... 123 K7
Gould Ter HACK E8 * 74 D4
Goulston St WCHPL E1 .... 13 L4
Goulton Rd CLPT E5 .... 74 E3
Gourley Pl SEVS/STOTM N15 .... 56 A4
Gourley St SEVS/STOTM N15 .... 56 A4
Gourock Rd ELTH/MOT SE9 .... 135 F4
Govan St BETH E2 .... 74 C7
Govier Cl SRTFD E15 .... 76 C6
Gowan Av FUL/PGN SW6 .... 107 H7
Gowan Rd WLSDN NW10 .... 69 K6
Gower Cl CLAP SW4 .... 129 H5
Gower Ms GWRST WC1E 11 H3
Gower Pl GWRST WC1E 4 F9
Gower Rd FSTGT E7 .... 76 E5
ISLW TW7 .... 104 A5
Gower St GWRST WC1E 11 G1
Gower's Wk WCHPL E1 .... 92 C5
Gowland Pl BECK BR3 .... 166 C1
Gowlett Rd PECK SE15 .... 131 H2
Gowrie Rd BTSEA SW11 .... 129 F2
Gowrie Rd CROY/NA CR0 .... 165 H6
Graburn Wy E/WMO/HCT KT8 .... 157 J2
Grace Av BXLYHN DA7 .... 137 G1
Gracechurch St BANK EC3V 13 H6
Grace Cl EDGW HA8 .... 36 B7
ELTH/MOT SE9 .... 153 H2
Gracedale Rd
STRHM/NOR SW16 .... 148 B4
Gracefield Gdns
STRHM/NOR SW16 .... 148 E2
Grace Jones Cl HACK E8 .... 74 B5
Grace Ms BECK BR3 .... 151 K4
Grace Pl BOW E3 .... 93 K2
Grace Rd CROY/NA CR0 .... 164 D5
Graces Aly WCHPL E1 * 92 C5
Graces Ms STJWD NW8 * 2 E7
Grace's Ms CMBW SE5 .... 130 E1

Grace's Rd CMBW SE5 .... 131 F1
Grace St BOW E3 .... 93 K2
The Gradient SYD SE26 .... 150 C3
Graduate Pl STHWK SE1 .... 19 J3
Graeme Rd EN EN1 .... 30 A1
Graemesdyke Av
  MORT/ESHN SW14 .... 125 J2
Grafton Cl HSLWW TW4 .... 122 D7
  WEA W13 .... 85 G5
  WPK KT4 .... 173 G2
Grafton Ct EBED/NFELT TW14 .... 121 F7
Grafton Crs CAMTN NW1 .... 72 B5
Grafton Gdns BCTR RM8 .... 80 A1
  FSBYPK N4 .... 55 J3
Grafton Ms FITZ W1T 10 E1
Grafton Park Rd WPK KT4 .... 173 G1
Grafton Pl CAMTN NW1 .... 5 G8
Grafton Rd ACT W3 .... 86 E6
  BCTR RM8 .... 80 A1
  CROY/NA CR0 .... 164 B7
  ENC/FH EN2 .... 29 F7
  HRW HA1 .... 48 C4
  KTTN NW5 .... 72 A4
  NWMAL KT3 .... 160 B3
  WPK KT4 .... 173 G1
Grafton Sq CLAP SW4 .... 129 H2
Grafton St CONDST W1S 10 D7
Grafton Ter HAMP NW3 .... 71 K4
Grafton Wy E/WMO/HCT KT8 .... 156 E3
  FITZ W1T 10 E2
Grafton Yd KTTN NW5 .... 72 B5
Graham Av MTCM CR4 .... 148 A7
  WEA W13 .... 104 C1
Graham Cl CROY/NA CR0 .... 179 J1
Grahame Park Wy MLHL NW7 .... 37 G6
Graham Gdns SURB KT6 .... 159 F7
Graham Rd BXLYHS DA6 .... 137 G3
  CHSWK W4 .... 106 A2
  HACK E8 .... 74 C5
  HDN NW4 .... 51 K5
  HPTN TW12 .... 142 A3
  KTN/HRWW/WS HA3 .... 48 C1
  MTCM CR4 .... 148 A7
  PLSTW E13 .... 94 E1
  SEVS/STOTM N15 .... 55 H3
  WIM/MER SW19 .... 146 D6
Graham St IS N1 .... 6 C4
Graham Ter BFN/LL DA15 * 136 C1
  BGVA SW1W 16 A6
Grainger Cl NTHLT UB5 .... 66 C4
Grainger Rd ISLW TW7 .... 124 A1
  WDGN N22 .... 41 J7
Gramer Cl WAN E11 .... 76 B1
Grampian Cl BELMT SM2 .... 175 G6
  HYS/HAR UB3 .... 101 G6
Grampian Gdns CRICK NW2 .... 52 C7
Gramsci Wy CAT SE6 .... 151 K2
Granada St TOOT SW17 .... 147 K4
Granard Av PUT/ROE SW15 .... 126 E4
Granard Rd BTSEA SW11 .... 128 B2
Granary Cl ED N9 .... 30 E6
Granary Rd WCHPL E1 .... 92 D3
Granary Sq IS N1 .... 73 G5
Granary St CAMTN NW1 .... 5 G4
Granby Rd ELTH/MOT SE9 .... 134 E2
  WOOL/PLUM SE18 .... 115 G2
Granby St BETH E2 .... 7 M9
Granby Ter CAMTN NW1 .... 4 E6
Grand Av BRYLDS KT5 .... 159 H7
  FARR EC1M 12 D2
  MUSWH N10 .... 54 A3
  WBLY HA9 .... 68 D4
Grand Av East WBLY HA9 .... 68 D4
Grand Depot Rd
  WOOL/PLUM SE18 .... 115 F4
Grand Dr NWDGN UB2 .... 103 H1
  RYNPK SW20 .... 161 F3
Granden Rd
  STRHM/NOR SW16 * 163 K1
Grandison Rd BTSEA SW11 .... 128 E4
  WPK KT4 .... 174 A1
Grand Junction Whf IS N1 * 6 E6
Grand Pde FSBYPK N4 * 55 H5
  MORT/ESHN SW14 * 125 J3
  SURB KT6 * 159 H7
  WBLY HA9 * 68 D1
Grand Union Canal Wk
  BTFD TW8 .... 104 D5
  MV/WKIL W9 .... 8 B2
  NTHLT UB5 .... 83 K3
  WDR/YW UB7 .... 100 E1
  WLSDN NW10 .... 86 D1
Grand Union Crs HACK E8 * 74 C7
Grand Union Wk
  CAMTN NW1 * 4 D2
Grand Wk WCHPL E1 * 93 G3
Granfield St BTSEA SW11 * 108 C7
  WPK KT4 .... 174 A1
Grange Av EBAR EN4 .... 27 J7
  KTN/HRWW/WS HA3 .... 49 H1
  NFNCH/WDSPK N12 .... 39 G4
  SNWD SE25 .... 165 F1
  TRDG/WHET N20 .... 26 C6
  WFD IG8 .... 44 E5
  WHTN TW2 .... 142 E1
Grangecliffe Gdns SNWD SE25 .... 165 F1
Grange Cl BFN/LL DA15 .... 155 G2
  E/WMO/HCT KT8 .... 157 G3
  HEST TW5 .... 102 E4
  HYS/HAR UB3 .... 82 C4
  WFD IG8 .... 44 E6
Grange Ct ALP/SUD HA0 * 67 J2
  BELMT SM2 * 175 F6
  HRW HA1 * 67 F2
  NTHLT UB5 .... 83 G1
  PIN HA5 * 47 J2
  WLGTN SM6 * 176 B2
Grangecourt Rd
  STNW/STAM N16 .... 56 A7
Grange Crs THMD SE28 .... 97 J5
Grangedale Cl NTHWD HA6 .... 32 C7
Grange Dr CHST BR7 .... 153 G3
Grange Farm Cl
  RYLN/HDSTN HA2 .... 66 C1
Grange Gdns HAMP NW3 .... 71 G2
  PIN HA5 .... 47 K3
  SNWD SE25 .... 165 F1
  STHGT/OAK N14 .... 28 D7
Grange Gv IS N1 .... 73 J5
Grange Hl EDGW HA8 .... 36 E4
  SNWD SE25 .... 165 F1
Grangehill Pl ELTH/MOT SE9 .... 134 E2
Grangehill Rd ELTH/MOT SE9 .... 134 E3
Grange Houses HBRY N5 * 73 J3
Grange La DUL SE21 .... 150 B1
Grange Ms FELT TW13 .... 140 B2
Grangemill Rd CAT SE6 .... 151 J2
Grangemill Wy CAT SE6 .... 151 J1
Grange Pk EA W5 .... 86 A7
Grange Park Av WCHMH N21 .... 29 H6
Grange Park Pl RYNPK SW20 .... 145 K6
Grange Park Rd LEY E10 .... 57 K7
  THHTH CR7 .... 164 E2

Grange Pl KIL/WHAMP NW6 .... 2 A2
Grange Rd BARN SW13 .... 106 D7
  BELMT SM2 .... 174 E6
  BORE WD6 .... 24 D1
  BUSH WD23 .... 21 J4
  CHSGTN KT9 .... 172 A6
  CHSWK W4 .... 105 J4
  E/WMO/HCT KT8 .... 157 G3
  EA W5 .... 85 K7
  EDGW HA8 .... 37 F5
  HCT N6 .... 54 A5
  HRW HA1 .... 49 G5
  HYS/HAR UB3 .... 82 C4
  IL IG1 .... 78 C5
  KUT/HW KT1 .... 159 F2
  LEY E10 .... 57 J7
  PLSTW E13 .... 94 D2
  RYLN/HDSTN HA2 .... 66 D1
  SNWD SE25 .... 164 E3
  STHL UB1 .... 102 D1
  STHWK SE1 .... 19 K4
  TOTM N17 .... 42 C5
  WALTH E17 .... 57 G4
  WLSDN NW10 .... 69 K5
Grange Rd CROY/NA CR0 .... 179 J1
  HTH N3 .... 52 D1
Gravel Hill Cl BXLYHS DA6 .... 137 J4
Gravel La WCHPL E1 .... 13 L4
Gravel Rd HAYES BR2 .... 181 J1
  WHTN TW2 .... 123 K7
Gravelwood Cl CHST BR7 .... 154 C2
Gravenel Gdns TOOT SW17 * 147 J4
Graveney Gv PGE/AN SE20 .... 150 E6
Graveney Rd TOOT SW17 .... 147 J3
Gravesend Rd SHB W12 .... 87 J6
Gray Av BCTR RM8 .... 62 B7
Gray Gdns RAIN RM13 .... 81 J5
Grayham Crs NWMAL KT3 .... 160 A3
Grayham Rd NWMAL KT3 .... 160 A3
Grayland Cl BMLY BR1 .... 153 H7
Grayling Cl CAN/RD E16 .... 94 C3
Grayling Ct EA W5 * 85 K7
Grayling Rd STNW/STAM N16 .... 73 K1
Grayling Sq BETH E2 * 92 C2
Grays Cots STMC/STPC BR5 * 155 J7
Grayscroft Rd
  STRHM/NOR SW16 .... 148 D6
Grays Farm Rd
  STMC/STPC BR5 .... 155 H7
Grayshott Rd BTSEA SW11 .... 129 F2
Gray's Inn Rd FSBYW WC1X 5 K7
Gray's Inn Sq GINN WC1R 12 A2
Grayswood Gdns
  RYNPK SW20 .... 160 E1
Gray's Yd MHST W1U * 10 B5
Graywood Ct
  NFNCH/WDSPK N12 .... 39 G4
Grazebrook Rd
  STNW/STAM N16 .... 73 K1
Grazeley Cl BXLYHS DA6 .... 137 K4
Great Amwell La
  CEND/HSY/T N8 .... 55 F2
Great Benty WDR/YW UB7 .... 100 B3
Great Brownings DUL SE21 .... 150 B3
Great Bushey Dr
  TRDG/WHET N20 .... 27 F1
Great Cambridge Jct
  PLMGR N13 * 41 J4
Great Cambridge Rd EN EN1 .... 30 C4
  UED N18 .... 41 K4
Great Castle St REGST W1B 10 D4
Great Central Av RSLP HA4 .... 65 G4
Great Central St CAMTN NW1 .... 9 L2
Great Central Wy WBLY HA9 .... 68 D2
Great Chapel St
  SOHO/SHAV W1D 11 G4
Great Chart St BTSEA SW11 .... 128 B2
Great Chertsey Rd CHSWK W4 .... 106 A7
  FELT TW13 .... 141 K2
Great Church La HMSMTH W6 .... 107 G4
Great College St WEST SW1P 17 J3
Great Cross Av GNWCH SE10 .... 113 H6
Great Cullings ROMW/RG RM7 .... 81 G1
Great Cumberland Ms
  MBLAR W1H 9 L5
Great Cumberland Pl
  MBLAR W1H 9 L4
Great Dover St STHWK SE1 .... 19 G3
Great Eastern Rd SRTFD E15 .... 76 B6
Great Eastern St SDTCH EC2A 7 J7
Great Eastern Wharf
  BTSEA SW11 .... 108 D6
Great Elms Rd HAYES BR2 .... 168 B3
Great Fld CDALE/KGS NW9 .... 37 G7
Greatfield Av EHAM E6 .... 95 K3
Greatfield Cl ARCH N19 .... 72 C3
  BROCKY SE4 .... 132 D3
Greatfields Rd BARK IG11 .... 78 D7
Great Galley Cl BARK IG11 .... 97 H2
Great Gardens Rd
  EMPK RM11 .... 63 K5
Great Gatton Cl CROY/NA CR0 .... 166 B6
Great George St STJSPK SW1H 17 H2
Great Gv BUSH WD23 .... 22 B3
Great Guildford St STHWK SE1 .... 12 F8
Greatham Rd BUSH WD23 .... 21 H2
Great Harry Dr ELTH/MOT SE9 .... 154 A2
Great James St STJWD NW8 .... 11 L2
Great Marlborough St
  REGST W1B 10 E5
Great Maze Pond STHWK SE1 .... 13 H9
Great New St
  FLST/FETLN EC4A * 12 B4
Great North Rd BAR EN5 .... 26 D1
  EFNCH N2 .... 53 J3
Great North Way (Barnet
  By-Pass) HDN NW4 .... 37 K7
Greatorex St WCHPL E1 .... 92 C4
Great Ormond St
  BMSBY WC1N 11 K2
Great Percy St FSBYW WC1X 5 M7
Great Peter St WEST SW1P 17 G4
Great Portland St GTPST W1W 10 D2
Great Pulteney St
  SOHO/CST W1F 10 F6
Great Queen St DART DA1 .... 139 J5
  HOL/ALD WC2B 11 K4
Great Russell St RSQ WC1B 11 H3
Great St Thomas Apostle
  BLKFR EC4V 12 F6
Great Scotland Yd
  WHALL SW1A 11 J9
Great Smith St WEST SW1P 17 H3
Great South-West Rd
  EBED/NFELT TW14 .... 121 F7
  HSLWW TW4 .... 122 A1
Great Spilmans EDUL SE22 .... 131 F4
Great Strd CDALE/KGS NW9 .... 51 H1
Great Suffolk St STHWK SE1 .... 12 D9
Great Sutton St FSBYE EC1V 12 D1
Great Swan Aly LOTH EC2R 13 G4
Great Thrift STMC/STPC BR5 .... 169 J4
Great Titchfield St
  GTPST W1W 10 D2
Great Tower St MON EC3R 13 J6
Great Trinity La BLKFR EC4V 12 F6
Great Turnstile HHOL WC1V * 11 M3
Great Western Rd NTGHL W11 .... 88 D4
Great West Rd BTFD TW8 .... 104 B6
  HEST TW5 .... 122 D1
  HMSMTH W6 .... 106 C4
  ISLW TW7 .... 103 K6
Great West Rd Chiswick
  CHSWK W4 .... 106 C4

Grassington Cl
  FBAR/BDGN N11 .... 40 A5
Grassington Rd SCUP DA14 .... 155 G3
Grassmount FSTH SE23 .... 150 D1
Grass Pk FNCH N3 .... 38 D7
Grassway WLGTN SM6 .... 176 C3
Grasvenor Av BAR EN5 .... 26 E5
Grately Wy PECK SE15 * 111 F6
Gratton Rd WKENS W14 .... 107 H2
Gratton Ter CRICK NW2 .... 70 B2
Graveley Av BORE WD6 .... 24 E3
Gravel Hl BXLYHS DA6 .... 137 J4
  CROY/NA CR0 .... 179 F5
Great West Road Ellesmere Rd
  CHSWK W4 .... 105 K5
Great West Road Hogarth La
  CHSWK W4 .... 106 A5
Great Winchester St
  OBST EC2N 13 H4
Great Windmill St
  SOHO/SHAV W1D 11 G7
Greatwood CHST BR7 .... 154 A6
Greaves Cl BARK IG11 .... 78 D6
Greaves Cots POP/IOD E14 * 93 G4
Greaves Pl TOOT SW17 .... 147 J3
Grebe Av YEAD UB4 .... 83 H5
Grebe Cl BARK IG11 .... 97 G3
  FSTGT E7 .... 76 D4
  WALTH E17 .... 43 G6
Grebe Ct SUT SM1 .... 174 D4
Grebe Ter KUT/HW KT1 * 159 F2
Grecian Crs NRWD SE19 .... 149 H5
Greek St SOHO/SHAV W1D 11 H5
Greenacre Cl NTHLT UB5 .... 65 K4
Greenacre Gdns WALTH E17 .... 58 A3
Greenacre Pl WLGTN SM6 .... 176 B1
Green Acres CROY/NA CR0 .... 178 B2
  SCUP DA14 .... 155 F3
Greenacres BUSH WD23 .... 34 D1
  ELTH/MOT SE9 .... 135 F5
Greenacres Dr STAN HA7 .... 35 H6
Greenacre Sq
  BERM/RHTH SE16 * 112 A1
Greenacre Wk
  STHGT/OAK N14 .... 40 D2
Green Arbour Ct STBT EC1A * 12 C4
Green Av MLHL NW7 .... 37 F3
  WEA W13 .... 104 C2
Greenaway Av UED N18 * 43 F1
Greenaway Gdns HAMP NW3 .... 71 F3
Green Bank
  NFNCH/WDSPK N12 .... 39 E3
  WAP E1W 92 D7
Greenbank Av ALP/SUD HA0 .... 67 F4
Greenbank Cl CHING E4 .... 44 A1
Greenbank Crs HDN NW4 .... 52 C3
Greenbay Rd CHARL SE7 .... 114 C6
Greenberry St STJWD NW8 .... 3 J6
Green Chain Wk BMLY BR1 .... 152 A4
  CHARL SE7 .... 114 C3
  ELTH/MOT SE9 .... 153 H1
  SYD SE26 .... 151 F5
  THMD SE28 .... 97 K7
  WELL DA16 .... 116 B7
Green Cl CAR SM5 .... 175 K1
  CDALE/KGS NW9 .... 50 E5
  FELT TW13 .... 141 J4
  GLDGN NW11 .... 53 G6
  HAYES BR2 .... 167 H2
Greencoat Pl WEST SW1P 16 F5
Greencoat Rw WEST SW1P 16 F4
Green Court Av CROY/NA CR0 .... 178 D1
Greencourt Av EDGW HA8 .... 36 C7
Green Court Gdns
  CROY/NA CR0 .... 178 D1
Greencourt Rd
  STMC/STPC BR5 .... 169 K4
Greencroft EDGW HA8 .... 36 E4
Greencroft Av RSLP HA4 .... 65 G1
Greencroft Gdns EN EN1 .... 30 A2
  KIL/WHAMP NW6 .... 2 B1
Greencroft Rd HEST TW5 .... 102 E7
Greendale EDUL SE22 .... 131 F4
Greendale Wy WCHMH N21 .... 29 H5
Green Dragon La BTFD TW8 .... 105 F4
  WCHMH N21 .... 29 H5
Green Dragon Yd WCHPL E1 .... 92 C4
Green Dr STHL UB1 .... 84 A7
Green End CHSGTN KT9 .... 171 K3
  WCHMH N21 .... 41 H1
Greenend Rd CHSWK W4 .... 106 B1
Greenfell Man DEPT SE8 * 112 C4
Green Ferry Wy WALTH E17 * 57 F3
Greenfield Av BRYLDS KT5 .... 159 J5
  OXHEY WD19 .... 33 J1
Greenfield Ct ELTH/MOT SE9 .... 153 J2
Greenfield Dr BMLY BR1 .... 168 B1
  EFNCH N2 .... 53 K3
Greenfield Gdns CRICK NW2 .... 70 C1
  DAGW RM9 .... 79 J7
  STMC/STPC BR5 .... 169 H6
Greenfield Rd DAGW RM9 .... 79 J7
  SEVS/STOTM N15 .... 56 A4
  WCHPL E1 .... 92 C4
Greenfields STHL UB1 .... 84 A6
Greenfield Wy
  RYLN/HDSTN HA2 .... 48 B2
Greenford Av HNWL W7 .... 84 E5
  STHL UB1 .... 83 K6
Greenford Gdns GFD/PVL UB6 .... 84 B2
Greenford Rd STHL UB1 .... 84 C6
  SUT SM1 .... 175 F3
Greengate GFD/PVL UB6 .... 67 H5
Greengate St PLSTW E13 .... 95 F1
Greenhalgh Wk EFNCH N2 .... 53 G3
Greenham Cl STHWK SE1 .... 18 A2
Greenham Crs CHING E4 .... 43 H5
Greenham Rd MUSWH N10 .... 54 A1
Greenhaven Dr THMD SE28 .... 97 H5
Greenheys Cl NTHWD HA6 .... 32 C7
Greenheys Dr SWFD E18 .... 58 D2
Greenhill HAMP NW3 .... 71 H3
  SUT SM1 .... 175 G1
  WBLY HA9 .... 68 D1
Green Hl WOOL/PLUM SE18 .... 114 E4
Greenhill Ct BAR EN5 * 27 F4
Greenhill Crs WATW WD18 .... 20 C5
Greenhill Gdns NTHLT UB5 .... 83 K1
Greenhill Gv MNPK E12 .... 77 J3
Greenhill Pde BAR EN5 * 27 F4
Greenhill Pk BAR EN5 .... 27 F4
  WLSDN NW10 .... 69 G1
Greenhill Rd HRW HA1 .... 48 E5
  WLSDN NW10 .... 69 G1
Greenhill's Rents FARR EC1M * 12 C2
Greenhills Ter IS N1 .... 73 K5
Greenhill Ter NTHLT UB5 .... 83 K1
  WOOL/PLUM SE18 .... 114 E4
Greenhill Wy HRW HA1 .... 48 E5
  WBLY HA9 .... 68 D1
Greenhithe Cl BFN/LL DA15 .... 135 K6
Greenholm Rd ELTH/MOT SE9 .... 135 G4
Green Hundred Rd PECK SE15 .... 111 H5
Greenhurst Rd WNWD SE27 .... 149 G4
Greenland Crs NWDGN UB2 .... 102 B2
Greenland Ms DEPT SE8 .... 112 A4
Greenland Pl CAMTN NW1 * 4 D3
Greenland Quay
  BERM/RHTH SE16 .... 112 A3
Greenland Rd BAR EN5 .... 26 A5
  CAMTN NW1 .... 4 D3
Greenlands La HDN NW4 .... 52 A1
Greenland Wy CROY/NA CR0 .... 163 J6
Green La BCTR RM8 .... 80 A1

CHSGTN KT9 .... 172 A7
  E/WMO/HCT KT8 .... 157 G4
  EDGW HA8 .... 36 C4
  ELTH/MOT SE9 .... 135 F7
  FELT TW13 .... 141 J4
  GDMY/SEVK IG3 .... 79 G3
  HDN NW4 .... 52 B4
  HNWL W7 .... 103 K1
  HSLWW TW4 .... 122 B4
  IL IG1 .... 78 D1
  MRDN SM4 .... 161 K5
  NTHWD HA6 .... 32 B6
  NWMAL KT3 .... 159 K4
  OXHEY WD19 .... 21 G7
  PGE/AN SE20 .... 151 F6
  STAN HA7 .... 35 H3
  SUN TW16 .... 140 D6
  THHTH CR7 .... 149 H7
  UX/CGN UB8 .... 82 A4
  WPK KT4 .... 160 E7
Green Lane Cots STAN HA7 * 35 H3
Green Lane Gdns THHTH CR7 .... 164 D1
Green Lanes FSBYPK N4 .... 55 H5
  HBRY N5 .... 73 J2
  HOR/WEW KT19 .... 173 G7
  PLMGR N13 .... 41 H4
  SEVS/STOTM N15 .... 55 H3
  WCHMH N21 .... 29 J6
Greenlaw Ct EA W5 * 85 K5
Greenlaw Gdns NWMAL KT3 .... 160 C6
Greenlawn La BTFD TW8 .... 104 E3
Green Lawns
  NFNCH/WDSPK N12 * 39 F3
  RSLP HA4 * 47 G7
Greenlaw St
  WOOL/PLUM SE18 .... 115 F2
Green Leaf Av WLGTN SM6 .... 176 D3
Greenleaf Cl
  BRXS/STRHM SW2 * 130 B6
Greenleafe Dr BARK/HLT IG6 .... 60 B2
Greenleaf Rd EHAM E6 .... 77 G1
  WALTH E17 .... 57 H2
Greenleaf Wy
  KTN/HRWW/WS HA3 .... 49 F3
Greenlea Pk WIM/MER SW19 * 147 J1
Green Leas SUN TW16 .... 140 D5
Green Leas Cl SUN TW16 .... 140 D5
Greenlink Wk RCH/KEW TW9 .... 105 J7
Green Man La
  EBED/NFELT TW14 .... 121 K3
  WEA W13 .... 85 G6
Greenman St IS N1 .... 6 E1
Greenmead Cl SNWD SE25 .... 165 H4
Green Moor Link WCHMH N21 .... 29 H6
Greenmoor Rd PEND EN3 .... 30 E1
Greenoak Pl EBAR EN4 .... 27 K1
Green Oaks NWDGN UB2 * 102 C3
Greenoak Wy WIM/MER SW19 .... 146 B4
Greenock Rd ACT W3 .... 105 J2
  STRHM/NOR SW16 .... 148 D7
Green Pde HSLW TW3 * 123 G5
Greenpark Wy GFD/PVL UB6 .... 66 E5
Green Pond Cl WALTH E17 .... 57 G2
Green Pond Rd WALTH E17 .... 57 F2
Green Rd STHGT/OAK N14 .... 28 B5
  TRDG/WHET N20 .... 39 G2
Greenroof Wy GNWCH SE10 .... 113 J2
Greens Ct NTGHL W11 * 88 D7
Green's Ct SOHO/CST W1F * 11 G6
Greenshank Cl WALTH E17 .... 43 G6
Greenside BCTR RM8 .... 79 J1
  BXLY DA5 .... 137 F2
Greenside Cl CAT SE6 .... 152 A1
  TRDG/WHET N20 .... 39 H1
Greenside Rd CROY/NA CR0 .... 164 B6
  SHB W12 .... 106 D2
Greenslade Av WFD IG8 .... 45 G5
Greenstead Av
  PUT/ROE SW15 .... 126 D4
  WFD IG8 .... 45 G5
Greenstead Gdns
  PUT/ROE SW15 .... 126 D4
  WFD IG8 .... 45 G5
Greenstone Ms WAN E11 .... 58 E5
Green St FSTGT E7 .... 77 F4
  MYFR/PKLN W1K * 9 M6
  PEND EN3 .... 30 E2
  SUN TW16 .... 140 E7
Greenstreet Hl NWCR SE14 * 132 A2
Greensward BUSH WD23 .... 22 B5
Green Ter CLKNW EC1R 6 A6
The Green ACT W3 .... 87 G5
  BXLYHN DA7 .... 117 F7
  CAR SM5 * 176 A3
  CROY/NA CR0 .... 179 K7
  ED N9 .... 42 C1
  FELT TW13 .... 141 F1
  HAYES BR2 .... 167 K6
  HEST TW5 .... 103 F1
  HGDN/ICK UB10 .... 64 A1
  HRW HA1 .... 67 G1
  MRDN SM4 .... 161 H3
  NWDGN UB2 .... 102 E1
  NWMAL KT3 .... 159 K2
  RCH/KEW TW9 .... 124 E4
  SCUP DA14 .... 155 G3
  SRTFD E15 .... 76 D5
  STHGT/OAK N14 .... 28 D6
  STMC/STPC BR5 .... 155 H6
  SUT SM1 .... 175 F2
  TOTM N17 .... 41 J5
  WAN E11 .... 59 F5
  WCHMH N21 .... 29 G7
  WDR/YW UB7 .... 100 A2
  WELL DA16 .... 135 K3
  WHTN TW2 .... 123 K7
  WIM/MER SW19 .... 146 A5
  WLGTN SM6 .... 176 A1
Green V BXLYHS DA6 .... 137 H4
  EA W5 .... 86 B5
Greenvale Rd ELTH/MOT SE9 .... 134 E3
Green Verges STAN HA7 .... 35 K6
Greenview Av BECK BR3 .... 166 B5
  CROY/NA CR0 .... 166 B5
Greenview Cl ACT W3 .... 87 G7
Green Vw CHSGTN KT9 .... 172 B6
Greenway Av WALTH E17 .... 58 B3
Green Wk DART DA1 .... 138 C3
  HDN NW4 .... 52 B4
  NWDGN UB2 .... 103 G4
  RSLP HA4 .... 46 D7
  STHWK SE1 .... 19 J5
  WFD IG8 .... 45 G5
Green Wy ELTH/MOT SE9 .... 134 C3
  HAYES BR2 .... 168 D5
Greenway BCTR RM8 .... 79 J1
  CHST BR7 .... 154 A4
  KTN/HRWW/WS HA3 .... 49 K4
  PIN HA5 .... 47 F1
  RYNPK SW20 .... 161 F3
  STHGT/OAK N14 .... 40 E1
  TRDG/WHET N20 .... 38 E2
  WLGTN SM6 .... 176 C3
  YEAD UB4 .... 83 F1

Greenway Av *WALTH* E17 ....58 B3
Greenway Cl
SEVS/STOTM N15 ....56 B3
CDALE/KGS NW9 ....51 F1
FBAR/BDGN N11 ....40 A3
FSBYPK N4 ....73 J1
TRDG/WHET N20 ....38 E1
Greenway Ct *IL* IG1 ....60 A7
SRTFD E15 ....94 C1
Greenway Gdns
CDALE/KGS NW9 ....50 E1
CROY/NA CR0 ....179 H2
GFD/PVL UB6 ....84 A2
Green Way Gdns
KTN/HRWW/WS HA3 ....48 B1
Greenways *BECK* BR3 ....166 D1
ESH/CLAY KT10 ....170 E3
NFNCH/WDSPK N12 * 39 G5
The Greenways *TWK* TW1 * ..124 B5
The Green Wy
KTN/HRWW/WS HA3 ....34 E7
The Greenway
CDALE/KGS NW9 ....51 F1
EHAM E6 ....96 A3
HSLWW TW4 ....122 E6
OLYMPICPK E20 ....75 K7
PIN HA5 ....47 K5
SRTFD E15 ....94 D1
Greenwell St *GTPST* W1W 10 D1
Greenwich Church St
GNWCH SE10 * 113 F5
Greenwich Crs *EHAM* E6 ......95 J4
Greenwich Foot Tnl
GNWCH SE10 ....113 F4
Greenwich Hts *CHARL* SE7 * ..114 D6
Greenwich High Rd
GNWCH SE10 ....112 E6
Greenwich House *LEW* SE13 ..133 G5
Greenwich Park St
GNWCH SE10 ....113 G5
Greenwich Quay *DEPT* SE8 * ..112 D5
Greenwich South St
GNWCH SE10 ....112 E7
Greenwich Vw *POP/IOD* E14 ..112 E2
Greenwood Av *DAGE* RM10 ....80 D3
Greenwood Cl *BFN/LL* DA15 ..155 G1
HYS/HAR UB3 ....83 J2
MRDN SM4 ....161 H3
STMC/STPC BR5 ....169 K5
THDIT KT7 ....158 B7
Greenwood Dr *CHING* E4 ......44 A4
Greenwood Gdns *PLMGR* N13 ..41 G2
IL IG6 ....54 C2
Greenwood La *HPTN* TW12 ....142 B4
Greenwood Pk
KUTN/CMB KT2 ....145 G6
Greenwood Pl *KTTN* NW5 ......72 B4
Greenwood Rd *CROY/NA* CR0 ..164 C6
HACK E8 ....74 C4
ISLW TW7 ....123 K2
MTCM CR4 ....163 J2
PLSTW E13 ....94 D1
THDIT KT7 ....158 B7
Greenwood Ter
WLSDN NW10 ....69 F7
Green Wrythe Crs *CAR* SM5 ..162 D7
Green Wrythe La *CAR* SM5 ....162 C5
Green Yd *FSBYW* WC1X 5 M9
Greet Rd *KTN/HRWW/WS* HA3 ..34 C7
Greet St *STHWK* SE1 ....12 B9
Greg Cl *LEY* E10 ....58 A5
Gregor Ms *BKHTH/KID* SE3 ..113 K6
Gregory Crs *ELTH/MOT* SE9 ..134 C6
Gregory Pl *KENS* W8 ....14 C1
Gregory Rd *CHDH* RM6 ....61 K3
NWDGN UB2 ....103 F2
Gregson Cl *BORE* WD6 ....24 E1
Greig Cl *CEND/HSY/T* N8 ......54 E4
Greig Ter *WALW* SE17 ....18 D9
Grenaby Av *CROY/NA* CR0 ....164 E6
Grenaby Rd *CROY/NA* CR0 ....164 E6
Grenada Rd *BKHTH/KID* SE3 ..114 B6
Grenade St *POP/IOD* E14 ......93 H6
Grenadier St *CAN/RD* E16 ......96 A7
Grena Gdns *RCH/KEW* TW9 ....125 G3
Grenard Cl *PECK* SE15 * 111 H6
Grena Rd *RCH/KEW* TW9 ......125 G3
Grendon Gdns *WBLY* HA9 ......68 C1
Grendon St *STJWD* NW8 ....3 J9
Grenfell Av *NTGHL* W11 ....63 H7
Grenfell Ct *MLHL* NW7 * 37 K5
Grenfell Gdns
KTN/HRWW/WS HA3 ....50 A6
NTGHL W11 ....88 B6
TOOT SW17 ....147 K5
Grennell Cl *SUT* SM1 ....175 H1
Grennell Rd *SUT* SM1 ....175 G1
Grenoble Gdns *PLMGR* N13 ....41 G5
BRYLDS KT5 ....159 K7
FNCH N3 ....38 D7
Grenville Gdns *WFD* IG8 ......45 G6
Grenville Ms *ARCH* N19 ....54 E7
HPTN TW12 ....142 B4
Grenville Pl *MLHL* NW7 ....37 F4
SKENS SW7 ....14 E5
Grenville Rd *ARCH* N19 ....54 C7
CROY/NA CR0 ....180 A7
Grenville St *BMSBY* WC1N 11 K1
Gresham Av *TRDG/WHET* N20 ..39 K1
Gresham Cl *BXLY* DA5 ....137 F5
ENC/FH EN2 ....29 J2
Gresham Dr *CHDH* RM6 ....61 H4
Gresham Gdns *GLDGN* NW11 ..52 C7
Gresham Rd *BECK* BR3 ....166 B1
BRXN/ST SW9 ....130 B2
CAN/RD E16 ....95 F5
EDGW HA8 ....36 B5
EHAM E6 ....95 K1
HPTN TW12 ....142 A5
HSLW TW3 ....103 H7
SNWD SE25 ....165 H3
WLSDN NW10 ....69 F4
Gresham St *CITYW* EC2V 12 E4
Gresham Wy *WIM/MER* SW19 ..146 E3
Gresley Cl *SEVS/STOTM* N15 * ..55 K3
WALTH E17 ....57 G5
Gresley Rd *ARCH* N19 ....54 C7
Gressenhall Rd
WAND/EARL SW18 ....127 J5
Gresse St *FITZ* W1T 11 G3
Gresswell St *FUL/PGN* SW6 ..107 G7
Gretton Rd *TOTM* N17 ....42 A6
Greville Cl *TWK* TW1 ....124 C6
Greville Ms *KIL/WHAMP* NW6 ..2 C4
Greville Pl *KIL/WHAMP* NW6 ....2 D5
RCHPK/HAM TW10 ....125 G5
WALTH E17 ....58 A3
Greville St *HCIRC* EC1N 12 B3
Grey Cl *GLDGN* NW11 ....53 G5
Greycoat Pl *WEST* SW1P 17 G4
Greycoat St *WEST* SW1P 17 G4
Greycot Rd *BECK* BR3 ....151 J4

Grey Eagle St *WCHPL* E1 ......13 M1
Greyfell Cl *STAN* HA7 ....35 H4
Greyhound Hl *HDN* NW4 ....51 J2
Greyhound La
STRHM/NOR SW16 ....148 E5
Greyhound Rd *HMSMTH* W6 ..107 G5
SUT SM1 ....175 G4
TOTM N17 ....56 A2
WLSDN NW10 ....87 K2
Greyhound Ter
STRHM/NOR SW16 ....148 C7
Greyhound Wy *DART* DA1 ....138 B4
Greyladies Gdns
GNWCH SE10 * 133 F1
Greys Park Cl *HAYES* BR2 ....181 G4
Greystead Rd *FSTH* SE23 ....131 K6
Greystoke Av *PIN* HA5 ....48 A2
Greystoke Cots *EA* W5 * 86 A3
Greystoke Gdns *EA* W5 ....86 A3
ENC/FH EN2 ....28 D3
Greystone Gdns *BARK/HLT* IG6 ..60 C1
KTN/HRWW/WS HA3 ....49 J5
Greywood St *STRHM/NOR* SW16 ..148 B5
Grierson Rd *FSTH* SE23 ......132 B5
Griffin Cl *WLSDN* NW10 ....69 K4
Griffin Manor Wy *THMD* SE28 ..115 J2
Griffin Rd *TOTM* N17 ....56 A1
WOOL/PLUM SE18 ....115 J4
Griffins Cl *WCHMH* N21 ....29 K7
Griffin Wy *THMD* SE28 ....115 K2
Griffith Cl *CHDH* RM6 ....61 J6
Griffiths Cl *WIM/MER* SW19 ..146 E6
Griggs Ap *IL* IG1 ....78 C1
Griggs Cl *IL* IG1 ....78 E3
Grigg's Pl *STHWK* SE1 ....19 K4
Griggs Rd *LEY* E10 ....58 A5
Grimsby Gv *CAN/RD* E16 ......96 B7
Grimsby St *WCHPL* E1 ....26 A2
Grimsdyke Rd *PIN* HA5 ....33 J6
Grimsel Pth *CMBW* SE5 ......110 C6
Grimshaw Cl *HGT* N6 * 54 A6
Grimshaw Wy *ROM* RM1 ......63 G4
Grimston Rd *FUL/PGN* SW6 ..127 J1
Grimwade Av *CROY/NA* CR0 ..178 C2
Grimwade Cl *PECK* SE15 ......131 J1
Grimwood Rd *TWK* TW1 ......124 A6
Grindall Cl *CROY/NA* CR0 ....177 H3
Grindal St *STHWK* SE1 ....18 A2
Grindleford Av
FBAR/BDGN N11 ....40 A1
Grindley Gdns *CROY/NA* CR0 * ..165 G5
Grinling Pl *DEPT* SE8 ....112 D5
Grinstead Rd *DEPT* SE8 ......112 B4
Grisle Cl *ED* N9 ....42 D3
Grittleton Av *WBLY* HA9 ....68 D5
Grittleton Rd *MV/WKIL* W9 ......2 A9
Grizedale Ter *FSTH* SE23 ......150 D1
Grocers' Hall Ct *LOTH* EC2R * ..13 G5
Groombridge Cl *WELL* DA16 ..136 B4
Groombridge Rd *HOM* E9 ......75 F6
Groom Cl *HAYES* BR2 ....168 A3
Groom Crs *WAND/EARL* SW18 ..128 C6
Groomfield Cl *TOOT* SW17 ....148 A3
Groom Pl *KTBR* SW1X 16 B3
Grooms Dr *PIN* HA5 ....46 E4
Grosmont Rd
WOOL/PLUM SE18 ....116 A4
Grosse Wy *PUT/ROE* SW15 ..126 E5
Grosvenor Av *CAR* SM5 ......175 K5
HBRY N5 ....73 J4
MORT/ESHN SW14 ....126 B2
RYLN/HDSTN HA2 ....48 B6
YEAD UB4 ....82 D1
Grosvenor Br *PIM* SW1V 16 D9
Grosvenor Cots *KTBR* SW1X ..16 A5
Grosvenor Ct
RKW/CH/CXG WD3 * 20 B4
Grosvenor Crs
CDALE/KGS NW9 ....50 C3
DART DA1 ....139 G4
KTBR SW1X 16 B2
Grosvenor Crescent Ms
KTBR SW1X 16 A2
Grosvenor Gdns *BGVA* SW1W ..16 D3
CRICK NW2 ....70 A5
GLDGN NW11 ....52 D5
KUTN/CMB KT2 ....143 K5
MORT/ESHN SW14 ....126 B2
MUSWH N10 ....54 C2
STHGT/OAK N14 ....28 E4
WFD IG8 ....44 E5
WLGTN SM6 ....176 C6
Grosvenor Gardens Ms East
BGVA SW1W * 16 D3
Grosvenor Gardens Ms North
BGVA SW1W 16 D3
Grosvenor Ga
MYFR/PKLN W1K 9 M7
Grosvenor Hl
MYFR/PKLN W1K 10 C1
WIM/MER SW19 ....146 C5
Grosvenor Pde *EA* W5 * 86 C7
Grosvenor Pk *CMBW* SE5 ....110 D6
Grosvenor Park Rd
WALTH E17 ....57 K5
Grosvenor Pl *KTBR* SW1X 16 B1
Grosvenor Ri East *WALTH* E17 ..57 K4
Grosvenor Rd *BCTR* RM8 ......62 B7
BELV DA17 ....117 G5
BORE WD6 ....24 C2
BTFD TW8 ....104 E5
BXLYHS DA6 ....136 E4
CHSWK W4 ....105 K4
ED N9 ....30 D7
FNCH N3 ....38 D6
FSTGT E7 ....77 F5
HNWL W7 ....85 G7
HSLWW TW4 ....122 E2
IL IG1 ....78 C2
LEY E10 ....58 A7
MUSWH N10 ....40 B7
NTHWD HA6 ....32 D4
NWDGN UB2 ....102 E2
PIM SW1V 16 D9
RCHPK/HAM TW10 ....125 F4
ROMW/RG RM7 ....63 F6
SNWD SE25 ....165 H3
STMC/STPC BR5 ....169 K5
TWK TW1 ....124 B5
WAN E11 ....59 F4
WAT WD17 ....21 G3
WLGTN SM6 ....176 C4
WWKM BR4 ....179 K1
Grosvenor Sq
MYFR/PKLN W1K 10 B6
Grosvenor St
MYFR/PKLN W1K 10 B6
Grosvenor Ter *CMBW* SE5 ....110 D6
Grosvenor V *RSLP* HA4 ....64 D1
Grosvenor Wy *TOOT* SW17 ..147 H2

Grosvenor Wharf Rd
POP/IOD E14 ....113 G3
Grote's Blds *BKHTH/KID* SE3 ..133 H1
Grote's Pl *BKHTH/KID* SE3 ....133 H1
Groton Rd *WAND/EARL* SW18 ..147 F1
Grotto Ct *STHWK* SE1 * 18 E1
Grotto Pas *MHST* W1U 10 A2
Grotto Rd *TWK* TW1 ....143 F1
Grove Av *FNCH* N3 ....38 E6
HNWL W7 ....84 E5
MUSWH N10 ....54 B1
PIN HA5 ....47 J3
SUT SM1 ....174 E5
TWK TW1 ....124 A7
Grove Bank *OXHEY* WD19 * 21 H7
Grovebury Cl *ERITH* DA8 ......118 A5
Grovebury Ct *STHGT/OAK* N14 ..28 C6
Grovebury Rd *ABYW* SE2 ......116 C1
Grove Cl *FSTH* SE23 ....132 A7
HAYES BR2 ....180 E1
KUT/HW KT1 ....159 G3
STHGT/OAK N14 * 28 B6
Grove Cots *CHEL* SW3 * 15 K9
CHSWK W4 ....106 B5
Grove Ct *E/WMO/HCT* KT8 ....157 J4
EA W5 * 86 A7
Grove Crs *CDALE/KGS* NW9 ....50 E3
FELT TW13 ....141 J3
KUT/HW KT1 ....159 F2
SWFD E18 ....45 F1
WOT/HER KT12 ....156 A6
Grove Crescent Rd *SRTFD* E15 ..76 B5
Grovedale Rd *ARCH* N19 ......72 D1
Grove Dwellings *WCHPL* E1 * ..92 E4
Grove End *KTTN* NW5 * 72 B3
SWFD E18 ....45 F1
Grove End La *ESH/CLAY* KT10 ..157 J1
Grove End Rd *STJWD* NW8 ......2 E6
Grove Farm Pk *NTHWD* HA6 ..32 B4
Grove Footpath *BRYLDS* KT5 ..159 F3
Grove Gdns *HDN* NW4 * 3 K8
STJWD NW8 ....3 J7
TEDD TW11 ....143 G3
Grove Green Rd *WAN* E11 ......76 A2
Grove Hall Rd *BUSH* WD23 ....21 J3
Groveherst Rd *DART* DA1 ....139 J2
Grove Hl *HRW* HA1 ....48 E6
SWFD E18 ....58 D1
Grove Hill Rd *CMBW* SE5 ......131 F2
HRW HA1 ....49 F6
Grove House Rd
CEND/HSY/T N8 ....54 E3
Groveland Av
STRHM/NOR SW16 ....149 F6
Groveland Ct *STP* EC4M 12 F5
Groveland Rd *BECK* BR3 ......166 C2
Grovelands *E/WMO/HCT* KT8 ..157 F3
Grovelands Cl *CMBW* SE5 ....131 F1
RYLN/HDSTN HA2 ....66 B2
Grovelands Ct
STHGT/OAK N14 ....28 D6
Grovelands Rd *PLMGR* N13 ....41 F3
SEVS/STOTM N15 ....56 C5
STMC/STPC BR5 ....155 G6
Groveland Wy *NWMAL* KT3 ..159 K4
Grove La *CMBW* SE5 ....110 E7
KUT/HW KT1 ....159 F3
Groveley Rd *SUN* TW16 ......140 D4
Grove Market Pl
ELTH/MOT SE9 ....134 E5
Grove Ms *HMSMTH* W6 ......107 F2
Grove Mill Pl *CAR* SM5 ......176 A2
Grove Pk *CDALE/KGS* NW9 ....50 E3
CMBW SE5 ....131 F1
WAN E11 ....59 F4
Grove Park Av *CHING* E4 ......43 K6
Grove Park Br *CHSWK* W4 ....105 K6
Grove Park Gdns *CHSWK* W4 ..105 J6
Grove Park Rd *CHSWK* W4 ....105 J6
ELTH/MOT SE9 ....153 F2
RAIN RM13 ....81 J7
SEVS/STOTM N15 ....56 A3
Grove Park Ter *CHSWK* W4 ..105 J6
Grove Pl *ACT* W3 ....86 E7
BAL SW12 ....129 G5
HAMP NW3 ....71 H2
Grove Rd *ACT* W3 ....86 E7
BARN SW13 ....126 C1
BELV DA17 ....117 G5
BOW E3 ....93 G1
BTFD TW8 ....104 D4
BXLYHN DA7 ....137 K3
CHDH RM6 ....61 J6
CHING E4 ....44 A2
CRICK NW2 ....70 A5
E/WMO/HCT KT8 ....157 J4
EA W5 ....85 K6
EBAR EN4 ....27 J2
EDGW HA8 ....36 C5
FBAR/BDGN N11 ....40 B4
HOM E9 ....75 F7
HSLW TW3 ....123 F3
ISLW TW7 ....103 K7
MTCM CR4 ....163 G1
NFNCH/WDSPK N12 ....39 H4
NTHWD HA6 ....32 B4
PIN HA5 ....47 K4
RCHPK/HAM TW10 ....125 G5
SEVS/STOTM N15 ....56 A4
SURB KT6 ....158 E4
SUT SM1 ....174 E5
SWFD E18 ....44 D1
THHTH CR7 ....164 B3
WALTH E17 ....57 K4
WAN E11 ....58 D6
WHTN TW2 ....142 D2
WIM/MER SW19 ....147 G6
Grover Rd *OXHEY* WD19 ......21 H5
Groveside Cl *ACT* W3 ....86 C5
CAR SM5 ....175 J1
Groveside Rd *CHING* E4 ......44 C2
Grovestile Waye
EBED/NFELT TW14 ....121 G6
Grove St *BERM/RHTH* SE16 ..112 C3
UED N18 ....42 B4
Grove Ter *KTTN* NW5 ....72 A2
STHL UB1 * 84 A6
TEDD TW11 ....143 G3
Grove Terrace Ms *KTTN* NW5 ..72 B2
The Grove *BXLYHS* DA6 ......136 E3
CDALE/KGS NW9 ....51 F4
CEND/HSY/T N8 ....54 D4
EA W5 ....85 K7
EDGW HA8 ....36 C3
ENC/FH EN2 ....29 G1
FNCH N3 ....38 E6
FSBYPK N4 ....55 F6
GFD/PVL UB6 ....84 C5
GLDGN NW11 ....52 C6
HGT N6 ....54 A7
ISLW TW7 ....103 K7
PLMGR N13 ....41 G3
SRTFD E15 ....76 C6

Grove V *CHST* BR7 ....154 A5
EDUL SE22 ....131 F3
Groveway *BCTR* RM8 ....79 J2
BRXN/ST SW9 ....110 A7
Grove Wy *ESH/CLAY* KT10 ....157 H6
WBLY HA9 ....68 E4
Grove Wood Cl *BMLY* BR1 ....169 F6
Grovewood Pl *WFD* IG8 ....45 K5
Grummant Rd *PECK* SE15 ....111 G7
Grundy St *POP/IOD* E14 ......93 K5
Gruneisen Rd *FNCH* N3 ......39 F6
Guardian Cl *EMPK* RM11 ......81 K1
Gubyon Av *HNHL* SE24 ......130 C4
Gudden Dr *CLPT* E5 ....74 D3
Guernsey Cl *HEST* TW5 ......103 F7
Guernsey Gv *HNHL* SE24 ....130 D5
Guernsey Rd *IS* N1 ....73 J5
LEY E10 ....58 B7
Guibal Rd *LEE/GVPK* SE12 ..133 K6
Guildersfield Rd
STRHM/NOR SW16 ....148 E6
Guildford Av *FELT* TW13 ......140 D1
Guildford Gv *GNWCH* SE10 ..112 E7
Guildford Rd *CROY/NA* CR0 ..164 E5
EHAM E6 ....95 J5
GDMY/SEVK IG3 ....78 E1
VX/NE SW8 ....109 K7
WALTH E17 ....44 A1
Guildhall Blds *CITYW* EC2V 12 F4
Guildhall Yd *CITYW* EC2V 12 F4
Guildhouse St *PIM* SW1V 16 E6
Guildown Av
NFNCH/WDSPK N12 ....39 F3
Guild Rd *CHARL* SE7 ....114 C4
ERITH DA8 ....118 C6
Guildsway *WALTH* E17 ....43 H7
Guilford Av *BRYLDS* KT5 ....159 G4
Guilford Pl *BMSBY* WC1N 11 L1
Guilford St *BMSBY* WC1N 11 L1
Guillemot Pl *WDGN* N22 * 55 F1
Guinness Cl *HOM* E9 ....75 G6
HYS/HAR UB3 ....101 G2
Guinness Ct *CROY/NA* CR0 * ..178 B1
Guinness Sq *STHWK* SE1 ......19 J4
Guinness Trust
STNW/STAM N16 * 56 B7
Guinness Trust Est *CHEL* SW3 ..15 L6
SRTFD E15 * 76 D7
Guion Rd *FUL/PGN* SW6 ......127 J1
Gulland Wk *IS* N1 * 73 J5
Gulliver Cl *NTHLT* UB5 ....65 K7
Gulliver Rd *BFN/LL* DA15 ....154 D1
Gulliver St *BERM/RHTH* SE16 ..112 C2
Gumleigh Rd *EA* W5 ....104 D3
Gumley Gdns *ISLW* TW7 ......124 B2
Gundulph Rd *HAYES* BR2 ....168 B2
Gunmakers La *BOW* E3 ....75 G7
Gunnell Cl *CROY/NA* CR0 ....165 G5
SYD SE26 ....150 C3
Gunner La *WOOL/PLUM* SE18 ..115 F4
Gunnersbury Ave (North Circular
Rd) *EA* W5 ....86 B6
Gunnersbury Cl *CHSWK* W4 * ..105 J4
Gunnersbury Crs *ACT* W3 ....105 G1
Gunnersbury Dr *EA* W5 ......105 G1
Gunnersbury Gdns *ACT* W3 ..105 G1
Gunnersbury La *ACT* W3 ......105 H1
Gunnersbury Ms *CHSWK* W4 ..105 J4
Gunners Gv *CHING* E4 ....44 A2
Gunners Rd *WAND/EARL* SW18 ..147 H1
Gunning St *WOOL/PLUM* SE18 ..115 K3
Gunstor Rd *STNW/STAM* N16 * ..74 A3
Gun St *WCHPL* E1 ....13 L3
Gunter Gv *EDGW* HA8 ....37 F7
WBPTN SW10 ....108 B5
Gunterstone Rd *WKENS* W14 ..107 H4
Gunthorpe St *WCHPL* E1 ......13 M3
Gunton Rd *CLPT* E5 ....74 D2
TOOT SW17 ....148 A5
Gunwhale Cl
BERM/RHTH SE16 ....93 F7
Gunyard Ms
WOOL/PLUM SE18 * 114 D6
Gurdon Rd *CHARL* SE7 ......113 K4
Gurnell Gv *WEA* W13 ....85 F3
Gurney Cl *BARK* IG11 ....78 B5
SRTFD E15 ....76 C4
WALTH E17 ....43 F7
Gurney Crs *CROY/NA* CR0 ....164 A2
Gurney Dr *EFNCH* N2 ....53 H3
Gurney Rd *CAR* SM5 ....176 B2
FUL/PGN SW6 ....128 B2
NTHLT UB5 ....83 F2
SRTFD E15 ....76 C4
Guthrie St *CHEL* SW3 ....15 J7
Gutter La *CITYW* EC2V 12 E4
Guyatt Gdns *MTCM* CR4 ......163 F1
Guy Barnett Gv
BKHTH/KID SE3 ....133 K2
Guy Rd *WLGTN* SM6 ....176 D2
Guyscliff Rd *LEW* SE13 ......133 F4
Guysfield Cl *RAIN* RM13 ......81 J7
Guysfield Dr *RAIN* RM13 ......81 J7
Guy St *STHWK* SE1 ....19 H1
Gwalior Rd *PUT/ROE* SW15 ..127 G2
Gwendolen Av
PUT/ROE SW15 ....127 F3
Gwendoline Av *PLSTW* E13 ....77 F7
Gwendwr Rd *WKENS* W14 ....107 H4
Gweneth Cots *EDGW* HA8 * ..36 C5
Gwillim Cl *BFN/LL* DA15 ......136 B5
Gwydor Rd *BECK* BR3 ....166 A3
Gwydyr Rd *HAYES* BR2 ......167 J2
Gwyn Cl *FUL/PGN* SW6 ......108 B6
Gwynne Av *CROY/NA* CR0 ..166 A6
Gwynne Park Av *WFD* IG8 ....45 K5
Gwynne Rd *BTSEA* SW11 ....128 C1
Gwynne Whf *CHSWK* W4 ....106 C5
Gylcote Cl *CMBW* SE5 ....130 E3
Gyles Pk *STAN* HA7 ....35 J7
Gyllyngdune Gdns
GDMY/SEVK IG3 ....79 F2
Gywnne Pl *FSBYW* WC1X 5 M8

H

Haarlem Rd *WKENS* W14 ......107 G2
Haberdasher Pl *IS* N1 * 7 H7
Haberdasher St *IS* N1 ....7 H8
Habington Cl *CMBW* SE5 * 110 E6
Habitat Cl *PECK* SE15 ....131 J1
Haccombe Rd
WIM/MER SW19 ....147 G5
Hackbridge Park Gdns
CAR SM5 ....175 K1

Hackbridge Rd *CAR* SM5 ....176 A1
Hackford Rd *BRXN/ST* SW9 ..110 A7
Hackford Wk *BRXN/ST* SW9 ..110 A7
Hackforth Cl *BAR* EN5 ....25 K4
Hackington Crs *BECK* BR3 ..151 J3
Hackney Cl *BORE* WD6 ....25 H5
Hackney Gv *HACK* E8 ....74 D5
Hackney Rd *BETH* E2 ....7 L7
Hackney Wick *HOM* E9 ....75 H5
Hadar Cl *TRDG/WHET* N20 ....26 E7
Haddenham Ct
OXHEY WD19 * 33 H2
Hadden Rd *THMD* SE28 ......115 K2
Hadden Wy *GFD/PVL* UB6 ....66 D5
Haddington Rd *BMLY* BR1 ..152 B2
Haddon Cl *BORE* WD6 ....24 C1
EN EN1 ....30 C5
NWMAL KT3 ....160 C4
Haddon Gv *BFN/LL* DA15 ....136 B6
Haddon Rd *SUT* SM1 ....175 F3
Haddo St *GNWCH* SE10 ......112 E5
Hadfield Cl *STHL* UB1 * 83 K7
Hadfield Rd
STWL/WRAY TW19 ....120 A5
Hadleigh Cl *RYNPK* SW20 ....161 J1
WCHPL E1 ....92 E3
Hadleigh Dr *BELMT* SM2 ......174 E7
Hadleigh Rd *ED* N9 ....30 D6
Hadleigh St *BETH* E2 ....92 E3
Hadley Cl *BORE* WD6 ....24 B4
WCHMH N21 ....29 G5
Hadley Common *BAR* EN5 ....27 G1
Hadley Gdns *CHSWK* W4 ....106 A4
NWDGN UB2 ....102 E4
Hadley Gn *BAR* EN5 ....26 E2
Hadley Green Rd *BAR* EN5 ....26 D2
Hadley Gn West *BAR* EN5 ....26 D2
Hadley Gv *BAR* EN5 ....26 C1
Hadley Pde *BAR* EN5 * 26 D2
Hadley Rdg *BAR* EN5 ....26 E2
Hadley Rd *BAR* EN5 ....27 F2
BELV DA17 ....117 G3
MTCM CR4 ....163 J3
Hadley St *KTTN* NW5 ....72 B5
Hadley Wy *WCHMH* N21 ......29 G5
Hadley Wood Rd *BAR* EN5 ....26 E1
Hadlow Pl *NRWD* SE19 ......150 C6
Hadlow Rd *SCUP* DA14 ......155 G3
WELL DA16 ....116 D3
Hadrian Cl *BOW* E3 * 75 J7
STWL/WRAY TW19 ....120 B6
Hadrian Est *BETH* E2 * 92 C1
Hadrian's Ride *EN* EN1 ....30 B4
Hadrian St *GNWCH* SE10 ....113 H4
Hadrian Wy *STWL/WRAY* TW19 ..120 A6
Hadyn Park Rd *SHB* W12 ....106 D1
Hafer Rd *BTSEA* SW11 ......128 E3
Hafton Rd *CAT* SE6 ....133 H7
Haggard Rd *TWK* TW1 ......124 C6
Hagger Ct *WALTH* E17 * 58 B2
Haggerston Rd *HACK* E8 ......7 L3
Hague St *BETH* E2 ....92 C2
Ha-Ha Rd *WOOL/PLUM* SE18 ..114 E5
Haig Rd *STAN* HA7 ....35 J4
UX/CGN UB8 ....82 A4
Haig Rd East *PLSTW* E13 ....95 G2
Haig Rd West *PLSTW* E13 ....95 G2
Haigville Gdns *BARK/HLT* IG6 ..60 B1
Hailes Cl *WIM/MER* SW19 ....147 G5
Hailey Rd *ERITHM* DA18 ......117 H1
Haimo Rd *ELTH/MOT* SE9 ....134 C4
Hainault Av *RYNPK* SW20 ....145 K6
Hainault Gore *CHDH* RM6 ....62 A4
Hainault Rd *CHDH* RM6 ......61 H2
CRW RM5 ....62 B2
WAN E11 ....58 A7
Hainford Cl *PECK* SE15 ......131 F1
Haining Cl *CHSWK* W4 ....105 H4
Hainthorpe Rd *WNWD* SE27 ..149 H2
Hainton Cl *WCHPL* E1 ....92 D5
Halberd Ms *CLPT* E5 * 74 D1
Halbutt St *DAGW* RM9 ....80 B3
Halcomb St *IS* N1 ....7 J4
Halcot Av *BXLYHS* DA6 ......137 J4
Halcrow St *WCHPL* E1 * 92 D4
Haldane Cl *MUSWH* N10 ......40 B6
Haldane Pl *WAND/EARL* SW18 ..128 A7
Haldane Rd *EHAM* E6 ....95 H2
FUL/PGN SW6 ....107 J5
STHL UB1 ....84 C6
THMD SE28 ....97 K6
Haldon Rd *WAND/EARL* SW18 ..127 J5
Hale Cl *CHING* E4 ....44 A2
EDGW HA8 ....36 E4
Hale Dr *MLHL* NW7 ....36 E5
Hale End *RSLP* HA4 ....46 E5
Hale End Rd *WALTH* E17 ......58 B1
Halefield Rd *TOTM* N17 ....42 C7
Hale Gdns *ACT* W3 ....86 C7
TOTM N17 ....56 C2
Hale Grove Gdns *MLHL* NW7 ..37 F4
Hale House
WOOL/PLUM SE18 * 114 D6
Hale La *EDGW* HA8 ....36 E4
MLHL NW7 ....37 F4
Halesowen Rd *MRDN* SM4 ..162 A6
Hales St *DEPT* SE8 ....112 D6
Hale St *POP/IOD* E14 ....93 K6
Halesworth Rd *LEW* SE13 ..132 E2
The Hale *CHING* E4 ....44 B6
TOTM N17 ....56 C2
Haley Rd *HDN* NW4 ....52 A5
Half Acre *BTFD* TW8 ....104 E5
Half Acre Ms *BTFD* TW8 * 104 E5
Half Acre Rd *HNWL* W7 ....84 E7
Half Moon Crs *IS* N1 ....5 M5
Half Moon La *HNHL* SE24 ....130 D5
Half Moon Pas *WCHPL* E1 ....13 M5
Half Moon St *MYFR/PICC* W1J ..10 D9
Halford Cl *EDGW* HA8 ....50 D1
Halford Rd *FUL/PGN* SW6 ....107 K5
LEY E10 ....58 B5
RCHPK/HAM TW10 ....125 F4
Halfway St *BFN/LL* DA15 ....135 K7
Haliburton Rd *TWK* TW1 ......124 B4
Haliday Wk *IS* N1 ....73 K5
Halifax Cl *TEDD* TW11 ....142 E5
Halifax St *SYD* SE26 ....150 D3
Halifax Rd *ENC/FH* EN2 ......29 J1

GFD/PVL UB6 .... 66 B7
Halifax St SYD SE26 .... 150 D2
Halifield Dr BELV DA17 .... 117 F2
Haling Gv SAND/SEL CR2 .... 177 J6
Haling Park Gdns SAND/SEL CR2 .... 177 H5
Haling Park Rd SAND/SEL CR2 .... 177 H5
Haling Rd SAND/SEL CR2 .... 177 K5
Halkin Ar KTBR SW1X 16 A3
Halkin Ms KTBR SW1X * 16 A3
Halkin Pl KTBR SW1X 16 A3
Halkin St KTBR SW1X 16 A3
Hallam Cl CHST BR7 .... 153 K4
  WATN WD24 .... 21 G1
Hallam Gdns PIN HA5 .... 33 J6
Hallam Ms GTPST W1W 10 D2
Hallam Rd BARN SW13 .... 126 E2
  SEVS/STOTM N15 .... 55 H3
Hallam St GTPST W1W 10 D2
Halland Wy NTHWD HA6 .... 32 B5
Hall Cl EA W5 .... 86 A4
Hall Ct TEDD TW11 .... 143 F4
Hall Dr SYD SE26 .... 150 E4
Halley Gdns LEW SE13 .... 133 G3
Halley Rd FSTGT E7 .... 77 G5
Halley St POP/IOD E14 .... 93 G4
Hall Farm Dr WHTN TW2 .... 123 J6
Hall Farm Dr WHTN TW2 .... 123 J6
Hallfield Est BAY/PAD W2 .... 8 D5
Halford Wy DART DA1 .... 139 F5
Hall Gdns CHING E4 .... 43 H3
Hall Ga STJWD NW8 .... 2 B7
Halliday Sq NWDGN UB2 .... 84 D7
Halliford St IS N1 .... 6 F1
Halliwell Rd BRXS/STRHM SW2 .... 130 A5
Halliwick Court Pde NFNCH/WDSPK N12 * 39 K4
Halliwick Rd MUSWH N10 .... 40 A4
Hall La CHING E4 .... 43 H5
  HDN NW4 .... 51 J1
  HYS/HAR UB3 .... 101 G6
Hallmead Rd SUT SM1 .... 175 F2
Hallowell Av CROY/NA CR0 .... 176 D5
Hallowell Cl MTCM CR4 .... 163 F2
Hallowell Gdns THHTH CR7 .... 164 D1
Hallowell Rd NTHWD HA6 .... 32 D6
Hallowes Crs OXHEY WD19 .... 32 E2
Hallowfield Wy MTCM CR4 .... 162 C2
Hallows Gv SUN TW16 .... 140 D4
Hall Pl BAY/PAD W2 .... 9 G1
Hall Place Crs BXLY DA5 .... 137 K4
Hall Rd CHDH RM6 .... 61 J5
  DART DA1 .... 139 J3
  EHAM E6 .... 77 K7
  GPK RM2 .... 63 K2
  ISLW TW7 .... 123 J4
  MV/WKIL W9 .... 2 F8
  SRTFD E15 .... 76 B3
  WLGTN SM6 .... 176 B7
Hall St FSBYE EC1V 6 B7
  NFNCH/WDSPK N12 .... 39 G4
Hallsville Rd CAN/RD E16 .... 94 D5
Hallswelle Pde GLDGN NW11 * 52 D5
Hallswelle Rd GLDGN NW11 .... 52 D4
The Hall BKHTH/KID SE3 .... 133 K2
Hall Vw ELTH/MOT SE9 .... 153 H1
Hallywell Crs EHAM E6 .... 95 K4
Halons Rd ELTH/MOT SE9 .... 135 F6
Halpin Pl WALW SE17 .... 19 H6
Halsbrook Rd BKHTH/KID SE3 .... 134 B2
Halsbury Cl STAN HA7 .... 35 H4
Halsbury Rd SHB W12 .... 87 K7
Halsbury Rd East NTHLT UB5 .... 66 C3
Halsbury Rd West NTHLT UB5 .... 66 B4
Halsend HYS/HAR UB3 * 83 F7
Halsey Rd WATW WD18 .... 21 F3
Halsey St CHEL SW3 .... 15 L5
Halsham Crs BARK IG11 .... 79 F5
Halsmere Rd CMBW SE5 .... 110 C7
Halstead Cl CROY/NA CR0 .... 177 J2
Halstead Gdns WCHMH N21 .... 29 K7
Halstead Rd EN EN1 .... 30 A3
  ERITH DA8 .... 118 B7
  WAN E11 .... 59 F4
  WCHMH N21 .... 29 K7
Halstow Rd GNWCH SE10 .... 113 K4
  WLSDN NW10 .... 88 B2
Halsway HYS/HAR UB3 .... 82 E7
Halter Cl BORE WD6 .... 25 F4
Halton Cl FBAR/BDGN N11 .... 39 K5
Halton Cross St IS N1 * 6 E3
Halton Pl IS N1 * 6 D2
Halton Rd IS N1 .... 6 B2
Halt Pde CDALE/KGS NW9 * 51 F3
Halt Robin La BELV DA17 .... 117 H3
Hambalt Rd CLAP SW4 .... 129 H4
Hamble Cl RSLP HA4 .... 64 C1
Hambledon Ct EA W5 * 86 A6
Hambledon Gdns SNWD SE25 .... 165 G2
Hambledon Pl DUL SE21 .... 131 G7
Hambledon Rd WAND/EARL SW18 .... 127 J6
Hambledown Rd BFN/LL DA15 .... 135 J6
Hamble St FUL/PGN SW6 .... 128 A2
Hambleton Cl WPK KT4 .... 174 A1
Hambro Av HAYES BR2 .... 167 K7
Hambrook Rd SNWD SE25 .... 165 J2
Hambro Rd STRHM/NOR SW16 .... 148 D5
Hambrough Rd STHL UB1 .... 83 J7
Ham Common RCHPK/HAM TW10 .... 143 K7
Ham Croft Cl FELT TW13 .... 140 D2
Hamden Crs DAGE RM10 .... 80 D2
Hamel Cl KTN/HRWW/WS HA3 .... 49 K3
Hameway EHAM E6 .... 96 A3
Ham Farm Rd RCHPK/HAM TW10 .... 143 K3
Hamfrith Rd SRTFD E15 .... 76 D5
Ham Gate Av RCHPK/HAM TW10 .... 144 A3
Hamilton Av BARK/HLT IG6 .... 60 B3
  CHEAM SM3 .... 174 C1
  ED N9 .... 30 C6
  ROM RM1 .... 63 F1
  SURB KT6 .... 172 C1
Hamilton Cl BERM/RHTH SE16 .... 112 B1
  EBAR EN4 .... 27 J3
  FELT TW13 .... 140 D4
  STJWD NW8 .... 3 G8
  TEDD TW11 .... 143 H5
  TOTM N17 .... 56 B2
Hamilton Ct EA W5 * 86 B6
Hamilton Crs HSLW TW3 .... 123 G4
  PLMGR N13 .... 41 G3
  RYLN/HDSTN HA2 .... 65 K2
Hamilton La HBRY N5 .... 73 H3
Hamilton Ms MYFR/PICC W1J * 16 C1
Hamilton Pde FELT TW13 * 140 E3

Hamilton Pk HBRY N5 .... 73 H3
Hamilton Pk West HBRY N5 .... 73 H3
Hamilton Rd MYFR/PKLN W1K 10 B9
  SUN TW16 .... 141 H4
Hamilton Rd BTFD TW8 .... 104 E5
  BXLYHN DA7 .... 137 F1
  CHSWK W4 .... 106 B2
  EA W5 .... 86 A6
  EBAR EN4 .... 27 J3
  ED N9 .... 30 C6
  EFNCH N2 .... 53 G2
  FELT TW13 .... 140 D3
  GLDGN NW11 .... 52 B6
  GPK RM2 .... 63 K4
  HRW HA1 .... 48 E4
  HYS/HAR UB3 .... 83 F6
  IL IG1 .... 78 B3
  OXHEY WD19 .... 33 F2
  SCUP DA14 .... 155 G3
  SRTFD E15 .... 94 C2
  STHL UB1 .... 83 K7
  THHTH CR7 .... 164 E2
  WALTH E17 .... 57 G1
  WHTN TW2 .... 123 K7
  WIM/MER SW19 .... 147 F6
  WLSDN NW10 .... 69 J4
  WNWD SE27 .... 149 K3
Hamilton Road Ms WIM/MER SW19 * 147 F6
Hamilton Sq NFNCH/WDSPK N12 * 39 G5
Hamilton St DEPT SE8 .... 112 D5
  WATW WD18 .... 21 G4
Hamilton Ter STJWD NW8 .... 2 E4
Hamilton Wy FNCH N3 .... 38 E5
  PLMGR N13 .... 41 H3
  WLGTN SM6 .... 176 D7
Hamlea Cl LEE/GVPK SE12 .... 133 K4
Hamlet Cl LEW SE13 .... 133 H3
Hamlet Gdns HMSMTH W6 .... 106 D3
Hamlet Rd NRWD SE19 .... 150 B6
Hamlet Sq CRICK NW2 .... 70 C2
Hamlets Wy BOW E3 .... 93 H3
The Hamlet CMBW SE5 .... 130 E2
Hamlet Wy STHWK SE1 .... 19 H2
Hamlin Crs PIN HA5 .... 47 G4
Hamlyn Cl EDGW HA8 .... 36 A2
Hamlyn Gdns NRWD SE19 .... 150 A6
Hammelton Rd BMLY BR1 .... 152 E7
Hammers La MLHL NW7 .... 37 J3
Hammersmith Br HMSMTH W6 .... 106 E4
Hammersmith Bridge Rd BARN SW13 .... 106 E4
Hammersmith Broadway HMSMTH W6 * 107 F3
Hammersmith Emb HMSMTH W6 * 107 F5
Hammersmith F/O HMSMTH W6 * 107 F4
Hammersmith Gv HMSMTH W6 * 107 F3
Hammersmith Rd HMSMTH W6 .... 107 G3
Hammersmith Ter HMSMTH W6 * 106 D4
Hammett Cl YEAD UB4 .... 83 H4
Hammett St TWRH EC3N 13 L6
Hammond Av MTCM CR4 .... 163 G1
Hammond Cl BAR EN5 .... 26 C4
  GFD/PVL UB6 .... 66 D4
  HPTN TW12 .... 142 A7
Hammond Rd EN EN1 .... 30 D2
  NWDGN UB2 .... 102 D2
Hammonds Cl BCTR RM8 .... 79 J2
Hammond St KTTN NW5 .... 72 C5
Hamond Cl SAND/SEL CR2 .... 177 H7
Hamonde Cl EDGW HA8 .... 36 D1
Hamond Sq IS N1 .... 7 J5
Ham Park Rd SRTFD E15 .... 76 D4
Hampden Av BECK BR3 .... 166 B1
Hampden Gurney St MBLAR W1H 9 L5
Hampden La TOTM N17 .... 42 B7
Hampden Rd ARCH N19 .... 72 D1
  BECK BR3 .... 166 B1
  CEND/HSY/T N8 .... 55 G3
  KTN/HRWW/WS HA3 .... 34 C7
  KUT/HW KT1 .... 159 H2
  MUSWH N10 .... 40 A4
  TOTM N17 .... 42 C7
Hampden Sq STHGT/OAK N14 .... 40 B2
Hampden Wy STHGT/OAK N14 .... 40 B2
Hampermill La OXHEY WD19 .... 20 E1
Hampshire Cl UED N18 .... 42 D4
Hampshire Hog La HMSMTH W6 * 106 E3
Hampshire Rd WDGN N22 .... 41 F6
Hampshire St KTTN NW5 .... 72 D5
Hampson Wy VX/NE SW8 .... 110 A7
Hampstead Cl THMD SE28 .... 97 H7
Hampstead Gdns GLDGN NW11 .... 52 E5
Hampstead Ga HAMP NW3 * 71 G4
Hampstead Gn HAMP NW3 .... 71 J4
Hampstead Gv HAMP NW3 .... 71 G3
Hampstead Hill Gdns HAMP NW3 .... 71 J3
Hampstead La HGT N6 .... 53 K6
Hampstead Rd CAMTN NW1 .... 4 E4
Hampstead Sq HAMP NW3 .... 71 G2
Hampstead Wy GLDGN NW11 .... 52 E5
Hampton Cl BORE WD6 .... 24 E4
  FBAR/BDGN N11 .... 40 A4
  KIL/WHAMP NW6 .... 2 A2
  RYNPK SW20 * 146 A6
Hampton Ct IS N1 .... 73 H5
Hampton Court Av E/WMO/HCT KT8 .... 157 J5
Hampton Court Crs E/WMO/HCT KT8 .... 157 J2
Hampton Court Est THDIT KT7 * 157 K4
Hampton Court Rd E/WMO/HCT KT8 .... 158 C2
  HPTN TW12 .... 157 J1
Hampton Court Wy ESH/CLAY KT10 .... 170 C6
Hampton La FELT TW13 .... 141 J3
Hampton Ri KTN/HRWW/WS HA3 .... 50 A5
Hampton Rd CHING E4 .... 43 H4
  CROY/NA CR0 .... 164 D5
  FSTGT E7 .... 77 F4
  IL IG1 .... 78 B3
  TEDD TW11 .... 142 D4
  WHTN TW2 .... 142 D2
  WPK KT4 .... 173 J1
Hampton Rd East FELT TW13 .... 141 K2
Hampton Rd West FELT TW13 .... 141 J1
Hampton St WALW SE17 .... 18 D6

Ham Ridings RCHPK/HAM TW10 .... 144 B4
Ham Shades Cl BFN/LL DA15 .... 155 F2
Ham St RCHPK/HAM TW10 .... 143 J5
The Ham BTFD TW8 .... 104 D6
Ham Vw CROY/NA CR0 .... 166 B5
Ham Yd SOHO/SHAV W1D * 11 A6
Hanameel St CAN/RD E16 .... 94 E7
Hana Ms CLPT E5 .... 74 E3
Hanbury Cl HDN NW4 .... 52 A2
Hanbury Ct HRW HA1 * 49 F5
Hanbury Dr WAN E11 .... 58 D6
  WCHMH N21 .... 29 F3
Hanbury Ms IS N1 .... 6 F4
Hanbury Rd ACT W3 .... 105 J1
  TOTM N17 .... 56 D1
Hanbury St WCHPL E1 .... 13 M2
Hancock Rd BOW E3 .... 94 A2
  NRWD SE19 .... 149 K5
Handa Wk IS N1 .... 73 J5
Hand Ct HHOL WC1V 11 M3
Handcroft Rd CROY/NA CR0 .... 164 B7
Handel Cl EDGW HA8 .... 36 B5
Handel Pde EDGW HA8 * 36 B5
Handel Pl WLSDN NW10 .... 69 F5
Handel St BMSBY WC1N 5 J8
Handel Wy EDGW HA8 .... 36 C6
Handen Rd LEE/GVPK SE12 .... 133 H4
Handforth Rd BRXN/ST SW9 .... 110 B6
  IL IG1 .... 78 B2
Handley Gv CRICK NW2 .... 70 B2
Handley Page Rd WLGTN SM6 .... 177 F6
Handley Rd HOM E9 .... 74 E6
Handowe Cl HDN NW4 .... 51 J3
Handside Cl WPK KT4 .... 161 G7
Handsworth Av CHING E4 .... 44 B5
Handsworth Cl OXHEY WD19 .... 32 E2
Handsworth Rd TOTM N17 .... 55 J5
Handtrough Wy BARK IG11 .... 96 B1
Hanford Cl WAND/EARL SW18 .... 127 K7
Hangar Ruding OXHEY WD19 .... 33 J2
Hanger Gn EA W5 .... 86 C3
Hanger La EA W5 .... 86 A1
Hanger La (North Circular Rd) EA W5 .... 86 A2
Hanger Vale La EA W5 .... 86 B4
Hanger View Wy ACT W3 .... 86 C5
Hankey Pl STHWK SE1 .... 19 H2
Hankins La MLHL NW7 .... 37 G1
Hanley Gdns FSBYPK N4 .... 55 F7
Hanley Pl BECK BR3 .... 151 J6
Hanley Rd FSBYPK N4 .... 54 E7
Hanmer Wk HOLWY N7 .... 73 F1
Hannah Cl BECK BR3 .... 166 E2
  WLSDN NW10 .... 68 E3
Hannah Mary Wy STHWK SE1 .... 111 H3
Hannay La ARCH N19 .... 54 D6
Hannell Rd FUL/PGN SW6 .... 107 H6
Hannen Rd WNWD SE27 * 149 H2
Hannibal Rd STWL/WRAY TW19 .... 120 B6
  WCHPL E1 .... 92 E4
Hannibal Wy CROY/NA CR0 .... 177 F4
Hannington Rd CLAP SW4 .... 129 G2
Hanno Cl WLGTN SM6 .... 176 D6
Hanover Av CAN/RD E16 .... 94 E7
  FELT TW13 .... 121 K7
Hanover Cir HYS/HAR UB3 .... 82 A5
Hanover Cl CHEAM SM3 .... 174 C3
  RCH/KEW TW9 .... 105 H6
Hanover Dr CHST BR7 .... 154 C3
Hanover Gdns LBTH SE11 .... 110 B5
  BARK/HLT IG6 .... 60 D7
Hanover Ga STJWD NW8 .... 3 K8
Hanover Pk PECK SE15 .... 111 H7
Hanover Rd SEVS/STOTM N15 .... 56 B3
  WIM/MER SW19 .... 147 G6
  WLSDN NW10 .... 70 A6
Hanover Sq CONDST W1S 10 D5
Hanover Steps BAY/PAD W2 * 9 K5
Hanover St CONDST W1S 10 D5
  CROY/NA CR0 .... 177 H2
Hanover Ter CAMTN NW1 .... 3 L8
Hanover Terrace Ms CAMTN NW1 .... 3 K8
Hanover Wy BXLYHS DA6 .... 136 E3
Hanover Yd IS N1 * 6 D5
Hansard Ms WKENS W14 .... 107 G1
Hans Crs KTBR SW1X 15 L3
Hanselin Cl STAN HA7 .... 35 F4
Hansen Dr WCHMH N21 .... 29 F4
Hanshaw Dr EDGW HA8 .... 37 F7
Hansler Gv E/WMO/HCT KT8 .... 157 J4
Hansler Rd EDUL SE22 .... 131 G4
Hansol Rd BXLYHS DA6 .... 137 F4
Hansom Ter BMLY BR1 * 153 F7
Hanson Cl BAL SW12 .... 129 G6
  BECK BR3 .... 151 K5
  MORT/ESHN SW14 .... 125 K2
  WDR/YW UB7 .... 100 C2
Hanson Gdns STHL UB1 .... 102 D1
Hanson St GTPST W1W 10 E2
Hans Pl KTBR SW1X 15 L3
Hans Rd CHEL SW3 .... 15 L3
Hans St KTBR SW1X 15 M4
Hanway Pl FITZ W1T 11 G4
Hanway Rd HNWL W7 .... 84 D5
Hanway St FITZ W1T 11 G4
Hanworth Rd FELT TW13 .... 122 K3
  HPTN TW12 .... 141 K3
  HSLW TW3 .... 123 G2
  HSLWW TW4 .... 122 E6
  SUN TW16 .... 140 E6
Hanworth Ter HSLW TW3 .... 123 G3
Hapgood Cl GFD/PVL UB6 .... 66 D4
Harben Pde HAMP NW3 * 3 G1
Harben Rd KIL/WHAMP NW6 .... 2 F1
Harberson Rd BAL SW12 .... 129 G1
  SRTFD E15 .... 76 D7
Harberton Rd ARCH N19 .... 54 C1
Harbet Rd BAY/PAD W2 .... 9 H3
  UED N18 .... 43 F4
Harbex Cl BXLY DA5 .... 137 J6
Harbinger Rd POP/IOD E14 .... 112 E3
Harbledown Rd FUL/PGN SW6 .... 107 K7
Harbord Cl CMBW SE5 .... 130 E1
Harbord St FUL/PGN SW6 .... 107 G7
Harborne Cl OXHEY WD19 .... 33 G4
Harborough Av BFN/LL DA15 .... 135 K6
Harborough Rd STRHM/NOR SW16 .... 149 F3
Harbour Av WBPTN SW10 .... 108 B7
Harbour Cl MTCM CR4 .... 148 A7
Harbour Exchange Sq POP/IOD E14 .... 112 E1
Harbour Rd CMBW SE5 .... 130 D2
Harbridge Av PUT/ROE SW15 .... 126 C6
Harbury Rd CAR SM5 .... 175 J7
Harbut Rd BTSEA SW11 .... 128 C3
Harcastle Cl YEAD UB4 .... 83 J4

Harcombe Rd STNW/STAM N16 .... 74 A2
Harcourt Av BFN/LL DA15 .... 136 D5
  EDGW HA8 .... 36 E2
  MNPK E12 .... 77 K3
  WLGTN SM6 .... 176 B3
Harcourt Blds EMB EC4Y * 12 A6
Harcourt Cl ISLW TW7 .... 124 C2
Harcourt Fld WLGTN SM6 .... 176 B3
Harcourt Ms GPK RM2 .... 63 H4
Harcourt Rd BROCKY SE4 .... 132 C3
  BUSH WD23 .... 22 C5
  BXLYHS DA6 .... 137 F3
  SRTFD E15 .... 94 D1
  THHTH CR7 .... 164 A5
  WDGN N22 .... 40 D7
  WIM/MER SW19 .... 146 E6
  WLGTN SM6 .... 176 B3
Harcourt St MBLAR W1H 9 K3
Harcourt Ter WBPTN SW10 .... 14 D8
Hardcastle Cl CROY/NA CR0 .... 165 H5
Hardcourts Cl WWKM BR4 .... 179 K5
Hardel Wk BRXS/STRHM SW2 .... 130 B6
Hardens Manorway WOOL/PLUM SE18 .... 114 C2
Harders Rd PECK SE15 .... 131 J1
Hardess St HNHL SE24 .... 130 D2
Hardie Cl WLSDN NW10 .... 69 F4
Hardie Rd DAGE RM10 .... 80 E2
Harding Cl CROY/NA CR0 .... 178 B2
  KUTN/CMB KT2 .... 144 B2
  WALW SE17 .... 18 D9
Hardinge Crs WOOL/PLUM SE18 .... 115 H2
Hardinge Rd UED N18 .... 42 A4
  WLSDN NW10 .... 70 A1
Hardinge St WCHPL E1 .... 92 E5
  WOOL/PLUM SE18 .... 115 G2
Harding Rd BXLYHN DA7 .... 137 G1
Hardings La PGE/AN SE20 .... 151 F5
Hardman Rd CHARL SE7 .... 114 A4
  KUTN/CMB KT2 .... 159 F1
Hardwick Cl STAN HA7 .... 35 J4
Hardwicke Av HEST TW5 .... 103 F7
Hardwicke Ms FSBYW WC1X * 5 M8
Hardwicke Rd CHSWK W4 .... 105 K3
  PLMGR N13 .... 40 E4
  RCHPK/HAM TW10 .... 143 J5
Hardwicke St BARK IG11 .... 78 C7
Hardwick Gn WEA W13 .... 85 H4
Hardwick Pl STRHM/NOR SW16 .... 148 C6
Hardwick's Sq WAND/EARL SW18 .... 127 K4
Hardwick St CLKNW EC1R 6 A8
Hardwidge St STHWK SE1 .... 19 J1
Hardy Av CAN/RD E16 .... 94 E7
  DART DA1 .... 139 G5
  RSLP HA4 .... 65 F4
Hardy Cl BAR EN5 .... 26 C4
  BERM/RHTH SE16 .... 112 A1
  PIN HA5 .... 47 H6
Hardy Cots GNWCH SE10 * 113 G5
Hardy Cv DART DA1 .... 139 K3
Hardy Pas WDGN N22 .... 41 F7
Hardy Rd BKHTH/KID SE3 .... 113 J5
  CHING E4 .... 43 H5
  WIM/MER SW19 .... 147 F6
Hardys Ms E/WMO/HCT KT8 .... 157 K3
Harebell Dr EHAM E6 .... 96 A4
Hare & Billet Rd BKHTH/KID SE3 .... 113 G7
Hare Ct EMB EC4Y * 12 A5
Harecourt Rd IS N1 .... 73 J5
Haredale Rd HNHL SE24 .... 130 D3
Haredon Cl FSTH SE23 .... 131 K6
Harefield ESH/CLAY KT10 .... 170 C4
Harefield Av BELMT SM2 .... 174 C7
Harefield Ms BROCKY SE4 .... 132 C2
Harefield Rd BROCKY SE4 .... 132 C2
  CEND/HSY/T N8 .... 54 D4
  SCUP DA14 .... 155 K1
  STRHM/NOR SW16 .... 149 F6
Hare Hall La GPK RM2 .... 63 K3
Hare La ESH/CLAY KT10 .... 170 D5
Hare Marsh BETH E2 .... 92 C3
Harepit Cl SAND/SEL CR2 .... 177 H6
Hare Rw BETH E2 .... 92 D1
Haresfield Rd DAGE RM10 .... 80 C5
Hare St WOOL/PLUM SE18 .... 115 F2
Hare Wk IS N1 .... 7 K6
Harewood Av CAMTN NW1 .... 9 K1
  NTHLT UB5 .... 65 H6
  STJWD NW8 .... 3 K9
Harewood Cl NTHLT UB5 .... 65 K6
Harewood Dr CLAY IG5 .... 59 K1
Harewood Pl CONDST W1S 10 D5
Harewood Rd ISLW TW7 .... 104 A6
  OXHEY WD19 .... 33 F1
  SAND/SEL CR2 .... 178 A5
  WIM/MER SW19 .... 147 J5
Harewood Rw CAMTN NW1 .... 9 K2
Harewood Ter NWDGN UB2 .... 102 E3
Harfield Gdns CMBW SE5 .... 131 F2
Harfield Rd SUN TW16 .... 156 C1
Harford Cl CHING E4 .... 31 K6
Harford Rd CHING E4 .... 31 K6
Harford St WCHPL E1 .... 93 G3
Harford Wk EFNCH N2 .... 53 H3
Harglaze Ter CDALE/KGS NW9 * 51 G2
Hargood Cl KTN/HRWW/WS HA3 .... 50 A5
Hargood Rd BKHTH/KID SE3 .... 114 B7
Hargrave Pk ARCH N19 .... 72 C1
Hargrave Pl KTTN NW5 .... 72 C1
Hargrave Rd ARCH N19 .... 72 C1
Hargwyne St BRXN/ST SW9 .... 130 A2
Haringey Rd CEND/HSY/T N8 .... 54 E3
Haringey Rd CEND/HSY/T N8 .... 54 E3
Harington Ter UED N18 * 41 K3
Harkett Cl KTN/HRWW/WS HA3 .... 49 F1
Harland Av BFN/LL DA15 .... 154 D2
  CROY/NA CR0 .... 178 B2
Harland Cl WIM/MER SW19 .... 162 A2
Harland Rd LEE/GVPK SE12 .... 133 K1
Harlech Gdns HEST TW5 .... 102 B5
  PIN HA5 .... 47 H6
Harlech Rd STHGT/OAK N14 .... 40 E2
Harlequin Av BTFD TW8 .... 104 B5
Harlequin Cl ISLW TW7 .... 123 K4
  YEAD UB4 .... 83 H4
Harlequin Ct EA W5 * 85 J6
Harlequin Rd TEDD TW11 .... 143 H6
The Harlequin WAT WD17 * 21 G3
Harlescott Rd PECK SE15 .... 132 A3
Harlesden Gdns WLSDN NW10 .... 69 H7
Harlesden La WLSDN NW10 .... 69 J7
Harlesden Rd WLSDN NW10 .... 69 H7
Harley Cl ALP/SUD HA0 .... 67 K5
Harley Crs HRW HA1 .... 48 D3
Harley Gdns WBPTN SW10 .... 14 F8
Harley Gv BOW E3 .... 93 H2
Harley Pl CAVSQ/HST W1G 10 C3
Harley Rd HAMP NW3 .... 3 H1
  HRW HA1 .... 48 D3
  WLSDN NW10 .... 87 G2
Harley Vls WLSDN NW10 * 87 G2
Harlinger St WOOL/PLUM SE18 .... 114 C2
Harlington Cl HYS/HAR UB3 .... 101 F6
Harlington Rd BXLYHN DA7 .... 137 G2
Harlington Rd East EBED/NFELT TW14 .... 122 A6
Harlington Rd West EBED/NFELT TW14 .... 122 A5
Harlow Rd PLMGR N13 .... 41 K2
  RAIN RM13 .... 81 H7
Harlyn Dr PIN HA5 .... 47 F2
Harman Av WFD IG8 .... 44 D6
Harman Cl CHING E4 .... 44 B3
  CRICK NW2 .... 70 C2
  STHWK SE1 * 111 H4
Harman Dr BFN/LL DA15 .... 136 A5
  CRICK NW2 .... 70 C2
Harman Ri IL IG1 .... 78 E3
Harman Rd EN EN1 .... 30 B4
Harmondsworth La WDR/YW UB7 .... 100 B5
Harmondsworth Rd WDR/YW UB7 .... 100 B2
Harmony Cl GLDGN NW11 .... 52 C4
  WLGTN SM6 .... 176 E7
Harmony Pl STHWK SE1 .... 19 M7
Harmony Wy BMLY BR1 .... 167 K1
  HDN NW4 .... 52 A3
Harmood Gv CAMTN NW1 .... 4 C1
Harmood St CAMTN NW1 .... 4 C1
Harmsworth Ms STHWK SE1 .... 18 B4
Harmsworth St WALW SE17 .... 18 C8
Harmsworth Wy TRDG/WHET N20 .... 26 D7
Harness Rd THMD SE28 .... 116 B1
Harold Av BELV DA17 .... 117 G4
  HYS/HAR UB3 .... 101 J2
Harold Ct CEND/HSY/T N8 .... 55 F4
  CHING E4 .... 44 C4
  NRWD SE19 .... 149 K6
  PLSTW E13 .... 77 F2
  SEVS/STOTM N15 .... 56 B4
  SUT SM1 .... 175 H3
  SWFD E18 .... 44 E7
  WAN E11 .... 58 C7
  WLSDN NW10 .... 87 F2
Haroldstone Rd WALTH E17 .... 57 F4
Harpenden Rd MNPK E12 .... 77 G1
  WNWD SE27 .... 149 H1
Harper Rd EHAM E6 .... 95 K5
  STHWK SE1 .... 18 F3
Harpers Yd ISLW TW7 * 124 A1
Harp Island Cl WLSDN NW10 .... 69 F1
Harp La MON EC3R 13 J7
Harpley Sq WCHPL E1 .... 92 E3
Harpour Rd BARK IG11 .... 78 C5
Harp Rd HNWL W7 .... 85 F3
Harpsden St BTSEA SW11 .... 109 F7
Harpur Ms BMSBY WC1N 11 L2
Harpur St BMSBY WC1N 11 L2
Harraden Rd BKHTH/KID SE3 .... 114 B7
Harrier Cl HCH RM12 .... 81 K5
Harrier Ms THMD SE28 .... 115 J1
Harrier Rd CDALE/KGS NW9 .... 51 G2
Harriers Cl EA W5 .... 86 A6
Harrier Wy EHAM E6 .... 95 K4
Harries Rd YEAD UB4 .... 83 G3
Harriet Cl HACK E8 .... 74 C7
Harriet Gdns CROY/NA CR0 .... 178 C1
Harriet St KTBR SW1X 15 M2
Harriet Tubman Cl BRXS/STRHM SW2 .... 130 B6
Harriet Wk KTBR SW1X 15 M2
Harriet Wy BUSH WD23 .... 22 D6
Harringay Gdns CEND/HSY/T N8 .... 55 H3
Harringay Rd SEVS/STOTM N15 .... 55 H4
Harrington Cl CROY/NA CR0 .... 176 E1
  WLSDN NW10 .... 69 F2
Harrington Ct NKENS W10 * 88 D2
Harrington Gdns SKENS SW7 .... 14 C6
Harrington Hi CLPT E5 .... 56 D7
Harrington Rd SKENS SW7 .... 15 G5
  SNWD SE25 .... 165 H3
  WAN E11 .... 58 C7
Harrington Sq CAMTN NW1 .... 4 E6
Harrington St CAMTN NW1 .... 4 E6
Harrington Wy WOOL/PLUM SE18 .... 114 C2
Harriott Cl GNWCH SE10 .... 113 J3
Harris Cl HSLW TW3 .... 103 F7
Harrison Cl NTHWD HA6 .... 32 A5
  TRDG/WHET N20 .... 27 J7
Harrison Dr BMLY BR1 .... 169 G3
Harrison Rd DAGE RM10 .... 80 D5
  WLSDN NW10 .... 69 F7
Harrison's Ri CROY/NA CR0 .... 177 H2
Harrisons Whf PUR RM19 .... 119 K4
Harrison St STPAN WC1H 5 K8
Harris Rd BXLYHN DA7 .... 117 F7
  DAGW RM9 .... 80 B4
Harris St CMBW SE5 .... 110 E6
  WALTH E17 .... 57 H6
Harris Wy SUN TW16 .... 140 C7
Harrods Gn EDGW HA8 * 36 C4
Harrogate Rd OXHEY WD19 .... 33 G2
Harrold Rd BCTR RM8 .... 79 H4
Harrow Av EN EN1 .... 30 B5
Harroway Rd BTSEA SW11 .... 128 C1
Harrowby St MBLAR W1H 9 K4
Harrow Cl CHSGTN KT9 .... 171 K6
Harrowdene Cl ALP/SUD HA0 .... 67 K3
Harrowdene Gdns TEDD TW11 .... 143 G6
Harrowdene Rd ALP/SUD HA0 .... 67 K3
Harrow Dr ED N9 .... 30 B7
Harrowes Meade EDGW HA8 .... 36 C2
Harrow Fields Gdns HRW HA1 .... 66 E2
Harrowgate Rd HOM E9 .... 75 G5
Harrow Gn WAN E11 .... 76 C2
Harrow La POP/IOD E14 .... 94 A6
Harrow Manor Wy ABYW SE2 .... 116 D2
Harrow Pk HRW HA1 .... 66 E1
Harrow Pl WCHPL E1 .... 13 K4
Harrow Rd ALP/SUD HA0 .... 67 G3
  CAR SM5 .... 175 J5
  EBED/NFELT TW14 .... 120 D7
  IL IG1 .... 78 C3
  MV/WKIL W9 .... 8 A1
  WAN E11 .... 76 C2
  WBLY HA9 .... 68 C2
  WLSDN NW10 .... 87 K2

Harrow Rd F/O BAY/PAD W2 9 H3
Harrow St CAMTN NW1 * 9 K2
Harrow Vw HGDN/ICK UB10 82 A2
HRW HA1 48 D3
HYS/HAR UB3 82 E6
RYLN/HDSTN HA2 48 D2
Harrow View Rd EA W5 85 H3
Harrow Wy OXHEY WD19 33 J2
Harrow Weald Pk
KTN/HRWW/WS HA3 34 D5
Harry Cl THHTH CR7 164 D5
Harry Zeital Wy CLPT E5 74 E1
Hartcliff Ct HNWL W7 * 104 A1
Hart Cl CROY/NA CR0 177 H2
Harte Rd HSLW TW3 122 E1
Hartfield Av BORE WD6 24 C3
NTHLT UB5 83 F1
Hartfield Cl BORE WD6 24 C4
Hartfield Crs WIM/MER SW19 146 D6
WWKM BR4 180 E2
Hartfield Gv PGE/AN SE20 150 D7
Hartfield Rd CHSGTN KT9 171 K4
WIM/MER SW19 146 D5
WWKM BR4 180 E3
Hartfield Ter BOW E3 93 J1
Hartford Av
KTN/HRWW/WS HA3 49 G2
Hartforde Rd BORE WD6 24 C1
Hartford Rd BXLY DA5 137 H5
HOR/WEW KT19 172 C5
Hart Gv EA W5 86 C7
STHL UB1 84 A4
Hartham Cl HOLWY N7 72 E4
ISLW TW7 104 B7
Hartham Rd HOLWY N7 72 E4
ISLW TW7 104 A7
TOTM N17 56 B1
Harting Rd ELTH/MOT SE9 153 J3
Hartington Cl HRW HA1 66 E3
Hartington Rd CAN/RD E16 95 F5
CHSWK W4 105 J6
NWDGN UB2 * 102 D2
TWK TW1 124 C6
VX/NE SW8 109 K7
WALTH E17 57 G5
WEA W13 85 H6
Hartismere Rd FUL/PGN SW6 107 J6
Hartlake Rd HOM E9 75 F5
Hartland Cl EDGW HA8 36 C1
WCHMH N21 29 J5
Hartland Dr EDGW HA8 36 C1
RSLP HA4 65 F2
Hartland Rd CAMTN NW1 4 C1
FBAR/BDGN N11 39 K4
HCH RM12 81 J1
HPTN TW12 142 B3
ISLW TW7 124 B2
KIL/WHAMP NW6 88 D1
MRDN SM4 161 K6
SRTFD E15 76 D6
Hartland Rd Arches
CAMTN NW1 * 4 B1
Hartlands Cl BXLY DA5 137 G5
The Hartlands HEST TW5 102 A5
Hartland Wy CROY/NA CR0 179 G1
MRDN SM4 161 J6
Hartley Av EHAM E6 77 J7
MLHL NW7 37 H4
Hartley Cl BMLY BR1 168 E1
MLHL NW7 37 H4
Hartley Rd CROY/NA CR0 164 D6
WAN E11 58 D7
WELL DA16 116 D6
Hartley St BETH E2 92 E2
Hartmann Rd CAN/RD E16 95 H7
Hartnoll St HOLWY N7 73 F4
Harton Cl BMLY BR1 153 H7
Harton Rd ED N9 42 D1
Harton St DEPT SE8 112 D7
Hartsbourne Av BUSH WD23 34 C1
Hartsbourne Cl BUSH WD23 34 D1
Hartsbourne Rd BUSH WD23 34 D1
Harts Cl BUSH WD23 22 A1
Hartscroft CROY/NA CR0 179 G7
Harts Gv WFD IG8 44 E4
Hartshorn Gdns EHAM E6 96 A3
Harts La BARK IG11 78 B6
Hart's La NWCR SE14 112 B6
Hartslock Dr ABYW SE2 116 E1
Hartsmead Rd ELTH/MOT SE9 153 K1
Hartspring La BUSH WD23 22 A1
Hart Sq MRDN SM4 * 162 A4
Hart St MON EC3R 13 K6
Hartsway PEND EN3 30 D3
Hartswood Cl BUSH WD23 22 A1
Hartswood Gdns SHB W12 * 106 C2
Hartswood Gn BUSH WD23 34 D1
Hartswood Rd SHB W12 106 C1
Hartsworth Cl PLSTW E13 94 D1
Hartville Rd
WOOL/PLUM SE18 115 K3
Hartwell Cl BRXS/STRHM SW2 130 A7
Hartwell Dr CHING E4 44 A5
Hartwell St HACK E8 74 B5
Harvard Hl CHSWK W4 105 J4
Harvard Rd CHSWK W4 105 J4
ISLW TW7 103 K7
LEW SE13 133 F4
Harvel Crs ABYW SE2 116 E4
Harvest Bank Rd WWKM BR4 180 E2
Harvesters Cl ISLW TW7 123 J4
Harvest La THDIT KT7 158 B5
Harvest Rd BUSH WD23 22 B3
FELT TW13 140 E3
Harvey Dr HPTN TW12 142 B7
Harvey Gdns CHARL SE7 114 B4
Harvey Rd CEND/HSY/T N8 55 F4
CMBW SE5 110 E7
HSLWW TW4 122 E6
IL IG1 78 B4
NTHLT UB5 65 G6
WAN E11 58 C7
Harvey's La ROMW/RG RM7 81 F1
Harvey St IS N1 7 H4
Harvill Rd SCUP DA14 155 K4
Harvington Wk HACK E8 * 74 C6
Harvist Rd KIL/WHAMP NW6 88 C1
Harwell Cl RSLP HA4 46 B7
Harwood Av BMLY BR1 168 A1
MTCM CR4 162 D2
Harwood Cl ALP/SUD HA0 67 K3
NFNCH/WDSPK N12 39 J5
Harwood Ms FUL/PGN SW6 * 108 A6
Harwood Rd FUL/PGN SW6 107 K6
Harwoods Rd WATW WD18 20 E3
Harwood Ter FUL/PGN SW6 108 A7
Hascombe Ter CMBW SE5 * 130 E1
Haselbury Rd UED N18 42 A3
Haseley End FSTH SE23 * 131 K6
Haselrigge Rd CLAP SW4 129 J3
Haseltine Rd SYD SE26 151 H3
Haselwood Dr ENC/FH EN2 29 H3
Haskard Rd DAGW RM9 79 K3
Hasker St CHEL SW3 15 K5
Haslam Av CHEAM SM3 161 H7
Haslam Cl HGDN/ICK UB10 64 A1
IS N1 6 B1
Haslam St PECK SE15 111 G7
Haslemere Av EBAR EN4 27 K7
HDN NW4 52 B5
HEST TW5 122 B1
HNWL W7 104 B2
MTCM CR4 162 C1
WAND/EARL SW18 147 F1
Haslemere Cl HPTN TW12 141 K4
WLGTN SM6 176 E4
Haslemere Gdns FNCH N3 52 D2
Haslemere Heathrow Est
HSLWW TW4 * 122 A1
Haslemere Rd BXLYHN DA7 137 G1
CEND/HSY/T N8 54 E6
GDMY/SEVK IG3 79 F1
THHTH CR7 164 C4
WCHMH N21 41 H1
Hasler Cl THMD SE28 97 H6
Hasluck Gdns BAR EN5 27 G5
Hassard St BETH E2 7 M6
Hassendean Rd
BKHTH/KID SE3 114 A5
Hassett Rd HOM E9 75 F5
Hassocks Cl SYD SE26 150 D2
Hassocks Rd
STRHM/NOR SW16 148 D7
Hassock Wd HAYES BR2 181 H3
Hassop Rd CRICK NW2 70 B3
Hasted Rd CHARL SE7 114 C4
Hastings Av BARK/HLT IG6 60 C3
Hastings Cl ALP/SUD HA0 67 J3
BAR EN5 27 G3
PECK SE15 * 111 H6
Hastings Dr SURB KT6 158 D5
Hastings Pl CROY/NA CR0 165 G7
Hastings Rd CROY/NA CR0 165 G7
FBAR/BDGN N11 40 C4
GPK RM2 63 K4
HAYES BR2 168 D7
TOTM N17 * 55 K2
WEA W13 85 H6
Hastings St STPAN WC1H 5 J8
Hastings Ter
SEVS/STOTM N15 * 55 J4
Hastings Wy BUSH WD23 21 J3
Hastings St WOOL/PLUM SE18 115 H2
Hastoe Cl YEAD UB4 83 J3
Hatcham Park Ms NWCR SE14 112 A7
Hatcham Park Rd NWCR SE14 112 A7
Hatcham Rd PECK SE15 111 K5
Hatchard Rd ARCH N19 72 D1
Hatchcroft HDN NW4 51 K2
Hatchers Ms STHWK SE1 19 K2
Hatchett Rd
EBED/NFELT TW14 121 F7
Hatch Gv CHDH RM6 62 A3
Hatch La CHING E4 44 B3
WDR/YW UB7 100 A6
Hatch Pl KUTN/CMB KT2 144 B4
Hatch Rd STRHM/NOR SW16 163 K1
Hatchwoods WFD IG8 44 D3
Hatcliffe Cl BKHTH/KID SE3 133 J2
Hatcliffe St GNWCH SE10 113 J4
Hatfield Cl BARK/HLT IG6 60 B2
BELMT SM2 174 E7
MTCM CR4 * 162 C3
Hatfield Ct BKHTH/KID SE3 * 113 K6
Hatfield Rd CHSWK W4 106 A1
HNWL W7 85 G7
SRTFD E15 76 C4
Hatfields STHWK SE1 12 B8
Hathaway Cl HAYES BR2 168 E7
RSLP HA4 64 D3
STAN HA7 35 G4
Hathaway Crs MNPK E12 77 K5
Hathaway Gdns CHDH RM6 61 K4
WEA W13 85 F4
Hathaway Rd CROY/NA CR0 164 C6
Hatherleigh Cl CHSGTN KT9 171 K4
MLHL NW7 38 B6
MRDN SM4 161 K3
Hatherleigh Rd RSLP HA4 64 E1
Hatherley Crs BFN/LL DA15 155 G1
Hatherley Gdns
CEND/HSY/T N8 54 E5
EHAM E6 95 H2
Hatherley Gv BAY/PAD W2 8 C4
Hatherley Ms WALTH E17 57 J3
Hatherley Rd RCH/KEW TW9 105 G7
SCUP DA14 155 G2
WALTH E17 57 H3
Hatherley St WEST SW1P 16 F6
Hathern Gdns ELTH/MOT SE9 154 A3
Hatherop Rd HPTN TW12 141 K6
Hathorne Cl PECK SE15 131 J1
Hathorne Ter ARCH N19 * 54 D7
Hathway St PECK SE15 131 K1
Hatley Av BARK/HLT IG6 60 C3
Hatley Cl FBAR/BDGN N11 39 K4
Hatley Rd FSBYPK N4 73 F1
Hat & Mitre Ct FARR EC1M 12 D1
Hatteraick St
BERM/RHTH SE16 111 K1
Hattersfield Cl BELV DA17 117 G3
Hatters La WATW WD18 20 B5
Hatton Cl WOOL/PLUM SE18 115 J6
Hatton Cross Est
HTHAIR TW6 * 121 J3
Hatton Gdn HCIRC EC1N 12 B2
Hatton Gdns MTCM CR4 162 E4
Hatton Gn EBED/NFELT TW14 121 K3
Hatton Gv WDR/YW UB7 * 100 A1
Hatton Pl HCIRC EC1N 12 B1
Hatton Rd CROY/NA CR0 164 B7
EBED/NFELT TW14 121 F6
HTHAIR TW6 121 J3
Hatton Rd North HTHAIR TW6 101 G7
Hatton Rw STJWD NW8 * 9 H1
Hatton St STJWD NW8 9 H1
Hatton Wall HCIRC EC1N 12 A2
Haunch of Venison Yd
OXSTW W1C * 10 C5
Havana Cl ROM RM1 63 G4
Havana Rd WIM/MER SW19 146 E1
Havannah St POP/IOD E14 112 D1
Havant Rd WALTH E17 58 A2
Havelock Cl SHB W12 * 87 K6
Havelock Pl HRW HA1 48 E5
Havelock Rd BELV DA17 * 117 G3
CROY/NA CR0 178 B1
DART DA1 138 E6
HAYES BR2 168 B3
KTN/HRWW/WS HA3 48 E2
NWDGN UB2 102 D2
TOTM N17 56 C1
WIM/MER SW19 147 G4
Havelock St IL IG1 78 B1
IS N1 5 K3
Havelock Ter VX/NE SW8 109 G6
Havelock Wk FSTH SE23 131 K7
Haven Cl ELTH/MOT SE9 153 K2
ESH/CLAY KT10 170 E1
SCUP DA14 155 J5
WIM/MER SW19 146 B2
YEAD UB4 82 C4
Haven Ct BRYLDS KT5 * 159 G5
Haven Gn EA W5 85 K5
Havenhurst Ri ENC/FH EN2 29 G1
Haven La EA W5 86 A5
Havens Ms BOW E3 93 H4
Haven St CAMTN NW1 * 4 C2
Havenswood Ct
KUTN/CMB KT2 144 D5
The Haven RCH/KEW TW9 125 H2
SUN TW16 140 E6
Havenwood WBLY HA9 68 D2
Haverfield Est BTFD TW8 105 F5
Haverfield Gdns
RCH/KEW TW9 105 H6
Haverfield Rd BOW E3 93 G2
Haverford Wy EDGW HA8 36 B7
Havergal Vls
SEVS/STOTM N15 * 55 H3
Haverhill Rd BAL SW12 129 H7
Havering Dr ROM RM1 63 G3
Havering Gdns CHDH RM6 61 J4
Havering Rd ROM RM1 63 F1
Havering St WCHPL E1 93 F5
Havering Wy BARK IG11 97 H2
Haversham Cl TWK TW1 124 E6
Haversham Pl HGT N6 71 K1
Haverstock Hl HAMP NW3 71 J5
Haverstock Pl FSBYE EC1V 6 B6
Haverstock Rd KTTN NW5 72 A4
Haverstock St IS N1 6 D6
Havil St CMBW SE5 111 F7
Havisham Pl NRWD SE19 149 H5
Hawarden Gv HNHL SE24 130 D6
Hawarden Hl CRICK NW2 69 J2
Hawarden Rd WALTH E17 57 F3
Hawbridge Rd WAN E11 58 B7
Hawes Cl NTHWD HA6 32 D6
Hawes La WWKM BR4 167 F7
Hawes Rd BMLY BR1 153 F7
UED N18 42 D5
Hawes St IS N1 6 D2
Hawgood St BOW E3 93 J4
Hawkdene CHING E4 31 K5
Hawke Park Rd WDGN N22 55 H2
Hawke Pl BERM/RHTH SE16 * 112 A1
Hawke Rd NRWD SE19 149 K5
Hawker Pl WALTH E17 58 A1
Hawker Rd CROY/NA CR0 177 F5
Hawkesbury Rd
PUT/ROE SW15 126 E4
Hawkesfield Rd FSTH SE23 151 G1
Hawkesley Cl TWK TW1 143 G3
Hawkes Rd EBED/NFELT TW14 121 K6
MTCM CR4 147 J7
Hawkesworth Cl NTHWD HA6 32 C6
Hawkhurst Rd
STRHM/NOR SW16 148 D6
Hawkhurst Wy NWMAL KT3 160 A4
WWKM BR4 179 K1
Hawkins Cl BORE WD6 24 E1
EDGW HA8 37 F4
HRW HA1 48 D6
Hawkins Rd TEDD TW11 143 H5
WLSDN NW10 69 G6
Hawkins Ter CHARL SE7 114 D4
Hawkins Wy CAT SE6 151 J4
Hawkley Gdns WNWD SE27 149 H1
Hawkridge Cl CHDH RM6 61 J5
Hawksbrook La BECK BR3 166 E5
Hawkshaw Cl
BRXS/STRHM SW2 129 K6
Hawkshead Cl BMLY BR1 152 C6
Hawkshead Rd CHSWK W4 106 B2
WLSDN NW10 * 69 H6
Hawkshill Cl ESH/CLAY KT10 170 A5
Hawkshill Pl ESH/CLAY KT10 * 170 A5
Hawkslade Rd PECK SE15 132 A4
Hawksley Rd STNW/STAM N16 73 K2
Hawks Ms GNWCH SE10 * 113 F6
Hawksmoor Cl EHAM E6 95 J5
WOOL/PLUM SE18 115 K4
Hawksmoor Ms WCHPL E1 92 D6
Hawksmoor St HMSMTH W6 107 G5
Hawksmouth CHING E4 31 K6
Hawks Rd KUT/HW KT1 159 G1
Hawkstone Est
BERM/RHTH SE16 111 K3
Hawkstone Rd
BERM/RHTH SE16 111 K3
Hawkwell Wk IS N1 * 6 F3
Hawkwood Crs CHING E4 31 K5
Hawkwood La CHST BR7 154 C7
Hawkwood Mt CLPT E5 56 D7
Hawlands Dr PIN HA5 47 J6
Hawley Cl HPTN TW12 141 K5
Hawley Crs CAMTN NW1 4 D2
Hawley Ms CAMTN NW1 4 C1
Hawley Rd CAMTN NW1 4 C1
UED N18 43 F4
Hawley St CAMTN NW1 4 C2
Hawstead Rd CAT SE6 132 E5
Hawthorn Av PLMGR N13 40 E4
RAIN RM13 99 K3
THHTH CR7 149 H7
Hawthorn Centre HRW HA1 49 F3
Hawthorn Cl HEST TW5 102 A6
HPTN TW12 142 A4
STMC/STPC BR5 169 J5
Hawthorn Ct ASHF TW15 140 A6
Hawthorn Crs TOOT SW17 148 A4
Hawthornden Cl
NFNCH/WDSPK N12 39 J5
Hawthorndene Cl HAYES BR2 180 D1
Hawthorndene Rd HAYES BR2 180 E1
Hawthorn Dr
RYLN/HDSTN HA2 48 A5
WWKM BR4 180 C3
Hawthorne Av BOW E3 75 H7
CAR SM5 176 A6
KTN/HRWW/WS HA3 49 G5
MTCM CR4 162 C1
RSLP HA4 47 F5
Hawthorne Cl BMLY BR1 168 E2
IS N1 74 A5
Hawthorne Ct
STWL/WRAY TW19 * 120 A6
Hawthorne Crs WDR/YW UB7 100 C1
Hawthorne Gv
CDALE/KGS NW9 50 E6
Hawthorne Rd BMLY BR1 168 E2
UED N18 42 B5
WALTH E17 57 J2
Hawthorne Wy ED N9 42 B1
STWL/WRAY TW19 120 A6
Hawthorn Farm Av
NTHLT UB5 65 J7
Hawthorn Gdns EA W5 104 E2
Hawthorn Gv PGE/AN SE20 150 D7
Hawthorn Hatch BTFD TW8 104 C6
Hawthorn Ms MLHL NW7 38 C7
Hawthorn Pl ERITH DA8 117 K4
HYS/HAR UB3 * 82 D6
Hawthorn Rd BTFD TW8 104 C6
BXLYHS DA6 * 137 G3
CEND/HSY/T N8 54 D2
DART DA1 139 G7
FELT TW13 121 K7
SUT SM1 175 H4
WFD IG8 45 G3
WLGTN SM6 176 B6
WLSDN NW10 69 J6
Hawthorns WFD IG8 44 E2
The Hawthorns EW KT17 173 H5
Hawthorn Ter BFN/LL DA15 136 A5
Hawthorn Wk NKENS W10 88 C3
Hawtrey Av NTHLT UB5 83 H1
Hawtrey Dr RSLP HA4 46 E6
Hawtrey Rd HAMP NW3 3 J2
Haxted Rd BMLY BR1 153 F7
Hayburn Wy HCH RM12 63 H7
Hay Cl BORE WD6 24 E1
SRTFD E15 76 C6
Haycroft Gdns WLSDN NW10 69 J7
Haycroft Rd
BRXS/STRHM SW2 129 K4
SURB KT6 171 K1
Hay Currie St POP/IOD E14 93 K5
Hayday Rd CAN/RD E16 94 E3
Hayden Dell BUSH WD23 21 K5
Hayden's Pl NTGHL W11 88 D5
Hayden Wy CRW RM5 62 E1
Haydock Av NTHLT UB5 66 A5
Haydock Gn NTHLT UB5 66 A5
Haydon Cl CDALE/KGS NW9 50 E3
EN EN1 30 A5
Haydon Dell Farm
BUSH WD23 * 21 K6
Haydon Dr PIN HA5 46 E3
Haydon Park Pas
WIM/MER SW19 147 F4
Haydon Park Rd
WIM/MER SW19 146 E4
Haydon Rd BCTR RM8 79 J1
OXHEY WD19 21 J5
Haydon's Rd WIM/MER SW19 147 F4
Haydon St TWRH EC3N 13 L6
Haydon Wk WCHPL E1 13 L5
Haydon Wy WAND/EARL SW18 128 B3
Hayes Cha WWKM BR4 167 G5
Hayes Cl HAYES BR2 180 E1
Hayes Crs CHEAM SM3 174 B3
GLDGN NW11 52 D4
Hayes Dr RAIN RM13 81 K6
Hayes End Dr YEAD UB4 82 B4
Hayes End Rd YEAD UB4 82 B3
Hayesford Park Dr HAYES BR2 167 J4
Hayes Gdn HAYES BR2 180 E1
Hayes Gv EDUL SE22 131 G2
Hayes Hl HAYES BR2 167 H7
Hayes Hill Rd HAYES BR2 167 J7
Hayes La BECK BR3 167 G2
HAYES BR2 167 K5
Hayes Mead Rd HAYES BR2 167 H7
Hayes Pl CAMTN NW1 9 K1
Hayes Rd HAYES BR2 167 K3
NWDGN UB2 102 A3
Hayes St HAYES BR2 168 A7
Hayes Wy BECK BR3 167 F3
Hayes Wood Av HAYES BR2 168 A7
Hayfield Cl BUSH WD23 22 B3
Hayfield Pas WCHPL E1 92 E3
Haygarth Pl WIM/MER SW19 146 B4
Haygreen Cl KUTN/CMB KT2 144 D5
Hay Hl MYFR/PICC W1J 10 D7
Hayland Cl CDALE/KGS NW9 51 F3
Hay La CDALE/KGS NW9 51 F3
Hayles St LBTH SE11 18 C5
Haylett Gdns KUT/HW KT1 * 158 E3
Hayling Av FELT TW13 140 E2
Hayling Cl STNW/STAM N16 74 A4
Hayling Rd OXHEY WD19 32 D2
Hayman Crs YEAD UB4 82 B1
Haymarket STJS SW1Y 11 G7
Haymeads Dr ESH/CLAY KT10 170 C5
Haymer Gdns WPK KT4 173 J2
Haymerle Rd PECK SE15 111 H5
Haymill Cl GFD/PVL UB6 85 F2
Hayne Rd BECK BR3 151 H7
Haynes Cl BKHTH/KID SE3 133 H2
FBAR/BDGN N11 40 A2
TOTM N17 42 D6
Haynes Dr ED N9 42 D2
Haynes La NRWD SE19 150 A5
Haynes Rd ALP/SUD HA0 68 A6
Hayne St STBT EC1A 12 D2
Haynt Wk RYNPK SW20 161 H2
Hay's La STHWK SE1 13 J8
Haysleigh Gdns PGE/AN SE20 165 H1
Hay's Ms MYFR/PICC W1J 10 C7
Haysoms Cl ROM RM1 63 G3
Haystall Cl YEAD UB4 82 C1
Hay St BETH E2 74 C7
Hayter Rd BRXS/STRHM SW2 129 K4
Hayton Cl HACK E8 74 B5
Hayward Cl DART DA1 138 A4
WIM/MER SW19 147 F6
Hayward Gdns
PUT/ROE SW15 127 F5
Hayward Rd THDIT KT7 158 A7
TRDG/WHET N20 39 G1
Haywards Cl CHDH RM6 61 J4
Hayward's Pl CLKNW EC1R * 12 C1
Haywood Cl PIN HA5 47 H1
Haywood Rd HAYES BR2 168 C3
Hazel Av WDR/YW UB7 100 D2
Hazelbank BRYLDS KT5 159 K7
Hazelbank Rd CAT SE6 152 B1
Hazelbourne Rd BAL SW12 129 G5
Hazelbury Cl WIM/MER SW19 161 K1
Hazelbury Gn ED N9 42 A2
Hazelbury La ED N9 42 A2
Hazel Cl BTFD TW8 * 104 C6
CDALE/KGS NW9 51 H1
CROY/NA CR0 166 A6
HCH RM12 81 K2
MTCM CR4 163 J3
PLMGR N13 41 K2
WHTN TW2 123 H6
Hazelcroft PIN HA5 34 A5
Hazeldean Rd WLSDN NW10 69 F6
Hazeldene Dr PIN HA5 47 G2
Hazeldene Gdns
HGDN/ICK UB10 64 A7
Hazeldene Rd GDMY/SEVK IG3 79 H1
WELL DA16 136 D1
Hazeldon Rd BROCKY SE4 132 B4
Hazel Dr ERITH DA8 118 D7
Hazeleigh Gdns WFD IG8 45 J4
Hazel Gdns EDGW HA8 36 D3
Hazelgreen Cl WCHMH N21 29 H7
Hazel Gv ALP/SUD HA0 68 A7
CHDH RM6 62 A2
EN EN1 * 30 C5
FELT TW13 121 K7
SYD SE26 151 F3
Hazelhurst BECK BR3 152 B7
Hazelhurst Rd TOOT SW17 147 G3
Hazellville Rd ARCH N19 54 D6
Hazel Md BAR EN5 25 K4
Hazelmere Cl
EBED/NFELT TW14 121 G5
NTHLT UB5 83 K1
Hazelmere Dr NTHLT UB5 83 K1
Hazelmere Gdns EMPK RM11 63 K4
Hazelmere Rd
KIL/WHAMP NW6 2 A4
NTHLT UB5 83 K1
STMC/STPC BR5 169 H3
Hazelmere Wk NTHLT UB5 83 K1
Hazelmere Wy HAYES BR2 167 K5
Hazel Rd ERITH DA8 118 D7
SRTFD E15 * 76 C4
WLSDN NW10 87 K2
Hazel Rw
NFNCH/WDSPK N12 * 39 H4
Hazeltree La NTHLT UB5 83 J2
Hazel Wk HAYES BR2 169 F5
Hazel Wy CHING E4 43 H5
STHWK SE1 19 L5
Hazelwood Av MRDN SM4 162 A3
Hazelwood Cl CLPT E5 75 G2
EA W5 105 F1
RYLN/HDSTN HA2 48 B3
Hazelwood Ct SURB KT6 159 F5
Hazelwood Dr PIN HA5 47 F1
Hazelwood La PLMGR N13 41 G3
Hazelwood Rd EN EN1 30 B5
RKW/CH/CXG WD3 20 A5
WALTH E17 57 G4
Hazlebury Rd FUL/PGN SW6 128 A1
Hazledean Rd CROY/NA CR0 177 K1
Hazledene Rd CHSWK W4 105 K5
Hazlemere Gdns WPK KT4 160 D7
Hazlewell Rd PUT/ROE SW15 127 F4
Hazlewood Crs NKENS W10 88 C3
Hazlitt Cl FELT TW13 141 J3
Hazlitt Ms WKENS W14 * 107 H2
Hazlitt Rd WKENS W14 107 H2
Heacham Av HGDN/ICK UB10 64 A2
Headcorn Rd BMLY BR1 152 D4
THHTH CR7 164 A3
TOTM N17 42 B6
Headfort Pl KTBR SW1X 16 B2
Headingley Dr BECK BR3 151 J5
Headington Rd
WAND/EARL SW18 128 B7
Headlam Rd CLAP SW4 129 J5
Headlam St WCHPL E1 92 D3
Headley Ap GNTH/NBYPK IG2 60 A4
Headley Av WLGTN SM6 177 F4
Headley Cl CHSGTN KT9 172 C5
Headley Dr CROY/NA CR0 180 A6
GNTH/NBYPK IG2 60 B5
Heads Ms NTGHL W11 8 A5
Headstone Dr HRW HA1 48 D3
KTN/HRWW/WS HA3 48 E2
Headstone Gdns
RYLN/HDSTN HA2 48 C3
Headstone La
RYLN/HDSTN HA2 48 B1
Headstone Pde HRW HA1 * 48 D3
Headstone Rd HRW HA1 48 E4
Head St WCHPL E1 93 F5
Headway Cl
RCHPK/HAM TW10 143 J3
The Headway EW KT17 173 H7
Heald St NWCR SE14 112 C7
Healey Rd WATW WD18 20 D5
Healey St CAMTN NW1 * 72 B5
Hearne Rd CHSWK W4 105 H4
Hearn Ri NTHLT UB5 65 H7
Hearn Rd ROM RM1 63 H5
Hearn's Blds WALW SE17 19 H6
Hearnshaw St POP/IOD E14 93 G5
Hearn St SDTCH EC2A 13 K1
Hearnville Rd BAL SW12 129 F7
Heatham Pk WHTN TW2 124 A6
Heath Av BXLYHN DA7 116 E5
Heathbourne Rd BUSH WD23 34 E1
Heath Brow HAMP NW3 71 G2
Heath Cl EA W5 86 B3
GLDGN NW11 53 F6
GPK RM2 63 J2
HYS/HAR UB3 101 G6
SAND/SEL CR2 177 H5
Heathclose Av DART DA1 138 E6
Heathclose Rd DART DA1 138 D7
Heathcote Av CLAY IG5 59 K1
Heathcote Gv CHING E4 44 A2
Heathcote Rd TWK TW1 124 C5
Heathcote St BMSBY WC1N 5 L9
Heathcroft EA W5 86 B3
Heathcroft Av SUN TW16 140 D6
Heathcroft Gdns WALTH E17 44 B7
Heathdale Av HSLWW TW4 122 D2
Heathdene Dr BELV DA17 117 J3
Heathdene Rd
STRHM/NOR SW16 149 F6
WLGTN SM6 176 B6
Heath Dr BELMT SM2 175 G7
HAMP NW3 71 F3
RYNPK SW20 161 F3
Heathedge SYD SE26 * 150 D1
Heathend Rd BXLY DA5 138 B7
Heather Av ROM RM1 63 F1
Heatherbank CHST BR7 169 F1
ELTH/MOT SE9 134 E1
Heatherbank Cl DART DA1 138 B5
Heather Cl EHAM E6 96 A5
HOLWY N7 73 F2
HPTN TW12 141 K7
ISLW TW7 123 J4
LEW SE13 133 G5
VX/NE SW8 129 G2
Heatherdale Cl
KUTN/CMB KT2 144 C5
Heatherdene Cl MTCM CR4 162 C3
NFNCH/WDSPK N12 39 G7
Heather Dr DART DA1 138 D6
ENC/FH EN2 29 H1
ROM RM1 63 F1
Heatherfold Wy PIN HA5 46 D2
Heather Gdns BELMT SM2 174 E5
GLDGN NW11 52 C5
ROM RM1 63 F1
Heather Gln ROM RM1 63 F1
Heatherlands SUN TW16 140 E5
Heatherlea Gv WPK KT4 161 F7
Heatherley Dr CLAY IG5 59 K2
Heather Park Dr
ALP/SUD HA0 68 C6
Heather Park Pde
ALP/SUD HA0 * 68 B6

Heather Pl ESH/CLAY KT10 170 B3
Heather Ri BUSH WD23 21 K1
Heather Rd CHING E4 43 H5
CRICK NW2 69 H1
LEE/GVPK SE12 152 E1
Heatherset Cl ESH/CLAY KT10 170 C4
Heatherset Gdns
STRHM/NOR SW16 149 F6
Heatherside Rd
HOR/WEW KT19 173 F6
SCUP DA14 155 J2
The Heathers
STWL/WRAY TW19 120 C6
Heather Wk EDGW HA8 36 D4
NKENS W10 88 C3
Heather Wy SAND/SEL CR2 179 F7
STAN HA7 35 F5
Heatherwood Cl MNPK E12 77 F1
Heatherwood Dr YEAD UB4 82 B1
Heathfield CHING E4 44 A2
CHST BR7 154 C5
HRW HA1 * 49 F6
Heathfield Av
WAND/EARL SW18 128 C6
Heathfield Cl CAN/RD E16 95 H4
HAYES BR2 181 G4
OXHEY WD19 21 G6
Heathfield Dr MTCM CR4 147 J6
Heathfield Gdns CHSWK W4 105 K4
CROY/NA CR0 * 177 J3
GLDGN NW11 52 B5
WAND/EARL SW18 128 C5
Heathfield La CHST BR7 154 C5
Heathfield North WHTN TW2 123 K6
Heathfield Pk CRICK NW2 70 A5
Heathfield Park Dr CHDH RM6 61 H4
Heathfield Ri RSLP HA4 46 A6
Heathfield Rd ACT W3 105 J1
BMLY BR1 152 D6
BUSH WD23 21 J3
BXLYHS DA6 137 G3
HAYES BR2 181 G4
SAND/SEL CR2 177 K4
WAND/EARL SW18 128 B5
Heathfield South WHTN TW2 124 A6
Heathfield Sq
WAND/EARL SW18 128 C6
Heathfield Ter CHSWK W4 105 K4
WOOL/PLUM SE18 115 K5
Heathfield V SAND/SEL CR2 179 F7
Heath Gdns DART DA1 * 139 F7
TWK TW1 124 A7
Heathgate GLDGN NW11 53 F5
Heathgate Pl HAMP NW3 71 K3
Heath Gv PGE/AN SE20 150 E6
SUN TW16 140 D6
Heath Hurst Rd HAMP NW3 71 J3
Heathhurst Rd SAND/SEL CR2 178 A7
Heathland Rd
STNW/STAM N16 56 A7
Heathlands Cl TWK TW1 143 F1
Heathlands Ct HSLWW TW4 122 D4
Heathlands Ri DART DA1 138 E6
Heathlands Wy HSLWW TW4 122 D4
Heath La BKHTH/KID SE3 133 G1
DART DA1 138 E7
Heathlee Rd BKHTH/KID SE3 133 J3
DART DA1 138 B5
Heathley End CHST BR7 154 C5
Heath Ldg BUSH WD23 * 22 D7
Heathman's Rd FUL/PGN SW6 107 J7
Heath Md WIM/MER SW19 146 B2
Heath Park Dr BMLY BR1 168 D2
Heath Park Rd GPK RM2 63 J4
Heath Ri HAYES BR2 167 K5
PUT/ROE SW15 127 G5
Heath Rd BXLY DA5 137 K7
CHDH RM6 61 K6
DART DA1 138 C5
HGDN/ICK UB10 82 A3
HRW HA1 48 C6
HSLW TW3 123 H3
OXHEY WD19 21 H6
THHTH CR7 164 D2
TWK TW1 124 A7
VX/NE SW8 129 G1
Heath's Cl EN EN1 29 K1
Heathside ESH/CLAY KT10 170 E2
HAMP NW3 71 H3
HSLWW TW4 122 E6
Heath Side STMC/STPC BR5 169 H7
Heathside Av BXLYHN DA7 137 F1
Heathside Cl ESH/CLAY KT10 170 E2
GNTH/NBYPK IG2 60 D4
NTHWD HA6 32 B4
Heathside Rd NTHWD HA6 32 B3
Heathstan Rd SHB W12 87 J5
Heath St DART DA1 139 G6
HAMP NW3 71 G3
The Heath HNWL W7 * 103 K1
Heath Vw EFNCH N2 53 G3
Heathview Av DART DA1 138 B5
Heath View Cl EFNCH N2 53 G3
Heathview Crs DART DA1 138 D6
Heath View Dr ABYW SE2 116 E5
Heathview Gdns
PUT/ROE SW15 127 F6
Heathview Rd THHTH CR7 164 B3
Heath Vls WAND/EARL SW18 * 128 B7
WOOL/PLUM SE18 116 A4
Heathville Rd ARCH N19 54 E6
Heathwall St BTSEA SW11 128 E2
Heath Wy ERITH DA8 117 K7
Heathway BKHTH/KID SE3 113 K6
CROY/NA CR0 179 H2
DAGW RM9 80 B3
NWDGN UB2 * 102 C3
WFD IG8 45 G3
Heathwood Gdns CHARL SE7 114 D3
Heathwood Wk BXLY DA5 138 B7
Heaton Cl CHING E4 44 A2
Heaton Rd MTCM CR4 148 A6
PECK SE15 131 J2
Heaven Tree Cl IS N1 73 J4
Heaver Rd BTSEA SW11 * 128 C2
Heavitree Cl
WOOL/PLUM SE18 115 J4
Heavitree Rd
WOOL/PLUM SE18 115 J4
Hebden Ter TOTM N17 42 A5
Hebdon Rd TOOT SW17 147 J2
Heber Rd CRICK NW2 70 B4
EDUL SE22 131 G5
Hebron Rd HMSMTH W6 106 E2
Hecham Cl WALTH E17 57 G1
Heckfield Pl FUL/PGN SW6 107 K6
Heckford Cl WATW WD18 20 A5
Heckford St WAP E1W 93 F6
Hector Cl ED N9 42 C1
Hector St WOOL/PLUM SE18 * 115 K3
Heddington Gv HOLWY N7 73 F4
Heddon Cl ISLW TW7 124 B3
Heddon Court Av EBAR EN4 27 K4
Heddon Court Pde
EBAR EN4 * 28 A4
Heddon Rd EBAR EN4 27 K4
Heddon St CONDST W1S 10 E7
Hedge La PLMGR N13 41 H2
Hedgeley REDBR IG4 59 K3
Hedgemans Rd DAGW RM9 79 K6
Hedgemans Wy DAGW RM9 80 A5
Hedgerley Gdns GFD/PVL UB6 84 C1
Hedgerow La BAR EN5 25 K4
Hedger's Gv HOM E9 * 75 G5
Hedger St LBTH SE11 18 C5
Hedgeside Rd NTHWD HA6 32 A4
Hedgewood Gdns CLAY IG5 60 A3
Hedgley Ms LEE/GVPK SE12 133 J4
Hedgley St LEE/GVPK SE12 133 J4
Hedingham Cl IS N1 6 E2
Hedingham Rd BCTR RM8 79 H4
Hedley Rd WHTN TW2 123 F6
Hedley Rw HBRY N5 73 K4
Heenan Cl BARK IG11 78 C5
Heene Rd ENC/FH EN2 29 K1
Heidegger Crs BARN SW13 106 E6
Heigham Rd EHAM E6 77 J6
Heighton Gdns CROY/NA CR0 177 H4
Heights Cl RYNPK SW20 145 K6
The Heights BECK BR3 * 152 A6
CHARL SE7 114 B4
NTHLT UB5 66 A4
Heiron St WALW SE17 110 C5
Helby Rd CLAP SW4 129 J5
Helder Gv LEE/GVPK SE12 133 J6
Helder St SAND/SEL CR2 177 K5
Heldmann Cl HSLW TW3 123 J3
Helena Pl HACK E8 74 D7
Helena Rd EA W5 85 K4
PLSTW E13 94 D1
WALTH E17 57 J4
WLSDN NW10 69 K4
Helena Sq BERM/RHTH SE16 93 G6
Helen Av EBED/NFELT TW14 122 A6
Helen Cl DART DA1 138 E6
E/WMO/HCT KT8 157 G3
EFNCH N2 53 G2
Helenslea Av GLDGN NW11 52 D7
Helen's Pl BETH E2 92 E2
Helen St WOOL/PLUM SE18 115 G3
Helford Cl RSLP HA4 64 C1
Helgiford Gdns SUN TW16 140 C6
Helios Rd WLGTN SM6 163 F7
Helix Gdns BRXS/STRHM SW2 130 A5
Helix Rd BRXS/STRHM SW2 130 A5
Hellings St WAP E1W 92 C7
Helme Cl WIM/MER SW19 146 D4
Helmet Rw FSBYE EC1V 6 F9
Helmore Rd BARK IG11 79 F6
Helmsdale Cl YEAD UB4 * 83 J3
Helmsdale Rd
STRHM/NOR SW16 148 C7
Helmsley Pl HACK E8 74 D6
Helmsley St HACK E8 74 D6
Helperby Rd WLSDN NW10 69 G6
Helsinki Sq BERM/RHTH SE16 112 B2
Helston Cl PIN HA5 33 K6
Helvetia St CAT SE6 151 H1
Hemans St VX/NE SW8 109 J6
Hemery Rd GFD/PVL UB6 66 D4
Hemingford Cl
NFNCH/WDSPK N12 39 H4
Hemingford Rd CHEAM SM3 174 A3
IS N1 5 M3
Heming Rd EDGW HA8 36 D5
Hemington Av
FBAR/BDGN N11 39 K4
Hemlock Cl STRHM/NOR SW16 163 J1
Hemlock Rd SHB W12 87 H6
Hemmen La HYS/HAR UB3 82 D6
Hemming Cl HPTN TW12 142 A7
Hemmings Cl SCUP DA14 155 H1
Hemmingsmead
HOR/WEW KT19 172 E5
Hemming St WCHPL E1 92 C3
Hemmingway Cl KTTN NW5 72 A3
Hempstead Cl BKHH IG9 44 E1
Hempstead Rd WALTH E17 58 B2
WAT WD17 20 E1
Hemp Wk WALW SE17 19 H5
Hemsby Rd CHSGTN KT9 172 B5
Hemstal Rd KIL/WHAMP NW6 2 A1
Hemsted Rd ERITH DA8 118 B7
Hemswell Dr CDALE/KGS NW9 37 G7
Hemsworth St IS N1 7 J5
Henbury Wy OXHEY WD19 33 H2
Henchman St SHB W12 87 H5
Hendale Av HDN NW4 51 J2
Henderson Cl EMPK RM11 81 K1
WLSDN NW10 68 E5
Henderson Dr DART DA1 139 K3
STJWD NW8 3 G9
Henderson Rd CROY/NA CR0 164 E5
ED N9 30 D7
FSTGT E7 77 G5
WAND/EARL SW18 128 D6
YEAD UB4 82 E2
Hendham Rd TOOT SW17 147 J1
Hendon Av FNCH N3 38 C7
Hendon Gv HOR/WEW KT19 172 C7
Hendon Hall Ct HDN NW4 * 52 B2
Hendon La FNCH N3 52 C2
Hendon Park Rw
GLDGN NW11 * 52 D5
Hendon Rd ED N9 42 C1
Hendon Ter ASHF TW15 * 140 B5
Hendon Wy CRICK NW2 52 B6
STWL/WRAY TW19 120 A4
Hendon Wood La MLHL NW7 25 J7
Hendren Cl GFD/PVL UB6 66 D4
Hendre Rd STHWK SE1 19 K6
Hendrick Av BAL SW12 128 E5
Heneage St WCHPL E1 13 M2
Henfield Cl ARCH N19 54 C7
BXLY DA5 137 H5
Henfield Rd WIM/MER SW19 146 D7
Hengelo Gdns MTCM CR4 162 C3
Hengest Av ESH/CLAY KT10 171 G2
Hengist Rd ERITH DA8 117 K6
LEE/GVPK SE12 134 A6
Hengist Wy HAYES BR2 167 G3
Hengrave Rd FSTH SE23 131 K6
Hengrove Ct BXLY DA5 137 F7
Henley Av CHEAM SM3 174 C2
Henley Cl BERM/RHTH SE16 * 111 K1
GFD/PVL UB6 * 84 C1
ISLW TW7 104 A7
Henley Dr KUTN/CMB KT2 145 H6
STHWK SE1 19 M5
Henley Gdns CHDH RM6 62 A4
PIN HA5 47 F2
Henley Rd CAN/RD E16 114 E1
IL IG1 78 C3
UED N18 42 A3
WLSDN NW10 70 A7
Henley St BTSEA SW11 129 F1
Henley Wy FELT TW13 141 H4
Hennel Cl FSTH SE23 150 E2
Hennessy Rd ED N9 42 E1
Henniker Gdns EHAM E6 95 H2
Henniker Ms CHEL SW3 15 G9
Henniker Rd SRTFD E15 76 B4
Henningham Rd TOTM N17 41 K7
Henning St BTSEA SW11 108 D7
Henrietta Cl DEPT SE8 112 D5
Henrietta Ms BMSBY WC1N 5 K9
Henrietta Pl CAVSQ/HST W1G 10 C4
Henrietta St COVGDN WC2E 11 K6
SRTFD E15 76 A4
Henriques St WCHPL E1 92 C5
Henry Addlington Cl EHAM E6 96 B4
Henry Cooper Wy
ELTH/MOT SE9 153 H2
Henry Darlot Dr MLHL NW7 38 B4
Henry Dickens Ct NTGHL W11 88 B6
Henry Doulton Dr TOOT SW17 148 A3
Henry Jackson Rd
PUT/ROE SW15 127 G2
Henry Macaulay Av
KUTN/CMB KT2 143 K7
Henry Peters Dr TEDD TW11 142 E4
Henry Rd EBAR EN4 27 H4
EHAM E6 95 J1
FSBYPK N4 55 J7
Henry's Av WFD IG8 44 D4
Henryson Rd BROCKY SE4 132 D4
Henry St BMLY BR1 153 F7
Henry Tate Ms
STRHM/NOR SW16 149 G4
Hensby Ms OXHEY WD19 21 J5
Henshall St IS N1 73 K5
Henshawe Rd BCTR RM8 79 K2
Henshaw St WALW SE17 19 G5
Henslowe Rd EDUL SE22 131 H4
Henson Av CRICK NW2 70 A4
Henson Pl NTHLT UB5 65 G7
Henstridge Pl STJWD NW8 3 J5
Henty Cl BTSEA SW11 108 D6
Henty Wk PUT/ROE SW15 126 E4
Henville Rd BMLY BR1 153 F7
Henwick Rd ELTH/MOT SE9 134 C2
Henwood Side WFD IG8 45 K5
Hepburn Gdns HAYES BR2 167 J7
Hepple Cl ISLW TW7 124 C1
Hepscott Rd HOM E9 75 J5
Hepworth Gdns BARK IG11 79 G4
Hepworth Rd
STRHM/NOR SW16 148 E6
Herald Gdns WLGTN SM6 176 B2
Heralds Pl LBTH SE11 18 C5
Herald St BETH E2 92 D3
Herbal Hl CLKNW EC1R 12 B1
Herbert Crs KTBR SW1X 15 M3
Herbert Gdns CHDH RM6 61 K6
CHSWK W4 105 J5
WLSDN NW10 87 K1
Herbert Ms BRXS/STRHM SW2 130 B5
Herbert Pl ISLW TW7 123 J1
WOOL/PLUM SE18 115 G5
Herbert Rd BXLYHN DA7 137 F1
CDALE/KGS NW9 51 J5
FBAR/BDGN N11 40 E6
GDMY/SEVK IG3 78 E1
HAYES BR2 168 C4
KUT/HW KT1 159 G2
MNPK E12 77 J3
SEVS/STOTM N15 56 B4
STHL UB1 83 K7
WALTH E17 57 H6
WIM/MER SW19 146 D6
WOOL/PLUM SE18 115 G6
Herbert St KTTN NW5 72 A5
PLSTW E13 94 E1
Herbrand St BMSBY WC1N 11 J1
STPAN WC1H 5 J9
Hercules Pl HOLWY N7 72 E2
Hercules Rd STHWK SE1 17 M4
Hercules St HOLWY N7 72 E2
Hereford Av EBAR EN4 40 C1
Hereford Gdns IL IG1 59 J6
PIN HA5 47 J4
WHTN TW2 * 123 H7
Hereford Ms BAY/PAD W2 8 B4
Hereford Pl NWCR SE14 * 112 C6
Hereford Retreat PECK SE15 111 H6
Hereford Rd ACT W3 86 E6
BAY/PAD W2 8 B5
BOW E3 93 H1
EA W5 104 D2
FELT TW13 122 B7
WAN E11 59 F4
Hereford Sq SKENS SW7 14 F6
Hereford St BETH E2 92 C3
Hereford Wy CHSGTN KT9 171 J4
Herent Dr CLAY IG5 59 K2
Heretage Cl BRXN/ST SW9 130 C2
Hereward Gdns PLMGR N13 41 G4
Hereward Rd TOOT SW17 147 J3
Herga Ct WAT WD17 20 E1
Herga Rd KTN/HRWW/WS HA3 49 F3
Heriot Av CHING E4 43 J1
Heriot Rd HDN NW4 52 A4
Heriots Cl STAN HA7 35 G3
Heritage Av CDALE/KGS NW9 51 H2
Heritage Cl SUN TW16 140 E7
Heritage Hl HAYES BR2 181 G4
Heritage Pl
WAND/EARL SW18 * 128 C5
Heritage Vw HRW HA1 67 F2
Herkomer Cl BUSH WD23 22 B5
Herkomer Rd BUSH WD23 22 A4
Herlwyn Av RSLP HA4 64 C2
Herlwyn Gdns TOOT SW17 147 K3
Herm Cl ISLW TW7 103 H6
Hermes Cl MV/WKIL W9 8 A1
Hermes St IS N1 6 A6
Hermes Wy WLGTN SM6 176 D6
Herminston Av CEND/HSY/T N8 54 E4
Hermitage Cl ABYW SE2 116 D2
ENC/FH EN2 29 H1
ESH/CLAY KT10 171 G5
RCHPK/HAM TW10 * 124 E4
SWFD E18 58 D3
Hermitage Cots STAN HA7 * 34 E4
Hermitage Gdns CRICK NW2 70 E2
NRWD SE19 149 J6
Hermitage La CRICK NW2 70 E2
CROY/NA CR0 165 G6
STRHM/NOR SW16 149 F6
UED N18 41 K4
Hermitage Rd FSBYPK N4 55 J6
NRWD SE19 149 J6
Hermitage Rw HACK E8 * 74 C4
Hermitage St BAY/PAD W2 9 G3
The Hermitage BARN SW13 * 106 C7
FELT TW13 * 140 D2
FSTH SE23 131 K7
KUT/HW KT1 * 158 E3
LEW SE13 * 133 F1
RCHPK/HAM TW10 125 F4
Hermitage Wk SWFD E18 58 D3
Hermitage Wall WAP E1W 92 C7
Hermitage Wy STAN HA7 35 G7
Hermit Pl KIL/WHAMP NW6 2 C4
Hermit Rd CAN/RD E16 94 D3
Hermit St FSBYE EC1V 6 C7
Hermon Gv HYS/HAR UB3 82 E7
Hermon Hl WAN E11 58 E3
Herndon Rd
WAND/EARL SW18 128 B4
Herne Cl HYS/HAR UB3 82 D5
WLSDN NW10 69 F4
Herne Ct BUSH WD23 * 22 C7
Herne Hl HNHL SE24 130 D4
Herne Hill Rd HNHL SE24 130 D2
Herne Ms UED N18 42 C3
Herne Pl HNHL SE24 130 C5
Herne Rd BUSH WD23 22 B5
SURB KT6 171 K1
Heron Cl WALTH E17 57 H1
WLSDN NW10 69 G5
Heron Ct HAYES BR2 168 B3
KUT/HW KT1 * 159 F2
Heron Crs SCUP DA14 154 E3
Herondale SAND/SEL CR2 179 F7
Herondale Av
WAND/EARL SW18 128 C7
Heron Dr FSBYPK N4 73 J1
Heron Flight Av HCH RM12 81 J6
Herongate Rd MNPK E12 77 G1
Heron Hl BELV DA17 117 G3
Heron Ms IL IG1 78 B1
Heron Pl BERM/RHTH SE16 93 G7
Heron Quays POP/IOD E14 93 J7
Heron Rd CROY/NA CR0 * 165 F7
HNHL SE24 130 D3
TWK TW1 124 B3
Heronsforde WEA W13 85 J5
Heronsgate EDGW HA8 36 C4
Herons Lea HGT N6 * 53 K5
Heronslea Dr STAN HA7 36 A4
Herons Pl ISLW TW7 124 C2
Herons Ri EBAR EN4 27 J3
Heron Wk NTHWD HA6 32 C3
Heron Wy
EBED/NFELT TW14 121 K3
Herrick Rd HBRY N5 73 J2
Herrick St WEST SW1P 17 H6
Herries St NKENS W10 88 C1
Herringham Rd CHARL SE7 114 B2
Herrongate Cl EN EN1 30 A1
Hersant Cl WLSDN NW10 69 J7
Herschell Rd FSTH SE23 132 A6
Hersham Cl PUT/ROE SW15 126 D6
Hershell Ct
MORT/ESHN SW14 * 125 J3
Hertford Av
MORT/ESHN SW14 126 A4
Hertford Cl EBAR EN4 27 H2
Hertford Ct STAN HA7 * 35 K6
Hertford End Ct
NTHWD HA6 * 32 C4
Hertford Pl FITZ W1T 10 E1
Hertford Rd BARK IG11 78 A6
EBAR EN4 27 G2
ED N9 30 D7
EFNCH N2 53 J2
GNTH/NBYPK IG2 60 E5
IS N1 7 K3
PEND EN3 30 E2
Hertford Road High St
PEND EN3 30 E5
Hertford St MYFR/PICC W1J 10 C8
Hertford Wy MTCM CR4 163 K3
Hertslet Rd HOLWY N7 73 F2
Hertsmere Rd POP/IOD E14 93 J6
Hertswood Ct BAR EN5 * 26 C3
Hervey Cl FNCH N3 38 E7
Hervey Park Rd WALTH E17 57 G3
Hesa Rd HYS/HAR UB3 82 E5
Hesewall Cl CLAP SW4 129 H1
Hesketh Pl NTGHL W11 88 C6
Hesketh Rd FSTGT E7 76 E2
Heslop Rd BAL SW12 128 E7
Hesper Ms ECT SW5 14 C7
Hesperus Crs POP/IOD E14 112 E3
Hessel Rd WEA W13 104 B1
Hessel St WCHPL E1 92 D5
Hesselyn Dr RAIN RM13 81 K6
Hestercombe Av
FUL/PGN SW6 127 H1
Hesterman Wy CROY/NA CR0 163 K7
Hester Rd BTSEA SW11 108 D6
UED N18 42 C4
Hester Ter RCH/KEW TW9 125 H2
Heston Av HEST TW5 102 D6
Heston Grange La HEST TW5 102 E5
Heston Rd HEST TW5 103 F6
Heston St NWCR SE14 112 C7
Heswell Gn OXHEY WD19 * 32 E2
Hetherington Rd CLAP SW4 129 K3
Hetley Rd SHB W12 87 K7
Heton Gdns HDN NW4 51 J3
Hevelius Cl GNWCH SE10 113 J4
Hever Cft ELTH/MOT SE9 154 A3
Hever Gdns BMLY BR1 169 F1
Heverham Rd
WOOL/PLUM SE18 115 K3
Heversham Rd BXLYHN DA7 137 H1
Hevingham Dr CHDH RM6 61 J4
Hewens Rd HGDN/ICK UB10 82 A2
Hewer St NKENS W10 88 B4
Hewett Cl STAN HA7 35 H3
Hewett Rd BCTR RM8 79 K4
Hewett St SDTCH EC2A 13 K1
Hewish Rd UED N18 42 A3
Hewison St BOW E3 93 H1
Hewitt Av WDGN N22 55 H1
Hewitt Cl CROY/NA CR0 179 J2
Hewitt Rd CEND/HSY/T N8 55 G4
Hewlett Rd BOW E3 93 G1
The Hexagon HGT N6 53 K7
Hexal Rd CAT SE6 152 C2
Hexham Gdns ISLW TW7 104 B6
NTHLT UB5 65 K4
Hexham Rd BAR EN5 27 F3
MRDN SM4 162 A7
WNWD SE27 149 J1
Heybourne Rd TOTM N17 42 D6
Heybridge Av
STRHM/NOR SW16 149 F5
Heybridge Dr BARK/HLT IG6 60 D2
Heybridge Wy LEY E10 57 G6
Heyford Av RYNPK SW20 161 J2
VX/NE SW8 109 K6
Heyford Rd MTCM CR4 162 D1
Heyford Ter VX/NE SW8 109 K6
Heygate St WALW SE17 18 F5
Heygate St WALW SE17 18 E6
Heynes Rd BCTR RM8 79 J3
Heysham Dr OXHEY WD19 33 G4
Heysham La HAMP NW3 71 F2
Heysham Rd
SEVS/STOTM N15 55 K5
Heythorp St
WAND/EARL SW18 146 D1
Heywood Av CDALE/KGS NW9 37 G7
Heyworth Rd CLPT E5 74 D3
SRTFD E15 76 D3
Hibbert Rd
KTN/HRWW/WS HA3 49 F1
WALTH E17 57 H6
Hibbert St BTSEA SW11 128 B2
Hibernia Gdns HSLW TW3 123 F4
Hibernia Rd HSLW TW3 123 F3
Hichisson Rd PECK SE15 131 K4
Hicken Rd BRXS/STRHM SW2 130 A4
Hickin Cl CHARL SE7 114 C3
Hickin St POP/IOD E14 113 F2
Hickling Rd IL IG1 78 B4
Hickman Av CHING E4 44 A5
Hickman Cl CAN/RD E16 95 H4
Hickman Rd CHDH RM6 61 J6
Hickory Cl ED N9 30 C6
Hicks Av GFD/PVL UB6 84 D2
Hicks Cl BTSEA SW11 128 D2
Hicks St DEPT SE8 112 B4
Hidcote Gdns RYNPK SW20 160 E2
Hidden Cl E/WMO/HCT KT8 157 H3
Hide Pl WEST SW1P 17 G6
Hide Rd HRW HA1 48 D3
Higham Hill Rd WALTH E17 57 G2
Higham Ms NTHLT UB5 83 K3
Higham Pl WALTH E17 57 G2
Higham Rd TOTM N17 55 K2
WFD IG8 44 E5
Higham Station Av CHING E4 43 K5
The Highams WALTH E17 * 44 A7
Higham St WALTH E17 57 G1
Highbank Pl
WAND/EARL SW18 * 128 A7
Highbanks Cl WELL DA16 116 B6
Highbanks Rd PIN HA5 34 B5
Highbank Wy CEND/HSY/T N8 55 G5
Highbarrow Rd CROY/NA CR0 165 G7
High Beech SAND/SEL CR2 178 A6
Highbridge Rd BARK IG11 78 B7
Highbrook Rd BKHTH/KID SE3 134 C2
High Broom Crs WWKM BR4 166 E6
Highbury Av THHTH CR7 164 B1
Highbury Cl NWMAL KT3 159 K3
WWKM BR4 179 K1
Highbury Cnr IS N1 73 H5
Highbury Crs HBRY N5 73 G4
Highbury Est HBRY N5 73 J4
Highbury Gdns
GDMY/SEVK IG3 78 E1
Highbury Gra HBRY N5 73 H3
Highbury Gv HBRY N5 73 H4
Highbury Hl HBRY N5 73 H5
Highbury New Pk HBRY N5 73 H5
Highbury Pk HBRY N5 73 H3
Highbury Pl HBRY N5 73 H5
Highbury Qd HBRY N5 73 J2
Highbury Rd WIM/MER SW19 146 C4
Highbury Station Pde
HBRY N5 * 73 H5
Highbury Station Rd IS N1 * 73 G5
Highbury Ter HBRY N5 73 H4
Highbury Terrace Ms
HBRY N5 73 H4
High Cedar Dr RYNPK SW20 145 K6
Highclere Rd NWMAL KT3 160 A2
Highclere St SYD SE26 151 G3
Highcliffe Dr PUT/ROE SW15 126 C5
Highcliffe Gdns REDBR IG4 59 J4
Highcombe CHARL SE7 114 A5
Highcombe Cl ELTH/MOT SE9 134 C7
High Coombe Pl
KUTN/CMB KT2 145 F6
Highcroft CDALE/KGS NW9 51 G4
Highcroft Av ALP/SUD HA0 68 B6
Highcroft Gdns GLDGN NW11 52 D5
Highcroft Rd ARCH N19 54 E6
High Cross Rd TOTM N17 56 C2
Highcross Wy PUT/ROE SW15 126 D7
Highdaun Dr
STRHM/NOR SW16 164 A3
Highdown WPK KT4 173 G1
Highdown Rd PUT/ROE SW15 126 E5
High Dr NWMAL KT3 144 E7
High Elms WFD IG8 44 E4
High Elms Cl NTHWD HA6 32 A5
Highfield OXHEY WD19 33 K2
Highfield Av CDALE/KGS NW9 50 E4
ERITH DA8 117 J5
GFD/PVL UB6 66 E4
GLDGN NW11 52 B6
PIN HA5 47 K4
WBLY HA9 68 A2
Highfield Cl CDALE/KGS NW9 50 E4
LEW SE13 133 G5
NTHWD HA6 32 C7
SURB KT6 158 D7
WDGN N22 41 G7
Highfield Ct STHGT/OAK N14 28 C5
Highfield Crs NTHWD HA6 32 C7
Highfield Dr HAYES BR2 167 H3
HOR/WEW KT19 173 H6
WWKM BR4 179 K2
Highfield Gdns GLDGN NW11 52 C5
Highfield Hl NRWD SE19 149 K6
Highfield Rd ACT W3 86 D4
BMLY BR1 168 E3
BRYLDS KT5 159 K6
BUSH WD23 21 J4
BXLYHS DA6 137 G4
DART DA1 139 G6
FELT TW13 121 K7
GLDGN NW11 * 52 C5
ISLW TW7 104 A7
NTHWD HA6 32 C7
SUT SM1 175 J4
WCHMH N21 41 H1
WFD IG8 45 J6
Highfield Rd North DART DA1 139 C5
Highfield Rd South DART DA1 139 G6
Highfields Gv HGT N6 54 A7
High Foleys ESH/CLAY KT10 171 H6
High Garth ESH/CLAY KT10 170 C5
Highgate Av HGT N6 54 B6
Highgate Cl HGT N6 54 A6
Highgate Edge EFNCH N2 * 53 J4
Highgate High St HGT N6 54 A7
Highgate Hl ARCH N19 54 B7
Highgate Rd KTTN NW5 72 B3
Highgate Spinney
CEND/HSY/T N8 * 54 D5
Highgate Wk FSTH SE23 150 E1
Highgate West Hl HGT N6 54 A7
High Gv BMLY BR1 153 G7
WOOL/PLUM SE18 115 J6
Highgrove Cl CHST BR7 153 J7
FBAR/BDGN N11 40 A4
Highgrove Ms CAR SM5 175 J2

Highgrove Rd *BCTR* RM8....79 J4
Highgrove Wy *RSLP* HA4....46 E5
High Hill Ferry *CLPT* E5....56 D7
High Holborn *HHOL* WC1V....11 K4
Highland Av *DAGE* RM10....80 E2
 HNWL W7....84 E5
Highland Cots *WLGTN* SM6 *....176 B3
Highland Dr *BECK* BR3....151 K4
Highland Pk *FELT* TW13....140 D5
Highland Rd *BMLY* BR1....152 D7
 BXLYHS DA6....137 H3
 HAYES BR2....167 J1
 NRWD SE19....150 A5
 NTHWD HA6....46 A1
Highlands *OXHEY* WD19....21 G7
Highlands Av *ACT* W3....86 E6
 WCHMH N21....29 F4
Highlands Cl *FSBYPK* N4....54 E6
 HSLW TW3....103 G7
Highlands Gdns *IL* IG1....59 K7
Highlands Heath
 PUT/ROE SW15....127 F6
Highlands Rd *BAR* EN5....26 E4
The Highlands *BAR* EN5....26 E4
 EDGW HA8....50 D1
Highland Ter *LEW* SE13 *....132 E2
High La *HNWL* W7....84 D5
Highlea Cl *CDALE/KGS* NW9....37 G7
High Level Dr *SYD* SE26....150 C3
Highlever Rd *NKENS* W10....88 A4
High Limes *NRWD* SE19 *....150 A5
High Md *HRW* HA1....48 E4
Highmead *WOOL/PLUM* SE18....116 A6
High Md *MRDN* SM4....180 B1
Highmead Crs *ALP/SUD* HA0....68 B6
High Meadow Cl *PIN* HA5....47 F3
High Meadow Crs
 CDALE/KGS NW9....51 F4
High Meads Rd *CAN/RD* E16....95 H5
Highmore Rd *BKHTH/KID* SE3....118 K5
High Mt *HDN* NW4 *....51 J5
The High Pde
 STRHM/NOR SW16 *....148 E2
High Park Rd *RCH/KEW* TW9....105 H7
High Pth *WIM/MER* SW19....147 F2
High Point *WIM/MER* SE9 *....154 B2
High Rdg *MUSWH* N10 *....40 B7
High Rd *BUSH* WD23....22 D7
 CHDH RM6....61 K6
 EFNCH N2....53 J3
 FBAR/BDGN N11....40 B4
 FNCH N3....53 H1
 GDMY/SEVK IG3....61 G7
 IL IG1....78 B3
 KTN/HRWW/WS HA3....34 E7
 LEY E10....57 K5
 NFNCH/WDSPK N12....39 G6
 SEVS/STOTM N15....56 B4
 TOTM N17....56 B2
 TRDG/WHET N20....27 F6
 WBLY HA9....68 A4
 WDGN N22....41 F6
 WDGN N22....55 G2
 WLSDN NW10....69 G5
High Rd Eastcote *PIN* HA5....47 F4
High Rd Leyton *LEY* E10....75 K1
High Rd Leytonstone
 WAN E11....76 C2
High Road Woodford Gn
 WFD IG8....44 E3
Highshore Rd *PECK* SE15....131 G1
Highstead Crs *ERITH* DA8....118 B7
Highstone Av *WAN* E11....58 E5
High St *ACT* W3....86 E7
 BAR EN5....26 C2
 BARK/HLT IG6....60 C1
 BECK BR3....151 J7
 BELMT SM2....175 G6
 BMLY BR1....167 K1
 BTFD TW8....104 E5
 BUSH WD23....22 A5
 CAR SM5....175 K4
 CEND/HSY/T N8....54 E3
 CHEAM SM3....174 C5
 CROY/NA CR0....177 J2
 DART DA1....139 H5
 E/WMO/HCT KT8....157 F4
 EA W5....85 K6
 ESH/CLAY KT10....170 B3
 ESH/CLAY KT10....171 F5
 EW KT17....173 H7
 FBAR/BDGN N11....40 B4
 FELT TW13....140 D2
 HEST TW5....102 A5
 HPTN TW12....142 B7
 HRW HA1....48 E7
 HSLW TW3....123 G2
 HYS/HAR UB3....101 G5
 KTN/HRWW/WS HA3....48 C2
 KUT/HW KT1....143 J7
 MLHL NW7....37 K4
 NTHWD HA6....32 D7
 NWMAL KT3....160 B3
 PGE/AN SE20....150 E6
 PIN HA5....47 J2
 PLSTW E13....94 E1
 PUR RM19....119 K4
 ROM RM1....63 G4
 RSLP HA4....46 C6
 SCUP DA14....155 G3
 SNWD SE25....165 G3
 SRTFD E15....76 C6
 STHGT/OAK N14....28 D7
 STWL/WRAY TW19....120 A5
 SUT SM1....175 F5
 TEDD TW11....143 G4
 THDIT KT7....158 B5
 THHTH CR7....164 D3
 WALTH E17....57 H3
 WAN E11....59 F5
 WAT WD17....21 F2
 WBLY HA9....68 A3
 WDR/YW UB7....100 A5
 WHTN TW2....123 H6
 WIM/MER SW19....146 B4
 WWKM BR4....166 E1
High Street Collier's Wd
 WIM/MER SW19 *....147 H6
High Street Harlesden
 WLSDN NW10....69 G7
High Street Harlington
 HYS/HAR UB3....101 G6
High Street Ms
 WIM/MER SW19....146 C4
High St North *EHAM* E6....77 J7
High St South *EHAM* E6....95 K1
High Timber St *BLKFR* EC4V....12 C5
High Tor Cl *BMLY* BR1....153 F6
High Trees *BRXS/STRHM* SW2....130 B7
 CROY/NA CR0....166 B7
 EBAR EN4....27 J4
High Vw *PIN* HA5....47 G3

WATW WD18....20 D5
Highview Av *EDGW* HA8....36 E3
 WLGTN SM6....177 H4
High View Cl *NRWD* SE19....165 G1
Highview Gdns *EDGW* HA8....36 E4
 FBAR/BDGN N11....40 C4
 FNCH N3....52 C2
High View Rd *NRWD* SE19....149 K5
 SWFD E18....58 D1
Highview Ter *DART* DA1 *....139 J4
The Highway *BELMT* SM2....175 G7
 STAN HA7....35 F1
 WCHPL E1....92 C6
Highwood Av
 NFNCH/WDSPK N12....39 G3
Highwood Cl *EDUL* SE22....131 H7
Highwood Gdns *CLAY* IG5....59 H4
Highwood Gv *MLHL* NW7....37 H4
Highwood Hl *MLHL* NW7....37 H1
Highwood Rd *ARCH* N19....72 E2
Highworth Rd
 FBAR/BDGN N11....40 D5
Highworth St *CAMTN* NW1 *....9 K2
Hilary Av *MTCM* CR4....163 F2
Hilary Cl *ERITH* DA8....117 J7
 FUL/PGN SW6 *....108 A6
Hilary Rd *SHB* W12....87 H6
Hilberry Ct *BUSH* WD23....22 B6
Hilbert Rd *CHEAM* SM3....174 B3
Hilborough Cl
 WIM/MER SW19 *....147 G6
Hilborough Rd *HACK* E8 *....7 M2
Hilda Lockert Wk
 BRXN/ST SW9....130 C1
Hilda Rd *CAN/RD* E16....94 C3
 EHAM E6....77 H6
Hilda Ter *BRXN/ST* SW9 *....130 B1
Hildenborough Gdns
 BMLY BR1....152 C5
Hilden Dr *ERITH* DA8....118 E6
Hildenlea Pl *HAYES* BR2....167 H1
Hildreth St *BAL* SW12....129 F7
Hildyard Rd *FUL/PGN* SW6....14 H8
Hiley Rd *WLSDN* NW10....88 A2
Hilfield La *GSTN* WD25....22 C1
Hilgrove Rd *KIL/WHAMP* NW6....2 F2
Hiliary Gdns *STAN* HA7....49 J1
Hillary Crs *WOT/HER* KT12....156 B7
Hillary Dr *ISLW* TW7....124 A3
Hillary Ri *BAR* EN5....26 E3
Hillary Rd *NWDGN* UB2....103 F2
Hillbeck Cl *PECK* SE15....111 K6
Hillbeck Wy *GFD/PVL* UB6....66 D7
Hillborne Cl *HYS/HAR* UB3....101 K4
Hillborough Cl
 WIM/MER SW19 *....147 G6
Hillbrook Rd *TOOT* SW17....147 K3
Hill Brow *BMLY* BR1....153 H7
 DART DA1....138 C5
Hillbrow *NWMAL* KT3....160 C2
Hillbrow Rd *BMLY* BR1....152 C6
 ESH/CLAY KT10....170 C3
Hillbury Av
 KTN/HRWW/WS HA3....49 H4
Hillbury Rd *TOOT* SW17....148 B2
Hill Cl *BAR* EN5....26 A4
 CHST BR7....154 B4
 CRICK NW2....69 K2
 GLDGN NW11....52 E5
 HRW HA1....48 E7
 STAN HA7....35 H3
Hillcote Av *STRHM/NOR* SW16....149 G6
Hillcourt Av
 NFNCH/WDSPK N12....39 F5
Hillcourt Rd *EDUL* SE22....131 J5
Hill Crs *BRYLDS* KT5....159 G4
 BXLY DA5....137 K7
 HRW HA1....49 G4
 TRDG/WHET N20....27 G1
 WPK KT4....174 A1
Hill Crest *SURB* KT6 *....159 F6
 BFN/LL DA15....136 B6
Hillcrest *HGT* N6....54 A6
 HNHL SE24 *....130 D3
 WCHMH N21....29 H7
Hillcrest Av *EDGW* HA8....36 D3
 GLDGN NW11....52 C4
 PIN HA5....47 H3
Hillcrest Cl *BECK* BR3....166 C5
 SYD SE26....150 C3
Hill Crest Gdns *CRICK* NW2....69 J2
Hillcrest Gdns *ESH/CLAY* KT10....171 F2
 FNCH N3....52 C3
Hillcrest Rd *ACT* W3....86 C7
 BMLY BR1....152 E3
 DART DA1....138 B6
 EA W5....86 A4
 EMPK RM11....63 J6
 WALTH E17....58 B1
Hillcrest Vw *BECK* BR3....166 C5
Hillcroft Av *PIN* HA5....47 K5
Hillcroft Crs *EA* W5....85 K5
 OXHEY WD19....21 F7
 RSLP HA4....65 H2
 WBLY HA9....68 B3
Hillcroft Rd *EHAM* E6....96 B4
Hillcroome Rd *BELMT* SM2....175 H5
Hillcross Av *MRDN* SM4....161 H5
Hilldale Rd *SUT* SM1....174 D3
Hilldown Rd *HAYES* BR2....167 H7
 STRHM/NOR SW16....148 E6
Hill Dr *CDALE/KGS* NW9....50 D7
 STRHM/NOR SW16....164 A2
Hilldrop Crs *HOLWY* N7....72 D4
Hilldrop Est *HOLWY* N7....72 D4
Hilldrop La *HOLWY* N7....72 D4
Hilldrop Rd *BMLY* BR1....152 E5
 HOLWY N7....72 D4
Hill End *WOOL/PLUM* SE18....115 F7
Hillersdon Av *BARN* SW13....126 D1
 EDGW HA8....36 A4
Hillery Cl *WALW* SE17....19 H6
Hill Farm Rd *NKENS* W10....88 A4
Hillfield Av *ALP/SUD* HA0....68 A6
 CDALE/KGS NW9....51 G4
 CEND/HSY/T N8....55 F3
 MRDN SM4....162 D5
Hillfield Cl *RYLN/HDSTN* HA2....48 C3
Hillfield La South *BUSH* WD23....22 E5
Hillfield Ms *CEND/HSY/T* N8....55 F3
Hillfield Pde *MRDN* SM4....162 C5
Hillfield Pk *MUSWH* N10....54 B2
 WCHMH N21....41 G1
Hillfield Park Ms *MUSWH* N10....54 B3
Hillfield Rd *HPTN* TW12....141 K6
 KIL/WHAMP NW6....70 D4
Hill Gardens Craven
 BAY/PAD W2 *....8 E6
Hillgate Pl *KENS* W8....8 A8

Hillgate St *KENS* W8....8 A8
Hill Gv *FELT* TW13....141 K1
 ROM RM1....63 G2
Hill House Av *STAN* HA7....35 F5
Hill House Cl *WCHMH* N21....29 G6
Hill House Dr *HPTN* TW12....142 A7
Hill House Rd
 STRHM/NOR SW16....149 F4
Hilliard Rd *NTHWD* HA6....32 D7
Hilliard's Ct *WAP* E1W *....92 E7
Hillier Cl *BAR* EN5....27 F5
Hillier Gdns *CROY/NA* CR0....177 G4
Hillier Pl *CHSGTN* KT9....171 K5
Hillier Rd *BTSEA* SW11....128 E5
Hillier's La *CROY/NA* CR0....176 C2
Hillingdon Av
 STWL/WRAY TW19....120 B7
Hillingdon Rd *BXLYHN* DA7....137 K2
 WALW SE17....110 C5
Hillingdon Trail
 HGDN/ICK UB10....64 A5
 HYS/HAR UB3....101 K4
 RSLP HA4....46 A4
Hill La *RSLP* HA4....46 A7
Hillman Dr *NKENS* W10....88 A3
Hillman St *HACK* E8....74 D5
Hillmarton Rd *HOLWY* N7....72 E4
Hillmarton Ter *HOLWY* N7 *....72 E4
Hillmont Rd *ESH/CLAY* KT10....170 E2
Hillmore Gv *SYD* SE26....151 F4
Hillreach *WOOL/PLUM* SE18....114 E4
Hill Ri *ED* N9....30 D5
 ESH/CLAY KT10....171 H1
 FSTH SE23....132 B1
 GFD/PVL UB6....66 C7
 GLDGN NW11....53 F3
 RCHPK/HAM TW10....124 E4
 RSLP HA4....46 A7
Hillrise Rd *ARCH* N19....54 E6
Hill Rd *ALP/SUD* HA0....67 H2
 CAR SM5....175 J4
 HRW HA1....49 G4
 MTCM CR4....148 B1
 MUSWH N10....39 K7
 NTHWD HA6....32 B5
 PIN HA5....47 J5
 STJWD NW8....2 F3
 SUT SM1....175 F4
Hillsboro Rd *EDUL* SE22....131 F4
Hillsborough Gn
 OXHEY WD19 *....32 E2
Hillsgrove Cl *WELL* DA16....116 D6
Hillside *BAR* EN5 *....25 J4
 BAR EN5....27 G4
 CDALE/KGS NW9....51 F3
 ESH/CLAY KT10 *....170 B4
 WIM/MER SW19....146 B5
 WLSDN NW10....69 F7
Hillside Av *BORE* WD6....24 D3
 FBAR/BDGN N11....39 K5
 WBLY HA9....68 B3
 WFD IG8....45 G4
Hillside Cl *MRDN* SM4....161 H3
 STJWD NW8....2 D4
 WFD IG8....45 G5
Hillside Crs *NTHWD* HA6....32 E7
 OXHEY WD19....21 H5
 RYLN/HDSTN HA2....66 C1
Hillside Dr *EDGW* HA8....36 C5
Hillside Gdns *BAR* EN5....26 C3
 BRXS/STRHM SW2 *....149 G1
 EDGW HA8....36 B3
 FBAR/BDGN N11 *....40 C5
 HGT N6....54 A5
 KTN/HRWW/WS HA3....50 A1
 NTHWD HA6....32 E6
 WALTH E17....58 B2
 WLGTN SM6....176 C6
Hillside Gv *MLHL* NW7....37 J6
 STHGT/OAK N14....28 D6
Hillside La *HAYES* BR2....180 E7
Hillside Ri *NTHWD* HA6....32 E7
Hillside Rd *BELMT* SM2....174 D6
 BRXS/STRHM SW2....149 F1
 BUSH WD23....21 J4
 CROY/NA CR0....177 H4
 DART DA1....138 D5
 EA W5....86 A4
 HAYES BR2....167 J4
 NTHWD HA6....32 E6
 SEVS/STOTM N15....56 A5
 STHL UB1....84 A4
 SURB KT6....159 G4
Hillsleigh Rd *KENS* W8....88 D7
Hills Ms *EA* W5 *....86 A6
Hills Pl *SOHO/SHAV* W1D....10 E5
Hillstowe St *CLPT* E5....74 E1
Hill St *MYFR/PICC* W1J....10 B8
 RCH/KEW TW9....124 E4
Hill Top *CHEAM* SM3....161 J6
 GLDGN NW11....53 F3
Hilltop *WALTH* E17 *....57 K2
Hilltop Rd *WLSDN* NW10 *....69 H6
Hilltop Cots *SYD* SE26 *....150 D3
Hilltop Gdns *DART* DA1....139 J4
 HDN NW4....51 K1
Hill Top Vw *WFD* IG8 *....45 K5
Hilltop Wy *STAN* HA7....35 G2
Hillview *RYNPK* SW20....145 K6
Hillview Av
 KTN/HRWW/WS HA3....50 A4
Hillview Cl *PIN* HA5....33 K5
 WBLY HA9....68 B1
Hillview Crs *IL* IG1....59 K5
 ORP BR6....169 K7
Hill View Dr *THMD* SE28....96 E7
 WELL DA16....135 K1
Hill View Gdns
 CDALE/KGS NW9....51 F4
Hillview Gdns *HDN* NW4....52 B3
 RYLN/HDSTN HA2....48 A2
Hill View Rd *ESH/CLAY* KT10....171 H3
 TWK TW1....124 B5
Hillview Rd *CHST* BR7....154 A4
 MLHL NW7....38 B3
 PIN HA5....33 K4
 SUT SM1....175 G2
Hillway *CDALE/KGS* NW9....51 G7
 HGT N6....72 A2
Hillworth *BECK* BR3 *....166 E1
Hillworth Rd
 BRXS/STRHM SW2....130 B6
Hillyard Rd *HNWL* W7....84 E4
Hillyard St *BRXN/ST* SW9....110 B7
Hillyfield *WALTH* E17....57 G1
Hillyfield Cl *HOM* E9....75 G4
Hilly Flds *BROCKY* SE4 *....132 D3
Hilly Fields Crs *BROCKY* SE4....132 D3
Hilsea St *CLPT* E5....74 E3
Hilton Av *NFNCH/WDSPK* N12....39 H4
Himalayan Wy *WATW* WD18....20 D5

Himley Rd *TOOT* SW17....147 J4
Hinchley Cl *ESH/CLAY* KT10....171 F2
Hinchley Dr *ESH/CLAY* KT10....171 F2
Hinchley Wy *ESH/CLAY* KT10....171 G2
Hinckley Rd *PECK* SE15....131 H3
Hind Ct *FLST/FETLN* EC4A....12 B5
Hinde Ms *MHST* W1U *....10 B4
Hinde St *MHST* W1U....10 B4
Hindes Rd *HRW* HA1....48 E4
Hinde St *MHST* W1U *....10 B4
Hindhead Gdns *NTHLT* UB5....83 H1
Hindhead Wy *WLGTN* SM6....176 E4
Hindmans Rd *EDUL* SE22....131 H4
Hindmans Wy *DAGW* RM9....98 B2
Hindmarsh Cl *WCHPL* E1 *....92 C6
Hindrey Rd *CLPT* E5....74 D4
Hindsley's Pl *FSTH* SE23....150 E1
Hinkler Rd
 KTN/HRWW/WS HA3....49 K2
Hinksey Pth *ABYW* SE2....116 E2
Hinstock Rd
 WOOL/PLUM SE18....115 H5
Hinton Av *HSLWW* TW4....122 C3
Hinton Cl *ELTH/MOT* SE9....134 D7
Hinton Rd *BRXN/ST* SW9....130 C2
 UED N18....42 A3
 WLGTN SM6....176 C5
Hippodrome Pl *NTGHL* W11....88 C6
Hirst Crs *WBLY* HA9....68 A1
Hitcham Rd *WALTH* E17....57 H6
Hitchin La *STAN* HA7....35 K6
Hithe Gv *BERM/RHTH* SE16....111 K2
Hitherbroom Rd
 HYS/HAR UB3....82 E7
Hither Farm Rd
 BKHTH/KID SE3....134 B2
Hitherfield Rd *BCTR* RM8....80 A1
 STRHM/NOR SW16....149 F1
Hither Green La *LEW* SE13....133 F4
Hitherwell Dr
 KTN/HRWW/WS HA3....34 D7
Hitherwood Dr *NRWD* SE19....150 B3
Hive Cl *BUSH* WD23....34 D1
Hive Rd *BUSH* WD23....34 D1
Hoadly Rd *STRHM/NOR* SW16....148 D2
Hobart Cl *TRDG/WHET* N20....39 J1
 YEAD UB4....83 H3
Hobart Dr *YEAD* UB4....83 H3
Hobart Gdns *THHTH* CR7....164 E2
Hobart La *YEAD* UB4....83 H3
Hobart Pl *BGVA* SW1W....16 C4
 RCHPK/HAM TW10....125 G6
Hobart Rd *BARK/HLT* IG6....60 C1
 DAGW RM9....79 K3
 WPK KT4....173 K2
 YEAD UB4....83 H3
Hobbayne Rd *HNWL* W7....84 D5
Hobbes Wk *PUT/ROE* SW15....126 E4
Hobbs Gn *EFNCH* N2....53 G2
Hobbs Pl *IS* N1....7 J4
Hobbs Place Est *IS* N1....7 J5
Hobbs Rd *WNWD* SE27....149 J3
Hobby St *PEND* EN3....31 F4
Hobday St *POP/IOD* E14....93 K5
Hoblands End *CHST* BR7....154 E5
Hobsons Pl *WCHPL* E1 *....92 C4
Hobury St *WBPTN* SW10....108 B5
Hocker St *BETH* E2 *....7 L9
Hockett Cl *DEPT* SE8....112 B2
Hockley Av *EHAM* E6....95 J1
Hockley Dr *CRICK* NW2....70 D2
Hockley Ms *BARK* IG11....96 E1
Hocroft Av *CRICK* NW2....70 D2
Hocroft Rd *CRICK* NW2....70 D2
Hocroft Wk *CRICK* NW2....70 D2
Hodder Dr *GFD/PVL* UB6....85 F1
Hoddesdon Rd *BELV* DA17....117 H4
Hodes Rw *HAMP* NW3....71 K3
Hodford Rd *GLDGN* NW11....52 D6
Hodges Wy *WATW* WD18....20 D5
Hodgkins Ms *STAN* HA7....35 H4
Hodister Cl *CMBW* SE5....110 D6
Hodnet Gv *BERM/RHTH* SE16....111 K3
Hodson Cl *RYLN/HDSTN* HA2....65 K2
Hoe St *WALTH* E17....57 J4
The Hoe *OXHEY* WD19....33 H1
Hoffmann Gdns
 SAND/SEL CR2....178 C5
Hoffman Sq *IS* N1 *....7 H7
Hofland Rd *WKENS* W14....107 H2
Hogan Ms *BAY/PAD* W2....9 G2
Hogarth Av *ASHF* TW15....140 A6
Hogarth Cl *CAN/RD* E16....95 H4
 EA W5....86 A4
Hogarth Crs *CROY/NA* CR0....164 D6
 WIM/MER SW19....147 H7
Hogarth Gdns *HEST* TW5....103 F6
Hogarth Hl *GLDGN* NW11....52 D3
Hogarth Pl *ECT* SW5 *....14 C6
Hogarth Rd *BCTR* RM8....79 H4
 ECT SW5....14 C6
 EDGW HA8....50 C1
Hogarth Ter *CHSWK* W4 *....106 B5
Hogarth Wy *HPTN* TW12....142 C7
Hogg La *BORE* WD6....23 G3
Hogshead Pas *WAP* E1W *....92 D6
Hogsmill La *KUT/HW* KT1....159 G2
Hogsmill Wy *HOR/WEW* KT19....172 E4
Holbeach Cl *CDALE/KGS* NW9 *....37 G7
Holbeach Gdns *BFN/LL* DA15....135 K5
Holbeach Rd *CAT* SE6....132 D6
Holbeck Rw *PECK* SE15....111 H6
Holbein Ga *NTHWD* HA6....32 C4
Holbein Ms *BGVA* SW1W....16 A7
Holbein Pl *BGVA* SW1W....16 A6
Holberton Gdns *WLSDN* NW10....87 K2
Holborn *GINN* WC1R....12 A3
 HCIRC EC1N....12 A3
Holborn Circ *HCIRC* EC1N....12 B3
Holborn Pl *HHOL* WC1V....11 L3
Holborn Rd *PLSTW* E13....95 F3
Holborn Viad *STBT* EC1A....12 C3
Holborn Wy *MTCM* CR4....162 E1
Holbrooke Ct *HOLWY* N7....72 E2
Holbrook La *CHST* BR7....154 D6
Holbrook Rd *SRTFD* E15....94 D1
Holbrook Wy *HAYES* BR2....168 E5
Holburne Gdns
 BKHTH/KID SE3....114 C7
Holburne Rd *BKHTH/KID* SE3....114 B7
Holcombe Hl *MLHL* NW7....37 J2
Holcombe Rd *IL* IG1....60 A6
 TOTM N17....56 B2
Holcombe St *HMSMTH* W6....106 E4
Holcote Cl *BELV* DA17....117 F2
Holcroft Rd *HOM* E9....74 E6
Holden Av *CDALE/KGS* NW9....50 E7
 NFNCH/WDSPK N12....39 F4
Holdenby Rd *BROCKY* SE4....132 B4

Holden Cl *BCTR* RM8....79 H2
Holdenhurst Av *FNCH* N3....39 F6
Holden Rd
 NFNCH/WDSPK N12....39 F3
Holden St *BTSEA* SW11....129 F1
Holder Cl *NFNCH/WDSPK* N12....39 G4
Holdernesse Rd *ISLW* TW7....104 B7
 TOOT SW17....147 K2
Holderness Wy *WNWD* SE27....149 H4
Holders Hill Av *HDN* NW4....52 B1
Holders Hill Crs *HDN* NW4....52 B1
Holders Hill Dr *HDN* NW4....52 B2
Holders Hill Gdns *HDN* NW4....52 C4
Holders Hill Pde *MLHL* NW7 *....38 C2
Holders Hill Rd *HDN* NW4....52 B1
Holford Rd *FSBYW* WC1X *....5 L7
Holford St *HAMP* NW3....71 G2
Holford St *FSBYW* WC1X....6 A7
Holford Wy *PUT/ROE* SW15....126 D5
Holford Yd *FSBYW* WC1X *....6 A6
Holgate Av *BTSEA* SW11....128 C2
Holgate Rd *DAGE* RM10....80 C4
Holgate St *CHARL* SE7....114 C2
Holland Av *BELMT* SM2....174 E6
 RYNPK SW20....145 H7
Holland Cl *BAR* EN5....27 H4
 HAYES BR2....180 C1
 ROMW/RG RM7....62 A4
 STAN HA7....35 H4
Holland Dr *FSTH* SE23....151 G2
Holland Gdns *BTFD* TW8....105 G4
 WKENS W14....107 H2
Holland Gv *BRXN/ST* SW9....110 B6
Holland Pk *NTGHL* W11....88 D7
Holland Park Av
 GDMY/SEVK IG3....60 E5
 NTGHL W11....88 C5
Holland Park Gdns
 WKENS W14....107 H1
Holland Park Ms *NTGHL* W11....88 D7
Holland Park Rd *WKENS* W14....107 J2
Holland Pas *IS* N1 *....6 E3
Holland Pl *KENS* W8....14 C1
Holland Rd *ALP/SUD* HA0....67 K5
 EHAM E6....77 K7
 SNWD SE25....165 H4
 SRTFD E15....94 C2
 WKENS W14....107 G1
 WLSDN NW10....69 J6
The Hollands *WPK* KT4....160 C7
Holland St *KENS* W8....14 B1
 STHWK SE1....12 D8
Holland Villas Rd *WKENS* W14....107 H1
Holland Wk *STAN* HA7....35 G4
Holland Rd *STNW/STAM* N16....73 K1
Hollar Rd *STNW/STAM* N16....74 B2
Hollen St *SOHO/CST* W1F....10 F5
Holles Cl *HPTN* TW12....142 A5
Holles St *OXSTW* W1C....10 D4
Holley Rd *ACT* W3....106 C1
Hollickwood Av
 NFNCH/WDSPK N12....39 K5
Holliday Sq *BTSEA* SW11....128 C2
Hollidge Wy *DAGE* RM10....80 D5
Hollies Av *BFN/LL* DA15....155 F1
Hollies Cl *STRHM/NOR* SW16....149 G5
 TWK TW1....143 F1
Hollies End *NWMAL* KT3....37 K4
Hollies Rd *EA* W5....104 D3
The Hollies *BAR* EN5 *....25 J4
 KTN/HRWW/WS HA3....49 G3
Hollies Wy *BAL* SW12 *....129 F6
Holligrave Rd *BMLY* BR1....152 E7
Hollingbourne Av
 BXLYHN DA7....117 G7
Hollingbourne Gdns *WEA* W13....85 G3
Hollingbourne Rd *HNHL* SE24....130 D4
Hollingsworth Rd
 CROY/NA CR0....178 D5
Hollington Crs *NWMAL* KT3....160 C5
Hollington Rd *EHAM* E6....95 K2
 TOTM N17....56 C1
Hollingworth Cl
 E/WMO/HCT KT8....156 E3
Hollingworth Rd
 STMC/STPC BR5....169 G6
Hollman Gdns
 STRHM/NOR SW16....149 H5
Holloway La *WDR/YW* UB7....100 C4
Holloway Rd *ARCH* N19....72 D1
 EHAM E6....95 K2
 HOLWY N7....73 F3
Holloway St *HSLW* TW3....123 G2
The Hollow *WFD* IG8....44 D3
Holly Av *STAN* HA7....50 A1
 WOT/HER KT12....156 C7
Holly Bank *MUSWH* N10 *....54 C3
Hollybank Cl *HPTN* TW12....142 A4
Hollybrake Cl *CHST* BR7....154 D6
Hollybush Cl
 KTN/HRWW/WS HA3....34 E7
 OXHEY WD19....21 H6
 WAN E11....58 E4
Hollybush Gdns *BETH* E2....92 D2
Hollybush Hl *WAN* E11....58 B6
Hollybush La *HPTN* TW12....141 K6
Hollybush Pl *BETH* E2....92 D2
Hollybush Rd *KUTN/CMB* KT2....144 A4
Hollybush St *PLSTW* E13....95 F2
Hollybush Ter *NRWD* SE19 *....150 A5
Holly Bush V *HAMP* NW3 *....71 G3
Holly Cl *BECK* BR3....167 F3
 BKHH IG9....45 G1
 FELT TW13....141 J4
 SUN TW16....156 A2
 WLGTN SM6....176 B6
 WLSDN NW10....69 G6
Holly Crs *BECK* BR3....166 C4
 WFD IG8....44 B6
Hollycroft Av *HAMP* NW3....70 D2
 WBLY HA9....68 A1
Hollycroft Cl *SAND/SEL* CR2....178 A4
 WDR/YW UB7....100 D5
Hollycroft Gdns *WDR/YW* UB7....100 D5
Hollydale Cl *NTHLT* UB5....66 B4
Hollydale Dr *HAYES* BR2....181 K2
Hollydale Rd *PECK* SE15....131 K1
Hollydown Wy *WAN* E11....76 B2
Holly Dr *CHING* E4....31 K6
Holly Farm Rd *NWDGN* UB2....102 D4
Hollyfield Av *FBAR/BDGN* N11....39 K4
Hollyfield Rd *BRYLDS* KT5....159 G6
Holly Gdns *BXLYHN* DA7....137 K3
 WDR/YW UB7....100 C1
Hollygrove Cl *HSLW* TW3....122 E3
Holly Hedge Ter *LEW* SE13....133 G4
Holly HI *HAMP* NW3....71 G3
 WCHMH N21....29 F5

Holly Hill Rd *BELV* DA17 ...... 117 J4
Holly Lodge Gdns *HGT* N6 ...... 72 A1
Hollymead *CAR* SM5 ...... 175 G2
Holly Mt *HAMP* NW3 * 71 H1
Hollyport Rd *GNWCH* SE10 ...... 113 F7
Holly Pk *FNCH* N3 ...... 52 D2
   FSBYPK N4 ...... 54 E6
Holly Park Gdns *FNCH* N3 ...... 52 E2
Holly Park Rd
   FBAR/BDGN N11 ...... 40 A4
   HNWL W7 ...... 85 F7
Holly Rd *CHSWK* W4 * 106 A3
   DART DA1 ...... 139 G2
   HPTN TW12 ...... 142 C5
   HSLW TW3 ...... 123 G3
   TWK TW1 ...... 124 B7
   WAN E11 ...... 58 D6
Hollytree CI *WIM/MER* SW19 ...... 127 G5
Hollytree Pde *SCUP* DA14 * 155 J4
Hollyview CI *HDN* NW4 ...... 51 J5
Holly VIs *HMSMTH* W6 * 106 E2
Holly Wk *HAMP* NW3 ...... 71 G4
Holly Wy *MTCM* CR4 ...... 163 J3
Hollywood Gdns *YEAD* UB4 ...... 83 F5
Hollywood Ms *WBPTN* SW10 ...... 14 F9
Hollywood Rd *CHING* E4 ...... 43 G4
   WBPTN SW10 ...... 14 E9
Hollywoods *CROY/NA* CR0 ...... 179 H7
Hollywood Wy *ERITH* DA8 ...... 118 E6
   WFD IG8 ...... 44 B6
Holman Ct *EW* KT17 * 173 J7
Holman Rd *BTSEA* SW11 ...... 128 B1
   HOR/WEW KT19 ...... 172 E6
Holmbridge Gdns *PEND* EN3 ...... 31 F5
Holmbrook Dr *HDN* NW4 ...... 52 B4
Holmbury Ct *BUSH* WD23 ...... 34 E1
Holmbury Ct *MTCM* CR4 * 163 G3
Holmbury Gdns *HYS/HAR* UB3 ...... 82 D7
Holmbury Gv *SAND/SEL* CR2 ...... 179 F6
Holmbury Mnr *SCUP* DA14 * 155 G3
Holmbury Pk *BMLY* BR1 ...... 153 J6
Holmbury Vw *CLPT* E5 ...... 56 D7
Holmbush Rd *PUT/ROE* SW15 ...... 127 H5
Holmcote Gdns *HBRY* N5 ...... 73 J4
Holmcroft Wy *HAYES* BR2 ...... 168 E4
Holmdale CI *BORE* WD6 ...... 24 B1
Holmdale Gdns *HDN* NW4 ...... 52 B4
Holmdale Rd *CHST* BR7 ...... 154 C4
   KIL/WHAMP NW6 ...... 70 E4
Holmdale Ter
   SEVS/STOTM N15 ...... 56 A5
Holmdene Av *HNHL* SE24 ...... 130 D4
   MLHL NW7 ...... 37 J5
   RYLN/HDSTN HA2 ...... 48 B2
Holmdene CI *BECK* BR3 * 167 F1
Holmdene Ct *BMLY* BR1 ...... 168 D2
Holmead Rd *FUL/PGN* SW6 ...... 108 A6
Holmebury CI *BUSH* WD23 * 34 E1
Holme Ct *ISLW* TW7 * 124 B2
Holme Lacey Rd
   LEE/GVPK SE12 ...... 133 J5
Holme Pk *BORE* WD6 ...... 24 B1
Holme Rd *EHAM* E6 ...... 77 J7
Holmes Av *MLHL* NW7 ...... 38 C4
   WALTH E17 ...... 57 H2
Holmes CI *EDUL* SE22 ...... 131 H3
Holmesdale Av
   MORT/ESHN SW14 ...... 125 J2
Holmesdale CI *SNWD* SE25 ...... 165 G2
Holmesdale Rd *BXLYHN* DA7 ...... 136 E1
   CROY/NA CR0 ...... 164 E4
   HGT N6 ...... 54 B6
   RCH/KEW TW9 ...... 105 G7
   SNWD SE25 ...... 165 F3
   TEDD TW11 ...... 143 J6
Holmesley Rd *FSTH* SE23 ...... 132 B5
Holmes Rd *KTTN* NW5 ...... 72 B4
   TWK TW1 ...... 143 F1
   WIM/MER SW19 ...... 147 G6
Holmes Ter *STHWK* SE1 ...... 18 A1
Holme Wy *STAN* HA7 ...... 35 F5
Holmewood Gdns
   BRXS/STRHM SW2 ...... 130 A6
Holmewood Rd
   BRXS/STRHM SW2 ...... 129 K6
   SNWD SE25 ...... 165 F2
Holmfield Av *HDN* NW4 ...... 52 B4
Holmhurst Rd *BELV* DA17 ...... 117 J4
Holmleigh Av *DART* DA1 ...... 139 F3
Holmleigh Rd
   STNW/STAM N16 ...... 56 A7
Holm Oak CI *PUT/ROE* SW15 ...... 127 J5
Holm Oak Pk *WATW* WD18 ...... 26 D4
Holmsdale Gv *BXLYHN* DA7 ...... 138 B1
Holmshaw CI *SYD* SE26 ...... 151 G3
Holmside Ri *OXHEY* WD19 ...... 33 F2
Holmside Rd *BAL* SW12 ...... 129 F5
Holmsley CI *NWMAL* KT3 ...... 160 C5
Holmstall Av *EDGW* HA8 ...... 50 C1
Holmstall Pde *EDGW* HA8 * 50 C1
Holmwood CI *BELMT* SM2 ...... 174 B7
   NTHLT UB5 ...... 66 B5
   RYLN/HDSTN HA2 ...... 48 C2
Holmwood Gdns *FNCH* N3 ...... 52 E1
   WLGTN SM6 ...... 176 B5
Holmwood Gv *MLHL* NW7 ...... 37 F4
Holmwood Rd *BELMT* SM2 ...... 174 A7
   CHSGTN KT9 ...... 172 A4
   GDMY/SEVK IG3 ...... 78 E1
Holmwood VIs *CHARL* SE7 ...... 113 K4
   MRDN SM4 ...... 161 K5
Holness Rd *SRTFD* E15 ...... 76 D5
Holroyd Rd *ESH/CLAY* KT10 ...... 171 F7
   PUT/ROE SW15 ...... 127 F3
Holstein Wy *ERITH* DA18 ...... 116 E2
Holstock Rd *IL* IG1 ...... 78 C1
Holsworth CI
   RYLN/HDSTN HA2 ...... 48 C2
Holsworthy Sq *FSBYW* WC1X * 11 M1
Holsworthy Wy *CHSGTN* KT9 ...... 171 J4
Holt CI *BORE* WD6 ...... 24 B3
   MUSWH N10 ...... 54 A4
   THMD SE28 ...... 97 H6
Holton St *WCHPL* E1 ...... 93 F3
Holt Rd *ALP/SUD* HA0 ...... 67 H2
   CAN/RD E16 ...... 95 J7
The Holt *MRDN* SM4 * 161 K4
   WLGTN SM6 ...... 176 C3
Holtwhite Av *ENC/FH* EN2 ...... 29 J1
Holwell PI *PIN* HA5 ...... 47 J3
Holwood Park Av *ORP* BR6 ...... 181 K3
Holwood PI *CLAP* SW4 * 129 J3
Holybourne Av
   PUT/ROE SW15 ...... 126 D6
Holyoake Ct
   BERM/RHTH SE16 ...... 112 B1
Holyoake Wk *EA* W5 ...... 85 J3
   EFNCH N2 ...... 53 G2
Holyoak Rd *LBTH* SE11 ...... 18 C5
Holyport Rd *FUL/PGN* SW6 ...... 107 F6

Holyrood Av
   RYLN/HDSTN HA2 ...... 65 J3
Holyrood Gdns *EDGW* HA8 ...... 50 D1
Holyrood Ms *CAN/RD* E16 ...... 94 E7
Holyrood Rd *BAR* EN5 ...... 27 G5
Holyrood St *STHWK* SE1 ...... 13 J1
Holywell CI
   BERM/RHTH SE16 * 111 J4
   BKHTH/KID SE3 ...... 113 K5
   STWL/WRAY TW19 ...... 120 B7
Holywell La *SDTCH* EC2A 7 K9
Holywell Rd *WATW* WD18 ...... 20 E4
Holywell Wy *SDTCH* EC2A 13 J1
Holywell Wy
   STWL/WRAY TW19 ...... 120 B7
Home CI *CAR* SM5 ...... 175 K1
   NTHLT UB5 ...... 83 K2
Home Ct *FELT* TW13 * 121 K7
   SURB KT6 * 158 E4
Homecroft Rd *SYD* SE26 ...... 150 E4
   WDGN N22 ...... 41 H7
Home Farm CI *ESH/CLAY* KT10 ...... 170 B5
   THDIT KT7 ...... 158 A6
Homefarm Rd *HNWL* W7 ...... 84 E5
Homefield Av
   GNTH/NBYPK IG2 ...... 60 E4
Homefield CI *WLSDN* NW10 ...... 68 E5
   YEAD UB4 ...... 83 H3
Homefield Gdns *EFNCH* N2 ...... 53 H2
   WIM/MER SW19 ...... 146 B5
Homefield Ms *BECK* BR3 * 151 J7
Homefield Pk *SUT* SM1 ...... 175 F5
Homefield PI *CROY/NA* CR0 * 178 B1
Homefield Rd *ALP/SUD* HA0 ...... 67 G3
   BMLY BR1 ...... 153 G7
   BUSH WD23 ...... 22 A4
   CHSWK W4 ...... 106 C3
   EDGW HA8 ...... 37 F5
   WIM/MER SW19 ...... 146 C5
   WOT/HER KT12 ...... 156 A6
Homefield St *IS* N1 * 7 J6
The Homefield *MRDN* SM4 * 161 K3
Home Gdns *DAGE* RM10 ...... 80 E2
   DART DA1 ...... 139 H5
Homeland Dr *BELMT* SM2 ...... 175 F7
Homelands Dr *NRWD* SE19 ...... 150 A6
Homeleigh Rd *PECK* SE15 ...... 132 A4
Home Md *STAN* HA7 ...... 35 J7
Homemead *CROY/NA* CR0 ...... 163 H5
   HAYES BR2 ...... 168 A4
Home Park Ct *KUT/HW* KT1 * 158 E3
Home Park Rd
   WIM/MER SW19 ...... 146 D3
Home Park Ter *KUT/HW* KT1 ...... 158 E1
Home Park Wk *KUT/HW* KT1 ...... 158 E4
Homer CI *BXLYHN* DA7 ...... 117 K7
Homer Dr *POP/IOD* E14 ...... 112 D3
Homer Rd *BTSEA* SW11 ...... 128 D1
Homer Rd *CROY/NA* CR0 ...... 166 A5
   HOM E9 ...... 75 G5
Homer Rw *CAMTN* NW1 ...... 9 K3
Homersham Rd *KUT/HW* KT1 ...... 159 H1
Homer St *MBLAR* W1H 9 K3
Homerton Gv *HOM* E9 ...... 75 F4
Homerton High St *HOM* E9 ...... 74 E4
Homerton Rd *HOM* E9 ...... 75 H4
Homerton Rw *HOM* E9 ...... 74 E4
Homerton Ter *HOM* E9 ...... 74 E5
Homesdale CI *WAN* E11 ...... 58 E4
Homesdale Rd *HAYES* BR2 ...... 168 B3
   ORP BR6 ...... 169 K6
Homesfield *GLDGN* NW11 ...... 52 E4
Homestall Rd *EDUL* SE22 ...... 131 K4
Homestead Paddock
   STHGT/OAK N14 ...... 28 B4
Homestead Pk *CRICK* NW2 ...... 69 H2
Homestead Rd *BCTR* RM8 ...... 80 B1
   FUL/PGN SW6 ...... 107 J6
The Homestead *DART* DA1 ...... 139 F6
Homewaters Av *SUN* TW16 ...... 140 D7
Homewillow CI *WCHMH* N21 ...... 29 H5
Homewood CI *HPTN* TW12 ...... 141 K5
Homewood Crs *CHST* BR7 ...... 154 E5
Homewood Rd
   SNWD SE25 ...... 165 F4
Honduras St *FSBYE* EC1V 6 E9
Honeybourne Rd
   KIL/WHAMP NW6 ...... 71 F4
Honeybourne Wy
   STMC/STPC BR5 ...... 169 H7
Honeybrook Rd *BAL* SW12 ...... 129 H6
Honey CI *DAGE* RM10 ...... 80 E5
Honeyfield Ms *FSTH* SE23 ...... 151 F2
Honeyman CI *CRICK* NW2 ...... 70 B6
Honeypot CI *CDALE/KGS* NW9 ...... 50 B3
Honeypot La *CDALE/KGS* NW9 ...... 50 E3
   STAN HA7 ...... 50 D3
Honeysett Rd *TOTM* N17 ...... 56 B1
Honeysuckle CI *STHL* UB1 ...... 83 J6
Honeysuckle Gdns
   CROY/NA CR0 ...... 166 A6
Honeywell Rd *BTSEA* SW11 ...... 128 D5
Honeywood CI *ISLW* TW7 * 124 B3
   WLSDN NW10 ...... 87 H1
Honeywood Wk *CAR* SM5 ...... 175 K3
Honister CI *STAN* HA7 ...... 35 H1
Honister Gdns *STAN* HA7 ...... 35 H6
Honister PI *STAN* HA7 ...... 35 H6
Honiton Rd *MLHL* NW7 ...... 38 B6
   PECK SE15 ...... 131 K1
Honiton Rd *KIL/WHAMP* NW6 ...... 2 A3
   ROMW/RG RM7 ...... 63 F5
   WELL DA16 ...... 136 A1
Honley Rd *CAT* SE6 ...... 132 E6
Honnor Gdns *ISLW* TW7 * 123 J1
Honor Oak Pk *FSTH* SE23 ...... 131 K6
Honor Oak Ri *FSTH* SE23 ...... 131 K5
Honor Oak Rd *FSTH* SE23 ...... 131 K7
Hood Av *MORT/ESHN* SW14 ...... 125 K4
   STHGT/OAK N14 ...... 28 B4
Hood CI *CROY/NA* CR0 ...... 164 C7
Hoodcote Gdns *WCHMH* N21 ...... 29 H6
Hood Rd *RAIN* RM13 ...... 81 G7
   RYNPK SW20 ...... 145 H6
Hooker's Rd *WALTH* E17 ...... 57 F2
Hooking Gn *RYLN/HDSTN* HA2 ...... 48 B4
Hook La *WELL* DA16 ...... 136 A4
Hook Ri North *SURB* KT6 ...... 172 B2
Hook Ri South *CHSGTN* KT9 ...... 172 B3
   HOR/WEW KT19 ...... 172 B2
   SURB KT6 ...... 172 B2
Hooks Hall Dr *DAGE* RM10 ...... 80 E2
Hookstone Wy *WFD* IG8 ...... 45 H6
The Hook *BAR* EN5 ...... 27 H5
Hook Underpass (Kingston
   By-Pass) *SURB* KT6 ...... 171 K2
Hook Wk *EDGW* HA8 ...... 36 E5
Hooper Rd *CAN/RD* E16 ...... 94 E5
Hoopers Ms *BUSH* WD23 ...... 22 B7

Hooper's Ms *ACT* W3 * 86 E7
Hooper St *WCHPL* E1 ...... 92 C6
Hoop La *GLDGN* NW11 ...... 52 D6
Hop Ct *ALP/SUD* HA0 * 67 J2
Hope CI *BTFD* TW8 ...... 105 F4
   CHDH RM6 ...... 61 K3
   IS N1 ...... 73 J5
   LEE/GVPK SE12 ...... 153 F2
   SUT SM1 ...... 175 G4
Hopedale Rd *CHARL* SE7 ...... 114 A5
Hopefield Av
   KIL/WHAMP NW6 ...... 88 C1
Hope Gdns *ACT* W3 ...... 105 J1
Hope La *ELTH/MOT* SE9 ...... 154 B2
Hope Pk *BMLY* BR1 ...... 152 D6
Hopes CI *HEST* TW5 ...... 103 F5
Hope Sq *LVPST* EC2M * 13 J3
Hope St *BTSEA* SW11 ...... 128 C2
Hopetown St *WCHPL* E1 * 13 M3
Hopewell St *CMBW* SE5 ...... 110 E6
Hopewell Yd *CMBW* SE5 ...... 110 E6
Hop Gdns *CHCR* WC2N 11 J7
Hopgood St *SHB* W12 ...... 88 A7
Hopkins CI *MUSWH* N10 ...... 40 A6
Hopkins Ms *SRTFD* E15 ...... 76 D7
Hopkinsons PI *CAMTN* NW1 ...... 3 M3
Hopkins Rd *LEY* E10 ...... 57 K6
Hopkins St *SOHO/CST* W1F 10 F5
Hoppers Rd *WCHMH* N21 ...... 41 G1
Hoppett Rd *CHING* E4 ...... 44 C2
Hopping La *IS* N1 * 73 H5
Hoppingwood Av *NWMAL* KT3 ...... 160 B2
Hoppner Rd *YEAD* UB4 ...... 82 B1
Hop St *GNWCH* SE10 ...... 113 J3
Hopton Gdns *NWMAL* KT3 ...... 160 D5
Hopton Pde
   STRHM/NOR SW16 * 148 E4
Hopton Rd *STRHM/NOR* SW16 ...... 148 E4
   WOOL/PLUM SE18 ...... 115 G2
Hoptons Gdns *STHWK* SE1 * 12 D8
Hopton St *STHWK* SE1 ...... 12 D7
Hoptree CI
   NFNCH/WDSPK N12 * 39 F3
Hopwood CI *TOOT* SW17 ...... 147 F3
Hopwood Rd *WALW* SE17 ...... 19 H9
Hopwood Wk *HACK* E8 * 74 C6
Horace Av *ROMW/RG* RM7 ...... 63 F7
Horace Rd *BARK/HLT* IG6 ...... 60 C2
   FSTGT E7 ...... 77 F3
   KUT/HW KT1 ...... 159 G2
Horatio PI *POP/IOD* E14 * 113 F1
Horatio St *BETH* E2 ...... 7 M6
Horatius Wy *CROY/NA* CR0 ...... 177 F5
Horbury Crs *NTGHL* W11 ...... 8 A7
Horbury Ms *NTGHL* W11 ...... 88 D6
Horder Rd *FUL/PGN* SW6 ...... 107 H7
Hordle Prom East *PECK* SE15 ...... 111 G6
Hordle Prom North
   PECK SE15 ...... 111 G6
Hordle Prom West *PECK* SE15 ...... 111 F6
Horley CI *BXLYHS* DA6 ...... 137 H4
Horley Rd *ELTH/MOT* SE9 ...... 153 J3
Hormead Rd *MV/WKIL* W9 ...... 88 D3
Hornbeam CI *IL* IG1 ...... 78 D4
   LBTH SE11 ...... 18 A5
   MLHL NW7 ...... 37 H2
   NTHLT UB5 ...... 65 K4
Hornbeam Gdns *BTFD* TW8 ...... 104 C6
Hornbeam Gdns *NWMAL* KT3 ...... 160 C5
Hornbeam Gv *CHING* E4 ...... 44 C2
Hornbeam La *BKHH* IG9 ...... 45 J2
   YEAD UB4 ...... 83 G4
Hornbeam Sq *BOW* E3 ...... 75 H7
Hornbeams Ri
   FBAR/BDGN N11 ...... 40 A5
Hornbeam Wy *HAYES* BR2 ...... 169 F5
Hornbuckle CI
   RYLN/HDSTN HA2 ...... 66 D1
Hornby CI *HAMP* NW3 ...... 3 H1
Horncastle CI *LEE/GVPK* SE12 ...... 133 K6
Horncastle Rd *LEE/GVPK* SE12 ...... 133 K6
Hornchurch CI
   KUTN/CMB KT2 ...... 143 K4
Hornchurch Rd *HCH* RM12 ...... 63 J3
Horndean CI *PUT/ROE* SW15 ...... 126 D7
Horne House *CHARL* SE7 * 114 A7
Horner La *MTCM* CR4 ...... 162 C1
The Hornets *WATW* WD18 ...... 21 F3
Horne Wy *PUT/ROE* SW15 ...... 127 F1
Hornfair Rd *CHARL* SE7 ...... 114 C5
Hornford Wy *ROMW/RG* RM7 ...... 63 G6
Horniman Dr *FSTH* SE23 ...... 131 J7
Horniman Gdns *FSTH* SE23 * 131 J7
Horning CI *ELTH/MOT* SE9 ...... 153 J3
Horn La *ACT* W3 ...... 86 E7
   GNWCH SE10 ...... 113 K3
   WFD IG8 ...... 44 E6
Horn Link Wy *GNWCH* SE10 ...... 113 K2
Horn Park CI *LEE/GVPK* SE12 ...... 134 A4
Horn Park La *LEE/GVPK* SE12 ...... 134 A4
Hornscroft CI *BARK* IG11 ...... 78 E6
Horns End PI *PIN* HA5 ...... 47 G3
Hornsey Chambers *CLPT* E5 * 74 D1
Hornsey La *HGT* N6 ...... 54 C6
Hornsey Lane Est *ARCH* N19 * 54 C6
Hornsey Lane Gdns *HGT* N6 ...... 54 C6
Hornsey Park Rd
   CEND/HSY/T N8 ...... 55 F2
Hornsey Ri *ARCH* N19 ...... 54 D6
Hornsey Rise Gdns *ARCH* N19 ...... 54 D6
Hornsey Rd *ARCH* N19 ...... 54 C6
   HOLWY N7 ...... 73 F2
Hornsey St *HOLWY* N7 ...... 73 F3
Hornshay St *PECK* SE15 ...... 111 K5
Horns Rd *BARK/HLT* IG6 ...... 60 C4
Hornton PI *KENS* W8 ...... 14 B2
Hornton St *KENS* W8 ...... 14 B2
Horsa Rd *ERITH* DA8 ...... 117 K6
   LEE/GVPK SE12 ...... 134 B6
Horsebridges CI *DAGW* RM9 ...... 80 A7
Horsecroft Rd *EDGW* HA8 ...... 37 F6
Horse Fair *KUT/HW* KT1 ...... 158 E1
Horseferry PI *GNWCH* SE10 ...... 113 F5
Horseferry Rd *POP/IOD* E14 ...... 93 G5
   WEST SW1P 17 G4
Horse Guards Av *WHALL* SW1A 11 J9
Horse Guards Rd
   WHALL SW1A 11 H9
Horse Leaze *EHAM* E6 ...... 96 A5
Horsell Rd *HBRY* N5 ...... 73 G4
   STMC/STPC BR5 ...... 155 G7
Horselydown La *STHWK* SE1 ...... 19 L1
Horsenden Av *GFD/PVL* UB6 ...... 66 E4
Horsenden Crs *GFD/PVL* UB6 ...... 67 F4
Horsenden La North
   GFD/PVL UB6 ...... 66 E5
Horsenden La South
   GFD/PVL UB6 ...... 67 G7
Horseshoe CI *CRICK* NW2 ...... 69 K1
   POP/IOD E14 ...... 113 F4
Horse Shoe Crs *NTHLT* UB5 ...... 84 A1
Horseshoe La *ENC/FH* EN2 ...... 29 J2
   TRDG/WHET N20 ...... 26 B7

Horseshoe Ms
   BRXS/STRHM SW2 ...... 129 K3
Horse Yd *IS* N1 * 6 B3
Horsfeld Gdns *ELTH/MOT* SE9 ...... 134 D4
Horsfeld Rd *ELTH/MOT* SE9 ...... 134 C4
Horsford Rd
   BRXS/STRHM SW2 ...... 130 A4
Horsham Av
   NFNCH/WDSPK N12 ...... 39 J4
Horsham Rd *BXLYHS* DA6 ...... 137 H5
   EBED/NFELT TW14 ...... 121 F5
Horsley Dr *CROY/NA* CR0 ...... 180 A6
   KUTN/CMB KT2 ...... 143 K4
Horsley Rd *BMLY* BR1 ...... 153 F7
   CHING E4 ...... 44 A1
Horsley St *WALW* SE17 ...... 19 G9
Horsmans PI *DART* DA1 * 139 H6
Horsman St *CMBW* SE5 ...... 110 D5
Horsmonden CI *ORP* BR6 ...... 169 K6
Horsmonden Rd *BROCKY* SE4 ...... 132 C4
Hortensia Rd *WBPTN* SW10 ...... 108 A6
Horticultural PI *CHSWK* W4 * 106 A4
Horton Av *CRICK* NW2 ...... 70 C3
Horton La *HOR/WEW* KT19 ...... 172 D7
Horton Rd *HACK* E8 ...... 74 D5
Horton St *LEW* SE13 ...... 132 E2
Horton Wy *CROY/NA* CR0 ...... 166 A4
Hortus Rd *NWDGN* UB2 ...... 102 E1
   CHING E4 ...... 44 A2
Hosack Rd *TOOT* SW17 ...... 147 K1
Hoser Av *LEE/GVPK* SE12 ...... 152 E1
Hosier La *STBT* EC1A 12 C3
Hoskins CI *CAN/RD* E16 ...... 95 G5
   HYS/HAR UB3 ...... 101 G5
Hoskins St *GNWCH* SE10 ...... 113 G4
Hospital Bridge Rd
   WHTN TW2 ...... 123 F6
Hospital Rd *HSLW* TW3 ...... 123 F2
   LEY E10 ...... 58 B5
Hospital Wy *LEW* SE13 ...... 133 G5
Hotham CI *E/WMO/HCT* KT8 ...... 157 F2
Hotham Rd *PUT/ROE* SW15 ...... 127 F2
Hotham Road Ms
   WIM/MER SW19 * 147 G6
Hotham St *SRTFD* E15 ...... 76 C6
Hothfield PI *BERM/RHTH* SE16 * 111 K2
Hotspur Rd *NTHLT* UB5 ...... 84 A1
Hotspur St *LBTH* SE11 ...... 18 A7
Houblon Rd
   RCHPK/HAM TW10 ...... 125 F4
Houghton CI *HACK* E8 * 74 B5
   HPTN TW12 ...... 141 J5
Houghton Rd
   SEVS/STOTM N15 ...... 56 B3
Houghton St *LINN* WC2A * 11 M5
Houlder Crs *CROY/NA* CR0 ...... 177 H4
Houndsden Rd *WCHMH* N21 ...... 29 F5
Houndsditch *HDTCH* EC3A 13 K4
Houndsfield Rd *ED* N9 ...... 30 D6
Hounslow Av *HSLW* TW3 ...... 123 G4
Hounslow Gdns *HSLW* TW3 ...... 123 G4
Hounslow Rd
   EBED/NFELT TW14 ...... 122 A4
   WHTN TW2 ...... 123 G6
Houseman Wy *CMBW* SE5 * 110 E6
Houston PI *ESH/CLAY* KT10 ...... 157 J7
Houston Rd *FSTH* SE23 ...... 151 G1
   SURB KT6 ...... 158 C5
Hove Av *WALTH* E17 ...... 57 H4
Hoveden Rd *CRICK* NW2 ...... 70 B4
Hove Gdns *SUT* SM1 ...... 162 A7
Hoveton Rd *THMD* SE28 ...... 97 J5
Howard Av *BXLY* DA5 ...... 136 D7
Howard CI *ACT* W3 ...... 86 D5
   BUSH WD23 ...... 22 E6
   CRICK NW2 ...... 70 C3
   FBAR/BDGN N11 ...... 40 A1
   HPTN TW12 ...... 142 C6
Howard Dr *BORE* WD6 ...... 25 F4
Howard Rd *BARK* IG11 ...... 78 D7
   BMLY BR1 ...... 152 E6
   CRICK NW2 ...... 70 B3
   DART DA1 ...... 139 K5
   EHAM E6 ...... 95 K1
   IL IG1 ...... 78 B3
   ISLW TW7 ...... 124 A2
   NWMAL KT3 ...... 160 B2
   PGE/AN SE20 ...... 150 E7
   SEVS/STOTM N15 ...... 56 A5
   SNWD SE25 ...... 165 H4
   STAN HA7 ...... 35 J4
   STHL UB1 ...... 84 B5
   STNW/STAM N16 ...... 73 K3
   SURB KT6 ...... 159 G5
   WALTH E17 ...... 57 J2
   WAN E11 ...... 76 C2
Howards CI *PIN* HA5 * 47 F1
Howards Crest CI *BECK* BR3 ...... 167 F1
Howard's La *PUT/ROE* SW15 ...... 127 F3
Howard's Rd *PLSTW* E13 ...... 94 E2
Howard St *THDIT* KT7 ...... 158 C6
Howards Yd
   WAND/EARL SW18 ...... 128 A6
Howard Wk *EFNCH* N2 ...... 53 G3
Howard Wy *BAR* EN5 ...... 26 B4
Howarth Rd *ABYW* SE2 ...... 116 B4
Howberry CI *EDGW* HA8 ...... 35 K5
Howberry Rd *STAN* HA7 ...... 35 K5
   THHTH CR7 ...... 149 K5
Howbury La *ERITH* DA8 ...... 138 D1
Howbury Rd *PECK* SE15 ...... 131 K2
Howcroft Crs *FNCH* N3 ...... 38 E6
Howcroft La *GFD/PVL* UB6 ...... 84 D2
Howden CI *THMD* SE28 ...... 97 J6
Howden Rd *SNWD* SE25 ...... 165 G1
Howden St *PECK* SE15 ...... 131 H2
Howell CI *CHDH* RM6 ...... 61 K4
Howell Wk *STHWK* SE1 ...... 18 D6
Howerd Wy
   WOOL/PLUM SE18 ...... 114 D7
Howes CI *FNCH* N3 ...... 52 E2
Howfield PI *TOTM* N17 * 56 B2
Howgate Rd
   MORT/ESHN SW14 ...... 126 A2
Howick PI *WESTW* SW1E 16 F4
Howie St *BTSEA* SW11 ...... 108 D6
Howitt CI *HAMP* NW3 ...... 71 J5
Howitt Rd *HAMP* NW3 ...... 71 J5
Howitts CI *ESH/CLAY* KT10 ...... 170 A5
Howland Ct *PIN* HA5 ...... 34 A5
Howland Ms East *FITZ* W1T 10 F2
Howland St *FITZ* W1T 10 F2
Howland Wy
   BERM/RHTH SE16 ...... 112 B1
Howletts La *RSLP* HA4 ...... 46 A5
Howletts Rd *HNHL* SE24 ...... 130 D5
Howley PI *BAY/PAD* W2 ...... 8 F2
Howley Rd *CROY/NA* CR0 ...... 177 J2
Howsman Rd *BARN* SW13 ...... 106 D5
Howson Rd *BROCKY* SE4 ...... 132 B3
Howson Ter
   RCHPK/HAM TW10 ...... 125 F5
How's St *BETH* E2 ...... 7 L5
Howton PI *BUSH* WD23 ...... 22 D7
Hoxton Market *IS* N1 * 7 J8

Hoxton Sq *IS* N1 ...... 7 J8
Hoxton St *IS* N1 ...... 7 J4
Hoylake Gdns *MTCM* CR4 ...... 163 H2
   OXHEY WD19 ...... 33 H3
   RSLP HA4 ...... 47 J1
Hoylake Rd *ACT* W3 ...... 87 G5
Hoyland CI *PECK* SE15 * 111 J6
Hoyle Rd *TOOT* SW17 ...... 147 J4
Hoy St *CAN/RD* E16 ...... 94 D5
Hubbard Dr *CHSGTN* KT9 ...... 171 J5
Hubbard Rd *WNWD* SE27 ...... 149 J3
Hubbard St *SRTFD* E15 ...... 76 C7
Hubert Gv *BRXN/ST* SW9 ...... 129 K2
Hubert Rd *EHAM* E6 ...... 95 H2
   RAIN RM13 ...... 99 H2
Huddart St *BOW* E3 ...... 93 H4
Huddleston CI *BETH* E2 * 92 E1
Huddlestone Rd *CRICK* NW2 ...... 69 K5
   FSTGT E7 ...... 76 D3
Huddleston Rd *HOLWY* N7 ...... 72 C2
Hudson CI *SHB* W12 * 87 K6
Hudson PI *WOOL/PLUM* SE18 ...... 115 H4
Hudson Rd *BXLYHN* DA7 ...... 137 G1
   HYS/HAR UB3 ...... 101 G5
Huggins PI *BRXS/STRHM* SW2 ...... 130 A7
Hughan Rd *SRTFD* E15 ...... 76 B4
Hugh Dalton Av *FUL/PGN* SW6 ...... 107 J5
Hughenden Av
   KTN/HRWW/WS HA3 ...... 49 H4
Hughenden Gdns *NTHLT* UB5 ...... 83 G2
Hughenden Rd *WPK* KT4 ...... 160 D7
Hughes CI *NFNCH/WDSPK* N12 * 39 G4
Hughes Rd *ASHF* TW15 ...... 140 A6
   HYS/HAR UB3 ...... 83 F6
Hughes Ter *CAN/RD* E16 * 94 D4
Hughes Wk *CROY/NA* CR0 ...... 164 D6
Hugh Gaitskell CI
   FUL/PGN SW6 * 107 J5
Hugh Ms *PIM* SW1V 16 D7
Hugh PI *WEST* SW1P 16 F6
Hugo Gdns *RAIN* RM13 ...... 81 H5
Hugo Rd *FUL/PGN* SW6 ...... 128 A2
Hugo Rd *ARCH* N19 ...... 72 C3
Huguenot PI
   WAND/EARL SW18 ...... 128 B4
   WCHPL E1 ...... 13 M2
Huitt Sq *BTSEA* SW11 * 128 C2
Hullbridge Ms *IS* N1 ...... 7 F2
Hull CI *BERM/RHTH* SE16 * 93 F7
Hull St *FSBYE* EC1V 6 E8
Hulme PI *STHWK* SE1 ...... 18 F2
Hulse Av *BARK* IG11 ...... 78 E5
Hulverston CI *BELMT* SM2 ...... 175 F7
Humber Dr *NKENS* W10 ...... 88 B3
Humber Rd *BKHTH/KID* SE3 ...... 113 J5
   CRICK NW2 ...... 69 K1
   DART DA1 ...... 139 H5
Humberstone Rd *PLSTW* E13 ...... 95 G2
Humbolt Rd *HMSMTH* W6 ...... 107 H5
Humes Av *HNWL* W7 ...... 104 A2
Hume Wy *RSLP* HA4 ...... 46 E5
Humphrey CI *CLAY* IG5 * 45 K7
Humphrey St *STHWK* SE1 ...... 19 L7
Humphries CI *DAGW* RM9 ...... 80 B3
Hundred Acre
   CDALE/KGS NW9 ...... 51 H1
Hungerford Rd *HOLWY* N7 ...... 72 D5
Hungerford St *WCHPL* E1 * 92 D5
Hunsdon CI *DAGW* RM9 ...... 80 A5
Hunsdon Rd *NWCR* SE14 ...... 112 A6
Hunslett St *BETH* E2 * 92 E1
Hunston Rd *MRDN* SM4 ...... 162 A7
Hunt CI *BKHTH/KID* SE3 * 133 K1
   NTGHL W11 ...... 88 B7
Hunter CI *BAL* SW12 ...... 129 F7
   BORE WD6 ...... 25 F4
   STHWK SE1 ...... 19 H4
   WGTN SM6 ...... 176 E6
Hunter Ct *CMBW* SE5 * 130 E3
Huntercrombe Gdns
   OXHEY WD19 ...... 33 G4
Hunter Rd *RYNPK* SW20 ...... 146 A7
   THHTH CR7 ...... 164 E2
Hunters CI *BXLY* DA5 ...... 137 K5
Hunters Gv *HYS/HAR* UB3 ...... 82 E7
   KTN/HRWW/WS HA3 ...... 49 J3
Hunters Hall Rd *DAGE* RM10 ...... 80 C3
Hunters HI *RSLP* HA4 ...... 65 G2
Hunters Meadow *NRWD* SE19 ...... 150 A3
Hunters Rd *CHSGTN* KT9 ...... 172 A2
   IL IG1 ...... 78 B4
Hunters Sq *DAGE* RM10 ...... 80 C3
Hunter St *BMSBY* WC1N 5 K9
Hunters Wy *CROY/NA* CR0 ...... 178 A3
Hunting CI *ESH/CLAY* KT10 ...... 170 A3
Huntingdon CI *MTCM* CR4 ...... 163 K3
   NTHLT UB5 ...... 66 C4
Huntingdon Gdns *CHSWK* W4 ...... 105 K6
   WPK KT4 ...... 174 A2
Huntingdon Rd *ED* N9 ...... 30 E7
   EFNCH N2 ...... 53 H2
Huntingdon St *CAN/RD* E16 ...... 94 D5
   IS N1 ...... 5 M1
Huntingfield *CROY/NA* CR0 ...... 179 H6
Huntingfield Rd
   PUT/ROE SW15 ...... 126 D5
Hunting Gate CI *ENC/FH* EN2 ...... 29 G2
Hunting Gate Dr *CHSGTN* KT9 ...... 172 A6
Hunting Gate Ms *SUT* SM1 ...... 175 F2
   WHTN TW2 ...... 123 K7
Huntings Rd *DAGE* RM10 ...... 80 C5
Huntington CI *BXLY* DA5 ...... 137 J7
Huntland CI *RAIN* RM13 ...... 99 K4
Huntley St *STWL/WRAY* TW19 ...... 120 B6
Huntley St *GWRST* WC1E 10 F1
Huntley Wy *RYNPK* SW20 * 160 D1
Huntly Dr *FNCH* N3 ...... 38 E5
Huntly Rd *SNWD* SE25 ...... 165 F3
Hunton St *WCHPL* E1 ...... 92 C4
Hunt Rd *NWDGN* UB2 ...... 103 F2
Hunt's CI *BKHTH/KID* SE3 ...... 133 K1
Hunt's La *SRTFD* E15 ...... 94 A1
Huntsman St *FELT* TW13 ...... 141 F1
Huntsman St *WALW* SE17 ...... 19 J6
Hunts Md *PEND* EN3 ...... 31 F2
Huntsmoor Rd
   HOR/WEW KT19 ...... 173 F4
Huntspill St *TOOT* SW17 ...... 147 G2
Hunts Slip Rd *DUL* SE21 ...... 150 A1
Huntsworth Ms *CAMTN* NW1 ...... 3 L9
Hurdwick PI *CAMTN* NW1 * 4 E4
Hurley Crs *BERM/RHTH* SE16 ...... 93 F1
Hurley Rd *GFD/PVL* UB6 ...... 84 B4
Hurlingham Gdns
   FUL/PGN SW6 ...... 127 J2
Hurlingham Rd *BXLYHN* DA7 ...... 117 G6
   FUL/PGN SW6 ...... 127 J1

Hurlingham Sq
FUL/PGN SW6 * 127 K2
Hurlock St HBRY N5 73 H2
Hurlstone Rd SNWD SE25 164 E4
Hurn Court Rd HSLWW TW4 122 C1
Huron Rd TOOT SW17 148 A1
Hurren Cl BKHTH/KID SE3 133 H2
Hurricane House
WOOL/PLUM SE18 * 114 D6
Hurricane Rd WLGTN SM6 176 E6
Hurry Cl SRTFD E15 76 C6
Hurst Av CHING E4 43 J2
HGT N6 54 C5
Hurstbourne ESH/CLAY KT10 171 F5
Hurstbourne Gdns BARK IG11 78 D5
Hurstbourne Rd FSTH SE23 132 B7
Hurst Cl CHING E4 43 J2
CHSGTN KT9 172 C4
GLDGN NW11 53 F5
HAYES BR2 167 J7
NTHLT UB5 65 K5
Hurstcourt Rd SUT SM1 162 A7
Hurstdene Av HAYES BR2 167 J7
Hurstdene Gdns
SEVS/STOTM N15 56 A6
Hurstfield HAYES BR2 167 K4
Hurstfield Crs YEAD UB4 82 C4
Hurstfield Rd
E/WMO/HCT KT8 157 F2
Hurst La ABYW SE2 116 E4
E/WMO/HCT KT8 157 H3
Hurstleigh Gdns CLAY IG5 45 K7
Hurst Pl ABYW SE2 116 D4
DART DA1 * 139 F5
Hurst Ri BAR EN5 26 E2
Hurst Rd BFN/LL DA15 155 H1
BXLY DA5 137 F7
CROY/NA CR0 177 K4
E/WMO/HCT KT8 157 F2
ERITH DA8 117 K6
WALTH E17 57 K2
WCHMH N21 29 G7
WOT/HER KT12 156 C3
Hurst Springs BXLY DA5 137 F7
Hurst St HNHL SE24 130 C5
Hurst View Rd SAND/SEL CR2 178 A6
Hurst Wy SAND/SEL CR2 178 A5
Hurstway Rd NTGHL W11 * 88 B6
Hurstway Wk NTGHL W11 * 88 B6
Hurstwood Av BXLY DA5 137 F7
ERITH DA8 118 B7
SWFD E18 59 F3
Hurstwood Dr BMLY BR1 168 E2
Hurstwood Rd GLDGN NW11 52 C3
Hurtwood Rd WOT/HER KT12 156 E6
Huson Cl HAMP NW3 3 J1
Hussain Cl HRW HA1 67 F3
Hussars Cl HSLWW TW4 122 D2
Husseywell Crs HAYES BR2 167 K7
Hutching's St POP/IOD E14 112 D1
Hutchings Wk GLDGN NW11 53 F3
Hutchins Cl SRTFD E15 76 A6
Hutchinson Ter WBLY HA9 67 K2
Hutchins Rd THMD SE28 97 G6
Hutton Cl GFD/PVL UB6 66 D4
WFD IG8 45 F5
Hutton Gv
NFNCH/WDSPK N12 39 F4
Hutton La
KTN/HRWW/WS HA3 34 C6
Hutton Rw EDGW HA8 36 E6
Hutton St EMB EC4Y 12 B5
Hutton Wk
KTN/HRWW/WS HA3 34 C6
Huxbear St BROCKY SE4 132 C4
Huxley UED N18 * 41 K4
Huxley Cl NTHLT UB5 83 J1
Huxley Dr CHDH RM6 61 H6
Huxley Gdns WLSDN NW10 86 B2
Huxley Pde UED N18 * 41 K4
Huxley Pl PLMGR N13 41 H3
Huxley Rd LEY E10 76 A1
UED N18 41 K3
WELL DA16 136 A2
Huxley Sayze UED N18 * 41 K4
Huxley St NKENS W10 88 C2
Hyacinth Cl HPTN TW12 142 A5
IL IG1 78 B5
Hyacinth Rd PUT/ROE SW15 126 D7
Hyde Cl BAR EN5 26 D2
PLSTW E13 94 E1
Hyde Crs CDALE/KGS NW9 51 G4
Hyde Estate Rd
CDALE/KGS NW9 51 H4
Hyde Farm Ms BAL SW12 129 J7
Hydefield Cl WCHMH N21 29 K7
Hydefield Ct ED N9 42 A1
Hyde Gv DART DA1 139 J1
Hyde La BTSEA SW11 108 D7
Hyde Park Av WCHMH N21 41 J1
Hyde Park Cnr
MYFR/PICC W1J 16 B1
Hyde Park Crs BAY/PAD W2 9 J5
Hyde Park Gdns BAY/PAD W2 9 H6
WCHMH N21 29 J7
Hyde Park Gardens Ms
BAY/PAD W2 9 H6
Hyde Park Ga SKENS SW7 14 E2
Hyde Park Gate Ms
SKENS SW7 * 14 F2
Hyde Park Pl BAY/PAD W2 9 K6
Hyde Park Sq BAY/PAD W2 9 J5
Hyde Park Square Ms
BAY/PAD W2 9 J5
Hyde Park St BAY/PAD W2 9 J6
Hyderabad Wy SRTFD E15 76 C6
Hyde Rd BXLYHN DA7 137 G1
IS N1 7 H4
RCHPK/HAM TW10 125 G4
WAT WD17 20 E2
Hydeside Gdns ED N9 42 B1
Hyde's Pl IS N1 6 C1
Hyde St DEPT SE8 112 D5
Hyde Ter ASHF TW15 140 C5
The Hyde CDALE/KGS NW9 * 51 F3
Hydethorpe Av ED N9 42 B1
Hydethorpe Rd BAL SW12 129 H7
Hyde V GNWCH SE10 113 F6
Hyde Wk MRDN SM4 161 K6
Hyde Wy ED N9 42 B1
HYS/HAR UB3 101 J3
Hyland Cl EMPK RM11 63 K6
Hylands Rd WALTH E17 58 B1
Hyland Wy EMPK RM11 63 K6
Hylton St WOOL/PLUM SE18 116 A3
Hyndewood FSTH SE23 * 151 F2
Hyndman St PECK SE15 111 J5
Hynton Rd BCTR RM8 79 J1
Hyperion Pl HOR/WEW KT19 173 F7
Hyrstdene SAND/SEL CR2 177 H3
Hyson Rd BERM/RHTH SE16 111 J4
Hythe Av BXLYHN DA7 117 F6
Hythe Cl UED N18 42 C3
Hythe Rd THHTH CR7 164 E1
WLSDN NW10 87 H2
Hythe St DART DA1 139 H4
Hyver Hl BAR EN5 25 F5

I

Ibbotson Av CAN/RD E16 94 D5
Ibbott St WCHPL E1 92 E3
Iberian Av WLGTN SM6 176 D3
Ibis La CHSWK W4 105 K7
Ibis Wy YEAD UB4 83 H5
Ibscott Cl DAGE RM10 80 E5
Ibsley Gdns PUT/ROE SW15 126 D7
Ibsley Wy EBAR EN4 27 J4
Iceland Rd BOW E3 75 J7
Ickburgh Est CLPT E5 * 74 D1
Ickburgh Rd CLPT E5 74 D2
Ickenham Cl RSLP HA4 64 B1
Ickenham Rd RSLP HA4 46 B7
Ickleton Rd ELTH/MOT SE9 153 J3
Icknield Dr GNTH/NBYPK IG2 60 B4
Ickworth Park Rd WALTH E17 57 G3
Ida Rd SEVS/STOTM N15 55 K4
Ida St POP/IOD E14 94 A5
Iden Cl HAYES BR2 167 H2
Idlecombe Rd TOOT SW17 148 A5
Idmiston Rd SRTFD E15 76 D4
WNWD SE27 149 J2
WPK KT4 160 C6
Idmiston Sq WPK KT4 160 C6
Idol La MON EC3R 13 J7
Idonia St DEPT SE8 112 C6
Iffley Rd HMSMTH W6 106 E2
Ifield Rd WBPTN SW10 14 D9
Ightham Rd ERITH DA8 117 H6
Ilbert St NKENS W10 88 C2
Ilchester Gdns BAY/PAD W2 8 C6
Ilchester Pl WKENS W14 107 J2
Ilchester Rd BCTR RM8 79 H4
Ildersly Gv DUL SE21 149 K1
Ilderton Rd PECK SE15 111 K5
Ilex Cl SUN TW16 156 B1
Ilex Rd WLSDN NW10 69 H5
Ilex Wy STRHM/NOR SW16 149 G4
Ilford Hl IL IG1 78 A2
MNPK E12 77 K3
Ilford La IL IG1 78 B3
Ilfracombe Gdns CHDH RM6 61 H6
Ilfracombe Rd BMLY BR1 152 D2
Iliffe St WALW SE17 18 D7
Iliffe Yd WALW SE17 18 D7
Ilkley Cl NRWD SE19 * 149 K5
Ilkley Ct FBAR/BDGN N11 40 A5
Ilkley Rd CAN/RD E16 95 G4
OXHEY WD19 33 H4
Illingworth Wy EN EN1 30 A4
Ilmington Rd
KTN/HRWW/WS HA3 49 K5
Ilminster Gdns BTSEA SW11 128 D3
Imber Cl STHGT/OAK N14 28 C6
Imber Cross THDIT KT7 158 A5
Imber Gv ESH/CLAY KT10 157 J6
Imber Park Rd ESH/CLAY KT10 157 J7
Imber St IS N1 7 G4
Imperial Av STNW/STAM N16 * 74 A3
Imperial Cl CRICK NW2 69 K4
RYLN/HDSTN HA2 48 A5
Imperial College Rd
SKENS SW7 15 G4
Imperial Crs FUL/PGN SW6 128 B1
Imperial Dr RYLN/HDSTN HA2 48 A6
Imperial Gdns MTCM CR4 163 G2
Imperial Ms EHAM E6 95 H1
Imperial Pl BORE WD6 * 24 D2
CHST BR7 154 A7
Imperial Rd
EBED/NFELT TW14 121 H6
FUL/PGN SW6 108 A7
WDGN N22 40 E6
Imperial Sq FUL/PGN SW6 108 A7
Imperial St BOW E3 94 A2
Imperial Wy CHST BR7 154 C2
CROY/NA CR0 177 F5
KTN/HRWW/WS HA3 50 A5
Imre Cl SHB W12 87 K7
Inca Dr ELTH/MOT SE9 135 G6
Inchmery Rd CAT SE6 151 K1
Inchwood CROY/NA CR0 179 K3
Independent Pl HACK E8 74 B4
Independents Rd
BKHTH/KID SE3 133 J2
Inderwick Rd CEND/HSY/T N8 55 F5
Indescon Ct POP/IOD E14 112 E1
India St TWRH EC3N 13 L5
India Wy SHB W12 87 K6
Indigo Ms POP/IOD E14 * 94 A6
STNW/STAM N16 73 K2
Indus Rd CHARL SE7 114 B6
Infant House
WOOL/PLUM SE18 * 114 D6
Ingal Rd PLSTW E13 94 E3
Ingate Pl VX/NE SW8 109 G7
Ingatestone Rd MNPK E12 59 G7
SNWD SE25 165 J4
WFD IG8 45 F6
Ingelow Rd VX/NE SW8 129 G1
Ingersoll Rd SHB W12 87 K7
Ingestre Pl SOHO/CST W1F 10 F5
Ingestre Rd FSTGT E7 76 E3
KTTN NW5 72 B3
Ingham Cl SAND/SEL CR2 179 F7
Ingham Rd KIL/WHAMP NW6 70 E3
SAND/SEL CR2 178 E7
Inglebert St CLKNW EC1R 6 A7
Ingleborough St
BRXN/ST SW9 130 B1
Ingleby Dr HRW HA1 66 D2
Ingleby Rd DAGE RM10 80 D5
HOLWY N7 72 E2
IL IG1 60 B7
Ingleby Wy CHST BR7 154 A4
WLGTN SM6 176 D7
Ingle Cl PIN HA5 47 K2
Ingledew Rd
WOOL/PLUM SE18 115 J4
Inglefield Sq WAP E1W * 92 D7
Inglehurst Gdns REDBR IG4 59 K4
Inglemere Rd FSTH SE23 151 F2
TOOT SW17 147 K6
Ingleside Cl BECK BR3 151 J6
Ingleside Gv BKHTH/KID SE3 113 J5
Inglethorpe St FUL/PGN SW6 107 G7
Ingleton Av WELL DA16 136 B4
Ingleton Rd CAR SM5 175 J7
UED N18 42 C5
Ingleton St BRXN/ST SW9 130 B1
Ingleway NFNCH/WDSPK N12 39 H5
Inglewood CROY/NA CR0 179 G7
Inglewood Cl POP/IOD E14 112 D3
Inglewood Copse BMLY BR1 168 D1
Inglewood Ms SURB KT6 159 H7
Inglewood Rd BXLYHN DA7 138 A3
KIL/WHAMP NW6 70 E4
Inglis Rd CROY/NA CR0 165 G7
EA W5 86 B6
Inglis St CMBW SE5 110 C7
Ingram Av GLDGN NW11 53 G6
Ingram Cl LBTH SE11 17 M5
STAN HA7 35 J4
Ingram Rd DART DA1 139 H7
EFNCH N2 53 J3
THHTH CR7 149 J7
Ingram Wy GFD/PVL UB6 66 D7
Ingrave Rd ROM RM1 63 F3
Ingrave St BTSEA SW11 128 C2
Ingrebourne Rd RAIN RM13 99 K3
Ingress St CHSWK W4 106 B4
Inigo Jones Rd CHARL SE7 114 C6
Inkerman Rd KTTN NW5 72 B5
Inks Gn CHING E4 44 A4
Inkwell Cl NFNCH/WDSPK N12 39 G2
Inman Rd WAND/EARL SW18 128 B6
WLSDN NW10 69 G7
Inmans Rw WFD IG8 44 E3
Inner Cir CAMTN NW1 4 A8
Inner Park Rd
WIM/MER SW19 146 B1
Inner Ring East HTHAIR TW6 120 E2
Innes Cl RYNPK SW20 161 H1
Innes Gdns PUT/ROE SW15 126 E5
Innes St PECK SE15 111 F6
Innes Yd CROY/NA CR0 177 J2
Inniskilling Rd PLSTW E13 95 G1
Innovation Cl ALP/SUD HA0 68 A7
Inskip Cl LEY E10 75 K1
Inskip Rd BCTR RM8 61 K7
Institute Pl HACK E8 74 D4
Instone Rd DART DA1 139 G6
Integer Gdns WAN E11 * 58 B6
International Av HEST TW5 102 B4
International Wy SUN TW16 140 C7
Inver Ct BAY/PAD W2 8 D5
Inveresk Gdns WPK KT4 173 H2
Inverforth Cl HAMP NW3 71 G1
Inverforth Rd
FBAR/BDGN N11 40 B4
Inverine Rd CHARL SE7 114 A4
Invermore Pl
WOOL/PLUM SE18 115 H3
Inverness Gdns KENS W8 8 C9
Inverness Ms BAY/PAD W2 8 D6
Inverness Pl BAY/PAD W2 8 D6
Inverness Rd HSLW TW3 122 E3
NWDGN UB2 102 D3
UED N18 42 D4
WPK KT4 161 G7
Inverness St CAMTN NW1 4 C3
Inverness Ter BAY/PAD W2 8 D7
WDGN N22 * 41 H7
Inverton Rd PECK SE15 132 A3
Invicta Cl CHST BR7 154 A4
EBED/NFELT TW14 121 J7
Invicta Gv NTHLT UB5 83 K2
Invicta Pde SCUP DA14 * 155 H3
Invicta Plaza STHWK SE1 12 C8
Invicta Rd BKHTH/KID SE3 113 K6
Inville Rd WALW SE17 19 H8
Inwood Av HSLW TW3 123 H2
Inwood Cl CROY/NA CR0 179 G1
Inwood Rd HSLW TW3 123 H3
Inworth St BTSEA SW11 128 D1
Inworth Wk IS N1 * 6 E3
Iona Cl CAT SE6 132 D6
MRDN SM4 162 A6
Ion Sq BETH E2 * 92 C1
Ipswich Rd TOOT SW17 148 A5
Ireland Cl EHAM E6 95 K4
Ireland Pl WDGN N22 40 E6
Irene Ms HNWL W7 * 85 F7
Irene Rd FUL/PGN SW6 107 K7
Ireton Cl MUSWH N10 40 A6
Ireton St BOW E3 93 J3
Iris Av BXLY DA5 137 F5
Iris Cl CROY/NA CR0 166 A7
EHAM E6 95 J4
SURB KT6 * 159 G6
Iris Crs BXLYHN DA7 117 G5
Iris Rd HOR/WEW KT19 172 D4
Iris Wy CHING E4 43 H5
Iron Bridge Cl NWDGN UB2 84 C7
WLSDN NW10 69 G4
Iron Bridge Rd South
WDR/YW UB7 100 D1
Iron Mill La DART DA1 138 C3
Iron Mill Pl DART DA1 138 C3
Iron Mill Rd WAND/EARL SW18 128 A5
Ironmonger La CITYW EC2V 13 G5
Ironmonger Rw FSBYE EC1V 6 F8
Ironmongers Pl POP/IOD E14 112 D3
Ironside Cl BERM/RHTH SE16 112 A1
Irvine Av KTN/HRWW/WS HA3 49 G2
Irvine Cl POP/IOD E14 93 K4
TRDG/WHET N20 39 J1
Irving Av NTHLT UB5 65 H7
Irving Gv BRXN/ST SW9 130 A1
Irving Ms IS N1 73 J5
Irving Rd WKENS W14 107 G2
Irving St LSQ/SEVD WC2H 11 H7
Irving Wy CDALE/KGS NW9 51 H4
Irwell Est BERM/RHTH SE16 * 111 K1
Irwin Av WOOL/PLUM SE18 115 K6
Irwin Gdns WLSDN NW10 69 K7
Isaac Wy STHWK SE1 18 F1
Isabella Cl STHGT/OAK N14 28 C6
Isabella Ct
RCHPK/HAM TW10 * 125 G5
Isabella Ms IS N1 74 A5
Isabella Pl KUTN/CMB KT2 144 B4
Isabella Rd HOM E9 * 74 E4
Isabella St STHWK SE1 12 C9
Isabel St BRXN/ST SW9 110 A7
Isambard Ms POP/IOD E14 113 F2
Isambard Pl BERM/RHTH SE16 92 E7
Isham Rd STRHM/NOR SW16 163 K1
Isis Cl PUT/ROE SW15 127 F3
RSLP HA4 46 A5
Isis St WAND/EARL SW18 147 G1
Island Farm Av
E/WMO/HCT KT8 156 E4
Island Farm Rd
E/WMO/HCT KT8 156 E4
Island Rd BERM/RHTH SE16 112 A3
MTCM CR4 147 K6
Island Rw POP/IOD E14 93 H5
Isla Rd WOOL/PLUM SE18 115 H5
Islay Gdns HSLWW TW4 122 C4
Islay Wk IS N1 * 73 J5
Islay Whf POP/IOD E14 * 94 A4
Isledon Rd HOLWY N7 73 G2
Islehurst Cl CHST BR7 154 A7
Islington Gn IS N1 6 C4
Islington High St IS N1 6 C5
Islington Park Ms IS N1 6 C1
Islington Park St IS N1 6 B1
Islip Gdns EDGW HA8 37 F5
NTHLT UB5 65 J6
Islip Manor Rd NTHLT UB5 65 J6
Islip St KTTN NW5 72 C4
Ismailia Rd FSTGT E7 77 F6
Isom Cl PLSTW E13 95 F2
Issa Rd HSLW TW3 122 E3
Ivanhoe Dr
KTN/HRWW/WS HA3 49 H1
Ivanhoe Rd CMBW SE5 131 G2
HSLWW TW4 122 C2
Ivatt Pl WKENS W14 107 J4
Ivatt Wy SEVS/STOTM N15 55 H2
Iveagh Av WLSDN NW10 86 C1
Iveagh Cl HOM E9 75 F7
WLSDN NW10 86 C1
Ivedon Rd WELL DA16 136 D1
Ive Farm Cl LEY E10 75 J1
Ive Farm La LEY E10 75 J1
Iveley Rd CLAP SW4 129 H1
Ivere Dr BAR EN5 27 F5
Iverhurst Cl BXLYHS DA6 136 E4
Iverna Ct KENS W8 14 B3
Iverna Gdns
EBED/NFELT TW14 121 G4
KENS W8 14 B3
Iverson Rd KIL/WHAMP NW6 70 D5
Ivers Wy CROY/NA CR0 179 K6
Ives Gdns ROM RM1 63 H3
Ives Rd CAN/RD E16 94 C4
Ives St CHEL SW3 15 K5
Ivimey St BETH E2 * 92 C2
Ivinghoe Cl EN EN1 30 A1
Ivinghoe Rd BCTR RM8 79 H4
BUSH WD23 22 D5
Ivor Gv ELTH/MOT SE9 135 G7
Ivor Pl CAMTN NW1 9 L1
Ivor St CAMTN NW1 4 E2
Ivory Ct FELT TW13 121 K7
Ivorydown BMLY BR1 152 E3
Ivybridge Cl TWK TW1 124 B5
Ivychurch Cl PGE/AN SE20 150 D6
Ivy Church La WALW SE17 * 19 L7
Ivy Cl DART DA1 139 K5
PIN HA5 47 G6
RYLN/HDSTN HA2 65 K3
SUN TW16 156 B1
Ivy Ct BERM/RHTH SE16 * 111 H4
Ivy Crs CHSWK W4 105 K3
Ivydale Rd CAR SM5 175 K1
PECK SE15 132 A4
Ivyday Gv STRHM/NOR SW16 149 F2
Ivydene E/WMO/HCT KT8 156 E4
Ivydene Cl SUT SM1 175 G3
Ivy Gdns CEND/HSY/T N8 54 E5
MTCM CR4 163 J2
Ivyhouse Rd DAGW RM9 79 K5
Ivy La HSLWW TW4 122 E3
Ivymount Rd WNWD SE27 149 G2
Ivy Rd BROCKY SE4 132 C3
CAN/RD E16 94 E5
CRICK NW2 70 A3
HSLW TW3 123 G3
STHGT/OAK N14 28 C6
SURB KT6 * 172 C1
TOOT SW17 147 J4
WALTH E17 57 J5
Ivy St IS N1 7 J5
Ivy Wk DAGW RM9 80 A5
NTHWD HA6 * 32 C7
Ixworth Pl CHEL SW3 15 J6
Izane Rd BXLYHS DA6 137 G3

J

Jacaranda Cl NWMAL KT3 160 B2
Jacaranda Gv HACK E8 7 M1
Jackass La HAYES BR2 181 F5
Jack Clow Rd SRTFD E15 94 C1
Jack Cornwell St MNPK E12 78 A3
Jack Dash Wy EHAM E6 95 J3
Jack Jones Wy DAGW RM9 80 B7
Jackman Ms WLSDN NW10 69 G2
Jackman St HACK E8 74 D7
Jackson Cl HOM E9 75 F6
Jackson Rd BARK IG11 78 D7
EBAR EN4 27 H5
HAYES BR2 181 J1
HOLWY N7 73 F3
Jackson's La HGT N6 54 A6
Jackson's Pl CROY/NA CR0 164 E7
Jackson St WOOL/PLUM SE18 115 F5
Jackson's Wy CROY/NA CR0 179 J2
Jackson Wy HOR/WEW KT19 172 C7
NWDGN UB2 103 G1
Jack Walker Ct HBRY N5 73 H3
Jacobs Cl DAGE RM10 80 D3
Jacob St STHWK SE1 19 M1
Jacob's Well Ms MHST W1U 10 B4
Jacqueline Cl NTHLT UB5 65 J7
Jacqueline Creft Ter HGT N6 * 54 A5
Jacqueline Vls WALTH E17 * 58 A4
Jade Cl BCTR RM8 61 J7
CAN/RD E16 95 H5
CRICK NW2 52 B6
Jade Ter KIL/WHAMP NW6 * 2 F1
Jaffe Rd IL IG1 60 C7
Jaffray Rd HAYES BR2 168 C3
Jaggard Wy BAL SW12 128 E6
Jago Cl WOOL/PLUM SE18 115 H5
Jago Wk CMBW SE5 110 E6
Jamaica Rd BERM/RHTH SE16 111 H2
STHWK SE1 19 M2
THHTH CR7 164 C5
Jamaica St WCHPL E1 92 E4
James Av BCTR RM8 62 B7
CRICK NW2 70 A4
James Bedford Cl PIN HA5 47 G1
James Cl BUSH WD23 21 J4
GLDGN NW11 * 52 C5
GPK RM2 63 J4
PLSTW E13 94 E1
James Collins Cl MV/WKIL W9 88 D3
James Gdns TOTM N17 41 J6
James Joyce Wk
BRXN/ST SW9 130 C3
James La WAN E11 58 D5
Jameson St KENS W8 8 B8
James Pl TOTM N17 42 B7
James Rd DART DA1 138 D6
James St BARK IG11 78 C6
COVGDN WC2E 11 K6
EN EN1 30 B4
HSLW TW3 123 J2
MHST W1U 10 B5
Jamestown Rd CAMTN NW1 4 C3
Jamestown Wy POP/IOD E14 94 B6
James Voller Wy WCHPL E1 92 E5
James Watt Wy ERITH DA8 118 B5
James Wy OXHEY WD19 33 H3
James Yd CHING E4 * 44 B5
Jamuna Cl POP/IOD E14 93 G4
Jane St WCHPL E1 92 D5
Janet St POP/IOD E14 112 D2
Janeway Pl BERM/RHTH SE16 111 J1
Janeway St BERM/RHTH SE16 111 H1
Janson Cl SRTFD E15 76 C4
WLSDN NW10 69 F2
Janson Rd SRTFD E15 76 C4
Jansons Rd SEVS/STOTM N15 56 A2
Japan Crs FSBYPK N4 55 F7
Japan Rd CHDH RM6 61 K5
Jardine Rd WAP E1W 93 F6
Jarrett Cl BRXS/STRHM SW2 130 C7
Jarrow Cl MRDN SM4 162 A4
Jarrow Rd BERM/RHTH SE16 111 K3
CHDH RM6 61 J5
TOTM N17 56 D3
Jarrow Wy HOM E9 75 H3
Jarvis Cl BAR EN5 26 B4
BARK IG11 78 D7
Jarvis Rd EDUL SE22 131 F3
SAND/SEL CR2 177 K5
Jasmin Cl NTHWD HA6 32 D7
Jasmine Cl IL IG1 78 B4
STHL UB1 83 J6
Jasmine Ct LEE/GVPK SE12 133 K5
Jasmine Gdns CROY/NA CR0 179 K2
RYLN/HDSTN HA2 66 A1
Jasmine Gv PGE/AN SE20 150 D7
Jasmine Rd HOR/WEW KT19 172 D5
ROMW/RG RM7 81 G1
Jasmine Ter WDR/YW UB7 100 D1
Jasmin Rd HOR/WEW KT19 172 D4
Jason Wk ELTH/MOT SE9 154 A3
Jasper Rd CAN/RD E16 95 H5
NRWD SE19 150 B5
Javelin Wy NTHLT UB5 83 H2
Jay Gdns CHST BR7 153 K3
Jay Ms SKENS SW7 14 F2
Jean Batten Cl WLGTN SM6 177 F6
Jebb Av BRXS/STRHM SW2 129 K5
Jebb St BOW E3 93 J1
Jedburgh Rd PLSTW E13 95 G2
Jedburgh St BTSEA SW11 129 F3
Jeddo Ms SHB W12 106 C1
Jeddo Rd SHB W12 106 C1
Jefferson Cl GNTH/NBYPK IG2 60 B4
WEA W13 104 C2
Jeffrey's Pl CAMTN NW1 4 E1
Jeffreys Rd CLAP SW4 129 K1
PEND EN3 31 H3
Jeffrey's St CAMTN NW1 4 D1
Jeffs Cl HPTN TW12 * 142 B5
Jeffs Rd SUT SM1 174 D3
Jeger Av BETH E2 7 L4
Jeken Rd ELTH/MOT SE9 134 B3
Jelf Rd BRXS/STRHM SW2 130 B4
Jellicoe Gdns STAN HA7 35 F5
Jellicoe Rd TOTM N17 41 K6
WATW WD18 20 E5
Jemmett Cl KUTN/CMB KT2 144 D7
Jem Paterson Ct HRW HA1 * 66 E3
Jengar Cl SUT SM1 175 F3
Jenkins La BARK IG11 96 B1
Jenkins Rd PLSTW E13 95 F3
Jenner Av ACT W3 87 F4
Jenner Cl SCUP DA14 155 G3
Jenner Pl BARN SW13 106 E5
Jenner Rd STNW/STAM N16 74 B1
Jenner Wy HOR/WEW KT19 172 C7
Jennett Rd CROY/NA CR0 177 G2
Jennifer Rd BMLY BR1 152 D2
Jennings Cl SURB KT6 158 D6
Jennings Rd EDUL SE22 131 G5
Jennings Wy BAR EN5 26 A2
Jenningtree Rd ERITH DA8 118 E6
Jenningtree Wy BELV DA17 117 K1
Jenny Hammond Cl WAN E11 76 D2
Jenson Wy NRWD SE19 150 B6
Jenton Av BXLYHN DA7 117 F7
Jephson Rd FSTGT E7 77 G6
Jephson St CMBW SE5 110 E7
Jephtha Rd WAND/EARL SW18 127 K5
Jerdan Pl FUL/PGN SW6 107 K6
Jeremiah St POP/IOD E14 93 K5
Jeremy's Gn UED N18 42 D3
Jermyn St STJS SW1Y 10 E8
Jerningham Av CLAY IG5 60 B1
Jerningham Rd NWCR SE14 132 B1
Jerome St WCHPL E1 13 L2
Jerrard St LEW SE13 132 E2
Jerrold St IS N1 * 7 K6
Jersey Av KTN/HRWW/WS HA3 49 H1
Jersey Dr STMC/STPC BR5 169 J5
Jersey Rd CAN/RD E16 95 G4
HEST TW5 103 G6
HNWL W7 104 B1
HSLW TW3 103 G7
IL IG1 78 B3
ISLW TW7 103 H6
LEY E10 58 B7
RAIN RM13 81 J6
TOOT SW17 148 B6
Jersey St BETH E2 92 D2
Jersey Vls HNWL W7 * 103 K1
Jerusalem Pas CLKNW EC1R 12 C1
Jerviston Gdns
STRHM/NOR SW16 149 G5
Jervois House
WOOL/PLUM SE18 * 114 D6
Jesmond Av WBLY HA9 68 B5
Jesmond Cl MTCM CR4 163 G2
Jesmond Dene HAMP NW3 * 71 G5
Jesmond Rd CROY/NA CR0 165 G6
Jesmond Wy STAN HA7 36 A4
Jessam Av CLPT E5 56 D7
Jessamine Rd HNWL W7 84 E7
Jesse Rd LEY E10 58 A7
Jessett Cl ERITH DA8 118 A3
Jessica Rd WAND/EARL SW18 128 B5
Jessop Av NWDGN UB2 102 E3
Jessop Sq POP/IOD E14 * 93 J7
Jessops Wy CROY/NA CR0 163 H5
Jessup Cl WOOL/PLUM SE18 115 H3
Jetstar Wy NTHLT UB5 83 J2
Jevington Wy LEE/GVPK SE12 134 A7
Jewel Rd WALTH E17 57 J2
Jewry St TWRH EC3N 13 L5
Jews Rw WAND/EARL SW18 128 A3
Jews Wk SYD SE26 150 D3
Jeymer Av WLSDN NW10 69 K4
Jeymer Dr GFD/PVL UB6 66 C7
Jeypore Rd WAND/EARL SW18 128 B6
Jillian Cl HPTN TW12 142 A6
Jim Bradley Cl
WOOL/PLUM SE18 115 F3
Jim Veal Dr HOLWY N7 72 E5
Joan Crs ELTH/MOT SE9 134 C6
Joan Gdns BCTR RM8 80 A1
Joan Rd BCTR RM8 80 A1

Joan St STHWK SE1 .... 12 C9
Jocelyn Rd RCH/KEW TW9 .... 125 F2
Jocelyn St PECK SE15 .... 111 M2
Jockey's Flds FSBYW WC1X 11 H4
Jodane St DEPT SE8 .... 112 C2
Jodrell Cl BOW E3 .... 104 B7
Jodrell Rd BOW E3 .... 75 H7
Joel St PIN HA5 .... 46 E2
Johanna St STHWK SE1 * 18 A3
John Adam St CHCR WC2N 11 K8
John Aird Ct BAY/PAD W2 .... 8 F2
John Archer Wy WAND/EARL SW18 .... 128 C5
John Ashby Cl BRXS/STRHM SW2 .... 129 K5
John Austin Cl KUTN/CMB KT2 .... 144 B7
John Bradshaw Rd STHGT/OAK N14 .... 28 D7
John Burns Dr BARK IG11 .... 78 E7
John Campbell Rd STNW/STAM N16 .... 74 A4
John Carpenter St EMB EC4Y 12 B6
John Felton Rd BERM/RHTH SE16 * 111 H1
John Fisher St WCHPL E1 .... 92 C6
John Goodchild Wy KUT/HW KT1 .... 159 J2
John Harrison Wy BERM/RHTH SE16 .... 112 A4
GNWCH SE10 .... 113 J2
John Islip St WEST SW1P 17 H7
John Lamb Ct KTN/HRWW/WS HA3 .... 34 E1
John Maurice Cl WALW SE17 .... 19 G5
John McKenna Wk BERM/RHTH SE16 * 111 H2
John Parker Sq BTSEA SW11 * 128 C2
John Penn St LEW SE13 .... 112 E7
John Perrin Pl KTN/HRWW/WS HA3 * 50 A6
John Prince's St CAVSQ/HST W1G 10 C4
John Roll Wy BERM/RHTH SE16 .... 111 H2
John Ruskin St CMBW SE5 .... 110 C6
John's Av HDN NW4 .... 52 A3
John's Cl ASHF TW15 .... 140 A4
John Silkin La DEPT SE8 .... 112 A4
John's La MRDN SM4 .... 162 B4
John's Ms BMSBY WC1N 11 M1
John Smith Av FUL/PGN SW6 .... 107 J6
John Smith Ms POP/IOD E14 .... 94 B6
Johnson Cl HACK E8 .... 74 C7
Johnson Rd CROY/NA CRO 164 E6
HAYES BR2 .... 168 C4
HEST TW5 .... 101 J7
WLSDN NW10 .... 69 F7
Johnson's Cl CAR SM5 .... 175 K2
Johnson's Ct FLST/FETLN EC4A 12 B5
Johnsons Dr HPTN TW12 .... 142 C7
Johnson's Pl PIM SW1V 16 F8
Johnson St NWDGN UB2 .... 102 B2
WCHPL E1 .... 92 E5
Johnsons Wy WLSDN NW10 .... 86 D3
John Spencer Sq IS N1 * 73 H5
Johns Pl WCHPL E1 .... 92 D5
John's Ter CROY/NA CRO 165 F7
Johnston Cl BRXN/ST SW9 .... 110 A7
Johnstone Ter EHAM E6 * 95 K2
Johnstone Ter CRICK NW2 .... 70 B2
Johnston Rd WFD IG8 .... 44 E4
John St BMSBY WC1N 11 M1
EN EN1 .... 30 B4
HSLW TW3 .... 123 D1
SNWD SE25 .... 165 H3
SRTFD E15 .... 76 D7
John Trundle Highwalk BARB EC2Y * 12 E2
John Watkin Cl HOR/WEW KT19 .... 172 D1
John Wesley Cl EHAM E6 * 95 K2
John William Cl KUTN/CMB KT2 * 144 A7
John Williams Cl NWCR SE14 .... 112 A5
John Wilson St WOOL/PLUM SE18 .... 115 F3
John Wooley Cl LEW SE13 * 133 H3
Joiner's Arms Yd CMBW SE5 * 110 E7
Joiner St STHWK SE1 .... 13 H9
Jollys La YEAD UB4 .... 83 H4
Jonathan St LBTH SE11 .... 17 L7
Jones Rd PLSTW E13 .... 95 F3
Jonson Cl MTCM CR4 .... 163 G3
YEAD UB4 .... 82 E4
Jordan Cl RYLN/HDSTN HA2 .... 65 K2
Jordan Rd GFD/PVL UB6 .... 67 H7
Jordans Cl DAGE RM10 .... 80 D3
Jordans Ms WHTN TW2 .... 142 E1
Joseph Av ACT W3 .... 87 F5
Joseph Hardcastle Cl NWCR SE14 .... 112 A6
Josephine Av BRXS/STRHM SW2 .... 130 A4
Joseph Locke Wy ESH/CLAY KT10 .... 170 A1
Joseph Powell Cl BAL SW12 .... 129 H5
Joseph Ray Rd WAN E11 .... 76 C1
Joseph St BOW E3 .... 93 H4
Joseph Trotter Cl CLKNW EC1R 6 B8
Joshua Cl MUSWH N10 .... 54 A6
SAND/SEL CR2 .... 177 H6
Joshua St POP/IOD E14 .... 94 A5
Joslings Cl SHB W12 .... 87 J6
Joubert St BTSEA SW11 .... 128 E1
Jowett St PECK SE15 .... 111 G6
Joyce Av UED N18 .... 42 B4
Joyce Green La ERITH DA8 .... 119 C7
Joydon Dr CHDH RM6 .... 61 H1
Joyners Cl DAGW RM9 .... 80 B3
Jubilee Av CHING E4 .... 44 A5
ROMW/RG RM7 .... 62 E4
WHTN TW2 .... 123 H7
Jubilee Cl CDALE/KGS NW9 .... 51 F5
KUT/HW KT1 .... 143 J7
ROMW/RG RM7 .... 62 D4
WLSDN NW10 .... 87 G1
Jubilee Crs ED N9 .... 30 C1
Jubilee Dr RSLP HA4 .... 65 H3
Jubilee Gdns STHL UB1 .... 84 A4
Jubilee Pl CHEL SW3 .... 15 K7
Jubilee Rd CHEAM SM3 .... 174 B6
GFD/PVL UB6 .... 67 H7
Jubilee St WCHPL E1 .... 92 E5
Jubilee Ter FUL/PGN SW6 * 127 J6
The Jubilee GNWCH SE10 * 112 C6
Jubilee Vls ESH/CLAY KT10 * 157 K7
Jubilee Wy CHSGTN KT9 .... 172 D2
EBED/NFELT TW14 .... 121 K7
SCUP DA14 .... 155 G1

WIM/MER SW19 .... 147 F7
Judd St STPAN WC1H 5 J8
Jude St CAN/RD E16 .... 94 D5
Judge Heath La HYS/HAR UB3 .... 82 A5
Judges' Wk HAMP NW3 .... 71 G2
Judge Wk ESH/CLAY KT10 .... 170 E6
Juer St BTSEA SW11 .... 108 D6
Jules Thorn Av EN EN1 .... 30 C2
Julia Gdns BARK IG11 .... 97 K1
Juliana Cl EFNCH N2 .... 53 G2
Julian Av ACT W3 .... 86 D6
Julian Cl BAR EN5 .... 27 F2
Julian Hl HRW HA1 .... 66 E1
Julian Pl POP/IOD E14 .... 112 E4
Julian Tayler Pth FSTH SE23 * 150 D1
Julien Rd EA W5 .... 104 D2
Juliette Rd PLSTW E13 .... 94 E1
Juliette Wy SOCK/AV RM15 .... 119 J1
Julius Caesar Wy STAN HA7 * 35 J2
Julius Nyerere Cl IS N1 .... 5 M4
Junction Ap BTSEA SW11 .... 128 D2
Junction Ms BAY/PAD W2 * 9 H3
Junction Pl BAY/PAD W2 * 9 H4
Junction Rd ARCH N19 .... 72 C2
ASHF TW15 .... 140 A4
DART DA1 .... 139 G5
EA W5 .... 104 D3
ED N9 .... 30 C7
HRW HA1 .... 48 D5
PLSTW E13 .... 77 F7
ROM RM1 .... 63 H3
SAND/SEL CR2 .... 177 K5
TOTM N17 .... 56 C2
Junction Rd East CHDH RM6 .... 62 A6
Junction Rd West CHDH RM6 .... 61 M7
Juniper Cl BAR EN5 .... 26 B4
CHSGTN KT9 .... 172 B6
HOR/WEW KT19 .... 173 F7
WBLY HA9 .... 68 B4
Juniper Ct CHDH RM6 .... 61 H5
KTN/HRWW/WS HA3 * 35 F1
NTHWD HA6 * 32 E7
Juniper Crs CAMTN NW1 4
Juniper Dr WAND/EARL SW18 .... 128 B3
Juniper Gdns MTCM CR4 .... 148 C7
SUN TW16 .... 140 D5
Juniper La EHAM E6 .... 95 J4
Juniper Rd IL IG1 .... 78 A3
Juniper St WCHPL E1 .... 92 E6
Juniper Wy HYS/HAR UB3 .... 82 B6
Juno Wy NWCR SE14 .... 112 A5
Jupiter Wy HOLWY N7 .... 73 F5
Jupp Rd SRTFD E15 .... 76 B6
Jupp Rd West SRTFD E15 .... 76 B7
Justice Wk CHEL SW3 .... 108 D5
Justin Cl BTFD TW8 .... 104 E6
Justin Rd CHING E4 .... 43 H5
Jute La PEND EN3 .... 31 G1
Jutland Cl ARCH N19 .... 54 E7
Jutland Rd CAT SE6 .... 133 F6
PLSTW E13 .... 94 E3
Jutsums Av ROMW/RG RM7 .... 62 D5
Jutsums La ROMW/RG RM7 .... 62 D5
Juxon Cl KTN/HRWW/WS HA3 * 34 B7
Juxon St LBTH SE11 .... 17 M5

K

Kaduna Cl PIN HA5 .... 47 F4
Kaine Pl CROY/NA CRO 166 C6
Kale Rd ERITH DA18 .... 116 E1
Kambala Rd BTSEA SW11 .... 128 C1
Kamrans Pl EDGW HA8 .... 50 B1
Kangley Bridge Rd SYD SE26 .... 151 H4
Kaplan Dr WCHMH N21 .... 29 F4
Kara Wy CRICK NW2 .... 70 B3
Karen Cl RAIN RM13 .... 99 G1
Karen Ct BMLY BR1 .... 152 D7
ELTH/MOT SE9 .... 134 B4
Karenza Ct WBLY HA9 * 49 J6
Karma Wy RYLN/HDSTN HA2 .... 48 A7
Kashgar Rd WOOL/PLUM SE18 .... 116 A4
Kashmir Rd CHARL SE7 .... 114 C6
Kassala Rd BTSEA SW11 .... 108 E7
Kates Cl BAR EN5 .... 25 J4
Katharine St CROY/NA CRO 177 J2
Katherine Cl BERM/RHTH SE16 .... 93 F7
Katherine Gdns ELTH/MOT SE9 .... 134 C3
Katherine Rd EHAM E6 .... 77 H6
Katherine Sq NTGHL W11 * 88 C7
Kathleen Av ACT W3 .... 86 E4
ALP/SUD HA0 .... 68 A6
Kathleen Rd BTSEA SW11 .... 128 E2
Kayemoor Rd BELMT SM2 .... 175 J6
Kay Rd BRXN/ST SW9 .... 129 K1
Kays Ter SRTFD E18 * 58 D1
Kay St BETH E2 .... 92 C1
SRTFD E15 .... 76 B6
WELL DA16 .... 116 C2
Kean St HOL/ALD WC2B 11 L5
Keatley Gn CHING E4 .... 43 H5
Keats Av CAN/RD E16 .... 95 F7
Keats Cl BKHTH/KID SE3 .... 114 B6
BORE WD6 .... 24 C3
PEND EN3 .... 31 H4
STHWK SE1 .... 19 M1
WAN E11 .... 59 F4
WIM/MER SW19 .... 147 H5
YEAD UB4 .... 82 E4
Keats Est STNW/STAM N16 * 74 B1
Keats Gv HAMP NW3 .... 71 J3
Keats Pde ED N9 .... 42 C1
Keats Rd BELV DA17 .... 117 K2
LEY E10 .... 57 K6
WELL DA16 .... 115 K7
Keats Wy CROY/NA CRO 165 K5
GFD/PVL UB6 .... 84 B4
WDR/YW UB7 .... 100 C3
Keble Cl NTHLT UB5 .... 66 C4
WPK KT4 .... 160 C7
Keble Pl BARN SW13 .... 106 E5
Keble St TOOT SW17 .... 147 G3
Kechill Gdns HAYES BR2 .... 167 K6
Kedleston Wk BETH E2 .... 92 D2
Keeble Cl WOOL/PLUM SE18 * 115 H5
Keedonwood Rd BMLY BR1 .... 152 C5
Keel Cl BARK IG11 .... 97 J1
BERM/RHTH SE16 .... 93 F7
Keele Cl WATN WD24 .... 21 G1
Keeley Rd CROY/NA CRO 177 J1
Keeley St HOL/ALD WC2B 11 L5
Keeling Rd ELTH/MOT SE9 .... 134 C4
Keely Cl EBAR EN4 .... 27 J4
Keemor Cl WOOL/PLUM SE18 * 115 F6
Keens Cl STRHM/NOR SW16 .... 148 D4
Keen's Rd CROY/NA CRO 177 J3
Keen's Yd IS N1 * 73 H5

Keepers Ms TEDD TW11 .... 143 J5
The Keep BKHTH/KID SE3 .... 133 K1
KUTN/CMB KT2 .... 144 B5
Keesey St WALW SE17 .... 19 G9
Keeton's Rd BERM/RHTH SE16 .... 111 J2
Keevil Dr WIM/MER SW19 .... 127 G6
Keighley Cl HOLWY N7 .... 72 E3
Keightley Dr ELTH/MOT SE9 .... 135 H7
Keildon Rd BTSEA SW11 .... 128 E3
Keir Hardie Est CLPT E5 * 56 D7
Keir Hardie Wy BARK IG11 .... 79 G6
YEAD UB4 * 82 E2
Keith Connor Cl VX/NE SW8 .... 129 G2
Keith Gv SHB W12 .... 106 D1
Keith Rd BARK IG11 .... 96 D1
HYS/HAR UB3 .... 101 J1
WALTH E17 .... 43 H7
Kelbrook Rd BKHTH/KID SE3 .... 134 E1
Kelburn Wy RAIN RM13 .... 99 J2
Kelceda Cl CRICK NW2 .... 69 J1
Kelf Gv HYS/HAR UB3 .... 82 D5
Kelfield Gdns NKENS W10 .... 88 B5
Kelfield Ms NKENS W10 .... 88 B4
Kelland Cl CEND/HSY/T N8 * 54 D4
Kelland Rd PLSTW E13 .... 94 E3
Kellaway Rd BKHTH/KID SE3 .... 134 B1
Keller Crescent MNPK E12 .... 77 H3
Kellerton Rd LEW SE13 .... 133 H4
Kellett Rd BRXS/STRHM SW2 .... 130 B3
Kelling Gdns CROY/NA CRO 164 C6
Kellino St TOOT SW17 .... 147 K3
Kellner Rd THMD SE28 .... 116 A2
Kell St STHWK SE1 .... 18 D3
Kelly Av PECK SE15 .... 111 G6
Kelly Cl BORE WD6 .... 25 F1
WLSDN NW10 .... 69 F2
Kelly Ms MV/WKIL W9 * 88 D4
Kelly Rd MLHL NW7 .... 38 C5
Kelly St CAMTN NW1 .... 72 B5
Kelly Wy CHDH RM6 .... 62 A4
Kelman Cl CLAP SW4 .... 129 J1
Kelmore Gv EDUL SE22 .... 131 H3
Kelmscott Cl WALTH E17 .... 43 H7
WATW WD18 .... 20 E5
Kelmscott Crs WATW WD18 .... 20 E4
Kelmscott Gdns SHB W12 .... 106 D2
Kelmscott Rd BTSEA SW11 .... 128 D4
Kelross Rd HBRY N5 .... 73 H3
Kelsall Cl BKHTH/KID SE3 .... 134 A1
Kelsall Ms RCH/KEW TW9 .... 105 J2
Kelsey La BECK BR3 .... 166 D2
Kelsey Park Av BECK BR3 .... 166 E1
Kelsey Park Rd BECK BR3 .... 166 D1
Kelsey Sq BECK BR3 .... 166 D1
Kelsey St BETH E2 .... 92 C3
Kelsey Wy BECK BR3 .... 166 D2
Kelso Pl KENS W8 .... 14 C3
Kelso Rd CAR SM5 .... 162 B6
Kelston Rd BARK/HLT IG6 .... 60 B1
Kelton Vls KUT/HW KT1 * 159 L1
Kelvedon Cl KUTN/CMB KT2 .... 144 C5
Kelvedon Rd FUL/PGN SW6 .... 107 J6
Kelvin Av PALM N13 .... 41 F5
TEDD TW11 .... 142 E5
Kelvinbrook E/WMO/HCT KT8 .... 157 G2
Kelvin Cl HOR/WEW KT19 .... 172 C5
Kelvin Crs KTN/HRWW/WS HA3 .... 34 E6
Kelvin Dr TWK TW1 .... 124 C5
Kelvin Gdns CROY/NA CRO 163 K6
STHL UB1 .... 84 A5
Kelvin Gv CHSGTN KT9 .... 171 K2
SYD SE26 .... 150 D2
Kelvington Cl CROY/NA CRO 166 B6
Kelvington Rd PECK SE15 .... 132 A4
Kelvin Pde ORP BR6 .... 169 K7
Kelvin Rd HBRY N5 .... 73 H3
WELL DA16 .... 136 B2
Kember St IS N1 * 5 L1
Kemble Dr HAYES BR2 .... 181 J2
Kemble Rd CROY/NA CRO 177 H2
FSTH SE23 .... 132 A7
TOTM N17 .... 42 C7
Kemble St HOL/ALD WC2B 11 L5
Kemerton Rd BECK BR3 .... 166 E1
CMBW SE5 .... 130 D2
CROY/NA CRO 165 G6
Kemey's St HOM E9 .... 75 G4
Kemnal Rd CHST BR7 .... 154 C5
Kempe Rd KIL/WHAMP NW6 .... 88 B1
Kemp Gdns CROY/NA CRO 164 D5
Kemplay Rd HAMP NW3 .... 71 H3
Kemp Pl BUSH WD23 .... 22 A5
Kemps Dr NTHWD HA6 .... 32 D6
POP/IOD E14 .... 93 J6
Kempsford Gdns ECT SW5 .... 14 B8
Kempsford Rd LBTH SE11 .... 18 B6
Kempshott Rd STRHM/NOR SW16 .... 148 G6
Kempson Rd FUL/PGN SW6 .... 107 K6
Kempthorne Rd DEPT SE8 .... 112 B3
Kempton Av NTHLT UB5 .... 66 A5
SUN TW16 .... 141 F7
Kempton Cl ERITH DA8 .... 117 K5
HGDN/ICK UB10 .... 64 A3
Kempton Pk SUN TW16 .... 141 G7
Kempton Rd EHAM E6 .... 77 K7
Kempton Wk CROY/NA CRO 166 B5
Kempt St WOOL/PLUM SE18 .... 115 F5
Kemsing Cl BXLY DA5 .... 137 F6
THHTH CR7 * 164 C3
Kemsing Rd GNWCH SE10 .... 113 K4
Kenbury St CMBW SE5 .... 130 D1
Kenchester Cl VX/NE SW8 .... 109 K6
Kencot Wy ERITH DA18 .... 117 G1
Kendal Av ACT W3 .... 86 A4
BARK IG11 .... 78 E7
UED N18 .... 41 K3
Kendal Cl BRXN/ST SW9 .... 110 C6
EBED/NFELT TW14 .... 121 J7
TRDG/WHET N20 .... 39 J1
WFD IG8 .... 44 D1
YEAD UB4 .... 82 C1
Kendal Ct ACT W3 .... 86 A4
Kendal Cft CHDH RM6 .... 61 K5
Kendale Rd BMLY BR1 .... 152 C4
Kendal Gdns SUT SM1 .... 175 G1
UED N18 .... 41 K3
Kendal Pde UED N18 * 41 K3
Kendall Av BECK BR3 .... 166 B1
SAND/SEL CR2 .... 177 J7
Kendall Pl MHST W1U 10 A3
Kendall Rd BECK BR3 .... 166 B1
ISLW TW7 .... 124 B1
WOOL/PLUM SE18 .... 114 D7
Kendalmere Cl MUSWH N10 .... 40 B7
Kendal Pl PUT/ROE SW15 .... 127 H4
Kendal Rd WLSDN NW10 .... 69 J2
Kendal Steps BAY/PAD W2 * 9 K5
Kendal St BAY/PAD W2 .... 9 K5
Kender St NWCR SE14 .... 111 K6
Kendoa Rd CLAP SW4 .... 129 J3

Kendon Cl WAN E11 .... 59 F4
Kendra Hall Rd SAND/SEL CR2 .... 177 H6
Kendrey Gdns WHTN TW2 .... 123 K5
Kendrick Ms SKENS SW7 .... 15 G5
Kendrick Pl SKENS SW7 .... 15 G6
Kenelm Cl HRW HA1 .... 67 G2
Kenerne Dr BAR EN5 .... 26 C4
Kenilford Rd BAL SW12 .... 129 G6
Kenilworth Av RYLN/HDSTN HA2 .... 65 K3
WALTH E17 .... 57 J1
WIM/MER SW19 .... 146 E4
Kenilworth Dr BORE WD6 .... 24 E2
Kenilworth Gdns GDMY/SEVK IG3 .... 79 F1
OXHEY WD19 .... 33 G4
STHL UB1 .... 83 K2
WOOL/PLUM SE18 .... 135 H5
YEAD UB4 .... 82 D4
Kenilworth Rd BOW E3 .... 93 G1
EA W5 .... 86 A7
EDGW HA8 .... 36 E1
EW KT17 .... 173 J5
KIL/WHAMP NW6 .... 70 D7
PGE/AN SE20 .... 151 F7
STMC/STPC BR5 .... 169 H5
Kenilworth Ter BELMT SM2 * 174 E6
Kenley Av CDALE/KGS NW9 .... 37 G2
Kenley Cl BXLY DA5 .... 137 H6
CHST BR7 .... 169 K2
EBAR EN4 .... 27 J3
Kenley Gdns THHTH CR7 .... 164 C3
Kenley Rd KUT/HW KT1 .... 159 L1
TWK TW1 .... 124 B5
WIM/MER SW19 .... 161 K1
Kenley Wk CHEAM SM3 .... 174 B3
NTGHL W11 * 88 C7
Kenlor Rd TOOT SW17 .... 147 H4
TOTM N17 .... 56 B1
Kenmare Dr MTCM CR4 .... 147 K6
TOTM N17 .... 56 B1
Kenmare Gdns PLMGR N13 .... 41 J3
Kenmare Rd THHTH CR7 .... 164 A5
Kenmere Gdns ALP/SUD HA0 .... 68 C7
Kenmere Rd WELL DA16 .... 136 D1
Kenmont Gdns WLSDN NW10 .... 87 K2
Kenmore Av KTN/HRWW/WS HA3 .... 49 G4
Kenmore Crs YEAD UB4 .... 82 D1
Kenmore Gdns EDGW HA8 .... 50 D1
Kenmore Rd KTN/HRWW/WS HA3 .... 49 K2
HACK E8 .... 74 D4
Kenmure Rd HACK E8 .... 74 D4
Kennacraig Cl CAN/RD E16 .... 95 F7
Kennard Rd FBAR/BDGN N11 .... 39 K4
SRTFD E15 .... 76 B6
Kennard St BTSEA SW11 .... 109 F7
CAN/RD E16 .... 95 K7
Kennedy Av PEND EN3 .... 30 E5
Kennedy Cl MTCM CR4 .... 163 F1
PIN HA5 .... 33 K5
PLSTW E13 .... 94 E1
STMC/STPC BR5 .... 169 J7
Kennedy Rd BARK IG11 .... 78 E7
HNWL W7 .... 84 E4
Kennedy Wk WALW SE17 * 19 H6
Kennet Cl BTSEA SW11 .... 128 C3
Kennet Dr YEAD UB4 .... 83 J3
Kenneth Av IL IG1 .... 78 B3
Kenneth Crs CRICK NW2 .... 69 K4
Kenneth Gdns STAN HA7 .... 35 G5
Kenneth More Rd IL IG1 .... 78 B2
Kenneth Rd CHDH RM6 .... 61 K6
Kennet Rd DART DA1 .... 138 D2
ISLW TW7 .... 124 A2
MV/WKIL W9 .... 88 D3
Kennet Sq MTCM CR4 .... 147 J7
Kennet St WAP E1W 92 C7
Kennett Wharf La BLKFR EC4V 12 F6
Kenninghall Rd CLPT E5 .... 74 D2
UED N18 .... 43 F4
Kenning St BERM/RHTH SE16 .... 111 K1
Kennings Wy LBTH SE11 .... 18 B7
Kennington Gdns KUT/HW KT1 * 158 E9
Kennington La LBTH SE11 .... 17 M8
Kennington Park Gdns LBTH SE11 .... 18 C9
Kennington Park Pl LBTH SE11 .... 18 B8
Kennington Park Rd LBTH SE11 .... 18 C7
Kenny Dr CAR SM5 .... 176 A7
Kenrick Pl MHST W1U 10 A2
Kensal Rd NKENS W10 .... 88 C3
Kensal Whf NKENS W10 * 88 C3
Kensington Av MNPK E12 .... 77 J5
THHTH CR7 .... 149 G7
WATW WD18 .... 20 D3
Kensington Church Ct KENS W8 .... 14 C2
Kensington Church St KENS W8 .... 8 B8
Kensington Church Wk KENS W8 * 14 C1
Kensington Cl FBAR/BDGN N11 * 40 A4
Kensington Ct KENS W8 .... 14 D3
Kensington Court Gdns KENS W8 * 14 D3
Kensington Court Ms KENS W8 * 14 D3
Kensington Court Pl KENS W8 .... 14 D3
Kensington Dr WFD IG8 .... 59 H1
Kensington Gdns IL IG1 .... 59 K7
Kensington Gardens Sq BAY/PAD W2 .... 8 E5
Kensington Ga KENS W8 .... 14 E3
Kensington Hall Gdns WKENS W14 * 107 J4
Kensington High St KENS W8 .... 107 H3
Kensington MI KENS W8 .... 8 B8
Kensington Palace Gdns KENS W8 .... 8 C6
Kensington Park Gdns NTGHL W11 .... 88 D6
Kensington Park Ms NTGHL W11 * 88 D5
Kensington Park Rd NTGHL W11 .... 88 D5
Kensington Pl KENS W8 .... 8 A9
Kensington Rd KENS W8 .... 14 C1
NTHLT UB5 .... 84 A2
ROMW/RG RM7 .... 62 E5
Kensington Sq KENS W8 .... 14 D2
Kensington Ter SAND/SEL CR2 * 177 K6
Kent Av DAGW RM9 .... 98 C3
WEA W13 .... 85 H4

WELL DA16 .... 136 A4
Kent Cl MTCM CR4 .... 163 K3
Kent Ct CDALE/KGS NW9 .... 51 G1
Kent Dr EBAR EN4 .... 28 A3
TEDD TW11 .... 142 E4
Kentford Wy NTHLT UB5 .... 65 J7
Kent Gdns RSLP HA4 .... 46 E5
WEA W13 .... 85 H4
Kent Gate Wy CROY/NA CRO 179 H5
Kent House La BECK BR3 .... 151 G5
Kent House Rd BECK BR3 .... 151 F6
Kentish Rd BELV DA17 .... 117 H3
Kentish Town Rd CAMTN NW1 .... 4 D1
Kentish Wy BMLY BR1 .... 168 A2
Kentlea Rd THMD SE28 .... 115 K1
Kentmere Rd WOOL/PLUM SE18 .... 115 K3
Kenton Av HRW HA1 .... 49 F6
STHL UB1 .... 84 A6
SUN TW16 .... 156 C1
Kenton Gdns KTN/HRWW/WS HA3 .... 49 J3
Kenton La KTN/HRWW/WS HA3 .... 35 F6
KTN/HRWW/WS HA3 .... 49 J2
Kenton Park Av KTN/HRWW/WS HA3 .... 49 K3
Kenton Park Cl KTN/HRWW/WS HA3 .... 49 K3
Kenton Park Crs KTN/HRWW/WS HA3 .... 49 K3
Kenton Park Pde KTN/HRWW/WS HA3 * 49 J4
Kenton Park Rd KTN/HRWW/WS HA3 .... 49 K3
Kenton Rd HOM E9 .... 75 F5
KTN/HRWW/WS HA3 .... 49 K5
Kenton St STPAN WC1H 5 J9
Kenton Wy YEAD UB4 .... 82 C2
Kent Pas CAMTN NW1 .... 3 L9
Kent Rd CHSWK W4 .... 105 K2
DAGE RM10 .... 80 D4
DART DA1 .... 139 G5
E/WMO/HCT KT8 .... 157 H3
KUT/HW KT1 .... 158 E2
RCH/KEW TW9 .... 105 H6
WCHMH N21 .... 29 K7
WWKM BR4 .... 166 E7
Kent St BETH E2 .... 7 M5
PLSTW E13 .... 95 F2
Kent Ter CAMTN NW1 .... 3 K8
Kent View Gdns GDMY/SEVK IG3 .... 78 E1
Kent Wy SURB KT6 .... 172 A5
Kentwell Cl BROCKY SE4 * 132 B5
Kentwode Gn BARN SW13 .... 106 D6
Kent Yd SKENS SW7 .... 15 K2
Kenver Av NFNCH/WDSPK N12 .... 39 H5
Kenway CRW RM5 .... 62 E1
Ken Wy WBLY HA9 .... 68 E1
Kenway Rd ECT SW5 .... 14 C6
Kenwood Cl HAMP NW3 .... 53 J5
WDR/YW UB7 .... 100 D5
Kenwood Dr BECK BR3 .... 167 F2
Kenwood Gdns CLAY IG5 .... 60 A3
SWFD E18 .... 59 F2
Kenwood Rd ED N9 .... 42 C1
HGT N6 .... 53 K5
Kenworthy Rd HOM E9 .... 75 G4
Kenwyn Dr CRICK NW2 .... 69 G2
Kenwyn Rd CLAP SW4 .... 129 J3
DART DA1 .... 139 G4
RYNPK SW20 .... 146 A2
Kenya Rd CHARL SE7 .... 114 C6
Kenyngton Dr SUN TW16 .... 140 E4
Kenyngton Pl KTN/HRWW/WS HA3 .... 49 J4
Kenyon St FUL/PGN SW6 .... 107 G7
Keogh Rd SRTFD E15 .... 76 C5
Kepler Rd CLAP SW4 .... 129 K3
Keppel Rd DAGW RM9 .... 80 A3
EHAM E6 .... 77 K6
Keppel St GWRST WC1E 11 J2
Kerbela St BETH E2 .... 92 C3
Kerbey St POP/IOD E14 .... 93 K5
Kerfield Crs CMBW SE5 .... 110 E7
Kerfield Pl CMBW SE5 .... 110 E7
Kerri Cl BAR EN5 .... 26 A3
Kerrison Pl EA W5 .... 85 K7
Kerrison Rd BTSEA SW11 .... 128 D2
EA W5 .... 85 K7
SRTFD E15 .... 76 B7
Kerry Av SOCK/AV RM15 .... 119 J1
STAN HA7 .... 35 J3
Kerry Cl CAN/RD E16 .... 95 F5
PLMGR N13 .... 41 F1
Kerry Ct STAN HA7 .... 35 K3
Kerry Pth NWCR SE14 .... 112 C5
Kerry Rd NWCR SE14 .... 112 C5
Kersfield Rd PUT/ROE SW15 .... 127 G5
WAND/EARL SW18 .... 127 H6
Kershaw Cl WAND/EARL SW18 .... 128 C5
Kershaw Rd DAGE RM10 .... 80 C2
Kersley Ms BTSEA SW11 .... 108 E7
Kersley Rd STNW/STAM N16 .... 74 A2
Kersley St BTSEA SW11 .... 128 E1
Kerswell Cl SEVS/STOTM N15 .... 56 A4
Kerwick Cl HOLWY N7 * 5 K1
Keslake Rd KIL/WHAMP NW6 .... 88 B1
Kessock Cl TOTM N17 .... 56 D4
Keston Av HAYES BR2 .... 181 H2
Keston Cl UED N18 .... 30 A6
WELL DA16 .... 116 D6
Keston Gdns HAYES BR2 .... 181 G2
Keston Ms WAT WD17 .... 21 F1
Keston Park Cl HAYES BR2 .... 181 K3
Keston Rd PECK SE15 .... 131 G2
THHTH CR7 .... 164 A5
TOTM N17 .... 55 K2
Kestrel Av EHAM E6 .... 95 J4
HNHL SE24 .... 130 C4
Kestrel Cl CDALE/KGS NW9 .... 51 G1
HCH RM12 .... 81 K4
KUTN/CMB KT2 .... 143 K3
WLSDN NW10 .... 69 F4
Kestrel Pl NWCR SE14 * 112 B5
Kestrel Wy CROY/NA CRO 180 B7
HYS/HAR UB3 .... 101 G1
Keswick Av PUT/ROE SW15 .... 145 G4
WIM/MER SW19 .... 161 K1
Keswick Cl SUT SM1 .... 175 G3
Keswick Gdns REDBR IG4 .... 59 J4
RSLP HA4 .... 46 A4
WBLY HA9 .... 68 A4
Keswick Ms EA W5 .... 105 F1
Keswick Rd BXLYHN DA7 .... 137 H1
PUT/ROE SW15 .... 127 H4
WHTN TW2 .... 123 G5
WWKM BR4 .... 180 C1

Kettering St
 STRHM/NOR SW16 .....148 B5
Kett Gdns BRXS/STRHM SW2 .130 A4
Kettlebaston Rd LEY E10 .....57 H7
Kettlewell Cl FBAR/BDGN N11 .40 A5
Kevelioc Rd TOTM N17 .....41 J7
Kevin Cl HSLWW TW4 .....122 C1
Kew Br RCH/KEW TW9 .....105 H5
Kew Bridge Arches
 CHSWK W4 * 105 H5
Kew Bridge Ct BTFD TW8 .....105 H4
Kew Bridge Rd BTFD TW8 .....105 G5
Kew Crs CHEAM SM3 .....174 C2
Kewferry Rd NTHWD HA6 .....32 A3
Kew Foot Rd RCH/KEW TW9 .125 F3
Kew Gardens Rd
 RCH/KEW TW9 .....105 G6
Kew Gn RCH/KEW TW9 .....105 G5
Kew Meadow Pth
 RCH/KEW TW9 .....105 J6
Kew Riverside Pk
 RCH/KEW TW9 .....125 F3
Kew Rd RCH/KEW TW9 .....105 J6
Key Cl WCHPL E1 .....92 D3
Keyes Rd CRICK NW2 .....70 B4
 DART DA1 .....139 J4
Keymer Rd BRXS/STRHM SW2 .149 F1
Keynes Cl EFNCH N2 .....53 K2
Keynsham Av WFD IG8 .....44 C3
Keynsham Gdns
 ELTH/MOT SE9 .....134 D4
Keynsham Rd ELTH/MOT SE9 .134 C4
 MRDN SM4 .....162 A7
Keysham Av HEST TW5 .....101 K7
Keystone Crs IS N1 .....5 K6
Keystone Pas BORE WD6 .....24 C2
Keywood Dr SUN TW16 .....140 E5
Keyworth Cl CLPT E5 .....75 G3
Keyworth St STHWK SE1 .....18 D3
Kezia St DEPT SE8 .....112 B4
Khama Rd TOOT SW17 .....147 J3
Khartoum Rd IL IG1 .....78 B4
 PLSTW E13 .....95 F2
 TOOT SW17 .....147 H3
Khyber Rd BTSEA SW11 .....128 D1
Kibworth St VX/NE SW8 .....110 A6
Kidbrooke Gdns
 BKHTH/KID SE3 .....133 K1
Kidbrooke La ELTH/MOT SE9 .134 D3
Kidbrooke Park Cl
 BKHTH/KID SE3 .....114 A7
Kidbrooke Park Rd
 BKHTH/KID SE3 .....134 A3
Kidbrooke Wy BKHTH/KID SE3 .134 A1
Kidderminster Pl
 CROY/NA CR0 .....164 C7
Kidderminster Rd
 CROY/NA CR0 .....164 C7
Kidd Pl CHARL SE7 .....114 D4
Kiffen St SDTCH EC2A 7 F4
Kilberry Cl ISLW TW7 .....103 J7
Kilburn Br KIL/WHAMP NW6 * .2 A4
Kilburn High Rd
 KIL/WHAMP NW6 .....2 B3
Kilburn La NKENS W10 .....88 B2
Kilburn Park Rd KIL/WHAMP NW6 .2 A8
Kilburn Pl KIL/WHAMP NW6 .2 A4
Kilburn Priory
 KIL/WHAMP NW6 .....2 B4
Kilburn Sq KIL/WHAMP NW6 .2 A4
Kilburn V KIL/WHAMP NW6 .....2 A4
Kildare Cl RSLP HA4 .....47 G7
Kildare Gdns BAY/PAD W2 .....8 B4
Kildare Rd CAN/RD E16 .....94 E4
Kildare Ter BAY/PAD W2 .....8 B4
Kildoran Rd CLAP SW4 .....129 K4
Kildowan Rd GDMY/SEVK IG3 .61 G7
Kilgour Rd FSTH SE23 .....132 B5
Kilkie St FUL/PGN SW6 .....128 B1
Killarney Rd
 WAND/EARL SW18 .....128 B5
Killburns Mill Cl WLGTN SM6 .176 B1
Killearn Rd CAT SE6 .....133 G7
Killester Gdns WPK KT4 .....173 K3
Killick St IS N1 .....5 L4
Killieser Av
 BRXS/STRHM SW2 .....148 E1
Killip Cl CAN/RD E16 .....94 D5
Killowen Av NTHLT UB5 .....66 C4
Killowen Rd HOM E9 * 75 F5
Killyon Rd VX/NE SW8 .....129 H1
Kilmaine Rd FUL/PGN SW6 .107 H6
Kilmarnock Rd OXHEY WD19 .33 H4
Kilmarsh Rd HMSMTH W6 .107 F3
Kilmartin Av
 STRHM/NOR SW16 .....164 B2
Kilmartin Rd GDMY/SEVK IG3 .79 G1
Kilmartin Wy HCH RM12 .....81 K4
Kilmington Rd BARN SW13 .106 D5
Kilmorey Gdns TWK TW1 .....124 C3
Kilmorey Rd TWK TW1 .....124 C3
Kilmorie Rd FSTH SE23 .....132 B7
Kiln Cl HYS/HAR UB3 .....101 G5
Kilner St POP/IOD E14 .....93 J4
Kiln Ms TOOT SW17 .....147 H4
Kiln Pl KTTN NW5 .....72 A3
Kilnside ESH/CLAY KT10 .....171 G4
Kiln Wy NTHWD HA6 .....32 C5
Kilpatrick Wy YEAD UB4 .....83 J4
Kilravock St NKENS W10 .....88 C2
Kilross Rd EBED/NFELT TW14 .121 G7
Kilsha Rd WOT/HER KT12 .156 A5
Kimball Gdns FUL/PGN SW6 .107 H7
Kimbell Pl BKHTH/KID SE3 .134 B3
Kimberley Av EHAM E6 .....95 J1
 GNTH/NBYPK IG2 .....60 D5
 PECK SE15 .....131 J1
 ROMW/RG RM7 .....62 D5
Kimberley Ct
 KIL/WHAMP NW6 .....70 C7
Kimberley Dr SCUP DA14 .....155 K1
Kimberley Gdns EN EN1 .....30 B2
 FSBYPK N4 .....55 H4
Kimberley Rd BECK BR3 .....166 A1
 BRXN/ST SW9 .....129 K1
 CAN/RD E16 .....94 D3
 CROY/NA CR0 .....164 C5
 KIL/WHAMP NW6 .....70 C7
 TOTM N17 .....56 C1
 WALTH E17 .....43 G7
 WAN E11 .....76 B1
Kimber Rd WAND/EARL SW18 .127 K6
Kimble Cl WATW WD18 * 20 C5
Kimble Crs BUSH WD23 .....22 C6
Kimble Rd WIM/MER SW19 .147 H5
Kimbolton Cl LEE/GVPK SE12 .133 J5
Kimbolton Gn BORE WD6 .....24 E3
Kimmeridge Gdns
 ELTH/MOT SE9 .....153 J3

Kimmeridge Rd
 ELTH/MOT SE9 .....153 J3
Kimpton Park Wy
 CHEAM SM3 .....174 D1
Kimpton Rd CHEAM SM3 .....174 D2
 CMBW SE5 .....110 E7
Kinburn St
 BERM/RHTH SE16 * 112 A1
Kincaid Rd PECK SE15 .....111 J6
Kincardine Gdns
 MV/WKIL W9 * 8 A1
Kinch Gv WBLY HA9 .....50 B6
Kinder Cl THMD SE28 .....97 J6
Kinder St WCHPL E1 .....92 D5
Kinderton Cl STHGT/OAK N14 .28 C7
Kinfauns Rd
 BRXS/STRHM SW2 .....149 G1
 GDMY/SEVK IG3 .....61 H7
Kingaby Gdns RAIN RM13 .....81 J6
King Alfred Av CAT SE6 .....151 J3
King Arthur Cl PECK SE15 .....111 K6
King Charles Crs BRYLDS KT5 .159 G6
King Charles I Island
 WHALL SW1A 11 J8
King Charles Rd BRYLDS KT5 .159 G6
King Charles St WHALL SW1A .17 H1
King Charles Ter WAP E1W * .92 D6
King Charles Wk
 WIM/MER SW19 * 127 H7
Kingcup Cl CROY/NA CR0 .....166 A7
King David La WCHPL E1 .....92 E6
Kingdom St BAY/PAD W2 .....8 E4
Kingdon Rd KIL/WHAMP NW6 .70 E5
King Edward Av DART DA1 .....139 K4
King Edward Dr CHSGTN KT9 .172 A2
King Edward III Ms
 BERM/RHTH SE16 .....111 J1
King Edward Pl BUSH WD23 .21 K3
King Edward Rd BAR EN5 .....26 E3
 LEY E10 .....58 A7
 OXHEY WD19 .....21 J5
 ROM RM1 .....63 H5
 WALTH E17 .....57 G2
King Edward's Gdns ACT W3 .86 C7
King Edward's Gv TEDD TW11 .143 H5
King Edwards Pl ACT W3 * 86 C7
King Edward's Rd RSLP HA4 .46 B7
 BARK IG11 .....78 D7
 ED N9 .....30 D6
 HACK E8 .....74 D7
 PEND EN3 .....31 F2
King Edward St STBT EC1A .12 E4
Kingfield Rd EA W5 .....85 K3
Kingfield St POP/IOD E14 .113 F3
Kingfisher Cl
 KTN/HRWW/WS HA3 .....35 F6
 THMD SE28 .....97 J6
Kingfisher Dr
 RCHPK/HAM TW10 .....143 J3
Kingfisher Ms LEW SE13 .....132 E4
Kingfisher Pl WDGN N22 * 55 F1
Kingfisher St EHAM E6 .....95 J4
Kingfisher Wy BECK BR3 .....166 A4
 WLSDN NW10 * 69 F5
King Gdns CROY/NA CR0 .....177 H4
King Garth Ms FSTH SE23 * .131 K4
King George Av BUSH WD23 .22 B5
 CAN/RD E16 .....95 H5
 GNTH/NBYPK IG2 .....60 D5
 WOT/HER KT12 .....156 C7
King George Cl
 ROMW/RG RM7 .....62 E2
 SUN TW16 .....140 C4
King Georges Av WATW WD18 .20 C4
King George Sq
 RCHPK/HAM TW10 .....125 G5
King George St GNWCH SE10 .113 F6
King George VI Av MTCM CR4 .162 E3
Kingham Cl NTGHL W11 .....107 H1
 WAND/EARL SW18 .....128 B6
King Harolds Wy BXLYHN DA7 .116 E6
King Henry Ms HRW HA1 * .48 E7
King Henry's Dr
 CROY/NA CR0 .....180 A7
King Henry's Reach
 HMSMTH W6 .....107 F5
King Henry's Rd HAMP NW3 .3 J2
 KUT/HW KT1 .....159 J2
King Henry St
 STNW/STAM N16 .....74 A4
King Henry's Wk IS N1 .....74 A5
King Henry's Yd
 STNW/STAM N16 .....74 A4
King Henry Ter WAP E1W * .92 D6
King James Ct STHWK SE1 .18 E3
King James St STHWK SE1 .18 D2
King John Ct SDTCH EC2A 7 K9
King John St WCHPL E1 .....93 F4
King John's Wk
 ELTH/MOT SE9 .....134 D6
Kinglake Est WALW SE17 * 19 J7
Kinglake St WALW SE17 .....19 J8
Kinglet Cl FSTGT E7 .....76 E5
Kingly Ct REGST W1B 10 F6
Kingly St REGST W1B 10 E5
King & Queen Cl
 ELTH/MOT SE9 * 153 J3
King & Queen St WALW SE17 .18 F7
King & Queen Whf
 BERM/RHTH SE16 * 93 G7
Kingsand Rd LEE/GVPK SE12 .152 E1
King's Arms Yd LOTH EC2R .13 G4
Kingsash Dr YEAD UB4 * 83 J3
Kings Av BAL SW12 .....129 J7
 BMLY BR1 .....152 D5
 CAR SM5 .....175 J6
 CHDH RM6 .....62 B5
 CLAP SW4 .....129 J6
 EA W5 .....85 K5
 MUSWH N10 .....54 A2
 NWMAL KT3 .....160 C3
 WATW WD18 .....20 D5
King's Av GFD/PVL UB6 .....84 B5
 HSLW TW3 .....103 G1
 SUN TW16 .....140 D4
 WCHMH N21 .....29 H7
 WFD IG8 .....45 G4
King's Bench St STHWK SE1 .18 D1
King's Bench Wk EMB EC4Y .12 B5
Kingsbridge Av ACT W3 .....105 G1
Kingsbridge Ct POP/IOD E14 *.112 D2
Kingsbridge Crs STHL UB1 .83 K4
Kingsbridge Dr MLHL NW7 .38 B2
Kingsbridge Rd BARK IG11 .96 D1
 MRDN SM4 .....161 G6
 NKENS W10 .....88 A5
 NWDGN UB2 .....102 E3
 WOT/HER KT12 .....156 A6
Kingsbury Gn
 CDALE/KGS NW9 * 50 E4

Kingsbury Rd
 CDALE/KGS NW9 .....50 C4
 IS N1 .....74 A5
Kingsbury Ter IS N1 .....74 A5
Kings tha E/WMO/HCT KT8 .157 H2
Kingsclere Cl PUT/ROE SW15 .126 D6
Kingsclere Pl ENC/FH EN2 .....29 J1
Kingscliffe Gdns
 WIM/MER SW19 .....127 J7
Kings Cl DART DA1 .....138 E3
 HDN NW4 .....52 B3
 LEY E10 .....57 K6
 NTHWD HA6 .....32 D5
 THDIT KT7 .....158 B5
 WATW WD18 .....21 G3
 WOT/HER KT12 .....156 A7
Kings College Rd RSLP HA4 .46 B7
King's College Rd HAMP NW3 .3 H1
Kingscote Rd CHSWK W4 .....106 A2
 CROY/NA CR0 .....165 J6
 NWMAL KT3 .....160 A2
Kingscote St BLKFR EC4V .12 C6
Kings Ct PLSTW E13 .....77 F7
King's Ct STHWK SE1 * 18 D1
Kingscourt Rd
 STRHM/NOR SW16 .....148 D2
King's Crs FSBYPK N4 .....73 J2
Kingscroft Rd CRICK NW2 .70 D5
King's Cross Br IS N1 * 5 J7
King's Cross Rd FSBYW WC1X .5 L7
Kingsdale Gdns NTGHL W11 .88 B7
Kingsdale Rd PGE/AN SE20 .151 F6
 WOOL/PLUM SE18 .....116 A5
Kingsdown Av ACT W3 .....87 G6
 SAND/SEL CR2 .....177 J7
 WEA W13 .....104 C1
Kingsdown Cl
 BERM/RHTH SE16 * 111 J4
 NKENS W10 .....88 B5
Kingsdowne Ct EA W5 * 86 A6
Kingsdown Rd SURB KT6 .159 F6
 ARCH N19 .....72 E2
 CHEAM SM3 .....174 C4
 WAN E11 .....76 C2
Kingsdown Wy HAYES BR2 .167 K5
Kingsd Dr BRYLDS KT5 .....159 H6
 EDGW HA8 .....36 B3
 WBLY HA9 .....68 D1
King's Dr THDIT KT7 .....158 C5
Kingsend RSLP HA4 .....46 B7
Kingsend Ct RSLP HA4 * 46 C7
Kings Farm WALTH E17 * .43 H1
Kings Farm Av
 RCHPK/HAM TW10 .....125 H3
Kingsfield Av
 RYLN/HDSTN HA2 .....48 B3
Kingsfield Ct OXHEY WD19 .21 H5
Kingsfield Rd HRW HA1 * 48 D6
 OXHEY WD19 .....21 H6
Kingsfield Ter DART DA1 * .139 J5
Kingsford St KENTISH TOWN NW5 .71 K4
Kingsford Wy EHAM E6 .....95 K4
Kings Gdns IL IG1 .....60 D7
 KIL/WHAMP NW6 * 2 A2
Kingsgate WBLY HA9 .....68 E2
Kingsgate Av FNCH N3 .....52 E2
Kingsgate Cl BXLYHN DA7 .117 F7
Kingsgate Est IS N1 * 74 A5
Kings Gate Ms
 CEND/HSY/T N8 .....55 F4
Kingsgate Pl
 KIL/WHAMP NW6 .....2 A2
Kingsgate Rd
 KIL/WHAMP NW6 .....2 A1
 KUT/HW KT1 .....144 F7
Kingsground ELTH/MOT SE9 .134 C6
Kings Gv ROM RM1 .....63 H4
King's Gv PECK SE15 .....111 J6
Kings Hall Ms LEW SE13 * .133 F2
Kings Hall Rd BECK BR3 .....151 G5
Kings Head Hl CHING E4 .....31 K1
King's Hwy WOOL/PLUM SE18 .115 K4
Kingshill Av
 KTN/HRWW/WS HA3 .....49 H3
 NTHLT UB5 .....83 F7
 WPK KT4 .....160 D6
 YEAD UB4 .....82 C2
Kingshill Cl YEAD UB4 * 82 C2
Kingshill Ct BAR EN5 * 26 C3
Kingshill Dr
 KTN/HRWW/WS HA3 .....49 H1
Kingshold Rd HOM E9 .....74 E6
Kingsholm Gdns
 ELTH/MOT SE9 .....134 C3
Kingshurst Rd LEE/GVPK SE12 .133 K6
Kings Keep HAYES BR2 * .167 J4
 KUT/HW KT1 * 159 F3
Kingsland Gn
 STNW/STAM N16 .....74 A5
Kingsland High St HACK E8 .74 B5
Kingsland Pas HACK E8 * 74 A5
Kingsland Rd BETH E2 .....7 L4
 HACK E8 .....7 L1
 PLSTW E13 .....95 G2
King's La SUT SM1 .....175 H4
Kingslawn Cl PUT/ROE SW15 .126 E4
Kingsleigh Cl BTFD TW8 .104 E5
Kingsleigh Pl MTCM CR4 .162 E2
Kingsley Av BORE WD6 .....24 B1
 DART DA1 .....139 K4
 HSLW TW3 .....123 H1
 STHL UB1 .....84 A6
 SUT SM1 .....175 H3
 WEA W13 .....85 G5
Kingsley Cl DAGE RM10 .....80 D3
 GLDGN NW11 .....53 C6
Kingsley Ct EDGW HA8 * 36 D1
Kingsley Dr WPK KT4 .....173 H1
Kingsley Gdns CHING E4 .....43 J4
Kingsley Ms CHST BR7 .....154 B5
 IL IG1 .....78 B1
 KENS W8 .....14 D4
 WAP E1W * 92 D6
Kingsley Pl HGT N6 .....54 A6
Kingsley Rd CROY/NA CR0 .164 B7
 FSTGT E7 .....76 E6
 HSLW TW3 .....123 H1
 KIL/WHAMP NW6 .....70 D7
 PIN HA5 .....47 K3
 PLMGR N13 .....41 G3
 RYLN/HDSTN HA2 .....66 C3
 WALTH E17 .....58 A1
 WIM/MER SW19 .....147 F4
Kingsley St BTSEA SW11 .....128 E2
Kingsley Wy EFNCH N2 .....53 G5
 GLDGN NW11 .....53 G5

Kingsmead BAR EN5 .....26 E3
 RCHPK/HAM TW10 .....125 G5
Kingsmead Av
 CDALE/KGS NW9 .....51 F7
 ED N9 .....30 D7
 MTCM CR4 .....163 H2
 ROM RM1 .....63 G5
 SUN TW16 .....156 B2
 SURB KT6 .....172 C1
 WPK KT4 .....173 K2
Kingsmead Cl BFN/LL DA15 .155 C1
 HOR/WEW KT19 .....173 F6
 TEDD TW11 .....143 H5
Kingsmead Dr NTHLT UB5 .65 K6
Kingsmead Pde NTHLT UB5 * .65 K6
Kings Mead Pk
 ESH/CLAY KT10 .....170 E6
Kingsmead Rd
 BRXS/STRHM SW2 .....149 G1
Kings Mead Wy HOM E9 .75 G3
Kingsmere Cl PUT/ROE SW15 .127 G2
Kingsmere Pl
 STNW/STAM N16 .....55 K7
Kingsmere Rd
 WIM/MER SW19 .....146 B1
King's Ms BMSBY WC1N 11 M1
 CLAP SW4 * 129 K4
King's Quay WBPTN SW10 * .108 B7
Kings Reach EMB EC4Y * .12 B6
 WHALL SW1A 11 K9
Kings Ride Ga
 RCHPK/HAM TW10 .....125 H3
Kingsridge Gdns DART DA1 .139 H6
Kings Rd BAR EN5 .....26 A2
 CHEL SW3 .....108 C5
 EA W5 .....85 K4
 FELT TW13 .....122 B7
 MTCM CR4 .....163 F2
 RCHPK/HAM TW10 .....125 G5
 RYLN/HDSTN HA2 .....65 K1
 WDGN N22 .....41 F7
 WDR/YW UB7 .....100 C1
 WLSDN NW10 .....69 K6
King's Rd BARK IG11 .....78 C6
 CHEL SW3 .....15 L7
 FUL/PGN SW6 .....108 B6
 KUTN/CMB KT2 .....144 B6
 MORT/ESHN SW14 .....126 A2
 PLSTW E13 .....77 G7
 ROM RM1 .....63 H4
 SNWD SE25 .....165 H2
 SURB KT6 .....158 F7
 TEDD TW11 .....142 D4
 TOTM N17 .....42 B7
 TWK TW1 .....124 C5
 UED N18 * 42 C4
 WAN E11 .....58 C6
 WIM/MER SW19 .....146 E5
King's Scholars' Pas
 PIM SW1V * 16 E4
King Stairs Cl
 BERM/RHTH SE16 .....111 J1
King's Ter CAMTN NW1 .....4 E4
Kingsthorpe Rd SYD SE26 .151 F3
Kingston Av CHEAM SM3 .174 C2
 EBED/NFELT TW14 .....121 H5
Kingston By-Pass
 ESH/CLAY KT10 .....170 E2
 RYNPK SW20 .....160 D1
Kingston Cl CHDH RM6 .....62 A2
 NTHLT UB5 .....65 K6
 TEDD TW11 .....143 H5
Kingston Crs BECK BR3 .....151 H7
Kingston Gdns CROY/NA CR0 .176 C2
Kingston Ga KUTN/CMB KT2 .144 A6
Kingston Hall Rd KUT/HW KT1 .158 E2
Kingston Hl KUTN/CMB KT2 .144 C7
Kingston Hill Av CHDH RM6 .62 A2
Kingston Hill Pl
 KUTN/CMB KT2 .....144 E3
Kingston House Est
 SURB KT6 * 158 C5
Kingston La TEDD TW11 .....143 G4
 WDR/YW UB7 .....100 C1
Kingston Ldg NWMAL KT3 * .160 B3
Kingston Pl
 KTN/HRWW/WS HA3 .....35 F6
Kingston Rd BRYLDS KT5 .172 D1
 EBAR EN4 .....27 H4
 ED N9 .....42 C1
 HOR/WEW KT19 .....173 F3
 IL IG1 .....78 C3
 KUT/HW KT1 .....159 J2
 NWDGN UB2 .....102 E1
 NWMAL KT3 .....160 A3
 PUT/ROE SW15 .....126 E2
 ROM RM1 .....63 H3
 RYNPK SW20 .....161 G1
 TEDD TW11 .....143 H5
 WIM/MER SW19 .....146 B6
Kingston Sq NRWD SE19 .149 K4
Kingston V PUT/ROE SW15 .145 F3
Kingstown St CAMTN NW1 .....4 B3
King St CITYW EC2V 12 F5
 COVGDN WC2E 11 J6
 EFNCH N2 .....53 H2
 HMSMTH W6 .....106 D3
 NWDGN UB2 .....102 D2
 PLSTW E13 .....95 F4
 RCH/KEW TW9 .....124 E4
 TOTM N17 .....42 B7
 TWK TW1 .....124 B7
 WATW WD18 .....21 G4
 WHALL SW1A 10 F9
King Street Cloisters
 HMSMTH W6 * 106 E3
King Street Pde TWK TW1 * .124 B7
Kingswater Pl BTSEA SW11 * .108 D6
Kings Wy CROY/NA CR0 .....177 G4
 HRW HA1 .....48 E3
Kingsway HOL/ALD WC2B .11 L5
 HYS/HAR UB3 .....82 C7

 MORT/ESHN SW14 .....125 J2
 NFNCH/WDSPK N12 .....39 G5
 NWMAL KT3 .....161 H3
 PEND EN3 .....30 D4
 STMC/STPC BR5 .....169 J4
 STWL/WRAY TW19 .....120 A7
 WBLY HA9 .....68 B3
 WWKM BR4 .....180 C5
Kingsway Av SAND/SEL CR2 .178 C5
Kingsway Crs
 RYLN/HDSTN HA2 .....48 C3
Kingsway Pde
 STNW/STAM N16 * 73 K2
Kingsway Pl CLKNW EC1R * .6 B9
Kingsway Rd CHEAM SM3 .174 C6
Kingswear Rd KTTN NW5 .....72 B2
 RSLP HA4 .....64 E1
Kingswood Av BELV DA17 .117 G3
 HAYES BR2 .....167 H2
 HPTN TW12 .....142 B5
 HSLW TW3 .....122 E1
 KIL/WHAMP NW6 .....70 C1
 THHTH CR7 .....164 B4
Kingswood Cl ASHF TW15 .140 A3
 BAR EN5 .....27 G5
 EN EN1 .....30 A4
 NWMAL KT3 .....160 C5
 STMC/STPC BR5 .....169 J6
 SURB KT6 .....159 F6
 VX/NE SW8 .....109 K6
Kingswood Dr BELMT SM2 .175 F7
 CAR SM5 .....162 E7
 DUL SE21 .....150 A3
Kingswood Pk FNCH N3 .....52 D1
Kingswood Pl LEW SE13 .....133 H3
Kingswood Rd
 BRXS/STRHM SW2 .....129 K5
 CHSWK W4 .....105 K2
 GDMY/SEVK IG3 .....61 G7
 HAYES BR2 .....167 H2
 PGE/AN SE20 .....150 E5
 WBLY HA9 .....68 C2
 WIM/MER SW19 .....146 D7
Kingswood Ter CHSWK W4 * .105 K2
Kingsworth Cl BECK BR3 .166 B4
Kingsworthy Cl KUT/HW KT1 .159 G1
Kings Yd PUT/ROE SW15 * .127 G3
 SRTFD E15 * 75 J5
Kingthorpe Rd WLSDN NW10 .69 F6
Kingthorpe Ter
 WLSDN NW10 * 69 F6
Kingweston Cl CRICK NW2 .70 C2
King William La GNWCH SE10 .113 H4
King William St CANST EC4R .13 H7
King William Wk GNWCH SE10 .113 F5
Kingwood Rd FUL/PGN SW6 .107 H6
Kinlet Rd WOOL/PLUM SE18 .115 H6
Kinloch Dr CDALE/KGS NW9 .51 G3
Kinloch St HOLWY N7 .....73 F2
Kinloss Gdns FNCH N3 .....52 D2
Kinloss Rd CAR SM5 .....162 B6
Kinnaird Av BMLY BR1 .....152 D5
 CHSWK W4 .....105 K6
Kinnaird Cl BMLY BR1 .....152 D5
Kinnaird Wy WFD IG8 .....45 K5
Kinnear Rd SHB W12 .....106 C1
Kinnerton Pl North
 KTBR SW1X * 15 M2
Kinnerton Pl South
 KTBR SW1X * 15 M2
Kinnerton St KTBR SW1X .16 A2
Kinnerton Yd KTBR SW1X * .16 A2
Kinnoul Rd HMSMTH W6 .107 H5
Kinross Av WPK KT4 .....173 J1
Kinross Cl
 KTN/HRWW/WS HA3 .....50 B3
 SUN TW16 .....140 D4
Kinross Dr SUN TW16 .....140 D4
Kinross Ter WALTH E17 .....57 H1
Kinsale Rd PECK SE15 .....131 H2
Kinsella Gdns WIM/MER SW19 .145 H2
Kintyre Cl STRHM/NOR SW16 .164 A1
Kinveachy Gdns CHARL SE7 .114 D4
Kinver Rd SYD SE26 .....150 E3
Kipling Dr WIM/MER SW19 .147 H5
Kipling Est STHWK SE1 .....19 H2
Kipling Rd BXLYHN DA7 .....117 F7
Kipling St STHWK SE1 .....19 H2
Kipling Ter ED N9 * 41 K2
Kippington Dr ELTH/MOT SE9 .134 C7
Kirby Cl HOR/WEW KT19 .173 H4
 NTHWD HA6 .....32 D5
Kirby Est BERM/RHTH SE16 * .111 J2
Kirby Gv STHWK SE1 .....19 J1
Kirby St HCIRC EC1N 12 B2
Kirchen Rd WEA W13 .....85 H6
Kirkcaldy Gn OXHEY WD19 * .33 G2
Kirkdale SYD SE26 .....150 D1
Kirkdale Cnr SYD SE26 .....150 E3
Kirkdale Rd WAN E11 .....58 C7
Kirkfield Cl WEA W13 .....85 H6
Kirkham Rd EHAM E6 .....95 J5
Kirkham St WOOL/PLUM SE18 .115 K5
Kirkland Av CLAY IG5 .....60 A1
Kirkland Cl BFN/LL DA15 .135 K5
Kirkland Ter BECK BR3 .....151 J5
Kirkland Wk HACK E8 .....74 B5
Kirk La WOOL/PLUM SE18 .115 H6
Kirkleas Rd SURB KT6 .....159 F7
Kirklees Rd BCTR RM8 .....79 J4
 THHTH CR7 .....164 B4
Kirkley Rd WIM/MER SW19 .146 E7
Kirkly Cl SAND/SEL CR2 .178 A7
Kirkmichael Rd POP/IOD E14 .94 A5
Kirk Rd WALTH E17 .....57 H5
Kirkside Rd BKHTH/KID SE3 .113 K5
Kirkstall Av TOTM N17 .....55 K3
Kirkstall Gdns
 BRXS/STRHM SW2 .....129 K7
Kirkstall Rd BRXS/STRHM SW2 .129 K7
Kirkstead Ct CLPT E5 * 75 G2
Kirkstone Wy BMLY BR1 .152 C6
Kirkton Rd SEVS/STOTM N15 .56 A3
Kirkwall Pl BETH E2 * 92 E2
Kirkwood Rd PECK SE15 .....131 J1
Kirk Rd WEA W13 .....85 H6
Kirrane Cl NWMAL KT3 .....160 C4
Kirtley Rd SYD SE26 .....151 G3
Kirtling St VX/NE SW8 .....109 H6
Kirton Cl CHSWK W4 .....106 A3
Kirton Gdns BETH E2 .....7 L5
Kirton Ldg
 WAND/EARL SW18 * 128 A5
Kirton Rd PLSTW E13 .....95 G1
Kirton Wk EDGW HA8 .....36 E6
Kirwyn Wy CMBW SE5 .....110 D6
Kitcat Ter BOW E3 .....93 J2
Kitchener Rd EFNCH N2 .....53 J2
 FSTGT E7 .....77 F5

THHTH CR7 .... 164 E2
TOTM N17 .... 56 U1
WALTH E17 .... 43 K7
Kite Pl BETH E2 * 92 C2
Kite Yd BTSEA SW11 * 108 E7
Kitley Gdns NRWD SE19 .... 150 D7
Kitson Rd BARN SW13 .... 106 D7
CMBW SE5 .... 110 C6
Kittiwake Rd WBLY UB5 .... 83 H1
Kittiwake Wy YEAD UB4 .... 83 H4
Kitto Rd NWCR SE14 .... 132 K1
Kiver Rd ARCH N19 .... 72 D1
Kiwi Ter EHAM E6 .... 96 A2
Klea Av CLAP SW4 .... 129 H5
Knapdale Cl FSTH SE23 .... 150 D1
Knapmill Rd CAT SE6 .... 151 J1
Knapmill Wy CAT SE6 .... 151 J1
Knapp Cl WLSDN NW10 .... 69 G5
Knapp Rd BOW E3 .... 93 J3
Knapton Ms TOOT SW17 .... 148 A5
Knaresborough Dr
WAND/EARL SW18 .... 128 A7
Knaresborough Pl ECT SW5 .... 14 C5
Knatchbull Rd CMBW SE5 .... 130 C1
WLSDN NW10 .... 69 F7
Knebworth Av WALTH E17 .... 43 J7
Knebworth Pth BORE WD6 * 25 F3
Knebworth Rd
STNW/STAM N16 * 74 A3
Knee Hl ABYW SE2 .... 116 D4
Knee Hill Crs ABYW SE2 .... 116 D3
Kneller Gdns ISLW TW7 .... 123 J5
Kneller Rd BROCKY SE4 .... 132 B3
NWMAL KT3 .... 160 B6
WHTN TW2 .... 123 F5
Knevett Ter HSLW TW3 .... 123 F3
Knight Cl BCTR RM8 .... 79 J1
Knighten St WAP E1W * 92 D7
Knighthead Point
POP/IOD E14 * 112 D1
Knightland Rd CLPT E5 .... 74 D1
Knighton Cl ROMW/RG RM7 .... 63 F5
SAND/SEL CR2 .... 177 H7
WFD IG8 .... 45 F3
Knighton Dr WFD IG8 .... 45 F3
Knighton La BKHH IG9 .... 45 F1
Knighton Park Rd SYD SE26 .... 151 F4
Knighton Rd FSTGT E7 .... 76 E2
ROMW/RG RM7 .... 62 E5
Knightrider Ct BLKFR EC4V * 12 D5
Knightrider St BLKFR EC4V 12 E6
Knight's Av EA W5 .... 105 F1
Knightsbridge SKENS SW7 .... 15 K2
Knightsbridge Gdns
ROMW/RG RM7 .... 63 F4
Knightsbridge Gn
KTBR SW1X * 15 L2
Knights Chambers ED N9 * 42 C2
Knights Cl E/WMO/HCT KT8 .... 156 E4
Knights Hl WNWD SE27 .... 149 H4
Knight's Hill Sq WNWD SE27 .... 149 H3
Knights Manor Wy
DART DA1 .... 139 J5
Knight's Pk KUT/HW KT1 .... 159 F2
Knight's Pl WHTN TW2 .... 123 K7
Knights Rd CAN/RD E16 .... 94 E7
STAN HA7 .... 35 J3
Knights Wk LBTH SE11 .... 18 C6
Knightswood Cl EDGW HA8 .... 36 E1
Knightswood Rd RAIN RM13 .... 99 H1
Knightwood Crs
NWMAL KT3 .... 160 B5
Knivet Rd FUL/PGN SW6 .... 107 K5
Knockholt Rd ELTH/MOT SE9 .... 134 C4
Knole Cl CROY/NA CRO * 165 K5
Knole Rd DART DA1 .... 138 D6
The Knole ELTH/MOT SE9 .... 154 A3
Knoll Cl NTHLT UB5 .... 46 C1
Knoll Dr STHGT/OAK N14 .... 28 A6
Knollmead BRYLDS KT5 .... 159 K2
Knoll Rd BXLY DA5 .... 137 H6
SCUP DA14 .... 155 H4
WAND/EARL SW18 .... 128 A4
Knolls Cl WPK KT4 .... 173 K2
The Knoll BECK BR3 .... 151 K7
EA W5 .... 85 J4
HAYES BR2 .... 180 E1
PIN HA5 * 47 H1
Knollys Cl
STRHM/NOR SW16 * 149 H2
Knolly's Cl
STRHM/NOR SW16 .... 149 G2
Knolly's Rd
STRHM/NOR SW16 .... 149 G2
Knotley Wy WWKM BR4 .... 179 K1
Knottisford St BETH E2 .... 93 F2
Knotts Green Ms LEY E10 .... 57 K5
Knotts Green Rd LEY E10 .... 57 K5
Knowle Av BXLYHN DA7 .... 117 F6
Knowle Cl BRXN/ST SW9 .... 130 B2
Knowle Rd HAYES BR2 .... 181 J1
WHTN TW2 .... 123 K7
Knowles Hill Crs LEW SE13 .... 133 G4
Knowlton Gn HAYES BR2 .... 167 J4
Knowl Wy BORE WD6 .... 24 A4
Knowsley Av STHL UB1 .... 84 B7
Knowsley Rd BTSEA SW11 .... 128 E1
Knox Rd FSTGT E7 .... 76 E5
Knox St CAMTN NW1 .... 9 L2
Knoyle St NWCR SE14 .... 112 B5
Kohat Rd WIM/MER SW19 .... 147 F4
Koh-I-Noor Av BUSH WD23 .... 22 A5
Kossuth St GNWCH SE10 .... 113 H4
Kramer Ms ECT SW5 .... 14 B8
Kreedman Wk HACK E8 * 74 C4
Kuala Gdns
STRHM/NOR SW16 .... 149 F7
Kydbrook Cl
STMC/STPC BR5 .... 169 H6
Kylemore Cl EHAM E6 .... 95 H1
Kylemore Rd
KIL/WHAMP NW6 .... 2 A1
Kymberley Rd HRW HA1 * 48 E5
Kyme Rd ROM RM1 .... 63 H5
Kynance Gdns STAN HA7 .... 35 J7
Kynance Ms SKENS SW7 .... 14 C3
Kynance Pl KENS W8 .... 14 E4
Kynaston Av THHTH CR7 .... 164 D4
Kynaston Cl
KTN/HRWW/WS HA3 .... 34 D6
Kynaston Crs THHTH CR7 .... 164 D4
Kynaston Rd BMLY BR1 .... 152 E4
STNW/STAM N16 .... 74 A2
THHTH CR7 .... 164 D4
Kynaston Wd
KTN/HRWW/WS HA3 .... 34 D6
Kynersley Cl CAR SM5 .... 175 K2
Kynoch Rd UED N18 .... 42 E4
Kyrle Rd BTSEA SW11 .... 129 F5
Kyverdale Rd
STNW/STAM N16 .... 56 B6

L

Laburnham Cl BAR EN5 .... 26 D2
Laburnum Av DART DA1 .... 139 F7
ED N9 .... 42 A1
HCH RM12 .... 81 J1
SUT SM1 .... 175 J2
TOTM N17 .... 41 K6
Laburnum Cl ALP/SUD HA0 .... 68 C3
CHING E4 .... 43 H5
PECK SE15 .... 111 K6
Laburnum Ct STAN HA7 .... 35 J3
Laburnum Crs SUN TW16 .... 141 F7
Laburnum Gdns CROY/NA CRO 166 A7
Laburnum Gv
CDALE/KGS NW9 .... 50 E6
HSLW TW3 .... 122 E3
NWMAL KT3 .... 160 A1
RSLP HA4 .... 46 B5
STHL UB1 .... 83 K3
WCHMH N21 .... 41 J1
Laburnum Pl ELTH/MOT SE9 * 135 F4
Laburnum Rd HYS/HAR UB3 .... 101 J3
MTCM CR4 .... 163 F1
WIM/MER SW19 .... 147 G6
Laburnum St BETH E2 .... 7 L1
Laburnum Wy HAYES BR2 .... 169 H6
STWL/WRAY TW19 .... 120 C2
Lacebark Cl BFN/LL DA15 .... 136 A6
Lacewing Cl PLSTW E13 .... 94 E2
Lacey Cl ED N9 .... 42 C1
Lacey Dr BCTR RM8 .... 79 J2
EDGW HA8 .... 36 A3
HPTN TW12 .... 141 K7
Lacey Ms BOW E3 .... 93 J1
Lackington St SDTCH EC2A 13 H2
Lacock Cl WIM/MER SW19 .... 147 G5
Lacon Rd EDUL SE22 .... 131 H3
Lacrosse Wy
STRHM/NOR SW16 .... 148 D7
Lacy Rd PUT/ROE SW15 .... 127 G3
Ladas Rd WNWD SE27 .... 149 J4
Ladbroke Crs NTGHL W11 .... 88 C5
Ladbroke Gdns NTGHL W11 .... 88 D6
Ladbroke Gv NKENS W10 .... 88 B3
NTGHL W11 .... 88 C6
Ladbroke Ms NTGHL W11 .... 88 C7
Ladbroke Rd EN EN1 .... 30 B5
NTGHL W11 .... 88 D7
Ladbroke Sq NTGHL W11 .... 88 D6
Ladbroke Ter NTGHL W11 .... 88 D6
Ladbroke Wk NTGHL W11 .... 88 D7
Ladbrook Cl BMLY BR1 .... 152 E5
PIN HA5 .... 47 K4
Ladbrooke Crs SCUP DA14 .... 155 K2
Ladbrook Rd SNWD SE25 .... 164 E2
Ladderstile Ride
KUTN/CMB KT2 .... 144 D4
Ladderswood Wy
FBAR/BDGN N11 .... 40 C4
Lady Alesford Av STAN HA7 .... 35 H4
Lady Booth Rd KUT/HW KT1 .... 159 F1
Ladycroft Rd LEW SE13 .... 132 E2
Ladycroft Wk STAN HA7 .... 35 K7
Lady Forsdyke Wy
HOR/WEW KT19 .... 172 C7
Ladygate La RSLP HA4 .... 46 A3
Ladygrove CROY/NA CRO 179 G7
Lady Harewood Wy
HOR/WEW KT19 .... 172 C7
Lady Hay WPK KT4 .... 173 H1
Lady Margaret Rd KTTN NW5 .... 72 B4
STHL UB1 .... 83 K6
Ladymount WLGTN SM6 .... 176 D3
Lady's Cl WATW WD18 * 21 G3
Ladyship Ter EDUL SE22 * 131 J6
Ladysmith Av EHAM E6 .... 95 J1
GNTH/NBYPK IG2 .... 60 D5
Ladysmith Cl MLHL NW7 .... 37 J6
Ladysmith Rd CAN/RD E16 .... 94 D2
ELTH/MOT SE9 .... 135 F5
EN EN1 .... 30 B1
KTN/HRWW/WS HA3 .... 48 E1
TOTM N17 .... 56 C1
Lady Somerset Rd KTTN NW5 .... 72 B3
Ladywell Cl BROCKY SE4 .... 132 D4
Ladywell Rd LEW SE13 .... 132 D4
Ladywell St SRTFD E15 .... 76 D7
Ladywell Water Tower
BROCKY SE4 * 132 C2
Ladywood Av STMC/STPC BR5 .... 169 K4
Ladywood Rd SURB KT6 .... 172 C1
Lafone Av FELT TW13 .... 122 B7
Lafone St STHWK SE1 .... 19 L1
Lagado Ms BERM/RHTH SE16 .... 93 F7
Lagonda Wy DART DA1 .... 139 F3
Laidlaw Dr WCHMH N21 .... 29 F4
Laing Dean NTHLT UB5 .... 65 G7
Laings Av MTCM CR4 .... 162 E1
Lainlock Pl HSLW TW3 .... 103 G2
Lainson St WAND/EARL SW18 .... 127 K6
Lairdale Cl DUL SE21 .... 130 D7
Lairs Cl HOLWY N7 * 72 E5
Laitwood Rd BAL SW12 .... 129 G2
Lake Av BMLY BR1 .... 152 E5
Lake Cl BCTR RM8 .... 79 K2
Lakedale Rd
WOOL/PLUM SE18 .... 115 K4
Lake Dr BUSH WD23 .... 34 C1
Lakefield Rd WDGN N22 .... 55 H1
Lake Gdns DAGE RM10 .... 80 C4
RCHPK/HAM TW10 .... 143 H1
WLGTN SM6 .... 176 B2
Lakehall Gdns THHTH CR7 .... 164 C4
Lakehall Rd THHTH CR7 .... 164 C4
Lake House Rd WAN E11 .... 76 D2
Lakehurst Rd HOR/WEW KT19 .... 173 G4
Lakeland Cl
KTN/HRWW/WS HA3 .... 34 D5
Lakenheath STHGT/OAK N14 .... 28 D4
Lake Ri ROM RM1 .... 63 H2
Lake Rd CHDH RM6 .... 61 K3
CROY/NA CRO 179 H1
DAGW RM9 .... 98 D2
LEY E10 .... 57 K6
WIM/MER SW19 .... 146 D4
Lakeside BECK BR3 .... 166 E2
ENC/FH EN2 .... 28 D3
HOR/WEW KT19 .... 173 H5
WEA W13 .... 85 J5
WLGTN SM6 .... 176 B3
Lakeside Av REDBR IG4 .... 59 H3
THMD SE28 .... 97 G7
Lakeside Cl BFN/LL DA15 .... 136 D4
RSLP HA4 .... 46 B3
SNWD SE25 .... 165 H1
Lakeside Crs EBAR EN4 .... 27 K4
Lakeside Dr ESH/CLAY KT10 .... 170 C5
HAYES BR2 .... 181 J2
WLSDN NW10 .... 86 B2
Lakeside Rd PLMGR N13 .... 41 F3
WKENS W14 .... 107 G2
Lakeside Wy WBLY HA9 .... 68 C3
Lakes Rd HAYES BR2 .... 181 G4
Lakeswood Rd
STMC/STPC BR5 .... 169 G5
Lake Vw EDGW HA8 .... 36 B4
Lake View Est BOW E3 * 93 F1
Lakeview Rd WELL DA16 .... 136 C4
WNWD SE27 .... 149 G4
Lakis Cl HAMP NW3 .... 71 G3
Laleham Av MLHL NW7 .... 37 F2
Laleham Ct SUT SM1 * 175 G4
Laleham Rd CAT SE6 .... 133 F6
Lalor St FUL/PGN SW6 .... 127 H1
Lambarde Av ELTH/MOT SE9 .... 154 A3
Lamb Cl NTHLT UB5 .... 83 J2
Lamberhurst Rd BCTR RM8 .... 62 A7
WNWD SE27 .... 149 G3
Lambert Av RCH/KEW TW9 .... 125 H2
Lambert Ct BUSH WD23 .... 21 H3
Lambert Jones Ms
BARB EC2Y * 12 E2
Lambert Rd
BRXS/STRHM SW2 .... 129 K4
CAN/RD E16 .... 95 F5
NFNCH/WDSPK N12 .... 39 H4
Lambert's Pl CROY/NA CRO 164 E7
Lambert's Rd BRYLDS KT5 .... 159 F4
Lambert St IS N1 .... 6 A2
Lambert Wy
NFNCH/WDSPK N12 .... 39 G4
Lambeth Br WEST SW1P 17 K5
Lambeth High St STHWK SE1 .... 17 L6
Lambeth Hl BLKFR EC4V 12 E6
Lambeth Palace Rd
STHWK SE1 .... 17 L4
Lambeth Rd CROY/NA CRO 164 B7
STHWK SE1 .... 18 A4
Lambeth Wk LBTH SE11 .... 17 M5
PECK SE15 .... 131 G1
Lambkins Ms WALTH E17 .... 58 A3
Lamble St HAMP NW3 .... 71 K3
Lambley Rd DAGW RM9 .... 79 H5
Lambole Pl HAMP NW3 .... 71 J5
Lambole Rd HAMP NW3 .... 71 J5
Lambourn Cl HNWL W7 .... 104 A1
KTTN NW5 * 72 C3
SAND/SEL CR2 .... 177 H7
Lambourne Av
WIM/MER SW19 .... 146 D3
Lambourne Gdns BARK IG11 .... 79 F6
CHING E4 .... 43 J1
EN EN1 .... 30 B1
Lambourne Gv
BERM/RHTH SE16 .... 112 A4
KUT/HW KT1 .... 159 J1
Lambourne Pl BKHTH/KID SE3 .... 114 A1
GDMY/SEVK IG3 .... 78 E1
WAN E11 .... 58 A6
Lambourn Rd VX/NE SW8 .... 129 G2
Lambrook Ter FUL/PGN SW6 .... 107 H7
Lambs Cl ED N9 .... 42 C1
Lamb's Conduit Pas
FSBYW WC1X 11 L2
Lamb's Conduit St
BMSBY WC1N 11 L1
Lambscroft Av ELTH/MOT SE9 .... 153 G2
Lambs Meadow WFD IG8 .... 59 H1
Lambs Ms IS N1 .... 6 C4
Lambs Ter ED N9 * 41 K1
Lamb St WCHPL E1 .... 13 L2
Lambs Wk ENC/FH EN2 .... 29 J1
Lamb Wk STHWK SE1 .... 19 J2
Lambton Pl NTGHL W11 * 88 D6
Lambton Rd ARCH N19 .... 54 E7
RYNPK SW20 .... 146 A7
Lamerock Rd BMLY BR1 .... 152 D3
Lamerton Rd BARK/HLT IG6 .... 60 B1
Lamerton St DEPT SE8 .... 112 D5
Lamford Cl TOTM N17 .... 41 K6
Lamington St HMSMTH W6 .... 106 E3
Lamlash St LBTH SE11 .... 18 C5
Lammas Av MTCM CR4 .... 163 F1
Lammas La ESH/CLAY KT10 .... 170 A3
Lammas Park Gdns EA W5 .... 85 J7
Lammas Rd HOM E9 .... 75 G1
LEY E10 .... 57 F1
RCHPK/HAM TW10 .... 143 J3
WATW WD18 .... 21 G4
Lammermoor Rd BAL SW12 * 129 G6
Lamont Rd WBPTN SW10 .... 108 C5
Lamont Road Pas
WBPTN SW10 * 108 C5
Lamorbey Cl BFN/LL DA15 .... 155 F1
Lamorbey Pk BFN/LL DA15 * 136 C7
Lamorna Cl WALTH E17 .... 58 A1
Lamorna Gv STAN HA7 .... 35 K7
Lampard Gv STNW/STAM N16 .... 56 B7
Lampern Sq BETH E2 * 92 C2
Lampeter Sq HMSMTH W6 .... 107 H5
Lamplighter Cl WCHPL E1 .... 92 E3
Lampmead Rd LEE/GVPK SE12 .... 133 H4
Lamport Cl WOOL/PLUM SE18 .... 114 E3
Lampton Av HSLW TW3 .... 103 F7
Lampton House Cl
WIM/MER SW19 .... 146 B3
Lampton Park Rd HSLW TW3 .... 123 G1
Lampton Rd HSLW TW3 .... 123 G2
Lamson Rd RAIN RM13 .... 99 H3
Lanacre Av CDALE/KGS NW9 .... 37 H7
EDGW HA8 .... 37 F7
Lanadron Cl ISLW TW7 .... 124 A1
Lanark Cl EA W5 .... 85 J4
Lanark Pl MV/WKIL W9 .... 2 F9
Lanark Rd MV/WKIL W9 .... 2 F7
Lanbury Rd PECK SE15 .... 132 A3
Lancashire Ct
MYFR/PKLN W1K 10 C6
Lancaster Av BARK IG11 .... 78 E6
MTCM CR4 .... 163 K4
WAN E11 .... 59 F3
WIM/MER SW19 .... 146 B4
WNWD SE27 .... 149 H1
Lancaster Cl CDALE/KGS NW9 .... 37 H7
HAYES BR2 .... 167 J4
IS N1 .... 7 K2
STWL/WRAY TW19 .... 120 B3
TOTM N17 * 42 C6
WPK KT4 .... 160 E7
Lancaster Dr HAMP NW3 .... 71 J5
HCH RM12 .... 81 K4
POP/IOD E14 .... 94 A7
Lancaster Gdns KUTN/CMB KT2 .... 143 K4
Lancaster Gdn
WIM/MER SW19 .... 146 C4
Lancaster Ga BAY/PAD W2 .... 8 E7
Lancaster Gv HAMP NW3 .... 71 J5
Lancaster House
WOOL/PLUM SE18 * 114 D6
Lancaster Ms BAY/PAD W2 .... 8 E6
RCHPK/HAM TW10 .... 125 F5
WAND/EARL SW18 .... 128 A4
Lancaster Pk
RCHPK/HAM TW10 .... 125 F4
Lancaster Pl TPL/STR WC2R * 11 L6
TWK TW1 .... 124 B5
WIM/MER SW19 .... 146 B4
Lancaster Rd EBAR EN4 .... 27 H3
FBAR/BDGN N11 .... 40 D5
FSBYPK N4 .... 55 G6
FSTGT E7 .... 76 E6
NKENS W10 .... 88 B5
NTHLT UB5 .... 66 C5
RYLN/HDSTN HA2 .... 48 A4
SNWD SE25 .... 165 G1
STHL UB1 .... 83 J6
UED N18 .... 42 B4
WALTH E17 .... 57 F1
WAN E11 .... 76 C1
WIM/MER SW19 .... 146 B4
WLSDN NW10 .... 69 H4
Lancaster Stables
HAMP NW3 * 71 J5
Lancaster St STHWK SE1 .... 18 C2
Lancaster Ter BAY/PAD W2 .... 9 G6
Lancaster Wy WPK KT4 .... 161 F6
Lancaster West NTGHL W11 * 88 C5
Lancastrian Rd WLGTN SM6 .... 176 E6
Lancefield St NKENS W10 .... 88 D2
Lancell St STNW/STAM N16 .... 74 A1
Lancelot Av ALP/SUD HA0 .... 67 K3
Lancelot Crs ALP/SUD HA0 .... 67 K3
Lancelot Gdns EBAR EN4 .... 28 A6
Lancelot Pde ALP/SUD HA0 * 68 A4
Lancelot Pl SKENS SW7 .... 15 L2
Lancelot Rd ALP/SUD HA0 .... 67 K3
WELL DA16 .... 136 B3
Lance Rd HRW HA1 .... 48 C6
Lancer Sq KENS W8 .... 14 C1
Lancey Cl CHARL SE7 .... 114 C3
Lanchester Rd HGT N6 .... 53 K4
Lanchester Wy NWCR SE14 .... 111 K7
Lancing Gdns ED N9 .... 30 B7
Lancing Rd CROY/NA CRO 164 A5
FELT TW13 .... 140 D1
GNTH/NBYPK IG2 .... 60 D5
WEA W13 .... 85 H6
Lancing St CAMTN NW1 .... 5 G7
Landale Gdns DART DA1 .... 139 F7
Landau Ter HAYES BR2 .... 181 J3
Landau Wy ERITH DA8 .... 119 G4
Landcroft Rd EDUL SE22 .... 131 G5
Landells Rd EDUL SE22 .... 131 G5
Landford Rd PUT/ROE SW15 .... 127 F2
Landgrove Rd
WIM/MER SW19 .... 146 E4
Landleys Flds HOLWY N7 * 72 D4
Landmann Wy NWCR SE14 .... 112 A5
Landon Pl KTBR SW1X 15 L3
Landons Cl POP/IOD E14 .... 94 A7
Landor Rd BRXN/ST SW9 .... 129 K2
Landor Wk SHB W12 .... 106 D1
Landra Gdns WCHMH N21 .... 29 H5
Landridge Rd FUL/PGN SW6 .... 127 H1
Landrock Rd CEND/HSY/T N8 .... 54 E5
Landscape Rd WFD IG8 .... 45 F6
Landseer Av MNPK E12 .... 78 A4
Landseer Cl EDGW HA8 .... 50 C1
EMPK RM11 .... 63 K7
WIM/MER SW19 .... 147 G7
Landseer Rd ARCH N19 .... 72 E2
EN EN1 .... 30 C4
NWMAL KT3 .... 160 A6
SUT SM1 .... 174 E5
Land's End BORE WD6 .... 23 J4
Landstead Rd
WOOL/PLUM SE18 .... 115 J6
Lane Ap MLHL NW7 * 38 C4
Lane Cl CRICK NW2 .... 69 K2
Lane End BXLYHN DA7 .... 137 J2
Lane Gdns BUSH WD23 .... 22 E7
ESH/CLAY KT10 .... 171 F6
Lane Ms MNPK E12 .... 78 A3
Lanercost Gdns
STHGT/OAK N14 .... 28 E5
Lanercost Rd
BRXS/STRHM SW2 .... 149 G1
Laneside CHST BR7 .... 154 B4
EDGW HA8 .... 36 E4
Laneside Av BCTR RM8 .... 62 B6
The Lane BKHTH/KID SE3 .... 133 K2
STJWD NW8 .... 2 E6
Laneway PUT/ROE SW15 .... 126 E4
Lanfranc Rd BOW E3 .... 93 G1
Lanfrey Pl WKENS W14 .... 107 J4
Langbourne Av HGT N6 .... 72 A1
Langbourne Wy
ESH/CLAY KT10 .... 171 F5
Langbrook Rd BKHTH/KID SE3 .... 134 C2
Langcroft Cl CAR SM5 .... 175 K2
Langdale Av MTCM CR4 .... 162 E2
Langdale Cl BCTR RM8 .... 61 J7
MORT/ESHN SW14 .... 125 J3
WALW SE17 .... 18 E9
Langdale Crs BXLYHN DA7 .... 117 H7
Langdale Dr YEAD UB4 .... 82 C1
Langdale Gdns HCH RM12 .... 81 J4
Langdale Pde MTCM CR4 * 162 E1
Langdale Rd GNWCH SE10 .... 113 F6
THHTH CR7 .... 164 B3
Langdale St WCHPL E1 * 92 D5
Langdale Ter BORE WD6 * 25 F2
Langdon Cr WLSDN NW10 .... 69 G7
Langdon Crs EHAM E6 .... 96 A1
Langdon Dr CDALE/KGS NW9 .... 50 E7
Langdon House
WOOL/PLUM SE18 * 114 D6
Langdon Pk TEDD TW11 .... 143 J6
Langdon Park Rd HGT N6 .... 54 B6
Langdon Pl MORT/ESHN SW14 .... 125 K2
Langdon Rd EHAM E6 .... 78 A7
HAYES BR2 .... 168 A2
MRDN SM4 .... 162 B4
Langdon Shaw SCUP DA14 .... 155 F4
Langdon Wk MRDN SM4 .... 162 B4
Langdon Wy STHWK SE1 * 111 H3
Langford Cl HACK E8 .... 74 C4
SEVS/STOTM N15 .... 56 A5
STJWD NW8 .... 2 F5
Langford Crs EBAR EN4 .... 27 K3
Langford Gn CMBW SE5 .... 131 F2
Langford Pl SCUP DA14 .... 155 G2
STJWD NW8 .... 2 F6
Langford Rd EBAR EN4 .... 27 K3
FUL/PGN SW6 .... 128 A1
WFD IG8 .... 45 G5
Langfords BKHH IG9 .... 45 J1
Langfords Wy CROY/NA CRO 179 G7
Langham Ct RSLP HA4 * 65 F4
Langham Dr GDMY/SEVK IG3 .... 61 H5
Langham Gdns ALP/SUD HA0 .... 67 J3
EDGW HA8 .... 36 E6
RCHPK/HAM TW10 .... 143 H3
WCHMH N21 .... 29 G4
WEA W13 .... 85 H6
Langham House Cl
RCHPK/HAM TW10 .... 143 K3
Langham Pde
SEVS/STOTM N15 * 55 J2
Langham Park Pl HAYES BR2 .... 167 J1
Langham Pl CHSWK W4 .... 106 B5
REGST W1B 10 D3
SEVS/STOTM N15 .... 55 J2
Langham Rd EDGW HA8 .... 36 E6
RYNPK SW20 .... 146 A7
SEVS/STOTM N15 .... 55 J2
TEDD TW11 .... 143 H4
Langham St GTPST W1W 10 E3
REGST W1B 10 D3
Langhedge Cl UED N18 .... 42 B5
Langhedge La UED N18 .... 42 B4
Langholm Cl BAL SW12 .... 129 J6
Langholme BUSH WD23 .... 22 C7
Langhorn Dr WHTN TW2 .... 123 K6
Langhorne Rd DAGE RM10 .... 80 C6
Langland Ct NTHWD HA6 .... 32 A6
Langland Crs STAN HA7 .... 49 K1
Langland Dr PIN HA5 .... 33 J6
Langland Gdns CROY/NA CRO 179 H1
HAMP NW3 .... 71 F4
Langler Rd WLSDN NW10 .... 88 A1
Langley Av RSLP HA4 .... 65 F1
SURB KT6 .... 158 E7
WPK KT4 .... 174 B1
Langley Ct BECK BR3 * 166 E3
COVGDN WC2E 11 J6
Langley Crs DAGW RM9 .... 79 J6
EDGW HA8 .... 36 E2
HYS/HAR UB3 .... 101 J5
WAN E11 .... 59 F6
Langley Dr ACT W3 .... 105 J2
WAN E11 .... 59 F5
Langley Gdns DAGW RM9 .... 79 K6
STMC/STPC BR5 .... 169 G5
Langley Gv NWMAL KT3 .... 160 A1
Langley La VX/NE SW8 .... 17 K9
Langley Pk MLHL NW7 .... 37 G5
Langley Park Rd BELMT SM2 .... 175 G5
Langley Pl WPK KT4 .... 174 B1
Langley Rd BECK BR3 .... 166 B3
ISLW TW7 .... 124 A1
SAND/SEL CR2 .... 179 F7
SURB KT6 .... 159 F6
WELL DA16 .... 116 D5
WIM/MER SW19 .... 146 D7
Langley St LSQ/SEVD WC2H 11 J5
Langley Wy WWKM BR4 .... 167 G7
Langley Wd BECK BR3 * 167 F5
Langmead Dr BUSH WD23 .... 22 D7
Langmead St WNWD SE27 .... 149 H3
Langport Ct WOT/HER KT12 .... 156 B7
Langridge Ms HPTN TW12 .... 141 K5
Langroyd Rd TOOT SW17 .... 147 K1
Langside Av PUT/ROE SW15 .... 126 C3
Langside Crs STHGT/OAK N14 .... 40 D2
Langstone Wy MLHL NW7 .... 38 B6
Langston Hughes Cl
HNHL SE24 * 130 C3
Lang St WCHPL E1 .... 92 E3
Langthorn Ct LOTH EC2R * 13 H4
Langthorne Rd WAN E11 .... 76 B2
Langthorne St FUL/PGN SW6 .... 107 G6
Langton Av EHAM E6 .... 96 A2
TRDG/WHET N20 .... 27 G6
Langton Cl FSBYW WC1X 5 M8
Langton Gv NTHWD HA6 .... 32 A4
Langton Ri EDUL SE22 .... 131 F3
Langton Rd BRXN/ST SW9 .... 110 C6
CRICK NW2 .... 70 A2
E/WMO/HCT KT8 .... 157 H4
KTN/HRWW/WS HA3 .... 34 C6
Langton St WBPTN SW10 .... 108 B5
Langton Wy BKHTH/KID SE3 .... 113 K6
CROY/NA CRO 178 A3
NTHLT UB5 .... 83 H1
Langtry Wk STJWD NW8 .... 2 F2
Langwood Cha TEDD TW11 .... 143 J5
Langworth Dr YEAD UB4 .... 83 F5
Lanhill Rd MV/WKIL W9 .... 2 A9
Lanier Rd LEW SE13 .... 133 F5
Lanigan Dr HSLW TW3 .... 123 G4
Lankaster Gdns EFNCH N2 .... 39 H7
Lankers Dr RYLN/HDSTN HA2 .... 47 K5
Lankton Cl BECK BR3 .... 152 A7
Lannock Rd HYS/HAR UB3 .... 82 D7
Lannoy Rd ELTH/MOT SE9 .... 135 H7
Lanrick Rd POP/IOD E14 .... 94 B4
Lanridge Rd ABYW SE2 .... 116 E2
Lansbury Av BARK IG11 .... 79 G6
CHDH RM6 .... 62 A4
EBED/NFELT TW14 .... 122 A5
UED N18 .... 41 K4
Lansbury Cl WLSDN NW10 .... 68 E4
Lansbury Crs DART DA1 .... 139 K4
Lansbury Dr YEAD UB4 .... 82 D2
Lansbury Gdns POP/IOD E14 * 94 B5
Lanscombe Wk VX/NE SW8 * 109 K6
Lansdell Rd MTCM CR4 .... 163 F1
Lansdown Cl WOT/HER KT12 .... 156 B7
Lansdowne Av BXLYHN DA7 .... 116 D6
ORP BR6 .... 169 G7
Lansdowne Cl BRYLDS KT5 .... 172 C1
TWK TW1 .... 124 A7
Lansdowne Copse WPK KT4 * 173 J1
Lansdowne Ct WPK KT4 .... 173 J1
Lansdowne Crs NTGHL W11 .... 88 C6
Lansdowne Dr HACK E8 .... 74 D5
Lansdowne Gdns VX/NE SW8 .... 109 K7
Lansdowne Gn VX/NE SW8 .... 109 K6
Lansdowne Gv WLSDN NW10 .... 69 G3
Lansdowne Hl WNWD SE27 .... 149 H2
Lansdowne La CHARL SE7 .... 114 C4
Lansdowne Ms CHARL SE7 .... 114 C4
NTGHL W11 .... 88 D7
Lansdowne Ms WBPTN SW10 .... 88 D7
STHWK SE1 .... 18 E3
Lansdowne Ri NTGHL W11 .... 88 C6
Lansdowne Rd BMLY BR1 .... 152 E6
CHING E4 .... 31 J7
CROY/NA CRO 164 D7
FNCH N3 .... 38 D6
GDMY/SEVK IG3 .... 78 E1
HACK E8 .... 74 C5
HOR/WEW KT19 .... 172 E6
HSLW TW3 .... 123 G2
MUSWH N10 .... 54 B1
NTGHL W11 .... 88 C6
RYNPK SW20 .... 146 A6

STAN HA7 ... 35 J5
SWFD E18 ... 58 E2
TOTM N17 ... 42 C7
WALTH E17 ... 57 J5
WAN E11 ... 76 D1
Lansdowne Ter BMSBY WC1N * ... 11 K1
Lansdowne Wk NTGHL W11 ... 88 C7
Lansdowne Wy VX/NE SW8 ... 109 K7
Lansdowne Wood Cl
WNWD SE27 ... 149 H2
Lansdown Rd FSTGT E7 ... 77 G6
SCUP DA14 ... 155 H2
Lansfield Av UED N18 ... 42 C3
Lantern Cl ALP/SUD HA0 ... 67 K4
PUT/ROE SW15 ... 126 D3
Lanterns Ct POP/IOD E14 ... 112 D2
Lantern Wy WDR/YW UB7 ... 100 B1
Lant St STHWK SE1 ... 18 E1
Lanvanor Rd PECK SE15 ... 131 K1
Lapford Cl MV/WKIL W9 * ... 88 D3
Lapse Wood Wk FSTH SE23 ... 131 J7
Lapstone Gdns
KTN/HRWW/WS HA3 ... 49 J5
Lapwing Cl ERITH DA8 * ... 118 E6
Lapwing Ter FSTGT E7 ... 77 H4
Lapwing Wy YEAD UB4 ... 83 H5
Lapworth Ct BAY/PAD W2 * ... 8 D2
Lara Cl CHSGTN KT9 ... 172 A6
LEW SE13 ... 133 F5
Larbert Rd STRHM/NOR SW16 ... 148 C7
Larch Av ACT W3 ... 87 G7
Larch Cl BAL SW12 ... 148 B1
DEPT SE8 ... 112 C5
FBAR/BDGN N11 ... 40 A4
PLSTW E13 ... 95 G3
Larch Crs HOR/WEW KT19 ... 172 D5
YEAD UB4 ... 83 G3
Larch Dr CHSWK W4 * ... 105 H4
Larches Av MORT/ESHN SW14 ... 126 A3
The Larches BUSH WD23 ... 21 J4
PLMGR N13 ... 41 J3
Larch Gv NFNCH/WDSPK N12 ... 39 F4
Larch Rd CRICK NW2 ... 70 A3
DART DA1 ... 139 G7
LEY E10 ... 75 J1
Larch Tree Wy CROY/NA CR0 ... 179 J2
Larch Wy HAYES BR2 ... 169 F6
Larchwood Rd
ELTH/MOT SE9 ... 154 D1
Larcombe Cl CROY/NA CR0 ... 178 B3
Larcom St WALW SE17 ... 18 F6
Larden Rd ACT W3 ... 106 B1
Largewood Av SURB KT6 ... 172 C1
Larken Cl BUSH WD23 ... 22 C7
Larken Dr BUSH WD23 ... 22 C7
Larkfield Av
KTN/HRWW/WS HA3 ... 49 H2
Larkfield Rd RCH/KEW TW9 ... 125 F3
SCUP DA14 ... 155 F2
Larkhall La CLAP SW4 ... 129 J1
Larkhall Ri CLAP SW4 ... 129 H2
Larkham Cl FELT TW13 ... 140 C2
Larkhill Ter
WOOL/PLUM SE18 * ... 115 F6
Lark Rw BETH E2 ... 74 E7
Larkshall Crs CHING E4 ... 44 A3
Larkshall Rd CHING E4 ... 44 A4
Larkspur Cl CDALE/KGS NW9 ... 50 D4
TOTM N17 ... 41 K6
Larkspur Gv EDGW HA8 ... 36 E3
Larkswood Cl ERITH DA8 ... 118 D7
Larkswood Ri PIN HA5 ... 47 G3
Larkswood Rd CHING E4 ... 43 J3
Lark Wy CAR SM5 ... 162 D6
Larkway Cl CDALE/KGS NW9 ... 51 F3
Larnach Rd HMSMTH W6 ... 107 G5
Larne Rd RSLP HA4 ... 46 D6
Larner Rd ERITH DA8 ... 118 B6
Larpent Av PUT/ROE SW15 ... 127 F4
Larwood Cl GFD/PVL UB6 ... 66 D4
Lascelles Av HRW HA1 ... 48 D6
Lascelles Cl WAN E11 ... 76 B1
Lascott's Rd WDGN N22 ... 41 F5
Lassa Rd ELTH/MOT SE9 ... 134 D4
Lassell St GNWCH SE10 ... 113 G4
Lasseter Pl BKHTH/KID SE3 ... 113 H5
Latchett Rd SWFD E18 ... 45 F7
Latchingdon Gdns WFD IG8 ... 45 J5
Latchmere Cl
RCHPK/HAM TW10 ... 144 A4
Latchmere La KUTN/CMB KT2 ... 144 B5
Latchmere Rd BTSEA SW11 ... 128 E1
KUTN/CMB KT2 ... 144 A5
Latchmere St BTSEA SW11 ... 128 E1
Lateward Rd BTFD TW8 ... 104 E5
Latham Cl EHAM E6 ... 95 J5
TWK TW1 ... 124 A6
Latham Rd BXLYHS DA6 ... 137 H4
Latham's Wy CROY/NA CR0 ... 164 A7
Lathkill Cl EN EN1 ... 30 C6
Lathom Rd EHAM E6 ... 77 K6
Latimer Av EHAM E6 ... 77 K7
Latimer Cl PIN HA5 ... 33 G7
WATW WD18 ... 20 C6
WPK KT4 ... 173 K3
Latimer Gdns PIN HA5 ... 33 G7
Latimer Pl NKENS W10 ... 88 A4
Latimer Rd ED N9 ... 42 C1
BAR EN5 ... 27 F2
CROY/NA CR0 * ... 177 H2
FSTGT E7 ... 77 F3
NKENS W10 ... 88 A4
SEVS/STOTM N15 ... 56 A5
TEDD TW11 ... 143 F4
WIM/MER SW19 ... 147 F5
Latona Rd PECK SE15 ... 111 H5
Lattimer Pl CHSWK W4 ... 106 B6
Latton Cl ESH/CLAY KT10 ... 170 B3
WOT/HER KT12 ... 156 E6
Latymer Gdns FNCH N3 * ... 52 C1
Latymer Rd ED N9 ... 42 B1
Latymer Wy ED N9 ... 41 K1
Laubin Cl TWK TW1 ... 124 C3
Lauder Cl NTHLT UB5 ... 83 H1
Lauderdale Dr
RCHPK/HAM TW10 ... 143 K2
Lauderdale Pde
MV/WKIL W9 * ... 2 C8
Lauderdale Pl BARB EC2Y * ... 12 E3
Lauderdale Rd MV/WKIL W9 * ... 2 D8
Laud St CROY/NA CR0 ... 177 J2
LBTH SE11 ... 17 L7
Laughton Rd NTHLT UB5 ... 83 H1
Launcelot Rd BMLY BR1 ... 152 E3
Launceston Gdns
GFD/PVL UB6 ... 67 J7
Launceston Pl KENS W8 ... 14 E3
Launceston Rd GFD/PVL UB6 ... 67 J7
Launch St POP/IOD E14 ... 113 F2
Launders Ga ACT W3 * ... 105 J1

Laundress La
STNW/STAM N16 ... 74 C2
Laundry Ms FSTH SE23 ... 132 A6
Laundry Rd HMSMTH W6 ... 107 H5
Laura Cl EN EN1 ... 30 A4
WAN E11 ... 59 G4
Lauradale Rd EFNCH N2 ... 53 K3
Laura Pl CLPT E5 ... 74 E3
Laura Ter FSBYPK N4 * ... 73 H1
Laurel Av TWK TW1 ... 124 A7
Laurel Bank
NFNCH/WDSPK N12 * ... 39 G3
Laurel Bank Gdns
FUL/PGN SW6 ... 127 J1
Laurel Cl BFN/LL DA15 ... 155 G2
DART DA1 ... 139 F7
OXHEY WD19 ... 21 H6
TOOT SW17 ... 147 J4
Laurel Crs CROY/NA CR0 ... 179 J2
ROMW/RG RM7 ... 63 G7
Laurel Dr WCHMH N21 ... 29 G6
Laurel Gdns BMLY BR1 ... 168 D3
CHING E4 ... 31 K6
HNWL W7 ... 84 E7
HSLWW TW4 ... 122 D3
MLHL NW7 ... 37 F2
Laurel Gv PGE/AN SE20 ... 150 D6
SYD SE26 ... 151 F4
Laurel La WDR/YW UB7 ... 100 B3
Laurel Pk KTN/HRWW/WS HA3 ... 35 F6
Laurel Rd BARN SW13 ... 126 D1
HPTN TW12 ... 142 D4
RYNPK SW20 ... 145 K7
The Laurels BRXN/ST SW9 * ... 110 C6
BUSH WD23 * ... 34 E1
Laurel St HACK E8 ... 74 B5
Laurel Vw NFNCH/WDSPK N12 ... 39 F2
Laurel Vls HNWL W7 * ... 103 K1
Laurel Wy SWFD E18 ... 58 D5
TRDG/WHET N20 ... 38 E2
Laurence Ms SHB W12 ... 106 D1
Laurence Pountney HI
CANST EC4R ... 13 G6
Laurence Pountney La
CANST EC4R ... 13 G6
Laurie Gv NWCR SE14 ... 112 B7
Laurie Rd HNWL W7 ... 84 E4
Laurier Rd CROY/NA CR0 ... 165 G6
KTTN NW5 ... 72 B2
Laurimel Cl STAN HA7 ... 35 H5
Laurino Pl BUSH WD23 ... 34 C1
Lauriston Rd HOM E9 ... 75 F6
WIM/MER SW19 ... 146 B5
Lausanne Rd CEND/HSY/T N8 ... 55 G3
PECK SE15 ... 111 K7
Lavell St STNW/STAM N16 ... 74 A2
Lavender Av CDALE/KGS NW9 ... 50 E7
MTCM CR4 ... 147 J7
WPK KT4 ... 174 A2
Lavender Cl CAR SM5 ... 176 A3
CHEL SW3 ... 108 C5
HAYES BR2 ... 168 D5
Lavender Ct E/WMO/HCT KT8 ... 157 G2
Lavender Gdns BTSEA SW11 ... 128 E3
KTN/HRWW/WS HA3 ... 34 E5
Lavender Gv HACK E8 ... 74 C7
MTCM CR4 ... 147 J7
Lavender Hl BTSEA SW11 ... 128 E2
ENC/FH EN2 ... 29 G1
Lavender Pl IL IG1 ... 78 B4
Lavender Ri WDR/YW UB7 ... 100 D1
Lavender Rd BERM/RHTH SE16 ... 93 G7
BTSEA SW11 ... 128 C2
CROY/NA CR0 ... 164 A5
HOR/WEW KT19 ... 172 D4
SUT SM1 ... 175 H3
WLGTN SM6 ... 176 D4
Lavender Sweep BTSEA SW11 ... 128 E3
Lavender Ter BTSEA SW11 * ... 128 D2
Lavender V WLGTN SM6 ... 176 D5
Lavender Wk BTSEA SW11 ... 128 E3
Lavender Wy CROY/NA CR0 ... 166 A5
Lavengro Rd WNWD SE27 ... 149 J1
Lavenham Rd
WAND/EARL SW18 ... 146 D1
Lavernock Rd BXLYHN DA7 ... 137 H1
Lavers Rd STNW/STAM N16 ... 74 A2
Laverstoke Gdns
PUT/ROE SW15 ... 126 C6
Laverton Ms ECT SW5 * ... 14 C6
Laverton Pl ECT SW5 ... 14 C6
Lavidge Rd ELTH/MOT SE9 ... 153 J1
Lavina Gv IS N1 ... 5 L2
Lavington Cl HOM E9 ... 75 H5
Lavington Rd CROY/NA CR0 ... 177 F2
WEA W13 ... 85 H7
Lavington St STHWK SE1 ... 12 D9
Lavinia Rd DART DA1 ... 139 J5
Lawdon Gdns CROY/NA CR0 ... 177 H3
Lawford Gdns DART DA1 ... 139 F4
Lawford Rd CHSWK W4 ... 105 K6
IS N1 ... 7 J2
KTTN NW5 ... 72 C5
Lawless St POP/IOD E14 ... 93 K6
Lawley St CLPT E5 ... 74 E3
Lawn Cl BMLY BR1 ... 153 F6
EN EN1 ... 30 B6
NWMAL KT3 ... 160 B1
RSLP HA4 ... 64 B1
Lawn Crs RCH/KEW TW9 ... 125 H1
Lawn Farm Gv CHDH RM6 ... 62 A3
Lawn Gdns HNWL W7 ... 84 E7
Lawn House Cl POP/IOD E14 ... 113 F1
Lawn La VX/NE SW8 ... 17 K9
Lawn Rd BECK BR3 ... 151 H6
HAMP NW3 ... 71 K4
Lawns Ct WBLY HA9 * ... 68 C1
The Lawns BELMT SM2 ... 174 E6
BKHTH/KID SE3 * ... 133 J2
CHING E4 ... 43 J4
NRWD SE19 ... 149 K7
PIN HA5 ... 48 B6
SCUP DA14 ... 155 H3
Lawnswood BAR EN5 * ... 26 C4
Lawn Ter BKHTH/KID SE3 ... 133 H2
The Lawn NWDGN UB2 ... 103 F4
Lawn V PIN HA5 ... 47 J1
Lawrence Av MLHL NW7 ... 37 G4
MNPK E12 ... 78 A3
NWMAL KT3 ... 160 A5
PLMGR N13 ... 41 H3
WALTH E17 ... 57 F1
WLSDN NW10 ... 69 F7
Lawrence Blds
STNW/STAM N16 ... 74 B2
Lawrence Campe Cl
TRDG/WHET N20 ... 39 H2
Lawrence Cl SEVS/STOTM N15 ... 56 A2
SHB W12 ... 87 K6
Lawrence Ct MLHL NW7 ... 37 G4
OXHEY WD19 * ... 33 H1
Lawrence Crs DAGE RM10 ... 80 D2

EDGW HA8 ... 50 C1
Lawrence Dr HGDN/ICK UB10 ... 64 A3
Lawrence Gdns MLHL NW7 ... 37 H2
Lawrence Hl CHING E4 ... 43 J1
Lawrence Hill Gdns DART DA1 ... 139 F5
Lawrence Hill Rd DART DA1 ... 139 F5
Lawrence La CITYW EC2V * ... 12 F5
Lawrence Pde ISLW TW7 * ... 124 C2
Lawrence Pl IS N1 ... 5 K3
Lawrence Rd EA W5 ... 104 D3
EHAM E6 ... 77 J7
ERITH DA8 ... 117 J6
GPK RM2 ... 63 K4
HPTN TW12 ... 141 K6
HSLWW TW4 ... 122 B3
PIN HA5 ... 47 H4
PLSTW E13 ... 77 F7
RCHPK/HAM TW10 ... 143 H3
SEVS/STOTM N15 ... 56 A3
SNWD SE25 ... 165 G3
UED N18 ... 42 D3
WWKM BR4 ... 180 E3
YEAD UB4 ... 82 A1
Lawrence St CAN/RD E16 ... 94 D4
CHEL SW3 ... 108 D5
MLHL NW7 ... 37 H3
Lawrence Wy WLSDN NW10 ... 68 E2
Lawrence Yd
SEVS/STOTM N15 ... 56 A3
Lawrie Park Av SYD SE26 ... 150 D4
Lawrie Park Crs SYD SE26 ... 150 D4
Lawrie Park Gdns SYD SE26 ... 150 D4
Lawrie Park Rd SYD SE26 ... 150 E5
Laws Cl SNWD SE25 ... 164 E3
Lawson Cl CAN/RD E16 ... 95 G4
IL IG1 ... 78 D4
WIM/MER SW19 ... 146 B2
Lawson Gdns DART DA1 ... 139 G4
PIN HA5 ... 46 E3
Lawson Rd DART DA1 ... 139 G3
STHL UB1 ... 83 K3
WOOL/PLUM SE18 ... 114 E2
Lawton Rd BOW E3 ... 93 G2
EBAR EN4 ... 27 H2
LEY E10 ... 58 A7
Laxcon Cl WLSDN NW10 ... 69 F4
Laxley Cl CMBW SE5 ... 110 C6
Laxton Pl CAMTN NW1 ... 4 D9
Layard Rd BERM/RHTH SE16 ... 111 J3
THHTH CR7 ... 164 E1
Layard Sq BERM/RHTH SE16 ... 111 J3
Laycock St IS N1 ... 73 G5
Layer Gdns ACT W3 ... 86 C6
Layfield Cl HDN NW4 ... 51 K6
Layfield Crs HDN NW4 ... 51 K6
Layfield Rd HDN NW4 ... 51 K6
Layhams Rd WWKM BR4 ... 180 C3
Laymarsh Cl BELV DA17 ... 117 G2
Laymead Cl NTHLT UB5 ... 65 J5
Laystall St FSBYW WC1X ... 12 A1
Layton Crs CROY/NA CR0 ... 177 G4
Layton Pl RCH/KEW TW9 ... 105 H7
Layton Rd BTFD TW8 ... 104 E4
HSLW TW3 ... 123 G3
Layzell Wk ELTH/MOT SE9 ... 134 C7
Lazenby Ct COVGDN WC2E * ... 11 J6
Leabank Cl HRW HA1 ... 66 E2
Leabank Sq HOM E9 ... 75 J5
Leabank Vw SEVS/STOTM N15 ... 56 C5
Leabourne Rd
STNW/STAM N16 ... 56 C5
Lea Bridge Rd LEY E10 ... 75 F1
WALTH E17 ... 58 A4
Lea Cl BUSH WD23 ... 22 B4
WHTN TW2 ... 122 E7
Lea Cots MTCM CR4 * ... 163 F1
Lea Crs RSLP HA4 ... 64 D3
Leacroft Av BAL SW12 ... 128 E6
Leacroft Cl WCHMH N21 ... 41 H1
Leadale Av CHING E4 ... 43 J1
Leadale Rd STNW/STAM N16 ... 56 C5
leadbeaters Cl
FBAR/BDGN N11 ... 39 K4
Leadenhall Pl BANK EC3V ... 13 J5
Leadenhall St BANK EC3V ... 13 J5
Leader Av MNPK E12 ... 78 A4
The Leadings WBLY HA9 ... 68 E2
Leaf Cl NTHWD HA6 ... 32 B6
Leaf Gv WNWD SE27 ... 149 G4
Leafield Cl STRHM/NOR SW16 ... 149 H5
Leafield Rd RYNPK SW20 ... 161 J2
SUT SM1 ... 174 E1
Leafy Gv HAYES BR2 ... 181 G4
Leafy Oak Rd LEE/GVPK SE12 ... 153 G3
Leafy Wy CROY/NA CR0 ... 178 B1
Lea Gdns WBLY HA9 ... 68 A4
Leagrave St CLPT E5 ... 74 E2
Lea Hall Gdns LEY E10 * ... 57 J7
Lea Hall Rd LEY E10 ... 57 J7
Leahurst Rd LEW SE13 ... 133 G4
Leake St STHWK SE1 ... 17 M1
Lealand Rd SEVS/STOTM N15 ... 56 B5
Leaming Cl MNPK E12 ... 77 J4
Leamington Av BMLY BR1 ... 153 G3
MRDN SM4 ... 161 J3
WALTH E17 ... 57 J4
Leamington Cl BMLY BR1 ... 153 G3
HSLW TW3 ... 123 H4
Leamington Crs
RYLN/HDSTN HA2 ... 65 J2
Leamington Gdns
GDMY/SEVK IG3 ... 79 F1
Leamington Pk ACT W3 ... 87 F4
Leamington Pl YEAD UB4 ... 82 D3
Leamington Road Vls
NTGHL W11 ... 88 D4
Leamore St HMSMTH W6 ... 106 E3
Leamouth Rd EHAM E6 ... 95 J5
POP/IOD E14 ... 94 B5
Leander Rd BRXS/STRHM SW2 ... 130 A5
NTHLT UB5 ... 84 A1
THHTH CR7 ... 164 A3
Learner Dr RYLN/HDSTN HA2 ... 66 A1
Lea Rd BECK BR3 ... 166 D1
ENC/FH EN2 ... 29 J1
NWDGN UB2 ... 102 D3
Learoyd Gdns EHAM E6 ... 96 A6
Leas Cl CHSGTN KT9 ... 172 B6
Leas Dl ELTH/MOT SE9 ... 154 A4
Leas Gn CHST BR7 ... 155 F5
Leaside Av MUSWH N10 ... 54 A2
Leaside Rd CLPT E5 ... 56 E7
Leasowes Rd LEY E10 ... 57 J7
The Leas BUSH WD23 ... 21 K1
Leathart Cl HCH RM12 ... 81 K6
Leatherbottle Gn
ERITHM DA18 ... 117 G2
Leather Cl MTCM CR4 ... 163 F1
Leatherdale St WCHPL E1 * ... 93 F3
Leather Gdns SRTFD E15 ... 76 C7
Leatherhead Cl
STNW/STAM N16 ... 56 A7

Leatherhead Rd CHSGTN KT9 ... 171 K6
Leather La HCIRC EC1N ... 12 A2
Leathermarket Ct STHWK SE1 ... 19 J2
Leathermarket St STHWK SE1 ... 19 J2
Leather Rd
BERM/RHTH SE16 * ... 112 A3
Leathersellers Cl BAR EN5 * ... 26 C2
Leather St WAP E1W ... 93 F6
Leathsale Rd
RYLN/HDSTN HA2 ... 66 B2
Leathwaite Rd BTSEA SW11 ... 128 E3
Leathwell Rd DEPT SE8 ... 132 E1
Lea V DART DA1 ... 138 A3
Lea Valley Rd CHING E4 ... 31 H5
Lea Valley Wk CLPT E5 ... 56 D6
UED N18 ... 43 F3
Leaveland Cl BECK BR3 ... 166 D3
Leaver Gdns GFD/PVL UB6 ... 84 D1
Leavesden Rd STAN HA7 ... 35 G5
Leaway CLPT E5 ... 56 E7
Lebanon Av FELT TW13 ... 141 H4
Lebanon Gdns
WAND/EARL SW18 ... 127 K5
Lebanon Pk TWK TW1 ... 124 C6
Lebanon Rd CROY/NA CR0 ... 165 F7
WAND/EARL SW18 ... 127 K4
Lebrun Sq BKHTH/KID SE3 ... 134 A3
Lechmere Ap WFD IG8 ... 59 G1
Lechmere Rd CRICK NW2 ... 69 K5
Leckford Rd
WAND/EARL SW18 ... 147 G1
Leckhampton Pl
BRXS/STRHM SW2 ... 130 B6
Leckwith Av ABYW SE2 ... 117 F5
Lecky St SKENS SW7 ... 15 G7
Leconfield Av BARN SW13 ... 126 C2
Leconfield Rd HBRY N5 ... 73 K3
Leda Rd WOOL/PLUM SE18 ... 114 E2
Ledbury Ms North
NTGHL W11 ... 8 A6
Ledbury Ms West NTGHL W11 ... 8 A6
Ledbury Rd CROY/NA CR0 ... 177 J3
NTGHL W11 ... 88 D5
Ledbury St PECK SE15 ... 111 H6
Ledrington Rd NRWD SE19 ... 150 B5
Ledway Dr WBLY HA9 ... 50 B6
Lee Av CHDH RM6 ... 62 A5
Lee Church St LEW SE13 ... 133 H3
Lee Cl WALTH E17 ... 43 F7
Lee Conservancy Rd HOM E9 ... 75 H4
Leecroft Rd BAR EN5 ... 26 C4
Leeds Rd IL IG1 ... 60 D7
Leeds St UED N18 ... 42 C4
Lee High Rd LEW SE13 ... 133 G3
Leeke St FSBYW WC1X ... 5 L7
Leeland Rd WEA W13 ... 85 G7
Leeland Ter WEA W13 ... 85 G7
Leeland Wy WLSDN NW10 ... 69 G3
Leemount Cl HDN NW4 * ... 52 B3
Lee Pk BKHTH/KID SE3 ... 133 J3
Lee Park Wy ED N9 ... 43 H4
UED N18 ... 43 H4
Lee Rd BKHTH/KID SE3 ... 133 J2
EN EN1 ... 30 C5
GFD/PVL UB6 ... 67 J7
MLHL NW7 ... 38 B6
WIM/MER SW19 ... 147 F7
Lees Av NTHWD HA6 ... 32 D7
Leeside BAR EN5 ... 26 C4
Leeside Crs GLDGN NW11 ... 52 C5
Leeside Rd TOTM N17 ... 42 E5
Leeson Rd HNHL SE24 * ... 130 B4
Leesons Hl CHST BR7 ... 169 K2
Leeward Gdns
WIM/MER SW19 ... 146 C5
Leeway DEPT SE8 ... 112 C4
Leeway Cl PIN HA5 ... 33 K6
The Leeways CHEAM SM3 * ... 174 C5
Leewood Cl LEE/GVPK SE12 ... 133 J5
Lefevre Wk BOW E3 ... 75 H7
Leffern Rd SHB W12 ... 106 D1
Lefroy Rd SHB W12 ... 106 C1
Left Side STHGT/OAK N14 * ... 28 D7
Legard Rd HBRY N5 ... 73 H2
Legatt Rd ELTH/MOT SE9 ... 134 C4
Leggatt Rd SRTFD E15 ... 94 A1
Legge St LEW SE13 ... 133 F4
Leghorn Rd WLSDN NW10 ... 87 J1
WOOL/PLUM SE18 ... 115 J4
Legion Cl IS N1 ... 6 B1
Legion Ct MRDN SM4 ... 161 K5
Legion Ter BOW E3 ... 75 J7
Legion Wy
NFNCH/WDSPK N12 ... 39 J6
Legon Av ROMW/RG RM7 ... 62 E7
legrace Av HSLWW TW4 ... 122 C1
Leicester Av MTCM CR4 ... 163 K3
Leicester Cl WPK KT4 ... 174 A3
Leicester Gdns
GDMY/SEVK IG3 ... 60 E6
Leicester Pl LSO/SEVD WC2H * ... 11 H6
Leicester Rd BAR EN5 ... 27 F4
CROY/NA CR0 ... 165 F6
EFNCH N2 ... 53 J2
WAN E11 ... 59 F4
WLSDN NW10 ... 69 F6
Leicester Sq LSO/SEVD WC2H * ... 11 H7
Leigham Av
STRHM/NOR SW16 ... 148 E2
Leigham Cl STRHM/NOR SW16 ... 149 G2
Leigham Court Rd
STRHM/NOR SW16 ... 149 F2
Leigham Dr ISLW TW7 ... 103 K6
Leigham Hall Pde
STRHM/NOR SW16 * ... 148 E2
Leigham V STRHM/NOR SW16 ... 149 G2
Leigh Cl NWMAL KT3 ... 160 A3
Leigh Ct BORE WD6 * ... 25 F1
RYLN/HDSTN HA2 * ... 48 E7
Leigh Crs CROY/NA CR0 ... 179 K6
Leigh Gdns WLSDN NW10 ... 88 A1
Leigh Hunt Dr
STHGT/OAK N14 ... 28 D7
Leigh Orchard Cl
STRHM/NOR SW16 ... 149 G2
Leigh Pl FELT TW13 ... 122 B7
WELL DA16 ... 136 B1
Leigh Rd EHAM E6 ... 78 A6
HBRY N5 ... 73 H3
HSLW TW3 ... 123 J3
LEY E10 ... 58 A6
Leigh Rodd OXHEY WD19 ... 33 J2
Leigh St STPAN WC1H ... 5 J8
The Leigh KUTN/CMB KT2 ... 145 G7

Leighton Av MNPK E12 ... 78 A4
PIN HA5 ... 47 J2
Leighton Cl EDGW HA8 ... 50 C1
Leighton Crs KTTN NW5 ... 72 C4
Leighton Gdns WLSDN NW10 ... 87 K1
Leighton Gv KTTN NW5 ... 72 C4
Leighton Pl KTTN NW5 ... 72 C4
Leighton Rd EN EN1 ... 30 B4
KTN/HRWW/WS HA3 ... 48 D1
KTTN NW5 ... 72 C4
WEA W13 ... 104 B1
Leighton St CROY/NA CR0 ... 164 C7
Leila Parnell Pl CHARL SE7 ... 114 B5
Leinster Av MORT/ESHN SW14 ... 125 K2
Leinster Gdns BAY/PAD W2 ... 8 E7
Leinster Ms BAY/PAD W2 ... 8 E7
Leinster Pl BAY/PAD W2 ... 8 E7
Leinster Rd MUSWH N10 ... 54 B3
Leinster Sq BAY/PAD W2 ... 8 B5
Leinster Ter BAY/PAD W2 ... 8 E6
Leisure Wy
NFNCH/WDSPK N12 ... 39 H6
Leith Cl CDALE/KGS NW9 ... 51 F1
Leithcote Gdns
STRHM/NOR SW16 ... 149 F3
Leithcote Pth
STRHM/NOR SW16 ... 149 F2
Leith Hl STMC/STPC BR5 ... 155 G7
Leith Rd WDGN N22 ... 41 H7
Leith Towers BELMT SM2 * ... 175 F6
Leith Yd KIL/WHAMP NW6 * ... 2 B3
Lela Av HSLWW TW4 ... 122 A1
Lelitia Cl HACK E8 ... 74 C7
Leman St WCHPL E1 ... 13 M5
Le May Av LEE/GVPK SE12 ... 153 F2
Lemark Cl STAN HA7 ... 35 J5
Lemmon Rd GNWCH SE10 ... 113 H5
Lemna Rd WAN E11 ... 58 C6
Lemonwell Dr ELTH/MOT SE9 ... 135 G4
Lemsford Cl SEVS/STOTM N15 ... 56 C5
Lemsford Ct BORE WD6 ... 24 E4
FSBYPK N4 ... 42 E1
Lena Crs ED N9 ... 42 E1
Lena Gdns HMSMTH W6 ... 107 F2
Lena Kennedy Cl CHING E4 ... 44 A5
Lendal Ter CLAP SW4 ... 129 J2
Lenelby Rd SURB KT6 ... 159 H7
Len Freeman Pl FUL/PGN SW6 ... 107 J5
Lenham Rd BXLYHN DA7 ... 117 G5
LEE/GVPK SE12 ... 133 J3
SUT SM1 ... 175 F3
THHTH CR7 ... 164 E1
Lennard Av WWKM BR4 ... 180 C1
Lennard Cl WWKM BR4 ... 180 C1
Lennard Rd CROY/NA CR0 ... 164 D7
HAYES BR2 ... 168 E7
PGE/AN SE20 ... 151 F5
SYD SE26 ... 150 E5
Lennard Ter PGE/AN SE20 * ... 151 F5
Lennon Rd CRICK NW2 ... 70 A4
Lennox Cl ROM RM1 ... 63 H5
Lennox Gdns CROY/NA CR0 ... 177 H3
IL IG1 ... 59 K7
WLSDN NW10 ... 69 H3
Lennox Gardens Ms
KTBR SW1X ... 15 L4
Lennox Rd FSBYPK N4 ... 73 F1
WALTH E17 ... 57 H5
Lenor Cl BXLYHS DA6 ... 137 F3
Lensbury Wy ABYW SE2 ... 116 E2
Lens Rd FSTGT E7 ... 77 G6
Lenthall Rd HACK E8 ... 7 M1
Lenthorp Rd GNWCH SE10 ... 113 J3
Lentmead Rd BMLY BR1 ... 152 D2
Lenton Ri RCH/KEW TW9 ... 125 F2
Lenton St WOOL/PLUM SE18 ... 115 J3
Lenton Ter FSBYPK N4 * ... 73 G1
Leof Crs CAT SE6 ... 151 K4
Leominster Rd MRDN SM4 ... 162 B5
Leominster Wk MRDN SM4 ... 162 B5
Leonard Av MRDN SM4 ... 162 B4
ROMW/RG RM7 ... 63 F7
Leonard Crs KENS W8 * ... 14 A3
Leonard Pl HAYES BR2 * ... 181 J2
STNW/STAM N16 ... 74 A3
Leonard Rd CHING E4 ... 43 J5
ED N9 ... 42 B2
FSTGT E7 ... 76 E3
NWDGN UB2 ... 102 C2
STRHM/NOR SW16 ... 148 C7
Leonard St CAN/RD E16 ... 95 J7
SDTCH EC2A ... 7 H9
Leonora Tyson Ms DUL SE21 ... 149 K1
Leontine Cl PECK SE15 ... 111 H6
Leopold Av WIM/MER SW19 ... 146 D4
Leopold Ms HOM E9 ... 74 E7
Leopold Rd EA W5 ... 86 B7
EFNCH N2 ... 53 H2
UED N18 ... 42 D4
WALTH E17 ... 57 J4
WIM/MER SW19 ... 146 D3
WLSDN NW10 ... 69 G6
Leopold St BOW E3 ... 93 H4
Leo St PECK SE15 ... 111 J6
Leppoc Rd CLAP SW4 ... 129 J4
Leroy St STHWK SE1 ... 19 J5
Lerry Cl WKENS W14 ... 107 J5
Lescombe Cl FSTH SE23 ... 151 G2
Lescombe Rd FSTH SE23 ... 151 G2
Lesley Cl BXLY DA5 ... 137 J6
Leslie Gdns BELMT SM2 ... 174 E6
Leslie Gv CROY/NA CR0 ... 165 F7
Leslie Grove Pl CROY/NA CR0 * ... 165 F7
Leslie Park Rd CROY/NA CR0 ... 165 F7
Leslie Rd CAN/RD E16 ... 95 F5
EFNCH N2 ... 53 H2
WAN E11 ... 76 B3
Lesney Pk ERITH DA8 ... 118 A5
Lesney Park Rd ERITH DA8 ... 118 A5
Lessar Av CLAP SW4 ... 129 H4
Lessingham Av TOOT SW17 ... 147 K3
IL IG5 ... 60 B3
Lessing St FSTH SE23 ... 132 B6
Lessington Av ROMW/RG RM7 ... 62 E5
Lessness Av BXLYHN DA7 ... 116 E6
Lessness Pk BELV DA17 ... 117 G4
Lessness Rd MRDN SM4 ... 162 B5
Lester Av SRTFD E15 ... 94 C3
Lestock Cl SNWD SE25 ... 165 H2
Leston Cl RAIN RM13 ... 99 K2
Leswin Pl STNW/STAM N16 ... 74 B2
Leswin Rd STNW/STAM N16 ... 74 B2
Letchford Gdns WLSDN NW10 ... 87 J2
Letchford Ms WLSDN NW10 * ... 87 J2
Letchford Ter
KTN/HRWW/WS HA3 * ... 34 B7
Letchworth Av
EBED/NFELT TW14 ... 121 J6
Letchworth Cl HAYES BR2 ... 167 K4
OXHEY WD19 ... 33 H4
Letchworth Dr HAYES BR2 ... 167 K4
Letchworth St TOOT SW17 ... 147 K3
Letterstone Rd FUL/PGN SW6 ... 107 J6
Lettice St FUL/PGN SW6 ... 127 J1

Lett Rd BRXN/ST SW9....110 A7
  SRTFD E15....76 B6
Leucha Rd WALTH E17....57 G4
Levana Cl WIM/MER SW19....127 K1
Levehurst Wy CLAP SW4....129 K1
Levendale Rd FSTH SE23....151 G1
Leven Cl OXHEY WD19 *....33 H4
Leven Rd POP/IOD E14....94 A4
Leven Wy HYS/HAR UB3....82 C5
Leverett St CHEL SW3....15 G5
Leverholme Gdns
  ELTH/MOT SE9....154 A3
Leverson St
  STRHM/NOR SW16....148 C5
Leverton Pl KTTN NW5....72 C4
Leverton St KTTN NW5....72 C4
Levett Gdns GDMY/SEVK IG3....79 F3
Levett Rd BARK IG11....78 E5
Levine Gdns BARK IG11....97 K1
Lewes Cl NTHLT UB5....66 A5
Lewesdon Cl WIM/MER SW19....127 G7
Lewes Rd BMLY BR1....168 C1
  NFNCH/WDSPK N12....39 J4
Leweston Pl STNW/STAM N16....56 B6
Lewgars Av CDALE/KGS NW9....50 E5
Lewing Cl ORP BR6....169 K7
Lewin Rd BXLYHS DA6....137 F3
  MORT/ESHN SW14....126 A2
  STRHM/NOR SW16....148 D5
Lewin Ter EBED/NFELT TW14....121 F7
Lewis Av WALTH E17....43 J7
Lewis Cl STHGT/OAK N14....28 C6
Lewis Crs WLSDN NW10....69 F4
Lewis Gdns EFNCH N2....53 H1
  SEVS/STOTM N15....56 B6
Lewis Gv LEW SE13....133 F3
Lewisham High St LEW SE13....132 E4
Lewisham Hi LEW SE13....133 F1
Lewisham Pk LEW SE13....132 E5
Lewisham Rd LEW SE13....133 F1
Lewisham Wy BROCKY SE4....132 C4
Lewis Pl HACK E8....74 C4
Lewis Rd MTCM CR4....162 D1
  RCH/KEW TW9 *....124 E4
  SCUP DA14....155 J2
  STHL UB1....102 D1
  SUT SM1....175 F3
  WELL DA16....136 D2
Lewis St CAMTN NW1....4 D1
Lewiston Cl WPK KT4....160 E6
Lewis Wy DAGE RM10....80 D5
Lexden Dr CHDH RM6....61 H5
Lexden Rd ACT W3....86 D6
  MTCM CR4....163 J3
Lexham Gdns KENS W8....14 B5
Lexham Ms KENS W8....14 A6
Lexington Cl BORE WD6....24 B2
Lexington Pl KUT/HW KT1....143 K7
Lexington St SOHO/CST W1F....10 F5
Lexington Wy BAR EN5....26 B3
Lexton Gdns BAL SW12....129 J7
Leyborne Av WEA W13....104 D1
Leyborne Pk RCH/KEW TW9....105 H7
Leybourne Av HAYES BR2....167 K4
Leybourne Rd CAMTN NW1 *....4 D2
  CDALE/KGS NW9....50 C4
  HGDN/ICK UB10....64 A7
  WAN E11....58 D7
Leybourne St CAMTN NW1 *....4 C2
Leyburn Cl WALTH E17....58 A3
Leyburn Gdns CROY/NA CR0....178 A1
Leyburn Gv UED E18....42 C1
Leyburn House CHARL SE7 *....114 D6
Leyburn Rd UED N18....42 C1
Leycroft Gdns ERITH DA8....118 E7
Leyden St WCHPL E1....13 L3
Leyes Rd CAN/RD E16....95 H6
Leyfield WPK KT4....173 G1
Leyland Av PEND EN3....31 G1
Leyland Gdns WFD IG8....45 G4
Leyland Rd LEE/GVPK SE12....133 J4
Leylang Rd NWCR SE14....112 A6
Leys Av DAGE RM10....80 E6
Leys Cl DAGE RM10....80 E6
  HRW HA1....48 D3
Leysdown Av BXLYHN DA7....137 K3
Leysdown Rd ELTH/MOT SE9....153 J1
Leysfield Rd SHB W12....106 D1
Leys Gdns EBAR EN4....28 A4
Leyspring Rd WAN E11....58 D7
The Leys EFNCH N2....53 G3
  KTN/HRWW/WS HA3....50 B5
Ley St IL IG1....78 B1
Leyswood Dr
  GNTH/NBYPK IG2....60 E4
Leythe Rd ACT W3....105 K1
Leyton Gra LEY E10....75 J1
Leyton Green Rd LEY E10....58 A5
Leyton Park Rd LEY E10....76 A1
Leyton Rd SRTFD E15....76 B5
  WIM/MER SW19....147 G6
Leytonstone Rd SRTFD E15....76 C5
Leywick St SRTFD E15....94 C1
Liardet St NWCR SE14....112 B5
Liberia Rd HBRY N5....73 H5
Liberty Av WIM/MER SW19....147 H7
Liberty Cl UED N18....42 B3
  WPK KT4....161 F7
Liberty Ms WDGN N22....41 H7
Liberty St BRXN/ST SW9....110 A7
Libra Rd BOW E3....75 H7
  PLSTW E13....76 E1
Library Pde WLSDN NW10 *....69 G7
Library St STHWK SE1....18 D2
Library Wy WHTN TW2....123 H6
Lichfield Cl EBAR EN4....27 K2
Lichfield Gdns
  RCH/KEW TW9 *....125 F4
Lichfield Gv FNCH N3....38 E7
Lichfield Rd BCTR RM8....79 H5
  BOW E3....93 G2
  CRICK NW2....70 C3
  ED N9....30 C7
  EHAM E6....95 H2
  HSLWW TW4....122 B2
  NTHWD HA6....46 D2
  RCH/KEW TW9....105 F7
  WFD IG8....44 C4
Lidbury Rd MLHL NW7....38 D5
Lidcote Gdns BRXN/ST SW9 *....130 B1
Liddall Wy WDR/YW UB7....100 C1
Liddell Cl KTN/HRWW/WS HA3....49 K4
Liddell Gdns WLSDN NW10....69 J1
Liddell Rd KIL/WHAMP NW6....70 E5
Lidding Rd
  KTN/HRWW/WS HA3....49 K4
Liddington Rd SRTFD E15....76 D7
Liddon Rd BMLY BR1....168 B2
  PLSTW E13....95 F2
Liden Cl LEY E10....57 H6
Lidfield Rd STNW/STAM N16....73 K3

Lidgate Rd CMBW SE5 *....111 G6
Lidgould Gv RSLP HA4....46 E5
Lidiard Rd WAND/EARL SW18....147 G1
Lidlington Pl CAMTN NW1....4 F6
Lido Sq TOTM N17....55 K1
Lidyard Rd ARCH N19....54 C7
Liffler Rd WOOL/PLUM SE18....115 K4
Lifford St PUT/ROE SW15....127 G3
Lightcliffe Rd PLMGR N13....41 G3
Lighterman Ms WCHPL E1....93 F5
Lighterman's Rd POP/IOD E14....112 D1
Lightfoot Rd CEND/HSY/T N8....54 E4
Lightley Cl ALP/SUD HA0....68 B7
Ligonier St BETH E2....7 L9
Lilac Cl CHING E4....43 H5
Lilac Gdns CROY/NA CR0....179 J2
  EA W5....104 E2
  HYS/HAR UB3....82 C5
  ROMW/RG RM7....63 G7
Lilac Pl LBTH SE11....17 L6
Lilac St SHB W12....87 J6
Lilah Ms HAYES BR2....167 H1
Lilburne Gdns ELTH/MOT SE9....134 D4
Lilburne Rd ELTH/MOT SE9....134 D4
Lile Crs HNWL W7....84 E4
Lilestone St STJWD NW8....3 J9
Liliord St CMBW SE5....130 C1
Lilian Barker Cl
  LEE/GVPK SE12....133 K4
Lilian Board Wy GFD/PVL UB6....66 D4
Lilian Gdns WFD IG8....45 F7
Lilian Rd STRHM/NOR SW16....148 B7
Lillechurch Rd BCTR RM8....79 H5
Lilleshall Rd MRDN SM4....162 C4
Lilley Cl WAP E1W *....92 C7
Lilley La MLHL NW7 *....37 G4
Lillian Av ACT W3....105 H1
Lillian Rd BARN SW13....106 D5
Lillie Rd FUL/PGN SW6....107 G5
Lilleshall Rd CLAP SW4....129 G2
Lillie Yd FUL/PGN SW6....14 A9
Lillington Gardens Est
  PIM SW1V....16 F6
Lilliput Av NTHLT UB5....65 J7
Lilliput Rd ROMW/RG RM7....63 F6
Lily Cl WKENS W14....107 H3
Lily Dr WDR/YW UB7....100 A3
Lily Pl FARR EC1M....12 B2
Lily Rd WALTH E17....57 J5
Lilyville Rd FUL/PGN SW6....107 J7
Lime Cl BKHH IG9....45 H1
  BMLY BR1....168 D3
  KTN/HRWW/WS HA3....49 G1
  OXHEY WD19....27 J1
  PIN HA5....46 D2
  ROMW/RG RM7....62 E3
  WAP E1W....92 C7
Lime Crs SUN TW16....156 B1
Limecroft Cl HOR/WEW KT19....173 F6
Limedene Cl PIN HA5....33 H7
Lime Gv BFN/LL DA15....136 A5
  CHING E4....43 H5
  HYS/HAR UB3....82 B6
  NWMAL KT3....160 A2
  RSLP HA4....47 F5
  SHB W12....107 F1
  TRDG/WHET N20....26 C7
  TWK TW1....124 A5
The Limes Av FBAR/BDGN N11....40 B4
Limes Cl CAR SM5....175 K1
  FBAR/BDGN N11 *....40 C4
Limesdale Gdns EDGW HA8....50 E1
Limes Field Rd
  MORT/ESHN SW14....126 B2
Limesford Rd PECK SE15....132 A3
Limes Gdns WAND/EARL SW18....127 K5
Limes Gv LEW SE13....133 F3
Limes Rd BECK BR3....166 E1
  CROY/NA CR0....164 E5
The Limes CMBW SE5 *....131 F2
  PUR RM19....119 K4
  WAND/EARL SW18 *....127 K5
Limestone Wk ERITH DA18....116 E1
Lime St FENCHST EC3M....13 J6
  WALTH E17....57 G3
Lime Street Pas BANK EC3V *....13 J5
Limes Wk EA W5....104 E1
  PECK SE15....131 K3
Lime Tree Av ESH/CLAY KT10....157 J7
Limetree Cl BRXS/STRHM SW2....130 A7
Lime Tree Ct PIN HA5 *....34 A6
Lime Tree Gv CROY/NA CR0....179 H2
Limetree Pl MTCM CR4....148 B7
Lime Tree Rd HEST TW5....103 G7
Lime Tree Ter CAT SE6 *....132 C7
Lime Tree Wk BUSH WD23....22 E7
  WWKM BR4....180 D5
Lime Wk SRTFD E15 *....76 C7
Limewood Cl BECK BR3....167 F4
  WALTH E17....57 H3
  WEA W13....85 H5
Limewood Rd ERITH DA8....117 K6
Limpsfield Av THHTH CR7....164 A4
  WIM/MER SW19....146 A1
Linacre Cl PECK SE15....131 J2
Linacre Rd CRICK NW2....69 K5
Linchmere Rd LEE/GVPK SE12....133 J6
Lincoln Av RYLN/HDSTN HA2....47 K6
  STHGT/OAK N14....40 C3
  WHTN TW2....142 C1
  WIM/MER SW19....146 B1
Lincoln Cl ERITH DA8....118 C1
  GFD/PVL UB6....66 C2
  RYLN/HDSTN HA2....47 K6
Lincoln Dr OXHEY WD19....33 G2
Lincoln Est BOW E3....93 J3

Lincoln Fld BUSH WD23....21 K2
Lincoln Gdns IL IG1....59 J6
Lincoln Ms KIL/WHAMP NW6....70 D7
  SEVS/STOTM N15....55 J3
Lincoln Pde EFNCH N2 *....53 J2
Lincoln Rd ALP/SUD HA0....67 K5
  EFNCH N2....53 J2
  EN EN1....30 A3
  ERITH DA8....138 C1
  FELT TW13....141 K2
  FSTGT E7....77 H5
  MTCM CR4....163 K4
  NTHWD HA6....46 D2
  NWMAL KT3....159 K2
  PEND EN3....30 D4
  PLSTW E13....95 F3
  RYLN/HDSTN HA2....47 K4
  SCUP DA14....155 H4
  SNWD SE25....165 J2
  SWFD E18....59 F2
  WPK KT4....160 D7
Lincoln's Inn Flds LINN WC2A....11 L4
The Lincolns MLHL NW7....37 H2
Lincoln St CHEL SW3....15 L6
  WAN E11....76 C1
Lincoln Ter BELMT SM2 *....174 E6
  SUN TW16....140 C7
Lincombe Rd BMLY BR1....152 D2
Lindal Crs ENC/FH EN2....28 E4
Lindales The TOTM N17....42 B5
Lindal Rd BROCKY SE4....132 C4
Lindbergh Rd WLGTN SM6....176 E7
Linden Av DART DA1....139 F7
  HSLW TW3....123 G4
  RSLP HA4....46 E7
  THHTH CR7....164 C3
  WBLY HA9....68 B4
  WLSDN NW10....88 B1
Linden Cl RSLP HA4....46 E7
  STAN HA7....35 H4
  STHGT/OAK N14....28 C5
  THDIT KT7....158 A6
Linden Cots WIM/MER SW19 *....146 C5
Linden Crs GFD/PVL UB6....67 F5
  KUT/HW KT1....159 G1
  WFD IG8....45 F5
Lindenfield CHST BR7....169 G1
Linden Gdns BAY/PAD W2....8 A6
  CHSWK W4....106 A4
  ENC/FH EN2....28 E4
Linden Gv NWMAL KT3....160 B2
  PECK SE15....131 J2
  SYD SE26....150 E5
  TEDD TW11....143 F4
Linden Lea EFNCH N2....53 G4
  PIN HA5 *....33 K6
Linden Leas WWKM BR4....180 B1
Linden Ms BAY/PAD W2....8 A6
  IS N1....73 K4
Linden Pl MTCM CR4....162 D3
Linden Rd FBAR/BDGN N11....39 K1
  HPTN TW12....142 A7
  MUSWH N10....54 B3
  SEVS/STOTM N15....55 J3
The Lindens CHSWK W4....105 K7
  CROY/NA CR0....180 A5
  NFNCH/WDSPK N12 *....39 H4
  WALTH E17 *....57 K3
Linden St ROMW/RG RM7....63 F3
Linden Wk ARCH N19....72 C2
Linden Wy STHGT/OAK N14....28 C5
Lindfield Rd CROY/NA CR0....165 G5
  EA W5....85 J3
Lindfield St POP/IOD E14....93 J5
Lindhill Cl PEND EN3....31 F1
Lindisfarne Md HOM E9....75 G3
Lindisfarne Rd BCTR RM8....79 J2
  RYNPK SW20....145 J6
Lindley Est PECK SE15 *....111 H6
Lindley Pl RCH/KEW TW9....105 H7
Lindley Rd LEY E10....75 K1
Lindley St WCHPL E1....92 E4
Lindore Rd BTSEA SW11....128 E3
Lindores Rd CAR SM5....162 B6
Lindo St PECK SE15....131 K1
Lind Rd SUT SM1....175 G4
Lindrop St FUL/PGN SW6....128 B1
Lindsay Cl CHSGTN KT9....172 A6
  STWL/WRAY TW19....120 A4
Lindsay Dr
  KTN/HRWW/WS HA3....50 A5
  HPTN TW12....142 C6
  WPK KT4....173 K1
Lindsay Sq PIM SW1V....17 H7
Lindsell St GNWCH SE10....113 F7
Lindsey Cl BMLY BR1....168 C2
  MTCM CR4....163 K3
Lindsey Gdns
  EBED/NFELT TW14 *....121 G6
Lindsey Ms IS N1....6 E1
Lindsey Rd BCTR RM8....79 J2
Lindsey St FARR EC1M....12 D2
Lind St DEPT SE8....132 E1
Lindum Rd TEDD TW11....143 J6
Lindway WNWD SE27....149 H4
Linfield Cl HDN NW4....52 A2
Linford Rd WALTH E17....58 A2
Linford St VX/NE SW8....109 H7
Lingards Rd LEW SE13....133 F3
Lingey Cl BFN/LL DA15....155 F1
Lingfield Av KUT/HW KT1....159 F3
Lingfield Cl EN EN1....30 A5
  NTHWD HA6....32 C6
Lingfield Crs ELTH/MOT SE9....135 J3
Lingfield Gdns ED N9....30 D6
Lingfield Rd WIM/MER SW19....146 B5
  WPK KT4....174 A2
Lingham St BRXN/ST SW9....129 K1
Lingholm Wy BAR EN5....26 B4
Ling Rd CAN/RD E16....94 E4
  ERITH DA8....117 K5
Lingwell Rd TOOT SW17....147 J2
Lingwood Gdns ISLW TW7....103 K6
Lingwood Rd CLPT E5....56 C6
Linhope St CAMTN NW1....3 L9
Linfield E/WMO/HCT KT8....157 F2
Linkfield Rd ISLW TW7....124 A1
Linklea Cl CDALE/KGS NW9....37 G6
Link Rd DAGW RM9....98 D2
  EBED/NFELT TW14....121 J6
  FBAR/BDGN N11....40 A3
  MNPK E12....77 J1
  WATN WD24....21 H3
  WLGTN SM6....176 B7
Links Av GPK RM2....63 K3
  MRDN SM4....161 K3
Links Dr BORE WD6....24 B2
  TRDG/WHET N20....26 E7

Links Gdns STRHM/NOR SW16....149 G6
Linkside NFNCH/WDSPK N12....38 D5
  NWMAL KT3....160 B1
Linkside Cl ENC/FH EN2....29 F2
  ENC/FH EN2....29 F2
Links Rd ACT W3....86 C5
  CRICK NW2....69 H1
  TOOT SW17....148 A5
  WFD IG8....44 E4
  WWKM BR4....167 F7
Links Side ENC/FH EN2....29 F2
The Links WALTH E17....57 G3
Link St HOM E9....74 E5
Links Vw DART DA1....139 F7
  FNCH N3....38 D6
Links View Cl STAN HA7....35 G5
Linksview Ct HPTN TW12 *....142 D3
Links View Rd CROY/NA CR0....179 J2
  HPTN TW12....142 C4
Links Wy BECK BR3....166 D5
  NTHWD HA6....32 A7
  RKW/CH/CXG WD3....20 A2
  TOOT SW17....147 K5
Linksway HDN NW4....52 B1
  NTHWD HA6....32 B7
Links Yd WCHPL E1....13 M2
The Link ACT W3....86 C5
  ALP/SUD HA0....49 J7
  CRICK NW2....51 J7
  NTHLT UB5....65 K4
  PIN HA5....47 G5
Link Wy HAYES BR2....168 D6
  RCHPK/HAM TW10....143 H1
Linkway BCTR RM8....79 J3
  FSBYPK N4....55 J6
  NWMAL KT3....160 B3
  PIN HA5....33 H7
  RYNPK SW20....160 E2
The Linkway BAR EN5....26 E5
  BELMT SM2....175 G7
Linkwood Wk CAMTN NW1 *....5 H1
Linley Crs ROMW/RG RM7....62 D2
Linley Rd TOTM N17....56 A1
Linnell Cl GLDGN NW11....53 F5
Linnell Dr GLDGN NW11....53 F5
Linnell Rd CMBW SE5....131 F1
  UED N18....42 C4
Linnet Cl BUSH WD23....22 C7
  ED N9....31 H1
  THMD SE28....97 J6
Linnet Ms BAL SW12....129 F6
Linnett Cl CHING E4....44 A3
Linom Rd CLAP SW4....129 K3
Linscott Rd CLPT E5....74 E3
Linsdell Rd BARK IG11....78 C7
Linsey St BERM/RHTH SE16....111 H3
Linslade Cl HSLWW TW4....122 D4
  PIN HA5....47 F2
Linstead St KIL/WHAMP NW6....2 B1
Linstead Wy
  WAND/EARL SW18....127 H6
Linster Gv BORE WD6....24 E4
Lintaine Cl HMSMTH W6 *....107 H5
Linthorpe Av ALP/SUD HA0....67 J5
Linthorpe Rd EBAR EN4....27 J2
  STNW/STAM N16....56 A6
Linton Av BORE WD6....24 B1
Linton Cl CAR SM5....162 E6
  CHARL SE7....114 B4
  WELL DA16....116 B7
Linton Ct ROM RM1....63 G1
Linton Gdns EHAM E6....95 J5
Linton Gv WNWD SE27....149 H4
Linton Rd BARK IG11....78 C6
Linton St IS N1....6 F4
Lintott Ct STWL/WRAY TW19....120 A4
Linver Rd FUL/PGN SW6....127 J1
Linwood Cl CMBW SE5....131 G1
Linzee Rd CEND/HSY/T N8....54 E3
Lion Av TWK TW1....124 A7
Lion Cl BROCKY SE4....132 D5
Lionel Gdns ELTH/MOT SE9....134 C4
Lionel Ms NKENS W10 *....88 C4
Lionel Rd ELTH/MOT SE9....134 C4
Lionel Rd North BTFD TW8....105 F2
Lionel Rd South BTFD TW8....105 H3
Lion Gate Gdns RCH/KEW TW9....125 G2
Lion Gate Ms
  WAND/EARL SW18....127 K6
Lion Mills BETH E2 *....92 C1
Lion Park Av CHSGTN KT9....172 C3
Lion Rd BXLYHS DA6....137 F3
  CROY/NA CR0....164 D4
  ED N9....42 C1
  EHAM E6....95 K4
  TWK TW1....124 A7
Lions Cl LEE/GVPK SE12....153 G2
Lion Wy BTFD TW8....104 E6
Lion Wharf Rd ISLW TW7....124 C2
Liphook Cl HCH RM12....81 H1
Liphook Crs FSTH SE23....131 K6
Liphook Rd OXHEY WD19....33 H3
Lipton Av WNWD SE27....142 C1
Lisbon Cl WALTH E17....57 H1
Lisburne Rd HAMP NW3....71 K3
Lisford St PECK SE15....111 G7
Lisgar Ter WKENS W14....107 J3
Liskeard Cl CHST BR7....154 C5
Liskeard Gdns BKHTH/KID SE3....113 K7
Lisle Cl TOOT SW17....148 B3
Lisle St LSQ/SEVD WC2H....11 H6
Lismore Wk IS N1 *....73 J5
Lismore Cl WIM/MER SW19....146 D4
Lismore Circ KTTN NW5....71 K4
Lismore Cl ISLW TW7....124 B1
Lismore Rd SAND/SEL CR2....178 A5
  TOTM N17....55 K2
Lissant Cl SURB KT6....158 D6
Lissenden Gdns KTTN NW5....72 A3
Lisson Gv CAMTN NW1....9 J1
Lisson St CAMTN NW1....9 J3
  STJWD NW8....3 H9
Lister Cl ACT W3....87 F4
  MTCM CR4....147 J6
Lister Gdns UED N18....41 J4
Lister Rd WAN E11....58 C7
Liston Rd CLAP SW4....129 H2
  TOTM N17....42 C7
Liston Wy WFD IG8....45 G6
Listowel Cl BRXN/ST SW9....110 B6
Listowel Rd DAGE RM10....80 C1
Listria Pk STNW/STAM N16....74 A1
Litchfield Av MRDN SM4....161 J6
  SRTFD E15....76 C5
Litchfield Gdns WLSDN NW10....69 J5
Litchfield Rd SUT SM1....175 G4
Litchfield St LSQ/SEVD WC2H....11 H5
Litchfield Wy GLDGN NW11....53 F4
Lithgow's Rd HTHAIR TW6....121 H3
Lithos Rd HAMP NW3....71 F5
The Little Acre BECK BR3....166 D2
Little Albany St CAMTN NW1....4 D9
Little Argyll St REGST W1B *....10 E5

Little Benty WDR/YW UB7....100 A4
Little Birches BFN/LL DA15....154 E1
The Little Boltons
  WBPTN SW10....14 D7
Little Bornes DUL SE21....150 A3
Littlebrook Cl CROY/NA CR0....166 A7
  DART DA1....139 K4
Little Brownings FSTH SE23....150 D1
Littlebury Rd CLAP SW4 *....129 J2
Little Bury St ED N9....30 A6
Little Bushey La BUSH WD23....22 A2
Little Cedars
  NFNCH/WDSPK N12....39 G3
Little Chester St KTBR SW1X....16 C3
Little Cloisters WEST SW1P....17 J3
Littlecombe Cl
  PUT/ROE SW15....127 G5
Little Common STAN HA7....35 G2
Littlecote Cl WIM/MER SW19....127 G6
Littlecote Pl PIN HA5....33 J7
Little Cottage Pl
  GNWCH SE10....112 E6
Little Ct WWKM BR4....180 C1
Littlecroft ELTH/MOT SE9....135 F2
Littledale ABYW SE2....116 B5
Little Deans Yd WEST SW1P....17 J3
Little Dimocks BAL SW12....148 B1
Little Dorrit Ct STHWK SE1....18 F1
Little Ealing La W5....104 D3
Little Edward St
  CAMTN NW1 *....4 D7
Little Elms HYS/HAR UB3....101 H6
Little Essex St
  TPL/STR WC2R *....12 A6
Little Ferry Rd TWK TW1 *....124 C3
Littlefield Cl ARCH N19....72 C3
  KUT/HW KT1....159 F1
Littlefield Rd EDGW HA8....36 E6
Little Friday Rd CHING E4....44 C1
Little Gearies BARK/HLT IG6....60 B3
Little George St WEST SW1P *....17 J2
Little Gn RCH/KEW TW9....124 E3
Little Green St KTTN NW5 *....72 B3
Little Gv BUSH WD23....22 B3
Littlegrove EBAR EN4....27 J5
Little Heath CHARL SE7....114 D5
  CHDH RM6....61 H3
Little Heath Rd BXLYHN DA7....117 G7
Littleheath Rd SAND/SEL CR2....178 D7
Little Ilford La MNPK E12....77 K3
Littlejohn Rd HNWL W7....85 F5
Little Marlborough St
  REGST W1B *....10 E5
Little Martins BUSH WD23....22 B4
Littlemead ESH/CLAY KT10....170 D3
Littlemede ELTH/MOT SE9....153 K2
Littlemoor Rd IL IG1....78 D2
Littlemore Rd ABYW SE2....116 B1
Little Moss La PIN HA5....47 J1
Little Newport St
  LSQ/SEVD WC2H....11 H6
Little Orchard Cl PIN HA5 *....47 J1
Little Oxhey La OXHEY WD19....33 J4
Little Park Dr FELT TW13....141 H1
Little Park Gdns ENC/FH EN2....29 J2
Little Portland St REGST W1B....10 D4
Little Potters BUSH WD23....22 D6
Little Queens Rd TEDD TW11....143 F5
Little Queen St DART DA1....139 J4
Little Redlands BMLY BR1....168 D1
Little Rd HYS/HAR UB3....101 J1
Littlers Cl WIM/MER SW19....147 H7
Little Russell St
  NOXST/BSQ WC1A....11 J3
Little St James's St
  WHALL SW1A....10 E9
Little St Leonards
  MORT/ESHN SW14....125 K2
Little Smith St WEST SW1P....17 H3
Little Somerset St
  TWRH EC3N....13 L5
Littlestone Cl BECK BR3....151 J3
Little Strd CDALE/KGS NW9....51 H1
Little Stream Cl NTHWD HA6....32 C4
Little Thrift STMC/STPC BR5....169 H3
Little Titchfield St
  GTPST W1W....10 D3
Littleton Crs HRW HA1....67 F1
Littleton Rd ASHF TW15....140 A6
  HRW HA1....67 F1
Littleton St WAND/EARL SW18....147 G1
Little Trinity La BLKFR EC4V....12 F6
Little Turnstile HHOL WC1V....11 L3
Littlewood LEW SE13....133 F4
Little Wood Cl
  STMC/STPC BR5....155 G7
Littlewood Cl WEA W13....104 B3
Littleworth Av ESH/CLAY KT10....170 D4
Littleworth Common Rd
  ESH/CLAY KT10....170 D2
Littleworth La ESH/CLAY KT10....170 D3
Littleworth Pl ESH/CLAY KT10....170 D3
Littleworth Rd ESH/CLAY KT10....170 D4
Livermere Rd HACK E8....7 L1
Liverpool Gv WALW SE17....19 G8
Liverpool Rd CAN/RD E16....94 C4
  EA W5....104 E1
  IS N1....6 B3
  KUTN/CMB KT2....144 C6
  LEY E10....58 A5
  THHTH CR7....164 D2
  WATW WD18....21 F4
Liverpool St LVPST EC2M....13 J3
Livesey Cl KUT/HW KT1....159 G2
  THMD SE28....115 H2
Livesey Pl STHWK SE1 *....111 H5
Livingstone Rd BTSEA SW11....128 C2
  HSLW TW3....123 H3
  PLMGR N13....40 E5
  STHL UB1....83 H6
  THHTH CR7....164 E1
  WALTH E17....57 K5
  WPK KT4....174 A2

Lizban St BKHTH/KID SE3....114 A6
Llanelly Rd CRICK NW2....70 D1
Llanover Rd WBLY HA9....67 K2
  WOOL/PLUM SE18....115 F5
Llanthony Rd MRDN SM4....162 C5
Llanvanor Rd CRICK NW2....70 D1
Lloyd Av STRHM/NOR SW16....148 E7
Lloyd Baker St FSBYW WC1X....5 M8
Lloyd Ct PIN HA5....47 H4
Lloyd Park Av CROY/NA CR0....178 B3
Lloyd Rd DAGW RM9....80 B5
  EHAM E6....77 K7
  WALTH E17....57 F3
  WPK KT4....174 A2
Lloyd's Av FENCHST EC3M....13 K5
Lloyd's Pl BKHTH/KID SE3 *....133 H1

Lloyd Sq FSBYW WC1X 6 A7
Lloyd's Rw CLKNW EC1R 6 B8
Lloyd St FSBYW WC1X 6 A7
Lloyds Wy BECK BR3 .....166 B4
Lloyd Thomas Ct WDGN N22 * 41 F4
Lloyd Vls BROCKY SE4 .....132 D1
Loampit Hl LEW SE13 .....132 D1
Loampit V LEW SE13 .....132 E2
Loanda Cl HACK E8 .....7 L3
Loates La WAT WD17 .....21 G2
Loats Rd BRXS/STRHM SW2 .....129 K5
Locarno Rd ACT W3 .....86 E7
  GFD/PVL UB6 .....84 C3
Lochaber Rd LEW SE13 .....133 H3
Lochaline St HMSMTH W6 .....107 F5
Lochan Cl YEAD UB4 .....83 J3
Lochinvar St BAL SW12 .....129 G6
Lochmere Cl ERITH DA8 .....117 J5
Lochnagar St POP/IOD E14 .....94 A4
Lock Cha BKHTH/KID SE3 .....133 H2
Lock Cl NWDGN UB2 .....103 H1
Locke Cl RAIN RM13 .....81 H5
Lockesfield Pl POP/IOD E14 .....112 A3
Lockesley St SURB KT6 * 158 E5
Locket Rd
  KTN/HRWW/WS HA3 .....49 F1
Locket Road Ms
  KTN/HRWW/WS HA3 .....48 E1
Lockfield Av PEND EN3 .....31 G1
Lockgate Cl HOM E9 .....75 H4
Lockhart Cl HOLWY N7 .....73 F5
  PEND EN3 .....30 D4
Lockhart St BOW E3 .....93 H3
Lockhurst St CLPT E5 .....75 F3
Lockington Rd VX/NE SW8 .....109 G7
Lock Keepers Cots
  TOTM N17 * 56 D3
  SEVS/STOTM N15 .....56 C5
Lockmead Rd LEW SE13 .....133 F2
Lock's La MTCM CR4 .....148 A7
Locksley Est POP/IOD E14 .....93 H5
Locksley St POP/IOD E14 .....93 H4
Locksmeade Rd
  RCHPK/HAM TW10 .....143 H3
Lockton St WLSN W11 * 88 B5
Lockwood Cl EBAR EN4 .....27 K3
  SYD SE26 .....151 F3
Lockwood Pl CHING E4 .....43 J5
Lockwood Sq
  BERM/RHTH SE16 .....111 J2
  WALTH E17 .....57 F1
Lockyer St STHWK SE1 .....19 H2
Locomotive Dr
  EBED/NFELT TW14 .....121 K6
Locton St BOW E3 * 75 H7
Loddiges Rd HOM E9 .....74 E6
Loder St PECK SE15 .....111 K6
Lodge Av BCTR RM8 .....79 H4
  BORE WD6 .....24 B4
  CROY/NA CRO 177 F2
  DAGW RM9 .....79 G7
  DART DA1 .....139 F5
  GPK RM2 .....63 J4
  KTN/HRWW/WS HA3 .....50 A3
Lodge Cl EDGW HA8 .....36 B5
  ISLW TW7 .....104 C7
  UED N18 .....41 J4
  WLGTN SM6 .....163 F7
Lodge Ct ALP/SUD HA0 * 68 A4
Lodge Dr PLMGR N13 .....41 G3
Lodge End RKW/CH/CXG WD3 .....20 B3
Lodge Gdns BECK BR3 .....166 C4
Lodge Hl REDBR IG4 .....59 J3
  WELL DA16 .....116 C6
Lodgehill Park Cl
  RYLN/HDSTN HA2 .....66 B1
Lodge La BXLY DA5 .....136 E5
  CROY/NA CRO 179 K6
  NFNCH/WDSPK N12 .....39 G4
Lodge Mansions Pde
  PLMGR N13 * 41 G3
Lodge Ms HBRY N5 * 73 J3
Lodge Pl SUT SM1 .....175 F4
Lodge Rd BMLY BR1 .....153 G8
  CROY/NA CRO 164 C5
  HDN NW4 .....52 A3
  RKW/CH/CXG WD3 .....20 B3
  STJWD NW8 .....3 H8
  SUT SM1 .....175 F4
  WLGTN SM6 .....176 B4
The Lodge SHB W12 * 107 G1
Lodge Vls WFD IG8 .....44 D6
Lodore Gdns CDALE/KGS NW9 .....51 G4
Lodore St POP/IOD E14 .....94 A5
Lofthouse Pl CHSGTN KT9 .....171 J5
Loftie St BERM/RHTH SE16 .....111 H1
Lofting Rd IS N1 .....6 A2
Loftus Rd BARK IG11 .....78 C5
  SHB W12 .....87 K7
Loftus Vls SHB W12 * 87 K7
Logan Cl HSLWW TW4 .....14 A5
Logan Ms KENS W8 * 14 C4
  ROM RM1 .....63 G4
Logan Pl ECT SW5 .....14 C4
Logan Rd ED N9 .....42 D1
  WBLY HA9 .....68 A1
The Logans BAR EN5 * 26 B2
Logs Hl CHST BR7 .....153 J7
Logs Hill Cl CHST BR7 .....153 J7
Loisworth Cl WCHPL E1 .....13 L3
Loman St STHWK SE1 .....18 D1
Lomas Cl CROY/NA CRO 180 A6
Lomas Dr HACK E8 .....7 M1
Lombard Av GDMY/SEVK IG3 .....60 E7
  MANHO EC4N 13 H6
Lombard La EMB EC4Y * 12 B5
Lombard Rd BTSEA SW11 .....128 C1
  FBAR/BDGN N11 .....40 B4
  WIM/MER SW19 .....162 A1
  BANK EC3V 13 H5
Lombard Vls
  FBAR/BDGN N11 * 40 B4
Lombard Wall CHARL SE7 .....114 A3
Lombardy Pl BAY/PAD W2 * 8 C7
Lomond Cl ALP/SUD HA0 .....68 A6
  SEVS/STOTM N15 .....56 A3
Lomond Gdns SAND/SEL CR2 .....179 G6
Lomond Gv CMBW SE5 .....110 E6
Loncroft Rd CMBW SE5 .....19 K3
Londesborough Rd
  STNW/STAM N16 .....74 A3
London Br CANST EC4R 13 H7
London Bridge St STHWK SE1 .....13 H9
London Bridge Wk
  STHWK SE1 * 13 H8
Londonderry Pde
  ERITH DA8 * 118 A6
London Flds HACK E8 * 74 D6

London Fields East Side
  HACK E8 .....74 D6
London Fields West Side
  HACK E8 .....74 C6
London La BMLY BR1 .....152 D6
  HACK E8 .....74 D6
London Loop BAR EN5 .....25 K6
  HAYES BR2 .....180 D3
  ORP BR6 .....169 G2
  SAND/SEL CR2 .....178 E6
London Ms BAY/PAD W2 * 9 J5
London Rd BARK IG11 .....78 B6
  BMLY BR1 .....152 D6
  BUSH WD23 .....21 K5
  CHEAM SM3 .....174 B1
  CROY/NA CRO 164 C7
  DART DA1 .....138 A4
  ENC/FH EN2 .....29 K3
  EW KT17 .....173 H7
  FSTH SE23 .....131 K7
  HRW HA1 .....66 B3
  ISLW TW7 .....123 K1
  KUTN/CMB KT2 .....159 G1
  MRDN SM4 .....161 K4
  MTCM CR4 .....162 D3
  PLSTW E13 .....94 E1
  PUR RM19 .....119 K4
  ROMW/RG RM7 .....62 C5
  SOCK/AV RM15 .....119 K1
  STAN HA7 .....35 K3
  STHWK SE1 .....18 D3
  STRHM/NOR SW16 .....164 A1
  THHTH CR7 .....164 B5
  TOOT SW17 .....147 K6
  TWK TW1 .....124 B6
  WBLY HA9 .....68 A4
  WLGTN SM6 .....176 B3
London Stile CHSWK W4 .....105 H4
London St BAY/PAD W2 .....9 J5
  FENCHST EC3M * 13 K6
London Ter BETH E2 * 92 C1
London Wall CITYW EC2V 12 F3
  LVPST EC2M 13 H4
London Wall Blds LVPST EC2M 13 H3
Lonesome Wy MTCM CR4 .....148 B7
Long Acre CHCR WC2N 11 J6
  COVGDN WC2E 11 J5
Long Acre Ct WEA W13 * 85 G4
Longacre Pl CAR SM5 * 176 A5
Longacre Rd WALTH E17 .....44 B1
Longbeach Rd BTSEA SW11 .....128 E2
Longboat Rw STHL UB1 .....83 K5
Longbridge Rd BARK IG11 .....78 D5
  BCTR RM8 .....79 G3
Longbridge Wy LEW SE13 .....133 F4
Longcliffe Pth OXHEY WD19 .....32 E2
Long Ct PUR RM19 .....119 K3
Longcroft ELTH/MOT SE9 .....154 A2
Long Cft OXHEY WD19 .....21 F6
Longcrofte Rd EDGW HA8 .....35 K6
Longdown Rd CAT SE6 .....151 J3
Long Dr ACT W3 .....87 G5
  GFD/PVL UB6 .....66 D7
  RSLP HA4 .....65 H3
  WDR/YW UB7 * 100 B1
Long Elmes
  KTN/HRWW/WS HA3 .....34 B7
Longfellow Rd WALTH E17 .....57 H5
  WCHPL E1 * 93 G2
  WPK KT4 .....160 D7
Longfellow Wy STHWK SE1 * 19 M6
Long Fld CDALE/KGS NW9 .....37 G6
Longfield BMLY BR1 .....152 D7
Longfield Av EA W5 .....85 J6
  EMPK RM11 .....63 H6
  MLHL NW7 .....37 J6
  WALTH E17 .....57 G5
  WBLY HA9 .....50 A7
  WLGTN SM6 .....176 B4
Longfield Crs SYD SE26 .....150 E2
Longfield Dr
  MORT/ESHN SW14 .....125 J4
  MTCM CR4 .....147 J7
Longfield Est STHWK SE1 .....19 M5
Longfield Rd EA W5 .....85 J5
Longfield St
  WAND/EARL SW18 .....127 K6
Longford Av
  EBED/NFELT TW14 .....121 H5
  STHL UB1 .....84 A6
  STWL/WRAY TW19 .....120 B7
Longford Cl FELT TW13 .....141 J2
  HPTN TW12 .....142 A3
  YEAD UB4 .....83 H6
Longford Ct HOR/WEW KT19 .....172 E3
  HPTN TW12 .....142 B5
Longford Gdns SUT SM1 .....175 G2
  YEAD UB4 .....83 H6
Longford Rd WHTN TW2 .....123 F7
Longford St CAMTN NW1 .....4 D9
Longford Wy
  STWL/WRAY TW19 .....120 B7
Longhayes Av CHDH RM6 .....61 K2
Longheath Gdns
  CROY/NA CRO 165 K4
Longhedge St BTSEA SW11 .....129 F1
Longhill Rd CAT SE6 .....152 B1
Longhook Gdns NTHLT UB5 .....82 E1
Longhurst Rd CROY/NA CRO 165 J5
  LEW SE13 .....133 H4
Longland Dr TRDG/WHET N20 .....39 F2
Longlands Park Crs
  BFN/LL DA15 .....154 E2
Longlands Rd BFN/LL DA15 .....154 E2
Long La BXLYHN DA7 .....117 F6
  CROY/NA CRO 165 K5
  FNCH N3 .....39 F7
  STBT EC1A 12 D2
  STHWK SE1 .....19 H2
  STWL/WRAY TW19 .....120 C7
Longleat Rd EN EN1 .....30 A4
Longleigh La ABYW SE2 .....116 D5
Longley Av ALP/SUD HA0 .....68 B7
  HRW HA1 .....48 D6
  TOOT SW17 .....147 J5
Long Leys CHING E4 .....43 J5
Longley St STHWK SE1 .....111 H4
Longley Wy CRICK NW2 .....70 A2
Longmans Cl WATW WD18 .....20 A5
Long Mark Rd CAN/RD E16 .....95 H4
Longmarsh La THMD SE28 .....96 E7
Long Md CDALE/KGS NW9 .....37 H1
Longmead BMLY BR1 .....169 F1
Longmead Dr SCUP DA14 .....155 K2
Long Meadow KTTN NW5 * 72 D5
Long Meadow Cl WWKM BR4 .....167 F6
Longmeadow Rd
  BFN/LL DA15 .....135 K7
Longmead Rd HYS/HAR UB3 .....82 D1

  THDIT KT7 .....157 K6
  TOOT SW17 .....147 K4
Longmoore St PIM SW1V 16 E5
Longmore Av BAR EN5 .....27 G5
Lonnnor Rd WCHPL E1 .....93 F2
Long Pond Rd BKHTH/KID SE3 .....113 H5
Long Reach Rd BARK IG11 .....97 F3
Longreach Rd ERITH DA8 .....118 E6
Longridge La STHL UB1 .....84 B6
Longridge Rd ECT SW5 .....14 A6
Long Rd CLAP SW4 .....129 H3
Longshaw Rd CHING E4 .....44 B3
Longshore DEPT SE8 .....112 C3
Longstaff Crs
  WAND/EARL SW18 .....127 K5
Longstaff Rd
  WAND/EARL SW18 .....127 K5
Longstone Av WLSDN NW10 .....69 H6
Longstone Rd TOOT SW17 .....148 B4
Long St BETH E2 .....7 L6
Longthornton Rd
  STRHM/NOR SW16 .....163 H1
Longton Av SYD SE26 .....150 C3
Longton Gv SYD SE26 .....150 D3
Longville Rd LBTH SE11 .....18 C5
Long Wk NWMAL KT3 .....159 K2
  STHWK SE1 .....19 K3
  WOOL/PLUM SE18 .....115 G5
Longwood Ct WPK KT4 .....173 J1
Longwood Dr PUT/ROE SW15 .....126 D5
Longwood Gdns CLAY IG5 .....59 K3
Longworth Cl THMD SE28 .....97 K5
Long Yd BMSBY WC1N 11 L1
The Loning CDALE/KGS NW9 .....51 H3
Lonsdale Av EHAM E6 .....95 H3
  ROMW/RG RM7 .....62 E5
  WBLY HA9 .....68 A4
Lonsdale Cl EHAM E6 .....95 J3
  ELTH/MOT SE9 .....153 H2
  UX/CGN UB8 .....82 A5
Lonsdale Crs GNTH/NBYPK IG2 .....60 B5
Lonsdale Dr ENC/FH EN2 .....28 D3
Lonsdale Dr North
  ENC/FH EN2 .....28 E4
Lonsdale Gdns THHTH CR7 .....164 A3
  RCH/KEW TW9 * 105 H7
Lonsdale Ms NTGHL W11 .....88 D5
  RCH/KEW TW9 * 105 H7
Lonsdale Pl IS N1 .....6 A1
Lonsdale Rd BARN SW13 .....106 C6
  BXLYHN DA7 .....137 G1
  CHSWK W4 .....106 C3
  KIL/WHAMP NW6 .....70 D7
  NTGHL W11 .....88 D5
  NWDGN UB2 .....102 C3
  SNWD SE25 .....165 J3
  WAN E11 .....58 D6
Lonsdale Sq IS N1 * 6 B2
Loobert Rd SEVS/STOTM N15 .....56 A2
Looe Gdns BARK/HLT IG6 .....60 B1
Loop Rd CHST BR7 .....154 C5
Lopen Rd UED N18 .....42 A3
Loraine Cl PEND EN3 .....30 E4
Loraine Cots HOLWY N7 * 73 F3
Loraine Rd CHSWK W4 .....105 J5
  HOLWY N7 .....73 F3
Lord Av CLAY IG5 .....59 K3
Lord Chancellor Wk
  KUTN/CMB KT2 .....144 E7
Lordell Pl WIM/MER SW19 .....146 A5
Lord Hills Rd BAY/PAD W2 .....8 D2
Lord Holland La
  BRXN/ST SW9 * 130 B1
Lord Knyvett Cl
  STWL/WRAY TW19 .....120 A5
Lord Knyvetts Ct
  STWL/WRAY TW19 * 120 B5
Lord Napier Pl HMSMTH W6 .....106 D4
Lord North St WEST SW1P 17 J4
Lord Roberts Ms
  FUL/PGN SW6 * 108 A6
Lords Cl DUL SE21 .....149 J1
  FELT TW13 .....141 J1
Lordship Gv STNW/STAM N16 .....73 K1
Lordship La EDUL SE22 .....131 G5
  TOTM N17 .....41 J7
  WDGN N22 .....55 G1
Lordship Pk STNW/STAM N16 .....73 K1
Lordship Park Ms
  STNW/STAM N16 .....73 J1
Lordship Pl CHEL SW3 * 108 D5
Lordship Rd NTHLT UB5 .....65 J6
  STNW/STAM N16 .....55 K7
Lordship Ter STNW/STAM N16 .....73 K1
Lordsmead Rd TOTM N17 .....42 A7
Lord St CAN/RD E16 .....95 J7
  WAT WD17 .....21 G2
Lords Vw STJWD NW8 .....3 J7
Lord Warwick St
  WOOL/PLUM SE18 .....114 E2
Lorenzo St FSBYW WC1X 5 L7
Loretto Gdns
  KTN/HRWW/WS HA3 .....50 A3
Lorian Cl NFNCH/WDSPK N12 .....39 F3
Loring Rd ISLW TW7 .....124 A1
  TRDG/WHET N20 .....39 J1
Loris Rd HMSMTH W6 .....107 F2
Lorn Ct BRXN/ST SW9 .....130 B1
Lorne Av CROY/NA CRO 166 A6
Lorne Cl STJWD NW8 .....3 J8
Lorne Gdns CROY/NA CRO 166 A6
  NTGHL W11 .....107 G1
  WAN E11 .....59 G3
Lorne Rd FSBYPK N4 .....55 F7
  FSTGT E7 .....77 F3
  KTN/HRWW/WS HA3 .....49 F1
  RCHPK/HAM TW10 .....125 G4
  WALTH E17 .....57 J4
Lorne Ter FNCH N3 * 52 D1
Lorn Rd BRXN/ST SW9 .....130 A1
Lorraine Pk
  KTN/HRWW/WS HA3 .....34 E6
Lorrimore Rd WALW SE17 .....110 C5
Lorrimore Sq WALW SE17 .....18 C9
Loseberry Rd ESH/CLAY KT10 .....170 D4
Lothair Rd EA W5 .....104 E1
Lothair Rd North FSBYPK N4 .....55 H5
Lothair Rd South FSBYPK N4 .....55 G6
Lothbury LOTH EC2R 13 G4
Lothian Av YEAD UB4 .....83 F4
Lothian Cl ALP/SUD HA0 .....67 G3
Lothian Rd BRXN/ST SW9 .....110 C7
Lothrop St NKENS W10 .....88 C2
Lots Rd WBPTN SW10 .....108 B6
Loubet St TOOT SW17 .....147 K5
Loudoun Av BARK/HLT IG6 .....60 B4
Loudoun Rd STJWD NW8 .....2 F2
Loughborough Pk
  BRXN/ST SW9 .....130 C3
Loughborough Rd
  BRXN/ST SW9 .....130 B1
Loughborough St LBTH SE11 .....17 M7
Lough Rd HOLWY N7 .....73 F5
Louisa Cl HOM E9 .....74 E6
Louisa St WCHPL E1 .....93 F4

Louise Bennett Cl
  HNHL SE24 * 130 C3
Louise Gdns RAIN RM13 .....99 G3
Louise Rd SRTFD E15 .....76 C5
Louis Gdns CHST BR7 .....153 K5
Louisville Rd TOOT SW17 .....148 A2
Louvaine Rd BTSEA SW11 .....128 C3
Lovage Ap EHAM E6 .....95 J4
Lovat Cl CRICK NW2 .....69 H2
Lovat La FENCHST EC3M 13 J6
Lovatt Cl EDGW HA8 .....36 D5
Loveday Rd WEA W13 .....85 H7
Lovegrove St STHWK SE1 .....111 H4
Lovegrove Wk POP/IOD E14 .....94 A7
Lovekyn Cl KUTN/CMB KT2 .....159 F1
Lovelace Av HAYES BR2 .....169 F5
Lovelace Gdns BARK IG11 .....79 G3
  SURB KT6 .....158 E6
Lovelace Gn ELTH/MOT SE9 .....134 E2
Lovelace Rd DUL SE21 .....149 J1
  EBAR EN4 .....27 J6
  SURB KT6 .....158 D6
Lovelace Vls THDIT KT7 * 158 C5
Love La BXLY DA5 .....137 H5
  CHEAM SM3 .....174 C5
  CITYW EC2V 12 F4
  MRDN SM4 .....161 K6
  NORTH N17 .....162 D2
  PIN HA5 .....47 J2
  SNWD SE25 .....165 J2
  SURB KT6 .....171 K1
  TOTM N17 .....42 B6
  WFD IG8 .....45 K5
  WOOL/PLUM SE18 .....115 F3
Lovel Av WELL DA16 .....136 B1
Lovelinch Cl PECK SE15 .....111 K5
Lovell Pl BERM/RHTH SE16 .....112 B2
Lovell Rd RCHPK/HAM TW10 .....143 J2
  STHL UB1 .....84 B5
Lovell Wk RAIN RM13 .....81 J5
Loveridge Ms
  KIL/WHAMP NW6 .....70 D5
Loveridge Rd
  KIL/WHAMP NW6 .....70 D5
Lovett Dr CAR SM5 .....162 B6
Lovett Rd WLSDN NW10 .....68 E4
Lovett Wy WLSDN NW10 .....68 D4
Love Wk CMBW SE5 .....130 E1
Lowbrook Rd IL IG1 .....78 B3
Lowden Rd ED N9 .....30 D4
  HNHL SE24 .....130 C3
  STHL UB1 .....83 J6
Lowe Av CAN/RD E16 .....94 E4
Lowell St POP/IOD E14 .....93 G5
Lowen Rd RAIN RM13 .....99 F1
Lower Addiscombe Rd
  CROY/NA CRO 164 E7
Lower Addison Gdns
  WKENS W14 .....107 H1
Lower Belgrave St
  BGVA SW1W 16 C4
Lower Broad St DAGE RM10 .....80 C7
Lower Camden CHST BR7 .....153 K7
Lower Church St
  CROY/NA CRO * 177 H1
Lower Clapton Rd CLPT E5 .....74 D3
  HACK E8 .....74 D4
Lower Clarendon Wk
  NTGHL W11 * 88 C5
Lower Common South
  PUT/ROE SW15 .....126 E2
Lower Coombe St
  CROY/NA CRO 177 J3
Lower Derby Rd WAT WD17 .....21 G3
Lower Downs Rd
  RYNPK SW20 .....146 B7
Lower Gravel Rd HAYES BR2 .....168 D7
Lower Green Gdns WPK KT4 .....160 D7
Lower Green West MTCM CR4 .....162 D2
Lower Grosvenor Pl
  BGVA SW1W 16 C3
Lower Grove Rd
  RCHPK/HAM TW10 .....125 G5
Lower Hall La CHING E4 .....43 G4
Lower Hampton Rd
  SUN TW16 .....156 C1
Lower Ham Rd
  KUTN/CMB KT2 .....143 K5
Lower High St WAT WD17 .....21 G3
Lower James St
  SOHO/CST W1F * 10 F6
Lower John St SOHO/CST W1F 10 F6
Lower Kenwood Av
  ENC/FH EN2 .....28 C4
Lower Kings Rd
  KUTN/CMB KT2 .....144 A6
Lower Lea Crossing
  POP/IOD E14 .....94 C6
Lower Maidstone Rd
  FBAR/BDGN N11 .....40 C5
Lower Mardyke Av
  RAIN RM13 .....98 E1
Lower Marsh STHWK SE1 .....18 A2
Lower Marsh La BRYLDS KT5 .....159 G3
Lower Merton Ri HAMP NW3 .....3 J2
Lower Morden La MRDN SM4 .....161 F5
Lower Mortlake Rd
  RCH/KEW TW9 .....125 F3
Lower Paddock Rd
  OXHEY WD19 .....21 J5
Lower Park Rd BELV DA17 .....117 H2
  FBAR/BDGN N11 .....40 C4
Lower Queen's Rd BKHH IG9 .....45 J1
Lower Richmond Rd
  PUT/ROE SW15 .....127 G2
  RCH/KEW TW9 .....125 H2
Lower Rd BELV DA17 .....117 J2
  BERM/RHTH SE16 .....111 K1
  ERITH DA8 .....118 A3
  RYLN/HDSTN HA2 .....66 D1
  SUT SM1 .....175 G4
Lower Robert St CHCR WC2N 11 K7
Lower Sand Hills SURB KT6 .....158 E6
Lower Sloane St BGVA SW1W 15 M6
Lower Station Rd DART DA1 .....138 B5
Lower Strd CDALE/KGS NW9 .....51 H1
Lower Sunbury Rd
  E/WMO/HCT KT8 .....156 E1
Lower Tail OXHEY WD19 .....33 J2
Lower Teddington Rd
  KUT/HW KT1 .....143 K7
Lower Ter HAMP NW3 .....71 G2
Lower Thames St MON EC3R 13 J7
Lower Tub BUSH WD23 .....22 D6
Lower Wood Rd
  ESH/CLAY KT10 .....171 G5
Loweswater Cl WBLY HA9 .....67 K1
Lowfield Rd ACT W3 .....86 E5
  KIL/WHAMP NW6 .....2 A1
Lowfield St DART DA1 .....139 H6
Low Hall Cl CHING E4 .....31 J6

Low Hall La WALTH E17 .....57 G5
Lowick Rd HRW HA1 .....48 E3
Lowland Gdns ROMW/RG RM7 .....62 D3
Lowlands Dr
  STWL/WRAY TW19 .....120 A4
Lowlands Rd HRW HA1 .....48 E6
  PIN HA5 .....47 G6
Lowman Rd HOLWY N7 .....73 F3
Lowndes Cl KTBR SW1X 16 B4
Lowndes Ct SOHO/CST W1F * 10 E5
Lowndes Ms
  STRHM/NOR SW16 .....148 E1
Lowndes Pl KTBR SW1X 16 A4
Lowndes Sq KTBR SW1X 15 M3
Lowndes St KTBR SW1X 15 M3
Lowood St WCHPL E1 .....92 D6
Lowry Cl ERITH DA8 .....118 A3
Lowry Crs MTCM CR4 .....162 D1
Lowry Rd BCTR RM8 .....79 H4
Lowson Gv OXHEY WD19 .....21 J6
Lowswood Cl NTHWD HA6 .....32 A7
Lowther Cl BORE WD6 .....24 B4
Lowther Dr ENC/FH EN2 .....28 E4
Lowther Hl FSTH SE23 .....132 B6
Lowther Man BARN SW13 * 106 D7
Lowther Rd BARN SW13 .....106 C7
  HOLWY N7 .....73 G4
  KUTN/CMB KT2 .....144 B2
  STAN HA7 .....50 C1
  WALTH E17 .....57 G1
Lowth Rd CMBW SE5 .....130 D1
Loxford Av EHAM E6 .....95 H1
Loxford La IL IG1 .....78 C4
Loxford Rd BARK IG11 .....78 B5
Loxham Rd CHING E4 .....43 K6
Loxham St STPAN WC1H * 5 K8
Loxley Cl SYD SE26 .....151 F4
Loxley Rd HPTN TW12 .....141 K3
  WAND/EARL SW18 .....128 C7
Loxton Rd FSTH SE23 .....132 A7
Loxwood Cl
  EBED/NFELT TW14 .....121 G7
Loxwood Rd TOTM N17 .....56 A2
Lubbock Rd CHST BR7 .....154 A7
Lubbock St NWCR SE14 .....111 K6
Lucan Pl CHEL SW3 .....15 J6
Lucas Av PLSTW E13 .....77 F7
  RYLN/HDSTN HA2 .....66 A1
Lucas Gdns EFNCH N2 .....53 G2
Lucas Rd PGE/AN SE20 .....150 E5
Lucas Sq GLDGN NW11 .....52 E5
Lucas St BROCKY SE4 .....132 D1
Lucerne Cl PLMGR N13 .....40 E2
Lucerne Gv WALTH E17 .....58 B3
Lucerne Ms KENS W8 * 8 B1
Lucerne Rd HBRY N5 .....73 H3
  THHTH CR7 .....164 C4
Lucey Rd BERM/RHTH SE16 .....111 H2
Lucey Wy BERM/RHTH SE16 .....111 H2
Lucien Rd TOOT SW17 .....148 A3
  WIM/MER SW19 .....147 F1
Lucknow St
  WOOL/PLUM SE18 .....115 K6
Lucorn Cl LEE/GVPK SE12 .....133 J5
Luddesdon Rd ERITH DA8 .....117 H6
Ludford Cl CROY/NA CRO 177 H3
Ludgate Broadway
  BLKFR EC4V * 12 D5
Ludgate Circ STP EC4M 12 D5
Ludgate Hl STP EC4M 12 D5
Ludgate Sq STP EC4M * 12 D5
Ludham Cl THMD SE28 .....97 J5
Ludlow Cl HAYES BR2 * 167 K2
  RYLN/HDSTN HA2 .....65 K3
Ludlow Md OXHEY WD19 .....33 F2
Ludlow Rd EA W5 .....85 J3
  FELT TW13 .....140 E2
Ludlow St FSBYE EC1V * 6 E9
Ludlow Wy EFNCH N2 .....53 G3
  RKW/CH/CXG WD3 .....20 D6
Ludovick Wk PUT/ROE SW15 .....126 B3
Luffield Rd ABYW SE2 .....116 C2
Luffman Rd LEE/GVPK SE12 .....153 F2
Lugard Rd PECK SE15 .....131 J1
Lugg Ap MNPK E12 .....78 A2
Luke St SDTCH EC2A 7 J9
Lukin Crs CHING E4 .....44 B2
Lukin St WCHPL E1 .....92 E5
Lullingstone Cl
  STMC/STPC BR5 .....155 H6
Lullingstone Crs
  STMC/STPC BR5 .....155 G6
Lullingstone La BELV DA17 .....117 G5
Lullingstone Rd BELV DA17 .....117 G5
Lullingstone Garth BMLY BR1 .....152 C6
  BORE WD6 .....24 E4
  NFNCH/WDSPK N12 .....38 D2
Lullington Rd DAGW RM9 .....80 A6
  PGE/AN SE20 .....150 C6
Lulot Gdns ARCH N19 .....72 B1
Lulworth Av HEST TW5 .....103 G7
  WBLY HA9 .....49 J6
Lulworth Cl RYLN/HDSTN HA2 .....65 J1
Lulworth Crs MTCM CR4 .....162 D1
Lulworth Dr PIN HA5 .....47 H5
Lulworth Gdns
  RYLN/HDSTN HA2 .....65 J1
Lulworth Rd ELTH/MOT SE9 .....153 J1
  PECK SE15 .....131 J1
  WELL DA16 .....136 A1
Lulworth Waye YEAD UB4 .....83 F5
Lumen Rd WBLY HA9 .....67 K1
Lumley Cl BELV DA17 .....117 H5
Lumley Gdns CHEAM SM3 .....174 C4
Lumley Rd CHEAM SM3 .....174 C5
Lumley St OXSTW W1C 10 B5
Luna Rd THHTH CR7 .....164 D2
Lundin Wk OXHEY WD19 .....33 H3
Lundy Dr HYS/HAR UB3 .....101 H3
Lundy Wk IS N1 * 73 J5
Lunham Rd NRWD SE19 .....150 A5
Lupin Cl BRXS/STRHM SW2 .....149 H1
  CROY/NA CRO 166 A7
  ROMW/RG RM7 .....81 F1
  WDR/YW UB7 .....100 A4
Lupton Cl LEE/GVPK SE12 .....153 F2
Lupton St KTTN NW5 .....72 C3
Lupus St PIM SW1V 16 D8
Lurgan Av HMSMTH W6 .....107 G5
Lurline Gdns BTSEA SW11 .....109 G7
Luscombe Gv VX/NE SW8 .....109 K6
Lushington Rd CAT SE6 .....151 K4
  WLSDN NW10 .....87 K1
Lushington Ter HACK E8 * 74 C4
Luther Cl EDGW HA8 .....36 E1
Luther King Cl WALTH E17 .....57 G5
Luther Ms TEDD TW11 .....143 F4
Luther Rd TEDD TW11 .....143 F4
Luton Pl GNWCH SE10 .....113 F6
Luton Rd PLSTW E13 .....94 E3
  SCUP DA14 .....155 J2
  WALTH E17 .....57 H3

Luton St STJWD NW8 9 H1
Luttrell Av PUT/ROE SW15 126 E4
Lutwyche Rd FSTH SE23 151 H1
Luxborough La CHIG IG7 45 K3
Luxborough St CAMTN NW1 10 A1
MHST W1U 10 A2
Luxemburg Ms SRTFD E15 76 C4
Luxemburg Gdns
HMSMTH W6 107 G3
Luxfield Rd ELTH/MOT SE9 134 D7
Luxford St BERM/RHTH SE16 112 A3
Luxmore St BROCKY SE4 112 C7
Luxor St CMBW SE5 130 D2
Lyall Av DUL SE21 150 A3
Lyall Ms KTBR SW1X 16 A4
Lyall Ms West KTBR SW1X * 16 A4
Lyall St KTBR SW1X 16 A4
Lyal Rd BOW E3 93 G1
Lycett Pl SHB W12 106 D1
Lych Gate Wk HYS/HAR UB3 82 D6
Lyconby Gdns CROY/NA CR0 166 B6
Lydd Cl BFN/LL DA15 154 E2
Lydden Gv WAND/EARL SW18 128 A6
Lydden Rd WAND/EARL SW18 128 A6
Lydd Rd BXLYHN DA7 117 G6
Lydeard Rd EHAM E6 77 K6
Lydford Cl STNW/STAM N16 74 A4
Lydford Rd CRICK NW2 70 B5
MV/WKIL W9 88 D3
SEVS/STOTM N15 55 K4
Lydhurst Av
BRXS/STRHM SW2 149 F1
Lydia Rd ERITH DA8 118 C5
Lydney Cl WIM/MER SW19 146 C1
Lydon Rd CLAP SW4 129 H2
Lydstep Rd CHST BR7 154 A3
Lyford Rd WAND/EARL SW18 128 C6
Lyford St WOOL/PLUM SE18 114 D3
Lygon Pl BGVA SW1W * 16 C4
Lyham Cl BRXS/STRHM SW2 129 K5
Lyham Rd BRXS/STRHM SW2 129 K5
Lyle Cl MTCM CR4 163 F6
Lyme Farm Rd LEE/GVPK SE12 133 K3
Lyme Gv HOM E9 74 E6
Lymer Av NRWD SE19 150 B4
Lyme Rd WELL DA16 116 C7
Lymescote Gdns SUT SM1 174 E1
Lyme St CAMTN NW1 4 E2
Lyme Ter CAMTN NW1 4 E2
Lyminge Cl SCUP DA14 155 F3
Lyminge Gdns
WAND/EARL SW18 128 D7
Lymington Av WDGN N22 55 G1
Lymington Cl
STRHM/NOR SW16 163 J1
Lymington Dr RSLP HA4 64 B1
Lymington Gdns
HOR/WEW KT19 173 H4
Lymington Rd BCTR RM8 61 K7
KIL/WHAMP NW6 * 71 F5
Lyminster Cl YEAD UB4 83 J4
Lympstone Gdns PECK SE15 111 H6
Lynbridge Gdns PLMGR N13 41 H3
Lynbrook Cl RAIN RM13 99 F1
Lynbrook Gv PECK SE15 111 F6
Lynchen Cl HEST TW5 101 K7
Lyncourt BKHTH/KID SE3 * 133 G1
Lyncroft Av PIN HA5 47 H4
Lyncroft Gdns EW KT17 173 H7
HSLW TW3 123 H4
KIL/WHAMP NW6 70 E4
WEA W13 104 D1
Lyndale CRICK NW2 70 D2
THDIT KT7 * 157 K6
Lyndale Av CRICK NW2 70 D2
Lyndale Cl BKHTH/KID SE3 113 J5
Lyndale Hampton Court Wy
ESH/CLAY KT10 157 K6
Lyndhurst Av BRYLDS KT5 159 J7
MLHL NW7 37 G5
NFNCH/WDSPK N12 39 K5
PIN HA5 33 F7
STHL UB1 84 B7
STRHM/NOR SW16 163 J1
WHTN TW2 122 E7
Lyndhurst Cl BXLYHN DA7 137 J2
CROY/NA CR0 178 B2
WLSDN NW10 69 F2
Lyndhurst Ct BELMT SM2 * 174 E6
Lyndhurst Dr LEY E10 58 A6
NWMAL KT3 160 B5
Lyndhurst Gdns BARK IG11 78 E5
EN EN1 30 A3
FNCH N3 38 C7
GNTH/NBYPK IG2 60 D5
HAMP NW3 71 H4
PIN HA5 33 F7
Lyndhurst Gv CMBW SE5 131 F1
Lyndhurst Leys HAYES BR2 * 167 G1
Lyndhurst Prior SNWD SE25 * 165 F2
Lyndhurst Rd BXLYHN DA7 137 J2
CHING E4 44 A6
GFD/PVL UB6 84 B3
HAMP NW3 71 H4
THHTH CR7 164 B3
UED N18 42 C3
WDGN N22 41 G5
Lyndhurst Sq PECK SE15 111 G7
Lyndhurst Ter HAMP NW3 71 H4
Lyndhurst Wy BELMT SM2 174 E7
PECK SE15 111 G7
Lyndon Av BFN/LL DA15 136 A4
PIN HA5 33 J5
WLGTN SM6 176 A2
Lyndon Rd BELV DA17 117 H3
Lyndon Yd TOOT SW17 147 F3
Lyne Crs WALTH E17 43 H7
Lynegrove Av ASHF TW15 140 A4
Lyneham Wk CLPT E5 * 75 G4
Lynette Av CLAP SW4 129 G5
Lynford Cl BAR EN5 25 H4
EDGW HA8 36 E7
Lynford Gdns EDGW HA8 36 D2
GDMY/SEVK IG3 79 F1
Lynford Ter ED N9 * 30 B7
Lynhurst Crs HGDN/ICK UB10 64 A6
Lynhurst Rd HGDN/ICK UB10 64 A6
Lynmere Rd WELL DA16 136 C1
Lyn Ms STNW/STAM N16 * 74 B3
Lynmouth Av EN EN1 30 B5
MRDN SM4 161 G6
Lynmouth Dr RSLP HA4 65 F1
Lynmouth Gdns GFD/PVL UB6 67 H7
HEST TW5 102 C7
Lynmouth Rd EFNCH N2 53 K2
GFD/PVL UB6 67 H7
STNW/STAM N16 56 B7
WALTH E17 57 G5
Lynn Cl ASHF TW15 140 B4
KTN/HRWW/WS HA3 48 D1
Lynnett Rd BCTR RM8 79 K1
Lynne Wk ESH/CLAY KT10 170 C4
Lynne Wy NTHLT UB5 83 H1
Lynn Ms WAN E11 76 C1
Lynn Rd BAL SW12 129 G6
GNTH/NBYPK IG2 60 D6
WAN E11 76 C1
Lynscott Wy SAND/SEL CR2 177 H7
Lynstead Cl BMLY BR1 168 B1
Lynsted Cl BXLYHS DA6 137 J4
Lynsted Ct BECK BR3 166 B1
Lynsted Gdns ELTH/MOT SE9 134 C3
Lynton Av CDALE/KGS NW9 51 H3
NFNCH/WDSPK N12 39 H3
WEA W13 85 G5
Lynton Cl CHSGTN KT9 172 A3
ISLW TW7 124 A3
WLSDN NW10 69 G4
Lynton Crs GNTH/NBYPK IG2 60 B5
Lynton Est STHWK SE1 19 M6
Lynton Gdns EN EN1 30 A6
FBAR/BDGN N11 40 D5
Lynton Md TRDG/WHET N20 38 E2
Lynton Rd ACT W3 86 C6
CEND/HSY/T N8 54 D4
CHING E4 43 K4
CROY/NA CR0 164 B5
KIL/WHAMP NW6 70 D7
NWMAL KT3 160 A4
RYLN/HDSTN HA2 65 J1
STHWK SE1 19 M6
Lynton Ter ACT W3 * 86 E5
Lynwood Cl RYLN/HDSTN HA2 65 J2
SWFD E18 45 G7
Lynwood Dr NTHWD HA6 32 C7
WPK KT4 173 J1
Lynwood Gdns CROY/NA CR0 177 F3
STHL UB1 83 K5
Lynwood Gv ORP BR6 169 K6
WCHMH N21 29 G7
Lynwood Rd EA W5 85 K2
THDIT KT7 171 F1
TOOT SW17 147 K2
Lynwood Ter
WIM/MER SW19 * 146 D7
Lyon Meade STAN HA7 35 J7
Lyon Park Av ALP/SUD HA0 68 A5
Lyon Rd HRW HA1 49 F5
ROM RM1 63 H6
WIM/MER SW19 147 G7
Lyonsdown Av BAR EN5 27 G5
Lyonsdown Rd BAR EN5 27 G4
Lyons Pl STJWD NW8 9 G1
Lyon St IS N1 5 L2
Lyons Wk WKENS W14 107 H3
Lyon Wy GFD/PVL UB6 66 E7
Lyric Dr GFD/PVL UB6 84 B3
Lyric Ms SYD SE26 150 E3
Lyric Rd BARN SW13 106 C7
Lysander CDALE/KGS NW9 * 37 H7
Lysander Gdns SURB KT6 159 G5
Lysander Gv ARCH N19 54 D7
Lysander Ms ARCH N19 54 C7
Lysander Rd CROY/NA CR0 177 F5
RSLP HA4 64 B1
Lysias Rd BAL SW12 129 F5
Lysia St FUL/PGN SW6 107 G6
Lysons Wk PUT/ROE SW15 * 126 D4
Lytchet Rd BMLY BR1 152 E6
Lytchgate Cl SAND/SEL CR2 178 A6
Lytcott Dr E/WMO/HCT KT8 156 E2
Lytcott Gv EDUL SE22 131 G4
Lytham Av OXHEY WD19 33 H4
Lytham Cl THMD SE28 98 A5
Lytham St WALW SE17 19 G8
Lyttelton Rd EFNCH N2 53 G6
LEY E10 75 K2
Lyttleton Cl HAMP NW3 3 J2
Lyttleton Rd
CEND/HSY/T N8 * 55 G2
Lytton Av PLMGR N13 41 G1
Lytton Cl EFNCH N2 53 H4
NTHLT UB5 65 K6
Lytton Gdns WLGTN SM6 176 D3
Lytton Gv PUT/ROE SW15 127 G4
Lytton Rd BAR EN5 27 G3
GPK RM2 63 K4
PIN HA5 33 J6
WAN E11 58 C6
Lyveden Rd BKHTH/KID SE3 114 A6
TOOT SW17 147 J5

M

Maberley Crs NRWD SE19 150 C6
Maberley Rd BECK BR3 166 A2
NRWD SE19 150 B7
Mabledon Pl CAMTN NW1 5 H8
Mablethorpe Rd
FUL/PGN SW6 107 H6
Mabley St HOM E9 75 G4
Macaret Cl TRDG/WHET N20 27 F6
Macarthur Cl FSTGT E7 76 E5
WBLY HA9 68 D5
Macarthur Ter CHARL SE7 * 114 C5
Macaulay Av ESH/CLAY KT10 170 E1
Macaulay Rd CLAP SW4 129 G2
EHAM E6 95 H1
Macbean St
WOOL/PLUM SE18 115 F2
Macbeth St HMSMTH W6 106 E4
Macclesfield Br STJWD NW8 3 K5
Macclesfield Rd FSBYE EC1V 6 E7
SNWD SE25 165 J4
Macclesfield St
SOHO/SHAV W1D * 11 H6
Macdonald Av DAGE RM10 80 D2
Macdonald Rd ARCH N19 72 C1
FBAR/BDGN N11 39 K4
FSTGT E7 76 E3
WALTH E17 58 A1
Macduff Rd BTSEA SW11 109 F7
Mace Cl WAP E1W 92 D7
Mace St BETH E2 93 F1
Macfarlane La ISLW TW7 104 A5
Macfarlane Rd SHB W12 88 A7
Mac Farren Pl CAMTN NW1 10 B1
Macgregor Rd CAN/RD E16 95 G4
Machell Rd PECK SE15 131 K2
Mackay Rd VX/NE SW8 129 G2
Mackennal St STJWD NW8 3 K6
Mackenzie Cl SHB W12 87 K6
Mackenzie Rd BECK BR3 166 A1
HOLWY N7 73 F5
Mackeson Rd HAMP NW3 * 71 K3
Mackie Rd BRXS/STRHM SW2 130 B6
Mackintosh La HOM E9 75 F4
Macklin St HOL/ALD WC2B * 11 K4
Macks Rd BERM/RHTH SE16 111 H2
Mackworth St CAMTN NW1 4 E7
Maclean Rd FSTH SE23 132 B5
Macleod House CHARL SE7 * 114 D6
Macleod Rd WCHMH N21 28 E4
Macleod St WALW SE17 18 F8
Maclise Rd WKENS W14 107 H2
Macmillan Wy TOOT SW17 148 B3
Macoma Rd
WOOL/PLUM SE18 115 J5
Macoma Ter
WOOL/PLUM SE18 115 J5
Maconochies Rd
POP/IOD E14 * 112 E4
Macquarie Wy POP/IOD E14 112 E3
Macroom Rd MV/WKIL W9 88 D2
Maddams St BOW E3 93 K3
Maddison Cl EFNCH N2 53 G1
TEDD TW11 143 F5
Maddocks Cl SCUP DA14 155 K5
Maddock Wy WALW SE17 110 C5
Maddox St CONDST W1S 10 D6
Madeira Av BMLY BR1 152 C7
Madeira Gv WFD IG8 45 G5
Madeira Rd MTCM CR4 162 E3
PLMGR N13 41 H3
STRHM/NOR SW16 148 E4
WAN E11 58 B7
Madeleine Ct CHDH RM6 61 J5
Madeley Rd EA W5 85 K5
Madeline Gv IL IG1 78 D4
Madeline Rd PGE/AN SE20 150 C6
Madge Gill Wy EHAM E6 77 J7
Madge Hl HNWL W7 * 84 E6
Madinah Rd HACK E8 74 C4
Madison Cl BELMT SM2 175 H6
Madison Crs BXLYHN DA7 116 D6
Madison Gdns BXLYHN DA7 116 D6
Madoc Cl CRICK NW2 70 D1
Madras Pl HOLWY N7 73 G5
Madras Rd IL IG1 78 B3
Madrid Rd BARN SW13 106 D7
Madron St WALW SE17 19 K7
Mafeking Av BTFD TW8 105 F5
EHAM E6 95 H1
GNTH/NBYPK IG2 60 D6
Mafeking Rd CAN/RD E16 94 D3
EN EN1 30 B2
TOTM N17 56 C1
Magazine Ga BAY/PAD W2 * 9 K8
Magdala Av ARCH N19 72 C1
Magdala Rd ISLW TW7 124 B2
SAND/SEL CR2 177 K6
Magdalene Gdns EHAM E6 96 A3
Magdalen Rd
WAND/EARL SW18 128 B7
Magdalen St STHWK SE1 13 J9
Magee St LBTH SE11 18 A9
Magellan Bvd CAN/RD E16 96 C6
Magellan Pl POP/IOD E14 112 D3
Magnaville Rd BUSH WD23 22 E6
Magnet Rd WBLY HA9 67 K1
Magnin Cl HACK E8 74 C7
Magnolia Cl KUTN/CMB KT2 144 D5
LEY E10 75 J1
Magnolia Ct
KTN/HRWW/WS HA3 50 B6
Magnolia Gdns EDGW HA8 36 E3
Magnolia Pl CLAP SW4 * 129 K4
EA W5 * 85 K4
Magnolia Rd CHSWK W4 105 J5
Magnolia St WDR/YW UB7 100 A3
Magnolia Wy HOR/WEW KT19 172 E4
Magnolia Whf CHSWK W4 * 105 J5
Magpie Cl CDALE/KGS NW9 51 G1
FSTGT E7 76 D4
Magpie Hall Cl HAYES BR2 168 D5
Magpie Hall La HAYES BR2 168 D6
Magpie Hall Rd STAN HA7 34 E1
Magpie Pl NWCR SE14 * 112 B5
Magri Wk WCHPL E1 92 E4
Maguire Dr RCHPK/HAM TW10 143 J3
Maguire St STHWK SE1 19 M1
Mahlon Av RSLP HA4 65 F4
Mahogany Cl
BERM/RHTH SE16 93 G7
Maida Av BAY/PAD W2 8 F2
CHING E4 31 K6
Maida Rd BELV DA17 117 H2
Maida V MV/WKIL W9 2 D6
STJWD NW8 3 G9
Maida Vale Rd DART DA1 138 D4
Maida Wy CHING E4 31 K6
Maiden Erlegh Av BXLY DA5 137 F7
Maiden La CAMTN NW1 5 H1
COVGDN WC2E 11 K6
DART DA1 138 D3
STHWK SE1 12 F9
Maiden Rd SRTFD E15 76 C6
Maidenstone Hl GNWCH SE10 113 F7
Maidstone Av CRW RM5 62 E1
Maidstone Buildings Ms
STHWK SE1 12 F9
Maidstone Rd
FBAR/BDGN N11 40 D5
SCUP DA14 155 K5
Main Av EN EN1 30 B4
NTHWD HA6 32 A2
Main Barracks
WOOL/PLUM SE18 * 114 E4
Main Dr GFD/PVL UB6 * 85 G2
WBLY HA9 67 K2
Mainridge Rd CHST BR7 154 A3
Main Rd ROM RM1 63 H3
SCUP DA14 154 E2
STMC/STPC BR5 155 J7
Main St FELT TW13 141 H4
Maise Webster Cl
STWL/WRAY TW19 * 120 A6
Maismore St PECK SE15 111 H5
The Maisonettes SUT SM1 * 174 D4
Maitland Cl GNWCH SE10 112 E6
HSLWW TW4 122 E2
Maitland Park Rd HAMP NW3 71 K5
Maitland Park Vls HAMP NW3 71 K5
Maitland Rd PGE/AN SE20 151 F5
SRTFD E15 76 D5
Majendie Rd
WOOL/PLUM SE18 115 J4
Major Cl BRXN/ST SW9 130 C2
Major Draper St
WOOL/PLUM SE18 115 G2
Major Rd BERM/RHTH SE16 * 111 H2
SRTFD E15 76 A4
Makepeace Av HGT N6 72 A1
Makepeace Rd NTHLT UB5 83 J1
WAN E11 58 E3
Makins St CHEL SW3 15 K6
Malabar St POP/IOD E14 112 D1
Malam Gdns POP/IOD E14 93 K6
Malan Sq RAIN RM13 81 K5
Malbrook Rd PUT/ROE SW15 126 E3
Malcolm Cl PGE/AN SE20 * 150 E6
Malcolm Ct STAN HA7 35 J4
Malcolm Crs HDN NW4 51 J4
Malcolm Dr SURB KT6 158 E7
Malcolm Pl BETH E2 92 E3
Malcolm Rd PGE/AN SE20 150 E6
SNWD SE25 165 H5
WCHPL E1 92 E3
WIM/MER SW19 146 C5
Malcolms Wy
STHGT/OAK N14 * 28 C4
Malcolm Wy WAN E11 58 E4
Malden Av GFD/PVL UB6 66 E5
SNWD SE25 165 J3
Malden Flds BUSH WD23 21 H4
Malden Green Av WPK KT4 160 C7
Malden Hl NWMAL KT3 160 C3
Malden Hill Gdns NWMAL KT3 160 C2
Malden Pk NWMAL KT3 160 C5
Malden Pl KTTN NW5 72 A4
Malden Rd BORE WD6 24 C2
CHEAM SM3 174 B3
KTTN NW5 71 K4
NWMAL KT3 160 B4
WAT WD17 21 F1
Malden Wy NWMAL KT3 160 A5
Maldon Cl CMBW SE5 * 131 F2
IS N1 6 E3
Maldon Rd ACT W3 86 E6
ED N9 42 B2
ROMW/RG RM7 62 E6
WLGTN SM6 176 B4
Maldon Wk WFD IG8 45 G5
Malet St GWRST WC1E 11 G1
Maley Av WNWD SE27 149 H1
Malford Gv SWFD E18 58 D2
Malfort Rd CMBW SE5 131 F2
Malham Cl FBAR/BDGN N11 40 A5
Malham Rd FSTH SE23 132 A7
Malham Ter UED N18 * 42 D5
Malins Cl BAR EN5 * 25 K4
Malkin Wy WATW WD18 20 C3
Mallams Ms BRXN/ST SW9 130 B2
Mallard Cl BAR EN5 * 27 H5
DART DA1 139 J4
HNWL W7 103 K1
KIL/WHAMP NW6 2 B4
WHTN TW2 123 F6
Mallard Ct WALTH E17 * 58 B2
Mallard Pl TWK TW1 143 G2
WDGN N22 * 55 F1
Mallards Ct OXHEY WD19 33 K2
Mallards Rd BARK IG11 97 G2
WFD IG8 45 F6
Mallard Wk BECK BR3 166 A4
Mallard Wy CDALE/KGS NW9 50 E6
NTHWD HA6 32 A6
WLGTN SM6 176 C7
Mall Chambers KENS W8 * 8 B8
Mallet Dr NTHLT UB5 65 K4
Mallet Rd LEW SE13 133 G5
Malling Cl CROY/NA CR0 * 165 K5
Malling Gdns MRDN SM4 162 B5
Malling Wy HAYES BR2 167 J6
Mallinson Rd BTSEA SW11 128 D4
CROY/NA CR0 176 D2
Mallord St CHEL SW3 15 H9
Mallory Cl BROCKY SE4 132 B3
POP/IOD E14 93 K3
Mallory Ct LEE/GVPK SE12 134 A6
Mallory Gdns EBAR EN4 28 A6
Mallory St STJWD NW8 9 K1
Mallow Cl CROY/NA CR0 166 A7
Mallow Md MLHL NW7 38 C6
Mallow St FSBYE EC1V 7 G9
Mall Rd HMSMTH W6 106 E4
The Mall BTFD TW8 * 104 E5
BXLYHS DA6 * 137 H3
EA W5 86 A6
EMPK RM11 63 K7
KTN/HRWW/WS HA3 50 B5
MORT/ESHN SW14 125 K4
SRTFD E15 * 76 B6
STHGT/OAK N14 40 E2
SURB KT6 158 E4
WHALL SW1A 16 E1
Mall Vls HMSMTH W6 * 106 E4
Malmains Cl BECK BR3 167 G4
Malmains Wy BECK BR3 167 F3
Malmesbury Cl PIN HA5 46 D3
Malmesbury Rd BOW E3 93 H1
CAN/RD E16 94 C4
MRDN SM4 162 B6
SWFD E18 44 D7
Malmesbury Ter CAN/RD E16 94 D4
Malmesbury West Est
BOW E3 93 H2
Malory Cl BECK BR3 166 B1
Malpas Dr PIN HA5 47 H4
Malpas Rd BROCKY SE4 132 C1
DAGW RM9 79 K5
HACK E8 74 D5
Malta Rd LEY E10 57 J7
Malta St FSBYE EC1V 6 C9
Maltby Rd CHSGTN KT9 172 C5
Maltby St STHWK SE1 19 L2
Malthouse Dr CHSWK W4 106 C5
FELT TW13 141 H4
Maltings Cl BOW E3 94 A2
Maltings Pl FUL/PGN SW6 108 A7
STHWK SE1 19 K1
The Maltings ROM RM1 63 H6
SNWD SE25 * 165 F2
Malting Wy ISLW TW7 124 A2
Malton Ms NKENS W10 * 88 C5
WOOL/PLUM SE18 115 K5
Malton Rd NKENS W10 88 C5
Malton St WOOL/PLUM SE18 115 K5
Maltravers St TPL/STR WC2R 11 M6
Malt St STHWK SE1 111 H5
Malva Cl WAND/EARL SW18 128 A4
Malvern Av BXLYHN DA7 117 F6
CHING E4 44 B6
RYLN/HDSTN HA2 65 J2
Malvern Cl BUSH WD23 22 C5
MTCM CR4 163 H2
NKENS W10 88 D4
SURB KT6 159 F7
Malvern Dr FELT TW13 141 H4
GDMY/SEVK IG3 79 F3
WFD IG8 45 G4
Malvern Gdns CRICK NW2 70 C1
KTN/HRWW/WS HA3 50 A3
Malvern Ms KIL/WHAMP NW6 2 A8
Malvern Pl MV/WKIL W9 * 88 D2
Malvern Rd CEND/HSY/T N8 55 F2
EHAM E6 77 J7
HACK E8 74 C6
HPTN TW12 142 A7
HYS/HAR UB3 101 H6
KIL/WHAMP NW6 2 A7
MV/WKIL W9 * 88 D2
SURB KT6 172 A1
THHTH CR7 164 B3
TOTM N17 56 C2
WAN E11 76 C1
Malvern Ter ED N9 30 B7
IS N1 6 A3
Malvern Wy WEA W13 85 H4
Malwood Rd BAL SW12 129 G5
Malyons Rd LEW SE13 132 E4
Malyons Ter LEW SE13 132 E4
Managers St POP/IOD E14 * 94 A7
Manaton Cl PECK SE15 131 J2
Manaton Crs STHL UB1 84 A5
Manbey Gv SRTFD E15 76 C5
Manbey Park Rd SRTFD E15 76 C5
Manbey Rd SRTFD E15 * 76 C5
Manbey St SRTFD E15 76 C5
Manbre Rd HMSMTH W6 107 F5
Manbrough Av EHAM E6 96 A2
Manchester Ct CAN/RD E16 95 F5
Manchester Dr NKENS W10 * 88 C3
Manchester Gv POP/IOD E14 113 F4
Manchester Ms MHST W1U 10 A3
Manchester Rd POP/IOD E14 113 F4
SEVS/STOTM N15 55 K5
THHTH CR7 164 D2
Manchester Sq MBLAR W1H 10 A4
Manchester St MHST W1U 10 A3
Manchester Wy DAGE RM10 * 80 D3
Manchuria Rd BTSEA SW11 129 F5
Manciple St STHWK SE1 19 H2
Mandalay Rd CLAP SW4 129 H4
Mandarin Wy YEAD UB4 83 H5
Mandela Cl WLSDN NW10 68 E6
Mandela Pl WATN WD24 21 H1
Mandela Rd CAN/RD E16 94 E5
Mandela St BRXN/ST SW9 110 B6
CAMTN NW1 4 F3
Mandela Wy STHWK SE1 19 K5
Mandeville Cl WIM/MER SW19 146 C6
Mandeville Ct CHING E4 43 G3
Mandeville Dr SURB KT6 158 E7
Mandeville Pl MHST W1U 10 B4
Mandeville Rd ISLW TW7 124 B1
NTHLT UB5 65 K6
STHGT/OAK N14 40 B1
Mandeville St CLPT E5 75 G2
Mandrake Rd TOOT SW17 147 K2
Mandrake Wy SRTFD E15 * 76 C6
Mandrell Rd
BRXS/STRHM SW2 129 K4
Manette St LSQ/SEVD WC2H 11 H5
Manfred Rd PUT/ROE SW15 127 J4
Manger Rd HOLWY N7 72 E5
Mangold Wy ERITHM DA18 116 E2
Manilla St POP/IOD E14 112 D1
Manister Rd ABYW SE2 116 B2
Manley Ct STNW/STAM N16 74 B2
Manley St CAMTN NW1 4 A3
Mann Cl CROY/NA CR0 177 J2
Manningford Cl FSBYE EC1V * 6 C7
Manning Gdns CROY/NA CR0 165 J6
KTN/HRWW/WS HA3 49 K6
Manning Pl RCHPK/HAM TW10 125 G5
Manning Rd DAGE RM10 80 C5
WALTH E17 57 G3
Manningtree Cl
WIM/MER SW19 127 H7
Manningtree Rd RSLP HA4 65 F3
Manningtree St WCHPL E1 92 C5
Mannin Rd CHDH RM6 61 H6
Mannock Cl CDALE/KGS NW9 51 F2
Mannock Ms SWFD E18 45 F7
Mannock Rd DART DA1 139 J2
WDGN N22 55 H2
Mann's Cl ISLW TW7 124 A4
Manns Rd EDGW HA8 36 C5
Manoel Rd WHTN TW2 142 C1
Manor Av BROCKY SE4 132 C1
HSLWW TW4 122 C2
NTHLT UB5 65 K6
Manorbrook BKHTH/KID SE3 133 K3
Manor Cl BAR EN5 26 C3
CDALE/KGS NW9 50 D3
DAGE RM10 81 F5
DART DA1 138 A3
MLHL NW7 * 37 F4
ROM RM1 63 J4
RSLP HA4 46 D7
THMD SE28 97 J5
WPK KT4 160 B7
Manor Cots NTHWD HA6 32 D7
Manor Cottages Ap
EFNCH N2 53 G1
Manor Ct ACT W3 * 105 H3
E/WMO/HCT KT8 * 157 F3
HRW HA1 * 49 F5
KUTN/CMB KT2 * 144 C7
WBLY HA9 * 68 A4
Manor Court Rd HNWL W7 84 E6
Manor Crs BRYLDS KT5 159 H5
Manor Cft EDGW HA8 * 36 C5
Manordene Cl THDIT KT7 158 B7
Manordene Rd THMD SE28 97 J5
Manor Dr BRYLDS KT5 159 H5
ESH/CLAY KT10 171 F2
FELT TW13 141 H4
HOR/WEW KT19 173 G5
MLHL NW7 37 F4
STHGT/OAK N14 28 B6
TRDG/WHET N20 39 J2
WBLY HA9 68 B3
Manor Dr North NWMAL KT3 160 A6
The Manor Dr WPK KT4 160 B7
Manor Est BERM/RHTH SE16 111 J3
Manor Farm Cl WPK KT4 160 B7
Manor Farm Dr CHING E4 44 C1
Manor Farm Rd ALP/SUD HA0 85 K1
STRHM/NOR SW16 164 B1
Manorfield Cl ARCH N19 72 C3
Manor Gdns ACT W3 105 H3
CLAP SW4 * 129 H1
HOLWY N7 72 E2
HPTN TW12 142 B6
RCH/KEW TW9 125 G3
RSLP HA4 65 G4
RYNPK SW20 161 J1
SAND/SEL CR2 178 B5
SUN TW16 140 E7
Manor Ga NTHLT UB5 65 J6
Manorgate Rd KUTN/CMB KT2 144 C7
Manor Gv BECK BR3 166 E1
PECK SE15 111 K5
RCH/KEW TW9 125 H3
Manor Hall Av HDN NW4 52 A1
Manor Hall Dr HDN NW4 52 B1
Manor Hall Gdns LEY E10 57 J7
Manor House Dr
KIL/WHAMP NW6 70 B6
Manor House Wy ISLW TW7 124 C2
Manor La FELT TW13 140 E1
HYS/HAR UB3 101 G5
LEE/GVPK SE12 133 H5
SUN TW16 156 A1
SUT SM1 175 G4
Manor Lane Ter LEW SE13 133 H3
Manor Ms BROCKY SE4 132 C1
KIL/WHAMP NW6 2 B5
Manor Mt FSTH SE23 131 K7
Manor Pde HRW HA1 * 49 F5

STNW/STAM N16 * 74 B1
Manor Pk CHST BR7 169 J1
LEW SE13 133 G4
RCH/KEW TW9 125 G3
Manor Park Cl WWKM BR4 166 E7
Manor Park Crs EDGW HA8 36 C5
Manor Park Dr
RYLN/HDSTN HA2 48 B2
Manor Park Gdns EDGW HA8 36 C4
Manor Park Rd CHST BR7 154 C7
EFNCH N2 53 G2
MNPK E12 77 H3
SUT SM1 175 G4
WLSDN NW10 69 G7
WWKM BR4 166 E7
Manor Pl BORE WD6 * 24 E2
CHST BR7 169 J1
EBED/NFELT TW14 121 K7
MTCM CR4 163 H2
SUT SM1 175 F4
WALW SE17 18 D8
Manor Rd BAR EN5 26 C3
BARK IG11 79 F5
BECK BR3 166 D1
BELMT SM2 174 D6
BFN/LL DA15 155 F2
BXLY DA5 137 J7
CAN/RD E16 94 C4
CHDH RM6 61 K5
DAGE RM10 80 E5
DART DA1 138 B3
E/WMO/HCT KT8 157 J3
ENC/FH EN2 29 K1
ERITH DA8 118 C5
HRW HA1 49 G5
HYS/HAR UB3 82 E5
LEY E10 57 J6
MTCM CR4 163 H2
RCH/KEW TW9 125 G2
ROM RM1 63 J4
RSLP HA4 46 B7
RYNPK SW20 161 J1
SNWD SE25 165 H3
SRTFD E15 94 C2
STNW/STAM N16 56 A7
TEDD TW11 143 G4
TOTM N17 42 C7
WALTH E17 57 G1
WDGN N22 40 E5
WEA W13 85 G6
WHTN TW2 142 C1
WLGTN SM6 176 B3
WWKM BR4 166 E7
Manor Rd North
ESH/CLAY KT10 171 F2
WLGTN SM6 176 B3
Manor Rd South
ESH/CLAY KT10 170 E3
Manorside BAR EN5 26 C3
Manor Sq BCTR RM8 79 J1
Manor V BTFD TW8 104 D4
Manor Vw FNCH N3 53 F1
Manor Wy WPK KT4 160 B7
BECK BR3 166 D2
BKHTH/KID SE3 133 K3
BORE WD6 24 E3
BXLY DA5 137 H7
BXLYHN DA7 138 A2
CDALE/KGS NW9 51 G3
CHING E4 44 B3
Manorway EN EN1 30 A6
Manor Wy FSTH SE23 131 K6
HAYES BR2 168 D5
MTCM CR4 163 H2
NWDGN UB2 102 C3
RAIN RM13 99 G3
RSLP HA4 46 C6
RYLN/HDSTN HA2 48 B3
SAND/SEL CR2 178 A5
STMC/STPC BR5 169 H3
Manorway WFD IG8 45 G4
The Manor Wy WLGTN SM6 176 B3
Manresa Rd CHEL SW3 15 H7
Mansard Beeches TOOT SW17 148 A4
Mansard Cl HCH RM12 81 J1
PIN HA5 47 H2
Manse Cl HYS/HAR UB3 101 G5
Mansel Gv WALTH E17 43 J7
Mansell Rd ACT W3 87 F7
GFD/PVL UB6 84 B4
Mansell St WCHPL E1 13 M5
Mansel Rd WIM/MER SW19 146 C5
Mansergh Cl CHARL SE7 114 D6
Manse Rd STNW/STAM N16 74 B2
Manser Rd RAIN RM13 99 G2
Mansfield Av EBAR EN4 27 K5
RSLP HA4 47 F7
SEVS/STOTM N15 55 K3
Mansfield Cl ED N9 30 C5
Mansfield Dr YEAD UB4 82 C3
Mansfield Hl CHING E4 31 K7
Mansfield Ms CAVSQ/HST W1G 10 C3
Mansfield Rd ACT W3 86 D3
CHSGTN KT9 171 J4
HAMP NW3 71 K4
IL IG1 78 A1
SAND/SEL CR2 177 K5
WALTH E17 57 H3
WAN E11 59 F5
Mansfield St CAVSQ/HST W1G 10 C3
Mansford St BETH E2 92 C1
Manship Rd MTCM CR4 148 A7
Mansion Cl BRXN/ST SW9 110 B7
Mansion Gdns HAMP NW3 71 F2
Mansion House Pl
MANHO EC4N * 13 G5
Mansion House St
MANHO EC4N 13 G5
Manson Ms SKENS SW7 14 F6
Manson Pl SKENS SW7 15 G6
Manstead Gdns CHDH RM6 61 J6
RAIN RM13 99 K5
Manston Av NWDGN UB2 103 F3
Manston Cl PGE/AN SE20 150 E7
Manstone Rd CRICK NW2 70 C4
Manston Gv KUTN/CMB KT2 143 K4
Manston Wy HCH RM12 81 K5
Manthorpe Rd
WOOL/PLUM SE18 115 H4
Mantilla Rd TOOT SW17 148 A3
Mantle Rd BROCKY SE4 132 B2
Mantlet Cl STRHM/NOR SW16 148 C6
Mantle Wy SRTFD E15 76 C6
Manton Av HNWL W7 104 A1
Manton Cl HYS/HAR UB3 82 C6
Manton Rd ABYW SE2 116 B3
Mantua St BTSEA SW11 128 C2
Mantus Rd WCHPL E1 92 E3
Manus Wy TRDG/WHET N20 39 G1
Manville Gdns TOOT SW17 148 B1
Manville Rd TOOT SW17 148 A1
Manwood Rd BROCKY SE4 132 C4
Manwood St CAN/RD E16 95 K7
Many Gates BAL SW12 148 B1
Mapesbury Ms
CDALE/KGS NW9 51 J5
Mapesbury Rd CRICK NW2 70 C5
Mapeshill Pl CRICK NW2 70 A5
Mape St BETH E2 92 D3
Maple Av ACT W3 87 G7
CHING E4 43 H5
RYLN/HDSTN HA2 66 B1
Maple Cl BKHH IG9 45 H2
BUSH WD23 21 J1
CLAP SW4 129 J5
FNCH N3 38 E5
HCH RM12 81 K2
HPTN TW12 141 K5
MTCM CR4 148 B7
RSLP HA4 47 F5
STMC/STPC BR5 169 J4
STNW/STAM N16 56 C5
YEAD UB4 83 H2
Maple Ct ASHF TW15 140 B5
HACK E8 * 74 C5
NWMAL KT3 160 A2
Maple Crs BFN/LL DA15 136 B5
Maplecroft Cl EHAM E6 95 H5
Mapledale Av CROY/NA CR0 178 D2
Mapledene Est HACK E8 * 74 C6
Mapledene Rd HACK E8 7 M1
Maple Gdns EDGW HA8 37 G6
Maple Gv BTFD TW8 104 C6
CDALE/KGS NW9 50 E6
EA W5 104 E2
STHL UB1 83 K4
Maplehurst Cl KUT/HW KT1 159 F3
Maple Leaf Dr BFN/LL DA15 136 A7
Mapleleafe Gdns
BARK/HLT IG6 60 B2
Maple Leaf Sq
BERM/RHTH SE16 * 112 A1
Maple Ms KIL/WHAMP NW6 * 2 C5
STRHM/NOR SW16 149 F4
Maple Pl FITZ W1T 10 F2
TOTM N17 42 C6
Maple Rd DART DA1 139 F7
PGE/AN SE20 150 D7
SURB KT6 158 E4
WAN E11 58 C5
YEAD UB4 83 G2
Maples Pl WCHPL E1 * 92 D4
Maplestead Rd
BRXS/STRHM SW2 130 A6
DAGW RM9 79 H7
The Maples ESH/CLAY KT10 * 171 G6
KUT/HW KT1 * 143 J6
Maple St BETH E2 92 C1
FITZ W1T 10 E2
ROMW/RG RM7 62 E3
Maplethorpe Rd THHTH CR7 164 B3
Mapleton Cl HAYES BR2 167 K4
Mapleton Crs
WAND/EARL SW18 128 A5
Mapleton Rd CHING E4 44 A2
EN EN1 30 D1
WAND/EARL SW18 127 K5
Maple Tree Pl BKHTH/KID SE3 114 D7
Maple Wk NKENS W10 * 88 B3
Maple Wy FELT TW13 140 E2
Maplin Cl WCHMH N21 29 F5
Maplin Rd CAN/RD E16 94 E5
Maplin St BOW E3 93 H2
Mapperley Dr WFD IG8 44 C6
Marabou Cl MNPK E12 77 J4
Maran Wy ERITHM DA18 116 E2
Marathon Wy THMD SE28 97 F7
Marban Rd MV/WKIL W9 88 D2
Marble Cl ACT W3 86 D7
Marble Dr CRICK NW2 52 B6
Marble Hill Cl TWK TW1 124 C6
Marble Hill Gdns TWK TW1 124 C6
Marble Quay WAP E1W 13 M8
Marbrook Ct LEE/GVPK SE12 153 G2
Marcella Rd BRXN/ST SW9 130 B1
Marcet Rd DART DA1 139 F4
Marchant Cl MLHL NW7 37 G5
Marchant Rd WAN E11 76 B1
Marchant St NWCR SE14 112 B5
Marchbank Rd WKENS W14 107 J5
Marchmont Gdns
RCHPK/HAM TW10 125 F4
Marchmont Rd
RCHPK/HAM TW10 125 G4
WLGTN SM6 176 C7
Marchmont St BMSBY WC1N 5 J9
STPAN WC1H 5 J9
March Rd TWK TW1 124 A6
Marchside Cl HEST TW5 102 C7
Marchwood Cl CMBW SE5 111 F6
Marchwood Crs EA W5 85 J5
Marcia Rd STHWK SE1 19 K6
Marcilly Rd WAND/EARL SW18 128 C4
Marconi Pl FBAR/BDGN N11 40 B3
Marconi Rd LEY E10 57 J7
Marconi Wy STHL UB1 84 B5
Marcon Pl HACK E8 74 D5
Marco Rd HMSMTH W6 106 E2
Marcus Garvey Ms EDUL SE22 131 J5
Marcus Garvey Wy HNHL SE24 130 B3
Marcus Rd DART DA1 138 D6
Marcus St SRTFD E15 76 C7
WAND/EARL SW18 128 A5
Marcus Ter WAND/EARL SW18 128 A5
Mardale Dr CDALE/KGS NW9 51 F4
Mardell Rd CROY/NA CR0 166 A4
Marden Av HAYES BR2 167 K5
Marden Crs BXLY DA5 137 K4
CROY/NA CR0 164 A5
Marden Rd CROY/NA CR0 164 A5
ROM RM1 63 G5
TOTM N17 56 A1
Marden Sq BERM/RHTH SE16 111 J2
Marder Rd WEA W13 104 B1
Mardyke Cl RAIN RM13 98 E1
Marechal Niel Av BFN/LL DA15 154 D2
Marechal Niel Pde
SCUP DA14 * 154 D2
Maresfield CROY/NA CR0 178 A2
Maresfield Gdns HAMP NW3 71 G4
Mare St HACK E8 74 D7
Marfield Cl WPK KT4 160 D7
Marfleet Cl CAR SM5 175 J1
Margaret Av CHING E4 31 K5
Margaret Bondfield Av
BARK IG11 79 G6
Margaret Cl GPK RM2 63 K4
Margaret Gardner Dr
ELTH/MOT SE9 153 K1
Margaret Ingram Cl
FUL/PGN SW6 * 107 J5
Margaret Lockwood Cl
KUT/HW KT1 * 159 G3
Margaret Rd BXLY DA5 136 E5
EBAR EN4 27 H3
GPK RM2 63 K4
STNW/STAM N16 * 56 B7
WAN E11 58 B5
Margaret Rutherford Pl
BAL SW12 129 H7
Margaret St GTPST W1W 10 E4
REGST W1B 10 D4
Margaretta Ter CHEL SW3 15 J9
Margaretting Rd MNPK E12 77 G1
Margaret Wy REDBR IG4 59 J5
Margate Rd
BRXS/STRHM SW2 129 K4
Margeholes OXHEY WD19 33 J1
Margery Park Rd FSTGT E7 76 E5
Margery Rd BCTR RM8 79 K2
Margery St CLKNW EC1R 6 A8
Margin Dr WIM/MER SW19 146 B4
Margravine Gdns
HMSMTH W6 107 G4
Margravine Rd HMSMTH W6 107 G5
Marguerite Vls RYNPK SW20 * 145 K6
Marham Dr CDALE/KGS NW9 51 G1
Marham Gdns MRDN SM4 162 B5
WAND/EARL SW18 128 D7
Maria Cl STHWK SE1 111 H3
Marian Cl YEAD UB4 83 H3
Marian Pl BETH E2 92 D1
Marian Rd STRHM/NOR SW16 148 C7
Marian St BETH E2 * 92 D1
Marian Wy WLSDN NW10 69 H6
Maria Ter WCHPL E1 93 F4
Maria Theresa Cl NWMAL KT3 160 A4
Maricas Av
KTN/HRWW/WS HA3 34 D7
Marie Curie CMBW SE5 * 111 F7
Marie Lloyd Wk HACK E8 * 74 C5
Mariette Wy WLGTN SM6 176 E7
Marigold Aly STHWK SE1 12 C7
Marigold Cl STHL UB1 83 J6
Marigold Rd TOTM N17 42 E6
Marigold St BERM/RHTH SE16 111 J1
Marigold Wy CROY/NA CR0 166 A7
Marina Ap YEAD UB4 83 J4
Marina Av NWMAL KT3 160 E5
Marina Dr DART DA1 139 K7
WELL DA16 135 K1
Marina Gdns ROMW/RG RM7 62 D4
Marina Pl KUT/HW KT1 158 E1
Marina Wy TEDD TW11 143 K6
Marine Ct PUR RM19 119 J3
Marine Dr BARK IG11 97 G3
WOOL/PLUM SE18 114 E3
Marinefield Rd FUL/PGN SW6 128 A1
Mariner Gdns
RCHPK/HAM TW10 143 H2
Mariner Rd MNPK E12 78 A3
Mariners Ms POP/IOD E14 113 G3
Marine St BERM/RHTH SE16 111 H2
Marion Gv WFD IG8 44 C4
Marion Ms DUL SE21 149 K2
Marion Rd MLHL NW7 37 J4
THHTH CR7 164 D4
Marischal Rd LEW SE13 133 G2
Maritime Quay POP/IOD E14 112 D4
Maritime St BOW E3 93 H3
Marius Rd TOOT SW17 148 A1
Marjorie Gv BTSEA SW11 128 E3
Mark Av CHING E4 31 K5
Mark Cl BXLYHN DA7 117 F7
HAYES BR2 181 J3
STHL UB1 84 A7
Markeston Gn OXHEY WD19 33 H3
Market Chambers
ENC/FH EN2 * 29 K2
Market Est HOLWY N7 72 E5
Market La EDGW HA8 36 E7
SHB W12 * 107 F1
Market Link ROM RM1 63 G3
Market Ms MYFR/PICC W1J 10 C9
Market Pde BMLY BR1 * 152 E7
ED N9 * 42 C1
EW KT17 * 173 H7
FELT TW13 * 141 J1
LEY E10 * 57 K5
SCUP DA14 * 155 G3
SNWD SE25 * 165 H3
STNW/STAM N16 * 56 C7
WALTH E17 * 57 H2
Market Pl ACT W3 86 E7
BERM/RHTH SE16 * 111 H3
BTFD TW8 104 D6
BXLYHS DA6 137 H3
DART DA1 139 H6
EFNCH N2 53 H2
GTPST W1W 10 E4
KUT/HW KT1 * 158 E1
ROM RM1 63 G4
WAT WD17 21 G3
Market Rd HOLWY N7 72 E5
RCH/KEW TW9 125 H2
Market Sq ED N9 42 D1
Market St EHAM E6 95 K1
WATW WD18 21 F3
WOOL/PLUM SE18 115 F3
Market Ter BTFD TW8 * 105 F5
The Market CAR SM5 * 162 B7
HNWL W7 * 104 A1
PECK SE15 * 131 H1
RCH/KEW TW9 * 124 E4
SUT SM1 * 162 B7
Market Yard Ms STHWK SE1 19 J3
Markfield Gdns CHING E4 31 K6
Markfield Rd
SEVS/STOTM N15 56 C3
Markham Cl BORE WD6 24 B2
Markham Pl CHEL SW3 * 15 L7
Markham Sq CHEL SW3 15 L7
Markham St CHEL SW3 15 K7
Markhole Cl HPTN TW12 141 K6
Markhouse Av WALTH E17 57 G5
Markhouse Pas WALTH E17 57 H5
Markhouse Rd WALTH E17 57 H5
Mark La MON EC3R 13 K6
Markmanor Av WALTH E17 57 G6
Mark Rd WDGN N22 55 H1
Marksbury Av RCH/KEW TW9 125 H2
Marks Rd ROMW/RG RM7 62 E4
Mark St SDTCH EC2A 7 J9
SRTFD E15 76 C6
Mark Ter RYNPK SW20 * 146 A6
Markwade Cl MNPK E12 59 H7
The Markway SUN TW16 156 B1
Markwell Cl SYD SE26 150 D3
Markyate Rd BCTR RM8 79 H4
Marlands Rd CLAY IG5 59 J2
Marlborogh Rd ISLW TW7 104 C7
Marlborough Av EDGW HA8 36 D2
HACK E8 74 C7
RSLP HA4 46 A5
STHGT/OAK N14 40 C2
Marlborough Cl
TRDG/WHET N20 39 K2
WALW SE17 18 D6
WIM/MER SW19 147 J5
Marlborough Ct REGST W1B * 10 E6
Marlborough Crs CHSWK W4 106 A2
HYS/HAR UB3 101 G6
Marlborough Dr BUSH WD23 21 K3
CLAY IG5 59 J2
Marlborough Gdns
TRDG/WHET N20 39 K2
Marlborough Ga BAY/PAD W2 9 G7
Marlborough Gv STHWK SE1 111 H4
Marlborough Hl HRW HA1 48 E3
STJWD NW8 2 F4
Marlborough La CHARL SE7 114 B5
Marlborough Ms
BRXS/STRHM SW2 130 A3
Marlborough Pde
FSBYPK N4 * 55 J7
Marlborough Park Av
BFN/LL DA15 136 B7
Marlborough Pl STJWD NW8 2 E6
Marlborough Rd ARCH N19 72 E1
BCTR RM8 79 J3
CHING E4 43 K5
CHSWK W4 105 K4
DART DA1 139 F5
EA W5 104 E1
ED N9 30 B7
FELT TW13 141 H1
FSTGT E7 77 G6
HAYES BR2 168 B3
HPTN TW12 142 A5
NWDGN UB2 102 B2
RCHPK/HAM TW10 125 F5
ROMW/RG RM7 62 C3
SAND/SEL CR2 177 J6
SRTFD E15 * 76 C3
SUT SM1 174 E2
SWFD E18 58 E2
WATW WD18 21 F3
WDGN N22 41 F6
WELL DA16 136 E2
WHALL SW1A 10 F9
WIM/MER SW19 147 J5
WOOL/PLUM SE18 115 G2
Marlborough St CHEL SW3 15 J6
Marlborough Yd ARCH N19 72 D1
Marler Rd FSTH SE23 132 C7
Marley Av BXLYHN DA7 116 E5
Marley Cl GFD/PVL UB6 84 A2
SEVS/STOTM N15 55 H3
Marley Rd BERM/RHTH SE16 * 112 A3
Marlin Cl SUN TW16 140 C5
Marlingdene Cl HPTN TW12 142 A5
Marlings Cl CHST BR7 169 K3
Marlings Park Av CHST BR7 169 K2
Marlins Cl SUT SM1 * 175 G4
Marlins Meadow WATW WD18 20 B5
The Marlins NTHWD HA6 32 D5
Marloes Cl ALP/SUD HA0 67 K3
Marloes Rd KENS W8 14 C3
Marlow Av PUR RM19 119 K3
Marlow Cl PGE/AN SE20 165 J2
Marlow Ct CDALE/KGS NW9 51 H2
Marlow Crs TWK TW1 124 A5
Marlow Dr CHEAM SM3 174 B2
Marlowe Cl CHST BR7 154 D5
Marlowe Rd WALTH E17 58 A3
Marlowe Sq MTCM CR4 163 H3
The Marlowes DART DA1 138 A3
STJWD NW8 3 G4
Marlowe Wy CROY/NA CR0 176 E1
Marlow Gdns HYS/HAR UB3 101 G2
Marlow Rd EHAM E6 95 K2
NWDGN UB2 102 E2
PGE/AN SE20 165 J2
Marlow Wy BERM/RHTH SE16 112 A1
Marl Rd WAND/EARL SW18 128 A3
Marlton St GNWCH SE10 113 J4
Marlwood Cl BFN/LL DA15 154 E1
Marmadon Rd
WOOL/PLUM SE18 116 A3
Marmion Ap CHING E4 43 J3
Marmion Av CHING E4 43 H3
Marmion Cl CHING E4 43 H3
Marmion Ms BTSEA SW11 * 129 F2
Marmion Rd BTSEA SW11 129 F3
Marmont Rd PECK SE15 111 H7
Marmora Rd EDUL SE22 131 K5
Marmot Rd HSLWW TW4 122 C2
Marne Av FBAR/BDGN N11 40 B3
WELL DA16 136 B2
Marnell Wy HSLWW TW4 122 C2
Marne St NKENS W10 88 C2
Marney Rd BTSEA SW11 129 F3
Marnfield Crs
BRXS/STRHM SW2 130 A7
Marnham Av CRICK NW2 70 C3
Marnham Crs GFD/PVL UB6 84 B1
Marnock Rd BROCKY SE4 132 C4
Maroon St POP/IOD E14 93 G4
Maroons Wy CAT SE6 151 J4
Marquess Rd IS N1 73 K5
Marquess Rd South IS N1 * 73 J5
Marquis Cl ALP/SUD HA0 68 B6
Marquis Rd CAMTN NW1 72 D5
FSBYPK N4 55 F7
WDGN N22 41 F5
Marrabon Cl BFN/LL DA15 136 B7
Marrick Cl PUT/ROE SW15 126 D3
Married Quarters EDGW HA8 * 36 D6
Marriner Ct HYS/HAR UB3 * 82 C6
Marriot Rd MUSWH N10 39 K7
Marriott Cl EBED/NFELT TW14 121 G5
Marriott Rd BAR EN5 26 B2
DART DA1 139 K6
FSBYPK N4 55 F7
SRTFD E15 76 C7
Marriotts Cl CDALE/KGS NW9 51 H5
Marriotts Yd BAR EN5 * 26 B2
Marryat Cl HSLWW TW4 122 E3
Marryat Pl WIM/MER SW19 146 C3
Marryat Rd WIM/MER SW19 146 B4
Marryfields Wy CAT SE6 132 E6
Marsala Rd LEW SE13 132 E3
Marsden Gdns DART DA1 139 J1
Marsden Rd ED N9 42 D1
PECK SE15 131 G2
Marsden St KTTN NW5 72 A5
Marshall Cl FBAR/BDGN N11 40 B3
HRW HA1 48 D6
HSLWW TW4 122 E4
WAND/EARL SW18 128 B5
Marshall Dr YEAD UB4 82 D4
Marshall Est MLHL NW7 * 37 J3
Marshall Rd LEY E10 75 K3
TOTM N17 41 K7
Marshalls Dr ROM RM1 63 G2
Marshalls Gv
WOOL/PLUM SE18 114 D3
Marshall's Pl
BERM/RHTH SE16 19 M4
Marshalls Rd ROMW/RG RM7 63 F3
Marshall's Rd SUT SM1 175 F3
Marshall St SOHO/CST W1F 10 F5
Marshalsea Rd STHWK SE1 18 F1
Marsham Cl CHST BR7 * 154 B4
Marsham St WEST SW1P 17 H5
Marsh Av MTCM CR4 162 E1
Marshbrook Cl
BKHTH/KID SE3 134 C2
Marsh Cl MLHL NW7 37 H2
Marsh Dr CDALE/KGS NW9 51 H5
Marsh Farm Rd WHTN TW2 124 A7
Marshfield St POP/IOD E14 113 F2
Marsh Green Rd DAGE RM10 80 C7
Marsh Hl HOM E9 75 G4
Marsh La LEY E10 75 H1
MLHL NW7 37 G2
STAN HA7 35 J4
TOTM N17 42 D6
Marsh Rd ALP/SUD HA0 85 K2
PIN HA5 47 J3
Marshside Cl ED N9 30 E7
Marsh St DART DA1 139 K2
POP/IOD E14 * 112 E3
Marsh Wall POP/IOD E14 112 D1
Marsh Wy RAIN RM13 99 F5
Marsland Cl WALW SE17 18 D8
Marston Av CHSGTN KT9 172 A5
DAGE RM10 80 C2
Marston Cl DAGE RM10 80 C2
KIL/WHAMP NW6 2 F1
Marston Ct WOT/HER KT12 * 156 B7
Marston Rd CLAY IG5 59 J1
TEDD TW11 143 H4
Marston Wy NRWD SE19 149 H6
Marsworth Av PIN HA5 33 H7
Marsworth Cl WATW WD18 * 20 C5
YEAD UB4 83 J4
Martaban Rd
STNW/STAM N16 74 A1
Martello St HACK E8 74 D6
Martell Rd DUL SE21 149 K2
Martel Pl HACK E8 74 B5
Marten Rd WALTH E17 57 J1
Martens Av BXLYHN DA7 137 K3
Martens Cl BXLYHN DA7 137 K3
Martham Cl THMD SE28 97 K6
Martha Rd SRTFD E15 76 C5
Martha's Blds FSBYE EC1V 7 G9
Martha St WCHPL E1 92 E5
Marthorne Crs
KTN/HRWW/WS HA3 48 D1
Martin Bowes Rd
ELTH/MOT SE9 134 E2
Martin Cl ED N9 31 F7
Martin Crs CROY/NA CR0 164 A7
Martindale MORT/ESHN SW14 125 K4
Martindale Av CAN/RD E16 94 E6
Martindale Rd BAL SW12 129 G6
HSLWW TW4 122 D2
Martin Dene BXLYHS DA6 137 G4
Martin Dr NTHLT UB5 65 K4
RAIN RM13 99 K3
Martineau Cl ESH/CLAY KT10 170 D3
Martineau Dr TWK TW1 124 C3
Martineau Rd HBRY N5 73 H3
Martingales Cl
RCHPK/HAM TW10 143 K2
Martin Gdns BCTR RM8 79 J3
Martin Gv MRDN SM4 161 K2
Martin La CANST EC4R 13 H6
Martin Ri BXLYHS DA6 137 G4
Martin Rd BCTR RM8 79 J3
Martins Cl WWKM BR4 180 B1
Martins Mt BAR EN5 26 E3
Martins Pl THMD SE28 96 E7
Martin's Rd HAYES BR2 167 H1
The Martins SYD SE26 150 D4
WBLY HA9 * 68 B2
Martin St THMD SE28 96 E7
Martins Wk MUSWH N10 * 40 A7
THMD SE28 96 E7
Martin Wy MRDN SM4 161 H2
Martlet Gv NTHLT UB5 83 H2
Martlett Ct HOL/ALD WC2B 11 K5
Martley Dr GNTH/NBYPK IG2 60 B4
Martock Cl
KTN/HRWW/WS HA3 49 G3
Martock Gdns
FBAR/BDGN N11 39 K4
Marton Cl CAT SE6 151 J2
Marton Rd STNW/STAM N16 * 74 A1
Martys Yd HAMP NW3 * 71 H3
Marvell Av YEAD UB4 82 E4
Marvels Cl LEE/GVPK SE12 153 F1
Marvels La LEE/GVPK SE12 153 F1
Marville Rd FUL/PGN SW6 107 J6
Marvin St HACK E8 * 74 D5
Marwell Cl ROM RM1 63 J5
WWKM BR4 180 D1
Marwood Cl WELL DA16 136 C2
Marwood Dr MLHL NW7 38 B6
Mary Adelaide Cl
PUT/ROE SW15 145 G2
Mary Ann Blds DEPT SE8 112 D5
Maryat Sq FUL/PGN SW6 107 H7
Maryatt Av RYLN/HDSTN HA2 66 B1
Marybank WOOL/PLUM SE18 114 E3
Mary Cl KTN/HRWW/WS HA3 50 B3
Mary Datchelor Cl CMBW SE5 110 E7
Mary Gn STJWD NW8 * 2 D3
Maryland Pk SRTFD E15 76 C4
Maryland Rd MV/WKIL W9 8 B1
SRTFD E15 76 B4
THHTH CR7 149 H7
WDGN N22 41 G5
Maryland Sq SRTFD E15 76 C4
Marylands Rd MV/WKIL W9 8 B1
Maryland St SRTFD E15 76 B4
Maryland Wk IS N1 * 6 E3
Mary Lawrencson Pl
BKHTH/KID SE3 113 K6
Marylebone F/O BAY/PAD W2 9 J3
Marylebone High St
CAVSQ/HST W1G 10 B3
Marylebone La MHST W1U 10 B4
Marylebone Ms
CAVSQ/HST W1G 10 B3
Marylebone Pas GTPST W1W 10 F4
Marylebone Rd CAMTN NW1 9 M1
MBLAR W1H 9 K2
Marylebone St
CAVSQ/HST W1G 10 B3
Marylee Wy LBTH SE11 17 M6
Mary Neuner Rd WDGN N22 55 F2
Maryon Gv CHARL SE7 114 D3
Maryon Ms HAMP NW3 71 J3
Maryon Rd CHARL SE7 114 D3
Mary Peters Dr GFD/PVL UB6 66 D4
Mary Pl NTGHL W11 88 C6
Mary Rose Cl HPTN TW12 142 A7
Maryrose Wy
TRDG/WHET N20 27 H7
Mary Seacole Cl HACK E8 * 7 L3
Mary Secole Cl HACK E8 * 7 L3
Mary's Ter TWK TW1 124 B6

Mary St *CAN/RD* E16......**94** D4
  IS N1......**6** F4
Mary Ter *CAMTN* NW1......**4** F4
Mary Wy *OXHEY* WD19......**33** G3
Masbro' Rd *WKENS* W14......**107** G2
Mascalls Rd *CHARL* SE7......**114** B5
Mascotts Cl *CRICK* NW2......**69** K2
Masefield Av *BORE* WD6......**24** D4
  STAN HA7......**35** F4
  STHL UB1......**84** A6
Masefield Cl *ERITH* DA8......**118** C7
Masefield Crs *STHGT/OAK* N14......**28** C2
Masefield Gdns *EHAM* E6......**96** A3
Masefield La *YEAD* UB4......**83** F3
Masefield Rd *HPTN* TW12......**141** K3
Masefield Wy
  STWL/WRAY TW19......**120** D4
Mashie Rd *ACT* W3......**87** G5
Mashiters Wk *ROM* RM1......**63** G3
Maskall Cl *BRXS/STRHM* SW2 *......**130** B3
Maskell Rd *TOOT* SW17......**147** G2
Maskelyne Cl *BTSEA* SW11......**108** D7
Mason Cl *BERM/RHTH* SE16......**111** H4
  BORE WD6......**25** F1
  BXLYHN DA7......**137** J2
  CAN/RD E16......**94** E6
  HPTN TW12......**141** H7
  RYNPK SW20......**146** B7
Mason Ct *WBLY* HA9 *......**68** C1
Mason Rd *SUT* SM1......**175** F4
  WFD IG8......**44** C3
Mason's Arms Ms
  CONDST W1S *......**10** D5
Masons Av
  KTN/HRWW/WS HA3......**48** D2
Mason's Av *CITYW* EC2V......**13** G4
  CROY/NA CR0......**177** J2
Masons Ct *EW* KT17 *......**173** H7
Masons Hl *BMLY* BR1......**167** K2
  WOOL/PLUM SE18......**115** G5
Mason's Pl *FSBYE* EC1V......**6** D7
  MTCM CR4......**147** K7
Mason St *WALW* SE17......**19** H5
  STJS SW1Y......**10** F8
Masons Yd *FSBYE* EC1V......**6** E9
Massey Cl *FBAR/BDGN* N11......**40** B4
Massie Rd *HACK* E8......**74** C5
Massingberd Wy *TOOT* SW17......**148** B3
Massinger St *WALW* SE17 *......**19** J6
Massingham St *WCHPL* E1......**93** F3
Masson Av *RSLP* HA4......**65** G5
Masterman Rd *EHAM* E6......**95** J2
Masters Cl *STRHM/NOR* SW16......**148** C5
Masters Dr *BERM/RHTH* SE16......**111** J4
Master's St *WCHPL* E1......**93** F4
Masthouse Ter *POP/IOD* E14......**112** D3
Mast House Ter
  POP/IOD E14......**112** D3
Mastmaker Rd *POP/IOD* E14......**112** D1
Mast Quay *WOOL/PLUM* SE18......**114** E2
Maswell Park Crs *HSLW* TW3......**123** H4
Maswell Park Rd *HSLW* TW3......**123** G4
Matara Ms *WALW* SE17......**18** C7
Matcham Rd *WAN* E11......**76** C2
Matchless Dr
  WOOL/PLUM SE18......**115** F6
Matfield Cl *HAYES* BR2......**167** K4
Matfield Rd *BELV* DA17......**117** H5
Matham Gv *EDUL* SE22......**131** F3
Matham Rd *E/WMO/HCT* KT8......**157** J4
Matheson Rd *WKENS* W14......**107** J3
Mathews Av *EHAM* E6......**96** A1
Mathews Park Av *SRTFD* E15......**76** D5
Mathews Yd
  LSO/SEYD WC2H *......**11** J3
Mathieson Ct *STHWK* SE1 *......**18** D2
Matilda Cl *NRWD* SE19......**149** K6
Matilda Gdns *BOW* E3......**93** J1
Matilda St *IS* N1......**5** M4
  HNHL SE24......**130** D3
Matlock Cl *BAR* EN5......**26** B4
  OXHEY WD19......**33** G2
Matlock Crs *CHEAM* SM3......**174** C3
  OXHEY WD19......**33** G2
Matlock Pl *CHEAM* SM3......**174** C3
Matlock Rd *LEY* E10......**58** A5
Matlock St *POP/IOD* E14......**93** G5
Matlock Wy *NWMAL* KT3......**145** F7
Mattellen Cl *WIM/MER* SW19......**146** C1
Matthew Cl *NKENS* W10 *......**88** B3
Matthew Ct *MTCM* CR4......**163** J4
Matthews Rd *GFD/PVL* UB6......**66** D4
Matthews St *BTSEA* SW11......**128** E1
Matthias Rd *STNW/STAM* N16......**73** K4
Mattingly Wy *PECK* SE15......**111** G6
Mattison Rd *FSBYPK* N4......**55** G5
Mattock La *WEA* W13......**85** H7
Maud Cashmore Wy
  WOOL/PLUM SE18......**114** E3
Maude Rd *CMBW* SE5......**131** F1
  WALTH E17......**57** G4
Maudesville Cots *HNWL* W7 *......**84** E7
Maude Ter *WALTH* E17......**57** G3
Maud Gdns *BARK* IG11......**97** F1
  PLSTW E13......**94** D1
Maudlins Gn *WAP* E1W *......**92** C7
Maud Rd *LEY* E10......**76** A2
  PLSTW E13......**94** D1
Maudslay Rd *ELTH/MOT* SE9......**134** E2
Maud St *CAN/RD* E16......**94** D4
Maud Wilkes Cl *KTTN* NW5......**72** C4
Maugham Wy *ACT* W3......**105** K2
Mauleverer Rd
  BRXS/STRHM SW2......**129** K4
Maundeby Wk *WLSDN* NW10 *......**69** G6
Maunder Rd *HNWL* W7......**84** E7
Maunsel St *WEST* SW1P......**17** H6
Maurice Av *WDGN* N22......**55** H1
Maurice Browne Cl
  MLHL NW7......**38** A4
Maurice St *SHB* W12......**87** K5
Maurice Wk *GLDGN* NW11......**53** G5
Maurier Cl *NTHLT* UB5......**65** G7
Mauritius Rd *GNWCH* SE10......**113** H3
Maury Rd *STNW/STAM* N16......**74** C1
Mauveine Gdns *HSLW* TW3......**123** F3
Mavelstone Rd *BMLY* BR1......**153** H7
Maverton Rd *BOW* E3......**75** J7
Mavis Av *HOR/WEW* KT19......**173** G4
Mavis Cl *HOR/WEW* KT19......**173** G4
Mawbey Pl *STHWK* SE1......**19** M8
Mawbey St *VX/NE* SW8......**109** K6
Mawney Cl *ROMW/RG* RM7......**62** D1
Mawney Rd *ROMW/RG* RM7......**62** D1
Mawson Cl *RYNPK* SW20......**161** H1
Mawson La *CHSWK* W4......**106** C5
Maxey Gdns *DAGW* RM9......**80** A3
Maxey Rd *DAGW* RM9......**80** A3
  WOOL/PLUM SE18......**115** H3
Maxfield Cl *TRDG/WHET* N20......**27** G6
Maxilla Wk *NKENS* W10......**88** B5
Maximfeldt Rd *ERITH* DA8......**118** B4

Maxim Rd *DART* DA1......**138** B4
  ERITH DA8......**118** B4
  WCHMH N21......**29** G5
Maxted Pk *HRW* HA1......**48** E6
Maxted Rd *PECK* SE15......**131** G2
Maxwell Cl *CROY/NA* CR0......**163** K7
  HYS/HAR UB3......**82** E6
Maxwell Ri *OXHEY* WD19......**21** J3
Maxwell Rd *ASHF* TW15......**140** A5
  BORE WD6......**24** D1
  FUL/PGN SW6......**108** A6
  NTHWD HA6......**32** B6
  WDR/YW UB7......**100** B3
  WELL DA16......**136** B3
Maxwelton Av *MLHL* NW7......**37** F4
Maxwelton Cl *MLHL* NW7......**37** F4
Maya Cl *PECK* SE15......**131** J1
Mayall Cl *STHWK* SE1 *......**12** F9
Mayall Rd *HNHL* SE24......**130** C4
Maya Pl *FBAR/BDGN* N11......**40** D6
Maya Rd *EFNCH* N2......**53** G3
Maybank Av *ALP/SUD* HA0......**67** G4
  HCH RM12......**81** K4
  SWFD E18......**59** F1
Maybank Gdns *PIN* HA5......**46** E4
Maybank Rd *SWFD* E18......**45** G7
May Bate Av *KUTN/CMB* KT2......**143** F7
Mayberry Pl *BRYLDS* KT5......**159** G6
Maybourne Cl *SYD* SE26......**150** D4
Maybury Cl *STMC/STPC* BR5......**169** G4
Maybury Gdns *WLSDN* NW10......**69** K5
Maybury Ms *HGT* N6......**54** C6
Maybury Rd *BARK* IG11......**97** G1
  PLSTW E13......**95** G3
Maybury St *TOOT* SW17......**147** J4
Maychurch Cl *STAN* HA7......**35** K6
May Cl *CHSGTN* KT9......**172** B5
Maycock Gv *NTHWD* HA6......**32** D5
Maycroft *PIN* HA5......**47** F1
Maycross Av *MRDN* SM4......**161** J3
Mayday Gdns *BKHTH/KID* SE3......**134** D1
Mayday Rd *THHTH* CR7......**164** C5
Maydwell Ldg *BORE* WD6......**24** B1
Mayerne Rd *ELTH/MOT* SE9......**134** C4
Mayesbrook Rd *BARK* IG11......**79** G1
  GDMY/SEVK IG3......**79** G2
Mayesford Rd *CHDH* RM6......**61** J6
Mayes Rd *WDGN* N22......**55** F1
Mayeswood Rd
  LEE/GVPK SE12......**153** G3
Mayfair Av *BXLYHN* DA7......**116** E7
  CHDH RM6......**61** K5
  IL IG1......**77** K1
  WHTN TW2......**123** H6
  WPK KT4......**160** D7
Mayfair Cl *BECK* BR3......**151** K7
  SURB KT6......**159** F7
Mayfair Gdns *TOTM* N17......**41** J5
  WFD IG8......**44** E6
Mayfair Ms *CAMTN* NW1 *......**3** M2
Mayfair Rd *DART* DA1......**139** G4
Mayfair Ter *STHGT/OAK* N14......**28** D6
Mayfare *RKW/CH/CXG* WD3......**20** B4
Mayfield *BXLYHN* DA7......**137** G2
Mayfield Av *CHSWK* W4......**106** B3
  KTN/HRWW/WS HA3......**49** H4
  NFNCH/WDSPK N12......**39** G3
  STHGT/OAK N14......**40** C1
  WEA W13......**104** C2
  WFD IG8......**44** E5
Mayfield Cl *CLAP* SW4......**129** J4
  PGE/AN SE20......**150** D7
  THDIT KT7......**158** C7
Mayfield Crs *ED* N9......**30** D5
  THHTH CR7......**164** A3
Mayfield Dr *PIN* HA5......**47** K3
Mayfield Gdns *HDN* NW4......**52** B5
  HNWL W7......**84** D5
Mayfield Rd *ACT* W3......**86** D6
  BCTR RM8......**61** J7
  BELMT SM2......**175** H5
  BELV DA17......**117** K3
  BMLY BR1......**168** D4
  CEND/HSY/T N8......**55** F5
  CHING E4......**44** A1
  HACK E8......**7** L2
  PEND EN3......**31** F1
  PLSTW E13......**94** D3
  SAND/SEL CR2......**177** K7
  SHB W12......**106** B1
  WALTH E17......**57** G1
  WIM/MER SW19......**146** D7
Mayflower Cl
  BERM/RHTH SE16......**112** A3
  RSLP HA4......**46** A5
Mayflower St
  BERM/RHTH SE16......**111** K1
Mayfly Cl *PIN* HA5......**47** G6
Mayford Cl *BAL* SW12......**128** K6
  BECK BR3......**166** A2
Mayford Rd *BAL* SW12......**128** K6
May Gdns *ALP/SUD* HA0......**85** J2
Maygood St *IS* N1......**5** M5
Maygreen Crs *EMPK* RM11......**63** J5
Maygrove Rd
  KIL/WHAMP NW6......**70** D5
Mayhew Cl *CHING* E4......**43** J2
Mayhill Rd *BAR* EN5......**26** C4
  CHARL SE7......**114** A5
Maylands Av *HCH* RM12......**81** K4
Maylands Dr *SCUP* DA14......**155** K2
Maylands Rd *OXHEY* WD19......**33** G3
Maynard Cl *ERITH* DA8......**118** D6
  FUL/PGN SW6......**108** A6
  SEVS/STOTM N15......**56** A4
Maynard Rd *WALTH* E17......**58** A4
Maynards Quay *WAP* E1W *......**92** F6
Maynooth Gdns *CAR* SM5......**162** E6
Mayola Rd *CLPT* E5......**74** E3
Mayo Rd *CROY/NA* CR0......**164** E4
  WLSDN NW10......**69** G5
Mayow Rd *SYD* SE26......**151** F3
Mayplace Av *DART* DA1......**138** D3
Mayplace Cl *BXLYHN* DA7......**137** J2
Mayplace La
  WOOL/PLUM SE18......**115** G5
Mayplace Rd East
  BXLYHN DA7......**137** J2
Mayplace Rd West
  BXLYHN DA7......**137** H3
Maypole Crs *ERITH* DA8......**119** K4
May Rd *CHING* E4......**43** J5
  PLSTW E13......**94** E1
  WHTN TW2......**123** J7
Mayroyd Av *SURB* KT6......**172** C1

May's Buildings Ms
  GNWCH SE10......**113** G6
Mays Cl *CHCR* WC2N......**11** J7
May's Hill Rd *HAYES* BR2......**167** H1
Mays La *BAR* EN5......**25** K6
  BAR EN5......**26** D4
Maysoule Rd *BTSEA* SW11......**128** C3
Mays Rd *TEDD* TW11......**142** C4
Mayston Ms *BKHTH/KID* SE3......**113** K4
May St *WKENS* W14......**107** J4
Mayswood Gdns *DAGE* RM10......**80** E5
Maythorne Dr *WATW* WD18......**20** C3
Maythorne Cots *LEW* SE13......**133** G5
Mayton St *HOLWY* N7......**73** F2
Maytree Cl *EDGW* HA8......**36** E2
  RAIN RM13......**99** G1
Maytree Cl *MTCM* CR4......**163** F2
Maytree La *STAN* HA7......**35** F5
Maytree Wk
  BRXS/STRHM SW2 *......**149** G1
Mayville Est
  STNW/STAM N16 *......**74** A4
Mayville Rd *IL* IG1......**78** B4
  WAN E11......**76** C1
Maywood Cl *BECK* BR3......**151** K6
Maze Hl *MLHL/WHAMP* NW6 *......**2** B2
  GNWCH SE10......**113** H5
Mazenod Av *KIL/WHAMP* NW6......**2** B2
Maze Rd *RCH/KEW* TW9......**105** H6
McAdam Dr *ENC/FH* EN2......**29** H1
McAuley Cl *ELTH/MOT* SE9......**135** F4
  STHWK SE1......**18** A3
McCall Cl *CLAP* SW4......**129** K1
McCall Crs *CHARL* SE7......**114** D4
McCarthy Rd *FELT* TW13......**141** H4
McCoid Wy *STHWK* SE1......**18** E2
McCrone Ms *HAMP* NW3......**71** H5
McCudden Rd *DART* DA1......**139** J2
McCullum Rd *BOW* E3......**75** H7
McDermott Cl *BTSEA* SW11......**128** D1
McDermott Rd *PECK* SE15......**131** H2
McDonough Cl *CHSGTN* KT9......**172** A3
McDougall Ct *RCH/KEW* TW9......**125** H1
McDowall Cl *CAN/RD* E16......**94** D4
McDowall Rd *CMBW* SE5......**110** D7
McEntee Av *WALTH* E17......**43** G7
McEwan Wy *SRTFD* E15 *......**76** B7
McGrath Rd *SRTFD* E15......**76** D4
McGregor Rd *NTGHL* W11......**88** D5
McIntosh Cl *ROM* RM1......**63** G2
  CROY/NA CR0......**179** G1
  HAYES BR2......**167** J5
  RSLP HA4......**65** J2
McIntosh Rd *ROM* RM1......**63** G2
McKay Rd *RYNPK* SW20......**145** K6
McKellar Cl *BUSH* WD23......**34** C1
McKerrell Rd *PECK* SE15......**111** H7
McKillop Wy *SCUP* DA14......**155** J6
McLeod Rd *ABYW* SE2......**116** D3
McLeod's Ms *SKENS* SW7......**14** D4
McMillan St *DEPT* SE8......**112** D5
McNair Rd *NWDGN* UB2......**103** F2
McNeil Rd *CMBW* SE5......**131** F1
McNicol Dr *WLSDN* NW10......**86** E1
McRae La *MTCM* CR4......**162** E6
Mead Cl *CAMTN* NW1 *......**4** B1
  GPK RM2......**63** J1
  KTN/HRWW/WS HA3......**34** D7
Mead Cl *CDALE/KGS* NW9......**50** D7
Mead Crs *CHING* E4......**44** A3
  DART DA1......**139** G2
  SUT SM1......**175** J3
Meadcroft Rd *LBTH* SE11......**110** B5
Meade Cl *CHSWK* W4......**105** H5
Meadfield *EDGW* HA8......**36** D1
Mead Fld *RYLN/HDSTN* HA2 *......**65** K2
Meadfoot Rd
  STRHM/NOR SW16......**148** C7
Meadgate Av *WFD* IG8......**45** J4
Mead Gv *CHDH* RM6......**61** K2
Mead House La *YEAD* UB4......**82** B3
Meadhurst Pk *SUN* TW16......**140** C5
Meadlands Dr
  RCHPK/HAM TW10......**143** K1
Meadow Av *CROY/NA* CR0......**166** A5
Meadowbank *BKHTH/KID* SE3......**133** J2
  BRYLDS KT5......**159** G5
  HAMP NW3......**3** L2
  OXHEY WD19......**21** G6
  WCHMH N21......**29** F5
Meadowbank Cl
  FUL/PGN SW6......**107** G6
  ISLW TW7......**103** K7
Meadowbank Gdns
  HSLWW TW4......**121** K1
Meadowbank Rd
  CDALE/KGS NW9......**51** F6
Meadowbanks *BAR* EN5......**25** H4
Meadow Cl *BAR* EN5......**26** D5
  BARK IG11......**79** F6
  BXLYHS DA6......**137** G4
  CAT SE6......**151** K4
  CHING E4......**31** K7
  CHST BR7......**154** D4
  ESH/CLAY KT10......**171** F2
  HOM E9......**75** H4
  HSLWW TW4......**123** F5
  NTHLT UB5......**84** A1
  RCHPK/HAM TW10......**125** F7
  RSLP HA4......**46** D5
  RYNPK SW20......**161** F3
Meadowcourt Rd
  BKHTH/KID SE3......**133** J3
Meadow Cft *BMLY* BR1......**168** E2
Meadowcroft *BUSH* WD23 *......**22** B6
Meadowcroft Cl *PLMGR* N13 *......**41** H1
Meadowcroft Rd *PLMGR* N13......**41** H1
Meadow Dr *HDN* NW4......**52** A1
  MUSWH N10......**54** A2
Meadowford Cl *THMD* SE28......**97** G6
Meadow Gdns *EDGW* HA8......**36** D5
Meadow Garth *WLSDN* NW10......**68** E5
Meadow Hl *NWMAL* KT3......**160** B5
Meadowlands *BAR* EN5......**25** H4
Meadow La *LEE/GVPK* SE12......**153** G2
Meadowlea Cl *WDR/YW* UB7......**100** A5
Meadow Ms *VX/NE* SW8......**110** A5
Meadow Pl *CHSWK* W4......**106** B1
  VX/NE SW8......**109** K6
Meadow Rd *ASHF* TW15......**140** A4
  BARK IG11......**79** F6
  BORE WD6......**24** B1
  BUSH WD23......**22** B5
  DAGW RM9......**80** B5
  ESH/CLAY KT10......**170** A4
  FELT TW13......**141** H1
  HAYES BR2......**152** C7
  PIN HA5......**47** H3
  ROMW/RG RM7......**62** G7
  STHL UB1......**83** K6
  SUT SM1......**175** J3
  VX/NE SW8......**110** A5
  WIM/MER SW19......**147** G6
Meadow Rw *STHWK* SE1......**18** F4
Meadows End *SUN* TW16......**140** E7

Meadows End *SUN* TW16......**140** E7
  DART DA1......**139** H7
  TWK TW1......**124** B7
Meadowside Rd *BELMT* SM2......**174** C7
Meadow Stile *CROY/NA* CR0......**177** J2
Meadowsweet Cl *CAN/RD* E16......**95** H4
  NWMAL KT3......**161** F4
The Meadow *CHST* BR7......**154** C5
The Meadow Vw *BFN/LL* DA15......**136** C5
  HRW HA1......**48** D7
Meadowview Rd *BXLY* DA5......**137** F5
  CAT SE6......**151** J3
  HOR/WEW KT19......**173** G7
Meadow View Rd *THHTH* CR7......**164** C4
  YEAD UB4......**82** B3
Meadow Wk *DAGW* RM9......**80** B5
  HOR/WEW KT19......**173** G5
  SWFD E18......**58** E3
  WLGTN SM6......**176** B2
Meadow Wy *CDALE/KGS* NW9......**51** F4
  CHSGTN KT9......**172** A4
  RSLP HA4......**47** G5
  WBLY HA9......**68** A3
Meadow Waye *HEST* TW5......**102** D6
The Meadow Wy
  KTN/HRWW/WS HA3......**34** E7
Mead Pl *CROY/NA* CR0......**164** C7
  HOM E9......**74** E5
Mead Plat *WLSDN* NW10......**68** E5
Mead Rd *CHST* BR7......**154** C5
  DART DA1......**139** G7
  EDGW HA8......**36** C5
  RCHPK/HAM TW10......**143** J2
Mead Rw *STHWK* SE1......**18** A3
Meadside Cl *BECK* BR3......**151** G7
Meads La *GDMY/SEVK* IG3......**61** F6
Meads Rd *WDGN* N22......**55** H1
The Meads *CHEAM* SM3......**174** B3
  EDGW HA8......**37** F5
  MRDN SM4 *......**162** D4
The Mead *BECK* BR3......**167** F1
  EFNCH N2......**53** J1
  OXHEY WD19......**33** J2
  WEA W13......**85** H4
  WLGTN SM6......**176** D5
  WWKM BR4......**180** B1
Meadvale Rd *CROY/NA* CR0......**165** G6
  EA W5......**85** H3
Mead Wy *BUSH* WD23......**21** J1
  CROY/NA CR0......**179** G1
  HAYES BR2......**167** J5
  RSLP HA4......**65** J2
Meadway *BAR* EN5......**26** E3
  BECK BR3......**152** A7
  BRYLDS KT5......**159** K7
  ESH/CLAY KT10......**170** B7
  GDMY/SEVK IG3......**78** E3
  GLDGN NW11......**53** F5
  GPK RM2......**63** J1
  RYNPK SW20......**161** F1
  STHGT/OAK N14......**40** D1
  WFD IG8......**45** G4
  WHTN TW2......**123** J7
Meadway Cl *BAR* EN5......**26** E2
  GLDGN NW11......**53** F5
  PIN HA5......**34** B5
Meadway Ct *EA* W5 *......**86** B4
Meadway Gdns *RSLP* HA4......**46** B5
The Meadway *BKHTH/KID* SE3......**133** G1
Meaford Wy *PGE/AN* SE20......**150** D6
Meanley Rd *MNPK* E12......**77** J4
Meard St *SOHO/CST* W1F......**11** G5
Meath Crs *BETH* E2......**93** F2
Meath Rd *IL* IG1......**78** C2
  SRTFD E15......**94** D1
Meath St *BTSEA* SW11......**109** G7
Mecklenburgh Pl
  BMSBY WC1N......**5** L9
Mecklenburgh Sq
  BMSBY WC1N......**5** L9
Mecklenburgh St
  BMSBY WC1N......**5** L9
Medburn St *CAMTN* NW1......**5** G5
Medcroft Gdns
  MORT/ESHN SW14......**125** K3
Medebourne Cl
  BKHTH/KID SE3......**133** K2
Medesenge Wy *PLMGR* N13......**41** H5
Medfield St *PUT/ROE* SW15......**126** D6
Medhurst Cl *BOW* E3......**93** G1
Median Rd *CLPT* E5......**74** E4
Medici Cl *GDMY/SEVK* IG3......**61** G5
Medina Av *ESH/CLAY* KT10......**170** E2
Medina Rd *HOLWY* N7......**73** G2
Medland Cl *WLGTN* SM6......**163** F7
Medlar Cl *NTHLT* UB5......**83** H1
Medlar St *CMBW* SE5......**110** D7
Medley Rd *KIL/WHAMP* NW6......**70** E5
Medora Rd *BRXS/STRHM* SW2......**130** A6
  ROMW/RG RM7......**63** F3
Medusa Rd *CAT* SE6......**132** E5
Medway Cl *CROY/NA* CR0......**165** K5
  IL IG1......**78** C4
Medway Dr *GFD/PVL* UB6......**85** F1
Medway Gdns *ALP/SUD* HA0......**67** G3
Medway Pde *GFD/PVL* UB6 *......**85** F1
Medway Rd *BOW* E3......**93** G1
  DART DA1......**138** D2
Medway St *WEST* SW1P......**17** G4
Medwin St *CLAP* SW4......**130** A3
Meerbrook Rd *BKHTH/KID* SE3......**134** B2
Meeson Rd *SRTFD* E15......**76** D7
Meeson St *CLPT* E5......**75** G3
Meesons Whf *SRTFD* E15 *......**94** A1
Meeting Aly *WAT* WD17 *......**21** G3
Meeting Field Pth *HOM* E9......**74** E5
Meeting House Aly
  WAP E1W *......**92** D7
Meeting House La *PECK* SE15......**111** J7
Mehetabel Rd *HOM* E9......**74** E5
Meister Cl *IL* IG1......**60** D7
Melanda Cl *CHST* BR7......**153** K4
Melanie Cl *BXLYHN* DA7......**117** F7
Melba Wy *LEW* SE13......**114** C7
Melbourne Av *PIN* HA5......**48** B2
  WDGN N22......**55** F1
  WEA W13......**85** G7
Melbourne Cl *ORP* BR6......**169** K6
  WLGTN SM6......**176** C4
Melbourne Gdns *CHDH* RM6......**62** A4
Melbourne Gv *EDUL* SE22......**131** F3
Melbourne Ms *BRXN/ST* SW9......**110** B7
  CAT SE6......**133** F6
Melbourne Pl *HOL/ALD* WC2B......**11** M5
Melbourne Rd *BUSH* WD23......**22** B5
  EHAM E6......**77** K1
  IL IG1......**60** B7
  LEY E10......**58** A6
  TEDD TW11......**143** J5
  WALTH E17......**57** G3
  WIM/MER SW19......**146** D7
  WLGTN SM6......**176** B4

Melbourne Sq *BRXN/ST* SW9 *......**110** B7
Melbourne Ter *EDUL* SE22 *......**131** F3
  FUL/PGN SW6 *......**108** A6
Melbourne Wy *EN* EN1......**30** B4
Melbury Av *NWDGN* UB2......**103** G2
Melbury Cl *CHST* BR7......**153** K5
  ESH/CLAY KT10......**171** H5
Melbury Ct *KENS* W8......**107** H2
Melbury Dr *CMBW* SE5......**111** F6
Melbury Gdns *RYNPK* SW20......**145** K7
Melbury Rd
  KTN/HRWW/WS HA3......**50** B4
  WKENS W14......**107** J2
Melbury Ter *CAMTN* NW1......**9** K1
Melcombe Gdns
  KTN/HRWW/WS HA3......**50** B5
Melcombe Pl *CAMTN* NW1......**9** M1
Melcombe St *CAMTN* NW1......**9** M1
Meldex Cl *MLHL* NW7......**38** A5
Meldon Cl *FUL/PGN* SW6......**108** A7
Meldone Cl *BRYLDS* KT5......**159** J5
Meldrum Rd *GDMY/SEVK* IG3......**79** G1
Melfield Gdns *CAT* SE6......**151** K3
Melford Av *BARK* IG11......**78** E5
Melford Cl *CHSGTN* KT9......**172** B4
Melford Rd *EDUL* SE22......**131** H7
  EHAM E6......**95** K3
  IL IG1......**78** D1
  WALTH E17......**57** G3
  WAN E11......**76** C1
Melfort Av *THHTH* CR7......**164** C2
Melfort Rd *THHTH* CR7......**164** C2
Melgund Rd *HBRY* N5......**73** G4
Melina Cl *HYS/HAR* UB3......**82** A4
Melina Pl *STJWD* NW8......**3** G2
Melina Rd *SHB* W12......**106** E1
Melior Pl *STHWK* SE1......**19** J1
Melior St *STHWK* SE1......**19** J2
Meliot Rd *CAT* SE6......**152** B1
Meller Cl *CROY/NA* CR0......**176** E2
Mellifont Cl *MRDN* SM4......**162** C5
Melling St *WOOL/PLUM* SE18......**115** K5
Mellish Gdns *WFD* IG8......**44** E4
Mellish St *POP/IOD* E14......**112** D2
Mellison Rd *TOOT* SW17......**147** J4
Melliss Av *RCH/KEW* TW9......**105** J7
Mellitus St *SHB* W12......**87** H5
Mellor Cl *WOT/HER* KT12......**156** E6
Mellow La East
  HGDN/ICK UB10......**82** A3
Mellows Rd *CLAY* IG5......**59** K2
  WLGTN SM6......**176** D4
Mells Crs *ELTH/MOT* SE9......**153** K3
Mell St *GNWCH* SE10......**113** H4
Melody La *HBRY* N5......**73** H4
Melody Rd *WAND/EARL* SW18......**128** B5
Melon Pl *KENS* W8 *......**14** B1
Melon Rd *PECK* SE15......**111** H7
  WAN E11......**76** C2
Melrose Av *BORE* WD6......**24** D4
  CRICK NW2......**70** A4
  DART DA1......**138** B6
  GFD/PVL UB6......**84** B1
  MTCM CR4......**148** B6
  STRHM/NOR SW16......**164** A2
  WDGN N22......**41** H7
  WHTN TW2......**123** G7
  WIM/MER SW19......**146** D1
Melrose Cl *GFD/PVL* UB6......**84** B1
  LEE/GVPK SE12......**133** K7
  YEAD UB4......**82** E4
Melrose Dr *STHL* UB1......**84** A7
Melrose Gdns *EDGW* HA8......**50** D2
  HMSMTH W6......**107** F2
  NWMAL KT3......**160** A2
Melrose Ms *NWMAL* KT3......**160** A2
Melrose Rd *BARN* SW13......**126** C1
  PIN HA5......**47** K3
  WAND/EARL SW18......**127** J5
  WIM/MER SW19......**161** K1
Melrose Ter *HMSMTH* W6......**107** F1
Melrose Vls *BECK* BR3 *......**166** C1
Melsa Rd *MRDN* SM4......**162** B5
Melthorpe Gdns
  BKHTH/KID SE3......**114** C7
Melton Cl *RSLP* HA4......**47** G7
Melton Flds *HOR/WEW* KT19......**173** F7
Melton Gdns *ROM* RM1......**63** H6
Melton Pl *HOR/WEW* KT19......**173** F7
Melton St *CAMTN* NW1......**4** F8
  RYNPK SW20......**145** J6
  SAND/SEL CR2......**178** A5
Melville Av *GFD/PVL* UB6......**67** F4
  RYNPK SW20......**145** J6
  SAND/SEL CR2......**178** A3
Melville Cl *HGDN/ICK* UB10......**64** B2
Melville Ct *DEPT* SE8......**112** A3
Melville Gdns *PLMGR* N13......**41** H4
Melville Rd *BARN* SW13......**106** C7
  RAIN RM13......**99** J3
  SCUP DA14......**155** J1
  WALTH E17......**57** H3
  WLSDN NW10......**69** G6
Melville Villas Rd *ACT* W3......**87** F7
Melvin Rd *PGE/AN* SE20......**150** E7
Memel St *STLK* EC1Y......**12** E1
Memess Path
  WOOL/PLUM SE18 *......**115** F5
Memorial Av *MNPK* E12......**77** J1
  SRTFD E15......**94** C2
Memorial Cl *HEST* TW5......**102** E5
Memorial Sq *KUT/HW* KT1......**158** E1
Mendez Wy *PUT/ROE* SW15......**126** D5
Mendip Cl *HYS/HAR* UB3......**101** G3
  SYD SE26......**151** J3
  WPK KT4......**174** A1
Mendip Dr *CRICK* NW2......**70** C1
Mendip Houses *BETH* E2 *......**92** E2
Mendip Rd *BTSEA* SW11......**128** B2
  BUSH WD23......**22** D5
  EMPK RM11......**63** K6
  ERITH DA8......**118** B7
  GNTH/NBYPK IG2......**60** C4
Mendora Rd *FUL/PGN* SW6......**107** H6
Menelik Rd *CRICK* NW2......**70** C3
Menlo Gdns *NRWD* SE19......**149** K6
Menon Dr *ED* N9......**42** D2
Menotti St *BETH* E2 *......**92** C3
Mentmore Cl
  KTN/HRWW/WS HA3......**49** J5
Mentmore Ter *HACK* E8......**74** D6
Meon Rd *ACT* W3......**105** K1
Meopham Rd *MTCM* CR4......**148** C7
Mepham Crs
  KTN/HRWW/WS HA3......**34** C6
Mepham Gdns
  KTN/HRWW/WS HA3......**34** C6
Mepham St *STHWK* SE1......**11** M9
Mera Dr *BXLYHN* DA7......**137** H3
Merantun Wy
  WIM/MER SW19......**147** G7
Merbury Cl *LEW* SE13......**133** F4
  THMD SE28......**96** D7
Merbury Rd *THMD* SE28......**96** D7
Merbury St *WOOL/PLUM* SE18......**115** G2
Mercator Pl *POP/IOD* E14......**112** D4

Mercator Rd *LEW* SE13 ....133 G3
Mercer Cl *THDIT* KT7 ....158 A6
Merceron Houses *BETH* E2 * 92 C3
Merceron St *WCHPL* E1 ....92 D3
Mercer Pl *PIN* HA5 ....47 G1
Mercers Cl *GNWCH* SE10 ....113 J3
Mercers Cots *WCHPL* E1 * 93 D5
Mercers Ms *ARCH* N19 ....72 D5
Mercers Pl *HMSMTH* W6 ....107 F3
Mercers Rd *ARCH* N19 ....72 D2
Mercer St *LSQ/SEVD* WC2H 11 J3
Merchants Cl *SNWD* SE25 ....165 H3
Merchant St *BOW* E3 ....93 H2
Merchland Rd *ELTH/MOT* SE9 ....135 H7
Mercia Gv *LEW* SE13 ....133 F2
Mercier Rd *PUT/ROE* SW15 ....127 H4
Mercury Gdns *ROM* RM1 ....63 G3
Mercury House
HYS/HAR UB3 * 101 J1
Mercury Wy *NWCR* SE14 ....112 A5
Mercy Ter *LEW* SE13 ....132 E4
Merebank La *WLGTN* SM6 ....177 F4
Mere Cl *WIM/MER* SW19 ....127 G6
Meredith Cl *PIN* HA5 ....33 H4
Meredith Ms *BROCKY* SE4 ....132 C3
Meredith St *CLKNW* EC1R 6 A4
PLSTW E13 ....94 E2
Meredyth Rd *BARN* SW13 ....126 D1
Mere End *CROY/NA* CR0 ....166 A6
Mere Rd *ABYW* SE2 ....116 D1
Mereside Pk *ASHF* TW15 * 140 A3
Meretone Cl *BROCKY* SE4 ....132 B3
Merevale Crs *MRDN* SM4 ....162 B5
Mereway Rd *WHTN* TW2 ....123 J7
Merewood Cl *BMLY* BR1 ....169 F1
Merewood Gdns
CROY/NA CR0 ....166 A6
Merewood Rd *BXLYHN* DA7 ....137 K1
Mereworth Cl *HAYES* BR2 ....167 J4
Mereworth Dr
WOOL/PLUM SE18 ....115 G6
Meriden Cl *BMLY* BR1 ....153 H6
Meridian Cl *MLHL* NW7 ....37 F3
Meridian Rd *CHARL* SE7 ....114 C6
Meridian Sq *SRTFD* E15 ....76 B6
Meridian Wy *UED* N18 ....42 E5
Merifield Rd *ELTH/MOT* SE9 ....134 B3
Merino Cl *WAN* E11 ....59 G3
Merivale Rd *HRW* HA1 ....48 C6
PUT/ROE SW15 ....127 H3
Merlewood Dr *CHST* BR7 ....153 K7
Merley Ct *CDALE/KGS* NW9 ....50 E7
Merlin Cl *CROY/NA* CR0 ....178 A3
MTCM CR4 ....162 D2
NTHLT UB5 ....83 G2
WLGTN SM6 ....177 F5
Merlin Crs *EDGW* HA8 ....36 B7
Merlin Gdns *CHSGTN* KT9 ....171 K4
Merlin Gv *BECK* BR3 ....166 C3
Merlin Rd *MNPK* E12 ....77 J1
WELL DA16 ....136 B3
Merlin Rd North *WELL* DA16 ....136 B3
Merlins Av *RYLN/HDSTN* HA2 ....65 K2
Merlin St *FSBYW* WC1X 6 A4
Mermagen Dr *RAIN* RM13 ....81 K6
Mermaid Ct *STHWK* SE1 ....19 G1
Merredene St
BRXS/STRHM SW2 ....130 A5
Merriam Av *HOM* E9 ....75 H5
Merriam Cl *CHING* E4 ....44 A4
Merrick Rd *NWDGN* UB2 ....102 E3
Merrick Sq *STHWK* SE1 ....19 G3
Merridene *WCHMH* N21 ....29 H5
Merrielands Crs *DAGW* RM9 ....98 B3
Merrilees Rd *BFN/LL* DA15 ....135 K6
Merrilyn Cl *ESH/CLAY* KT10 ....171 G5
Merriman Rd *BKHTH/KID* SE3 ....114 B7
Merrion Av *STAN* HA7 ....35 K4
Merritt Gdns *CHSGTN* KT9 ....171 J5
Merritt Rd *BROCKY* SE4 ....132 C4
Merrivale *STHGT/OAK* N14 ....28 D5
Merrivale Av *REDBR* IG4 ....59 H3
Merrow Rd *BELMT* SM2 ....174 B7
Merrow St *WALW* SE17 ....19 G8
Merrow Wy *CROY/NA* CR0 ....180 A5
Merrydown Wy *CHST* BR7 ....153 J7
Merryfield *BKHTH/KID* SE3 ....133 J1
Merryfield Gdns *STAN* HA7 ....35 J4
Merryfield Wy *CAT* SE6 ....132 E6
Merryhill Mt *BUSH* WD23 ....22 B7
Merryhill Rd *BUSH* WD23 ....22 A6
Merryhills Dr *ENC/FH* EN2 ....28 D3
Merryweather Ct *DART* DA1 ....139 J5
Merryweather Ct
NWMAL KT3 * 160 B4
Mersey Rd *WALTH* E17 ....57 H2
Mersham Dr *CDALE/KGS* NW9 ....50 C4
Mersham Pl *PGE/AN* SE20 ....150 D7
THHTH CR7 ....164 E1
Mersham Rd *THHTH* CR7 ....164 E1
Merten Rd *RDBR* RM6 ....62 A6
Merton Av *CHSWK* W4 ....106 C3
NTHLT UB5 ....66 C4
Merton Gdns *STMC/STPC* BR5 ....169 G4
Merton Hall Gdns
RYNPK SW20 ....146 C7
Merton Hall Rd
WIM/MER SW19 ....146 C7
Merton High St
WIM/MER SW19 ....147 G6
Merton La *HGT* N6 ....71 K1
Merton Pl *WIM/MER* SW19 * 147 G7
Merton Ri *HAMP* NW3 ....3 J1
Merton Rd *BARK* IG11 ....79 F6
GDMY/SEVK IG3 ....61 K6
RYLN/HDSTN HA2 ....48 C7
SNWD SE25 ....165 G4
WALTH E17 ....58 A4
WAND/EARL SW18 ....127 K7
WATW WD18 ....21 F3
WIM/MER SW19 ....147 G6
Merton Wy *E/WMO/HCT* KT8 ....157 H3
Mertoun Ter *MBLAR* W1H * 9 L1
Merttins Rd *PECK* SE15 ....132 A3
Meru Cl *KTTN* NW5 ....72 A3
Mervan Rd *BRXS/STRHM* SW2 ....130 B3
Mervyn Av *ELTH/MOT* SE9 ....154 C2
Mervyn Rd *WEA* W13 ....104 B2
Meryfield Cl *BORE* WD6 ....24 B1
Messaline Av *ACT* W3 ....86 E5
Messent Rd *ELTH/MOT* SE9 ....134 B4
Messeter Pl *ELTH/MOT* SE9 ....135 F5
Messina Av *KIL/WHAMP* NW6 ....2 A2
Meteor St *BTSEA* SW11 ....129 F4
Meteor Wy *WLGTN* SM6 ....176 E6

Methley St *LBTH* SE11 ....18 B8
Methuen Cl *EDGW* HA8 ....36 C6
Methuen Pk *MUSWH* N10 ....54 B1
Methuen Rd *BELV* DA17 ....117 J3
BXLYHS DA6 ....137 G3
EDGW HA8 ....36 C6
Methwold Rd *NKENS* W10 ....88 B4
Metropolitan Cl *POP/IOD* E14 ....93 J4
Metropolitan Rd *WATW* WD18 ....20 C3
Metropolitan Station Ap
WATW WD18 ....20 D3
Metropolitan Whf *WAP* E1W * 92 E7
Mews North *BGVA* SW1W 16 C4
Mews Pl *WFD* IG8 ....44 E3
Mews St *WAP* E1W 13 M8
The Mews *BECK* BR3 ....151 J7
CEND/HSY/T N8 ....55 G3
NFNCH/WDSPK N12 * 39 H4
REDBR IG4 ....59 H4
ROM RM1 ....63 G3
STRHM/NOR SW16 * 149 F7
TWK TW1 * 124 C5
WATW WD18 * 21 H1
Mexfield Rd *PUT/ROE* SW15 ....127 J4
Meyer Rd *ERITH* DA8 ....117 K5
Meymott St *STHWK* SE1 ....12 C9
Meynell Crs *HOM* E9 ....75 F6
Meynell Gdns *HOM* E9 ....75 F6
Meynell Rd *HOM* E9 ....75 F6
Meyrick Rd *BTSEA* SW11 ....128 C2
WLSDN NW10 ....69 J5
Mezen Cl *NTHWD* HA6 ....32 B4
Miah Ter *WAP* E1W * 92 C7
Micawber St *IS* N1 ....6 E7
Michael Gaynor Cl *HNWL* W7 ....85 F7
Michaelmas Cl *RYNPK* SW20 ....161 F2
Michael Rd *FUL/PGN* SW6 ....108 A7
SNWD SE25 ....165 F2
WAN E11 ....58 C7
Michaels Cl *LEW* SE13 ....133 H2
Micheldever
LEE/GVPK SE12 ....133 H5
Micheldever Rd
LEE/GVPK SE12 ....133 H5
Michelham Gdns *TWK* TW1 ....143 F2
Micheldale Dr *RCH/KEW* TW9 ....125 F3
Michel Wk *WOOL/PLUM* SE18 ....115 H4
Michigan Av *MNPK* E12 ....77 J3
Michleham Down
NFNCH/WDSPK N12 ....38 D3
Mickleham Gdns *CHEAM* SM3 ....174 C5
Mickleham Rd
STMC/STPC BR5 ....155 F7
Mickleham Wy *CROY/NA* CR0 ....180 B6
Micklethwaite Rd
FUL/PGN SW6 ....107 K5
Midcroft *RSLP* HA4 ....46 C7
Middle Dartrey Wk
WBPTN SW10 * 108 B6
Middle Dene *MLHL* NW7 ....37 F2
Middlefield *STJWD* NW8 ....3 G3
Middlefielde *WEA* W13 ....85 H4
Middlefields *CROY/NA* CR0 ....179 G7
WEA W13 ....85 H4
Middle Furlong *BUSH* WD23 ....22 B3
Middle Green Cl *BRYLDS* KT5 ....159 G5
Middleham Gdns *UED* N18 ....42 C5
Middleham Rd *UED* N18 ....42 C5
Middle La *CEND/HSY/T* N8 ....54 E4
TEDD TW11 ....143 F5
Middle Lane Ms
CEND/HSY/T N8 ....54 E4
Middle Park Av *ELTH/MOT* SE9 ....134 C5
Middle Rd *EBAR* EN4 ....27 J5
PLSTW E13 ....94 E1
RYLN/HDSTN HA2 ....66 D1
STRHM/NOR SW16 ....163 H1
Middle Rw *NKENS* W10 ....88 C3
Middlesborough Rd *UED* N18 ....42 C5
Middlesex Cl *STHL* UB1 ....84 B3
Middlesex Pl *HOM* E9 ....74 E5
Middlesex Rd *MTCM* CR4 ....163 K4
Middlesex St *WCHPL* E1 ....13 L3
Middle St *CROY/NA* CR0 ....177 J1
STBT EC1A 12 E2
Middle Temple La *EMB* EC4Y 12 A5
Middleton Av *CHING* E4 ....43 H3
GFD/PVL UB6 ....84 D1
SCUP DA14 ....155 J5
Middleton Cl *CHING* E4 ....43 H2
Middleton Dr
BERM/RHTH SE16 ....112 A1
PIN HA5 ....46 E2
Middleton Gdns
GNTH/NBYPK IG2 ....60 B5
Middleton Ms *HOLWY* N7 ....72 E4
Middleton Ms *HOLWY* N7 ....72 E4
Middleton Rd *CAR* SM5 ....162 D6
GLDGN NW11 ....52 E6
HACK E8 ....7 L2
HYS/HAR UB3 ....82 B4
NWMAL KT3 ....159 K2
Middleton St *BETH* E2 ....92 D2
Middleton Wy *LEW* SE13 ....133 G3
Middleway *GLDGN* NW11 ....53 F4
Middle Wy *STRHM/NOR* SW16 ....163 J1
The Middle Wy
KTN/HRWW/WS HA3 ....49 F1
Middle Yd *STHWK* SE1 ....13 J8
Midfield Av *BXLYHN* DA7 ....137 K2
Midfield Wy *STMC/STPC* BR5 ....155 H7
Midford Pl *FITZ* W1T * 10 F1
Midholm *GLDGN* NW11 ....53 F3
WBLY HA9 ....50 D7
Midholm Cl *GLDGN* NW11 * 53 F3
Midholm Rd *CROY/NA* CR0 ....179 G1
Midhope St *STPAN* WC1H 5 J7
Midhurst Av *CROY/NA* CR0 ....164 B6
MUSWH N10 ....54 A2
Midhurst Cl *HCH* RM12 ....81 J3
Midhurst Gdns
HGDN/ICK UB10 ....64 A6
Midhurst Hl *BXLYHS* DA6 ....137 H4
Midhurst Pde *MUSWH* N10 * 54 A2
Midhurst Rd *WEA* W13 ....104 B1
Midhurst Wy *CLPT* E5 ....74 C3
Midland Arches *CRICK* NW2 * 69 K1
Midland Crs *HAMP* NW3 ....71 G5
Midland Rd *CAMTN* NW1 ....5 H4
LEY E10 ....58 A6
Midland Ter *CRICK* NW2 ....70 B2
WLSDN NW10 ....87 G3
Midlothian Rd *BOW* E3 ....93 H4
Midmoor Rd *BAL* SW12 ....129 H7
WIM/MER SW19 ....146 B7
Midship Cl *BERM/RHTH* SE16 * 93 F7
Midship Point *POP/IOD* E14 * 112 D1
Midstrath Rd *WLSDN* NW10 ....69 G3
Midsummer Av *HSLWW* TW4 ....122 E3
Midway *CHEAM* SM3 ....161 J6
Midwinter Cl *WELL* DA16 ....136 B2
Midwood Cl *CRICK* NW2 ....69 J2
Mighell Av *REDBR* IG4 ....59 H4
Milan Rd *STHL* UB1 ....102 E1

Milborne Gv *WBPTN* SW10 ....14 F8
Milborne St *HOM* E9 ....74 E5
Milborough Crs
LEE/GVPK SE12 ....133 G5
Milbourne La *ESH/CLAY* KT10 ....170 C4
Milbrook *ESH/CLAY* KT10 ....170 C4
Milcote St *STHWK* SE1 ....18 C2
Mildenhall Rd *CLPT* E5 ....74 E3
Mildmay Av *IS* N1 ....73 K5
Mildmay Gv North *IS* N1 ....73 K4
Mildmay Gv South *IS* N1 ....73 K4
Mildmay Pk *IS* N1 ....73 K4
Mildmay Pl *STNW/STAM* N16 ....74 A4
IS N1 ....73 K4
ROMW/RG RM7 ....62 E5
Mildmay Rd *IS* N1 ....73 K5
ROMW/RG RM7 ....62 E5
Mildred Av *BORE* WD6 ....24 C1
HYS/HAR UB3 ....101 J3
NTHLT UB5 ....66 B4
WATW WD18 ....20 D7
Mildred Cl *DART* DA1 ....139 K5
Mildred Rd *ERITH* DA8 ....118 B4
Mile End Pl *WCHPL* E1 * 93 F3
Mile End Rd *WCHPL* E1 ....92 E4
The Mile End *WALTH* E17 ....43 F7
Mile Rd *CROY/NA* CR0 ....163 F7
WLGTN SM6 ....163 F7
Miles Dr *THMD* SE28 ....96 E7
Milespit Hl *MLHL* NW7 ....37 K4
Miles Pl *BRYLDS* KT5 * 159 G3
Miles Rd *CEND/HSY/T* N8 ....54 E2
MTCM CR4 ....162 D2
Miles St *VX/NE* SW8 ....109 K5
Milestone Cl *BELMT* SM2 ....175 H5
ED N9 ....42 C1
Milestone Rd *NRWD* SE19 ....149 K5
Miles Wy *TRDG/WHET* N20 ....39 J1
Milfoil St *SHB* W12 ....87 J6
Milford Cl *ABYW* SE2 ....117 F5
Milford Gdns *ALP/SUD* HA0 ....67 K4
CROY/NA CR0 ....165 K4
EDGW HA8 ....36 C6
Milford Gv *SUT* SM1 ....175 G3
Milford La *TPL/STR* WC2R 12 A6
Milford Ms *STRHM/NOR* SW16 ....149 F2
Milford Rd *STHL* UB1 ....84 A6
WEA W13 ....85 H7
Milk St *BMLY* BR1 ....153 F4
CAN/RD E16 ....96 C7
CITYW EC2V 12 F4
Milkwell Gdns *WFD* IG8 ....45 F6
Milkwell Yd *CMBW* SE5 ....110 D7
Milkwood Rd *HNHL* SE24 ....130 C4
Milk Yd *WAP* E1W 92 E6
Millais Av *MNPK* E12 ....78 A4
Millais Gdns *EDGW* HA8 ....50 C1
Millais Rd *EN* EN1 ....30 C5
NWMAL KT3 ....160 B6
WAN E11 ....76 A3
Millais Wy *HOR/WEW* KT19 ....172 E3
Millard Cl *STNW/STAM* N16 ....74 A4
Millard Rd *DEPT* SE8 ....112 C4
Millars Meadow
BKHTH/KID SE3 ....133 J3
Millbank *WEST* SW1P 17 H6
Millbank Est *WEST* SW1P 17 H6
Millbank Wy *LEE/GVPK* SE12 ....133 K4
Millbourne Rd *FELT* TW13 ....141 J3
Mill Br *BAR* EN5 ....26 D4
Millbrook Av *ELTH/MOT* SE9 ....135 J3
Millbrook Gdns *CHDH* RM6 ....62 A5
GPK RM2 ....63 G1
Millbrook Rd *BRXN/ST* SW9 ....130 C2
ED N9 ....30 D7
Mill Cl *CAR* SM5 * 176 A1
WDR/YW UB7 ....100 A2
Mill Ct *WDR/YW* UB7 ....122 D7
Millennium Br *STHWK* SE1 ....12 E7
Millennium Cl *CAN/RD* E16 ....94 E5
Millennium Dr *POP/IOD* E14 ....113 G2
Millennium Pl *BETH* E2 * 92 D1
Millennium Sq *STHWK* SE1 ....19 L1
Millennium Wy *GNWCH* SE10 ....113 H1
Millennium Whf *POP/IOD* E14 ....113 G2
Miller Cl *BMLY* BR1 ....152 E4
MTCM CR4 ....162 E6
Miller Rd *CROY/NA* CR0 ....164 A7
WIM/MER SW19 ....147 H5
Miller's Av *HACK* E8 ....74 B4
Millers Cl *DART* DA1 ....139 G6
MLHL NW7 ....37 J3
Miller's Ct *CHSWK* W4 * 106 C4
Millers Green Cl *ENC/FH* EN2 ....29 H2
Miller's Ter *HACK* E8 ....74 B4
Miller St *CAMTN* NW1 ....4 E5
Miller's Wy *HMSMTH* W6 ....107 F1
Millers Yd *FNCH* N3 ....39 F7
Miller Wk *STHWK* SE1 ....12 B9
Millet Rd *GFD/PVL* UB6 ....84 B2
Mill Farm Av *SUN* TW16 ....140 C6
Mill Farm Cl *PIN* HA5 ....47 G1
Mill Farm Crs *HSLWW* TW4 ....122 D7
Millfield *SUN* TW16 ....140 B7
Millfield Av *WALTH* E17 ....43 G7
Millfield La *HGT* N6 ....71 K1
Millfield Pl *HGT* N6 ....72 A1
Millfield Rd *EDGW* HA8 ....50 E1
HSLWW TW4 ....122 D7
Millfields Rd *CLPT* E5 ....74 E3
Mill Gdns *SYD* SE26 ....150 D3
Mill Gn *MTCM* CR4 ....163 F6
Mill Green Rd *MTCM* CR4 ....163 F6
Millgrove St *BTSEA* SW11 ....109 F7
Millharbour *POP/IOD* E14 ....112 E2
Millhaven Cl *CHDH* RM6 ....61 H5
Mill HI *BARN* SW13 ....126 D1
Mill Hill Gv *ACT* W3 ....86 D7
Mill Hill Rd *ACT* W3 ....105 J1
BARN SW13 ....126 D1
Mill Hill Ter *ACT* W3 ....86 D7
Millhouse Pl *WNWD* SE27 ....149 H3
Millicent Gv *PLMGR* N13 ....41 H4
Millicent Rd *LEY* E10 ....57 H7
Milligan St *POP/IOD* E14 ....93 H6
Milling Rd *EDGW* HA8 ....37 F6
Millington Rd *HYS/HAR* UB3 ....101 H3
Mill La *CAR* SM5 ....176 A3
CHDH RM6 ....62 A5
CHING E4 ....31 K2
CRICK NW2 ....70 C2
CROY/NA CR0 ....177 G2
EW KT17 ....173 G6
KIL/WHAMP NW6 ....70 E4
WFD IG8 ....44 D5
WOOL/PLUM SE18 ....115 F4
Millman Ms *BMSBY* WC1N * 11 L1
Millman Pl *BMSBY* WC1N * 11 L1
Millman St *BMSBY* WC1N 11 L1
Millmark Gv *NWCR* SE14 ....132 B1
Millmarsh La *PEND* EN3 ....31 H1
Mill Mead Rd *TOTM* N17 ....56 D2

Mill Pl *CHST* BR7 ....154 A7
DART DA1 ....138 D3
KUT/HW KT1 ....159 G2
POP/IOD E14 ....93 G5
Mill Plat *ISLW* TW7 ....124 B1
Mill Plat Av *ISLW* TW7 ....124 B1
Mill Pond Cl *VX/NE* SW8 ....109 J6
Millpond Est
BERM/RHTH SE16 * 111 J1
Mill Pond Rd *DART* DA1 ....139 H6
Mill Rdg *EDGW* HA8 ....36 B4
Mill Rd *CAN/RD* E16 ....95 F7
ERITH DA8 ....117 K6
ESH/CLAY KT10 ....170 C4
IL IG1 ....78 A2
WDR/YW UB7 ....100 A2
WHTN TW2 ....142 C1
WIM/MER SW19 ....147 G6
Mill Rw *BXLY* DA5 ....137 J6
IS N1 ....7 K4
Mills Gv *HDN* NW4 ....52 B2
POP/IOD E14 ....94 A4
Millshot Cl *FUL/PGN* SW6 ....107 F7
Millshott Cl *WHALL* SW1A * 11 H8
Millside *CAR* SM5 ....175 K1
Millside Pl *ISLW* TW7 ....124 C1
Millson Cl *TRDG/WHET* N20 ....39 H1
Mills Rw *CHSWK* W4 ....106 A3
Millstone Cl *SRTFD* E15 ....76 B5
Millstream Cl *PLMGR* N13 ....41 G4
Millstream Rd *STHWK* SE1 ....19 L2
Mill St *CONDST* W1S 10 D6
KUT/HW KT1 ....159 F2
STHWK SE1 ....19 M2
Mill V *HAYES* BR2 ....167 K2
Mill View Cl *EW* KT17 ....173 H6
Mill View Gdns *CROY/NA* CR0 ....179 F2
Millwall Dock Rd
POP/IOD E14 ....112 D2
Millway *MLHL* NW7 ....37 G4
Millway Gdns *NTHLT* UB5 ....65 K5
Millwood Rd *HSLW* TW3 ....123 H4
Millwood St *NKENS* W10 ....88 C4
Mill Yd *WCHPL* E1 ....92 C6
Milman Cl *PIN* HA5 ....47 H2
Milman Rd *KIL/WHAMP* NW6 ....88 B1
Milman's St *WBPTN* SW10 ....108 C5
Milne Fld *PIN* HA5 ....34 A4
Milne Gdns *ELTH/MOT* SE9 ....134 D4
Milner Ct *BUSH* WD23 ....22 B5
Milner Dr *WHTN* TW2 ....123 J6
Milner Pl *IS* N1 ....6 B2
KUT/HW KT1 ....158 E2
Milner Rd *BCTR* RM8 ....79 J1
KUT/HW KT1 ....158 E2
MRDN SM4 ....162 C4
SRTFD E15 ....94 C2
THHTH CR7 ....164 E2
WIM/MER SW19 ....147 F7
Milner Sq *IS* N1 ....6 B1
Milner St *CHEL* SW3 ....15 L5
Milnthorpe Rd *CHSWK* W4 ....106 A5
Milo Rd *EDUL* SE22 ....131 G5
Milroy Wk *STHWK* SE1 ....12 C8
Milson Rd *WKENS* W14 ....107 H2
Milton Av *BAR* EN5 ....26 D4
CDALE/KGS NW9 ....50 D2
CROY/NA CR0 ....164 E6
EHAM E6 ....77 H1
HCH RM12 ....81 H1
HGT N6 ....54 C6
SUT SM1 ....175 H2
WLSDN NW10 ....69 F7
Milton Cl *EFNCH* N2 ....53 G5
STHWK SE1 ....19 L6
SUT SM1 ....175 H2
YEAD UB4 ....82 E5
Milton Court Rd *NWCR* SE14 ....112 B5
Milton Crs *GNTH/NBYPK* IG2 ....60 D6
Milton Dr *BORE* WD6 ....24 D3
Milton Gdns
STWL/WRAY TW19 ....120 C7
Milton Gv *FBAR/BDGN* N11 ....40 C4
STNW/STAM N16 ....73 K3
Milton Pk *HGT* N6 ....54 C6
Milton Rd *ACT* W3 ....87 F7
BELV DA17 ....117 H3
CDALE/KGS NW9 ....51 J1
CROY/NA CR0 ....164 E6
HGT N6 ....54 C6
HNHL SE24 ....130 C4
HNWL W7 ....85 F6
HPTN TW12 ....142 A4
HRW HA1 ....48 E3
MLHL NW7 ....37 J4
MORT/ESHN SW14 ....126 A2
MTCM CR4 ....148 A6
ROM RM1 ....63 J5
SEVS/STOTM N15 ....55 H2
SUT SM1 ....174 E2
WALTH E17 ....57 J3
WELL DA16 ....116 A7
WIM/MER SW19 ....147 G5
WLGTN SM6 ....176 C5
Milton St *BARB* EC2Y 13 G2
Milton Wy *WDR/YW* UB7 ....100 C3
Milverton Gdns
GDMY/SEVK IG3 ....79 F1
Milverton Rd
KIL/WHAMP NW6 ....70 A6
Milverton St *LBTH* SE11 ....18 B8
Milverton Wy *ELTH/MOT* SE9 ....154 A3
Milward St *WCHPL* E1 ....92 D4
Mimosa Rd *YEAD* UB4 ....83 G4
Minard Rd *CAT* SE6 ....133 H6
Mina Rd *WALW* SE17 ....19 K8
WIM/MER SW19 ....146 E7
Minchenden Crs
STHGT/OAK N14 ....40 C2
Mincing La *MON* EC3R 13 J6
Minden Rd *CHEAM* SM3 ....174 C1
PGE/AN SE20 ....150 D7
Minehead Rd
RYLN/HDSTN HA2 ....66 A2
STRHM/NOR SW16 ....149 F4
Mineral Cl *BAR* EN5 ....26 A5
Mineral St *WOOL/PLUM* SE18 ....115 K3
Minera Ms *BGVA* SW1W 16 C6
Minerva Cl *BRXN/ST* SW9 ....110 B6
SCUP DA14 ....154 E3
Minerva Rd *CHING* E4 ....43 K6
KUT/HW KT1 ....159 G1
WLSDN NW10 ....86 E3
Minerva St *BETH* E2 ....92 D1
Minet Av *WLSDN* NW10 ....87 G1
Minet Dr *HYS/HAR* UB3 ....83 F7
Minet Gdns *HYS/HAR* UB3 ....83 F7
WLSDN NW10 ....87 G1

Minet Rd *BRXN/ST* SW9 ....130 C1
Minford Gdns *WKENS* W14 ....107 G1
Ming St *POP/IOD* E14 * 93 J6
Minimax Cl *EBED/NFELT* TW14 ....121 K5
Ministry Wy *ELTH/MOT* SE9 ....153 K1
Mink Ct *HSLWW* TW4 ....122 B1
Minniedale *BRYLDS* KT5 ....159 G4
Minnow Wk *WALW* SE17 ....19 K6
Minories *TWRH* EC3N 13 L5
Minshull Pl *BECK* BR3 ....151 J5
Minshull St *VX/NE* SW8 * 109 J7
Minson Rd *HOM* E9 ....75 F7
Minstead Gdns
PUT/ROE SW15 ....126 C6
Minstead Wy *NWMAL* KT3 ....160 B5
Minster Av *SUT* SM1 ....174 E1
Minster Ct *MON* EC3R * 13 J6
Minster Dr *CROY/NA* CR0 ....178 A3
Minster Gdns
E/WMO/HCT KT8 ....156 E3
Minster Rd *BMLY* BR1 ....153 F6
CRICK NW2 ....70 C4
Minster Wk *CEND/HSY/T* N8 * 54 E3
Minstrel Gdns *BRYLDS* KT5 ....159 G3
Mintern Cl *PLMGR* N13 ....41 H2
Minterne Av *NWDGN* UB2 ....103 F3
Minterne Rd
KTN/HRWW/WS HA3 ....50 B4
Minterne Waye *YEAD* UB4 ....83 G5
Mintern St *IS* N1 ....7 H5
Minton Ms *KIL/WHAMP* NW6 ....71 F5
Mint Rd *WLGTN* SM6 ....176 B4
Mint St *STHWK* SE1 ....18 E1
Mint Wk *CROY/NA* CR0 ....177 J2
Mirabel Rd *FUL/PGN* SW6 ....107 J6
Miranda Cl *WCHPL* E1 ....92 E4
Miranda Rd *ARCH* N19 ....54 C7
Mirfield St *CHARL* SE7 ....114 C2
Miriam Rd *WOOL/PLUM* SE18 ....115 K4
Mirren Cl *RYLN/HDSTN* HA2 ....65 K3
Miskin Rd *DART* DA1 ....139 F6
Missenden Cl
EBED/NFELT TW14 ....121 J7
Missenden Gdns *MRDN* SM4 ....162 B5
Mission Gv *WALTH* E17 ....57 G4
Mission Pl *PECK* SE15 ....111 H7
Mistletoe Cl *CROY/NA* CR0 ....166 A7
Misty's Fld *WOT/HER* KT12 ....156 B7
Mitali Pas *WCHPL* E1 ....92 C5
Mitcham La
STRHM/NOR SW16 ....148 C5
Mitcham Pk *MTCM* CR4 ....162 D3
Mitcham Rd *CROY/NA* CR0 ....163 K5
EHAM E6 ....95 J2
GDMY/SEVK IG3 ....61 F6
TOOT SW17 ....147 K4
Mitchellbrook Wy
WLSDN NW10 ....69 F5
Mitchell Cl *ABYW* SE2 ....116 D4
BELV DA17 ....117 K2
Mitchell Rd *PLMGR* N13 ....41 H4
Mitchell St *FSBYE* EC1V 6 E9
Mitchell Wy *BMLY* BR1 ....152 E7
WLSDN NW10 ....68 E5
Mitchison Rd *IS* N1 ....73 K5
Mitchley Rd *TOTM* N17 ....56 C2
Mitford Rd *ARCH* N19 ....72 E1
Mitre Cl *BELMT* SM2 ....175 G6
Mitre Rd *SRTFD* E15 ....94 C1
STHWK SE1 ....18 B1
Mitre Sq *HDTCH* EC3A 13 L5
Mitre St *HDTCH* EC3A 13 L5
The Mitre *POP/IOD* E14 ....93 H6
Mitre Wy *NKENS* W10 ....87 K4
Moat Cl *ELTH/MOT* SE9 * 134 E5
Moat Crs *FNCH* N3 ....53 F2
Moat Cft *WELL* DA16 ....136 D2
Moat Dr *HRW* HA1 ....48 C3
PLSTW E13 ....95 G1
RSLP HA4 ....46 C6
Moat Farm Rd *NTHLT* UB5 ....65 K5
Moatfield Rd *BUSH* WD23 ....22 B4
Moat La *ERITH* DA8 ....118 D7
Moat Pl *ACT* W3 ....86 D5
BRXN/ST SW9 ....130 A2
Moat Side *FELT* TW13 ....141 G3
PEND EN3 ....30 E3
The Moat *NWMAL* KT3 ....145 G7
Moberly Rd *CLAP* SW4 ....129 J6
Modbury Gdns *KTTN* NW5 ....72 A5
Model Cots *MORT/ESHN* SW14 ....125 K2
WEA W13 ....104 C1
Model Farm Cl *ELTH/MOT* SE9 ....153 J2
Moelyn Ms *HRW* HA1 ....49 G4
Moffat Rd *PLMGR* N13 ....40 E5
THHTH CR7 ....164 D1
TOOT SW17 ....147 J3
Mogden La *ISLW* TW7 ....124 A4
Mohmmad Khan Rd
WAN E11 * 58 D7
Moiety Rd *POP/IOD* E14 ....112 D1
Moira Cl *TOTM* N17 ....56 A1
Moira Rd *ELTH/MOT* SE9 ....134 E3
Moir Cl *SAND/SEL* CR2 ....178 C7
Mole Abbey Gdns
E/WMO/HCT KT8 ....157 F2
Mole Ct *HOR/WEW* KT19 ....172 E3
Molember Ct *E/WMO/HCT* KT8 ....157 K4
Molember Rd
E/WMO/HCT KT8 ....157 K4
Molescroft *ELTH/MOT* SE9 ....154 C3
Molesey Av *E/WMO/HCT* KT8 ....156 E3
Molesey Dr *CHEAM* SM3 ....174 C1
Molesey Park Av
E/WMO/HCT KT8 ....157 G4
Molesey Park Cl
E/WMO/HCT KT8 ....157 H4
Molesey Park Rd
E/WMO/HCT KT8 ....157 G4
Molesey Rd *E/WMO/HCT* KT8 ....157 G4
WOT/HER KT12 ....156 D7
Molesford Rd *FUL/PGN* SW6 ....107 K7
Molesham Cl *E/WMO/HCT* KT8 ....157 G2
Molesham Wy
E/WMO/HCT KT8 ....157 G3
Molesworth St *LEW* SE13 ....133 F2
Mollison Av *PEND* EN3 ....31 J4
Mollison Dr *WLGTN* SM6 ....176 E6
Mollison Wy *EDGW* HA8 ....50 C1
Molly Huggins Cl *BAL* SW12 ....129 J6
Molyneux Dr *TOOT* SW17 ....148 B3
Molyneux St *MBLAR* W1H * 9 J2
Monarch Cl *EBED/NFELT* TW14 ....121 H6
RAIN RM13 ....99 J1
WWKM BR4 ....180 D3
Monarch Dr *CAN/RD* E16 ....95 H4
Monarch Ms
STRHM/NOR SW16 ....149 G4
Monarch Pde *MTCM* CR4 * 162 E1
Monarch Pl *BKHH* IG9 ....45 G1
Monarch Rd *BELV* DA17 ....117 H2
Monarchs Wy *RSLP* HA4 ....46 C7

Monarch's Wy RSLP HA4 * ... 46 B7
Monarch Wy GNTH/NBYPK IG2 ... 60 D5
Mona Rd PECK SE15 ... 131 K1
Monastery Gdns ENC/FH EN2 ... 29 K1
Mona St CAN/RD E16 ... 94 D4
Monaveen Gdns E/WMO/HCT KT8 ... 157 G2
Monck's Rw WAND/EARL SW18 * ... 127 J5
Monck St WEST SW1P ... 17 J5
Monclar Rd CMBW SE5 ... 130 E8
Moncorvo Cl SKENS SW7 ... 15 J2
Moncrieff Cl EHAM E6 ... 95 J5
Moncrieff St PECK SE15 ... 131 H1
Monday Aly STNW/STAM N16 ... 74 B2
Mondial Wy HYS/HAR UB3 ... 101 H6
Monega Rd FSTGT E7 ... 77 G5
  MNPK E12 ... 77 H5
Money La WDR/YW UB7 ... 100 A2
Monica Cl WATN WD24 ... 21 H1
Monier Rd BOW E3 ... 75 J6
Monivea Rd BECK BR3 ... 151 H6
Monk Dr CAN/RD E16 ... 94 E6
Monkfrith Wy STHGT/OAK N14 ... 28 B5
Monkham's Av WFD IG8 ... 45 F4
Monkham's Av WFD IG8 ... 45 F3
Monkham's La WFD IG8 ... 45 F3
Monkleigh Rd MRDN SM4 ... 161 H6
Monks Av BAR EN5 ... 27 G5
  E/WMO/HCT KT8 ... 156 E3
Monks Cl ABYW SE2 ... 116 E3
  ENC/FH EN2 ... 29 J1
  RSLP HA4 ... 65 H3
  RYLN/HDSTN HA2 * ... 66 A7
Monks Crs WOT/HER KT12 ... 156 A7
Monksdene Gdns SUT SM1 ... 175 F2
Monks Dr ACT W3 ... 86 C4
Monksmead BORE WD6 ... 24 E3
Monks Orchard Rd BECK BR3 ... 166 D1
Monks Pk WBLY HA9 ... 68 D5
Monks Park Gdns WBLY HA9 ... 68 D5
Monks Rd ENC/FH EN2 ... 29 J1
Monk St WOOL/PLUM SE18 ... 115 F3
Monks Wy BECK BR3 ... 166 D5
  GLDGN NW11 ... 52 D3
  STMC/STPC BR5 ... 169 H7
Monkswood Gdns BORE WD6 ... 25 F4
  CLAY IG5 ... 60 A2
Monk Ter FSTH SE23 ... 151 H1
Monkton St LBTH SE11 ... 17 K6
Monkville Av GLDGN NW11 ... 52 D3
Monkville Pde GLDGN NW11 * ... 52 D3
Monkwood Cl BARB EC2Y ... 12 F3
Monmouth Av KUT/HW KT1 ... 143 J6
  SWFD E18 ... 59 F3
Monmouth Cl CHSWK W4 ... 106 A2
  MTCM CR4 ... 163 K2
  WELL DA16 ... 136 B3
Monmouth Gv BTFD TW8 ... 105 F3
Monmouth Pl BAY/PAD W2 * ... 8 C4
Monmouth Rd BAY/PAD W2 ... 8 C5
  DAGW RM9 ... 80 B4
  ED N9 ... 42 D1
  EHAM E6 ... 95 K2
  HYS/HAR UB3 ... 101 H3
  WAT WD17 ... 21 F2
Monmouth St LSO/SEVD WC2H ... 11 J5
Monnery Rd ARCH N19 ... 72 C2
Monnow Rd STHWK SE1 ... 111 H4
Mono La FELT TW13 ... 141 F1
Monoux Gv WALTH E17 ... 43 H7
Monroe Dr MORT/ESHN SW14 ... 125 J4
Monroe Gdns KTN/HRWW/WS HA3 ... 34 E6
Monro Gv HOR/WEW KT19 ... 172 E7
Monsell Rd FSBYPK N4 ... 73 H2
Monson Rd NWCR SE14 ... 112 A6
  WLSDN NW10 ... 87 J1
Mons Wy HAYES BR2 ... 168 D5
Montacute Rd BUSH WD23 ... 22 E6
  CAT SE6 ... 132 C6
  CROY/NA CR0 ... 180 A7
  MRDN SM4 ... 162 C6
Montagu Crs UED N18 ... 42 D3
Montague Av BROCKY SE4 ... 132 C3
  HNWL W7 ... 85 F7
Montague Cl BAR EN5 ... 26 E3
  STHWK SE1 ... 13 G8
Montague Gdns EA W5 ... 86 C6
Montague Hall Pl BUSH WD23 ... 22 C4
Montague Pl CEND/HSY/T N8 ... 55 F4
  CROY/NA CR0 ... 164 C7
  HACK E8 ... 74 C4
  HNWL W7 ... 104 A1
  HSLW TW3 ... 123 G2
  NWDGN UB2 ... 102 D3
  RCHPK/HAM TW10 ... 125 F5
  SEVS/STOTM N15 * ... 56 C3
  WAN E11 ... 76 D1
  WEA W13 ... 85 H5
  WIM/MER SW19 ... 147 F6
Montague Sq PECK SE15 ... 111 K6
Montague St RSQ WC1B ... 11 J2
  STBT EC1A ... 12
Montague Ter HAYES BR2 * ... 167 K3
Montague Waye NWDGN UB2 ... 102 D2
Montagu Gdns UED N18 ... 42 D3
  WLGTN SM6 ... 176 C3
Montagu Man MHST W1U ... 9 M3
Montagu Ms North MBLAR W1H ... 9 M3
Montagu Ms South MBLAR W1H ... 9 M4
Montagu Ms West MBLAR W1H ... 9 L4
Montagu Pl ED N9 ... 42 E2
  HDN NW4 ... 51 J3
  UED N18 ... 42 D4
Montagu Rw MHST W1U ... 9 M3
Montagu Sq MBLAR W1H ... 9 M3
Montagu St MBLAR W1H ... 9 M4
Montaigne Cl WEST SW1P ... 17 H6
Montalt Rd WFD IG8 ... 44 D4
Montana Gdns SUT SM1 ... 175 G4
  SYD SE26 ... 151 H4
Montana Rd RYNPK SW20 ... 146 A7
  TOOT SW17 ... 148 A2
Montbelle Rd ELTH/MOT SE9 ... 154 B3
Montcalm Cl HAYES BR2 ... 167 K5
  YEAD UB4 ... 83 F2
Montcalm Rd CHARL SE7 ... 114 C6
Montclare St BETH E2 ... 7 L8
Monteagle Av BARK IG11 ... 78 C5
Monteagle Wy PECK SE15 ... 131 J2
Montefiore St VX/NE SW8 ... 129 G1
Montem Rd FSTH SE23 ... 132 C6

NWMAL KT3 ... 160 B3
Montem St FSBYPK N4 ... 55 F7
Montenotte Rd CEND/HSY/T N8 ... 54 C4
Montesole Ct PIN HA5 * ... 47 G1
Montesquieu Ter CAN/RD E16 * ... 94 D5
Montford Pl LBTH SE11 ... 18 A8
Montfort Pl WIM/MER SW19 ... 127 G7
Montgomerie Ms FSTH SE23 ... 131 K6
Montgomery Av ESH/CLAY KT10 ... 170 E1
Montgomery Cl BFN/LL DA15 ... 135 K4
  MTCM CR4 * ... 163 K3
Montgomery Gdns BELMT SM2 ... 175 H6
Montgomery Rd CHSWK W4 ... 105 K3
  EDGW HA8 ... 36 B5
Montgomery St POP/IOD E14 ... 93 K7
Montholme Rd BTSEA SW11 ... 128 E5
Monthorpe Rd WCHPL E1 ... 92 C4
Montolieu Gdns PUT/ROE SW15 ... 126 E4
Montpelier Av BXLY DA5 ... 136 E6
  EA W5 ... 85 J4
Montpelier Gdns CHDH RM6 ... 61 J6
  EHAM E6 ... 95 H2
Montpelier Gv KTTN NW5 ... 72 C4
Montpelier Ms SKENS SW7 ... 15 K3
Montpelier Pl SKENS SW7 ... 15 K3
  WCHPL E1 ... 92 E5
Montpelier Ri GLDGN NW11 ... 52 C6
  WBLY HA9 ... 49 K7
Montpelier Rd EA W5 ... 85 K4
  FNCH N3 ... 39 G7
  PECK SE15 ... 111 J7
  SUT SM1 ... 175 G3
Montpelier Rw BKHTH/KID SE3 ... 133 J1
  TWK TW1 ... 124 C6
Montpelier Sq SKENS SW7 ... 15 K3
Montpelier St SKENS SW7 ... 15 K2
Montpelier Ter SKENS SW7 ... 15 K2
Montpelier V BKHTH/KID SE3 * ... 133 J1
Montpelier Wk SKENS SW7 ... 15 K3
Montpelier Wy GLDGN NW11 ... 52 C6
Montrave Rd PGE/AN SE20 ... 150 E5
Montreal Pl HOL/ALD WC2B ... 11 L6
Montreal Rd IL IG1 ... 60 C6
Montrell Rd BRXS/STRHM SW2 ... 129 K7
Montrose Av BFN/LL DA15 ... 136 B6
  EDGW HA8 ... 51 F1
  KIL/WHAMP NW6 ... 88 C1
  WELL DA16 ... 135 J2
  WHTN TW2 ... 123 G6
Montrose Crs ALP/SUD HA0 ... 68 A5
  NFNCH/WDSPK N12 ... 39 F3
Montrose Gdns MTCM CR4 ... 162 E2
  SUT SM1 ... 175 F1
Montrose Pl KTBR SW1X ... 16 B2
Montrose Rd EBED/NFELT TW14 ... 121 G5
  KTN/HRWW/WS HA3 ... 48 E1
Montrose Vls HMSMTH W6 * ... 106 D4
Montrose Wy FSTH SE23 ... 132 A7
Montserrat Av WFD IG8 ... 44 B6
Montserrat Cl NRWD SE19 ... 149 K4
Montserrat Rd PUT/ROE SW15 ... 127 H3
Monument Wy TOTM N17 ... 56 B2
Monza St WAP E1W ... 92 E6
Moodkee St BERM/RHTH SE16 ... 111 K1
Moody St WCHPL E1 ... 93 G3
Moon Ct LEE/GVPK SE12 * ... 133 K3
Moon La BAR EN5 ... 26 D2
Moon St IS N1 ... 6 B2
Moorcroft EDGW HA8 * ... 36 D7
Moorcroft Gdns HAYES BR2 ... 168 D4
Moorcroft Rd STRHM/NOR SW16 ... 148 E2
Moorcroft Wy PIN HA5 ... 47 J4
Moordown WOOL/PLUM SE18 ... 115 F7
Moore Cl MORT/ESHN SW14 ... 125 K2
  MTCM CR4 ... 163 G1
Moore Crs DAGW RM9 ... 79 H7
Moorefield Rd TOTM N17 ... 56 B2
Mooreland Rd BMLY BR1 ... 152 D6
Moore Park Rd FUL/PGN SW6 ... 108 A6
Moore St CHEL SW3 ... 15 L5
Moore Wy BELMT SM2 ... 174 E7
Moorey Cl SRTFD E15 ... 76 D7
Moorfield Av EA W5 ... 85 K3
Moorfield Rd CHSGTN KT9 ... 172 A4
  ENC/FH EN2 ... 29 J1
  IL IG1 ... 78 D7
  PGE/AN SE20 ... 151 F6
  SUT SM1 ... 175 G4
  WALTH E17 ... 57 J4
Moorfields LVPST EC2M ... 13 G3
Moorfields Highwalk BARB EC2Y ... 13 G3
Moorgate LOTH EC2R ... 13 G4
Moorgate Pl LOTH EC2R * ... 13 G4
Moorhead Wy BKHTH/KID SE3 ... 134 A2
Moorhen Cl ERITH DA8 ... 118 E5
Moorhouse Rd BAY/PAD W2 ... 8 A4
  KTN/HRWW/WS HA3 ... 49 K2
The Moorings BUSH WD23 ... 21 J3
  CHSWK W4 * ... 105 H5
Moorland Cl WHTN TW2 ... 123 F6
Moorland Rd BRXN/ST SW9 ... 130 C3
Moorlands Av MLHL NW7 ... 37 K5
Moor La BARB EC2Y ... 13 G3
  CHSGTN KT9 ... 172 B4
Moor Lane Crossing WATW WD18 ... 20 A6
Moormead Dr HOR/WEW KT19 ... 173 G4
Moor Mead Rd TWK TW1 ... 124 B5
Moor Park Gdns KUTN/CMB KT2 ... 145 G6
  NTHWD HA6 * ... 32 A1
Moor Park Rd NTHWD HA6 ... 32 B5
Moorside Rd BMLY BR1 ... 152 C3
Moor St SOHO/SHAV W1D ... 11 H5
Moortown Rd OXHEY WD19 ... 33 G3
Moor Vw WATW WD18 ... 20 A6
Morant Pl POP/IOD E14 ... 93 J6
Mora Rd CRICK NW2 ... 70 A3
Mora St FSBYE EC1V ... 6 F8
Morat St BRXN/ST SW9 ... 110 A7
Moravian Pl WBPTN SW10 ... 108 C5
Moravian St BETH E2 ... 92 E2
Moray Av HYS/HAR UB3 ... 82 D1
Moray Cl EDGW HA8 * ... 36 D1
Moray Ms HOLWY N7 ... 73 F1
Moray Rd HOLWY N7 ... 73 F1
Morcambe St WALW SE17 ... 18 F6
Mordaunt Gdns DAGW RM9 ... 80 A6
Mordaunt Rd WLSDN NW10 ... 69 F7
Mordaunt St BRXN/ST SW9 ... 130 A2

Morden Ct MRDN SM4 ... 162 A3
Morden Court Pde MRDN SM4 * ... 162 A2
Morden Gdns GFD/PVL UB6 ... 67 F4
  MTCM CR4 ... 162 C3
Morden Hall Rd MRDN SM4 ... 162 A2
Morden Hl LEW SE13 ... 133 F1
Morden La LEW SE13 ... 133 F1
Morden Rd BKHTH/KID SE3 ... 133 K1
  CHDH RM6 ... 62 A5
  MTCM CR4 ... 162 C3
  WIM/MER SW19 ... 162 A1
Morden Road Ms BKHTH/KID SE3 ... 133 K1
Morden St LEW SE13 ... 112 E7
Morden Wy CHEAM SM3 ... 161 K6
Morden Wharf Rd GNWCH SE10 ... 113 H2
Mordon Rd GDMY/SEVK IG3 ... 61 F6
Mordred Rd CAT SE6 ... 152 C1
Morecambe Cl HCH RM12 ... 81 K4
  WCHPL E1 * ... 93 F4
Morecambe Gdns STAN HA7 ... 35 K3
Morecambe St POP/IOD E14 ... 112 K4
  WALW SE17 ... 19 J8
More Cl CAN/RD E16 ... 94 D5
  WKENS W14 ... 107 G3
Morecoombe Cl KUTN/CMB KT2 ... 144 D3
Moree Wy UED N18 ... 42 C3
Moreland Cots BOW E3 * ... 93 J1
Moreland Wy CHING E4 ... 43 K2
More La ESH/CLAY KT10 ... 170 B2
Morella Rd BTSEA SW11 ... 128 E6
More London Riverside STHWK SE1 ... 13 K9
Moremead Rd CAT SE6 ... 151 H3
Morena St CAT SE6 ... 132 E6
Moresby Av BRYLDS KT5 ... 159 J6
Moresby Rd CLPT E5 ... 56 D7
Mores Gdn CHEL SW3 * ... 108 C5
Moreton Cl CLPT E5 ... 74 E1
  MLHL NW7 ... 38 A5
  SEVS/STOTM N15 ... 55 K5
Moreton Gdns WFD IG8 ... 45 J4
Moreton Pl PIM SW1V ... 16 F7
Moreton Rd SAND/SEL CR2 ... 177 K4
  SEVS/STOTM N15 ... 55 K5
  WPK KT4 ... 173 J1
Moreton St PIM SW1V ... 16 F7
Moreton Ter PIM SW1V ... 16 F7
Moreton Terrace Ms South PIM SW1V ... 16 F7
Morford Cl RSLP HA4 ... 47 F5
Morford Wy RSLP HA4 ... 47 F5
Morgan Av WALTH E17 ... 58 B3
Morgan Cl DAGE RM10 ... 80 C6
  NTHWD HA6 ... 32 D4
Morgan Rd BMLY BR1 ... 152 E6
  HOLWY N7 ... 73 G4
  NKENS W10 ... 88 D4
Morgan's La HYS/HAR UB3 ... 82 B4
  STHWK SE1 ... 13 J9
Morgan St BOW E3 ... 93 G2
  CAN/RD E16 ... 94 D4
Morgan Wy WFD IG8 ... 45 J5
Moriarty Cl BMLY BR1 ... 169 G3
Moriarty Rd HOLWY N7 ... 72 E3
Morie St WAND/EARL SW18 ... 128 A3
Morieux Rd LEY E10 ... 57 H7
Moring Rd TOOT SW17 ... 148 A3
Morkyns Wk DUL SE21 ... 150 A3
Morland Av CROY/NA CR0 ... 165 F7
  DART DA1 ... 138 C4
Morland Cl GLDGN NW11 ... 53 F7
  HPTN TW12 ... 141 K4
  MTCM CR4 ... 162 D2
Morland Est HACK E8 * ... 74 C6
Morland Gdns STHL UB1 ... 84 B7
  WLSDN NW10 ... 69 F6
Morland Ms IS N1 ... 6 B2
Morland Rd CROY/NA CR0 ... 165 G6
  DAGE RM10 ... 80 C6
  IL IG1 ... 78 B1
  KTN/HRWW/WS HA3 ... 50 A4
  PGE/AN SE20 ... 151 F6
  SUT SM1 ... 175 G4
  WALTH E17 ... 57 F4
Morley Av CHING E4 ... 44 B6
  UED N18 ... 42 C3
  WDGN N22 ... 41 H7
Morley Crs EDGW HA8 ... 36 E1
  RSLP HA4 ... 65 G1
Morley Crs East STAN HA7 ... 49 J2
Morley Crs West STAN HA7 ... 49 J3
Morley Rd BARK IG11 ... 78 D7
  CHDH RM6 ... 62 A4
  CHEAM SM3 ... 161 J7
  CHST BR7 ... 154 C7
  LEW SE13 ... 133 F3
  LEY E10 ... 58 A7
  SRTFD E15 ... 94 D1
  TWK TW1 ... 124 E5
Morley St STHWK SE1 ... 18 B3
Morna Rd CMBW SE5 ... 130 D1
Morning La HOM E9 ... 74 E5
Morningside Rd WPK KT4 ... 173 K1
Mornington Av HAYES BR2 ... 168 B3
  IL IG1 ... 60 A6
  WKENS W14 ... 107 J3
Mornington Crs CAMTN NW1 ... 4 E5
  HEST TW5 ... 102 A7
Mornington Gv BOW E3 ... 93 J2
Mornington Ms CMBW SE5 ... 110 D7
Mornington Pl CAMTN NW1 * ... 4 E4
Mornington Rd ASHF TW15 ... 140 A4
  GFD/PVL UB6 ... 84 B4
  WAN E11 ... 58 D7
  WFD IG8 ... 44 D3
Mornington St CAMTN NW1 ... 4 D4
Mornington Ter CAMTN NW1 ... 4 D3
Mornington Wk RCHPK/HAM TW10 ... 143 J3
Morocco St STHWK SE1 ... 19 J2
Morpeth Gv HOM E9 ... 75 F7
Morpeth Rd HOM E9 ... 74 E7
Morpeth St BETH E2 ... 93 F2
Morpeth Ter WEST SW1P ... 16 E4
Morpeth Wk TOTM N17 * ... 42 D6
Morphou Rd MLHL NW7 ... 38 C4
Morrab Gdns GDMY/SEVK IG3 ... 79 F2
Morrel Cl BAR EN5 ... 27 G2
Morrells Yd LBTH SE11 ... 18 B7
Morris Av MNPK E12 ... 77 K4
Morris Bishop Ter HGT N6 * ... 54 A5
Morris Cl CROY/NA CR0 ... 166 B5
Morris Ct CHING E4 ... 43 K2
Morris Gdns DART DA1 ... 139 K4

WAND/EARL SW18 ... 127 K6
Morrish Rd BRXS/STRHM SW2 ... 129 K6
Morrison Av CHING E4 ... 43 J7
  TOTM N17 ... 56 A2
Morrison Rd BARK IG11 ... 98 A1
  YEAD UB4 ... 83 F2
Morrison St BTSEA SW11 ... 129 F2
Morris Pl FSBYPK N4 ... 73 G2
Morris Rd BCTR RM8 ... 80 B1
  ISLW TW7 ... 124 A2
  POP/IOD E14 ... 93 K4
  SRTFD E15 ... 76 C3
Morris St WCHPL E1 ... 92 D5
Morriston Cl OXHEY WD19 ... 33 G4
Morse Cl PLSTW E13 ... 94 E2
Morshead Rd MV/WKIL W9 ... 2 B8
Morson Rd PEND EN3 ... 31 G5
Morteyne Rd TOTM N17 ... 41 K7
Mortham St SRTFD E15 ... 76 C3
Mortimer Cl BUSH WD23 ... 22 B5
  CRICK NW2 ... 70 D2
  STRHM/NOR SW16 ... 148 D1
Mortimer Crs KIL/WHAMP NW6 ... 2
  WPK KT4 ... 173 F2
Mortimer Dr EN EN1 ... 29 K4
Mortimer Pl KIL/WHAMP NW6 ... 2
Mortimer Rd EHAM E6 ... 95 K2
  ERITH DA8 ... 118 A5
  IS N1 ... 7 K1
  MTCM CR4 ... 147 K7
  WEA W13 ... 85 J5
  WLSDN NW10 ... 88 A2
Mortimer Sq NTGHL W11 ... 88 B6
Mortimer St GTPST W1W ... 10 D4
Mortimer Ter KTTN NW5 * ... 72 B3
Mortlake Cl CROY/NA CR0 ... 176 E2
Mortlake Dr MTCM CR4 ... 147 J7
Mortlake High St MORT/ESHN SW14 ... 126 A2
Mortlake Rd CAN/RD E16 ... 95 F5
  IL IG1 ... 78 C3
  MORT/ESHN SW14 ... 125 J2
  RCH/KEW TW9 ... 105 H6
Morton Cl CLAP SW4 ... 129 J5
  WCHPL E1 ... 92 E5
  WLGTN SM6 ... 177 F6
Morton Crs STHGT/OAK N14 ... 40 D3
Morton Gdns WLGTN SM6 ... 176 C4
Morton Ms ECT SW5 ... 14 C6
Morton Pl STHWK SE1 ... 18 A4
Morton Rd IS N1 ... 6 F2
  MRDN SM4 ... 162 C4
  SRTFD E15 ... 76 D6
Morton Wy STHGT/OAK N14 ... 40 C2
Morvale Cl BELV DA17 ... 117 G3
Morval Rd BRXS/STRHM SW2 ... 130 B4
Morven Cl TOOT SW17 ... 147 K2
Morville St BOW E3 ... 93 J1
Morwell St RSQ WC1B ... 11 G3
Moscow Pl BAY/PAD W2 ... 8 C6
Moscow Rd BAY/PAD W2 ... 8 C6
Moselle Av WDGN N22 ... 55 G1
Moselle Cl CEND/HSY/T N8 ... 55 F2
Moselle Pl TOTM N17 * ... 42 B6
Moselle St TOTM N17 ... 42 B6
Mossborough Cl NFNCH/WDSPK N12 ... 39 F5
Mossbury Rd BTSEA SW11 ... 128 D2
Moss Cl PIN HA5 ... 47 K1
  WCHPL E1 ... 92 C4
Mossdown Cl BELV DA17 ... 117 H3
Mossford Gn BARK/HLT IG6 ... 60 B2
Mossford La BARK/HLT IG6 ... 60 C1
Mossford St BOW E3 ... 93 H3
Moss Gdns FELT TW13 ... 140 E1
  SAND/SEL CR2 ... 179 F6
Moss Hall Crs NFNCH/WDSPK N12 ... 39 F5
Moss Hall Gv NFNCH/WDSPK N12 ... 39 F5
Moss La PIN HA5 ... 47 K2
  ROM RM1 ... 63 H5
Mosslea Rd HAYES BR2 ... 168 C4
  PGE/AN SE20 ... 150 E5
Mossop St CHEL SW3 ... 15 K5
Moss Rd DAGE RM10 ... 80 C6
Mossville Gdns MRDN SM4 ... 161 J2
Moston Cl HYS/HAR UB3 ... 101 J4
Mostyn Av WBLY HA9 ... 68 B4
Mostyn Gdns WLSDN NW10 ... 88 B2
Mostyn Gv BOW E3 ... 93 H1
Mostyn Rd BRXN/ST SW9 ... 110 B7
  BUSH WD23 ... 22 C4
  EDGW HA8 ... 37 F6
  WIM/MER SW19 ... 161 J2
Mosul Wy HAYES BR2 ... 168 D5
Motcomb St KTBR SW1X ... 16 A3
Moth Cl WLGTN SM6 ... 176 E6
The Mothers Sq CLPT E5 * ... 74 D3
Moth House WOOL/PLUM SE18 * ... 114 D6
Motley Av SDTCH EC2A *
Motley St VX/NE SW8 ... 129 H1
Motspur Pk NWMAL KT3 ... 160 C5
Mottingham Gdns ELTH/MOT SE9 ... 134 C7
Mottingham La LEE/GVPK SE12 ... 134 B7
Mottingham Rd ED N9 ... 31 F6
  ELTH/MOT SE9 ... 153 J2
Mottisfont Rd ABYW SE2 ... 116 C2
Moulins Rd HOM E9 ... 74 E6
Moulton Av HSLW TW3 ... 122 D1
Moundfield Rd STNW/STAM N16 ... 56 C5
Mountacre Cl SYD SE26 ... 150 B3
Mount Adon Pk EDUL SE22 ... 131 H6
Mountague Pl POP/IOD E14 ... 94 A6
Mount Angelus Rd PUT/ROE SW15 ... 126 C6
Mount Ararat Rd RCHPK/HAM TW10 ... 125 F4
Mount Ash Rd SYD SE26 ... 150 D2
Mount Av CHING E4 ... 43 J2
  EA W5 ... 85 K4
  STHL UB1 ... 84 A5
Mountbatten Cl NRWD SE19 ... 150 A4
  WOOL/PLUM SE18 ... 115 K5
Mountbatten Ct BKHH IG9 ... 45 H1
Mountbel Rd STAN HA7 ... 49 G1
Mount Cl BMLY BR1 ... 153 J1
  CAR SM5 ... 176 A7
  EBAR EN4 ... 28 A3
Mountcombe Cl SURB KT6 ... 159 F6
Mount Cots BXLYHS DA6 * ... 137 F3
Mount Culver Av SCUP DA14 ... 155 K5
Mount Dr RYLN/HDSTN HA2 ... 48 A1
  WBLY HA9 ... 68 E1

Mount Echo Dr CHING E4 ... 31 K7
Mount Ephraim La STRHM/NOR SW16 ... 148 D2
Mount Ephraim Rd STRHM/NOR SW16 ... 148 D2
Mountfield Cl CAT SE6 ... 133 G6
Mountfield Rd EA W5 ... 85 K5
  EHAM E6 ... 96 A1
  FNCH N3 ... 52 E2
Mountfield Ter CAT SE6 ... 133 G6
Mountfort Ter IS N1 * ... 6 A1
Mount Gdns SYD SE26 ... 150 D2
Mount Gv EDGW HA8 ... 36 E2
Mountgrove Rd HBRY N5 ... 73 J2
Mount Holme THDIT KT7 ... 158 C6
Mounthurst Rd HAYES BR2 ... 167 K6
Mountington Park Cl KTN/HRWW/WS HA3 ... 49 K5
Mountjoy Cl ABYW SE2 ... 116 C1
Mount Ms HPTN TW12 ... 142 B7
Mount Mills FSBYE EC1V * ... 6 D8
Mount Nod Rd STRHM/NOR SW16 ... 149 F3
Mount Pde EBAR EN4 * ... 27 J3
Mount Pk CAR SM5 ... 176 A7
Mount Park Av HRW HA1 ... 66 D1
  SAND/SEL CR2 ... 177 H7
Mount Park Crs EA W5 ... 85 K5
Mount Park Rd EA W5 ... 85 K4
  HRW HA1 ... 66 D1
  PIN HA5 ... 46 E4
Mount Pl ACT W3 ... 86 D7
Mount Pleasant ALP/SUD HA0 ...
  EBAR EN4 ... 27 J3
  FSBYW WC1X ... 11 M1
  HRW HA1 ... 66 E2
  RSLP HA4 ... 65 G3
  WNWD SE27 ... 149 J3
Mount Pleasant Crs FSBYPK N4 * ... 55 F6
Mount Pleasant Hl CLPT E5 ... 74 D1
Mount Pleasant La CLPT E5 ... 56 D7
Mount Pleasant Pl WOOL/PLUM SE18 ... 115 J3
Mount Pleasant Rd DART DA1 ... 139 J3
  EA W5 ... 85 J3
  LEW SE13 ... 133 F5
  NWMAL KT3 ... 159 K2
  TOTM N17 ... 56 A2
  WALTH E17 ... 57 G1
  WLSDN NW10 ... 70 A6
Mount Pleasant Vls FSBYPK N4 ... 55 F6
Mount Ri FSTH SE23 ... 150 E1
Mount Rd BCTR RM8 ... 62 B7
  BXLYHS DA6 ... 137 F4
  CHSGTN KT9 ... 172 B3
  CRICK NW2 ... 69 K2
  DART DA1 ... 138 C5
  EBAR EN4 ... 27 J4
  FELT TW13 ... 141 J2
  HDN NW4 ... 51 J5
  HYS/HAR UB3 ... 101 K1
  MTCM CR4 ... 162 C1
  NRWD SE19 ... 149 K5
  NWMAL KT3 ... 160 A2
  WIM/MER SW19 ... 146 E1
Mount Rw MYFR/PKLN W1K ... 10 C7
Mountside KTN/HRWW/WS HA3 ... 35 F7
  STAN HA7 ... 35 G7
Mounts Pond Rd BKHTH/KID SE3 ... 133 G1
  LEW SE13 ... 133 G1
The Mount Sq HAMP NW3 * ... 71 G3
Mount Stewart Av KTN/HRWW/WS HA3 ... 49 K5
Mount St MYFR/PKLN W1K ... 10 A7
Mount Ter WCHPL E1 ... 92 D4
The Mount BMLY BR1 * ... 153 J7
  BXLYHS DA6 * ... 137 F4
  CLPT E5 ... 74 D1
  ESH/CLAY KT10 ... 170 A5
  EW KT17 ... 173 K5
  HAMP NW3 ... 71 G3
  NTHLT UB5 * ... 66 B4
  NWMAL KT3 ... 160 C2
  TRDG/WHET N20 ... 39 G1
  WBLY HA9 ... 68 E1
Mount Vw NWDGN UB2 * ... 102 C3
Mountview MLHL NW7 ... 37 K2
  NTHWD HA6 ... 32 E5
Mountview Cl HAMP NW3 ... 53 G7
Mount View Rd CDALE/KGS NW9 ... 51 F3
  ESH/CLAY KT10 ... 171 H6
  FSBYPK N4 ... 55 F6
Mount Vls WNWD SE27 ... 149 H2
Mount Wy CAR SM5 ... 176 A7
Mountwood E/WMO/HCT KT8 ... 157 F3
Movers La BARK IG11 ... 78 D7
Mowatt Cl ARCH N19 ... 54 D7
Mowbray Gdns NTHLT UB5 * ... 66 A5
Mowbray Rd BAR EN5 ... 27 G3
  EDGW HA8 ... 36 C5
  KIL/WHAMP NW6 ... 88 C1
  NRWD SE19 ... 150 B7
  RCHPK/HAM TW10 ... 143 J2
Mowbrays Cl CRW RM5 ... 62 E1
Mowlem St BETH E2 ... 92 D1
Mowll St BRXN/ST SW9 ... 110 B6
Moxon Cl PLSTW E13 ... 94 D1
Moxon St BAR EN5 ... 26 D2
Moye Cl BETH E2 ... 74 C1
Moyers Rd LEY E10 ... 58 A6
Moylan Rd HMSMTH W6 ... 107 H5
Moyne Pl WLSDN NW10 ... 86 C2
Moynihan Dr WCHMH N21 ... 28 E4
Moys Cl CROY/NA CR0 ... 163 J5
Moyser Rd STRHM/NOR SW16 ... 148 B4
Mozart St NKENS W10 ... 88 D2
Muchelney Rd MRDN SM4 ... 162 B5
Muggeridge Cl SAND/SEL CR2 ... 177 K4
Muggeridge Rd DAGE RM10 ... 80 D3
Muirdown Av MORT/ESHN SW14 ... 125 K3
Muir Dr WAND/EARL SW18 ... 128 C5
Muirfield ACT W3 ... 87 G5
Muirfield Cl BERM/RHTH SE16 ... 111 J4
  OXHEY WD19 ... 33 G4
Muirfield Crs POP/IOD E14 ... 112 E2
Muirfield Gn OXHEY WD19 ... 33 G3
Muirfield Rd OXHEY WD19 ... 33 F3
Muirkirk Rd CAT SE6 ... 133 G6
Muir Rd CLPT E5 ... 74 C3
Muir St CAN/RD E16 ... 95 K7
Mulberry Av STWL/WRAY TW19 ... 120 B7
Mulberry Cl CEND/HSY/T N8 ... 54 E4
  CHEL SW3 ... 108 C5
  CHING E4 ... 43 H1

EBAR EN4 ... 27 H3
GPK RM2 ... 63 K3
HDN NW4 ... 52 A2
HOR/WEW KT19 ... 172 E7
NTHLT UB5 ... 83 J1
STRHM/NOR SW16 ... 148 C3
Mulberry Crs BTFD TW8 ... 104 C6
WDR/YW UB7 ... 100 D1
Mulberry Dr PUR RM19 ... 119 J3
Mulberry La CROY/NA CR0 ... 165 C7
Mulberry Ms NWCR SE14 ... 112 C7
Mulberry Pde WDR/YW UB7 ... 100 D2
Mulberry Pl ELTH/MOT SE9 ... 134 C3
HMSMTH W6 ... 106 D4
Mulberry Rd HACK E8 ... 7 L2
Mulberry St WCHPL E1 ... 92 C5
Mulberry Wk CHEL SW3 ... 15 H9
Mulberry Wy BARK/HLT IG6 ... 60 C3
BELV DA17 ... 117 K1
SWFD E18 ... 59 F1
Mulgrave Rd BELMT SM2 ... 175 F5
CROY/NA CR0 ... 177 K2
EA W5 ... 85 K2
HRW HA1 ... 67 C1
WKENS W14 ... 107 J5
WLSDN NW10 ... 69 H3
WOOL/PLUM SE18 ... 114 E3
Mulholland Cl MTCM CR4 ... 163 G1
Mulkern Rd ARCH N19 ... 54 D7
Mullards Cl MTCM CR4 ... 162 E7
Mullet Gdns BETH E2 ... 92 C2
Mullins Pth MORT/ESHN SW14 ... 126 A2
Mullion Cl KTN/HRWW/WS HA3 ... 34 B3
Mullion Wk OXHEY WD19 ... 33 H3
Mull Wk IS N1 ... 73 J5
Mulready St STJWD NW8 ... 9 J1
Multi Wy ACT W3 ... 106 B1
Mumford Ct CITYW EC2V ... 12 F4
Mumford Rd HNHL SE24 ... 130 C4
Muncaster Rd CLAP SW4 ... 129 J4
Muncies Ms CAT SE6 ... 152 A1
Mundania Rd EDUL SE22 ... 131 J5
Munday Rd CAN/RD E16 ... 94 E5
Munden St WKENS W14 ... 107 H3
Mundesly Cl OXHEY WD19 ... 33 G3
Mundford Rd CLPT E5 ... 74 E1
Mundon Gdns IL IG1 ... 60 D7
Mund St WKENS W14 ... 107 J4
Mundy St IS N1 ... 7 J7
Mungo-Park Cl BUSH WD23 * ... 34 C1
Mungo Park Rd RAIN RM13 ... 81 J5
Munnings Gdns ISLW TW7 ... 123 J4
Munro Dr FBAR/BDGN N11 ... 40 C5
Munroe Ter WBPTN SW10 ... 108 C6
Munro Ms NKENS W10 ... 88 C4
Munro Ter WBPTN SW10 ... 108 C5
Munro Wy CLPT E5 ... 74 C3
Munslow Gdns SUT SM1 ... 175 G3
Munster Av HSLWW TW4 ... 122 D3
Munster Ct FUL/PGN SW6 ... 127 J1
Munster Gdns PLMGR N13 ... 41 J3
Munster Ms FUL/PGN SW6 ... 107 J6
Munster Rd FUL/PGN SW6 ... 107 H6
TEDD TW11 ... 143 J5
Munster Sq CAMTN NW1 ... 4 D8
Munton Rd WALW SE17 ... 18 F6
Murchison Av BXLY DA5 ... 136 E7
Murchison Rd LEY E10 ... 76 A1
Murdock Cl CAN/RD E16 ... 94 D5
Murdock St PECK SE15 ... 111 J6
Murfett Cl WIM/MER SW19 ... 146 C1
Muriel Av WATW WD18 ... 21 G4
Muriel St IS N1 ... 5 M4
Murillo Rd LEW SE13 ... 133 G3
Murphy St STHWK SE1 ... 18 A2
Murray Av BMLY BR1 ... 168 A2
HSLW TW3 ... 123 G4
Murray Cl THMD SE28 ... 96 E7
Murray Crs PIN HA5 ... 33 H7
Murray Gv IS N1 ... 7 G6
Murray House WOOL/PLUM SE18 * ... 114 D4
Murray Ms CAMTN NW1 ... 5 G1
Murray Rd EA W5 ... 104 D3
NTHWD HA6 ... 32 C7
RCHPK/HAM TW10 ... 143 H1
WIM/MER SW19 ... 146 B5
Murray Sq CAN/RD E16 ... 94 E5
Murray Ter CAMTN NW1 ... 4 F1
Murray Ter HAMP NW3 ... 71 G3
Musard Rd HMSMTH W6 ... 107 H5
Musbury St WCHPL E1 ... 92 E5
Muscatel Pl CMBW SE5 ... 111 F7
PECK SE15 ... 131 G2
Muscovy St MON EC3R ... 13 K7
Museum St NOXST/BSQ WC1A ... 11 J3
Museum St ACT W3 ... 105 H1
Musgrave Crs FUL/PGN SW6 ... 107 K6
Musgrave Rd ISLW TW7 ... 104 A7
Musgrove Rd NWCR SE14 ... 112 A7
Musjid Rd BTSEA SW11 ... 128 C1
Musquash Wy HSLWW TW4 ... 122 B1
Muston Rd CLPT E5 ... 74 D1
Muswell Av MUSWH N10 ... 54 B1
Muswell Hl MUSWH N10 ... 54 B2
Muswell Hill Broadway MUSWH N10 ... 54 B2
Muswell Hill Pl MUSWH N10 ... 54 B3
Muswell Hill Rd HGT N6 ... 54 A5
Muswell Ms MUSWH N10 ... 54 B2
Muswell Rd MUSWH N10 ... 54 B1
Mutrix Rd KIL/WHAMP NW6 ... 2 B3
Mutter Rd CLAP SW4 ... 129 J5
Mutton Pl CAMTN NW1 ... 72 A5
Muybridge Rd NWMAL KT3 ... 159 K1
Myatt Rd BRXN/ST SW9 ... 110 C7
Mycenae Rd BKHTH/KID SE3 ... 113 K5
Myddelton Gdns WCHMH N21 ... 29 J6
Myddelton Pk TRDG/WHET N20 ... 39 H2
Myddelton Pas CLKNW EC1R ... 6 B7
Myddleton Av CEND/HSY/T N8 ... 54 E3
Myddleton Av CLKNW EC1R ... 6 B7
Myddleton Cl CLKNW EC1R ... 6 B7
Myddleton Av FSBYPK N4 ... 73 H1
Myddleton Cl STAN HA7 ... 35 G1
Myddleton Rd WDGN N22 ... 40 E6
Myers La NWCR SE14 ... 112 A5
Mylis Cl SYD SE26 ... 150 D3
Mylne Cl HMSMTH W6 * ... 106 D4
Mylne St IS N1 ... 6 A6
Myra St ABYW SE2 ... 116 B4
Myrdle St WCHPL E1 ... 92 C5
Myron Pl LEW SE13 ... 133 F2
Myrna Cl WIM/MER SW19 ... 147 J6
Myrtle Aly WOOL/PLUM SE18 ... 115 F3
Myrtle Av EBED/NFELT TW14 ... 121 H3
RSLP HA4 ... 46 E6

Myrtleberry Cl HACK E8 * ... 74 B5
Myrtle Cl EBAR EN4 ... 27 K7
ERITH DA8 ... 118 B6
WDR/YW UB7 ... 100 C3
Myrtledene Rd ABYW SE2 ... 116 B4
Myrtle Gdns HNWL W7 ... 84 B1
Myrtle Gv NWMAL KT3 ... 159 K1
Myrtle Rd ACT W3 ... 86 E7
CROY/NA CR0 ... 179 J2
EHAM E6 ... 77 J7
HPTN TW12 ... 142 C5
HSLW TW3 ... 123 H1
IL IG1 ... 78 B1
PLMGR N13 ... 41 J2
SUT SM1 ... 175 G4
WALTH E17 ... 57 G5
Myrtleside Cl NTHWD HA6 ... 32 B6
Myrtle St IS N1 ... 7 J6
Myrtle Wk IS N1 ... 7 J6
Mysore Rd BTSEA SW11 ... 128 E3
Myton Rd DUL SE21 ... 149 K2

N

Nadine St CHARL SE7 ... 114 B4
Nagle Cl WALTH E17 ... 58 B1
Nag's Head La WELL DA16 ... 136 C2
Nags Head Rd PEND EN3 ... 30 E3
Nairne Gv HNHL SE24 ... 130 E4
Nairn Gn OXHEY WD19 ... 32 E2
Nairn Rd RSLP HA4 ... 65 G5
Nairn St POP/IOD E14 ... 94 A4
Nallhead Rd FELT TW13 ... 141 G4
Namba Roy Cl STRHM/NOR SW16 ... 149 F3
Namton Dr THHTH CR7 ... 164 A3
Nan Clark's La MLHL NW7 ... 37 H1
Nancy Downs OXHEY WD19 ... 21 G6
Nankin St POP/IOD E14 ... 93 J5
Nansen Rd BTSEA SW11 ... 129 F3
Nansen Village NFNCH/WDSPK N12 * ... 39 F3
Nantes Cl WAND/EARL SW18 ... 128 B3
Nant Rd CRICK NW2 ... 70 C1
Nant St BETH E2 ... 92 D2
Naoroji St FSBYW WC1X ... 6 A8
Napier Av FUL/PGN SW6 ... 127 J2
POP/IOD E14 ... 112 D4
Napier Cl DEPT SE8 ... 112 C6
EMPK RM11 ... 63 K7
WDR/YW UB7 ... 100 C2
WKENS W14 ... 107 J2
Napier Ct LEE/GVPK SE12 ... 153 F1
Napier Gv IS N1 ... 6 F6
Napier Pl WKENS W14 ... 107 J2
Napier Rd ALP/SUD HA0 ... 67 K4
ASHF TW15 ... 140 B6
BELV DA17 ... 117 G3
EHAM E6 ... 78 A7
HAYES BR2 ... 168 A2
ISLW TW7 ... 124 B3
PEND EN3 ... 31 F5
SAND/SEL CR2 ... 177 K6
SNWD SE25 ... 165 J3
SRTFD E15 ... 94 C1
TOTM N17 ... 56 A2
WAN E11 ... 76 C2
WKENS W14 ... 107 J2
WLSDN NW10 ... 87 K2
Napier Ter IS N1 ... 6 C2
Napier Wk ASHF TW15 ... 140 B6
Napoleon Rd CLPT E5 ... 74 D2
TWK TW1 * ... 124 C6
Napton Cl YEAD UB4 ... 83 J3
Narbonne Av CLAP SW4 ... 129 H4
Narboro Ct ROM RM1 ... 63 J5
Narborough Cl HGDN/ICK UB10 ... 64 A1
Narborough St FUL/PGN SW6 ... 128 A1
Narcissus Rd KIL/WHAMP NW6 ... 70 E4
Narford Rd CLPT E5 ... 74 C2
Narrow Boat Cl THMD SE28 ... 115 J1
Narrow St ACT W3 ... 86 D7
POP/IOD E14 ... 93 G6
Narrow Wy HAYES BR2 ... 168 D5
Nascot Pl WAT WD17 ... 21 F1
Nascot Rd WAT WD17 ... 21 F1
Nascot St SHB W12 ... 88 A5
WAT WD17 ... 21 F1
Naseby Cl ISLW TW7 ... 103 K7
KIL/WHAMP NW6 ... 2 F1
Naseby Rd CLAY IG5 ... 45 K7
DAGE RM10 ... 80 D2
NRWD SE19 ... 149 K5
Nash Cl BORE WD6 ... 24 B3
SUT SM1 ... 175 H2
Nash Gn BMLY BR1 ... 152 E6
Nash La HAYES BR2 ... 180 E5
Nash Rd BROCKY SE4 ... 132 B3
CHDH RM6 ... 61 K3
ED N9 ... 42 E1
Nash St CAMTN NW1 ... 4 D7
Nash Wy KTN/HRWW/WS HA3 ... 49 H5
Nasmyth St HMSMTH W6 ... 106 E2
Nassau Rd BARN SW13 ... 106 C7
Nassau St GTPST W1W ... 10 E3
Nassington Rd HAMP NW3 ... 71 J3
Natalie Cl EBED/NFELT TW14 ... 121 C6
Natalie Ms WHTN TW2 ... 142 D2
Natal Rd FBAR/BDGN N11 ... 40 E4
IL IG1 ... 78 B3
STRHM/NOR SW16 ... 148 D5
THHTH CR7 ... 164 E2
Nathaniel Cl WCHPL E1 ... 13 M3
Nathans Rd ALP/SUD HA0 ... 67 J1
Nathan Wy ABYW SE2 ... 116 A2
THMD SE28 ... 116 A2
National Ter BERM/RHTH SE16 * ... 111 J1
Naval Rw POP/IOD E14 ... 94 A6
Navarino Gv HACK E8 ... 74 C5
Navarino Rd HACK E8 ... 74 C5
Navarre Rd EHAM E6 ... 95 J1
Navarre St BETH E2 ... 7 L9
Navestock Cl WALTH E17 * ... 44 A2
Navestock Crs WFD IG8 ... 45 G7
Navestock Ho WFD IG8 * ... 45 G6
Navigator Dr NWDGN UB2 ... 103 H3
Navy St CLAP SW4 ... 129 J2
Nayim Pl HACK E8 ... 74 D5
Naylor Gv PEND EN3 ... 31 F4
Naylor Rd PECK SE15 ... 111 J6
TRDG/WHET N20 ... 39 G1
Nazareth Cl PECK SE15 ... 131 J1
Nazrul St BETH E2 ... 7 L7
Neal Av STHL UB1 ... 83 K3
Neal Cl NTHWD HA6 ... 32 E7
Nealden St BRXN/ST SW9 ... 130 A2
Neale Cl EFNCH N2 ... 53 G2

Neal St LSO/SEVD WC2H ... 11 J5
WATW WD18 ... 21 G4
Neal Ter FSTH SE23 * ... 132 A7
Near Acre CDALE/KGS NW9 ... 37 H2
Neasden Cl WLSDN NW10 ... 69 G4
Neasden La WLSDN NW10 ... 69 G3
Neasham Rd BCTR RM8 ... 79 H4
Neate St CMBW SE5 ... 19 L8
Neath Gdns MRDN SM4 ... 162 B5
Neathouse Pl PIM SW1V ... 16 E6
Neats Acre RSLP HA4 ... 46 B6
Neatscourt Rd EHAM E6 ... 95 H4
Neckinger BERM/RHTH SE16 ... 19 M3
Neckinger Est BERM/RHTH SE16 ... 19 M3
Neckinger St STHWK SE1 ... 19 M2
Nectarine Wy LEW SE13 ... 132 E1
Needham Rd NTGHL W11 ... 8 A5
Needleman St BERM/RHTH SE16 ... 112 A1
Neeld Crs HDN NW4 ... 51 K4
WBLY HA9 ... 68 C4
Neil Cl ASHF TW15 ... 140 A4
Neils Yd LSO/SEVD WC2H * ... 11 J5
Nelgarde Rd CAT SE6 ... 132 D6
Nella Rd HMSMTH W6 ... 107 G5
Nelldale Rd BERM/RHTH SE16 ... 111 J3
Nello James Gdns WNWD SE27 ... 149 K3
Nelson Cl CROY/NA CR0 ... 164 C7
EBED/NFELT TW14 * ... 121 J7
KIL/WHAMP NW6 ... 2 A1
WOT/HER KT12 ... 156 A7
Nelson Gdns BETH E2 ... 92 C2
HSLW TW3 ... 123 F5
Nelson Grove Rd WIM/MER SW19 ... 147 F7
Nelson Mandela Cl MUSWH N10 ... 53 K1
Nelson Mandela Rd BKHTH/KID SE3 ... 134 B2
Nelson Pl IS N1 ... 6 D6
Nelson Rd BELV DA17 ... 117 G4
CEND/HSY/T N8 ... 55 F4
CHING E4 ... 43 K5
DART DA1 ... 139 F5
ED N9 ... 42 D2
GNWCH SE10 ... 113 F5
HAYES BR2 ... 168 B3
HRW HA1 ... 48 D6
HTHAIR TW6 ... 100 C7
NWMAL KT3 ... 160 A4
PEND EN3 ... 31 F5
RAIN RM13 ... 99 H1
SCUP DA14 ... 155 G3
SEVS/STOTM N15 ... 56 A3
STAN HA7 ... 35 J5
WAN E11 ... 58 E3
WHTN TW2 ... 123 F5
WIM/MER SW19 ... 147 F6
Nelson Sq STHWK SE1 ... 18 C1
Nelson Rw CLAP SW4 ... 129 J3
Nelson St CAN/RD E16 ... 94 D6
EHAM E6 ... 78 A7
WCHPL E1 ... 92 D5
Nelson Ter FSBYE EC1V ... 6 D6
Nelson Wk HOR/WEW KT19 ... 172 C7
Nemoure Rd ACT W3 ... 86 E6
Nene Gdns FELT TW13 ... 141 K1
Nene Rd HTHAIR TW6 ... 100 E7
Nepaul Rd BTSEA SW11 ... 128 D1
Nepean St PUT/ROE SW15 ... 126 D5
Neptune Cl RAIN RM13 ... 99 J4
Neptune Ct BORE WD6 * ... 24 C2
Neptune Rd HRW HA1 ... 48 D5
HTHAIR TW6 * ... 101 F7
Neptune St BERM/RHTH SE16 ... 111 K2
Nesbit Cl BKHTH/KID SE3 ... 133 H2
Nesbit Rd ELTH/MOT SE9 ... 134 C3
Nesbitts Aly BAR EN5 * ... 26 D2
Nesbitt Sq NRWD SE19 * ... 150 A6
Nesham St WAP E1W ... 92 C7
Ness Rd ERITH DA8 ... 119 G5
Ness St BERM/RHTH SE16 ... 111 H2
Nesta Rd WFD IG8 ... 44 D5
Nestle's Av HYS/HAR UB3 ... 101 J3
Nestor Av WCHMH N21 ... 29 H5
Netheravon Cl CHSWK W4 ... 106 C3
HNWL W7 ... 85 F7
Netheravon Rd South CHSWK W4 ... 106 C5
Netherbury Rd EA W5 ... 104 E2
Netherby Gdns ENC/FH EN2 ... 28 E3
Netherby Rd FSTH SE23 ... 131 K6
Nether Ct FNCH N3 ... 38 E6
Nether Ct MLHL NW7 * ... 38 C5
Nethercourt Av FNCH N3 ... 38 E5
Netherfield Gdns BARK IG11 ... 78 D5
Netherfield Rd NFNCH/WDSPK N12 ... 39 F4
TOOT SW17 ... 148 A2
Netherford Rd VX/NE SW8 ... 129 H1
Netherhall Gdns HAMP NW3 ... 71 G4
Netherhall Wy HAMP NW3 ... 71 G3
Netherheys Dr SAND/SEL CR2 ... 177 J6
Netherlands Rd BAR EN5 ... 27 H5
Netherleigh Cl HGT N6 ... 54 B7
Netherpark Dr GPK RM2 ... 63 H1
Nether St FNCH N3 ... 38 E6
Netherton Gv WBPTN SW10 ... 108 B5
Netherton Rd SEVS/STOTM N15 ... 55 K5
TWK TW1 ... 124 B4
Netherwood Pl HMSMTH W6 * ... 107 G2
Netherwood Rd WKENS W14 ... 107 G2
Netherwood St KIL/WHAMP NW6 ... 70 D6
Netley Cl CHEAM SM3 ... 174 B4
CROY/NA CR0 ... 180 A6
Netley Dr WOT/HER KT12 ... 156 E6
Netley Gdns MRDN SM4 ... 162 B6
Netley Rd BTFD TW8 ... 105 F5
GNTH/NBYPK IG2 ... 60 D5
MRDN SM4 ... 162 B6
WALTH E17 ... 57 H4
Netley St CAMTN NW1 ... 4 E8
Nettlecombe Cl BELMT SM2 ... 175 F7
Nettleden Av WBLY HA9 ... 68 C5
Nettlefold Pl WNWD SE27 ... 149 H2
Nettlestead Cl BECK BR3 ... 151 H6
Nettleton Rd HTHAIR TW6 ... 100 E7
NWCR SE14 ... 112 A7
Nettlewood Rd STRHM/NOR SW16 ... 148 D6
Neuchatel Rd CAT SE6 ... 151 H1
Nevada Cl NWMAL KT3 ... 159 K3
Nevada St GNWCH SE10 ... 113 F6
Nevern Pl ECT SW5 ... 14 B6
Nevern Rd ECT SW5 ... 14 A6
Nevern Sq ECT SW5 ... 14 B6
Nevil Cl NTHWD HA6 ... 32 B5
Neville Av NWMAL KT3 ... 145 F7

Neville Cl ACT W3 ... 105 K1
BFN/LL DA15 ... 155 F3
CAMTN NW1 ... 5 H6
HSLW TW3 ... 123 H1
KIL/WHAMP NW6 ... 88 D1
PECK SE15 ... 111 H6
WAN E11 ... 76 D2
Neville Dr EFNCH N2 ... 53 G5
Neville Gdns BCTR RM8 ... 79 K2
Neville Gill Cl WAND/EARL SW18 ... 127 K5
Neville Pl WDGN N22 ... 41 F7
Neville Rd BCTR RM8 ... 79 K1
CROY/NA CR0 ... 164 E6
EA W5 ... 85 K3
FSTGT E7 ... 76 E6
KIL/WHAMP NW6 ... 88 D1
KUT/HW KT1 ... 159 H1
RCHPK/HAM TW10 ... 143 J2
Neville St SKENS SW7 ... 15 G7
Neville Ter SKENS SW7 * ... 15 G7
Neville Wk CAR SM5 ... 162 D6
Nevill Rd STNW/STAM N16 ... 74 A3
Nevill Wy LOU IG10 * ... 45 J1
Nevin Dr CHING E4 ... 31 K7
Nevinson Cl WAND/EARL SW18 ... 128 C5
Nevis Rd TOOT SW17 ... 148 A1
New Acres Rd THMD SE28 ... 96 E7
Newall Rd HTHAIR TW6 ... 101 F7
Newark Ct WOT/HER KT12 ... 156 B7
Newark Crs WLSDN NW10 ... 87 F2
Newark Gn BORE WD6 ... 25 F2
Newark Knok EHAM E6 ... 96 A5
Newark Rd SAND/SEL CR2 ... 177 K5
Newark St WCHPL E1 ... 92 D4
Newark Wy HDN NW4 ... 51 J2
New Ash Cl EFNCH N2 ... 53 H2
New Barn Cl WLGTN SM6 ... 177 F5
New Barns Av MTCM CR4 ... 163 J3
New Barn St PLSTW E13 ... 94 E3
Newbery Rd ERITH DA8 ... 118 C7
Newbiggin Pth OXHEY WD19 ... 33 G3
Newbold Cots WCHPL E1 * ... 92 E5
Newbolt Av CHEAM SM3 ... 174 A4
Newbolt Rd STAN HA7 ... 35 F5
New Bond St MYFR/PICC W1J * ... 10 D6
Newborough Gn NWMAL KT3 ... 160 A3
New Brent St HDN NW4 ... 52 A4
New Bridge St EMB EC4Y ... 12 C5
New Broad St LVPST EC2M ... 13 H3
New Broadway EA W5 ... 85 K6
Newburgh Rd ACT W3 ... 86 E7
Newburgh St SOHO/CST W1F ... 10 E5
New Burlington Ms CONDST W1S ... 10 E6
New Burlington Pl CONDST W1S ... 10 E6
New Burlington St CONDST W1S ... 10 E6
Newbury Cl NTHLT UB5 ... 65 K5
Newbury Gdns HOR/WEW KT19 ... 173 H3
Newbury Ms KTTN NW5 ... 72 A5
Newbury Rd CHING E4 ... 44 A5
CNTH/NBYPK IG2 ... 60 D5
HAYES BR2 ... 167 K2
HTHAIR TW6 ... 100 C7
Newbury Wy NTHLT UB5 ... 65 J5
New Butt La DEPT SE8 * ... 112 D6
Newby Cl EN EN1 ... 30 A1
Newby Pl POP/IOD E14 ... 94 A6
Newby St VX/NE SW8 ... 129 G2
Newcastle Cl FLST/FETLN EC4A ... 12 C4
Newcastle Rw CLKNW EC1R * ... 12 B1
New Cavendish St CAVSQ/HST W1G ... 10 B3
GTPST W1W ... 10 E2
New Change STP EC4M ... 12 E5
New Charles St FSBYE EC1V * ... 6 D7
New Church Rd CMBW SE5 ... 110 D6
New City Rd PLSTW E13 ... 95 G2
New Clock Tower Pl HOLWY N7 * ... 72 E5
New Cl FELT TW13 ... 141 J4
WIM/MER SW19 ... 162 B2
New College Ms IS N1 * ... 6 B1
New College Pde HAMP NW3 * ... 71 G5
Newcombe Gdns HSLWW TW4 ... 122 E3
Newcombe Pk ALP/SUD HA0 ... 68 B7
MLHL NW7 ... 37 G4
Newcome Gdns STRHM/NOR SW16 ... 148 E3
Newcomen Rd BTSEA SW11 ... 128 C2
WAN E11 ... 76 D2
Newcomen St STHWK SE1 ... 19 G1
New Compton St LSO/SEVD WC2H * ... 11 H5
New Ct EMB EC4Y * ... 12 A6
NTHLT UB5 ... 66 B4
Newcourt St STJWD NW8 ... 3 J4
New Crane Pl WAP E1W * ... 92 E7
New Crescent Yd WLSDN NW10 * ... 87 H1
New Cross Rd NWCR SE14 ... 111 K6
Newdales Cl ED N9 ... 42 C1
Newdene Av NTHLT UB5 ... 83 H1
Newdigate STRHM/NOR SW16 ... 149 G3
Newell St POP/IOD E14 ... 93 H6
New End HAMP NW3 ... 71 G3
New End Sq HAMP NW3 ... 71 H3
Newent Cl CAR SM5 ... 162 E7
PECK SE15 ... 111 F6
New Era Est IS N1 * ... 7 J4
New Farm Av HAYES BR2 ... 167 K3
New Farm La NTHWD HA6 ... 32 C7
New Ferry Ap WOOL/PLUM SE18 ... 115 F2
New Fetter La FLST/FETLN EC4A ... 12 B4
Newfield Cl HPTN TW12 ... 142 A7
Newfield Ri CRICK NW2 ... 69 J2
Newgate CROY/NA CR0 ... 164 D7
New Garden Dr WDR/YW UB7 * ... 100 B1
Newgate Cl FELT TW13 ... 141 J1
Newgate St CHING E4 ... 44 D2
STBT EC1A ... 12 D4
New Globe Wk STHWK SE1 ... 12 E8
New Goulston St WCHPL E1 ... 13 L4
New Green Pl BRXS/STRHM SE27 ... 130 B6
NRWD SE19 ... 150 A5
Newham's Rw STHWK SE1 * ... 19 L2
Newham Wy CAN/RD E16 ... 94 C4
EHAM E6 ... 95 J4

Newhaven Cl HYS/HAR UB3 ... 101 J3
Newhaven Crs ASHF TW15 ... 140 B4
Newhaven Gdns ELTH/MOT SE9 ... 134 C3
Newhaven La CAN/RD E16 ... 94 D4
Newhaven Rd SNWD SE25 ... 164 E4
New Heston Rd HEST TW5 ... 102 E6
Newhouse Av CHDH RM6 ... 61 K2
Newhouse Cl NWMAL KT3 ... 160 B6
Newhouse Wk MRDN SM4 ... 162 B6
Newick Cl BXLY DA5 ... 137 J5
Newick Rd CLPT E5 ... 74 D2
Newing Gn BMLY BR1 ... 153 H6
Newington Barrow Wy HOLWY N7 ... 73 F2
Newington Butts WALW SE17 ... 18 D6
Newington Cswy STHWK SE1 ... 18 E3
Newington Gn IS N1 ... 73 K4
Newington Green Rd IS N1 ... 73 K4
New Inn Broadway SDTCH EC2A * ... 7 K9
New Inn Sq SDTCH EC2A * ... 7 K9
New Inn St SDTCH EC2A ... 7 K9
New Inn Yd SDTCH EC2A ... 7 K9
New Kelvin Av TEDD TW11 ... 142 E5
New Kent Rd WALW SE17 ... 18 F5
New King's Rd FUL/PGN SW6 ... 107 K7
New King St DEPT SE8 ... 112 D5
Newland Cl PIN HA5 ... 33 J5
Newland Gdns WEA W13 ... 104 B1
Newland Rd CEND/HSY/T N8 ... 54 E2
Newlands Av THDIT KT7 ... 157 K7
Newlands Cl ALP/SUD HA0 ... 67 J5
EDGW HA8 ... 36 A2
NWDGN UB2 ... 102 D4
Newlands Pk SYD SE26 ... 150 E5
Newlands Pl BAR EN5 ... 26 B4
Newlands Quay WAP E1W ... 92 E6
Newlands Rd STRHM/NOR SW16 ... 163 K1
WFD IG8 ... 44 D1
The Newlands WLGTN SM6 ... 176 C6
Newland St CAN/RD E16 ... 95 H7
Newlands Wy CHSGTN KT9 ... 171 J4
Newlands Woods CROY/NA CR0 ... 179 H7
Newling Cl EHAM E6 ... 95 K5
Newling Est BETH E2 * ... 7 M7
New London St MON EC3R * ... 13 K6
New Lydenburg St CHARL SE7 ... 114 B2
Newlyn Gdns RYLN/HDSTN HA2 ... 47 K6
Newlyn Rd BAR EN5 ... 26 D3
TOTM N17 ... 42 B7
WELL DA16 ... 136 A1
Newman Ms WDGN N22 ... 41 F6
Newman Rd BMLY BR1 ... 152 E7
CROY/NA CR0 ... 164 A6
HYS/HAR UB3 ... 83 F6
PLSTW E13 ... 95 F2
WALTH E17 ... 57 F4
Newmans La SURB KT6 ... 158 E5
Newman's Rw LINN WC2A * ... 11 M3
Newman's Wy EBAR EN4 ... 27 G1
Newmarket Av NTHLT UB5 ... 66 A4
New Mill Rd STMC/STPC BR5 ... 155 J7
Newminster Ct ENC/FH EN2 * ... 29 H1
Newminster Rd MRDN SM4 ... 162 B5
New Mount St SRTFD E15 ... 76 B6
Newnham Av RSLP HA4 ... 47 G7
Newnham Cl NTHLT UB5 ... 66 C5
THHTH CR7 ... 164 D1
Newnham Gdns NTHLT UB5 ... 66 C5
Newnham Gn WDGN N22 * ... 41 G7
Newnham Ms WDGN N22 * ... 41 G7
Newnhams Cl BMLY BR1 ... 168 E2
Newnham Ter STHWK SE1 ... 18 A3
Newnham Wy KTN/HRWW/WS HA3 ... 50 A4
New North Pl SDTCH EC2A * ... 7 J9
New North Rd IS N1 ... 6 F3
BMSBY WC1N ... 11 L2
Newnton Cl FSBYPK N4 ... 55 K6
New Oak Rd EFNCH N2 ... 53 G1
New Oxford St NOXST/BSQ WC1A ... 11 H4
New Park Cl NTHLT UB5 ... 65 J5
New Park Est UED N18 ... 42 E4
New Park Rd ASHF TW15 ... 140 A4
BRXS/STRHM SW2 ... 129 K6
New Place Sq BERM/RHTH SE16 ... 111 J2
New Plaistow Rd SRTFD E15 ... 76 C7
New Pond Pde RSLP HA4 * ... 64 E2
Newport Av POP/IOD E14 ... 94 B6
Newport Ct LSO/SEVD WC2H * ... 11 H6
Newport Md OXHEY WD19 * ... 33 H3
Newport Pl SOHO/SHAV W1D * ... 11 H6
Newport Rd HTHAIR TW6 ... 100 D7
ACT W3 ... 105 K1
BARN SW13 ... 106 D7
HTHAIR TW6 ... 100 D7
LEY E10 ... 76 B1
WALTH E17 ... 57 G3
YEAD UB4 ... 82 B4
Newport St LBTH SE11 ... 17 L6
Newquay Crs RYLN/HDSTN HA2 ... 65 J1
Newquay Gdns OXHEY WD19 ... 33 F1
Newquay Rd CAT SE6 ... 151 K1
New Quebec St MBLAR W1H ... 9 M5
New River Av CEND/HSY/T N8 ... 55 F2
New River Crs PLMGR N13 ... 41 H3
New River Wy FSBYPK N4 ... 55 K6
New Rd ABYW SE2 ... 116 E3
BORE WD6 ... 23 K5
BTFD TW8 ... 104 E5
CEND/HSY/T N8 ... 54 D4
CHING E4 ... 43 K3
DAGE RM10 ... 98 C1
E/WMO/HCT KT8 ... 157 F2
EBED/NFELT TW14 ... 121 G5
ED N9 ... 42 D1
ESH/CLAY KT10 ... 170 C4
FELT TW13 ... 141 J4
GDMY/SEVK IG3 ... 78 E1
HRW HA1 ... 67 F3
HSLW TW3 ... 123 G3
HYS/HAR UB3 ... 101 F6
KUTN/CMB KT2 ... 144 C6
MLHL NW7 ... 38 C5
MNPK E12 ... 77 J3
MTCM CR4 ... 163 F7
RAIN RM13 ... 99 J3
RCHPK/HAM TW10 ... 143 J3
TOTM N17 ... 42 B7
UX/CGN UB8 ... 82 A1
WAT WD17 ... 21 G3
WCHPL E1 ... 92 C4

WDGN N22 ... 41 J7
WELL DA16 ... 136 C1
New Road Hl HAYES BR2 ... 181 J7
New Rw CHCR WC2N ... 11 J6
Newry Rd TWK TW1 ... 124 C3
Newsholme Dr WCHMH N21 ... 29 H4
New Spring Gardens Wk
  STHWK SE1 * ... 17 K8
New Sq EBED/NFELT TW14 ... 121 F7
  LINN WC2A ... 11 M4
Newstead Cl
  NFNCH/WDSPK N12 ... 39 J5
Newstead Ct NTHLT UB5 * ... 83 J2
Newstead Rd LEE/GVPK SE12 ... 133 J2
Newstead Wk CAR SM5 ... 162 B6
Newstead Wy
  WIM/MER SW19 ... 146 B3
New St LVPST EC2M ... 13 K3
  WAT WD17 ... 21 G3
New Street Hl BMLY BR1 ... 153 F4
New Street Sq
  FLST/FETLN EC4A ... 12 B4
Newton Av ACT W3 ... 105 K1
  MUSWH N10 ... 40 A7
Newton Cl RYLN/HDSTN HA2 ... 66 A1
  WALTH E17 ... 57 G5
Newton Crs BORE WD6 ... 24 E3
Newton Gv CHSWK W4 ... 106 B2
Newton Park Pl CHST BR7 ... 153 K6
Newton Pl POP/IOD E14 ... 112 D3
Newton Rd ALP/SUD HA0 ... 68 B6
  BAY/PAD W2 ... 8 B5
  CRICK NW2 ... 70 A3
  HTHAIR TW6 ... 100 B7
  ISLW TW7 ... 124 A1
  KTN/HRWW/WS HA3 ... 34 E7
  SEVS/STOTM N15 ... 56 B4
  SRTFD E15 ... 76 B4
  WELL DA16 ... 136 B2
  WIM/MER SW19 ... 146 C6
Newtons Cl RAIN RM13 ... 81 G6
Newton's Yd
  WAND/EARL SW18 ... 127 K4
Newton Ter HAYES BR2 ... 168 C5
  WDGN N22 ... 41 J7
Newton Wk EDGW HA8 ... 36 E7
Newton Wy UED N18 ... 41 K4
New Tower Blds WAP E1W * ... 92 D7
Newtown St BTSEA SW11 ... 109 G7
New Trinity Rd EFNCH N2 ... 53 H2
New Union Cl POP/IOD E14 ... 113 F2
New Union St BARB EC2Y ... 13 C3
New Vis TOTM N17 * ... 42 C7
New Wanstead WAN E11 ... 58 E5
New Way Rd CDALE/KGS NW9 ... 51 G3
New Wharf Rd IS N1 ... 5 K5
New Zealand Wy RAIN RM13 ... 99 H2
Niagara Av EA W5 ... 104 D3
Niagara Cl IS N1 ... 6 F5
Nibthwaite Rd HRW HA1 ... 48 E3
Nicholas Cl GFD/PVL UB6 ... 84 B1
Nicholas Gdns EA W5 ... 85 K1
Nicholas La MANHO EC4N ... 13 H6
Nicholas Rd BCTR RM8 ... 80 B1
  BORE WD6 ... 24 B5
  CROY/NA CR0 ... 176 E3
  WCHPL E1 ... 92 E3
Nicholas Wy NTHWD HA6 ... 32 A4
Nicholay Rd ARCH N19 ... 54 D7
Nichol Cl STHGT/OAK N14 ... 28 D7
Nicholes Rd HSLW TW3 ... 123 F3
Nichol La BMLY BR1 ... 152 E1
Nichollsfield Wk HOLWY N7 ... 72 E4
Nicholl St BETH E2 ... 74 C7
Nichols Cl FSBYPK N4 * ... 55 G7
Nichols Gn EA W5 ... 86 A4
Nicholson Dr BUSH WD23 ... 22 C7
Nicholson House CHARL SE7 * ... 114 D6
Nicholson Rd CROY/NA CR0 ... 165 G7
Nicholson St STHWK SE1 * ... 12 C9
Nickelby Cl THMD SE28 ... 97 J5
Nickols Wk WAND/EARL SW18 ... 128 A3
Nicola Cl KTN/HRWW/WS HA3 ... 48 D1
  SAND/SEL CR2 ... 177 J5
Nicol Cl TWK TW1 ... 124 C5
Nicoll Pl HDN NW4 ... 51 K5
Nicoll Rd WLSDN NW10 ... 69 G7
Nicoll Wy BORE WD6 ... 25 F5
Nicosia Rd WAND/EARL SW18 ... 128 D6
Niederwald Rd SYD SE26 ... 151 G3
Nield Rd HYS/HAR UB3 ... 101 J1
Nigel Cl NTHLT UB5 ... 65 J7
Nigel Fisher Wy CHSGTN KT9 ... 171 J6
Nigel Ms IL IG1 ... 78 B3
Nigel Playfair Av HMSMTH W6 ... 106 E3
Nigel Rd FSTGT E7 ... 77 G4
  PECK SE15 ... 131 H2
Nigeria Rd CHARL SE7 ... 114 B6
Nightingale Av CHING E4 ... 44 C4
Nightingale Cl CAR SM5 ... 176 A1
  CHING E4 ... 44 C3
  CHSWK W4 ... 105 K5
  PIN HA5 ... 47 G4
Nightingale Ct SUT SM1 ... 175 G4
Nightingale Dr
  HOR/WEW KT19 ... 172 D5
Nightingale Gv LEW SE13 ... 133 G4
Nightingale La BAL SW12 ... 129 F5
  BMLY BR1 ... 168 B1
  CEND/HSY/T N8 ... 54 E3
  RCHPK/HAM TW10 ... 125 F6
  WAN E11 ... 59 F4
Nightingale Ms KUT/HW KT1 * ... 158 E2
  LBTH SE11 ... 18 B5
Nightingale Pl WBPTN SW10 ... 14 F9
  WOOL/PLUM SE18 ... 115 G5
Nightingale Rd BUSH WD23 ... 22 B4
  CAR SM5 ... 175 K2
  CLPT E5 ... 74 D2
  E/WMO/HCT KT8 ... 157 G4
  ED N9 ... 30 E6
  HNWL W7 ... 85 F7
  HPTN TW12 ... 142 A5
  IS N1 ... 73 J5
  STMC/STPC BR5 ... 169 H5
  WDGN N22 ... 41 G6
  WLSDN NW10 ... 87 H1
  WOT/HER KT12 * ... 156 A7
Nightingale Sq BAL SW12 ... 129 F6
The Nightingales
  STWL/WRAY TW19 ... 120 C7
Nightingale V
  WOOL/PLUM SE18 ... 115 F5
Nightingale Wk BAL SW12 ... 129 H5
Nightingale Wy EHAM E6 ... 95 J4
Nightingale Av HRW HA1 ... 49 F6
Nile Cl STNW/STAM N16 ... 74 B2
Nile Rd PLSTW E13 ... 95 G1
Nile St IS N1 ... 7 G7

Nile Ter PECK SE15 ... 19 M8
Nimmo Dr BUSH WD23 ... 22 D6
Nimrod Cl NTHLT UB5 ... 83 H2
Nimrod Pas IS N1 ... 74 A5
Nimrod Rd STRHM/NOR SW16 ... 148 B5
Nina Mackay Cl SRTFD E15 * ... 76 C7
Nine Acres Cl HYS/HAR UB3 ... 101 F2
  MNPK E12 ... 77 J3
Nine Elms Cl
  EBED/NFELT TW14 ... 121 J7
Nine Elms La VX/NE SW8 ... 109 H6
Nineteenth Rd MTCM CR4 ... 163 K3
Ninth Av HYS/HAR UB3 ... 82 E6
Nipper Aly KUT/HW KT1 ... 159 F1
Nisbett Wk SCUP DA14 ... 155 G3
Nithdale Rd
  WOOL/PLUM SE18 ... 115 G6
Nithsdale Gv HCDN/ICK UB10 ... 64 A2
Niton Cl BAR EN5 ... 26 B5
Niton Rd RCH/KEW TW9 ... 125 H2
Niton St FUL/PGN SW6 ... 107 G6
No1 St WOOL/PLUM SE18 ... 115 G2
No2 St WOOL/PLUM SE18 ... 115 G2
Nobel Dr HYS/HAR UB3 ... 101 H6
Nobel Rd UED N18 ... 42 E3
Noble Cnr HEST TW5 * ... 103 F7
Noble St CITYW EC2V ... 12 E4
  ACT W3 ... 86 C5
  EHAM E6 ... 95 J3
  IS N1 ... 6 C5
Noel Sq SOHO/CST W1F * ... 10 F1
Nolan Wy CLPT E5 ... 74 C3
Nolton Pl EDGW HA8 ... 36 B7
Nonsuch Pl CHEAM SM3 * ... 174 B6
Norbiton Av KUT/HW KT1 ... 159 H1
  KUTN/CMB KT2 ... 144 C7
Norbiton Common Rd
  KUT/HW KT1 ... 159 J2
Norbreck Pde EA W5 ... 86 A2
Norbroke St SHB W12 ... 87 H6
Norburn St NKENS W10 ... 88 C4
Norbury Av HSLW TW3 ... 123 J4
  STRHM/NOR SW16 ... 149 F1
  THHTH CR7 ... 164 B1
Norbury Cl STRHM/NOR SW16 ... 149 G1
Norbury Court Rd
  STRHM/NOR SW16 ... 163 K1
Norbury Crs
  STRHM/NOR SW16 ... 164 B1
Norbury Cross
  STRHM/NOR SW16 ... 163 K2
Norbury Gdns CHDH RM6 ... 61 K4
Norbury Hill STRHM/NOR SW16 ... 149 G6
Norbury Ri STRHM/NOR SW16 ... 163 K2
Norbury Rd CHING E4 ... 43 J5
  THHTH CR7 ... 164 D1
Norbury Vls KUT/HW KT1 * ... 159 H1
Norcombe Gdns
  KTN/HRWW/WS HA3 ... 49 J5
Norcott Cl YEAD UB4 ... 83 C3
Norcott Rd STNW/STAM N16 ... 74 C1
Norcroft Gdns EDUL SE22 ... 131 H6
Norcutt Rd WHTN TW2 ... 123 K7
Nordenfeldt Rd ERITH DA8 ... 118 A4
Norfolk Av PLMGR N13 ... 41 H5
  SEVS/STOTM N15 ... 56 B5
Norfolk Cl DART DA1 ... 139 K5
  EBAR EN4 ... 28 A3
  EFNCH N2 ... 53 J2
  PLMGR N13 ... 41 H5
  TWK TW1 * ... 124 C5
Norfolk Ct BAR EN5 * ... 26 C3
Norfolk Crs BAY/PAD W2 ... 9 J4
  BFN/LL DA15 ... 135 K6
  BXLYHN DA7 ... 117 G7
Norfolk House Rd
  STRHM/NOR SW16 ... 148 D2
Norfolk Ms NKENS W10 ... 88 C4
Norfolk Pl BAY/PAD W2 ... 9 H4
  WELL DA16 ... 136 B1
Norfolk Rd BAR EN5 ... 26 E2
  BARK IG11 ... 78 E6
  DAGE RM10 ... 80 D4
  EHAM E6 ... 77 K7
  ESH/CLAY KT10 ... 170 E4
  FELT TW13 ... 122 B7
  GDMY/SEVK IG3 ... 60 E7
  HRW HA1 ... 48 B4
  PEND EN3 ... 30 D2
  ROMW/RG RM7 ... 62 E5
  STJWD NW8 ... 3 H4
  THHTH CR7 ... 164 D1
  WALTH E17 ... 43 F7
  WIM/MER SW19 ... 147 K6
  WLSDN NW10 ... 69 G6
Norfolk Rw STHWK SE1 ... 17 L5
Norfolk Sq BAY/PAD W2 ... 9 H5
Norfolk Square Ms
  BAY/PAD W2 ... 9 H5
Norfolk St FSTGT E7 ... 76 E4
Norgrove St BAL SW12 ... 129 F7
Norhyrst Av SNWD SE25 ... 165 G2
Norland Pl NTGHL W11 ... 88 C7
Norland Rd NTGHL W11 ... 88 B7
Norlands Crs CHST BR7 ... 154 B7
Norlands Ga CHST BR7 * ... 154 B7
Norland Sq NTGHL W11 ... 88 C7
Norley V PUT/ROE SW15 ... 126 D7
Norlington Rd LEY E10 ... 58 A7
Norman Av FELT TW13 ... 141 J1
  STHL UB1 ... 83 J6
  TWK TW1 ... 124 C6
  WDGN N22 ... 41 J7
Normanby Cl PUT/ROE SW15 ... 127 J4
Normanby Rd WLSDN NW10 ... 69 H4
Norman Cl ROMW/RG RM7 ... 62 E2
Norman Crs HEST TW5 ... 102 C6
  PIN HA5 ... 33 G7
Normand Gdns WKENS W14 * ... 107 H5
Normand Ms WKENS W14 ... 107 H5
Normand Rd WKENS W14 ... 107 J5
Normandy Av BAR EN5 ... 26 D4
Normandy Cl SYD SE26 ... 151 G2
Normandy Dr HYS/HAR UB3 ... 82 A5
Normandy Rd BRXN/ST SW9 ... 110 B7
Normandy Ter CAN/RD E16 ... 95 F5
Normandy Wy ERITH DA8 ... 118 D7
Normanhurst Av
  BXLYHN DA7 ... 136 E1
  WELL DA16 ... 135 K3
Normanhurst Dr TWK TW1 ... 124 C4
Normanhurst Rd
  BRXS/STRHM SW2 ... 149 F1
Norman Rd ASHF TW15 ... 140 B5
  BELV DA17 ... 117 J3
  DART DA1 ... 139 H7
  EHAM E6 ... 95 K3
  EMPK RM11 ... 63 H4
  GNWCH SE10 ... 112 E6
  IL IG1 ... 78 B4

SEVS/STOTM N15 ... 56 B4
SUT SM1 ... 174 E4
THHTH CR7 ... 164 C4
WAN E11 ... 76 C1
WIM/MER SW19 ... 147 G6
Normans Cl WDGN N22 * ... 41 J7
  WLSDN NW10 ... 69 F5
Normansfield Av KUT/HW KT1 ... 143 J1
Normansfield Cl BUSH WD23 ... 22 B6
Normanshire Dr CHING E4 ... 43 J3
Normans Md WLSDN NW10 ... 69 F5
Norman Ter
  KIL/WHAMP NW6 * ... 70 D4
Normanton Av
  WAND/EARL SW18 ... 146 E1
Normanton Pk CHING E4 ... 44 C2
Normanton Rd SAND/SEL CR2 ... 178 A5
Normanton St STRHM/NOR SW16 ... 149 F1
Norman Wy ACT W3 ... 86 D4
  STHGT/OAK N14 ... 40 C1
Normington Cl
  STRHM/NOR SW16 ... 149 G4
Norrice Lea EFNCH N2 ... 53 H4
Norris Wy DART DA1 ... 138 C2
Norris Cl EBAR EN4 ... 27 K4
Norroy Rd PUT/ROE SW15 ... 127 G3
Norrys Cl EBAR EN4 ... 27 K4
Norrys Rd EBAR EN4 ... 27 K3
Norseman Cl GDMY/SEVK IG3 ... 61 H7
Norseman Wy GFD/PVL UB6 ... 66 B7
Norstead Pl PUT/ROE SW15 ... 145 J1
North Access Rd WALTH E17 ... 57 J1
North Acre CDALE/KGS NW9 ... 37 G7
Northall Rd BXLYHN DA7 ... 137 K1
Northampton Gv IS N1 ... 73 K4
Northampton Pk IS N1 ... 73 J5
Northampton Rd
  CLKNW EC1R ... 6 B9
  CROY/NA CR0 ... 178 C1
  PEND EN3 ... 31 G3
Northampton Rw
  CLKNW EC1R * ... 6 B9
Northampton Sq FSBYE EC1V ... 6 E1
Northanger Rd
  STRHM/NOR SW16 ... 148 E5
North Ap NTHWD HA6 ... 32 A1
North Audley St
  MYFR/PKLN W1K ... 10 A3
North Av CAR SM5 ... 176 A6
  HYS/HAR UB3 ... 82 E6
  RCH/KEW TW9 ... 105 H7
  RYLN/HDSTN HA2 ... 48 B5
  STHL UB1 ... 83 K6
  UED N18 ... 42 C3
  WEA W13 ... 85 H5
North Bank STJWD NW8 ... 3 H9
Northbank Rd WALTH E17 ... 58 A1
North Birkbeck Rd WAN E11 ... 76 B2
Northborough Rd
  STRHM/NOR SW16 ... 163 K1
North Boundary Rd
  MNPK E12 ... 77 H1
Northbourne HAYES BR2 ... 167 K6
Northbourne Rd CLAP SW4 ... 129 J3
Northbrook Dr NTHWD HA6 ... 32 C7
Northbrook Rd BAR EN5 ... 26 C5
  CROY/NA CR0 ... 164 E4
  IL IG1 ... 78 A1
  LEW SE13 ... 133 G4
  WDGN N22 ... 40 E5
North Carriage Dr
  BAY/PAD W2 ... 9 K6
Northchurch Rd IS N1 ... 7 H1
  WBLY HA9 ... 68 C5
Northchurch Ter IS N1 ... 7 J2
North Circular PLMGR N13 ... 41 G4
  WALTH E17 ... 43 K7
North Circular Rd BARK IG11 ... 78 A6
  CHING E4 ... 43 G5
  CRICK NW2 ... 69 G2
  EFNCH N2 ... 53 G1
  GLDGN NW11 ... 52 C5
  IL IG1 ... 59 H5
  MNPK E12 ... 78 A4
  NFNCH/WDSPK N12 ... 39 J6
  REDBR IG4 ... 59 G2
  WLSDN NW10 ... 86 B1
Northcliffe Cl WPK KT4 ... 173 G6
Northcliffe Dr
  TRDG/WHET N20 ... 26 D7
North Cl BAR EN5 ... 26 A4
  BXLYHS DA6 ... 136 E3
  DAGE RM10 ... 80 C7
  EBED/NFELT TW14 ... 121 G5
  MRDN SM4 ... 161 H3
The North Colonnade
  POP/IOD E14 ... 93 K7
North Common Rd EA W5 ... 86 A6
Northcote Av BRYLDS KT5 ... 159 H6
  EA W5 ... 86 A6
  ISLW TW7 ... 124 B4
  STHL UB1 ... 83 J6
Northcote Rd BTSEA SW11 ... 128 D3
  CROY/NA CR0 ... 164 E5
  NWMAL KT3 ... 159 K2
  SCUP DA14 ... 154 E3
  TWK TW1 ... 124 B4
  WALTH E17 ... 57 G3
  WLSDN NW10 ... 69 G6
Northcott Av WDGN N22 ... 40 E7
North Countess Rd
  WALTH E17 ... 57 H1
Northcourt FITZ W1T ... 10 E1
North Crs CAN/RD E16 ... 94 B3
  FNCH N3 ... 52 D1
  GWRST WC1E ... 11 G2
Northcroft Rd
  HOR/WEW KT19 ... 173 G6
  WEA W13 ... 104 C1
North Cross Rd BARK/HLT IG6 ... 60 C3
  EDUL SE22 ... 131 G4
North Dene HSLW TW3 ... 103 G7
  MLHL NW7 ... 37 F2
Northdene Gdns
  SEVS/STOTM N15 ... 56 A5
Northdown Gdns
  GNTH/NBYPK IG2 ... 60 D4
Northdown Rd EMPK RM11 ... 63 K6
  WELL DA16 ... 135 K3
Northdown St IS N1 ... 5 L6
North Dr BECK BR3 ... 166 E3
  HSLW TW3 ... 123 H1
  RSLP HA4 ... 46 B6
  STRHM/NOR SW16 ... 148 C3
North End CROY/NA CR0 ... 177 J2
  HAMP NW3 ... 71 G1
North End Av HAMP NW3 ... 71 G1
North End Crs WKENS W14 ... 107 J3

North End Rd FUL/PGN SW6 ... 107 K6
  GLDGN NW11 ... 52 E7
  WBLY HA9 ... 68 C2
  WKENS W14 ... 107 H3
North End Wy HAMP NW3 ... 71 G1
Northern Av ED N9 ... 42 B1
Northernhay Wk MRDN SM4 ... 161 H3
Northern Perimeter Rd
  HTHAIR TW6 ... 101 H3
Northern Perimeter Rd (West)
  HTHAIR TW6 ... 100 B7
Northern Relief Rd BARK IG11 ... 78 C6
North Eyot Gdns
  HMSMTH W6 * ... 106 C4
Northey St POP/IOD E14 ... 93 G6
Northfield Av PIN HA5 ... 47 H3
  WEA W13 ... 104 C1
Northfield Cl BMLY BR1 ... 153 J7
  HYS/HAR UB3 ... 101 J2
Northfield Crs CHEAM SM3 ... 174 C3
Northfield Pde
  HYS/HAR UB3 * ... 101 J2
Northfield Pk HYS/HAR UB3 ... 101 J2
Northfield Rd DAGW RM9 ... 80 B3
  EBAR EN4 ... 27 J2
  ED N9 ... 30 D4
  EHAM E6 ... 77 K5
  HEST TW5 ... 102 C6
  PEND EN3 ... 30 D5
  STNW/STAM N16 ... 56 A6
  WEA W13 ... 104 C1
Northfields WAND/EARL SW18 ... 127 K3
Northfields Rd ACT W3 ... 86 E4
North Gdns WIM/MER SW19 ... 147 H6
Northgate Dr
  CDALE/KGS NW9 ... 51 G5
North Gv HGT N6 ... 54 A6
  SEVS/STOTM N15 ... 55 K4
North Hl HGT N6 ... 53 K5
North Hill Av HGT N6 ... 53 K5
North Hyde Gdns
  HYS/HAR UB3 ... 101 K2
North Hyde La NWDGN UB2 ... 102 D4
North Hyde Rd HYS/HAR UB3 ... 101 H2
North Hyde Whf
  NWDGN UB2 * ... 102 B3
Northiam NFNCH/WDSPK N12 ... 38 E3
Northiam St HACK E8 ... 74 D7
North La TEDD TW11 ... 143 F5
North Lodge Cl
  PUT/ROE SW15 * ... 127 G4
North Ms BMSBY WC1N ... 11 M1
North Mt TRDG/WHET N20 * ... 39 G1
Northolm EDGW HA8 ... 37 F3
Northolme Gdns EDGW HA8 ... 36 C7
Northolme Rd HBRY N5 ... 73 J3
Northolt Av RSLP HA4 ... 65 F4
Northolt Gdns GFD/PVL UB6 ... 67 F4
Northolt Rd HTHAIR TW6 ... 100 B7
  RYLN/HDSTN HA2 ... 66 B3
Northover BMLY BR1 ... 152 D2
North Pde CHSGTN KT9 ... 172 B4
  EDGW HA8 * ... 50 C1
  STHL UB1 * ... 84 A5
North Pk ELTH/MOT SE9 ... 134 E5
North Pas WAND/EARL SW18 ... 127 K4
North Peckham Est
  PECK SE15 ... 111 G6
North Pl MTCM CR4 ... 147 K6
  TEDD TW11 ... 143 F5
Northpoint Cl SUT SM1 ... 175 G2
North Pole La HAYES BR2 ... 180 E5
North Pole Rd SHB W12 ... 88 A5
Northport St IS N1 ... 7 H4
North Ri BAY/PAD W2 * ... 9 K5
North Rd BELV DA17 ... 117 J2
  BMLY BR1 ... 153 F7
  BTFD TW8 ... 105 F5
  CHDH RM6 ... 62 A4
  DART DA1 ... 138 C5
  EA W5 ... 104 E2
  EBED/NFELT TW14 ... 121 G5
  ED N9 ... 30 D7
  EDGW HA8 ... 36 D7
  GDMY/SEVK IG3 ... 78 E1
  HEST TW5 ... 102 B5
  HGT N6 ... 54 A6
  HOLWY N7 ... 72 E5
  HYS/HAR UB3 ... 82 B4
  RCH/KEW TW9 ... 125 H1
  STHL UB1 ... 84 A6
  SURB KT6 ... 158 E5
  WDR/YW UB7 ... 100 C2
  WIM/MER SW19 ... 147 G5
  WWKM BR4 ... 166 E1
  WLSDN NW10 ... 87 F1
North Rw MYFR/PKLN W1K ... 9 M6
North Several
  BKHTH/KID SE3 * ... 133 G1
Northside Rd BMLY BR1 ... 152 E7
North Side Wandsworth
  Common
  WAND/EARL SW18 ... 128 A4
Northspur Rd SUT SM1 ... 174 E2
North Sq ED N9 ... 42 D1
  GLDGN NW11 ... 52 E4
Northstead Rd
  BRXS/STRHM SW2 ... 149 G3
North St BARK IG11 ... 78 B6
  BMLY BR1 ... 152 E7
  BXLYHN DA7 ... 137 H3
  CAR SM5 ... 175 K3
  CLAP SW4 ... 129 G2
  DART DA1 ... 139 G6
  HDN NW4 ... 52 A4
  ISLW TW7 ... 124 B2
  PLSTW E13 ... 95 F1
  ROM RM1 ... 63 F3
North Tenter St WCHPL E1 ... 13 M5
North Ter SKENS SW7 ... 15 G4
Northumberland Aly
  FENCHST EC3M * ... 13 K4
Northumberland Av
  CHCR WC2N ... 11 J8
  ISLW TW7 ... 104 A7
  MNPK E12 ... 59 G2
  WELL DA16 ... 135 K3
Northumberland Cl
  ERITH DA8 ... 117 K5
  STWL/WRAY TW19 ... 120 B5
Northumberland Crs
  EBED/NFELT TW14 ... 121 H5
Northumberland Gdns
  BMLY BR1 ... 169 F4
  ED N9 ... 42 B1
  MTCM CR4 ... 163 J4

Northumberland Gv
  TOTM N17 ... 42 D6
Northumberland Pk
  ERITH DA8 ... 117 K6
  TOTM N17 ... 42 C6
Northumberland Pl
  BAY/PAD W2 ... 8 C5
Northumberland Rd BAR EN5 ... 27 G5
  EHAM E6 ... 95 J5
  RYLN/HDSTN HA2 ... 47 K4
  WALTH E17 ... 57 J6
Northumberland St
  CHCR WC2N ... 11 J8
Northumberland Wy
  ERITH DA8 ... 117 K7
Northumbria St POP/IOD E14 ... 93 J5
North Verbena Gdns
  HMSMTH W6 * ... 106 D4
North Vw EA W5 ... 85 J2
  PIN HA5 ... 47 G6
  WIM/MER SW19 ... 146 A5
Northview Crs WLSDN NW10 ... 69 H3
Northview Dr WFD IG8 ... 59 H1
Northview Pde HOLWY N7 * ... 72 E2
North View Rd
  CEND/HSY/T N8 ... 54 D2
North Vls CAMTN NW1 ... 72 D5
North Wk CROY/NA CR0 ... 179 K4
North Wy CDALE/KGS NW9 ... 50 D2
  ED N9 ... 42 E1
  FBAR/BDGN N11 ... 40 C5
  PIN HA5 ... 47 G3
Northway GLDGN NW11 ... 53 F4
  MRDN SM4 ... 161 H6
  WLGTN SM6 ... 176 C3
Northway Crs MLHL NW7 ... 37 F3
Northway Rd CMBW SE5 ... 130 D2
  CROY/NA CR0 ... 165 G5
Northways Pde HAMP NW3 * ... 3 G1
North Weald La
  KUTN/CMB KT2 ... 143 K4
North Wharf Rd BAY/PAD W2 ... 9 G3
Northwick Av
  KTN/HRWW/WS HA3 ... 49 G5
Northwick Cir
  KTN/HRWW/WS HA3 ... 49 H6
Northwick Cl STJWD NW8 ... 3 G9
Northwick Park Rd HRW HA1 ... 49 F6
Northwick Rd ALP/SUD HA0 ... 67 K7
  OXHEY WD19 ... 33 G3
Northwick Ter STJWD NW8 ... 3 G9
Northwold Dr PIN HA5 ... 47 G2
Northwold Rd
  STNW/STAM N16 ... 74 C1
Northwood Av HCH RM12 ... 81 J3
Northwood Gdns CLAY IG5 ... 60 A2
  GFD/PVL UB6 ... 67 F4
  NFNCH/WDSPK N12 ... 39 H4
Northwood Pl ERITH DA18 ... 117 G2
Northwood Rd CAR SM5 ... 176 A5
  FSTH SE23 ... 132 C7
  HGT N6 ... 54 B6
  HTHAIR TW6 ... 100 A7
  THHTH CR7 ... 164 D1
Northwood Wy NTHWD HA6 ... 32 E6
North Woolwich Rd
  CAN/RD E16 ... 94 E7
North Worple Wy
  MORT/ESHN SW14 ... 126 A2
Norton Av BRYLDS KT5 ... 159 J6
Norton Cl CHING E4 ... 43 J4
Norton Folgate WCHPL E1 ... 13 K1
Norton Gdns
  STRHM/NOR SW16 ... 163 K1
Norton Rd ALP/SUD HA0 ... 67 J4
  DAGE RM10 ... 81 F5
  WALTH E17 ... 57 F4
Norval Gn BRXN/ST SW9 * ... 130 B1
Norval Rd ALP/SUD HA0 ... 67 G1
Norway Ga BERM/RHTH SE16 ... 112 B2
Norway Pl POP/IOD E14 ... 93 H5
Norway St GNWCH SE10 ... 112 E5
Norwich Crs CHDH RM6 ... 61 H4
Norwich Ms GDMY/SEVK IG3 ... 61 G7
Norwich Rd FSTGT E7 ... 76 E4
  GFD/PVL UB6 ... 66 C1
  NTHWD HA6 ... 46 D7
  THHTH CR7 ... 164 D1
Norwich St FLST/FETLN EC4A ... 12 A4
Norwood Wk EDGW HA8 ... 50 B1
Norwood Av ALP/SUD HA0 ... 68 B7
  ROMW/RG RM7 ... 63 F6
Norwood Cl CRICK NW2 ... 70 C2
  NWDGN UB2 ... 103 F3
  WHTN TW2 ... 142 D1
Norwood Dr
  RYLN/HDSTN HA2 ... 47 K5
Norwood Gdns NWDGN UB2 ... 102 E3
  YEAD UB4 ... 83 G3
Norwood Green Rd
  NWDGN UB2 ... 103 F3
Norwood High St WNWD SE27 ... 149 H2
Norwood Park Rd
  WNWD SE27 ... 149 J4
Norwood Rd HNHL SE24 ... 130 C7
  NWDGN UB2 ... 102 D2
  WNWD SE27 ... 149 H1
Notley St CMBW SE5 ... 110 E6
Notson Rd SNWD SE25 ... 165 J3
Notting Barn Rd NKENS W10 ... 88 B3
Nottingdale Sq NTGHL W11 ... 88 B7
Nottingham Av CAN/RD E16 ... 95 G4
Nottingham Ct
  LSQ/SEVD WC2H ... 11 J5
Nottingham Pl CAMTN NW1 ... 10 A1
Nottingham Rd ISLW TW7 ... 124 A1
  LEY E10 ... 58 A5
  SAND/SEL CR2 ... 177 J3
  TOOT SW17 ... 128 E7
Nottingham St MHST W1U ... 10 A1
Nottingham Ter CAMTN NW1 ... 10 A1
Notting Hill Ga NTGHL W11 ... 8 B8
Nova Ms CHEAM SM3 ... 161 H6
Nova Rd CROY/NA CR0 ... 164 C7
Novar Rd ELTH/MOT SE9 ... 135 H1
Novello St FUL/PGN SW6 ... 107 K7
Nowell Rd BARN SW13 ... 106 D5
Nower Hl PIN HA5 ... 47 K3
Noyna Rd TOOT SW17 ... 147 K2
Nubia Wy BMLY BR1 ... 152 C3
Nuding Cl LEW SE13 ... 132 D2
Nugent Rd ARCH N19 ... 54 E7
  SNWD SE25 ... 165 G2
Nugents Ct PIN HA5 * ... 33 J7
Nugent's Pk PIN HA5 ... 33 J7
Nugent Ter STJWD NW8 ... 2 E4
Nun Ct LOTH EC2R * ... 13 G4
Nuneaton Rd DAGW RM9 ... 79 K6
Nunhead Crs PECK SE15 ... 131 J2
Nunhead Gv PECK SE15 ... 131 J2
Nunhead La PECK SE15 ... 131 J2
Nunnington Cl ELTH/MOT SE9 ... 153 J2

Nunn's Rd ENC/FH EN2 ... 29 J1
Nupton Dr BAR EN5 ... 26 A5
Nurse EDGW HA8 ... 36 E7
Nursery Av BXLYHN DA7 ... 137 G2
  CROY/NA CR0 ... 179 F1
  FNCH N3 ... 53 F1
Nursery CI BROCKY SE4 ... 132 C1
  CHDH RM6 ... 61 K5
  CROY/NA CR0 ... 179 F1
  EBED/NFELT TW14 ... 122 A6
  OXHEY WD19 ... 21 F7
  PUT/ROE SW15 ... 127 G4
  WFD IG8 ... 45 F4
Nursery Gdns CHST BR7 ... 154 B5
  HPTN TW12 ... 141 K3
  HSLWW TW4 ... 122 K4
Nursery La BETH E2 ... 7 L4
  FSTGT E7 ... 76 E5
  NKENS W10 ... 88 A4
Nurserymans Rd
  FBAR/BDGN N11 ... 40 A1
Nursery Rd BRXN/ST SW9 ... 130 A3
  EFNCH N2 ... 39 H7
  HOM E9 ... 74 E5
  MNPK E12 ... 77 J1
  MTCM CR4 ... 162 D2
  PIN HA5 ... 47 F2
  STHGT/OAK N14 ... 28 C6
  SUN TW16 ... 140 E7
  SUT SM1 ... 175 G3
  THHTH CR7 ... 164 E3
  WIM/MER SW19 ... 146 C6
Nursery Rw BAR EN5 *
  WALW SE17 ... 19 G6
Nursery St TOTM N17 ... 42 B6
The Nursery ERITH DA8 ... 118 C6
Nursery Wk HDN NW4 ... 51 K2
  ROMW/RG RM7 ... 63 F6
Nurstead Rd ERITH DA8 ... 117 H6
Nutbourne St NKENS W10 ... 88 B2
Nutbrook St PECK SE15 ... 131 G2
Nutbrowne Rd DAGW RM9 ... 80 B7
Nutcroft Rd PECK SE15 ... 111 J6
  UED N18 ... 42 C5
Nutfield CI CAR SM5 ... 175 J2
  UED N18 ...
Nutfield Gdns GDMY/SEVK IG3 ... 79 F1
  NTHLT UB5 ... 83 C1
Nutfield Rd CRICK NW2 ... 69 J1
  EDUL SE22 ... 131 G4
  SRTFD E15 ... 76 A3
  THHTH CR7 ... 164 C3
Nutford PI MBLAR W1H ... 9 K4
Nuthatch CI
  STWL/WRAY TW19 ... 120 C7
Nuthatch Gdns THMD SE28 ... 115 J1
Nuthurst Av
  BRXS/STRHM SW2 ... 149 F1
Nutley Ter HAMP NW3 ... 71 H5
Nutmead CI BXLY DA5 ... 137 K2
Nutmeg CI CAN/RD E16 ... 94 C3
Nutmeg La POP/IOD E14 ... 94 B5
Nuttall St IS N1 ... 7 K5
Nutter La WAN E11 ... 59 G4
Nutt Gv EDGW HA8 ... 35 K1
Nutt St PECK SE15 ... 111 G6
Nutwell St TOOT SW17 ... 147 J4
Nuxley Rd BELV DA17 ... 117 G5
Nyanza St WOOL/PLUM SE18 ... 115 J5
Nylands Av RCH/KEW TW9 ... 125 H1
Nymans Gdns RYNPK SW20 ... 160 E2
Nynehead St NWCR SE14 ... 112 B6
Nyon Gv CAT SE6 ... 151 H1
Nyssa CI WFD IG8 ... 45 K5
Nyton CI ARCH N19 ... 54 E7

O

Oak Av CEND/HSY/T N8 ... 54 E3
  CROY/NA CR0 ... 179 J1
  HEST TW5 ... 102 C6
  HPTN TW12 ... 141 F4
  MUSWH N10 ... 40 B6
  TOTM N17 ... 41 K6
  WDR/YW UB7 ... 100 D2
Oakbank CROY/NA CR0 ... 180 A5
Oakbank Av WOT/HER KT12 ... 156 E6
Oakbank Gv HNHL SE24 ... 130 D3
Oakbrook CI BMLY BR1 ... 153 F3
Oakbury Rd FUL/PGN SW6 ... 128 A1
Oak CI DART DA1 ... 138 B3
  STHGT/OAK N14 ... 28 B6
Oakcombe CI NWMAL KT3 ... 145 C7
Oak Cottage CI CAT SE6 ... 133 H7
Oak Crs CAN/RD E16 ... 94 C4
Oakcroft CI PIN HA5 ... 47 F1
  LEW SE13 ... 133 G4
Oakcroft Rd CHSGTN KT9 ... 172 B3
  LEW SE13 ... 133 G4
Oakcroft Vls CHSGTN KT9 ... 172 B3
Oakdale STHGT/OAK N14 ... 28 B7
Oakdale Av
  KTN/HRWW/WS HA3 ... 50 A4
  NTHWD HA6 ... 46 E1
Oakdale CI OXHEY WD19 ... 33 G3
Oakdale Gdns CHING E4 ... 44 A4
Oakdale Rd FSBYPK N4 ... 55 J5
  FSTGT E7 ... 77 F6
  HOR/WEW KT19 ... 173 F7
  OXHEY WD19 ... 33 G2
  PECK SE15 ... 131 K2
  STRHM/NOR SW16 ... 148 E4
  SWFD E18 ... 58 B3
  WAN E11 ... 76 B1
Oakdale Wy MTCM CR4 ... 163 F6
Oakdene WEA W13 ... 85 H4
Oakdene Av CHST BR7 ... 154 A4
  ERITH DA8 ... 117 K5
  THDIT KT7 ... 158 B7
Oak Dene CI EMPK RM11 ... 63 K6
Oakdene CI PIN HA5 ... 33 K6
Oakdene Dr BRYLDS KT5 ... 159 K6
Oakdene Ms CHEAM SM3 ... 161 J7
Oakdene Pk FNCH N3 ... 38 D6
Oakden St LBTH SE11 ... 18 B5
Oaken Dr ESH/CLAY KT10 ... 171 F5
Oaken La ESH/CLAY KT10 ... 170 E4
Oakenshaw Av SURB KT6 ... 159 F6
Oakeshott Av HGT N6 ... 72 A2
Oakey La STHWK SE1 ... 18 A3
Oak Farm BORE WD6 ... 24 E4
Oakfield CHING E4 ... 43 K4
Oakfield Av
  KTN/HRWW/WS HA3 ... 49 H2
Oakfield CI NWMAL KT3 ... 160 C4
  RSLP HA4 ... 47 F7
Oakfield Ct BORE WD6 * ... 24 D3
Oakfield Gdns BECK BR3 ... 166 D4
  CAR SM5 ... 162 D7
  GFD/PVL UB6 ... 84 D3
  UED N18 ... 42 A3

Oakfield La HAYES BR2 ... 181 G3
  EHAM E6 ... 77 J7
  FNCH N3 ... 39 F7
  FSBYPK N4 ... 55 C5
  IL IG1 ... 78 B2
  PGE/AN SE20 ... 150 D6
  STHGT/OAK N14 ... 40 E1
  WALTH E17 ... 57 G1
Oakfields Rd GLDGN NW11 ... 52 C5
Oakfield St WBPTN SW10 ... 14 E9
Oakford Rd KTTN NW5 ... 72 C3
Oak Gdns CROY/NA CR0 ... 179 J1
  EDGW HA8 ... 50 D1
Oak Gv CRICK NW2 ... 70 B3
  RSLP HA4 ... 47 F7
  SUN TW16 ... 141 F6
  WWKM BR4 ... 180 A1
Oak Grove Rd PGE/AN SE20 ... 150 E7
Oakhall Dr SUN TW16 ... 140 D7
Oak Hall Rd WAN E11 ... 59 F5
Oakham CI CAT SE6 ... 151 H1
Oakham Dr HAYES BR2 ... 167 K3
Oakhampton Rd MLHL NW7 ... 38 B7
Oakhill ESH/CLAY KT10 ... 171 C5
  WFD IG8 ... 44 B6
Oakhill Av HAMP NW3 ... 71 F3
  PIN HA5 ... 47 J1
Oak Hill Crs SURB KT6 ... 159 F6
  WFD IG8 ... 44 C6
Oak Hill Gdns WFD IG8 ... 44 C7
Oak Hill Gv SURB KT6 ... 159 F5
Oak Hill Pk HAMP NW3 ... 71 F3
Oak Hill Park Ms HAMP NW3 ... 71 F3
Oakhill PI PUT/ROE SW15 ... 127 K4
Oak Hill Rd SURB KT6 ... 159 F5
Oakhill Rd BECK BR3 ... 167 F1
  PUT/ROE SW15 ... 127 K4
  STRHM/NOR SW16 ... 148 E7
  SUT SM1 ... 175 F2
Oak Hill Wy HAMP NW3 ... 71 F3
Oakhouse Rd BXLYHS DA6 ... 137 H4
Oakhurst Av BXLYHN DA7 ... 117 F6
  EBAR EN4 ... 27 J4
Oakhurst CI CHST BR7 ... 153 K7
  KUTN/CMB KT2 ... 144 B6
  TEDD TW11 ... 142 E4
  WALTH E17 ... 58 C3
Oakhurst Gdns BXLYHN DA7 ... 117 F6
  WALTH E17 ... 58 C3
Oakhurst Gv EDUL SE22 ... 131 H3
Oakhurst PI WATW WD18 * ... 20 D3
Oakhurst Rd HOR/WEW KT19 ... 172 E5
Oakington Av HYS/HAR UB3 ... 101 C3
  RYLN/HDSTN HA2 ... 48 A6
  WBLY HA9 ... 68 B2
Oakington CI SUN TW16 ... 156 B1
Oakington Dr SUN TW16 ... 156 B1
Oakington Manor Dr
  WBLY HA9 ... 68 C4
Oakington Rd MV/WKIL W9 ... 2 B9
Oakington Wy
  CEND/HSY/T N8 ... 54 E5
Oakland PI BKHH IG9 ... 44 E1
Oakland Rd SRTFD E15 ... 76 C3
Oaklands WCHMH N21 ... 41 F1
Oaklands Av BFN/LL DA15 ... 136 A6
  ED N9 ... 30 D5
  ESH/CLAY KT10 ... 157 J7
  ISLW TW7 ... 104 A5
  OXHEY WD19 ... 21 F7
  ROM RM1 ... 63 G2
  THHTH CR7 ... 164 B3
  WWKM BR4 ... 179 K2
Oaklands CI ALP/SUD HA0 ... 67 K4
  BXLYHS DA6 ... 137 G4
  CHSGTN KT9 ... 171 J3
  STMC/STPC BR5 ... 169 K5
Oaklands Ga NTHWD HA6 ... 32 C5
Oaklands Gv SHB W12 ... 87 J7
Oaklands La BAR EN5 ... 25 K3
Oaklands Ms CRICK NW2 ... 70 B3
Oaklands Park Av IL IG1 ... 78 C1
Oaklands PI CLAP SW4 ... 129 J3
Oaklands Rd BMLY BR1 ... 152 E6
  BXLYHS DA6 ... 137 G3
  CRICK NW2 ... 70 B3
  HNWL W7 ... 104 A1
  MORT/ESHN SW14 ... 126 A2
  WCHMH N21 ... 29 F1
Oaklands Wy WLGTN SM6 ... 176 D6
Oakland Wy HOR/WEW KT19 ... 173 F5
Oak La EFNCH N2 ... 53 H1
  FBAR/BDGN N11 ... 40 D5
  ISLW TW7 ... 123 K3
  POP/IOD E14 ... 93 H6
  TWK TW1 ... 124 B6
  WFD IG8 ... 44 B3
Oakleafe Gdns BARK/HLT IG6 ... 60 B2
Oakleigh Av EDGW HA8 ... 50 D1
  SURB KT6 ... 159 H7
  TRDG/WHET N20 ... 27 H1
Oakleigh CI TRDG/WHET N20 ... 39 K2
Oakleigh Ct EDGW HA8 * ... 50 E1
Oakleigh Crs TRDG/WHET N20 ... 39 J2
Oakleigh Dr
  RKW/CH/CXG WD3 ... 20 A5
Oakleigh Gdns EDGW HA8 ... 36 B4
  TRDG/WHET N20 ... 27 G7
Oakleigh Ms TRDG/WHET N20 ... 39 G1
Oakleigh Park Av CHST BR7 ... 169 F1
Oakleigh Pk North
  TRDG/WHET N20 ... 27 H7
Oakleigh Pk South
  TRDG/WHET N20 ... 27 J7
  PIN HA5 ... 33 K5
Oakleigh Rd North
  TRDG/WHET N20 ... 39 H1
Oakleigh Rd South
  FBAR/BDGN N11 ... 40 A3
Oakleigh Wy MTCM CR4 ... 163 A7
  SURB KT6 ... 159 H7
Oakley Av BARK IG11 ... 79 F6
  CROY/NA CR0 ... 176 E3
  EA W5 ... 86 C6
Oakley CI CHING E4 ... 44 A3
  EHAM E6 ... 95 J5
  HNWL W7 ... 84 E6
  ISLW TW7 ... 123 J1
Oakley Ct MTCM CR4 * ... 163 J7
Oakley Dr CAT SE6 ... 151 J7
  ELTH/MOT SE9 ... 135 J7
  HAYES BR2 ... 181 J2
Oakley Gdns CEND/HSY/T N8 ... 55 F4
  CHEL SW3 ... 15 K9
Oakley Pk BXLY DA5 ... 136 D6
Oakley PI STHWK SE1 ... 19 L8
Oakley Rd HAYES BR2 ... 181 J2

HRW HA1 ... 48 E5
IS N1 ... 7 G1
  SNWD SE25 ... 165 J4
Oakley Sq CAMTN NW1 ... 4 E5
Oakley St CHEL SW3 ... 15 G9
Oakley Yd BETH E2 * ... 7 M9
Oak Lodge CI STAN HA7 ... 35 J4
Oak Lodge Dr WWKM BR4 ... 166 A7
Oaklodge Wy MLHL NW7 ... 37 H5
Oakmead Av HAYES BR2 ... 167 J5
Oakmeade PIN HA5 ... 34 A5
Oakmead Gdns EDGW HA8 ... 37 F3
Oakmead PI MTCM CR4 ... 147 J7
Oakmead Rd BAL SW12 ... 129 G7
  CROY/NA CR0 ... 163 J5
Oakmere Rd ABYW SE2 ... 116 B3
Oak Park Gdns
  WIM/MER SW19 ... 127 G7
Oakridge Dr EFNCH N2 ... 53 H3
Oakridge Rd BMLY BR1 ... 152 C3
Oak Ri BKHH IG9 ... 45 H1
Oak Rd EA W5 ... 85 K6
  ERITH DA8 ... 117 K6
  NWMAL KT3 ... 160 A1
Oak Rw MTCM CR4 ... 163 G5
Oaks Av CRW RM5 ... 62 E1
  FELT TW13 ... 141 J1
  NRWD SE19 ... 150 A4
  WPK KT4 ... 173 K3
Oaksford Av SYD SE26 ... 150 D2
Oaks Gv CHING E4 ... 44 C1
Oakshade Rd BMLY BR1 ... 152 B3
Oakshaw Rd
  WAND/EARL SW18 ... 128 A6
Oaks La CROY/NA CR0 ... 178 C2
  GNTH/NBYPK IG2 ... 60 E3
Oak Sq BRXN/ST SW9 ... 130 A1
Oaks Rd CROY/NA CR0 ... 178 A4
  STWL/WRAY TW19 ... 120 A4
The Oaks CHSGTN KT9 ... 171 J2
  FELT TW13 ... 141 J1
  HAYES BR2 * ... 169 F5
  MRDN SM4 ... 161 H3
  NFNCH/WDSPK N12 ... 39 J3
  OXHEY WD19 ... 21 G7
  RSLP HA4 ... 46 D7
  WFD IG8 ... 44 C6
  WOOL/PLUM SE18 ... 115 H4
  YEAD UB4 ... 82 A1
Oak St ROMW/RG RM7 ... 62 E4
Oaks Wy CAR SM5 ... 175 K6
  SURB KT6 ... 171 K1
Oakthorpe Rd PLMGR N13 ... 41 G4
Oaktree Av PLMGR N13 ... 41 G2
Oak Tree CI EA W5 * ... 85 J6
  STAN HA7 ... 35 J6
Oak Tree Ct BORE WD6 * ... 23 K5
Oak Tree Dell CDALE/KGS NW9 ... 50 E4
Oak Tree Dr TRDG/WHET N20 ... 27 F7
Oak Tree Gdns BMLY BR1 ... 153 F4
Oaktree Gv IL IG1 ... 78 D4
Oak Tree Rd STJWD NW8 ... 3 H9
Oakview Gv CROY/NA CR0 ... 166 B7
Oakview Rd CAT SE6 ... 151 K4
Oak Village HAMP NW3 ... 72 A3
Oak Vls GLDGN NW11 * ... 52 D4
Oak Wy ACT W3 ... 87 G7
  CROY/NA CR0 ... 166 A6
  STHGT/OAK N14 ... 28 A6
  EBED/NFELT TW14 ... 121 H7
Oakway HAYES BR2 ... 167 G1
  RYNPK SW20 ... 161 F5
Oakway CI BXLY DA5 ... 137 F5
Oakways ELTH/MOT SE9 ... 135 G5
Oakwood Av BECK BR3 ... 167 F1
  BORE WD6 ... 24 D3
  CHSGTN KT9 ... 172 A6
  HAYES BR2 ... 168 A2
  MTCM CR4 ... 162 C1
  STHGT/OAK N14 ... 28 C6
Oakwood CI CHST BR7 ... 153 G5
  LEW SE13 ... 133 G6
  STHGT/OAK N14 ... 28 C5
  WFD IG8 ... 45 J5
Oakwood Ct WKENS W14 ... 107 J2
Oakwood Crs GFD/PVL UB6 ... 67 G5
  WCHMH N21 ... 29 F5
Oakwood Dr BXLYHN DA7 ... 137 K3
  EDGW HA8 ... 36 E6
Oakwood Gdns
  GDMY/SEVK IG3 ... 79 F1
  SUT SM1 ... 174 E1
Oakwood La WKENS W14 ... 107 J2
Oakwood Pde
  STHGT/OAK N14 * ... 28 C4
Oakwood Park Cots
  WCHMH N21 * ... 29 F5
Oakwood Park Rd
  STHGT/OAK N14 ... 28 D5
Oakwood PI CROY/NA CR0 ... 164 B5
Oakwood Rd CROY/NA CR0 ... 164 B5
  GLDGN NW11 ... 52 E4
  PIN HA5 ... 47 F1
  RYNPK SW20 ... 145 J7
Oakworth Rd NKENS W10 ... 88 A4
Oak Yd WAT WD17 * ... 21 G3
Oarsman PI E/WMO/HCT KT8 ... 157 K3
Oates CI HAYES BR2 ... 167 G2
Oatland Ri WALTH E17 ... 57 G1
Oat La CITYW EC2V ... 12 E4
Oban CI PLSTW E13 ... 95 G3
Oban Rd PLSTW E13 ... 95 G2
  THHTH CR7 ... 164 E3
Oban St POP/IOD E14 ... 94 B5
Oberstein Rd BTSEA SW11 ... 128 C3
Oborne CI HNHL SE24 ... 130 C4
Observatory Gdns KENS W8 ... 14 A1
Observatory Rd
  MORT/ESHN SW14 ... 125 K3
  SKENS SW7 ... 15 G3
Observer Dr WATW WD18 ... 20 C3
Occupation La EA W5 ... 104 E3
  WOOL/PLUM SE18 ... 115 G7
Occupation Rd WALW SE17 ... 18 F7
  WATW WD18 ... 21 F4
  WEA W13 ... 104 C1
Ocean St WCHPL E1 ... 93 F4
Ockendon Ms IS N1 * ... 73 K5
Ockendon Rd IS N1 ... 73 K5
Ockham Dr GFD/PVL UB6 ... 66 E5
  STMC/STPC BR5 ... 155 G6
Ockley Rd CROY/NA CR0 ... 164 A6
  STRHM/NOR SW16 ... 148 E3
Octagon Ar LVPST EC2M * ... 13 J3
Octavia CI MTCM CR4 ... 162 D4
Octavia Rd ISLW TW7 ... 124 A1
Octavia St BTSEA SW11 ... 108 D7

Octavia Ms CRICK NW2 * ... 69 K5
Octavia Rd ISLW TW7 ... 124 A1
Octavia St BTSEA SW11 ... 108 D7
Octavius St DEPT SE8 ... 112 D6
October PI HDN NW4 ... 52 B2
Odard Rd E/WMO/HCT KT8 ... 157 F3
Odell CI BARK IG11 ... 79 F6
Odell Wk LEW SE13 ... 132 E2
Odeon Pde ELTH/MOT SE9 * ... 134 D3
  GFD/PVL UB6 ... 67 H5
  HOLWY N7 * ... 72 E2
  ISLW TW7 * ... 123 K1
Odessa Rd FSTGT E7 ... 76 D3
  WLSDN NW10 ... 87 J1
Odessa St BERM/RHTH SE16 ... 112 C2
Odger St BTSEA SW11 ... 128 E1
Odhams Wk
  LSO/SEVD WC2H * ... 11 J3
Odsey Vls FSBYPK N4 * ... 55 G5
Offa's Md HOM E9 ... 75 G3
Offenham Rd ELTH/MOT SE9 ... 153 K3
Offerton Rd CLAP SW4 ... 129 H2
Offham Slope
  NFNCH/WDSPK N12 ... 38 D1
Offley PI ISLW TW7 ... 123 J1
Offley Rd BRXN/ST SW9 ... 110 B6
Offord CI TOTM N17 ... 42 C6
Offord Rd IS N1 ... 5 M1
Offord St HOLWY N7 ... 5 L1
Ogilby St WOOL/PLUM SE18 ... 114 D3
Oglander Rd PECK SE15 ... 131 G3
Ogle St GTPST W1W ... 10 E2
Oglethorpe Rd DAGE RM10 ... 80 B2
Ohio Rd PLSTW E13 ... 94 D3
Oil Mill La HMSMTH W6 ... 106 D4
Okeburn Rd TOOT SW17 ... 148 A4
Okehampton CI
  NFNCH/WDSPK N12 ... 39 H4
Okehampton Rd
  WLSDN NW10 ... 70 A7
Olaf St NTGHL W11 ... 88 B6
Old Bailey STP EC4M ... 12 D5
Old Barn CI BELMT SM2 ... 174 C6
Old Barn Wy BXLYHN DA7 ... 138 A3
Old Barrack Yd KTBR SW1X ... 16 A1
Old Bellgate Whf
  POP/IOD E14 ... 112 D2
Oldberry Rd EDGW HA8 ... 37 F5
Old Bethnal Green Rd
  BETH E2 ... 92 D2
Old Bond St CONDST W1S ... 10 E7
Oldborough Rd ALP/SUD HA0 ... 67 J1
Old Brewery Ms HAMP NW3 ... 71 H3
Old Bridge CI NTHLT UB5 ... 84 A1
Old Bridge St KUT/HW KT1 ... 158 E1
Old Broad St OBST EC2N ... 13 H5
Old Bromley Rd BMLY BR1 ... 152 B4
Old Brompton Rd ECT SW5 ... 14 B8
Old Bldgs LINN WC2A ... 12 A4
Old Burlington St
  CONDST W1S ... 10 E6
Old Castle St WCHPL E1 ... 13 L4
Old Cavendish St OXSTW W1C ... 10 C4
Old Chestnut Av
  ESH/CLAY KT10 ... 170 A5
Old Church La
  CDALE/KGS NW9 ... 68 E7
  GFD/PVL UB6 ... 85 G2
  STAN HA7 ... 35 H5
Old Church Pth
  ESH/CLAY KT10 ... 170 B3
Old Church Rd CHING E4 ... 43 J4
  WCHPL E1 ... 93 F5
Old Church St CHEL SW3 ... 15 H8
Old Claygate La
  ESH/CLAY KT10 ... 171 G5
Old Compton St
  SOHO/SHAV W1D ... 11 G6
Old Cote Dr HEST TW5 ... 103 F5
Old Court PI KENS W8 ... 14 C1
The Old Ctyd BMLY BR1 ... 153 F7
Old Dairy Ms BAL SW12 ... 129 F7
  KTTN NW5 * ... 72 B5
Old Deer Pk RCH/KEW TW9 ... 125 G2
Old Deer Park Gdns
  RCH/KEW TW9 ... 125 F2
Old Devonshire Rd BAL SW12 ... 129 G6
Old Dock CI RCH/KEW TW9 ... 105 H5
Old Dover Rd BKHTH/KID SE3 ... 113 K6
Old Farm Av BFN/LL DA15 ... 135 J7
  STHGT/OAK N14 ... 28 C6
Old Farm CI HSLWW TW4 ... 122 E3
Old Farm Rd EFNCH N2 ... 39 H7
  HPTN TW12 ... 141 K5
  WDR/YW UB7 ... 100 A1
Old Farm Rd East
  BFN/LL DA15 ... 155 G2
Old Farm Rd West
  BFN/LL DA15 ... 155 F1
Oldfield CI BMLY BR1 ... 168 E3
  GFD/PVL UB6 ... 66 E4
  STAN HA7 ... 35 G4
Oldfield Farm Gdns
  GFD/PVL UB6 ... 66 D7
Oldfield Gv BERM/RHTH SE16 ... 112 A3
Oldfield La North
  GFD/PVL UB6 ... 66 D7
Oldfield La South
  GFD/PVL UB6 ... 84 C2
Oldfield Ms HGT N6 ... 54 C7
Oldfield Rd ACT W3 ... 106 E1
  BMLY BR1 ... 168 E3
  BXLYHN DA7 ... 137 F1
  HPTN TW12 ... 141 K7
  STNW/STAM N16 ... 74 A2
  WIM/MER SW19 ... 146 C5
  WLSDN NW10 ... 69 H6
Oldfields Circ NTHLT UB5 ... 66 C5
Oldfields Rd SUT SM1 ... 174 D1
Old Fish Street HI
  BLKFR EC4V * ... 12 E6
Old Fleet La FLST/FETLN EC4A ... 12 C4
Old Fold Vw BAR EN5 ... 26 A2
Old Ford Lock BOW E3 * ... 75 J6
Old Ford Rd BETH E2 ... 92 E1
  BOW E3 ... 75 J7
Old Forge CI STAN HA7 ... 35 G3
Old Forge Ms SHB W12 ... 106 E1
Old Forge Rd ARCH N19 ... 72 D1
Old Forge Wy SCUP DA14 ... 155 H3
Old Gannon CI NTHWD HA6 ... 32 A4
Old Gloucester St
  BMSBY WC1N ... 11 K2
Old Hall CI PIN HA5 ... 33 J1
Old Hall Dr PIN HA5 ... 33 J1
Oldham Ter ACT W3 ... 86 E7
Old Hatch Mnr RSLP HA4 ... 46 D6
Old HI CHST BR7 ... 154 A7
Oldhill St STNW/STAM N16 ... 56 C7
Old Homesdale Rd HAYES BR2 ... 168 A3

Old Hospital CI BAL SW12 * ... 128 E7
Old House CI WIM/MER SW19 ... 146 C4
Old House Gdns TWK TW1 * ... 124 D5
Old Howletts La RSLP HA4 ... 46 B5
Old Jamaica Rd
  BERM/RHTH SE16 ... 111 H2
Old James St PECK SE15 ... 131 J2
Old Jewry LOTH EC2R * ... 13 G5
Old Kenton La
  CDALE/KGS NW9 ... 50 D4
Old Kent Rd PECK SE15 ... 111 J5
  STHWK SE1 ... 19 J5
Old Kingston Rd WPK KT4 ... 172 E2
Old Lodge Wy STAN HA7 ... 35 G4
Old London Rd
  KUTN/CMB KT2 ... 159 F1
Old Maiden La WPK KT4 ... 173 G1
Old Manor Dr ISLW TW7 ... 123 H5
Old Manor Rd NWDGN UB2 ... 102 C3
Old Manor Wy BXLYHN DA7 ... 138 A1
  CHST BR7 ... 153 K4
Old Manor Yd ECT SW5 * ... 14 B7
Old Marylebone Rd
  CAMTN NW1 ... 9 K3
Old Mill CI SWFD E18 ... 59 G2
Old Mill Ct WOOL/PLUM SE18 ... 115 J5
Old Mitre Ct EMB EC4Y * ... 12 B5
Old Montague St WCHPL E1 ... 92 C4
Old Nichol St BETH E2 ... 7 L9
Old North St FSBYW WC1X * ... 11 L2
Oak Common La
  WLSDN NW10 ... 87 G3
Old Oak La WLSDN NW10 ... 87 H2
Old Oak Rd ACT W3 ... 87 H6
Old Orch SUN TW16 ... 141 G7
The Old Orch HAMP NW3 * ... 71 K3
Old Palace La RCH/KEW TW9 ... 124 D4
Old Palace Rd CROY/NA CR0 ... 177 J2
Old Palace Yd RCH/KEW TW9 ... 124 D4
  WHALL SW1A ... 17 J3
Old Paradise St LBTH SE11 ... 17 L5
Old Park Av BAL SW12 ... 129 F5
  ENC/FH EN2 ... 29 J3
Old Park Gv ENC/FH EN2 ... 29 J3
Old Park La MYFR/PKLN W1K ... 10 B9
Old Park Ms HEST TW5 ... 102 E6
Old Park Ridings WCHMH N21 ... 29 H5
Old Park Rd ABYW SE2 ... 116 B4
  ENC/FH EN2 ... 29 H2
  PLMGR N13 ... 41 F2
Old Park Rd South
  ENC/FH EN2 ... 29 H3
Old Park Vw ENC/FH EN2 ... 29 G3
Old Pearson St GNWCH SE10 ... 112 E6
Old Perry St CHST BR7 ... 154 E6
Old Post Office La
  BKHTH/KID SE3 ... 134 A2
Old Pound Ct ISLW TW7 * ... 104 B7
Old Pye St WEST SW1P ... 17 G3
Old Quebec St MBLAR W1H ... 9 M5
Old Queen St STJSPK SW1H ... 17 H2
Old Rectory Gdns EDGW HA8 ... 36 C5
Old Redding
  KTN/HRWW/WS HA3 ... 34 D4
Oldridge Rd BAL SW12 ... 129 F6
Old Rd DART DA1 ... 138 D3
  LEW SE13 ... 133 H3
Old Royal Free Sq IS N1 ... 6 A4
Old Ruislip Rd NTHLT UB5 ... 83 G1
Old's Ap WATW WD18 ... 20 A7
Old School CI BECK BR3 ... 166 A1
Old School Crs FSTGT E7 ... 76 E5
Old School PI CROY/NA CR0 ... 177 G3
Old Schools La EW KT17 ... 173 H7
Old School Sq THDIT KT7 ... 158 A5
Old School Ter CHEAM SM3 * ... 174 B6
Old Seacoal La STP EC4M ... 12 C5
Old South CI PIN HA5 ... 33 H7
Old South Lambeth Rd
  VX/NE SW8 * ... 109 K6
Old Sq LINN WC2A ... 11 M4
Old Stable Ms HBRY N5 ... 73 J2
Old Station Gdns
  TEDD TW11 * ... 143 G5
Old Station Rd HYS/HAR UB3 ... 101 J2
The Old Station Yd
  WALTH E17 * ... 58 C4
Oldstead Rd BMLY BR1 ... 152 B3
Old St PLSTW E13 ... 95 F1
  STLK EC1Y ... 7 H9
Old Studio CI CROY/NA CR0 ... 164 E6
Old Swan Yd CAR SM5 ... 175 K3
Old Town CLAP SW4 ... 129 H2
  CROY/NA CR0 ... 177 H2
Old Tramyard
  WOOL/PLUM SE18 ... 115 K3
Old Woolwich Rd
  GNWCH SE10 ... 113 G5
Old York Rd
  WAND/EARL SW18 ... 128 A4
O'Leary Sq WCHPL E1 ... 92 E4
Olga St BOW E3 ... 93 G1
Olinda Rd STNW/STAM N16 ... 56 B5
Oliphant St NKENS W10 ... 88 C2
Olive Gv SEVS/STOTM N15 ... 55 J3
Oliver Av SNWD SE25 ... 165 G2
Oliver CI CHSWK W4 ... 105 J5
Oliver Gdns EHAM E6 ... 95 J4
Oliver Gv SNWD SE25 ... 165 G3
Oliver Ms PECK SE15 ... 131 H1
Olive Rd CRICK NW2 ... 70 A3
  DART DA1 ... 139 G7
  EA W5 ... 104 E2
  PLSTW E13 ... 95 G2
  WIM/MER SW19 * ... 147 G6
Oliver Rd LEY E10 ... 75 K2
  NWMAL KT3 ... 159 K1
  RAIN RM13 ... 81 H7
  SUT SM1 ... 175 H3
  WALTH E17 ... 58 A4
Oliver's Yd STLK EC1Y ... 7 H8
Olive St ROMW/RG RM7 ... 63 F4
Ollerton Gn BOW E3 ... 93 J7
Ollerton Rd FBAR/BDGN N11 ... 40 D4
Olley CI WLGTN SM6 ... 176 E6
Ollgar CI SHB W12 ... 87 H7
Olliffe St POP/IOD E14 ... 113 F2
Olmar St STHWK SE1 ... 111 H5
Olney Rd WALW SE17 ... 18 E9
Olron Crs BXLYHS DA6 ... 136 E4
Olven Rd WOOL/PLUM SE18 ... 115 H6
Olveston Wk CAR SM5 ... 162 C5
Olwen Ms PIN HA5 ... 47 H1
Olyffe Av WELL DA16 ... 136 B1
Olyffe Dr BECK BR3 ... 152 A7
Olympia Wy WKENS W14 ... 107 H2
Olympic Wy GFD/PVL UB6 ... 66 C2
  WBLY HA9 ... 68 C2
Olympus Sq CLPT E5 ... 74 D2
Oman Av CRICK NW2 ... 70 A4
O'Meara St STHWK SE1 ... 12 F9
Omega PI IS N1 ... 5 K6

Omega St NWCR SE14 ....112 C7
Ommaney Rd NWCR SE14 ...112 A7
Omnibus Wy WALTH E17....57 J1
Ondine Rd PECK SE15 ....131 G3
Onega Gn RCHPK/HAM SE16..142 E2
One Tree Cl FSTH SE23....131 K5
Ongar Cl CHDH RM6.......61 J4
Ongar Rd FUL/PGN SW6....14 B9
Ongar Wy RAIN RM13......88 J6
Onra Rd WALTH E17.......57 J6
Onslow Cl CHING E4.......44 B1
   NKENS W10............88 D2
Onslow Crs CHST BR7.....154 B7
   SKENS SW7............15 G6
Onslow Dr SCUP DA14.....155 K2
Onslow Gdns MUSWH N10...54 B4
   SKENS SW7............15 G6
   SWFD E18.............59 F2
   THDIT KT7............157 H7
   WCHMH N21............29 C4
   WLGTN SM6............176 C6
Onslow Ms East SKENS SW7..15 G6
Onslow Ms West SKENS SW7..15 G6
Onslow Pde STHGT/OAK N14*..28 B7
Onslow Rd CROY/NA CR0....164 B6
   NWMAL KT3............160 D3
   RCHPK/HAM TW10.......125 F4
Onslow Sq SKENS SW7......15 G5
Onslow St CLKNW EC1R.....12 B1
Onslow Wy THDIT KT7......157 K7
Ontario St STHWK SE1.....18 D4
Ontario Wy POP/IOD E14...93 J6
On The Hl OXHEY WD19.....33 J1
Onyx Ms SRTFD E15........76 C7
Opal Cl CAN/RD E16.......95 H5
Opal Ms WLSDN NW6.......70 D7
Opal St LBTH SE11........18 C6
Openshaw Rd ABYW SE2....116 C3
Openview WAND/EARL SW18..128 B7
Ophir Ter PECK SE15......111 H7
Opossum Wy HSLWW TW4....122 E2
Oppenheim Rd LEW SE13...133 F1
Oppidans Rd HAMP NW3.....3 L2
Optima Pk DART DA1.......138 D2
Orange Gv WAN E11.......76 C2
Orange Hill Rd EDGW HA8..36 E6
Orange Pl BERM/RTH SE16..111 K2
Orangery La ELTH/MOT SE9..134 E4
The Orangery
   RCHPK/HAM TW10.......143 J1
Orange St LSQ/SEVD WC2H..11 H7
   WAP E1W..............92 C7
Oransay Rd IS N1.........73 J5
Oratory La CHEL SW3*.....15 H7
Orbain Rd FUL/PGN SW6....107 H6
Orbel St BTSEA SW11......108 D7
Orb St WALW SE17.........19 G6
Orchard Av ASHF TW15.....140 A5
   BELV DA17............117 F5
   CROY/NA CR0..........179 G1
   DART DA1.............138 E6
   EBED/NFELT TW14......121 G4
   FNCH N3..............52 E2
   HEST TW5.............102 D6
   MTCM CR4.............163 F7
   NWMAL KT3............160 B1
   STHGT/OAK N14........28 C5
   STHL UB1.............83 J7
   THDIT KT7............158 B7
   TRDG/WHET N20........39 H1
Orchard Cl ALP/SUD HA0...68 A7
   ASHF TW15............140 A5
   BORE WD6.............24 B3
   BUSH WD23............22 D7
   BXLYHN DA7...........117 F3
   CHING E4.............43 J3
   CRICK NW2............69 J2
   EDGW HA8.............36 A5
   FSTH SE23............131 K5
   HOR/WEW KT19 *.......172 D5
   IS N1................6 F2
   NKENS W10............88 C4
   NTHLT UB5............46 A6
   RSLP HA4.............46 A6
   RYNPK SW20...........161 F3
   THDIT KT7............158 C7
   WAT WD17.............20 D1
   WOT/HER KT12.........156 A6
Orchard Cots HYS/HAR UB3*..101 H1
   KUTN/CMB KT2*........144 C2
Orchard Ct WLGTN SM6.....176 B4
   WPK KT4 *............160 D7
Orchard Crs EDGW HA8.....36 E4
   EN EN1...............30 B1
Orchard Dr BKHTH/KID SE3..133 H1
   EDGW HA8.............36 B4
Orchard Gdns CHSGTN KT9..172 A3
Orchard Ga CDALE/KGS NW9..51 G3
   ESH/CLAY KT10........157 J7
   GFD/PVL UB6..........67 H5
Orchard Gv CROY/NA CR0...166 B6
   EDGW HA8.............36 C7
   KTN/HRWW/WS HA3......50 B2
   PGE/AN SE20..........150 C7
Orchard Hl DART DA1......138 B4
   LEW SE13.............112 E7
Orchard La E/WMO/HCT KT8..157 J5
   RYNPK SW20...........145 K7
   WFD IG8..............45 G3
Orchardleigh Av PEND EN3..30 E1
Orchardmede WCHMH N21...29 K5
Orchard Ms IS N1.........7 H2
   TOOT SW17............147 G2
Orchard Pl POP/IOD E14...94 C6
   TOTM N17.............56 B3
Orchard Ri CROY/NA CR0...166 B7
   KUTN/CMB KT2.........144 E7
   PIN HA5..............46 D2
   RCHPK/HAM TW10.......125 J3
Orchard Ri East BFN/LL DA15..135 K4
Orchard Ri West BFN/LL DA15..135 H4
Orchard Rd BAR EN5.......26 C3
   BELV DA17............117 H3
   BMLY BR1.............153 G7
   BTFD TW8.............104 D5
   CHSGTN KT9...........172 A3
   DAGE RM10............80 C7
   FELT TW13............121 K7
   HGT N6...............54 B6
   HPTN TW12............141 K6
   HSLWW TW4............122 E4
   HYS/HAR UB3..........82 D6
   KUT/HW KT1...........159 F1
   PEND EN3.............30 E1
   RCH/KEW TW9..........125 H2
   ROMW/RG RM7..........62 D3
   SCUP DA14............154 E3
   SUN TW16.............141 F6
   SUT SM1..............174 D4
   TWK TW1..............124 B4
   WELL DA16............136 C2

Orchard Sq WKENS W14 *...107 J4
Orchard St DART DA1......139 H5
   MBLAR W1H............10 A5
   WALTH E17............57 G5
   WLSDN NW10...........69 H3
Orchard Ter EN EN1 *.....30 C5
Orchid Cl CHSGTN KT9.....171 J6
   EHAM E6..............95 J4
   LEW SE13.............133 G4
   STHL UB1.............83 J5
Orchid Gdns HSLWW TW4....122 E3
Orchard Vls SCUP DA14....155 J5
Orchard Wy CROY/NA CR0...166 B6
   EN EN1...............30 A2
   ESH/CLAY KT10........170 C5
   SUT SM1..............175 H5
Orchid Ct STHGT/OAK N14..28 A7
Orchid Rd STHGT/OAK N14..28 C5
Orchid St SHB W12........87 J6
Orde Hall St BMSBY WC1N..11 L1
Ordell Rd BOW E3.........93 H1
Ordnance Cl FELT TW13....140 D1
Ordnance Crs GNWCH SE10..113 G1
Ordnance Hl STJWD NW8....3 H4
Ordnance Ms STJWD NW8....3 H5
Ordnance Rd CAN/RD E16...94 D4
   WOOL/PLUM SE18.......115 F5
Oregano Dr POP/IOD E14...94 B5
Oregon Av MNPK E12......77 K3
Oregon Cl NWMAL KT3.....159 K3
Oregon Sq ORP BR6.......169 J7
Orestes Ms KIL/WHAMP NW6..70 E4
Orford Gdns TWK TW1......143 F1
Orford Rd CAT SE6.......151 K2
   SWFD E18.............59 F2
   WALTH E17............57 J4
Oriel Cl MTCM CR4.......163 J3
Oriel Ct HAMP NW3.......71 G3
Oriel Dr BARN SW13.......107 F5
Oriel Gdns CLAY IG5......59 K2
Oriel Rd HOM E9.........75 F5
Oriel Wy NTHLT UB5......66 B6
Oriental Rd CAN/RD E16...95 H7
Orient St LBTH SE11......18 C5
Orient Wy CLPT E5........75 F2
   LEY E10..............75 J1
Oriole Wy THMD SE28.....97 H6
Orion Rd MUSWH N10......40 A5
Orion Wy NTHWD HA6......32 D3
Orissa Rd WOOL/PLUM SE18..115 K4
Orkney St BTSEA SW11.....129 F1
Orlando Rd CLAP SW4......129 H2
Orleans Cl ESH/CLAY KT10..170 D1
Orleans Rd NRWD SE19.....149 K5
   TWK TW1..............124 C6
Orleston Ms HOLWY N7....73 G5
Orleston Rd HOLWY N7.....73 G5
Orley Farm Rd HRW HA1....66 E2
Ormanton Rd SYD SE26....150 C3
Orme Ct BAY/PAD W2......8 C7
Orme Court Ms BAY/PAD W2*..8 C7
Orme La BAY/PAD W2......8 C7
Ormeley Rd BAL SW12.....129 G6
Orme Rd KUT/HW KT1......159 J1
   SUT SM1..............174 E5
Ormerod Gdns MTCM CR4...163 F1
Ormesby Cl THMD SE28....97 K6
Ormesby Wy
   KTN/HRWW/WS HA3......50 B5
Orme Square Ga BAY/PAD W2..8 C7
Ormiston Gv SHB W12.....87 J7
Ormiston Rd GNWCH SE10..113 K4
Ormond Av HPTN TW12.....142 B7
Ormond Cl BMSBY WC1N....11 K2
Ormond Crs HPTN TW12....142 B6
Ormond Dr HPTN TW12.....142 B6
Ormonde Av HOR/WEW KT19..173 F7
Ormonde Ga CHEL SW3.....15 L8
Ormonde Pl BCVA SW1W....16 B6
Ormonde Rd
   MORT/ESHN SW14.......125 J2
   NTHWD HA6............32 B3
Ormonde Ter STJWD NW8...3 M4
Ormond Rd ARCH N19......54 E7
   RCHPK/HAM TW10.......124 D4
Ormond Yd STJS SW1Y.....10 F8
Ormsby BELMT SM2 *......175 F6
Ormsby Gdns GFD/PVL UB6..84 C1
Ormsby Pl STNW/STAM N16..74 B2
Ormsby St BETH E2........7 L5
Ormside St PECK SE15.....111 K5
Ormskirk Rd OXHEY WD19...33 H3
Ornan Rd HAMP NW3.......71 J4
Oronsay Ms IS N1 *.......73 J5
Orphanage Rd WAT WD17...21 G1
Orpheus St CMBW SE5......110 E7
Orpington Gdns UED N18...42 A2
Orpington Rd CHST BR7....169 K2
   WCHMH N21............29 G2
Orpwood Cl HPTN TW12....141 K5
Orsett Ms BAY/PAD W2 *...8 D5
Orsett St LBTH SE11......17 M7
   WFD IG8..............45 J2
Orsman Rd IS N1..........7 J4
Orton St WAP E1W.........92 C7
Orville Rd BTSEA SW11....128 C1
Orwell Cl HYS/HAR UB3....82 C6
Orwell Ct WANH WD24 *....21 H2
Orwell Rd PLSTW E15......95 G1
Osbaldeston Rd
   STNW/STAM N16........74 C1
Osberton Rd LEE/GVPK SE12..133 K4
Osbert St WEST SW1P.....17 G6
Osborn Cl HACK E8.......74 C7
Osborne Av STWL/WRAY TW19..120 B7
Osborne Cl BECK BR3.....166 B3
   EBAR EN4.............27 K2
   EMPK RM11............63 K5
   FELT TW13............141 J5
Osborne Ct EA W5 *.......86 A4
Osborne Gv WALTH E17....57 H3
Osborne Ms WALTH E17....57 H4
Osborne Rd ACT W3.......105 J2
   BELV DA17............117 G4
   CRICK NW2............69 K3
   EMPK RM11............63 K5
   FSBYPK N4............55 G7
   FSTGT E7.............77 H4
   HOM E9...............75 H5
   HSLW TW3.............123 G1
   KUTN/CMB KT2.........144 A6
   LEY E10..............75 K2

PEND EN3 ....31 G1
   PLMGR N13............41 G2
   STHL UB1.............84 C5
   THHTH CR7............164 D1
Osborne Sq DAGW RM9.....80 B3
Osborne Ter TOOT SW17 *..148 A4
Osborne Wy CHSGTN KT9...172 A3
Osborn Gdns MLHL NW7....38 B6
Osborn La FSTH SE23.....132 B6
Osborn St WCHPL E1......13 M3
Osborn Ter BKHTH/KID SE3..133 J3
Osbourne Ct
   RYLN/HDSTN HA2.......48 B3
Oscar Faber Pl IS N1 *...7 K2
Oscar St BROCKY SE4.....132 C1
Oseney Crs KTTN NW5.....72 C5
Osgood Av ORP BR6.......169 K7
Osgood Gdns ORP BR6.....169 K7
Osier Ct STPAN WC1H *....5 J7
Osiers Rd WAND/EARL SW18..127 K3
The Osiers RKW/CH/CXG WD3..20 A4
Osier St WCHPL E1.......92 E3
Osier Wy LEY E10........75 K2
   MTCM CR4.............162 D4
Oslac Rd CAT SE6........151 K4
Osman Cl SEVS/STOTM N15..55 K5
Osman Rd ED N9..........42 C2
   HMSMTH W6............107 F2
Osmond Cl RYLN/HDSTN HA2..66 C1
Osmond Gdns WLGTN SM6...176 C4
Osmund St SHB W12.......87 H5
Osnaburgh St CAMTN NW1...4 D9
Osnaburgh Ter CAMTN NW1..4 D9
Osney Wk CAR SM5........162 A5
Osprey Cl EHAM E6.......95 J4
   HAYES BR2............168 D7
   SUT SM1..............174 D4
   WALTH E17............43 G5
   WAN E11..............58 E3
   WDR/YW UB7...........100 A1
Osprey Est BERM/RTH SE16..30 D4
Osprey Ms PEND EN3......30 D4
Ospringe Cl PGE/AN SE20..150 E6
Ospringe Rd KTTN NW5....72 C3
Osram Rd WBLY HA9.......67 K2
Ossian Rd FSBYPK N4.....55 F6
Ossier Ms CHSWK W4......106 C3
Ossington Blds MHST W1U *..10 A3
Ossington Cl BAY/PAD W2..8 B7
Ossington St BAY/PAD W2..8 B7
Ossory Rd STHWK SE1.....111 H4
Ossulston St CAMTN NW1...5 H6
Ossulton Pl EFNCH N2....53 G2
Ossulton Wy EFNCH N2....53 G3
Ostade Rd BRXS/STRHM SW2..130 A6
Osten Ms SKENS SW7......14 D4
Osterberg Rd DART DA1...139 J3
Osterley Av ISLW TW7....103 J6
Osterley Cl STMC/STPC BR5..155 J7
Osterley Crs ISLW TW7...103 K7
Osterley Gdns THHTH CR7..164 D1
Osterley La NWDGN UB2...102 E3
Osterley Park Rd
   HNWL W7.............103 K1
Osterley Rd ISLW TW7....103 K6
   STNW/STAM N16........74 A3
Ostlers Dr ASHF TW15....140 A4
Ostliffe Rd PLMGR N13...41 H4
Oswald Rd STHL UB1......83 J7
Oswald's Md HOM E9......75 G3
Oswald St CLPT E5.......75 F2
Oswald Ter CRICK NW2 *...70 A2
Osward CROY/NA CR0......179 H7
Osward Pl ED N9.........42 C1
Osward Rd BAL SW12......147 K1
Oswin St LBTH SE11......18 D5
Oswyth Rd CMBW SE5......131 H1
Otford Cl BMLY BR1......169 F2
   BXLY DA5.............137 J3
   PGE/AN SE20..........150 E7
Otford Crs BROCKY SE4...132 C5
Othello Cl LBTH SE11....18 D6
Otis St BOW E3..........94 A2
Otley Dr GNTH/NBYPK IG2..60 B5
Otley Rd CAN/RD E16.....95 G5
Otley Ter CLPT E5.......74 E1
Otley Wy OXHEY WD19.....33 G2
Ottawa Gdns DAGE RM10...81 F6
Ottaway St CLPT E5......74 D2
Otterbourne Rd CHING E4..44 B2
   CROY/NA CR0..........177 J1
Otterburn Gdns ISLW TW7..104 B6
Otterburn St TOOT SW17..147 K5
Otter Cl SRTFD E15......76 A7
Otterden St CAT SE6.....151 J3
Otter Rd GFD/PVL UB6....84 C3
Otto Cl CAT SE6.........151 J1
   SYD SE26.............150 D1
Ottoman Ter WAT WD17....21 G2
Otto St WALW SE17.......110 C5
Otway Gdns BUSH WD23....22 E6
Oulton Cl THMD SE28.....79 J5
Oulton Crs BARK IG11....79 F5
Oulton Rd SEVS/STOTM N15..55 K4
Oulton Wy OXHEY WD19....33 K3
Oundle Av BUSH WD23.....22 C5
Ouseley Rd BAL SW12.....128 E7
Outer Cir CAMTN NW1.....3 J6
Outgate Rd WLSDN NW10...69 H6
Outram Pl IS N1.........5 K3
Outram Rd CROY/NA CR0...178 B1
   EHAM E6..............77 J7
   WDGN N22.............40 D7
Outwich St HDTCH EC3A *..13 K4
Oval Ct EDGW HA8 *......36 E6
Oval Pl VX/NE SW8.......110 A6
Oval Rd BARK IG11.......78 C7
   CAMTN NW1............4 C3
   CROY/NA CR0..........177 K1
Oval Rd North DAGE RM10..80 D7
Oval Rd South DAGE RM10..98 D1
The Oval BETH E2........92 D1
   BFN/LL DA15..........136 B6
Oval Wy LBTH SE11.......17 M8
Overbrae BECK BR3.......151 J5
Overbrook Wk EDGW HA8...36 C6
Overbury Av BECK BR3....166 E2
Overbury Rd FSBYPK N4...55 F5
Overbury St CLPT E5.....75 F3
Overcliff Rd BROCKY SE4..132 A2
Overcourt Cl BFN/LL DA15..136 C5
Overdale Av NWMAL KT3...159 K1
Overdale Rd EA W5.......104 D2
Overdown Rd CAT SE6.....151 J4
Overhill Cots MTCM CR4 *..163 F1
Overhill Rd EDUL SE22...131 H6
   PUR/KEN CR8..........177 G7
Overhill Wy BECK BR3....167 G4
Overlea Rd CLPT E5......56 C6
Overmead ELTH/MOT SE9...135 J3
Overstand Cl BECK BR3...166 D4
Overstone Gdns
   CROY/NA CR0..........166 C6

Overstone Rd HMSMTH W6..107 F3
   BELMT SM2............174 E5
   BRXN/ST SW9..........130 B1
   LEY E10..............57 G7
   STHGT/OAK N14........28 E4
Overton's Yd CROY/NA CR0..177 J2
Overy Liberty DART DA1...139 H6
Overy St DART DA1.......139 J5
Ovesdon Av RYLN/HDSTN HA2..47 K7
Ovett Cl NRWD SE19......150 A5
Ovex Cl POP/IOD E14.....113 F2
Ovington Gdns CHEL SW3...15 K4
Ovington Ms CHEL SW3....15 K4
Ovington Sq CHEL SW3....15 K4
Ovington St CHEL SW3....15 K4
Owen Cl CROY/NA CR0.....164 E5
   NTHLT UB5............65 J5
   THMD SE28............97 J7
   YEAD UB4.............83 F2
Owen Gdns WFD IG8.......45 J5
Owenite St ABYW SE2.....116 C3
Owen Rd PLMGR N13......41 J4
Owens Ms WAN E11.......76 C1
Owen St FSBYE EC1V......6 C6
Owens Rw FSBYE EC1V....6 C6
Owens Wy FSTH SE23.....132 B6
Owen Wy WLSDN NW10....68 E5
Owgan Cl CMBW SE5......110 E6
Oxberry Av FUL/PGN SW6..127 H1
Oxendon St
   SOHO/SHAV W1D *......11 G7
Oxenford St PECK SE15...131 G2
Oxenpark Av WBLY HA9....50 A6
Oxestalls Rd DEPT SE8...112 B4
Oxford Av HEST TW5......103 F4
   HYS/HAR UB3..........101 J6
   RYNPK SW20...........161 H1
   STHGT/OAK N14........28 E4
Oxford Cl ASHF TW15.....140 A6
   ED N9................42 D1
   GPK RM2..............63 J4
   MTCM CR4.............163 H2
   NTHWD HA6............32 A3
Oxford Crs NWMAL KT3....160 A5
Oxford Dr RSLP HA4......65 G1
   STHWK SE1............19 M1
Oxford Gdns CHSWK W4....105 H4
   NKENS W10............88 B5
   TRDG/WHET N20........27 H7
   WCHMH N21............29 J6
Oxford Ga HMSMTH W6.....107 G3
Oxford Ms BXLY DA5......137 H7
Oxford Rd CAR SM5......175 J5
   EA W5...............85 K6
   ED N9...............42 D1
   FSBYPK N4............55 G7
   HRW HA1.............48 C5
   IL IG1..............78 C4
   KIL/WHAMP NW6........2 B5
   KTN/HRWW/WS HA3......49 F2
   NRWD SE19............149 K5
   PEND EN3.............30 D4
   PUT/ROE SW15.........127 H3
   SCUP DA14............155 H4
   SRTFD E15............76 B5
   TEDD TW11............142 D4
   WFD IG8..............45 H4
   WLGTN SM6............176 C4
Oxford Rd North CHSWK W4..105 J4
Oxford Rd South CHSWK W4..105 H4
Oxford Rw SUN TW16......156 B2
Oxford Sq BAY/PAD W2.....9 J5
Oxford St OXSTW W1C.....10 A5
Oxford Wk STHL UB1......83 K7
Oxford Wy FELT TW13.....141 H3
Oxgate Court Pde
   CRICK NW2............69 K1
Oxgate Gdns CRICK NW2...69 J1
Oxgate La CRICK NW2.....69 J1
Oxhawth Crs HAYES BR2...169 F4
Oxhey Av OXHEY WD19.....21 H6
Oxhey Dr NTHWD HA6......33 F4
Oxhey La OXHEY WD19.....21 H6
   PIN HA5..............34 A1
Oxhey Ridge Cl NTHWD HA6..32 E4
Oxhey Rd OXHEY WD19.....21 G6
Oxleas EHAM E6..........96 B5
Oxleas Cl WELL DA16.....135 J1
Oxleay Rd RYLN/HDSTN HA2..48 A7
Oxleigh Cl NWMAL KT3....160 B4
Oxley Cl STHWK SE1......19 M7
Oxleys Rd CRICK NW2.....69 K2
Oxlow La DAGW RM9......80 B3
Oxonian St EDUL SE22....131 G3
Oxtoby Wy STRHM/NOR SW16..148 D7
Oyster Catchers Cl
   CAN/RD E16...........95 F5
Oyster Rw WCHPL E1......92 E5
Ozolins Wy CAN/RD E16...94 D5

P

Pablo Neruda HNHL SE24...130 C3
Pace Pl WCHPL E1........92 D5
Pacific Cl EBED/NFELT TW14..121 H7
Pacific Rd CAN/RD E16....94 E5
Packington Rd ACT W3....105 K3
Packington Sq IS N1.....6 E4
Packington St IS N1.....6 D4
Packmores Rd ELTH/MOT SE9..135 J4
Padbury Cl EBED/NFELT TW14..121 G7
Padbury Ct BETH E2......7 M8
Paddenswick Rd
   HMSMTH W6............106 D2
Paddington Gn BAY/PAD W2..9 H3
Paddington St MHST W1U..10 A2
Paddock Cl BKHTH/KID SE3..133 K2
   OXHEY WD19...........21 J5
   SYD SE26.............151 F3
   WPK KT4..............160 B1
Paddock Gdns NRWD SE19..150 A5
Paddock La BAR EN5......25 G3
Paddock Rd BXLYHS DA6...137 F3
   CRICK NW2............69 J1
   RSLP HA4.............65 H2
Paddocks Cl RYLN/HDSTN HA2..66 B1
The Paddocks EA W5 *....104 A2
   EBAR EN4.............27 K2
   MLHL NW7 *...........38 D5

WBLY HA9 ....68 D1
   PUT/ROE SW15.........127 F6
Padelford La STAN HA7...35 G1
Padfield Rd BRXN/ST SW9..130 D2
Padley Cl CHSGTN KT9....172 B4
Padnall Rd CHDH RM6.....61 K6
Padstow Rd ENC/FH EN2...29 H1
Padstow Wk FELT TW13....140 E1
Padua Rd PGE/AN SE20....150 E7
Pagden St VX/NE SW8.....109 G7
Pageant Crs
   BERM/RTH SE16........93 H7
Pageant Wk CROY/NA CR0..178 A2
Page Av WBLY HA9.......68 E2
Page Cl DAGW RM9.......80 A4
   HPTN TW12............141 J5
   KTN/HRWW/WS HA3......50 B5
Page Crs CROY/NA CR0....177 H4
   ERITH DA8............118 C6
Page Green Rd
   SEVS/STOTM N15.......56 C4
Page Green Ter
   SEVS/STOTM N15.......56 C4
Page Heath La BMLY BR1..168 C2
Page Heath Vls BMLY BR1..168 C2
Pagehurst Rd CROY/NA CR0..165 H4
Page Meadow MLHL NW7...37 J6
Page Rd EBED/NFELT TW14..121 G5
Page's La MUSWH N10.....54 A1
Page St MLHL NW7........37 H5
   WEST SW1P............17 H5
Page's Wk STHWK SE1.....106 B5
Page's Yd CHSWK W4 *....106 B5
Paget Av SUT SM1.......175 H2
Paget Cl HPTN TW12......142 D3
Paget Gdns CHST BR7.....154 B7
Paget La ISLW TW7.......123 J2
Paget Pl KUTN/CMB KT2 *..144 E5
   THDIT KT7............158 A7
Paget Ri WOOL/PLUM SE18..115 F6
Paget Rd HGDN/ICK UB10..82 A3
   IL IG1...............78 B3
   STNW/STAM N16........55 K7
Paget St FSBYE EC1V.....6 C7
Paget Ter WOOL/PLUM SE18..115 G5
Pagnell St NWCR SE14....112 C6
Pagoda Av RCH/KEW TW9...125 G2
Pagoda Gdns BKHTH/KID SE3..133 G1
Pagoda Gv WNWD SE27....149 J3
Paignton Rd RSLP HA4....65 F2
   SEVS/STOTM N15.......56 A5
Paines Cl PIN HA5.......47 J2
Paine's La PIN HA5......47 J1
Pain's Cl MTCM CR4......163 G1
Painsthorpe Rd
   STNW/STAM N16........74 A2
Painters Ms BERM/RTH SE16..111 H3
Painters Rd GNTH/NBYPK IG2..61 G2
Paisley Rd CAR SM5......162 A5
   WDGN N22............41 H7
Paisley Ter CAR SM5.....162 A3
Pakeman St HOLWY N7.....73 F2
Pakenham Cl BAL SW12....129 F7
Pakenham St FSBYW WC1X..5 M8
Palace Av KENS W8.......8 D9
Palace Court Gdns
   MUSWH N10...........54 C2
Palace Gardens Ms KENS W8..8 C8
Palace Gardens Ter KENS W8..8 B8
Palace Ga KENS W8......8 C9
Palace Gates Rd WDGN N22..40 E7
Palace Gn CROY/NA CR0...179 H6
   KENS W8.............8 C9
Palace Gv BMLY BR1......153 F7
   NRWD SE19............150 B6
Palace Ms FUL/PGN SW6 *..107 J6
   WALTH E17............57 H3
Palace Pde WALTH E17 *...57 H3
Palace Pl BCVA SW1W.....16 E3
Palace Rd BMLY BR1......153 F7
   BRXS/STRHM SW2.......130 A7
   CEND/HSY/T N8........54 D4
   E/WMO/HCT KT8........157 J4
   FBAR/BDGN N11........40 E6
   KUT/HW KT1...........158 E4
   NRWD SE19............150 B6
   RSLP HA4.............65 J4
Palace Sq NRWD SE19.....150 B6
Palace St WESTW SW1E....16 E3
Palace Vw BMLY BR1......168 A2
   CROY/NA CR0..........179 H3
   LEE/GVPK SE12........152 E1
Palace View Rd CHING E4..43 K4
Palamos Rd LEY E10......57 J7
Palatine Av STNW/STAM N16..74 A3
Palatine Rd STNW/STAM N16..74 A3
Palemead Cl FUL/PGN SW6..107 G7
Palermo Rd WLSDN NW10..87 J1
Palestine Gv WIM/MER SW19..147 H7
Palewell Common Dr
   MORT/ESHN SW14......126 A4
Palewell Pk
   MORT/ESHN SW14......126 A4
Palfrey Pl VX/NE SW8....110 A6
Palgrave Av STHL UB1....84 A6
Palgrave Gdns CAMTN NW1..3 K9
Palgrave Rd SHB W12.....106 C2
Palissy St BETH E2......7 L8
Pallet Wy WOOL/PLUM SE18..114 D7
Palliser Dr RAIN RM13...99 J4
Palliser Rd WKENS W14...107 H4
Pall Ml STJS SW1Y.......11 G8
Pall Ml East STJS SW1Y..11 G8
Palmar Crs BXLYHN DA7...137 H2
Palmar Rd BXLYHN DA7...137 H1
Palm Av SCUP DA14......155 K5
Palm Cl LEY E10.........75 K2
Palmeira Rd BXLYHN DA7..136 E2
Palmer Av BUSH WD23....22 B5
   CHEAM SM3............174 A4
Palmer Cl HEST TW5......103 F7
   NTHLT UB5............65 J5
   WWKM BR4............180 B1
Palmer Crs KUT/HW KT1...159 F2
Palmer Dr BMLY BR1......169 F4
Palmer Gdns BAR EN5.....26 B4
Palmer Pl HOLWY N7......73 G4
Palmer Rd BCTR RM8......61 K7
   PLSTW E13............95 F3
Palmers Rd BETH E2......93 F1
   MORT/ESHN SW14......125 J2
   STRHM/NOR SW16......164 A1
Palmer's Rd FBAR/BDGN N11..40 C4
Palmerston Ct BKHH IG9..45 G1
Palmerston Crs PLMGR N13..41 F4

WOOL/PLUM SE18 115 H5
Palmerston Gv
WIM/MER SW19 146 E6
Palmerston Rd ACT W3 105 K2
BKHH IG9 45 G1
CAR SM5 175 K3
CROY/NA CR0 164 E4
FSTGT E7 77 F4
HSLW TW3 103 H7
KIL/WHAMP NW6 70 D6
KTN/HRWW/WS HA3 49 F2
MORT/ESHN SW14 125 K3
SUT SM1 175 G4
WALTH E17 57 H3
WDGN N22 41 F6
WHTN TW2 123 K5
WIM/MER SW19 146 E6
Palmerston Wy VX/NE SW8 * 109 G6
Palmer St STJSPK SW1H 16 F3
Palmers Whf KUT/HW KT1 * 158 E1
Palm Gv EA W5 105 F2
Palm Rd ROMW/RG RM7 62 E4
Pamela Ct
NFNCH/WDSPK N12 * 39 F5
Pamela Gdns PIN HA5 47 F4
Pampisford Rd SAND/SEL CR2 177 H7
Pams Wy HOR/WEW KT19 173 F4
Pancras La MANHO EC4N 12 F5
Pancras Rd CAMTN NW1 5 G5
KCROSS N1C 5 J6
Pancras Wy BOW E3 93 J1
Pandian Wy KTTN NW5 72 D5
Pandora Rd KIL/WHAMP NW6 70 E5
Panfield Ms GNTH/NBYPK IG2 60 A5
Panfield Rd ABYW SE2 116 B1
Pangbourne Av NKENS W10 * 88 A4
Pangbourne Dr STAN HA7 35 K4
Panhard Pl STHL UB1 84 D6
Pank Av BAR EN5 27 H4
Pankhurst Av CAN/RD E16 * 95 F7
Pankhurst Cl ISLW TW7 124 A2
NWCR SE14 112 A6
Pankhurst Pl WATN WD24 21 G2
Pankhurst Rd WOT/HER KT12 156 B6
Pankridge OXHEY WD19 * 33 H1
Panmuir Rd RYNPK SW20 145 K7
Panmure Cl HBRY N5 73 H3
Panmure Rd SYD SE26 150 D2
Pan Peninsula Sq
POP/IOD E14 112 E1
Pansy Gdns SHB W12 87 J6
Panther Dr WLSDN NW10 69 F4
Pantiles Cl PLMGR N13 41 H4
The Pantiles BMLY BR1 168 D2
BUSH WD23 22 D7
BXLYHN DA7 117 G6
Panton Cl CROY/NA CR0 164 C7
Panton St STJS SW1Y 11 H7
Panyers Gdns DAGE RM10 80 D2
Paper Blds EMB EC4Y * 12 B6
Papermill Cl CAR SM5 176 A3
Papermill La DART DA1 139 G3
Papermill Pl WALTH E17 57 G1
Papillons Wk BKHTH/KID SE3 133 K1
Papworth Gdns HOLWY N7 73 F4
Papworth Wy
BRXS/STRHM SW2 130 B6
Parade Ms BRXS/STRHM SW2 149 H1
Parade Ter CDALE/KGS NW9 * 51 J5
The Parade BROCKY SE4 * 112 C7
BTSEA SW11 * 128 C3
CAR SM5 * 175 K4
CROY/NA CR0 * 163 K5
DART DA1 * 138 C4
EA W5 * 85 K5
EDUL SE22 * 131 F2
ESH/CLAY KT10 170 E5
FSBYPK N4 * 73 G1
GFD/PVL UB6 * 67 H5
KUT/HW KT1 * 159 F1
OXHEY WD19 33 H2
PGE/AN SE20 * 150 E7
RCH/KEW TW9 * 125 H2
SUN TW16 140 D6
SUT SM1 * 174 D2
SYD SE26 * 150 D3
WAT WD17 21 F2
WLGTN SM6 * 177 F4
Paradise Pas HOLWY N7 73 F4
Paradise Rd CLAP SW4 129 K1
RCH/KEW TW9 125 F4
Paradise Rw BETH E2 * 92 D2
Paradise St BERM/RHTH SE16 111 J1
Paradise Wk CHEL SW3 15 L9
Paragon Cl CAN/RD E16 94 E5
Paragon Gv BRYLDS KT5 159 G5
Paragon Ms STHWK SE1 19 H5
Paragon Pl BKHTH/KID SE3 133 J1
Paragon Rd HACK E8 74 D5
The Paragon BKHTH/KID SE3 133 K1
Parbury Ri CHSGTN KT9 172 A5
Parbury Rd FSTH SE23 132 B5
Parchmore Rd THHTH CR7 164 C1
Parchmore Wy THHTH CR7 164 C1
Pardoe Rd LEY E10 57 K6
Pardoner St STHWK SE1 19 H3
Pardon St FSBYE EC1V 6 D9
Parfett St WCHPL E1 92 C4
Parfitt Cl HAMP NW3 53 G7
Parfrey St HMSMTH W6 107 F5
Parham Dr GNTH/NBYPK IG2 60 B5
Paris Gdn STHWK SE1 12 C8
Parish Cl HCH RM12 81 K1
Parish Gate Dr BFN/LL DA15 135 K5
Parish La PGE/AN SE20 151 F5
Parish Whf WOOL/PLUM SE18 114 D3
Park Ap BERM/RHTH SE16 * 111 K2
WELL DA16 136 C3
Park Av BARK IG11 78 C5
BMLY BR1 152 E5
BUSH WD23 21 H3
CAR SM5 176 A5
CRICK NW2 69 K5
EHAM E6 78 A7
EN EN1 29 K4
FNCH N3 39 F7
GLDGN NW11 53 F7
HSLW TW3 123 G5
IL IG1 60 A7
MORT/ESHN SW14 126 A3
ORP BR6 181 K1
PLMGR N13 41 G2
RSLP HA4 46 C5
SRTFD E15 76 C5
STHL UB1 102 E1
UED N18 42 C3
WATW WD18 20 E2
WDGN N22 54 E1
WFD IG8 45 F4
WLSDN NW10 86 B2
WWKM BR4 180 A1
Park Av East EW KT17 173 J5
Park Avenue Ms MTCM CR4 148 B6
Park Av North
CEND/HSY/T N8 54 D3
WLSDN NW10 69 K4
Park Avenue Rd TOTM N17 42 D6
Park Av South
CEND/HSY/T N8 54 D3
Park Av West EW KT17 173 J5
Park Cha WBLY HA9 68 B3
Park Cl BUSH WD23 21 H2
CAR SM5 175 K5
CRICK NW2 69 J2
HOM E9 74 E7
HPTN TW12 142 C7
HSLW TW3 123 H4
KTN/HRWW/WS HA3 34 E7
KUTN/CMB KT2 144 C7
NFNCH/WDSPK N12 * 39 H3
SKENS SW7 * 15 L2
WKENS W14 107 J2
WLSDN NW10 86 B2
Park Cots FNCH N3 * 52 D1
Park Ct DUL SE21 * 149 K2
NWMAL KT3 160 A3
SYD SE26 * 150 D5
WBLY HA9 68 A4
Park Crs BORE WD6 24 B2
EMPK RM11 63 J6
ENC/FH EN2 29 K3
ERITH DA8 117 K5
FNCH N3 39 F6
KTN/HRWW/WS HA3 34 E7
REGST W1B 10 C1
WHTN TW2 123 J7
Park Crescent Ms East
GTPST W1W 10 D1
Park Crescent Ms West
CAVSQ/HST W1G 10 C1
Park Cft EDGW HA8 36 E7
Parkcroft Rd LEE/GVPK SE12 133 J6
Parkdale Crs WPK KT4 173 F2
Parkdale Rd
WOOL/PLUM SE18 115 K4
Park Dr ACT W3 105 H2
CHARL SE7 114 D4
DAGE RM10 80 E2
GLDGN NW11 53 F7
KTN/HRWW/WS HA3 34 D5
MORT/ESHN SW14 126 A4
ROM RM1 63 F3
RYLN/HDSTN HA2 48 A6
WCHMH N21 29 J5
Park End BMLY BR1 152 D7
HAMP NW3 71 J3
Park End Rd ROM RM1 63 G3
Parker Cl CAN/RD E16 95 J7
CAR SM5 175 K5
Parker Ms HOL/ALD WC2B * 11 K4
Parke Rd BARN SW13 106 D7
Parker Rd CROY/NA CR0 177 J3
Parker's Rw STHWK SE1 19 M2
Parker St CAN/RD E16 95 J7
HOL/ALD WC2B 11 K4
Parker Ter FSTH SE23 151 H1
Park Farm Cl EFNCH N2 53 G2
PIN HA5 47 F4
Park Farm Rd BMLY BR1 153 H7
KUTN/CMB KT2 144 A6
Parkfield Av FELT TW13 140 E2
MORT/ESHN SW14 126 B3
NTHLT UB5 83 H1
RYLN/HDSTN HA2 48 C1
Parkfield Cl EDGW HA8 36 D5
NTHLT UB5 83 J1
Parkfield Crs FELT TW13 140 E2
RSLP HA4 65 J1
RYLN/HDSTN HA2 48 C1
Parkfield Dr NTHLT UB5 83 H1
Parkfield Gdns
RYLN/HDSTN HA2 48 B2
Parkfield Pde FELT TW13 * 140 E2
Parkfield Rd CLAP SW4 129 J5
FELT TW13 140 E2
NTHLT UB5 83 J1
NWCR SE14 112 C7
RYLN/HDSTN HA2 66 C2
WLSDN NW10 69 J6
Parkfields CROY/NA CR0 166 C7
PUT/ROE SW15 127 F3
Parkfields Av CDALE/KGS NW9 51 F7
RYNPK SW20 145 K7
Parkfields Cl CAR SM5 176 A3
Parkfields Rd KUTN/CMB KT2 144 B4
Parkfield St IS N1 6 B5
Parkfield Wy HAYES BR2 168 E5
Park Gdns CDALE/KGS NW9 50 D2
ERITH DA8 118 A3
KUTN/CMB KT2 144 B4
Parkgate BKHTH/KID SE3 133 J2
Park Ga EA W5 85 K4
EFNCH N2 53 H2
WCHMH N21 29 F6
Parkgate Cl KUTN/CMB KT2 144 D5
Park Gate Ct HPTN TW12 * 142 C4
Parkgate Gdns
MORT/ESHN SW14 126 A4
Parkgate Ms HGT N6 54 C6
Parkgate Rd BTSEA SW11 108 D6
WLGTN SM6 176 A4
Park Gates
RYLN/HDSTN HA2 * 66 A3
Park Gv BMLY BR1 153 F7
BXLYHN DA7 137 K3
EDGW HA8 36 B4
FBAR/BDGN N11 40 D6
SRTFD E15 76 E7
Park Grove Rd WAN E11 76 C1
Park Hall Rd DUL SE21 149 K1
EFNCH N2 53 J3
Parkham St BTSEA SW11 108 C7
Park Hl BMLY BR1 168 D3
CAR SM5 175 K5
CLAP SW4 129 J4
EA W5 85 K4
FSTH SE23 150 D1
RCHPK/HAM TW10 125 G5
Park Hill Cl CAR SM5 175 J4
Park Hill Ri CROY/NA CR0 178 A1
Park Hill Rd CROY/NA CR0 178 A3
HAYES BR2 167 H1
WLGTN SM6 176 B6
Parkhill Rd BFN/LL DA15 154 E2
BXLY DA5 137 G6
HAMP NW3 71 K4
Park Hill Wk HAMP NW3 71 K4
Parkholme Rd HACK E8 74 C5
Park House Gdns TWK TW1 124 D4
Parkhouse St CMBW SE5 110 E6
Parkhurst Gdns BXLY DA5 137 H6
Parkhurst Rd BXLY DA5 137 H6
FBAR/BDGN N11 40 A3
HOLWY N7 72 E3
MNPK E12 78 A3
SUT SM1 175 H3
TOTM N17 56 C1
WALTH E17 * 57 G3
WDGN N22 41 F6
Parkland Av ROM RM1 63 G1
Parkland Gv ISLW TW7 104 A7
Parkland Md BMLY BR1 169 F2
Parkland Ms CHST BR7 154 D6
Parkland Rd WDGN N22 55 F1
WFD IG8 45 F6
Parklands BRYLDS KT5 159 G4
BUSH WD23 * 22 C5
HGT N6 54 B6
Parklands Cl GNTH/NBYPK IG2 60 C6
MORT/ESHN SW14 125 K4
Parklands Dr FNCH N3 52 C2
Parklands Pde HEST TW5 * 122 C1
Parklands Rd
STRHM/NOR SW16 148 B4
Parklands Wy WPK KT4 173 G1
Park La CAR SM5 176 A3
CHDH RM6 61 K5
CHEAM SM3 174 C5
CROY/NA CR0 177 K2
EMPK RM11 63 J6
HCH RM12 81 K5
HEST TW5 101 K6
MYFR/PICC W1J 16 B1
OXSTW W1C 9 M6
RCH/KEW TW9 124 E3
RYLN/HDSTN HA2 66 B2
SRTFD E15 * 76 A7
STAN HA7 35 G2
TEDD TW11 143 F5
TOTM N17 42 B6
UED N18 42 B2
WBLY HA9 68 B3
YEAD UB4 82 C4
Park Lane Cl TOTM N17 42 C6
Parklea Cl CDALE/KGS NW9 37 G7
Parkleigh Rd WIM/MER SW19 162 A1
Parkleys RCHPK/HAM TW10 143 K3
Parkleys Pde
RCHPK/HAM TW10 * 143 K3
Parklodge Av WDR/YW UB7 100 C1
Park Md BFN/LL DA15 136 B4
Parkmead PUT/ROE SW15 126 E5
Park Md RYLN/HDSTN HA2 66 B2
Parkmead Gdns MLHL NW7 37 H5
Park Ms CEND/HSY/T N8 54 E5
GNWCH SE10 113 J4
NKENS W10 88 C1
RAIN RM13 81 J5
STWL/WRAY TW19 120 C6
Park Pde ACT W3 * 105 H2
HYS/HAR UB3 * 82 C5
WLSDN NW10 87 H1
Park Piazza LEW SE13 133 G5
Park Pl ACT W3 105 H3
BMLY BR1 * 153 F7
EA W5 85 K7
HPTN TW12 142 C5
IS N1 7 H3
POP/IOD E14 93 J7
WBLY HA9 68 B3
WHALL SW1A 10 E9
Park Place Vls BAY/PAD W2 8 F2
Park Ridings CEND/HSY/T N8 55 G2
Park Ri KTN/HRWW/WS HA3 34 E7
Park Rise Rd FSTH SE23 132 B7
Park Rd ALP/SUD HA0 68 A5
BAR EN5 26 D3
BECK BR3 151 H6
BMLY BR1 153 F7
BRYLDS KT5 159 G5
BUSH WD23 22 A5
CDALE/KGS NW9 51 F6
CEND/HSY/T N8 54 D4
CHEAM SM3 174 C5
CHST BR7 154 B5
CHSWK W4 106 A5
DART DA1 139 K6
E/WMO/HCT KT8 157 H3
EBAR EN4 27 H3
EFNCH N2 53 H2
ESH/CLAY KT10 170 B3
FBAR/BDGN N11 40 D6
FELT TW13 141 H3
HDN NW4 51 K5
HNWL W7 85 F6
HPTN TW12 142 C4
HSLW TW3 123 H4
IL IG1 78 D2
ISLW TW7 104 C7
KUT/HW KT1 143 J7
KUTN/CMB KT2 144 B4
LEY E10 57 J7
MNPK E12 59 F7
NWMAL KT3 160 A3
PLSTW E13 77 G7
RCHPK/HAM TW10 125 G5
SNWD SE25 165 F3
SRTFD E15 76 E7
STHGT/OAK N14 28 D6
STJWD NW8 3 K8
SUN TW16 141 F6
TEDD TW11 143 F5
TWK TW1 124 D5
UED N18 42 B3
WALTH E17 57 H4
WIM/MER SW19 147 H5
WLGTN SM6 176 B4
WLSDN NW10 * 69 G7
YEAD UB4 82 C4
Park Rd East ACT W3 105 K1
Park Rd North ACT W3 105 J1
CHSWK W4 106 A5
Park Rw GNWCH SE10 113 G5
Park Royal Rd WLSDN NW10 86 E2
Parkshot RCH/KEW TW9 124 E3
Park Side BKHH IG9 45 F1
CRICK NW2 69 J2
HYS/HAR UB3 * 82 C6
Parkside BECK BR3 * 166 E1
BKHTH/KID SE3 * 113 J6
CHEAM SM3 174 C5
FNCH N3 39 F7
HPTN TW12 142 D4
MLHL NW7 37 J5
OXHEY WD19 * 21 G5
SCUP DA14 155 H1
WIM/MER SW19 146 B4
Parkside Av BMLY BR1 168 D3
BXLYHN DA7 138 A1
ROM RM1 63 F1
WIM/MER SW19 146 B4
Parkside Cl PGE/AN SE20 150 E6
Parkside Crs BRYLDS KT5 159 K5
HOLWY N7 * 73 G2
Parkside Cross BXLYHN DA7 138 B1
Parkside Dr EDGW HA8 36 C2
WAT WD17 20 C1
Parkside Est HOM E9 * 75 F7
Parkside Gdns EBAR EN4 27 K7
WIM/MER SW19 146 B3
Parkside Pde DART DA1 * 138 C1
Parkside Rd BELV DA17 117 J3
HSLW TW3 123 G4
NTHWD HA6 32 D4
Parkside St BTSEA SW11 109 F7
Parkside Ter UED N18 * 41 K3
Parkside Wy
RYLN/HDSTN HA2 48 B3
Park Sq East CAMTN NW1 4 C9
Park Square Ms CAMTN NW1 10 C1
Park Sq West CAMTN NW1 4 C9
Parkstead Rd PUT/ROE SW15 126 D4
Park Steps BAY/PAD W2 * 9 K6
Parkstone Av UED N18 42 B4
Parkstone Rd PECK SE15 * 131 H1
WALTH E17 58 A2
Park St CROY/NA CR0 177 J2
MYFR/PKLN W1K 10 A7
STHWK SE1 12 E8
TEDD TW11 142 E5
Park Ter CAR SM5 * 175 J2
WPK KT4 160 D7
The Park CAR SM5 175 K4
EA W5 85 K7
GLDGN NW11 53 F7
HGT N6 54 A6
SCUP DA14 155 F4
Parkthorne Cl
RYLN/HDSTN HA2 * 48 B5
Parkthorne Dr
RYLN/HDSTN HA2 48 A5
Parkthorne Rd BAL SW12 129 J6
Park Vw ACT W3 86 E4
NWMAL KT3 160 C2
PIN HA5 48 A1
WBLY HA9 68 D4
WCHMH N21 29 F6
Park View Cl CAR SM5 175 K6
Park View Ct
NFNCH/WDSPK N12 * 39 J3
Park View Crs
FBAR/BDGN N11 40 B3
Parkview Crs WPK KT4 161 F7
Park View Dr MTCM CR4 162 C1
Park View Est HBRY N5 * 73 J3
Parkview Gdns CLAY IG5 59 K3
Park View Gdns HDN NW4 52 A4
WDGN N22 * 41 G7
Parkview Ms RAIN RM13 99 K4
Park View Rd EA W5 86 A4
ELTH/MOT SE9 135 G7
FNCH N3 39 F7
PIN HA5 33 F5
STHL UB1 84 A7
TOTM N17 56 C2
WELL DA16 136 D2
CRICK NW2 69 H3
Parkview Rd CROY/NA CR0 165 H7
Park Village East CAMTN NW1 4 C5
Park Village West
CAMTN NW1 4 C5
Park Vls TOOT SW17 * 147 J4
Parkville Rd FUL/PGN SW6 107 J6
Park Vis GNWCH SE10 113 G5
Park Vista Apartments
CAN/RD E16 94 D2
Park Wk WBPTN SW10 14 F9
Parkwat Crs SRTFD E15 76 B4
Park Wy E/WMO/HCT KT8 157 G2
EBED/NFELT TW14 122 A6
EDGW HA8 36 D7
ENC/FH EN2 29 G1
GLDGN NW11 52 D5
RSLP HA4 46 E7
TRDG/WHET N20 39 K3
Parkway CAMTN NW1 4 C4
CROY/NA CR0 180 A7
ERITHM DA18 117 F2
GDMY/SEVK IG3 79 F2
GPK RM2 63 H1
RAIN RM13 99 H3
RYNPK SW20 161 G3
STHGT/OAK N14 40 E1
WFD IG8 45 G4
The Parkway HEST TW5 101 K5
NTHLT UB5 83 H3
NWDGN UB2 102 A2
YEAD UB4 83 G6
Park West Pl BAY/PAD W2 9 K4
Parkwood BECK BR3 151 J6
Parkwood Av ESH/CLAY KT10 157 H7
Parkwood Ms HGT N6 54 B5
Parkwood Rd BXLY DA5 137 G6
ISLW TW7 104 A7
WIM/MER SW19 146 D4
Parliament Ct WCHPL E1 * 13 K3
Parliament Hl HAMP NW3 71 J3
Parliament Hill Flds
KTTN NW5 * 72 A2
Parliament Ms
MORT/ESHN SW14 125 K1
Parliament Sq WEST SW1P 17 J2
Parliament St WHALL SW1A 17 J1
Parma Crs BTSEA SW11 128 E3
Parmiter St BETH E2 92 D1
Parnell Cl EDGW HA8 36 D3
SHB W12 106 E2
Parnell Rd BOW E3 75 H7
Parnell Wy
KTN/HRWW/WS HA3 35 H7
Parnham Cl BMLY BR1 169 G2
Parnham St POP/IOD E14 * 93 G5
Parolles Rd ARCH N19 54 C7
Paroma Rd BELV DA17 117 H2
Parr Av EW KT17 173 K7
Parr Cl ED N9 42 D3
Parr Rd EHAM E6 77 H7
STAN HA7 35 K7
Parrs Cl SAND/SEL CR2 177 K7
Parr's Pl HPTN TW12 142 A6
Parr St IS N1 7 G5
Parry Av EHAM E6 95 K5
Parry Cl EW KT17 173 J6
Parry Pl WOOL/PLUM SE18 115 G3
Parry Rd NKENS W10 88 C2
SNWD SE25 165 F2
Parry St VX/NE SW8 17 K9
Parsifal Rd KIL/WHAMP NW6 70 E4
Parsloes Av DAGW RM9 80 A4
Parsonage Cl HYS/HAR UB3 82 D5
Parsonage Gdns ENC/FH EN2 29 J1
Parsonage La ENC/FH EN2 29 K1
Parsonage Manorway
BELV DA17 117 H5
Parsonage St POP/IOD E14 113 F3
Parsons Crs EDGW HA8 36 C2
Parsons Gn FUL/PGN SW6 107 K7
Parsons Green La
FUL/PGN SW6 107 K7
Parsons Gv EDGW HA8 36 C2
Parsons Md E/WMO/HCT KT8 157 H2
Parson's Md CROY/NA CR0 164 C7
Parsons Rd PLSTW E13 95 G1
Parson St HDN NW4 52 A2
Parthenia Rd FUL/PGN SW6 107 K7
Partingdale La MLHL NW7 38 B4
Partington Cl ARCH N19 54 D7
Partridge Cl BAR EN5 26 A5
BUSH WD23 * 22 C7
CAN/RD E16 95 H4
STAN HA7 36 A3
Partridge Gn ELTH/MOT SE9 154 A2
Partridge Rd HPTN TW12 141 K5
SCUP DA14 154 E2
Partridge Sq EHAM E6 95 J4
Partridge Wy WDGN N22 40 E7
Pasadena Cl HYS/HAR UB3 101 K1
Pascal St VX/NE SW8 109 J6
Pascoe Rd LEW SE13 133 G4
Pasley Cl WALW SE17 18 D8
Pasquier Rd WALTH E17 57 G2
Passey Pl ELTH/MOT SE9 134 E5
Passfield Dr POP/IOD E14 93 K4
Passmore Gdns
FBAR/BDGN N11 40 D5
Passmore St BGVA SW1W 16 A6
Pasteur Cl CDALE/KGS NW9 51 G1
Pasteur Gdns UED N18 41 J4
Paston Cl WLGTN SM6 176 C2
Paston Crs LEE/GVPK SE12 134 A6
Pastor St LBTH SE11 18 D5
Pasture Cl ALP/SUD HA0 67 H2
BUSH WD23 22 C6
Pasture Rd ALP/SUD HA0 67 H1
CAT SE6 133 H7
DAGW RM9 80 B4
Pastures Pth WAN E11 58 C7
The Pastures OXHEY WD19 21 F6
TRDG/WHET N20 26 D7
Patcham Ter VX/NE SW8 109 G7
Patching Wy YEAD UB4 83 J4
Paternoster Sq STP EC4M 12 D5
Pater St KENS W8 14 A4
Pates Manor Dr
EBED/NFELT TW14 121 G6
Pathfield Rd
STRHM/NOR SW16 148 D5
The Path WIM/MER SW19 147 F7
The Pathway OXHEY WD19 21 H7
Patience Rd BTSEA SW11 128 D1
Patio Cl CLAP SW4 129 J5
Patmore St VX/NE SW8 109 H7
Patmos Rd BRXN/ST SW9 110 C6
Paton Cl BOW E3 93 J2
Patricia Ct WELL DA16 116 C6
Patricia Vls TOTM N17 * 42 D7
Patrick Rd PLSTW E13 95 G2
Patriot Sq BETH E2 92 D1
Patrol Pl CAT SE6 132 E5
Patshull Pl KTTN NW5 72 C5
Patshull Rd KTTN NW5 72 C5
Pattenden Rd CAT SE6 132 C7
Patten Rd WAND/EARL SW18 128 D6
Patterdale Cl BMLY BR1 152 C5
Patterdale Rd PECK SE15 111 K6
Patterson Rd NRWD SE19 150 B5
Pattina Wk BERM/RHTH SE16 93 G7
Pattison Rd CRICK NW2 70 E2
Paul Cl SRTFD E15 76 C6
Paulet Rd CMBW SE5 130 C1
Paulet Wy WLSDN NW10 * 69 G6
Paul Gdns CROY/NA CR0 178 B1
Paulhan Rd
KTN/HRWW/WS HA3 49 K3
Paulin Dr WCHMH N21 29 G6
Pauline Crs WHTN TW2 123 H7
Paul Julius Cl POP/IOD E14 94 B6
Paul Robeson Cl EHAM E6 96 A2
Paul St SDTCH EC2A 7 J9
SRTFD E15 76 C7
Paultons Sq CHEL SW3 15 H9
Paultons St CHEL SW3 108 C5
Pauntley St ARCH N19 54 C7
Paveley Dr BTSEA SW11 108 D6
Paveley St STJWD NW8 3 K8
Pavement Sq CROY/NA CR0 165 H7
The Pavement CLAP SW4 129 H3
EA W5 * 105 F2
TEDD TW11 * 143 H6
WAN E11 * 58 A7
WIM/MER SW19 * 146 D5
WNWD SE27 * 149 J3
Pavet Cl DAGE RM10 80 D5
Pavilion Ldg
RYLN/HDSTN HA2 * 48 D7
Pavilion Ms FNCH N3 52 E1
Pavilion Pde SHB W12 * 88 A5
Pavilion Rd IL IG1 59 K6
KTBR SW1X 15 M2
Pavilion St KTBR SW1X 15 M4
The Pavilion VX/NE SW8 * 109 J6
Pavilion Wy EDGW HA8 36 E6
RSLP HA4 65 G1
Pavillion Sq TOOT SW17 147 J2
Pavillion Ter SHB W12 * 88 A5
Pawleyne Cl PGE/AN SE20 150 E6
Pawsey Cl PLSTW E13 76 E7
Pawson's Rd THHTH CR7 164 D5
Paxford Rd ALP/SUD HA0 67 H1
Paxton Cl RCH/KEW TW9 125 G1
WOT/HER KT12 156 B6
Paxton Pl WNWD SE27 150 A3
Paxton Rd BMLY BR1 152 E6
CHSWK W4 106 B5
FSTH SE23 151 G2
TOTM N17 42 B6
Paxton Ter PIM SW1V 16 D9
Payne Cl BARK IG11 78 E6
Paynell Ct BKHTH/KID SE3 133 H2
Payne Rd BOW E3 93 K1
Paynesfield Av
MORT/ESHN SW14 126 A2
Paynesfield Rd BUSH WD23 23 F6
Payne St DEPT SE8 112 C5
Paynes Wk HMSMTH W6 107 H5
Payzes Gdns WFD IG8 * 44 D5
Peabody Av PIM SW1V 16 C7
Peabody Cl CROY/NA CR0 165 K7
GNWCH SE10 * 112 E7
PIM SW1V 16 D8
Peabody Cots HNHL SE24 * 130 D6
Peabody Est BTSEA SW11 * 128 D3
CLKNW EC1R * 12 B1
CMBW SE5 * 110 E7
HMSMTH W6 * 107 F4
HNHL SE24 130 C6
NKENS W10 * 88 A4
STHWK SE1 * 12 B8
STLK EC1Y * 12 F1
TOTM N17 * 42 A7
Peabody Hl DUL SE21 130 C7
Peabody Sq IS N1 * 6 E3
Peabody Ter CLKNW EC1R * 12 B1
Peace Cl GFD/PVL UB6 66 D7
SNWD SE25 165 F3

STHGT/OAK N14 .... 28 B4
Peace Dr WAT WD17 .... 20 E2
Peace Gv WBLY HA9 .... 68 D2
Peace St WOOL/PLUM SE18 .... 115 H5
Peaches CI BELMT SM2 .... 174 C6
Peach Gv WAN E11 .... 76 B3
Peach Rd FELT TW13 .... 121 K7
  NKENS W10 .... 88 B2
Peachum Rd BKHTH/KID SE3 .... 113 J6
Peachy CI EDGW HA8 .... 36 C5
Peacock Av
  EBED/NFELT TW14 .... 121 G7
Peacock CI BCTR RM8 .... 61 J7
  CHING E4 .... 43 H4
  MLHL NW7 .... 38 C4
Peacock St WALW SE17 .... 18 D6
Peacock Yd WALW SE17 .... 18 D6
Peaketon Av REDBR IG4 .... 59 H4
Peak Hill SYD SE26 .... 150 E3
Peak Hill Av SYD SE26 .... 150 E3
Peak Hill Gdns SYD SE26 * 150 E3
The Peak SYD SE26 .... 150 E2
Peal Gdns WEA W13 .... 85 G2
Peall Rd CROY/NA CR0 .... 164 A5
Pearce CI MTCM CR4 .... 163 F1
Pearcefield Av FSTH SE23 .... 131 K3
Pearcroft Rd CDALE/KGS NW9 .... 51 J3
  NWCR SE14 .... 112 B6
Pearl CI CRICK NW2 .... 52 B6
  EHAM E6 .... 96 A5
Pearl Rd WALTH E17 .... 57 J2
Pearl St WAP E1W 92 D7
Pearman St STHWK SE1 .... 18 B3
Pear PI STHWK SE1 * 18 A1
Pear Rd WAN E11 .... 76 B2
Pearscroft Ct FUL/PGN SW6 .... 108 A7
Pearscroft Rd FUL/PGN SW6 .... 128 A1
Pearse St PECK SE15 .... 111 F5
Pearson CI BAR EN5 .... 27 F2
Pearson's NWCR SE14 .... 112 D7
Pearson's Rd NWCR SE14 * 112 D7
Pearson St BETH E2 .... 7 L5
Pearson Wy MTCM CR4 .... 148 A7
Pears Rd HSLW TW3 .... 123 H2
Peartree Av TOOT SW17 .... 147 K5
Peartree CI MTCM CR4 .... 162 D1
Pear Tree CI CHSGTN KT9 .... 172 *
  ERITH DA8 .... 118 A4
  MTCM CR4 .... 162 D1
Peartree Ct HAYES BR2 .... 168 C4
Pear Tree Ct CLKNW EC1R 12 B1
Peartree Gdns BCTR RM8 .... 79 H4
  ROMW/RG RM7 .... 62 D2
Peartree La WAP E1W * 92 E6
Pear Tree Rd ASHF TW15 .... 140 A4
Peartree Rd EN EN1 .... 30 A2
Pear Tree St FSBYE EC1V 6 D9
Peartree Wy GNWCH SE10 .... 113 K3
Pearwood Cots STAN HA7 * 35 J1
Peary PI BETH E2 .... 92 E2
Pease CI HCH RM12 .... 81 K6
Peasmead Ter CHING E4 * 44 A3
Peatfield CI BFN/LL DA15 .... 154 E2
Pebworth Rd HRW HA1 .... 67 G1
Peckarmans Wd SYD SE26 .... 150 C2
Peckford PI BRXN/ST SW9 .... 130 B1
Peckham High St PECK SE15 .... 111 H7
Peckham Hill St PECK SE15 .... 111 H7
Peckham Park Rd PECK SE15 .... 111 H6
Peckham Rye EDUL SE22 .... 131 H3
Pecks Yd WCHPL E1 * 13 L2
Peckwater St KTTN NW5 .... 72 C4
Pedlars Wk HOLWY N7 .... 72 E4
Pedley Rd BCTR RM8 .... 61 J7
Pedley St WCHPL E1 .... 92 C3
Pedro St CLPT E5 .... 75 F2
Peek Crs WIM/MER SW19 .... 146 B4
Peel CI CHING E4 .... 43 K1
  ED N9 .... 42 C2
  CLAY IG5 .... 59 J2
Peel Dr CDALE/KGS NW9 .... 51 J3
  CLAY IG5 .... 59 J2
Peel Gv BETH E2 .... 92 E1
Peel Pas KENS W8 * 8 A8
Peel PI CLAY IG5 .... 59 J2
Peel Prec KIL/WHAMP NW6 .... 88 D1
Peel Rd ALP/SUD HA0 .... 67 J2
  KTN/HRWW/WS HA3 .... 49 F2
  SWFD E18 .... 44 D7
Peel St KENS W8 .... 8 A9
Peerglow Est PEND EN3 * 30 E4
Peerless St FSBYE EC1V 7 G8
Pegamoid Rd UED N18 .... 42 E2
Pegasus CI STNW/STAM N16 * 73 K3
Pegasus PI BTFD TW8 .... 105 G4
Pegasus PI FUL/PGN SW6 .... 107 K7
  LBTH SE11 .... 18 B9
Pegasus Rd CROY/NA CR0 .... 177 G5
Pegasus Wy FBAR/BDGN N11 .... 40 B5
Pegg Rd HEST TW5 .... 102 C6
Pegley Gdns LEE/GVPK SE12 .... 152 E1
Pegwell St WOOL/PLUM SE18 .... 115 K6
Pekin St POP/IOD E14 .... 93 J5
Peldon Wk IS N1 * 6 C3
Pelham Av BARK IG11 .... 79 F7
Pelham CI CMBW SE5 .... 131 F2
Pelham Cots BXLY DA5 .... 137 J2
Pelham PI SKENS SW7 .... 15 J5
Pelham Rd BXLYHN DA7 .... 137 G2
  IL IG1 .... 78 D1
  PGE/AN SE20 .... 165 K1
  SEVS/STOTM N15 .... 56 B3
  SWFD E18 .... 59 F2
  WDGN N22 .... 55 G1
  WIM/MER SW19 .... 146 D6
Pelhams CI ESH/CLAY KT10 .... 170 A3
Pelham St SKENS SW7 .... 15 H5
Pelhams Wk ESH/CLAY KT10 .... 170 A2
Pelier St WALW SE17 .... 18 F9
Pelinore Rd CAT SE6 .... 152 C1
Pellant Rd FUL/PGN SW6 .... 107 H6
Pellatt Gv WDGN N22 .... 41 G7
Pellatt Rd EDUL SE22 .... 131 G4
  WBLY HA9 .... 68 A1
Pellerin Rd STNW/STAM N16 .... 74 A4
Pellings CI HAYES BR2 .... 167 H1
Pelling St POP/IOD E14 .... 93 H5
Pellipar CI PLMGR N13 .... 41 G2
Pellipar Rd WOOL/PLUM SE18 .... 114 D4
Pellow CI BAR EN5 .... 26 D5
Pelly Rd PLSTW E13 .... 94 E1
  SRTFD E15 .... 76 C4
Pelter St BETH E2 .... 7 L7
Pelton Rd GNWCH SE10 .... 113 H4
Pembar Av WALTH E17 * 57 G2

Pemberley Cha
  HOR/WEW KT19 .... 172 D4
Pemberley CI HOR/WEW KT19 .... 172 D4
Pember Rd WLSDN NW10 .... 88 B2
Pemberton CI
  STWL/WRAY TW19 .... 120 B7
Pemberton Gdns ARCH N19 .... 72 C2
  CHDH RM6 .... 62 A4
Pemberton PI ESH/CLAY KT10 .... 170 C2
  HACK E8 .... 74 D6
Pemberton Rd
  E/WMO/HCT KT8 .... 157 H3
  FSBYPK N4 .... 55 H4
Pemberton Rw
  FLST/FETLN EC4A 12 A4
Pemberton Ter ARCH N19 .... 72 C2
Pembridge Av WHTN TW2 .... 122 J1
Pembridge Crs NTGHL W11 .... 88 D6
Pembridge Gdns BAY/PAD W2 .... 8 A7
Pembridge Ms NTGHL W11 .... 8 A6
Pembridge PI NTGHL W11 .... 8 A7
Pembridge Rd NTGHL W11 .... 8 A7
Pembridge Sq BAY/PAD W2 .... 8 A7
Pembridge Vls BAY/PAD W2 .... 8 A6
Pembroke Av BRYLDS KT5 .... 159 J4
  IS N1 .... 5 K3
  KTN/HRWW/WS HA3 .... 49 G3
  PIN HA5 .... 47 H7
Pembroke CI ERITH DA8 .... 117 K3
  KTBR SW1X 16 D2
Pembroke Gdns DAGE RM10 .... 80 D2
  KENS W8 .... 107 J2
Pembroke Gardens CI
  KENS W8 .... 107 J2
Pembroke Ms KENS W8 * 14 A4
  MUSWH N10 .... 40 A7
Pembroke Pde ERITH DA8 * 117 K3
Pembroke Pde EDGW HA8 .... 36 C6
Pembroke Rd BMLY BR1 .... 168 A1
  CEND/HSY/T N8 .... 54 E3
  EHAM E6 .... 95 K4
  ERITH DA8 .... 117 K4
  GDMY/SEVK IG3 .... 61 F7
  GFD/PVL UB6 .... 84 B3
  MTCM CR4 .... 163 F1
  MUSWH N10 .... 40 A7
  NTHWD HA6 .... 32 A2
  PLMGR N13 .... 41 J2
  RSLP HA4 .... 46 C7
  SEVS/STOTM N15 .... 56 B4
  SNWD SE25 .... 165 F3
  WALTH E17 .... 57 K4
  WBLY HA9 .... 67 K2
Pembroke Sq KENS W8 .... 14 A3
Pembroke St IS N1 .... 5 K2
Pembroke Ter STJWD NW8 * 3 H2
Pembroke Vls KENS W8 .... 14 A4
Pembroke Wk KENS W8 .... 14 A4
Pembry Ms BTSEA SW11 * 128 C3
Pembury Av WPK KT4 .... 160 D6
Pembury CI CLPT E5 * 74 D4
  HAYES BR2 .... 167 J6
Pembury Crs HYS/HAR UB3 .... 101 G5
Pembury PI BXLYHN DA7 .... 117 F6
  CLPT E5 .... 74 D4
  SNWD SE25 .... 165 H3
  TOTM N17 .... 42 B7
Pemdevon Rd CROY/NA CR0 .... 164 B6
Pemell CI WCHPL E1 .... 92 E3
Pemerich CI HYS/HAR UB3 * 101 J4
Pempath PI WBLY HA9 .... 67 K1
Penally PI IS N1 .... 7 H3
Penang St WAP E1W 92 D7
Penard Rd NWDGN UB2 .... 103 F2
Penarth St PECK SE15 .... 111 K5
Penates ESH/CLAY KT10 .... 170 C4
Penberth Rd CAT SE6 .... 133 F7
Penbury Rd NWDGN UB2 .... 102 E4
Pencombe Ms NTGHL W11 .... 88 D6
Pencraig Wy PECK SE15 .... 111 J5
Pencroft Dr DART DA1 .... 139 G6
Pendall CI EBAR EN4 .... 27 J3
Penda Rd ERITH DA8 .... 117 J6
Pendarves Rd RYNPK SW20 .... 146 A1
Penda's Md HOM E9 .... 75 G3
Pendell Av HYS/HAR UB3 .... 101 J6
Pendennis Rd
  STRHM/NOR SW16 .... 148 E3
  TOTM N17 .... 55 K5
Penderel Rd HSLW TW3 .... 123 F4
Penderry Ri CAT SE6 .... 152 B1
Penderyn Wy HOLWY N7 .... 72 D3
Pendle Rd STRHM/NOR SW16 .... 148 B5
Pendlestone Rd WALTH E17 .... 57 K4
Pendlewood CI EA W5 .... 85 J4
Pendolino Wy ALP/SUD HA0 .... 68 C6
Pendragon Rd BMLY BR1 .... 152 E2
Pendrell Rd NWCR SE14 .... 132 B2
Pendrell St WOOL/PLUM SE18 .... 115 J5
Pendula Dr YEAD UB4 .... 83 H4
Pendulum Ms HACK E8 .... 74 B4
Penerley Rd CAT SE6 .... 132 E7
  RAIN RM13 .... 99 K4
Penfold CI CROY/NA CR0 .... 177 G2
Penfold La BXLY DA5 .... 136 E7
Penfold PI BAY/PAD W2 .... 9 J2
Penfold Rd ED N9 .... 31 F7
Penfold St STJWD NW8 .... 9 H1
Penford Gdns ELTH/MOT SE9 .... 134 C2
Penford St CMBW SE5 .... 130 C1
Pengarth Rd BXLY DA5 .... 136 E4
Penge La PGE/AN SE20 .... 150 E6
Penge Rd PLSTW E13 .... 77 G6
  SNWD SE25 .... 165 H2
Penhall Rd CHARL SE7 .... 114 C3
Penhill Rd BXLY DA5 .... 136 D6
Penifather La GFD/PVL UB6 .... 84 D2
Peninsular CI
  EBED/NFELT TW14 .... 121 G5
Peninsular Park Rd
  CHARL SE7 .... 113 K4
Penistone Rd
  STRHM/NOR SW16 .... 148 E6
Penketh Dr HRW HA1 .... 66 D1
Penmon Rd ABYW SE2 .... 116 B2
Pennack Rd PECK SE15 .... 111 G5
Pennant Ms KENS W8 .... 14 C5
Pennant Ter WALTH E17 .... 57 H1
Pennard Rd SHB W12 .... 107 F1
The Pennards SUN TW16 .... 156 B1
Penn CI GFD/PVL UB6 .... 84 B1
  KTN/HRWW/WS HA3 .... 49 G3
Penner CI WIM/MER SW19 .... 146 C1
Penners Gdns SURB KT6 .... 159 F6
Pennethorne CI HOM E9 .... 74 E7
Pennethorne Rd PECK SE15 .... 111 J6

Penney CI DART DA1 .... 139 G6
Penn Gdns CHST BR7 .... 169 G1
Pennine Dr CRICK NW2 .... 70 B1
Pennine La CRICK NW2 .... 70 C1
Pennine Pde CRICK NW2 * 70 C1
Pennine Wy BXLYHN DA7 .... 118 B7
  HYS/HAR UB3 .... 101 G6
Pennington Dr WCHMH N21 .... 28 E4
Pennington St WAP E1W 92 D6
Pennington Wy
  LEE/GVPK SE12 .... 153 F1
Penniston CI TOTM N17 .... 55 J1
Penniwell CI EDGW HA8 .... 36 B3
Penn La BXLY DA5 .... 136 E5
Penn Rd HOLWY N7 .... 72 E4
Penn St IS N1 .... 7 H4
Penny CI RAIN RM13 .... 99 J2
Pennycroft CROY/NA CR0 .... 179 G6
Pennyfields POP/IOD E14 .... 93 J6
Penny Ms WAND/EARL SW18 .... 127 K5
Pennymoor Wk MV/WKIL W9 .... 88 D3
Pennyroyal Av EHAM E6 .... 96 A5
Penpoll Rd HACK E8 .... 74 D5
Penpool La WELL DA16 .... 136 C2
Penrhyn Av WALTH E17 .... 43 J7
Penrhyn Crs
  MORT/ESHN SW14 .... 125 K3
  WALTH E17 .... 43 J7
Penrhyn Gdns KUT/HW KT1 .... 158 E3
Penrhyn Gv WALTH E17 .... 43 J7
Penrhyn Rd KUT/HW KT1 .... 159 F2
Penrith CI BECK BR3 .... 151 K7
  PUT/ROE SW15 .... 127 H4
Penrith Crs HCH RM12 .... 81 J4
Penrith PI WNWD SE27 .... 149 H1
Penrith Rd NWMAL KT3 .... 160 A3
  SEVS/STOTM N15 .... 55 K4
  THHTH CR7 .... 164 D1
Penrith St STRHM/NOR SW16 .... 148 C5
Penrose Av OXHEY WD19 .... 33 J1
Penrose Gv WALW SE17 .... 18 E8
Penrose Ho WALW SE17 .... 18 E8
Penryn St CAMTN NW1 .... 5 G5
Pensbury PI VX/NE SW8 .... 129 H1
Pensbury St VX/NE SW8 .... 129 H1
Penscroft Gdns BORE WD6 .... 25 F3
Pensford Av RCH/KEW TW9 .... 125 H1
Penshurst Av BFN/LL DA15 .... 136 B5
Penshurst Gdns EDGW HA8 .... 36 D5
Penshurst Gn HAYES BR2 .... 167 J4
Penshurst Rd BXLYHN DA7 .... 117 G7
  HOM E9 .... 75 F6
  THHTH CR7 .... 164 C4
  TOTM N17 .... 42 B6
Penshurst Wy BELMT SM2 .... 174 E6
Pensilver CI EBAR EN4 * 27 J3
Penstemon CI FNCH N3 .... 38 E5
Penta Ct BORE WD6 * 24 C1
Pentelow Gdns
  EBED/NFELT TW14 .... 121 K5
Pentire Rd WALTH E17 .... 44 B7
Pentland Av EDGW HA8 .... 36 D1
Pentland CI EDGW HA8 .... 42 E1
  GLDGN NW11 .... 70 C1
Pentland PI NTHLT UB5 .... 65 J7
Pentland Rd BUSH WD23 .... 22 C5
  KIL/WHAMP NW6 .... 2 A1
Pentlands CI MTCM CR4 .... 163 G2
Pentland St WAND/EARL SW18 .... 128 B5
Pentlow St PUT/ROE SW15 .... 127 F1
Pentney Rd BAL SW12 .... 129 H7
  RYNPK SW20 .... 146 C2
Penton Gv IS N1 .... 6 A6
Penton PI WALW SE17 .... 18 D6
Penton Ri IS N1 .... 5 M7
Penton St IS N1 .... 6 A5
Pentonville Rd IS N1 .... 5 L6
Pentridge St PECK SE15 .... 111 G6
Pentyre Av UED N18 .... 41 K4
Penwerris Av ISLW TW7 .... 103 H6
Penwith Rd WAND/EARL SW18 .... 147 F1
Penwortham Rd
  STRHM/NOR SW16 .... 148 B5
Penylan PI EDGW HA8 .... 36 C6
Penywern Rd ECT SW5 .... 14 B7
Penzance PI NTGHL W11 .... 88 C7
Penzance St NTGHL W11 .... 88 C7
Peony Gdns SHB W12 .... 87 J6
Pepler Ms CMBW SE5 .... 19 L8
Peploe Rd KIL/WHAMP NW6 .... 88 B1
Pepper CI EHAM E6 .... 95 K4
Peppercorn CI THHTH CR7 .... 164 E1
Peppermead Sq LEW SE13 .... 132 D4
Peppermint CI CROY/NA CR0 .... 163 K6
Peppermint PI WAN E11 .... 76 C2
Pepper St POP/IOD E14 .... 112 E2
  STHWK SE1 .... 18 E1
Peppie CI STNW/STAM N16 .... 74 A1
Pepys Crs BAR EN5 .... 26 A4
  CAN/RD E16 .... 94 E7
Pepys Est DEPT SE8 .... 112 B3
Pepys Park Est DEPT SE8 .... 112 C3
Pepys Rd NWCR SE14 .... 132 A1
  RYNPK SW20 .... 161 F1
Pepys St TWRH EC3N 13 K6
Perceval Av HAMP NW3 .... 71 J4
Percheron Rd BORE WD6 .... 25 F5
Perch St HACK E8 .... 74 B3
Percival Ct TOTM N17 .... 42 B6
Percival Gdns CHDH RM6 .... 61 J5
Percival Rd EN EN1 .... 30 B3
  FELT TW13 .... 140 D1
  MORT/ESHN SW14 .... 125 K3
Percival St FSBYE EC1V 6 C9
Percival Wy HOR/WEW KT19 .... 172 E3
Percy Bryant Rd SUN TW16 .... 140 C6
Percy Bush Rd WDR/YW UB7 .... 100 C3
Percy Gdns PEND EN3 .... 31 F4
  WPK KT4 .... 160 B1
  YEAD UB4 .... 82 C2
Percy Ms FITZ W1T 11 G3
Percy Rd BXLYHN DA7 .... 137 F1
  CAN/RD E16 .... 94 C4
  GDMY/SEVK IG3 .... 79 F2
  HPTN TW12 .... 142 A6
  ISLW TW7 .... 124 B3
  MTCM CR4 .... 163 F6
  NFNCH/WDSPK N12 .... 39 G4
  PGE/AN SE20 .... 151 F7
  ROMW/RG RM7 .... 62 D2
  SHB W12 .... 106 D1
  SNWD SE25 .... 165 H4
  WAN E11 .... 58 E6
  WATW WD18 .... 21 F3
  WCHMH N21 .... 29 J6
  WHTN TW2 .... 123 G7
Percy St FITZ W1T 11 G3
Percy Ter BMLY BR1 * 169 G1
Percy Wy WHTN TW2 .... 123 H7

Peregrine CI WLSDN NW10 .... 69 F4
Peregrine Ct WELL DA16 .... 116 A7
Peregrine Gdns CROY/NA CR0 .... 179 G1
Peregrine Rd TOTM N17 .... 41 G7
Peregrine Wy
  WIM/MER SW19 .... 146 A6
Perendale Dr SHPTN TW17 .... 140 A7
Perham Rd WKENS W14 .... 107 H4
Peridot St EHAM E6 .... 95 J4
Perifield DUL SE21 .... 130 D7
Perimeade Rd GFD/PVL UB6 .... 85 J2
Periton Rd ELTH/MOT SE9 .... 134 C3
Perivale Gdns WEA W13 .... 85 H3
Perivale La GFD/PVL UB6 .... 85 G2
Perivale Village
  GFD/PVL UB6 * 85 J2
Periwood Crs GFD/PVL UB6 .... 67 G2
Perkin CI ALP/SUD HA0 .... 67 H4
  HSLW TW3 .... 123 G3
Perkin's Rents WEST SW1P 17 G3
Perkins Rd BARK/HLT IG6 .... 60 D4
Perkins Sq STHWK SE1 .... 12 F8
Perks CI BKHTH/KID SE3 .... 133 H1
Perpins Rd ELTH/MOT SE9 .... 135 K5
Perran Rd BRXS/STRHM SW2 .... 149 H1
Perrers Rd HMSMTH W6 .... 106 E2
Perrin Rd ALP/SUD HA0 .... 67 G3
Perrin's Ct HAMP NW3 * 71 G3
Perrin's Wk HAMP NW3 .... 71 G3
Perran Ct SEVS/STOTM N15 * 56 A5
Perryfield Wy
  CDALE/KGS NW9 .... 51 H5
  RCHPK/HAM TW10 .... 143 H1
Perry Gdns ED N9 .... 42 A2
Perry Garth NTHLT UB5 .... 65 G1
Perry Gv DART DA1 .... 139 K3
Perry HI CAT SE6 .... 151 H1
Perry How WPK KT4 .... 160 C7
Perry Mnr CHST BR7 .... 154 E5
Perrymans Farm Rd
  GNTH/NBYPK IG2 .... 60 D5
  ENC/FH EN2 .... 22 C5
Perrymead St FUL/PGN SW6 .... 107 K7
Perryn Rd ACT W3 .... 87 F5
  BERM/RHTH SE16 .... 111 J2
Perry Ri FSTH SE23 .... 151 G2
Perry Rd DAGW RM9 .... 98 B4
Perry St CHST BR7 .... 154 E5
  DART DA1 .... 138 B2
Perry V FSTH SE23 .... 150 E1
Persant Rd CAT SE6 .... 152 C2
Perseverance PI
  BRXN/ST SW9 .... 110 B6
Pershore CI GNTH/NBYPK IG2 .... 60 B4
Pershore Gv CAR SM5 .... 162 C5
Pert CI MUSWH N10 .... 40 B6
Perth Av CDALE/KGS NW9 .... 51 F6
  YEAD UB4 .... 83 G3
Perth CI NTHLT UB5 .... 66 A5
  NWMAL KT3 .... 160 A4
Perth Rd BARK IG11 .... 96 E1
  BECK BR3 .... 167 F1
  FSBYPK N4 .... 55 G7
  GNTH/NBYPK IG2 .... 60 B5
  IL IG1 .... 60 C6
  LEY E10 .... 57 G7
  PLSTW E13 .... 95 F1
  WDGN N22 .... 41 H7
Perth Ter GNTH/NBYPK IG2 .... 60 C6
Perwell Av RYLN/HDSTN HA2 .... 47 K7
Petavel Rd TEDD TW11 .... 142 E5
Peter Av WLSDN NW10 .... 69 K6
Peterboat CI GNWCH SE10 .... 113 H3
Peterborough Ms
  FUL/PGN SW6 .... 127 K1
Peterborough Rd CAR SM5 .... 162 D5
  FUL/PGN SW6 .... 127 K1
  HRW HA1 .... 48 E7
  LEY E10 .... 58 A4
Peterborough Vls
  FUL/PGN SW6 .... 108 A7
Petergate BTSEA SW11 .... 128 B3
Peters CI BCTR RM8 .... 61 K7
  STAN HA7 .... 35 K5
  WELL DA16 .... 135 K1
Petersfield CI UED N18 .... 41 J4
Petersfield Ri PUT/ROE SW15 .... 126 E7
Petersfield Rd ACT W3 .... 105 K1
Petersham CI
  RCHPK/HAM TW10 .... 143 K1
  SUT SM1 .... 174 D4
Petersham Gdns SKENS SW7 .... 14 E2
Petersham La SKENS SW7 .... 14 E3
Petersham Ms SKENS SW7 .... 14 E3
Petersham PI SKENS SW7 .... 14 E2
Petersham Rd
  RCHPK/HAM TW10 .... 143 K2
Petersham Ter
  CROY/NA CR0 * 176 E2
Peter's HI BLKFR EC4V 12 E6
Peterstone Rd ABYW SE2 .... 116 C1
Peterstow CI WIM/MER SW19 .... 146 C1
Peter St SOHO/CST W1F 11 G6
Peterwood Wy CROY/NA CR0 .... 177 F1
Petherton Rd HBRY N5 .... 73 J4
Petiver CI HOM E9 * 74 E6
Petley Rd HMSMTH W6 .... 107 F5
Peto PI CAMTN NW1 .... 4 D9
Peto St North CAN/RD E16 .... 94 D6
Petrie CI CRICK NW2 .... 70 C5
Petros Gdns
  KIL/WHAMP NW6 * 71 G5
Petro St South CAN/RD E16 .... 94 D6
Pettacre CI THMD SE28 .... 115 H2
Pett CI EMPK RM11 .... 63 K6
Petticoat La WCHPL E1 .... 13 K3
Petticoat Sq WCHPL E1 .... 13 L4
Petticoat Tower WCHPL E1 * 13 L4
Pettits Bvd ROM RM1 .... 63 G1
Pettits CI ROM RM1 .... 63 G1
Pettits La ROM RM1 .... 63 G2
Pettits PI DAGE RM10 .... 80 C4
Pettits Rd DAGE RM10 .... 80 C4
Pettiward CI PUT/ROE SW15 .... 127 F3
Pettley Gdns ROMW/RG RM7 .... 63 F4
Pettman Crs THMD SE28 .... 115 J3
Pett's Hill NTHLT UB5 .... 66 B4
  RYLN/HDSTN HA2 .... 66 B4
Pett St WOOL/PLUM SE18 .... 114 D3
Petts Wood Rd
  STMC/STPC BR5 .... 169 J4
Petty France WESTW SW1E 16 E3
Petty Wales MON EC3R 13 J7
Petworth Gdns
  HGDN/ICK UB10 .... 64 A7
  RYNPK SW20 .... 160 E2
Petworth Rd BXLYHS DA6 .... 137 H4
  NFNCH/WDSPK N12 .... 39 J4

Petworth St BTSEA SW11 .... 108 D7
Petworth Wy HCH RM12 .... 81 H4
Petyt PI CHEL SW3 * 108 D5
Petyward CHEL SW3 .... 15 K6
Pevensey Av EN EN1 .... 30 A1
  FBAR/BDGN N11 .... 40 E4
Pevensey CI ISLW TW7 .... 103 H7
Pevensey Rd FELT TW13 .... 122 D7
  FSTGT E7 .... 76 E3
  TOOT SW17 .... 147 H3
Peverel EHAM E6 .... 96 A5
Peveret CI FBAR/BDGN N11 * 40 B4
Peveril Dr TEDD TW11 .... 142 D4
Pewsey CI CHING E4 .... 43 J4
Peyton PI GNWCH SE10 .... 113 F6
Pharaoh CI MTCM CR4 .... 162 E6
Pheasant CI CAN/RD E16 .... 95 F5
Phelp St WALW SE17 .... 19 G8
Phelps Wy HYS/HAR UB3 .... 101 J3
Phene St CHEL SW3 .... 15 K9
Philbeach Gdns ECT SW5 .... 14 A7
Philchurch PI WCHPL E1 * 92 C5
Philimore CI
  WOOL/PLUM SE18 .... 115 K4
Philip Av ROMW/RG RM7 .... 63 F7
Philip Gdns CROY/NA CR0 .... 179 H1
Philip La SEVS/STOTM N15 .... 55 K3
Philippa Gdns ELTH/MOT SE9 .... 134 C4
Philip Rd RAIN RM13 .... 99 G2
Philips CI CAR SM5 .... 163 F7
Philip St PLSTW E13 .... 94 E3
Philip Wk PECK SE15 .... 131 H2
Phillimore Gdns
  KENS W8 .... 14 A3
  WLSDN NW10 .... 70 A7
Phillimore Gardens CI
  KENS W8 * 14 A3
Phillimore PI KENS W8 .... 14 A3
Phillimore Wk KENS W8 .... 14 A3
Phillipp St IS N1 .... 7 K4
Phillips CI DART DA1 .... 138 C5
Philpot La FENCHST EC3M 13 J6
Philpot St WCHPL E1 * 92 D5
Phineas Pett Rd
  ELTH/MOT SE9 .... 134 D2
Phipp's Bridge Rd
  WIM/MER SW19 .... 162 B1
Phipps Ms BCVA SW1W 16 C4
Phipp St SDTCH EC2A 7 J9
Phoebeth Rd LEW SE13 .... 132 C4
Phoenix CI HACK E8 * 7 L1
  NTHWD HA6 .... 32 D3
  WALTH E17 .... 57 H1
  WWKM BR4 .... 180 B1
Phoenix Ct BTFD TW8 .... 105 F4
  POP/IOD E14 .... 112 D3
Phoenix Dr HAYES BR2 .... 181 H2
Phoenix Pk BTFD TW8 * 104 E4
Phoenix PI DART DA1 .... 139 G6
  FSBYW WC1X 5 M9
Phoenix Rd CAMTN NW1 .... 5 G7
  PGE/AN SE20 .... 150 E5
Phoenix St LSO/SEVD WC2H 11 H5
Phoenix Wy HEST TW5 .... 102 C5
Phoenix Wharf Rd
  STHWK SE1 .... 19 M2
Phyllis Av NWMAL KT3 .... 160 E4
Picardy Manorway
  BELV DA17 .... 117 J2
Picardy Rd BELV DA17 .... 117 H4
Picardy St BELV DA17 .... 117 H2
Piccadilly MYFR/PICC W1J 10 E8
Piccadilly Ar MYFR/PICC W1J * 10 E8
Piccadilly Circ REGST W1B 10 F7
Pickard CI STHGT/OAK N14 .... 28 D7
Pickard St FSBYE EC1V 6 D7
Pickering Av EHAM E6 .... 96 A1
Pickering Gdns CROY/NA CR0 .... 165 G6
  FBAR/BDGN N11 .... 40 A5
Pickering Ms BAY/PAD W2 .... 8 D4
Pickering PI WHALL SW1A * 10 F9
Pickering St IS N1 .... 6 D3
Pickets CI BUSH WD23 .... 22 D7
Pickets St BAL SW12 .... 129 G6
Pickett Cft STAN HA7 .... 35 K7
Pickett's Lock La ED N9 .... 42 E1
Pickford CI BXLYHN DA7 .... 137 F1
Pickford La BXLYHN DA7 .... 137 F1
Pickford Rd BXLYHN DA7 .... 137 F2
Pickfords Whf IS N1 * 6 E6
Pickhurst Av CHING E4 .... 44 B5
Pickhurst Gn HAYES BR2 .... 180 E1
Pickhurst La HAYES BR2 .... 167 F6
Pickhurst Md HAYES BR2 .... 167 F6
Pickhurst Pk HAYES BR2 .... 167 F4
Pickhurst Ri WWKM BR4 .... 167 F6
Pickwick CI HSLWW TW4 .... 122 D4
Pickwick Ms UED N18 .... 42 A4
Pickwick PI HRW HA1 .... 48 E6
Pickwick Rd DUL SE21 .... 130 E6
Pickwick St STHWK SE1 .... 18 E2
Pickwick Wy CHST BR7 .... 154 C5
Pickworth CI VX/NE SW8 * 109 K6
Picton PI MHST W1U 10 B5
  SURB KT6 .... 159 H7
Picton St CMBW SE5 .... 110 E6
Pied Bull Yd IS N1 * 5 J4
Piedmont Rd
  WOOL/PLUM SE18 .... 115 J4
Pier Head WAP E1W * 92 D7
Piermont PI BMLY BR1 .... 168 C1
Piermont Rd EDUL SE22 .... 131 J4
Pierpoint Ar IS N1 * 6 C5
Pierrepoint Ar IS N1 .... 6 C5
Pierrepoint Rd ACT W3 .... 86 D6
Pierrepoint Rw IS N1 * 6 C5
Pier Rd CAN/RD E16 .... 114 E1
  EBED/NFELT TW14 .... 122 A4
  ERITH DA8 .... 118 B5
Pier St POP/IOD E14 .... 113 F3
Pier Ter WAND/EARL SW18 .... 128 A3
Pier Wy THMD SE28 .... 115 J2
Pigeon La HPTN TW12 .... 142 A3
Pigott St POP/IOD E14 .... 93 J5
Pike CI BMLY BR1 .... 153 F4
Pike Rd MLHL NW7 .... 37 F3
Pike's End PIN HA5 .... 47 F3
Pikestone CI YEAD UB4 * 83 J3
Pilgrimage St STHWK SE1 .... 19 G2
Pilgrim HI WNWD SE27 .... 149 J3
Pilgrims CI NTHLT UB5 .... 66 D4
  PLMGR N13 .... 41 F3
Pilgrims Ct DART DA1 .... 139 K4
Pilgrim's La HAMP NW3 .... 71 H3
Pilgrims Ms POP/IOD E14 .... 94 B6
Pilgrim's PI HAMP NW3 * 71 H3
Pilgrim's Ri EBAR EN4 .... 27 J4
Pilgrim St BLKFR EC4V 12 C5
Pilgrims Wy ARCH N19 .... 54 D7
  SAND/SEL CR2 * 178 B4
  WBLY HA9 .... 50 D7
Pilgrim's Wy SAND/SEL CR2 .... 178 B5
Pilkington Rd PECK SE15 .... 131 J1
Pilot CI DEPT SE8 .... 112 C5
Pilsden CI WIM/MER SW19 * 127 G7
Piltdown Rd OXHEY WD19 .... 33 H3

Pilton Pl WALW SE17 .... 18 F7
Pimlico Rd BGVA SW1W 16 A7
Pinchin & Johnsons Yd
WCHPL E1 * 92 C6
Pinchin St WCHPL E1 .... 92 C6
Pincott Pl BROCKY SE4 .... 132 A2
Pincott Rd BXLYHS DA6 .... 137 H4
WIM/MER SW19 .... 147 G6
Pindar St SDTCH EC2A 13 J2
Pindock Ms MV/WKIL W9 .... 8 D1
Pine Apple Cl WESTW SW1E * ... 16 B3
Pine Av SRTFD E15 .... 76 B4
WWKM BR4 .... 166 E7
Pine Cl LEY E10 .... 75 J1
PGE/AN SE20 .... 150 E7
STAN HA7 .... 35 H5
STHGT/OAK N14 .... 28 C6
Pine Coombe CROY/NA CR0 ...... 179 F3
Pinecroft
KTN/HRWW/WS HA3 .... 50 B4
WOOL/PLUM SE18 .... 116 B6
Pinecroft Crs BAR EN5 .... 26 C3
Pinefield Cl POP/IOD E14 * 93 J6
Pine Gdns BRYLDS KT5 .... 159 H5
RSLP HA4 .... 47 F7
Pine Gv ORP BR6 .... 181 K3
FSBYPK N4 .... 72 E1
TRDG/WHET N20 .... 26 D7
WIM/MER SW19 .... 146 D4
Pinelands Cl BKHTH/KID SE3 * . 113 J6
Pinelees Ct
MORT/ESHN SW14 * 125 K3
Pinemartin Cl CRICK NW2 .... 70 A2
Pine Rdg CAR SM5 .... 176 A7
Pine Rd CRICK NW2 .... 70 A3
FBAR/BDGN N11 .... 40 A1
Pines Cl NTHWD HA6 .... 32 C5
Pines Rd BMLY BR1 .... 168 D1
The Pines BORE WD6 .... 24 B1
NRWD SE19 * 149 H5
STHGT/OAK N14 .... 28 C4
WFD IG8 .... 44 E2
Pine St CLKNW EC1R 6 A3
Pine Tree Cl HEST TW5 .... 102 A7
Pine Tree Wy LEW SE13 * 132 E2
Pine Wk BRYLDS KT5 .... 159 H5
Pine Wd SUN TW16 .... 140 E7
Pinewood Av BFN/LL DA15 ...... 135 K7
PIN HA5 .... 34 B1
RAIN RM13 .... 99 K3
Pinewood Cl CROY/NA CR0 ...... 179 G2
NTHWD HA6 .... 32 C4
ORP BR6 .... 169 J7
PIN HA5 .... 34 B5
Pinewood Gv WEA W13 .... 85 G5
Pinewood Ldg BUSH WD23 * 22 D7
Pinewood Ms
STWL/WRAY TW19 .... 120 A5
Pinewood Pl HOR/WEW KT19 ... 173 F6
Pinewood Rd ABYW SE2 .... 116 E5
FELT TW13 .... 141 F2
HAYES BR2 .... 167 K3
Pinfold Rd BUSH WD23 .... 21 K4
STRHM/NOR SW16 .... 148 E3
Pinglestone Cl WDR/YW UB7 ... 100 B6
Pinkcoat Cl FELT TW13 .... 141 F2
Pinkwell Av HYS/HAR UB3 .... 101 G3
Pinkwell La HYS/HAR UB3 .... 101 G3
Pinley Gdns DAGW RM9 .... 79 H7
Pinnacle Hl BXLYHN DA7 .... 137 J3
Pinnacle Hl North
BXLYHN DA7 .... 137 J2
Pinnell Rd ELTH/MOT SE9 .... 134 C3
Pinner Ct PIN HA5 * 48 A3
Pinner Gn PIN HA5 .... 47 G1
Pinner Gv PIN HA5 .... 47 J3
Pinner Hl PIN HA5 .... 33 F6
Pinner Hill Rd PIN HA5 .... 33 F7
Pinner Park Av
RYLN/HDSTN HA2 .... 48 C1
Pinner Park Gdns
RYLN/HDSTN HA2 .... 48 C1
Pinner Rd HRW HA1 .... 48 B4
NTHWD HA6 .... 32 D7
OXHEY WD19 .... 21 H5
PIN HA5 .... 47 K3
Pinner Vw HRW HA1 .... 48 C1
Pinn Wy RSLP HA4 .... 46 B6
Pintail Cl EHAM E6 .... 95 J4
Pintail Rd WFD IG8 .... 45 F6
Pintail Wy YEAD UB4 .... 83 H4
Pinto Cl BORE WD6 * 25 F5
Pinto Wy BKHTH/KID SE3 .... 134 A4
Pioneer Cl POP/IOD E14 .... 94 A4
SHB W12 .... 87 K5
Pioneer St PECK SE15 .... 111 H7
Pioneer Wy SHB W12 .... 88 A6
WATW WD18 .... 20 D5
Piper Cl HOLWY N7 .... 73 F5
Piper Rd KUT/HW KT1 .... 159 H2
Pipers Gdns CROY/NA CR0 .... 166 B6
Pipers Gn CDALE/KGS NW9 ...... 50 E4
Pipers Green La STAN HA7 .... 36 A2
Piper Wy IL IG1 .... 60 D7
Pipewell Rd CAR SM5 .... 162 D5
Pippin Cl CRICK NW2 .... 69 J2
CROY/NA CR0 .... 166 C7
Pippins Cl WDR/YW UB7 .... 100 B2
Piquet Rd PGE/AN SE20 .... 165 K1
Pirbright Crs CROY/NA CR0 ..... 180 A5
Pirbright Rd
WAND/EARL SW18 .... 127 J7
Pirie Cl CMBW SE5 .... 130 E2
Pirie St CAN/RD E16 .... 95 F7
Pitcairn Rd MTCM CR4 .... 147 K6
Pitchford St SRTFD E15 .... 76 B6
Pitfield Crs THMD SE28 .... 97 G7
Pitfield St IS N1 .... 7 H3
Pitfield Wy WLSDN NW10 .... 68 E5
Pitfold Rd LEE/GVPK SE12 .... 133 K6
Pitlake CROY/NA CR0 .... 177 H1
Pitman St CMBW SE5 .... 110 D6
Pitsea Pl WCHPL E1 * 93 F5
Pitsea St WCHPL E1 .... 93 F5
Pitshanger La EA W5 .... 85 H3
Pitt Crs WIM/MER SW19 .... 147 F3
Pittman Gdns IL IG1 .... 78 C4
Pitt Rd RYLN/HDSTN HA2 .... 66 C1
THHTH CR7 .... 164 D4
Pitts Head Ms
MYFR/PICC W1J 10 B9
Pittsmead Av HAYES BR2 .... 167 K6
Pitt St KENS W8 .... 14 B1
Pittville Gdns SNWD SE25 .... 165 H2
Pixley St POP/IOD E14 .... 93 H5
Pixton Wy CROY/NA CR0 .... 179 G7
Place Farm Av ORP BR6 .... 169 J7
Plaistow Gv BMLY BR1 .... 153 F6
SRTFD E15 .... 76 D7
Plaistow La BMLY BR1 .... 152 E6
Plaistow Park Rd PLSTW E13 ... 95 F1
Plaistow Rd SRTFD E15 .... 76 D7

Plane St SYD SE26 .... 150 D2
Plane Tree Crs FELT TW13 .... 141 F2
Plantagenet Cl WPK KT4 .... 173 F3
Plantagenet Gdns CHDH RM6 ... 61 K6
Plantagenet Pl CHDH RM6 .... 61 K6
Plantain Gdns WAN E11 * 76 B2
Plantain Pl STHWK SE1 .... 19 G1
Plantation Rd ERITH DA8 .... 118 D7
The Plantation
BKHTH/KID SE3 .... 133 K4
Plashet Gv EHAM E6 .... 77 G7
Plashet Rd PLSTW E13 .... 76 E7
Plassy Rd CAT SE6 .... 132 E6
Platina St SDTCH EC2A 7 H9
Platinum Ct ROMW/RG RM7 ..... 62 D2
Plato Rd BRXS/STRHM SW2 ..... 129 K3
Platt's La HAMP NW3 .... 70 E2
Platt St CAMTN NW1 .... 5 G5
Plawsfield Rd BECK BR3 .... 151 F7
Plaxtol Cl BMLY BR1 .... 153 G7
Plaxtol Rd ERITH DA8 .... 117 H6
Playfair St HMSMTH W6 * 107 F4
Playfield Av CRW RM5 .... 44 E1
Playfield Crs EDUL SE22 .... 131 F4
Playfield Rd EDGW HA8 .... 50 E1
Playford Rd FSBYPK N4 .... 73 F1
Playgreen Wy CAT SE6 .... 151 J3
Playground Cl STHWK SE1 * 18 E1
Playhouse Yd BLKFR EC4V 12 C5
Plaza Pde ALP/SUD HA0 * 68 A3
Plaza Wk CDALE/KGS NW9 .... 50 E2
Pleasance Rd PUT/ROE SW15 ... 126 E3
The Pleasance PUT/ROE SW15 . 126 E3
Pleasant Gv CROY/NA CR0 .... 179 H2
Pleasant Pl IS N1 .... 6 D2
Pleasant Vw ERITH DA8 .... 118 B4
Pleasant Wy ALP/SUD HA0 ...... 85 J1
Plender St CAMTN NW1 .... 4 E4
Pleshey Rd ARCH N19 .... 72 D3
Plesman Wy WLGTN SM6 * 176 E7
Plevna Crs SEVS/STOTM N15 ... 56 A5
Plevna Rd ED N9 .... 42 C2
HPTN TW12 .... 142 B7
Plevna St POP/IOD E14 .... 113 F2
Pleydell Av HMSMTH W6 .... 106 C2
NRWD SE19 .... 150 B6
Pleydell Est FSBYE EC1V * 6 E4
Pleydell Gdns NRWD SE19 * 150 B5
Pleydell St EMB EC4Y 12 B5
Plimsoll Cl POP/IOD E14 .... 93 K5
Plimsoll Rd FSBYPK N4 .... 73 H2
Plough Cl WLSDN NW10 .... 87 K2
Plough Farm Cl RSLP HA4 .... 46 B3
Plough La CROY/NA CR0 .... 176 E3
EDUL SE22 .... 131 G5
PUR/KEN CR8 .... 176 E7
TEDD TW11 .... 143 G4
WIM/MER SW19 .... 147 F4
WLGTN SM6 .... 176 E3
Plough Lane Cl WLGTN SM6 .... 176 E4
Ploughmans Cl CAMTN NW1 .... 5 G3
Ploughmans End ISLW TW7 ..... 123 J4
Plough Pl FLST/FETLN EC4A 12 B4
Plough Rd BTSEA SW11 .... 128 C2
HOR/WEW KT19 .... 173 F6
Plough St WCHPL E1 * 92 C5
Plough Ter BTSEA SW11 .... 128 C3
Plough Wy BERM/RTHE SE16 ... 112 B3
Plough Yd SDTCH EC2A 13 K1
Plover Wy BERM/RTHE SE16 .... 112 B2
YEAD UB4 .... 83 H5
Plowden Bldgs EMB EC4Y * 12 A5
Plowman Cl UED N18 .... 41 K4
Plowman Wy BCTR RM8 .... 61 J7
Plumbers Rw WCHPL E1 .... 92 C4
Plumbridge St GNWCH SE10 * .. 113 F7
Plum Cl FELT TW13 .... 121 F7
Plum Garth BTFD TW8 .... 104 E3
Plumtree La WALTH E17 * 44 A7
Plummer La MTCM CR4 .... 147 K7
Plummer Rd CLAP SW4 .... 129 J6
Plumpton Wy CAR SM5 .... 175 J2
Plumstead Common Rd
WOOL/PLUM SE18 .... 115 H5
Plumstead High St
WOOL/PLUM SE18 .... 115 J3
Plumstead Rd
WOOL/PLUM SE18 .... 115 H3
Plumtree Cl DAGE RM10 .... 80 D5
WLGTN SM6 .... 176 D6
Plumtree Ct FLST/FETLN EC4A 12 B4
Plymouth Rd BMLY BR1 .... 153 F7
CAN/RD E16 .... 94 E4
Plymouth Whf POP/IOD E14 ..... 113 G3
Plympton Av
KIL/WHAMP NW6 .... 70 D6
Plympton Cl BELV DA17 * 117 F2
Plympton Pl STJWD NW8 * 9 J1
Plympton Rd
KIL/WHAMP NW6 .... 70 D6
Plympton St STJWD NW8 .... 9 J1
Plymstock Rd WELL DA16 .... 116 D6
Pocklington Ct
CDALE/KGS NW9 * 51 G1
Pocock Av WDR/YW UB7 .... 100 C3
Pocock St STHWK SE1 .... 18 C2
Podmore Rd
WAND/EARL SW18 .... 128 B3
Poet's Rd HBRY N5 .... 73 K4
Poets Wy HRW HA1 .... 48 E3
Pointalls Cl FNCH N3 .... 53 G1
Point Cl GNWCH SE10 .... 113 F7
Pointer Cl THMD SE28 .... 97 K5
Pointers Cl POP/IOD E14 .... 112 E4
Point Hl GNWCH SE10 .... 113 F7
Point Pl WBLY HA9 .... 68 D6
Point Pleasant
WAND/EARL SW18 .... 127 K3
Point Wharf La BTFD TW8 .... 104 E6
Poland St SOHO/SHAV W1D 10 F4
Polebrook Rd BKHTH/KID SE3 . 134 B2
Polecroft La CAT SE6 .... 151 H1
Polesden Gdns RYNPK SW20 ... 160 E2
Polesworth Rd DAGW RM9 .... 98 B1
Polish War Memorial Rbt
RSLP HA4 .... 65 C5
Pollard Cl CAN/RD E16 .... 94 E6
HOLWY N7 .... 73 F3
Pollard Rd MRDN SM4 .... 162 C4
TRDG/WHET N20 .... 39 J1
Pollard Rw BETH E2 .... 92 C2
Pollards Crs
STRHM/NOR SW16 .... 163 K1
Pollards Hl East
STRHM/NOR SW16 .... 164 A1
Pollards Hl North
STRHM/NOR SW16 .... 164 A1
Pollards Hl South
STRHM/NOR SW16 .... 163 K2
Pollards Hl West
STRHM/NOR SW16 .... 163 K2

Pollard St BETH E2 * 92 C1
Pollards Wood Rd
STRHM/NOR SW16 .... 163 K1
Pollen St CONDST W1S 10 D5
Pollitt Dr STJWD NW8 .... 3 G9
Polperro Ms LBTH SE11 .... 18 B5
Polsted Rd CAT SE6 .... 132 C6
Polthorne Gv
WOOL/PLUM SE18 .... 115 H3
Polworth Rd
STRHM/NOR SW16 .... 148 E4
Polygon Rd CAMTN NW1 .... 5 G6
The Polygon CLAP SW4 * 129 H3
Polytechnic St
WOOL/PLUM SE18 .... 115 F3
Pomell Wy WCHPL E1 .... 13 M4
Pomeroy Cl TWK TW1 .... 124 C3
Pomeroy St NWCR SE14 .... 111 K6
Pomfret Rd CMBW SE5 .... 130 C2
Pomoja La ARCH N19 .... 72 E1
Pond Cl BKHTH/KID SE3 .... 133 K1
NFNCH/WDSPK N12 .... 39 J3
Pond Cottage La BECK BR3 ...... 166 D7
Pond Cots DUL SE21 .... 131 F7
Ponder St HOLWY N7 .... 5 L1
Pond Farm Est CLPT E5 * 74 E2
Pondfield Rd DAGE RM10 .... 80 D4
HAYES BR2 .... 167 H7
Pond Gn RSLP HA4 .... 64 C1
Pond Hill Gdns CHEAM SM3 .... 174 C5
Pond Lees Cl DAGE RM10 .... 81 F6
Pond Md DUL SE21 .... 130 E5
Pond Pl CHEL SW3 .... 15 J6
Pond Rd BKHTH/KID SE3 .... 133 J2
SRTFD E15 .... 94 C1
Pondside Av WPK KT4 .... 161 F7
Pondside Cl HYS/HAR UB3 .... 101 G6
Pond St HAMP NW3 .... 71 H4
Pond Wy TEDD TW11 .... 143 J5
Pondwood Ri ORP BR6 .... 169 K6
Ponder St WCHPL E1 * 92 D5
Ponsard Rd WLSDN NW10 .... 87 K2
Ponsford St HOM E9 .... 74 E5
Ponsonby Pl WEST SW1P 17 H7
Ponsonby Rd PUT/ROE SW15 .. 126 E6
Ponsonby Ter WEST SW1P 17 H7
Pontefract Rd BMLY BR1 .... 152 E4
Ponton Rd VX/NE SW8 .... 109 J6
Pont St KTBR SW1X 15 L4
Pont Street Ms KTBR SW1X 15 L4
Pool Cl BECK BR3 .... 151 J4
E/WMO/HCT KT8 .... 156 E4
Pool Ct CAT SE6 .... 151 J1
Poole Cl RSLP HA4 .... 64 C1
Poole Court Rd HSLWW TW4 ... 122 C1
Poole Rd HOM E9 .... 75 F5
HOR/WEW KT19 .... 173 F5
Pooles Bldgs FSBYW WC1X * ... 12 A1
Pooles La WBPTN SW10 .... 108 B6
Pooles Pk FSBYPK N4 .... 73 G1
Poole St IS N1 .... 7 G4
Poole Wy YEAD UB4 * 82 C3
Pooley Dr MORT/ESHN SW14 ... 125 K2
Poolmans St
BERM/RTHE SE16 .... 112 A1
Pool Rd E/WMO/HCT KT8 .... 156 E4
HRW HA1 .... 48 D6
Poolsford Rd CDALE/KGS NW9 . 51 G3
Poonah St WCHPL E1 .... 92 E5
Pope Cl EBED/NFELT TW14 ..... 121 J7
WIM/MER SW19 * 147 H5
Pope Rd HAYES BR2 .... 168 C4
Popes Av WHTN TW2 .... 142 E1
Popes Dr FNCH N3 .... 38 E7
Popes Gv CROY/NA CR0 .... 179 H2
Pope's Gv WHTN TW2 .... 142 E1
Popes La EA W5 .... 104 E2
Pope's Rd BRXN/ST SW9 .... 130 B3
Pope St STHWK SE1 .... 19 K2
Popham Cl FELT TW13 .... 141 J2
Popham Gdns
RCH/KEW TW9 * 125 J2
Popham Rd IS N1 .... 6 E3
Popham St IS N1 .... 6 E3
Popinjays Rw CHEAM SM3 * 174 B4
Poplar Av MTCM CR4 .... 147 K7
NWDGN UB2 .... 103 G2
Poplar Bath St POP/IOD E14 * .. 93 K6
Poplar Cl HOM E9 * 75 H4
PIN HA5 .... 33 H7
Poplar Court Pde TWK TW1 * ... 124 D5
Poplar Crs HOR/WEW KT19 ..... 172 E5
Poplar Farm Cl
HOR/WEW KT19 .... 172 E5
Poplar Gdns NWMAL KT3 .... 160 A1
HMSMTH W6 .... 107 F1
NWMAL KT3 .... 160 A1
WBLY HA9 .... 49 J4
Poplar Gv FBAR/BDGN N11 ..... 40 A5
HMSMTH W6 .... 107 F1
NWMAL KT3 .... 160 A2
WBLY HA9 .... 49 J4
Poplar High St POP/IOD E14 .... 93 K6
Poplar La BECK BR3 .... 166 E4
Poplar Ms SHB W12 * 88 A7
Poplar Mt BELV DA17 .... 117 J3
Poplar Pl BAY/PAD W2 .... 8 C6
HYS/HAR UB3 .... 82 E6
THMD SE28 .... 97 J7
Poplar Rd ASHF TW15 .... 140 A4
CHEAM SM3 .... 161 J7
ESH/CLAY KT10 .... 171 G3
HNHL SE24 .... 130 D3
MNPK E12 .... 77 J2
WIM/MER SW19 .... 161 K1
Poplar Rd South
WIM/MER SW19 .... 161 K2
Poplars Cl RSLP HA4 .... 46 C7
The Poplars STHGT/OAK N14 ... 28 B4
Poplar St ROMW/RG RM7 .... 62 E3
Poplar Vw WBLY HA9 * 67 K1
Poplar Wk CROY/NA CR0 .... 177 J1
HNHL SE24 .... 130 D3
Poppleton Rd WAN E11 .... 58 C5
Poppy Cl BELV DA17 .... 117 J2
NTHLT UB5 .... 65 K5
WLGTN SM6 .... 163 F7
Poppy Dr PEND EN3 .... 30 D3
Poppy La CROY/NA CR0 .... 165 K6
Porchester Garden Ms
BAY/PAD W2 * 8 D5
Porchester Gdns BAY/PAD W2 .. 8 C5
Porchester Ga BAY/PAD W2 * ... 8 D7
Porchester Md BECK BR3 .... 151 K5
Porchester Pl BAY/PAD W2 ...... 9 J5
Porchester Rd BAY/PAD W2 ..... 8 D4
KUT/HW KT1 .... 159 J1
Porchester Sq BAY/PAD W2 ..... 8 D4
Porchester Square Ms
BAY/PAD W2 * 8 D4
Porchester Ter BAY/PAD W2 .... 8 D4
Porchester Ter North
BAY/PAD W2 .... 8 D4

Porch Wy TRDG/WHET N20 ...... 39 K2
Porcupine Cl ELTH/MOT SE9 ... 153 J1
Porden Rd BRXS/STRHM SW2 .. 130 A3
Porlock Av RYLN/HDSTN HA2 .. 48 C7
Porlock Rd EN EN1 .... 30 B6
Porlock St STHWK SE1 .... 19 H1
Porrington Cl CHST BR7 .... 153 K7
Portal Cl RSLP HA4 .... 64 C3
WNWD SE27 .... 149 G2
Portal Wy ACT W3 .... 87 F4
Portbury Cl PECK SE15 .... 111 H7
Portcullis Lodge Rd EN EN1 .... 29 K2
Portelet Rd WCHPL E1 .... 93 F2
Porten Houses WKENS W14 * ... 107 H2
Porten Rd WKENS W14 .... 107 H2
Porters Av DAGW RM9 .... 79 H5
Porter Sq ARCH N19 .... 54 E7
Porter St MHST W1U 9 M2
STHWK SE1 .... 12 F8
Porters Wk WAP E1W * 92 D6
Porters Wy WDR/YW UB7 .... 100 C3
Porteus Rd BAY/PAD W2 .... 8 F3
Portgate Cl MV/WKIL W9 .... 88 D3
Porthcawe Rd SYD SE26 .... 151 J3
Porthkerry Av WELL DA16 .... 136 B3
Portia Wy BOW E3 .... 93 H3
The Porticos CHEL SW3 * 108 C4
Portinscale Rd
PUT/ROE SW15 .... 127 H4
Portland Av BFN/LL DA15 .... 136 B5
NWMAL KT3 .... 160 C6
STNW/STAM N16 .... 56 B7
Portland Cl CHDH RM6 .... 62 A4
WPK KT4 .... 160 E6
Portland Cots CROY/NA CR0 * .. 163 J6
Portland Crs ELTH/MOT SE9 .... 153 J1
FELT TW13 .... 140 B3
STAN HA7 .... 49 K1
Portland Crs West STAN HA7 ... 49 K2
Portland Gdns CHDH RM6 .... 61 K4
FSBYPK N4 .... 55 H5
Portland Gv VX/NE SW8 .... 110 A7
Portland Ms SOHO/CST W1F ... 10 F5
Portland Pl REGST W1B 10 C1
SNWD SE25 .... 165 H3
Portland Ri FSBYPK N4 .... 55 H7
Portland Rd BMLY BR1 .... 153 J1
ELTH/MOT SE9 .... 153 J1
KUT/HW KT1 .... 159 F2
MTCM CR4 .... 162 D1
NTGHL W11 .... 88 C6
NWDGN UB2 .... 102 E2
SEVS/STOTM N15 .... 56 A3
SNWD SE25 .... 165 H3
YEAD UB4 .... 82 C2
Portland Sq WAP E1W * 92 D7
Portland St WALW SE17 .... 19 G8
Portland Ter RCH/KEW TW9 * .. 124 E3
Portman Av
MORT/ESHN SW14 .... 126 A2
Portman Cl BXLY DA5 .... 138 B7
BXLYHS DA6 .... 136 E2
MBLAR W1H 10 A4
Portman Dr WFD IG8 .... 59 H1
Portman Gdns
CDALE/KGS NW9 .... 51 F2
Portman Ga CAMTN NW1 * 9 K1
Portman Ms South
MBLAR W1H 10 A5
Portman Pl BETH E2 .... 92 E2
Portman Sq KUT/HW KT1 .... 159 G1
Portman Sq MBLAR W1H 9 M4
Portman St MBLAR W1H 10 A5
Portmeadow Wk ABYW SE2 ..... 116 E1
Portmeers Cl WALTH E17 * 57 H5
Portnall Rd MV/WKIL W9 .... 88 D1
Portnoi Cl ROM RM1 .... 63 F1
Portobello Rd NTGHL W11 .... 88 C5
Portobello Ms NTGHL W11 * 8 A7
Portobello Rd NKENS W10 .... 88 B6
NTGHL W11 .... 88 C6
Portpool La FSBYW WC1X 12 A2
Portree St POP/IOD E14 .... 94 B5
Portsdown Av GLDGN NW11 .... 52 D5
Portsdown Ms GLDGN NW11 ... 52 D5
Portsea Ms BAY/PAD W2 .... 9 K5
Portsea Pl BAY/PAD W2 .... 9 K5
Portslade Rd VX/NE SW8 .... 129 H1
Portsmouth Av THDIT KT7 .... 158 B6
Portsmouth Ms CAN/RD E16 .... 95 F6
Portsmouth Rd
ESH/CLAY KT10 .... 170 A5
KUT/HW KT1 .... 158 E2
PUT/ROE SW15 .... 126 E6
THDIT KT7 .... 158 C6
Portsmouth St LINN WC2A 11 L4
Portsoken St TWRH EC3N 13 L6
Portugal Gdns WHTN TW2 * 142 C1
Portugal St LINN WC2A 11 M3
Portway RAIN RM13 .... 81 J7
SRTFD E15 .... 76 D7
Portway Crs EW KT17 .... 173 J7
Portway Gdns
WOOL/PLUM SE18 .... 114 C7
Postern Gn ENC/FH EN2 .... 29 G1
The Postern BARB EC2Y * 12 F3
Post La WHTN TW2 .... 123 J7
Postmill Cl CROY/NA CR0 .... 178 E2
Post Office Ap FSTGT E7 .... 77 F4
Post Office Wy VX/NE SW8 .... 109 J6
Post Rd NWDGN UB2 .... 103 G2
Postway Ms IL IG1 * 78 B2
Potier St STHWK SE1 .... 19 H4
Potter Cl MTCM CR4 .... 163 G1
The Potteries BAR EN5 * 26 E4
Potterne Cl WIM/MER SW19 * .. 127 G6
Potters Cl CROY/NA CR0 .... 166 B7
PECK SE15 * 111 F6
Potters Flds STHWK SE1 .... 13 K9
Potters Gv NWMAL KT3 .... 159 K3
Potters Heights Cl PIN HA5 ...... 33 F6
Potter's La BAR EN5 .... 26 E3
STRHM/NOR SW16 * 148 E5
Potters Ms BORE WD6 .... 23 K5
Potter's Rd BAR EN5 .... 27 F3
Potter St NTHWD HA6 .... 32 E7
Potter Street HI PIN HA5 .... 33 F5
Pottery La NTGHL W11 .... 88 C7
Pottery Rd BTFD TW8 .... 105 F5
BXLY DA5 .... 137 J7
Pottery St BERM/RTHE SE16 * . 111 J1
Pott St BETH E2 .... 92 D2
Poulett Gdns TWK TW1 .... 143 F1
Poulett Rd EHAM E6 .... 95 K1
Poulter Pk MRDN SM4 * 162 D5
Poulters Wd HAYES BR2 .... 181 H4
Poulton Av SUT SM1 .... 175 H2

Poultry LOTH EC2R 13 G5
Pound Cl SURB KT6 .... 158 D7
Pound Farm Cl
ESH/CLAY KT10 .... 157 J7
Pound La WLSDN NW10 .... 69 J5
Pound Pl ELTH/MOT SE9 .... 135 F5
Pound St CAR SM5 .... 175 K4
Pountney Rd BTSEA SW11 .... 129 F2
Powder Mill La WHTN TW2 ...... 122 D4
Powell Cl EDGW HA8 .... 36 B5
Powell Gdns DAGE RM10 .... 80 C3
Powell Rd CLPT E5 .... 74 D2
Power Rd CHSWK W4 .... 105 H3
Powers Ct TWK TW1 .... 124 E6
Powerscroft Rd CLPT E5 .... 74 E3
SCUP DA14 .... 155 J5
Powis Ct BUSH WD23 * 22 D7
Powis Gdns GLDGN NW11 .... 52 D6
NTGHL W11 .... 88 D5
Powis Ms NTGHL W11 .... 88 D5
Powis PI BMSBY WC1N 11 K1
Powis Rd BOW E3 .... 93 K2
Powis Sq NTGHL W11 .... 88 D5
Powis St WOOL/PLUM SE18 .... 115 F3
Powis Ter NTGHL W11 .... 88 D5
Powlett Pl CAMTN NW1 .... 4 B1
Pownall Gdns HSLW TW3 .... 123 G3
Pownall Rd HACK E8 .... 74 C7
HSLW TW3 .... 123 G3
Pownsett Ter IL IG1 * 78 C4
Powster Rd BMLY BR1 .... 152 E4
Powys Cl BXLYHN DA7 .... 116 E5
Powys Ct BORE WD6 .... 25 F2
Powys La PLMGR N13 .... 40 E3
Poynders Rd CLAP SW4 .... 129 H6
Poynings Av ARCH N19 .... 72 C2
Poynings Wy
NFNCH/WDSPK N12 .... 38 E4
Poyntell Crs CHST BR7 .... 154 D7
Poynter Rd EN EN1 .... 30 B4
Poynton Rd TOTM N17 .... 56 C1
Poyntz Rd BTSEA SW11 .... 128 E1
Poyser St BETH E2 .... 92 D1
Praed Ms BAY/PAD W2 .... 9 H4
Praed St BAY/PAD W2 .... 9 H4
Pragel St PLSTW E13 .... 95 F1
Pragnell Rd LEE/GVPK SE12 ... 153 F1
Prague Pl BRXS/STRHM SW2 ... 129 K4
Prah Rd FSBYPK N4 .... 73 C1
Prairie St VX/NE SW8 .... 129 F1
Pratt Ms CAMTN NW1 .... 4 E4
Pratt St CAMTN NW1 .... 4 E3
Pratt Wk LBTH SE11 .... 17 M5
Prayle Gv CRICK NW2 .... 52 B7
Prebend Gdns HMSMTH W6 .... 106 C3
Prebend St IS N1 .... 6 E2
Precinct Rd HYS/HAR UB3 .... 82 E6
The Precinct IS N1 * 6 E4
Premiere Pl POP/IOD E14 * 93 J6
Premier Park Rd
WLSDN NW10 .... 86 D1
Premier Pl WATW WD18 * 20 D4
Prendergast Rd
BKHTH/KID SE3 .... 133 H2
Prentis Rd
STRHM/NOR SW16 .... 148 D3
Prentiss Ct CHARL SE7 .... 114 C3
Presburg Rd NWMAL KT3 .... 160 B4
Prescelly Pl EDGW HA8 .... 36 B7
Prescot St WCHPL E1 .... 13 M5
Prescott Av STMC/STPC BR5 ... 169 G5
Prescott Cl EMPK RM11 .... 63 K7
Prescott Pl CLAP SW4 .... 129 J2
Presentation Ms
BRXS/STRHM SW2 .... 149 F1
Presidents Dr WAP E1W 92 D7
President St FSBYE EC1V * 6 E7
Prespa Cl ED N9 .... 42 E1
Press Rd WLSDN NW10 .... 69 F2
Prestage Wy POP/IOD E14 .... 94 A6
Prestbury Rd FSTGT E7 .... 77 G6
Prestbury Sq ELTH/MOT SE9 ... 153 K3
Prested Rd BTSEA SW11 .... 128 D3
Preston Av CHING E4 .... 44 B5
Preston Cl STHWK SE1 .... 19 J5
WHTN TW2 .... 142 E3
Preston Ct BAR EN5 .... 27 G3
WOT/HER KT12 .... 156 B7
Preston Dr BXLYHN DA7 .... 116 E7
HOR/WEW KT19 .... 173 G5
WAN E11 .... 59 G4
Preston Gdns IL IG1 .... 59 J5
WLSDN NW10 .... 69 G5
Preston Hl
KTN/HRWW/WS HA3 .... 50 A6
Preston Pl CRICK NW2 .... 69 J5
Preston Rd
KTN/HRWW/WS HA3 .... 50 A6
NRWD SE19 .... 149 H5
RYNPK SW20 .... 145 G6
WAN E11 .... 58 C5
WBLY HA9 .... 68 A1
Prestons Rd WWKM BR4 .... 180 E2
Preston's Rd POP/IOD E14 .... 94 A4
Preston Vls KUT/HW KT1 * 159 G1
Preston Waye
KTN/HRWW/WS HA3 .... 50 A7
Prestwick Ter CLAP SW4 * 129 H3
Prestwich Cl NWDGN UB2 .... 102 D4
Prestwick Rd OXHEY WD19 ..... 33 G4
Prestwood Av
KTN/HRWW/WS HA3 .... 49 J3
Prestwood Cl
KTN/HRWW/WS HA3 .... 49 H3
WOOL/PLUM SE18 .... 116 B6
Prestwood Gdns
CROY/NA CR0 .... 164 D6
Prestwood St IS N1 * 6 F6
Pretoria Av WALTH E17 .... 57 G3
Pretoria Pde BROCKY SE4 * 132 C1
Pretoria Rd CAN/RD E16 .... 94 D2
IL IG1 .... 78 B3
LEY E10 .... 58 B7
ROMW/RG RM7 .... 62 D3
STRHM/NOR SW16 .... 148 B5
TOTM N17 .... 42 B5
WATW WD18 .... 20 D3
Pretoria Rd North UED N18 ...... 42 B5
Prevost Rd FBAR/BDGN N11 .... 40 A1
Price Cl MLHL NW7 .... 38 C5
TOOT SW17 .... 147 K2
Price Rd CROY/NA CR0 .... 177 H4
Price's St STHWK SE1 .... 12 D9
Pricklers Hl BAR EN5 .... 27 F4
Prickley Wd HAYES BR2 .... 167 J7
Priddy's Yd CROY/NA CR0 .... 177 J1
Prideaux Pl ACT W3 .... 87 F6
FSBYW WC1X 5 M7
Prideaux Rd BRXN/ST SW9 ...... 129 K2
Pridham Rd THHTH CR7 .... 164 E3
Priestfield Rd FSTH SE23 .... 151 G2

Priestlands Park Rd BFN/LL DA15 ... 155 F2
Priestley Cl STNW/STAM N16 * ... 56 B6
Priestley Gdns CHDH RM6 ... 61 H5
Priestley Rd MTCM CR4 ... 163 F1
Priestley Wy CRICK NW2 ... 51 J7
WALTH E17 ... 57 F2
Priest Park Av RYLN/HDSTN HA2 ... 66 A1
Priests Av ROM RM1 ... 63 F1
Priests Br MORT/ESHN SW14 ... 126 B2
Prima Rd BRXN/ST SW9 ... 110 B6
Primrose Av GDMY/SEVK IG3 ... 61 G6
Primrose Cl BOW E3 ... 93 J1
CAT SE6 ... 152 A4
FNCH N3 ... 53 F1
RYLN/HDSTN HA2 ... 65 K2
WLGTN SM6 ... 163 G7
Primrose Dr WDR/YW UB7 ... 100 A3
Primrose Gdns BUSH WD23 ... 22 C4
HAMP NW3 ... 71 J5
RSLP HA4 ... 65 G4
Primrose Hl EMB EC4Y ... 12 B5
Primrose Hill Rd HAMP NW3 ... 3 L2
Primrose Hill Studios CAMTN NW1 ... 4 A3
Primrose La CROY/NA CR0 ... 165 K6
Primrose Ms CAMTN NW1 * ... 3 M2
Primrose Rd ISLW TW7 ... 124 A1
Primrose Rd LEY E10 ... 57 K7
SWFD E18 ... 59 H1
Primrose Sq HOM E9 ... 74 E6
Primrose St SDTCH EC2A ... 13 J1
Primrose Wk KT17 ... 173 H6
NWCR SE14 ... 112 B6
Primrose Wy ALP/SUD HA0 ... 85 K1
Primula St SHB W12 ... 87 H3
Prince Albert Rd STJWD NW8 ... 3 J1
Prince Arthur Ms HAMP NW3 ... 71 G3
Prince Arthur Rd HAMP NW3 ... 71 G3
Prince Charles Dr HDN NW4 ... 52 A6
Prince Charles Rd BKHTH/KID SE3 ... 113 J7
Prince Charles Wy WLGTN SM6 ... 176 B2
Prince Consort Dr CHST BR7 ... 154 D4
Prince Consort Rd SKENS SW7 ... 15 G4
Princedale Rd NTGHL W11 ... 88 C7
Prince Edward Rd HOM E9 ... 75 H5
Prince George Av STHGT/OAK N14 ... 28 C4
Prince George Rd STNW/STAM N16 ... 74 A3
Prince George's Av RYNPK SW20 ... 161 F1
Prince Georges Rd WIM/MER SW19 ... 147 H2
Prince Henry Rd CHARL SE7 ... 114 C7
Prince Imperial Rd CHST BR7 ... 154 B6
WOOL/PLUM SE18 ... 114 E7
Prince John Rd ELTH/MOT SE9 ... 134 D4
Princelet St WCHPL E1 ... 13 M2
Prince of Orange La GNWCH SE10 ... 113 F6
Prince of Wales Cl HDN NW4 ... 51 K3
Prince of Wales Dr BTSEA SW11 ... 108 D7
VX/NE SW8 ... 109 G6
Prince of Wales Ga SKENS SW7 ... 15 G3
Prince of Wales Pas CAMTN NW1 * ... 4 E8
Prince of Wales Rd BKHTH/KID SE3 ... 113 J7
CAN/RD E16 ... 95 G5
KTTN NW5 ... 72 A4
Prince of Wales' Rd SUT SM1 ... 175 H1
Prince of Wales Ter CHSWK W4 ... 106 B4
KENS W8 ... 14 D2
Prince Regent La CAN/RD E16 ... 95 G5
Prince Regent Ms CAMTN NW1 * ... 4 E8
Prince Regent Rd HSLW TW3 ... 123 G2
Prince Rupert Rd SNWD SE25 ... 165 F4
Prince Rupert Rd ELTH/MOT SE9 ... 134 E3
Princes Ar MYFR/PICC W1J * ... 10 F8
Princes Av ACT W3 ... 105 H2
CAR SM5 ... 175 K6
CDALE/KGS NW9 ... 50 C3
FNCH N3 ... 39 F7
MUSWH N10 ... 54 A1
PLMGR N13 ... 41 G4
STMC/STPC BR5 ... 169 K4
SURB KT6 ... 172 C1
WATW WD18 ... 20 C3
WDGN N22 ... 40 D7
WFD IG8 ... 45 F7
Princes Av GFD/PVL UB6 ... 84 B3
Princes Cl CDALE/KGS NW9 ... 50 C3
EDGW HA8 ... 36 C4
SCUP DA14 ... 155 K2
Prince's Cl HPTN TW12 ... 142 D3
Princes Ct WBLY HA9 ... 68 A4
Princes Dr HRW HA1 ... 48 E2
Princes Gdns ACT W3 ... 86 C4
EA W5 ... 85 J3
SKENS SW7 ... 15 H3
Princes Ga SKENS SW7 ... 15 H3
Prince's Ga SKENS SW7 ... 15 G2
Princes Gate Ct SKENS SW7 ... 15 G2
Princes Gate Ms SKENS SW7 ... 15 H3
Princes La MUSWH N10 ... 54 A2
Princes Ms HMSMTH W6 ... 106 E4
HSLW TW3 ... 123 F3
Prince's Ms BAY/PAD W2 ... 8 C6
Princes Pde GLDGN NW11 * ... 52 C5
Princes Pk RAIN RM13 ... 81 J6
Princes Park Av GLDGN NW11 ... 52 C5
HYS/HAR UB3 ... 82 B5
Princes Park Cir HYS/HAR UB3 ... 82 B6
Princes Park Cl HYS/HAR UB3 ... 82 B6
Princes Park La HYS/HAR UB3 ... 82 B6
Princes Park Pde HYS/HAR UB3 ... 82 B6
Princes Pl NTGHL W11 ... 88 C7
Prince's Pln HAYES BR2 ... 168 D6
Princes Ri LEW SE13 ... 133 F1
Princes Riverside Rd BERM/RHTH SE16 ... 93 F7
Princes Rd BARK/HLT IG6 ... 60 D3
BKHH IG9 ... 45 G1
DART DA1 ... 138 E6
FELT TW13 ... 140 D2
KUTN/CMB KT2 ... 144 C7
PGE/AN SE20 ... 151 F5
RCH/KEW TW9 ... 105 G7
ROM RM1 ... 63 J4
TEDD TW11 ... 142 D5
UED N18 ... 42 E3

WEA W13 ... 85 H7
Prince's Rd MORT/ESHN SW14 ... 126 A2
TEDD TW11 ... 142 D5
WIM/MER SW19 ... 146 E5
Princess Alice Wy THMD SE28 ... 115 J1
Princess Av WBLY HA9 ... 68 A1
Princess Crs FSBYPK N4 ... 73 H1
Princesses Pde DART DA1 * ... 138 C4
Princess La RSLP HA4 ... 46 C7
Princess Louise Cl BAY/PAD W2 ... 9 H2
Princess May Rd STNW/STAM N16 ... 74 A3
Princess Ms HAMP NW3 ... 71 H5
Princess Sq BAY/PAD W2 * ... 8 E6
Princess Rd CAMTN NW1 ... 4 A3
CROY/NA CR0 ... 164 D5
KIL/WHAMP NW6 ... 2 A6
Princess St REGST W1B ... 10 D5
STHWK SE1 ... 18 D4
SUT SM1 ... 175 H3
TOTM N17 ... 42 A5
Prince's St LOTH EC2R ... 13 G5
Prince's Ter PLSTW E13 ... 77 F7
Prince St DEPT SE8 ... 112 C5
WAT WD17 ... 21 G2
Prince Vw DART DA1 ... 139 K7
Princes Wy BKHH IG9 ... 45 G1
CROY/NA CR0 ... 177 F4
RSLP HA4 ... 65 J3
WIM/MER SW19 ... 127 H3
WWKM BR4 ... 180 D3
Prince's Yd IS N1 * ... 5 M4
NTGHL W11 ... 88 C7
Princethorpe Rd SYD SE26 ... 151 F3
Princeton St GINN WC1R ... 11 L3
Pringle Gdns STRHM/NOR SW16 ... 148 C3
Printers Inn Ct FLST/FETLN EC4A ... 12 A4
Printinghouse La HYS/HAR UB3 ... 101 H1
Printing House Yd BETH E2 * ... 7 K8
Priolo Rd CHARL SE7 ... 114 B4
Prior Av BELMT SM2 ... 175 J6
Prior Bolton St IS N1 ... 73 H5
Prioress Rd WNWD SE27 ... 149 H2
Prioress St STHWK SE1 ... 19 H4
Prior Rd IL IG1 ... 78 A2
Priors Cft WALTH E17 ... 57 G1
Priors Fld NTHLT UB5 ... 65 J5
Priors Gdns RSLP HA4 ... 65 G4
Prior St GNWCH SE10 ... 113 F6
Priory Av ALP/SUD HA0 ... 67 J3
CEND/HSY/T N8 ... 54 D3
CHEAM SM3 ... 174 B3
CHING E4 ... 43 H2
CHSWK W4 ... 106 B3
STMC/STPC BR5 ... 169 J5
WALTH E17 ... 57 J4
Priory Cl ALP/SUD HA0 ... 67 J3
BECK BR3 ... 166 B2
CHING E4 ... 43 H2
CHST BR7 ... 153 K7
DART DA1 ... 139 F4
FNCH N3 ... 38 D7
HPTN TW12 ... 141 K7
HYS/HAR UB3 ... 83 F6
RSLP HA4 ... 46 D7
STHGT/OAK N14 ... 28 A4
SUN TW16 ... 140 E6
SWFD E18 ... 44 E7
TRDG/WHET N20 ... 26 D6
WIM/MER SW19 ... 147 F7
Priory Cots EA W5 * ... 86 A3
Priory Crs ALP/SUD HA0 ... 67 J3
CHEAM SM3 ... 174 B3
NRWD SE19 ... 149 J6
Priory Ct BLKFR EC4V * ... 12 D5
VX/NE SW8 ... 109 J7
WALTH E17 ... 57 H1
Priory Dr ABYW SE2 ... 116 E4
STAN HA7 ... 35 F7
Priory Field Dr EDGW HA8 ... 36 D3
Priory Gdns ALP/SUD HA0 ... 67 J3
ASHF TW15 ... 140 B4
BARN SW13 ... 126 C2
CHSWK W4 ... 106 B3
DART DA1 ... 139 G4
HGT N6 ... 54 B5
HPTN TW12 ... 141 K7
SNWD SE25 ... 165 G3
Priory Green Est IS N1 ... 5 G5
Priory Gv VX/NE SW8 ... 109 K7
Priory Hl ALP/SUD HA0 ... 67 G3
DART DA1 ... 139 G5
Priory La E/WMO/HCT KT8 ... 157 H3
PUT/ROE SW15 ... 126 C4
Priory Leas ELTH/MOT SE9 * ... 134 D7
Priory Ms BKHTH/KID SE3 ... 133 J2
Priory Park Rd ALP/SUD HA0 ... 67 G3
KIL/WHAMP NW6 ... 70 D7
Priory Pl DART DA1 ... 139 G5
Priory Rd BARK IG11 ... 78 D6
CEND/HSY/T N8 ... 54 D3
CHEAM SM3 ... 174 B3
CHSGTN KT9 ... 172 A2
CHSWK W4 ... 106 A2
CROY/NA CR0 ... 164 B6
DART DA1 ... 139 G3
EHAM E6 ... 77 H1
HPTN TW12 ... 141 K6
HSLW TW3 ... 123 H4
KIL/WHAMP NW6 ... 2 C2
MUSWH N10 ... 54 C3
RCH/KEW TW9 ... 105 H5
Priory St BOW E3 ... 93 K2
Priory Ter KIL/WHAMP NW6 ... 2 C2
The Priory BKHTH/KID SE3 ... 133 J2
Priory Vw BUSH WD23 ... 22 E6
Priory Vls FBAR/BDGN N11 * ... 39 K5
Priory Wy HYS/HAR UB3 ... 82 B6
NWDGN UB2 ... 102 C2
RYLN/HDSTN HA2 ... 48 B3
WDR/YW UB7 ... 100 B3
Pritchard's Rd BETH E2 ... 92 C1
Priter Rd BERM/RHTH SE16 * ... 111 H2
Private Rd EN EN1 ... 29 K4
Probert Rd BRXS/STRHM SW2 ... 130 B4
Probyn Rd BRXS/STRHM SW2 ... 149 H1
Procter St GINN WC1R ... 11 L3
Proctor Cl MTCM CR4 ... 148 A7
Proctors Cl EBED/NFELT TW14 ... 121 H7
Progress Wy CROY/NA CR0 ... 177 H1
EN EN1 ... 30 C4
WDGN N22 ... 41 G1
Promenade Approach Rd CHSWK W4 ... 106 B6

The Promenade CHSWK W4 ... 106 B7
EDGW HA8 * ... 36 C4
Prospect Cl BELV DA17 ... 117 H3
BUSH WD23 ... 22 D6
HSLW TW3 ... 102 E7
RSLP HA4 ... 47 H6
SYD SE26 ... 150 D3
Prospect Cots WAND/EARL SW18 ... 127 K3
Prospect Crs WHTN TW2 ... 123 H6
Prospect Hl WALTH E17 ... 57 K3
Prospect Pl CHSWK W4 ... 106 A4
CRICK NW2 ... 70 D2
CRW RM5 ... 62 E1
EFNCH N2 ... 53 H3
HAYES BR2 ... 168 A2
RYNPK SW20 ... 145 K6
WAP E1W ... 92 E7
Prospect Ring EFNCH N2 ... 53 H2
Prospect Rd BAR EN5 ... 26 E3
CRICK NW2 ... 70 D2
SURB KT6 ... 158 D6
WFD IG8 ... 45 G4
Prospect St BERM/RHTH SE16 ... 111 J1
Prospect V WOOL/PLUM SE18 ... 114 D3
Prospero Rd ARCH N19 ... 54 D7
Protea Cl CAN/RD E16 ... 94 D3
Prothero Gdns HDN NW4 ... 51 K4
Prothero Rd FUL/PGN SW6 ... 107 H6
Prout Gv WLSDN NW10 ... 69 G3
Prout Rd CLPT E5 ... 74 D2
Provence St IS N1 ... 6 E5
Providence Av RYLN/HDSTN HA2 ... 48 A5
Providence Cl HOM E9 * ... 75 F7
Providence Ct MYFR/PKLN W1K ... 10 B6
Providence La HYS/HAR UB3 ... 101 G5
Providence Pl IS N1 ... 6 C4
Providence Row BETH E2 ... 92 D2
Providence Sq STHWK SE1 ... 19 J1
Providence Yd BETH E2 * ... 92 C2
Provincial Ter PGE/AN SE20 * ... 151 F6
Provost Est IS N1 ... 7 G7
Provost Rd HAMP NW3 ... 3 K1
Provost St FSBYE EC1V ... 7 G8
Prowse Av BUSH WD23 ... 34 C1
Prowse Pl CAMTN NW1 ... 4 E1
Pruden Cl STHGT/OAK N14 ... 40 C1
Prusom St WAP E1W ... 92 D7
Pudding La MON EC3R ... 13 H6
Pudding Mill La SRTFD E15 ... 75 K7
Puddle Dock BLKFR EC4V ... 12 D6
Puffin Cl BARK IG11 ... 97 H2
BECK BR3 ... 166 A4
Pulborough Rd WAND/EARL SW18 ... 127 J6
Pulborough Wy HSLWW TW4 ... 122 B3
Pulford Rd SEVS/STOTM N15 ... 55 K5
Pulham Av EFNCH N2 ... 53 G3
Puller Rd BAR EN5 ... 26 B1
Pulleyns Av EHAM E6 ... 95 J2
Pullman Gdns PUT/ROE SW15 ... 127 F5
Pullman Ms LEE/GVPK SE12 ... 153 F2
Pullman Pl ELTH/MOT SE9 ... 134 D4
Pulross Rd BRXN/ST SW9 ... 130 A2
Pulteney Cl BOW E3 ... 75 H7
ISLW TW7 ... 124 B2
Pulteney Rd SWFD E18 ... 59 F2
Pulton Pl FUL/PGN SW6 ... 107 K6
Puma Ct WCHPL E1 ... 13 L2
Pump Aly BTFD TW8 ... 104 E6
Pump Cl NTHLT UB5 ... 84 A1
Pump Ct EMB EC4Y * ... 12 A5
Pump House Cl HAYES BR2 ... 167 J1
Pump House Ms WCHPL E1 * ... 92 C6
Pumping Station Rd CHSWK W4 ... 106 B6
Pump La HYS/HAR UB3 ... 101 K1
NWCR SE14 ... 111 K6
Punderson's Gdns BETH E2 ... 92 D2
Purbeck Av NWMAL KT3 ... 160 C5
Purbeck Dr CRICK NW2 ... 70 B1
Purbeck Rd EMPK RM11 ... 63 J6
Purbrook St STHWK SE1 ... 19 K3
Purcell Crs FUL/PGN SW6 ... 107 G6
Purcell Ms WLSDN NW10 ... 69 G6
Purcell Rd GFD/PVL UB6 ... 84 B4
Purcells Ave EDGW HA8 ... 36 C4
Purcell St IS N1 ... 7 J5
Purcers Cross Rd FUL/PGN SW6 ... 107 J7
Purchese St CAMTN NW1 ... 5 G5
Purdy St BOW E3 ... 93 K3
Purelake Ms LEW SE13 * ... 133 G2
Purfleet Industrial Access Rd SOCK/AV RM15 ... 119 K2
Purkis Cl UX/CGN UB8 ... 82 A6
Purland Cl BCTR RM8 ... 62 B7
Purland Rd THMD SE28 ... 116 A2
Purleigh Av WFD IG8 ... 45 J5
Purley Av CRICK NW2 ... 70 C1
Purley Cl CLAY IG5 ... 60 A1
Purley Pl IS N1 ... 6 C1
Purley Rd ED N9 ... 41 K2
SAND/SEL CR2 ... 177 K6
Purley Wy CROY/NA CR0 ... 177 G7
Purlings Rd BUSH WD23 ... 22 B4
Purneys Rd ELTH/MOT SE9 ... 134 C3
Purrett Rd WOOL/PLUM SE18 ... 116 A4
Pursers Cross Rd FUL/PGN SW6 ... 107 J7
Pursewardens Cl WEA W13 ... 85 J7
Pursley Rd MLHL NW7 ... 37 K6
Purves Rd WLSDN NW10 ... 87 K2
Puteaux Ho BETH E2 * ... 93 F1
Putney Br PUT/ROE SW15 ... 127 H2
Putney Bridge Ap FUL/PGN SW6 ... 127 H2
Putney Bridge Rd PUT/ROE SW15 ... 127 H3
Putney Common PUT/ROE SW15 ... 127 F2
Putney Ex PUT/ROE SW15 * ... 127 G3
Putney Heath PUT/ROE SW15 ... 126 E5
Putney Heath La PUT/ROE SW15 ... 127 G5
Putney High St PUT/ROE SW15 ... 127 H3
Putney Hl PUT/ROE SW15 ... 127 G5
Putney Park Av PUT/ROE SW15 ... 126 D3
Putney Park La PUT/ROE SW15 ... 126 E3

Pymmes Brook Trail EBAR EN4 ... 27 K6
ED N9 ... 42 D2
Pymmes Cl PLMGR N13 ... 41 F4
TOTM N17 ... 42 D7
Pymmes Gdns North ED N9 ... 42 B2
Pymmes Gdns South ED N9 ... 42 B2
Pymmes Green Rd FBAR/BDGN N11 ... 40 B3
Pymmes Rd PLMGR N13 ... 40 E4
Pymms Brook Dr EBAR EN4 ... 27 J3
Pyne Rd SURB KT6 ... 159 H7
Pynham Cl ABYW SE2 ... 116 B2
Pynnacles Cl STAN HA7 ... 35 H4
Pyrland Rd HBRY N5 ... 73 K4
RCHPK/HAM TW10 ... 125 G5
Pyrmont Gv WNWD SE27 ... 149 H2
Pyrmont Rd CHSWK W4 ... 105 H5
Pytchley Crs NRWD SE19 ... 149 J5
Pytchley Rd EDUL SE22 ... 131 F2

Q

The Quadrangle BAY/PAD W2 * ... 9 J4
HNHL SE24 * ... 130 E3
WBPTN SW10 * ... 108 B7
Quadrant Ar REGST W1B ... 10 F7
Quadrant Cl HDN NW4 * ... 51 K4
Quadrant Gv KTTN NW5 ... 71 K4
Quadrant Rd RCH/KEW TW9 ... 124 E3
THHTH CR7 ... 164 C3
The Quadrant BELMT SM2 ... 175 J7
BXLYHN DA7 ... 116 E6
EDGW HA8 * ... 36 C5
NKENS W10 ... 88 B3
RCH/KEW TW9 ... 124 E3
RYLN/HDSTN HA2 * ... 48 C3
RYNPK SW20 ... 146 C7
Quad Rd WBLY HA9 * ... 67 K2
Quaggy Wk BKHTH/KID SE3 ... 133 K3
Quainton St WLSDN NW10 ... 69 F2
Quaker La NWDGN UB2 ... 103 F2
Quakers Course CDALE/KGS NW9 ... 37 H7
Quakers La ISLW TW7 ... 104 B6
Quakers Pl FSTGT E7 ... 77 H4
Quaker St WCHPL E1 ... 13 L1
Quakers Wk WCHMH N21 ... 29 K5
Quality Ct LINN WC2A ... 12 A4
Quantock Gdns CRICK NW2 ... 70 B1
Quantock Ms PECK SE15 ... 131 H1
Quantock Rd BXLYHN DA7 ... 138 B3
Quarles Park Rd CHDH RM6 ... 61 H5
Quarrendon St FUL/PGN SW6 ... 107 K7
Quarr Rd CAR SM5 ... 162 C5
Quarry Ms PUR RM19 ... 119 K3
Quarry Park Rd SUT SM1 ... 174 D5
Quarry Ri SUT SM1 ... 174 D5
Quarry Rd WAND/EARL SW18 ... 128 B5
Quatre Ports CHING E4 ... 44 B4
Quay House POP/IOD E14 * ... 112 D1
Quebec Ms MBLAR W1H ... 9 M5
Quebec Rd GNTH/NBYPK IG2 ... 60 C6
YEAD UB4 ... 83 C4
Quebec Wy BERM/RHTH SE16 ... 112 A1
Queen Adelaide Rd PGE/AN SE20 ... 150 E5
Queen Anne Av HAYES BR2 ... 167 K2
Queen Anne Dr ESH/CLAY KT10 ... 170 E6
Queen Anne Ga BXLYHN DA7 ... 136 E2
Queen Anne Ms CAVSO/HST W1G ... 10 D3
Queen Anne Rd HOM E9 ... 75 F5
Queen Annes Cl WHTN TW2 ... 142 D2
Queen Anne's Gdns CHSWK W4 ... 106 B2
EA W5 ... 105 F1
EN EN1 ... 30 A5
MTCM CR4 ... 162 E2
Queen Anne's Ga STJSPK SW1H ... 17 G2
Queen Anne's Gv CHSWK W4 ... 106 B2
EA W5 ... 105 F1
ED N9 ... 29 K6
EN EN1 ... 30 A5
Queen Anne's Pl EN EN1 ... 30 A5
Queen Anne's Sq STHWK SE1 ... 111 H3
Queen Anne St CAVSO/HST W1G ... 10 C3
Queen Anne Ter WAP E1W * ... 92 D6
Queen Borough Gdns CHST BR7 ... 154 D5
Queenborough Gdns GNTH/NBYPK IG2 ... 60 A3
Queen Caroline Est HMSMTH W6 ... 107 F4
Queen Caroline St HMSMTH W6 ... 107 F3
Queen Elizabeth Blds EMB EC4Y * ... 12 A6
Queen Elizabeth College GNWCH SE10 ... 113 F6
Queen Elizabeth Gdns MRDN SM4 ... 161 K3
Queen Elizabeth Rd KUTN/CMB KT2 ... 159 G1
WALTH E17 ... 57 G2
Queen Elizabeth's Cl STNW/STAM N16 ... 73 K1
Queen Elizabeth's Dr STHGT/OAK N14 ... 28 E7
Queen Elizabeth St STHWK SE1 ... 19 K1
Queen Elizabeth's Wk STNW/STAM N16 ... 73 K1
WLGTN SM6 ... 176 D3
Queen Mother Ga BARN SW13 ... 106 D7
Queenhithe BLKFR EC4V ... 12 F6
Queen Isabella Wy STBT EC1A ... 12 D4
Queen Margaret's Gv IS N1 ... 74 A4
Queen Mary Av RYNPK SW20 ... 161 G1
SWFD E18 ... 44 E1
Queen Mary Cl ROM RM1 ... 63 H5
SURB KT6 ... 172 C2
Queen Mary's Av CAR SM5 ... 175 K6
WATW WD18 ... 20 C3
Queen Mother Ga MYFR/PICC W1J ... 10 B9
Queens Acre CHEAM SM3 ... 174 B6
Queens Av FELT TW13 ... 141 G3
KTN/HRWW/WS HA3 ... 49 H2
MUSWH N10 ... 54 A3
TRDG/WHET N20 ... 39 H1
WATW WD18 ... 20 C3

WCHMH N21 ... 29 H7
WFD IG8 ... 45 F4
Queensberry Ms West SKENS SW7 * ... 15 G5
Queensberry Pl MNPK E12 ... 77 H3
SKENS SW7 ... 15 G5
Queensberry Wy SKENS SW7 * ... 15 G5
Queensborough Ms BAY/PAD W2 * ... 8 E6
Queensborough Pas BAY/PAD W2 * ... 8 E6
Queensborough Studios BAY/PAD W2 * ... 8 E6
Queensborough Ter BAY/PAD W2 ... 8 D6
Queensbridge Pk ISLW TW7 ... 123 K5
Queensbridge Rd HACK E8 ... 7 M4
Queensbury Rd ALP/SUD HA0 ... 86 D7
CDALE/KGS NW9 ... 51 F6
Queensbury St IS N1 ... 6 C1
Queens Circ VX/NE SW8 ... 109 G6
Queens Cl ESH/CLAY KT10 ... 170 A3
Queen's Cl EDGW HA8 ... 36 C4
WLGTN SM6 ... 176 B4
Queens Club Gdns WKENS W14 ... 107 H5
Queen's Club Gdns WKENS W14 ... 107 H5
Queens Club Ter WKENS W14 * ... 107 J5
Queenscourt WBLY HA9 ... 68 A3
Queen's Crs RCHPK/HAM TW10 ... 125 G4
Queen's Crs KTTN NW5 ... 72 A4
Queenscroft Rd ELTH/MOT SE9 ... 134 C4
Queensdale Crs NTGHL W11 ... 88 B7
Queensdale Pl NTGHL W11 ... 88 C7
Queensdale Rd NTGHL W11 ... 88 B7
Queensdale Wk NTGHL W11 ... 88 C7
Queens Down Rd CLPT E5 ... 74 D3
Queens Dr BRYLDS KT5 ... 159 H6
LEY E10 ... 57 J6
Queen's Dr EA W5 ... 86 B5
FSBYPK N4 ... 73 H1
THDIT KT7 ... 158 B5
Queen's Elm Sq CHEL SW3 ... 15 G8
Queens Gdns HDN NW4 ... 52 A4
RAIN RM13 ... 99 F1
Queen's Gdns BAY/PAD W2 ... 8 E6
EA W5 ... 85 J4
HEST TW5 ... 102 D7
Queens Garth FSTH SE23 * ... 150 E1
Queens Ga SKENS SW7 ... 14 F2
Queen's Ga SKENS SW7 ... 14 F2
Queens Gate Gdns CHST BR7 ... 154 D7
Queensgate Gdns PUT/ROE SW15 ... 126 E3
Queen's Gate Gdns SKENS SW7 ... 14 E4
Queen's Gate Ms SKENS SW7 ... 14 F4
Queensgate Pl KIL/WHAMP NW6 ... 2 A2
Queen's Gate Pl SKENS SW7 ... 14 F4
Queen's Gate Place Ms SKENS SW7 ... 14 F4
Queen's Gv STJWD NW8 ... 3 G3
Queen's Head St IS N1 ... 6 D4
Queens Keep TWK TW1 * ... 124 D5
Queensland Av UED N18 ... 41 J5
WIM/MER SW19 ... 147 F7
Queensland Cl WALTH E17 ... 57 H1
Queensland Rd HOLWY N7 ... 73 G3
Queens La MUSWH N10 ... 54 B2
Queens Md EDGW HA8 ... 36 B5
Queensmead STJWD NW8 ... 3 H3
Queen's Mead Rd HAYES BR2 ... 167 J1
Queensmere Cl WIM/MER SW19 ... 146 B1
Queensmere Rd WIM/MER SW19 ... 146 B1
Queen's Ms BAY/PAD W2 ... 8 C6
Queensmill Rd FUL/PGN SW6 ... 107 F6
Queens Pde CEND/HSY/T N8 * ... 55 H3
CRICK NW2 * ... 70 A4
EA W5 * ... 86 B5
FBAR/BDGN N11 * ... 39 K4
HDN NW4 * ... 51 K4
Queens Parade Cl FBAR/BDGN N11 * ... 39 K4
Queens Park Gdns FELT TW13 * ... 140 D2
Queen's Pl MRDN SM4 ... 161 K3
WAT WD17 ... 21 G2
Queens Prom KUT/HW KT1 ... 158 E3
Queen Sq BMSBY WC1N ... 11 K1
Queen's Ride BARN SW13 ... 126 D3
Queen's Ri RCHPK/HAM TW10 ... 125 G5
Queens Rd BAR EN5 ... 26 B2
ERITH DA8 ... 118 B3
HYS/HAR UB3 ... 82 C5
MRDN SM4 ... 161 K3
WDR/YW UB7 ... 100 C3
Queen's Rd BARK IG11 ... 78 C6
BECK BR3 ... 166 B1
BKHH IG9 ... 45 F1
BMLY BR1 ... 167 K1
CHST BR7 ... 154 B5
CROY/NA CR0 ... 164 C5
EA W5 ... 86 A5
ED N9 ... 42 D1
EN EN1 ... 30 A3
FBAR/BDGN N11 ... 40 E6
FELT TW13 ... 122 A7
FNCH N3 ... 39 G7
HDN NW4 ... 52 A3
HPTN TW12 ... 142 B3
HSLW TW3 ... 123 G2
KUTN/CMB KT2 ... 144 C6
MORT/ESHN SW14 ... 126 A2
MTCM CR4 ... 162 C2
NWDGN UB2 ... 102 D3
NWMAL KT3 ... 160 C3
PECK SE15 ... 111 K7
PLSTW E13 ... 77 F7
RCHPK/HAM TW10 ... 143 F4
TEDD TW11 ... 143 F5
THDIT KT7 ... 157 K4
TWK TW1 ... 124 A7
WALTH E11 ... 58 C5
WALTH E17 ... 57 H4
WAT WD17 ... 21 G2
WELL DA16 ... 136 C1
WIM/MER SW19 ... 146 E5
WLGTN SM6 ... 176 B4
Queen's Rd West PLSTW E13 ... 94 E1
Queens Rw WALW SE17 ... 19 G9
Queens Rd WALW SE17 ... 19 G9
Queens Ter ISLW TW7 ... 124 B3
PLSTW E13 ... 77 F7
THDIT KT7 ... 158 B5
TWK TW1 * ... 124 B7
WCHPL E1 ... 92 E3
Queen's Ter ISLW TW7 ... 124 B3

STJWD NW8 3 G4
Queens Terrace Cots
HNWL W7 * 103 K1
Queensthorpe Ms SYD SE26 * 151 F3
Queensthorpe Rd SYD SE26 151 F3
Queenstown Gdns RAIN RM13 99 H2
Queenstown Rd VX/NE SW8 129 G1
Queen St BXLYHN DA7 137 G2
CROY/NA CR0 177 J3
ERITH DA8 * 118 B5
MYFR/PICC W1J 10 C8
ROMW/RG RM7 63 F5
STP EC4M 12 F5
TOTM N17 42 A5
Queen Street Pl CANST EC4R 12 F7
Queensville Rd BAL SW12 129 J6
Queens Wk CDALE/KGS NW9 68 E1
HRW HA1 48 E3
RSLP HA4 65 G2
Queen's Wk EA W5 85 J3
Queens Walk Ter RSLP HA4 * 65 G2
The Queens Wk STHWK SE1 13 K8
Queens Wy FELT TW13 141 G3
HDN NW4 52 A4
Queensway BAY/PAD W2 8 D4
CROY/NA CR0 177 F5
PEND EN3 30 E3
STMC/STPC BR5 169 H4
SUN TW16 156 A1
WWKM BR4 180 E3
Queens Well Av
TRDG/WHET N20 39 J3
Queen's Whf HMSMTH W6 107 F4
Queenswood Av HPTN TW12 142 B5
HSLW TW3 122 E1
THHTH CR7 164 B4
WALTH E17 44 A7
WLGTN SM6 176 D3
Queenswood Gdns WAN E11 58 E7
Queenswood Pk FNCH N3 52 C1
Queenswood Rd BFN/LL DA15 136 A4
FSTH SE23 151 G2
Queen's Wood Rd HGT N6 54 B5
Queen's Yd FITZ W1T 10 F1
Queen Victoria Av
ALP/SUD HA0 67 K6
Queen Victoria St BLKFR EC4V 12 C6
Queen Victoria Ter
WAP E1W * 92 D6
Quemerford Rd HOLWY N7 73 F4
Quentin Pl LEW SE13 133 H2
Quentin Rd LEW SE13 133 H2
Quernmore Cl BMLY BR1 152 E5
Quernmore Rd BMLY BR1 152 E5
FSBYPK N4 55 G5
Querrin St FUL/PGN SW6 128 B1
Quex Ms KIL/WHAMP NW6 2 B3
Quex Rd KIL/WHAMP NW6 2 B3
Quick Rd CHSWK W4 106 B4
Quicks Rd WIM/MER SW19 147 F6
Quick St IS N1 6 D6
Quickswood HAMP NW3 3 K1
Quiet Nook HAYES BR2 181 H2
Quill St EA W5 86 A2
FSBYPK N4 73 G2
Quilp St STHWK SE1 18 E1
Quilters Pl ELTH/MOT SE9 135 H7
Quilter St BETH E2 92 C2
WOOL/PLUM SE18 116 A4
Quince Rd LEW SE13 132 E1
Quinnel Cl WOOL/PLUM SE18 116 A4
Quinnell Cl WOOL/PLUM SE18 116 A4
Quinta Dr BAR EN5 25 K4
Quintin Av RYNPK SW20 146 C7
Quinton Cl BECK BR3 167 F2
HEST TW5 102 A6
WLGTN SM6 176 B3
Quinton Rd THDIT KT7 158 B7
Quinton St WAND/EARL SW18 147 G1
Quixley St POP/IOD E14 94 B6
Quorn Rd EDUL SE22 131 F3

R

Rabbit Rw KENS W8 * 8 B8
Rabbits Rd MNPK E12 77 J3
Rabournmead Dr NTHLT UB5 65 J4
Raby Rd NWMAL KT3 160 A3
Raby St POP/IOD E14 * 93 G5
Raccoon Wy HSLWW TW4 122 B1
Rachel Cl BARK/HLT IG6 60 D3
Rackham Cl WELL DA16 136 C1
Rackham Ms
STRHM/NOR SW16 148 C5
Racton Rd FUL/PGN SW6 107 K5
Radbourne Av EA W5 104 D3
Radbourne Cl CLPT E5 75 F3
Radbourne Ct
KTN/HRWW/WS HA3 * 49 H5
Radbourne Crs WALTH E17 58 B2
Radbourne Rd BAL SW12 129 H6
Radcliffe Av WLSDN NW10 87 J1
Radcliffe Gdns CAR SM5 175 J6
Radcliffe Rd CROY/NA CR0 178 B1
KTN/HRWW/WS HA3 49 G1
STHWK SE1 19 K3
WCHMH N21 29 H7
Radcliffe Sq PUT/ROE SW15 127 G5
Radcliffe Wy NTHLT UB5 83 H2
Radcot St LBTH SE11 18 B8
Raddington Rd NKENS W10 88 C4
Radfield Wy BFN/LL DA15 135 J6
Radford Est WLSDN NW10 * 87 G2
Radford Rd LEW SE13 133 F5
Radford Wy BARK IG11 97 F2
Radipole Rd FUL/PGN SW6 107 J7
Radius Pk EBED/NFELT TW14 * 121 J3
Radland Rd CAN/RD E16 94 E5
Radlet Av SYD SE26 150 D2
Radlett Cl FSTGT E7 76 D5
Radlett Pl STJWD NW8 3 J4
Radlett Rd WAT WD17 21 G2
Radley Av GDMY/SEVK IG3 79 F3
Radley Cl EBED/NFELT TW14 121 J7
Radley Ct BERM/RHTH SE16 112 A1
Radley Gdns
KTN/HRWW/WS HA3 50 A3
Radley Ms KENS W8 14 B4
Radley Rd TOTM N17 56 A1
Radley's La SWFD E18 58 E1
Radleys Md DAGE RM10 80 D5
Radley Sq CLPT E5 * 74 E1
Radley Ter CAN/RD E16 94 D4
Radlix Rd LEY E10 57 J7
Radnor Av HRW HA1 48 E4
WELL DA16 136 C4
Radnor Cl CHST BR7 154 E5
MTCM CR4 163 K4
Radnor Crs REDBR IG4 59 K4
WOOL/PLUM SE18 116 B6
Radnor Gdns TWK TW1 143 F1
Radnor Hall BORE WD6 * 24 A4
Radnor Ms BAY/PAD W2 9 H5
Radnor Pl BAY/PAD W2 9 J5
Radnor Rd HRW HA1 48 D4
KIL/WHAMP NW6 70 C7
PECK SE15 111 H6
TWK TW1 124 A7
Radnor St FSBYE EC1V 6 F8
Radnor Ter WKENS W14 107 J3
Radnor Wk CHEL SW3 15 K8
CROY/NA CR0 166 B6
Radnor Wy WLSDN NW10 86 D3
Radstock Av
KTN/HRWW/WS HA3 49 G2
Radstock Cl FBAR/BDGN N11 40 A4
Radstock St BTSEA SW11 * 108 D6
Raebarn Gdns BAR EN5 25 K4
Raeburn Av BRYLDS KT5 159 J6
DART DA1 138 E4
Raeburn Cl GLDGN NW11 53 G5
KUT/HW KT1 143 K6
Raeburn Rd BFN/LL DA15 135 K5
EDGW HA8 50 C1
YEAD UB4 82 B1
Raeburn St BRXS/STRHM SW2 129 K3
Rafford Wy BMLY BR1 168 A1
Raggleswood CHST BR7 154 A7
Raglan Cl HSLWW TW4 122 D4
Raglan Ct SAND/SEL CR2 177 H4
Raglan Gdns OXHEY WD19 21 F7
Raglan Rd BELV DA17 117 G3
EN EN1 30 A6
HAYES BR2 168 B3
WALTH E17 58 A4
WOOL/PLUM SE18 115 H4
Raglan St KTTN NW5 72 B5
Raglan Ter RYLN/HDSTN HA2 * 66 B3
Raglan Vls WALTH E17 * 58 A4
Raglan Wy NTHLT UB5 66 C5
Ragley Cl ACT W3 105 K1
Railey Ms KTTN NW5 72 C4
Railshead Rd ISLW TW7 124 C3
Railton Rd HNHL SE24 130 B4
Railway Ap FSBYPK N4 55 G5
HRW HA1 49 F3
STHWK SE1 13 G8
TWK TW1 124 B6
WLGTN SM6 * 176 B5
Railway Ar BRXN/ST SW9 * 130 B3
Railway Av BERM/RHTH SE16 111 K1
Railway Cots HMSMTH W6 * 107 F1
SRTFD E15 * 94 C1
WIM/MER SW19 * 147 F3
Railway Gv NWCR SE14 112 C6
Railway Pl BELV DA17 117 H2
Railway Ri EDUL SE22 131 F3
Railway Rd TEDD TW11 142 E3
Railway Side BARN SW13 126 B2
Railway Station Whf
LEY E10 * 57 G7
Railway St CHDH RM6 61 J7
IS N1 5 K6
Railway Ter FELT TW13 121 K7
LEW SE13 132 E4
WALTH E17 44 A7
Rainborough Cl WBLY HA9 68 E5
Rainbow Av POP/IOD E14 112 E4
Rainbow Ct OXHEY WD19 21 G5
Rainbow Quay
BERM/RHTH SE16 112 B2
Rainbow St CMBW SE5 111 F6
Raine St WAP E1W 92 D7
Rainham Cl BTSEA SW11 128 D5
ELTH/MOT SE9 135 K5
Rainham Rd RAIN RM13 99 J2
WLSDN NW10 88 A2
Rainham Rd North
DAGE RM10 80 D1
Rainham Rd South
DAGE RM10 80 E5
Rainhill Wy BOW E3 93 J2
Rainsborough Av DEPT SE8 112 B3
Rainsford Rd WLSDN NW10 86 C2
Rainsford St BAY/PAD W2 9 J4
Rainsford Wy HCH RM12 63 J7
Rainton Rd CHARL SE7 113 K4
Rainville Rd HMSMTH W6 107 F5
Raisins Hl PIN HA5 47 F2
Raith Av STHGT/OAK N14 40 D2
Raleigh Av WLGTN SM6 176 D3
YEAD UB4 83 F4
Raleigh Cl ERITH DA8 118 C5
HDN NW4 52 A4
PIN HA5 47 H6
RSLP HA4 64 D1
Raleigh Dr BRYLDS KT5 159 K7
ESH/CLAY KT10 170 D4
TRDG/WHET N20 39 J2
Raleigh Gdns
BRXS/STRHM SW2 130 A5
MTCM CR4 162 E1
Raleigh Ms IS N1 6 D4
Raleigh Rd CEND/HSY/T N8 55 G3
ENC/FH EN2 29 K3
FELT TW13 140 D1
NWDGN UB2 102 D4
PGE/AN SE20 151 F6
RCH/KEW TW9 125 G2
Raleigh St IS N1 6 D4
Raleigh Wy FELT TW13 141 G4
STHGT/OAK N14 28 D7
Ralph Perring Ct BECK BR3 166 D3
Ralston St CHEL SW3 15 L8
Ralston Wy OXHEY WD19 33 H1
Rama Cl STRHM/NOR SW16 148 E6
Ramac Wy CHARL SE7 114 A3
Rama La NRWD SE19 150 B6
Rambler Cl STRHM/NOR SW16 148 C3
Rame Cl TOOT SW17 148 A4
Ramilles Cl BRXS/STRHM SW2 129 K5
Ramillies Pl SOHO/CST W1F 10 E5
Ramillies Rd BFN/LL DA15 136 C5
CHSWK W4 106 A2
MLHL NW7 37 G1
Ramillies St SOHO/SHAV W1D 10 E5
Ramones Ter MTCM CR4 * 163 H3
Rampart St WCHPL E1 92 D5
Ram Pas KUT/HW KT1 158 E1
Rampayne St PIM SW1V 17 G7
Rampton Cl CHING E4 43 J2
Ramsay Rd ACT W3 105 K2
FSTGT E7 76 D3
Ramscroft Cl ED N9 30 A6
Ramsdale Rd TOOT SW17 148 A4
Ramsden Ga BAL SW12 * 129 G6
Ramsden Rd BAL SW12 129 F6
ERITH DA8 118 A6
FBAR/BDGN N11 39 K4
Ramsey Cl CDALE/KGS NW9 51 H5
GFD/PVL UB6 66 D4
Ramsey Rd THHTH CR7 164 A5
Ramsey St BETH E2 92 C3
Ramsey Wk IS N1 73 K5
Ramsey Wy STHGT/OAK N14 28 C6
Ramsgate Cl CAN/RD E16 95 F7
Ramsgate St HACK E8 * 74 B5
Ramsgill Ap GNTH/NBYPK IG2 61 F3
Ramsgill Dr GNTH/NBYPK IG2 61 F4
Rams Gv CHDH RM6 62 A3
Ramulis Dr YEAD UB4 83 H3
Rancliffe Gdns ELTH/MOT SE9 134 D3
Rancliffe Rd EHAM E6 95 J1
Randall Av CRICK NW2 69 G1
Randall Cl BTSEA SW11 108 D7
ERITH DA8 117 K5
Randall Pl GNWCH SE10 113 F6
Randall Rd LBTH SE11 17 L7
Randall Rw LBTH SE11 17 L6
Randell's Rd IS N1 5 K3
Randisbourne Gdns CAT SE6 * 151 K2
Randle Rd RCHPK/HAM TW10 143 J3
Randlesdown Rd CAT SE6 151 J3
Randolf Rd HAYES BR2 168 E7
Randolph Ap CAN/RD E16 95 G5
Randolph Av MV/WKIL W9 2 C6
Randolph Cl BXLYHN DA7 137 K2
KUTN/CMB KT2 * 144 E4
Randolph Crs MV/WKIL W9 8 E1
Randolph Gdns
KIL/WHAMP NW6 2 C6
Randolph Gv CHDH RM6 61 J4
Randolph Ms MV/WKIL W9 8 F1
Randolph Rd MV/WKIL W9 8 E1
STHL UB1 * 102 E1
WALTH E17 * 57 K4
Randolph St CAMTN NW1 4 E2
Randon Cl RYLN/HDSTN HA2 48 B1
Ranelagh Av BARN SW13 126 D1
FUL/PGN SW6 127 J2
Ranelagh Cl EDGW HA8 36 C3
Ranelagh Dr EDGW HA8 36 C3
TWK TW1 124 C3
Ranelagh Gdns CHSWK W4 105 K6
FUL/PGN SW6 127 J2
IL IG1 60 A7
WAN E11 59 G4
Ranelagh Gv BGVA SW1W 16 B7
Ranelagh Pl NWMAL KT3 160 B4
Ranelagh Rd ALP/SUD HA0 67 K4
EA W5 104 E1
EHAM E6 78 A7
PIM SW1V 16 F8
SRTFD E15 76 C7
STHL UB1 83 H7
TOTM N17 56 A2
WAN E11 76 C3
WDGN N22 41 F7
WLSDN NW10 87 H1
Ranfurly Rd SUT SM1 174 E1
Rangefield Rd BMLY BR1 152 C4
Rangemoor Rd
SEVS/STOTM N15 56 B4
Rangeworth Pl BFN/LL DA15 155 F2
Rangoon St TWRH EC3N * 13 L5
Rankin Cl CDALE/KGS NW9 51 G2
Ranleigh Gdns BXLYHN DA7 117 G6
Ranmere St BAL SW12 129 G7
Ranmoor Cl HRW HA1 48 D3
Ranmoor Gdns HRW HA1 48 D3
Ranmore Av CROY/NA CR0 178 B2
Ranmore Rd BELMT SM2 174 B7
Rannoch Cl EDGW HA8 36 D1
Rannoch Rd HMSMTH W6 107 F5
Rannock Av CDALE/KGS NW9 51 G7
Ransom Cl OXHEY WD19 21 G6
Ransom Rd CHARL SE7 * 114 B4
Ranston St CAMTN NW1 9 J2
Ranulf Rd CRICK NW2 70 D3
Ranwell Cl BOW E3 * 75 H7
Ranworth Cl ERITH DA8 138 B1
Ranworth Rd ED N9 42 E1
Ranyard Cl CHSGTN KT9 172 B2
Raphael Av ROM RM1 63 H2
Raphael Cl KUT/HW KT1 158 E3
Raphael Dr THDIT KT7 158 A7
WATN WD24 21 H1
Raphael St SKENS SW7 15 L2
Rapier Cl PUR RM19 119 J3
Rasper Rd TRDG/WHET N20 39 G1
Rastell Av BRXS/STRHM SW2 148 D1
Ratcliffe Cl LEE/GVPK SE12 133 K6
Ratcliffe Cross St WCHPL E1 * 93 F5
Ratcliffe La POP/IOD E14 93 G5
Ratcliff Rd FSTGT E7 77 G4
Rathbone Pl FITZ W1T 11 G3
Rathbone Sq CROY/NA CR0 * 177 J3
Rathbone St CAN/RD E16 94 D4
FITZ W1T 10 F3
Rathcoole Av CEND/HSY/T N8 55 F4
Rathcoole Gdns
CEND/HSY/T N8 55 F4
Rathfern Rd CAT SE6 132 C7
Rathgar Av WEA W13 85 H7
Rathgar Cl FNCH N3 52 D1
Rathgar Rd BRXN/ST SW9 130 C2
Rathmell Dr CLAP SW4 129 J5
Rathmore Rd CHARL SE7 114 A4
Rattray Rd BRXS/STRHM SW2 130 B3
Raul Rd PECK SE15 131 H1
Raveley St KTTN NW5 72 C3
Ravencroft Crs ELTH/MOT SE9 153 K2
Ravenet St BTSEA SW11 109 G7
Ravenfield Rd TOOT SW17 147 K2
Ravenhill Rd PLSTW E13 77 G7
Ravenna Rd PUT/ROE SW15 127 G4
Ravenor Park Rd
GFD/PVL UB6 84 B2
Raven Rd SWFD E18 59 G1
Raven Rw WCHPL E1 92 D4
Ravens Ait SURB KT6 * 158 E4
Ravensbourne Av HAYES BR2 152 B7
STWL/WRAY TW19 120 B7
Ravensbourne Gdns
WEA W13 85 H4
Ravensbourne Pk CAT SE6 132 D6
Ravensbourne Park Crs
CAT SE6 132 C6
Ravensbourne Pl LEW SE13 132 E1
Ravensbourne Rd BMLY BR1 167 K2
CAT SE6 132 C6
DART DA1 138 D2
TWK TW1 124 D5
Ravensbury Av MRDN SM4 162 B4
Ravensbury Gv MTCM CR4 162 C3
Ravensbury La MTCM CR4 162 C3
Ravensbury Rd
WAND/EARL SW18 147 F1
Ravensbury Ter
WAND/EARL SW18 147 F1
Ravenscar Rd BMLY BR1 152 C3
SURB KT6 172 B1
Ravens Cl CDALE/KGS NW9 51 H1
EN EN1 30 A1
HAYES BR2 167 J1
SURB KT6 158 E5
Ravenscourt SUN TW16 140 D7
Ravenscourt Av HMSMTH W6 106 D3
Ravenscourt Cl DEN/HRF UB9 46 A6
Ravenscourt Gdns
HMSMTH W6 106 C3
Ravenscourt Pk HMSMTH W6 106 D3
Ravenscourt Pl HMSMTH W6 106 E3
Ravenscourt Rd HMSMTH W6 106 E3
Ravenscourt Sq HMSMTH W6 106 D2
Ravenscraig Rd
FBAR/BDGN N11 40 B3
Ravenscroft Av GLDGN NW11 52 D6
WBLY HA9 50 A7
Ravenscroft Cl CAN/RD E16 94 E4
Ravenscroft Cots BAR EN5 * 26 E5
Ravenscroft Pk BAR EN5 26 B2
Ravenscroft Rd BECK BR3 165 K1
CAN/RD E16 94 E4
CHSWK W4 105 K3
Ravenscroft St BETH E2 7 M6
Ravensdale Av
NFNCH/WDSPK N12 39 G3
Ravensdale Gdns NRWD SE19 149 K6
Ravensdale Rd HSLWW TW4 122 D2
STNW/STAM N16 56 B6
Ravensdon St LBTH SE11 18 B8
Ravensfield DAGW RM9 79 K3
Ravensfield Gdns
HOR/WEW KT19 173 G4
Ravenshaw St
KIL/WHAMP NW6 70 D4
Ravenshill CHST BR7 154 B7
Ravenshurst Av HDN NW4 52 A3
Ravenside Cl UED N18 43 F4
Ravenslea Rd BAL SW12 128 E6
Ravensleigh Gdns BMLY BR1 152 E4
Ravensmead Rd HAYES BR2 152 B6
Ravensmede Wy CHSWK W4 106 C3
Ravens Ms LEE/GVPK SE12 * 133 K4
Ravenstone Rd
CDALE/KGS NW9 * 51 H5
CEND/HSY/T N8 55 F2
Ravenstone St BAL SW12 129 F7
Ravens Wy LEE/GVPK SE12 133 K4
Ravenswood BXLY DA5 137 F7
Ravenswood Av SURB KT6 172 B1
WWKM BR4 167 F7
Ravenswood Ct
KUTN/CMB KT2 * 144 E5
Ravenswood Crs
RYLN/HDSTN HA2 65 K1
WWKM BR4 167 F7
Ravenswood Gdns ISLW TW7 103 K7
Ravenswood Pk NTHWD HA6 32 E5
Ravenswood Rd BAL SW12 129 G6
CROY/NA CR0 177 H2
WALTH E17 58 A3
Ravensworth Rd
ELTH/MOT SE9 153 K3
WLSDN NW10 * 87 K2
Ravey St SDTCH EC2A 7 J9
Ravine Gv WOOL/PLUM SE18 115 K5
Rav Pinter Cl STNW/STAM N16 56 A6
Rawlings Cl BECK BR3 167 F4
Rawlings Crs WBLY HA9 68 D2
Rawlings St CHEL SW3 15 L5
Rawlins Cl FNCH N3 52 C2
SAND/SEL CR2 179 H6
Rawnsley Av MTCM CR4 162 C4
Rawreth Wk IS N1 * 6 F3
Rawson St BTSEA SW11 109 F7
Rawsthorne Cl CAN/RD E16 95 K7
Rawstorne Pl FSBYE EC1V * 6 C7
Rawstorne St FSBYE EC1V 6 C7
Ray Bell Ct BROCKY SE4 * 132 C1
Raydean Rd BAR EN5 26 E4
Raydons Gdns DAGW RM9 80 A3
Raydons Rd DAGW RM9 80 A4
Raydon St ARCH N19 72 B1
Rayfield Cl HAYES BR2 168 D5
Rayford Av LEE/GVPK SE12 133 J6
Rayford Cl DART DA1 139 F4
Ray Gdns BARK IG11 97 G1
STAN HA7 35 H4
Ray Lamb Wy ERITH DA8 118 E5
Rayleas Cl WOOL/PLUM SE18 115 G7
Rayleigh Av TEDD TW11 142 E5
Rayleigh Cl PLMGR N13 41 K2
Rayleigh Ct KUT/HW KT1 159 H1
Rayleigh Ri SAND/SEL CR2 178 A5
Rayleigh Rd CAN/RD E16 95 F7
PLMGR N13 41 J2
WFD IG8 45 G6
WIM/MER SW19 146 D7
Ray Lodge Rd WFD IG8 45 G5
Raymead Av THHTH CR7 164 B4
Raymere Gdns
WOOL/PLUM SE18 115 J6
Raymond Av SWFD E18 58 D2
WEA W13 104 B2
Raymond Blds GINN WC1R * 11 M2
Raymond Cl SYD SE26 150 E4
Raymond Rd BECK BR3 166 B3
GNTH/NBYPK IG2 60 D6
PLSTW E13 77 G6
WIM/MER SW19 146 C5
Raymond Wy
ESH/CLAY KT10 * 171 G5
Raymouth Rd
BERM/RHTH SE16 111 J3
Rayne Ct SWFD E18 58 D3
Rayners Cl ALP/SUD HA0 67 K4
Rayners Gdns NTHLT UB5 83 F2
Rayners La PIN HA5 47 K6
Rayner's Rd PUT/ROE SW15 127 H4
Raynes Av WAN E11 59 G6
Raynes Pk RYNPK SW20 161 F1
Raynham Av UED N18 42 C5
Raynham Rd HMSMTH W6 106 E3
UED N18 42 C4
Raynham Ter UED N18 42 C4
Raynor Cl STHL UB1 83 K7
Raynor Pl IS N1 6 F3
Raynton Cl RYLN/HDSTN HA2 47 J6
YEAD UB4 82 D3
Raynton Dr YEAD UB4 82 C1
Ray Rd E/WMO/HCT KT8 157 G4
Rays Av UED N18 42 E3
Rays Rd UED N18 42 E3
WWKM BR4 167 F6
Ray St CLKNW EC1R * 12 B1
Ray Street Br CLKNW EC1R * 12 B1
Raywood Cl HYS/HAR UB3 101 F6
Reachview Cl CAMTN NW1 4 F2
Read Cl THDIT KT7 158 B6
Reading La HACK E8 74 D5
Reading Rd NTHLT UB5 66 B4
SUT SM1 175 G4
Reading Wy MLHL NW7 38 B4
Reads Cl IL IG1 78 B2
Reapers Cl CAMTN NW1 5 G3
Reapers Wy ISLW TW7 123 J4
Reardon Pth WAP E1W 92 D7
Reardon St WAP E1W 92 D7
Reaston St NWCR SE14 111 K6
Reckitt Rd CHSWK W4 106 B4
Record St PECK SE15 111 K5
Recovery St TOOT SW17 147 J4
Recreation Av ROMW/RG RM7 62 E4
Recreation Rd HAYES BR2 167 J1
NWDGN UB2 102 D3
SYD SE26 151 F3
Recreation Wy MTCM CR4 163 K2
Rectar Pl ARCH N19 72 B1
Rector St IS N1 6 E4
Rectory Cl CHING E4 43 J2
DART DA1 138 B3
FNCH N3 38 D7
RYNPK SW20 161 F1
SCUP DA14 155 H3
STAN HA7 35 H5
SURB KT6 158 D7
Rectory Field Crs CHARL SE7 114 B6
Rectory Gdns BECK BR3 * 151 J7
CEND/HSY/T N8 54 E3
CHST BR7 * 154 C7
NTHLT UB5 65 K7
Rectory Gn BECK BR3 151 H7
Rectory Gv CLAP SW4 129 H2
CROY/NA CR0 177 H1
HPTN TW12 141 K3
Rectory La BUSH WD23 22 A5
EDGW HA8 36 C5
SCUP DA14 155 J4
STAN HA7 35 H4
SURB KT6 158 D7
TOOT SW17 148 A4
WLGTN SM6 176 C3
Rectory Orch WIM/MER SW19 146 C3
Rectory Park Av NTHLT UB5 83 K2
Rectory Pl CHST BR7 * 154 C7
WOOL/PLUM SE18 115 F3
Rectory Rd BARN SW13 126 D1
BECK BR3 151 J7
DAGE RM10 80 C5
HAYES BR2 181 H6
HSLWW TW4 122 A1
HYS/HAR UB3 82 E5
MNPK E12 77 K4
NWDGN UB2 102 E2
STNW/STAM N16 74 B2
SUT SM1 174 E2
WALTH E17 57 K3
Rectory Sq WCHPL E1 93 F4
Reculver Ms UED N18 42 C3
Reculver Rd
BERM/RHTH SE16 112 A4
Red Anchor Cl CHEL SW3 108 C5
Redan Pl BAY/PAD W2 8 C5
Redan St WKENS W14 107 G2
Redan Ter CMBW SE5 130 C1
Red Barracks Rd
WOOL/PLUM SE18 114 E3
Redberry Gv SYD SE26 150 E2
Redbourne Av FNCH N3 38 E7
Redbourne Dr THMD SE28 97 K5
Redbridge Gdns CMBW SE5 111 F6
Redbridge La East REDBR IG4 59 H5
Redbridge La West WAN E11 59 F5
Redburn St CHEL SW3 15 L9
Redbury Cl RAIN RM13 99 K3
Redcar Cl NTHLT UB5 66 B4
Redcar St CMBW SE5 * 110 D6
Redcastle Cl WAP E1W 92 E6
Red Cedars Rd ORP BR6 169 K6
Redchurch St BETH E2 7 L9
WCHPL E1 7 L9
Redcliffe Cl ECT SW5 14 C8
Redcliffe Gdns IL IG1 60 A7
WBPTN SW10 14 D8
Redcliffe Ms WBPTN SW10 14 D8
Redcliffe Pl WBPTN SW10 108 B5
Redcliffe Rd WBPTN SW10 14 E8
Redcliffe Sq WBPTN SW10 14 C9
Redcliffe St WBPTN SW10 14 D9
Redclose Av MRDN SM4 161 K4
Redclyffe Rd PLSTW E13 77 G7
Redcroft Rd STHL UB1 84 C6
Redcross Wy STHWK SE1 18 F1
Reddings Av BUSH WD23 22 B4
Reddings Cl MLHL NW7 37 H3
The Reddings BORE WD6 24 B2
MLHL NW7 37 H2
Reddington Cl SAND/SEL CR2 177 K7
Reddins Rd PECK SE15 111 H6
Reddons Rd BECK BR3 151 G6
Reddy Rd ERITH DA8 118 C5
Rede Pl BAY/PAD W2 8 B5
Redesdale Gdns ISLW TW7 104 B6
Redesdale St CHEL SW3 15 L9
Redfern Av HSLWW TW4 123 F6
Redfern Rd CAT SE6 133 F6
WLSDN NW10 69 G6
Redfield La ECT SW5 14 C5
Redford Av THHTH CR7 164 A3
WLGTN SM6 176 E5
Redford Cl FELT TW13 140 D1
Redford Wk IS N1 * 6 D3
Redgate Dr HAYES BR2 181 F1
Redgate Ter PUT/ROE SW15 127 G5
Redgrave Cl CROY/NA CR0 165 G5
Redgrave Rd PUT/ROE SW15 127 G2
Redgrave Ter BETH E2 * 92 C2
Redhall Ter EA W5 * 86 C6
Red Hl CHST BR7 154 A4
Redhill Dr EDGW HA8 50 D1
Redhill St CAMTN NW1 4 D6
Red House La BXLYHS DA6 136 E3
Red House Rd CROY/NA CR0 163 J5
Red House Sq IS N1 6 F1
Redington Gdns HAMP NW3 71 F3
Redington Rd HAMP NW3 71 F2
Redland Gdns
E/WMO/HCT KT8 * 156 E3
Redlands Wy
BRXS/STRHM SW2 129 K6
Red La ESH/CLAY KT10 171 G5
Redleaf Cl BXLYHN DA7 117 H5
Redlees Cl ISLW TW7 124 B3
Red Lion Cl WALW SE17 19 G9
Red Lion Ct FLST/FETLN EC4A 12 B4
HSLW TW3 * 123 G2
Red Lion Hl EFNCH N2 53 H1
Red Lion La WOOL/PLUM SE18 115 F7
Red Lion Pde PIN HA5 * 47 J2
Red Lion Pl
WOOL/PLUM SE18 * 115 F7
Red Lion Rd SURB KT6 172 B1
Red Lion Rw CMBW SE5 110 D5
Red Lion Sq GINN WC1R 11 L3
WAND/EARL SW18 * 127 K4
Red Lion St GINN WC1R 11 L3
RCH/KEW TW9 124 E4
Red Lion Yd
MYFR/PKLN W1K * 10 B8
Red Lodge Rd WWKM BR4 167 F7

Redman Cl NTHLT UB5 ....83 G1
Redman's Rd WCHPL E1 ....92 E4
Redmead La WAP E1W 92 C7
Redmead Rd HYS/HAR UB3 ....101 H3
Redmore Rd HMSMTH W6 * 106 E3
Red Pl MYFR/PKLN W1K 10
Redpoll Wy ERITHM DA18 ....116 E2
Redriffe Rd PLSTW E13 ....76 D7
Redriff Rd BERM/RHTH SE16 ....112 B2
  ROMW/RG RM7 ....62 D1
Red Rd BORE WD6 ....24 B2
Redroofs Cl BECK BR3 ....151 K7
Redruth Cl WDGN N22 ....41 F6
Redruth Gdns ESH/CLAY KT10...171 F6
Redruth Rd HOM E9 ....74 E7
Redsan Cl SAND/SEL CR2 ....177 K6
Redstart Cl EHAM E6 ....95 J4
  NWCR SE14 * 112 B6
Redston Rd CEND/HSY/T N8 ....54 D3
Redvers Cl WDGN N22 ....55 G1
Redvers St IS N1 ....7 K7
Redwald Rd CLPT E5 ....75 F3
Redway Dr WHTN TW2 ....123 H6
Redwing Ms CMBW SE5 ....130 D1
Redwing Rd WLGTN SM6 ....176 E6
Redwood Cl
  BERM/RHTH SE16 ....93 G7
  BFN/LL DA15 ....136 B7
  BOW E3 ....93 J1
  OXHEY WD19 ....33 G3
  STHGT/OAK N14 ....28 D6
Redwood Gdns CHING E4 ....31 K5
Redwood Gv EA W5 ....104 D2
Redwood Ms ASHF TW15 * 140 B6
  VX/NE SW8 ....129 G2
Redwood Wy BAR EN5 ....26 B4
Reece Ms SKENS SW7 ....15 G5
Reed Cl CAN/RD E16 ....94 E4
  LEE/GVPK SE12 ....133 K4
Reede Rd DAGE RM10 ....80 C5
Reede Wy DAGE RM10 ....80 D5
Reedham Cl TOTM N17 ....56 D3
Reedham St PECK SE15 ....131 H1
Reedholm Vls
  STNW/STAM N16 ....73 K3
Reed Pl BTSEA SW11 ....128 D3
  CLAP SW4 ....129 J3
Reed Pond Wk GPK RM2 ....63 H1
Reed Rd TOTM N17 ....56 B1
Reeds Crs WATN SW24 ....21 G1
Reeds Pl CAMTN NW1 ....4 B1
Reedworth St LBTH SE11 ....18 B6
Reenglass Rd STAN HA7 * 35 K3
Rees Dr STAN HA7 ....36 A3
Rees Gdns CROY/NA CR0 ....165 G5
Reesland Cl MNPK E12 ....78 A5
Rees St IS N1 ....6 F1
Reets Farm Cl
  CDALE/KGS NW9 ....51 G5
Reeves Av CDALE/KGS NW9...51 F5
Reeves Cnr CROY/NA CR0 * ...177 H1
Reeves Ms MYFR/PKLN W1K 10 A7
Reeves Rd BOW E3 ....93 K3
  WOOL/PLUM SE18 ....115 G5
Reform Rw TOTM N17 ....56 B1
Reform St BTSEA SW11 ....128 E1
Regal Cl EA W5 ....85 K4
  WCHPL E1 ....92 C4
Regal Ct MTCM CR4 ....162 E2
  UED N18 ....42 B4
Regal Crs WLGTN SM6 ....176 B2
Regal Dr FBAR/BDGN N11 ....40 B4
Regal La CAMTN NW1 ....4 A1
Regal Rw PECK SE15 ....111 K7
Regal Wy KTN/HRWW/WS HA3...50 A5
Regan Wy IS N1 ....7 H3
Regarth Av ROM RM1 ....4 A5
Regency Cl EN EN1 ....29 K4
  HPTN TW12 ....141 K4
Regency Crs HDN NW4 ....52 A2
Regency Dr RSLP HA4 ....46 A2
Regency Lawn KTTN NW5 * ...72 B2
Regency Ms BECK BR3 ....152 A1
  WLSDN NW10 ....69 J5
Regency Pde HAMP NW3 * 3 G2
Regency Pl WEST SW1P 17 G5
Regency St WEST SW1P 17 H5
Regency Ter HGT N6 * 53 K5
  SEVS/STOTM N15 ....56 A4
  SKENS SW7 ....15 G7
Regency Wk CROY/NA CR0 ....166 B5
Regency Wy BXLYHS DA6 ....136 E2
Regeneration Rd
  BERM/RHTH SE16 ....112 A3
Regent Cl HSLWW TW4 ....102 A2
  KTN/HRWW/WS HA3 ....50 A5
  NFNCH/WDSPK N12 ....39 G4
Regent Gdns GDMY/SEVK IG3...61 G5
Regent Pde BELMT SM2 * 175 G5
  STNW/STAM N16 * 56 B6
Regent Pl CROY/NA CR0 ....165 G7
  WIM/MER SW19 ....147 G4
Regent Rd BRYLDS KT5 ....159 G4
  HNHL SE24 ....130 C5
Regents Av PLMGR N13 ....41 G4
Regents Bridge Gdns
  VX/NE SW8 ....109 K5
Regents Cl SAND/SEL CR2 ....178 A5
  YEAD UB4 ....82 C4
Regents Dr HAYES BR2 ....181 H4
Regents Ms STJWD NW8 ....2 A2
Regent's Park Rd
  CAMTN NW1 ....3 M3
  FNCH N3 ....52 D2
Regent's Park Ter
  CAMTN NW1 ....4 C3
Regents Plaza
  KIL/WHAMP NW6 * 2 C5
Regent Sq BELV DA17 ....117 J3
  BOW E3 ....93 K2
  STPAN WC1H 5 K8
Regent's Rw BETH E2 ....74 C7
Regent St CHSWK W4 ....105 H4
  REGST W1B 10 D4
  STJS SW1Y 11 G7
  WLSDN NW10 ....88 B2
Regents Whf IS N1 * 5 L5
Reginald Rd DEPT SE8 ....112 D6
  FSTGT E7 ....76 E6
  NTHWD HA6 ....32 D7
Reginald Sq DEPT SE8 ....112 D6
Regina Rd FSBYPK N4 ....55 F7
  NWDGN UB2 ....102 D3
  SNWD SE25 ....165 H2
  WEA W13 ....85 G7
Regina Ter WEA W13 ....85 G7
Regis Rd KTTN NW5 ....72 B4
Regnart Blds CAMTN NW1 * ...4 F9
Reid Cl HYS/HAR UB3 ....82 C5
  PIN HA5 ....46 E2

Reidhaven Rd
  WOOL/PLUM SE18 ....115 K3
Reigate Av SUT SM1 ....162 A7
Reigate Rd BMLY BR1 ....152 C5
  GDMY/SEVK IG3 ....79 F1
Reigate Wy WLGTN SM6 ....176 E3
Reighton Rd CLPT E5 ....74 C2
Reinckendorf Av
  ELTH/MOT SE9 ....135 H4
Reizel Cl STNW/STAM N16 ....56 B7
Relay Rd SHB W12 ....88 A6
Relf Rd PECK SE15 ....131 H2
Reliance Ar BRXN/ST SW9 * 130 B3
Relton Ms SKENS SW7 ....15 K3
Rembrandt Cl BGVA SW1W 16 A7
  POP/IOD E14 ....113 G2
Rembrandt Ct
  HOR/WEW KT19 ....173 H5
Rembrandt Rd EDGW HA8 * 50 C1
  LEW SE13 ....133 H3
Remington Rd EHAM E6 ....95 J5
  SEVS/STOTM N15 ....55 K5
Remington St IS N1 ....6 C2
Remnant St HOL/ALD WC2B 11 L4
Remus Rd BOW E3 ....75 J6
Renaissance Wk GNWCH SE10..113 J2
Rendle Cl CROY/NA CR0 ....165 G4
Rendlesham Rd CLPT E5 ....74 C3
Renforth St BERM/RHTH SE16..111 K1
Renfrew Cl EHAM E6 ....96 A6
Renfrew Rd HSLWW TW4 ....122 C1
  KUTN/CMB KT2 ....144 E6
  LBTH SE11 ....18 C5
Renmuir St TOOT SW17 ....147 K5
Rennell St LEW SE13 ....133 F2
Renness Rd WALTH E17 ....57 G2
Rennets Cl ELTH/MOT SE9 ....135 J4
Rennets Wood Rd
  ELTH/MOT SE9 ....135 J4
Rennie Est BERM/RHTH SE16...111 J3
Rennie St STHWK SE1 ....12 C8
Renown Cl CROY/NA CR0 ....164 C7
Rensburg Rd WALTH E17 ....57 F4
Rensburg Vls WALTH E17 * 57 F4
Renshaw Cl BELV DA17 ....117 G5
Renters Av HDN NW4 ....52 A5
Renton Cl BRXS/STRHM SW2 *..130 A4
Renwick Rd BARK IG11 ....97 H3
Repens Wy YEAD UB4 ....83 H3
Rephidim St STHWK SE1 ....19 H4
Replingham Rd
  WAND/EARL SW18 ....127 J3
Reporton Rd FUL/PGN SW6 ....107 H7
Repository Rd
  WOOL/PLUM SE18 ....114 E5
Repton Av ALP/SUD HA0 ....67 J3
  GPK RM2 ....63 J2
  HYS/HAR UB3 ....101 G3
Repton Cl CAR SM5 ....175 J4
Repton Ct BECK BR3 ....151 K7
Repton Dr GPK RM2 ....63 J3
Repton Gdns GPK RM2 ....63 J2
Repton Gv CLAY IG5 ....45 K7
Repton Rd
  KTN/HRWW/WS HA3 ....50 B3
  POP/IOD E14 ....93 K6
Repton St POP/IOD E14 ....93 G5
Reservoir Cl THHTH CR7 ....164 E2
Reservoir Rd BROCKY SE4 ....132 B1
  RSLP HA4 ....46 A4
  STHGT/OAK N14 ....28 C4
Resham Cl NWDGN UB2 ....102 B2
Resolution Wy DEPT SE8 ....112 D6
Restell Cl BKHTH/KID SE3 ....113 H5
Restmor Wy CAR SM5 ....176 A1
  WLGTN SM6 ....176 A1
Reston Pl KENS W8 ....14 E2
Restons Crs ELTH/MOT SE9 ....135 J6
Restory Rd CAN/RD E16 ....95 H6
Restormel Cl HSLW TW3 ....123 F4
Retford St BETH E2 * 7 L7
  IS N1 * 7 K6
Retingham Wy CHING E4 ....43 K1
Retreat Cl
  KTN/HRWW/WS HA3 ....49 J4
Retreat Pl HOM E9 ....74 E5
Retreat Rd RCH/KEW TW9 ....124 E4
The Retreat BRYLDS KT5 ....159 G5
  CDALE/KGS NW9 ....51 F4
  MORT/ESHN SW14 ....126 B2
  RYLN/HDSTN HA2 ....48 A6
  THHTH CR7 ....164 E3
  TWK TW1 ....124 B7
  WPK KT4 ....173 K1
Reunion Rw WAP E1W * 92 D6
Reveley Sq BERM/RHTH SE16..112 B1
Revell Ri WOOL/PLUM SE18....116 A5
Revell Rd KUT/HW KT1 ....159 J1
  SUT SM1 ....174 D5
Revelon Rd BROCKY SE4 ....132 B3
Revelstoke Rd
  WIM/MER SW19 ....146 C2
Reventlow Rd ELTH/MOT SE9..135 H7
Reverdy Rd STHWK SE1 ....111 H3
Reverend Cl RYLN/HDSTN HA2..66 B2
Revere Wy HOR/WEW KT19 ....173 G7
Revesby Rd CAR SM5 ....162 D5
Review Rd CRICK NW2 ....69 H1
  DAGE RM10 ....98 D1
Rewell St FUL/PGN SW6 ....108 B6
Rewley Rd CAR SM5 ....162 C5
Rex Pl MYFR/PKLN W1K 10 A7
Reydon Av WAN E11 ....59 G5
Reynard Cl BMLY BR1 ....168 E2
Reynard Dr NRWD SE19 ....150 B6
Reynard Pl NWCR SE14 * 112 B5
Reynardson Rd TOTM N17 ....41 J6
Reynolah Gdns CHARL SE7 ....114 A4
Reynolds Av CHDH RM6 ....61 J6
  CHSGTN KT9 ....172 A6
  MNPK E12 ....78 A4
Reynolds Cl CAR SM5 ....162 E7
  GLDGN NW11 ....53 F6
  WIM/MER SW19 ....147 H7
Reynolds Dr EDGW HA8 ....50 B3
Reynolds Pl BKHTH/KID SE3..114 A6
  RCHPK/HAM TW10 ....125 G5
Reynolds Rd CHSWK W4 ....105 K2
  NWMAL KT3 ....160 A6
  PECK SE15 ....131 K4
  YEAD UB4 ....83 G3
Reynolds Wy CROY/NA CR0 ...178 A3
Rheidol Ms IS N1 ....6 D1
Rheidol Ter IS N1 ....6 C1
Rheingold Wy WLGTN SM6 ....176 E7
Rheola Cl TOTM N17 ....42 B7
Rhoda St BETH E2 ....7 M9
Rhodes St HOLWY N7 ....73 F4
Rhodes Wy WATN WD24 ....21 H1
Rhodesia Rd BRXN/ST SW9 ...129 K1
  WAN E11 ....76 B1
Rhodeswell Rd POP/IOD E14 ...93 G4
Rhodrons Av CHSGTN KT9 ...172 A4

Rhondda Gv BOW E3 ....93 G2
Rhyl Rd GFD/PVL UB6 ....85 F1
Rhyl St KTTN NW5 ....72 A5
Rhys Av FBAR/BDGN N11 ....40 D6
Rialto Rd MTCM CR4 ....163 F1
Ribble Cl WFD IG8 ....45 G5
Ribblesdale Av
  FBAR/BDGN N11 ....39 K5
  NTHLT UB5 ....66 B5
Ribblesdale Rd
  CEND/HSY/T N8 ....55 F3
  STRHM/NOR SW16 ....148 B4
Ribbon Dance Ms CMBW SE5...110 E7
Ribchester Av GFD/PVL UB6 ...85 F2
Ribston Cl HAYES BR2 ....168 E7
Ricardo St POP/IOD E14 ....93 K5
Ricards Rd WIM/MER SW19 ...146 D4
Rice Pde STMC/STPC BR5 * ...169 J4
Richard Cl WOOL/PLUM SE18..114 D3
Richard House Dr
  CAN/RD E16 ....95 H5
Richards Av ROMW/RG RM7 ...62 E4
Richards Cl BUSH WD23 ....22 D6
  HRW HA1 ....49 G4
  HYS/HAR UB3 ....101 G4
Richards Cots CAR SM5 * 175 K4
Richards Fld HOR/WEW KT19..173 F7
Richardson Cl HACK E8 * 7 L2
Richardson Gdns DAGE RM10...80 D5
Richardson Rd SRTFD E15 * ...94 C1
Richardson's Ms FITZ W1T * ...10 E1
Richards Pl CHEL SW3 ....15 K5
Richbell Pl FSBYW WC1X 11 L2
Richborne Ter VX/NE SW8 ....110 A6
Richborough Rd CRICK NW2 ...70 B3
Richens Cl HSLW TW3 ....123 J1
Riches Rd IL IG1 ....78 C1
Richfield Rd BUSH WD23 ....22 C6
Richford Ga HMSMTH W6 * ...107 F2
Richford Rd SRTFD E15 * 76 D7
Richford St HMSMTH W6 ....107 F1
Richill Ldg WHTN TW2 * 123 F5
Richlands Av EW KT17 ....173 J3
Richmer Rd ERITH DA8 ....118 D6
Richmond Av CHING E4 ....44 B4
  EBED/NFELT TW14 ....121 H5
  IS N1 ....5 M3
  RYNPK SW20 ....146 C7
Richmond Br TWK TW1 ....124 E4
Richmond Blds
  SOHO/SHAV W1D 11 G5
Richmond Cl BORE WD6 ....25 F4
  WALTH E17 ....57 H5
Richmond Crs CHING E4 ....44 B4
  ED N9 ....30 C7
  IS N1 ....5 M3
Richmond Dr WAT WD17 ....20 C1
Richmond Gdns HDN NW4 ....51 J4
  KTN/HRWW/WS HA3 ....35 F6
Richmond Ga KUTN/CMB KT2..144 A6
  RCHPK/HAM TW10 ....125 F6
Richmond Gn CROY/NA CR0 ...176 D2
Richmond Gv IS N1 ....6 C2
Richmond Hl
  RCHPK/HAM TW10 ....125 F5
Richmond Ms
  SOHO/SHAV W1D 11 G5
Richmond Pde TWK TW1 * 124 D5
Richmond Park Rd
  KUTN/CMB KT2 ....144 A6
  MORT/ESHN SW14 ....125 K4
Richmond Pl
  WOOL/PLUM SE18 ....115 H3
Richmond Rd BAR EN5 ....27 F3
  CROY/NA CR0 ....176 D2
  EA W5 ....105 F1
  EFNCH N2 * 53 G1
  FBAR/BDGN N11 ....40 E5
  FSTGT E7 ....77 F4
  HACK E8 ....7 L1
  IL IG1 ....78 C2
  ISLW TW7 ....124 B2
  KUTN/CMB KT2 ....143 K4
  ROM RM1 ....63 H5
  RYNPK SW20 ....145 K7
  SEVS/STOTM N15 ....56 A5
  THHTH CR7 ....164 C3
  TWK TW1 ....124 B7
  WAN E11 ....76 B1
Richmond St PLSTW E13 ....94 E1
Richmond Ter WHALL SW1A ...17 J1
Richmond Vls WALTH E17 * ...43 J1
Richmond Wy
  RKW/CH/CXG WD3 ....20 A3
  SHB W12 ....107 G1
  WAN E11 ....76 B1
Richmount Gdns
  BKHTH/KID SE3 ....133 K3
Rich St POP/IOD E14 ....93 H6
Rickard Cl BRXS/STRHM SW2..130 B7
  HDN NW4 ....51 J3
  WDR/YW UB7 ....100 A2
Rickards Cl SURB KT6 ....172 A1
Rickett St FUL/PGN SW6 ....14 B9
Rickman St WCHPL E1 ....92 E3
Rickmansworth Rd
  NTHWD HA6 ....32 B6
  PIN HA5 ....47 F1
  WATW WD18 ....20 C3
Rick Roberts Wy SRTFD E15 ...76 B7
Rickthorne Rd ARCH N19 ....72 E1
Ridding La GFD/PVL UB6 ....67 F4
Riddons Rd LEE/GVPK SE12...153 G2
Rideout St WOOL/PLUM SE18..114 E3
Rider Cl BFN/LL DA15 ....135 K5
The Ride BTFD TW8 ....104 C4
  PEND EN3 ....30 E2
Ridgdale St BOW E3 ....93 J1
Ridge Av DART DA1 ....138 C5
  WCHMH N21 ....29 J6
Ridgebrook Rd
  BKHTH/KID SE3 ....134 B3
Ridge Cl CDALE/KGS NW9 ....51 F3
  HDN NW4 ....52 B1
  THMD SE28 ....115 J1
Ridgecroft Cl BXLY DA5 ....137 K3
Ridge Hl GLDGN NW11 ....52 C7
Ridgemead Cl
  STHGT/OAK N14 ....40 C1
Ridgemont Gdns EDGW HA8...36 E3
Ridgemount Av CROY/NA CR0..179 F1
Ridgemount Cl PGE/AN SE20..150 D6
Ridgemount Gdns
  ENC/FH EN2 ....29 H2
Ridge Rd CEND/HSY/T N8 ....55 F5
  CHEAM SM3 ....161 J1
  CRICK NW2 ....70 D2
  MTCM CR4 ....148 B6
  WCHMH N21 ....29 K7
Ridges Yd CROY/NA CR0 ....177 H2
Ridge Ter WCHMH N21 * 29 H7
The Ridge BAR EN5 ....26 D4

  BRYLDS KT5 ....159 H4
  BXLY DA5 ....137 G6
  WHTN TW2 ....123 J6
Ridgeview Cl BAR EN5 ....26 B5
Ridgeview Rd
  TRDG/WHET N20 ....39 F2
  FELT TW13 ....141 J4
Ridgeway HAYES BR2 ....180 E1
  WFD IG8 ....45 G3
Ridgeway Av EBAR EN4 ....27 K5
Ridgeway Dr BMLY BR1 ....153 F2
Ridgeway East BFN/LL DA15..136 A4
Ridgeway Gdns HGT N6 ....54 C6
  REDBR IG4 ....59 J4
Ridgeway Rd ISLW TW7 ....103 K6
Ridgeway Rd North ISLW TW7..103 K5
The Ridgeway ACT W3 ....105 H2
  CDALE/KGS NW9 ....51 F3
  CROY/NA CR0 ....177 F2
  EBAR/BDGN N11 ....39 K3
  FNCH N3 ....39 F6
  GLDGN NW11 ....52 D7
  GPK RM2 ....63 J3
  KTN/HRWW/WS HA3 ....49 J3
  MLHL NW7 ....37 K4
  RSLP HA4 ....46 D6
  RYLN/HDSTN HA2 ....47 K4
  STAN HA7 ....35 J3
  STHGT/OAK N14 ....40 D1
Ridgeway West BFN/LL DA15...135 K4
Ridgewell Cl DAGE RM10 ....80 D7
  IS N1 ....6 D1
  SYD SE26 ....151 H3
Ridgmount Gdns
  GWRST WC1E 11 G2
Ridgmount Rd
  WAND/EARL SW18 ....128 A4
Ridgmount St GWRST WC1E ...11 G2
Ridgway RCHPK/HAM TW10 *...125 F5
  WIM/MER SW19 ....146 A6
Ridgway Gdns
  WIM/MER SW19 ....146 B6
Ridgway Pl WIM/MER SW19 ...146 C5
Ridgway Rd BRXN/ST SW9 ...130 C2
The Ridgway BELMT SM2 ....175 H6
Ridgwell Rd CAN/RD E16 ....95 G4
Riding House St GTPST W1W...10 D3
Ridings Av WCHMH N21 ....29 H4
Ridings Cl HGT N6 ....54 C6
The Ridings BRYLDS KT5 ....159 H4
  EA W5 ....86 B3
  EBAR EN4 ....27 H4
  EW KT17 ....173 H7
  SUN TW16 ....140 E7
The Riding GLDGN NW11 ....52 D6
Ridley Av WEA W13 ....104 C2
Ridley Cl BARK IG11 ....79 F6
Ridley Rd FSTGT E7 ....77 F3
  HACK E8 ....74 B4
  HAYES BR2 ....167 J2
  WELL DA16 ....116 C7
  WIM/MER SW19 ....147 F6
  WLSDN NW10 ....87 J1
Ridsdale Rd PGE/AN SE20 ....150 D7
Riefield Rd ELTH/MOT SE9 ...135 H4
Riesco Dr CROY/NA CR0 ....178 B5
Riffel Rd CRICK NW2 ....70 A4
Rifle Pl NTGHL W11 ....88 B7
Rifle Range La HRW HA1 ....49 F7
Rifle St POP/IOD E14 ....93 K4
Rigault Rd FUL/PGN SW6 ....127 H1
Rigby Cl CROY/NA CR0 ....177 G1
Rigby La HYS/HAR UB3 ....101 F1
Rigby Ms IL IG1 ....78 A1
Rigden St POP/IOD E14 ....93 K5
Rigeley Rd WLSDN NW10 ....87 J2
Rigg Ap LEY E10 ....75 F6
Rigge Pl CLAP SW4 ....129 J3
Riggindale Rd
  STRHM/NOR SW16 ....148 D4
Right Side STHGT/OAK N14 * ...28 D7
Riley Rd STHWK SE1 ....19 L3
Riley St WBPTN SW10 ....108 C6
Rinaldo Rd BAL SW12 ....129 G6
Ring Cl BMLY BR1 ....153 F6
Ringcroft St HOLWY N7 ....73 G4
Ringer's Rd BMLY BR1 ....167 K2
Ringford Rd
  WAND/EARL SW18 ....127 J4
Ringlet Cl CAN/RD E16 ....95 F4
Ringlewell Cl EN EN1 ....30 D1
Ringmer Av FUL/PGN SW6 ....107 H7
Ringmer Pl WCHMH N21 ....29 K4
Ringmer Wy BMLY BR1 ....168 E4
Ringmore Ri FSTH SE23 ....131 J6
Ring Rd SHB W12 ....88 A7
Ringslade Rd WDGN N22 ....55 F1
Ringstead Rd CAT SE6 ....132 E6
  SUT SM1 ....175 H3
Ring Wy FBAR/BDGN N11 * ...40 C5
Ringway NWDGN UB2 ....102 C4
Ringwood Av BECK BR3 ....151 G6
Ringwood Cl PIN HA5 * 47 G2
  EFNCH N2 ....53 K2
Ringwood Gdns
  PUT/ROE SW15 ....145 J1
  POP/IOD E14 ....112 D3
Ringwood Rd WALTH E17 ....57 H5
Ringwood Wy HPTN TW12 ....142 A3
  WCHMH N21 ....29 H6
Ripley Cl BMLY BR1 ....168 E4
  CROY/NA CR0 ....180 A5
Ripley Gdns
  MORT/ESHN SW14 ....126 A2
Ripley Ms WAN E11 ....58 C5
Ripley Rd BELV DA17 ....117 H3
  CAN/RD E16 ....95 G5
  GDMY/SEVK IG3 ....78 E1
  HPTN TW12 ....142 A6
Ripley Vls EA W5 ....85 J5
Ripon Cl NTHLT UB5 ....66 A4
Ripon Gdns CHSGTN KT9 ....171 K4
  IL IG1 ....59 J5
Ripon Rd ED N9 ....30 D6
  TOTM N17 ....55 K2
  WOOL/PLUM SE18 ....115 G5
Ripon Wy BORE WD6 ....24 E4
Rippersley Rd WELL DA16 ....116 B7
Ripple Rd BARK IG11 ....78 C7
  BARK IG11 ....79 H7
  DAGE RM9 ....98 A1
Ripplevale Gv IS N1 ....5 M2
Rippolson Rd
  WOOL/PLUM SE18 ....116 A4
Ripston Rd ASHF TW15 ....140 B4
Risborough Cl MUSWH N10 *...54 B2
Risborough Dr WPK KT4 ....160 D6
Risborough St STHWK SE1 * ...18 D1
Risdon St BERM/RHTH SE16..111 K1
Risebridge Rd GPK RM2 ....63 H1
Risedale Rd BXLYHN DA7 ....137 J2

Riseldine Rd FSTH SE23 ....132 B5
Rise Park Pde ROM RM1 ....63 G1
The Rise BORE WD6 ....24 B4
  BXLY DA5 ....136 D6
  DART DA1 ....138 A4
  EDGW HA8 ....36 D4
  GFD/PVL UB6 ....67 G4
  MLHL NW7 ....37 H5
  PLMGR N13 ....41 G3
  SAND/SEL CR2 ....178 E7
  WAN E11 ....58 E4
  WLSDN NW10 ....69 F2
Rising Hill Cl NTHWD HA6 *...32 A5
Risinghill St IS N1 ....6 A5
Risingholme Cl BUSH WD23 ...22 B6
  KTN/HRWW/WS HA3 ....34 E7
Risingholme Rd
  KTN/HRWW/WS HA3 ....48 E1
The Risings WALTH E17 ....58 B3
Risley Av TOTM N17 ....41 H4
Rita Rd VX/NE SW8 ....109 K6
Ritches Rd SEVS/STOTM N15...55 J5
Ritchie Rd CROY/NA CR0 ....165 J5
Ritchie St IS N1 ....6 B5
Ritchings Av WALTH E17 ....57 G3
Ritherdon Rd TOOT SW17 ....148 A1
Ritson Rd HACK E8 ....74 C5
Ritter St WOOL/PLUM SE18 ...115 F5
Rivaz Pl HOM E9 ....74 E5
Rivenhall Gdns SWFD E18 ....58 D3
River Av PLMGR N13 ....41 H2
  THDIT KT7 ....158 B6
Riverbank E/WMO/HCT KT8 ..157 K3
River Bank THDIT KT7 ....158 A4
  WCHMH N21 ....29 J6
Riverbank Rd BMLY BR1 ....152 E2
Riverbank Wy BTFD TW8 ....104 D5
River Barge Cl POP/IOD E14 ...113 F1
River Cl NWDGN UB2 ....103 H1
  RAIN RM13 ....99 K4
  RSLP HA4 ....46 D5
  WAN E11 ....59 G5
River Ct PUR RM19 ....119 J3
Rivercourt Rd HMSMTH W6 ...106 E3
River Crane Wy FELT TW13 ...141 K1
Riverdale Rd
  WAND/EARL SW18 ....128 A3
Riverdale Gdns TWK TW1 ....124 D4
Riverdale Rd BXLY DA5 ....137 G6
  ERITH DA8 ....117 J4
  FELT TW13 ....141 J3
  TWK TW1 ....124 D4
  WOOL/PLUM SE18 ....116 A4
Riverdene EDGW HA8 ....36 E3
Riverdene Rd IL IG1 ....78 A2
River Front EN EN1 ....29 K2
River Gdns CAR SM5 ....176 A1
  EBED/NFELT TW14 ....122 A4
River Grove Pk BECK BR3 ....151 H7
Riverhead Cl WALTH E17 ....57 F1
Riverholme Dr
  HOR/WEW KT19 ....173 F7
River La RCHPK/HAM TW10 ...124 E7
  KUT/HW KT1 * 158 E4
Rivermead E/WMO/HCT KT8..157 H3
Rivermead Rd UED N18 * 43 F4
River Meads Av WHTN TW2 ...142 B2
Rivernook Cl WOT/HER KT12..156 A4
Riverpark Gdns HAYES BR2 ...152 B6
River Park Rd WDGN N22 ....55 F1
River Pl IS N1 ....6 E2
River Reach TEDD TW11 ....143 J4
River Rd BARK IG11 ....96 E2
  THDIT KT7 ....158 B4
Riversdale Rd HBRY N5 ....73 H2
  THDIT KT7 ....158 B4
Riversfield Rd EN EN1 ....30 A2
Riverside CHARL SE7 ....114 A2
  HDN NW4 ....51 K6
  RCH/KEW TW9 ....105 H5
  RCH/KEW TW9 ....124 E4
  SUN TW16 ....156 C1
  TWK TW1 ....124 C7
Riverside Av E/WMO/HCT KT8..157 J2
Riverside Cl CLPT E5 ....56 E7
  HNWL W7 ....84 E3
  KUT/HW KT1 ....158 E3
  ROMW/RG RM7 ....63 F2
  WLGTN SM6 ....176 B2
Riverside Ct CHING E4 ....31 K5
Riverside Dr CHSWK W4 ....106 A6
  ESH/CLAY KT10 ....170 A3
  GLDGN NW11 ....52 C5
  MTCM CR4 ....162 D4
  RCHPK/HAM TW10 ....143 H2
Riverside Gdns ALP/SUD HA0..86 A1
  ENC/FH EN2 ....29 J1
  HMSMTH W6 ....106 E4
Riverside Ms CROY/NA CR0 *..176 E2
Riverside Pl
  FBAR/BDGN N11 * 40 C2
  STWL/WRAY TW19 ....120 A5
Riverside Rd IL IG1 ....78 B2
  OXHEY WD19 ....21 F5
  SEVS/STOTM N15 ....56 C5
  SRTFD E15 ....94 A1
  STWL/WRAY TW19 ....120 A4
  TOOT SW17 ....147 F3
The Riverside
  E/WMO/HCT KT8 ....157 J2
Riverside Vls SURB KT6 * 158 E5
Riverside Wk ISLW TW7 ....123 K2
  KUT/HW KT1 ....158 E3
Riverside Yd TOOT SW17 ....147 F3
Riverstone Cl
  RYLN/HDSTN HA2 ....66 D1
River St CLKNW EC1R 6 A7
Riverton Cl MV/WKIL W9 * ...88 D2
Riverview Gdns BARN SW13...106 E5
River View Gdns TWK TW1 ...143 F1
Riverview Gv CHSWK W4 ....105 J5
Riverview Pk CAT SE6 ....151 J1
Riverview Rd CHSWK W4 ....105 J6
  HOR/WEW KT19 ....172 E3
River Wk SUN TW16 ....156 C1
River Wy WHTN TW2 ....142 B1
  GNWCH SE10 ....113 J2
  HOR/WEW KT19 ....172 E5
Riverway PLMGR N13 ....41 G3
River Whf BELV DA17 * 118 A1
Riverwood La CHST BR7 ....169 J1
Rivington Av WFD IG8 ....59 H1
Rivington Crs MLHL NW7 ....37 G6
Rivington Pl FSBYE EC1V * ...7 K8
Rivington St SDTCH EC2A 7 K8
Rivington Wk HACK E8 * 74 C7
Rivulet Rd TOTM N17 ....41 H6
Rixon St HOLWY N7 ....73 G2
Rixsen Rd MNPK E12 ....77 J3
Roach Rd BOW E3 ....75 J6
Roads Pl ARCH N19 ....72 E1

Roan St GNWCH SE10 ... 113 F5
Robarts St STAN HA7 ... 47 F4
Robb Rd STAN HA7 ... 35 G5
Robert Adam St MHST W1U ... 10 H1
Robert St BETH E2 ... 92 C2
Robert Cl AM/WKIL W9 ... 8 F1
Robert Dashwood Wy WALW SE17 ... 18 E6
Robert Keen Cl PECK SE15 ... 111 H7
Robert Lowe Cl NWCR SE14 ... 112 A6
Roberton Dr BMLY BR1 ... 168 B1
Robertsbridge Rd CAR SM5 ... 162 A6
Roberts Cl CHEAM SM3 ... 174 B6
DAGE RM10 ... 80 C5
ELTH/MOT SE9 ... 135 J7
THHTH CR7 ... 164 E2
Roberts Ct CHSGTN KT9 ... 171 K4
PGE/AN SE20 ... 150 E7
WLSDN NW10 ... 69 G5
Roberts House WOOL/PLUM SE18 * ... 114 D8
Roberts Ms KTBR SW1X * ... 16 A1
Robertson St VX/NE SW8 ... 129 C1
Robert Sq LEW SE13 * ... 133 F3
Robert St BELV DA17 ... 117 H4
MLHL NW7 ... 38 C4
WALTH E17 ... 43 K7
WATW WD18 ... 21 G3
Robert St CAMTN NW1 ... 4 D7
CHCR WC2N ... 11 K7
CROY/NA CR0 ... 177 J2
WOOL/PLUM SE18 ... 115 J3
Robeson St BOW E3 ... 93 H4
Robina Rd BXLYHS DA6 ... 136 F5
NTHWD HA6 ... 46 D1
Robin Cl FELT TW13 ... 141 H4
MLHL NW7 ... 37 G2
Robin Gv BTFD TW8 ... 104 D5
HGT N6 ... 72 A1
KTN/HRWW/WS HA3 ... 50 B5
Robin Hill Dr CHST BR7 ... 153 J7
Robinhood Cl MTCM CR4 ... 163 H3
Robin Hood Dr KTN/HRWW/WS HA3 ... 35 F6
Robin Hood Gdns POP/IOD E14 * ... 94 A6
Robin Hood La BXLYHS DA6 ... 137 H4
POP/IOD E14 ... 94 A6
PUT/ROE SW15 ... 145 J2
SUT SM1 ... 174 E4
Robinhood La MTCM CR4 ... 163 H3
Robin Hood Rd PUT/ROE SW15 ... 145 G3
WIM/MER SW19 ... 145 J3
Robin Hood Wy GFD/PVL UB6 ... 67 J5
PUT/ROE SW15 ... 145 G3
Robinia Cl PGE/AN SE20 ... 150 C7
Robinia Crs LEY E10 ... 75 K1
Robin La HDN NW4 ... 52 B2
Robinscroft Ms GNWCH SE10 * ... 113 F7
Robins Gv WWKM BR4 ... 180 E2
Robinson Rd ENC/FH EN2 ... 29 J2
WAN E11 ... 81 K6
Robinson Crs BUSH WD23 ... 22 C7
Robinson Rd BETH E2 ... 92 E1
DAGE RM10 ... 80 C3
TOOT SW17 ... 147 J5
Robinson's Cl WEA W13 ... 85 G4
Robinson St CHEL SW3 ... 15 L9
Robinswood Ms HBRY N5 ... 73 H4
Robinwood Pl PUT/ROE SW15 ... 145 F3
Rob Pascoe La DAGW RM9 ... 98 A2
Robsart St BRXN/ST SW9 ... 130 A1
Robson Av WLSDN NW10 ... 69 J6
Robson Cl EHAM E6 ... 95 J5
ENC/FH EN2 ... 29 H1
Robson Rd WNWD SE27 ... 149 H2
Rocastle Rd BROCKY SE4 ... 132 B4
Roch Av EDGW HA8 ... 50 B1
Rochdale Rd ABYW SE2 ... 116 C4
WALTH E17 ... 57 J6
Rochdale Wy DEPT SE8 * ... 112 D6
Rochelle Cl BTSEA SW11 ... 128 C3
Rochelle St BETH E2 ... 7 L8
Rochemont Wk HACK E8 * ... 7 M4
Roche Rd STRHM/NOR SW16 ... 148 E7
Rochester Av BMLY BR1 ... 168 A1
FELT TW13 ... 140 D1
PLSTW E13 ... 77 G1
Rochester Cl BFN/LL DA15 ... 136 C5
STRHM/NOR SW16 * ... 148 E6
Rochester Dr BXLY DA5 ... 137 H5
PIN HA5 ... 47 H4
Rochester Gdns CROY/NA CR0 ... 178 A2
IL IG1 ... 59 K6
Rochester Ms CAMTN NW1 * ... 4 F1
EA W5 ... 104 D3
Rochester Pde FELT TW13 * ... 140 D1
Rochester Pl CAMTN NW1 ... 72 C5
Rochester Rd CAMTN NW1 ... 72 C5
CAR SM5 ... 175 K3
DART DA1 ... 139 G6
HCH RM12 ... 81 K6
NTHWD HA6 ... 46 D2
Rochester Rw WEST SW1P ... 16 F5
Rochester Sq CAMTN NW1 * ... 4 F1
Rochester St WEST SW1P ... 17 G4
Rochester Ter CAMTN NW1 ... 72 C5
Rochester Wk STHWK SE1 * ... 13 G8
Rochester Wy BKHTH/KID SE3 ... 114 A4
DART DA1 ... 138 B6
ELTH/MOT SE9 ... 134 C4
Rochester Way Relief Rd ELTH/MOT SE9 ... 134 D4
Roche Wk CAR SM5 ... 162 C5
Rochford Av CHDH RM6 ... 61 J4
Rochford Cl EHAM E6 ... 95 H1
HCH RM12 ... 81 K5
Rochford Wk HACK E8 * ... 74 C6
Rochford Wy CROY/NA CR0 ... 163 K5
Rock Av MORT/ESHN SW14 ... 126 A2
Rockbourne Rd FSTH SE23 ... 132 A7
Rock Cl MTCM CR4 ... 162 C1
Rockell's Pl EDUL SE22 ... 131 J5
Rock Gdns GFD/PVL UB6 ... 85 H1
Rock Grove Wy BERM/RHTH SE16 ... 111 H3
Rockhall Rd CRICK NW2 ... 70 B3
Rockhampton Rd SAND/SEL CR2 ... 178 A5
STRHM/NOR SW16 ... 149 C3
Rock Hl DUL SE21 ... 150 B3
Rockingham Av EMPK RM11 ... 63 K5
Rockingham Cl PUT/ROE SW15 ... 126 C3
Rockingham Ga BUSH WD23 ... 22 C5
Roma Read Cl PUT/ROE SW15 ... 126 E6
Rockingham St STHWK SE1 ... 18 E4
Rockland Rd PUT/ROE SW15 ... 127 H3
Rocklands Dr KTN/HRWW/WS HA3 ... 49 H1
Rockley Rd SHB W12 ... 107 G1

Rockmount Rd NRWD SE19 ... 149 K5
WOOL/PLUM SE18 ... 116 A6
Rocks La BARN SW13 ... 126 D2
Rock St FSBYPK N4 ... 73 G1
Rockware Av GFD/PVL UB6 ... 66 E7
Rockways BAR EN5 ... 25 H5
Rockwell Gdns NRWD SE19 ... 150 A3
Rockwell Rd DAGE RM10 ... 80 D3
Rocombe Crs FSTH SE23 * ... 131 K6
Rocque La BKHTH/KID SE3 ... 133 J2
Rodborough Rd GLDGN NW11 ... 52 E6
Roden Gdns CROY/NA CR0 ... 165 F5
Roden St HOLWY N7 ... 73 F2
IL IG1 ... 78 A2
Rodeo Cl ERITH DA8 ... 118 E7
Roderick Rd HAMP NW3 ... 71 K3
Rodgers Cl BORE WD6 ... 23 K5
Roding La North WFD IG8 ... 59 J1
Roding La South REDBR IG4 ... 59 H3
Roding Ms WAP E1W ... 92 C7
Roding Rd CLPT E5 ... 75 F3
EHAM E6 ... 96 B4
Roding St IS N1 ... 5 M5
Rodings Rw BAR EN5 * ... 26 C3
Rodmarton St MHST W1U ... 9 M3
Rodmell Cl YEAD UB4 ... 83 J3
Rodmell Slope NFNCH/WDSPK N12 ... 38 D4
Rodmere St GNWCH SE10 ... 113 H4
Rodney Cl CROY/NA CR0 ... 164 C7
NWMAL KT3 ... 160 B4
PIN HA5 ... 47 J6
WOT/HER KT12 * ... 156 B7
Rodney Gdns PIN HA5 ... 47 F4
WWKM BR4 ... 180 E3
Rodney Pl STHWK SE1 ... 18 F5
WALTH E17 ... 57 G1
WIM/MER SW19 ... 147 G2
Rodney Rd MTCM CR4 ... 162 D1
NWMAL KT3 ... 160 B4
STHWK SE1 ... 18 F6
WALW SE17 ... 19 G6
WAN E11 ... 59 F3
WHTN TW2 ... 123 F6
Rodney St IS N1 ... 5 M5
Rodway Rd BMLY BR1 ... 153 F7
PUT/ROE SW15 ... 126 D6
Rodwell Cl RSLP HA4 * ... 47 G1
Rodwell Rd EDUL SE22 ... 131 G5
Roebuck Cl FELT TW13 ... 141 F3
Roebuck Rd CHSGTN KT9 ... 172 C4
Roedean Crs PUT/ROE SW15 ... 126 B5
Roe End CDALE/KGS NW9 ... 50 E3
Roe Gn CDALE/KGS NW9 ... 50 E4
Roehampton Cl PUT/ROE SW15 ... 126 D3
Roehampton Dr CHST BR7 ... 154 C5
Roehampton Ga PUT/ROE SW15 ... 126 B5
Roehampton High St PUT/ROE SW15 ... 126 D6
Roehampton La PUT/ROE SW15 ... 126 E7
Roehampton V PUT/ROE SW15 ... 145 H2
Roe La CDALE/KGS NW9 ... 50 D3
Roe Rd WLGTN SM6 ... 176 E5
Rofant Rd NTHWD HA6 ... 32 C5
Roffey St POP/IOD E14 ... 113 F1
Rogers Gdns DAGE RM10 ... 80 C4
Rogers Rd CAN/RD E16 ... 94 D5
DAGE RM10 ... 80 C4
TOOT SW17 ... 147 H3
Rogers Ruff NTHWD HA6 ... 32 A7
Roger St BMSBY WC1N ... 11 M1
Rogers Wk NFNCH/WDSPK N12 ... 39 F2
Rojack Rd FSTH SE23 ... 132 A7
Rokeby Gdns WFD IG8 ... 44 E7
Rokeby Pl RYNPK SW20 ... 145 K6
Rokeby Rd BROCKY SE4 * ... 132 C1
Rokeby St SRTFD E15 ... 76 C7
Rokesby Cl WELL DA16 ... 135 J1
Rokesby Pl ALP/SUD HA0 ... 67 K4
Rokesly Av CEND/HSY/T N8 ... 54 E4
Roland Gdns SKENS SW7 ... 14 F7
Roland Ms WCHPL E1 * ... 93 F4
Roland Rd WALTH E17 ... 58 B3
Roland Wy SKENS SW7 ... 14 F7
WALW SE17 ... 19 H8
WPK KT4 ... 173 H1
Roles Gv CHDH RM6 ... 61 K3
Rolfe Cl EBAR EN4 ... 27 J3
Rolinsden Wy HAYES BR2 ... 181 H3
Rollesby Rd CHSGTN KT9 ... 172 C5
Rollesby Wy THMD SE28 ... 97 J6
Rolleston Av STMC/STPC BR5 ... 169 G6
Rolleston Cl STMC/STPC BR5 ... 169 G6
Rolleston Rd SAND/SEL CR2 ... 177 K6
Roll Gdns GNTH/NBYPK IG2 ... 60 A4
Rollins St PECK SE15 ... 111 K5
Rollit Crs HSLW TW3 ... 123 F4
Rollit St HOLWY N7 * ... 73 G4
Rollscourt Av HNHL SE24 ... 130 D4
Rolls Park Av CHING E4 ... 43 J5
Rolls Park Rd CHING E4 ... 43 K4
Rolls Rd STHWK SE1 ... 19 L8
Rolls Royce Cl WLGTN SM6 ... 176 E6
Rolt St DEPT SE8 ... 112 C5
NWCR SE14 ... 112 B5
Rolvenden Gdns BMLY BR1 ... 153 H7
Rolvenden Pl TOTM N17 ... 42 D7
Roman Cl ACT W3 ... 105 J1
EBED/NFELT TW14 ... 122 B4
RAIN RM13 ... 99 F1
Romanfield Rd BRXS/STRHM SW2 ... 130 A6
Romanhurst Av HAYES BR2 ... 167 H3
Romanhurst Gdns HAYES BR2 ... 167 H3
Roman Ri NRWD SE19 ... 149 K5
Roman Rd BETH E2 ... 93 F1
BOW E3 ... 93 J1
CHSWK W4 ... 106 C3
CRICK NW2 ... 70 A7
EHAM E6 ... 95 H3
IL IG1 ... 78 B4
MUSWH N10 ... 40 B6
Roman Sq THMD SE28 ... 97 G7
Roman Wy CROY/NA CR0 ... 177 H1
DART DA1 ... 138 B4
EN EN1 ... 30 B4
HOLWY N7 ... 73 F5
Romany Gdns CHEAM SM3 ... 161 K6
Romany Ri STMC/STPC BR5 ... 169 H6
Roma Rd WALTH E17 ... 57 G2
Romberg Rd TOOT SW17 ... 148 A2
Romborough Gdns LEW SE13 ... 133 F4
Romborough Wy LEW SE13 ... 133 F4
Rom Crs ROMW/RG RM7 ... 63 G6

Romeland BORE WD6 ... 23 K5
Romero Cl BRXN/ST SW9 ... 130 A2
Romero Sq BKHTH/KID SE3 ... 134 B3
Romeyn Rd STRHM/NOR SW16 ... 149 F2
Romford Rd FSTGT E7 ... 76 E5
MNPK E12 ... 77 K3
SRTFD E15 ... 76 D5
Romford St WCHPL E1 ... 92 C4
Romilly Dr OXHEY WD19 ... 33 J3
Romilly Rd FSBYPK N4 ... 73 H1
Romilly St SOHO/SHAV W1D ... 11 H6
Rommany Rd WNWD SE27 ... 149 K3
Romney Cl ASHF TW15 ... 140 A4
CHSGTN KT9 ... 172 A3
GLDGN NW11 ... 53 G7
NWCR SE14 ... 111 K6
RYLN/HDSTN HA2 ... 48 A6
TOTM N17 ... 42 D7
Romney Dr BMLY BR1 ... 153 H4
RYLN/HDSTN HA2 ... 48 A6
Romney Rd GNWCH SE10 ... 113 F5
NWMAL KT3 ... 160 A5
WOOL/PLUM SE18 ... 115 H2
YEAD UB4 ... 82 B1
Romney Rw CRICK NW2 * ... 70 B1
Romney St WEST SW1P ... 17 H4
Romola Rd HNHL SE24 ... 130 C7
Romsey Rd DAGW RM9 ... 79 K7
WEA W13 ... 85 G6
Romside Pl ROMW/RG RM7 ... 63 G2
Rom Valley Wy ROMW/RG RM7 ... 63 G5
Ronald Av SRTFD E15 ... 94 C2
Ronald Cl BECK BR3 ... 166 C4
Ronalds Rd BMLY BR1 ... 152 E7
HBRY N5 ... 73 G4
Ronaldstone Rd BFN/LL DA15 ... 135 K5
Rona Rd HAMP NW3 ... 71 L2
Ronart St KTN/HRWW/WS HA3 ... 49 F2
Rona Wk IS N1 * ... 73 L5
Rondu Rd CRICK NW2 ... 70 C4
Ronelaan Rd SURB KT6 ... 172 B1
Roneo Cnr ROMW/RG RM7 ... 63 H7
Roneo Link HCH RM12 ... 63 H7
Ron Green Ct ERITH DA8 ... 118 A4
Ron Leighton Wy EHAM E6 ... 77 J1
Ronnie La BCTR RM8 ... 79 J1
Ron Todd Cl DAGE RM10 ... 98 C2
Ronver Rd LEE/GVPK SE12 ... 133 K7
Rood La FENCHST EC3M ... 13 K6
Rookby Ct WCHMH N21 ... 41 H1
Rook Cl WBLY HA9 ... 68 D2
Rookeries Cl FELT TW13 ... 141 F2
Rookery Dr CHST BR7 ... 154 A7
Rookery La HAYES BR2 ... 168 C5
Rookery Rd CLAP SW4 ... 129 H3
The Rookery STRHM/NOR SW16 * ... 149 F5
Rookery Wy CDALE/KGS NW9 ... 51 H4
Rookfield Cl MUSWH N10 ... 54 C3
Rookfield Cl MUSWH N10 ... 54 C3
Rookley Cl BELMT SM2 ... 175 F7
Rooks Ter WDR/YW UB7 * ... 100 B1
Rookstone Rd TOOT SW17 ... 147 K4
Rookwood Av NWMAL KT3 ... 160 D3
WLGTN SM6 ... 176 D3
Rookwood Gdns CHING E4 * ... 44 C1
Rookwood Rd STNW/STAM N16 ... 56 C6
Roosevelt Wy DAGE RM10 ... 81 F5
Rootes Dr NKENS W10 ... 88 B3
Ropemaker Rd BERM/RHTH SE16 ... 112 B1
Ropemaker's Flds POP/IOD E14 * ... 93 H6
Ropemaker St BARB EC2Y ... 13 G2
Roper La STHWK SE1 ... 19 K2
Ropers Av CHING E4 ... 44 A4
Ropers Orch CHEL SW3 * ... 108 C5
Roper St ELTH/MOT SE9 ... 134 E4
Ropery St MTCM CR4 ... 163 F1
Rope St BERM/RHTH SE16 ... 112 B2
Ropewalk Gdns WCHPL E1 ... 92 C5
Ropley St BETH E2 ... 92 C1
Rosa Alba Ms HBRY N5 ... 73 J3
Rosaline Rd FUL/PGN SW6 ... 107 H6
Rosaline Ter FUL/PGN SW6 * ... 107 H6
Rosamond St SYD SE26 ... 150 D2
Rosamond Vls MORT/ESHN SW14 * ... 126 A3
Rosamund Cl SAND/SEL CR2 ... 177 A3
Rosamun Rd NWDGN UB2 ... 102 D3
Rosary Cl HSLW TW3 ... 122 D1
Rosary Gdns BUSH WD23 ... 22 C6
SKENS SW7 ... 14 F6
Rosary Ga BTSEA SW11 ... 109 G6
Rosaville Rd FUL/PGN SW6 ... 107 J6
Roscoe St STLK EC1Y ... 12 F1
Roscoff Cl EDGW HA8 ... 36 D7
Roseacre Cl WEA W13 ... 85 H4
Roseacre Rd WELL DA16 ... 136 C2
Rose Aly STHWK SE1 ... 12 F8
Roseary Cl WDR/YW UB7 ... 100 B3
Rose Av MRDN SM4 ... 162 A4
MTCM CR4 ... 147 K7
SWFD E18 ... 59 F1
Rosebank PGE/AN SE20 ... 150 D6
Rosebank Av WCHMH N21 ... 29 G7
ALP/SUD HA0 ... 67 G3
Rose Bank Cl NFNCH/WDSPK N12 ... 39 J4
Rosebank Cl TEDD TW11 ... 143 G5
Rosebank Est BOW E3 ... 93 H1
Rosebank Gdns ACT W3 ... 87 F5
BOW E3 * ... 93 H1
Rosebank Gv WALTH E17 ... 57 H2
Rosebank Rd HNWL W7 ... 103 K2
WALTH E17 ... 57 J5
Rosebank Wk CAMTN NW1 ... 5 M1
Rosebank Wy ACT W3 ... 87 F5
Rosebery Av BFN/LL DA15 ... 135 K5
Rosebery Av CLKNW EC1R ... 12 A1
MNPK E12 ... 77 J5
NWMAL KT3 ... 160 C1
RYLN/HDSTN HA2 ... 65 D1
THHTH CR7 ... 164 D1
TOTM N17 ... 56 C1
Rosebery Cl MRDN SM4 ... 161 G5
Rosebery Gdns CEND/HSY/T N8 ... 54 E4
SUT SM1 ... 175 F3
WEA W13 ... 85 G5
Rosebery Ms MUSWH N10 ... 54 C1
Rosebery Pde EW KT17 * ... 173 H7

Rosebery Rd BUSH WD23 ... 22 B7
CLAP SW4 ... 129 K5
HSLW TW3 ... 123 H4
KUT/HW KT1 ... 159 H4
MUSWH N10 ... 54 C1
SUT SM1 ... 174 D7
Rosebine Av WHTN TW2 ... 123 H8
Rosebriars ESH/CLAY KT10 ... 170 A5
Rosebury Rd FUL/PGN SW6 ... 128 A1
Rosebury V RSLP HA4 ... 64 E1
Rose Ct WCHPL E1 ... 13 M3
Rosecourt Rd CROY/NA CR0 ... 164 A5
Rosecroft Av HAMP NW3 ... 70 E2
Rose Croft Gdns CRICK NW2 ... 69 J2
Rosecroft Gdns WHTN TW2 ... 123 J7
Rosecroft Rd STHL UB1 ... 84 A3
Rosecroft Wk ALP/SUD HA0 ... 67 K4
PIN HA5 ... 47 H3
Rose & Crown Yd STJS SW1Y * ... 10 F9
Rosedale CROY/NA CR0 ...
Rosedale Cl ABYW SE2 ... 116 C2
HNWL W7 ... 104 A1
STAN HA7 ... 35 H5
Rosedale Dr DAGW RM9 ... 79 H6
Rosedale Gdns DAGW RM9 ... 79 H6
Rosedale Pl CROY/NA CR0 ... 166 A6
Rosedale Rd DAGW RM9 ... 79 H6
EW KT17 ... 173 J4
FSTGT E7 ... 77 G4
RCH/KEW TW9 ... 125 F3
ROM RM1 ... 63 G2
Rosedene Av CROY/NA CR0 ... 163 K6
GFD/PVL UB6 ... 84 A2
MRDN SM4 ... 161 K4
STRHM/NOR SW16 ... 148 E7
Rosedene Gdns GNTH/NBYPK IG2 ... 60 A3
Rosedew Rd HMSMTH W6 ... 107 G5
Rose End WPK KT4 ... 161 H7
Rosefield Rd POP/IOD E14 ... 93 K6
Rosefield Cl CAR SM5 ... 175 J4
Rosefield Gdns POP/IOD E14 ... 93 K6
Rose Garden Cl EDGW HA8 ... 36 A5
Rose Gdns EA W5 ... 104 E2
FELT TW13 ... 140 E1
STHL UB1 ... 84 A3
STWL/WRAY TW19 ... 120 A6
WATW WD18 ... 20 E4
Rose Gln CDALE/KGS NW9 ... 51 F3
ROMW/RG RM7 ... 63 G7
Rosehart Ms NTGHL W11 ... 8 B6
Rosehatch Av CHDH RM6 ... 61 K3
Roseheath Rd HSLWW TW4 ... 122 E4
Rosehill ESH/CLAY KT10 ... 171 G5
HPTN TW12 ... 142 A7
Rose Hl SUT SM1 ... 175 F1
Rosehill Av SUT SM1 ... 162 B7
Rosehill Court Pde MRDN SM4 * ... 162 B6
Rosehill Gdns GFD/PVL UB6 ... 67 G5
SUT SM1 ... 175 F1
Rose Hill Pk West SUT SM1 ... 162 B7
Rosehill Rd WAND/EARL SW18 ... 128 B5
Rose Joan Ms KIL/WHAMP NW6 ... 70 E2
Roseland Cl TOTM N17 ... 41 K6
Rose La CHDH RM6 ... 62 A3
Rose Lawn BUSH WD23 ... 22 C7
Roseleigh Av HBRY N5 ... 73 H3
Roseleigh Cl TWK TW1 ... 124 E5
Rosemary Av E/WMO/HCT KT8 ... 157 G2
ED N9 ... 30 D7
FNCH N3 ... 53 F1
HSLWW TW4 ... 122 C1
ROM RM1 ... 63 H2
Rosemary Cl CROY/NA CR0 ... 163 K6
Rosemary Dr POP/IOD E14 ... 94 B5
REDBR IG4 ... 59 H4
CHSGTN KT9 ... 172 A3
Rosemary La MORT/ESHN SW14 ... 125 K2
Rosemary Rd PECK SE15 ... 111 G6
TOOT SW17 ... 147 G2
WELL DA16 ... 116 A7
Rosemary St IS N1 ... 7 G2
Rosemead CDALE/KGS NW9 ... 51 H5
Rosemead Av FELT TW13 ... 140 D1
MTCM CR4 ... 163 H2
WBLY HA9 ... 68 A4
Rosemere Pl HAYES BR2 ... 167 H3
Rose Ms UED N18 ... 42 D3
Rosemont Av NFNCH/WDSPK N12 ... 39 G5
Rosemont Rd ACT W3 ... 86 D6
HAMP NW3 ... 71 G5
NWMAL KT3 ... 159 K2
RCHPK/HAM TW10 ... 125 F5
Rosemoor St CHEL SW3 ... 15 K6
Rosemount Cl WFD IG8 ... 45 K5
Rosemount Dr BMLY BR1 ... 168 E3
Rosemount Rd ALP/SUD HA0 ... 68 A1
WEA W13 ... 85 G5
Rosenau Crs BTSEA SW11 ... 108 E7
Rosenau Rd DUL SE21 ... 149 J1
HNHL SE24 ... 130 D4
Roseneath Av WCHMH N21 ... 29 H7
Roseneath Pl STRHM/NOR SW16 * ... 149 G3
Roseneath Rd BTSEA SW11 ... 129 F6
Roseneath Wk EN EN1 ... 30 B3
Rosens Wk EDGW HA8 ... 36 D2
Rosenthal Rd CAT SE6 ... 132 E5
Rosenthorpe Rd PECK SE15 ... 132 A4
Rose Park Cl YEAD UB4 ... 83 H3
Roserton St POP/IOD E14 ... 113 F1
The Rosery CROY/NA CR0 ... 166 A5
Rose St COVGDN WC2E ... 11 J6
Rosethorn Cl BAL SW12 ... 129 H6
Rosetree Pl HPTN TW12 ... 142 A7
Rosetta Cl VX/NE SW8 ... 109 K6
Roseveare Rd LEE/GVPK SE12 ... 153 F3
Roseville Av HSLW TW3 ... 123 F4
Roseville Rd HYS/HAR UB3 ... 101 K6
Rosevine Rd RYNPK SW20 ... 146 A1
Rose Wk BRYLDS KT5 ... 159 J4
WWKM BR4 ... 180 A1
Rose Wy DUL SE21 ... 131 F5
EDGW HA8 ... 36 E2
Rosewell Cl PGE/AN SE20 ... 150 D6
Rosewood Av GFD/PVL UB6 ... 67 G4
HCH RM12 ... 81 J2
Rosewood Cl SCUP DA14 ... 155 G2
Rosewood Ct KUTN/CMB KT2 ... 144 C5
Rosewood Gv SUT SM1 ... 175 G1

Rosewood Ter PGE/AN SE20 * ... 150 E6
Rosher Cl SRTFD E15 ... 76 B6
Rosina St HOM E9 ... 75 F5
Roskell Rd PUT/ROE SW15 ... 127 G2
Roslin Rd ACT W3 ... 105 J2
Roslin Wy BMLY BR1 ... 152 E4
Roslyn Cl MTCM CR4 ... 162 C1
Roslyn Gdns GPK RM2 ... 63 H1
Roslyn Ms SEVS/STOTM N15 * ... 56 A4
Roslyn Rd SEVS/STOTM N15 ... 55 K4
Rosmead Rd NTGHL W11 ... 88 C6
Rosoman Pl CLKNW EC1R ... 6 B9
Rosoman St CLKNW EC1R ... 6 B8
Rossall Cl EMPK RM11 ... 63 J5
Rossall Crs WLSDN NW10 ... 86 B2
Ross Av BCTR RM8 ... 80 B1
Ross Cl HYS/HAR UB3 ... 101 G3
KTN/HRWW/WS HA3 ... 34 C6
NTHLT UB5 ... 66 D3
Rossdale SUT SM1 ... 175 J4
Rossdale Dr CDALE/KGS NW9 ... 50 E7
ED N9 ... 30 E5
Rossdale Rd PUT/ROE SW15 ... 127 F3
Rosse Ms BKHTH/KID SE3 ... 114 A7
Rossendale Cl CLPT E5 ... 74 D1
Rossendale Wy CAMTN NW1 ... 4 F2
Rossetti Ms STJWD NW8 ... 3 H3
Rossetti Rd BERM/RHTH SE16 ... 111 J4
Ross House CHARL SE7 * ... 114 D6
Rossignol Gdns CAR SM5 ... 176 A1
Rossindel Rd HSLW TW3 ... 123 F4
Rossington St CLPT E5 ... 56 C6
Rossiter Cl NRWD SE19 ... 149 J6
Rossiter Flds BAR EN5 ... 26 C5
Rossiter Rd BAL SW12 ... 129 G7
Rossland Cl BXLYHS DA6 ... 137 H4
Rosslyn Av BARN SW13 ... 126 B2
BCTR RM8 ... 62 B3
CHING E4 ... 44 D3
EBAR EN4 ... 27 H5
EBED/NFELT TW14 ... 121 K5
Rosslyn Cl HYS/HAR UB3 ... 82 B6
SUN TW16 ... 140 C5
WWKM BR4 ... 180 D2
Rosslyn Crs HRW HA1 ... 49 F3
WBLY HA9 ... 68 A3
Rosslyn Hl HAMP NW3 ... 71 H4
Rosslyn Park Ms HAMP NW3 ... 71 H4
Rosslyn Rd BARK IG11 ... 78 D6
TWK TW1 ... 124 D5
WALTH E17 ... 58 A3
WATW WD18 ... 21 F2
Rossmore Cl CAMTN NW1 ... 9 K1
PEND EN3 ... 31 F3
Rossmore Rd CAMTN NW1 ... 3 K9
Ross Pde WLGTN SM6 ... 176 B5
Ross Rd DART DA1 ... 138 C5
SNWD SE25 ... 165 F2
WHTN TW2 ... 123 H7
WLGTN SM6 ... 176 C5
Ross Wy ELTH/MOT SE9 ... 134 D2
NTHWD HA6 ... 32 D3
Rossway Dr BUSH WD23 ... 22 C4
Rosswood Gdns WLGTN SM6 ... 176 C5
Rostella Rd TOOT SW17 ... 147 H3
Rostrevor Av SEVS/STOTM N15 ... 56 B5
Rostrevor Gdns NWDGN UB2 ... 102 D4
Rostrevor Rd FUL/PGN SW6 ... 107 J7
WIM/MER SW19 ... 146 E4
Rotary St STHWK SE1 ... 18 C3
Rothbury Rd RAIN RM13 ... 99 K4
Rothbury Cots GNWCH SE10 * ... 113 H3
Rothbury Gdns ISLW TW7 ... 104 B6
Rothbury Rd HOM E9 ... 75 H6
Rotherfield Rd CAR SM5 ... 176 A3
Rotherfield St IS N1 ... 6 F1
Rotherham Wk STHWK SE1 * ... 12 C8
Rotherhill Av STRHM/NOR SW16 ... 148 D5
Rotherhithe New Rd BERM/RHTH SE16 ... 111 J4
Rotherhithe Old Rd BERM/RHTH SE16 ... 112 A3
Rotherhithe St BERM/RHTH SE16 ... 112 B1
Rotherhithe Tnl BERM/RHTH SE16 ... 111 K1
Rothermere Rd CROY/NA CR0 ... 177 F4
Rotherwick Hl EA W5 ... 86 B3
Rotherwick Rd GLDGN NW11 ... 52 E6
Rotherwood Cl RYNPK SW20 ... 146 C2
Rotherwood Rd PUT/ROE SW15 ... 127 G2
Rothery St IS N1 * ... 6 D3
Rothery Ter BRXN/ST SW9 * ... 110 C6
Rothesay Av GFD/PVL UB6 ... 66 D5
RCHPK/HAM TW10 ... 125 J3
RYNPK SW20 ... 161 H1
Rothesay Rd SNWD SE25 ... 164 E3
Rothsay St STHWK SE1 ... 19 J3
Rothsay Wk POP/IOD E14 * ... 112 D3
Rothschild Rd CHSWK W4 ... 105 K3
Rothschild St WNWD SE27 ... 149 H3
Rothwell Gdns DAGW RM9 ... 79 J6
Rothwell Rd DAGW RM9 ... 79 J7
Rothwell St CAMTN NW1 * ... 3 M1
Rotterdam Dr POP/IOD E14 ... 113 F2
Rouel Rd BERM/RHTH SE16 ... 111 H2
Rougemont Av MRDN SM4 ... 161 K4
The Roughs NTHWD HA6 ... 32 C2
Roundaway Rd CLAY IG5 ... 59 K1
Roundel Cl BROCKY SE4 ... 132 C3
Round Gv CROY/NA CR0 ... 166 A6
Roundhay Cl FSTH SE23 ... 151 F1
Roundhill Dr ENC/FH EN2 ... 29 F3
Roundtable Rd BMLY BR1 ... 152 D2
Roundtree Rd ALP/SUD HA0 ... 67 H4
Roundways RSLP HA4 ... 64 D2
The Roundway ESH/CLAY KT10 ... 171 F5
TOTM N17 ... 41 J7
WATW WD18 ... 20 D5
Roundwood CHST BR7 ... 169 G1
Roundwood Av STKPK UB11 ... 82 A7
Roundwood Cl RSLP HA4 ... 46 B6
Roundwood Pk WLSDN NW10 ... 69 J7
Roundwood Rd WLSDN NW10 ... 69 H5
Roundwood Ter STNW/STAM N16 ... 56 C6
Rounton Rd BOW E3 ... 93 J3
Roupell Rd BRXS/STRHM SW2 ... 130 A7
Roupell St STHWK SE1 ... 12 B9
Rousden St CAMTN NW1 ... 4 F2
Rousebarn La RKW/CH/CXG WD3 ... 20 A2
Rouse Gdns DUL SE21 ... 150 A3
Routemaster Cl PLSTW E13 ... 95 F2
Routh Ct EBED/NFELT TW14 ... 121 F7
Routh Rd WAND/EARL SW18 ... 128 D6

Routh St EHAM E6 ...95 K4
Rowallan Rd FUL/PGN SW6 ...107 H6
Rowan Av CHING E4 ...43 H5
Rowan Cl ALP/SUD HA0 ...67 G2
  EA ...105 F1
  IL IG1 ...78 D3
  NWMAL KT3 ...160 B1
  STAN HA7 ...35 H5
  STRHM/NOR SW16 ...148 C7
Rowan Crs DART DA1 ...139 F7
  STRHM/NOR SW16 ...148 C7
Rowan Dr CDALE/KGS NW9 ...51 J2
Rowan Pl HYS/HAR UB3 ...82 D6
Rowan Rd BTFD TW8 ...104 C6
  BXLYHN DA7 ...137 F2
  HMSMTH W6 ...107 G3
  STRHM/NOR SW16 ...163 H1
  WDR/YW UB7 ...100 H3
The Rowans PLMGR N13 ...41 J2
  SUN TW16 ...140 D4
Rowan Ter HMSMTH W6 ...107 G3
  PGE/AN SE20 ...150 C2
  WIM/MER SW19 ...146 C6
Rowantree Cl WCHMH N21 ...29 K1
Rowantree Ms ENC/FH EN2 ...29 H1
Rowantree Rd ENC/FH EN2 ...29 H1
  WCHMH N21 ...29 K1
Rowan Wk EFNCH N2 ...53 G5
  HAYES BR2 ...181 K2
  NKENS W10 * ...88 C3
Rowan Wy CHDH RM6 ...61 J2
Rowanwood Av BFN/LL DA15 ...136 B2
Rowben Cl TRDG/WHET N20 ...27 F7
Rowberry Cl FUL/PGN SW6 ...107 G6
Rowcross St STHWK SE1 ...19 L7
Rowdell Rd NTHLT UB5 ...66 A7
Rowden Pde CHING E4 * ...43 H5
Rowden Rd BECK BR3 ...151 G7
  CHING E4 ...43 K5
  HOR/WEW KT19 ...172 E3
Rowditch La BTSEA SW11 ...129 F1
Rowdon Av WLSDN NW10 ...69 K6
Rowdown Crs CROY/NA CR0 ...180 B7
Rowdowns Rd DAGW RM9 ...80 B7
Rowe Gdns BARK IG11 ...97 F1
Rowe La HOM E9 ...74 E4
Rowena Crs BTSEA SW11 ...128 D1
Rowe Wk RYLN/HDSTN HA2 ...66 A2
Rowfant Rd TOOT SW17 ...148 A1
Rowhill Rd CLPT E5 ...74 D3
Rowington Cl BAY/PAD W2 ...8 C2
Rowland Av
  KTN/HRWW/WS HA3 ...49 J2
Rowland Av SYD SE26 ...150 D2
Rowland Hill Av TOTM N17 ...41 J6
Rowland Hill St HAMP NW3 ...71 J4
Rowland Pl NTHWD HA6 * ...32 C6
Rowlands Av PIN HA5 ...34 A5
Rowlands Cl HGT N6 * ...54 A5
  MLHL NW7 ...37 J6
Rowlands Rd BCTR RM8 ...80 B2
Rowland Wy ASHF TW15 ...140 A6
  WIM/MER SW19 ...147 F7
Rowley Av BFN/LL DA15 ...136 B5
Rowley Cl ALP/SUD HA0 ...86 A1
  OXHEY WD19 ...21 J5
Rowley Cots WKENS W14 * ...107 J3
Rowley Green Rd BAR EN5 ...25 J4
Rowley La BORE WD6 ...25 F1
Rowley Rd SEVS/STOTM N15 ...55 J4
Rowley Wy STJWD NW8 ...2 D3
Rowlheys Pl WDR/YW UB7 ...100 H2
Rowlls Rd KUT/HW KT1 ...159 G2
Rowney Gdns DAGW RM9 ...79 J5
Rowney Rd DAGW RM9 ...79 H5
Rowntree Clifford Cl
  PLSTW E13 ...95 F3
Rowntree Cl
  KIL/WHAMP NW6 * ...70 E5
Rowntree Rd WHTN TW2 ...123 K7
Rowse Cl SRTFD E15 ...76 A7
Rowsley Av HDN NW4 ...52 A2
Rowstock Gdns HOLWY N7 ...72 D5
Rowton Av HRW HA1 ...115 H6
  ISLW TW7 ...104 A4
Roxborough Av HRW HA1 ...48 D6
Roxborough Pk HRW HA1 ...48 D4
Roxbourne Cl NTHLT UB5 ...65 H5
Roxburgh Rd WNWD SE27 ...149 H4
Roxburn Wy RSLP HA4 ...64 D2
Roxby Pl FUL/PGN SW6 ...14 B9
Roxeth Green Av
  RYLN/HDSTN HA2 ...66 B3
Roxeth Gv RYLN/HDSTN HA2 ...66 B3
Roxeth Hl RYLN/HDSTN HA2 ...66 D1
Roxley Rd LEW SE13 ...132 E5
Roxton Gdns CROY/NA CR0 ...179 H5
Roxwell Rd BARK IG11 ...97 G1
  SHB W12 ...106 D1
Roxwell Wy WFD IG8 ...45 G6
Roxy Av CHDH RM6 ...61 K6
Royal Albert Wy EHAM E6 ...95 K6
Royal Av CONDST W1S ...10 E7
Royal Arsenal West
  WOOL/PLUM SE18 * ...115 F4
Royal Av CHEL SW3 ...15 L7
  WPK KT4 ...173 G1
Royal Circ WNWD SE27 ...149 G2
Royal Cl DEPT SE8 ...112 C5
  GDMY/SEVK IG3 ...61 G6
  STNW/STAM N16 ...56 A7
  WIM/MER SW19 ...146 B1
  WPK KT4 ...173 G1
Royal College St CAMTN NW1 ...4 F3
Royal Connaught Dr
  BUSH WD23 ...21 K3
Royal Ct BANK EC3V ...13 H5
  ELTH/MOT SE9 * ...134 E7
  EN EN1 * ...30 A5
  WATW WD18 ...6 F4
Royal Crs GNTH/NBYPK IG2 ...60 D5
  NTGHL W11 ...11 G7
  RSLP HA4 ...65 J3
Royal Crescent Ms
  NTGHL W11 ...107 G1
Royal Docks Rd EHAM E6 ...96 B4
Royal Dr FBAR/BDGN N11 ...40 A7
Royal Herbert Pavilions
  WOOL/PLUM SE18 * ...114 E7
Royal Hl GNWCH SE10 ...113 F6
Royal Hospital Rd CHEL SW3 ...15 L9
Royal Ms BAL SW12 ...129 G6
Royal Mint Pl WCHPL E1 ...13 M6
Royal Mint St WCHPL E1 ...13 M6
Royal Naval Pl NWCR SE14 ...112 C6
Royal Oak Ms TEDD TW11 * ...143 G4
Royal Oak Pl EDUL SE22 ...131 J5
Royal Oak Rd BXLYHS DA6 ...137 G4
  HACK E8 ...74 D5
Royal Oak Yd STHWK SE1 ...19 J2

Royal Opera Ar STJS SW1Y * ...11 G8
Royal Orchard Cl
  WAND/EARL SW18 ...127 H6
Royal Pde BKHTH/KID SE3 ...133 J1
  CHST BR7 ...154 C6
  FUL/PGN SW6 * ...107 H6
Royal Pl GNWCH SE10 ...113 F6
  LBTH SE11 ...18 C3
  SCUP DA14 ...155 K2
  TEDD TW11 ...142 D4
Royal Route WBLY HA9 ...68 B3
Royal St STHWK SE1 ...17 M3
Royal Victor Pl BOW E3 ...93 F1
Roycraft Av BARK IG11 ...97 F1
Roycroft Cl
  BRXS/STRHM SW2 * ...130 B7
  SWFD E18 ...45 F7
Roydene Rd
  WOOL/PLUM SE18 ...115 K5
Roy Gdns GNTH/NBYPK IG2 ...60 E3
Roy Gv HPTN TW12 ...142 B5
Royle Cl GPK RM2 ...63 K4
Royle Crs WEA W13 ...85 G3
Roy Sq POP/IOD E14 ...93 G6
Royston Av CHING E4 ...43 J4
  SUT SM1 ...175 H2
  WLGTN SM6 ...176 D3
Royston Cl HEST TW5 ...102 A7
Royston Gdns IL IG1 ...59 H5
Royston Gv PIN HA5 ...33 K5
Royston Park Rd PIN HA5 ...33 K5
Royston Rd DART DA1 ...138 C5
  PGE/AN SE20 ...151 F7
  RCHPK/HAM TW10 ...125 F4
The Roystons BRYLDS KT5 ...159 J4
Royston St BETH E2 ...92 E1
Rozel Rd VX/NE SW8 ...129 H1
Rubastic Rd NWDGN UB2 ...102 B2
Rubens Rd NTHLT UB5 ...83 G1
Rubens St CAT SE6 ...151 H1
Ruby Cl CLPT E5 ...75 F2
Ruby Ms WALTH E17 * ...57 J2
Ruby Rd WALTH E17 ...57 J2
Ruby Sq PECK SE15 ...111 J3
Ruby Triangle PECK SE15 * ...111 J3
Ruckholt Cl LEY E10 ...75 K2
Ruckholt Rd LEY E10 ...76 A2
Rucklidge Av WLSDN NW10 ...87 H1
Rudall Crs HAMP NW3 ...71 H3
Ruddington Cl CLPT E5 ...75 G3
Ruddock Cl EDGW HA8 ...36 E6
Ruddstreet Cl
  WOOL/PLUM SE18 ...115 G3
Rudgwick Ter STJWD NW8 * ...3 K4
Rudland Rd BXLYHN DA7 ...137 J2
Rudloe Rd BAL SW12 ...129 H6
Rudolf Pl VX/NE SW8 ...109 K5
Rudolph Rd BUSH WD23 ...22 A5
  KIL/WHAMP NW6 ...2 B1
  PLSTW E13 ...94 D1
Rudyard Gv EDGW HA8 ...36 C5
Ruffetts Cl SAND/SEL CR2 ...178 C6
The Ruffetts SAND/SEL CR2 ...178 B6
Ruffle Cl WDR/YW UB7 ...100 B1
Rufford Cl
  KTN/HRWW/WS HA3 ...49 G5
Rufford St IS N1 ...5 K3
Rufford Street Ms IS N1 ...5 K2
Rufus Cl RSLP HA4 ...65 H2
Rufus St FSBYE EC1V ...7 J7
Rugby Av ALP/SUD HA0 ...67 J3
  ED N9 ...30 B7
  GFD/PVL UB6 ...66 D5
Rugby Cl HRW HA1 ...48 E3
Rugby Gdns DAGW RM9 ...79 J5
Rugby La BELMT SM2 ...174 B7
Rugby Rd CDALE/KGS NW9 ...50 D3
  CHSWK W4 ...106 B1
  DAGW RM9 ...79 H6
  TWK TW1 ...123 K5
Rugby St BMSBY WC1N ...11 L1
Rugg St POP/IOD E14 ...93 J6
Ruislip Cl GFD/PVL UB6 ...84 B3
Ruislip Ct RSLP HA4 * ...64 D1
Ruislip Rd GFD/PVL UB6 ...84 A2
  NTHLT UB5 ...83 J2
Ruislip Rd East GFD/PVL UB6 ...84 C3
Ruislip St TOOT SW17 ...147 K3
Rumbold Rd FUL/PGN SW6 ...108 A6
Rum Cl WAP E1W ...92 D6
Rumsey Cl HPTN TW12 ...141 K5
Rumsey Ms BRXN/ST SW9 ...130 A2
Runbury Cir CDALE/KGS NW9 ...69 F7
Runcorn Cl TOTM N17 ...56 D3
Runcorn Pl NTGHL W11 ...88 C6
Rundell Crs HDN NW4 ...51 K4
Runes Cl MTCM CR4 ...162 C3
Runnelfield HRW HA1 ...66 E2
Runnymede WIM/MER SW19 ...147 H1
Runnymede Cl WHTN TW2 ...123 G6
Runnymede Crs
  STRHM/NOR SW16 ...148 D7
Runnymede Gdns
  GFD/PVL UB6 ...84 D1
  HSLW TW3 ...123 G5
  WHTN TW2 ...123 G6
Runnymede Rd WHTN TW2 ...123 G5
Runway Cl CDALE/KGS NW9 ...51 H1
The Runway RSLP HA4 ...65 F4
Rupack St BERM/RHTH SE16 * ...111 K1
Rupert Av WBLY HA9 ...68 A4
Rupert Ct E/WMO/HCT KT8 * ...157 F3
  SOHO/SHAV W1D ...11 G6
Rupert Gdns BRXN/ST SW9 ...130 C1
Rupert Rd ARCH N19 ...72 D2
  CHSWK W4 ...106 B3
  KIL/WHAMP NW6 ...88 D1
Rupert St SOHO/SHAV W1D ...11 G6
Rural Cl EMPK RM11 ...63 K7
Rural Wy STRHM/NOR SW16 ...148 B6
Rusbridge Cl HACK E8 ...74 C4
Ruscoe Rd CAN/RD E16 ...94 D5
Ruscombe Wy
  EBED/NFELT TW14 ...121 J6
Rusham Rd BAL SW12 ...128 E6
Rushbridge Cl CROY/NA CR0 ...164 D5
Rushbrook Crs WALTH E17 ...43 H7
Rushbrook Rd ELTH/MOT SE9 ...154 C1
Rush Common Ms
  BRXS/STRHM SW2 ...129 K6
Rushcroft Rd
  BRXS/STRHM SW2 ...130 B3
  CHING E4 ...43 K6
Rushden Cl NRWD SE19 ...149 K6
Rushdene ABYW SE2 ...116 D2
Rushdene Av EBAR EN4 ...27 J6
Rushdene Cl NTHLT UB5 ...83 F1
Rushdene Crs NTHLT UB5 ...83 F1
Rushdene Rd PIN HA5 ...47 G5
Rushden Gdns CLAY IG5 ...60 A2
  MLHL NW7 ...38 A5

Rushdon Cl ROM RM1 ...63 J4
Rushett Cl THDIT KT7 ...158 C7
Rushett Rd THDIT KT7 ...158 C6
Rushey Cl NWMAL KT3 ...160 A3
Rushey Gn CAT SE6 ...132 E6
Rushey Hl ENC/FH EN2 ...29 F5
Rushford Rd BROCKY SE4 ...132 C5
Rush Green Gdns
  ROMW/RG RM7 ...62 E7
Rush Green Rd
  ROMW/RG RM7 ...62 E7
Rushgrove Av
  CDALE/KGS NW9 ...51 H3
Rushgrove Pde
  CDALE/KGS NW9 * ...51 H3
Rushgrove St
  WOOL/PLUM SE18 ...114 E3
Rush Hill Ms BTSEA SW11 ...129 F2
Rush Hill Rd BTSEA SW11 ...129 F2
Rushley Cl HAYES BR2 ...181 H5
Rushmead BETH E2 ...92 D2
  RCHPK/HAM TW10 ...143 F2
Rushmead Cl CROY/NA CR0 ...178 B3
Rushmere Ct WPK KT4 ...173 J1
Rushmere Pl WIM/MER SW19 ...146 B4
Rushmon Pl CHEAM SM3 ...174 C5
Rushmon Vls NWMAL KT3 * ...160 C3
Rushmoor Cl PIN HA5 ...47 F3
Rushmore Cl BMLY BR1 ...168 D2
Rushmore Ct WATW WD18 * ...20 C5
Rushmore Crs CLPT E5 ...74 E3
Rushmore Gv NRWD SE19 ...150 A4
Rushmore Rd PUT/ROE SW15 ...127 G6
Rushout Av
  KTN/HRWW/WS HA3 ...49 H5
Rushton St IS N1 ...7 H5
Rushworth St STHWK SE1 ...18 D1
Rushy Meadow La CAR SM5 ...175 J1
Ruskin Av EBED/NFELT TW14 ...121 J6
  MNPK E12 ...77 J3
  RCH/KEW TW9 ...105 H6
  WELL DA16 ...136 B2
Ruskin Cl GLDGN NW11 ...53 F5
Ruskin Dr WELL DA16 ...136 B2
  WPK KT4 ...173 K1
Ruskin Gdns EA W5 ...85 K3
  KTN/HRWW/WS HA3 ...50 B4
Ruskin Gv DART DA1 ...139 K4
  WELL DA16 ...136 B1
Ruskin Rd BELV DA17 ...117 H3
  CAR SM5 ...176 A4
  CROY/NA CR0 ...177 H1
  ISLW TW7 ...124 A2
  SEVS/STOTM N15 ...56 B4
  STHL UB1 ...83 J7
  TOTM N17 ...42 B7
Ruskin Wk ED N9 ...42 C1
  HAYES BR2 ...168 D5
  HNHL SE24 ...130 D4
Ruskin Wy WIM/MER SW19 ...162 C1
Rusland Park Rd HRW HA1 ...48 E3
Rusper Cl CRICK NW2 ...70 A2
  STAN HA7 ...35 J3
Rusper Rd DAGW RM9 ...79 J5
  WDGN N22 ...55 H1
Russel Cl BECK BR3 ...166 E2
Russell Av WDGN N22 ...55 H1
Russell Cl BKHTH/KID SE3 ...114 B6
  BXLYHN DA7 ...137 H3
  CHSWK W4 ...106 C5
  DART DA1 ...138 D2
  NTHWD HA6 ...32 A4
  RSLP HA4 ...65 G1
  WLSDN NW10 ...68 E6
Russell Ct BAR EN5 * ...27 G3
  WHALL SW1A ...10 F9
Russell Gdns GLDGN NW11 ...52 C5
  RCHPK/HAM TW10 ...143 J1
  TRDG/WHET N20 ...39 J1
  WDR/YW UB7 ...100 D4
  WKENS W14 ...107 H2
Russell Gardens Ms
  WKENS W14 ...107 H1
Russell Gv BRXN/ST SW9 ...110 B7
  MLHL NW7 ...37 G4
Russell Kerr Cl CHSWK W4 * ...105 K6
Russell La TRDG/WHET N20 ...39 K1
Russell Pde GLDGN NW11 * ...52 C5
Russell Pl HAMP NW3 ...71 J4
Russell Rd CAN/RD E16 ...94 E5
  CDALE/KGS NW9 ...51 H5
  CEND/HSY/T N8 ...54 D5
  CHING E4 ...43 H3
  MTCM CR4 ...162 D2
  NTHLT UB5 ...66 C4
  NTHWD HA6 ...32 A2
  SEVS/STOTM N15 ...56 A4
  TRDG/WHET N20 ...39 J1
  WALTH E17 ...57 H2
  WDGN N22 ...55 F1
  WHTN TW2 ...124 A5
  WIM/MER SW19 ...146 E6
  WKENS W14 ...107 H2
Russell Sq RSQ WC1B ...11 J1
Russell St HOL/ALD WC2B ...11 L5
Russell Wy OXHEY WD19 ...21 F6
  SUT SM1 ...175 F4
Russet Cl HGDN/ICK UB10 ...82 A3
Russet Crs HOLWY N7 ...73 F4
Russet Dr CROY/NA CR0 ...166 B7
Russets Cl CHING E4 ...44 B3
Russia Dock Rd
  BERM/RHTH SE16 * ...93 G7
Russia La BETH E2 ...92 E1
Russia Rw CITYW EC2V ...12 F5
Rusthall Av CHSWK W4 ...106 A2
Rusthall Cl CROY/NA CR0 ...165 K5
Rustic Av STRHM/NOR SW16 ...148 B6
Rustic Pl ALP/SUD HA0 ...67 K3
Rustington Wk CHEAM SM3 ...161 J6
Ruston Av BRYLDS KT5 ...159 J6
Ruston Gdns STHGT/OAK N14 ...28 A5
Ruston Ms NTGHL W11 ...88 C5
Ruston Rd WOOL/PLUM SE18 ...114 D2
Ruston St BOW E3 ...75 H7
Rust Sq CMBW SE5 ...110 E6
Rutford Rd STRHM/NOR SW16 ...148 E4
Ruth Cl STAN HA7 ...50 B2
Rutherford Cl BELMT SM2 ...175 H5
  BORE WD6 ...24 E1
Rutherford St WEST SW1P ...17 G5
Rutherford Wy BUSH WD23 ...22 D7
  WBLY HA9 ...68 C3
Rutherglen Rd ABYW SE2 ...116 B5
Rutherwyke Cl EW KT17 ...173 J5
Ruthin Cl CDALE/KGS NW9 ...51 G5
Ruthin Rd BKHTH/KID SE3 ...113 K5
Ruthven St HOM E9 ...75 F7
Rutland Av BFN/LL DA15 ...136 B6
Rutland Cl BXLY DA5 ...136 E7
  CHSGTN KT9 ...172 B5

  DART DA1 ...139 G6
  MORT/ESHN SW14 ...125 J2
  WIM/MER SW19 ...147 J5
Rutland Ct CHST BR7 ...154 A7
  SKENS SW7 * ...15 K2
Rutland Dr MRDN SM4 ...161 K6
  RCHPK/HAM TW10 ...143 J1
Rutland Gdns BCTR RM8 ...79 J3
  CROY/NA CR0 ...178 A3
  FSBYPK N4 ...55 H5
  SKENS SW7 ...15 K2
  WEA W13 ...85 G4
Rutland Gardens Ms
  SKENS SW7 ...15 K2
Rutland Ga BELV DA17 ...117 J4
  HAYES BR2 ...167 J3
  SKENS SW7 ...15 J2
Rutland Gate Ms SKENS SW7 * ...15 J2
Rutland Gv HMSMTH W6 ...106 E4
Rutland Ms STJWD NW8 ...2 D4
Rutland Ms South
  SKENS SW7 * ...15 J3
Rutland Pk CAT SE6 ...151 H1
  CRICK NW2 ...70 A5
Rutland Pl BUSH WD23 ...22 D7
  FARR EC1M * ...12 D2
Rutland Rd FSTGT E7 ...77 H6
  HOM E9 ...74 E5
  HRW HA1 ...48 C5
  HYS/HAR UB3 ...101 G3
  IL IG1 ...78 B3
  STHL UB1 ...84 A3
  WALTH E17 ...57 J5
  WAN E11 ...59 F4
  WHTN TW2 ...142 D1
Rutland St SKENS SW7 ...15 K3
Rutland Wk CAT SE6 ...151 H1
Rutley Cl WALW SE17 ...18 C9
Rutlish Rd WIM/MER SW19 ...146 E6
Rutter Gdns MTCM CR4 ...162 C3
Rutters Cl WDR/YW UB7 ...100 D1
Rutt's Ter NWCR SE14 ...112 A7
The Rutts BUSH WD23 ...22 D7
Ruvigny Gdns PUT/ROE SW15 ...127 G2
Ruxley Cl HOR/WEW KT19 ...172 E4
  SCUP DA14 ...155 K5
Ruxley Crs ESH/CLAY KT10 ...171 H6
Ruxley La ESH/CLAY KT10 ...172 A4
Ruxley Ms HOR/WEW KT19 ...172 E4
Ruxley Rdg ESH/CLAY KT10 ...171 G6
Ruxley Towers
  ESH/CLAY KT10 * ...171 G6
Ryan Cl BKHTH/KID SE3 ...134 A3
  RSLP HA4 ...47 F7
Ryan Ct OXHEY WD19 ...21 J6
Ryan Dr BTFD TW8 ...104 B5
Rycroft Wy TOTM N17 * ...56 B2
Rydal Cl HDN NW4 ...38 C7
Rydal Crs GFD/PVL UB6 ...85 H2
Rydal Dr BXLYHN DA7 ...137 H7
  WWKM BR4 ...180 C1
Rydal Gdns CDALE/KGS NW9 ...51 G4
  HSLW TW3 ...123 F5
  PUT/ROE SW15 ...145 G4
  WBLY HA9 ...49 J7
Rydal Mt HAYES BR2 * ...167 J3
Rydal Rd STRHM/NOR SW16 ...148 D4
Rydal Wy PEND EN3 ...30 E5
  RSLP HA4 ...65 G3
Ryde Pl TWK TW1 ...124 D5
Ryder Av LEY E10 ...57 K6
Ryder Cl BUSH WD23 ...22 B5
Ryder Dr BERM/RHTH SE16 ...111 J4
Ryder Gdns RAIN RM13 ...81 H5
Ryder St STJS SW1Y ...10 F8
Ryder Yd STJS SW1Y ...10 F8
Ryde Vale Rd BAL SW12 ...148 B1
Rydon Ms WIM/MER SW19 ...146 A6
Rydon St IS N1 ...6 F3
Rydston Cl HOLWY N7 ...5 K1
Rye Cl BXLY DA5 ...137 J5
Ryecotes Md DUL SE21 ...131 F7
Ryecroft Av CLAY IG5 ...60 B1
  WHTN TW2 ...123 F7
Ryecroft Crs BAR EN5 ...25 K4
Ryecroft Rd LEW SE13 ...133 F4
  STMC/STPC BR5 ...169 J5
  STRHM/NOR SW16 ...149 G5
Ryecroft St FUL/PGN SW6 ...108 A7
Ryedale EDUL SE22 ...131 J5
Ryefield Av HGDN/ICK UB10 ...64 A7
Ryefield Crs PIN HA5 * ...46 E1
Ryefield Pde NTHWD HA6 * ...46 E1
Ryefield Rd NRWD SE19 ...149 J5
Rye Hill Pk PECK SE15 ...131 K3
Ryelands Crs LEE/GVPK SE12 ...134 B5
Rye La PECK SE15 ...131 H1
Rye Rd PECK SE15 ...132 A3
The Rye STHGT/OAK N14 ...28 C6
Rye Wk PUT/ROE SW15 ...127 G4
Rye Wy EDGW HA8 ...36 B5
Ryfold Rd WIM/MER SW19 ...146 E2
Ryhope Rd FBAR/BDGN N11 ...40 B3
Ryland Cl FELT TW13 ...140 D3
Rylandes Rd CRICK NW2 ...69 J2
  SAND/SEL CR2 ...178 D7
Ryland Rd KTTN NW5 ...72 B5
Rylett Crs SHB W12 ...106 C2
Rylett Rd SHB W12 ...106 C1
Rylston Rd FUL/PGN SW6 ...107 J5
  PLMGR N13 ...41 G2
Rymer Rd CROY/NA CR0 ...165 F6
Rymer St HNHL SE24 ...130 C5
Rymill St CAN/RD E16 ...96 A7
Rysbrack St CHEL SW3 ...15 L3
Rythe Cl CHSGTN KT9 ...171 J6
Rythe Ct THDIT KT7 ...158 B6
Rythe Rd ESH/CLAY KT10 ...170 D4
Ryves Cots MTCM CR4 ...163 F1

S

Saddlescombe Wy
  NFNCH/WDSPK N12 ...38 E1
Sadler Cl MTCM CR4 ...162 E1
Sadlers Gate Ms
  PUT/ROE SW15 ...127 F2
Sadlers Ride E/WMO/HCT KT8 ...157 H1
Saffron Av POP/IOD E14 ...94 B6
Saffron Cl CROY/NA CR0 ...163 K5
  GLDGN NW11 ...52 D4
Saffron Hl HCIRC EC1N ...12 B1
Saffron Rd CRW RM5 ...63 F1
Saffron St HCIRC EC1N ...12 B2
Saffron Wy SURB KT6 ...158 E7
Sage Cl EHAM E6 ...95 K4
Sage Ms EDUL SE22 ...131 G4
Sage St WCHPL E1 ...92 E6
Sage Wy FSBYW WC1X ...5 L8
Saigasso Cl CAN/RD E16 ...95 H5
Sail St LBTH SE11 ...17 M5
Sainfoin Rd TOOT SW17 ...148 A1
Sainsbury Rd NRWD SE19 ...150 A4
St Agatha's Gv CAR SM5 ...162 E7
St Agnes Cl HOM E9 * ...74 E7
St Agnes Pl LBTH SE11 ...110 C5
St Agnes Well STLK EC1Y ...7 H9
St Aidan's Rd EDUL SE22 ...131 J5
  WEA W13 ...104 C1
St Albans Av CHSWK W4 ...106 A3
  FELT TW13 ...141 H4
St Alban's Av EHAM E6 ...95 K2
St Albans Crs WDGN N22 ...41 G7
St Albans Farm
  EBED/NFELT TW14 * ...122 B4
St Alban's Gdns TEDD TW11 ...143 G4
St Albans Gv KENS W8 * ...14 D3
St Alban's Gv CAR SM5 ...162 E6
  KENS W8 ...14 D3
St Albans La GLDGN NW11 ...52 E7
St Alban's Ms BAY/PAD W2 ...9 H2
St Alban's Pl IS N1 ...6 C4
St Alban's Rd DART DA1 ...139 F5
  KTTN NW5 ...72 A2
  WFD IG8 ...44 E6
  WLSDN NW10 ...69 G7
St Alban's St STJS SW1Y ...11 G7
St Albans Ter HMSMTH W6 ...107 H5
St Alfege Pas GNWCH SE10 ...113 F5
St Alfege Rd CHARL SE7 ...114 C5
St Alphage Gdns BARB EC2Y ...12 F3
St Alphage Highwalk
  BARB EC2Y ...12 F3
St Alphage Wk EDGW HA8 * ...50 E1
St Alphege Rd ED N9 ...30 E6
St Alphonsus Rd CLAP SW4 ...129 H3
St Amunds Cl CAT SE6 ...151 J3
St Andrews Av ALP/SUD HA0 ...67 G3
  HCH RM12 ...81 H4
St Andrews Cl
  BERM/RHTH SE16 * ...111 J4
  RSLP HA4 ...65 H1
  STAN HA7 * ...49 J1
  THDIT KT7 ...158 C7
  THMD SE28 ...97 K5
  WIM/MER SW19 ...147 F5
St Andrew's Cl CRICK NW2 * ...69 J2
  ISLW TW7 ...103 J7
  NFNCH/WDSPK N12 * ...39 G3
St Andrew's Ct
  WAND/EARL SW18 ...147 G1
St Andrews Dr STAN HA7 ...35 J7
St Andrew's Gv
  STNW/STAM N16 ...55 K7
St Andrew's Hl BLKFR EC4V ...12 D5
St Andrews Ms
  BKHTH/KID SE3 ...113 K6
St Andrew's Ms
  STNW/STAM N16 ...56 A7
St Andrew's Pl CAMTN NW1 ...4 C9
  CDALE/KGS NW9 ...51 F7
St Andrews Rd ACT W3 ...87 G5
  CROY/NA CR0 ...177 J3
  EN EN1 ...30 A2
  GLDGN NW11 ...52 D5
  HNWL W7 ...103 K1
  IL IG1 ...59 K6
  PLSTW E13 ...95 F2
  SURB KT6 ...158 E5
  WALTH E17 ...58 C1
  WAN E11 ...58 C5
  WKENS W14 ...107 H5
  WLSDN NW10 ...69 K5
St Andrews Rd CAR SM5 ...175 J2
St Andrew's Ter
  OXHEY WD19 * ...33 G4
St Andrew St HCIRC EC1N ...12 B3
St Andrews Wy BOW E3 ...93 K3
St Anna Rd BAR EN5 * ...26 B4
St Anne's Av
  STWL/WRAY TW19 ...120 A6
St Annes Cl OXHEY WD19 ...33 G3
St Anne's Cl HGT N6 ...72 A3
St Annes Ct SOHO/CST W1F ...11 G5
St Annes Gdns WLSDN NW10 ...86 B2
St Anne's Pas POP/IOD E14 * ...93 H5
St Anne's Rd ALP/SUD HA0 ...67 K4
  LEY E10 ...76 B1
St Anne's Rw POP/IOD E14 ...93 H5
St Anne St POP/IOD E14 ...93 H5
St Ann's BARK IG11 ...78 C7
St Anns Ct HDN NW4 * ...51 K2
St Ann's Crs
  WAND/EARL SW18 ...128 A5
St Ann's Gdns KTTN NW5 ...72 A5
St Ann's Park Rd
  WAND/EARL SW18 ...128 B5
St Anns Rd BARN SW13 * ...126 C1
St Ann's Rd BARK IG11 ...78 C7
  ED N9 ...42 B1
  HRW HA1 ...48 E5
  NTGHL W11 ...88 B5
  SEVS/STOTM N15 ...55 J4
St Ann's Ter STJWD NW8 ...3 H5
St Ann's Vl WAND/EARL SW18 ...128 A6
St Ann's Wy CROY/NA CR0 ...177 H5
St Anselms Rd HYS/HAR UB3 ...101 J1
St Anthony's Av WFD IG8 ...45 G5
St Anthonys Cl TOOT SW17 ...147 J1
St Anthony's Cl WAP E1W * ...92 C7
St Anthony's Ct ORP BR6 ...169 G7

St Anthony's Wy EBED/NFELT TW14 121 J3
St Antony's Rd FSTGT E7 77 F6
St Arvans Rd CROY/NA CR0 178 A2
St Asaph Rd BROCKY SE4 132 A2
St Aubyn's Av HSLW TW3 123 F4
WIM/MER SW19 146 A4
St Aubyn's Rd NRWD SE19 150 B5
St Audrey Av BXLYHN DA7 137 H1
St Augustine's Av EA W5 86 A1
HAYES BR2 168 D4
SAND/SEL CR2 177 J6
WBLY HA9 68 A2
St Augustine's Rd BELV DA17 117 G3
CAMTN NW1 5 G1
St Austell Cl EDGW HA8 50 B1
St Austell Rd LEW SE13 133 F1
St Awdry's Rd BARK IG11 78 D6
St Barnabas Cl BECK BR3 167 F1
EDUL SE22 131 F3
St Barnabas Gdns E/WMO/HCT KT8 157 F4
St Barnabas Ms BGVA SW1W 16 A5
St Barnabas Rd MTCM CR4 148 A6
SUT SM1 175 H4
WALTH E17 57 J5
WFD IG8 45 F7
St Barnabas Ter HOM E9 75 F4
St Barnabas Vs VX/NE SW8 109 K7
St Bartholomew's Cl SYD SE26 150 E3
St Bartholomew's Rd EHAM E6 77 J7
St Benets Cl TOOT SW17 147 J1
St Benet's Gv CAR SM5 162 B6
St Bernards CROY/NA CR0 178 A6
St Bernards Rd WNWD SE27 149 K3
St Bernard's Rd EHAM E6 77 H1
St Blaise Av BMLY BR1 168 A1
St Botolph St TWRH EC3N 13 L4
St Bride's Av EDGW HA8 36 B7
St Brides Cl ERITHM DA18 116 E1
St Bride St FLST/FETLN EC4A 12 C4
St Catherines Cl CHSGTN KT9 171 K5
TOOT SW17 147 J1
St Catherines Ct FELT TW13 121 K7
St Catherines Dr NWCR SE14 132 A4
St Catherines Ms CHEL SW3 15 L5
St Catherines Rd CHING E4 43 J1
RSLP HA4 46 A4
St Chads Cl SURB KT6 158 D6
St Chad's Gdns CHDH RM6 62 A6
St Chad's Pl FSBYW WC1X 5 K7
St Chad's Rd CHDH RM6 62 A5
St Chad's St STPAN WC1H 5 K7
St Charles Cl NKENS W10 88 C4
St Charles Sq NKENS W10 88 B4
St Christophers Dr HYS/HAR UB3 83 F6
St Christopher's Ms WLGTN SM6 176 C4
St Christopher's Pl MHST W1U 10 B3
St Clair Cl CLAY IG5 59 K1
St Clair Dr WPK KT4 173 K2
St Clair Rd PLSTW E13 95 F1
St Clair's Rd CROY/NA CR0 178 A1
St Clare St TWRH EC3N 13 L5
St Clements Cl PUR RM19 119 K3
St Clement's La LINN WC2A 11 M5
St Clements Yd EDUL SE22 131 G4
St Cloud Rd WNWD SE27 149 J3
St Crispins Cl HAMP NW3 71 J3
St Crispin's Cl STHL UB1 83 K5
St Cross St HCIRC EC1N 12 B2
St Cuthberts Gdns PIN HA5 33 K6
St Cuthberts Rd PLMGR N13 41 G5
St Cuthbert's Rd CRICK NW2 70 D5
St Cyprian's St TOOT SW17 147 K3
St Davids Cl BERM/RHTH SE16 111 J4
WBLY HA9 68 A2
St David's Cl WWKM BR4 166 E6
St David's Dr EDGW HA8 36 B7
St Davids Ms BOW E3 93 G2
St David's Pl HDN NW4 51 K6
St Davids Rd POP/IOD E14 112 G4
St Denis Rd WNWD SE27 149 J3
St Dionis Rd FUL/PGN SW6 127 J7
MNPK E12 77 J2
St Donatt's Rd NWCR SE14 112 C7
St Dunstan's Av ACT W3 87 F6
St Dunstans Cl HYS/HAR UB3 101 J3
St Dunstan's Gdns ACT W3 87 F6
St Dunstan's Hl MON EC3R 13 J7
SUT SM1 174 C5
St Dunstan's La MON EC3R 13 J7
St Dunstans Rd FSTGT E7 77 F5
St Dunstan's Rd FELT TW13 140 D2
HMSMTH W6 107 G4
HNWL W7 103 K1
HSLWW TW4 122 A2
SNWD SE25 165 G3
St Edmunds Av RSLP HA4 46 B5
St Edmunds Cl ERITHM DA18 116 E1
TOOT SW17 147 J1
St Edmund's Cl STJWD NW8 3 L4
St Edmunds Dr STAN HA7 35 G7
St Edmund's La WHTN TW2 123 G6
St Edmunds Rd DART DA1 139 J2
ED N9 30 C6
St Edmund's Rd IL IG1 59 K5
St Edmunds Sq BARN SW13 107 F5
St Edmund's Ter STJWD NW8 3 K4
St Edward's Cl GLDGN NW11 52 E5
St Edwards Wy ROM RM1 63 F4
St Elmo Rd SHB W12 106 B1
St Elmos Rd BERM/RHTH SE16 112 B1
St Erkenwald Ms BARK IG11 78 D7
St Erkenwald Rd BARK IG11 78 D7
St Ervans Rd NKENS W10 88 C4
St Faith's Rd DUL SE21 130 C4
St Fidelis' Rd ERITH DA8 118 A3
St Fillans Rd CAT SE6 133 F7
St Francis Cl OXHEY WD19 21 F7
St Gabriel's Cl WAN E11 59 F7
St Gabriel's Rd CRICK NW2 70 B4
St George's Av CDALE/KGS NW9 50 E3
EA W5 104 E1
FSTGT E7 77 F6
HOLWY N7 72 D3
STHL UB1 83 K6
St George's Circ STHWK SE1 18 C3
St Georges Cl HRW HA1 67 G2
THMD SE28 97 K5
VX/NE SW8 109 H7
St George's Cl GLDGN NW11 52 D5
St George's Dr OXHEY WD19 33 J2

PIM SW1V 16 D6
St Georges Flds BAY/PAD W2 9 K6
St George's Gdns SURB KT6 172 D1
St Georges Gv TOOT SW17 147 H2
St Georges Industrial Est KUTN/CMB KT2 143 K4
St George's Ms CHSWK W4 105 K5
DEPT SE8 112 C3
St Georges Ms HAMP NW3 3 M2
St Georges Pde CAT SE6 151 H1
St Georges Rd BMLY BR1 168 E1
CHSWK W4 106 A1
DAGW RM9 80 A4
STMC/STPC BR5 169 J5
St George's Rd BECK BR3 151 K1
FELT TW13 141 H3
FSTGT E7 77 F6
GLDGN NW11 52 D5
HNWL W7 85 F7
IL IG1 59 K6
KUTN/CMB KT2 144 B6
LEY E10 76 A2
MTCM CR4 163 G2
PLMGR N13 41 F1
RCH/KEW TW9 125 G2
SCUP DA14 155 K5
STHWK SE1 18 C4
TWK TW1 124 C4
WIM/MER SW19 146 D5
WLGTN SM6 176 B4
St Georges Rd West BMLY BR1 168 D1
St Georges Sq NWMAL KT3 160 B2
St George's Sq FSTGT E7 77 F6
PIM SW1V 17 G7
St George's Square Ms PIM SW1V 17 G8
St Georges Ter PECK SE15 111 H6
St Georges Ter CAMTN NW1 3 M2
St George St CONDST W1S 10 D5
St Georges Wk CROY/NA CR0 177 J2
St George's Wy PECK SE15 111 F5
St Gerards Cl CLAP SW4 129 H4
St German's Pl BKHTH/KID SE3 113 K7
St German's Rd FSTH SE23 132 B1
St Giles Av DAGE RM10 80 D6
HGDN/ICK UB10 64 A3
St Giles Churchyard BARB EC2Y 12 F3
St Giles Circ SOHO/SHAV W1D 11 H4
St Giles Cl DAGE RM10 80 D6
HEST TW5 102 D6
St Giles Ct LSO/SEVD WC2H 11 H4
St Giles High St NOXST/BSQ WC1A 11 H4
St Giles Pas LSO/SEVD WC2H 11 H5
St Gothard Rd WNWD SE27 149 K3
St Gregory Cl RSLP HA4 65 G3
St Helena Rd BERM/RHTH SE16 112 A3
St Helena St FSBYW WC1X 6 A8
St Helena Ter RCH/KEW TW9 124 E4
St Helens THDIT KT7 157 K6
St Helens Cl RAIN RM13 99 J3
St Helen's Crs STRHM/NOR SW16 149 F7
St Helens Gdns NKENS W10 88 B5
St Helen's Pl LEY E10 57 G6
St Helen's Pl HDTCH EC3A 13 J4
St Helens Rd ERITHM DA18 116 E1
St Helen's Rd IL IG1 59 K5
STRHM/NOR SW16 164 A1
WEA W13 85 H7
St Heller Av MRDN SM4 162 B6
St Heliers Av HSLWW TW4 123 F4
St Heliers Rd LEY E10 57 K5
St Hildas Cl KIL/WHAMP NW6 70 B7
TOOT SW17 147 H1
St Hilda's Rd BARN SW13 106 E5
St Hughes Cl TOOT SW17 147 H1
St Hugh's Rd PGE/AN SE20 150 D7
St Ivians Dr GPK RM2 63 J2
St James' Av SUT SM1 174 E4
TRDG/WHET N20 39 K4
St James' Av WEA W13 85 G7
St James Cl EBAR EN4 27 H2
STJWD NW8 3 L5
TRDG/WHET N20 39 J2
St James' Cl NWMAL KT3 160 C4
RSLP HA4 65 G1
St James' Ct WESTW SW1E 16 F3
St James Gdns CHDH RM6 61 H3
St James Pl DART DA1 139 G5
St James Ms POP/IOD E14 113 F2
St James Rd CAR SM5 175 J2
St James' Rd KUT/HW KT1 159 F2
WESTW SW1E
St James's Av BECK BR3 166 B2
BETH E2 92 E1
HPTN TW12 142 C4
St James's Chambers STJS SW1Y 10 F8
St James's Cots RCH/KEW TW9 124 E4
St James's Ct KUT/HW KT1 159 F2
WESTW SW1E 16 F3
St James's Crs BRXN/ST SW9 130 B2
St James's Dr BAL SW12 128 E7
St James's Gdns CAMTN NW1 4 B1
NTGHL W11 88 B7
St James's Gv BTSEA SW11 128 E1
St James's La MUSWH N10 54 B3
St James's Market STJS SW1Y 11 G7
St James's Ms WALTH E17 57 K4
St James's Pk CROY/NA CR0 164 D6
St James's Pl WHALL SW1A 10 E8
St James's Rd BERM/RHTH SE16 111 H4
CROY/NA CR0 164 D6
HPTN TW12 142 B4
St James's Rw CHSGTN KT9 171 K5
St James St WALTH E17 57 J5
WHALL SW1A 10 E8
St James's Ter STJWD NW8 3 L4

St James's Terrace Ms STJWD NW8 3 L4
St James Ter BAL SW12 129 F7
St James Wk CLKNW EC1R 6 C9
St Jerome's Gv UX/CGN UB8 82 A5
St Joan's Rd ED N9 42 B1
St John Cl FUL/PGN SW6 107 K6
St John's Av FBAR/BDGN N11 39 K4
PUT/ROE SW15 127 G4
WLSDN NW10 69 H7
St John's Church Rd HOM E9 74 E4
St Johns Cl STHGT/OAK N14 28 C5
St John's Cl FUL/PGN SW6 107 K6
RAIN RM13 99 G1
WBLY HA9 68 A4
St Johns Cots PGE/AN SE20 150 E6
St John's Crs BRXN/ST SW9 130 B2
St Johns Dr WOT/HER KT12 156 A7
St John's Dr WAND/EARL SW18 128 A7
St John's Est IS N1 7 H6
St John's Gdns NTGHL W11 88 C6
St John's Gv ARCH N19 72 C1
BARN SW13 126 C1
RCH/KEW TW9 124 E3
St John's Hl BTSEA SW11 128 D3
St John's Hill Gv BTSEA SW11 128 C3
St Johns Pde SCUP DA14 155 H3
St John's Pk BKHTH/KID SE3 113 J6
St Johns Pl FARR EC1M 12 C1
St Johns Rd CNTH/NBYPK IG2 60 E6
NWMAL KT3 159 K2
STMC/STPC BR5 169 J5
St John's Rd BARK IG11 78 E7
BTSEA SW11 128 D3
CAN/RD E16 94 E5
CAR SM5 175 J2
CHING E4 43 K2
CROY/NA CR0 177 H2
E/WMO/HCT KT8 157 J3
EHAM E6 77 J7
ERITH DA8 118 A4
FELT TW13 141 A4
GLDGN NW11 52 D5
HRW HA1 49 F5
ISLW TW7 124 A1
KUT/HW KT1 158 D1
NWDGN UB2 102 D2
PGE/AN SE20 150 E6
RCH/KEW TW9 125 F3
SCUP DA14 155 H3
SEVS/STOTM N15 56 A5
SUT SM1 174 E1
WALTH E17 57 K1
WAT WD17 21 F1
WBLY HA9 67 K3
WELL DA16 136 C2
WIM/MER SW19 146 C6
St John's Sq FARR EC1M 12 C1
St John's Ter FSTGT E7 77 F5
NKENS W10 88 B3
WOOL/PLUM SE18 115 H5
St John St FSBYE EC1V 6 C6
St Johns Vls KENS W8 14 D4
St John's Vls ARCH N19 72 C1
St John's Wy ARCH N19 54 D7
St John's Wood High St STJWD NW8 3 H6
St John's Wood Pk STJWD NW8 3 H5
St John's Wood Rd STJWD NW8 3 C9
St John's Wood Ter STJWD NW8 3 J5
St Josephs Cl NKENS W10 88 C4
St Joseph's Dr STHL UB1 83 J7
St Josephs Gv HDN NW4 51 K3
St Joseph's Rd ED N9 30 D6
St Joseph's St VX/NE SW8 109 G7
St Joseph's V BKHTH/KID SE3 133 C1
St Jude's Rd BETH E2 92 D1
St Jude St STNW/STAM N16 74 A4
St Julian's Cl STRHM/NOR SW16 149 G3
St Julian's Farm Rd WNWD SE27 149 G3
St Julian's Rd KIL/WHAMP NW6 70 D6
St Katharine's Prec CAMTN NW1 4 C5
St Katharine's Wy WAP E1W 13 M8
St Katherines Rd ERITHM DA18 116 E1
St Katherines Wk NTGHL W11 88 B6
St Keverne Rd ELTH/MOT SE9 153 J5
St Kilda Rd WEA W13 104 B1
St Kilda's Rd HRW HA1 48 E5
STNW/STAM N16 55 K7
St Kitts Ter NRWD SE19 150 A4
St Laurence Cl KIL/WHAMP NW6 70 A1
St Lawrence Cots POP/IOD E14 94 A7
St Lawrence Dr PIN HA5 47 F4
St Lawrence St POP/IOD E14 94 A7
St Lawrence Ter NKENS W10 88 C4
St Lawrence Wy BRXN/ST SW9 130 B1
St Leonards Av KTN/HRWW/WS HA3 49 J4
St Leonard's Av CHING E4 44 B5
St Leonards Cl BUSH WD23 21 J3
WELL DA16 136 B2
St Leonards Gdns IL IG1 78 C4
St Leonard's Gdns HEST TW5 102 D6
St Leonards Rd MORT/ESHN SW14 125 K2
St Leonard's Rd CROY/NA CR0 177 H1
ESH/CLAY KT10 171 F5
POP/IOD E14 94 A5
SURB KT6 158 E5
THDIT KT7 158 B5
WEA W13 85 H6
WLSDN NW10 87 F3
St Leonard's Sq KTTN NW5 72 A5
SURB KT6 158 E4
St Leonard's St BOW E3 93 K2
St Leonard's Ter CHEL SW3 15 L8
St Leonards Wk STRHM/NOR SW16 149 F7
St Leonards Wy EMPK RM11 63 K7
St Loo Av CHEL SW3 15 K9
St Louis Rd WNWD SE27 149 J3

St Loy's Rd TOTM N17 56 A1
St Lucia Dr SRTFD E15 76 D7
St Luke's Av CLAP SW4 129 J3
IL IG1 78 B3
St Luke's Cl SNWD SE25 165 H5
St Luke's Est FSBYE EC1V 7 H9
St Luke's Ms NTGHL W11 88 D5
St Luke's Rd NTGHL W11 88 D4
St Lukes's Cl FSBYE EC1V 6 F9
St Luke's Sq CAN/RD E16 94 D5
St Luke's St CHEL SW3 15 K7
St Lukes Yd MV/WKIL W9 88 D1
St Malo Av ED N9 42 E2
St Margarets BARK IG11 78 D7
KUTN/CMB KT2 144 E4
St Margarets Av BFN/LL DA15 154 D7
CHEAM SM3 174 C2
RYLN/HDSTN HA2 66 C2
SEVS/STOTM N15 55 H3
St Margarets Ct PUT/ROE SW15 126 E3
St Margaret's Crs PUT/ROE SW15 126 E4
St Margaret's Dr TWK TW1 124 C4
St Margaret's Gv TWK TW1 124 B5
WAN E11 76 D2
WOOL/PLUM SE18 115 H5
St Margarets Ms KUTN/CMB KT2 144 E4
St Margarets Rd BROCKY SE4 132 C5
EDGW HA8 36 D4
RSLP HA4 46 B6
St Margaret's Rd BROCKY SE4 132 C5
EHAM E6 77 J7
HNWL W7 103 K1
MNPK E12 77 K1
TOTM N17 56 A2
TWK TW1 124 C4
WLSDN NW10 88 B1
St Margaret's Ter WOOL/PLUM SE18 115 H5
St Margaret St WEST SW1P 17 J2
St Mark's Cl FUL/PGN SW6 107 K7
BAR EN5 27 F2
St Mark's Crs CAMTN NW1 4 B3
St Marks Ga HOM E9 75 G6
St Mark's Gv WBPTN SW10 108 A6
St Mark's Hl SURB KT6 159 F5
St Mark's Pl DAGE RM10 80 C5
NTGHL W11 88 C5
WIM/MER SW19 146 D5
St Mark's Rd HACK E8 74 B4
EN EN1 30 E4
HAYES BR2 168 C2
HNWL W7 103 K1
MTCM CR4 162 E1
NKENS W10 88 B4
NTGHL W11 88 C5
SNWD SE25 165 H3
TEDD TW11 143 H6
St Mark's Sq CAMTN NW1 4 A3
St Mark St WCHPL E1 13 M5
St Marks Vls FSBYPK N4 73 F1
St Martin-in-the-Fields CHCR WC2N 11 J7
St Martins NTHWD HA6 32 B4
St Martins Ap RSLP HA4 46 C6
St Martin's Av EHAM E6 95 H1
St Martin's Cl ERITHM DA18 116 E1
OXHEY WD19 33 G3
St Martin's Cl CAMTN NW1 4 B3
St Martin's Ct CHCR WC2N 11 J6
St Martins La BECK BR3 166 E4
St Martin's La CHCR WC2N 11 J7
St Martins le Grand STBT EC1A 12 E4
St Martin's Pl CHCR WC2N 11 J7
St Martin's Rd BRXN/ST SW9 130 A1
DART DA1 139 J5
ED N9 42 D1
EFNCH N2 39 H7
St Martin's St LSO/SEVD WC2H 11 H7
St Martin's Wy TOOT SW17 147 G2
St Mary Abbots Pl KENS W8 107 J2
St Mary Abbot's Pl KENS W8 107 J2
St Mary Abbots Ter WKENS W14 107 J2
St Mary At Hl MON EC3R 13 J7
St Mary Av WLGTN SM6 176 A2
St Mary Axe HDTCH EC3A 13 J5
St Marychurch St BERM/RHTH SE16 111 K1
St Mary Graces Ct WCHPL E1 13 M7
St Mary Rd WALTH E17 57 K3
St Marys BARK IG11 96 D1
St Marys Av MNPK E12 77 K1
St Mary's Av FNCH N3 52 C1
HAYES BR2 167 K2
NTHWD HA6 32 C4
STWL/WRAY TW19 120 A5
TEDD TW11 143 F5
WAN E11 59 F5
St Marys Ct WATW WD18 21 F4
St Mary's Cl CHSGTN KT9 172 B6
EW KT17 173 H6
TOTM N17 42 C7
St Marys Ct HMSMTH W6 106 C3
St Mary's Crs HDN NW4 51 K2
HYS/HAR UB3 82 D6
ISLW TW7 103 J6
STWL/WRAY TW19 120 A5
St Mary's Dr EBED/NFELT TW14 121 F6
St Marys Est BERM/RHTH SE16 111 K1
St Mary's Gdns LBTH SE11 18 B5
St Mary's Ga KENS W8 14 C4
St Mary's Gn BARN SW13 126 C2
CHSWK W4 105 J5
St Mary's Gv IS N1 73 H5
RCH/KEW TW9 125 G3
St Mary's Man BAY/PAD W2 8 F2
St Mary's Ms KIL/WHAMP NW6 2 C1
St Mary's Pth IS N1 6 C3
WCHPL E1 92 C4
St Mary's Pl KENS W8 14 C4
St Mary's Pl EA W5 104 E1
St Mary's Rd BXLY DA5 137 K2
CEND/HSY/T N8 54 E3
E/WMO/HCT KT8 157 J4
EBAR EN4 27 K6
ED N9 30 E6
GLDGN NW11 52 C6
HYS/HAR UB3 82 D6

LEY E10 76 A2
PECK SE15 111 K7
PLSTW E13 95 F1
SNWD SE25 165 F2
SURB KT6 158 D6
WATW WD18 21 F4
WIM/MER SW19 146 C4
WLSDN NW10 69 G7
WPK KT4 173 G1
St Marys Sq BAY/PAD W2 9 G2
EA W5 104 E1
St Marys Ter BORE WD6 23 K5
St Mary's Ter BAY/PAD W2 9 G2
St Mary St WOOL/PLUM SE18 114 D3
St Marys Vw KTN/HRWW/WS HA3 49 J4
WATW WD18 21 G3
St Mary's Wk HYS/HAR UB3 82 D6
LBTH SE11 18 B5
St Matthew's Av SURB KT6 159 F7
St Matthews Cl OXHEY WD19 21 H5
St Matthews Cl RAIN RM13 81 J6
St Matthews Dr BMLY BR1 168 E2
St Matthew's Rd BRXS/STRHM SW2 130 A4
EA W5 86 A1
St Matthew's Rw BETH E2 92 C2
St Matthew St WEST SW1P 17 G3
St Matthias Cl CDALE/KGS NW9 51 H4
St Maur Rd FUL/PGN SW6 107 J7
St Meddens CHST BR7 154 D6
St Mellion Cl THMD SE28 97 K5
St Merryn Cl WOOL/PLUM SE18 115 J6
St Michael's Aly BANK EC3V 13 H5
St Michael's Av ED N9 30 E6
St Michaels Av WBLY HA9 68 C5
St Michaels Cl BMLY BR1 168 D2
CAN/RD E16 95 H4
WPK KT4 173 H1
St Michael's Cl ERITHM DA18 116 E1
FNCH N3 52 E1
NFNCH/WDSPK N12 39 J4
St Michaels Cl GLDGN NW11 52 D6
St Michael's Crs PIN HA5 47 J5
St Michael's Gdns NKENS W10 88 C4
St Michael's Ms BGVA SW1W 16 A6
St Michael's Ri WELL DA16 116 C2
St Michael's Rd BRXN/ST SW9 130 A1
CRICK NW2 70 A3
CROY/NA CR0 164 D7
WELL DA16 136 C2
WLGTN SM6 176 C5
St Michael's St BAY/PAD W2 9 H3
St Michaels Ter HGT N6 54 A7
St Michael's Ter WDGN N22 40 E1
St Mildred's Ct LOTH EC2R 13 H5
St Mildreds Rd LEE/GVPK SE12 133 H6
St Nicholas Av HCH RM12 81 K2
St Nicholas Cl BORE WD6 23 K5
St Nicholas Glebe TOOT SW17 148 A5
St Nicholas Rd SUT SM1 175 F4
THDIT KT7 158 A5
WOOL/PLUM SE18 116 A4
St Nicholas Sq DEPT SE8 112 C4
St Nicholas Wy SUT SM1 175 F3
St Nicolas La CHST BR7 153 J7
St Ninian's Ct TRDG/WHET N20 39 K2
St Norbert Rd BROCKY SE4 132 B3
St Olaf's Rd FUL/PGN SW6 107 H6
St Olave's Rd EHAM E6 78 A7
St Olave's Wk STRHM/NOR SW16 163 H1
St Onge Pde EN EN1 29 K2
St Oswald's Pl LBTH SE11 17 L7
St Oswald's Rd STRHM/NOR SW16 149 H7
St Oswulf St WEST SW1P 17 H6
St Pancras Gdns CAMTN NW1 5 G5
KCROSS N1C 5 H4
St Pancras Station Forecourt KCROSS N1C 5 J4
St Pancras Wy CAMTN NW1 4 E1
St Paul's Av BERM/RHTH SE16 93 F7
CRICK NW2 69 K5
KTN/HRWW/WS HA3 50 A4
St Paul's Church Yd STP EC4M 12 E5
St Pauls Cl EA W5 105 G1
HYS/HAR UB3 101 G4
BORE WD6 24 A4
CAR SM5 162 D6
CHARL SE7 114 C4
CHSGTN KT9 171 K3
EA W5 105 G1
HSLW TW3 122 D1
St Paul's Cray Rd CHST BR7 154 D7
St Paul's Crs CAMTN NW1 5 F1
HDN NW4 52 A3
St Pauls Crs CAMTN NW1 5 F1
St Pauls Dr SRTFD E15 76 B4
St Pauls Ms CAMTN NW1 5 F1
St Paul's Pl IS N1 73 K5
St Pauls Ri PLMGR N13 41 H5
St Pauls Rd BARK IG11 78 C7
RCH/KEW TW9 125 G2
St Paul's Rd BTFD TW8 104 E5
ERITH DA8 117 K6
IS N1 73 H5
THHTH CR7 164 D2
TOTM N17 42 C6
St Pauls Ter WALW SE17 18 D9
St Paul St IS N1 6 E4
St Pauls Wy NFNCH/WDSPK N12 39 H2
St Paul's Wy BOW E3 93 J4
POP/IOD E14 93 H4
St Paul's Wood Hl STMC/STPC BR5 169 K5
St Peter's Av BETH E2 92 C1
UED N18 42 D3
WALTH E17 58 C2
St Petersburgh Ms BAY/PAD W2 8 C6
St Petersburgh Pl BAY/PAD W2 8 C6
St Peter's Cl CHST BR7 154 D6
CNTH/NBYPK IG2 60 E2
TOOT SW17 147 J1
St Peter's Cl BAR EN5 25 K4
BETH E2 92 C1
BUSH WD23 22 C6
RSLP HA4 65 H1
St Peters Cl BKHTH/KID SE3 133 J4
E/WMO/HCT KT8 157 H3
St Peter's Ct HDN NW4 52 A4
St Peters Gdns WNWD SE27 149 G2
St Peter's Gv HMSMTH W6 106 D3
St Peters Ms FSBYPK N4 55 H4

St Peter's Pl *MV/WKIL* W9 ... 8 C1
St Peters Rd *KUT/HW* KT1 ... 159 H1
St Peter's Rd *CROY/NA* CR0 ... 177 K3
 E/WMO/HCT KT8 ... 157 F1
 ED N9 ... 30 D7
 HMSMTH W6 * ... 106 D4
 STHL UB1 ... 84 A4
 TWK TW1 ... 124 C4
St Peter's Sq *BETH* E2 * ... 92 C1
 HMSMTH W6 ... 106 D4
St Peter's St *IS* N1 ... 6 D4
 SAND/SEL CR2 ... 177 K6
St Peter's St *FUL/PGN* SW6 ... 107 H6
St Peter's Vls *HMSMTH* W6 ... 106 D3
St Peters Wy *HYS/HAR* UB3 ... 101 G4
St Peter's Wy *EA* W5 ... 85 K4
 IS N1 ... 7 K2
St Philip's Av *WPK* KT4 ... 173 K5
St Philip Sq *VX/NE* SW8 * ... 129 G1
St Philip's Rd *HACK* E8 ... 74 C5
 SURB KT6 ... 158 E5
St Philip St *VX/NE* SW8 ... 129 G1
St Philip's Wy *IS* N1 ... 6 E3
St Quentin Av *DA16* ... 136 A2
St Quintin Av *NKENS* W10 ... 88 A4
St Quintin Gdns *NKENS* W10 ... 88 A4
St Quintin Rd *PLSTW* E13 ... 95 F2
St Raphael's Wy *WLSDN* NW10 ... 68 E4
St Regis Cl *MUSWH* N10 ... 54 B1
St Ronans Crs *WFD* IG8 ... 44 E6
St Rowans Vw *DART* DA1 ... 139 J4
St Rule St *VX/NE* SW8 ... 129 H1
St Saviours Ct *WDGN* N22 ... 54 D1
St Saviour's Est *STHWK* SE1 ... 19 L3
St Saviour's Rd
 BRXS/STRHM SW2 ... 130 A4
 CROY/NA CR0 ... 164 D5
Saints Cl *WNWD* SE27 ... 149 H3
Saints Dr *FSTGT* E7 ... 77 H4
St Silas Pl *KTTN* NW5 ... 72 A5
St Simon's Av *PUT/ROE* SW15 ... 127 F4
St Stephen's Av *SHB* W12 ... 87 K7
 WALTH E17 ... 58 A4
 WEA W13 ... 85 H5
St Stephens Cl *KTTN* NW5 * ... 71 K4
 STJWD NW8 ... 3 J4
St Stephen's Cl *STHL* UB1 ... 84 A4
 WALTH E17 ... 57 K4
St Stephen's Crs
 BAY/PAD W2 * ... 8 B4
 THHTH CR7 ... 164 B2
St Stephen's Gdns
 BAY/PAD W2 * ... 8 B4
 TWK TW1 ... 124 D5
St Stephen's Gv *LEW* SE13 ... 133 F2
St Stephens Ms *BAY/PAD* W2 ... 8 B3
St Stephens Pde *WHALL* SW1A ... 17 J1
St Stephens Rd *BAR* EN5 ... 26 B4
St Stephen's Rd *BOW* E3 ... 75 G7
 EHAM E6 ... 77 G6
 HSLW TW3 ... 123 F5
 WALTH E17 ... 57 K4
 WEA W13 ... 85 H5
St Stephens Ter *VX/NE* SW8 * ... 109 K6
St Stephen's Ter *VX/NE* SW8 ... 110 A6
St Stephens Wk *SKENS* SW7 ... 14 E5
St Swithin's La *MANHO* EC4N ... 13 G6
St Swithun's Wk *LEW* SE13 * ... 133 G2
St Theresas Cl *HOM* E9 ... 75 J3
St Theresa's Rd
 EBED/NFELT TW14 ... 121 J3
St Thomas Cl *SURB* KT6 ... 159 G7
St Thomas Dr *BXLY* DA5 ... 137 H6
St Thomas Dr *STMC/STPC* BR5 ... 169 H7
St Thomas' Dr *PIN* HA5 ... 33 J7
 STMC/STPC BR5 ... 169 H7
St Thomas Gdns *IL* IG1 ... 78 C5
St Thomas Rd *BELV* DA17 ... 117 K1
 CAN/RD E16 ... 94 E5
 STHGT/OAK N14 ... 28 D7
St Thomas' Gdns *KTTN* NW5 * ... 72 A5
St Thomas' Pl *HOM* E9 ... 74 E6
St Thomas's Gdns *KTTN* NW5 ... 72 A5
St Thomas's Pl *HOM* E9 ... 74 E6
St Thomas's Rd *FSBYPK* N4 ... 73 G1
 WLSDN NW10 ... 69 G7
St Thomas's Sq *HOM* E9 ... 74 D6
St Thomas St *CHSWK* W4 ... 105 K6
St Thomas' St *STHWK* SE1 ... 13 H9
St Thomas's Wy *FUL/PGN* SW6 ... 107 J6
St Ursula Gv *PIN* HA5 ... 47 H4
St Ursula Rd *STHL* UB1 ... 84 A5
St Vincent Cl *WNWD* SE27 ... 149 H4
St Vincents La *MLHL* NW7 ... 37 K3
St Vincent Rd *WHTN* TW2 ... 123 H5
St Vincents Av *DART* DA1 ... 139 K4
St Vincents Cots
 WATW WD18 * ... 21 F3
St Vincents La *MLHL* NW7 * ... 37 K3
St Vincents Rd *DART* DA1 ... 139 K5
St Vincent St *MHST* W1U ... 10 B3
St Wilfrid's Cl *EBAR* EN4 ... 27 J4
St Wilfrid's Rd *EBAR* EN4 ... 27 H4
St Winefride's Av *MNPK* E12 ... 77 K4
St Winifred's Rd *TEDD* TW11 ... 143 H5
Sakura Dr *WDGN* N22 ... 40 D7
Saladin Dr *PUR* RM19 ... 119 K3
Salamanca Pl *STHWK* SE1 ... 17 L6
Salamanca St *STHWK* SE1 ... 17 L6
Salamander Cl *KUTN/CMB* KT2 ... 143 J4
Salamander Quay
 KUT/HW KT1 * ... 143 K7
Salamons Wy *RAIN* RM13 ... 99 G3
Salcombe Dr *CHDH* RM6 ... 62 B5
 MRDN SM4 ... 161 G2
Salcombe Gdns *MLHL* NW7 ... 38 A5
Salcombe Rd
 STNW/STAM N16 ... 74 B4
 WALTH E17 ... 57 H6
Salcombe Wy *RSLP* HA4 ... 64 E1
Salcott Rd *BTSEA* SW11 ... 128 D4
 CROY/NA CR0 ... 176 E2
Salehurst Cl
 KTN/HRWW/WS HA3 ... 50 A4
Salehurst Rd *BROCKY* SE4 ... 132 C5
Salem Pl *CROY/NA* CR0 ... 177 J2
Salem Rd *BAY/PAD* W2 ... 8 D5
Sale Pl *BAY/PAD* W2 ... 9 J3
Sale St *BETH* E2 ... 92 C3
Salford Rd *BRXS/STRHM* SW2 ... 129 J7
Salhouse Cl *THMD* SE28 ... 97 J5
Salisbury Av *BARK* IG11 ... 78 D6
 FNCH N3 ... 52 D2
 SUT SM1 ... 174 D5
Salisbury Ct *WALW* SE17 ... 19 G5
 WPK KT4 ... 173 H2
Salisbury Ct *EMB* EC4Y ... 12 B5
Salisbury Gdns
 WIM/MER SW19 * ... 146 C6
Salisbury Pavement
 FUL/PGN SW6 * ... 107 K6
Salisbury Pl *BRXN/ST* SW9 ... 110 C6
 MBLAR W1H ... 9 L2
Salisbury Prom
 CEND/HSY/T N8 * ... 55 H4
Salisbury Rd *BAR* EN5 ... 26 C2

Salisbury Sq *EMB* EC4Y * ... 12 B5
Salisbury St *ACT* W3 ... 105 K1
 STJWD NW8 ... 9 J1
Salisbury Ter *PECK* SE15 ... 131 K2
Salisbury Wk *ARCH* N19 ... 72 C1
Salix Cl *SUN* TW16 ... 141 F6
Salix La *WFD* IG8 ... 45 J7
Sally Murray Cl *MNPK* E12 ... 78 A3
Salmond Cl *STAN* HA7 ... 35 G5
Salmon La *POP/IOD* E14 ... 93 G5
Salmon Ms *KIL/WHAMP* NW6 * ... 70 E4
Salmon Rd *BELV* DA17 ... 117 H4
 DART DA1 ... 139 J2
Salmons Rd *CHSGTN* KT9 ... 172 A5
 ED N9 ... 30 C7
Salmon St *CDALE/KGS* NW9 ... 50 D7
 POP/IOD E14 * ... 93 H5
Salomons Rd *PLSTW* E13 ... 95 G4
Salop Rd *WALTH* E17 ... 57 F5
Saltash Cl *SUT* SM1 ... 174 D3
Saltash Rd *WELL* DA16 ... 116 D7
Saltcoats Rd *CHSWK* W4 ... 106 B1
Saltcote Cl *DART* DA1 ... 138 B5
Saltcroft Cl *WBLY* HA9 ... 50 D7
Salter Cl *RYLN/HDSTN* HA2 ... 65 K3
Salterford Rd *TOOT* SW17 ... 148 A5
Salter Rd *BERM/RHTH* SE16 ... 93 F7
Salters' Hall Ct *MANHO* EC4N * ... 13 G6
Salters Rd *NKENS* W10 ... 88 B3
 WALTH E17 ... 58 B3
Salters Rw *IS* N1 * ... 73 K5
Salter St *POP/IOD* E14 ... 93 J6
 WLSDN NW10 ... 87 J2
Salterton Rd *HOLWY* N7 ... 72 E2
Saltford Cl *ERITH* DA8 ... 118 B4
Saltley Cl *EHAM* E6 ... 95 J5
Saltoun Rd *BRXS/STRHM* SW2 ... 130 B3
Saltram Cl *SEVS/STOTM* N15 ... 56 B3
Saltram Crs *MV/WKIL* W9 ... 2 A4
Saltwell St *POP/IOD* E14 ... 93 J6
Saltwood Gv *WALW* SE17 ... 19 G8
Salusbury Rd
 KIL/WHAMP NW6 ... 88 D1
Salvador *TOOT* SW17 ... 147 J4
Salvia Gdns *GFD/PVL* UB6 ... 85 G1
Salvin Rd *PUT/ROE* SW15 ... 127 G2
Salway Cl *WFD* IG8 ... 44 E6
Salway Rd *SRTFD* E15 ... 76 B5
Samantha Cl *WALTH* E17 ... 57 H6
Sam Bartram Cl *CHARL* SE7 ... 114 B4
Sambruck Ms *CAT* SE6 ... 132 E7
Samels Ct *HMSMTH* W6 ... 106 D4
Samford St *STJWD* NW8 ... 9 J1
Samira Cl *WALTH* E17 ... 57 H5
Samos Rd *PGE/AN* SE20 ... 165 J1
Sampson Av *BAR* EN5 ... 26 B4
Sampson Cl *BELV* DA17 ... 116 E2
Sampson St *WAP* E1W * ... 92 C7
Samson St *PLSTW* E13 ... 95 G1
Samuel Cl *HACK* E8 ... 7 M1
 NWCR SE14 ... 112 A5
 STAN HA7 ... 35 G5
 WOOL/PLUM SE18 ... 114 D3
Samuel Gray Gdns
 KUTN/CMB KT2 ... 143 K7
Samuel Lewis Trust Dwellings
 CMBW SE5 * ... 110 D7
 WKENS W14 * ... 107 H3
Samuel St *WOOL/PLUM* SE18 ... 114 E3
Sancroft Cl *CRICK* NW2 ... 69 K2
Sancroft Rd
 KTN/HRWW/WS HA3 ... 49 F1
Sancroft St *LBTH* SE11 ... 17 M7
Sanctuary Cl *DART* DA1 ... 139 F5
Sanctuary Ms *HACK* E8 ... 74 B5
Sanctuary Rd *HTHAIR* TW6 ... 120 D5
Sanctuary St *STHWK* SE1 ... 18 F2
The Sanctuary *BXLY* DA5 ... 136 E5
 WEST SW1P ... 17 H3
Sandall Cl *EA* W5 ... 86 A3
Sandall Rd *EA* W5 ... 86 A3
 KTTN NW5 ... 72 C5
Sandal Rd *NWMAL* KT3 ... 160 B3
 UED N18 ... 42 C4
Sandal St *SRTFD* E15 ... 76 C7
Sandalwood Cl *WCHPL* E1 ... 93 G3
Sandalwood Dr *RSLP* HA4 ... 46 A6
Sandalwood Rd *FELT* TW13 ... 141 F2
Sandbach Pl
 WOOL/PLUM SE18 ... 115 H3
Sandbourne Av
 WIM/MER SW19 ... 162 A4
Sandbourne Rd *NWCR* SE14 ... 132 B1
Sandbrook Cl *MLHL* NW7 ... 37 F5
Sandbrook Rd
 STNW/STAM N16 ... 74 A2
Sandby Gn *ELTH/MOT* SE9 ... 134 D2
Sandcliff Rd *ERITH* DA8 ... 118 A3
Sandcroft Cl *PLMGR* N13 ... 41 H5
Sandell's Av *ASHF* TW15 ... 140 A3
Sandell St *STHWK* SE1 ... 18 A1
Sanders Cl *HPTN* TW12 ... 142 C4
Sanders La *MLHL* NW7 ... 38 A6
Sanderson Cl *KTTN* NW5 ... 72 B3
Sanders Pde
 STRHM/NOR SW16 * ... 148 E5
Sanderstead Av *GLDGN* NW11 ... 70 C1
Sanderstead Cl *BAL* SW12 ... 129 H6
Sanderstead Rd *LEY* E10 ... 57 F6
 SAND/SEL CR2 ... 177 K6
Sandfield Gdns *THHTH* CR7 ... 164 C2
Sandfield Pl *THHTH* CR7 ... 164 D2
Sandfield Rd *THHTH* CR7 ... 164 C2
Sandford Av *WDGN* N22 ... 41 H6
Sandford Rd *BXLYHS* DA6 ... 137 F3
 EHAM E6 ... 95 J3
 HAYES BR2 ... 167 K3

Sandford Rw *WALW* SE17 ... 19 G7
Sandford St *FUL/PGN* SW6 ... 108 A6
Sandgate La
 WAND/EARL SW18 ... 128 D7
Sandgate Rd *WELL* DA16 ... 116 D6
Sandgate St *PECK* SE15 ... 111 J5
Sandhills *WLGTN* SM6 ... 176 D3
Sandhurst Av *BRYLDS* KT5 ... 159 J6
 RYLN/HDSTN HA2 ... 48 A6
Sandhurst Cl *SAND/SEL* CR2 ... 178 A7
Sandhurst Dr *GDMY/SEVK* IG3 ... 79 F3
Sandhurst Market *CAT* SE6 * ... 133 F7
Sandhurst Pde *CAT* SE6 * ... 133 F7
Sandhurst Rd *BFN/LL* DA15 ... 155 F2
 BXLY DA5 ... 136 E4
 CAT SE6 ... 133 G7
 CDALE/KGS NW9 ... 50 C2
 ED N9 ... 30 E5
Sandhurst Wy *SAND/SEL* CR2 ... 178 A6
Sandiford Rd *CHEAM* SM3 ... 174 D1
Sandiland Crs *HAYES* BR2 ... 180 E1
Sandilands *CROY/NA* CR0 ... 178 C2
Sandilands Rd *FUL/PGN* SW6 ... 108 A7
Sandison St *PECK* SE15 ... 131 G2
Sandling Ri *ELTH/MOT* SE9 ... 154 A2
Sandlings Cl *PECK* SE15 ... 131 J1
The Sandlings *WDGN* N22 ... 55 G1
Sandmartin Wy *WLGTN* SM6 ... 163 F7
Sandmere Rd *CLAP* SW4 ... 129 K3
Sandon Cl *ESH/CLAY* KT10 ... 157 J6
Sandow Crs *HYS/HAR* UB3 ... 101 J2
Sandown Av *DAGE* RM10 ... 80 E5
 ESH/CLAY KT10 ... 170 C4
Sandown Ct *BELMT* SM2 * ... 175 F6
 SYD SE26 * ... 150 D2
Sandown Ga *ESH/CLAY* KT10 ... 170 C3
Sandown Rd *ESH/CLAY* KT10 ... 170 C4
 SNWD SE25 ... 165 J4
Sandown Wy *NTHLT* UB5 ... 65 J5
Sandpiper Cl
 BERM/RHTH SE16 ... 112 C1
 WALTH E17 ... 43 F6
Sandpiper Dr *ERITH* DA8 ... 118 E6
Sandpiper Rd *SUT* SM1 ... 174 D4
Sandpiper Ter *CLAY* IG5 * ... 60 B7
Sandpit Pl *CHARL* SE7 ... 114 D4
Sandpit Rd *BMLY* BR1 ... 152 C4
 DART DA1 ... 139 F3
Sandpits Rd *CROY/NA* CR0 ... 179 F3
 RCHPK/HAM TW10 ... 124 E7
Sandra Cl *HSLW* TW3 ... 123 G4
 WDGN N22 ... 41 J7
Sandridge Cl *HRW* HA1 ... 48 D3
Sandridge St *ARCH* N19 ... 72 C1
Sandringham Av *RYNPK* SW20 ... 146 C2
Sandringham Cl *EN* EN1 ... 30 A1
 WIM/MER SW19 ... 127 G7
Sandringham Crs
 RYLN/HDSTN HA2 ... 66 A2
Sandringham Dr *WELL* DA16 ... 135 K1
Sandringham Gdns
 BARK/HLT IG6 ... 60 C2
 CEND/HSY/T N8 ... 54 E5
 E/WMO/HCT KT8 ... 157 F3
 HEST TW5 ... 101 K7
 NFNCH/WDSPK N12 ... 39 H5
Sandringham Ms *EA* W5 ... 85 K6
 HPTN TW12 ... 141 F7
Sandringham Rd *BARK* IG11 ... 79 F5
 BMLY BR1 ... 152 E4
 CRICK NW2 ... 69 K4
 FSTGT E7 ... 77 H4
 GLDGN NW11 ... 52 C6
 HACK E8 ... 74 B4
 HTHAIR TW6 ... 120 B4
 LEY E10 ... 58 B5
 NTHLT UB5 ... 66 A6
 THHTH CR7 ... 164 D4
 WDGN N22 ... 55 J2
 WPK KT4 ... 173 J2
Sandrock Pl *CROY/NA* CR0 ... 179 F3
Sandrock Rd *LEW* SE13 ... 132 D2
Sands End La *FUL/PGN* SW6 ... 108 A7
Sandstone La *CAN/RD* E16 ... 95 F6
Sandstone Pl *ARCH* N19 ... 72 B1
Sandstone Rd *LEE/GVPK* SE12 ... 153 F1
Sands Wy *WFD* IG8 ... 45 K5
Sandtoft Rd *CHARL* SE7 ... 114 A5
Sandwell Crs
 KIL/WHAMP NW6 ... 70 E5
Sandwich St *STPAN* WC1H ... 5 J8
Sandwick Cl *MLHL* NW7 ... 37 J6
Sandycombe Rd
 EBED/NFELT TW14 ... 121 K7
 RCH/KEW TW9 ... 125 H1
Sandycoombe Rd *TWK* TW1 ... 124 D5
Sandycroft *ABYW* SE2 ... 116 B5
Sandy Dr *EBED/NFELT* TW14 ... 121 H7
Sandy Hill Av
 WOOL/PLUM SE18 ... 115 G4
Sandy Hill La
 WOOL/PLUM SE18 ... 115 G3
Sandyhill Rd *IL* IG1 ... 78 B3
Sandy Hill Rd *WLGTN* SM6 ... 176 C7
 WOOL/PLUM SE18 ... 115 G4
Sandy La *BELMT* SM2 ... 174 C7
 BUSH WD23 ... 22 C2
 KTN/HRWW/WS HA3 ... 50 B5
 KUT/HW KT1 ... 143 H7
 MTCM CR4 ... 148 A7
 NTHWD HA6 ... 32 E4
 RCHPK/HAM TW10 ... 143 H3
 SCUP DA14 ... 155 K6
 TEDD TW11 ... 143 G6
 WOT/HER KT12 ... 156 A5
Sandy La North *WLGTN* SM6 ... 176 D4
Sandy La South *WLGTN* SM6 ... 176 C7
Sandy Ldg *PIN* HA5 * ... 34 A5
Sandy Lodge Ct *NTHWD* HA6 * ... 32 C4
Sandy Lodge La *NTHWD* HA6 ... 32 B2
Sandy Lodge Wy *NTHWD* HA6 ... 32 C5
Sandy Md *HOR/WEW* KT19 ... 172 C7
Sandymount Av *STAN* HA7 ... 35 J4
Sandy Rdg *CHST* BR7 ... 154 A5
Sandy Wy *CROY/NA* CR0 ... 179 H2
Sanford La *STNW/STAM* N16 ... 74 B1
Sanford St *NWCR* SE14 ... 112 B5
Sanford Ter *STNW/STAM* N16 ... 74 B2
Sanger Av *CHSGTN* KT9 ... 172 B4
Sangley Rd *CAT* SE6 ... 132 E6
 SNWD SE25 ... 165 F3
Sangora Rd *BTSEA* SW11 ... 128 C3
Sansom Rd *WAN* E11 ... 76 D1
Sansom St *CMBW* SE5 ... 110 E6
Sans Wk *CLKNW* EC1R ... 6 C9
Santley St *CLAP* SW4 ... 129 K3
Santos Rd *WAND/EARL* SW18 ... 127 K4

Saperton Wk *LBTH* SE11 ... 17 M5
Sapphire Cl *BCTR* RM8 ... 61 J7
Sapphire Rd *DEPT* SE8 ... 112 B3
 WLSDN NW10 ... 68 E7
Saracen Cl *CROY/NA* CR0 ... 164 E5
Saracen's Head Yd
 FENCHST EC3M ... 13 K5
Saracen St *POP/IOD* E14 ... 93 J5
Saratoga Rd *CLPT* E5 ... 74 E3
Sardinia St *HOL/ALD* WC2B ... 11 L5
Sarita Cl *KTN/HRWW/WS* HA3 ... 48 D1
Sark Cl *HEST* TW5 ... 103 F6
Sarnesfield Rd
 ENC/FH EN2 * ... 29 K3
Sarre Rd *CRICK* NW2 ... 70 D4
Sarsen Av *HSLW* TW3 ... 122 E1
Sarsfeld Rd *BAL* SW12 ... 128 E7
Sarsfield Rd *GFD/PVL* UB6 ... 85 H1
Sartor Rd *PECK* SE15 ... 132 A3
Sarum Ter *BOW* E3 * ... 93 H3
Satanita Cl *CAN/RD* E16 ... 95 H5
Satchell Md *CDALE/KGS* NW9 ... 37 H7
Satchwell Rd *BETH* E2 ... 92 C2
Sattar Ms *STNW/STAM* N16 * ... 73 K2
Sauls Gn *WAN* E11 ... 76 C2
Saunders Cl *IL* IG1 ... 60 D7
 POP/IOD E14 * ... 93 H6
Saunders Ness Rd
 POP/IOD E14 ... 113 G3
Saunders Rd
 WOOL/PLUM SE18 ... 116 A4
Saunders St *LBTH* SE11 ... 18 A5
Saunders Wy *THMD* SE28 ... 97 H6
Saunderton Rd *ALP/SUD* HA0 ... 67 H4
Saunton Av *HYS/HAR* UB3 ... 101 J6
Saunton Rd *HCH* RM12 ... 81 J1
Savage Gdns *EHAM* E6 ... 95 K5
 TWRH EC3N ... 13 K6
Savanah Cl *PECK* SE15 ... 111 G6
Savera Cl *NWDGN* UB2 ... 102 B2
Savernake Ct *STAN* HA7 * ... 35 J5
Savernake Rd *ED* N9 ... 30 C5
 HAMP NW3 ... 71 K3
Savery Dr *SURB* KT6 ... 158 C6
Savile Cl *NWMAL* KT3 ... 160 B4
 THDIT KT7 ... 158 A7
Savile Gdns *CROY/NA* CR0 ... 178 B1
Savile Rw *CONDST* W1S ... 10 E6
Saville Crs *ASHF* TW15 ... 140 B5
Saville Rd *CAN/RD* E16 ... 95 J7
 CHDH RM6 ... 62 B5
 CHSWK W4 ... 106 A2
 TWK TW1 ... 124 A7
Saville Rw *HAYES* BR2 ... 167 J7
Savill Gdns *RYNPK* SW20 ... 160 D2
Savill Rw *WFD* IG8 ... 44 D5
Savona Cl *WIM/MER* SW19 ... 146 B6
Savona St *VX/NE* SW8 ... 109 H6
Savoy Av *HYS/HAR* UB3 ... 101 H4
Savoy Cl *EDGW* HA8 ... 36 C4
 SRTFD E15 ... 76 C7
Savoy Ct *TPL/STR* WC2R ... 11 K7
Savoy Hl *TPL/STR* WC2R ... 11 L7
Savoy Ms *BRXN/ST* SW9 ... 129 K2
Savoy Pde *EN* EN1 * ... 30 A2
Savoy Pl *CHCR* WC2N ... 11 K7
Savoy Rw *DART* DA1 ... 139 F4
Savoy Rw *TPL/STR* WC2R ... 11 L7
Savoy Steps *TPL/STR* WC2R * ... 11 L7
Savoy St *TPL/STR* WC2R ... 11 L7
Savoy Wy *TPL/STR* WC2R ... 11 L6
Sawbill Cl *YEAD* UB4 ... 83 H4
Sawkins Cl *WIM/MER* SW19 ... 146 B1
Sawley Rd *SHB* W12 ... 87 J7
Saw Mill Wy *STNW/STAM* N16 ... 56 C5
Sawtry Cl *CAR* SM5 ... 162 C6
Sawyer Cl *ED* N9 ... 42 C1
Sawyers Cl *DAGE* RM10 ... 80 E5
Sawyer's Hl
 MORT/ESHN SW14 ... 125 K6
 RCHPK/HAM TW10 ... 125 G6
Sawyers Lawn *WEA* W13 ... 85 G5
Sawyer St *STHWK* SE1 ... 18 E1
Saxham Rd *BARK* IG11 ... 78 E7
Saxlingham Rd *CHING* E4 ... 44 B2
Saxon Av *FELT* TW13 ... 141 J1
Saxonbury Av *SUN* TW16 ... 156 A2
Saxonbury Cl *MTCM* CR4 ... 162 C2
Saxonbury Gdns *SURB* KT6 ... 158 D7
Saxon Cha *CEND/HSY/T* N8 ... 55 F6
Saxon Cl *SURB* KT6 ... 158 E5
 WALTH E17 ... 57 J6
Saxon Dr *ACT* W3 ... 86 D5
Saxonfield Cl
 BRXS/STRHM SW2 ... 130 A6
Saxon Rd *ASHF* TW15 ... 140 B5
 BMLY BR1 ... 152 D6
 BOW E3 ... 93 H1
 EHAM E6 ... 95 K3
 IL IG1 ... 78 B5
 KUTN/CMB KT2 ... 144 A7
 SNWD SE25 ... 164 E4
 STHL UB1 ... 83 J6
 WBLY HA9 ... 68 E2
 WDGN N22 ... 41 H7
Saxon Wy *STHGT/OAK* N14 ... 28 D5
Saxony Pde *HYS/HAR* UB3 ... 82 A4
Saxton Cl *LEW* SE13 ... 133 G2
Sayesbury La *UED* N18 ... 42 C4
Sayes Court St *DEPT* SE8 ... 112 C4
Scala St *FITZ* W1T ... 10 F2
Scales Rd *TOTM* N17 ... 56 B2
Scammell Wy *WATW* WD18 ... 20 D7
Scampton Rd
 STWL/WRAY TW19 ... 120 C5
Scandrett St *WAP* E1W * ... 92 D2
Scarba Wk *IS* N1 ... 73 K5
Scarborough Rd *ED* N9 ... 30 E6
 FSBYPK N4 ... 55 G6
 HTHAIR TW6 ... 121 F5
 WAN E11 ... 58 B7
Scarborough St *WCHPL* E1 ... 13 M5
Scarbrook Rd *CROY/NA* CR0 ... 177 J2
Scarle Rd *ALP/SUD* HA0 ... 67 K5
Scarlet Rd *CAT* SE6 ... 152 C2
Scarsbrook Rd
 BKHTH/KID SE3 ... 134 C2
Scarsdale Pl *KENS* W8 * ... 14 C3
Scarsdale Rd
 RYLN/HDSTN HA2 ... 66 C2
Scarsdale Vls *KENS* W8 ... 14 B4
Scarth Rd *BARN* SW13 ... 126 C2
Scawen Cl *CAR* SM5 ... 176 A3
Scawen Rd *DEPT* SE8 ... 112 B4
Scawfell St *BETH* E2 ... 7 M6
Scaynes Link
 NFNCH/WDSPK N12 ... 38 E3
Sceptre Rd *BETH* E2 ... 92 E2
Scholars Cl *BAR* EN5 ... 26 C3
Scholars Rd *BAL* SW12 ... 129 H7
Scholars Wy *GPK* RM2 ... 63 K4
Scholefield Rd *ARCH* N19 ... 72 D1

Schonfeld Sq
 STNW/STAM N16 ... 73 K1
Schoolbank Rd *GNWCH* SE10 ... 113 J3
School Crs *DART* DA1 ... 138 C3
Schoolgate Dr *MRDN* SM4 ... 162 A4
School House La *TEDD* TW11 ... 143 H6
Schoolhouse La *WAP* E1W * ... 93 F6
School La *BUSH* WD23 ... 22 D1
 KUT/HW KT1 ... 143 J7
 PIN HA5 * ... 47 J3
 SURB KT6 ... 159 G7
School Pas *KUT/HW* KT1 ... 159 G1
 STHL UB1 ... 83 K7
School Rd *CHST* BR7 ... 154 C7
 DAGE RM10 ... 80 C7
 E/WMO/HCT KT8 ... 157 F3
 HPTN TW12 ... 142 C5
 HSLW TW3 ... 123 J2
 KUT/HW KT1 * ... 143 J7
 MNPK E12 ... 77 K3
 WDR/YW UB7 ... 100 A5
 WLSDN NW10 ... 87 F3
School Road Av *HPTN* TW12 ... 142 C5
School Sq *GNWCH* SE10 ... 113 J2
School Wy *BCTR* RM8 ... 79 J2
Schoolway
 NFNCH/WDSPK N12 ... 39 H4
Schooner Cl *BARK* IG11 ... 97 H2
 BERM/RHTH SE16 ... 112 A1
 POP/IOD E14 ... 113 G2
Schubert Rd *BORE* WD6 ... 23 K5
 PUT/ROE SW15 ... 127 J4
Sclater St *WCHPL* E1 ... 7 L9
Scoble Pl *STNW/STAM* N16 ... 74 B3
Scoles Crs *BRXS/STRHM* SW2 ... 130 B7
Scope Wy *KUT/HW* KT1 ... 159 F3
Scoresby St *STHWK* SE1 ... 12 C9
Scorton Av *GFD/PVL* UB6 ... 85 G4
Scoter Cl *WFD* IG8 ... 45 F6
Scot Gv *PIN* HA5 ... 33 H6
Scotia Rd *BRXS/STRHM* SW2 ... 130 B6
Scotland Gn *TOTM* N17 ... 56 B1
Scotland Green Rd *PEND* EN3 ... 31 F4
Scotland Green Rd North
 PEND EN3 ... 31 F3
Scots Cl *STWL/WRAY* TW19 ... 120 A7
Scotsdale Cl *CHEAM* SM3 ... 174 C6
 STMC/STPC BR5 ... 169 K5
Scotsdale Rd *LEE/GVPK* SE12 ... 134 B4
Scotswood St *CLKNW* EC1R * ... 6 B9
Scotswood Wk *TOTM* N17 ... 42 C6
Scott Av *PUT/ROE* SW15 ... 127 H5
Scott Cl *HOR/WEW* KT19 ... 172 E6
 STRHM/NOR SW16 ... 149 F7
 WDR/YW UB7 ... 100 C3
Scott Crs *ERITH* DA8 ... 118 C7
 RYLN/HDSTN HA2 ... 48 B7
Scott Ellis Gdns *STJWD* NW8 ... 3 G8
Scottes La *BCTR* RM8 ... 61 K2
Scott Farm Cl *THDIT* KT7 ... 158 C7
Scott Gdns *HEST* TW5 ... 102 C6
Scott Lidgett Crs
 BERM/RHTH SE16 ... 111 H1
Scott Rd *EDGW* HA8 ... 50 D1
Scotts Av *HAYES* BR2 ... 167 G1
 SUN TW16 ... 140 C6
Scotts Dr *HPTN* TW12 ... 142 B6
Scotts Farm Rd
 HOR/WEW KT19 ... 172 E5
Scott's La *HAYES* BR2 ... 167 G2
Scotts Pas
 WOOL/PLUM SE18 * ... 115 G3
Scotts Rd *BMLY* BR1 ... 152 E6
 LEY E10 ... 58 A7
 NWDGN UB2 ... 102 B2
 SHB W12 ... 106 E1
Scott St *WCHPL* E1 ... 92 D3
Scotts Wy *SUN* TW16 ... 140 C6
Scottswood Cl *BUSH* WD23 ... 21 J1
Scottswood Rd *BUSH* WD23 ... 21 J1
Scott's Yd *MANHO* EC4N ... 13 G6
Scott Trimmer Wy *HSLW* TW3 ... 122 D1
Scottwell Dr *CDALE/KGS* NW9 ... 51 H4
Scoulding Rd *CAN/RD* E16 ... 94 D5
Scouler St *POP/IOD* E14 ... 94 B6
Scout Wy *MLHL* NW7 ... 37 F3
Scovell Crs *STHWK* SE1 * ... 18 E2
Scovell Rd *STHWK* SE1 ... 18 E2
Scrattons Ter *BARK* IG11 ... 97 K1
Scriven St *HACK* E8 ... 7 M3
Scrooby St *CAT* SE6 ... 132 E5
Scrubs La *WLSDN* NW10 ... 87 J2
Scrutton Cl *BAL* SW12 ... 129 J6
Scrutton St *SDTCH* EC2A ... 7 K9
Scutari Rd *EDUL* SE22 ... 131 J4
Scylla Crs *HTHAIR* TW6 ... 120 E6
Scylla Rd *HTHAIR* TW6 ... 120 E5
 PECK SE15 ... 131 J2
Seabright St *BETH* E2 ... 92 D2
Seabrook Dr *WWKM* BR4 ... 180 C1
Seabrook Gdns
 ROMW/RG RM7 ... 62 C6
Seabrook Rd *BCTR* RM8 ... 79 K2
Seaburn Cl *RAIN* RM13 ... 99 G2
Seacole Cl *ACT* W3 ... 87 F5
Seacourt Rd *ABYW* SE2 ... 116 E1
Seacroft Gdns *OXHEY* WD19 ... 33 H2
Seafield Rd *FBAR/BDGN* N11 ... 40 D3
Seaford Cl *RSLP* HA4 ... 46 C7
Seaford Rd *EN* EN1 ... 30 A3
 HTHAIR TW6 ... 120 A4
 SEVS/STOTM N15 ... 55 K4
 WALTH E17 ... 58 A1
 WEA W13 ... 85 H7
Seaforth Av *NWMAL* KT3 ... 160 E4
Seaforth Crs *HBRY* N5 ... 73 J4
Seaforth Gdns
 HOR/WEW KT19 ... 173 H5
 WCHMH N21 ... 29 F6
 WFD IG8 ... 45 G4
Seaforth Pl *WESTW* SW1E ... 16 F3
Seager Blds *DEPT* SE8 * ... 112 D7
Seagrave Cl *WCHPL* E1 * ... 93 F4
Seagrave Rd *FUL/PGN* SW6 ... 14 B9
Seagry Rd *WAN* E11 ... 58 E5
Seaguil La *CAN/RD* E16 ... 94 E6
Sealand Rd *HTHAIR* TW6 ... 120 D4
Seal St *HACK* E8 ... 74 B3
Searles Cl *BTSEA* SW11 ... 108 D7
Searles Dr *EHAM* E6 ... 96 B4
Searles Rd *STHWK* SE1 ... 19 H5
Sears St *CMBW* SE5 ... 110 E6
Seasons Cl *HNWL* W7 ... 84 E7
Seasprite Cl *NTHLT* UB5 ... 83 H2
Seaton Av *GDMY/SEVK* IG3 ... 78 E4
Seaton Cl *LBTH* SE11 ... 18 B7
 PLSTW E13 ... 94 E3
 PUT/ROE SW15 ... 126 E7
 WHTN TW2 ... 123 J5
Seaton Gdns *RSLP* HA4 ... 64 C2
Seaton Rd *ALP/SUD* HA0 ... 67 J7

DART DA1 .... 138 D6
HYS/HAR UB3 .... 101 G3
MTCM CR4 .... 162 D1
WELL DA16 .... 116 D6
WHTN TW2 .... 123 H5
Seaton St *UED* N18 .... 42 C4
Sebastian St *FSBYE* EC1V 6 D8
Sebastopol Rd *ED* N9 .... 42 C3
Sebbon St *IS* N1 .... 6 D2
Sebergham Gv *MLHL* NW7 ..... 37 J6
Sebert Rd *FSTGT* E7 .... 77 F4
Sebright Rd *BAR* EN5 .... 26 B1
Secker Crs
  KTN/HRWW/WS HA3 .... 34 C7
Secker St *STHWK* SE1 .... 12 A9
Second Av *ACT* W3 .... 87 H7
  CHDH RM6 .... 61 J4
  DAGE RM10 .... 98 D1
  EN EN1 .... 30 B4
  HDN NW4 .... 52 B3
  HYS/HAR UB3 .... 82 D7
  MNPK E12 .... 77 J3
  MORT/ESHN SW14 .... 126 B2
  NKENS W10 .... 88 C3
  PLSTW E13 .... 94 E2
  UED N18 .... 42 E4
  WALTH E17 .... 57 J4
  WBLY HA9 .... 68 A2
  WOT/HER KT12 .... 156 A5
Second Cross Rd *WHTN* TW2 ... 142 D1
Second Wy *WBLY* HA9 .... 68 D3
Sedan Wy *WALW* SE17 .... 19 J7
Sedcombe Cl *SCUP* DA14 ...... 155 H3
Sedding St *KTBR* SW1X 16 A5
Seddon Rd *MRDN* SM4 .... 162 C4
Seddon St *FSBYW* WC1X 5 L8
Sedgebrook Rd
  BKHTH/KID SE3 .... 134 C1
Sedgecombe Av
  KTN/HRWW/WS HA3 .... 49 J4
Sedgeford Rd *SHB* W12 .... 87 H7
Sedgehill Rd *CAT* SE6 .... 151 J4
Sedgemere Av *EFNCH* N2 ...... 53 G2
Sedgemere Rd *ABYW* SE2 ...... 116 D2
Sedgemoor Dr *DAGE* RM10 ..... 80 C3
Sedge Rd *TOTM* N17 .... 42 E6
Sedgeway *CAT* SE6 .... 133 J7
Sedgmoor Pl *CMBW* SE5 .... 111 F6
Sedgwick Rd *LEY* E10 .... 76 A1
Sedgwick St *HOM* E9 .... 75 F4
Sedleigh Rd
  WAND/EARL SW18 .... 127 J5
Sedlescombe Rd
  FUL/PGN SW6 .... 107 J5
Sedley *PL* OXSTW* W1C 10 C5
Sednem Ct *PECK* SE15 .... 131 H1
Sedum Cl *CDALE/KGS* NW9 ..... 50 B3
Seeley Dr *DUL* SE21 .... 150 A3
Seelig Av *CDALE/KGS* NW9 .... 51 J6
Seely Rd *TOOT* SW17 .... 148 A5
Seething La *TWRH* EC3N 13 K6
Seething Wells La *SURB* KT6 . 158 C5
Sefton Av
  KTN/HRWW/WS HA3 .... 34 D7
  MLHL NW7 .... 37 F4
Sefton Ct *ENC/FH* EN2 * 29 H1
Sefton Rd *CROY/NA* CR0 ...... 165 H7
Sefton St *PUT/ROE* SW15 ..... 127 F1
Sekforde St *CLKNW* EC1R 12 C1
Sekhon Ter *FELT* TW13 .... 142 A2
Selan Gdns *YEAD* UB4 .... 83 H4
Selborne Av *BXLY* DA5 .... 137 F7
  MNPK E12 .... 78 A5
  WALTH E17 .... 57 H4
Selborne Gdns *GFD/PVL* UB6 .. 85 G1
  HDN NW4 .... 51 J3
Selborne Rd *CMBW* SE5 .... 130 E1
  CROY/NA CR0 .... 178 A2
  IL IG1 .... 78 A1
  NWMAL KT3 .... 160 B1
  SCUP DA14 .... 155 H3
  STHGT/OAK N14 .... 40 E2
  WALTH E17 .... 57 H4
  WDGN N22 .... 41 F7
Selbourne Av *SURB* KT6 ...... 172 B1
Selby Cha *RSLP* HA4 .... 65 F1
Selby Cl *CHSGTN* KT9 .... 172 A6
  CHST BR7 .... 154 A5
Selby Gdns *STHL* UB1 .... 84 A3
Selby Gn *CAR* SM5 .... 162 D6
Selby Rd *ASHF* TW15 .... 140 A5
  CAR SM5 .... 162 D6
  EA W5 .... 85 H3
  PGE/AN SE20 .... 165 H1
  PLSTW E13 .... 95 F4
  TOTM N17 .... 42 B2
  WAN E11 .... 76 C2
Selby St *WCHPL* E1 .... 92 C3
Selden Rd *PECK* SE15 .... 131 K1
Selhurst Cl *WIM/MER* SW19 ... 127 G7
Selhurst New Rd *SNWD* SE25 .. 165 F5
Selhurst Pl *SNWD* SE25 ...... 165 F5
Selhurst Rd *ED* N9 .... 41 K2
  SNWD SE25 .... 165 F4
Selinas La *BCTR* RM8 .... 62 A6
Selkirk Dr *ERITH* DA8 .... 118 C7
Selkirk Rd *TOOT* SW17 .... 147 J3
  WHTN TW2 .... 142 C1
Sellers Hall Cl *FNCH* N3 .... 38 E6
Sellincourt Rd *TOOT* SW17 ... 147 J4
Sellindge Cl *BECK* BR3 ...... 151 H6
Sellons Av *WLSDN* NW10 ...... 69 H6
Sellwood Dr *BAR* EN5 .... 26 B4
Selsdon Av *SAND/SEL* CR2 .... 177 K5
Selsdon Cl *SURB* KT6 .... 159 F4
Selsdon Park Rd
  CROY/NA CR0 .... 179 G7
Selsdon Rd *CRICK* NW2 .... 69 H1
  PLSTW E13 .... 95 F7
  SAND/SEL CR2 .... 177 K5
  WAN E11 .... 58 C6
  WNWD SE27 .... 149 H2
Selsdon Wy *POP/IOD* E14 ..... 112 E2
Selsea Pl *STNW/STAM* N16 .... 74 A4
Selsey Crs *WELL* DA16 .... 116 E7
Selsey St *BOW* E3 .... 93 J4
Selvage La *MLHL* NW7 .... 37 F4
Selway Cl *PIN* HA5 .... 47 F3
Selwood Pl *SKENS* SW7 .... 15 G7
Selwood Rd *CHEAM* SM3 .... 161 J7
  CHSGTN KT9 .... 171 K3
  CROY/NA CR0 .... 178 D1
Selwood Ter *SKENS* SW7 ...... 15 G7
Selworthy Cl *WAN* E11 .... 58 E4
Selworthy Rd *CAT* SE6 .... 151 H2
Selwyn Av *CHING* E4 .... 44 A5
  GDMY/SEVK IG3 .... 61 G5
  RCH/KEW TW9 .... 125 G2
Selwyn Cl *HSLWW* TW4 .... 122 D3

Selwyn Ct *EDGW* HA8 .... 36 D6
Selwyn Crs *WELL* DA16 .... 136 C2
Selwyn Rd *BOW* E3 .... 93 H1
  NWMAL KT3 .... 160 A4
  PLSTW E13 .... 77 F7
  WLSDN NW10 .... 69 G6
Semley Pl *BGVA* SW1W 16 B6
  STRHM/NOR SW16 .... 164 A1
Semley Rd *STRHM/NOR* SW16 ... 163 K1
Senate St *PECK* SE15 .... 131 K1
Seneca Rd *THHTH* CR7 .... 164 D3
Senga Rd *WLGTN* SM6 .... 163 F7
Senhouse Rd *CHEAM* SM3 ...... 174 B2
Senior St *BAY/PAD* W2 .... 8 C2
Senlac Rd *LEE/GVPK* SE12 .... 134 A7
Sennen Rd *EN* EN1 .... 30 B6
Senrab St *WCHPL* E1 .... 93 F5
Sentamu Cl *HNHL* SE24 .... 130 C7
Sentinel Cl *NTHLT* UB5 ...... 83 J3
September Wy *STAN* HA7 ...... 35 H5
Sequoia Cl *BUSH* WD23 .... 22 D7
Sequoia Pk *PIN* HA5 .... 34 B5
Serbin Cl *LEY* E10 .... 58 A6
Serenaders Rd *BRXN/ST* SW9 .. 130 B1
Serjeant's Inn *EMB* EC4Y 12 B3
Serle St *LINN* WC2A 11 M4
Sermon La *BLKFR* EC4V 12 C5
Serpentine Rd *SKENS* SW7 .... 15 K1
Service Route No 1
  SRTFD E15 .... 76 B6
Service Route No 2
  SRTFD E15 .... 76 B6
Service Route No 3
  SRTFD E15 .... 76 B5
Serviden Dr *BMLY* BR1 .... 153 H7
Setchell Est *STHWK* SE1 ..... 19 L5
Setchell Rd *STHWK* SE1 ...... 19 L5
Setchell Wy *STHWK* SE1 ...... 19 L5
Seth St *BERM/RHTH* SE16 ..... 111 K1
Seton Gdns *DAGW* RM9 .... 79 J6
Settles St *WCHPL* E1 .... 92 C5
Settrington Rd *FUL/PGN* SW6 . 128 A1
Seven Acres *CAR* SM5 .... 175 J1
  NTHWD HA6 .... 32 B5
Seven Dials *LSO/SEVD* WC2H .. 11 J5
Sevenex Pde *WBLY* HA9 * 68 A4
Seven Kings Rd
  GDMY/SEVK IG3 .... 60 E7
Seven Kings Wy
  KUTN/CMB KT2 .... 143 K7
Sevenoaks Cl *BXLYHN* DA7 .... 137 K3
Sevenoaks Rd *BROCKY* SE4 .... 132 C5
Seven Seas Rd *HTHAIR* TW6 ... 121 F5
Seven Sisters Rd *FSBYPK* N4 . 73 H1
  HOLWY N7 .... 73 F2
  SEVS/STOTM N15 .... 55 K5
Seven Stars Yd *WCHPL* E1 * .. 13 M2
Seventh Av *HYS/HAR* UB3 ..... 82 E7
  MNPK E12 .... 77 K3
Severnake Cl *POP/IOD* E14 ... 112 D3
Severn Av *GPK* RM2 .... 63 K2
  NKENS W10 .... 88 C2
Severn Dr *ESH/CLAY* KT10 .... 171 G1
Severn Wy *WLSDN* NW10 .... 69 H4
Severus Rd *BTSEA* SW11 ...... 128 D3
Seville Ms *IS* N1 .... 7 J2
Seville St *KTBR* SW1X 15 M2
Sevington Rd *HDN* NW4 .... 51 K5
Sevington St *MV/WKIL* W9 .... 8 C1
Seward Rd *BECK* BR3 .... 166 A1
  HNWL W7 .... 104 B1
Sewardstone Rd *BETH* E2 ..... 92 E1
  CHING E4 .... 31 K3
Seward St *FSBYE* EC1V 6 D9
Sewdley St *CLPT* E5 .... 75 F2
Sewell St *PLSTW* E13 .... 94 E2
Sextant Av *POP/IOD* E14 ..... 113 F3
Sexton Cl *RAIN* RM13 .... 81 H7
Seymer Rd *ROM* RM1 .... 63 F2
Seymour Av *EW* KT17 .... 173 K7
  MRDN SM4 .... 161 G6
  TOTM N17 .... 56 C1
Seymour Cl *E/WMO/HCT* KT8 ... 157 H4
  PIN HA5 .... 33 K7
Seymour Dr *HAYES* BR2 .... 168 E7
Seymour Gdns *BROCKY* SE4 .... 132 B2
  BRYLDS KT5 .... 159 G4
  FELT TW13 .... 141 F3
  IL IG1 .... 59 K7
  RSLP HA4 .... 47 H7
  TWK TW1 .... 124 C5
Seymour Gv *OXHEY* WD19 ...... 21 G6
Seymour Ms *MBLAR* W1H 10 A4
Seymour Pl *MBLAR* W1H * 9 L3
  SNWD SE25 .... 165 J3
Seymour Rd *CAR* SM5 .... 176 A4
  CEND/HSY/T N8 .... 55 H4
  CHING E4 .... 31 K7
  CHSWK W4 .... 105 K3
  E/WMO/HCT KT8 .... 157 H4
  ED N9 .... 42 D1
  EHAM E6 .... 77 H7
  FNCH N3 .... 39 F6
  HPTN TW12 .... 142 C5
  KUT/HW KT1 .... 143 K7
  LEY E10 .... 57 F7
  MTCM CR4 .... 162 F6
  WAND/EARL SW18 .... 127 J5
  WIM/MER SW19 .... 146 B2
Seymour St *BAY/PAD* W2 ...... 9 J5
  MBLAR W1H 9 M5
  WOOL/PLUM SE18 .... 115 H4
Seymour Ter *PGE/AN* SE20 .... 150 D7
Seymour Vls *PGE/AN* SE20 .... 150 D7
Seymour Wk *WBPTN* SW10 ...... 14 E9
Seymour Wy *SUN* TW16 .... 140 C5
Seyssel St *POP/IOD* E14 ..... 113 F3
Shaa Rd *ACT* W3 .... 87 F6
Shacklegate La *TEDD* TW11 ... 142 E3
Shackleton Cl *FSTH* SE23 .... 150 D1
Shackleton Rd *STHL* UB1 ..... 83 K6
Shacklewell La *HACK* E8 ..... 74 B3
Shacklewell Rd
  STNW/STAM N16 .... 74 B3
Shacklewell Rw *HACK* E8 ..... 74 B3
Shacklewell St *BETH* E2 ..... 7 M8
Shadbolt Av *CHING* E4 .... 43 G4
Shadbolt Cl *WPK* KT4 .... 173 H1
Shad Thames *STHWK* SE1 ...... 13 L8
Shadwell Dr *NTHLT* UB5 ...... 83 K2
Shadwell Gdns *WCHPL* E1 * ... 92 E6
Shadwell Pierhead *WAP* E1W .. 92 E6
Shady Bush Cl *BUSH* WD23 .... 22 C6
Shady La *WATF* WD17 .... 21 F1
Shaef Wy *TEDD* TW11 .... 143 G6
Shafter Rd *DAGE* RM10 .... 98 D5
Shaftesbury Av *BAR* EN5 ..... 27 G3
  EBED/NFELT TW14 .... 121 K5
  KTN/HRWW/WS HA3 .... 49 K5
  LSO/SEVD WC2H 11 J4
  NWDGN UB2 .... 103 F3
  PEND EN3 .... 31 F1

RYLN/HDSTN HA2 .... 48 B7
  SOHO/SHAV W1D 11 G6
Shaftesbury Cir
  RYLN/HDSTN HA2 * 48 C7
Shaftesbury Ct
  RKW/CH/CXG WD3 * 20 A4
Shaftesbury Gdns
  WLSDN NW10 .... 87 G3
Shaftesbury Ms *CLAP* SW4 .... 129 H4
  KENS W8 * 14 A1
Shaftesbury Pde
  RYLN/HDSTN HA2 * 48 C7
Shaftesbury Pl *BARB* EC2Y * . 12 E3
Shaftesbury Rd *ARCH* N19 .... 54 E7
  BECK BR3 .... 166 C1
  CAR SM5 .... 162 C6
  FSTGT E7 .... 77 G6
  LEY E10 .... 57 J7
  RCH/KEW TW9 .... 125 F2
  ROM RM1 .... 63 H5
  UED N18 .... 42 A4
  WALTH E17 .... 57 K4
  WAT WD17 .... 21 F2
The Shaftesburys *BARK* IG11 . 96 C1
Shaftesbury St *IS* N1 .... 6 F6
Shaftesbury Ter
  HMSMTH W6 * 106 C3
Shaftesbury Wy *WHTN* TW2 .... 142 D2
Shaftesbury Waye *YEAD* UB4 .. 83 H4
Shafteswood Ct *TOOT* SW17 ... 147 K2
Shafto Ms *KTBR* SW1X 15 L4
Shafton Ms *HOM* E9 * 75 F7
Shafton Rd *HOM* E9 .... 75 F7
Shakespeare Av
  EBED/NFELT TW14 .... 121 K5
  FBAR/BDGN N11 .... 40 C4
  WLSDN NW10 .... 68 E7
  YEAD UB4 .... 82 E5
Shakespeare Crs *MNPK* E12 ... 77 K6
  WLSDN NW10 .... 69 F7
Shakespeare Dr *BORE* WD6 .... 24 C3
  KTN/HRWW/WS HA3 .... 50 B3
Shakespeare Gdns *EFNCH* N2 .. 53 K3
Shakespeare Rd *ACT* W3 ...... 86 E7
  BXLYHN DA7 .... 117 F7
  DART DA1 .... 139 K3
  FNCH N3 * 38 E7
  HNHL SE24 .... 130 C4
  HNWL W7 .... 85 F6
  MLHL NW7 .... 37 J3
  ROM RM1 .... 63 H5
  WALTH E17 .... 57 F1
Shakespeare Ter
  RCH/KEW TW9 * 125 H2
Shakespeare Wy *FELT* TW13 ... 141 G3
Shakspeare Ms
  STNW/STAM N16 .... 74 A3
Shakspeare Wk
  STNW/STAM N16 .... 74 A3
Shalbourne Sq *HOM* E9 .... 75 H5
Shalcomb St *WBPTN* SW10 ..... 108 B5
Shaldon Dr *MRDN* SM4 .... 161 H4
  RSLP HA4 .... 65 G2
Shaldon Rd *EDGW* HA8 .... 50 B1
Shalfleet Dr *NKENS* W10 ..... 88 B6
Shalford Ct *IS* N1 * 6 C5
Shalimar Gdns *ACT* W3 .... 86 E6
Shalimar Rd *ACT* W3 .... 86 E6
Shallons Rd *ELTH/MOT* SE9 ... 154 B3
Shalstone Rd
  MORT/ESHN SW14 .... 125 J2
Shalston Vls *SURB* KT6 ...... 159 G5
Shamrock Rd *CROY/NA* CR0 .... 164 A5
Shamrock St *CLAP* SW4 .... 129 J2
Shamrock Wy
  STHGT/OAK N14 .... 28 B7
Shandon Rd *CLAP* SW4 .... 129 H5
Shand St *STHWK* SE1 .... 19 K1
Shandy St *WCHPL* E1 .... 93 F4
Shanklin Gdns *OXHEY* WD19 ... 33 G3
Shanklin Rd *CEND/HSY/T* N8 .. 54 D4
  SEVS/STOTM N15 .... 56 C3
Shannon Cl *NWDGN* UB2 .... 102 C4
Shannon Gv *BRXN/ST* SW9 ..... 130 A3
Shannon Pl *STJWD* NW8 .... 3 K5
Shannon Wy *BECK* BR3 .... 151 K5
Shap Crs *CAR* SM5 .... 162 E7
Shapland Wy *PLMGR* N13 ...... 41 F4
Shapwick Cl *FBAR/BDGN* N11 .. 39 K4
Shardcroft Av *HNHL* SE24 .... 130 C4
Shardeloes Rd *BROCKY* SE4 ... 132 C4
  NWCR SE14 .... 132 C1
Shard's Sq *PECK* SE15 .... 111 H5
Sharland Cl *THHTH* CR7 ...... 164 B5
Sharman Ct *SCUP* DA14 .... 155 G3
Sharnbrooke Cl *WELL* DA16 ... 136 D2
Sharon Cl *SURB* KT6 .... 158 D7
Sharon Gdns *HOM* E9 .... 74 E7
Sharon Rd *CHSWK* W4 .... 106 A4
  PEND EN3 .... 31 G1
Sharples Hall St *CAMTN* NW1 . 3 M2
Sharps La *RSLP* HA4 .... 46 B6
Sharp Wy *DART* DA1 .... 139 J2
Sharratt St *PECK* SE15 ...... 111 K5
Sharsted St *WALW* SE17 ...... 18 C8
Sharvel La *YEAD* UB4 .... 82 A4
Shavers Pl *MYFR/PICC* W1J ... 11 H7
Shaw Av *BARK* IG11 .... 98 A1
Shawbrooke Rd
  ELTH/MOT SE9 .... 134 C3
Shawbury Cl *CDALE/KGS* NW9 .. 37 G1
Shawbury Rd *EDUL* SE22 ...... 131 G4
Shaw Cl *BUSH* WD23 .... 34 E1
  EMPK RM11 .... 63 K7
  THMD SE28 .... 97 H7
Shaw Crs *POP/IOD* E14 .... 93 G5
Shaw Dr *WOT/HER* KT12 .... 156 B6
Shawfield Pk *BMLY* BR1 ...... 168 C1
Shawfield St *CHEL* SW3 ...... 15 K8
Shawford Ct *PUT/ROE* SW15 * . 126 D6
Shawford Rd *HOR/WEW* KT19 ... 173 F5
Shaw Gdns *BARK* IG11 .... 98 A1
Shaw Rd *BMLY* BR1 .... 152 D2
  EDUL SE22 .... 131 F3
Shaws Cots *FSTH* SE23 * 151 G2
Shaw's Cots *FSTH* SE23 ...... 151 G2
Shaw Sq *WALTH* E17 .... 43 G7
The Shaw *CHST* BR7 * 154 C6
Shaw Wy *WLGTN* SM6 .... 176 E6
Shaxton Crs *CROY/NA* CR0 .... 180 A7
Sheaf Cots *THDIT* KT7 * 157 K7
Shearing Dr *CAR* SM5 .... 162 B6
Shearling Wy *HOLWY* N7 ...... 72 E5
Shearman Rd *BKHTH/KID* SE3 .. 133 J4
Shearwater Cl *BARK* IG11 .... 97 G2
Shearwater Rd *SUT* SM1 ...... 174 D4
Shearwood Crs *DART* DA1 ..... 138 C2
Sheaths Cots *THDIT* KT7 * ... 158 C6
Sheaveshill Av
  CDALE/KGS NW9 .... 51 G2
Sheaveshill Pde
  CDALE/KGS NW9 * 51 G2

Sheen Common Dr
  RCHPK/HAM TW10 .... 125 H3
Sheen Court Rd
  RCHPK/HAM TW10 .... 125 H3
Sheendale Rd *RCH/KEW* TW9 ... 125 G2
Sheenewood *SYD* SE26 .... 150 D4
Sheen Ga *MORT/ESHN* SW14 .... 125 K5
Sheen Gate Gdns
  MORT/ESHN SW14 .... 125 K3
Sheen Gv *IS* N1 .... 6 A3
Sheen La *MORT/ESHN* SW14 .... 125 K3
Sheen Pk *RCH/KEW* TW9 .... 125 F3
Sheen Rd *RCH/KEW* TW9 .... 125 F3
Sheen Wy *WLGTN* SM6 .... 177 F4
Sheen Wd *MORT/ESHN* SW14 .... 125 K5
Sheepcote Cl *HEST* TW5 ...... 101 K6
Sheepcote La *BTSEA* SW11 .... 128 E1
Sheepcote Rd *HRW* HA1 .... 49 F5
Sheepcotes Rd *CHDH* RM6 ..... 61 K3
Sheephouse Wy *NWMAL* KT3 .... 160 A7
Sheep La *HACK* E8 .... 74 D7
Sheep Walk Ms
  WIM/MER SW19 .... 146 B5
Sheerwater Rd *CAN/RD* E16 ... 95 H4
Sheffield Rd *HTHAIR* TW6 .... 121 F5
Sheffield St *LINN* WC2A * ... 11 L5
Sheffield Ter *KENS* W8 ...... 14 A1
Shefton Ri *NTHWD* HA6 .... 32 E6
Shelbourne Cl *PIN* HA5 ...... 47 K2
Shelbourne Rd *TOTM* N17 ..... 42 D7
Shelburne Dr *HSLWW* TW4 ..... 123 F5
Shelburne Rd *HOLWY* N7 ...... 73 F3
Shelbury Cl *SCUP* DA14 ...... 155 G2
Shelbury Rd *EDUL* SE22 ...... 131 J4
Sheldon Av *CLAY* IG5 .... 60 B1
  HGT N6 .... 53 K6
Sheldon Cl *LEE/GVPK* SE12 ... 134 A4
  PGE/AN SE20 .... 150 D7
Sheldon Pl *BETH* E2 .... 92 C1
Sheldon Rd *BXLYHN* DA7 ...... 117 G1
  CRICK NW2 .... 70 B3
  DAGW RM9 .... 80 A6
  UED N18 .... 42 A3
Sheldon Sq *BAY/PAD* W2 ...... 8 F3
Sheldon St *CROY/NA* CR0 ..... 177 J2
Sheldrake Cl *CAN/RD* E16 .... 95 K7
Sheldrake Pl *KENS* W8 .... 107 J1
Sheldrick Cl *MTCM* CR4 ...... 162 C1
Shelduck Cl *SRTFD* E15 ...... 76 D4
Sheldwich Ter *HAYES* BR2 * .. 168 D5
Shelford Ri *NRWD* SE19 ...... 150 A6
Shelford Rd *BAR* EN5 .... 26 A5
Shelgate Rd *BTSEA* SW11 ..... 128 E4
Shell Cl *HAYES* BR2 .... 168 D5
Shellduck Cl *CDALE/KGS* NW9 . 51 G1
Shelley Av *GFD/PVL* UB6 ..... 84 D2
  HCH RM12 .... 81 H1
  MNPK E12 .... 77 J5
Shelley Cl *EDGW* HA8 .... 36 C3
  GFD/PVL UB6 .... 84 D2
  NTHWD HA6 .... 32 D4
  PECK SE15 .... 131 J1
  YEAD UB4 .... 82 E4
Shelley Crs *HEST* TW5 .... 102 C7
  STHL UB1 .... 83 K5
Shelley Dr *WELL* DA16 .... 115 K7
Shelley Gdns *ALP/SUD* HA0 ... 67 J1
Shelley Rd *WLSDN* NW10 ...... 69 F7
Shellgrove Rd
  STNW/STAM N16 * 74 A4
Shellness Rd *CLPT* E5 .... 74 D4
Shell Rd *LEW* SE13 .... 132 E2
Shellwood Rd *BTSEA* SW11 .... 128 E1
Shelly Cl *BORE* WD6 .... 24 C3
Shelmerdine Cl *BOW* E3 ...... 93 J4
Shelson Av *FELT* TW13 .... 140 D2
Shelson Pde *FELT* TW13 * 140 D2
Shelton Rd *WIM/MER* SW19 .... 146 E7
Shelton St *LSO/SEVD* WC2H * . 11 J5
Shenfield Rd *WFD* IG8 .... 45 F6
Shenfield St *IS* N1 .... 7 K6
Shenley Av *RSLP* HA4 .... 64 C1
Shenley Rd *BORE* WD6 .... 24 C2
  CMBW SE5 .... 111 F7
  DART DA1 .... 139 K5
  HEST TW5 .... 102 D7
Shenstone Cl *DART* DA1 ...... 138 A4
Shepherd Cl *FELT* TW13 ...... 141 J3
Shepherdess Pl *FSBYE* EC1V .. 6 F7
Shepherdess Wk *IS* N1 .... 6 F5
Shepherd **Market**
  MYFR/PICC W1J 10 C9
Shepherd's Bush Gn *SHB* W12 . 107 F1
Shepherd's Bush Market
  SHB W12 .... 107 F1
Shepherd's Bush Pl
  SHB W12 * 107 G1
Shepherd's Bush Rd
  HMSMTH W6 .... 107 F2
Shepherds Cl *CHDH* RM6 ...... 61 K4
  STAN HA7 .... 35 H4
Shepherd's Cl *HGT* N6 .... 54 B5
Shepherds Gn *CHST* BR7 ...... 154 C6
Shepherd's La *HOM* E9 .... 75 F5
Shepherd's La *DART* DA1 ..... 138 D7
  THMD SE28 .... 96 E7
Shepherd's Leas
  ELTH/MOT SE9 * 135 J3
Shepherds Pl
  MYFR/PKLN W1K 10 A6
Shepherds Rd *WATW* WD18 ..... 20 D3
Shepherd's Rd *MYFR/PICC* W1J 10 C9
Shepherds Wk *BUSH* WD23 ..... 34 D1
  CRICK NW2 .... 69 J1
Shepherd's Wk *HAMP* NW3 ..... 71 H4
Shepherd's Wy *SAND/SEL* CR2 . 179 F6
Shepiston La *HYS/HAR* UB3 ... 100 E3
Shepley Cl *CAR* SM5 .... 176 A2
Sheppard Cl *KUT/HW* KT1 ..... 159 F3
Sheppard Dr
  BERM/RHTH SE16 .... 111 J4
Sheppard St *CAN/RD* E16 ..... 94 D3
Shepperton Rd *IS* N1 .... 6 F3
  STMC/STPC BR5 .... 169 H5
Sheppey Gdns *DAGW* RM9 ...... 79 J6
Sheppey Rd *DAGW* RM9 .... 79 H6
Sheppey Wk *IS* N1 .... 6 F1
Shepton Houses *BETH* E2 * ... 92 E2
Sherard Rd *ELTH/MOT* SE9 .... 134 D4
Sheraton Cl *BORE* WD6 .... 24 A4
Sheraton Ms *WATW* WD18 ...... 20 D4
Sheraton St *SOHO/CST* W1F * . 11 G5
  PEND EN3 .... 30 E1
Sherborne Cl *YEAD* UB4 ...... 83 G5
Sherborne Crs *CAR* SM5 ...... 162 D6
Sherborne Gdns
  CDALE/KGS NW9 .... 50 C2
  WEA W13 .... 85 H5

Sherborne La *MANHO* EC4N 13 G6
Sherborne Pl *NTHWD* HA6 ..... 32 B5
Sherborne Rd *CHEAM* SM3 ..... 174 E1
  CHSGTN KT9 .... 172 A4
  EBED/NFELT TW14 .... 121 G6
Sherborne St *IS* N1 .... 7 G1
Sherborne Vls *WEA* W13 * 85 H4
Sherboro Rd
  SEVS/STOTM N15 .... 56 B5
Sherbrooke Cl *BXLYHN* DA7 ... 137 H3
Sherbrooke Rd *FUL/PGN* SW6 .. 107 H6
Sherbrooke Ter
  FUL/PGN SW6 * 107 H6
Sherbrooke Wy *WPK* KT4 ...... 160 E6
Sherbrook Gdns *WCHMH* N21 ... 29 H6
Shere Cl *CHSGTN* KT9 .... 171 K4
Sheredan Rd *CHING* E4 .... 44 B4
Shere Rd *GNTH/NBYPK* IG2 .... 60 A4
Sherfield Cl *NWMAL* KT3 ..... 159 J3
Sherfield Gdns
  PUT/ROE SW15 .... 126 C5
Sheridan Ct *DART* DA1 .... 139 K3
  HSLWW TW4 .... 122 D4
Sheridan Crs *CHST* BR7 ...... 169 G1
Sheridan Gdns
  KTN/HRWW/WS HA3 .... 49 K5
Sheridan Ms *WAN* E11 .... 59 F5
Sheridan Pl *BMLY* BR1 .... 168 C3
  HPTN TW12 .... 142 B7
Sheridan Rd *BELV* DA17 ...... 117 H3
  BXLYHN DA7 .... 137 F2
  FSTGT E7 .... 76 D2
  MNPK E12 .... 77 J4
  OXHEY WD19 .... 21 H6
  RCHPK/HAM TW10 .... 143 J2
  WIM/MER SW19 .... 146 D7
Sheridan Ter *NTHLT* UB5 * ... 66 B4
Sheridan Wk *CAR* SM5 .... 175 K4
  GLDGN NW11 .... 52 E5
Sheridan Wy *BECK* BR3 .... 151 H7
Sheringham Av *MNPK* E12 ..... 77 K3
  ROMW/RG RM7 .... 62 E5
  STHGT/OAK N14 .... 28 D4
  WHTN TW2 .... 122 E7
Sheringham Dr *BARK* IG11 .... 79 F4
Sheringham Rd *HOLWY* N7 ..... 73 G5
  PGE/AN SE20 .... 165 J1
Sherington Av *PIN* HA5 ...... 34 A6
Sherington Rd
  BKHTH/KID SE3 .... 114 A5
Sherland Rd *TWK* TW1 .... 124 A7
Sherlock Ms *MHST* W1U 10 A2
Shermanbury Cl *ERITH* DA8 ... 118 C6
Sherman Gdns *CHDH* RM6 ...... 61 J5
Sherman Rd *BMLY* BR1 .... 152 E7
Shernhall St *WALTH* E17 ..... 58 A4
Sherrard Rd *FSTGT* E7 .... 77 H5
Sherrards Wy *BAR* EN5 .... 26 E4
Sherrick Green Rd
  WLSDN NW10 .... 69 K4
Sherriff Cl *ESH/CLAY* KT10 .. 170 B1
Sherriff Rd *KIL/WHAMP* NW6 .. 70 E5
Sherringham Av *FELT* TW13 ... 140 E2
  TOTM N17 .... 56 C2
Sherrock Gdns *HDN* NW4 ...... 51 J3
Sherry Ms *BARK* IG11 .... 78 D6
Sherwin Rd *NWCR* SE14 .... 112 A7
Sherwood *SURB* KT6 .... 171 K1
Sherwood Av *GFD/PVL* UB6 .... 66 E5
  RSLP HA4 .... 46 C5
  STRHM/NOR SW16 .... 148 D6
  SWFD E18 .... 59 F2
  YEAD UB4 .... 83 F3
Sherwood Cl *BXLY* DA5 .... 136 D5
  WALTH E17 .... 57 H1
  WEA W13 .... 85 H1
Sherwood Ct *MBLAR* W1H * 9 L3
Sherwood Gdns *BARK* IG11 .... 78 D6
  BERM/RHTH SE16 .... 111 H4
  POP/IOD E14 .... 112 D3
Sherwood House
  RYLN/HDSTN HA2 * 66 C2
Sherwood Park Av
  BFN/LL DA15 .... 136 B6
Sherwood Park Rd
  MTCM CR4 .... 163 H3
  SUT SM1 .... 174 E4
Sherwood Rd *BARK/HLT* IG6 ... 60 D3
  CROY/NA CR0 .... 165 J6
  HDN NW4 .... 52 A2
  HPTN TW12 .... 142 C4
  RYLN/HDSTN HA2 .... 66 C1
  WELL DA16 .... 135 K1
  WIM/MER SW19 .... 146 D6
Sherwoods Rd *OXHEY* WD19 .... 21 K6
Sherwood St *SOHO/CST* W1F ... 10 F6
  TRDG/WHET N20 .... 39 H2
Sherwood Ter
  TRDG/WHET N20 .... 39 H2
Sherwood Wy *WWKM* BR4 .... 180 A1
Shetland Cl *BORE* WD6 .... 25 F5
Shetland Rd *BOW* E3 .... 93 H1
Shield Dr *BTFD* TW8 .... 104 B5
Shieldhall St *ABYW* SE2 ..... 116 D3
Shield Rd *ASHF* TW15 .... 140 A3
Shifford Pth *FSTH* SE23 ..... 151 F2
Shillibeer Pl *MBLAR* W1H * .. 9 K3
Shillingford Cl *MLHL* NW7 ... 38 B6
Shillingford St *IS* N1 * 6 D3
Shilling Pl *HNWL* W7 * 85 G7
Shinfield St *SHB* W12 .... 88 A5
Shinglewell Rd *ERITH* DA8 ... 117 H6
Shinners Cl *SNWD* SE25 ...... 165 H4
Ship & Mermaid Rw
  STHWK SE1 .... 19 H1
Ship La *MORT/ESHN* SW14 ..... 125 K2
Shipman Rd *CAN/RD* E16 ...... 95 F5
  FSTH SE23 .... 151 F1
Ship St *DEPT* SE8 .... 112 D7
Ship Tavern Pas *BANK* EC3V .. 13 J6
Shipton Cl *BCTR* RM8 .... 79 K2
Shipton St *BETH* E2 .... 7 M7
Shipwright Rd
  BERM/RHTH SE16 .... 112 B1
Shipwright Yd *STHWK* SE1 * .. 13 J9
Shirburn Cl *FSTH* SE23 ...... 131 K6
Shirbutt St *POP/IOD* E14 .... 93 K6
Shirebrook Rd *BKHTH/KID* SE3 134 C1
Shire Ct *EW* KT17 .... 173 H6
Shirehall Cl *HDN* NW4 .... 52 B5
Shirehall Gdns *HDN* NW4 ..... 52 B5
Shirehall La *HDN* NW4 .... 52 B5
Shirehall Pk *HDN* NW4 .... 52 B5
Shire Horse Wy *ISLW* TW7 ... 124 A2
Shire La *ORP* BR6 .... 181 K6
Shiremeade *BORE* WD6 .... 24 B4
Shire Ms *WHTN* TW2 .... 123 G5
The Shires *RCHPK/HAM* TW10 .. 144 A3
Shirland Ms *MV/WKIL* W9 ..... 88 D2
Shirland Rd *MV/WKIL* W9 ..... 2 D1
Shirley Av *BXLY* DA5 .... 136 E6
  CROY/NA CR0 .... 165 K7

SUT SM1 175 J3
Shirley Church Rd
CROY/NA CR0 179 F2
Shirley Cl DART DA1 139 F3
HSLW TW3 123 H4
WALTH E17 * 57 K4
Shirley Crs BECK BR3 166 B3
Shirley Dr HSLW TW3 123 H4
Shirley Gdns BARK IG11 78 E5
HNWL W7 85 F7
Shirley Gv BTSEA SW11 129 F2
ED N9 30 E6
Shirley Hills Rd CROY/NA CR0 179 F4
Shirley Oaks Rd CROY/NA CR0 166 A7
Shirley Park Rd CROY/NA CR0 165 J7
Shirley Rd BFN/LL DA15 154 E2
CHSWK W4 106 A1
CROY/NA CR0 165 J7
ENC/FH EN2 29 J2
SRTFD E15 76 C6
WLGTN SM6 176 C7
Shirley Rw SNWD SE25 * 165 H1
Shirley St CAN/RD E16 94 D5
Shirley Wy CROY/NA CR0 179 H2
Shirlock Rd HAMP NW3 71 K3
Shirwell Cl MLHL NW7 38 B6
Shobden Rd TOTM N17 41 K7
Shobroke Cl CRICK NW2 70 A2
Shoebury Rd EHAM E6 77 K6
Shoe La FLST/FETLN EC4A 12 B4
Shooters Av
KTN/HRWW/WS HA3 49 J3
Shooters Hill Rd GNWCH SE10 113 H7
Shoot-Up Hl CRICK NW2 70 C5
Shops SYD SE26 * 151 F4
Shore Cl EBED/NFELT TW14 121 K6
HPTN TW12 141 J4
Shoreditch High St
FSBYE EC1V 7 K8
WCHPL E1 13 K2
Shore Gv FELT TW13 142 A1
Shoreham Cl CROY/NA CR0 165 K5
WAND/EARL SW18 128 A4
Shoreham Rd STMC/STPC BR5 155 H7
Shoreham Rd (East)
HTHAIR TW6 120 B4
Shoreham Rd (West)
HTHAIR TW6 120 B4
Shoreham Wy HAYES BR2 167 K5
Shore Pl HOM E9 74 E6
Shore Rd HOM E9 74 E6
Shore Wy BRXN/ST SW9 130 B1
Shorncliffe Rd STHWK SE1 19 L8
Shorndean St CAT SE6 133 F7
Shorne Cl BFN/LL DA15 136 C5
Shornefield Cl BMLY BR1 169 F2
Shorrolds Rd FUL/PGN SW6 107 K6
Shortcroft Rd EW KT17 173 H6
Shortcrofts Rd DAGW RM9 80 B5
Shorter St TWRH EC3N 13 L6
Shortgate
NFNCH/WDSPK N12 38 D3
Shortlands HMSMTH W6 107 G3
HYS/HAR UB3 101 G5
Shortlands Cl BELV DA17 117 G2
UED N18 41 K2
Shortlands Gdns HAYES BR2 167 H1
Shortlands Gv HAYES BR2 167 G2
Shortlands Rd HAYES BR2 167 G2
KUTN/CMB KT2 144 B6
LEY E10 57 K6
Short La STWL/WRAY TW19 120 C6
Short Rd CHSWK W4 106 B5
WAN E11 76 C1
Shorts Cft CDALE/KGS NW9 50 D3
Shorts Gdns
LSQ/SEVD WC2H * 11 J5
Shorts Rd CAR SM5 175 J3
Short St HDN NW4 52 A3
STHWK SE1 18 B1
Shortway ELTH/MOT SE9 134 D2
Short Wy NFNCH/WDSPK N12 39 J5
WHTN TW2 123 H6
Shotfield WLGTN SM6 176 B5
Shott Cl SUT SM1 175 G4
Shottendane Rd
FUL/PGN SW6 * 107 K7
Shottery Cl ELTH/MOT SE9 153 J2
Shottfield Av
MORT/ESHN SW14 126 B3
Shoulder of Mutton Aly
POP/IOD E14 93 G6
Shouldham St MBLAR W1H 9 K3
Showers Wy HYS/HAR UB3 82 E7
Shrapnel Cl WOOL/PLUM SE18 114 E6
Shrapnel Rd ELTH/MOT SE9 134 E2
Shrewsbury Av
KTN/HRWW/WS HA3 50 A3
MORT/ESHN SW14 125 K3
Shrewsbury Cl SURB KT6 172 A1
Shrewsbury Crs
WLSDN NW10 * 69 F7
Shrewsbury La
WOOL/PLUM SE18 115 G7
Shrewsbury Ms BAY/PAD W2 8 A4
Shrewsbury Rd BAY/PAD W2 8 A3
BECK BR3 166 B2
CAR SM5 162 D6
FBAR/BDGN N11 40 D5
FSTGT E7 77 H5
HTHAIR TW6 121 F5
Shrewsbury St NKENS W10 88 A3
Shrewton Rd TOOT SW17 * 147 K6
Shroffold Rd BMLY BR1 152 C3
Shropshire Cl MTCM CR4 163 K3
Shropshire Rd WDGN N22 41 F6
Shroton St CAMTN NW1 9 J2
The Shrubberies SWFD E18 58 E1
Shrubbery Gdns WCHMH N21 29 H6
Shrubbery Rd ED N9 42 C2
STHL UB1 83 K7
STRHM/NOR SW16 148 E3
The Shrubbery SURB KT6 * 159 F7
Shrubland Cl
TRDG/WHET N20 * 39 H1
Shrubland Gv WPK KT4 174 A2
Shrubland Rd HACK E8 74 C7
LEY E10 57 J6
WALTH E17 57 J4
Shrublands Av CROY/NA CR0 179 J3
Shrublands Cl SYD SE26 150 E2
TRDG/WHET N20 27 H7
Shrubsall Cl ELTH/MOT SE9 134 D7
Shubbery Cl IS N1 6 F3
Shuna Wk IS N1 * 73 K5
Shurland Av EBAR EN4 27 H5
Shurland Gdns PECK SE15 * 111 G6
Shuters Sq WKENS W14 * 107 J4
Shuttle Cl BFN/LL DA15 136 A6
Shuttlemead BXLY DA5 137 G6
Shuttle Rd DART DA1 138 D2
Shuttle St WCHPL E1 92 C3
Shuttleworth Rd BTSEA SW11 128 C1
Sibella Rd CLAP SW4 129 J1
Sibley Cl BMLY BR1 168 D4
BXLYHS DA6 137 F4
Sibley Ct UX/CGN UB8 82 A4
Sibley Gv EHAM E6 77 J6
MNPK E12 77 K6
Sibthorpe Rd LEE/GVPK SE12 134 A6
Sibthorp Rd MTCM CR4 * 162 E1
Sibton Rd CAR SM5 162 D6
Sicilian Av NOXST/BSQ WC1A * 11 K3
Sidbury St FUL/PGN SW6 107 H7
Sidcup By-Pass Rd SCUP DA14 155 G5
Sidcup Hl SCUP DA14 155 H4
Sidcup Hill Gdns SCUP DA14 * 155 J4
Sidcup Pl SCUP DA14 155 G4
Sidcup Rd ELTH/MOT SE9 134 C7
Siddeley Dr HSLWW TW4 122 D2
Siddons La CAMTN NW1 9 M1
Siddons Rd CROY/NA CR0 177 G2
FSTH SE23 151 G1
TOTM N17 42 C7
Side Rd WALTH E17 57 H4
Sidewood Rd ELTH/MOT SE9 135 J7
Sidford Pl STHWK SE1 17 M4
Sidings Ms HOLWY N7 73 G3
The Sidings WAN E11 58 A7
Sidmouth Av ISLW TW7 123 K1
Sidmouth Cl OXHEY WD19 33 F1
Sidmouth Dr RSLP HA4 64 E2
Sidmouth Ms STPAN WC1H 5 L8
Sidmouth Pde CRICK NW2 * 70 A6
Sidmouth Rd CRICK NW2 70 A6
LEY E10 76 A1
PECK SE15 111 G7
WELL DA16 116 D6
Sidmouth St STPAN WC1H 5 K8
Sidney Av PLMGR N13 41 F4
Sidney Elson Wy EHAM E6 96 A1
Sidney Gdns BTFD TW8 104 E5
Sidney Gv FSBYE EC1V 6 C6
Sidney Rd BECK BR3 166 B1
BRXN/ST SW9 130 A1
FSTGT E7 76 E2
RYLN/HDSTN HA2 48 C2
SNWD SE25 165 H4
TWK TW1 124 B5
WDGN N22 41 F6
WOT/HER KT12 156 A7
Sidney Sq WCHPL E1 * 92 E4
Sidney St WCHPL E1 92 D4
Sidworth St HACK E8 74 D6
Siebert Rd BKHTH/KID SE3 113 K5
Siemens Rd WOOL/PLUM SE18 114 C2
Sienna Cl CHSGTN KT9 171 K5
Sienna Ter CRICK NW2 * 69 J1
Sierra Dr DAGE RM10 98 D1
Sigdon Rd HACK E8 74 C4
The Sigers PIN HA5 47 F5
Signmakers Yd CAMTN NW1 * 4 D4
Sigrist Sq KUTN/CMB KT2 144 A7
Silbury Av MTCM CR4 147 J7
Silbury St IS N1 * 7 G7
Silecroft Rd BXLYHN DA7 117 H7
Silesia Blds HACK E8 74 D6
Silex St STHWK SE1 18 D2
Silk Cl LEE/GVPK SE12 133 K4
Silkfield Rd CDALE/KGS NW9 51 G4
Silkin Ms PECK SE15 111 H6
Silk Ms LBTH SE11 18 A8
Silk Mill Rd OXHEY WD19 21 F6
Silk Mills Pth LEW SE13 133 F2
Silkstream Pde EDGW HA8 * 36 E7
Silkstream Rd EDGW HA8 36 E7
Silk St BARB EC2Y 12 F2
Silsoe Rd WDGN N22 55 F2
Silver Birch Av CHING E4 43 H4
Silver Birch Cl CAT SE6 151 H2
FBAR/BDGN N11 40 A5
THMD SE28 97 G7
Silverbirch Wk HAMP NW3 * 71 K5
Silvercliffe Gdns EBAR EN4 27 J3
Silver Cl KTN/HRWW/WS HA3 34 D6
NWCR SE14 * 112 B6
Silver Crs CHSWK W4 105 J3
Silverdale ENC/FH EN2 28 E3
SYD SE26 150 E3
Silverdale Cl HNWL W7 84 E7
NTHLT UB5 65 K4
SUT SM1 174 D3
Silverdale Dr ELTH/MOT SE9 153 J1
HCH RM12 81 K4
SUN TW16 156 A1
Silverdale Gdns HYS/HAR UB3 101 K1
Silverdale Rd BUSH WD23 21 J4
BXLYHN DA7 137 J1
CHING E4 44 B5
HYS/HAR UB3 101 K1
STMC/STPC BR5 169 H3
Silverdene
NFNCH/WDSPK N12 * 39 F5
Silver Dene PUT/ROE SW15 * 127 F4
Silvergate HOR/WEW KT19 172 E4
Silverhall St ISLW TW7 124 B2
Silverholme Cl
KTN/HRWW/WS HA3 50 A6
Silver La WWKM BR4 180 B1
Silverleigh Rd THHTH CR7 164 A3
Silvermere Dr UED N18 * 43 F4
Silvermere Rd CAT SE6 132 D5
Silvermere Rw SNWD SE25 * 165 H1
Silver Pl SOHO/CST W1F 10 F5
Silver Rd LEW SE13 132 E2
NKENS W10 88 B6
Silver Spring Cl ERITH DA8 117 J5
Silverston Wy STAN HA7 35 J5
Silver St EN EN1 29 K2
UED N18 41 K3
Silverthorne Rd VX/NE SW8 129 G1
Silverthorn Gdns CHING E4 43 J1
Silverton Rd HMSMTH W6 107 G6
Silvertown Wy CAN/RD E16 94 D6
Silvertree La GFD/PVL UB6 84 D2
Silver Wy ROMW/RG RM7 62 D2
Silverwood Cl BECK BR3 151 J6
CROY/NA CR0 179 H7
NTHWD HA6 32 A7
Silvester Rd EDUL SE22 131 G4
Silvester St STHWK SE1 19 G2
Silwood Estate Regeneration
Area BERM/RHTH SE16 112 A4
Silwood St BERM/RHTH SE16 112 A4
Simmil Rd ESH/CLAY KT10 170 E4
Simmons Cl TRDG/WHET N20 27 J7
Simmons Dr BCTR RM8 80 A2
Simmons Ga ESH/CLAY KT10 170 C4
Simmons La CHING E4 44 B1
Simmons Rd
WOOL/PLUM SE18 115 G4
Simmons' Wy
TRDG/WHET N20 39 J1
Simms Cl CAR SM5 175 J1
Simms Gdns EFNCH N2 53 G1
Simms Rd STHWK SE1 111 H3
Simnel Rd LEE/GVPK SE12 134 A6
Simon Cl NTGHL W11 88 D6
Simonds Rd LEY E10 75 J1
Simone Cl BMLY BR1 153 H7
Simons Wk SRTFD E15 76 B4
Simpson Cl CROY/NA CR0 164 D5
WCHMH N21 29 F4
Simpson Dr ACT W3 87 F5
Simpson Rd HSLWW TW4 122 E5
RAIN RM13 81 H5
RCHPK/HAM TW10 143 J3
Simpson's Rd HAYES BR2 167 K2
POP/IOD E14 93 K6
Simpson St BTSEA SW11 128 D1
Simpson Wy SURB KT6 158 D5
Simrose Ct WAND/EARL SW18 127 K4
Sims Cl ROM RM1 63 H3
Sinclair Dr BELMT SM2 175 F7
Sinclair Gdns WKENS W14 107 G1
Sinclair Gv GLDGN NW11 52 B5
Sinclair Rd CHING E4 43 H4
WKENS W14 107 H2
Singapore Rd WEA W13 85 G7
Singer St FSBYE EC1V 7 H8
Singleton Cl CROY/NA CR0 164 D6
HCH RM12 81 H3
TOOT SW17 147 K6
Singleton Rd DAGW RM9 80 B4
Singleton Scarp
NFNCH/WDSPK N12 38 E4
Sinnott Rd WALTH E17 43 F7
Sion Rd TWK TW1 124 C7
Sipson Cl WDR/YW UB7 100 D5
Sipson La WDR/YW UB7 100 E5
Sipson Rd WDR/YW UB7 100 C3
Sipson Wy WDR/YW UB7 100 D6
Sir Abraham Dawes Cots
PUT/ROE SW15 * 127 H3
Sir Alexander Cl ACT W3 87 H7
Sir Cyril Black Wy
WIM/MER SW19 146 D6
Sirdar Rd MTCM CR4 148 A5
NTGHL W11 88 B6
WDGN N22 55 H2
Sir John Kirk Cl CMBW SE5 110 D6
Sir Thomas More Est
CHEL SW3 108 C5
Sirus Rd NTHWD HA6 32 E4
Sise La MANHO EC4N * 13 G5
Siskin Cl BORE WD6 24 C3
BUSH WD23 21 J3
Sisley Rd BARK IG11 78 E7
Sispara Gdns
WAND/EARL SW18 127 J5
Sissinghurst Cl BMLY BR1 152 C4
Sissinghurst Rd CROY/NA CR0 165 H6
Sister Mabels Wy PECK SE15 * 111 H6
Sisters Av BTSEA SW11 128 E3
Sistova Rd BAL SW12 129 G7
Sisulu Pl BRXN/ST SW9 130 B2
Sittingbourne Av EN EN1 29 K5
Sitwell Gv STAN HA7 35 F4
Siverst Cl NTHLT UB5 66 B5
Siviter Wy DAGE RM10 80 D6
Siward Rd HAYES BR2 168 A2
TOOT SW17 147 G2
TOTM N17 41 K7
Sixth Av HYS/HAR UB3 82 D7
MNPK E12 77 K3
NKENS W10 88 C3
Sixth Cross Rd WHTN TW2 142 C2
Skardu Rd CRICK NW2 70 C4
Skeena Hl WAND/EARL SW18 127 H6
Skeffington Rd EHAM E6 77 K7
Skeffington St
WOOL/PLUM SE18 115 H2
Skelbrook St
WAND/EARL SW18 147 F1
Skelgill Rd PUT/ROE SW15 127 J3
Skelley Rd SRTFD E15 76 D6
Skelton Cl HACK E8 * 74 B5
Skelton Rd FSTGT E7 76 E5
Skelton's La LEY E10 57 K6
Skelwith Rd HMSMTH W6 107 F5
Skerne Rd KUTN/CMB KT2 143 K7
Skerne Wk KUTN/CMB KT2 143 K7
Sketchley Gdns
BERM/RHTH SE16 112 A4
Sketty Rd EN EN1 30 B2
Skiers St SRTFD E15 76 C7
Skiffington Cl
BRXS/STRHM SW2 130 B7
Skinner Pl BGVA SW1W * 16 A6
Skinners La BLKFR EC4V 12 F6
HEST TW5 103 G7
Skinner St CLKNW EC1R 6 C9
FSBYE EC1V 6 C8
Skipsey Av EHAM E6 95 K2
Skipton Cl FBAR/BDGN N11 40 A5
Skipton Dr HYS/HAR UB3 101 F2
Skipworth Rd HOM E9 74 E7
Skylines POP/IOD E14 113 F1
Skylines Village
POP/IOD E14 * 113 F1
Sky Peals Rd WFD IG8 44 B6
Skyport Dr WDR/YW UB7 100 A6
Sladebrook Rd
BKHTH/KID SE3 134 C2
Sladedale Rd
WOOL/PLUM SE18 115 K4
Slade Gdns ERITH DA8 118 C7
Slade Green Rd ERITH DA8 118 C7
Sladen Pl CLPT E5 74 D3
Slades Cl ENC/FH EN2 29 G2
Slades Dr CHST BR7 154 C2
ELTH/MOT SE9 154 C3
Slades Gdns ENC/FH EN2 29 G1
Slades Hl ENC/FH EN2 29 G2
Slades Ri ENC/FH EN2 29 G2
The Slade WOOL/PLUM SE18 115 K5
Slade Wk WALW SE17 110 C5
Slade Wy MTCM CR4 148 A7
Slagrove Pl LEW SE13 132 D4
Slaidburn St WBPTN SW10 108 B5
Slaithwaite Rd LEW SE13 133 F3
Slaney Pl HOLWY N7 73 G4
Slaney Rd ROM RM1 63 G4
Slattery Rd FELT TW13 122 B7
Sleaford Gn OXHEY WD19 33 H2
Sleaford St VX/NE SW8 109 H6
Sledmere Ct
EBED/NFELT TW14 121 H7
Slievemore Cl CLAP SW4 129 J2
Slingsby Pl LSQ/SEVD WC2H 11 J6
Slippers Pl BERM/RHTH SE16 111 J2
Sloane Av CHEL SW3 15 K6
Sloane Ct East CHEL SW3 16 A7
Sloane Ct West CHEL SW3 15 M7
Sloane Gdns BGVA SW1W 16 A6
Sloane Sq BGVA SW1W 15 M6
Sloane St KTBR SW1X 15 M4
Sloane Ter KTBR SW1X 15 M5
Sloane Wk CROY/NA CR0 166 C5
Slocum Cl THMD SE28 97 J6
Slough La CDALE/KGS NW9 50 E5
Sly St WCHPL E1 * 92 D5
Smaldon Cl WDR/YW UB7 100 D2
Smallberry Av ISLW TW7 124 A1
Smallbrook Ms BAY/PAD W2 9 G5
Smalley Cl STNW/STAM N16 74 B2
Smallwood Rd TOOT SW17 147 H3
Smarden Cl BELV DA17 117 H4
Smart's Pl NOXST/BSQ WC1A 11 K4
UED N18 42 C4
Smart St BETH E2 93 F2
Smeaton Rd
WAND/EARL SW18 127 K6
WFD IG8 45 K4
Smeaton St WAP E1W 92 D7
Smedley St VX/NE SW8 129 J1
Smeed Rd BOW E3 75 J6
Smiles Pl LEW SE13 133 F1
Smith Cl BERM/RHTH SE16 93 F7
Smithfield St STBT EC1A 12 C3
Smithies Rd ABYW SE2 116 C3
Smith's Ct SOHO/SHAV W1D * 11 G6
Smithson Rd TOTM N17 41 K7
Smith Sq WEST SW1P 17 J4
Smith St BRYLDS KT5 159 G5
CHEL SW3 15 L7
WATW WD18 21 G3
Smith's Yd CROY/NA CR0 177 J2
Smith Ter CHEL SW3 15 L8
Smithwood Cl
WIM/MER SW19 127 H7
Smithy St WCHPL E1 92 E4
Smugglers Wy
WAND/EARL SW18 128 A3
Smyrk's Rd WALW SE17 19 K8
Smyrna Rd KIL/WHAMP NW6 2 A2
Smythe Cl ED N9 42 C2
Smythe St POP/IOD E14 93 K6
Snakes La EBAR EN4 28 B2
Snakes La East WFD IG8 45 G5
Snakes La West WFD IG8 44 E5
Snakey La FELT TW13 140 E3
Snaresbrook Dr STAN HA7 35 K3
Snaresbrook Rd WAN E11 58 C3
Snarsgate St NKENS W10 88 A4
Sneath Av GLDGN NW11 52 D6
Snell's Pk UED N18 42 B5
Sneyd Rd CRICK NW2 70 A4
Snipe Cl ERITH DA8 118 E6
Snowberry Cl SRTFD E15 76 B3
Snowbury Rd FUL/PGN SW6 128 A1
Snowden Dr CDALE/KGS NW9 51 G5
Snowdon Crs HYS/HAR UB3 101 F2
Snowdon Rd HTHAIR TW6 121 F5
Snowdown Cl PGE/AN SE20 150 E7
Snowdrop Cl HPTN TW12 142 A5
Snow Hl STBT EC1A 12 C3
Snowsfields STHWK SE1 19 H1
Snowshill Rd MNPK E12 77 J4
Snowy Fielder Waye
ISLW TW7 124 C1
Soames St PECK SE15 131 G2
Soames Wk NWMAL KT3 145 G7
Soane Cl EA W5 104 E1
Soaphouse La BTFD TW8 105 F6
Soho Sq SOHO/SHAV W1D 11 G4
Soho St SOHO/SHAV W1D 11 G4
Sojourner-Truth Cl HACK E8 74 D5
Solander Gdns WCHPL E1 92 D6
Solar Ct WATW WD18 * 20 D4
Solebay St WCHPL E1 93 G3
Solent Ri PLSTW E13 94 E2
Solent Rd KIL/WHAMP NW6 70 E4
Solna Av PUT/ROE SW15 127 F4
Solna Rd WCHMH N21 29 K7
Solomon Av UED N18 42 C3
Solomon's Pas PECK SE15 131 J3
Solon New Rd CLAP SW4 129 K3
Solon Rd BRXS/STRHM SW2 129 K3
Solway Cl HACK E8 74 B5
HSLWW TW4 122 D2
Solway Rd EDUL SE22 131 H3
WDGN N22 41 H7
Somaford Gv EBAR EN4 27 H5
Somali Rd CRICK NW2 70 D3
Somerby Rd BARK IG11 78 D6
Somercoates Cl EBAR EN4 27 J2
Somerfield Rd FSBYPK N4 73 H1
Somerfield St
BERM/RHTH SE16 112 A4
Somerford Cl PIN HA5 46 E3
Somerford Gv
STNW/STAM N16 74 B3
TOTM N17 42 C6
Somerford St WCHPL E1 * 92 D3
Somerford Wy
BERM/RHTH SE16 112 B1
Somerhill Av BFN/LL DA15 136 C6
Somerhill Rd WELL DA16 136 C1
Somerleyton Rd
BRXN/ST SW9 130 B3
Somersby Gdns REDBR IG4 59 K4
Somers Cl CAMTN NW1 5 G5
Somers Crs BAY/PAD W2 9 J5
Somerset Av CHSGTN KT9 171 K3
RYNPK SW20 160 E1
WELL DA16 136 A4
Somerset Cl CHEAM SM3 174 A2
NWMAL KT3 160 B5
TOTM N17 55 K1
WFD IG8 44 E7
Somerset Gdns HGT N6 54 A6
LEW SE13 132 E1
STRHM/NOR SW16 164 A2
TEDD TW11 142 E4
TOTM N17 * 42 A6
Somerset Rd BAR EN5 27 F4
BTFD TW8 104 D5
CHSWK W4 106 A2
DART DA1 138 E5
HDN NW4 52 A3
HRW HA1 48 C5
KUT/HW KT1 159 G1
STHL UB1 84 A4
TEDD TW11 142 E4
TOTM N17 56 B2
UED N18 42 B4
WALTH E17 57 J4
WEA W13 85 H7
WIM/MER SW19 146 B2
Somerset Sq WKENS W14 * 107 H2
Somerset Waye HEST TW5 102 D5
Somersham Rd BXLYHN DA7 137 F1
Somers Pl BRXS/STRHM SW2 130 A6
Somers Rd BRXS/STRHM SW2 130 A5
WALTH E17 57 H3
Somers Wy BUSH WD23 22 C6
Somerton Av RCH/KEW TW9 125 J2
Somerton Rd CRICK NW2 70 B2
PECK SE15 131 J3
Somertrees Av
LEE/GVPK SE12 153 F1
Somervell Rd
RYLN/HDSTN HA2 65 K4
Somerville Av BARN SW13 107 F5
Somerville Cl BRXN/ST SW9 110 A7
Somerville Rd CHDH RM6 61 J4
DART DA1 139 J5
PGE/AN SE20 151 F6
Sonderburg Rd HOLWY N7 73 F1
Sondes St WALW SE17 19 G9
Songhurst Cl CROY/NA CR0 164 A5
Sonia Cl OXHEY WD19 21 G6
Sonia Gdns HEST TW5 103 F6
NFNCH/WDSPK N12 39 G3
WLSDN NW10 69 H3
Sonning Gdns HPTN TW12 141 J5
Sonning Rd SNWD SE25 165 H5
Soper Cl CHING E4 43 H4
FSTH SE23 132 A7
Sophia Cl HOLWY N7 73 F5
Sophia Rd CAN/RD E16 95 F4
LEY E10 57 K7
Sophia Sq BERM/RHTH SE16 93 G6
Sopwith Av CHSGTN KT9 172 A4
Sopwith Cl KUTN/CMB KT2 144 B4
Sopwith Rd HEST TW5 102 B6
Sopwith Wy KUTN/CMB KT2 144 A7
VX/NE SW8 109 G6
Sorrel Bank CROY/NA CR0 * 179 G7
Sorrel Cl THMD SE28 97 G7
Sorrel Gdns EHAM E6 95 J4
Sorrel La POP/IOD E14 94 B5
Sorrell Cl BRXN/ST SW9 * 130 B1
NWCR SE14 112 B6
Sorrel Wk ROM RM1 63 H2
Sorrento Rd SUT SM1 175 F2
Sotheby Rd HBRY N5 73 J3
Sotheran Cl HACK E8 74 C7
Sotheron Rd WAT WD17 21 G1
Soudan Rd BTSEA SW11 108 E7
Souldern Rd WKENS W14 * 107 G2
Souldern St WATW WD18 21 F4
South Access Rd LEY E10 57 F6
South Africa Rd SHB W12 87 K6
Southall Ct STHL UB1 * 83 K6
Southall La HEST TW5 102 A5
Southall Pl STHWK SE1 19 G2
Southampton Blds
LINN WC2A * 12 A3
Southampton Gdns
MTCM CR4 163 K4
Southampton Ms CAN/RD E16 95 F7
Southampton Pl
NOXST/BSQ WC1A 11 K3
Southampton Rd HAMP NW3 71 K4
Southampton Rd East
HTHAIR TW6 120 C5
Southampton Rd West
HTHAIR TW6 120 C5
Southampton Rw
NOXST/BSQ WC1A 11 K2
RSQ WC1B 11 J2
Southampton St
COVGDN WC2E 11 K6
Southampton Wy CMBW SE5 110 E6
Southam St NKENS W10 88 C3
South Ap NTHWD HA6 32 B2
South Audley St
MYFR/PKLN W1K 10 B7
South Av CAR SM5 176 A6
CHING E4 31 K6
RCH/KEW TW9 * 125 H1
STHL UB1 83 K6
South Avenue Gdns STHL UB1 83 K6
South Bank STHWK SE1 12 B7
SURB KT6 159 F5
Southbank THDIT KT7 158 C6
South Bank Ter SURB KT6 * 159 F5
South Birkbeck Rd WAN E11 76 B2
South Black Lion La
HMSMTH W6 106 D4
South Bolton Gdns
WBPTN SW10 14 D7
Southborough Cl SURB KT6 158 E7
Southborough La HAYES BR2 168 D4
Southborough Rd BMLY BR1 168 D2
HOM E9 74 E7
SURB KT6 159 F7
Southborough Rd (The Lane)
SURB KT6 * 159 F7
South Boundary Rd
MNPK E12 77 K2
Southbourne HAYES BR2 167 K6
Southbourne Av
CDALE/KGS NW9 50 E1
Southbourne Cl PIN HA5 47 J6
Southbourne Crs HDN NW4 52 C3
Southbourne Gdns IL IG1 78 C4
LEE/GVPK SE12 134 A4
RSLP HA4 47 F7
Southbridge Pl CROY/NA CR0 177 J3
Southbridge Rd CROY/NA CR0 177 J3
Southbridge Wy NWDGN UB2 102 D1
Southbrook Rd
LEE/GVPK SE12 133 H5
STRHM/NOR SW16 148 E7
Southbury Av EN EN1 30 C3
RAIN RM13 99 K4
Southbury Rd EN EN1 30 B3
South Carriage Dr KTBR SW1X 15 M1
SKENS SW7 15 J2
Southchurch Rd EHAM E6 95 K1
South Cl BAR EN5 26 D2
BXLYHS DA6 136 E3
DAGE RM10 80 C7
HGT N6 54 B5
PIN HA5 47 K6
WDR/YW UB7 100 C2
WHTN TW2 142 A2
The South Colonnade
POP/IOD E14 93 J7
Southcombe St WKENS W14 107 H3
Southcote Av BRYLDS KT5 159 J6
FELT TW13 140 D1
Southcote Ri RSLP HA4 46 B6
Southcote Rd ARCH N19 72 C3
SNWD SE25 165 J4
WALTH E17 57 F4
South Countess Rd
WALTH E17 57 H2
South Crs CAN/RD E16 94 B3
Southcroft Av WELL DA16 135 K2
WWKM BR4 180 A1
Southcroft Rd TOOT SW17 148 A5
South Cross Rd BARK/HLT IG6 60 C4
South Croxted Rd DUL SE21 149 K2
Southdean Gdns
WIM/MER SW19 146 D1
South Dene MLHL NW7 37 F2
Southdown Av HNWL W7 104 B2
Southdown Crs
GNTH/NBYPK IG2 60 E4
RYLN/HDSTN HA2 48 C7
Southdown Dr RYNPK SW20 146 B6

Southdown Rd CAR SM5 ... 176 A7
  EMPK RM11 ... 63 K6
  RYNPK SW20 ... 146 B7
Southdown Vls
  SEVS/STOTM N15 * ... 55 H4
South Dr MNPK E12 ... 77 J2
  RSLP HA4 ... 46 C7
South Ealing Rd EA W5 ... 104 E1
South Eastern Av N9 ... 42 B2
South Eaton Pl BGVA SW1W ... 16 B5
South Eden Park Rd
  BECK BR3 ... 166 A4
South Edwardes Sq KENS W8 ... 107 J3
South End CROY/NA CR0 ... 177 J3
  KENS W8 ... 14 D3
Southend Cl ELTH/MOT SE9 ... 135 C5
Southend Crs ELTH/MOT SE9 ... 135 F5
Southend La CAT SE6 ... 151 J3
  SYD SE26 ... 151 H3
Southend Rd BECK BR3 ... 151 J7
  CLAY IG5 ... 59 J2
  EHAM E6 ... 77 K6
South End Rd HAMP NW3 ... 71 J3
  RAIN RM13 ... 81 J7
Southend Rd (North Circular)
  WALTH E17 ... 44 B7
Southend Rd (North Circular Rd)
  SWFD E18 ... 58 E1
South End Rw KENS W8 ... 14 D3
Southern Av
  EBED/NFELT TW14 ... 121 K7
  SNWD SE25 ... 165 G2
Southern Down FELT TW13 * ... 122 B7
Southerngate Wy NWCR SE14 ... 112 B6
Southern Gv BOW E3 ... 93 H2
Southern Perimeter Rd
  HTHAIR TW6 ... 121 F4
  STWL/WRAY TW19 ... 120 E3
Southern Rd EFNCH N2 ... 53 K3
  PLSTW E13 ... 95 F1
Southern Rw NKENS W10 ... 88 B3
Southern St IS N1 ... 5 L5
Southern Wy GNWCH SE10 ... 113 H3
  ROMW/RG RM7 ... 62 C5
Southerton Rd HMSMTH W6 * ... 107 F3
South Esk Rd FSTGT E7 ... 77 G5
Southey Rd BRXN/ST SW9 ... 110 B7
  SEVS/STOTM N15 ... 56 A4
  WIM/MER SW19 ... 146 E6
Southey St PGE/AN SE20 ... 151 F6
Southfield BAR EN5 ... 26 B5
Southfield Gdns TWK TW1 ... 143 F3
Southfield Pk
  RYLN/HDSTN HA2 ... 48 B3
  PEND EN3 ... 30 D5
Southfields E/WMO/HCT KT8 ... 157 K5
  HDN NW4 ... 51 K2
Southfields Ms
  WAND/EARL SW18 * ... 127 K5
Southfields Rd
  WAND/EARL SW18 ... 127 K5
South Gdns WBLY HA9 * ... 68 C3
  WIM/MER SW19 ... 147 H6
South Gate Av FELT TW13 ... 140 B3
Southgate Gv IS N1 ... 7 J2
Southgate Rd IS N1 ... 7 H2
  MNPK E12 ... 77 K1
South Gipsy Rd WELL DA16 ... 136 E2
South Gv HGT N6 ... 54 A7
  SEVS/STOTM N15 ... 55 K4
  WALTH E17 ... 57 H4
South Hall Dr RAIN RM13 ... 99 K4
South Hill CHST BR7 ... 153 K5
  NTHWD HA6 * ... 32 C7
South Hill Av
  RYLN/HDSTN HA2 ... 66 C2
South Hill Gv HRW HA1 ... 66 E3
South Hill Park Gdns
  HAMP NW3 ... 71 J3
South Hill Rd HAYES BR2 ... 167 H2
Southill La RSLP HA4 ... 46 E3
Southill Rd CHST BR7 ... 153 J6
Southill St POP/IOD E14 ... 93 K5
South Island Pl BRXN/ST SW9 ... 110 A6
South Kensington Station Ar
  SKENS SW7 ... 15 H5
South Lambeth Pl VX/NE SW8 * ... 17 K9
South Lambeth Rd
  VX/NE SW8 ... 17 K9
Southland Rd
  WOOL/PLUM SE18 ... 116 B6
Southlands Dr
  WIM/MER SW19 ... 146 B1
Southlands Gv BMLY BR1 ... 168 D2
Southlands Rd HAYES BR2 ... 168 C3
Southland Wy HSLW TW3 ... 123 J4
South La KUT/HW KT1 ... 158 E2
  NWMAL KT3 ... 160 A3
South La West NWMAL KT3 ... 160 A3
South Lodge Av MTCM CR4 ... 163 K3
South Lodge Crs ENC/FH EN2 ... 28 D3
South Lodge Dr
  STHGT/OAK N14 ... 28 D3
South Md CDALE/KGS NW9 ... 37 H7
  HOR/WEW KT19 ... 173 H6
Southmead Rd
  WIM/MER SW19 ... 127 H7
Southmere Dr ABYW SE2 ... 116 D1
South Molton La
  MYFR/PKLN W1K ... 10 C5
South Molton Rd CAN/RD E16 ... 94 E5
South Molton St
  MYFR/PKLN W1K ... 10 C5
Southmont Rd ESH/CLAY KT10 ... 170 E1
South Mt TRDG/WHET N20 * ... 39 G1
South Norwood Hl
  SNWD SE25 ... 150 A7
South Oak Rd STRHM/NOR SW16 ... 149 F3
Southold Ri ELTH/MOT SE9 ... 153 K2
Southolm St BTSEA SW11 ... 109 G7
Southover BMLY BR1 ... 152 E4
  NFNCH/WDSPK N12 ... 39 F4
South Pde CHEL SW3 ... 15 H7
  CHSWK W4 ... 106 A3
  EDGW HA8 * ... 50 C1
South Park Crs CAT SE6 ... 133 H7
  IL IG1 ... 78 D2
South Park Dr
  GDMY/SEVK IG3 ... 78 E4
South Park Gv NWMAL KT3 ... 159 K3
South Park Hill Rd
  SAND/SEL CR2 ... 177 K4
South Park Ms FUL/PGN SW6 ... 128 A2
South Park Rd IL IG1 ... 78 D3
  WIM/MER SW19 ... 146 E5
South Park Ter IL IG1 ... 78 D3
South Park Wy RSLP HA4 ... 65 G5

South Pl BRYLDS KT5 ... 159 G6
  LVPST EC2M ... 13 H3
  PEND EN3 ... 30 E4
South Place Ms LVPST EC2M ... 13 H3
Southport Rd
  WOOL/PLUM SE18 ... 115 J3
Southridge Pl RYNPK SW20 ... 146 B6
South Ri BAY/PAD W2 * ... 9 G6
  CAR SM5 ... 175 J7
South Rd CHDH RM6 ... 61 J4
  EA W5 ... 104 E3
  ED N9 ... 30 C7
  EDGW HA8 ... 36 D7
  ERITH DA8 ... 118 C5
  FELT TW13 ... 141 H4
  FSTH SE23 ... 151 F1
  HPTN TW12 ... 141 J5
  STHL UB1 ... 83 K7
  WDR/YW UB7 ... 100 D2
  WHTN TW2 ... 142 D2
  WIM/MER SW19 ... 147 H5
South Rw BKHTH/KID SE3 ... 133 K1
Southsea Av WATW WD18 ... 20 E3
Southsea Rd KUT/HW KT1 ... 159 F3
South Sea St
  BERM/RHTH SE16 ... 112 C2
South Side HMSMTH W6 ... 106 C2
  SEVS/STOTM N15 * ... 56 B3
Southside Common
  WIM/MER SW19 ... 146 B5
Southspring BFN/LL DA15 ... 135 J6
South Sq GINN WC1R ... 12 A3
  GLDGN NW11 ... 52 E5
South St BMLY BR1 ... 167 K1
  EMPK RM11 ... 63 J5
  ISLW TW7 ... 124 B2
  MYFR/PKLN W1K ... 10 B8
  PEND EN3 ... 31 F4
  RAIN RM13 ... 98 C1
  ROM RM1 ... 63 G5
South Tenter St WCHPL E1 ... 13 M6
South Ter SKENS SW7 ... 15 J5
  SURB KT6 ... 159 F5
  WDGN N22 ... 54 E1
South V HRW HA1 ... 66 E3
  NRWD SE19 ... 150 A5
Southvale Rd BKHTH/KID SE3 ... 133 H1
South Vale Rd SURB KT6 ... 172 A1
South Vw BMLY BR1 ... 168 B1
Southview Av WLSDN NW10 ... 69 H4
South View Cl BXLY DA5 ... 137 G5
Southview Ct SWFD E18 ... 148 A4
South View Ct NRWD SE19 * ... 149 J6
South View Crs
  GNTH/NBYPK IG2 ... 60 B5
Southview Dr SWFD E18 ... 59 F2
Southview Gdns WLGTN SM6 ... 176 C6
Southview Rd BMLY BR1 ... 152 B3
South View Rd
  CEND/HSY/T N8 ... 54 D2
  PIN HA5 ... 33 F5
Southviews SAND/SEL CR2 ... 179 F7
Southville VX/NE SW8 ... 109 J7
Southville Cl
  EBED/NFELT TW14 ... 121 H7
  HOR/WEW KT19 ... 173 F5
Southville Crs
  EBED/NFELT TW14 ... 121 H7
Southville Rd
  EBED/NFELT TW14 ... 121 H7
  THDIT KT7 ... 158 B6
South Wk WWKM BR4 ... 180 C2
Southwark Br CANST EC4R ... 12 F7
Southwark Bridge Rd
  STHWK SE1 ... 18 D3
Southwark Park Est
  BERM/RHTH SE16 * ... 111 J3
Southwark Park Rd
  BERM/RHTH SE16 ... 19 M5
Southwark Pl BMLY BR1 ... 168 E2
Southwark St STHWK SE1 ... 12 C8
Southwater Cl BECK BR3 ... 151 K6
  POP/IOD E14 ... 93 H5
South Wy CROY/NA CR0 ... 179 G2
  ED N9 ... 42 E1
  FBAR/BDGN N11 ... 40 C5
  RYLN/HDSTN HA2 ... 48 A3
  WBLY HA9 ... 68 B4
Southway GLDGN NW11 ... 53 F5
  HAYES BR2 ... 167 K6
  RYNPK SW20 ... 161 G3
  TRDG/WHET N20 ... 38 E2
  WLGTN SM6 ... 176 C3
Southway Cl SHB W12 ... 106 E1
Southwell Av NTHLT UB5 ... 66 A5
Southwell Gdns SKENS SW7 ... 14 E5
Southwell Grove Rd WAN E11 ... 76 C1
Southwell Rd CMBW SE5 ... 130 D2
  CROY/NA CR0 ... 164 B5
  KTN/HRWW/WS HA3 ... 49 K5
South Western Rd TWK TW1 ... 124 B5
South West India Dock Entrance
  POP/IOD E14 ... 113 F1
Southwest Rd WAN E11 ... 58 B7
South Wharf Rd BAY/PAD W2 ... 9 G4
Southwick Ms BAY/PAD W2 ... 9 H4
Southwick Pl BAY/PAD W2 ... 9 J5
Southwick St BAY/PAD W2 ... 9 H4
Southwold Dr BARK IG11 ... 79 G4
Southwold Rd BXLY DA5 ... 137 J5
  CLPT E5 ... 74 D1
Southwood Av HGT N6 ... 54 B6
  KUTN/CMB KT2 ... 144 E7
Southwood Cl BMLY BR1 ... 168 E3
  WPK KT4 ... 161 G2
Southwood Dr BRYLDS KT5 ... 159 K6
Southwood Gdns
  ESH/CLAY KT10 ... 171 G2
  GNTH/NBYPK IG2 ... 60 B3
Southwood La HGT N6 ... 54 A6
Southwood Lawn Rd HGT N6 ... 54 A6
Southwood Pk HGT N6 * ... 54 A6
Southwood Rd ELTH/MOT SE9 ... 154 B1
  THMD SE28 ... 97 H7
South Worple Wy
  MORT/ESHN SW14 ... 126 A2
Southy Ms CAN/RD E16 ... 94 E7
Sovereign Cl EA W5 ... 85 J4
  WAP E1W ... 92 D6
Sovereign Crs
  BERM/RHTH SE16 ... 93 G6
Sovereign Gv ALP/SUD HA0 ... 67 K2
Sovereign Ms BETH E2 * ... 7 L5
  EBAR EN4 ... 27 K2
Sovereign Pk WLSDN NW10 * ... 86 D3
Sovereign Pl HRW HA1 ... 49 F4
Sovereign Rd BARK IG11 ... 97 J2
Sowerby Cl ELTH/MOT SE9 ... 134 E4

Sowrey Av RAIN RM13 ... 81 H5
Space Waye
  EBED/NFELT TW14 ... 122 A4
Spafield St CLKNW EC1R ... 6 A9
Spa Green Est CLKNW EC1R * ... 6 B7
Spa Hl NRWD SE19 ... 149 K7
Spalding Cl EDGW HA8 ... 37 G6
Spalding Rd HDN NW4 ... 52 A5
  TOOT SW17 ... 148 B4
Spanby Rd BOW E3 ... 93 J3
Spaniards Cl GLDGN NW11 ... 53 G7
Spaniards End HAMP NW3 ... 53 G7
Spaniards Rd HAMP NW3 ... 71 G1
Spanish Pl MHST W1U * ... 10 B4
Spanish Rd WAND/EARL SW18 ... 128 B4
Sparkbridge Rd HRW HA1 ... 48 E3
Sparkes Cl HAYES BR2 ... 168 A3
Sparke Ter CAN/RD E16 * ... 94 D5
Sparkford Gdns
  FBAR/BDGN N11 ... 40 A4
Sparks Cl ACT W3 ... 87 F5
  BCTR RM8 ... 79 K1
  HPTN TW12 ... 141 J5
Spa Rd BERM/RHTH SE16 ... 19 L4
Sparrow Cl HPTN TW12 ... 141 H5
Sparrow Dr STMC/STPC BR5 ... 169 H7
Sparrow Farm Dr
  EBED/NFELT TW14 ... 122 B6
Sparrow Farm Rd EW KT17 ... 173 J5
Sparrow Green DAGE RM10 ... 80 D2
Sparrows Herne BUSH WD23 ... 22 B6
Sparrows La ELTH/MOT SE9 ... 135 H6
Sparrows Wy BUSH WD23 * ... 22 C6
Sparrows Wick BUSH WD23 ... 22 C6
Sparsholt Rd ARCH N19 ... 55 F7
  BARK IG11 ... 78 E7
Spartan Cl WLGTN SM6 ... 176 E6
Sparta St GNWCH SE10 ... 113 F7
Speakers Ct CROY/NA CR0 * ... 164 E7
Spearman St
  WOOL/PLUM SE18 * ... 115 F5
Spear Ms ECT SW5 ... 14 B6
Spears Rd ARCH N19 ... 54 E7
Speart La HEST TW5 ... 102 D6
Spectrum Pl WALW SE17 ... 19 G9
Spedan Cl HAMP NW3 ... 71 F2
Speedwell St DEPT SE8 ... 112 D6
Speedy Pl STPAN WC1H ... 5 J8
Speer Rd THDIT KT7 ... 158 A5
Speirs Cl NWMAL KT3 ... 160 C5
Spekehill ELTH/MOT SE9 ... 153 K2
Speke Rd THHTH CR7 ... 164 E1
Speldhurst Cl HAYES BR2 ... 167 J4
Speldhurst Rd CHSWK W4 ... 106 A2
  HOM E9 ... 75 F6
Spellbrook Wk IS N1 * ... 6 E3
Spelman St WCHPL E1 ... 92 C4
Spelthorne Gv SUN TW16 ... 140 D6
Spelthorne La ASHF TW15 ... 140 A6
Spence Cl BERM/RHTH SE16 ... 112 C1
Spencer Cl FNCH N3 ... 52 D1
  WFD IG8 ... 45 G4
  WLSDN NW10 ... 86 B2
Spencer Dr EFNCH N2 ... 53 G5
Spencer Gdns
  MORT/ESHN SW14 ... 125 K4
Spencer Hl WIM/MER SW19 ... 146 C5
Spencer Hill Rd
  WIM/MER SW19 ... 146 C6
Spencer House SURB KT6 * ... 159 F6
Spencer Ms CLAP SW4 ... 109 K7
  HMSMTH W6 ... 107 H5
Spencer Pk WAND/EARL SW18 ... 128 C4
  IS N1 ... 6 C1
  WEST SW1P ... 16 F4
Spencer Pl CROY/NA CR0 ... 164 E6
  IS N1 ... 6 C1
Spencer Ri KTTN NW5 ... 72 B3
Spencer Rd ACT W3 ... 86 E7
  ALP/SUD HA0 ... 67 J1
  BMLY BR1 ... 152 B2
  BTSEA SW11 ... 128 C3
  CEND/HSY/T N8 ... 55 F4
  CHSWK W4 ... 105 K6
  E/WMO/HCT KT8 ... 157 K3
  EHAM E6 ... 77 H7
  FBAR/BDGN N11 ... 40 B3
  HRW HA1 ... 48 E1
  ISLW TW7 ... 103 J7
  KTN/HRWW/WS HA3 ... 48 E1
  MTCM CR4 ... 162 E6
  RAIN RM13 ... 99 F2
  RYNPK SW20 ... 145 K7
  SAND/SEL CR2 ... 178 A4
  TOTM N17 ... 42 C7
  WALTH E17 ... 58 A1
  WHTN TW2 ... 142 E2
Spencer St FSBYE EC1V * ... 6 C8
  NWDGN UB2 ... 102 C2
Spencer Wk PUT/ROE SW15 ... 127 G3
  WCHPL E1 * ... 92 C5
Spenser Gv STNW/STAM N16 ... 74 A3
Spenser Ms DUL SE21 ... 130 E7
Spenser Rd HNHL SE24 ... 130 C4
Spenser St WESTW SW1E ... 16 F3
Spensley Wk STNW/STAM N16 * ... 73 K2
Speranza St
  WOOL/PLUM SE18 ... 116 A4
Sperling Rd TOTM N17 ... 56 B1
Spert St POP/IOD E14 ... 93 G6
Speyside STHGT/OAK N14 ... 28 C5
Spey St POP/IOD E14 ... 94 A4
Spezia Rd WLSDN NW10 ... 87 J1
Spicer Cl BRXN/ST SW9 ... 130 C1
  WOT/HER KT12 ... 156 B5
Spices Yd CROY/NA CR0 ... 177 J3
Spielman Rd DART DA1 ... 139 J3
Spigurnell Rd TOTM N17 ... 41 K7
Spikes Bridge Rd STHL UB1 ... 83 J6
Spindle Cl WOOL/PLUM SE18 ... 114 D2
Spindlewood Gdns
  CROY/NA CR0 ... 178 A3
Spindrift Av POP/IOD E14 ... 112 D3
Spinel Cl WOOL/PLUM SE18 ... 116 A4
Spinnaker Cl BARK IG11 ... 97 G2
Spinnells Rd RYLN/HDSTN HA2 ... 47 K4
Spinney Cl BECK BR3 ... 166 E3
  NWMAL KT3 ... 160 B4
  RAIN RM13 ... 99 G1
  WPK KT4 ... 173 H1
Spinney Gdns DAGW RM9 ... 80 B4
  ESH/CLAY KT10 ... 170 B2
  NRWD SE19 ... 150 B4
Spinney Oak BMLY BR1 ... 168 D1
The Spinneys BMLY BR1 ... 168 E1
The Spinney ALP/SUD HA0 ... 67 G2
  BAR EN5 ... 27 F1
  BARN SW13 ... 106 E5
  CHEAM SM3 ... 174 A4
  NFNCH/WDSPK N12 * ... 39 G3
  STAN HA7 ... 36 A3

  STRHM/NOR SW16 ... 148 C2
  SUN TW16 ... 140 E7
  WCHMH N21 ... 29 G6
Spirit Quay WAP E1W ... 92 C7
Spital Sq WCHPL E1 ... 13 L2
Spital St DART DA1 ... 139 G5
  WCHPL E1 ... 92 C4
Spital Yd WCHPL E1 * ... 13 L2
Spitfire Est HEST TW5 * ... 102 B4
Spitfire House
  WOOL/PLUM SE18 * ... 114 D6
Spitfire Rd WLGTN SM6 ... 177 F6
Spitfire Wy HEST TW5 ... 102 B4
Spode Wk KIL/WHAMP NW6 * ... 71 F4
Spondon Rd SEVS/STOTM N15 ... 56 C3
Spoonbill Wy YEAD UB4 ... 83 H4
Spooner Wk WLGTN SM6 ... 176 D4
Sportsbank St CAT SE6 ... 133 F6
Sportsman Pl BETH E2 ... 74 C7
Spottons Gv TOTM N17 ... 41 J7
Spout Hl CROY/NA CR0 ... 179 J4
Spratt Hall Rd WAN E11 ... 58 E5
Spray St WOOL/PLUM SE18 ... 115 G3
Spreighton Rd
  E/WMO/HCT KT8 ... 157 G3
Sprimont Pl CHEL SW3 ... 15 L7
Springall St PECK SE15 ... 111 J6
Springbank WCHMH N21 ... 29 F5
Springbank Rd LEW SE13 ... 133 H5
Springbank Wk CAMTN NW1 ... 5 G2
Springbourne Ct BECK BR3 ... 152 A7
Spring Bridge Rd EA W5 ... 85 K6
Spring Cl BAR EN5 ... 26 B4
  BCTR RM8 ... 61 K6
  BORE WD6 ... 24 C1
Springclose La CHEAM SM3 ... 174 C4
Spring Cnr FELT TW13 * ... 140 E2
Spring Cots SURB KT6 * ... 158 E4
Springcroft Av EFNCH N2 ... 53 K2
Spring Crofts BUSH WD23 ... 22 A4
Springdale Rd
  STNW/STAM N16 ... 73 K3
Spring Dr PIN HA5 ... 46 E5
Springfield BUSH WD23 ... 22 D7
  CLPT E5 ... 56 D7
Springfield Av
  HPTN TW12 ... 142 B5
  MUSWH N10 ... 54 C2
  RYNPK SW20 ... 161 J2
Springfield Cl
  NFNCH/WDSPK N12 ... 39 F4
  STAN HA7 ... 35 G2
Springfield Dr
  GNTH/NBYPK IG2 ... 60 C4
Springfield Gdns BMLY BR1 ... 168 E3
  CDALE/KGS NW9 ... 51 F4
  CLPT E5 ... 56 D7
  RSLP HA4 ... 47 F3
  WFD IG8 ... 45 G6
  WWKM BR4 ... 179 K1
Springfield Gv CHARL SE7 ... 114 B5
  SUN TW16 ... 140 E7
Springfield La
  KIL/WHAMP NW6 ... 2 B4
Springfield Mt
  CDALE/KGS NW9 ... 51 G4
Springfield Parade Ms
  PLMGR N13 ... 41 G3
Springfield Pl NWMAL KT3 ... 159 K3
Springfield Ri SYD SE26 ... 150 D3
Springfield Rd BMLY BR1 ... 168 E3
  BXLYHN DA7 ... 137 K2
  EHAM E6 ... 77 K6
  FBAR/BDGN N11 ... 40 C4
  HNWL W7 ... 84 E7
  HRW HA1 ... 48 E5
  KUT/HW KT1 ... 159 F5
  SEVS/STOTM N15 ... 56 C3
  SRTFD E15 ... 94 C2
  STJWD NW8 ... 2 E3
  SYD SE26 ... 150 D4
  TEDD TW11 ... 143 G4
  THHTH CR7 ... 149 J7
  WALTH E17 ... 57 H5
  WELL DA16 ... 136 C2
  WHTN TW2 ... 123 F7
  WIM/MER SW19 ... 146 D5
  WLGTN SM6 ... 176 B4
  YEAD UB4 ... 83 J7
Springfield Wk
  KIL/WHAMP NW6 ... 2 C4
Spring Gdns E/WMO/HCT KT8 ... 157 H4
  HBRY N5 ... 73 J4
  HCH RM12 ... 81 K3
  ROMW/RG RM7 ... 62 E4
  WFD IG8 ... 45 G6
  WHALL SW1A ... 11 J8
  WLGTN SM6 ... 176 C4
Spring Gv CHSWK W4 ... 105 H4
  HPTN TW12 ... 142 B7
  MTCM CR4 ... 148 A7
Spring Grove Crs HSLW TW3 ... 103 H7
Spring Grove Rd HSLW TW3 ... 103 H7
  RCHPK/HAM TW10 ... 125 G4
Springhead Rd ERITH DA8 ... 118 C5
Spring Hl CLPT E5 ... 56 C6
  SYD SE26 ... 150 E3
Springhill Cl CMBW SE5 ... 130 E2
Springhurst Cl CROY/NA CR0 ... 179 H3
Spring Lake STAN HA7 ... 35 H3
Spring La CLPT E5 ... 56 D6
  MUSWH N10 ... 54 A2
  SNWD SE25 ... 165 J5
Spring Ms MHST W1U * ... 9 M2
Spring Park Av CROY/NA CR0 ... 179 F1
Springpark Dr BECK BR3 ... 167 F2
  FSBYPK N4 ... 55 J7
Spring Park Rd CROY/NA CR0 ... 179 F1
Spring Pl BARK IG11 ... 96 C1
  KTTN NW5 ... 72 B4
Springpond Rd DAGW RM9 ... 80 A4
Spring Rd FELT TW13 ... 140 D2
Springrice Rd LEW SE13 ... 133 F5
Spring Shaw Rd
  STMC/STPC BR5 ... 155 G7
Spring St BAY/PAD W2 ... 9 G5
  EW KT17 ... 173 H7
Spring Tide Cl PECK SE15 * ... 111 H7
Spring V BXLYHN DA7 ... 137 J3
Springvale Av BTFD TW8 ... 104 E4
Spring V North DART DA1 ... 139 G6
Spring V South DART DA1 ... 139 G6
Springvale Ter WKENS W14 ... 107 G2
Spring Villa Rd EDGW HA8 ... 36 C6
Spring Vis WEA W13 * ... 85 G6
Spring Wk WCHPL E1 ... 92 C4
Springwater Cl
  WOOL/PLUM SE18 ... 115 G7
Springwell Av WLSDN NW10 ... 69 H7
Springwell Rd HEST TW5 ... 102 B7
  STRHM/NOR SW16 ... 149 F3
Springwood Cl BOW E3 ... 93 J1
Springwood Crs EDGW HA8 ... 36 E1
Springwood Wy ROM RM1 ... 63 J4

Sprowston Ms FSTGT E7 ... 76 E4
Sprowston Rd FSTGT E7 ... 76 E4
Sprucedale Gdns
  CROY/NA CR0 ... 179 F3
  WLGTN SM6 ... 176 E7
Spruce Hills Rd WALTH E17 ... 57 K1
Sprules Rd BROCKY SE4 ... 132 B1
Spurfield E/WMO/HCT KT8 ... 157 G2
Spurgeon Av NRWD SE19 ... 149 K7
Spurgeon Rd NRWD SE19 ... 149 K6
Spurgeon St STHWK SE1 ... 19 G4
Spurling Rd DAGW RM9 ... 80 B5
  EDUL SE22 * ... 131 G3
Spur Rd BARK IG11 ... 96 C2
  EBED/NFELT TW14 ... 122 A4
  EDGW HA8 ... 36 A3
  ISLW TW7 ... 104 B6
  SEVS/STOTM N15 * ... 55 H3
  STHWK SE1 ... 18 A1
  WHALL SW1A ... 16 E2
Spurstowe Rd HACK E8 ... 74 C5
Spurstowe Ter HACK E8 ... 74 C4
The Square CAR SM5 ... 176 A4
  HMSMTH W6 ... 107 F4
  IL IG1 ... 60 C3
  RCH/KEW TW9 ... 124 E4
  STKPK UB11 ... 82 B7
  WFD IG8 ... 44 E5
Squarey St TOOT SW17 ... 147 G2
Squire Gdns STJWD NW8 ... 3 G3
Squires Ct WIM/MER SW19 ... 146 E5
Squires La FNCH N3 ... 39 F7
Squire's Mt HAMP NW3 ... 71 H2
Squires Wk ASHF TW15 ... 140 B6
Squires Wood Dr CHST BR7 * ... 153 K6
Squirrel Cl HSLWW TW4 ... 122 B2
Squirrel Ms WEA W13 * ... 85 G6
Squirrels Cl
  NFNCH/WDSPK N12 ... 39 G3
Squirrels Gn WPK KT4 ... 173 H1
Squirrel's Heath Av GPK RM2 ... 63 K2
The Squirrels BUSH WD23 ... 22 D5
  LEW SE13 ... 133 G2
  PIN HA5 ... 47 K2
Squirries St BETH E2 ... 92 C2
Stable Cl KUTN/CMB KT2 ... 144 B5
  NTHLT UB5 ... 84 A1
Stable Ms TWK TW1 ... 124 A7
  WNWD SE27 ... 149 J4
Stables Wy LBTH SE11 ... 18 A7
Stable Wk EFNCH N2 ... 39 H7
  IS N1 ... 5 K5
Stable Wy NKENS W10 ... 88 A5
Stable Yard Rd WHALL SW1A ... 10 F9
Stacey Av UED N18 ... 42 E3
Stacey Cl LEY E10 ... 58 B4
Stacey St HOLWY N7 ... 73 G2
  LSO/SEVD WC2H ... 11 H5
Stackhouse St KTBR SW1X ... 15 L3
Stacy Pth CMBW SE5 * ... 111 F6
Staddon Ct BECK BR3 ... 166 A3
Staddon Ct BECK BR3 ... 166 A3
Stadium Rd HDN NW4 ... 51 K6
  WOOL/PLUM SE18 ... 114 E6
Stadium St WBPTN SW10 ... 108 B6
Stadium Wy DART DA1 ... 138 B4
  WATW WD18 ... 21 F4
  WBLY HA9 ... 68 B3
Staffa Rd LEY E10 ... 57 G7
Stafford Av CLAY IG5 ... 60 A1
Stafford Cl CHEAM SM3 ... 174 C5
  KIL/WHAMP NW6 ... 2 A4
  STHGT/OAK N14 ... 28 C4
  WALTH E17 ... 57 H5
Stafford Cross CROY/NA CR0 ... 177 F4
Stafford Gdns CROY/NA CR0 ... 177 F4
Stafford Pl RCHPK/HAM TW10 ... 125 G6
  WESTW SW1E ... 16 E3
Stafford Rd BOW E3 ... 93 H1
  CROY/NA CR0 ... 177 G3
  FSTGT E7 ... 77 G1
  KIL/WHAMP NW6 ... 2 A7
  KTN/HRWW/WS HA3 ... 34 C6
  NWMAL KT3 ... 159 K2
  RSLP HA4 ... 64 C3
  SCUP DA14 ... 154 E3
  WLGTN SM6 ... 176 C5
Staffordshire St PECK SE15 ... 111 H7
Stafford St CONDST W1S ... 10 E8
Stafford Ter KENS W8 ... 14 A3
Stag Cl EDGW HA8 ... 50 D1
Stag La BKHH IG9 ... 45 F1
  CDALE/KGS NW9 ... 50 E3
  EDGW HA8 ... 50 D1
  PUT/ROE SW15 ... 145 K2
Stag Pl WESTW SW1E ... 16 E3
Stags Wy ISLW TW7 ... 104 A5
Stainbank Rd MTCM CR4 ... 163 G2
Stainby Cl WDR/YW UB7 ... 100 B2
Stainby Rd TOTM N17 ... 56 B1
Stainer St STHWK SE1 ... 13 H9
Staines Av CHEAM SM3 ... 174 B1
Staines Rd EBED/NFELT TW14 ... 120 E7
  EBED/NFELT TW14 ... 122 C4
  IL IG1 ... 78 D3
  WHTN TW2 ... 142 B2
Staines Rd East SUN TW16 ... 140 E6
Staines Rd West ASHF TW15 ... 140 A6
Stainford Cl ASHF TW15 ... 140 B4
Stainforth Rd
  GNTH/NBYPK IG2 ... 60 D6
  WALTH E17 ... 57 J3
Staining La CITYW EC2V ... 12 F4
Stainmore Cl CHST BR7 ... 154 D7
Stainsbury St BETH E2 ... 92 E1
Stainsby Pl POP/IOD E14 * ... 93 J5
Stainsby Rd POP/IOD E14 ... 93 J5
Stainton Rd CAT SE6 ... 133 G6
Stalbridge St CAMTN NW1 ... 9 K2
Stalham St BERM/RHTH SE16 ... 111 J2
Stambourne Wy NRWD SE19 ... 150 B6
  WWKM BR4 ... 180 A2
Stambourne Woodland Wk
  NRWD SE19 ... 150 A6
Stamford Brook Av
  HMSMTH W6 ... 106 C3
Stamford Brook Gdns
  HMSMTH W6 ... 106 C3
Stamford Brook Rd
  HMSMTH W6 ... 106 C3
Stamford Cl HAMP NW3 * ... 71 F3
  KTN/HRWW/WS HA3 ... 34 D6
  SEVS/STOTM N15 ... 56 C3
  STHL UB1 ... 84 A6
Stamford Cots WBPTN SW10 * ... 108 A6
Stamford Ct HAYES BR2 ... 167 J3
Stamford Gdns DAGW RM9 ... 79 J6
Stamford Gv East
  STNW/STAM N16 ... 56 C7
Stamford Gv West
  STNW/STAM N16 ... 56 C7
Stamford Hl STNW/STAM N16 ... 56 B7
Stamford Rd DAGW RM9 ... 79 H6

EHAM E6. 77 J7
IS N1. 7 K1
SEVS/STOTM N15 56 C4
WAT WD17 21 F1
Stamford St STHWK SE1 12 A8
Stamp Pl BETH E2. 7 L6
Stanborough Cl HPTN TW12 141 K5
Stanborough Pas HACK E8. 74 B5
Stanborough Rd HSLW TW3 123 J2
Stanbridge Pl WCHMH N21. 41 H1
Stanbridge Rd PUT/ROE SW15. 127 F2
Stanbrook Rd ABYW SE2. 116 C1
Stanbury Rd HAMP NW3. 71 K5
Stanbury Rd PECK SE15. 111 J7
Stancroft CDALE/KGS NW9. 51 G3
Standale Gv RSLP HA4. 46 A4
Standard Pl SDTCH EC2A. 7 K8
Standard Rd BELV DA17. 117 H4
  BXLYHS DA6. 137 F3
  HSLW TW4 122 D2
  WLSDN NW10 86 E3
Standen Rd WAND/EARL SW18. 127 K6
Standfield Rd DAGE RM10. 80 C4
Standish Rd HMSMTH W6 106 D3
Stane Cl WIM/MER SW19. 147 F6
Stane Gv VX/NE SW8 129 J1
Stane Wy WOOL/PLUM SE18. 114 C6
Stanford Cl HPTN TW12 141 K5
  ROMW/RG RM7 62 D5
  RSLP HA4 46 A5
  WFD IG8 45 G5
Stanford Pl WALW SE17 19 J6
Stanford Rd FBAR/BDGN N11. 39 K4
  KENS W8 14 D4
  STRHM/NOR SW16 163 K1
Stanford St PIM SW1V 17 G6
Stanford Wy
  STRHM/NOR SW16 163 J1
Stangate Gdns STAN HA7 35 H3
Stanger Rd SNWD SE25 165 H3
Stanham Pl DART DA1. 138 D3
Stanham Rd DART DA1 139 F4
Stanhope Av FNCH N3 52 D2
  HAYES BR2 167 K2
  KTN/HRWW/WS HA3 34 D7
Stanhope Cl
  BERM/RHTH SE16 * 112 A1
Stanhope Gdns BCTR RM8 80 B2
  FSBYPK N4 55 H5
  HGT N6 54 B5
  IL IG1 78 C2
  MLHL NW7 37 H4
  SKENS SW7 14 F5
Stanhope Ga BAY/PAD W2 9 L6
  MYFR/PKLN W1K 10 B9
Stanhope Gv BECK BR3. 166 C4
Stanhope Ms East SKENS SW7. 14 F5
Stanhope Ms South
  SKENS SW7 14 F6
Stanhope Ms West
  SKENS SW7 14 F5
Stanhope Pde CAMTN NW1 4 D7
Stanhope Park Rd
  GFD/PVL UB6 84 C3
Stanhope Pl BAY/PAD W2 9 L5
Stanhope Rd BAR EN5 26 B5
  BCTR RM8 80 B1
  BFN/LL DA15 155 G3
  BXLYHN DA7 137 F1
  CAR SM5 176 A6
  CROY/NA CRO 178 A2
  GFD/PVL UB6 84 C5
  HGT N6 54 C5
  NFNCH/WDSPK N12 39 G4
  RAIN RM13 99 J1
  WALTH E17 57 K4
Stanhope Rw
  MYFR/PICC W1J * 10 C9
Stanhope St CAMTN NW1 4 E7
Stanhope Ter BAY/PAD W2 9 H6
  WHTN TW2 * 124 A6
Stanier Cl WKENS W14 107 J4
Stanlake Rd SHB W12 88 A7
Stanlake Vls SHB W12 88 A7
Stanley Av ALP/SUD HA0 68 A6
  BARK IG11 97 F2
  BCTR RM8 62 B7
  BECK BR3 167 F2
  GFD/PVL UB6 66 C7
  GPK RM2 63 J3
  NWMAL KT3 160 D4
Stanley Cl ALP/SUD HA0 68 A6
  ELTH/MOT SE9 135 J3
  GPK RM2 63 J3
  VX/NE SW8 110 A5
Stanley Crs NTGHL W11 88 D6
Staneycroft Cl ISLW TW7 103 K3
Stanley Gdns ACT W3 106 B1
  CRICK NW2 70 A4
  MTCM CR4 * 148 A5
  NTGHL W11 88 D6
  WLGTN SM6 176 C5
Stanley Gardens Rd
  TEDD TW11 142 E4
Stanley Gv CROY/NA CRO 164 B5
  VX/NE SW8 129 F1
Stanley Park Dr ALP/SUD HA0. 68 A6
Stanley Park Rd CAR SM5. 175 K6
  WLGTN SM6 176 B6
Stanley Pas KCROSS N1C 5 H6
Stanley Rd ACT W3 105 J2
  BELMT SM2 175 F5
  CAR SM5 175 K7
  CROY/NA CRO 164 B6
  ED N9 30 B7
  ERNCH N2 53 H3
  EN EN1 30 A2
  FBAR/BDGN N11 40 D5
  HAYES BR2 168 A3
  HSLW TW3 123 H3
  IL IG1 78 D1
  MNPK E12 77 J4
  MORT/ESHN SW14 125 J3
  MRDN SM4 161 K3
  MTCM CR4 148 A6
  MUSWH N10 40 B7
  NTHWD HA6 32 E7
  RYLN/HDSTN HA2 66 C1
  SCUP DA14 155 G2
  SEVS/STOTM N15 55 H3
  STHL UB1 83 J6
  SWFD E18 44 D7
  TEDD TW11 142 B4
  WALTH E17 57 K5
  WAT WD17 21 G2
  WBLY HA9 68 B5
  WHTN TW2 142 D2
  WIM/MER SW19 146 E6
Stanley Rd North RAIN RM13. 81 G7
Stanley Rd South RAIN RM13. 99 H1
Stanley Sq CAR SM5 175 K7
Stanley St DEPT SE8. 112 C6

Stanley Ter ARCH N19 * 72 E1
  BXLYHS DA6 * 137 H3
Stanmer St BTSEA SW11 108 D7
Stanmore Gdns
  RCH/KEW TW9 125 G2
  SUT SM1 175 G2
Stanmore Hl STAN HA7 35 H1
Stanmore Rd BELV DA17 117 K3
  RCH/KEW TW9 125 G2
  SEVS/STOTM N15 55 H3
  WAN E11 58 D7
Stanmore St IS N1. 5 L3
Stanmore Ter BECK BR3. 166 D1
Stannard Ms HACK E8 * 74 C5
Stannard Rd HACK E8 74 C5
Stannary Pl LBTH SE11 18 B8
Stannary St LBTH SE11 18 B9
Stannet Wy WLGTN SM6 176 C3
Stansbury Sq NKENS W10 88 C2
Stansfeld Rd EHAM E6 95 H5
Stansfield Rd BRXN/ST SW9 130 A2
  HSLW TW4 122 A1
Stansgate Rd DAGE RM10 80 C1
Stanstead Cl HAYES BR2 167 J4
Stanstead Gv CAT SE6 132 C5
Stanstead Rd FSTH SE23 132 A7
  WAN E11 59 F4
Stansted Cl HCH RM12 81 K5
Stansted Crs BXLY DA5 136 E7
Stanswood Gdns CMBW SE5 111 F6
Stanthorpe Cl
  STRHM/NOR SW16 * 148 E4
Stanthorpe Rd
  STRHM/NOR SW16 148 E4
Stanton Av TEDD TW11 142 E5
Stanton Cl HOR/WEW KT19 172 D4
  WPK KT4 161 G2
Stanton Rd BARN SW13 126 C1
  CROY/NA CRO 164 D6
  RYNPK SW20 161 G1
Stanton St PECK SE15 * 111 H7
Stanton Wy SYD SE26 151 H3
Stanway Gdns ACT W3 86 C7
  EDGW HA8 36 E5
Stanway St IS N1 7 K5
Stanwell Cl STWL/WRAY TW19. 120 A5
Stanwell Gdns
  STWL/WRAY TW19 120 A5
Stanwell Rd
  EBED/NFELT TW14 121 F6
  HTHAIR TW6 120 E6
Stanwick Rd WKENS W14 107 J3
Stanworth St STHWK SE1 19 L2
Stanwyn Rd ALP/SUD HA0 * 67 H2
Stapelfield Cl
  BRXS/STRHM SW2 * 129 K7
  PIN HA5. 33 J6
Stapleford Av
  GNTH/NBYPK IG2 60 E4
Stapleford Cl CHING E4 44 A2
  KUT/HW KT1 159 H1
  WIM/MER SW19 127 H7
Stapleford Rd ALP/SUD HA0 67 K6
Stapleford Wy BARK IG11 97 H2
Staplehurst Rd CAR SM5 175 J6
  LEW SE13 133 G4
Staple Inn HHOL WC1V 12 A3
Staples Cl BERM/RHTH SE16 93 G7
Staple St STHWK SE1 19 H2
Stapleton Crs RAIN RM13 81 J5
Stapleton Gdns CROY/NA CRO. 177 G4
Stapleton Hall Rd FSBYPK N4. 55 F6
Stapleton Rd BXLYHN DA7 117 G6
  TOOT SW17 148 A2
Stapleton Vls
  STNW/STAM N16 * 74 A3
Stapley Rd BELV DA17 117 H4
Stapylton Rd BAR EN5 26 C2
Starboard Wy POP/IOD E14. 112 D2
Starbuck Cl ELTH/MOT SE9 135 F6
Starch House La
  BARK/HLT IG6 60 D1
Star Cl PEND EN3 30 E5
Starcross St CAMTN NW1 4 F8
Star & Garter Hl
  RCHPK/HAM TW10 125 F4
Star Hl DART DA1 138 B4
Star La CAN/RD E16 94 C3
Starling Cl PIN HA5 47 G2
Starling Rd CROY/NA CRO 166 B5
Starmans Cl DAGW RM9 80 A7
Star Pl WAP E1W * 13 M7
Star Rd HGDN/ICK UB10 82 A3
  ISLW TW7 123 J1
  WKENS W14 107 J5
Star St BAY/PAD W2 9 H4
Starveall Cl WDR/YW UB7 100 C2
Star Yd LINN WC2A 12 A4
Staten Gdns TWK TW1 124 A7
Statham Gv STNW/STAM N16. 73 K2
  UED N18 41 K4
Station Ap ALP/SUD HA0 67 H5
  BAR EN5 27 G3
  BECK BR3 151 G7
  BELMT SM2 174 C6
  BKHH IG9 * 45 H3
  BKHTH/KID SE3 134 A2
  BXLY DA5 137 H6
  BXLYHN DA7 137 F1
  CAMTN NW1 * 10 A1
  CAR SM5 175 K3
  CHING E4 * 44 A6
  CHST BR7 153 J5
  CROY/NA CRO * 177 K1
  DART DA1 139 H5
  ESH/CLAY KT10 171 F2
  FBAR/BDGN N11 40 B4
  FSTGT E7 77 F3
  FUL/PGN SW6 * 127 G7
  GFD/PVL UB6 66 D6
  GLDGN NW11 * 52 B6
  HAYES BR2 167 K7
  HOR/WEW KT19 173 H6
  HPTN TW12 142 A7
  HYS/HAR UB3 101 J2
  KUT/HW KT1. 159 H1
  NFNCH/WDSPK N12 * 39 F3
  NTHWD HA6 32 D6
  OXHEY WD19 33 H2
  PIN HA5. 47 J3
  RCH/KEW TW9 105 H7
  RSLP HA4 46 C7
  RSLP HA4 64 A4
  SAND/SEL CR2 177 K7
  STRHM/NOR SW16 148 D4
  SUN TW16 140 D7
  SURB KT6 158 E5
  SWFD E18 * 59 F1
  SYD SE26 151 H4
  WALTH E17 57 J4
  WAN E11 58 E4
  WAN E11 * 76 C3

WATW WD18 * 20 D3
WELL DA16 136 A1
WFD IG8 45 F5
WLSDN NW10 87 H2
Station Approach Rd
  CHSWK W4 105 K6
Station Ar GTPST W1W * 10 E1
Station Av HOR/WEW KT19 173 G7
  NWMAL KT3 160 B2
  RCH/KEW TW9 105 H7
Station Blds HAYES BR2 * 167 K7
Station Chambers EA W5 * 86 C3
Station Cl HPTN TW12 142 B7
Station Cots WBPTN N22 * 54 E1
Station Crs ALP/SUD HA0 67 H5
  BKHTH/KID SE3 113 K4
  SEVS/STOTM N15 55 K3
Stationers Hall Ct STP EC4M * 12 D5
Station Est BECK BR3 * 166 A3
Station Estate Rd
  EBED/NFELT TW14 122 A7
Station Garage Ms
  STRHM/NOR SW16 * 148 D5
Station Gdns CHSWK W4 105 K6
Station Gv ALP/SUD HA0 68 A5
Station Hl HAYES BR2 180 E1
Station House Ms ED N9 42 C3
Station Pde ACT W3 * 86 C5
  BAL SW12 * 129 F7
  BARK IG11 78 C6
  BECK BR3 * 166 A3
  BELMT SM2 * 175 G5
  BMLY BR1 * 152 E7
  BXLYHN DA7 * 137 F1
  CHSWK W4 * 105 K6
  CLPT E5 * 74 D2
  CRICK NW2 70 A5
  EA W5 * 86 B7
  EBAR EN4 * 28 A3
  EBED/NFELT TW14 * 122 A6
  EDGW HA8 * 36 A6
  EHAM E6 * 77 J6
  HCH RM12 81 K3
  KTN/HRWW/WS HA3 * 49 H1
  NTHLT UB5 * 66 A4
  PLSTW E13 * 77 G7
  RCH/KEW TW9 * 105 H7
  ROM RM1 * 63 G5
  RYLN/HDSTN HA2 * 66 B3
  STHGT/OAK N14 28 D7
Station Pas PECK SE15 * 111 K7
  SWFD E18 59 F1
Station Ri TULSE SE27 131 H3
Station Rd BAR EN5 27 F4
  BARK/HLT IG6 60 D2
  BARN SW13 126 C1
  BCTR RM8 61 K7
  BELV DA17 117 H3
  BFN/LL DA15 155 G1
  BMLY BR1 152 E7
  BORE WD6 24 C3
  BXLYHN DA7 137 F2
  CAR SM5 175 K3
  CHSGTN KT9 172 A4
  CROY/NA CRO 164 D7
  DART DA1 138 C5
  EA W5. 86 B5
  EDGW HA8 36 C5
  ESH/CLAY KT10 170 D4
  FBAR/BDGN N11 40 B4
  FNCH N3 38 E7
  GPK RM2 63 K3
  HAYES BR2 167 K1
  HDN NW4 51 J5
  HNWL W7 84 E7
  HOLWY N7 72 C4
  HPTN TW12 142 B7
  HRW HA1 48 B4
  HSLW TW3 123 G2
  HYS/HAR UB3 101 H3
  IL IG1 78 B2
  KUT/HW KT1 143 K7
  KUTN/CMB KT2 144 C7
  LEW SE13 133 F2
  MLHL NW7 37 G5
  MNPK E12 77 H3
  NWMAL KT3 160 A2
  PGE/AN SE20 150 E5
  RYLN/HDSTN HA2 48 B4
  SCUP DA14 155 G3
  SNWD SE25 165 G3
  SUN TW16 140 E6
  TEDD TW11 143 G5
  THDIT KT7 158 A6
  TOTM N17 56 C2
  TWK TW1 124 A7
  WALTH E17 57 G5
  WAT WD17 21 F1
  WCHMH N21 29 H1
  WDGN N22 41 H1
  WDR/YW UB7 100 B1
  WIM/MER SW19 147 G7
  WLSDN NW10 87 H1
  WWKM BR4 167 F7
Station Rd North BELV DA17. 117 J3
Station Sq STMC/STPC BR5 169 H4
Station Sr SRTFD E15 76 B7
Station Ter CMBW SE5 110 D7
  WLSDN NW10 88 B1
Station Vw GFD/PVL UB6 66 D6
Station Vw BKHH IG9 * 45 H3
  CHEAM SM3 174 C6
  ESH/CLAY KT10 170 E5
Station Yd RSLP HA4 * 64 B1
  STHL UB1 * 102 E1
  TWK TW1 124 B6
Staunton Rd KUTN/CMB KT2. 144 B6
Staunton St DEPT SE8. 112 C5
Staveley Cl HOLWY N7 * 72 E3
  PECK SE15 111 K7
Staveley Gdns CHSWK W4 106 A7
Staveley Rd ASHF TW15 140 B5
  CHSWK W4 105 K5
Staverton Rd CRICK NW2 70 A5
Stave Yard Rd
  BERM/RHTH SE16 93 G7
Stavordale Rd CAR SM5 162 B6
  HBRY N5 73 H3
Stayner's Rd WCHPL E1 93 F3
Stayton Rd SUT SM1 174 E2
Steadfast Rd KUT/HW KT1 143 K7
Steam Farm La
  EBED/NFELT TW14 121 J3
Stean St HACK E8 7 M1
Stebbing Wy BARK IG11 97 G1
Stebondale St POP/IOD E14. 113 F4
Stedly SCUP DA14 * 155 G3
Steed Cl EMPK RM11 81 K1
Steedman St WALW SE17 18 E6
Steeds Rd MUSWH N10 39 K7

Steel Ap BARK IG11 97 H1
Steele Rd CHSWK W4 105 K2
  ISLW TW7 124 B3
  TOTM N17 56 A3
  WAN E11 76 C3
  WLSDN NW10 86 E1
Steele's Ms North
  HAMP NW3 * 71 K5
Steele's Ms South HAMP NW3. 71 K5
Steele's Rd HAMP NW3 71 K5
Steeles Studios HAMP NW3 * 71 K5
Steel's La WCHPL E1 92 E5
Steep Hl CROY/NA CRO 178 A3
  STRHM/NOR SW16 148 D2
Steeplands BUSH WD23 22 B6
Steeple Cl FUL/PGN SW6 127 H1
  WIM/MER SW19 146 C5
Steeplestone Cl UED N18 41 J4
Steeple Wk IS N1 * 6 F1
Steerforth St
  WAND/EARL SW18 147 F1
Steering Cl ED N9 30 E7
Steers Md MTCM CR4 147 K7
Steers Wy BERM/RHTH SE16 112 A1
Stelling Rd ERITH DA8 118 A6
Stellman Cl CLPT E5 74 C2
Stembridge Rd PGE/AN SE20. 165 J1
Stephan Cl HACK E8 74 C7
Stephen Av RAIN RM13 81 J5
Stephendale Rd
  FUL/PGN SW6 128 A2
Stephen Ms FITZ W1T 11 G3
Stephen Pl CLAP SW4 * 129 H2
Stephen Rd BXLYHN DA7 137 K2
Stephenson Cl WELL DA16 136 A1
Stephenson Rd HNWL W7 85 F5
  WALTH E17 57 G4
  WHTN TW2 123 F6
Stephenson St CAN/RD E16 94 C3
  WLSDN NW10 87 G2
Stephenson Wy BUSH WD23 21 J7
  CAMTN NW1 4 F9
Stephen's Rd SRTFD E15 76 C7
Stephen St FITZ W1T 11 G3
Stepney Cswy WCHPL E1 93 F5
Stepney Gn WCHPL E1 92 E4
Stepney High St WCHPL E1 93 F4
Stepney Wy MTCM CR4 * 148 A7
  WCHPL E1 92 D4
Sterling Av EDGW HA8 36 B3
Sterling Cl WLSDN NW10 69 J6
Sterling Gdns NWCR SE14 112 B6
Sterling Pl EA W5 * 105 F3
Sterling St SKENS SW7 15 K3
Sterling Way (North Circular)
  UED N18 41 K4
Stern Cl BARK IG11 97 J1
Sterndale Rd DART DA1 139 J6
  WKENS W14 107 G2
Sterne St SHB W12 107 H1
Sternhall La PECK SE15 131 H2
Sternhold Av
  BRXS/STRHM SW2 148 D1
Sterry Crs DAGE RM10 80 C4
Sterry Dr HOR/WEW KT19 173 G3
  THDIT KT7 157 K5
Sterry Gdns DAGE RM10 80 C5
Sterry Rd BARK IG11 79 F7
  DAGE RM10 80 C3
Sterry St STHWK SE1 19 H2
Steucers La FSTH SE23 132 B7
Steve Biko La CAT SE6 151 J3
Steve Biko Rd HOLWY N7 73 G2
Steve Biko Wy HSLW TW3 123 F2
Stevedale Rd WELL DA16 136 D1
Stevedore St WAP E1W 92 D7
Stevenage Rd EHAM E6 78 A4
  FUL/PGN SW6 107 G7
Stevens Av HOM E9 74 E5
Stevens Cl BECK BR3 151 J5
  HPTN TW12 141 K5
  PIN HA5. 47 G4
Stevens Gn BUSH WD23 22 C7
Stevens' La ESH/CLAY KT10 171 G6
Stevenson Cl BAR EN5 27 H5
  ERITH DA8 118 E6
Stevenson Crs
  BERM/RHTH SE16 111 H4
Stevens Rd BCTR RM8 79 H1
Stevens St STHWK SE1 19 K3
Steventon Rd SHB W12 87 H6
Stewart Cl CDALE/KGS NW9 * 50 E5
  CHST BR7 154 B4
  HPTN TW12 141 J5
Stewart Quay HYS/HAR UB3. 101 H1
Stewart Rd SRTFD E15 76 B3
Stewartsby Cl UED N18 41 J4
Stewart's Gv CHEL SW3 15 H7
Stewart's La VX/NE SW8 109 G6
Stewarts Rd VX/NE SW8 109 H6
Stewart St POP/IOD E14 113 F1
Steyne Rd ACT W3 86 D7
Steyning Gv ELTH/MOT SE9 153 K3
Steynings Wy
  NFNCH/WDSPK N12 38 E4
Steyning Wy HSLWW TW4 122 B3
Stickland Rd BELV DA17 * 117 H3
Stickleton Cl GFD/PVL UB6 84 B2
Stilecroft Gdns ALP/SUD HA0. 67 H2
Stile Hall Gdns CHSWK W4 105 H4
Stiles Cl ERITH DA8 118 E4
  HAYES BR2 168 E5
Stillingfleet Rd BARN SW13 106 D6
Stillington St WEST SW1P 16 F5
Stillness Rd FSTH SE23 132 B5
Stipularis Dr YEAD UB4 83 H3
Stirling Av PIN HA5 47 H5
  WLGTN SM6 176 E6
Stirling Cl RAIN RM13 99 K2
  SCUP DA14 154 E3
  STRHM/NOR SW16 148 C7
Stirling Gv HSLW TW3 123 H1
Stirling Rd ACT W3 105 J2
  BRXN/ST SW9 129 K1
  HYS/HAR UB3 83 F6
  KTN/HRWW/WS HA3 49 G2
  PLSTW E13 95 F1
  TOTM N17 42 C7
  WALTH E17 57 G2
  WDGN N22 41 H7
  WHTN TW2 123 G6
Stirling Wy BORE WD6 24 E4
  CROY/NA CRO 163 K6

Stockholm Rd
  BERM/RHTH SE16 111 K4
Stockholm Wy WAP E1W 92 C7
Stockhurst Cl PUT/ROE SW15. 127 F1
Stockingswater La PEND EN3. 31 G1
Stockland Rd ROMW/RG RM7. 63 F5
Stockley Farm Rd
  WDR/YW UB7 100 E2
Stockley Rd WDR/YW UB7 100 E2
Stock Orchard Crs
  HOLWY N7 73 F3
Stock Orchard St HOLWY N7. 73 F4
Stockport Rd
  STRHM/NOR SW16 148 D7
Stocksfield Rd WALTH E17 * 58 A2
Stocks Pl POP/IOD E14 93 H6
Stock St PLSTW E13 94 E1
Stockton Cl BAR EN5 27 G3
Stockton Gdns MLHL NW7 37 F2
  TOTM N17 41 J6
Stockton Rd TOTM N17 41 J6
  UED N18 42 C5
Stockwell Av BRXN/ST SW9. 130 A2
Stockwell Gdns BRXN/ST SW9. 130 A1
Stockwell La BRXN/ST SW9 130 A1
Stockwell Park Crs
  BRXN/ST SW9 130 A1
Stockwell Park Rd
  BRXN/ST SW9 110 A7
Stockwell Park Wk
  BRXN/ST SW9 130 A2
Stockwell Rd BRXN/ST SW9 130 A1
Stockwell St GNWCH SE10 113 F5
Stockwell Ter BRXN/ST SW9 110 A7
Stodart Rd PGE/AN SE20 150 E7
Stofield Gdns ELTH/MOT SE9. 153 H2
Stoford Cl WIM/MER SW19 127 H7
Stokenchurch St
  FUL/PGN SW6. 108 A7
Stoke Newington Church St
  STNW/STAM N16 73 K2
Stoke Newington Common
  STNW/STAM N16 74 B1
Stoke Newington High St
  STNW/STAM N16 74 B2
Stoke Newington Rd HACK E8. 74 B4
Stoke Pl WLSDN NW10 87 H2
Stoke Rd KUTN/CMB KT2. 144 E6
Stokesby Rd CHSGTN KT9 172 B5
Stokesley St SHB W12 87 H5
Stokes Ms TEDD TW11 143 G4
Stokes Rd CROY/NA CRO 166 A6
  EHAM E6 95 J3
Stoll Cl CRICK NW2 70 A2
Stonard Rd BCTR RM8 79 H4
  PLMGR N13 41 G2
Stondon Pk FSTH SE23 132 B5
Stonebridge Ms NRWD SE19. 149 J6
Stonebridge Pk WLSDN NW10. 69 F6
Stonebridge Rd
  SEVS/STOTM N15 56 A4
Stonebridge Wy WBLY HA9 68 D5
Stone Blds LINN WC2A 11 M3
Stonechat Sq EHAM E6 95 J4
Stone Cl BCTR RM8 80 B1
  CLAP SW4 129 H1
Stonecot Cl CHEAM SM3 161 H7
Stonecot Hl CHEAM SM3 161 H7
Stone Crs EBED/NFELT TW14 121 J6
Stonecroft Cl BAR EN5 25 K3
Stonecroft Rd ERITH DA8 117 K6
Stonecroft Wy CROY/NA CRO. 163 K6
Stonecrop Cl CDALE/KGS NW9. 51 F2
Stonecutter St
  FLST/FETLN EC4A. 12 C4
Stonefield Cl BXLYHN DA7 137 H2
  RSLP HA4 65 J3
Stonefield St IS N1 6 B3
Stonefield Wy CHARL SE7 114 C6
  RSLP HA4 65 H4
Stone Gv EDGW HA8 36 A3
  STAN HA7 36 A3
Stonegrove Gdns EDGW HA8. 36 A4
Stonehall Av IL IG1 59 J5
Stone Hall Gdns KENS W8 * 14 C4
Stone Hall Pl KENS W8 * 14 C4
Stone Hall Rd WCHMH N21 29 F6
Stoneham Rd
  FBAR/BDGN N11 40 C4
Stonehill Cl MORT/ESHN SW14. 126 A4
Stonehill Rd CHSWK W4 105 H4
  MORT/ESHN SW14 125 K4
Stonehills Ct DUL SE21 150 A2
Stonehorse Rd PEND EN3 30 E4
Stone House Ct LVPST EC2M 13 J3
Stoneleigh Av WPK KT4 173 J2
Stoneleigh Broadway
  EW KT17 173 J4
Stoneleigh Crs
  HOR/WEW KT19 173 J4
Stoneleigh Park Av
  CROY/NA CRO 166 A5
Stoneleigh Park Rd
  HOR/WEW KT19 173 H5
Stoneleigh Pl NTGHL W11 88 B6
Stoneleigh Rd BMLY BR1 169 G2
  CAR SM5 162 D6
  CLAY IG5 59 J2
  TOTM N17 56 B1
Stoneleigh St NTGHL W11 88 B6
Stoneleigh Ter ARCH N19 * 72 B1
Stonell's Rd TOOT SW17 147 G2
Stonemasons Cl
  SEVS/STOTM N15 * 55 K3
Stonenest St FSBYPK N4 55 F7
Stone Park Av BECK BR3 166 D3
Stone Pl WPK KT4 173 J1
Stone Rd HAYES BR2 167 J4
Stones End St STHWK SE1 18 E2
Stonewall EHAM E6 96 A4
Stonewood Rd ERITH DA8 118 B4
Stoney Aly WOOL/PLUM SE18. 115 F1
Stoneyard La POP/IOD E14 93 K6
Stoneycroft Cl LEE/GVPK SE12. 133 J6
Stoneycroft Rd WFD IG8 45 J5
Stoneydown Av WALTH E17 57 G3
Stoneydown WALTH E17 57 G3
Stoneyfields La EDGW HA8 36 E4
Stoney La HDTCH EC3A 13 K4
  NRWD SE19 150 B5
Stoney St STHWK SE1 13 G8
Stonhouse St CLAP SW4 129 H3
Stonnell's Rd BTSEA SW11 128 E4
Stonor Rd WKENS W14 107 J3
Stopes St PECK SE15 111 G6
Stopford Rd PLSTW E13 76 E7
  WALW SE17 * 18 D8
Store Rd CAN/RD E16 115 H1

Storers Quay POP/IOD E14 113 G3
Store St GWRST WC1E 11 G3
SRTFD E15 76 B4
Storey Rd HGT N6 53 K5
WALTH E17 57 H3
Storey's Ga STJSPK SW1H 17 H2
Stories Ms CMBW SE5 * 131 F1
Stories Rd CMBW SE5 131 F2
Stork Rd FSTGT E7 76 D5
Storksmead Rd EDGW HA8 37 G6
Storks Rd BERM/RHTH SE16 * 111 H2
Stormont Rd BTSEA SW11 129 F3
HGT N6 53 K6
Stormont Wy CHSGTN KT9 171 J4
Stormount Dr HYS/HAR UB3 101 F1
Storrington Rd CROY/NA CR0 165 G7
Story St IS N1 5 L2
Stothard St WCHPL E1 92 E3
Stott Cl WAND/EARL SW18 128 C5
Stoughton Av CHEAM SM3 174 B4
Stoughton Cl LBTH SE11 17 M6
PUT/ROE SW15 126 D7
Stour Av NWDGN UB2 103 F2
Stourcliffe St MBLAR W1H 9 L5
Stour Cl HAYES BR2 181 G3
Stourhead Cl WIM/MER SW19 127 G6
Stourhead Gdns RYNPK SW20 160 D2
Stour Rd BOW E3 75 J6
DAGE RM10 80 C1
DART DA1 138 D2
Stourton Av FELT TW13 141 K3
Stowage DEPT SE8 112 E5
The Stowage DEPT SE8 112 D5
Stow Crs WALTH E17 43 G7
Stowe Gdns ED N9 30 B7
Stowe Pl SEVS/STOTM N15 56 A2
Stowe Rd SHB W12 106 E1
Stox Md KTN/HRWW/WS HA3 34 D7
Stracey Rd WLSDN NW10 69 F7
Strachan Pl RYNPK SW20 146 A5
Stradbroke Gv CLAY IG5 59 J2
Stradbroke Rd HBRY N5 73 J3
Stradbroke Cl
RYLN/HDSTN HA2 65 K2
Stradella Rd HNHL SE24 130 D5
Strafford Rd ACT W3 105 K1
BAR EN5 26 C2
HSLW TW3 122 E2
TWK TW1 124 B6
Strafford St POP/IOD E14 112 D1
Strahan Rd BOW E3 93 G1
Straightsmouth GNWCH SE10 113 F6
The Straight NWDGN UB2 102 C1
Strait Rd EHAM E6 95 J6
Straker's Rd EDUL SE22 131 J3
Strand CHCR WC2N 11 K7
HOL/ALD WC2B 11 M5
TPL/STR WC2R 11 L6
Strand Dr RCH/KEW TW9 105 H6
Strandfield Cl
WOOL/PLUM SE18 115 K4
Strand-on-the-Green
CHSWK W4 105 H5
Strand Pl UED N18 42 A3
Strangways Ter WKENS W14 107 J2
Stranraer Wy IS N1 5 L2
Strasburg Rd BTSEA SW11 109 F7
Stratfield Park Cl
WCHMH N21 29 H6
Stratfield Rd BORE WD6 24 B2
Stratford Cl BARK IG11 79 G6
DAGE RM10 80 E6
Stratford Ct NWMAL KT3 160 A3
Stratford Gv PUT/ROE SW15 127 G3
Stratford House Av BMLY BR1 168 D2
Stratford Pl OXSTW W1C 10 C5
Stratford Rd HTHAIR TW6 120 E5
KENS W8 14 B4
NWDGN UB2 102 D3
PLSTW E13 76 E7
THHTH CR7 164 B3
WAT WD17 20 E1
YEAD UB4 83 F3
Stratford Studios KENS W8 14 B4
Stratford Vls CAMTN NW1 4 F1
Stratford Wy WAT WD17 20 D1
Strathan Cl WAND/EARL SW18 127 H5
Strathaven Rd LEE/GVPK SE12 134 A5
Strathblaine Rd BTSEA SW11 128 C4
Strathbrook Rd
STRHM/NOR SW16 149 F6
Strathcona Rd WBLY HA9 67 K1
Strathdale STRHM/NOR SW16 149 F4
Strathdon Dr TOOT SW17 147 H2
Strathearn Av HYS/HAR UB3 101 J6
WHTN TW2 123 H7
Strathearn Cots
TRDG/WHET N20 * 38 E2
Strathearn Pl BAY/PAD W2 9 J6
Strathearn Rd SUT SM1 174 E4
WIM/MER SW19 146 E4
Stratheden Rd
BKHTH/KID SE3 113 K7
Strathfield Gdns BARK IG11 78 D5
Strathleven Rd
BRXS/STRHM SW2 129 K4
Strathmore Gdns EDGW HA8 50 F1
FNCH N3 39 F7
HCH RM12 63 H7
Strathmore Rd CROY/NA CR0 164 D6
TEDD TW11 142 E3
WIM/MER SW19 146 E2
Strathnairn St STHWK SE1 111 H3
Strathray Gdns HAMP NW3 * 71 J5
Strath Ter BTSEA SW11 128 D3
Strathville Rd
WAND/EARL SW18 146 E1
Strathyre Av
STRHM/NOR SW16 164 B2
Stratton Av WLGTN SM6 176 D7
Stratton Cl BXLYHN DA7 137 F2
EDGW HA8 36 B5
HSLW TW3 102 E7
WIM/MER SW19 161 J1
WOT/HER KT12 * 156 B7
Strattondale St POP/IOD E14 113 F2
Stratton Dr BARK IG11 78 E4
Stratton Gdns STHL UB1 83 K5
Stratton Rd BXLYHN DA7 137 F2
WIM/MER SW19 161 K1
Stratton St MYFR/PICC W1J 10 D8
Strauss Rd CHSWK W4 * 106 A1
Strawberry Hl CHSGTN KT9 171 K5
Strawberry Hill Rd TWK TW1 143 F2
Strawberry La CAR SM5 175 K2
Strawberry Ter MUSWH N10 * 39 K7
Strawberry V EFNCH N2 39 H7
TWK TW1 143 F2
Streakes Field Rd CRICK NW2 69 J1
Streamdale ABYW SE2 116 C5
Stream La EDGW HA8 36 D5
Streamline Ms EDUL SE22 131 J7
Streamside Cl ED N9 30 B7
HAYES BR2 167 K3
Stream Wy BELV DA17 117 H5
Streatfeild Av EHAM E6 77 K7
Streatfield Rd
KTN/HRWW/WS HA3 49 J2
Streatham Cl
STRHM/NOR SW16 * 148 E1
Streatham Common
STRHM/NOR SW16 * 148 D6
Streatham Common North
STRHM/NOR SW16 149 F4
Streatham Common South
STRHM/NOR SW16 148 E5
Streatham Ct
STRHM/NOR SW16 148 E2
Streatham Gn
STRHM/NOR SW16 * 148 E3
Streatham High Rd
STRHM/NOR SW16 148 E6
Streatham Hl
BRXS/STRHM SW2 129 K7
Streatham Pl
BRXS/STRHM SW2 129 K6
Streatham Rd MTCM CR4 148 A7
Streatham St
NOXST/BSQ WC1A 11 J4
Streatham V
STRHM/NOR SW16 148 C6
Streathbourne Rd TOOT SW17 148 A1
Streatleigh Pde
STRHM/NOR SW16 * 148 E1
Streatley Pl HAMP NW3 71 H3
Streatley Rd KIL/WHAMP NW6 70 D6
Streeters La WLGTN SM6 176 D2
Streetfield Ms BKHTH/KID SE3 133 K1
Streimer Rd SRTFD E15 94 A1
Strelley Wy ACT W3 87 G6
Stretton Rd CROY/NA CR0 165 F6
RCHPK/HAM TW10 143 J1
Strickland Av DART DA1 139 J2
Strickland Rw
WAND/EARL SW18 128 C6
Strickland St DEPT SE8 132 D1
Stride Rd PLSTW E13 94 D1
Strimon Cl ED N9 42 E1
Stripling Wy WATW WD18 20 E5
Strode Cl MUSWH N10 40 A6
Strode Rd FSTGT E7 76 E3
FUL/PGN SW6 107 G6
TOTM N17 56 A1
WLSDN NW10 69 J5
Strond Green Gdns
CROY/NA CR0 165 K6
Strond Green Wy
CROY/NA CR0 165 K6
Strone Rd FSTGT E7 77 G5
MNPK E12 77 H5
Strone Wy YEAD UB4 83 J3
Strongbow Crs ELTH/MOT SE9 134 E4
Strongbow Rd ELTH/MOT SE9 134 E4
Stronsa Rd SHB W12 106 C1
Strood Av ROMW/RG RM7 63 F7
Stroud Crs PUT/ROE SW15 145 H2
Stroudes Cl WPK KT4 160 C6
Stroud Fld NTHLT UB5 65 J5
Stroud Ga RYLN/HDSTN HA2 66 B3
Stroud Green Rd FSBYPK N4 55 F7
Stroud Green Wy
CROY/NA CR0 165 J6
Stroud Rd SNWD SE25 165 H5
WIM/MER SW19 146 E2
Strouds Cl CHDH RM6 61 H4
Strout's Pl BETH E2 7 L7
Strutton Gnd STJSPK SW1H 17 G3
Strype St WCHPL E1 13 L3
Stuart Av CDALE/KGS NW9 51 J6
EA W5 105 G1
HAYES BR2 167 K7
RYLN/HDSTN HA2 65 K2
WOT/HER KT12 156 B7
Stuart Ct BORE WD6 23 K5
Stuart Crs CROY/NA CR0 179 H2
HYS/HAR UB3 82 A5
WDGN N22 41 F7
Stuart Evans Cl WELL DA16 136 D2
Stuart Gv TEDD TW11 142 E4
Stuart Mantle Wy ERITH DA8 118 A6
Stuart Pl MTCM CR4 147 K7
Stuart Rd ACT W3 86 E7
BARK IG11 79 F7
EBAR EN4 27 J6
KIL/WHAMP NW6 2 A8
KTN/HRWW/WS HA3 49 F2
PECK SE15 131 K3
RCHPK/HAM TW10 143 H1
THHTH CR7 164 D3
WELL DA16 116 C7
WIM/MER SW19 146 E2
Stubbs Cl CDALE/KGS NW9 50 E4
Stubbs Dr BERM/RHTH SE16 111 J4
Stubbs Wy WIM/MER SW19 147 H7
Stucley Pl CAMTN NW1 4 D2
Stucley Rd HEST TW5 103 H6
Studdridge St FUL/PGN SW6 127 K1
Studd St IS N1 6 C3
Studholme Ct HAMP NW3 * 70 E3
Studholme St PECK SE15 111 J6
Studio Ms HDN NW4 52 A3
Studio Pl KTBR SW1X 15 M2
The Studios BUSH WD23 22 A5
Studio Wy BORE WD6 24 E1
Studland Cl BFN/LL DA15 155 F2
Studland Rd HNWL W7 84 D5
KUTN/CMB KT2 144 A5
SYD SE26 151 F4
Studland St HMSMTH W6 106 E3
Studley Av CHING E4 44 B6
Studley Cl CLPT E5 75 G4
Studley Ct SCUP DA14 155 H4
Studley Dr REDBR IG4 59 H5
Studley Grange Rd HNWL W7 103 K2
Studley Rd CLAP SW4 109 K7
DAGW RM9 79 K6
FSTGT E7 77 F5
Stukeley Rd FSTGT E7 77 F6
Stukeley St HOL/ALD WC2B 11 K4
Stumps Hill La BECK BR3 151 J5
Sturdy Rd PECK SE15 131 J1
Sturge Av WALTH E17 43 K7
Sturgeon Rd WALW SE17 18 E8
Sturges Fld CHST BR7 154 D5
Sturgess Av HDN NW4 51 K6
Sturge St STHWK SE1 18 E2
Sturmer Wy HOLWY N7 73 F4
Sturminster Cl YEAD UB4 83 G5
Sturrock Cl SEVS/STOTM N15 55 K3
Sturry St POP/IOD E14 93 K5
Sturt St IS N1 6 F5
Stutfield St WCHPL E1 92 C5
Styles Gdns BRXN/ST SW9 130 C2
Styles Wy BECK BR3 167 F3
Sudbourne Rd
BRXS/STRHM SW2 129 K4
Sudbrooke Rd BAL SW12 128 E5
Sudbrook Gdns
RCHPK/HAM TW10 144 A2
Sudbrook La
RCHPK/HAM TW10 125 F7
Sudbury EHAM E6 96 A5
Sudbury Av ALP/SUD HA0 67 J2
Sudbury Court Dr HRW HA1 67 G2
Sudbury Court Rd HRW HA1 67 G2
Sudbury Crs ALP/SUD HA0 67 H4
BMLY BR1 152 E4
Sudbury Cft ALP/SUD HA0 67 F3
Sudbury Gdns CROY/NA CR0 178 A3
Sudbury Heights Av
GFD/PVL UB6 67 F4
Sudbury Hl HRW HA1 67 F2
Sudbury Hill Cl ALP/SUD HA0 67 F2
Sudbury Rd BARK IG11 79 F4
Sudeley St IS N1 6 D6
Sudlow Rd WAND/EARL SW18 127 K3
Sudrey St STHWK SE1 18 E2
Suez Av GFD/PVL UB6 85 F1
Suez Rd PEND EN3 31 G3
Suffield Rd CHING E4 43 K2
PGE/AN SE20 165 K1
SEVS/STOTM N15 * 56 B4
Suffolk Cl BORE WD6 25 F4
Suffolk La CANST EC4R 13 G6
Suffolk Park Rd WALTH E17 57 G3
Suffolk Rd BARK IG11 78 D6
BARN SW13 106 C6
DAGE RM10 80 D4
DART DA1 139 H5
GDMY/SEVK IG3 60 E5
PEND EN3 30 D4
PLSTW E13 94 D2
RYLN/HDSTN HA2 47 K5
SCUP DA14 155 J5
SEVS/STOTM N15 55 K5
SNWD SE25 165 G3
WLSDN NW10 69 G6
WPK KT4 173 H1
Suffolk St FSTGT E7 76 E4
STJS SW1Y 11 H8
Suffolk Vls
WAND/EARL SW18 * 127 K6
Sugar House La SRTFD E15 94 A1
Sugar Loaf Wk BETH E2 * 92 E2
Sugden Rd BTSEA SW11 129 F2
THDIT KT7 158 B7
Sugden Wy BARK IG11 97 F1
Sulgrave Gdns HMSMTH W6 107 F1
Sulgrave Rd HMSMTH W6 107 F1
Sulina Rd BRXS/STRHM SW2 129 K6
Sulivan Ct FUL/PGN SW6 127 K1
Sulivan Rd FUL/PGN SW6 127 K2
Sullivan Av CAN/RD E16 95 H4
Sullivan Cl BTSEA SW11 128 D2
DART DA1 138 E5
E/WMO/HCT KT8 157 F2
YEAD UB4 83 G4
Sullivan Rd LBTH SE11 18 B5
Sullivan Wy BORE WD6 23 J5
Sultan Rd WAN E11 59 F3
Sultan St BECK BR3 166 A1
CMBW SE5 110 D6
Sumatra Rd KIL/WHAMP NW6 70 E5
Sumburgh Rd BAL SW12 129 F5
Summer Av E/WMO/HCT KT8 157 K4
Summer Crossing THDIT KT7 158 A4
Summerene Cl
STRHM/NOR SW16 148 C6
Summerfield Av
KIL/WHAMP NW6 88 C1
NFNCH/WDSPK N12 39 J5
Summerfield La SURB KT6 171 K1
Summerfield Rd EA W5 85 H3
Summerfield St
LEE/GVPK SE12 133 J6
Summer Gdns
E/WMO/HCT KT8 157 K4
Summer Gv BORE WD6 23 K5
Summer Hl BORE WD6 24 C4
CHST BR7 169 F1
Summerhill Gv EN EN1 30 A5
Summerhill Rd DART DA1 139 G6
SEVS/STOTM N15 55 K3
Summerhill Wy MTCM CR4 148 A7
Summerhouse Av HEST TW5 102 D7
Summerhouse La
WDR/YW UB7 100 A5
Summerhouse Rd
STNW/STAM N16 74 A1
Summerland Gdns
MUSWH N10 54 B2
Summerlands Av ACT W3 86 E6
Summerlee Av EFNCH N2 53 K3
Summerlee Gdns EFNCH N2 53 K3
Summerley St
WAND/EARL SW18 147 F1
Summer Pl WATW WD18 * 20 D5
Summer Rd E/WMO/HCT KT8 157 J4
THDIT KT7 158 A4
Summersby Rd HGT N6 54 B5
Summers Cl BELMT SM2 174 E6
WBLY HA9 50 D7
Summerskille Cl ED N9 42 D1
Summers La
NFNCH/WDSPK N12 39 H6
Summers Rw
NFNCH/WDSPK N12 39 J5
Summers St CLKNW EC1R 12 A1
Summerstown TOOT SW17 147 G2
Summers Wd BORE WD6 * 24 D3
Summerton Wy THMD SE28 97 K6
Summer Trees SUN TW16 141 F7
Summerville Gdns SUT SM1 174 D5
Summerwood Rd ISLW TW7 124 A5
TWK TW1 124 A5
Summit Av CDALE/KGS NW9 51 F4
Summit Cl CDALE/KGS NW9 51 F3
EDGW HA8 36 C6
STHGT/OAK N14 40 C1
Summit Dr WFD IG8 59 H1
Summit Est
STNW/STAM N16 * 56 C6
Summit Rd NTHLT UB5 66 A6
WALTH E17 57 K3
Summit Wy NRWD SE19 150 A6
STHGT/OAK N14 40 B1
Sumner Av PECK SE15 * 111 G7
Sumner Gdns CROY/NA CR0 164 B7
Sumner Pl SKENS SW7 15 H6
Sumner Place Ms SKENS SW7 15 H6
Sumner Rd CROY/NA CR0 164 C7
HRW HA1 48 C6
PECK SE15 111 G7
Sumner Rd South
CROY/NA CR0 164 B7
Sumner St STHWK SE1 12 E8
Sumpter Cl HAMP NW3 71 G5
Sunbeam Crs NKENS W10 88 A3
Sunbeam Rd WLSDN NW10 86 E3
Sunbury Av MLHL NW7 37 F4
MORT/ESHN SW14 126 A3
Sunbury Ct BAR EN5 * 26 C3
SUN TW16 156 C1
Sunbury Court Rd SUN TW16 156 B1
Sunbury Gdns MLHL NW7 37 F4
Sunbury La BTSEA SW11 108 C7
Sunbury Rd CHEAM SM3 174 B2
FELT TW13 140 D2
Sunbury St WOOL/PLUM SE18 114 E2
Sunbury Wy FELT TW13 141 G4
Sun Ct ERITH DA8 138 C1
Suncroft Pl SYD SE26 150 E2
Sundeala Cl SUN TW16 140 E6
Sunderland Mt FSTH SE23 * 151 F1
Sunderland Rd EA W5 104 E2
FSTH SE23 132 A7
Sunderland Ter BAY/PAD W2 8 C4
Sunderland Wy MNPK E12 77 H1
Sundew Av SHB W12 87 J6
Sundew Ct ALP/SUD HA0 * 86 A1
Sundial Av SNWD SE25 165 G1
Sundial Rd MNPK E12 77 J2
Sundorne Rd CHARL SE7 114 A4
Sundown Rd ASHF TW15 140 A4
Sundridge Av BMLY BR1 153 H7
WELL DA16 135 J1
Sundridge Cl DART DA1 139 K5
Sundridge Pde BMLY BR1 * 153 F6
Sundridge Pl CROY/NA CR0 165 H7
Sundridge Rd CROY/NA CR0 165 G7
Sunfields Pl BKHTH/KID SE3 114 A6
Sun in Sands Rbt
BKHTH/KID SE3 113 K6
Sunken Rd CROY/NA CR0 178 E4
Sunkist Wy WLGTN SM6 176 E7
Sunland Av BXLYHS DA6 137 F3
Sun La BKHTH/KID SE3 114 A6
Sunleigh Rd ALP/SUD HA0 68 A7
Sunley Gdns GFD/PVL UB6 85 G1
Sunlight Cl WIM/MER SW19 * 147 G5
Sunlight Sq BETH E2 92 D2
Sunna Gdns SUN TW16 156 A1
Sunningdale STHGT/OAK N14 40 D4
Sunningdale Av ACT W3 87 G6
BARK IG11 78 D7
FELT TW13 141 J1
RAIN RM13 99 K3
RSLP HA4 47 G7
Sunningdale Cl
BERM/RHTH SE16 * 111 J4
STAN HA7 35 G6
SURB KT6 172 A1
THMD SE28 98 A5
Sunningdale Gdns
CDALE/KGS NW9 50 E4
KENS W8 14 B4
Sunningdale Ldg EDGW HA8 * 36 B4
Sunningdale Rd BMLY BR1 168 D3
RAIN RM13 81 J6
SUT SM1 174 D2
Sunningfield Rd HDN NW4 51 K2
Sunningfields Crs HDN NW4 51 K1
Sunninghill Ct ACT W3 * 105 K1
Sunninghill Rd LEW SE13 132 E1
Sunny Bank SNWD SE25 165 H2
Sunny Crs WLSDN NW10 68 E6
Sunnycroft Rd HSLW TW3 123 G1
SNWD SE25 165 H3
STHL UB1 84 A4
Sunnydale Gdns MLHL NW7 37 F5
Sunnydale Rd LEE/GVPK SE12 134 A4
Sunnydene Av CHING E4 44 B4
RSLP HA4 46 E7
Sunnydene Gdns
ALP/SUD HA0 67 J5
Sunnydene St SYD SE26 151 G3
Sunnyfield MLHL NW7 37 H3
Sunny Gardens Rd HDN NW4 52 A2
Sunny Hl HDN NW4 51 K2
Sunnyhill Cl CLPT E5 75 G3
Sunnyhill Rd
STRHM/NOR SW16 148 E3
Sunnyhurst Cl SUT SM1 174 E2
Sunnymead Av MTCM CR4 163 J2
Sunnymead Rd
CDALE/KGS NW9 51 F6
PUT/ROE SW15 126 E4
Sunnymede Av
HOR/WEW KT19 173 G7
Sunnymede Dr BARK/HLT IG6 60 B3
Sunny Nook Gdns
SAND/SEL CR2 177 K5
Sunny Pl HDN NW4 52 A3
Sunnyside CAT SE6 * 132 C6
CRICK NW2 70 D2
WOT/HER KT12 156 B4
Sunnyside Pl WIM/MER SW19 146 C5
Sunnyside Rd ARCH N19 54 D6
EA W5 85 K7
IL IG1 78 C2
LEY E10 57 J7
TEDD TW11 142 D3
Sunnyside Rd East ED N9 42 C2
Sunnyside Rd North ED N9 42 B2
Sunnyside Rd South ED N9 42 B2
Sunny Vw CDALE/KGS NW9 51 F4
Sunny Wy NFNCH/WDSPK N12 39 J6
Sun Pas BERM/RHTH SE16 111 H2
Sunray Av BRYLDS KT5 172 D1
HAYES BR2 168 D5
HNHL SE24 130 E3
WDR/YW UB7 100 A1
Sunrise Cl FELT TW13 141 K2
Sun Rd WKENS W14 107 J4
Sunset Av CHING E4 31 K7
WFD IG8 44 E4
Sunset Cl ERITH DA8 118 E6
Sunset Gdns SNWD SE25 165 F1
Sunset Rd HNHL SE24 130 D3
THMD SE28 97 G7
WIM/MER SW19 145 K4
Sunset Vw BAR EN5 26 C1
Sunshine Wy MTCM CR4 162 E1
Sun St SDTCH EC2A 13 H2
Surbiton Ct SURB KT6 158 D5
Surbiton Court Ms SURB KT6 158 E5
Surbiton Crs KUT/HW KT1 159 F3
Surbiton Hall Cl KUT/HW KT1 159 F3
Surbiton Hl Pk BRYLDS KT5 159 G4
Surbiton Hill Rd SURB KT6 159 F3
Surbiton Rd KUT/HW KT1 158 E3
Surlingham Cl THMD SE28 97 K6
Surma Cl WCHPL E1 92 C3
Surmans Cl DAGW RM9 79 J7
Surrendale Pl MV/WKIL W9 8 B1
Surrey Canal Rd PECK SE15 111 K5
Surrey Cl FNCH N3 52 C2
Surrey Crs CHSWK W4 105 H4
Surrey Gdns FSBYPK N4 55 J5
Surrey Gv SUT SM1 175 H2
WALW SE17 19 J8
Surrey La BTSEA SW11 108 D7
Surrey Ms WNWD SE27 150 A3
Surrey Mt FSTH SE23 131 J7
Surrey Quays Rd
BERM/RHTH SE16 111 K2
Surrey Rd BARK IG11 78 E6
DAGE RM10 80 D4
HRW HA1 48 C5
PECK SE15 132 A4
WWKM BR4 166 E7
Surrey Rw STHWK SE1 18 C1
Surrey Sq WALW SE17 19 J7
Surrey St CROY/NA CR0 177 J2
PLSTW E13 95 F2
TPL/STR WC2R 11 M6
Surrey Ter WALW SE17 19 K6
Surrey Water Rd
BERM/RHTH SE16 93 F7
Surridge Gdns NRWD SE19 149 K5
Surr St HOLWY N7 72 E4
Sury Basin KUTN/CMB KT2 144 A7
Susan Cl ROMW/RG RM7 62 E2
Susannah St POP/IOD E14 93 K5
Susan Rd BKHTH/KID SE3 134 A1
Susan Wd CHST BR7 154 A7
Sussex Av ISLW TW7 123 K2
Sussex Cl ARCH N19 * 72 E1
NWMAL KT3 160 B3
REDBR IG4 59 K5
TWK TW1 124 C5
Sussex Crs NTHLT UB5 66 A5
Sussex Gdns BAY/PAD W2 9 H4
CHSGTN KT9 171 K5
FSBYPK N4 55 J4
HGT N6 53 K4
Sussex Ga HGT N6 * 53 K4
Sussex Ms East BAY/PAD W2 * 9 H6
Sussex Ms West BAY/PAD W2 9 H6
Sussex Pl BAY/PAD W2 9 H5
CAMTN NW1 3 L9
HMSMTH W6 107 F4
NWMAL KT3 160 B3
Sussex Ring
NFNCH/WDSPK N12 38 E4
Sussex Rd CAR SM5 175 K5
DART DA1 139 K6
EHAM E6 96 A1
ERITH DA8 117 J6
HGDN/ICK UB10 64 A3
HRW HA1 48 C4
MTCM CR4 * 163 K4
NWDGN UB2 102 C2
NWMAL KT3 160 B3
SAND/SEL CR2 177 K5
SCUP DA14 155 H4
WWKM BR4 166 E7
Sussex Sq BAY/PAD W2 9 H6
Sussex St PIM SW1V 16 D8
PLSTW E13 95 F2
Sussex Ter PGE/AN SE20 * 150 E6
Sussex Wy ARCH N19 54 D7
EBAR EN4 28 B4
Sutcliffe Cl BUSH WD23 22 C3
GLDGN NW11 53 F4
Sutcliffe Rd WELL DA16 136 D1
WOOL/PLUM SE18 115 K5
Sutherland Av HYS/HAR UB3 101 K3
MV/WKIL W9 2 E8
MV/WKIL W9 8 B1
WEA W13 85 H5
WELL DA16 135 J3
Sutherland Cl BAR EN5 26 C3
Sutherland Ct
CDALE/KGS NW9 50 D3
Sutherland Dr
WIM/MER SW19 147 H7
Sutherland Gdns
MORT/ESHN SW14 126 B2
WPK KT4 160 E7
Sutherland Gv TEDD TW11 142 E4
WAND/EARL SW18 127 J6
Sutherland House
WALTH E17 * 57 G2
Sutherland Pl BAY/PAD W2 8 A4
Sutherland Rd BELV DA17 117 H2
BOW E3 93 H1
CHSWK W4 106 A5
CROY/NA CR0 164 B6
ED N9 30 C7
PEND EN3 31 F5
STHL UB1 83 K5
TOTM N17 42 C6
WALTH E17 57 F1
WEA W13 85 G5
Sutherland Rw PIM SW1V 16 D7
Sutherland Sq WALW SE17 18 E8
Sutherland St PIM SW1V 16 D7
Sutherland Vls WEA W13 * 85 G6
Sutherland Wk WALW SE17 18 F8
Sutlej Rd CHARL SE7 114 B6
Sutterton St HOLWY N7 73 F5
Sutton Cl BECK BR3 151 K7
CHSWK W4 * 105 K5
PIN HA5 46 E4
Sutton Common Rd
CHEAM SM3 161 J6
Sutton Ct BELMT SM2 175 G6
CHSWK W4 * 105 K5
EA W5 * 86 A7
Sutton Court Rd CHSWK W4 105 K5
PLSTW E13 95 G2
SUT SM1 175 G5
Sutton Crs BAR EN5 26 B4
Sutton Dene HSLW TW3 103 G7
Sutton Dwelling Est
CHEL SW3 15 J7
Sutton Est IS N1 * 6 C1
The Sutton Est IS N1 6 C2
Sutton Gdns CROY/NA CR0 165 G4
Sutton Gv SUT SM1 175 H4
Sutton Hall Rd HEST TW5 103 F6
Sutton La FARR EC1M 12 D1
HSLW TW3 122 E1
Sutton La North CHSWK W4 105 K4
Sutton La South CHSWK W4 105 K5
Sutton Park Rd SUT SM1 175 F5
Sutton Pl HOM E9 74 E4
Sutton Rd BARK IG11 96 E1
HEST TW5 103 F7
MUSWH N10 40 A7
PLSTW E13 94 D3
WALTH E17 43 F7
WAT WD17 21 G2
Sutton Rw SOHO/SHAV W1D 11 G4
Sutton Sq HEST TW5 102 E7
HOM E9 * 74 E4
Sutton St WCHPL E1 92 E5
Sutton Wy HEST TW5 102 E7
NKENS W10 88 A4
STLK EC1Y 12 F1
Swaby Rd WAND/EARL SW18 147 G1
Swaffield Rd
WAND/EARL SW18 128 B6
Swain Cl STRHM/NOR SW16 148 B5

Swain Rd THHTH CR7 164 D4
Swains Cl WDR/YW UB7 100 B1
Swain's La HGT N6 72 A2
Swainson Rd ACT W3 106 C1
Swains Rd MTCM CR4 147 K6
Swain St STJWD NW8 3 J9
Swaisland Rd DART DA1 138 E4
Swaislands Dr DART DA1 138 C4
Swaledale Cl FBAR/BDGN N11 40 A5
Swale Rd DART DA1 138 D2
Swallands Rd CAT SE6 151 J2
Swallow Cl BUSH WD23 22 B7
ERITH DA8 118 B7
NWCR SE14 111 K7
Swallow Ct RSLP HA4 * 47 G7
Swallowdale SAND/SEL CR2 179 F7
Swallow Dr NTHLT UB5 84 A1
WLSDN NW10 69 F5
Swallowfield Rd CHARL SE7 114 A4
Swallowfield Wy
HYS/HAR UB3 101 G1
Swallow Gdns
STRHM/NOR SW16 148 D4
Swallow Pl REGST W1B 10 D5
Swallow St EHAM E6 95 J4
REGST W1B 10 F7
Swanage Rd CHING E4 44 A6
WAND/EARL SW18 128 B5
Swanage Waye YEAD UB4 83 G5
Swan Ap EHAM E6 95 J4
Swanbridge Rd BXLYHN DA7 117 H7
Swan Cl CROY/NA CR0 * 165 F6
FELT TW13 141 J3
WALTH E17 43 G7
Swandon Wy
WAND/EARL SW18 128 A3
Swan Dr CDALE/KGS NW9 51 G1
Swanfield St BETH E2 7 L8
Swan Island TWK TW1 * 143 G2
Swan La CANST EC4R 13 G7
DART DA1 138 C6
TRDG/WHET N20 39 G2
Swanley Rd WELL DA16 116 D7
Swan Md STHWK SE1 19 J4
Swan Ms BRXN/ST SW9 130 A1
Swan Pas WCHPL E1 13 M7
Swan Pl BARN SW13 126 C1
Swan Rd BERM/RHTH SE16 111 K1
FELT TW13 141 J3
STHL UB1 84 B5
WDR/YW UB7 100 A1
WOOL/PLUM SE18 114 C2
Swanscombe Rd CHSWK W4 106 B4
NTGHL W11 88 B7
Swansea Rd HTHAIR TW6 121 F5
PEND EN3 30 E3
Swanston Pth OXHEY WD19 33 G2
Swan St ISLW TW7 124 C2
STHWK SE1 18 F2
Swanton Gdns
WIM/MER SW19 127 G7
Swanton Rd ERITH DA8 117 H6
Swan Wk CHEL SW3 15 L9
Swan Wy PEND EN3 31 F1
Swanwick Cl PUT/ROE SW15 126 C6
Swan Yd IS N1 73 H5
Swaton Rd BOW E3 93 J3
Swaylands Rd BELV DA17 117 H5
Swaythling Cl UED N18 42 D3
Swedenbourg Gdns
WCHPL E1 92 C6
Sweden Ga BERM/RHTH SE16 112 B3
Sweeney Crs STHWK SE1 19 M2
Sweet Briar Gn ED N9 42 B2
Sweet Briar Gv ED N9 42 B2
Sweet Briar Wk UED N18 42 B3
Sweetmans Av PIN HA5 47 H2
Sweets Wy TRDG/WHET N20 39 H1
Swete St PLSTW E13 94 E1
Sweyn Pl BKHTH/KID SE3 133 K1
Swift Cl HYS/HAR UB3 82 D5
RYLN/HDSTN HA2 66 B1
THMD SE28 97 H5
WALTH E17 43 G6
Swift Rd FELT TW13 141 H3
NWDGN UB2 102 E2
Swiftsden Wy BMLY BR1 152 C5
Swift St FUL/PGN SW6 107 H7
Swinbrook Rd NKENS W10 88 C4
Swinburne Crs CROY/NA CR0 165 K5
Swinburne Rd PUT/ROE SW15 126 D3
Swinderby Rd ALP/SUD HA0 68 A5
Swindon Cl GDMY/SEVK IG3 78 E1
Swindon Rd HTHAIR TW6 121 F4
Swindon St SHB W12 * 87 K7
Swinfield Cl FELT TW13 141 J3
Swinford Gdns BRXN/ST SW9 130 C2
Swingate La
WOOL/PLUM SE18 115 K6
Swinnerton St HOM E9 75 G4
Swinton Cl WBLY HA9 50 D7
Swinton Pl FSBYW WC1X 5 L7
Swinton St FSBYW WC1X 5 L7
Swires Shaw HAYES BR2 181 H3
Swiss Av WATW WD18 20 C3
Swiss Cl WATW WD18 20 C2
Swithland Gdns
ELTH/MOT SE9 153 K3
Swyncombe Av EA W5 104 C3
Swynford Gdns HDN NW4 51 J3
Sybil Phoenix Cl DEPT SE8 112 A4
Sybourn St WALTH E17 57 H6
Sycamore
RKW/CH/CXG WD3 20 A4
Sycamore Av BFN/LL DA15 136 A5
BOW E3 75 H7
EA W5 104 E2
HYS/HAR UB3 82 C6
Sycamore Cl ACT W3 87 G7
BUSH WD23 21 J1
CAN/RD E16 94 C3
CAR SM5 175 K3
EBAR EN4 27 H5
ED N9 42 C3
EDGW HA8 36 E3
FELT TW13 140 E2
NTHLT UB5 65 J7
SAND/SEL CR2 178 A4
Sycamore Gdns MTCM CR4 162 C1
SHB W12 106 E1
Sycamore Gv CAT SE6 133 F5
CDALE/KGS NW9 50 E6
GPK RM2 63 J1
NWMAL KT3 160 B2
PGE/AN SE20 150 C7
Sycamore Hl FBAR/BDGN N11 40 A5
Sycamore Ms CLAP SW4 129 H2
ERITH DA8 * 118 A4
Sycamore Rd DART DA1 139 G6
RKW/CH/CXG WD3 20 A4
WIM/MER SW19 146 A5
Sycamore St FSBYE EC1V 12 E1
Sycamore Wk NKENS W10 88 C3
Sycamore Wy TEDD TW11 143 J5
Sydcote DUL SE21 * 149 J1
Sydenham Av SYD SE26 150 D4
Sydenham Cl ROM RM1 63 H3
Sydenham Cots
LEE/GVPK SE12 * 153 G1
Sydenham Hl FSTH SE23 150 D1
SYD SE26 150 C2
Sydenham Pk SYD SE26 150 E2
Sydenham Park Rd SYD SE26 150 E2
Sydenham Ri FSTH SE23 150 D1
Sydenham Rd CROY/NA CR0 177 J1
SYD SE26 151 F4
Sydenham Station Ap
SYD SE26 150 E3
Sydmons Ct FSTH SE23 * 131 K6
Sydner Ms STNW/STAM N16 74 B3
Sydner Rd STNW/STAM N16 74 B3
Sydney Chapman Wy
BAR EN5 26 D1
Sydney Cl SKENS SW7 15 H6
Sydney Gv HDN NW4 52 A4
Sydney Ms CHEL SW3 15 H6
Sydney Pl SKENS SW7 15 H6
Sydney Rd ABYW SE2 116 E2
BARK/HLT IG6 60 C1
BXLYHS DA6 136 E3
CEND/HSY/T N8 55 G3
EBED/NFELT TW14 121 K7
ENC/FH EN2 29 K3
MUSWH N10 40 B7
RCH/KEW TW9 125 F3
RYNPK SW20 161 G1
SCUP DA14 154 E3
SUT SM1 174 E3
TEDD TW11 143 F4
WAN E11 59 F5
WATW WD18 20 C4
WEA W13 85 G7
WFD IG8 44 E3
Sydney St CHEL SW3 15 J7
Sydney Ter ESH/CLAY KT10 * 171 F5
Sylvan Av CHDH RM6 62 B5
MLHL NW7 37 G5
WDGN N22 41 G6
Sylvan Gdns SURB KT6 158 E6
Sylvan Gv CRICK NW2 70 B3
PECK SE15 111 J5
Sylvan Hl NRWD SE19 150 A7
Sylvan Rd FSTGT E7 76 E5
IL IG1 78 C1
NRWD SE19 150 B7
WALTH E17 * 57 J4
WAN E11 58 E4
Sylvan Ter PECK SE15 * 111 J6
Sylvan Wk BMLY BR1 168 E2
Sylvan Wy BCTR RM8 79 H3
WWKM BR4 180 C3
Sylverdale Rd CROY/NA CR0 177 H2
Sylvester Av CHST BR7 153 K5
Sylvester Pth HACK E8 * 74 D5
Sylvester Rd ALP/SUD HA0 67 J4
EFNCH N2 53 G1
HACK E8 * 74 D5
WALTH E17 * 57 H6
Sylvia Av PIN HA5 33 K5
Sylvia Gdns WBLY HA9 68 D6
Symes Ms CAMTN NW1 4 E5
Symington Ms HOM E9 75 F4
Symister Ms IS N1 7 J8
Symons Cl PECK SE15 131 K1
Symons St CHEL SW3 15 M6
KTBR SW1X 15 M6
Symphony Cl EDGW HA8 36 D6
Symphony Ms NKENS W10 88 C2
Syon Gate Wy BTFD TW8 104 B6
Syon La ISLW TW7 104 B6
Syon Pk ISLW TW7 * 124 C2
Syon Park Gdns ISLW TW7 104 A6

T

Tabard Garden Est
STHWK SE1 19 G1
Tabard St STHWK SE1 19 G2
Tabernacle Av PLSTW E13 94 E3
Tabernacle St SDTCH EC2A 13 H1
Tableer Av CLAP SW4 129 H4
Tabley Rd HOLWY N7 72 E3
Tabor Gdns CHEAM SM3 174 C5
Tabor Gv WIM/MER SW19 146 C6
Tabor Rd HMSMTH W6 106 E2
Tachbrook Rd
EBED/NFELT TW14 121 J6
NWDGN UB2 102 C3
Tachbrook St PIM SW1V 16 E7
Tack Ms BROCKY SE4 132 D2
Tadema Rd WBPTN SW10 108 B6
Tadmor St SHB W12 88 B7
Tadworth Av NWMAL KT3 160 C4
Tadworth Pde HCH RM12 81 K3
Tadworth Rd CRICK NW2 69 J1
Taeping St POP/IOD E14 112 E3
Taffy's How MTCM CR4 162 D2
Tait Ct BOW E3 75 H7
Tait Rd CROY/NA CR0 165 F6
Tait St WCHPL E1 92 D5
Takeley Cl CRW RM5 63 F1
Talacre Rd KTTN NW5 72 A5
Talbot Av EFNCH N2 53 H2
OXHEY WD19 21 J6
Talbot Cl SEVS/STOTM N15 56 B3
Talbot Ct BANK EC3V 13 H6
Talbot Crs HDN NW4 51 J4
Talbot Gdns GDMY/SEVK IG3 79 G1
Talbot Pl BKHTH/KID SE3 133 H1
Talbot Rd ALP/SUD HA0 67 K4
BAY/PAD W2 8 B4
CAR SM5 176 A4
DAGW RM9 80 B6
EDUL SE22 131 F3
EHAM E6 95 K1
FSTGT E7 76 E3
HGT N6 54 A5
ISLW TW7 124 B3
KTN/HRWW/WS HA3 49 F1
NTGHL W11 88 D5
NWDGN UB2 102 D3
SEVS/STOTM N15 56 B3
THHTH CR7 164 E3
WDGN N22 54 C1
WEA W13 * 85 G6
WHTN TW2 123 K7
Talbot Sq BAY/PAD W2 9 G5
Talbot Wk NTGHL W11 88 C5
WLSDN NW10 * 69 G5
Talbot Yd STHWK SE1 13 G9
Talcott Pth
BRXS/STRHM SW2 * 130 B7
Talehangers Cl BXLYHS DA6 136 E3
Talfourd Pl PECK SE15 111 G7
Talfourd Rd PECK SE15 111 G7
Talgarth Rd HMSMTH W6 * 107 F4
WKENS W14 107 H4
Talgarth Wk CDALE/KGS NW9 51 G4
Talisman Cl GDMY/SEVK IG3 61 H7
Talisman Sq SYD SE26 150 C3
Talisman Wy WBLY HA9 68 B2
Tallack Cl KTN/HRWW/WS HA3 34 E6
Tallack Rd LEY E10 57 H7
Tall Elms Cl HAYES BR2 167 J4
Tallis Cl CAN/RD E16 95 F5
Tallis Gv CHARL SE7 114 A5
Tallis St EMB EC4Y 12 B6
Tallis Vw WLSDN NW10 69 F5
Tallow Cl DAGW RM9 79 K5
Tallow Rd BTFD TW8 104 D5
Tall Trees STRHM/NOR SW16 164 A2
Talma Gdns WHTN TW2 123 K6
Talmage Cl FSTH SE23 131 K6
Talman Gv STAN HA7 35 K5
Talma Rd BRXS/STRHM SW2 130 B3
Talwin St BOW E3 93 K2
Tamar Cl BOW E3 * 75 H7
Tamarind Yd WAP E1W 92 C7
Tamarisk Sq SHB W12 87 H6
Tamar St CHARL SE7 114 D3
Tamesis Gdns WPK KT4 173 G1
Tamian Wy HSLWW TW4 122 B3
Tamworth Av WFD IG8 44 C5
Tamworth La MTCM CR4 163 G2
Tamworth Pk MTCM CR4 163 G3
Tamworth Pl CROY/NA CR0 * 177 J1
Tamworth Rd CROY/NA CR0 177 J1
Tamworth St FUL/PGN SW6 14 A9
Tancred Rd FSBYPK N4 55 H5
Tandridge Dr ORP BR6 169 J7
Tanfield Av CRICK NW2 69 H3
Tanfield Rd CROY/NA CR0 177 J3
Tangier Rd RCHPK/HAM TW10 125 H3
Tangleberry Cl BMLY BR1 168 E3
Tangle Tree Cl FNCH N3 53 F1
Tanglewood Cl CROY/NA CR0 178 E2
STAN HA7 34 E1
Tanglewood Wy FELT TW13 141 F2
Tangley Gv PUT/ROE SW15 126 C6
Tangley Park Rd HPTN TW12 * 141 K4
Tangmere Crs HCH RM12 81 K5
Tangmere Gdns NTHLT UB5 83 G1
Tangmere Gv KUTN/CMB KT2 143 K4
Tangmere Wy
CDALE/KGS NW9 51 G1
Tanhouse Fld KTTN NW5 * 72 D4
Tankerton Houses
STPAN WC1H * 5 K8
Tankerton Rd SURB KT6 172 B1
Tankerton St STPAN WC1H 5 K8
Tankerton Ter CROY/NA CR0 * 164 A6
Tankerville Rd
STRHM/NOR SW16 148 D6
Tank Hill Rd PUR RM19 119 K2
Tankridge Rd CRICK NW2 69 K1
The Tanneries WCHPL E1 * 92 E3
Tanners Cl WOT/HER KT12 156 A5
Tanners End La UED N18 42 A3
Tanner's Hl DEPT SE8 112 D7
Tanners La BARK/HLT IG6 60 C2
Tanners Ms DEPT SE8 112 C7
Tanner St BARK IG11 78 C5
STHWK SE1 19 K2
Tannery Cl CROY/NA CR0 166 A4
DAGE RM10 80 D2
Tannington Ter HBRY N5 73 G2
Tannsby Sq WNWD SE27 149 K3
Tannsfeld Rd SYD SE26 151 F4
Tansley Cl HOLWY N7 72 D4
Tanswell St STHWK SE1 * 18 A2
Tansy Cl EHAM E6 96 A5
Tantallon Rd BAL SW12 129 F7
Tant Av CAN/RD E16 94 D5
Tantony Gv CHDH RM6 61 K2
Tanworth Cl NTHWD HA6 32 A5
Tanworth Gdns PIN HA5 47 F1
Tan Yard La BXLY DA5 * 137 H6
Tanza Rd HAMP NW3 71 K3
Tapestry Cl BELMT SM2 175 F6
Taplow Ct MTCM CR4 162 D3
Taplow Rd PLMGR N13 41 J3
Taplow St IS N1 6 F6
Tappesfield Rd PECK SE15 131 K2
Tapping Cl KUTN/CMB KT2 * 144 C6
Tapp St WCHPL E1 92 D3
Tapster St BAR EN5 26 D2
Tara Ms CEND/HSY/T N8 54 E6
Taransay Wk IS N1 73 K5
Tara Ter BROCKY SE4 * 132 B2
Tarbert Rd EDUL SE22 131 F4
Tarbert Wk WCHPL E1 92 E6
Target Cl EBED/NFELT TW14 121 H5
Tariff Rd UED N18 42 C5
Tarleton Gdns FSTH SE23 131 J7
Tarling Cl SCUP DA14 155 H2
Tarling Rd CAN/RD E16 94 D5
EFNCH N2 39 G7
Tarling St WCHPL E1 92 E5
Tarnbank ENC/FH EN2 28 E4
Tarn St STHWK SE1 18 E4
Tarnwood Pk ELTH/MOT SE9 134 E7
Tarragon Cl NWCR SE14 112 B6
Tarragon Gv SYD SE26 151 F5
Tarrant Pl MBLAR W1H 9 L3
Tarriff Crs DEPT SE8 112 C3
Tarrington Cl
STRHM/NOR SW16 148 D3
Tarver Rd WALW SE17 18 D8
Tarves Wy GNWCH SE10 112 E6
Tash Pl FBAR/BDGN N11 * 40 B4
Tasker Cl HYS/HAR UB3 101 F6
Tasker Rd HAMP NW3 71 K4
Tasmania Ter UED N18 41 J5
Tasman Rd BRXN/ST SW9 129 K2
Tasso Rd HMSMTH W6 107 H5
Tate Gdns BUSH WD23 22 E6
Tate Rd CAN/RD E16 95 K7
SUT SM1 174 E4
Tatham Pl STJWD NW8 3 H5
Tatnell Rd FSTH SE23 132 B5
Tattersall Cl ELTH/MOT SE9 134 D4
Tatton Cl CAR SM5 163 F7
Tatton Crs CLPT E5 56 B6
Tatum Rd WLSDN NW10 68 E6
Tatum St WALW SE17 19 H6
Tauber Cl BORE WD6 24 B3
Tauheed Cl FSBYPK N4 73 J1
Taunton Av HSLW TW3 123 H1
RYNPK SW20 160 E1
Taunton Cl BXLYHN DA7 138 A2
CHEAM SM3 161 K7
Taunton Dr EFNCH N2 53 G1
ENC/FH EN2 29 G2
Taunton Ms CAMTN NW1 9 L1
Taunton Pl CAMTN NW1 3 L9
Taunton Rd GFD/PVL UB6 66 B6
LEE/GVPK SE12 133 H4
Taunton Wy STAN HA7 50 A1
Tavern Cl CAR SM5 162 D6
Taverners Cl NTGHL W11 88 C7
Taverner Sq HBRY N5 * 73 J3
Tavistock Av GFD/PVL UB6 85 G1
MLHL NW7 38 B6
WALTH E17 57 F2
Tavistock Cl
STNW/STAM N16 * 74 A4
Tavistock Ct COVGDN WC2E * 11 K6
Tavistock Crs MTCM CR4 163 K3
NTGHL W11 88 D4
Tavistock Gdns
GDMY/SEVK IG3 78 E3
Tavistock Gv CROY/NA CR0 164 E6
Tavistock Ms NTGHL W11 * 88 D5
Tavistock Pl STHGT/OAK N14 * 28 B5
STPAN WC1H 5 H9
Tavistock Rd CAR SM5 162 C7
CROY/NA CR0 164 E7
EDGW HA8 36 B7
FSBYPK N4 55 K5
HAYES BR2 167 K3
HGDN/ICK UB10 64 B4
NTGHL W11 88 D4
SRTFD E15 76 D5
SWFD E18 58 E2
WAN E11 76 D3
WELL DA16 116 D7
WLSDN NW10 87 H1
Tavistock Sq STPAN WC1H 5 H9
Tavistock St COVGDN WC2E 11 K6
HOL/ALD WC2B 11 L6
Tavistock Ter ARCH N19 72 D2
Taviton St STPAN WC1H 5 G9
Tavy Br ABYW SE2 116 D1
Tavy Cl LBTH SE11 18 B7
Tawney Rd THMD SE28 97 H6
Tawny Cl FELT TW13 140 E2
WEA W13 85 H7
Tawny Wy BERM/RHTH SE16 112 A3
Tayben Av WHTN TW2 123 K5
Taybridge Rd BTSEA SW11 129 F2
Tayburn Cl POP/IOD E14 94 A5
Tayfield Cl HGDN/ICK UB10 64 A2
Taylor Av RCH/KEW TW9 125 J1
Taylor Cl DEPT SE8 112 C5
HPTN TW12 142 C4
HSLW TW3 103 H7
TOTM N17 42 C6
Taylor Rd MTCM CR4 147 J6
WLGTN SM6 176 B4
Taylor's Blds
WOOL/PLUM SE18 115 G3
Taylors Cl SCUP DA14 155 F3
Taylors Ct FELT TW13 140 E1
Taylor's Gn ACT W3 * 87 G5
Taylors La WLSDN NW10 69 G5
Taylor's La SYD SE26 150 D3
WLSDN NW10 69 G6
Taylors Md MLHL NW7 * 37 J4
Taymount Ri FSTH SE23 150 E1
Tayport Cl IS N1 5 L2
Tayside Dr EDGW HA8 36 D2
Taywood Rd NTHLT UB5 83 J3
Teak Cl BERM/RHTH SE16 93 G7
Teal Cl CAN/RD E16 95 H4
Teal Dr NTHWD HA6 32 A6
Teale St BETH E2 92 C1
Tealing Dr HOR/WEW KT19 173 F3
Teal Pl SUT SM1 174 D4
Teal St GNWCH SE10 113 J2
Teasel Cl CROY/NA CR0 166 A7
Teasel Crs THMD SE28 96 E7
Teasel Wy SRTFD E15 94 C2
Tebworth Rd TOTM N17 42 B6
Teck Cl ISLW TW7 124 B1
Tedder Cl CHSGTN KT9 171 J4
RSLP HA4 64 E4
Tedder Rd SAND/SEL CR2 179 F6
Teddington Pk TEDD TW11 143 F4
Teddington Park Rd
TEDD TW11 143 F3
Tedworth Gdns CHEL SW3 15 L8
Tedworth Sq CHEL SW3 15 L8
Tees Av GFD/PVL UB6 84 E1
Teesdale Av ISLW TW7 104 B7
Teesdale Cl BETH E2 92 C1
Teesdale Gdns ISLW TW7 104 B7
SNWD SE25 165 F1
Teesdale Rd WAN E11 58 D5
Teesdale St BETH E2 92 D1
Teesdale Yd BETH E2 * 92 D1
The Tee ACT W3 87 G5
Teevan Cl CROY/NA CR0 165 H6
Teevan Rd CROY/NA CR0 165 H6
Teign Ms ELTH/MOT SE9 153 J1
Teignmouth Cl CLAP SW4 129 J3
EDGW HA8 50 B1
Teignmouth Gdns
GFD/PVL UB6 85 G1
Teignmouth Rd CRICK NW2 70 B4
WELL DA16 136 D1
Telcote Wy RSLP HA4 * 47 G6
Telegraph Hl HAMP NW3 71 F2
Telegraph La ESH/CLAY KT10 171 F3
Telegraph Ms GDMY/SEVK IG3 61 F7
Telegraph Pas
BRXS/STRHM SW2 129 K6
Telegraph Pl POP/IOD E14 112 E3
Telegraph Rd PUT/ROE SW15 126 E6
Telegraph St LOTH EC2R 13 G4
Telephone Pl WKENS W14 * 107 J5
Telferscot Rd BAL SW12 129 J7
Telford Av BRXS/STRHM SW2 129 J7
Telford Cl NRWD SE19 150 B5
WALTH E17 57 G6
Telford Dr WOT/HER KT12 156 B6
Telford Rd CDALE/KGS NW9 51 H5
ELTH/MOT SE9 154 D1
NKENS W10 88 C4
STHL UB1 84 B6
WHTN TW2 123 F6
Telford Rd (North Circular Rd)
FBAR/BDGN N11 40 C4
Telfords Yd WAP E1W * 92 C6
Telford Ter PIM SW1V 16 E9
Telford Wy ACT W3 87 G4
YEAD UB4 83 J4
Telham Rd EHAM E6 96 A1
Tell Gv EDUL SE22 131 G3
Tellisford ESH/CLAY KT10 170 B3
Tellson Av WOOL/PLUM SE18 114 D7
Temeraire Pl BTFD TW8 105 G4
Temeraire St
BERM/RHTH SE16 111 K1
Tempelhof Av HDN NW4 52 A6
Temperley Rd BAL SW12 129 F6
Tempest Wy RAIN RM13 81 J5
Templar Dr THMD SE28 97 K5
Templar Pl HPTN TW12 142 A6
Templars Av GLDGN NW11 52 D5
Templars Ct DART DA1 * 139 K4
Templars Crs FNCH N3 52 E1
Templars Dr
KTN/HRWW/WS HA3 * 34 D5
Templar St CMBW SE5 130 C1
Temple Av BCTR RM8 62 C7
CROY/NA CR0 179 H2
EMB EC4Y 12 B6
TRDG/WHET N20 27 H6
Temple Cl FNCH N3 52 D1
THMD SE28 115 H2
WAN E11 58 C6
WAT WD17 20 D1
Templecombe Rd HOM E9 74 E7
Templecombe Wy MRDN SM4 161 H4
Temple Dwellings BETH E2 * 92 D1
Temple Fortune Hl
GLDGN NW11 52 E4
Temple Fortune La
GLDGN NW11 52 D5
Temple Gdns BCTR RM8 79 K2
EMB EC4Y * 12 A6
GLDGN NW11 52 D5
WCHMH N21 * 41 H1
Temple Gv ENC/FH EN2 29 H2
GLDGN NW11 52 E5
Temple Hl DART DA1 139 J4
Temple Hill Sq DART DA1 139 J4
Temple La EMB EC4Y 12 B5
Templeman Rd HNWL W7 85 F4
Templemead Cl ACT W3 87 G5
Temple Mead Cl STAN HA7 35 H5
Temple Mills La SRTFD E15 76 A4
Temple Pde BAR EN5 * 27 H6
Temple Pl TPL/STR WC2R 11 M6
Temple Rd CEND/HSY/T N8 55 F3
CHSWK W4 105 K2
CRICK NW2 70 A3
CROY/NA CR0 177 K3
EA W5 104 E2
EHAM E6 77 J7
HSLW TW3 123 G3
Temple Sheen Rd
MORT/ESHN SW14 125 K3
Temple St BETH E2 92 D1
Temple Ter WDGN N22 * 55 G1
Templeton Av CHING E4 43 J3
Templeton Cl NRWD SE19 149 K7
STNW/STAM N16 * 74 A4
Templeton Pl ECT SW5 14 B6
Templeton Rd FSBYPK N4 55 K5
Temple Wy SUT SM1 175 H2
Templewood WEA W13 85 H4
Templewood Av HAMP NW3 71 F2
Templewood Gdns
HAMP NW3 71 F2
Temple Yd BETH E2 92 C2
Tempsford Av BORE WD6 25 F3
Tempsford Cl ENC/FH EN2 29 J2
Temsford Cl RYLN/HDSTN HA2 48 C1
Tenbury Cl FSTGT E7 77 H4
Tenbury Ct BAL SW12 129 J7
Tenby Av KTN/HRWW/WS HA3 49 H1
Tenby Cl CHDH RM6 62 A5
SEVS/STOTM N15 56 B3
Tenby Gdns NTHLT UB5 66 A5
Tenby Rd CHDH RM6 62 A5
EDGW HA8 36 B7
PEND EN3 30 E2
WALTH E17 57 G4
WELL DA16 116 E7
Tench St WAP E1W * 92 D7
Tenda Rd STHWK SE1 111 J3
Tendring Wy CHDH RM6 61 J4
Tenham Av BRXS/STRHM SW2 148 D1
Tenison Wy STHWK SE1 12 A9
Tenniel Cl BAY/PAD W2 8 E5
Tennison Av BORE WD6 24 D4
Tennison Rd SNWD SE25 165 G3
Tennis St STHWK SE1 19 G1
Tennyson Av CDALE/KGS NW9 50 E2
MNPK E12 77 J6
NWMAL KT3 160 E4
TWK TW1 124 A7
WAN E11 58 E6
Tennyson Cl
EBED/NFELT TW14 121 K5
PEND EN3 31 F4
WELL DA16 115 K7
Tennyson Rd DART DA1 139 K4
HNWL W7 85 F6
HSLW TW3 123 H1
KIL/WHAMP NW6 70 D7
LEY E10 57 K7
MLHL NW7 37 H4
PGE/AN SE20 151 F6
SRTFD E15 76 C6
WALTH E17 57 H5
WIM/MER SW19 147 G5
Tennyson St VX/NE SW8 129 G1
Tennyson Wy HCH RM12 63 H7
Tensing Rd NWDGN UB2 103 F2
Tentelow La NWDGN UB2 103 G2
Tenterden Cl ELTH/MOT SE9 153 K3
HDN NW4 52 B2
Tenterden Dr HDN NW4 52 B2
Tenterden Gdns CROY/NA CR0 165 H6
HDN NW4 52 B2
Tenterden Gv HDN NW4 52 A3
Tenterden Rd BCTR RM8 80 B1
CROY/NA CR0 165 H6
TOTM N17 42 B6
Tenterden St CONDST W1S 10 D5
Tenter Gnd WCHPL E1 13 L3
Tent Peg La STMC/STPC BR5 169 H4
Tent St WCHPL E1 92 D3
Teredo St LEW SE13 132 E1
Terling Cl WAN E11 76 D2
Terling Rd BCTR RM8 80 C1
Terling Wk IS N1 * 6 E3
Terminus Pl BGVA SW1W 16 D4
Terrace Gdns BARN SW13 126 C1
WAT WD17 21 F1
Terrace Rd HOM E9 75 F6
PLSTW E13 76 E7
WOT/HER KT12 156 A5
The Terrace BARN SW13 126 B1
BETH E2 * 92 E2
CHING E4 * 44 C2
DEPT SE8 * 112 C3
EFNCH N2 * 54 A3
FNCH N3 * 52 D1
FSTH SE23 * 132 B6
KIL/WHAMP NW6 2 A3
Terrace Vls HMSMTH W6 * 106 D4
Terrace Wk DAGW RM9 80 A4
Terrac St RCH/KEW TW9 125 G3
Terrapin Rd TOOT SW17 148 B2
Terretts Pl IS N1 6 C2
Terrick Rd WDGN N22 40 E7
Terrick St SHB W12 87 K5
Terrilands PIN HA5 47 K2
Terront Rd SEVS/STOTM N15 55 J4

Tessa Sanderson Wy
  GFD/PVL UB6 ....66 D4
Testerton Rd *NTGHL* W11 * 88 B6
Testerton Wk *NTGHL* W11 * 88 B6
Tetbury Pl *IS* N1 ....6 E7
Tetcott Rd *WBPTN* SW10 ....108 B6
Tetherdown *MUSWH* N10 ....54 A2
Tetty Wy *BMLY* BR1 ....167 K1
Teversham La *VX/NE* SW8 ....109 K7
Teviot Cl *WELL* DA16 ....116 C7
Teviot St *POP/IOD* E14 ....94 A4
Tewkesbury Av *FSTH* SE23 ....131 J7
  PIN HA5 ....47 J4
Tewkesbury Cl
  SEVS/STOTM N15 ....55 K5
Tewkesbury Gdns
  CDALE/KGS NW9 ....50 D4
Tewkesbury Rd *CAR* SM5 ....162 C1
  SEVS/STOTM N15 ....55 K6
  WEA W13 ....85 C7
Tewkesbury Ter
  FBAR/BDGN N11 ....40 C5
Tewson Rd *WOOL/PLUM* SE18 ..115 K4
Teynham Av *EN* EN1 ....29 K5
Teynham Gn *HAYES* BR2 ....167 K4
Teynton Ter *TOTM* N17 ....41 J7
Thackeray Av *TOTM* N17 ....56 C1
Thackeray Cl *ISLW* TW7 ....124 B1
  WIM/MER SW19 ....146 B6
Thackeray Dr *CHDH* RM6 ....61 H6
Thackeray Ms *HACK* E8 ....74 C5
Thackeray Rd *EHAM* E6 ....95 H1
  VX/NE SW8 ....129 G1
Thackeray St *KENS* W8 ....14 D3
Thakeham Cl *SYD* SE26 ....150 D4
Thalia Cl *GNWCH* SE10 ....113 G5
Thame Rd *BERM/RHTH* SE16 .....112 A1
Thames Av *DAGW* RM9 ....98 D3
  GFD/PVL UB6 ....85 F1
  WBPTN SW10 ....108 B7
  WPK KT4 ....161 F7
Thames Bank
  MORT/ESHN SW14 ....125 K1
Thamesbank Pl *THMD* SE28 ....97 J5
Thames Cir *POP/IOD* E14 ....112 D3
Thames Cl *HPTN* TW12 ....157 G1
  RAIN RM13 ....99 G5
Thames Crs *CHSWK* W4 ....106 B6
Thames Down Link
  BRYLDS KT5 ....159 K4
  HOR/WEW KT19 ....172 C6
  WPK KT4 ....173 J7
Thames Dr *RSLP* HA4 ....46 A3
Thames Eyot *TWK* TW1 * 143 G1
Thames Ga *DART* DA1 ....139 K4
Thamesgate Cl
  RCHPK/HAM TW10 ....143 H7
Thameside *TEDD* TW11 ....143 K6
Thames Meadow
  E/WMO/HCT KT8 ....157 F2
Thamesmere Dr *THMD* SE28 ......97 C6
Thames Pth *BARN* SW13 ....106 C2
  BERM/RHTH SE16 ....112 C2
  CHEL SW3 ....109 F5
  CLPT E5 ....75 F2
  E/WMO/HCT KT8 ....158 A3
  ISLW TW7 ....124 C1
  KUTN/CMB KT2 ....143 J4
  MORT/ESHN SW14 ....126 B1
  PIM SW1V 17 H8
  POP/IOD E14 ....112 D2
  RCH/KEW TW9 ....124 D4
  RCHPK/HAM TW10 ....143 C2
  SRTFD E15 ....93 K1
  SUN TW16 ....156 B3
  TPL/STR WC2R 11 M7
  TWK TW1 ....143 G1
  TWRH EC3N 13 K8
  VX/NE SW8 ....109 H5
Thames Pl *PUT/ROE* SW15 ....127 G2
Thames Quay *WBPTN* SW10 * ...108 B7
Thames Reach *KUT/HW* KT1 * ...143 K7
Thames Rd *BARK* IG11 ....97 G2
  CAN/RD E16 ....95 H7
  CHSWK W4 ....105 H5
  DART DA1 ....138 D2
Thames Side *KUT/HW* KT1 ....143 K7
  THDIT KT7 ....158 C5
Thames St *GNWCH* SE10 ....112 E5
  HPTN TW12 ....157 G1
  KUT/HW KT1 ....158 E1
  SUN TW16 ....156 A3
Thamesvale Cl *HSLW* TW3 ....123 F1
Thames Village *CHSWK* W4 ......105 K7
Thamley *PUR* RM19 ....119 K3
Thanescroft Gdns
  CROY/NA CR0 ....178 A2
Thanet Pl *HAYES* BR2 ....181 H2
Thanet Pl *CROY/NA* CR0 ....177 J3
Thanet Rd *BXLY* DA5 ....137 H6
  ERITH DA8 ....118 B6
Thanet St *STPAN* WC1H 5 J8
Thane Vls *HOLWY* N7 ....73 F2
Thant Cl *LEY* E10 ....75 K2
Tharp Rd *WLGTN* SM6 ....176 D4
Thatcham Gdns
  TRDG/WHET N20 ....27 G6
Thatcher Cl *WDR/YW* UB7 ....100 B1
Thatchers Wy *ISLW* TW7 ....123 J4
Thatches Gv *CHDH* RM6 ....62 A2
Thavies Inn *FLST/FETLN* EC4A 12 B4
Thaxted Pl *RYNPK* SW20 ....146 B6
Thaxted Rd *ELTH/MOT* SE9 .....154 C1
Thaxton Rd *WKENS* W14 ....107 J5
Thayers Farm Rd *BECK* BR3 ....151 H2
Thayer St *MHST* W1U 10 B4
Theatre Rd *SRTFD* SE15 ....76 B5
Theatre St *BTSEA* SW11 ....128 E2
Theberton St *IS* N1 ....6 B3
The Beverly *MRDN* SM4 ....161 F6
The Courtyard *HAYES* BR2 ......181 J5
Theed St *STHWK* SE1 ....12 A9
The Green *WIM/MER* SW19 ....146 B4
Thelma Gv *TEDD* TW11 ....143 G5
Theobald Crs
  KTN/HRWW/WS HA3 ....34 D7
Theobald Rd *CROY/NA* CR0 ......177 H1
  WALTH E17 ....57 H6
Theobald's Rd
  GINN WC1R 11 L2
Theobald St *BORE* WD6 ....24 B2
Theobald's Rd
  STHWK SE1 ....19 G4
Theodora Wy *PIN* HA5 ....46 D2
Theodore Rd *LEW* SE13 ....133 G5
Therapia La *CROY/NA* CR0 ....163 J6
Therapia Rd *EDUL* SE22 ....131 K5
Theresa Rd *HMSMTH* W6 ....106 D3
Theresa's Wk *SAND/SEL* CR2 ..177 K7
Thermopylae Ga *POP/IOD* E14 ..112 D3
Theseus Wk *IS* N1 * 6 D6
Thesiger Rd *PGE/AN* SE20 ....151 F6
Thessaly Rd *VX/NE* SW8 ....109 J7
Thetford Cl *PLMGR* N13 ....41 H5
Thetford Gdns *RAIN* RM13 ....81 G6
Thetford Rd *DAGW* RM9 ....79 K6
  NWMAL KT3 ....160 A5
Theydon Gdns *RAIN* RM13 ....81 G6
Theydon Rd *WFD* IG8 ....45 G5
Theydon St *WALTH* E17 ....74 E1
Theydon St *WALTH* E17 ....57 H6
Thicket Crs *SUT* SM1 ....175 G3
Thicket Gv *DAGW* RM9 ....79 J5
  PGE/AN SE20 ....150 C6
Thicket Rd *PGE/AN* SE20 ....150 D6
  SUT SM1 ....175 G3
Thicket Ter *PGE/AN* SE20 * 150 C6
Third Av *ACT* W3 ....87 H7
  CHDH RM6 ....61 J5
  DAGE RM10 ....80 D7
  EN EN1 ....30 B4
  HYS/HAR UB3 ....82 D7
  MNPK E12 ....77 J3
  NKENS W10 ....88 C2
  PLSTW E13 ....94 E2
  WALTH E17 ....57 J4
  WBLY HA9 ....67 K1
Third Cl *E/WMO/HCT* KT8 ....157 G3
Third Cross Rd *WHTN* TW2 ......142 D1
Thirleby Rd *EDGW* HA8 ....37 F7
  MLHL NW7 ....38 C4
  WEST SW1P 16 F4
Thirlmere Av *GFD/PVL* UB6 ....85 J2
Thirlmere Gdns *WBLY* HA9 ....49 J7
Thirlmere Ri *BMLY* BR1 ....152 D5
Thirlmere Rd *BXLYHN* DA7 ......137 K1
  MUSWH N10 ....40 B7
  STRHM/NOR SW16 ....148 D3
Thirsk Cl *NTHLT* UB5 ....66 A5
Thirsk Rd *BTSEA* SW11 ....129 F2
  MTCM CR4 ....148 A6
  SNWD SE25 ....164 E3
Thirza Rd *DART* DA1 ....139 J5
Thisilefield Cl *BXLY* DA5 ....136 E7
Thistlebrook *ABYW* SE2 ....116 D2
Thistlecroft Gdns *STAN* HA7 ....35 K7
Thistledene *THDIT* KT7 ....157 K5
Thistledene Av
  RYLN/HDSTN HA2 ....65 J2
Thistle Gv *WBPTN* SW10 ....14 F8
Thistlemead *CHST* BR7 ....169 G1
Thistlewaite Rd *CLPT* E5 ....74 D2
Thistlewood Cl *HOLWY* N7 ....73 F1
Thistleworth Cl *ISLW* TW7 ....103 J6
Thistley Cl
  NFNCH/WDSPK N12 ....39 J5
Thomas A Beckett Cl
  HRW HA1 ....67 F3
Thomas Baines Rd
  BTSEA SW11 ....128 C2
Thomas Cribb Ms *EHAM* E6 ....95 K5
Thomas Dean Rd *SYD* SE26 * ..151 H3
Thomas Dinwiddy Rd
  LEE/GVPK SE12 ....153 F1
Thomas Doyle St *STHWK* SE1 ...18 C5
Thomas Fyre Dr *BOW* E3 ....93 J1
Thomas Jacomb Pl
  WALTH E17 ....57 H3
Thomas' La *CAT* SE6 ....132 E6
Thomas Moore St *WAP* E1W 92 C6
Thomas Moore Wy *EFNCH* N2 ....53 G2
Thomas More Gdns
  ESH/CLAY KT10 ....170 A1
Thomas More St *WAP* E1W * 92 C6
Thomas North Ter
  CAN/RD E16 * 94 D4
Thomas Pl *KENS* W8 ....14 C4
Thomas Rd *POP/IOD* E14 ....93 H5
Thomas St *WOOL/PLUM* SE18 ..115 F3
Thomas Wall Cl *SUT* SM1 ....175 F4
Thompson Av *CMBW* SE5 ....110 D6
  RCH/KEW TW9 ....125 J2
Thompson Cl *CHEAM* SM3 ....161 K7
  IL IG1 ....78 C2
Thompson Rd *DAGW* RM9 ....80 B2
  EDUL SE22 ....131 G5
  HSLW TW3 ....123 G3
Thomson Crs *CROY/NA* CR0 ....164 B7
Thomson Rd
  KTN/HRWW/WS HA3 ....48 E2
Thomson Rd *BTSEA* SW11 ....111 H3
Thorburn Wy
  WIM/MER SW19 * 147 H7
Thoresby St *IS* N1 ....6 F7
Thorkhill Gdns *THDIT* KT7 ....158 B7
Thorkhill Rd *THDIT* KT7 ....158 C7
Thornaby Gdns *UED* N18 ....42 C5
Thorn Av *BUSH* WD23 ....22 C7
Thornbury Av *ISLW* TW7 ....103 J6
Thornbury Cl
  STNW/STAM N16 ....74 A4
Thornbury Gdns *BORE* WD6 ....24 E3
Thornbury Rd *CLAP* SW4 ....129 K5
  ISLW TW7 ....123 J1
Thornbury Sq *HGT* N6 ....54 C7
Thornby Rd *CLPT* E5 ....74 E2
Thorncliffe Rd *CLAP* SW4 ....129 J5
  NWDGN UB2 ....102 E4
Thorn Cl *HAYES* BR2 ....169 F5
  NTHLT UB5 ....85 K2
Thorncombe Rd *EDUL* SE22 .....131 F4
Thorn Ct *BELMT* SM2 * 175 F6
Thorncroft *EMPK* RM11 ....63 K5
Thorncroft Rd *SUT* SM1 ....175 F4
Thorncroft St *VX/NE* SW8 ....109 K6
Thorndean St
  WAND/EARL SW18 ....147 G1
Thorndene Av
  TRDG/WHET N20 ....28 A7
Thorndike Av *NTHLT* UB5 ....65 H7
Thorndike Cl *WBPTN* SW10 ......108 B6
Thorndike Rd *IS* N1 ....73 K5
Thorndike St *PIM* SW1V * 17 G6
Thorndon Gdns
  HOR/WEW KT19 ....173 G3
Thorndyke Ct *PIN* HA5 ....33 K6
Thorne Cl *ASHF* TW15 ....140 A6
  CAN/RD E16 ....94 E5
  ERITH DA8 ....117 J5
  ESH/CLAY KT10 ....171 H5
  WAN E11 ....76 C3
Thorneloe Gdns *CROY/NA* CR0 ..177 H4
Thorne Rd *VX/NE* SW8 ....109 K6
Thorne's Cl *BECK* BR3 ....167 F2
Thorne St *BARN* SW13 ....126 B2
Thornet Wood Rd *BMLY* BR1 ....169 F2
Thorney Crs *BTSEA* SW11 * 108 C6
Thorneycroft Cl
  WOT/HER KT12 ....156 B5
Thorney Hedge Rd
  CHSWK W4 ....105 J3
Thorney St *WEST* SW1P 17 H5
Thornfield Av *MLHL* NW7 ....38 C7
Thornfield Pde *MLHL* NW7 * 38 C6
Thornfield Rd *SHB* W12 ....106 E1
Thornford Rd *LEW* SE13 ....133 F4
Thorngate Rd *MV/WKIL* W9 ....2 B9
Thorngrove Rd *PLSTW* E13 ....77 F7
Thornham Gv *SRTFD* E15 ....76 B4
Thornham St *GNWCH* SE10 ......112 E5
Thornhaugh St *STPAN* WC1H 11 H1
Thornhill Av *SURB* KT6 ....172 A1
  WOOL/PLUM SE18 ....115 K6
Thornhill Bridge Whf *IS* N1 ....5 L4
Thornhill Crs *IS* N1 ....5 M2
Thornhill Gdns *BARK* IG11 ....78 E6
  LEY E10 ....75 K1
Thornhill Gv *IS* N1 ....6 A2
Thornhill Rd *CROY/NA* CR0 ......164 D6
  IS N1 ....6 A1
  LEY E10 ....75 K1
  NTHWD HA6 ....32 A3
  SURB KT6 ....172 A1
Thornhill Sq *IS* N1 ....5 M2
Thornlaw Rd *WNWD* SE27 ....149 G3
Thornley Cl *TOTM* N17 ....42 C6
Thornley Dr *RYLN/HDSTN* HA2 ...66 B1
Thornsbeach Rd *CAT* SE6 ....133 F7
Thornsett Pl *PGE/AN* SE20 ......165 J1
Thornsett Rd *PGE/AN* SE20 .....165 J1
  WAND/EARL SW18 ....147 F1
Thornsett Ter *PGE/AN* SE20 * ..165 J1
Thornton Av
  BRXS/STRHM SW2 ....129 J7
  CHSWK W4 ....106 B3
  CROY/NA CR0 ....164 A5
  WDR/YW UB7 ....100 C2
Thornton Cl *WDR/YW* UB7 ....100 C2
Thornton Dene *BECK* BR3 ....166 D1
Thornton Gdns *BAL* SW12 ....129 J7
Thornton Gv *PIN* HA5 ....34 A5
Thornton Hl *WIM/MER* SW19 ....146 C6
Thornton Pl *MBLAR* W1H 9 M2
Thornton Rd *BAL* SW12 ....129 J7
  BAR EN5 ....26 C2
  BELV DA17 * 117 J3
  BMLY BR1 ....152 E4
  CAR SM5 ....162 C7
  IL IG1 ....78 A3
  MORT/ESHN SW14 ....126 A2
  THHTH CR7 ....164 B4
  UED N18 ....42 E2
  WAN E11 ....76 B1
  WIM/MER SW19 ....146 B5
Thornton Rw *THHTH* CR7 ....164 B4
Thorntons Farm Av
  ROMW/RG RM7 ....80 E5
Thornton St *BRXN/ST* SW9 ......130 B1
Thornton Wy *GLDGN* NW11 ....53 F4
Thorntree Rd *CHARL* SE7 ....114 C4
Thornville Gv *MTCM* CR4 ....162 B1
Thornville St *DEPT* SE8 ....112 D7
Thornwood Cl *SWFD* E18 ....59 F1
Thornwood Rd *LEW* SE13 ....133 H4
Thorogood Gdns *SRTFD* E15 .....76 C4
Thorogood Wy *RAIN* RM13 ....81 G7
Thorold Rd *IL* IG1 ....78 A1
  WDGN N22 ....40 E6
Thorparch Rd *VX/NE* SW8 ....109 J7
Thorpebank Rd *SHB* W12 ....87 J7
Thorpe Cl *NKENS* W10 ....88 C5
  SYD SE26 * 151 F3
Thorpe Crs *OXHEY* WD19 ....21 F6
  WALTH E17 ....57 H1
Thorpedale Gdns
  GNTH/NBYPK IG2 ....60 B3
Thorpedale Rd *FSBYPK* N4 ....55 F7
Thorpe Hall Rd *WALTH* E17 ....44 A7
Thorpe Rd *BARK* IG11 ....78 D6
  EHAM E6 ....77 K7
  FSTGT E7 ....76 E2
  KUTN/CMB KT2 ....144 A7
  SEVS/STOTM N15 ....56 A5
  WALTH E17 ....58 A1
Thorpewood Av *SYD* SE26 ....150 D1
Thorpland Av *HGDN/ICK* UB10 ...64 A2
Thorsden Wy *NRWD* SE19 * 150 A4
Thorverton Rd *CRICK* NW2 ....70 C2
Thoydon Rd *BOW* E3 ....93 G1
Thrale Rd *STRHM/NOR* SW16 ..148 C4
Thrale St *STHWK* SE1 ....12 F9
Thrasher Cl *HACK* E8 * 7 L3
Thrawl St *WCHPL* E1 ....13 M5
Threadneedle St *LOTH* EC2R 13 H5
Three Colts La *BETH* E2 ....92 D3
Three Colt St *POP/IOD* E14 * 93 H6
Three Corners *BXLYHN* DA7 ....137 J1
Three Kings Yd
  MYFR/PKLN W1K 10 C6
Three Meadows Ms
  KTN/HRWW/WS HA3 ....35 F7
Three Mill La *BOW* E3 ....94 A2
Three Oak La *STHWK* SE1 ....19 L1
Three Valleys Wy *BUSH* WD23 ...21 H4
Threshers Pl *NTGHL* W11 ....88 C6
Thriftwood *SYD* SE26 ....150 E2
Thrift Farm La *BORE* WD6 ....24 E1
Thrigby Rd *CHSGTN* KT9 ....172 B5
Throckmorten Rd
  CAN/RD E16 ....95 F5
Throgmorton Av *OBST* EC2N 13 H4
Throgmorton St *OBST* EC2N 13 H4
Throwley Cl *ABYW* SE2 ....116 D2
Throwley Rd *SUT* SM1 ....175 F4
Throwley Wy *SUT* SM1 ....175 F3
Thrupp Cl *MTCM* CR4 ....163 G1
Thrush Gn *RYLN/HDSTN* HA2 ....48 A3
Thrush St *WALW* SE17 ....18 E7
Thunderer Rd *DAGW* RM9 ....98 A3
Thurbarn Rd *CAT* SE6 ....151 K4
Thurland Rd
  BERM/RHTH SE16 ....111 H2
Thurlby Cl *WFD* IG8 ....45 K4
Thurlby Rd *ALP/SUD* HA0 ....67 K5
  WNWD SE27 ....149 G3
Thurleigh Av *BAL* SW12 ....129 F5
Thurleigh Rd *BAL* SW12 ....128 D6
Thurleston Av *MRDN* SM4 ....161 H4
Thurlestone Av
  GDMY/SEVK IG3 ....79 F3
  NFNCH/WDSPK N12 ....39 K5
Thurlestone Rd *WNWD* SE27 ....149 G2
Thurloe Cl *SKENS* SW7 ....15 G5
Thurloe Gdns *ROM* RM1 ....63 G5
Thurloe Pl *SKENS* SW7 ....15 G5
Thurloe Place Ms
  SKENS SW7 * 15 G5
Thurloe Sq *SKENS* SW7 ....15 H5
Thurloe St *SKENS* SW7 ....15 G5
Thurlow Cl *CHING* E4 ....43 K5
Thurlow Gdns *ALP/SUD* HA0 * ...67 K4
Thurlow Hl *DUL* SE21 ....130 D7
Thurlow Park Rd *DUL* SE21 ......149 H1
Thurlow Rd *HAMP* NW3 ....71 H4
  HNWL W7 ....104 B1
Thurlow St *WALW* SE17 ....19 J8
Thurlow Ter *KTTN* NW5 ....71 K4
Thurlow Wk *WALW* SE17 ....19 J7
Thurlston Rd *RSLP* HA4 ....64 E2
Thurlstone Crs *CROY/NA* CR0 ..180 B6
Thursley Crs *CROY/NA* CR0 .....180 B6
Thursley Gdns
  WIM/MER SW19 ....146 B1
Thursley Rd *ELTH/MOT* SE9 .....153 K2
Thurso St *TOOT* SW17 ....147 H3
Thurstan Rd *RYNPK* SW20 ......145 K6
Thurston Rd *DEPT* SE8 ....132 D1
  STHL UB1 ....83 K5
Thurtle Rd *BETH* E2 ....7 M4
Thwaite Cl *ERITH* DA8 ....117 K5
Thyra Gv *NFNCH/WDSPK* N12 ...39 F5
Tibbatt's Rd *BOW* E3 ....93 K3
Tibbenham Pl *CAT* SE6 ....151 J1
Tibberton Sq *IS* N1 ....6 E2
Tibbets Cl *WIM/MER* SW19 ......127 G7
Tibbet's Ride *PUT/ROE* SW15 ..127 G6
Tiber Gdns *BOW* E3 ....75 J7
Tiber Gdns *IS* N1 * 5 K4
Ticehurst Cl *STMC/STPC* BR5 ..155 G6
Ticehurst Rd *FSTH* SE23 ....151 G1
Tickford Cl *ABYW* SE2 ....116 D1
Tidal Basin Rd *CAN/RD* E16 ....94 D6
Tide Cl *MTCM* CR4 ....148 A7
Tidenham Gdns *CROY/NA* CR0 ..178 A2
Tideswell Rd *CROY/NA* CR0 .....179 J2
  PUT/ROE SW15 ....127 F3
Tideway Cl *RCHPK/HAM* TW10 ..143 H5
Tideway Wk *VX/NE* SW8 * 109 H5
Tidey St *BOW* E3 ....93 J4
Tidford Rd *WELL* DA16 ....136 A1
Tidworth Rd *BOW* E3 ....93 J2
Tiepigs La *WWKM* BR4 ....180 C1
Tierney Rd *BRXS/STRHM* SW2 ..129 K7
Tierney Ter
  BRXS/STRHM SW2 ....129 K7
Tiger La *HAYES* BR2 ....168 A3
Tiger Wy *CLPT* E5 ....74 D3
Tigres Cl *ED* N9 ....42 E1
Tilbrook Rd *BKHTH/KID* SE3 ....134 B2
Tilbury Cl *PECK* SE15 ....111 G6
  PIN HA5 ....33 K6
Tilbury Rd *EHAM* E6 ....96 A1
  LEY E10 ....58 A6
Tildesley Rd *PUT/ROE* SW15 ...127 F5
Tilehouse Cl *BORE* WD6 ....24 B2
Tilehurst Rd *CHEAM* SM3 ....174 C4
  WAND/EARL SW18 ....128 C7
Tile Kiln La *HGT* N6 ....54 B7
Tileyard Rd *HOLWY* N7 ....5 J1
Tilford Av *CROY/NA* CR0 ....180 A6
Tilford Gdns *WIM/MER* SW19 ...127 G7
Tilia Cl *SUT* SM1 ....174 D4
Tilia Wk *BRXN/ST* SW9 ....130 C3
Tiller Rd *POP/IOD* E14 ....112 D2
Tillett Cl *WLSDN* NW10 ....68 E5
Tillett Wy *BETH* E2 ....92 C2
Tilley Rd *FELT* TW13 ....121 K7
Tillingbourne Gdns *FNCH* N3 ....52 D2
Tillingbourne Wy *FNCH* N3 ....52 D2
Tillingham Wy
  NFNCH/WDSPK N12 ....38 D3
Tilling Rd *CRICK* NW2 ....51 K7
Tilling Wy *WBLY* HA9 ....67 K2
Tillman St *WCHPL* E1 ....92 D5
Tilloch St *IS* N1 * 5 L1
Tillotson Rd *ED* N9 ....42 B1
  IL IG1 ....60 A6
  KTN/HRWW/WS HA3 ....34 B6
Tilney Gdns *IS* N1 ....73 K5
Tilney Rd *DAGW* RM9 ....80 B5
  NWDGN UB2 ....102 B3
Tilney St *MYFR/PKLN* W1K 10 B8
Tilson Cl *CMBW* SE5 ....111 F6
Tilson Gdns *BRXS/STRHM* SW2 ..129 K6
Tilson Rd *TOTM* N17 ....42 C7
Tilston Cl *WAN* E11 ....76 D2
Tilton St *FUL/PGN* SW6 ....107 H5
The Tiltwood *ACT* W3 ....86 E6
Tilt Yard Ap *ELTH/MOT* SE9 .....134 E5
Timber Cl *CHST* BR7 ....169 F1
Timbercroft *HOR/WEW* KT19 ....173 G3
Timbercroft La
  WOOL/PLUM SE18 ....115 K5
Timberland Cl *PECK* SE15 * 111 H6
Timberland Rd *WCHPL* E1 ....92 D5
Timber Mill Wy *CLAP* SW4 ....129 J2
Timber Pond Rd
  BERM/RHTH SE16 ....112 A1
Timberslip Dr *WLGTN* SM6 ......176 D7
The Timbers *CHEAM* SM3 * 174 C5
Timber St *FSBYE* EC1V * 6 E9
Timberwharf Rd
  SEVS/STOTM N15 ....56 C5
Time Sq *HACK* E8 * 74 B4
Times Sq *SUT* SM1 ....175 F4
Timms Cl *BMLY* BR1 ....168 E3
Timothy Cl *BXLYHS* DA6 ....137 F4
Tindal St *BRXN/ST* SW9 ....110 C7
Tinniswood Cl *HBRY* N5 ....73 G4
  HOLWY N7 ....73 G4
Tinsley Cl *SNWD* SE25 ....165 J2
Tinsley Rd *WCHPL* E1 ....92 E4
Tintagel Crs *EDUL* SE22 ....131 G3
Tintagel Dr *STAN* HA7 ....35 K4
Tintern Av *CDALE/KGS* NW9 ......50 D2
Tintern Cl *PUT/ROE* SW15 ....127 H4
  WIM/MER SW19 ....147 G6
Tintern Gdns *STHGT/OAK* N14 ..28 E5
Tintern Rd *CAR* SM5 ....162 C7
  WDGN N22 ....41 J7
Tintern St *CLAP* SW4 ....129 K3
Tintern Wy *RYLN/HDSTN* HA2 ...48 B3
Tinto Rd *CAN/RD* E16 ....94 E4
Tinwell Ms *BORE* WD6 ....25 F4
Tinworth St *LBTH* SE11 ....17 K7
Tipthorpe Rd *BTSEA* SW11 ......129 F2
Tipton Dr *CROY/NA* CR0 ....178 A3
Tiptree Cl *CHING* E4 ....44 A2
Tiptree Crs *CLAY* IG5 ....60 A1
Tiptree Dr *ENC/FH* EN2 ....29 K3
Tiptree Rd *RSLP* HA4 ....65 F3
Tirlemont Rd *SAND/SEL* CR2 ....177 J6
Tirrell Rd *CROY/NA* CR0 ....164 D5
Tisbury Rd *STRHM/NOR* SW16 ..163 K1
Tisdall Pl *WALW* SE17 ....19 H6
Titan Ct *BTFD* TW8 ....105 G4
Titchborne Rw *BAY/PAD* W2 ....9 L5
Titchfield Rd *CAR* SM5 ....162 C7
  STJWD NW8 ....3 K4
Titchfield Wk *CAR* SM5 ....162 B6
Titchwell Rd
  WAND/EARL SW18 ....128 C6
Tite St *CHEL* SW3 ....15 J9
Tithe Barn Cl *KUTN/CMB* KT2 ..144 B7
Tithe Barn Wy *NTHLT* UB5 ....83 F1
Tithe Cl *MLHL* NW7 ....37 J7
  WOT/HER KT12 ....156 A5
  YEAD UB4 ....82 D2
Tithe Ct *HDN* NW4 * 37 J7
Tithe Farm Av
  RYLN/HDSTN HA2 ....66 A2
Tithe Farm Cl
  RYLN/HDSTN HA2 ....66 A2
Tithe Wk *MLHL* NW7 ....37 J7
Titian Av *BUSH* WD23 ....22 E6
Titley Cl *CHING* E4 ....43 J4
Titmus Cl *UX/CGN* UB8 ....82 A5
Titmuss Av *THMD* SE28 ....97 H6
Titmuss St *SHB* W12 * 106 E1
Tiverton Av *CLAY* IG5 ....60 A2
Tiverton Cl *CROY/NA* CR0 ....165 G6
Tiverton Rd *ALP/SUD* HA0 ....86 A1
  EDGW HA8 ....50 B1
  HSLW TW3 ....123 G1
  RSLP HA4 ....64 E2
  SEVS/STOTM N15 ....55 K5
  UED N18 ....42 A4
  WLSDN NW10 ....70 B7
Tiverton St *STHWK* SE1 ....18 E3
Tiverton Wy *CHSGTN* KT9 ....171 J4
  MLHL NW7 ....38 B6
Tivoli Gdns *WOOL/PLUM* SE18 ..114 D3
Tivoli Rd *CEND/HSY/T* N8 ....54 D4
  HSLW TW4 ....122 D3
  WNWD SE27 ....149 J4
Toad La *HSLWW* TW4 ....122 D3
Tobago St *POP/IOD* E14 ....112 D1
Tobin Cl *HAMP* NW3 ....3 J1
Toby La *WCHPL* E1 ....93 G3
Toby Wy *SURB* KT6 ....172 D1
Tokenhouse Yd *LOTH* EC2R 13 G4
Token Yd *PUT/ROE* SW15 ....127 H3
Tokyngton Av *WBLY* HA9 ....68 C5
Toland Sq *PUT/ROE* SW15 ......126 D4
Tolcarne Dr *PIN* HA5 ....46 E1
Toley Av *KTN/HRWW/WS* HA3 ....50 A5
Tollbridge Cl *NKENS* W10 ....88 C3
Tollesbury Gdns *BARK/HLT* IG6 ..60 D2
Tollet St *WCHPL* E1 ....93 F3
Tollgate Dr *DUL* SE21 ....150 A1
  YEAD UB4 ....83 H6
Tollgate Gdns
  KIL/WHAMP NW6 ....2 C5
Tollgate Rd *CAN/RD* E16 ....95 G4
Tollhouse La *WLGTN* SM6 ....176 C5
Tollhouse Wy *ARCH* N19 ....72 C1
Tollington Pk *FSBYPK* N4 ....73 F1
Tollington Pl *FSBYPK* N4 ....73 F1
Tollington Rd *HOLWY* N7 ....73 F3
Tollington Wy *HOLWY* N7 ....72 E2
Tolmer's Sq *CAMTN* NW1 ....4 F9
Tolpits Cl *WATW* WD18 ....20 D4
Tolpits La *WATW* WD18 ....20 A7
Tolpuddle Av *PLSTW* E13 * 77 G7
Tolpuddle St *IS* N1 ....6 A5
Tolsford Rd *HACK* E8 ....74 D4
Tolson Rd *ISLW* TW7 ....124 B2
Tolverne Rd *RYNPK* SW20 ....146 A7
Tolworth Broadway
  SURB KT6 ....159 K6
Tolworth Cl *SURB* KT6 ....159 J7
Tolworth Gdns *CHDH* RM6 ....61 K4
Tolworth Park Rd *SURB* KT6 ....172 B1
**Tolworth Ri North (Kingston
  By-Pass)** *BRYLDS* KT5 ....159 K6
Tolworth Ri South
  BRYLDS KT5 ....159 K6
Tolworth Rd *SURB* KT6 ....172 A1
**Tolworth Underpass (Kingston
  By-Pass)** *SURB* KT6 ....172 C2
Tom Cribb Rd
  WOOL/PLUM SE18 ....115 H4
Tom Groves Cl *SRTFD* E15 ....76 B4
Tom Hood Cl *SRTFD* E15 ....76 B4
Tom Jenkinson Rd
  CAN/RD E16 ....94 E7
Tomlin's Gv *BOW* E3 ....93 J2
Tomlinson Cl *BETH* E2 ....7 M8
  CHSWK W4 ....105 J4
Tomlins Orch *BARK* IG11 ....78 C7
Tomlin's Ter *POP/IOD* E14 ....93 G5
Tom Mann Cl *BARK* IG11 ....78 E7
Tom Nolan Cl *SRTFD* E15 ....94 C1
Tompion St *FSBYE* EC1V * 6 C8
Tom Smith Cl *GNWCH* SE10 .....113 H5
Tonbridge Crs
  KTN/HRWW/WS HA3 ....50 A3
Tonbridge Rd
  E/WMO/HCT KT8 ....156 D3
Tonbridge St *STPAN* WC1H 5 J8
Tonfield Rd *CHEAM* SM3 ....161 J7
Tonge Cl *BECK* BR3 ....166 D4
Tonsley Hl *WAND/EARL* SW18 ..128 A4
Tonsley Pl *WAND/EARL* SW18 ..128 A4
Tonsley Rd *WAND/EARL* SW18 ..128 A4
Tonsley St *WAND/EARL* SW18 ..128 A4
Tonstall Rd *MTCM* CR4 ....163 F1
Tooke Cl *PIN* HA5 ....33 J7
Tookey Cl
  KTN/HRWW/WS HA3 ....50 A6
Took's Ct *FLST/FETLN* EC4A 12 A4
Tooley St *STHWK* SE1 ....13 H8
Toorack Rd
  KTN/HRWW/WS HA3 ....48 D1
Tooting Bec Gdns
  STRHM/NOR SW16 ....148 D3
Tooting Bec Rd *TOOT* SW17 .....148 A2
Tooting Gv *TOOT* SW17 ....147 J4
Tooting High St *TOOT* SW17 .....147 J5
Tooting Market *TOOT* SW17 * ...147 J4
Tootswood Rd *HAYES* BR2 ....167 H4
Topham Sq *TOTM* N17 ....41 J7
Topham St *CLKNW* EC1R * 6 A9
Topiary Sq *RCH/KEW* TW9 ......125 G2
Topley St *ELTH/MOT* SE9 ....134 B3
Topmast Point *POP/IOD* E14 * ..112 D1
Top Pk *BECK* BR3 ....167 H4
Topsfield Cl *CEND/HSY/T* N8 .....54 D4
Topsfield Pde
  CEND/HSY/T N8 * 54 E4
Topsfield Rd *CEND/HSY/T* N8 ....54 D4
Topsham Rd *TOOT* SW17 ....147 K2
Torbay Rd *KIL/WHAMP* NW6 ....70 D6
  RYLN/HDSTN HA2 ....65 J1
Torbay St *CAMTN* NW1 ....4 D2
Torbitt Wy *GNTH/NBYPK* IG2 .....61 F4
Torbridge Cl *EDGW* HA8 ....36 A6
Torcross Dr *FSTH* SE23 ....150 E1
Torcross Rd *RSLP* HA4 ....65 F2
Tor Gdns *KENS* W8 ....14 A1
Tor Gv *THMD* SE28 ....96 E7
Tormead Cl *SUT* SM1 ....174 E5
Tormount Rd
  WOOL/PLUM SE18 ....115 K5
Toronto Av *MNPK* E12 ....77 K3
Toronto Rd *IL* IG1 ....60 B7
Torquay Gdns *REDBR* IG4 ....59 H3
Torquay St *BAY/PAD* W2 ....8 E3
Torrens Rd *BRXS/STRHM* SW2 ..130 A4
  SRTFD E15 ....76 D5
Torrens Sq *SRTFD* E15 ....76 D5
Torrens St *FSBYE* EC1V 6 B6
Torres Sq *POP/IOD* E14 ....112 D4
Torrey Dr *BRXN/ST* SW9 ....130 B1

Torriano Av KTTN NW5 ... 72 D4
Torriano Cots KTTN NW5 ... 72 D4
Torridge Gdns PECK SE15 ... 131 K3
Torridge Rd THHTH CR7 ... 164 C4
Torridon Rd CAT SE6 ... 133 G7
Torrington Av
  NFNCH/WDSPK N12 ... 39 H4
Torrington Cl ESH/CLAY KT10 ... 170 E5
Torrington Dr
  RYLN/HDSTN HA2 ... 66 B3
Torrington Gdns
  FBAR/BDGN N11 ... 40 C5
  GFD/PVL UB6 ... 67 J7
Torrington Gv
  NFNCH/WDSPK N12 ... 39 J4
Torrington Pk
  NFNCH/WDSPK N12 ... 39 H3
Torrington Pl FITZ W1T ... 10 C1
  GWRST WC1E ... 11 G1
  WAP E1W ... 92 C7
Torrington Rd BCTR RM8 ... 82 B7
  ESH/CLAY KT10 ... 170 E5
  GFD/PVL UB6 ... 67 J7
  RSLP HA4 ... 64 B2
Torrington Sq CROY/NA CR0 * ... 164 E6
  STPAN WC1H ... 11 H1
Torrington Wy MRDN SM4 ... 161 K6
Tor Rd WELL DA16 ... 116 D7
Torr Rd PGE/AN SE20 ... 151 F6
Torver Rd HRW HA1 ... 48 E3
Torwood Rd PUT/ROE SW15 ... 126 D4
Tothill St STJSPK SW1H ... 17 G2
Totnes Rd WELL DA16 ... 116 C6
Totnes Vls FBAR/BDGN N11 * ... 40 C4
Totnes Wk EFNCH N2 ... 53 H3
Tottan Ter WCHPL E1 * ... 93 F5
Tottenhall Rd PLMGR N13 ... 41 G5
Tottenham Court Rd FITZ W1T ... 10 F1
Tottenham Gn East
  SEVS/STOTM N15 ... 56 B3
Tottenham Gn East South Side
  SEVS/STOTM N15 ... 56 B3
Tottenham La
  CEND/HSY/T N8 ... 54 E4
Tottenham Ms FITZ W1T * ... 10 A1
Tottenham Rd IS N1 ... 74 A5
Tottenham St FITZ W1T ... 10 F3
Totterdown St TOOT SW17 ... 147 K3
Totteridge Common ... 37 J1
Totteridge La
  TRDG/WHET N20 ... 38 E1
Totteridge Village
  TRDG/WHET N20 ... 26 C7
Totternhoe Cl
  KTN/HRWW/WS HA3 ... 49 J4
Totton Rd THHTH CR7 ... 164 B2
Toucan Cl WLSDN NW10 ... 86 C2
Toulmin St STHWK SE1 * ... 18 E2
Toulon St CMBW SE5 ... 110 D6
Tournay Rd FUL/PGN SW6 ... 107 J6
Toussaint Wk
  BERM/RHTH SE16 ... 111 H2
Tovil Cl PGE/AN SE20 ... 165 H1
Towcester Rd BOW E3 ... 93 K3
Tower Br WAP E1W ... 13 L8
Tower Bridge Ap TWRH EC3N ... 13 L6
Tower Bridge Ms
  ALP/SUD HA0 ... 67 F3
Tower Bridge Rd STHWK SE1 ... 19 J4
Tower Cl HAMP NW3 ... 71 H4
  PGE/AN SE20 ... 150 D6
Tower Ct LSQ/SEVD WC2H * ... 11 J5
Tower Gdns ESH/CLAY KT10 ... 171 G4
Tower Gardens Rd TOTM N17 ... 41 J7
  WALTH E17 ... 57 J2
Tower Hamlets Rd FSTGT E7 ... 76 D3
  WALTH E17 ... 57 J2
Tower Hl TWRH EC3N ... 13 L7
Tower Hill Ter MON EC3R * ... 13 K7
Tower La WBLY HA9 ... 67 K2
Tower Ms CLPT E5 ... 75 G3
  WALTH E17 ... 57 J3
Tower Mill Rd CMBW SE5 * ... 111 F6
Tower Park Rd DART DA1 ... 138 C4
Tower Pl MON EC3R ... 13 K7
Tower Ri RCH/KEW TW9 ... 125 F2
Tower Rd BELV DA17 ... 117 K3
  BXLYHN DA7 ... 137 J3
  DART DA1 ... 139 F6
  TWK TW1 ... 143 F2
  WLSDN NW10 ... 69 J7
Tower Royal MANHO EC4N * ... 12 F6
Towers Ct HGDN/ICK UB10 ... 82 A2
Towers Ct HGDN/ICK UB10 * ... 82 A2
Towers Pl RCH/KEW TW9 ... 125 F4
Towers Rd PIN HA5 ... 33 J7
  STHL UB1 ... 84 A3
Tower St LSQ/SEVD WC2H ... 11 J5
Tower Ter WDGN N22 ... 55 F1
Tower Vw BUSH WD23 ... 22 E6
  CROY/NA CR0 ... 166 D7
Towfield Rd FELT TW13 ... 141 K1
Towncourt Crs
  STMC/STPC BR5 ... 169 H4
Towncourt La
  STMC/STPC BR5 ... 169 J5
Towncourt Pth FSBYPK N4 ... 55 J7
Town End Cl KUT/HW KT1 * ... 158 F2
Towney Md NTHLT UB5 ... 83 K1
Town Farm Wy
  STWL/WRAY TW19 * ... 120 A6
Townfield Rd HYS/HAR UB3 ... 82 D7
Townfield Sq HYS/HAR UB3 ... 82 D7
Town Field Wy ISLW TW7 ... 124 B1
Town Hall Approach Rd
  SEVS/STOTM N15 ... 56 B3
Townhall Av CHSWK W4 ... 106 A4
Town Hall Pde
  BRXS/STRHM SW2 * ... 130 A3
Town Hall Rd BTSEA SW11 ... 128 E2
Townholm Crs HNWL W7 ... 104 A2
Town La STWL/WRAY TW19 ... 120 A5
Townley Ct SRTFD E15 ... 76 D5
Townley Rd BXLYHS DA6 ... 137 G4
  EDUL SE22 ... 131 G4
Townley St WALW SE17 ... 19 G7
Town Meadow BTFD TW8 ... 104 E6
Townmead Rd FUL/PGN SW6 ... 128 A2
  RCH/KEW TW9 ... 125 J2
Town Quay BARK IG11 ... 78 B7
Town Rd ED N9 ... 42 D1
Townsend Av
  SEVS/STOTM N15 ... 56 B4
Townsend La
  CDALE/KGS NW9 ... 51 F7
Townsend Ms
  WAND/EARL SW18 ... 147 G1
Townsend Rd
  SEVS/STOTM N15 ... 56 B4
  STHL UB1 ... 83 J7
  STJWD NW8 ... 3 J5
  WOOL/PLUM SE18 ... 115 G3
Townsend St WALW SE17 ... 19 H6
Townsend Wy NTHWD HA6 ... 32 D6

Townsend Yd HGT N6 ... 54 A7
Townshend Cl SCUP DA14 ... 155 H5
Townshend Est STJWD NW8 ... 3 J4
Townshend Rd CHST BR7 ... 154 B4
  RCH/KEW TW9 ... 125 G3
  STJWD NW8 ... 3 J3
Townshend Ter
  RCH/KEW TW9 ... 125 G3
Townson Av NTHLT UB5 ... 83 H1
Townson Wy NTHLT UB5 ... 82 E1
Town Whf ISLW TW7 * ... 124 C2
Towpath Rd UED N18 ... 43 F5
Towpath Wy CROY/NA CR0 ... 165 G5
Towton Rd WNWD SE27 ... 149 J1
Toynbec Cl CHST BR7 ... 154 B3
Toynbee Rd RYNPK SW20 ... 146 C7
Toynbee St WCHPL E1 ... 13 L3
Toyne Wy HGT N6 ... 53 K5
Tracey Av CRICK NW2 * ... 70 A4
Trade Cl PLMGR N13 ... 41 G3
Trader Rd EHAM E6 ... 96 B5
Tradescant Rd VX/NE SW8 ... 109 K6
Trading Estate Rd
  WLSDN NW10 * ... 86 E3
Trafalgar Av PECK SE15 ... 19 M8
  TOTM N17 ... 42 A5
  WPK KT4 ... 161 G1
Trafalgar Cl
  EBED/NFELT TW14 ... 121 J7
Trafalgar Gv GNWCH SE10 ... 113 G5
Trafalgar Ms HOM E9 * ... 75 H5
Trafalgar Pl UED N18 ... 42 C4
  WAN E11 ... 58 E3
Trafalgar Rd GNWCH SE10 ... 113 H4
  RAIN RM13 ... 99 H1
  WHTN TW2 ... 142 D1
  WIM/MER SW19 ... 147 F6
Trafalgar Sq STJS SW1Y * ... 11 J8
Trafalgar Ter HRW HA1 * ... 48 E6
Trafalgar Wy CROY/NA CR0 ... 177 J1
  POP/IOD E14 ... 94 A6
Trafford Cl THHTH CR7 ... 164 A4
Trahorn Cl WCHPL E1 ... 92 C3
Tram Cl HNHL SE24 ... 130 C2
Tramway Av ED N9 ... 30 D6
Tramway Ct PGE/AN SE20 ... 162 D3
Tramway Pth MTCM CR4 ... 162 D3
Tranby Ms HOM E9 ... 75 F4
Tranley Ms HAMP NW3 ... 71 J3
Tranmere Rd ED N9 ... 30 B6
  WAND/EARL SW18 ... 147 G1
  WHTN TW2 ... 123 G6
Tranquil La RYLN/HDSTN HA2 ... 48 A7
Tranquil Pas BKHTH/KID SE3 * ... 133 J1
Tranquil Ri ERITH DA8 ... 118 B4
Tranquil V BKHTH/KID SE3 ... 133 H1
Transept St CAMTN NW1 ... 9 J1
Transmere Rd
  STMC/STPC BR5 ... 169 H5
Transom Cl BERM/RHTH SE16 ... 112 B3
Transom Sq POP/IOD E14 ... 112 E4
Transport Av BTFD TW8 ... 104 B4
Tranton Rd BERM/RHTH SE16 ... 111 J2
Traps La NWMAL KT3 ... 160 B1
Travellers Wy HSLWW TW4 ... 122 B1
Travers Cl WALTH E17 ... 43 F1
Travers Rd HOLWY N7 ... 73 G2
Treacy Cl BUSH WD23 ... 34 C1
Treadgold St NTGHL W11 ... 88 B6
Treadway St BETH E2 ... 92 D1
Treaty St IS N1 ... 5 L4
Trebeck St MYFR/PICC W1J ... 10 D8
Trebovir Rd ECT SW5 ... 14 B7
Treby St BOW E3 ... 93 H3
Trecastle Wy HOLWY N7 ... 72 D3
Tredegar Rd BOW E3 ... 93 H1
  FBAR/BDGN N11 ... 40 D6
Tredegar Sq BOW E3 ... 93 H2
Trederwen Rd HACK E8 ... 74 C7
Tredown Rd SYD SE26 ... 150 E4
Tredwell Cl BRXS/STRHM SW2 ... 149 F1
  HAYES BR2 ... 168 C3
Tredwell Rd WNWD SE27 ... 149 H3
Tree Cl RCHPK/HAM TW10 ... 124 E7
Tree Av BARN SW13 ... 126 B2
Tree Rd CAN/RD E16 ... 95 G5
Treeside Cl WDR/YW UB7 ... 100 A3
Tree Top Ms DAGE RM10 ... 81 F5
Treetops Cl ABYW SE2 ... 117 F4
  NTHWD HA6 ... 32 B4
Tree View Cl NRWD SE19 ... 150 A7
Treewall Gdns BMLY BR1 ... 153 F3
Trefgarne Rd DAGE RM10 ... 80 C1
Trefoil Rd WAND/EARL SW18 ... 128 B4
Tregaron Av CEND/HSY/T N8 ... 54 E5
Tregaron Gdns NWMAL KT3 ... 160 B3
Tregarvon Rd BTSEA SW11 ... 129 F3
Tregenna Av
  RYLN/HDSTN HA2 ... 66 A3
Tregenna Cl STHGT/OAK N14 ... 28 C4
Trego Rd HOM E9 ... 75 J6
Tregothnan Rd BRXN/ST SW9 ... 129 K2
Tregunter Rd WBPTN SW10 ... 14 E9
Treherne Ct BRXN/ST SW9 * ... 110 C7
Trehern Rd MORT/ESHN SW14 ... 126 A2
Trehurst St CLPT E5 ... 75 G4
Trelawney Est HOM E9 * ... 74 E5
Trelawn Rd BRXS/STRHM SW2 ... 130 B4
  LEY E10 ... 76 A2
Trelawny Cl WALTH E17 ... 57 K3
Trellis Sq BOW E3 ... 93 H2
Treloar Gdns NRWD SE19 ... 149 K5
Trelwney Est HOM E9 * ... 74 E5
Tremadoc Rd CLAP SW4 ... 129 J3
Tremaine Cl BROCKY SE4 ... 132 D1
Tremaine Rd PGE/AN SE20 ... 165 J1
Trematon Pl TEDD TW11 ... 143 J6
Tremlett Gv ARCH N19 ... 72 C2
Tremlett Ms ARCH N19 * ... 72 C2
Trenance Gdns
  GDMY/SEVK IG3 ... 79 G2
Trenchard Av RSLP HA4 ... 65 F4
Trenchard Ct CDALE/KGS NW9 ... 37 G7
  STAN HA7 ... 35 H5
Trenchard St GNWCH SE10 ... 113 G4
Trenchold St VX/NE SW8 * ... 109 K5
Trenholme Rd PGE/AN SE20 ... 150 D6
Trenholme Ter PGE/AN SE20 ... 150 D6
Trenmar Gdns WLSDN NW10 ... 87 K2
Trent Av EA W5 ... 104 D2
Trent Ct WAN E11 ... 58 E4
Trent Gdns STHGT/OAK N14 ... 28 B5
Trentham St
  WAND/EARL SW18 ... 127 K7
Trent Pk EBAR EN4 ... 28 C1
Trent Rd BRXS/STRHM SW2 ... 130 A4
Trent Wy WPK KT4 ... 174 A2
  YEAD UB4 ... 82 C2
Trentwood Side ENC/FH EN2 ... 29 F2
Treport St WAND/EARL SW18 ... 128 A6
Tresco Cl BMLY BR1 ... 152 C5
Trescoe Gdns
  RYLN/HDSTN HA2 ... 47 J6
Tresco Gdns GDMY/SEVK IG3 ... 79 G1

Tresco Rd PECK SE15 ... 131 J3
Tresham Crs STJWD NW8 ... 3 J9
Tresham Rd BARK IG11 ... 79 F6
Tresilian Av WCHMH N21 ... 29 F4
Tressel Cl IS N1 ... 6 D2
Tressillian Crs BROCKY SE4 ... 132 D2
Tressillian Rd BROCKY SE4 ... 132 D3
Trestis Cl YEAD UB4 ... 83 H3
Treswell Rd DAGW RM9 ... 80 A7
Tretawn Gdns MLHL NW7 ... 37 G3
Tretawn Pk MLHL NW7 ... 37 G3
Trevanion Rd WKENS W14 * ... 107 H4
Treve Av HRW HA1 ... 48 C6
Trevelyan Av MNPK E12 ... 77 K3
Trevelyan Crs
  KTN/HRWW/WS HA3 ... 49 K6
Trevelyan Gdns
  WLSDN NW10 * ... 70 A7
Trevelyan Rd SRTFD E15 ... 76 C3
  TOOT SW17 ... 147 K5
Treveris St STHWK SE1 ... 12 D9
Treverton St NKENS W10 ... 88 B3
Treves Cl WCHMH N21 ... 29 F4
Treville St PUT/ROE SW15 ... 126 E6
Treviso Rd FSTH SE23 ... 151 F1
Trevithick Cl
  EBED/NFELT TW14 ... 121 J7
Trevithick Dr DART DA1 ... 139 J4
Trevithick St DEPT SE8 ... 112 D5
Trevone Gdns PIN HA5 ... 47 J5
Trevor Cl EBAR EN4 ... 27 H5
  HAYES BR2 ... 167 J6
  ISLW TW7 ... 124 A4
  KTN/HRWW/WS HA3 ... 35 F6
  NTHLT UB5 ... 83 G1
Trevor Crs RSLP HA4 ... 64 D3
Trevor Gdns EDGW HA8 ... 37 F7
  NTHLT UB5 ... 83 G1
  RSLP HA4 ... 64 D3
Trevor Pl SKENS SW7 ... 15 K2
Trevor Rd EDGW HA8 ... 37 F7
  HYS/HAR UB3 ... 101 H1
  WFD IG8 ... 44 E6
  WIM/MER SW19 ... 146 C6
Trevor Sq SKENS SW7 ... 15 K2
Trevor St SKENS SW7 ... 15 K2
Trevose Rd WALTH E17 ... 44 B7
Trevose Wy WATW WD18 ... 33 G2
Trewenna Dr CHSGTN KT9 ... 171 K4
Trewince Rd RYNPK SW20 ... 146 A7
Trewint St WAND/EARL SW18 ... 147 F1
Trewsbury Rd SYD SE26 ... 151 F4
Triandra Wy YEAD UB4 ... 83 H4
Triangle Pas EBAR EN4 * ... 27 G3
Triangle Pl CLAP SW4 ... 129 J3
Triangle Rd HACK E8 ... 74 D7
The Triangle BFN/LL DA15 * ... 136 B6
  HACK E8 ... 74 D7
  KUT/HW KT1 ... 159 K1
Triangle Wy ACT W3 ... 105 J2
Trident St BERM/RHTH SE16 ... 112 A3
Trident Wy NWDGN UB2 ... 102 A2
Trigon Rd VX/NE SW8 ... 110 A6
Trilby Rd FSTH SE23 ... 151 F1
Trim St NWCR SE14 ... 112 C5
Trinder Rd ARCH N19 ... 54 E7
  BAR EN5 ... 26 A4
Tring Av EA W5 ... 86 B7
  STHL UB1 ... 83 K5
  WBLY HA9 ... 68 C5
Tring Cl GNTH/NBYPK IG2 ... 60 C4
Trinidad Gdns DAGE RM10 ... 81 F6
Trinidad St POP/IOD E14 ... 93 H6
Trinity Av EFNCH N2 ... 53 H2
  EN EN1 ... 30 B5
Trinity Buoy Whf
  POP/IOD E14 * ... 94 B4
Trinity Church Rd BARN SW13 ... 106 E5
Trinity Church Sq STHWK SE1 ... 18 F3
Trinity Cl CLAP SW4 ... 129 H3
  HACK E8 ... 74 B5
  HAYES BR2 ... 168 D7
  HSLWW TW4 ... 122 D3
  LEW SE13 ... 133 G3
  NTHWD HA6 ... 32 C5
  SAND/SEL CR2 ... 178 A7
  WAN E11 ... 76 C1
Trinity Crs ELTH/MOT SE9 ... 135 C5
  TOOT SW17 ... 147 K1
Trinity Dr UX/CGN UB8 ... 82 A5
Trinity Est DEPT SE8 ... 112 C4
Trinity Gdns BRXN/ST SW9 ... 130 A3
  CAN/RD E16 ... 94 D4
  DART DA1 ... 139 G5
Trinity Gn WCHPL E1 * ... 92 E4
Trinity Gv GNWCH SE10 ... 113 F7
Trinity Hall Cl WATN WD24 ... 21 G1
Trinity Ms PGE/AN SE20 ... 165 J1
  WIM/MER SW19 ... 146 E5
Trinity Pde HSLW TW3 * ... 123 G2
Trinity Pk BXLYHS DA6 ... 137 F3
Trinity Pl BXLYHS DA6 ... 137 F3
Trinity Ri BRXS/STRHM SW2 ... 130 C6
Trinity Rd BARK/HLT IG6 ... 60 C2
  EFNCH N2 ... 53 H2
  RCH/KEW TW9 ... 125 G2
  STHL UB1 ... 83 J7
  TOOT SW17 ... 147 K1
  WAND/EARL SW18 ... 128 C5
  WDGN N22 ... 40 E7
  WIM/MER SW19 ... 146 E5
Trinity Sq TWRH EC3N ... 13 L6
Trinity St CAN/RD E16 ... 94 D4
  ENC/FH EN2 ... 29 J1
  STHWK SE1 ... 18 F2
Trinity Wy ACT W3 ... 87 G6
  CHING E4 ... 43 H5
Trio Pl STHWK SE1 ... 18 F2

Troy Town PECK SE15 ... 131 H2
Trubshaw Rd NWDGN UB2 ... 103 F2
Trueman Cl EDGW HA8 * ... 36 D6
Trulock Rd TOTM N17 ... 42 C6
Trumans Rd STNW/STAM N16 ... 74 A4
Trumpers Wy HNWL W7 ... 104 A2
Trumpington Rd FSTGT E7 ... 76 D3
Trump St CITYW EC2V ... 12 F5
Trundlers Wy BUSH WD23 ... 22 E7
Trundle St STHWK SE1 ... 18 E1
Trundleys Rd DEPT SE8 ... 112 B5
Trundley's Rd DEPT SE8 ... 112 A4
Trundley's Ter DEPT SE8 ... 112 A3
Truro Gdns IL IG1 ... 59 J6
Truro Rd WALTH E17 ... 57 H3
  WDGN N22 ... 40 E6
Truro St KTTN NW5 ... 72 A5
Truro Wy YEAD UB4 ... 82 C2
Trusdale Rd EHAM E6 ... 96 A5
Truslove Rd WNWD SE27 ... 149 G4
Trussley Rd HMSMTH W6 ... 107 F2
Trustons Gdns EMPK RM11 ... 63 J6
Tryfan Cl REDBR IG4 ... 59 H4
Tryon Crs HOM E9 ... 74 E7
Tryon St CHEL SW3 ... 15 L7
Trystings Cl ESH/CLAY KT10 ... 171 G5
Tubbs Rd WLSDN NW10 ... 87 H1
Tucker Rd RAIN RM13 ... 99 J5
Tudor Av GPK RM2 ... 63 J2
  HPTN TW12 ... 142 A5
  WPK KT4 ... 173 K2
Tudor Cl BRXS/STRHM SW2 * ... 130 A5
  CDALE/KGS NW9 ... 68 E1
  CHEAM SM3 ... 174 B4
  CHSGTN KT9 ... 172 A4
  CHST BR7 ... 153 K7
  DART DA1 ... 138 C7
  HAMP NW3 ... 71 J4
  HGT N6 ... 54 C6
  HPTN TW12 ... 142 D4
  MLHL NW7 ... 37 J5
  PIN HA5 ... 46 E4
  WFD IG8 ... 45 F4
  WLGTN SM6 ... 176 C6
Tudor Ct BORE WD6 ... 24 D1
  ELTH/MOT SE9 * ... 134 D3
  WALTH E17 ... 57 H6
Tudor Ct North WBLY HA9 ... 68 C4
Tudor Ct South WBLY HA9 ... 68 C4
Tudor Dr GPK RM2 ... 63 J3
  KUTN/CMB KT2 ... 144 A4
  MRDN SM4 ... 161 G5
  WOT/HER KT12 ... 156 A7
Tudor Est WLSDN NW10 ... 86 D1
Tudor Gdns ACT W3 ... 86 C4
  BARN SW13 ... 126 B2
  CDALE/KGS NW9 ... 68 E1
  GPK RM2 ... 63 J3
  TWK TW1 ... 124 A7
  WWKM BR4 ... 180 A2
Tudor Gv HOM E9 ... 74 E6
Tudor Ms WLSDN NW10 ... 69 J5
Tudor Pde ELTH/MOT SE9 * ... 134 D3
Tudor Pl MTCM CR4 ... 147 J6
  NRWD SE19 * ... 150 B6
Tudor Rd ASHF TW15 ... 140 B5
  BAR EN5 ... 26 E2
  BARK IG11 ... 79 F6
  BECK BR3 ... 167 F2
  CHING E4 ... 43 K5
  ED N9 ... 30 D6
  HACK E8 ... 74 D7
  HPTN TW12 ... 142 A6
  HSLW TW3 ... 123 J3
  KTN/HRWW/WS HA3 ... 48 C1
  KUTN/CMB KT2 ... 144 C6
  NRWD SE19 ... 150 B6
  PIN HA5 ... 47 G1
  PLSTW E13 ... 94 D2
  SNWD SE25 ... 165 J4
  STHL UB1 ... 83 J6
Tudor Sq HYS/HAR UB3 ... 82 B4
Tudor St EMB EC4Y ... 12 B5
Tudor Wy ACT W3 ... 105 H1
  STHGT/OAK N14 ... 28 D7
  STMC/STPC BR5 ... 169 F5
Tudor Well Cl STAN HA7 ... 35 H4
Tudway Rd BKHTH/KID SE3 ... 134 B3
Tufnail Rd DART DA1 ... 139 J4
Tufnell Park Rd HOLWY N7 ... 72 C3
Tufton Gdns E/WMO/HCT KT8 ... 157 G1
Tufton Rd CHING E4 ... 43 J3
Tufton St WEST SW1P ... 17 J3
Tugboat St THMD SE28 ... 115 K1
Tugela Rd CROY/NA CR0 ... 164 E5
Tugela St CAT SE6 ... 151 H1
Tulip Cl CROY/NA CR0 ... 166 A7
  EHAM E6 ... 95 J4
  HPTN TW12 ... 141 K5
  NWDGN UB2 ... 103 H1
Tulip Gdns CHING E4 * ... 44 B2
  IL IG1 ... 78 C6
Tulip Wy WDR/YW UB7 ... 100 A3
Tull St CAR SM5 ... 162 E6
Tulse Cl BECK BR3 ... 167 F2
Tulse Hl BRXS/STRHM SW2 ... 130 C7
Tulsemere Rd WNWD SE27 ... 149 J1
Tummons Gdns SNWD SE25 ... 165 F1
Tuncombe Rd UED N18 ... 42 A3
Tunis Rd SHB W12 ... 88 A7
Tunley Gn POP/IOD E14 ... 93 H4
Tunley Rd TOOT SW17 ... 148 A1
  WLSDN NW10 ... 69 G7
Tunmarsh La PLSTW E13 ... 95 F2
Tunnan Leys EHAM E6 ... 96 A5
Tunnel Av GNWCH SE10 ... 113 G2
Tunnel Gdns FBAR/BDGN N11 ... 40 C6
Tunnel Rd BERM/RHTH SE16 ... 111 K1
Tunnel Rd East WDR/YW UB7 ... 100 D7
Tunnel Rd West WDR/YW UB7 ... 100 D7
Tunstall Rd BRXN/ST SW9 ... 130 A3
  CROY/NA CR0 ... 165 F7
Tunstock Wy BELV DA17 ... 117 F2
Tunworth Cl CDALE/KGS NW9 ... 50 E5
Tunworth Crs PUT/ROE SW15 ... 126 C5
Tupelo Rd LEY E10 ... 75 K1
Tuppy St THMD SE28 ... 115 J2
Turene Cl WAND/EARL SW18 ... 128 C3
Turin Rd ED N9 ... 30 E6
Turin St BETH E2 ... 92 C2
Turkey Oak Cl NRWD SE19 ... 150 A7
Turks Rw CHEL SW3 ... 15 M7
Turle Rd FSBYPK N4 ... 73 F1
  STRHM/NOR SW16 ... 163 K1
Turlewray Cl FSBYPK N4 ... 55 F7
Turley Cl SRTFD E15 ... 76 C7
Turnagain La
  FLST/FETLN EC4A ... 12 C4
Turnage Rd BCTR RM8 ... 62 A7
Turnant Rd TOTM N17 ... 41 J7

Turnberry Cl
  BERM/RHTH SE16 * ... 111 J4
  HDN NW4 ... 52 B1
Turnberry Ct OXHEY WD19 * ... 33 G2
Turnberry Wy ORP BR6 ... 169 J7
Turnchapel Ms CLAP SW4 ... 129 G2
Turner Av MTCM CR4 ... 147 K5
  SEVS/STOTM N15 ... 56 A3
  WHTN TW2 ... 142 C2
Turner Cl BRXN/ST SW9 ... 110 C7
  GLDGN NW11 ... 53 F5
Turner Ct CMBW SE5 * ... 130 E3
  DART DA1 ... 139 F4
Turner Crs THHTH CR7 ... 164 C4
Turner Dr GLDGN NW11 ... 53 F5
Turner Ms BELMT SM2 ... 175 F6
Turner Rd BUSH WD23 ... 22 C3
  EDGW HA8 ... 50 A1
  NWMAL KT3 ... 160 A6
  WALTH E17 ... 58 A2
Turners Cl TRDG/WHET N20 ... 39 K2
Turners Meadow Wy
  BECK BR3 ... 151 H7
Turner's Rd BOW E3 ... 93 H4
Turner St CAN/RD E16 ... 94 D5
  WCHPL E1 ... 92 D4
Turners Wy CROY/NA CR0 ... 177 G1
Turner's Wd GLDGN NW11 ... 53 G2
Turneville Rd WKENS W14 ... 107 J5
Turney Rd DUL SE21 ... 130 E5
Turnham Green Ter
  CHSWK W4 ... 106 B3
Turnham Rd BROCKY SE4 ... 132 B4
Turnmill St FARR EC1M ... 12 D1
Turnpike Cl DEPT SE8 ... 112 C6
  WELL DA16 ... 136 B2
Turnpike La CEND/HSY/T N8 ... 55 G3
  SUT SM1 ... 175 G4
Turnpike Link CROY/NA CR0 ... 178 A1
Turnpike Ms
  CEND/HSY/T N8 ... 55 G2
Turnpike Pde
  SEVS/STOTM N15 * ... 55 H2
Turnpike Wy ISLW TW7 ... 104 B7
Turnstone Cl
  CDALE/KGS NW9 ... 51 G1
  PLSTW E13 ... 94 E2
Turnstone Ter WEA W13 * ... 85 F3
Turpentine La PIM SW1V ... 16 D7
Turpington Cl HAYES BR2 ... 168 D5
Turpington La HAYES BR2 ... 168 D4
Turpin La ERITH DA8 ... 118 D5
Turpin Rd EBED/NFELT TW14 ... 121 J5
Turpin's La WFD IG8 ... 45 K4
Turpins Yd CRICK NW2 * ... 70 B4
  GNWCH SE10 ... 113 F6
Turpin Wy WLGTN SM6 ... 176 B6
Turquand St WALW SE17 ... 18 F6
Turret Gv CLAP SW4 ... 129 H2
Turton Rd ALP/SUD HA0 ... 68 A4
Turville St BETH E2 ... 7 L9
Tuscan Rd WOOL/PLUM SE18 ... 115 J4
Tuskar St GNWCH SE10 ... 113 H4
Tweeddale Gv
  HGDN/ICK UB10 ... 64 A2
Tweeddale Rd CAR SM5 ... 162 C7
Tweedmouth Rd PLSTW E13 ... 95 F1
Tweedy Rd BMLY BR1 ... 152 E7
Twelvetrees Crs BOW E3 ... 94 A3
Twentyman Cl WFD IG8 ... 44 E4
Twickenham Br TWK TW1 ... 124 D4
Twickenham Cl CROY/NA CR0 ... 177 F2
Twickenham Gdns
  GFD/PVL UB6 ... 67 G4
  KTN/HRWW/WS HA3 ... 34 E6
Twickenham Rd FELT TW13 ... 141 J2
  ISLW TW7 ... 124 A3
  TEDD TW11 ... 143 G3
  WAN E11 ... 76 B1
Twig Folly Cl BETH E2 ... 93 F1
Twig Folly Whf BETH E2 * ... 93 F1
Twigg Cl ERITH DA8 ... 118 B6
Twilley St WAND/EARL SW18 ... 128 A6
Twine Cl BARK IG11 ... 97 H2
Twine Ct WCHPL E1 ... 92 E6
Twineham Gn
  NFNCH/WDSPK N12 ... 38 E3
Twine Ter BOW E3 * ... 93 H3
Twining Av WHTN TW2 ... 142 C2
Twinn Rd MLHL NW7 ... 38 C5
Twin Tumps Wy THMD SE28 ... 97 G6
Twisden Rd KTTN NW5 ... 72 B3
Twisleton Ct DART DA1 ... 139 G5
Twitten Gv BMLY BR1 ... 168 E2
Twybridge Wy WLSDN NW10 ... 68 G6
Twycross Ms GNWCH SE10 ... 113 H3
Twyford Abbey Rd
  WLSDN NW10 ... 86 B2
Twyford Av ACT W3 ... 86 C6
  EFNCH N2 ... 53 K2
Twyford Crs ACT W3 ... 86 B7
Twyford Pl CAR SM5 ... 162 C7
  IL IG1 ... 78 C2
  RYLN/HDSTN HA2 ... 66 B2
Twyford Pl IS N1 ... 5 L3
Twyford St IS N1 ... 5 L3
Tyas Rd CAN/RD E16 ... 94 D3
Tybenham Rd
  WIM/MER SW19 ... 161 K4
Tyberry Rd PEND EN3 ... 30 D2
Tyburn La HRW HA1 ... 48 E6
Tyburn Wy MBLAR W1H ... 9 M6
Tyers Ga STHWK SE1 ... 19 J2
Tyers St LBTH SE11 ... 17 L7
Tyers Ter LBTH SE11 ... 17 L7
Tyeshurst Cl ABYW SE2 ... 117 F4
Tylecroft Rd
  STRHM/NOR SW16 ... 163 K1
Tylehurst Gdns IL IG1 ... 78 C4
Tyler Cl BETH E2 ... 7 L5
  ERITH DA8 ... 118 D7
Tylers Ga KTN/HRWW/WS HA3 ... 50 A5
Tyler St GNWCH SE10 ... 113 H4
Tylney Av NRWD SE19 ... 150 B4
Tylney Rd BMLY BR1 ... 168 C1
  FSTGT E7 ... 77 G3
Tynan Cl EBED/NFELT TW14 ... 121 K7
Tyndale Ct IS N1 * ... 6 A1
Tyndale La IS N1 ... 6 A1
Tyndall Rd LEY E10 ... 76 A1
  WELL DA16 ... 136 A2
Tyneham Cl BTSEA SW11 ... 129 F2
Tyneham Rd BTSEA SW11 ... 129 F1
Tynemouth Cl EHAM E6 ... 96 B5
Tynemouth Rd MTCM CR4 ... 148 A6
  SEVS/STOTM N15 ... 56 B3
  WOOL/PLUM SE18 ... 115 K4
Tynemouth St
  SEVS/STOTM N15 * ... 56 D4
Tyne St WCHPL E1 ... 13 M4

Tynsdale Rd WLSDN NW10....69 G6
Type St BETH E2....93 F1
Tyrawley Rd FUL/PGN SW6....108 A4
Tyre La CDALE/KGS NW9 *....51 G3
Tyrell Cl HRW HA1....66 E3
Tyrone Rd EHAM E6....95 H3
Tyron Wy SCUP DA14....154 E3
Tyrrell Av WELL DA16....136 B4
Tyrrell Rd EDUL SE22....131 H3
Tyrrel Wy CDALE/KGS NW9 *....51 H6
Tyrwhitt Rd BROCKY SE4....132 D2
Tysoe St CLKNW EC1R....6 B8
  FSBYW WC1X....6 A8
Tyson Gdns FSTH SE23....131 K6
Tyson Rd FSTH SE23....131 K6
Tyssen Rd STNW/STAM N16 *....74 B2
Tyssen St HACK E8....74 B5
  IS N1....7 K5
Tytherton Rd ARCH N19....72 D2

U

Uamvar St POP/IOD E14....93 K4
Uckfield Gv MTCM CR4....148 A7
Udall St WEST SW1P....16 F6
Udney Park Rd TEDD TW11....143 G4
Uffington Rd WLSDN NW10....69 H7
  WNWD SE27....149 G3
Ufford Cl KTN/HRWW/WS HA3....34 B6
Ufford Rd KTN/HRWW/WS HA3....34 B6
Ufford St STHWK SE1....18 B1
Ufton Rd IS N1....7 J1
Uhura Sq STNW/STAM N16 *....74 A2
Ullathorne Rd STRHM/NOR SW16....148 C3
Ulleswater Vls STHGT/OAK N14....40 E3
Ulleswater Vls STHGT/OAK N14....40 E3
Ullin St POP/IOD E14....94 A4
Ullswater Cl BMLY BR1....152 C5
  PUT/ROE SW15....145 F3
  YEAD UB4....82 C1
Ullswater Ct RYLN/HDSTN HA2 *....48 A6
Ullswater Crs PUT/ROE SW15....145 F3
Ullswater Rd BARN SW13....106 D6
  WNWD SE27....149 H2
Ullswater Wy HCH RM12....81 J4
Ulster Gdns PLMGR N13....41 J3
Ulster Pl CAMTN NW1....10 C1
Ulundi Rd BKHTH/KID SE3....113 H5
Ulva Rd PUT/ROE SW15....127 G3
Ulverscroft Rd EDUL SE22....131 H4
Ulverston Rd WALTH E17....58 B1
Ulysses Rd KIL/WHAMP NW6....70 D4
Umberston St WCHPL E1 *....92 C5
Umbria St PUT/ROE SW15....126 D5
Umfreville Rd FSBYPK N4....55 H5
Undercliff Rd LEW SE13....132 D2
Underhill BAR EN5....26 E4
Underhill Ct BAR EN5 *....26 E4
Underhill Rd EDUL SE22....131 H4
Underhill St CAMTN NW1....4 D4
Underne Av STHGT/OAK N14....40 B1
Undershaft HDTCH EC3A....13 J5
Undershaw Rd BMLY BR1....152 C2
Underwood CROY/NA CR0....180 A5
Underwood Rd CHING E4....43 K4
  WCHPL E1....92 C3
  WFD IG8....45 H6
Underwood Rw IS N1....6 F7
Underwood St IS N1....6 F7
The Underwood ELTH/MOT SE9....153 K4
Undine Rd POP/IOD E14....112 E3
Undine St TOOT SW17....147 K4
Uneeda Dr GFD/PVL UB6....76 B3
Union Cl WAN E11....76 B1
Union Ct CLAP SW4 *....129 K1
  OBST EC2N....13 J4
Union Dr WCHPL E1 *....93 G3
Union Gv VX/NE SW8....129 J1
Union La ISLW TW7....104 B7
Union Pk GNWCH SE10....113 J4
Union Rd ALP/SUD HA0....68 A5
  CLAP SW4....129 J1
  CROY/NA CR0....164 D6
  FBAR/BDGN N11....40 D5
  HAYES BR2....168 C4
  NTHLT UB5....84 A1
  ROMW/RG RM7....63 F5
  VX/NE SW8....129 J1
Union Sq IS N1....6 E4
Union St BAR EN5....26 C3
  KUT/HW KT1....158 E1
  SRTFD E15....76 B7
  STHWK SE1....17 L7
Union Wk BETH E2....7 L7
Unity Cl CROY/NA CR0....179 K7
  NRWD SE19....149 J4
  WLSDN NW10....69 G5
Unity Ms CAMTN NW1....5 G5
Unity Wy WOOL/PLUM SE18....114 C2
University Av MLHL NW7....37 H4
University Gdns BXLY DA5....137 G6
University Pl ERITH DA8....117 J6
University Rd WIM/MER SW19....147 H5
University Wy CAN/RD E16....96 A6
  DART DA1....139 J2
Unwin Av EBED/NFELT TW14....121 H4
Unwin Cl PECK SE15....111 H5
Unwin Rd ISLW TW7....123 K2
  SKENS SW7....15 H3
Upbrook Ms BAY/PAD W2....8 F5
Upcerne Rd WBPTN SW10....108 B6
Upcroft Av EDGW HA8....36 E4
Updale Rd SCUP DA14....155 F4
Upfield CROY/NA CR0....178 D1
Upfield Rd HNWL W7....85 F3
Uphall Rd IL IG1....78 B4
Upham Park Rd CHSWK W4....106 B3
Uphill Dr CDALE/KGS NW9....50 E4
  MLHL NW7....37 G4
Uphill Gv MLHL NW7....37 G3
Uphill Rd MLHL NW7....37 G3
Upland Rd BELMT SM2....175 H6
  BXLYHN DA7....137 G2
  EDUL SE22....131 H6
  PLSTW E13....94 E3
  SAND/SEL CR2....177 K4
Uplands BECK BR3....166 D1
Uplands Rd MORT/ESHN SW14....125 J4
  WOOL/PLUM SE18....115 G6
Uplands Park Rd ENC/FH EN2....29 G1
  CEND/HSY/T N8....61 K2
  CHDH RM6....61 J4
  EBAR EN4....28 D1

WFD IG8....45 J6
The Uplands RSLP HA4....46 E7
Uplands Wy WCHMH N21....29 G4
Upminster Rd South RAIN RM13....99 J3
Upney La BARK IG11....79 F6
Upnor Wy WALW SE17....19 K7
Uppark Dr GNTH/NBYPK IG2....60 C5
Upper Abbey Rd BELV DA17....117 H3
Upper Addison Gdns WKENS W14....107 H1
Upper Bank St POP/IOD E14....93 K7
Upper Bardsey Wk IS N1 *....73 J5
Upper Belgrave St KTBR SW1X....16 B3
Upper Berenger Wk WBPTN SW10 *....108 C6
Upper Berkeley St MBLAR W1H....9 L5
Upper Beulah Hl NRWD SE19....150 A7
Upper Blantyre Wk WBPTN SW10 *....108 C6
Upper Brighton Rd SURB KT6....158 E5
Upper Brockley Rd BROCKY SE4....132 C1
Upper Brook St MYFR/PKLN W1K....10 A7
Upper Butts BTFD TW8....104 D5
Upper Caldy Wk IS N1 *....73 J5
Upper Camelford Wk NTGHL W11 *....88 C5
Upper Cavendish Av FNCH N3....52 E2
Upper Cheyne Rw CHEL SW3....108 D5
Upper Clapton Rd CLPT E5....74 D1
Upper Clarendon Wk NTGHL W11 *....88 C5
Upper Dartrey Wk WBPTN SW10 *....108 B6
Upper Dengie Wk IS N1 *....6 E1
Upper Elmers End Rd BECK BR3....166 B3
Upper Farm Rd E/WMO/HCT KT8....156 E3
Upper Gn East MTCM CR4....162 E1
Upper Gn West MTCM CR4....162 E1
Upper Grosvenor St MYFR/PKLN W1K....10 A7
Upper Grotto Rd TWK TW1....143 F1
Upper Gnd STHWK SE1....12 A8
Upper Gv SNWD SE25....165 F3
Upper Grove Rd BELV DA17....117 G5
Upper Gulland Wk IS N1 *....73 J5
Upper Ham Rd RCHPK/HAM TW10....143 K3
Upper Handa Wk IS N1 *....73 K5
Upper Harley St CAMTN NW1....10 B8
Upper Hawkwell Wk IS N1 *....6 F1
Upper Hitch OXHEY WD19....21 J7
Upper Holly Hill Rd BELV DA17....117 J4
Upper John St SOHO/CST W1F....10 F6
Upper Lismore Wk IS N1 *....73 J5
Upper Mi HMSMTH W6....106 D4
Upper Marsh STHWK SE1....17 M3
Upper Montagu St MBLAR W1H....9 L2
Upper Mulgrave Rd BELMT SM2....174 C6
Upper North St POP/IOD E14....93 J4
Upper Paddock Rd OXHEY WD19....21 J5
Upper Park Rd BELV DA17....117 J3
  BMLY BR1....153 F7
  FBAR/BDGN N11....40 B4
  HAMP NW3....71 K5
  KUTN/CMB KT2....144 C5
Upper Phillimore Gdns KENS W8....14 A2
Upper Rainham Rd HCH RM12....81 H3
Upper Rawreth St IS N1 *....6 F3
Upper Richmond Rd PUT/ROE SW15....126 E3
Upper Richmond Rd West MORT/ESHN SW14....126 A3
  RCHPK/HAM TW10....125 H3
Upper Rd PLSTW E13....94 E2
  WLGTN SM6....176 D4
Upper St Martin's La LSQ/SEVD WC2H....11 J5
Upper Selsdon Rd SAND/SEL CR2....178 B7
Upper Sheppey Wk IS N1 *....73 J5
Upper Sheridan Rd BELV DA17....117 H3
Upper Shirley Rd CROY/NA CR0....178 E2
Upper Sq ISLW TW7....124 B2
Upper St IS N1....6 B5
  IS N1....6 C1
Upper Sunbury Rd HPTN TW12....141 K7
Upper Sutton La HEST TW5....103 F7
Upper Tachbrook St PIM SW1V....16 E6
Upper Talbot St NTGHL W11 *....88 C5
Upper Teddington Rd KUT/HW KT1....143 J7
Upper Ter HAMP NW3....71 G2
Upper Thames St BLKFR EC4V....12 E6
Upper Tollington Pk FSBYPK N4....55 G7
Upperton Rd East PLSTW E13....95 G2
Upperton Rd West PLSTW E13....95 G2
Upper Tooting Pk TOOT SW17....147 K1
Upper Tooting Rd TOOT SW17....147 K3
Upper Town Rd STHL UB1....84 B3
Upper Tulse HI BRXS/STRHM SW2....130 A6
Upper Vernon Rd SUT SM1....175 H4
Upper Walthamstow Rd WALTH E17....58 B3
Upper Whistler Wk WBPTN SW10 *....108 B6
Upper Wickham La WELL DA16....136 C1
Upper Wimpole St CAVSO/HST W1G....10 B1
Upper Woburn Pl CAMTN NW1....5 H8
  STPAN WC1H....5 H9
Uppingham Av STAN HA7....49 J2
Upsdell Av PLMGR N13....41 G5
Upstall St CMBW SE5....110 C7
Upton Av FSTGT E7....76 E6
Upton Cl BXLY DA5....137 G5
  CRICK NW2....70 C2
Upton Dene BELMT SM2....175 F6
Upton Gdns KTN/HRWW/WS HA3....49 J5
Upton La FSTGT E7....77 F5
Upton Lodge Cl BUSH WD23....22 C6
Upton Park Rd FSTGT E7....77 F6

Upton Rd BXLYHS DA6....137 F3
  HSLW TW3....123 F2
  THHTH CR7....164 E1
  UED N18....42 C4
  WATW WD18....21 F3
  WOOL/PLUM SE18....115 H5
Upton Rd South BXLY DA5....137 G5
Upway NFNCH/WDSPK N12....39 J4
Upwood Rd LEE/GVPK SE12....133 K5
  STRHM/NOR SW16....148 E7
Urban Ms FSBYPK N4....55 H6
Urlwin St CMBW SE5....110 D5
Urlwin Wk BRXN/ST SW9....110 B7
Urmston Dr WIM/MER SW19....127 H7
Ursula Gould Wy POP/IOD E14....93 J4
Ursula Ms FSBYPK N4....55 J4
Ursula St BTSEA SW11....108 D7
Urswick Gdns DAGW RM9....80 A6
Urswick Rd CLPT E5....74 E4
  DAGW RM9....80 A6
Usborne Ms VX/NE SW8....110 A6
Usher Rd BOW E3....75 H7
Usk Rd BTSEA SW11....128 B3
Usk St BETH E2....93 F2
Uvedale Rd DAGE RM10....80 C2
  ENC/FH EN2....29 K4
Uverdale Rd WBPTN SW10....108 B6
Uxbridge Rd EA W5....86 A6
  FELT TW13....141 H1
  HGDN/ICK UB10....82 A3
  HNWL W7....84 E7
  HPTN TW12....142 B4
  KUT/HW KT1....158 E5
  SHB W12....87 J7
  STHL UB1....84 A7
  WEA W13....85 H5
  YEAD UB4....82 E5
Uxbridge Rd (Harrow Weald) KTN/HRWW/WS HA3....34 C6
Uxbridge Rd (Hatch End) PIN HA5....33 J7
Uxbridge Road High St STHL UB1....83 K7
Uxbridge Rd (Pinner) PIN HA5....47 H1
Uxbridge Rd (Stanmore) STAN HA7....35 F5
Uxbridge Rd The Broadway YEAD UB4....83 F3
Uxbridge St KENS W8....8 A8
Uxendon Crs WBLY HA9....50 A7
Uxendon HI WBLY HA9....50 B7

V

Valan Leas HAYES BR2....167 H2
Vale Av BORE WD6....24 D4
Vale Cl EFNCH N2....53 K2
  MV/WKIL W9....2 E8
  TWK TW1 *....143 G2
Vale Cots PUT/ROE SW15 *....145 G7
Vale Crs PUT/ROE SW15....145 G3
Vale Cft ESH/CLAY KT10....171 F6
  PIN HA5....47 J4
Vale Dr BAR EN5....26 D3
Vale End EDUL SE22....131 G3
Vale Gv ACT W3....87 F7
  FSBYPK N4....55 J4
Vale La ACT W3....86 C4
Valence Av BCTR RM8....79 K2
Valence Circ BCTR RM8....79 K2
Valence Wood Rd BCTR RM8....79 K2
Valencia Rd STAN HA7....35 J3
Valency Cl NTHWD HA6....32 D3
Valentia Pl BRXN/ST SW9....130 B3
Valentine Pl STHWK SE1....18 C1
Valentine Rd HOM E9 *....75 F5
  RYLN/HDSTN HA2....66 B2
Valentines Rd IL IG1....60 B7
Valentines Wy ROMW/RG RM7....81 G1
Vale of Health HAMP NW3....71 G2
Valerian Wy SRTFD E15....94 C2
Vale Ri GLDGN NW11....52 D7
  BUSH WD23....21 J4
  DART DA1....138 E7
  ESH/CLAY KT10....170 E7
  FSBYPK N4....55 J4
  FSTGT E7....77 F5
  HOR/WEW KT19....173 H3
  MTCM CR4....163 J2
  SUT SM1....175 H3
  WPK KT4....173 H2
Vale Rw HBRY N5....73 H2
Vale Royal HOLWY N7....5 J1
Vale St DUL SE21....130 B6
Valeswood Rd BMLY BR1....152 D4
Vale Ter FSBYPK N4....55 J5
The Vale ACT W3....87 F7
  CHEL SW3....15 C9
  CROY/NA CR0....179 F1
  EBED/NFELT TW14....122 A5
  GLDGN NW11....70 B2
  HEST TW5....102 D5
  MUSWH N10....40 A7
  RSLP HA4....65 G3
  SHB W12....87 H7
  STHGT/OAK N14....28 E6
  SUN TW16 *....140 E5

Valley Wk CROY/NA CR0....178 E1
  RKW/CH/CXG WD3....20 A4
Valliere Rd WLSDN NW10....87 J2
Valliers Wood Rd BFN/LL SE9....135 J7
Vallis Wy CHSGTN KT9....171 K5
  WEA W13....85 G4
Valmar Rd CMBW SE5....110 D7
Val McKenzie Av HOLWY N7....73 G2
Valnay St TOOT SW17....147 K4
Valognes Av WALTH E17....43 G7
Valonia Gdns WAND/EARL SW18....127 J5
Vambery Rd WOOL/PLUM SE18....115 H5
Vanbrugh Crs NTHLT UB5....83 G1
Vanbrugh Flds BKHTH/KID SE3....113 J5
Vanbrugh Hl GNWCH SE10....113 H4
  BKHTH/KID SE3....113 J5
Vanbrugh Pk BKHTH/KID SE3....113 J6
Vanbrugh Park Rd BKHTH/KID SE3....113 J5
Vanbrugh Park Rd West BKHTH/KID SE3....113 J5
Vanbrugh Rd CHSWK W4....106 A2
Vanbrugh Ter BKHTH/KID SE3....113 J7
Vanburgh Cl CAN/RD E16....95 H4
  ORP BR6....169 K7
Vancouver Man EDGW HA8 *....36 D7
Vancouver Rd EDGW HA8....36 D7
  FSTH SE23....151 G1
  RCHPK/HAM TW10....143 J3
  YEAD UB4....83 F3
Vanderbilt Rd WAND/EARL SW18....128 A7
Vanderbilt Vls SHB W12 *....107 G1
Vanderville Gdns EFNCH N2....53 H1
Vandome Cl CAN/RD E16....95 F5
Vandon Cl STJSPK SW1H....16 F3
Vandon St STJSPK SW1H....16 F3
Van Dyck Av NWMAL KT3....160 A6
Vandyke Cl PUT/ROE SW15....127 G5
Vandyke Cross ELTH/MOT SE9....134 D4
Vandy St SDTCH EC2A....13 J1
Vane Cl HAMP NW3....71 H4
  KTN/HRWW/WS HA3....50 B5
Vanessa Cl BELV DA17....117 H4
Vanessa Wy BXLY DA5....155 J3
Van Gogh Cl ISLW TW7....124 B2
Vanguard CDALE/KGS NW9 *....37 G6
Vanguard Cl CAN/RD E16....94 E4
  CROY/NA CR0....164 C7
  ROMW/RG RM7....62 D1
Vanguard St DEPT SE8....112 D7
Vanguard Wy CROY/NA CR0....178 B3
  HTHAIR TW6....121 H1
  WLGTN SM6....176 E6
Vanneck Sq PUT/ROE SW15 *....126 D4
Vanoc Gdns BMLY BR1....152 E3
Vanquish Cl WHTN TW2....123 F7
Vansittart Rd FSTGT E7....76 E3
Vansittart St NWCR SE14....112 B6
Vanston Pl FUL/PGN SW6....107 K6
Vantage Pl KENS W8....14 B4
Vant Rd TOOT SW17....147 K4
Varcoe Gdns HYS/HAR UB3....82 B5
Varcoe Rd BERM/RHTH SE16....111 J4
Vardens Rd BTSEA SW11....128 C3
Varden St WCHPL E1....92 D5
Vardon Cl ACT W3....87 F5
Varley Dr TWK TW1....124 C3
Varley Rd CAN/RD E16....95 F5
Varley Wy MTCM CR4....162 C1
Varna Rd FUL/PGN SW6....107 H6
  HPTN TW12....142 B7
Varndell St CAMTN NW1....4 E7
Varsity Dr TWK TW1....123 K4
Varsity Rw MORT/ESHN SW14....125 K1
Vartry Rd SEVS/STOTM N15....56 A5
Vassall Rd BRXN/ST SW9....110 B6
Vauban Est BERM/RHTH SE16....19 M4
Vauban St BERM/RHTH SE16....19 M4
Vaughan Av HDN NW4....51 J4
  HMSMTH W6....106 C3
Vaughan Est BETH E2 *....7 L7
Vaughan Gdns IL IG1....59 K6
Vaughan Rd CMBW SE5....130 D1
  HRW HA1....48 C6
  SRTFD E15....76 D5
  THDIT KT7....158 C6
  WELL DA16....136 A1
Vaughan St BERM/RHTH SE16....112 C1
Vaughan Wy WAP E1W *....92 C6
Vaughan Williams Cl DEPT SE8....112 D6
Vauxhall Br STHWK SE1....17 J8
Vauxhall Bridge Rd PIM SW1V....16 E4
  WEST SW1P....17 H7
Vauxhall Gdns SAND/SEL CR2....177 J5
Vauxhall Gv VX/NE SW8....17 K9
Vauxhall Pl DART DA1....139 H6
Vauxhall St LBTH SE11....17 M7
Vauxhall Wk LBTH SE11....17 L7
Vawdrey Cl WCHPL E1....92 E3
Veals Md MTCM CR4....147 J7
Vectis Gdns TOOT SW17....148 B5
Vectis Rd TOOT SW17....148 B5
Veda Rd LEW SE13....132 D3
Vega Crs NTHWD HA6....32 C5
Vega Rd BUSH WD23....22 C6
Veitch Cl EBED/NFELT TW14....121 J7
Veldene Wy RYLN/HDSTN HA2....65 K2
Vellum Dr CAR SM5....176 A2
Venables Cl DAGE RM10....80 D3
Venables St STJWD NW8....8 G2
Vencourt Pl HMSMTH W6....106 D3
Venetia Rd EA W5....104 E1
  FSBYPK N4....55 H5
Venette Cl RAIN RM13....99 K4
Venice Av WATW WD18....20 C3
Venner Rd SYD SE26....150 E5
Venners Cl BXLYHN DA7....138 B1
Venn St CLAP SW4....129 H3
Ventnor Av STAN HA7....35 H1
Ventnor Dr TRDG/WHET N20....39 F2
Ventnor Gdns BARK IG11....78 E5
Ventnor Rd BELMT SM2....175 F6
  NWCR SE14....112 A6
Ventnor Ter SEVS/STOTM N15 *....56 C3
Venture Cl BXLY DA5....137 F6
Venue St POP/IOD E14....93 K4
Venus Ms MTCM CR4....162 D2
Venus Rd WOOL/PLUM SE18....114 D2
Vera Av WCHMH N21....29 G4
Vera Ct OXHEY WD19....21 H6
Vera Lynn Cl FSTGT E7....76 E3
Verbena Cl CAN/RD E16....94 C3
Verbena Gdns HMSMTH W6....106 D4

Verdant La CAT SE6....133 H7
Verdayne Av CROY/NA CR0....166 A7
Verdun Rd BARN SW13....106 D6
  WOOL/PLUM SE18....116 B5
Vereker Rd WKENS W14....107 H4
Vere St CAVSO/HST W1G....10 C5
Vermont Cl ENC/FH EN2....29 H3
Vermont Rd NRWD SE19....149 K5
  SUT SM1....175 F2
  WAND/EARL SW18....80 A3
Verney Gdns DAGW RM9....80 A3
Verney Rd BERM/RHTH SE16....111 J4
  DAGW RM9....80 A3
Verney St WLSDN NW10....69 F2
Verney Wy BERM/RHTH SE16....111 J4
Vernham Rd WOOL/PLUM SE18....115 H5
Vernon Av MNPK E12....77 K3
  RYNPK SW20....161 G1
  WFD IG8....45 F5
Vernon Cl HOR/WEW KT19....172 E5
  STWL/WRAY TW19....120 B7
Vernon Crs EBAR EN4....28 A4
Vernon Dr STAN HA7....35 G7
Vernon Pl FSBYW WC1X....11 K3
Vernon Rd BOW E3....93 H1
  BUSH WD23....21 J4
  CEND/HSY/T N8....55 G2
  FELT TW13....140 D1
  GDMY/SEVK IG3....61 F7
  MORT/ESHN SW14....126 A2
  SRTFD E15....76 C6
  SUT SM1....175 G4
  WALTH E17....57 H3
  WAN E11....58 C7
Vernon Sq FSBYW WC1X....5 M7
Vernon St WKENS W14....107 H3
Vernon Yd NTGHL W11....88 D6
Veroan Rd BXLYHN DA7....137 F1
Verona Ct CHSWK W4....106 B4
Verona Dr SURB KT6....172 A1
Veronica Gdns STRHM/NOR SW16....148 C7
Veronica Rd TOOT SW17....148 B2
Veronique Gdns BARK/HLT IG6....60 C4
Verran Rd BAL SW12 *....129 G6
Versailles Rd PGE/AN SE20....150 C6
Verulam Av WALTH E17....57 H5
Verulam Ct CDALE/KGS NW9 *....51 J6
Verulam Rd GFD/PVL UB6....84 A3
Verulam St FSBYW WC1X....12 A2
Verwood Dr EBAR EN4....27 K2
Verwood Rd RYLN/HDSTN HA2....48 C1
Vespan Rd SHB W12....106 D1
Vesta Rd BROCKY SE4....132 B1
Vestris Rd FSTH SE23....151 F1
Vestry Ms CMBW SE5....111 F7
Vestry Rd CMBW SE5....111 F7
  WALTH E17....57 K4
Vestry St IS N1....7 G7
Vevey St CAT SE6....151 H1
Viaduct Pl BETH E2....92 D2
Viaduct St BETH E2....92 D2
The Viaduct MUSWH N10....54 B3
  SWFD E18....58 E1
Vian St LEW SE13....132 E2
Vibart Gdns BRXS/STRHM SW2....130 A6
Vibart St IS N1....5 K3
Vibia Cl STWL/WRAY TW19....120 A6
Vicarage Dr ERITH DA8....117 K5
  NTHLT UB5....65 K7
  RSLP HA4....46 B6
  WPK KT4....160 B7
Vicarage Ct BECK BR3 *....166 C2
Vicarage Crs BTSEA SW11....128 C1
Vicarage Dr BARK IG11....78 C6
  BECK BR3....151 J7
  MORT/ESHN SW14....126 A4
Vicarage Farm Rd HSLWW TW4....122 D1
Vicarage Flds WOT/HER KT12....156 B5
Vicarage Gdns KENS W8 *....14 B1
  MTCM CR4....162 D2
Vicarage Ga KENS W8....8 C9
Vicarage Gv CMBW SE5....110 E7
Vicarage La EHAM E6....95 K2
  IL IG1....60 D7
  SRTFD E15....76 C6
Vicarage Ms CHSWK W4 *....106 B5
Vicarage Pde SEVS/STOTM N15 *....55 J3
Vicarage Pk WOOL/PLUM SE18....115 H4
Vicarage Rd BXLY DA5....137 J7
  CROY/NA CR0....177 G2
  DAGE RM10....80 D6
  HCH RM12....63 J7
  HDN NW4....51 J5
  KUT/HW KT1....143 J7
  LEY E10....57 K6
  MORT/ESHN SW14....125 K4
  SRTFD E15....76 D6
  SUN TW16....140 D5
  SUT SM1....174 E3
  TEDD TW11....143 G4
  TOTM N17....42 C6
  WATW WD18....20 E4
  WFD IG8....45 J6
  WHTN TW2....123 J7
  WOOL/PLUM SE18....115 H4
Vicarage Wy RYLN/HDSTN HA2....48 A1
  WLSDN NW10....69 F2
Vicars Bridge Cl ALP/SUD HA0....86 A1
Vicar's Cl EN N1....30 A1
  HOM E9....74 E7
  SRTFD E15....76 E7
Vicars HI LEW SE13....132 E3
Vicars Oak Rd NRWD SE19....150 A5
Vicar's Rd KTTN NW5....72 A4
Viceroy Cl EFNCH N2....53 J3
Viceroy Pde EFNCH N2 *....53 J2
Viceroy Rd VX/NE SW8....109 K7
Vickers Cl WLGTN SM6....177 G6
Vickers La DART DA1....139 K2
Vickers Rd ERITH DA8....118 A4
Victor Gv ALP/SUD HA0....68 A6
Victoria Ar WESTW SW1E....16 D4
Victoria Av E/WMO/HCT KT8....157 G2
  EHAM E6....77 H1
  FNCH N3....38 D7
  HSLW TW3....123 F4
  SURB KT6....158 E6
  WBLY HA9....68 D5
  WLGTN SM6....176 A2
Victoria Cl E/WMO/HCT KT8....157 F2
  EBAR EN4....27 H4

HRW HA1 ... 49 F5
HYS/HAR UB3 ... 82 B5
Victoria Cots RCH/KEW TW9 ... 105 C2
WCHPL E1 * ... 92 C4
Victoria Crs WBLY HA9 ... 68 C5
Victoria Crs NRWD SE19 ... 150 A5
SEVS/STOTM N15 ... 56 A4
WIM/MER SW19 * ... 146 D6
Victoria Dock Rd CAN/RD E16 ... 94 D6
Victoria Dr WIM/MER SW19 ... 127 C2
Victoria Emb EMB EC4Y ... 12 B6
TPL/STR WC2R ... 11 L7
WHALL SW1A ... 17 K2
Victoria Embankment Gdns
CHCR WC2N * ... 11 K7
Victoria Gdns HEST TW5 ... 102 D7
NTGHL W11 ... 88 D7
Victoria Ga BAY/PAD W2 ... 9 H6
Victoria Gv KENS W8 ... 14 C3
NFNCH/WDSPK N12 ... 39 H4
Victoria Grove Ms
BAY/PAD W2 * ... 8 C7
HYS/HAR UB3 ... 101 G4
Victoria Ms KIL/WHAMP NW6 ... 2 A4
WAND/EARL SW18 ... 128 B7
Victorian Gv STNW/STAM N16 ... 74 A3
Victorian Rd STNW/STAM N16 ... 74 A2
Victoria Park Rd HOM E9 ... 74 E7
Victoria Park Sq BETH E2 ... 92 E2
Victoria Park Studios
HOM E9 * ... 74 E7
Victoria Pas WATW WD18 ... 21 F3
Victoria Ri RCH/KEW TW9 ... 124 E4
Victoria Ri CLAP SW4 ... 129 G2
Victoria Rd ACT W3 ... 87 F4
BARK IG11 ... 78 B5
BFN/LL DA15 ... 155 F2
BKHH IG9 ... 45 H1
BUSH WD23 ... 22 B7
BXLYHS DA6 ... 137 H3
CHST BR7 ... 154 A4
DAGE RM10 ... 80 E4
DART DA1 ... 139 G4
EA W5 ... 85 H4
EBAR EN4 ... 27 H3
ED N9 ... 42 B2
ERITH DA8 ... 118 B5
FELT TW13 ... 122 A4
FSBYPK N4 ... 55 F6
HAYES BR2 ... 168 C4
HDN NW4 ... 52 A3
KENS W8 ... 14 C4
KIL/WHAMP NW6 ... 2 D1
KUT/HW KT1 ... 159 G1
MLHL NW7 ... 37 H4
MORT/ESHN SW14 ... 126 A2
MTCM CR4 ... 147 J6
NWDGN UB2 ... 102 E2
PLSTW E13 ... 94 E1
ROM RM1 ... 63 H4
RSLP HA4 ... 46 E7
RSLP HA4 ... 65 F3
SEVS/STOTM N15 * ... 56 C3
SURB KT6 ... 158 E5
SUT SM1 ... 175 H4
SWFD E18 ... 59 F2
TEDD TW11 ... 143 G6
TWK TW1 ... 124 C6
UED N18 ... 42 B3
WALTH E17 ... 58 A1
WAN E11 ... 76 B3
WDGN N22 ... 40 D7
WIM/MER SW19 ... 147 J6
WLSDN NW10 ... 87 G3
Victoria Sq BCVA SW1W ... 16 D3
Victoria St BELV DA17 ... 117 H4
SRTFD E15 ... 76 C6
WESTW SW1E ... 16 D4
Victoria Ter EA W5 * ... 85 K7
FSBYPK N4 ... 55 F7
HRW HA1 ... 48 E7
Victoria Vls RCH/KEW TW9 ... 125 G2
Victoria Wy CHARL SE7 ... 114 A4
Victoria Works
STMC/STPC BR5 ... 169 H4
Victor Rd PGE/AN SE20 ... 151 F6
RYLN/HDSTN HA2 ... 48 C2
TEDD TW11 ... 142 E4
WLSDN NW10 ... 87 K2
Victors Dr HPTN TW12 * ... 141 J5
Victors Wy BAR EN5 ... 26 D2
Victor Vls ED N9 * ... 41 K2
Victory Av MRDN SM4 ... 162 B4
Victory Cl STWL/WRAY TW19 ... 120 D7
Victory Pk WBLY HA9 ... 67 K2
Victory Pl NRWD SE19 ... 150 A5
WALW SE17 ... 18 F5
Victory Rd RAIN RM13 ... 99 J1
WAN E11 ... 58 E3
WIM/MER SW19 ... 147 G6
Victory Road Ms
WIM/MER SW19 ... 147 G6
Victory Wy BERM/RHTH SE16 ... 112 B1
HEST TW5 ... 102 B4
ROMW/RG RM7 ... 62 D1
Vienna Cl WFD IG8 ... 59 H1
View Cl HGT N6 ... 53 K6
HRW HA1 ... 48 D3
View Crs CEND/HSY/T N8 ... 54 D4
Viewfield Cl
KTN/HRWW/WS HA3 ... 50 A5
Viewfield Rd BFN/LL DA15 ... 136 D7
WAND/EARL SW18 ... 127 J5
Viewland Rd
WOOL/PLUM SE18 ... 116 A4
View Rd HGT N6 ... 53 K6
The View ABYW SE2 ... 117 F4
Viga Rd WCHMH N21 ... 29 G5
Vigilant Cl SYD SE26 ... 150 C3
Vignoles Rd ROMW/RG RM7 ... 62 C6
Vigo St CONDST W1S ... 10 E7
Viking Cl BOW E3 ... 93 G1
Viking Gdns EHAM E6 ... 95 J4
Viking Pl LEY E10 ... 57 H7
Viking Rd STHL UB1 ... 83 J6
Viking Wy ERITH DA8 ... 117 K2
Villacourt Rd
WOOL/PLUM SE18 ... 116 B6
Village Cl CHING E4 ... 44 A4
HAMP NW3 * ... 71 H4
Village Green Rd DART DA1 ... 138 D3
Village Ms CDALE/KGS NW9 * ... 69 F1
Village Mt HAMP NW3 * ... 71 G3
Village Park Cl EN EN1 ... 30 A5
Village Rd EN EN1 ... 29 K5
FNCH N3 ... 52 C1
Village Rw BELMT SM2 * ... 174 E6
The Village CHARL SE7 ... 114 B5
HAMP NW3 * ... 71 G1
Village Wy BARK/HLT IG6 ... 60 C2

BECK BR3 ... 166 D3
DUL SE21 ... 130 E5
PIN HA5 ... 47 J6
WLSDN NW10 ... 69 F3
Village Wy East PIN HA5 ... 47 K6
Villa Rd BRXN/ST SW9 ... 130 B2
Villas Rd WOOL/PLUM SE18 ... 115 H3
Villa St WALW SE17 ... 19 H6
Villiers Av BRYLDS KT5 ... 159 G4
WHTN TW2 ... 122 E7
Villiers Cl BRYLDS KT5 ... 159 G3
LEY E10 ... 75 J1
Villiers Pth BERM/RHTH SE16 ... 112 B1
Villiers Rd BECK BR3 ... 166 A1
CRICK NW2 ... 69 J5
ISLW TW7 ... 123 K1
KUT/HW KT1 ... 159 G1
OXHEY WD19 ... 21 J5
STHL UB1 ... 83 K7
Villiers St CHCR WC2N ... 11 K8
Vimy Cl HSLWW TW4 ... 122 E4
Vimy Dr DART DA1 ... 139 J2
Vincam Cl WHTN TW2 ... 123 F6
Vincennes Est WNWD SE27 * ... 149 K3
Vincent Av BRYLDS KT5 ... 159 J5
Vincent Cl BAR EN5 ... 26 E2
BFN/LL DA15 ... 135 K7
ESH/CLAY KT10 ... 170 B2
HAYES BR2 ... 168 A3
WDR/YW UB7 ... 100 D5
Vincent Gdns CRICK NW2 ... 69 H2
Vincent Pde FSBYPK N4 * ... 54 E7
Vincent Rd ACT W3 ... 105 K2
ALP/SUD HA0 ... 68 B6
CHING E4 ... 44 B5
CROY/NA CR0 ... 165 F6
DAGW RM9 ... 80 A6
HSLWW TW4 ... 122 C2
KUT/HW KT1 ... 159 H1
SEVS/STOTM N15 ... 55 G1
WDGN N22 ... 55 G1
WOOL/PLUM SE18 ... 115 G3
Vincent Rw HPTN TW12 ... 142 C5
Vincents Cl BERM/RHTH SE16 ... 112 B1
Vincent Sq WDGN N22 * ... 55 G1
WEST SW1P ... 16 F5
Vincent St CAN/RD E16 ... 94 E4
WEST SW1P ... 17 G5
Vincent Ter IS N1 ... 6 C1
Vincent Vls
SEVS/STOTM N15 * ... 55 J3
Vince St FSBYE EC1V ... 7 J7
Vine Cl BRYLDS KT5 ... 159 G5
CLPT E5 ... 74 C3
SUT SM1 ... 175 G2
WDR/YW UB7 ... 100 D5
Vine Cots HNWL W7 * ... 84 E7
WCHPL E1 * ... 92 A5
Vine Gdns IL IG1 ... 78 C4
Vinegar St WAP E1W ... 92 D7
Vinegar Yd STHWK SE1 ... 19 J1
Vine HI CLKNW EC1R ... 12 A1
Vine La STHWK SE1 ... 13 K9
Vine Pl HSLW TW3 ... 123 G3
Vineries Cl WDR/YW UB7 ... 100 D5
The Vineries CAT SE6 ... 132 C6
EN EN1 ... 30 A2
STHGT/OAK N14 ... 28 C5
Vine Rd BARN SW13 ... 126 C2
E/WMO/HCT KT8 ... 157 H3
SRTFD E15 ... 76 D6
Vine Rw RCHPK/HAM TW10 * ... 125 F4
Viners Cl WOT/HER KT12 ... 156 B5
Vines Av FNCH N3 ... 39 F7
Vine Sq WKENS W14 * ... 107 J4
Vine St MYFR/PICC W1J ... 10 F7
ROMW/RG RM7 ... 62 E4
TWRH EC3N ... 13 L5
Vine Street Br FARR EC1M ... 12 B1
Vine Yd STHWK SE1 ... 18 F1
Vineyard Av MLHL NW7 ... 38 C6
Vineyard Cl CAT SE6 ... 132 D7
KUT/HW KT1 ... 159 G2
Vineyard Gv FNCH N3 ... 39 F7
Vineyard Hill Rd
WIM/MER SW19 ... 146 E3
Vineyard Ms CLKNW EC1R * ... 6 A9
Vineyard Pth
MORT/ESHN SW14 ... 126 A2
Vineyard Rd FELT TW13 ... 140 E2
Vineyard Rw KUT/HW KT1 ... 143 J7
The Vineyard
RCHPK/HAM TW10 ... 124 E4
Vineyard Wk CLKNW EC1R * ... 6 A9
Viney Bank CROY/NA CR0 ... 179 H7
Viney Rd LEW SE13 ... 132 E2
Vining St BRXS/STRHM SW2 ... 130 B3
Vinries Bank MLHL NW7 ... 37 K4
Vintage Ms CHING E4 ... 43 J5
Vintry Ms WALTH E17 ... 57 J3
Viola Av ABYW SE2 ... 116 C3
EBED/NFELT TW14 ... 122 B5
STWL/WRAY TW19 ... 120 B7
Viola Sq SHB W12 ... 87 H6
Violet Cl CAN/RD E16 ... 94 C3
CHEAM SM3 ... 161 H7
DEPT SE8 ... 112 C5
WLGTN SM6 ... 163 F7
Violet Gdns CROY/NA CR0 ... 177 H4
Violet Hl STJWD NW8 ... 2 B2
Violet La SAND/SEL CR2 ... 177 H4
Violet Rd BOW E3 ... 93 K3
SWFD E18 ... 59 F1
WALTH E17 ... 57 J5
Violet St BETH E2 ... 92 D3
Virgil St STHWK SE1 ... 17 M3
Virginia Cl HAYES BR2 ... 167 H2
NWMAL KT3 ... 159 K3
Virginia Gdns BARK/HLT IG6 ... 60 D1
Virginia Rd BETH E2 ... 7 L5
THHTH CR7 ... 149 H7
Virginia St WCHPL E1 * ... 92 C6
Viscount Cl FBAR/BDGN N11 ... 40 B4
Viscount Dr EHAM E6 ... 95 K4
Viscount Gv NTHLT UB5 ... 83 H2
Viscount Rd
STWL/WRAY TW19 ... 120 A6
Viscount St BARB EC2Y ... 12 E1
Viscount Wy HTHAIR TW6 ... 121 H3
Vista Av PEND EN3 ... 31 F1
Vista Dr REDBR IG4 ... 59 H4
The Vista ELTH/MOT SE9 ... 134 C5
Vista Wy KTN/HRWW/WS HA3 ... 50 A5
Viveash Cl HYS/HAR UB3 ... 101 J2
Vivian Av HDN NW4 ... 51 K4
WBLY HA9 ... 68 C3
Vivian Gdns OXHEY WD19 ... 32 E1
Vivian Gdns OXHEY WD19 ... 20 E7
WBLY HA9 ... 68 C3
Vivian Rd BOW E3 ... 93 G1

Vivian Sq PECK SE15 ... 131 J2
Vivian Wy EFNCH N2 ... 53 H4
Vivien Cl CHSGTN KT9 ... 172 A6
Vivienne Cl TWK TW1 ... 124 E5
Vixen Ms HACK E8 * ... 7 L3
Voce Rd WOOL/PLUM SE18 ... 115 J6
Voewood Cl NWMAL KT3 ... 160 C5
Voltaire Rd CLAP SW4 ... 129 J2
Volt Av WLSDN NW10 ... 87 F2
Volta Wy CROY/NA CR0 ... 164 A7
Voluntary Pl WAN E11 ... 58 E5
Vorley Rd ARCH N19 ... 72 C1
Voss Ct STRHM/NOR SW16 ... 148 E5
Voss St BETH E2 ... 92 C2
Voyagers Cl THMD SE28 ... 97 J5
Vulcan Cl EHAM E6 ... 96 A5
Vulcan Ga ENC/FH EN2 ... 29 G1
Vulcan Rd BROCKY SE4 ... 132 C1
Vulcan Ter BROCKY SE4 ... 132 C1
Vulcan Wy HOLWY N7 ... 73 F5
WLGTN SM6 ... 176 F7
Vyner Rd ACT W3 ... 87 F6
Vyner St BETH E2 ... 92 D1
The Vyne BXLYHN DA7 ... 137 J2
Vyse Cl BAR EN5 ... 26 A3

W

Wadbrook St KUT/HW KT1 ... 158 E1
Wadding St WALW SE17 ... 19 G6
Waddington Cl EN EN1 ... 30 A3
Waddington Rd SRTFD E15 ... 76 B4
Waddington St SRTFD E15 ... 76 B5
Waddington Wy NRWD SE19 ... 149 J7
Waddon Cl CROY/NA CR0 ... 177 G2
Waddon Court Rd
CROY/NA CR0 ... 177 G3
Waddon Marsh Wy
CROY/NA CR0 ... 164 A7
Waddon New Rd
CROY/NA CR0 ... 177 H2
Waddon Park Av
CROY/NA CR0 ... 177 G3
Waddon Rd CROY/NA CR0 ... 177 G2
Waddon Wy CROY/NA CR0 ... 177 G5
Wade House ABYW SE2 * ... 116 C1
Wade's Gv WCHMH N21 ... 29 G6
Wade's La TEDD TW11 ... 143 G4
Wadeson St BETH E2 ... 92 D1
Wade's Pl POP/IOD E14 ... 93 K6
Wadeville Av CHDH RM6 ... 62 A5
Wadeville Cl BELV DA17 ... 117 H4
Wadham Av WALTH E17 ... 43 K6
Wadham Gdns GFD/PVL UB6 ... 66 D5
HAMP NW3 ... 3 J3
Wadham Rd CHING E4 ... 44 A2
PUT/ROE SW15 ... 127 H3
WALTH E17 ... 43 K6
Wadhurst Cl PGE/AN SE20 ... 165 J1
Wadhurst Rd CHSWK W4 ... 106 A2
VX/NE SW8 ... 109 H7
Wadley Rd WAN E11 ... 58 C6
Wadsworth Cl GFD/PVL UB6 ... 85 J1
PEND EN3 ... 31 F4
Wadsworth Rd GFD/PVL UB6 ... 85 H1
Wager St BOW E3 ... 93 H3
Waghorn Rd
KTN/HRWW/WS HA3 ... 49 K2
PLSTW E13 ... 77 G7
Waghorn St PECK SE15 ... 131 H2
Wagner St PECK SE15 ... 111 K6
Wagstaff Gdns DAGW RM9 ... 79 J6
Wagtail Cl CDALE/KGS NW9 ... 51 G1
Wagtail Wk BECK BR3 ... 167 F4
Waid Cl DART DA1 ... 139 J5
Waights Ct KUTN/CMB KT2 ... 144 A7
Wainfleet Av CRW RM5 ... 62 E1
Wainford Cl WIM/MER SW19 ... 127 G7
Wainwright Gv ISLW TW7 ... 123 J3
Waite Davies Rd
LEE/GVPK SE12 ... 133 J6
Waite St CMBW SE5 ... 19 L9
Wakefield Gdns IL IG1 ... 59 J5
NRWD SE19 ... 150 A6
Wakefield Ms STPAN WC1H ... 5 J8
Wakefield Rd
FBAR/BDGN N11 ... 40 D4
RCHPK/HAM TW10 ... 124 E4
SEVS/STOTM N15 ... 56 B4
Wakefield St BMSBY WC1N ... 5 K9
EHAM E6 ... 77 J7
STPAN WC1H ... 5 K8
UED N18 ... 42 C4
Wakeford Cl CLAP SW4 ... 129 H4
Wakehams Hl PIN HA5 ... 47 K2
Wakeham St IS N1 ... 73 K5
Wakehurst Rd BTSEA SW11 ... 128 D4
Wakeling La ALP/SUD HA0 ... 67 H2
Wakeling Rd HNWL W7 ... 85 F4
Wakeling St POP/IOD E14 ... 93 G5
Wakelin Rd SRTFD E15 ... 94 C1
Wakeman Rd WLSDN NW10 ... 88 A2
Wakemans Hill Av
CDALE/KGS NW9 ... 51 F4
Wakering Rd BARK IG11 ... 78 C5
Wakerly Cl EHAM E6 ... 95 K5
Wakley St FSBYE EC1V ... 6 C7
Walberswick St VX/NE SW8 ... 109 K6
Walbrook MANHO EC4N ... 13 G6
Walburgh St WCHPL E1 * ... 92 D5
Walcorde Av WALW SE17 ... 18 F6
Walcot Rd PEND EN3 ... 31 H1
Walcot Sq LBTH SE11 ... 18 A5
Walcott St WEST SW1P * ... 16 F5
Waldeck Gv WNWD SE27 ... 149 H2
Waldeck Rd CHSWK W4 ... 105 H5
DART DA1 ... 139 J6
MORT/ESHN SW14 ... 125 K2
SEVS/STOTM N15 ... 55 H2
WEA W13 ... 85 H5
Waldegrave Gdns TWK TW1 ... 143 F1
Waldegrave Pk TWK TW1 ... 143 F3
Waldegrave Rd BCTR RM8 ... 79 J1
BMLY BR1 ... 168 D4
CEND/HSY/T N8 ... 55 G2
EA W5 ... 86 B6
NRWD SE19 ... 150 B6
TWK TW1 ... 143 F3
Waldegrove CROY/NA CR0 ... 178 B2
Waldemar Av FUL/PGN SW6 ... 107 H7
WEA W13 ... 85 J7
Waldemar Rd WIM/MER SW19 ... 146 E4
Walden Av CHST BR7 ... 153 K3
PLMGR N13 ... 41 J3
RAIN RM13 ... 99 F1
Walden Cl BELV DA17 ... 117 G4
Walden Gdns THHTH CR7 ... 164 A3
Walden Pde CHST BR7 * ... 153 K5
Walden Rd CHST BR7 ... 153 K5

TOTM N17 ... 41 K7
Waldenshaw Rd FSTH SE23 ... 131 K7
Walden St WCHPL E1 ... 92 D5
Walden Wy MLHL NW7 ... 38 A5
Waldo Cl CLAP SW4 ... 129 H4
Waldorf Cl SAND/SEL CR2 ... 177 H7
Waldo Rd BMLY BR1 ... 168 B2
WLSDN NW10 ... 87 J2
Waldram Crs FSTH SE23 ... 131 K7
Waldram Park Rd FSTH SE23 ... 132 A7
Waldrist Wy ERITHM DA18 ... 117 G1
Waldron Gdns HAYES BR2 ... 167 G2
Waldron Ms CHEL SW3 ... 15 H9
Waldron Rd RYLN/HDSTN HA2 ... 48 E7
WAND/EARL SW18 ... 147 G2
The Waldrons CROY/NA CR0 ... 177 J3
Waldron's Yd
RYLN/HDSTN HA2 ... 66 D1
Waldstock Rd THMD SE28 ... 97 G6
Waleran Cl STAN HA7 ... 35 F5
Walerand Rd LEW SE13 ... 133 F1
Wales Av CAR SM5 ... 175 J4
Wales Cl PECK SE15 ... 111 J6
Wales Farm Rd ACT W3 ... 87 F4
Waleton Acres WLGTN SM6 * ... 176 C5
Waley St WCHPL E1 * ... 93 F4
Walford Rd STNW/STAM N16 ... 74 A3
Walfrey Gdns DAGW RM9 ... 80 A6
Walham Green Ct
FUL/PGN SW6 * ... 108 A6
Walham Gv FUL/PGN SW6 ... 107 K6
Walham Ri WIM/MER SW19 ... 146 C5
Walham Yd FUL/PGN SW6 * ... 107 K6
Walkden Rd CHST BR7 ... 154 A3
Walker Cl CROY/NA CR0 ... 180 A6
DART DA1 ... 138 C2
EBED/NFELT TW14 ... 121 J6
FBAR/BDGN N11 ... 40 C3
HNWL W7 ... 84 E7
HPTN TW12 ... 141 K5
WOOL/PLUM SE18 ... 115 H4
Walker's Ct SOHO/CST W1F * ... 11 G6
DUL SE21 ... 130 D7
Walker's Pl PUT/ROE SW15 ... 127 H3
Walkerscroft Md CAT SE6 ... 151 K1
Walkford Wy CHARL SE7 ... 114 A3
Walkley Rd DART DA1 ... 138 E4
Wallace Cl THMD SE28 ... 97 K6
Wallace Crs CAR SM5 ... 175 K4
Wallace Rd IS N1 ... 73 J5
Wallbutton Rd BROCKY SE4 ... 132 B1
Wallcote Av CRICK NW2 ... 52 B7
Walled Garden Cl BECK BR3 ... 166 E3
Wall End Rd EHAM E6 ... 78 A6
Wallenger Av GPK RM2 ... 63 K2
Waller Dr NTHWD HA6 ... 32 E7
Waller Rd NWCR SE14 ... 112 A7
Wallers Cl DAGW RM9 ... 80 A7
WFD IG8 ... 45 K5
Wallflower St SHB W12 ... 87 H6
Wallgrave Rd ECT SW5 ... 14 B5
Wallhouse Rd ERITH DA8 ... 119 F6
Wallingford Av NKENS W10 ... 88 B4
Wallington Cl RSLP HA4 ... 46 A5
Wallington Rd
GDMY/SEVK IG3 ... 61 F6
Wallis Cl BTSEA SW11 ... 128 C2
EMPK RM11 ... 63 K7
Wallis Rd HOM E9 ... 75 H5
STHL UB1 ... 84 B5
Wallman Pl WDGN N22 * ... 41 F7
Wallorton Gdns
MORT/ESHN SW14 ... 126 A3
Wallside BARB EC2Y * ... 12 F3
Wall St IS N1 ... 73 K5
Wallwood Rd WAN E11 ... 58 B6
Wallwood St POP/IOD E14 ... 93 H4
Walmar Cl EN EN1 ... 43 K1
ROMW/RG RM7 ... 62 D1
Walmer Gdns WEA W13 ... 104 B1
Walmer Pl MBLAR W1H * ... 9 L2
Walmer Rd NTGHL W11 ... 88 C6
Walmer Ter WOOL/PLUM SE18 ... 115 H3
Walmgate Rd GFD/PVL UB6 ... 67 H7
Walmington Fold
NFNCH/WDSPK N12 ... 38 E5
Walm La CRICK NW2 ... 70 B4
Walney Wk IS N1 ... 73 J5
Walnut Av WDR/YW UB7 ... 100 D2
Walnut Cl BARK/HLT IG6 ... 60 D1
CAR SM5 ... 175 K4
DEPT SE8 ... 112 C5
HYS/HAR UB3 ... 82 C6
Walnut Ct EA W5 * ... 105 F1
Walnut Gdns SRTFD E15 ... 76 C4
Walnut Gn BUSH WD23 ... 21 K1
Walnut Gv EN EN1 ... 29 K4
Walnut Ms BELMT SM2 ... 175 G6
Walnut Rd LEY E10 ... 75 J1
Walnut Tree Av MTCM CR4 * ... 162 D2
Walnut Tree Cl BARN SW13 ... 106 C7
CHST BR7 ... 154 C7
Walnut Tree Rd BCTR RM8 ... 79 K1
BTFD TW8 ... 105 F5
ERITH DA8 ... 118 B4
GNWCH SE10 ... 113 H4
HEST TW5 ... 102 E5
Walnut Tree Wk LBTH SE11 ... 18 A5
RSLP HA4 ... 65 G5
Walnut Wy BKHH IG9 ... 45 J2
RSLP HA4 ... 65 G5
Walpole Av RCH/KEW TW9 ... 125 G1
Walpole Cl PIN HA5 ... 34 A5
WEA W13 ... 104 D1
Walpole Crs TEDD TW11 ... 143 F4
Walpole Gdns CHSWK W4 ... 105 K4
WHTN TW2 ... 142 E1
Walpole Ms STJWD NW8 * ... 3 G4
Walpole Pl TEDD TW11 ... 143 F4
Walpole Rd CROY/NA CR0 ... 177 K1
EHAM E6 ... 77 G6
HAYES BR2 ... 168 C4
SURB KT6 ... 159 F6
SWFD E18 ... 44 D7
TEDD TW11 ... 143 F4
TOTM N17 ... 55 J1
WALTH E17 ... 57 G3
WHTN TW2 ... 142 E1
WIM/MER SW19 ... 147 H5
Walrond Av WBLY HA9 ... 68 A4
Walsham Cl STNW/STAM N16 ... 56 C7
THMD SE28 ... 97 K6
Walsham Rd
EBED/NFELT TW14 ... 122 A6
NWCR SE14 ... 132 A1
Walsingham Gdns
HOR/WEW KT19 ... 173 G3
Walsingham Pk CHST BR7 ... 169 J1
Walsingham Rd CLAP SW4 ... 129 J4

CLPT E5 ... 74 C2
ENC/FH EN2 ... 29 K3
MTCM CR4 ... 162 E4
STMC/STPC BR5 ... 155 J7
WEA W13 * ... 85 G7
Walsingham Wk BELV DA17 ... 117 H5
Walter Rodney Cl MNPK E12 * ... 77 K5
Walters Cl HYS/HAR UB3 ... 101 J1
Walters Rd PEND EN3 ... 30 E4
Walter's Rd SNWD SE25 ... 165 F3
Walter St BETH E2 ... 93 F2
KUTN/CMB KT2 * ... 144 A7
Walters Wy FSTH SE23 ... 132 A5
Walters Yd BMLY BR1 ... 167 K1
Walter Ter WCHPL E1 ... 93 F5
Walterton Rd MV/WKIL W9 ... 88 D3
Walter Wk EDGW HA8 ... 36 E5
Waltham Av CDALE/KGS NW9 ... 50 C5
HYS/HAR UB3 ... 101 F2
Waltham Cl DART DA1 ... 138 D5
Waltham Dr EDGW HA8 ... 50 C1
Waltham Pk WALTH E17 ... 43 J6
Waltham Park Wy CHING E4 * ... 43 J6
Waltham Rd CAR SM5 ... 162 C7
NWDGN UB2 ... 102 D2
WFD IG8 ... 45 J5
Walthamstow Av CHING E4 ... 43 J6
Walthamstow Av (North
Circular) CHING E4 ... 43 G4
Waltham Wy CHING E4 ... 43 H2
Waltheof Av TOTM N17 ... 41 K7
Waltheof Gdns TOTM N17 ... 41 K7
Walton Av CHEAM SM3 ... 174 C2
NWMAL KT3 ... 160 C3
RYLN/HDSTN HA2 ... 65 K3
WBLY HA9 ... 68 C2
Walton Cl CRICK NW2 ... 69 K1
HRW HA1 ... 48 D3
VX/NE SW8 ... 109 K6
Walton Dr HRW HA1 ... 48 D3
WLSDN NW10 ... 69 F5
Walton Gdns ACT W3 ... 86 D5
FELT TW13 ... 140 D3
Walton Gn CROY/NA CR0 ... 179 K7
Walton Pl CHEL SW3 ... 15 K4
Walton Rd BUSH WD23 ... 21 H3
E/WMO/HCT KT8 ... 157 F3
HRW HA1 ... 48 D3
MNPK E12 ... 78 A3
PLSTW E13 ... 95 G1
SCUP DA14 ... 155 H2
SEVS/STOTM N15 * ... 56 B3
WOT/HER KT12 ... 156 C6
Walton St CHEL SW3 ... 15 K5
ENC/FH EN2 ... 29 K1
Walton Vls IS N1 * ... 7 K2
Walton Wy ACT W3 ... 86 D4
MTCM CR4 ... 163 H3
Walt Whitman Cl HNHL SE24 * ... 130 C3
Walverns Cl OXHEY WD19 ... 21 G5
Walworth Pl WALW SE17 ... 18 F8
Walworth Rd STHWK SE1 ... 18 E5
Walwyn Av BMLY BR1 ... 168 C2
Wanborough Dr
PUT/ROE SW15 ... 126 E7
Wanderer Dr BARK IG11 ... 97 H2
Wandle Bank CROY/NA CR0 ... 176 B2
WIM/MER SW19 ... 147 H5
Wandle Ct HOR/WEW KT19 ... 172 E3
Wandle Court Gdns
CROY/NA CR0 ... 176 B2
Wandle Rd CROY/NA CR0 ... 176 B2
MRDN SM4 ... 162 C4
TOOT SW17 ... 147 J1
WLGTN SM6 ... 176 B1
Wandle Side CROY/NA CR0 ... 177 F2
WLGTN SM6 ... 176 B2
Wandle Wy MTCM CR4 ... 162 E4
WAND/EARL SW18 ... 128 A7
Wandsworth Br
WAND/EARL SW18 ... 128 B2
Wandsworth Bridge Rd
FUL/PGN SW6 ... 108 A7
Wandsworth Common West
Side WAND/EARL SW18 ... 128 B4
Wandsworth High St
WAND/EARL SW18 ... 127 K4
VX/NE SW8 ... 129 J1
Wangey Rd CHDH RM6 ... 61 K6
Wanless Rd HNHL SE24 ... 130 D2
Wanley Rd CMBW SE5 ... 130 E3
Wanlip Rd PLSTW E13 ... 95 F3
Wansbeck Rd HOM E9 ... 75 H6
Wansdown Pl FUL/PGN SW6 ... 108 A6
Wansey St WALW SE17 ... 18 F6
Wansford Pk BORE WD6 ... 25 F3
Wansford Rd WFD IG8 ... 45 G7
Wanstead Cl BMLY BR1 ... 168 B1
Wanstead La IL IG1 ... 59 J3
Wanstead Park Av MNPK E12 ... 77 H1
Wanstead Park Rd IL IG1 ... 59 J6
Wanstead Pl WAN E11 ... 58 E5
Wanstead Rd BMLY BR1 ... 168 B1
Wansunt Rd BXLY DA5 ... 137 K7
Wantage Rd LEE/GVPK SE12 ... 133 J4
Wantz La RAIN RM13 ... 99 K3
Wantz Rd DAGE RM10 ... 80 D3
Wapping Dock St WAP E1W * ... 92 D7
Wapping High St WAP E1W ... 92 C7
Wapping La WAP E1W ... 92 D6
Wapping Wall WAP E1W ... 92 E7
Warbank La KUTN/CMB KT2 ... 145 H6
Warbeck Rd SHB W12 ... 87 K7
Warberry Rd WDGN N22 ... 55 F1
Warboys Ap KUTN/CMB KT2 ... 144 D5
Warboys Crs CHING E4 ... 44 A4
Warboys Rd KUTN/CMB KT2 ... 144 D5
Warburton Cl IS N1 ... 74 A5
KTN/HRWW/WS HA3 ... 34 D7
Warburton Rd HACK E8 ... 74 D7
WHTN TW2 ... 123 G7
Warburton St HACK E8 ... 74 D7
Warburton Ter WALTH E17 ... 43 K1
Wardalls Gv NWCR SE14 ... 111 K6
Ward Cl ERITH DA8 ... 118 A3
SAND/SEL CR2 ... 178 A4
Wardell Cl EDGW HA8 ... 37 G7
Wardell Fld CDALE/KGS NW9 ... 37 G7
Warden Av CROY/NA CR0 ... 179 K5
RYLN/HDSTN HA2 ... 47 K5
Warden Rd KTTN NW5 ... 72 A5
Wardens Gv STHWK SE1 ... 12 E9
Wardle St HOM E9 ... 75 F5
Wardley St WAND/EARL SW18 ... 128 A6
Wardo Av FUL/PGN SW6 ... 107 H7
Wardour Ms SOHO/CST W1F ... 10 F5
Wardour St SOHO/CST W1F ... 11 G5
Ward Rd ARCH N19 ... 72 C2
SRTFD E15 ... 76 B7
Wardrobe Pl BLKFR EC4V * ... 12 D5
The Wardrobe
RCH/KEW TW9 * ... 124 E4
Wards La BORE WD6 ... 23 H1

Wards Rd *GNTH/NBYPK* IG2....60 D6
Wards Wharf Ap *CAN/RD* E16.114 C1
Wareham Cl *HSLW* TW3....123 F3
Waremead Rd
 GNTH/NBYPK IG2....60 B8
Warepoint Dr *THMD* SE28....115 J1
Warfield Rd
 EBED/NFELT TW14....121 H6
 HPTN TW12....142 B4
 WLSDN NW10 *....88 B2
Warfield *WLSDN* NW10 *....88 B2
Wargrave Av
 SEVS/STOTM N15....56 B5
Wargrave Rd
 RYLN/HDSTN HA2....66 C2
 KTN/HRWW/WS HA3....49 F1
 SAND/SEL CR2....177 J1
Warham Rd *FSBYPK* N4....55 G4
Warham St *SE5*....110 C6
Waring Rd *SCUP* DA14....155 H5
Waring St *WNWD* SE27....149 J3
Warkworth Gdns *ISLW* TW7....104 B6
Warkworth Rd *TOTM* N17....41 K6
Warland Rd *WOOL/PLUM* SE18....115 J6
Warley Av *BCTR* RM8....62 B6
 WFD IG8....82 E5
Warley Rd *ED* N9....42 E1
 WFD IG8....45 F6
 YEAD UB4....82 E5
Warley St *BETH* E2....93 F2
Warlingham Rd *THHTH* CR7....164 C3
Warlock Rd *MV/WKIL* W9....88 D3
Warlters Cl *HOLWY* N7....72 K1
Warlters Rd *HOLWY* N7....72 K3
Warltersville Rd *ARCH* N19....54 E6
Warming Cl *CLPT* E5 *....75 F2
Warmington Rd *HNHL* SE24....130 D5
Warmington St *PLSTW* E13....94 E3
Warminster Gdns *SNWD* SE25....165 H1
Warminster Rd *SNWD* SE25....165 H1
Warminster Wy *MTCM* CR4....148 B7
Warmwell Av *CDALE/KGS* NW9....37 C7
Warndon St *BERM/RHTH* SE16....111 J1
Warneford Rd *OXHEY* WD19....21 J3
Warneford Rd
 KTN/HRWW/WS HA3....49 K2
Wateford St *HOM* E9....74 D7
Warne Pl *BFN/LL* DA15....136 C5
Warner Av *CHEAM* SM3....174 C1
Warner Cl *CDALE/KGS* NW9....51 H6
 HPTN TW12....141 K4
 HYS/HAR UB3....101 C6
 SRTFD E15....76 C4
Warner Pl *BETH* E2....92 C1
Warner Rd *BMLY* BR1....152 D6
 CEND/HSY/T N8....54 D3
 CMBW SE5....110 D7
 WALTH E17....57 G3
Warner St *CLKNW* EC1R....12 A1
Warner Ter *POP/IOD* E14 *....93 J4
Warner Yd *CLKNW* EC1R....12 A1
Warnham Court Rd *CAR* SM5....175 K6
Warnham Rd
 NFNCH/WDSPK N12....39 J4
Warple Ms *ACT* W3 *....106 B1
Warple Wy *ACT* W3....106 B1
 SHB W12....106 B1
Warren Av *BMLY* BR1....152 C6
 RCHPK/HAM TW10....125 J3
 SAND/SEL CR2....179 F6
 WAN E11 *....76 B2
Warren Cl *BXLYHS* DA6....137 H4
 ED N9....31 H1
 ESH/CLAY KT10....170 C3
 WBLY HA9....67 K1
 YEAD UB4....83 G4
Warren Ct *CHARL* SE7....114 B4
Warren Crs *ED* N9....30 B4
Warren Cutting
 KUTN/CMB KT2 *....145 F6
Warren Dr North *BRYLDS* KT5....159 J7
Warren Dr South *BRYLDS* KT5....159 K7
The Warren Dr *WAN* E11....59 J4
Warren Flds *STAN* HA7 *....35 J3
Warren Gv *BORE* WD6....25 F3
Warren La *STAN* HA7....35 C1
 WOOL/PLUM SE18....115 G2
Warren Lane Ga
 WOOL/PLUM SE18....115 G2
Warren Ms *FITZ* W1T....10 E1
Warren Pk *KUTN/CMB* KT2....144 E5
Warren Park Rd *SUT* SM1....175 H5
Warren Ri *KUTN/CMB* KT2....145 F3
Warren Rd *ASHF* TW15....140 C6
 BARK/HLT IG6....60 D4
 BUSH WD23....22 C7
 BXLYHS DA6....137 H4
 CHING E4....44 A1
 CRICK NW2....69 H1
 CROY/NA CR0....165 F7
 HAYES BR2....181 J2
 KUTN/CMB KT2....144 E5
 LEY E10....76 A2
 SCUP DA14....155 J2
 WAN E11....59 G5
 WHTN TW2....123 J5
 WIM/MER SW19....147 J5
Warrens Shawe La *EDGW* HA8....36 D1
Warren St *FITZ* W1T....10 E1
The Warren *BELMT* SM2....175 H7
 HEST TW5....102 E6
 MNPK E12....77 J3
 WPK KT4....173 F3
 YEAD UB4....82 E5
Warren Wy *EDGW* HA8....50 D1
Warren Wood Cl *HAYES* BR2....180 D1
Warriner Dr *ED* N9....42 C2
Warriner Gdns *BTSEA* SW11....108 E7
Warrington Crs *MV/WKIL* W9....8 E1
Warrington Gdns
 MV/WKIL W9....8 E1
Warrington Pl *POP/IOD* E14 *....94 A7
Warrington Rd *BCTR* RM8....79 K1
 CROY/NA CR0....177 H2
 HRW HA1....48 E4
 RCHPK/HAM TW10....124 E4
Warrington Sq *BCTR* RM8....79 K1
Warrior Cl *THMD* SE28....96 E7
Warrior Sq *MNPK* E12....78 A3
Warsaw Cl *RSLP* HA4....65 F5
Warspite Rd
 WOOL/PLUM SE18....114 D2
Warton Rd *SRTFD* E15....76 A7
Warwick Av *EDGW* HA8....36 D1
 MV/WKIL W9....8 D1
 RYLN/HDSTN HA2....65 K3
Warwick Cl *BUSH* WD23....22 E6

Warwick Ct *HHOL* WC1V....11 M5
Warwick House St
 SURB KT6....172 A1
Warwick Crs *BAY/PAD* W2....8 E1
 YEAD UB4....82 D3
Warwick Dene *EA* W5....86 A7
Warwick Dr *PUT/ROE* SW15....126 E2
 IL IG1....60 B7
 THDIT KT7....158 A4
 THHTH CR7 *....164 B3
 WKENS W14....107 J2
Warwick Gv *BRYLDS* KT5....159 C6
 CLPT E5....56 D7
Warwick La *STP* EC4M....12 D4
Warwick Pde
 KTN/HRWW/WS HA3 *....49 H1
Warwick Pl *BORE* WD6 *....25 F2
 EA W5....104 E1
 MV/WKIL W9....8 E2
 THDIT KT7 *....158 B5
Warwick Pl North *PIM* SW1V....16 E6
Warwick Rd *BAR* EN5....27 F2
 BORE WD6....25 F2
 CHING E4....43 J4
 EA W5....86 A7
 ECT SW5....14 A6
 FBAR/BDGN N11....40 D5
 HSLWW TW4....122 A2
 KUT/HW KT1....143 J7
 MNPK E12....77 J4
 NWDGN UB2....102 E2
 NWMAL KT3....159 K2
 PGE/AN SE20....165 J4
 SCUP DA14....155 H4
 SRTFD E15....76 D5
 SUT SM1....175 G4
 THDIT KT7....158 A4
 THHTH CR7....164 B2
 UED N18....42 A3
 WALTH E17....43 H7
 WAN E11....59 F4
 WELL DA16....136 D2
 WHTN TW2....123 K7
 WKENS W14....107 J3
Warwick Rw *WESTW* SW1E....16 E3
Warwickshire Rd
 STNW/STAM N16 *....74 A3
Warwick Sq *PIM* SW1V....16 E6
 STP EC4M *....12 D4
Warwick Square Ms
 PIM SW1V....16 E6
Warwick St *REGST* W1B....10 F6
Warwick Ter *WALTH* E17 *....58 B4
 WOOL/PLUM SE18....115 J5
Warwick Wy *PIM* SW1V....16 D7
 RKW/CH/CXG WD3....20 A3
Warwick Yd *STLK* EC1Y *....12 F1
Wasdale Rd *FSTH* SE23....132 A7
Watchfield Ct *CHSWK* W4 *....105 K4
The Watch
 NFNCH/WDSPK N12 *....39 G3
Watcombe Rd *SNWD* SE25....165 J4
Waterbank Rd *CAT* SE6....151 K3
Waterbeach Rd *DAGW* RM9....79 J5
Water Brook La *HDN* NW4....52 A4
Watercress Pl *IS* N1....7 M1
Waterdale Rd *ABYW* SE2....116 B5
Water End Cl *BORE* WD6....24 B1
Waterer Ri *WLGTN* SM6....176 D5
Waterfall Cots
 WIM/MER SW19....147 H5
Waterfall Rd *FBAR/BDGN* N11....40 B3
 WIM/MER SW19....147 H5
Waterfall Ter *TOOT* SW17....147 H2
Waterfield Cl *BELV* DA17....117 H2
 THMD SE28....97 H7
Waterfield Cots
 MORT/ESHN SW14 *....125 J3
Waterfield Gdns *SNWD* SE25....165 F3
Waterfields Wy *BUSH* WD23....22 A4
Waterford Rd *FUL/PGN* SW6....108 A6
Waterford Wy *WLGTN* NW10....69 K4
The Waterfront *BORE* WD6....23 H1
Water Gdns *STAN* HA7....35 H5
The Water Gdns *BAY/PAD* W2....9 J4
Watergate *EMB* EC4Y....12 C6
Watergate St *DEPT* SE8....112 D5
The Watergate *OXHEY* WD19....33 H1
Waterhall Av *CHING* E4....44 C3
Waterhall Cl *WALTH* E17....43 F7
Waterhead Rd *ERITH* DA8....118 B6
Waterhouse Cl *HMSMTH* W6....107 H4
Wateridge Cl *POP/IOD* E14....112 D2
Water La *CAMTN* NW1....4 D2
 ED N9....30 D7
 CDMY/SEVK IG3....79 F2
 KUT/HW KT1....143 K7
 MON EC3R....13 J7
 NWCR SE14....111 K6
 PUR RM19....119 K3
 SRTFD E15....76 C5
 TWK TW1....124 B7
 WAT WD17....21 G2
Water Lily Cl *NWDGN* UB2....103 H1
Waterloo Br *STHWK* SE1....11 M8
 TPL/STR WC2R....11 L7
Waterloo Cl
 EBED/NFELT TW14....121 J7
 HOM E9....74 E4
Waterloo Gdns *BETH* E2....92 E1
 ROMW/RG RM7....63 F5
Waterloo Pl *CAR* SM5 *....175 K2
 RCH/KEW TW9....105 H5
 STJS SW1Y....11 G8
Waterloo Rd *BARK/HLT* IG6....60 C1
 CRICK NW2....51 J6
 EHAM E6....77 G6
 LEY E10....57 J6
 ROMW/RG RM7....63 F4
 STHWK SE1....11 M8
 SUT SM1....175 G4
Waterloo Ter *IS* N1....6 C2
Waterlow Rd *ARCH* N19....54 C7
Waterman Cl *OXHEY* WD19....21 F5
Watermans Cl
 KUTN/CMB KT2 *....144 A6
Watermans Ms *EA* W5 *....86 A6
Waterman Sq *PGE/AN* SE20....150 E6
Waterman St *PUT/ROE* SW15....127 G2
Waterman Wy *WAP* E1W....92 D7
Watermead
 EBED/NFELT TW14....121 H7
Watermead La *CAR* SM5....162 E5

Watermeadow Cl *ERITH* DA8....118 E6
Watermeadow La
 FUL/PGN SW6....128 B1
Watermead Rd *CAT* SE6....152 B1
Watermead Wy *TOTM* N17....42 D7
Watermens Sq *PGE/AN* SE20 *....150 E6
Water Ms *PECK* SE15....131 K3
Watermill Cl
 RCHPK/HAM TW10....143 J2
Watermill La *UED* N18....42 A4
Water Mill Wy *FELT* TW13....141 K1
Watermill La *WIM/MER* SW19....147 J2
Watermint Quay
 STNW/STAM N16....56 C6
Water Rd *ALP/SUD* HA0....68 B7
Watersedge *HOR/WEW* KT19....172 E3
Water's Edge *FUL/PGN* SW6 *....107 C7
Watersfield Wy *EDGW* HA8....35 K4
Waterside *DART* DA1....138 B4
Waterside Cl *BECK* BR3....166 K4
Waterside Cl *BARK* IG11....79 G3
 BERM/RHTH SE16....111 H1
 BOW E3....75 H7
 NTHLT UB5....83 K2
 SHPTN TW17....140 H7
 SURB KT6....172 A1
 THMD SE28....97 F7
Waterside Ct *LEW* SE13 *....133 F3
Waterside Dr *WOT/HER* KT12....156 A4
Waterside Rd *NWDGN* UB2....103 F1
Waterside Wy *TOOT* SW17....147 G3
Watersmeet Wy *THMD* SE28....97 K5
Waterson Rd *BETH* E2....7 K7
Watersplash Cl *KUT/HW* KT1....159 F2
Watersplash La *HEST* TW5....102 A4
 HYS/HAR UB3....101 K3
Waters Rd *CAT* SE6....152 C2
 KUT/HW KT1....159 J1
Waters Sq *KUT/HW* KT1....159 J1
Water St *TPL/STR* WC2R....12 A6
Water Tower Hl *CROY/NA* CR0....177 K3
Water Tower Pl *IS* N1....6 B4
Waterway Av *LEW* SE13....132 E2
Waterworks La *CLPT* E5....75 F1
Waterworks Rd
 BRXS/STRHM SW2....129 K5
Watery La *HYS/HAR* UB3....101 G4
 NTHLT UB5....83 G1
 RYNPK SW20....161 J1
 STMC/STPC BR5....155 H5
Wates Wy *MTCM* CR4....162 E5
Wateville Rd *TOTM* N17....41 H4
Watford Cl *BTSEA* SW11....108 D7
Watford Field Rd
 WATW WD18....21 G4
Watford Heath *OXHEY* WD19....21 H6
Watford Heath Farm
 OXHEY WD19 *....21 H6
Watford House La *WAT* WD17....21 F2
Watford Rd *BORE* WD6....23 J5
 CAN/RD E16....94 E4
 HRW HA1....67 G2
 NTHWD HA6....32 D6
 RKW/CH/CXG WD3....20 B4
Watford Wy *HDN* NW4....51 J3
 MLHL NW7....37 F3
Watford Way (Barnet By-Pass)
 MLHL NW7....37 H4
Watkin Rd *WBLY* HA9....68 D2
Watkinson Rd *HOLWY* N7....73 F5
Watling Av *EDGW* HA8....36 E7
Watling Ct *STP* EC4M....12 F5
Watling Farm Cl *BORE* WD6....23 J1
Watlings Cl *CROY/NA* CR0....166 B5
Watling St *BORE* WD6....23 J2
 BXLYHS DA6....137 K4
 PECK SE15....111 F5
 STP EC4M....12 F5
Watlington Gv *SYD* SE26....151 G4
Watney Market *WCHPL* E1....92 D5
Watney Rd
 MORT/ESHN SW14....125 K2
Watneys Rd *CROY/NA* CR0....163 J4
Watney St *WCHPL* E1....92 D5
Watson Av *CHEAM* SM3....174 C1
 EHAM E6....78 A6
Watson Cl *STNW/STAM* N16....73 K4
 WIM/MER SW19....147 J5
Watson's Ms *CAMTN* NW1....9 K3
Watsons Rd *WDGN* N22....41 F7
Watson's St *DEPT* SE8....112 D6
Wattisfield Rd *CLPT* E5....74 E2
Watts Cl *SEVS/STOTM* N15....56 A4
Wattsdown Cl *PLSTW* E13....76 E7
Watts Gv *BOW* E3....93 J4
Watt's La *CHST* BR7....154 B7
 TEDD TW11....143 G4
Watts Rd *THDIT* KT7....158 B6
Watts St *PECK* SE15....111 C7
 WAP E1W....92 D7
Weirs Pas *CAMTN* NW1....5 J6
Weiss Rd *PUT/ROE* SW15....127 G2
Welbeck Av *BFN/LL* DA15....136 B7
 BMLY BR1....152 E3
 YEAD UB4....83 F3
Welbeck Cl *BORE* WD6....24 C2
 EW KT17....173 K6
 NWMAL KT3....160 C4
Welbeck Rd *CAR* SM5....162 D6
 EBAR EN4....27 H5
 EHAM E6....95 J2
 RYLN/HDSTN HA2....48 B7
 SUT SM1....175 H1
Welbeck Vls *WCHMH* N21 *....29 J7
Welbeck Wk *CAVSQ/HST* W1G....10 C4
Welby Ct *PLSTW* E13....95 G2
Welby St *CMBW* SE5....110 C7
Welch Pl *PIN* HA5 *....33 G7
Weldon Cl *RSLP* HA4....65 F5
Weldon Dr *E/WMO/HCT* KT8....156 K3
Welfare Rd *SRTFD* E15....76 C6
Welford Cl *CLPT* E5 *....75 F2
Welford Pl *WIM/MER* SW19....146 C3
Welham Rd *TOOT* SW17....148 A4
Welhouse Rd *CAR* SM5....162 D6
Wellacre Rd
 KTN/HRWW/WS HA3....49 H5
Wellan Cl *BFN/LL* DA15....136 C4
Welland Gdns *GFD/PVL* UB6....85 F1
Welland Ms *WAP* E1W....92 C7
Welland St *GNWCH* SE10....113 F5
Well Ap *BAR* EN5....26 A4
Wellby Cl *ED* N9....30 C7
Well Cl *RSLP* HA4....65 J2
 STRHM/NOR SW16....149 F3
Wellclose Sq *WCHPL* E1....92 C6
Wellcome Av *DART* DA1....139 H3
Well Cottage Cl *WAN* E11....59 G6
Well Ct *STP* EC4M....12 F5

Wavertree Rd
 BRXS/STRHM SW2....130 A7
 SWFD E18....58 E1
Waxlow Crs *STHL* UB1....84 A5
Waxlow Rd *WLSDN* NW10....86 E1
Waxlow Wy *NTHLT* UB5....83 K3
Waxwell La *PIN* HA5....47 H2
Wayborne Gv *RSLP* HA4....46 A5
Waye Av *HEST* TW5....101 K7
Wayfarer Rd *NTHLT* UB5....83 J2
Wayford St *BTSEA* SW11....128 D1
Wayland Av *HACK* E8....74 C4
Waylands *HYS/HAR* UB3....82 B4
Waylen Gdns *DART* DA1....139 J1
Waylett Pl *ALP/SUD* HA0 *....67 K3
 WNWD SE27....149 H2
Wayneflete Pl *ESH/CLAY* KT10....170 A2
Wayneflete Tower Av
 ESH/CLAY KT10....170 A2
Wayneflete Sq *NKENS* W10 *....88 B6
Wayneflete St
 WAND/EARL SW18....147 G1
Wayside *CROY/NA* CR0 *....179 K5
 GLDGN NW11....52 C7
 MORT/ESHN SW14....125 K3
Wayside Av *BUSH* WD23....22 D5
Wayside Cl *ROM* RM1....63 H2
 STHGT/OAK N14....28 C5
Wayside Ct *TWK* TW1....124 D5
Wayside Gdns *DAGE* RM10....80 C6
Wayside Gv *ELTH/MOT* SE9....153 K5
Wayside Ms *GNTH/NBYPK* IG2....60 B4
Weald Cl *BERM/RHTH* SE16....111 J4
 HAYES BR2....181 J1
Weald La *KTN/HRWW/WS* HA3....48 D1
Weald Ri *KTN/HRWW/WS* HA3....35 F6
Weald Sq *CLPT* E5 *....74 D1
Wealdstone Rd *CHEAM* SM3....174 D1
The Weald *CHST* BR7....153 K5
Weald Wy *ROMW/RG* RM7....62 D5
 YEAD UB4....82 D3
Wealdwood Gdns *PIN* HA5....34 B5
Weale Rd *CHING* E4....44 B2
Weald Ri *LEW* SE13....133 C3
Wearside Rd *LEW* SE13....132 E3
Weatherley Cl *BOW* E3....93 H4
Weaver Cl *CROY/NA* CR0....178 B3
 EHAM E6....96 B6
Weavers Cl *ISLW* TW7....123 K3
Weaver's La *STHWK* SE1....13 K9
Weaver Ter *FUL/PGN* SW6 *....107 K5
Weaver St *WCHPL* E1....92 C3
Weavers Wy *CAMTN* NW1....5 J1
Weaver Wk *WNWD* SE27....149 H3
Webb Cl *NKENS* W10....88 A3
Webber Cl *BORE* WD6....23 K5
 ERITH DA8....118 B6
Webber Rw *STHWK* SE1....18 B2
Webber St *STHWK* SE1....18 B1
Webb Est *CLPT* E5 *....56 C6
Webb Pl *WLSDN* NW10....87 H2
Webb Rd *BKHTH/KID* SE3....113 J5
Webbscroft Rd *DAGE* RM10....80 D3
Webbs Rd *YEAD* UB4....82 E2
Webb's Rd *BTSEA* SW11....128 E4
Webb St *STHWK* SE1....19 J4
Webster Gdns *EA* W5....85 K7
Webster Rd *BERM/RHTH* SE16....111 H2
 WAN E11....76 A2
Wedderburn Rd *BARK* IG11....78 D7
 HAMP NW3....71 H4
Wedgewood Cl
 KIL/WHAMP NW6 *....71 F2
Wedgwood Wy *NRWD* SE19....149 J6
Wedlake St *NKENS* W10....88 C3
Wedmore Gdns *ARCH* N19....72 E1
Wedmore Ms *ARCH* N19....72 D2
Wedmore Rd *GFD/PVL* UB6....84 D2
Wedmore St *ARCH* N19....72 D2
Weech Rd *KIL/WHAMP* NW6....70 E3
Weedington Rd *KTTN* NW5....72 A4
Weekley Sq *BTSEA* SW11....128 C2
Weigall Rd *LEE/GVPK* SE12....133 K3
Weighhouse St
 MYFR/PKLN W1K....10 B6
Weighton Rd
 KTN/HRWW/WS HA3....34 D7
 PGE/AN SE20....165 J1
Weihurst Gdns *SUT* SM1....175 H4
Weimar St *PUT/ROE* SW15....127 H2
Weirdale Av *TRDG/WHET* N20....39 K1
Weir Hall Av *UED* N18....41 K5
Weir Hall Gdns *UED* N18....41 K4
Weir Hall Rd *UED* N18....41 K5
Weir Rd *BAL* SW12....129 H7
 WIM/MER SW19....147 F2

Weller St *STHWK* SE1....18 E1
Wellesley Av *HMSMTH* W6....106 E2
 NTHWD HA6....32 D4
Wellesley Cl *CHARL* SE7 *....114 B4
Wellesley Ct *MV/WKIL* W9....2 E1
Wellesley Court Rd
 CROY/NA CR0 *....177 K1
Wellesley Crs *WHTN* TW2....142 E1
Wellesley Gv *CROY/NA* CR0....177 K1
Wellesley Pde *WHTN* TW2 *....142 E1
Wellesley Park Ms
 ENC/FH EN2....29 H1
Wellesley Pl *CAMTN* NW1 *....5 G8
 KTTN NW5....72 A4
Wellesley Rd *BELMT* SM2....175 G5
 CHSWK W4....105 J4
 CROY/NA CR0....164 D7
 HRW HA1....48 E4
 IL IG1....78 B1
 KTTN NW5....72 A4
 WALTH E17....57 J5
 WAN E11....58 E4
 WHTN TW2....142 E1
 WOOL/PLUM SE18....115 F6
Wellesley St *WCHPL* E1....93 F4
Wellesley Ter *IS* N1....6 F7
Wellfield Av *MUSWH* N10....54 B2
Wellfield Gdns *CAR* SM5....175 J7
Wellfield Rd
 STRHM/NOR SW16....148 E3
Wellfit St *HNHL* SE24....130 C2
Wellgarth *GFD/PVL* UB6....67 H5
Wellgarth Rd *GLDGN* NW11....53 F7
Well Gv *TRDG/WHET* N20....27 G7
Well Hall Pde *ELTH/MOT* SE9....134 E3
Well Hall Rd *ELTH/MOT* SE9....134 E3
Wellhouse La *BAR* EN5....26 A3
Wellhouse Rd *BECK* BR3....166 C3
Welling High St *WELL* DA16....136 C2
Wellings La *CHST* BR7....136 B5
Wellington Av *BFN/LL* DA15....136 B5
 CHING E4....43 J1
 ED N9....42 D2
 HSLW TW3....123 F4
 PIN HA5....33 K7
 SEVS/STOTM N15....56 B5
 WPK KT4....174 A2
Wellington Cl *DAGE* RM10....80 E6
 NTGHL W11....8 A5
 NWCR SE14....112 A7
 OXHEY WD19....33 J2
Wellington Dr *DAGE* RM10....80 E6
 WHTN TW2....142 D3
Wellington Gv *GNWCH* SE10....113 G6
Wellington Ms *CHARL* SE7....114 B5
 EDUL SE22....131 H3
 HOLWY N7....73 F5
 STRHM/NOR SW16....148 D2
Wellington Pde
 BFN/LL DA15 *....136 B4
 CRICK NW2 *....69 J1
Wellington Pas *WAN* E11....58 E4
Wellington Pl *EFNCH* N2 *....53 J4
 STJWD NW8....3 H7
Wellington Rd *BELV* DA17....117 G4
 BXLY DA5....136 E5
 CROY/NA CR0....164 C6
 DART DA1....139 F5
 EA W5....104 D3
 EBED/NFELT TW14....121 H4
 EHAM E6....77 K7
 EN EN1....30 A4
 FSTGT E7....76 D3
 HAYES BR2....168 B3
 HPTN TW12....142 D3
 KTN/HRWW/WS HA3....48 E2
 LEY E10....57 G7
 NKENS W10 *....88 B2
 PIN HA5....33 K7
 STJWD NW8....3 H6
 WALTH E17....57 G2
 WAN E11....58 E4
 WAT WD17....21 F1
 WIM/MER SW19....146 E1
Wellington Rd North
 HSLWW TW4....122 E2
Wellington Rd South
 HSLWW TW4....122 E3
Wellington Rw *BETH* E2....7 M7
Wellington Sq *CHEL* SW3....15 L7
 IS N1....5 K3
Wellington St *COVGDN* WC2E....11 K6
 WOOL/PLUM SE18....115 F3
Wellington Ter *BAY/PAD* W2....8 D7
 CEND/HSY/T N8 *....54 D3
 HRW HA1....48 D7
 WAP E1W *....92 D7
Wellington Wy *BOW* E3....93 J2
Welling Wy *ELTH/MOT* SE9....135 J2
 WELL DA16....135 K2
Well La *MORT/ESHN* SW14....125 K4
Wellmeadow Rd *CAT* SE6....133 H7
 HNWL W7....104 B3
 LEW SE13....133 H5
Well Rd *BAR* EN5....26 A4
 HAMP NW3....71 H2
Wells Cl *NTHLT* UB5....83 G2
 SAND/SEL CR2....178 A4
Wells Dr *CDALE/KGS* NW9....51 F7
Wellsfield *BUSH* WD23....21 J4
Wells Gdns *IL* IG1....59 J6
 RAIN RM13....81 H5
Wells House Rd *WLSDN* NW10....87 G4
Wellside Cl *BAR* EN5....26 A3
Wellside Gdns
 MORT/ESHN SW14....125 K3
Wells Ms *FITZ* W1T....10 F3
Wellsmoor Gdns *BMLY* BR1....169 F2
Wells Park Rd *SYD* SE26....150 C2
Wells Pl *CMBW* SE5....111 F6
 WAND/EARL SW18....128 B6
Wellspring Crs *WBLY* HA9....68 D2
Wellspring Ms *SYD* SE26....150 D2
Wellspring Wy *WAT* WD17....21 G3
Wells Ri *STJWD* NW8....3 L4
Wells Rd *BMLY* BR1....168 E1
 SHB W12....107 F1
Wells Sq *FSBYW* WC1X....5 L8
Wells St *FITZ* W1T....10 E3
Wells Ter *FSBYPK* N4....73 G1
The Wells *STHGT/OAK* N14....28 D6
Wellstones *WAT* WD17....21 F3
Well St *HOM* E9....74 E6
 SRTFD E15....76 C5
Wells Wy *SKENS* SW7....15 G3
Well Wk *HAMP* NW3....71 H2
Wellwood Rd *GDMY/SEVK* IG3....61 G2
Welsford St *STHWK* SE1....111 H4

Welsh Cl PLSTW E13 .... 94 E2
Welshpool St HACK E8 * 74 C7
Welshside CDALE/KGS NW9 * 51 L4
Welstead Wy CHSWK W4 .... 106 C2
Weltje Rd HMSMTH W6 .... 106 D4
Welton Rd WOOL/PLUM SE18 .... 115 K6
Welwyn Av EBED/NFELT TW14 .... 121 J5
Welwyn St BETH E2 .... 92 E2
Welwyn Wy YEAD UB4 .... 82 C3
Wembley Hill Rd WBLY HA9 .... 68 B4
Wembley Park Dr WBLY HA9 .... 68 B3
Wembley Rd HPTN TW12 .... 142 A7
Wembley Wy WBLY HA9 .... 68 C5
Wemborough Rd STAN HA7 .... 35 H7
Wembury Ms HGT N6 .... 54 B6
Wembury Rd HGT N6 .... 54 B6
Wemyss Rd BKHTH/KID SE3 .... 133 J1
Wendela Ct HRW HA1 .... 66 E2
Wendell Rd SHB W12 .... 106 C1
Wendling Rd SUT SM1 .... 162 C7
Wendon St BOW E3 .... 75 H7
Wendover Cl YEAD UB4 * 83 H3
Wendover Dr NWMAL KT3 .... 160 C5
Wendover Rd ELTH/MOT SE9 .... 134 C2
  HAYES BR2 .... 168 A3
  WLSDN NW10 .... 87 H1
Wendover Wy BUSH WD23 .... 22 C5
  WELL DA16 .... 136 B4
Wendy Cl EN EN1 .... 30 B5
Wendy Wy ALP/SUD HA0 .... 68 A7
Wenlock Gdns HDN NW4 * 51 J3
Wenlock Rd EDGW HA8 .... 36 D5
  IS N1 .... 6 E6
Wenlock St IS N1 .... 6 E6
Wennington Rd BOW E3 .... 93 F1
  RAIN RM13 .... 99 H4
Wensley Av WFD IG8 .... 44 D6
Wensley Cl ELTH/MOT SE9 .... 134 E5
  FBAR/BDGN N11 .... 40 A5
Wensleydale Av CLAY IG5 .... 59 J1
Wensleydale Gdns HPTN TW12 .... 142 B6
Wensleydale Pas HPTN TW12 .... 142 A7
Wensley Rd UED N18 .... 42 D5
Wentland Cl CAT SE6 .... 152 B1
Wentland Rd CAT SE6 .... 152 B1
Wentworth Av BORE WD6 .... 24 B4
  FNCH N3 .... 38 E6
Wentworth Cl FNCH N3 .... 39 F6
  HAYES BR2 .... 180 E1
  MRDN SM4 .... 161 K6
  SURB KT6 .... 171 K1
  THMD SE28 .... 97 K5
Wentworth Crs HYS/HAR UB3 .... 101 G2
  PECK SE15 .... 111 H6
Wentworth Dr DART DA1 .... 138 D6
  OXHEY WD19 .... 33 H4
  PIN HA5 .... 46 E4
Wentworth Gdns PLMGR N13 .... 41 H2
Wentworth Hl WBLY HA9 .... 50 B7
Wentworth Ms BOW E3 .... 93 G3
Wentworth Pk FNCH N3 .... 39 F6
Wentworth Pl STAN HA7 * 35 H5
Wentworth Rd BAR EN5 .... 26 A1
  CROY/NA CR0 .... 164 B6
  GLDGN NW11 .... 52 D5
  MNPK E12 .... 77 H3
  NWDGN UB2 .... 102 B3
Wentworth St WCHPL E1 .... 13 L4
Wentworth Wy PIN HA5 .... 47 H3
  RAIN RM13 .... 99 K2
Wenvoe Av BXLYHN DA7 .... 137 J1
Wepham Cl YEAD UB4 .... 83 H4
Wernbrook St WOOL/PLUM SE18 .... 115 H5
Werndee Rd SNWD SE25 .... 165 H3
Werneth Hall Rd CLAY IG5 .... 59 K2
Werrington St CAMTN NW1 .... 4 F6
Werter Rd PUT/ROE SW15 .... 127 H3
Wesleyan Pl KTTN NW5 .... 72 B3
Wesley Av CAN/RD E16 .... 94 E7
  HSLW TW3 .... 122 D1
  WLSDN NW10 .... 87 F2
Wesley Cl HOLWY N7 .... 73 F1
  RYLN/HDSTN HA2 .... 66 C1
  WALW SE17 .... 18 D6
Wesley Rd HYS/HAR UB3 .... 82 E6
  LEY E10 .... 58 A6
  WLSDN NW10 .... 68 E7
Wesley Sq NTGHL W11 .... 88 B5
Wesley St CAVSQ/HST W1G 10 B3
Wessex Av WIM/MER SW19 .... 161 K1
Wessex Cl GDMY/SEVK IG3 .... 60 E7
  KUT/HW KT1 .... 144 D7
  THDIT KT7 .... 171 F7
Wessex Ct BECK BR3 * 151 G7
Wessex Dr ERITH DA8 .... 138 B1
  PIN HA5 .... 33 K6
Wessex Gdns GLDGN NW11 .... 52 C7
Wessex La GFD/PVL UB6 .... 84 D1
Wessex St BETH E2 .... 92 E2
Wessex Ter MTCM CR4 * 162 D4
Wessex Wy GLDGN NW11 .... 52 C6
Wesson Md CMBW SE5 .... 110 D6
Westacott YEAD UB4 .... 82 C4
Westacott Cl ARCH N19 .... 54 D7
West Ap FNCH N3 .... 38 E5
West Arbour St WCHPL E1 .... 92 E5
West Av FNCH N3 .... 38 E5
  HDN NW4 .... 52 B4
  HYS/HAR UB3 .... 82 D6
  PIN HA5 .... 47 K5
  STHL UB1 .... 83 K6
  WALTH E17 .... 57 K4
  WLGTN SM6 .... 176 E4
West Avenue Rd WALTH E17 .... 57 J3
West Bank BARK IG11 .... 78 B7
  ENC/FH EN2 .... 29 J2
  STNW/STAM N16 .... 56 A6
Westbank Rd HPTN TW12 .... 142 C5
West Barnes La NWMAL KT3 .... 160 D4
Westbeech Rd WDGN N22 .... 55 G2
Westbere Dr STAN HA7 .... 35 K4
Westbere Rd CRICK NW2 .... 70 C3
Westbourne Av ACT W3 .... 87 F5
  CHEAM SM3 .... 174 C1
Westbourne Cl YEAD UB4 .... 83 G3
Westbourne Crs BAY/PAD W2 .... 9 G6
Westbourne Crescent Ms
  BAY/PAD W2 .... 9 G6
Westbourne Dr FSTH SE23 .... 132 A1
Westbourne Gdns
  BAY/PAD W2 .... 8 C4
Westbourne Ga BAY/PAD W2 .... 9 H6
Westbourne Gv BAY/PAD W2 .... 8 B5
  NTGHL W11 .... 8 A5
Westbourne Grove Ms
  NTGHL W11 .... 8 B5
Westbourne Grove Ter
  BAY/PAD W2 .... 8 C5
Westbourne Park Rd
  NTGHL W11 .... 8 A4

Westbourne Park Vls
  BAY/PAD W2 .... 8 B3
Westbourne Pl ED N1 * 42 D2
Westbourne Rd BXLYHN DA7 .... 116 E5
  CROY/NA CR0 .... 165 G5
  FELT TW13 .... 140 D2
  HOLWY N7 .... 73 F5
  SYD SE26 .... 151 F5
Westbourne Ter BAY/PAD W2 .... 8 E5
Westbourne Terrace Ms
  BAY/PAD W2 .... 8 E4
Westbourne Terrace Rd
  BAY/PAD W2 .... 8 E3
Westbridge Cl SHB W12 .... 87 J7
Westbridge Rd BTSEA SW11 .... 108 C7
Westbrook Av HPTN TW12 .... 141 K6
Westbrook Cl EBAR EN4 .... 27 H2
Westbrooke Crs WELL DA16 .... 136 D2
Westbrooke Rd BFN/LL DA15 .... 154 D1
  WELL DA16 .... 136 D2
Westbrook Rd BKHTH/KID SE3 .... 113 K7
  HEST TW5 .... 102 E6
  THHTH CR7 .... 149 K7
Westbury Ar WDGN N22 * 55 H2
Westbury Av ALP/SUD HA0 .... 68 A6
  ESH/CLAY KT10 .... 171 F5
  SEVS/STOTM N15 .... 55 J2
  STHL UB1 .... 84 A3
  WDGN N22 .... 55 H1
Westbury Cl RSLP HA4 .... 46 E6
Westbury Gv
  NFNCH/WDSPK N12 .... 38 E5
Westbury La BKHH IG9 .... 45 G1
Westbury Lodge Cl PIN HA5 * 47 H2
Westbury Pl BTFD TW8 .... 104 E5
Westbury Rd ALP/SUD HA0 .... 68 A6
  BARK IG11 .... 78 D7
  BECK BR3 .... 166 B2
  BMLY BR1 .... 153 H7
  CROY/NA CR0 .... 164 E5
  EA W5 .... 86 A5
  FBAR/BDGN N11 .... 40 E5
  FELT TW13 .... 122 C7
  FSTGT E7 .... 77 F4
  IL IG1 .... 78 A1
  NFNCH/WDSPK N12 .... 38 E5
  NTHWD HA6 .... 32 C3
  NWMAL KT3 .... 160 A3
  PGE/AN SE20 .... 151 F7
  WALTH E17 .... 57 J3
  WATW WD18 .... 21 F4
  WEA W13 .... 85 H6
Westbury Ter FSTGT E7 .... 77 F5
West Carriage Dr
  BAY/PAD W2 .... 9 H9
West Central St
  LSQ/SEVD WC2H 11 J4
West Chantry
  KTN/HRWW/WS HA3 .... 34 B7
Westchester Dr HDN NW4 .... 52 B2
Westcliffe Vls KUT/HW KT1 * 159 G1
West Cl BAR EN5 .... 25 K4
  EBAR EN4 .... 28 A3
  ED N9 .... 42 B2
  GFD/PVL UB6 .... 84 C1
  RAIN RM13 .... 99 K3
  WBLY HA9 .... 50 B7
Westcombe Av CROY/NA CR0 .... 163 K6
Westcombe Dr BAR EN5 .... 26 E4
Westcombe Hl
  BKHTH/KID SE3 .... 113 K5
Westcombe Lodge Dr
  YEAD UB4 .... 82 B4
Westcombe Park Rd
  BKHTH/KID SE3 .... 113 H5
Westcoombe Av
  RYNPK SW20 .... 145 H7
Westcote Ri RSLP HA4 .... 46 A6
Westcote Rd
  STRHM/NOR SW16 .... 148 C4
Westcott Cl BMLY BR1 * 168 C4
  CROY/NA CR0 .... 179 K7
  SEVS/STOTM N15 .... 56 B5
Westcott Crs HNWL W7 .... 84 E4
Westcott House
  POP/IOD E14 * 93 J6
Westcott Rd WALW SE17 .... 18 D9
West Ct ALP/SUD HA0 .... 67 J1
Westcroft Cl CRICK NW2 .... 70 C3
Westcroft Gdns MRDN SM4 .... 161 J2
Westcroft Ms HMSMTH W6 * 106 C3
Westcroft Sq HMSMTH W6 .... 106 D3
Westcroft Wy CRICK NW2 .... 70 C3
West Cross Route NTGHL W11 .... 88 B7
West Cross Wy BTFD TW8 .... 104 C5
Westdale Rd
  WOOL/PLUM SE18 .... 115 G5
Westdean Av LEE/GVPK SE12 .... 134 A7
Westdean Cl
  WAND/EARL SW18 .... 128 A5
Westdown Rd CAT SE6 .... 132 C6
  SRTFD E15 .... 76 A3
West Drayton Park Av
  WDR/YW UB7 .... 100 B2
West Drayton Rd
  UX/CGN UB8 .... 82 A4
  UX/CGN UB8 .... 82 A4
West Dr BELMT SM2 .... 174 B7
  KTN/HRWW/WS HA3 .... 34 D5
  STRHM/NOR SW16 .... 148 B3
West Drive Gdns
  KTN/HRWW/WS HA3 .... 34 D5
West Eaton Pl BGVA SW1W 16 A5
West Eaton Place Ms
  KTBR SW1X 16 A5
West Ella Rd WLSDN NW10 .... 69 G6
West End Av LEY E10 .... 58 A4
  PIN HA5 .... 47 H3
West End Cl WLSDN NW10 .... 68 E6
West End Ct PIN HA5 * 47 H3
West End Gdns NTHLT UB5 .... 83 G1
West End La BAR EN5 .... 26 B3
  HYS/HAR UB3 .... 101 F6
  KIL/WHAMP NW6 .... 2 B4
  PIN HA5 .... 47 H3
West End Rd NTHLT UB5 .... 65 G6
  RSLP HA4 .... 64 D2
  STHL UB1 .... 83 J7
Westerdale Rd GNWCH SE10 .... 113 K4
Westerfield Rd
  SEVS/STOTM N15 .... 56 B4
Westergate Rd ABYW SE2 .... 117 F5
Westerham Av ED N9 .... 41 K2
Westerham Dr BFN/LL DA15 .... 136 D5
Westerham Rd HAYES BR2 .... 181 H5
  LEY E10 .... 57 K5
Westerley Crs SYD SE26 * 151 H4
Western Av DAGE RM10 .... 80 E5
  EA W5 .... 86 A2
  GFD/PVL UB6 .... 66 A7

  GFD/PVL UB6 .... 85 F2
  GLDGN NW11 .... 52 B5
  RSLP HA4 .... 65 F6
Western Ct FNCH N3 * 38 E5
Western Gdns EA W5 .... 86 C6
Western Gtwy CAN/RD E16 .... 94 E6
Western La BAL SW12 .... 129 F6
Western Man BAR EN5 * 27 F4
Western Ms MV/WKIL W9 .... 88 D3
Western Pde BAR EN5 .... 26 E4
Western Pl BERM/RHTH SE16 .... 111 K1
Western Rd BRXN/ST SW9 .... 130 B2
  EA W5 .... 85 K6
  EFNCH N2 .... 53 K3
  MTCM CR4 .... 147 J7
  NWDGN UB2 .... 102 B3
  PLSTW E13 .... 77 F7
  ROM RM1 .... 63 G4
  SUT SM1 .... 174 E4
  WALTH E17 .... 58 A4
  WDGN N22 .... 55 F1
  WLSDN NW10 .... 86 E3
Western Ter HMSMTH W6 * 106 D4
Western Vw HYS/HAR UB3 .... 101 J1
Westernville Gdns
  GNTH/NBYPK IG2 .... 60 C5
Western Wy BAR EN5 .... 26 E5
  THMD SE28 .... 115 J2
Westferry Circ POP/IOD E14 .... 93 J7
Westferry Rd POP/IOD E14 .... 112 D2
Westfield Cl CDALE/KGS NW9 .... 50 E2
  FUL/PGN SW6 * 108 B6
  PEND EN3 .... 31 G2
  SUT SM1 .... 174 D3
  WBPTN SW10 .... 108 B6
Westfield Dr
  KTN/HRWW/WS HA3 .... 49 K4
Westfield Gdns CHDH RM6 .... 61 J5
  KTN/HRWW/WS HA3 .... 49 K3
Westfield Park Dr WFD IG8 .... 45 J5
Westfield Pk PIN HA5 .... 33 K6
Westfield Rd BECK BR3 .... 166 C1
  BXLYHN DA7 .... 137 K2
  CROY/NA CR0 .... 177 H1
  DAGW RM9 .... 80 A3
  MLHL NW7 .... 37 F3
  MTCM CR4 .... 162 D1
  SURB KT6 .... 158 E4
  SUT SM1 .... 174 D3
  WEA W13 .... 85 G7
  WOT/HER KT12 .... 156 D6
Westfields BARN SW13 .... 126 C6
Westfields Av BARN SW13 .... 126 B3
Westfields Rd ACT W3 .... 86 D4
Westfield St
  WOOL/PLUM SE18 .... 114 C2
Westfield Wy RSLP HA4 .... 64 C2
  WCHPL E1 .... 93 G2
West Gdns TOOT SW17 .... 147 J5
  WAP E1W 92 D6
Westgate Est
  EBED/NFELT TW14 * 120 E7
West Gate Ms WATW WD18 .... 20 C4
Westgate Rd BECK BR3 .... 152 A7
  DART DA1 .... 139 G5
  SNWD SE25 .... 165 J3
Westgate St HACK E8 .... 74 D7
Westgate Ter WBPTN SW10 .... 14 D8
Westglade Ct
  KTN/HRWW/WS HA3 .... 49 K4
West Green Pl GFD/PVL UB6 .... 66 D7
West Green Rd
  SEVS/STOTM N15 .... 55 H3
West Gv GNWCH SE10 .... 113 F7
  WFD IG8 .... 45 G5
Westgrove La GNWCH SE10 .... 113 F7
West Halkin St KTBR SW1X 16 A3
West Hallowes ELTH/MOT SE9 .... 134 C7
West Ham La SRTFD E15 .... 76 B6
West Hampstead Ms
  KIL/WHAMP NW6 .... 71 F3
West Harding St
  FLST/FETLN EC4A * 12 B4
West Hatch Mnr RSLP HA4 .... 46 D7
Westhay Gdns
  MORT/ESHN SW14 .... 125 J4
West Heath Av GLDGN NW11 .... 52 E7
West Heath Cl DART DA1 * 138 C5
  HAMP NW3 .... 70 E2
West Heath Dr GLDGN NW11 .... 52 E7
West Heath Gdns HAMP NW3 .... 70 E1
West Heath Rd ABYW SE2 .... 116 E5
  DART DA1 .... 138 C5
  HAMP NW3 .... 70 E1
West Hl DART DA1 .... 139 G5
  PUT/ROE SW15 .... 127 H5
  RYLN/HDSTN HA2 .... 66 E1
  SAND/SEL CR2 .... 178 A7
  WAND/EARL SW18 .... 127 K4
  WBLY HA9 .... 50 B7
  WIM/MER SW19 .... 127 G6
West Hill Dr DART DA1 .... 139 F5
Westhill Pk HGT N6 .... 71 K1
West Hill Ri DART DA1 .... 139 G5
West Hill Rd
  WAND/EARL SW18 .... 127 J5
West Hill Wy TRDG/WHET N20 .... 27 F7
Westholm GLDGN NW11 .... 53 F3
West Holme ERITH DA8 .... 117 K7
Westholme ORP BR6 .... 169 K6
Westholme Gdns RSLP HA4 .... 46 E7
Westhorne Av ELTH/MOT SE9 .... 134 B6
  LEE/GVPK SE12 .... 133 K6
Westhorpe Gdns HDN NW4 .... 52 A2
Westhorpe Rd PUT/ROE SW15 .... 127 F2
West House Cl
  WIM/MER SW19 .... 127 H7
Westhurst Dr CHST BR7 .... 154 B4
West India Av POP/IOD E14 .... 93 J7
West India Dock Rd
  POP/IOD E14 .... 93 K6
Westlake Cl PLMGR N13 .... 41 G2
  YEAD UB4 .... 83 J3
Westland Cl
  STWL/WRAY TW19 * 120 B5
Westland Dr HAYES BR2 .... 180 D1
Westland Pl FSBYE EC1V 7 G7
Westland Rd WAT WD17 * 21 F1
Westlands Cl HYS/HAR UB3 .... 101 K3
Westlands Ter BAL SW12 .... 129 H5
West La BERM/RHTH SE16 .... 111 J1
Westlea Rd HNWL W7 .... 104 B2
Westleigh Av PUT/ROE SW15 .... 127 F4
Westleigh Dr BMLY BR1 .... 168 D1
Westleigh Gdns EDGW HA8 .... 36 C7
West Ling RYLN/HDSTN HA2 .... 65 K2
Westlinton Cl MLHL NW7 .... 38 C5
West Lodge Av ACT W3 .... 86 C1
West Lodge Ct ACT W3 * 86 C1
Westmacott Dr
  EBED/NFELT TW14 .... 121 J6
  GFD/PVL UB6 .... 66 A7

West Md HOR/WEW KT19 .... 173 G5
Westmead PUT/ROE SW15 .... 126 E6
West Md RSLP HA4 .... 65 G3
Westmead Rd SUT SM1 .... 175 H3
Westmere Dr MLHL NW7 .... 37 F2
West Mersea Cl CAN/RD E16 .... 95 F7
West Ms PIM SW1V 16 D6
  TOTM N17 * 42 D6
Westminster Av THHTH CR7 .... 164 C1
Westminster Br
  WHALL SW1A 17 K2
Westminster Bridge Rd
  WHALL SW1A 17 K2
Westminster Cl
  EBED/NFELT TW14 .... 121 K7
  TEDD TW11 .... 143 G4
Westminster Dr PLMGR N13 .... 40 E4
Westminster Gdns BARK IG11 .... 96 E1
  BARK/HLT IG6 .... 60 D1
Westminster Rd ED N9 .... 30 D7
  HNWL W7 .... 84 E7
  SUT SM1 .... 175 H2
Westmoat Cl BECK BR3 .... 152 A6
Westmoor Rd ESH/CLAY KT10 .... 170 E1
Westmoor Gdns PEND EN3 .... 31 F1
Westmoor St CHARL SE7 .... 114 C3
Westmoreland Av WELL DA16 .... 135 J2
Westmoreland Dr BELMT SM2 .... 175 F7
Westmoreland Pl BMLY BR1 * 167 K2
  EA W5 .... 85 K4
  PIM SW1V 16 D8
Westmoreland Rd
  BARN SW13 .... 106 C7
  CMBW SE5 .... 18 F9
  HAYES BR2 .... 167 K4
  KTN/HRWW/WS HA3 .... 50 B3
  WALW SE17 .... 19 G9
  WWKM BR4 .... 167 H4
Westmoreland St
  CAVSQ/HST W1G 10 B3
Westmoreland Ter
  PGE/AN SE20 * 150 D6
  PIM SW1V 16 D7
Westmorland Cl MNPK E12 .... 77 H1
  TWK TW1 .... 124 C5
Westmorland Rd HRW HA1 .... 48 B4
  WALTH E17 .... 57 J6
Westmorland Wy MTCM CR4 .... 163 J5
Westmount Cl WPK KT4 .... 161 F7
Westmount Ct EA W5 * 86 B4
Westmount Rd
  ELTH/MOT SE9 .... 134 C2
West Oak BECK BR3 .... 152 B7
Westoe Rd ED N9 .... 42 D1
Weston Av E/WMO/HCT KT8 .... 156 E2
  THDIT KT7 .... 157 K6
Weston Dr STAN HA7 .... 35 H7
Weston Gdns ISLW TW7 .... 103 J7
Weston Gn DAGW RM9 .... 80 A3
  THDIT KT7 .... 170 E1
Weston Green Rd
  ESH/CLAY KT10 .... 157 J7
Weston Gv BMLY BR1 .... 152 D6
Weston Pk CEND/HSY/T N8 .... 54 E5
  KUT/HW KT1 .... 159 F1
  THDIT KT7 .... 157 K7
Weston Park Cl THDIT KT7 * 157 K7
Weston Ri FSBYW WC1X 5 M7
Weston Rd BMLY BR1 .... 152 D7
  CHSWK W4 .... 105 K2
  DAGW RM9 .... 80 A3
  ENC/FH EN2 .... 29 K1
  THDIT KT7 .... 157 K7
Weston St STHWK SE1 .... 19 H3
Westover Cl BELMT SM2 .... 175 F7
Westover Hl HAMP NW3 .... 70 E1
Westover Rd
  WAND/EARL SW18 .... 128 B5
Westow Hl NRWD SE19 .... 150 A5
Westow St NRWD SE19 .... 150 A5
West Pk ELTH/MOT SE9 .... 153 J1
West Park Av RCH/KEW TW9 .... 105 H7
West Park Cl CHDH RM6 .... 61 K4
  HEST TW5 .... 102 E5
West Park Rd NWDGN UB2 .... 84 C7
  RCH/KEW TW9 .... 105 H7
West Parkside GNWCH SE10 .... 113 H1
West Pl NWDGN UB2 * 103 H1
  WIM/MER SW19 .... 146 A4
Westpole Av EBAR EN4 .... 28 A3
Westport Rd PLSTW E13 .... 95 F3
Westport St WCHPL E1 .... 93 F5
West Poultry Av FARR EC1M 12 C2
West Quarters SHB W12 .... 87 J5
West Quay Dr YEAD UB4 .... 83 J4
West Ridge Gdns
  GFD/PVL UB6 .... 84 C1
West Ri BAY/PAD W2 * 9 K6
West Rd CHDH RM6 .... 62 A5
  CHEL SW3 .... 15 M9
  CLAP SW4 .... 129 J4
  EA W5 .... 86 A4
  EBAR EN4 .... 28 A7
  EBED/NFELT TW14 .... 121 G6
  KUTN/CMB KT2 .... 144 E7
  ROMW/RG RM7 .... 63 F6
  SRTFD E15 .... 76 D7
  TOTM N17 .... 42 D5
  WDR/YW UB7 .... 100 C2
West Rw NKENS W10 .... 88 C3
Westrow Dr BARK IG11 .... 79 G4
Westrow Gdns
  GDMY/SEVK IG3 .... 79 F1
West Sheen V RCH/KEW TW9 .... 125 G3
Westside HDN NW4 .... 51 K1
West Side Common
  WIM/MER SW19 .... 146 A4
West Smithfield STBT EC1A 12 C3
West Sq LBTH SE11 .... 18 C4
West St BETH E2 .... 92 D1
  BMLY BR1 .... 152 E7
  BXLYHN DA7 .... 137 G3
  CAR SM5 .... 175 K2
  CROY/NA CR0 .... 177 J3
  ERITH DA8 .... 118 A3
  HRW HA1 .... 48 D4
  LSQ/SEVD WC2H 11 H5
  SUT SM1 .... 175 F4
  WALTH E17 .... 57 K4
  WAN E11 .... 76 C2
  WAT WD17 .... 21 F1
West Street La CAR SM5 .... 175 K3
West Street Pl CROY/NA CR0 * 177 J3
West Temple Sheen
  MORT/ESHN SW14 .... 125 J4
West Tenter St WCHPL E1 .... 13 M5
West Ter BFN/LL DA15 * 135 K2
West Towers PIN HA5 .... 47 H5
West Vw EBED/NFELT TW14 .... 121 H6
Westview HNWL W7 .... 84 E5
Westview Cl NKENS W10 .... 88 A3
  WLSDN NW10 .... 69 H4

Westview Ct BORE WD6 * 23 K5
Westview Crs ED N9 .... 30 A6
Westview Dr WFD IG8 .... 59 H1
West View Gdns BORE WD6 .... 23 K5
West View Rd DART DA1 .... 139 J5
Westville Rd SHB W12 .... 106 D7
  THDIT KT7 .... 158 B6
West Wk EBAR EN4 .... 28 A7
  HYS/HAR UB3 .... 82 E7
Westward Rd CHING E4 .... 43 H4
Westward Wy
  KTN/HRWW/WS HA3 .... 50 A5
West Warwick Pl PIM SW1V * 16 D6
West Wy CROY/NA CR0 .... 179 G1
  EDGW HA8 .... 36 D5
  HEST TW5 .... 102 E1
  PIN HA5 .... 47 H2
  RSLP HA4 .... 46 D5
  STMC/STPC BR5 .... 169 J4
  UED N18 .... 41 K4
  WLSDN NW10 .... 69 F3
  WWKM BR4 .... 167 G3
Westway BAY/PAD W2 .... 8 A2
  NKENS W10 .... 88 B4
  RYNPK SW20 .... 160 E3
  SHB W12 .... 87 J6
Westway Cl RYNPK SW20 .... 160 E2
West Way Gdns CROY/NA CR0 .... 179 F1
Westways HOR/WEW KT19 .... 173 H3
Westwell Rd
  STRHM/NOR SW16 .... 148 E5
Westwell Road Ap
  STRHM/NOR SW16 .... 148 E5
Westwick Gdns HMSMTH W6 .... 107 G3
  HSLWW TW4 .... 122 A1
Westwood Av NRWD SE19 .... 149 J7
  RYLN/HDSTN HA2 .... 66 B3
Westwood Cl BMLY BR1 .... 168 C2
  ESH/CLAY KT10 .... 170 C2
Westwood Gdns BARN SW13 .... 126 C2
Westwood Hl SYD SE26 .... 150 C4
Westwood La WELL DA16 .... 136 B3
Westwood Pk FSTH SE23 .... 131 J6
Westwood Pl SYD SE26 * 150 C4
Westwood Rd BARN SW13 .... 126 C2
  GDMY/SEVK IG3 .... 61 F7
West Woodside BXLY DA5 .... 137 F7
Wetheral Dr STAN HA7 .... 35 H7
Wetherby Cl NTHLT UB5 .... 66 B5
Wetherby Gdns ECT SW5 .... 14 E5
Wetherby Ms ECT SW5 .... 14 D7
Wetherby Pl SKENS SW7 .... 14 E5
Wetherby Rd ENC/FH EN2 .... 29 J1
Wetherby Wy CHSGTN KT9 .... 172 A6
Wetherden St WALTH E17 .... 57 H6
Wetherell Rd HOM E9 .... 75 F7
Wetherill Rd MUSWH N10 .... 40 A4
Wexford Rd BAL SW12 .... 128 E6
Weybourne St
  WAND/EARL SW18 .... 147 G1
Weybridge Ct
  BERM/RHTH SE16 * 111 J4
Weybridge Rd THHTH CR7 .... 164 A3
Wey Ct HOR/WEW KT19 .... 172 E3
Weydown Cl WIM/MER SW19 .... 127 H7
Weyhill Rd WCHPL E1 * 92 C5
Weyland Rd BCTR RM8 .... 80 B2
Weyman Rd BKHTH/KID SE3 .... 114 B7
Weymouth Av ACT W3 .... 104 D2
  MLHL NW7 .... 37 G4
Weymouth Cl EHAM E6 .... 96 B5
Weymouth Ct BELMT SM2 * 175 F6
Weymouth Ms
  CAVSQ/HST W1G 10 B2
Weymouth Rd YEAD UB4 .... 82 C2
Weymouth St
  CAVSQ/HST W1G 10 B2
Weymouth Ter BETH E2 .... 7 L3
Weymouth Vls FSBYPK N4 * 73 F1
Weymouth Wk STAN HA7 .... 35 G5
Whadcoat St FSBYPK N4 .... 73 G1
Whalebone Av CHDH RM6 .... 62 B5
Whalebone Gv CHDH RM6 .... 62 B5
Whalebone La North
  CHDH RM6 .... 62 A3
Whalebone La South
  BCTR RM8 .... 62 B6
Whales Yd SRTFD E15 * 76 C6
Wharfdale Cl FBAR/BDGN N11 .... 40 A5
Wharfdale Rd IS N1 .... 5 K5
Wharfedale Gdns THHTH CR7 .... 164 A3
Wharfedale St WBPTN SW10 .... 14 C8
Wharf La POP/IOD E14 .... 93 H5
  TWK TW1 .... 124 B7
Wharf Pl BETH E2 .... 74 C7
Wharf Rd IS N1 .... 6 E6
  KCROSS N1C 5 H4
  PEND EN3 .... 31 G5
  SRTFD E15 .... 76 B7
Wharfside Rd POP/IOD E14 .... 94 C5
Wharf St CAN/RD E16 .... 94 C4
Wharf Ter PUT/ROE SW15 .... 127 H2
Wharncliffe Dr STHL UB1 .... 84 D7
Wharncliffe Gdns SNWD SE25 .... 165 F1
Wharncliffe Rd SNWD SE25 .... 165 G1
Wharton Cl WLSDN NW10 .... 69 G5
Wharton Cots FSBYW WC1X * 5 M8
Wharton Rd BMLY BR1 .... 153 F7
Wharton St FSBYW WC1X 5 M8
Whateley Rd EDUL SE22 .... 131 G4
  PGE/AN SE20 .... 151 F6
Whatley Av RYNPK SW20 .... 161 G2
Whatman Rd FSTH SE23 .... 132 A6
Wheastone Rd NKENS W10 .... 88 C4
Wheatfield Wy KUT/HW KT1 .... 159 F1
Wheathill Rd PGE/AN SE20 .... 165 J1
Wheatlands HEST TW5 .... 103 F5
Wheatlands Rd TOOT SW17 .... 148 A2
Wheatley Cl HDN NW4 .... 51 J1
Wheatley Crs HYS/HAR UB3 .... 82 E6
Wheatley Gdns ED N9 .... 42 A1
Wheatley Rd ISLW TW7 .... 124 A2
Wheatley St CAVSQ/HST W1G 10 B3
Wheatley Terrace Rd
  ERITH DA8 .... 118 C5
Wheatsheaf Cl NTHLT UB5 .... 65 H4
Wheat Sheaf Cl POP/IOD E14 .... 112 D3
Wheatsheaf La FUL/PGN SW6 .... 107 G6
  VX/NE SW8 .... 109 K6
Wheatsheaf Rd ROM RM1 .... 63 H5
Wheatsheaf Ter
  FUL/PGN SW6 .... 107 J6
Wheatstone Cl
  WIM/MER SW19 .... 147 H7
Wheatstone Rd NKENS W10 .... 88 C4
Wheeler Gdns IS N1 .... 5 K3
Wheeler La WCHPL E1 .... 13 L2
Wheeler Pl HAYES BR2 .... 168 A3
Wheelers Cross BARK IG11 .... 96 D1
Wheelers Dr RSLP HA4 .... 46 A5
Wheel Farm Dr DAGE RM10 .... 80 E2
Wheelock Cl ERITH DA8 .... 117 J6
Wheelright Cl BUSH WD23 .... 22 B5

Wheelwright St HOLWY N7 ... 5 L1
Whelan Wy WLGTN SM6 ... 176 D2
Wheler St WCHPL E1 ... 13 L1
Whellock Rd CHSWK W4 ... 106 B2
Whetstone Cl
  TRDG/WHET N20 ... 39 H1
Whetstone Pk LINN WC2A ... 11 L4
Whewell Rd ARCH N19 ... 72 E1
Whichcote St STHWK SE1 * ... 12 A9
Whidborne St STPAN WC1H ... 5 K8
Whimbrel Wy YEAD UB4 ... 83 H5
Whinchat Rd THMD SE28 ... 115 J2
Whinfell Cl STRHM/NOR SW16 ... 148 D4
Whinyates Rd ELTH/MOT SE9 ... 134 D2
Whippendell Cl
  STMC/STPC BR5 ... 155 H7
Whippendell Rd WATW WD18 ... 20 C4
Whippendell Wy
  STMC/STPC BR5 ... 155 H7
Whipps Cross Rd WAN E11 ... 58 C4
Whiskin St CLKNW EC1R ... 6 C8
Whistler Gdns EDGW HA8 ... 50 B1
Whistler Ms PECK SE15 ... 111 G6
Whistlers Av BTSEA SW11 * ... 108 C6
Whistler St HBRY N5 ... 73 H3
Whistler Wk WBPTN SW10 * ... 108 B6
Whiston Rd BETH E2 ... 7 L5
Whitacre Ms LBTH SE11 ... 18 B8
Whitbread Cl TOTM N17 ... 42 C7
Whitbread Rd BROCKY SE4 ... 132 B3
Whitburn Rd LEW SE13 ... 132 E4
Whitby Av WLSDN NW10 ... 86 D2
Whitby Gdns CDALE/KGS NW9 ... 50 C2
  SUT SM1 ... 175 H1
Whitby Pde RSLP HA4 * ... 65 G1
Whitby Rd RSLP HA4 ... 65 F2
  RYLN/HDSTN HA2 ... 66 C2
  SUT SM1 ... 175 H1
  WOOL/PLUM SE18 ... 114 E3
Whitby St WCHPL E1 ... 7 L9
Whitcher Cl NWCR SE14 ... 112 B5
Whitcher Pl CAMTN NW1 ... 72 C5
Whitchurch Av EDGW HA8 ... 36 A6
Whitchurch Cl EDGW HA8 ... 36 B5
Whitchurch Gdns EDGW HA8 ... 36 A6
Whitchurch La EDGW HA8 ... 36 A6
Whitchurch Pde EDGW HA8 * ... 36 C6
Whitchurch Rd NKENS W10 ... 88 B6
Whitcomb St
  SOHO/SHAV W1D ... 11 H7
Whitcome Ms RCH/KEW TW9 ... 105 J7
Whiteadder Wy POP/IOD E14 ... 112 E3
Whitear Wk SRTFD E15 ... 76 B5
Whitebarn La DAGE RM10 ... 80 C7
Whitebeam Av HAYES BR2 ... 169 F6
Whitebeam Cl VX/NE SW8 ... 110 A6
White Bear Pl HAMP NW3 * ... 71 H3
White Bear Yd CLKNW EC1R * ... 12 A1
White Bridge Av MTCM CR4 ... 162 C3
White Bridge Cl
  EBED/NFELT TW14 ... 121 J5
White Butts Rd RSLP HA4 ... 65 H2
Whitechapel High St
  TWRH EC3N ... 13 M4
Whitechapel Rd WCHPL E1 ... 92 C5
White Church La WCHPL E1 ... 92 C5
White City Cl SHB W12 ... 88 A6
White City Est SHB W12 ... 87 K6
White Conduit St IS N1 ... 6 B5
Whitecote Rd STHL UB1 ... 84 C5
White Craig Cl PIN HA5 ... 34 A4
Whitecroft Cl BECK BR3 ... 167 G3
Whitecroft Wy BECK BR3 ... 167 F3
Whitecross St STLK EC1Y ... 6 F9
Whitefield Av CRICK NW2 ... 52 A8
Whitefield Cl PUT/ROE SW15 ... 127 H5
Whitefoot La BMLY BR1 ... 152 B3
Whitefoot Ter BMLY BR1 ... 152 D2
Whitefriars Av
  KTN/HRWW/WS HA3 ... 48 E1
Whitefriars Dr
  KTN/HRWW/WS HA3 ... 48 E1
Whitefriars St EMB EC4Y ... 12 B5
White Gdns DAGE RM10 ... 80 C5
White Gate Gdns
  KTN/HRWW/WS HA3 ... 34 E6
White Gates THDIT KT7 ... 158 B6
Whitehall WHALL SW1A ... 11 J9
Whitehall Cl BORE WD6 ... 24 C3
Whitehall Ct WHALL SW1A ... 11 J9
Whitehall Crs CHSGTN KT9 ... 171 K4
Whitehall Gdns ACT W3 ... 86 C7
  CHSWK W4 ... 105 J5
  WHALL SW1A ... 11 J9
Whitehall La BKHH IG9 ... 44 E1
  ERITH DA8 ... 138 C1
Whitehall Pk ARCH N19 ... 54 C7
Whitehall Park Rd CHSWK W4 ... 105 J5
Whitehall Pl WHALL SW1A ... 11 J9
  WLGTN SM6 ... 176 B3
Whitehall Rd CHING E4 ... 44 C1
  HAYES BR2 ... 168 C4
  HNWL W7 ... 104 B1
  HRW HA1 ... 48 E6
  THHTH CR7 ... 164 B4
  WFD IG8 ... 44 E2
White Hart Av
  WOOL/PLUM SE18 ... 116 A2
White Hart La BARN SW13 ... 126 B1
  TOTM N17 ... 41 J6
White Hart Rd
  WOOL/PLUM SE18 ... 115 K3
White Hart St LBTH SE11 ... 18 B7
White Hart Ter TOTM N17 * ... 42 B6
White Hart Yd STHWK SE1 ... 13 G9
Whitehaven Cl HAYES BR2 ... 167 K3
Whitehaven St STJWD NW8 ... 9 J1
Whitehead Cl UED N18 ... 41 K4
  WAND/EARL SW18 ... 128 B6
Whiteheads Gv CHEL SW3 ... 15 K6
Whiteheath Av RSLP HA4 ... 46 A6
White Heron Ms TEDD TW11 * ... 143 F5
Whitehill Rd DART DA1 ... 138 D4
White Horse Hl CHST BR7 ... 154 A3
White Horse La SNWD SE25 ... 165 H3
White Horse Ms LBTH SE11 ... 18 B4
White Horse Ms PEND EN3 ... 31 F1
White Horse Rd EHAM E6 ... 95 K2
  WCHPL E1 ... 93 G5
White Horse St
  MYFR/PICC W1J ... 10 D9
White Horse Yd LOTH EC2R ... 13 G4
Whitehouse Av BORE WD6 ... 24 D3
White House Dr STAN HA7 ... 35 J3
Whitehouse Wy
  STHGT/OAK N14 ... 40 B1

Whitehurst Dr UED N18 * ... 43 F4
White Kennett St
  HDTCH EC3A ... 13 K4
Whitelands Crs
  WAND/EARL SW18 ... 127 H6
White Ledges WEA W13 ... 85 J5
Whitelegg Rd PLSTW E13 ... 94 D1
Whiteley Rd NRWD SE19 ... 149 K4
Whiteleys Wy FELT TW13 ... 142 A2
White Lion Ct LOTH EC2R ... 13 J5
  PECK SE15 * ... 111 K5
White Lion HI BLKFR EC4V ... 12 D6
White Lion St IS N1 ... 6 A6
White Ldg NRWD SE19 ... 149 H6
White Lodge Cl BELMT SM2 ... 175 G6
  EFNCH N2 ... 53 H5
  ISLW TW7 ... 124 B1
The White Ldg BAR EN5 * ... 26 C2
White Lyon Ct STBT EC1A ... 12 E2
White Oak Dr BECK BR3 ... 167 F1
White Oak Gdns BFN/LL DA15 ... 136 A6
White Orchards STAN HA7 ... 35 G4
  TRDG/WHET N20 ... 26 D6
White Post La HOM E9 ... 75 H6
White Post St NWCR SE14 ... 111 K6
White Rd SRTFD E15 ... 76 C6
Whites Av GNTH/NBYPK IG2 ... 60 E5
White's Grounds STHWK SE1 ... 19 K1
Whites Grounds Est
  STHWK SE1 * ... 19 K1
Whites Meadow BMLY BR1 * ... 169 J3
White's Rw WCHPL E1 ... 13 L3
White's Sq CLAP SW4 ... 129 J3
Whitestile Rd BTFD TW8 ... 104 D4
Whitestone La HAMP NW3 ... 71 G2
Whitestone Wk HAMP NW3 ... 71 G2
Whitestone Wy CROY/NA CR0 ... 177 G2
White St STHL UB1 ... 102 C1
Whitethorn Gdns
  CROY/NA CR0 ... 178 D1
  ENC/FH EN2 ... 29 K4
Whitethorn St BOW E3 ... 93 J3
White Tower Wy WCHPL E1 ... 93 G4
Whitewebbs Wy
  STMC/STPC BR5 ... 155 F7
Whitfield Ct RYNPK SW20 ... 161 G1
Whitfield Pl FITZ W1T ... 10 E1
Whitfield Rd BXLYHN DA7 ... 117 G6
  EHAM E6 ... 77 G6
  GNWCH SE10 ... 113 G7
Whitfield St FITZ W1T ... 10 F2
Whitford Gdns MTCM CR4 ... 162 E2
Whitgift Av SAND/SEL CR2 ... 177 J4
Whitgift St CROY/NA CR0 ... 177 J2
  STHWK SE1 ... 17 L5
Whitings Rd BAR EN5 ... 26 A4
Whitings Wy EHAM E6 ... 96 A4
Whitland Rd CAR SM5 ... 162 C7
Whitley Cl STWL/WRAY TW19 ... 120 B5
Whitley Rd TOTM N17 ... 56 A1
Whitlock Dr WIM/MER SW19 ... 127 H6
Whitman Rd WCHPL E1 ... 93 G3
Whitmead Cl SAND/SEL CR2 ... 177 K5
Whitmore Cl FBAR/BDGN N11 ... 40 B4
Whitmore Est IS N1 ... 7 K4
Whitmore Gdns WLSDN NW10 ... 88 A1
Whitmore Rd BECK BR3 ... 166 C2
  HRW HA1 ... 48 C6
  IS N1 ... 7 J4
Whitnell Wy PUT/ROE SW15 * ... 127 F4
Whitney Av REDBR IG4 ... 59 H3
Whitney Rd LEY E10 ... 57 K6
Whitstable Cl BECK BR3 ... 151 H1
Whitstable Pl CROY/NA CR0 ... 177 J3
Whitstone La BECK BR3 ... 166 E4
Whittaker Av RCH/KEW TW9 * ... 124 E4
Whittaker Rd CHEAM SM3 ... 174 D2
  EHAM E6 ... 77 H6
Whittaker St BGVA SW1W ... 16 A6
Whitta Rd MNPK E12 ... 77 H3
Whittell Gdns SYD SE26 ... 150 E2
Whittingstall Rd
  FUL/PGN SW6 ... 107 J7
Whittington Av BANK EC3V ... 13 J5
  YEAD UB4 ... 82 D4
Whittington Ms
  NFNCH/WDSPK N12 ... 39 G3
Whittington Rd WDGN N22 ... 40 E6
Whittington Wy PIN HA5 ... 47 J4
Whittlebury Cl CAR SM5 ... 175 K6
Whittle Cl STHL UB1 ... 84 B5
  WALTH E17 ... 57 G5
Whittle Rd HEST TW5 ... 102 B6
  NWDGN UB2 ... 103 J1
Whittlesea Rd
  KTN/HRWW/WS HA3 ... 34 C6
Whittlesey St STHWK SE1 ... 12 B9
Whitton Av East GFD/PVL UB6 ... 67 F4
Whitton Av West NTHLT UB5 ... 66 B4
Whitton Cl GFD/PVL UB6 ... 67 H5
Whitton Dene HSLW TW3 ... 123 G4
  ISLW TW7 ... 123 G4
Whitton Dr GFD/PVL UB6 ... 67 G5
Whitton Manor Rd
  WHTN TW2 ... 123 H5
Whitton Rd HSLW TW3 ... 123 G4
  WHTN TW2 ... 123 K5
Whitton Waye HSLW TW3 ... 123 F5
Whitwell Rd PLSTW E13 ... 94 E2
Whitworth Rd SNWD SE25 ... 165 F2
  WOOL/PLUM SE18 ... 115 F6
Whitworth St GNWCH SE10 ... 113 H4
Whorlton Rd PECK SE15 ... 131 H2
Whybridge Cl RAIN RM13 ... 81 G7
Whymark Av WDGN N22 ... 55 G2
Whytecroft HEST TW5 ... 102 C6
Whyteville Rd FSTGT E7 ... 77 F5
Wickersley Rd BTSEA SW11 ... 129 F1
Wickers Oake NRWD SE19 ... 150 B3
Wicker St WCHPL E1 * ... 92 C5
Wicket Rd GFD/PVL UB6 ... 85 G2
The Wicket CROY/NA CR0 ... 179 J4
Wickford St WCHPL E1 ... 92 E3
Wickford Wy WALTH E17 ... 57 F3
Wickham Av CHEAM SM3 ... 174 A4
  CROY/NA CR0 ... 179 G1
Wickham Cha WWKM BR4 ... 167 G6
Wickham Cl NWMAL KT3 ... 160 C4
  PEND EN3 ... 30 D2
  WCHPL E1 ... 92 E4
Wickham Ct WWKM BR4 ... 180 A1
Wickham Court Rd
  WWKM BR4 ... 180 A1
Wickham Crs WWKM BR4 ... 180 A1
Wickham Gdns BROCKY SE4 ... 132 C2
Wickham La ABYW SE2 ... 116 B5
Wickham Ms BROCKY SE4 ... 132 C1
Wickham Rd BECK BR3 ... 166 E2
  BROCKY SE4 ... 132 C2
  CHING E4 ... 44 A6
  CROY/NA CR0 ... 178 A1
  KTN/HRWW/WS HA3 ... 48 D1
Wickham St LBTH SE11 ... 17 L7

  WELL DA16 ... 116 B7
  WELL DA16 ... 135 K1
Wickham Wy BECK BR3 ... 167 F4
Wick La BOW E3 ... 93 J1
Wickliffe Av FNCH N3 ... 52 C1
Wickliffe Gdns WBLY HA9 ... 68 C1
Wicklow St FSBYW WC1X ... 5 L7
Wick Rd HOM E9 ... 75 F5
  TEDD TW11 ... 143 H6
Wicks Cl LEE/GVPK SE12 ... 153 H5
Wickwood St CMBW SE5 ... 130 C1
Widdenham Rd HOLWY N7 ... 73 F3
Widdicombe Av
  RYLN/HDSTN HA2 ... 65 J1
Widdin St SRTFD E15 ... 76 C6
Widecombe Gdns REDBR IG4 ... 59 J3
Widecombe Rd
  ELTH/MOT SE9 ... 153 J2
Widegate St WCHPL E1 ... 13 K3
Widenham Cl PIN HA5 ... 47 G4
Wide Wy MTCM CR4 ... 163 J2
Widgeon Cl CAN/RD E16 ... 95 F5
Widgeon Rd ERITH DA8 ... 118 E6
Widley Rd MV/WKIL W9 ... 2 B8
Widmore Lodge Rd BMLY BR1 ... 168 C1
Widmore Rd BMLY BR1 ... 168 A1
Wieland Rd NTHWD HA6 ... 32 E6
Wigeon Wy YEAD UB4 ... 83 H5
Wiggenhall Industrial Est
  WATW WD18 ... 21 G4
Wiggenhall Rd WATW WD18 ... 21 F4
Wiggins La RCHPK/HAM TW10 ... 143 J1
Wiggins Md CDALE/KGS NW9 ... 37 H6
Wigginton Av WBLY HA9 ... 68 C5
Wightman Rd
  CEND/HSY/T N8 ... 55 G3
  FELT TW13 ... 122 C7
Wigley Rd FELT TW13 ... 122 C7
Wigmore Pl MHST W1U * ... 10 C4
Wigmore Rd CAR SM5 ... 175 H1
Wigmore St MHST W1U ... 10 B4
Wigram Rd WAN E11 ... 59 G5
Wigram Sq WALTH E17 ... 58 A2
Wigston Cl UED N18 ... 42 A4
Wigston Rd PLSTW E13 ... 95 F3
Wigton Gdns STAN HA7 ... 36 A7
Wigton Pl LBTH SE11 ... 18 B8
Wigton Rd WALTH E17 ... 43 H7
Wilberforce Ms CLAP SW4 ... 129 J3
Wilberforce Rd
  CDALE/KGS NW9 ... 51 J5
  FSBYPK N4 ... 73 H1
Wilberforce Wk
  SRTFD E15 ... 76 C4
Wilberforce Wy
  WIM/MER SW19 ... 146 B5
Wilbraham Pl KTBR SW1X ... 16 A5
Wilbury Wy UED N18 ... 41 K4
Wilby Ms NTGHL W11 ... 88 D6
Wilcot Av OXHEY WD19 ... 21 J6
Wilcot Cl OXHEY WD19 ... 21 J6
Wilcox Cl VX/NE SW8 ... 109 K6
Wilcox Rd SUT SM1 * ... 175 F3
  TEDD TW11 ... 142 D3
  VX/NE SW8 ... 109 K6
Wildacres NTHWD HA6 ... 32 D3
Wild Ct HOL/ALD WC2B ... 11 L4
Wildcroft Gdns STAN HA7 ... 35 K5
Wildcroft Rd PUT/ROE SW15 ... 127 F6
Wilde Cl HACK E8 ... 7 M1
Wilde Pl PLMGR N13 ... 41 H5
  WAND/EARL SW18 ... 128 C6
Wilder Cl RSLP HA4 ... 47 F1
Wilderness Ms CLAP SW4 ... 129 G3
Wilderness Rd CHST BR7 ... 154 B6
The Wilderness
  E/WMO/HCT KT8 ... 157 H4
  HPTN TW12 * ... 142 B3
Wilde Rd ERITH DA8 ... 117 K6
Wilderton Rd
  STNW/STAM N16 ... 56 A6
Wildfell Rd CAT SE6 ... 132 E6
Wild Goose Dr NWCR SE14 ... 111 K7
Wild Hatch GLDGN NW11 ... 52 E5
Wild Oaks Cl NTHWD HA6 ... 32 D5
Wild's Rents STHWK SE1 ... 19 J3
Wild St HOL/ALD WC2B ... 11 K5
Wildwood NTHWD HA6 ... 32 B5
Wildwood Cl LEE/GVPK SE12 ... 133 J6
Wildwood Gv HAMP NW3 ... 53 G7
Wildwood Ri GLDGN NW11 ... 53 G7
Wildwood Rd GLDGN NW11 ... 53 F5
Wildwood Ter HAMP NW3 ... 53 G7
Wilford Cl ENC/FH EN2 * ... 29 K2
  NTHWD HA6 ... 32 B6
Wilfred Av RAIN RM13 ... 99 J4
Wilfred Owen Cl
  WIM/MER SW19 ... 147 G5
Wilfred St WESTW SW1E ... 16 E3
Wilfrid Gdns ACT W3 ... 86 E4
Wilkes Rd BTFD TW8 ... 105 F5
Wilkes St WCHPL E1 ... 13 M2
Wilkins Cl HYS/HAR UB3 ... 101 J4
  MTCM CR4 ... 147 J7
Wilkinson Gdns SNWD SE25 ... 150 A7
Wilkinson Rd CAN/RD E16 ... 95 G5
Wilkinson St VX/NE SW8 ... 110 A6
Wilkinson Wy CHSWK W4 ... 106 A1
Wilkin St KTTN NW5 ... 72 A5
Wilkin Street Ms KTTN NW5 ... 72 A5
Wilks Pl IS N1 ... 7 K6
Willan Rd TOTM N17 ... 55 K1
Willan Wall CAN/RD E16 ... 94 D6
Willard St VX/NE SW8 ... 129 G2
Willcocks Cl CHSGTN KT9 ... 172 A2
Willcott Rd ACT W3 ... 86 D7
Will Crooks Gdns
  ELTH/MOT SE9 ... 134 C3
Willenfield Rd WLSDN NW10 ... 86 D1
Willenhall Av BAR EN5 ... 27 G5
Willenhall Dr HYS/HAR UB3 ... 82 C6
Willenhall Rd
  WOOL/PLUM SE18 ... 115 G4
Willerfield Rd WLSDN NW10 ... 86 E2
Willersley Av BFN/LL DA15 ... 136 A7
Willersley Cl BFN/LL DA15 ... 136 A7
Willesden La
  KIL/WHAMP NW6 ... 70 B6
Willes Rd KTTN NW5 ... 72 B5
Willett Cl NTHLT UB5 ... 83 G2
  STMC/STPC BR5 ... 169 K5
Willett Pl THHTH CR7 ... 164 B4
Willett Wy STMC/STPC BR5 ... 169 K4
William Ash Cl DAGW RM9 ... 79 H5
William Barefoot Dr
  ELTH/MOT SE9 ... 154 A3
William Booth Rd
  PGE/AN SE20 ... 150 C7
William Carey Wy HRW HA1 ... 48 E5
William Cl EFNCH N2 ... 53 H1
  LEW SE13 ... 133 F2
  NWDGN UB2 ... 103 H1
William Dr STAN HA7 ... 35 G5

William Ellis Wy
  BERM/RHTH SE16 * ... 111 H2
William Foster La WELL DA16 ... 136 B1
William Gdns PUT/ROE SW15 ... 126 E4
William Guy Gdns BOW E3 ... 93 K2
William Margrie Cl
  PECK SE15 * ... 131 H1
William Ms KTBR SW1X ... 15 M2
William Morley Cl EHAM E6 ... 77 H7
William Morris Cl WALTH E17 ... 57 H2
William Morris Wy
  FUL/PGN SW6 ... 128 B2
William Rd CAMTN NW1 ... 4 E8
  SUT SM1 ... 175 G4
  WIM/MER SW19 ... 146 C6
Williams Av WALTH E17 ... 43 H7
William's Blds WCHPL E1 * ... 92 E3
Williams Cl CEND/HSY/T N8 * ... 54 D5
  FUL/PGN SW6 ... 107 H6
Williams Dr HSLW TW3 ... 123 F3
Williams Gv SURB KT6 ... 158 D5
  WDGN N22 ... 41 G7
Williams La MORT/ESHN SW14 ... 125 K1
  MRDN SM4 ... 162 B5
Williamson Cl GNWCH SE10 ... 113 J4
Williamson Rd FSBYPK N4 ... 55 H5
Williamson St HOLWY N7 * ... 72 E3
Williamson Wy RSLP HA4 ... 47 F2
Williams Rd NWDGN UB2 ... 102 D3
  WEA W13 ... 85 G7
Williams Rd WEA W13 * ... 85 G7
William St BARK IG11 ... 78 C6
  BUSH WD23 ... 21 K1
  CAR SM5 ... 175 J2
  KTBR SW1X ... 15 M2
  LEY E10 ... 57 K5
  TOTM N17 ... 42 B6
Willifield Wy GLDGN NW11 ... 52 E4
Willingale Cl WFD IG8 ... 45 H5
Willingdon Cl KTTN NW5 ... 72 C4
Willingham Cl KTTN NW5 ... 72 C4
Willingham Ter KTTN NW5 ... 72 C4
Willington Ct HOM E9 * ... 75 H5
Willington Rd BRXN/ST SW9 ... 129 K2
Willis Av BELMT SM2 ... 175 J5
Willis Rd CROY/NA CR0 ... 164 D6
  ERITH DA8 ... 117 K3
  SRTFD E15 ... 76 D1
Willis St POP/IOD E14 ... 93 K5
Willmore End WIM/MER SW19 * ... 147 F7
Willoughby Av CROY/NA CR0 ... 177 F3
Willoughby Dr RAIN RM13 ... 81 G6
Willoughby Gv TOTM N17 ... 42 D6
Willoughby La BMLY BR1 ... 153 G6
  TOTM N17 ... 42 D6
Willoughby Ms TOTM N17 ... 42 D6
Willoughby Park Rd
  TOTM N17 ... 42 D6
Willoughby Rd
  CEND/HSY/T N8 ... 55 G2
  HAMP NW3 ... 71 H3
  KUTN/CMB KT2 ... 144 B7
  TWK TW1 ... 124 D4
Willoughby Wy CHARL SE7 ... 114 A3
Willow Av BARN SW13 ... 126 C1
  BFN/LL DA15 ... 136 B5
Willow Bank
  RCHPK/HAM TW10 ... 143 H2
Willowbay Cl BAR EN5 ... 26 B5
Willowbrook HPTN TW12 ... 142 B4
Willowbrook Est PECK SE15 * ... 111 G6
Willowbrook Rd NWDGN UB2 ... 102 E2
  PECK SE15 ... 111 G5
  STWL/WRAY TW19 ... 120 B7
The Willow Centre MTCM CR4 ... 162 E4
Willow Cl BKHH IG9 ... 45 H2
  BTFD TW8 ... 104 D5
  BXLY DA5 ... 137 G5
  CAT SE6 ... 133 J7
  HAYES BR2 ... 168 E4
  HCH RM12 ... 81 K2
Willow Ct STAN HA7 * ... 35 K6
Willowcourt Av
  KTN/HRWW/WS HA3 ... 49 H4
Willow Dean PIN HA5 * ... 47 H1
Willow Dene BUSH WD23 ... 22 E6
  PIN HA5 ... 47 H1
Willowdene HCT N6 * ... 53 K6
Willowdene Cl WHTN TW2 ... 123 G6
Willow Dr BAR EN5 ... 26 C3
Willow End NTHWD HA6 ... 32 E5
  SURB KT6 ... 159 F7
  TRDG/WHET N20 ... 38 E1
Willowfields Cl
  WOOL/PLUM SE18 ... 115 K4
Willow Gdns HSLW TW3 ... 103 F7
  RSLP HA4 ... 64 D1
Willow Gv CHST BR7 ... 154 A5
  RSLP HA4 ... 64 D1
Willowhayne Dr
  WOT/HER KT12 ... 156 A6
Willowhayne Gdns WPK KT4 ... 174 A1
Willow La MTCM CR4 ... 162 E4
  WATW WD18 ... 20 E4
  WOOL/PLUM SE18 ... 114 E3
Willowmead Cl EA W5 ... 85 K4
Willowmere ESH/CLAY KT10 ... 170 C3
Willow Mt CROY/NA CR0 ... 178 A3
Willow Pl WEST SW1P ... 16 F5
Willow Rd CHDH RM6 ... 62 A5
  DART DA1 ... 139 F7
  EA W5 ... 105 F1
  EN EN1 ... 30 A1
  ERITH DA8 ... 118 D7
  HAMP NW3 ... 71 H3
  MNPK E12 ... 77 K2
  NWMAL KT3 ... 159 K3
  WLSDN NW10 ... 88 B6
Willows Av MRDN SM4 ... 162 A4
Willows Cl PIN HA5 ... 47 G1
Willows Ter WLSDN NW10 * ... 87 H1
The Willows BECK BR3 * ... 151 J5
  EBAR EN4 * ... 27 J5
  ESH/CLAY KT10 ... 170 E5
  OXHEY WD19 ... 21 F6
Willow St ROMW/RG RM7 ... 62 E3
  SDTCH EC2A ... 7 J9
Willow Ter PGE/AN SE20 * ... 150 D7
Willow Tree Cl BOW E3 ... 75 H7
  NTHLT UB5 ... 65 V5
  WAND/EARL SW18 ... 128 A7
  YEAD UB4 ... 83 G3
Willowtree Cl HGDN/ICK UB10 ... 64 A2
Willow Tree La YEAD UB4 ... 83 G3
Willow Tree Wk BMLY BR1 ... 153 F7
Willowtree Wy THHTH CR7 ... 149 G7
Willow Vw CHST BR7 ... 154 A5

  STHWK SE1 ... 19 K5
  WALTH E17 ... 57 H4
  WCHMH N21 ... 29 F5
Willow Wk ALP/SUD HA0 * ... 67 G2
  FNCH N3 ... 39 F6
  HOR/WEW KT19 ... 173 H5
  NTGHL W11 ... 88 B6
  SYD SE26 ... 150 D3
  WHTN TW2 ... 142 B1
Willow Wood Crs SNWD SE25 ... 165 F5
Will Rd KTTN NW5 ... 72 B5
Willrose Crs ABYW SE2 ... 116 C4
Wills Crs HSLW TW3 ... 123 G5
Wills Gv MLHL NW7 ... 37 J4
Wilman Gv HACK E8 ... 74 C6
Wilmar Cl YEAD UB4 ... 82 B3
Wilmar Gdns WWKM BR4 ... 166 E7
Wilmcote Cl KUTN/CMB KT2 ... 144 B4
Wilmer Crs KUTN/CMB KT2 ... 144 B4
Wilmer Gdns IS N1 ... 7 K4
Wilmer Lea Cl SRTFD E15 ... 76 A6
Wilmer Pl STNW/STAM N16 ... 74 B1
Wilmer Wy FBAR/BDGN N11 ... 40 D4
Wilmington Av CHSWK W4 ... 106 A6
Wilmington Gdns BARK IG11 ... 78 D6
Wilmington Sq FSBYW WC1X ... 6 A8
Wilmington St FSBYW WC1X ... 6 A8
Wilmot Cl PECK SE15 ... 111 H6
Wilmot Pl CAMTN NW1 ... 4 E1
  HNWL W7 ... 84 E7
Wilmot Rd CAR SM5 ... 175 K4
  DART DA1 ... 138 C4
  LEY E10 ... 75 K1
  TOTM N17 ... 55 K2
Wilmot St BETH E2 ... 92 D3
Wilmount St
  WOOL/PLUM SE18 ... 115 G3
Wilna Rd WAND/EARL SW18 ... 128 B6
Wilsham St NTGHL W11 ... 88 B7
Wilshaw Cl HDN NW4 ... 51 J2
Wilshaw St NWCR SE14 ... 112 D7
Wilsmere Dr
  KTN/HRWW/WS HA3 ... 34 E6
  NTHLT UB5 ... 65 J5
Wilson Av MTCM CR4 ... 147 K6
Wilson Cl SAND/SEL CR2 ... 177 K4
  WBLY HA9 ... 50 B6
Wilson Dr WBLY HA9 ... 50 B6
Wilson Gdns HRW HA1 ... 48 C6
Wilson Gv BERM/RHTH SE16 ... 111 J1
Wilson Rd CHSGTN KT9 ... 172 B5
  CMBW SE5 ... 110 E7
  IL IG1 ... 59 K6
  PLSTW E13 ... 95 H2
Wilson's Av TOTM N17 ... 56 B1
Wilson's Pl POP/IOD E14 ... 93 H5
Wilson St FSBYPK N4 ... 55 H1
  LVPST EC2M ... 13 H2
  WALTH E17 ... 58 A4
  WCHMH N21 ... 29 G6
Wilson Wk CHSWK W4 ... 106 C3
Wilstone Cl YEAD UB4 ... 83 J3
Wilthorne Gdns DAGE RM10 ... 80 D6
Wilton Av CHSWK W4 ... 106 B4
Wilton Cl WDR/YW UB7 ... 100 A5
Wilton Crs KTBR SW1X ... 16 A2
  WIM/MER SW19 ... 146 D7
Wilton Est HACK E8 * ... 74 C5
Wilton Gdns E/WMO/HCT KT8 ... 157 F2
  WOT/HER KT12 ... 156 C7
Wilton Gv NWMAL KT3 ... 160 C5
  WIM/MER SW19 ... 146 D6
Wilton Ms HACK E8 * ... 74 D5
  KTBR SW1X ... 16 A3
Wilton Pl KTBR SW1X ... 16 A1
Wilton Rd ABYW SE2 ... 116 D2
  EBAR EN4 ... 27 K3
  HSLW TW4 ... 122 C2
  MUSWH N10 ... 54 A1
  PIM SW1V ... 16 D4
  WIM/MER SW19 ... 147 J6
Wilton Rw KTBR SW1X ... 16 A2
Wilton Sq IS N1 ... 7 G3
Wilton St KTBR SW1X ... 16 B3
Wilton Ter KTBR SW1X ... 16 A3
Wilton Vls IS N1 * ... 7 G4
Wilton Wk FELT TW13 ... 141 F1
Wilton Wy HACK E8 ... 74 C5
Wiltshire Cl CHEL SW3 ... 15 K6
  MLHL NW7 * ... 37 H4
Wiltshire Gdns FSBYPK N4 ... 55 J5
  WHTN TW2 ... 123 H7
Wiltshire La PIN HA5 ... 46 E3
Wiltshire Rd BRXN/ST SW9 ... 130 B2
  THHTH CR7 ... 164 B2
Wiltshire Rw IS N1 ... 7 G4
Wilverley Crs NWMAL KT3 ... 160 B5
Wimbart Rd
  BRXS/STRHM SW2 * ... 130 A6
Wimbledon Br
  WIM/MER SW19 ... 146 D5
Wimbledon Hill Rd
  WIM/MER SW19 ... 146 C5
Wimbledon Park Rd
  WAND/EARL SW18 ... 127 J3
  WIM/MER SW19 ... 146 C2
Wimbledon Park Side
  PUT/ROE SW15 ... 126 E7
  WIM/MER SW19 ... 146 B1
Wimbledon Rd TOOT SW17 ... 147 G3
Wimbolt St BETH E2 ... 92 C2
Wimborne Av NWDGN UB2 ... 103 F3
  YEAD UB4 ... 83 F5
Wimborne Cl BKHH IG9 ... 45 G1
  LEE/GVPK SE12 ... 133 J4
  WPK KT4 ... 161 F7
Wimborne Dr EDGW HA8 ... 50 C2
  PIN HA5 ... 47 H6
Wimborne Gdns WEA W13 ... 85 H5
Wimborne Rd ED N9 ... 42 C1
  TOTM N17 ... 56 A1
Wimborne Wy BECK BR3 ... 166 A2
Wimbourne St IS N1 ... 7 G5
Wimpole Cl HAYES BR2 ... 168 B3
  KUT/HW KT1 ... 159 G1
Wimpole St CAVSQ/HST W1G ... 10 C3
Wimshurst Cl CROY/NA CR0 ... 163 K7
Wincanton Crs NTHLT UB5 ... 66 A4
Wincanton Gdns
  BARK/HLT IG6 ... 60 B2
Wincanton Rd CAR SM5 ... 175 H1
  WAND/EARL SW18 ... 127 J6
Winchcomb Gdns
  ELTH/MOT SE9 ... 134 C2
Winchelsea Av BXLYHN DA7 ... 117 G6
Winchelsea Cl PUT/ROE SW15 ... 127 G4
Winchelsea Rd FSTGT E7 ... 76 E3

TOTM N17....56 A2
WLSDN NW10....69 F7
Winchelsey Ri SAND/SEL CR2....178 B5
Winchendon Rd
FUL/PGN SW6....107 J6
TEDD TW11....142 E7
Winchester Av
CDALE/KGS NW9....50 B2
HEST TW5....102 E5
KIL/WHAMP NW6....70 C6
Winchester Cl EN EN1 *....30 A4
ESH/CLAY KT10....170 A3
HAYES BR2....167 J1
KUTN/CMB KT2....144 D6
LBTH SE11....18 A2
Winchester Dr PIN HA5....47 H4
Winchester Ms WPK KT4....174 E1
Winchester Pk HAYES BR2....167 J2
Winchester Pl HACK E8....74 B4
HGT N6....54 B7
Winchester Rd BXLYHN DA7....136 E3
CHING E4....44 A6
ED N9....30 D7
FELT TW13....141 K2
HAMP NW3....3 H1
HAYES BR2....167 J2
HGT N6....54 B7
HYS/HAR UB3....101 H6
IL IG1....78 D2
KTN/HRWW/WS HA3....50 A3
TWK TW1....124 C5
Winchester Sq STHWK SE1....13 G8
Winchester St ACT W3....86 E7
PIM SW1V....16 D7
Winchester Wk STHWK SE1....13 G8
Winchfield
KTN/HRWW/WS HA3....49 J5
Winchfield Rd SYD SE26....151 G4
Winchilsea Crs
E/WMO/HCT KT8....157 H1
Winchmore Hill Rd
STHGT/OAK N14....28 D7
Winchmore Vis WCHMH N21 *....29 F6
Winckley Cl
KTN/HRWW/WS HA3....50 B4
Wincott St LBTH SE11....18 B5
Wincrofts Dr ELTH/MOT SE9....135 K3
Windall Cl NRWD SE19....150 C7
Windborough Rd CAR SM5....176 A6
Windermere Av FNCH N3....52 E1
HCH RM12....81 J4
KIL/WHAMP NW6....70 C7
RSLP HA4....47 G4
WBLY HA9....49 J7
WIM/MER SW19....162 A2
Windermere Cl DART DA1....138 E7
EBED/NFELT TW14....121 H7
Windermere Gdns REDBR IG4....59 J4
Windermere Gv WBLY HA9....49 J7
Windermere Hall EDGW HA8 *....36 B4
Windermere Rd ARCH N19 *....72 C1
BXLYHN DA7....137 K1
CROY/NA CR0....165 G4
EA W5....104 D2
MUSWH N10....40 B7
PUT/ROE SW15....145 G3
STHL UB1....83 K4
STRHM/NOR SW16....148 C7
WWKM BR4....180 C1
Winders Rd BTSEA SW11....128 D1
Windfield Cl SYD SE26....151 F3
Windham Rd RCH/KEW TW9....125 G2
Winding Wy BCTR RM8....79 J2
Windlass Pl DEPT SE8....112 B3
Windlesham Gv
WIM/MER SW19....127 G7
Windley Cl FSTH SE23....150 E1
Windmill Cl LEW SE13....133 F1
STHWK SE1 *....111 H3
SUN TW16....140 E5
SURB KT6....158 D7
Windmill Dr CLAP SW4....129 G4
CRICK NW2....70 C2
Windmill Gdns ENC/FH EN2....29 G1
Windmill Gv CROY/NA CR0....164 D6
Windmill Hl ENC/FH EN2....29 H2
HAMP NW3 *....71 F3
RSLP HA4....46 D6
Windmill La BAR EN5....25 H5
BUSH WD23....22 E7
CFD/PVL UB6....84 C4
HAYES BR2....181 G3
ISLW TW7....103 K3
NWDGN UB2....103 H1
SRTFD E15....76 B5
SURB KT6....158 C6
Windmill Pas CHSWK W4....106 B3
Windmill Ri KUTN/CMB KT2....144 D6
Windmill Rd CHSWK W4....106 B3
CROY/NA CR0....164 D6
EA W5....104 D3
HPTN TW12....142 B4
MTCM CR4....163 H4
SUN TW16....140 C7
UED N18....41 K3
WAND/EARL SW18....128 C5
WIM/MER SW19....145 K4
Windmill Rd West SUN TW16....140 C7
Windmill Rw LBTH SE11....18 A8
Windmill St BUSH WD23....22 E7
FITZ W1T....11 G3
Windmill Wy RSLP HA4....46 D7
Windover Av CDALE/KGS NW9....51 F3
Windrose Cl BERM/RHTH SE16....112 A1
Windrush NWMAL KT3....159 J3
Windrush Cl BTSEA SW11 *....128 C3
CHSWK W4 *....105 K6
HACK E8....74 C6
TOTM N17....42 A7
Windrush La FSTH SE23....151 F2
Windrush Rd WLSDN NW10....69 F7
Windsor Av CHEAM SM3....174 C2
E/WMO/HCT KT8....157 F2
EDGW HA8....36 D3
NWMAL KT3....159 K4
WALTH E17....57 G1
WIM/MER SW19....147 G7
Windsor Cl CHST BR7....154 B4
FNCH N3....52 C1
NTHWD HA6....46 E1
RYLN/HDSTN HA2....66 A2
NRWD SE27....149 J3
Windsor Ct PIN HA5 *....47 F1
STHGT/OAK N14....28 C5
Windsor Crs RYLN/HDSTN HA2....48 A2
WBLY HA9....68 C2
Windsor Dr DART DA1....138 C5
EBAR EN4....27 K5
Windsor Gdns CROY/NA CR0....176 E2
HYS/HAR UB3....101 G2
MV/WKIL W9....8 A2
Windsor Gv WNWD SE27....149 J3

Windsor Ms CAT SE6....133 F7
Windsor Park Rd
HYS/HAR UB3....101 J6
Windsor Rd BAR EN5....26 B5
BCTR RM8....80 A2
BXLYHS DA6....137 F3
CHING E4....43 K3
CRICK NW2....69 K5
EA W5....86 A6
FNCH N3....52 C1
FSTGT E7....77 F4
HOLWY N7....72 E2
HSLWW TW4....122 A1
IL IG1....78 C3
KTN/HRWW/WS HA3....34 C7
KUTN/CMB KT2....144 A6
LEY E10....75 K1
NWDGN UB2....102 E2
PLMGR N13....41 G2
RCH/KEW TW9....125 G1
SUN TW16....140 E6
TEDD TW11....142 D4
THHTH CR7....164 C1
TOTM N17....56 C1
WAN E11....58 E2
WPK KT4....173 J1
The Windsors BKHH IG9....45 J1
Windsor St IS N1....6 C3
Windsor Ter IS N1....6 F7
Windsor Wk CMBW SE5....130 E1
Windsor Wy WKENS W14....107 G3
Windspoint Dr PECK SE15....111 J5
Windstock Cl
BERM/RHTH SE16....112 C2
Windus Rd STNW/STAM N16....56 B7
Windy Rdg BMLY BR1....153 J7
Windy Ridge Cl
WIM/MER SW19....146 B4
Wine Cl WAP E1W....92 E6
Wine Office Ct
FLST/FETLN EC4A....12 B4
Winery La KUT/HW KT1....159 G2
Winey Cl CHSGTN KT9....171 J6
Winforton St GNWCH SE10....113 F7
Winfrith Rd WAND/EARL SW18....128 B6
Wingate Crs CROY/NA CR0....163 K5
Wingate Rd HMSMTH W6....106 E2
IL IG1....78 B4
SCUP DA14....155 J4
Wingate Sq CLAP SW4....129 H3
Wingfield Ct WATW WD18 *....20 B5
Wingfield Ms PECK SE15....131 H2
Wingfield Rd KUTN/CMB KT2....144 B6
SRTFD E15....76 C4
WALTH E17....57 K4
Wingfield St PECK SE15....131 H2
Wingfield Wy RSLP HA4....65 F5
Wingford Rd
BRXS/STRHM SW2....129 K5
Wingmore Rd HNHL SE24....130 D2
Wingrave Rd HMSMTH W6....107 F5
Wingrove Rd CAT SE6....152 C1
Wings Cl SUT SM1....174 E3
Winifred Cl BAR EN5....25 H5
Winifred Pl
NFNCH/WDSPK N12....39 G4
DART DA1....138 E4
ERITH DA8....118 A4
HPTN TW12....142 A3
WIM/MER SW19....146 E7
Winifred St CAN/RD E16....95 K7
Winifred Ter EN EN1....30 B6
PLSTW E13....94 E1
Winkfield Rd WDGN N22....41 G7
Winkley St BETH E2....92 D1
Winkworth Cots WCHPL E1 *....92 E3
Winlaton Rd BMLY BR1....152 B3
Winmill Rd BCTR RM8....80 B2
Winn Common Rd
WOOL/PLUM SE18....115 K5
Winnett St SOHO/SHAV W1D....11 C1
Winnington Cl EFNCH N2....53 H5
Winnington Rd EFNCH N2....53 H6
Winn Rd LEE/GVPK SE12....133 K7
Winns Av WALTH E17....57 H2
Winns Ms STNW/STOTM N15....56 A3
Winns Ter WALTH E17....57 J1
Winsbeach WALTH E17....58 B2
Winscombe Crs EA W5....85 K3
Winscombe St ARCH N19....72 B1
Winscombe Wy STAN HA7....35 G4
Winsford Rd CAT SE6....151 H2
Winsford Ter UED N18 *....41 K4
Winsham Gv BTSEA SW11....129 F4
Winslade Rd
BRXS/STRHM SW2....129 K4
Winsland Ms BAY/PAD W2....9 A4
Winsland St BAY/PAD W2....9 A4
Winsley St GTPST W1W....10 E4
Winslow Cl PIN HA5....47 F5
WLSDN NW10....69 G2
Winslow Gv CHING E4....44 C1
Winslow Rd HMSMTH W6....107 F5
Winslow Wy FELT TW13....141 H2
Winsor Ter EHAM E6....96 A4
Winstanley Rd BTSEA SW11....128 C2
Winstead Gdns DAGE RM10....80 E4
Winston Av CDALE/KGS NW9....51 G1
Winston Cl
KTN/HRWW/WS HA3....35 F5
ROMW/RG RM7....62 E3
Winston Ct
KTN/HRWW/WS HA3....34 B6
Winston House SURB KT6 *....159 F4
Winston Rd STNW/STAM N16....73 K3
Winston Wy IL IG1....78 B2
Winter Av EHAM E6....77 J1
Winterbourne Rd BCTR RM8....79 J1
CAT SE6....132 C7
THHTH CR7....164 B3
Winter Box Wk
RCHPK/HAM TW10....125 F3
Winterburn Cl
FBAR/BDGN N11....40 A5
Winterfold Cl WIM/MER SW19....146 C1
Winters Rd THDIT KT7....158 C6
Winterstoke Rd FSTH SE23....131 H7
Winterton Pl WBPTN SW10....14 F9
Winterwell Rd
BRXS/STRHM SW2....129 K4
Winthorpe Rd PUT/ROE SW15....127 H3
Winthrop St WCHPL E1....92 D4
Winton Av FBAR/BDGN N11....40 A5
Winton Cl ED N9....31 F6
Winton Dr RKW/CH/CXG WD3....20 A4
Winton Gdns EDGW HA8....36 B6
The Wintons BUSH WD23 *....22 D7
Winton Wy STRHM/NOR SW16....149 G4
Wirral Wood Cl CHST BR7....154 A5

Wisbeach Rd CROY/NA CR0....164 E4
Wisborough Rd
SAND/SEL CR2....178 B7
Wisdons Cl DAGE RM10....62 D1
Wise La MLHL NW7....37 H5
WDR/YW UB7....100 A3
Wiseman Rd LEY E10 *....75 J1
Wise Rd SRTFD E15....76 A1
Wiseton Rd TOOT SW17....128 D7
Wishart Rd BKHTH/KID SE3....114 C7
Wishaw Wk FBAR/BDGN N11....40 E5
Wisley Rd BTSEA SW11....128 E4
STMC/STPC BR5....155 G6
Wisteria Cl IL IG1....78 B3
MLHL NW7....37 H5
Wisteria Rd LEW SE13....133 G3
Witanhurst La HGT N6....54 A7
Witan St BETH E2....92 D2
Witham Rd DAGE RM10....80 C4
GPK RM2....63 K4
ISLW TW7....103 J7
PGE/AN SE20....165 K2
WEA W13....85 G7
Witherby Cl CROY/NA CR0....178 A4
Witherington Rd HBRY N5 *....73 G4
Withers Md CDALE/KGS NW9....37 H7
Witherston Wy
ELTH/MOT SE9....154 A1
Withycombe Rd
WIM/MER SW19....127 G5
Withy La RSLP HA4....46 A4
Withy Md CHING E4....44 B2
Witley Crs CROY/NA CR0....180 A5
Witley Gdns NWDGN UB2....102 E3
Witley Rd ARCH N19....72 C1
Witney Cl PIN HA5....33 J6
Witney Pth FSTH SE23....151 F2
Wittenham Wy CHING E4....44 B2
Wittering Cl KUTN/CMB KT2....143 K4
Wittersham Rd BMLY BR1....152 D4
Wivenhoe Cl PECK SE15....131 H2
Wivenhoe Ct HSLW TW3....122 E3
Wivenhoe Rd BARK IG11....97 G1
Wiverton Rd SYD SE26....150 E5
Wix Rd DAGW RM9....79 K7
Wix's La CLAP SW4....129 G3
Woburn WEA W13 *....85 H4
Woburn Av HCH RM12....81 J3
Woburn Cl BUSH WD23....22 C5
THMD SE28....97 K5
WIM/MER SW19....147 G5
Woburn Pl STPAN WC1H....5 J9
Woburn Rd CAR SM5....162 D7
CROY/NA CR0....164 D7
Woburn Sq STPAN WC1H....11 H1
Woburn Wk STPAN WC1H....5 H8
Wodeham Gdns WCHPL E1....92 C4
Wodehouse Av CMBW SE5....111 G7
Wodehouse Rd DART DA1....139 K3
Woffington Cl TEDD TW11....143 J4
Woking Cl PUT/ROE SW15....126 C3
Woldham Pl HAYES BR2....168 B3
Woldham Rd HAYES BR2....168 B3
Wolfe Cl HAYES BR2....167 K5
YEAD UB4....83 F2
Wolfe Crs CHARL SE7....114 C4
Wolferton Rd MNPK E12....77 K3
Wolfington Rd WNWD SE27....149 H3
Wolfram Cl LEE/GVPK SE13....133 H4
Wolftencroft Cl BTSEA SW11....128 D2
Wollaston Cl STHWK SE1....18 D5
Wolmer Cl EDGW HA8....36 C3
Wolmer Gdns EDGW HA8....36 C2
Wolseley Av
WAND/EARL SW18....146 E1
Wolseley Gdns CHSWK W4....105 J5
Wolseley Rd CEND/HSY/T N8....54 D5
CHSWK W4....105 K4
FSTGT E7....77 F6
KTN/HRWW/WS HA3....48 E2
MTCM CR4....163 F6
ROMW/RG RM7....63 F6
WDGN N22....41 F7
Wolseley St STHWK SE1....19 M2
Wolsey Av EHAM E6....96 A2
THDIT KT7....158 A4
WALTH E17....57 H2
Wolsey Cl HSLW TW3....123 H3
KUTN/CMB KT2....144 D7
NWDGN UB2....103 H2
RYNPK SW20....145 K6
WPK KT4....173 J3
Wolsey Crs CROY/NA CR0....180 A7
MRDN SM4....161 J6
Wolsey Dr KUTN/CMB KT2....144 A5
Wolsey Gdns EDGW HA8....37 F6
WOT/HER KT12....156 C7
Wolsey Gv EDGW HA8....37 F6
ESH/CLAY KT10....170 C5
Wolsey Ms KTTN NW5....72 C5
Wolsey Rd E/WMO/HCT KT8....157 J3
EN EN1....30 D1
ESH/CLAY KT10....170 B3
HPTN TW12....142 B5
IS N1....73 K4
NTHWD HA6....32 A1
SUN TW16....140 D6
Wolsey St WCHPL E1....92 E4
Wolsey Wy CHSGTN KT9....172 C4
Wolsley Cl DART DA1....138 A4
Wolstonbury
NFNCH/WDSPK N12....38 C4
Wolvercote Rd ABYW SE2....116 E1
Wolverley St BETH E2 *....92 D2
Wolverton Av
KUTN/CMB KT2....144 C7
Wolverton Gdns EA W5....85 H5
HMSMTH W6....107 G3
Wolverton Rd STAN HA7....35 H5
Wolverton Wy
STHGT/OAK N14....28 C4
Wolves La WDGN N22....41 G6
Womersley Rd
CEND/HSY/T N8....55 F5
Wonersh Wy BELMT SM2....174 B7
Wonford Cl KUTN/CMB KT2....145 G7
Wontner Cl IS N1....73 J2
Wontner Rd BAL SW12....129 G5
Woodall Cl CHSGTN KT9....171 J4
Woodall Rd PEND EN3....31 F5
Woodbank Rd BMLY BR1....152 D2
Woodbastwick Rd SYD SE26....151 F4
Woodberry Av
RYLN/HDSTN HA2....48 C3
WCHMH N21....41 G1
Woodberry Cl
MLHL NW7....38 B6
SUN TW16....140 E5
Woodberry Crs MUSWH N10....54 B2
Woodberry Down FSBYPK N4....55 J7
Woodberry Gdns
NFNCH/WDSPK N12....39 G5
Woodberry Gv
NFNCH/WDSPK N12....39 G5
FSBYPK N4....55 J6

Woodberry Wy
NFNCH/WDSPK N12....39 G5
CHING E4....44 A1
Woodbine Gv PGE/AN SE20....150 D6
Woodbine La WPK KT4....173 K2
Woodbine Pl WAN E11....58 K2
Woodbines Av KUT/HW KT1....158 F2
Woodbine Ter HOM E9....74 E5
Woodborough Rd
PUT/ROE SW15....126 E3
Woodbourne Av
STRHM/NOR SW16....148 D2
Woodbourne Dr
ESH/CLAY KT10....171 F5
Woodbourne Gdns
WLGTN SM6....176 B6
Woodbridge Cl HOLWY N7....73 F1
BARK IG11....79 F4
Woodbridge St CLKNW EC1R....6 C9
Woodbrook Rd ABYW SE2....116 B5
Woodburn Cl HDN NW4....52 B4
Woodbury Cl CROY/NA CR0....178 B1
WAN E11....59 F3
Woodbury Gdns
LEE/GVPK SE12....152 A3
Woodbury Park Rd WEA W13....85 H3
Woodbury Rd WALTH E17....57 K3
Woodbury St TOOT SW17....147 J4
Woodchurch Sq SCUP DA14....154 D2
Woodchurch Cl SCUP DA14....153 H6
Woodchurch Rd
KIL/WHAMP NW6....2 D1
Wood Cl BETH E2....92 C3
CDALE/KGS NW9....51 F6
HRW HA1....48 D6
Woodclyffe Dr CHST BR7....169 F1
Woodcock Dell Av
KTN/HRWW/WS HA3....49 J6
Woodcock Hl
KTN/HRWW/WS HA3....49 J5
Woodcocks CAN/RD E16....95 G4
Woodcombe Crs FSTH SE23....131 K7
Woodcot Cl PEND EN3....30 E5
Woodcote Av HCH RM12....81 J3
MLHL NW7....38 A5
THHTH CR7....164 C3
WLGTN SM6....176 B7
Woodcote Cl KUTN/CMB KT2....144 B4
PEND EN3....30 E5
Woodcote Dr ORP BR6....169 J6
Woodcote Ms WLGTN SM6....176 B5
Woodcote Pl WNWD SE27 *....149 H4
Woodcote Rd WAN E11....58 E6
WLGTN SM6....176 B5
Wood Crest BELMT SM2 *....175 G6
Woodcroft ELTH/MOT SE9....153 K2
GFD/PVL UB6....67 G5
WCHMH N21....29 F7
Woodcroft Av MLHL NW7....37 G6
STAN HA7....35 G7
Woodcroft Ms DEPT SE8....112 B3
THHTH CR7....164 C4
Wood Dene PECK SE15 *....111 J7
Wood Dr CHST BR7....153 J5
Wooden Bridge Ter
WNWD SE27 *....149 H2
Wood End HYS/HAR UB3....82 A5
Wood End Av
RYLN/HDSTN HA2....66 B5
Woodend ESH/CLAY KT10....170 C1
NRWD SE19....149 J5
SUT SM1....175 G1
Wood End Av
RYLN/HDSTN HA2....66 B5
Wood End Cl NTHLT UB5....66 D4
Woodend Gdns ENC/FH EN2....28 E3
Wood End Gdns NTHLT UB5....66 C4
Wood End Gn YEAD UB4....82 D4
Wood End Green Rd
HYS/HAR UB3 *....82 A5
Wood End La NTHLT UB5....66 B5
Wood End Rd HRW HA1....66 A4
Wood End Rd WALTH E17....58 A1
The Wood End WLGTN SM6....176 B7
Wood End Wy NTHLT UB5....66 C4
Wooder Gdns FSTGT E7....76 D3
Wooderson Cl SNWD SE25....165 F3
Woodfall Av BAR EN5....26 D4
Woodfall Dr DART DA1....138 C3
Woodfall Rd FSBYPK N4....55 G7
Woodfall St CHEL SW3....15 L8
Woodfarrs CMBW SE5....130 E3
Wood Fld HAMP NW3 *....71 K4
Woodfield Av ALP/SUD HA0....67 J2
CAR SM5....176 A5
CDALE/KGS NW9....51 G3
EA W5....85 J3
NTHWD HA6....32 C3
STRHM/NOR SW16....148 D2
Woodfield Cl EN EN1....30 A3
NRWD SE19....149 J6
Woodfield Crs EA W5....85 J3
Woodfield Dr EBAR EN4....28 A7
GPK RM2....63 J3
Woodfield Gdns NWMAL KT3....160 C4
Woodfield Gv
STRHM/NOR SW16....148 D2
Woodfield La
STRHM/NOR SW16....148 D2
Woodfield Pl MV/WKIL W9....88 D3
Woodfield Ri BUSH WD23....22 D6
Woodfield Rd EA W5....85 J3
HSLWW TW4....122 A1
MV/WKIL W9....88 D4
THDIT KT7....171 J7
Woodfields WATW WD18 *....21 G3
Woodfield Wy
FBAR/BDGN N11....40 D6
Woodford Av
GNTH/NBYPK IG2....59 K4
Woodford Bridge Rd
REDBR IG4....59 H2
Woodford Crs PIN HA5....47 F1
Woodford New Rd
WALTH E17....58 C2
Woodford Pl WBLY HA9....50 A7
Woodford Rd FSTGT E7....77 F3
SWFD E18....58 E3
WAT WD17....21 F1
Woodgate Av CHSGTN KT9....171 K4
Woodgate Crs NTHWD HA6....32 E5
Woodgate Dr
STRHM/NOR SW16....148 D2
Woodger Cl SHB W12....107 F9
Woodget Cl EHAM E6....95 J5
Woodgrange Av EA W5....86 B7
EN EN1....30 D5
KTN/HRWW/WS HA3....49 J4
NFNCH/WDSPK N12....39 H5
Woodgrange Cl
KTN/HRWW/WS HA3....49 J4
Woodgrange Gdns EN EN1....30 D5
Woodgrange Rd FSTGT E7....76 E4

Woodgrange Ter EN EN1 *....30 C5
PIN HA5....33 J7
Woodhall Av DUL SE21....150 B3
PIN HA5....33 J7
Woodhall Dr DUL SE21....150 B3
PIN HA5....33 H7
Woodhall Ga PIN HA5....33 H6
Woodhall La OXHEY WD19....33 H2
Woodham Rd CAT SE6....152 A2
Woodhatch Cl EHAM E6....95 J4
Woodhaven Gdns
BARK/HLT IG6....60 C3
Woodhayes Rd
WIM/MER SW19....146 A5
Woodheyes Rd WLSDN NW10....69 G4
Woodhill WOOL/PLUM SE18....114 D3
Woodhill Crs
KTN/HRWW/WS HA3....49 K5
Woodhouse Av GFD/PVL UB6....85 F1
Woodhouse Cl EDUL SE22....131 H3
GFD/PVL UB6....85 F1
HYS/HAR UB3....101 H2
Woodhouse Eaves
NTHWD HA6....32 A4
Woodhouse Gv FSTGT E7....77 F3
Woodhouse Rd
NFNCH/WDSPK N12....39 G5
WAN E11....76 D2
Woodhurst Av
STMC/STPC BR5....169 H5
Woodhurst Rd ABYW SE2....116 B3
ACT W3....86 E7
Woodies La NWMAL KT3....160 A5
Woodington Cl ELTH/MOT SE9....135 F5
Woodknoll Dr CHST BR7....153 K7
Woodland Ap GFD/PVL UB6....67 G5
Woodland Av MNPK E12....77 J2
Woodland Cl CDALE/KGS NW9....51 F5
HOR/WEW KT19....173 G5
NRWD SE19....150 A5
WFD IG8....45 F2
Woodland Ct GLDGN NW11 *....52 C4
Woodland Crs
BERM/RHTH SE16....112 A1
GNWCH SE10....113 H5
Woodland Gdns ISLW TW7....123 K2
MUSWH N10....54 B5
Woodland Gv CROY/NA CR0....177 G6
GNWCH SE10....113 H4
Woodland Hl NRWD SE19....150 A5
Woodland Ms
STRHM/NOR SW16....148 E2
Woodland Ri GFD/PVL UB6....67 G5
MUSWH N10....54 B3
Woodland Rd
FBAR/BDGN N11....40 B4
NRWD SE19....150 A4
THHTH CR7....164 B3
Woodlands BXLYHS DA6....137 J4
GLDGN NW11....52 C4
RYLN/HDSTN HA2....48 A3
RYNPK SW20....161 F3
Woodlands Av ACT W3....86 D7
BFN/LL DA15....135 K7
CHDH RM6....62 A5
FNCH N3....39 G7
NWMAL KT3....145 F7
RSLP HA4....65 G7
WAN E11....59 F7
WPK KT4....173 G1
Woodlands Cl BMLY BR1....168 E1
BORE WD6....24 C1
ESH/CLAY KT10....171 F6
GLDGN NW11....52 C4
Woodlands Dr STAN HA7....35 F5
SUN TW16....156 B1
Woodlands Gdns
WALTH E17....58 C3
Woodlands Gv ISLW TW7....123 K1
Woodlands Pde ASHF TW15....140 A5
Woodlands Park Rd
GNWCH SE10....113 H5
SEVS/STOTM N15....55 J4
Woodlands Rd BARN SW13....126 C2
BMLY BR1....168 E1
BUSH WD23....21 J3
BXLYHN DA7....137 F2
ED N9....30 E7
HRW HA1....49 F4
IL IG1....78 C2
ISLW TW7....123 J1
ROM RM1....63 H2
STHL UB1....83 H7
SURB KT6....158 E6
WALTH E17....58 A2
WAN E11....76 C1
Woodlands St LEW SE13....133 G6
The Woodlands
BRXN/ST SW9 *....110 C6
ESH/CLAY KT10....170 C1
HRW HA1....66 C1
ISLW TW7....124 A1
LEW SE13....133 G6
NRWD SE19....149 K6
STAN HA7 *....35 H4
STHGT/OAK N14....28 B7
WLGTN SM6....176 B7
Woodland St HACK E8 *....74 B5
Woodlands Wy
PUT/ROE SW15....127 J4
Woodland Ter CHARL SE7....114 D3
Woodland Wk HAMP NW3....71 J4
HOR/WEW KT19....172 C5
Woodland Wy ABYW SE2....116 E3
BRYLDS KT5....172 D1
CROY/NA CR0....166 B7
MLHL NW7....37 G5
MRDN SM4....161 J3
MTCM CR4....148 A6
STMC/STPC BR5....169 H5
WCHMH N21....41 G1
WFD IG8....45 F2
WWKM BR4....180 A2
Wood La BCTR RM8....80 C1
CDALE/KGS NW9....51 F6
DAGW RM9....80 A2
HCH RM12....81 J2
HGT N6....54 B5
ISLW TW7....103 K5
MUSWH N10....54 C4
RSLP HA4....64 B6
SHB W12....88 A6
STAN HA7....35 H2
WFD IG8....44 D4
Woodlawn Cl PUT/ROE SW15....127 J4
Woodlawn Crs WHTN TW2....142 B1
Woodlawn Dr FELT TW13....141 H1
Woodlawn Rd FUL/PGN SW6....107 G6
Woodlea Dr HAYES BR2....167 H4
Woodlea Gv NTHWD HA6....32 A5
Woodlea Rd STNW/STAM N16....74 A2
Woodleigh Av
NFNCH/WDSPK N12....39 J5

Woodleigh Gdns STRHM/NOR SW16 ....148 E2
Woodley Cl TOOT SW17 ....147 K6
Woodley La SUT SM1 ....175 J2
Wood Lodge Gdns BMLY BR1 ....153 J6
Wood Lodge La WWKM BR4 ....180 A2
Woodman Ms RCH/KEW TW9 ....105 J7
Woodmans Gv WLSDN NW10 ....69 H4
Woodmansterne Rd CAR SM5 ....175 J7
  STRHM/NOR SW16 ....148 D4
Wood Md TOTM N17 * 42 C5
Woodmere ELTH/MOT SE9 ....134 E6
Woodmere Av CROY/NA CRO 166 A6
  CROY/NA CRO 166 A6
Woodmere Cl BTSEA SW11 ....129 F2
  CROY/NA CRO 166 A6
Woodmere Gdns CROY/NA CRO 166 A6
Woodmere Wy BECK BR3 ....167 G4
Woodmill Rd CLPT E5 ....74 E1
Woodnook Rd STRHM/NOR SW16 ....148 B4
Woodpecker Cl BUSH WD23 ....22 C7
  ED N9 ....30 D5
  KTN/HRWW/WS HA3 ....35 F5
Woodpecker Ms LEW SE13 ....133 C3
Woodpecker Mt CROY/NA CRO 179 G7
Woodquest Av HNHL SE24 ....130 C4
Wood Ride STMC/STPC BR5 ....169 J3
Woodridge Av NTHWD HA6 ....32 C5
Woodridings Av PIN HA5 ....33 K7
Woodridings Cl PIN HA5 ....33 K6
Woodriffe Rd WAN E11 ....58 B6
Wood Ri PIN HA5 ....46 E4
Wood Rd WLSDN NW10 ....68 E6
Woodrow WOOL/PLUM SE18 ....114 D3
Woodrow Av YEAD UB4 ....82 D4
Woodrow Cl GFD/PVL UB6 ....67 H6
Woodrow Ct TOTM N17 * 42 D6
Woodrush Cl NWCR SE14 ....112 B6
Woodrush Wy CHDH RM6 ....61 K3
Woodseer St WCHPL E1 ....13 M2
Woodsford Sq WKENS W14 ....107 H1
Woodshire Rd DAGE RM10 ....80 D2
Woodshots Meadow WATW WD18 ....20 B4
Woodside BKHH IG9 ....45 G1
  BORE WD6 ....24 B3
  GLDGN NW11 ....52 E4
  WIM/MER SW19 ....146 D4
Woodside Av ALP/SUD HA0 ....68 A7
  CHST BR7 ....154 C4
  ESH/CLAY KT10 ....157 K6
  HGT N6 ....53 K4
  NFNCH/WDSPK N12 ....39 G3
  SNWD SE25 ....165 J5
Woodside Cl EA W5 * 86 A7
  CROY/NA CRO 165 H6
Woodside Court Rd CROY/NA CRO 165 H6
Woodside Crs BFN/LL DA15 ....154 B2
Woodside End ALP/SUD HA0 ....68 A7
Woodside Gdns CHING E4 ....43 K4
  TOTM N17 ....56 B1
Woodside Grange Rd NFNCH/WDSPK N12 ....39 F3
Woodside Gn SNWD SE25 ....165 H5
Woodside Gv NFNCH/WDSPK N12 ....39 G2
Woodside La BXLY DA5 ....136 E5
  TRDG/WHET N20 ....39 F2
Woodside Pde BFN/LL DA15 * 154 B2
Woodside Pk SNWD SE25 ....165 H5
Woodside Park Av NFNCH/WDSPK N12 ....39 F3
Woodside Park Rd NFNCH/WDSPK N12 ....39 F3
Woodside Pl ALP/SUD HA0 ....68 A7
Woodside Rd BFN/LL DA15 ....154 B2
  BMLY BR1 ....168 D4
  BXLYHN DA7 ....138 A3
  KUTN/CMB KT2 ....144 A6
  NTHWD HA6 ....32 D6
  NWMAL KT3 ....160 A1
  PLSTW E13 ....95 G3
  SNWD SE25 ....165 J5
  SUT SM1 ....175 G2
  WDGN N22 ....41 G6
  WFD IG8 ....44 E3
Woodside Wy CROY/NA CRO 165 H5
  MTCM CR4 ....148 B7
Wood's Ms MYFR/PKLN W1K 9 M6
Woodsome Rd KTTN NW5 ....72 A2
Wood's Pl STHWK SE1 ....19 K4
Woodspring Rd WIM/MER SW19 ....146 C1
Wood's Rd PECK SE15 ....111 J7
Woodstead Gv EDGW HA8 ....36 A5
The Woods NTHWD HA6 ....32 E4
Woodstock Av CHEAM SM3 ....161 J6
  GLDGN NW11 ....52 C6
  ISLW TW7 ....124 B4
  STHL UB1 ....83 K2
  WEA W13 ....104 B2
Woodstock Cl BXLY DA5 ....137 G3
  STAN HA7 ....50 A1
Woodstock Crs ED N9 ....30 D5
Woodstock Gdns BECK BR3 ....151 K7
  CDMY/SEVK IG3 ....79 G1
  YEAD UB4 ....82 D4
Woodstock Gra W5 * 86 A7
Woodstock Gv SHB W12 ....107 H1
Woodstock La North SURB KT6 ....171 J1
Woodstock La South ESH/CLAY KT10 ....171 H4
Woodstock Ms CAVSQ/HST W1G 10 B3
Woodstock Ri CHEAM SM3 ....161 J6
  BUSH WD23 ....22 E6
  CAR SM5 ....176 A4
  CHSWK W4 ....106 B3
  CROY/NA CRO 177 K4
  FSBYPK N4 ....55 G7
  FSTGT E7 ....77 G6
  GLDGN NW11 ....52 D6
  WALTH E17 ....58 B1
Woodstock St CAN/RD E16 ....96 C5
  OXSTW W1C 10 C5
Woodstock Ter POP/IOD E14 ....93 K6
Woodstone Av EW KT17 ....173 J4

KUT/HW KT1 ....143 K7
MTCM CR4 ....163 F6
WALTH E17 ....58 A2
Woodsyre SYD SE26 ....150 B3
Wood Ter CRICK NW2 * 69 H1
Woodthorpe Rd PUT/ROE SW15 ....126 E3
Woodtree Cl HDN NW4 ....52 A1
Wood V FSTH SE23 ....131 J7
Woodvale Av SNWD SE25 ....165 G2
Woodvale Wy GLDGN NW11 ....70 E6
Woodview Av CHING E4 ....44 A3
Woodview Cl PUT/ROE SW15 ....145 F3
Woodville Cl LEE/GVPK SE12 ....133 K4
  TEDD TW11 ....143 G3
Woodville Court Ms WAT WD17 * 20 E1
Woodville Gdns BARK/HLT IG6 ....60 B2
  EA W5 ....86 A5
  RSLP HA4 ....46 A6
  SURB KT6 * 158 E6
Woodville Gv WELL DA16 * 136 B2
Woodville Rd BARK IG11 ....27 G2
  EA W5 ....86 A5
  GLDGN NW11 ....52 C6
  KIL/WHAMP NW6 * 88 D1
  MRDN SM4 ....161 K5
  RCHPK/HAM TW10 ....143 H2
  STNW/STAM N16 ....74 A4
  SWFD E18 ....59 F1
  THHTH CR7 ....164 E2
  WALTH E17 ....57 G4
  WAN E11 ....58 D7
Woodville St WOOL/PLUM SE18 ....114 D3
Woodward Av HDN NW4 ....51 J4
Woodward Cl ESH/CLAY KT10 ....171 F5
Woodwarde Rd EDUL SE22 ....131 F5
Woodward Gdns DAGW RM9 ....79 J6
  STAN HA7 ....35 F5
Woodward Rd DAGW RM9 ....79 H6
Woodway Crs HRW HA1 ....49 G5
Woodwaye OXHEY WD19 ....21 G6
Woodwell St WAND/EARL SW18 ....128 B4
Wood Whf GNWCH SE10 ....112 E5
Woodyard Cl KTTN NW5 ....72 A4
Woodyard La DUL SE21 ....131 F6
Woodyates Rd LEE/GVPK SE12 ....133 K5
Woolacombe Rd BKHTH/KID SE3 ....134 B1
Woolacombe Wy HYS/HAR UB3 ....101 H3
Woolbrook Rd DART DA1 ....138 B5
Wooler St WALW SE17 ....19 G8
Woolf Cl THMD SE28 ....97 H7
Woolf Ms STPAN WC1H 5 J9
Woollaston Rd FSBYPK N4 ....55 H5
Woollett Cl DART DA1 ....138 D3
Woolmead Av CDALE/KGS NW9 ....51 J6
Woolmerdine Ct BUSH WD23 ....21 H2
Woolmer Gdns UED N18 ....42 C5
Woolmer Rd UED N18 ....42 C4
Woolmore St POP/IOD E14 ....94 A6
Woolneigh St FUL/PGN SW6 ....128 A2
Woolridge Cl EBED/NFELT TW14 ....121 F7
Woolridge Wy HOM E9 * 74 E6
Wool Rd RYNPK SW20 ....145 K5
Woolstaplers Wy BERM/RHTH SE16 ....111 H2
Woolston Cl WALTH E17 * 57 F1
Woolstone Rd FSTH SE23 ....151 G1
Woolwich Church St WOOL/PLUM SE18 ....114 D2
Woolwich Common WOOL/PLUM SE18 ....115 F5
Woolwich Foot Tnl CAN/RD E16 ....115 F1
Woolwich High St WOOL/PLUM SE18 ....115 F2
Woolwich Manorway CAN/RD E16 ....115 G1
Woolwich Manor Wy EHAM E6 ....95 K3
Woolwich New Rd WOOL/PLUM SE18 ....115 F4
Woolwich Rd ABYW SE2 ....116 E5
  BXLYHN DA7 ....137 J2
  CHARL SE7 ....114 B3
  CNWCH SE10 ....113 K4
Wooster Gdns POP/IOD E14 ....94 B5
Wootton Gv FNCH N3 ....38 E7
Wootton St STHWK SE1 ....18 B1
Worbeck Rd PGE/AN SE20 ....165 J1
Worcester Av TOTM N17 ....42 C6
Worcester Cl CRICK NW2 ....69 J2
  CROY/NA CRO 179 H1
  MTCM CR4 ....163 F1
Worcester Crs MLHL NW7 ....37 G2
  WFD IG8 ....45 G3
Worcester Dr CHSWK W4 ....106 B2
Worcester Gdns GFD/PVL UB6 ....66 C5
  IL IG1 ....59 J6
  WPK KT4 ....173 G2
Worcester Ms KIL/WHAMP NW6 * 71 F5
Worcester Park Rd WPK KT4 ....172 E2
Wordsworth Av GFD/PVL UB6 ....84 D1
  MNPK E12 ....77 K4
  WALTH E17 ....57 F1
  WIM/MER SW19 ....146 D4
Wordsworth Dr CHEAM SM3 ....173 J3
Wordsworth Gdns BORE WD6 ....24 C4
Wordsworth Pde CEND/HSY/T N8 * 55 H3
Wordsworth Pl HAMP NW3 ....71 K4
Wordsworth Rd HPTN TW12 ....141 K3
  PGE/AN SE20 ....151 F6
  STHWK SE1 ....19 L6
  STNW/STAM N16 ....74 A3
  WELL DA16 ....115 K7
  WLGTN SM6 ....176 C5
Wordsworth Wk GLDGN NW11 ....52 D3
Wordsworth Wy DART DA1 ....139 K3
  WDR/YW UB7 ....100 B3
Worfield St BTSEA SW11 ....108 D6
Worgan St BERM/RHTH SE16 ....112 A2
  LBTH SE11 ....17 L7
Worland Rd SRTFD E15 ....76 C6
Worlds End Est WBPTN SW10 * 108 C6
World's End La WCHMH N21 ....29 F4
Worlds End Pas WBPTN SW10 * 108 C6
Worlidge St HMSMTH W6 ....107 F4

Worlingham Rd EDUL SE22 ....131 G3
Wormholt Rd SHB W12 ....87 J7
Wormholt Ter SHB W12 * 87 J7
Wormwood St OBST EC2N 13 J4
Wornington Rd NKENS W10 ....88 C4
Woronzow Rd STJWD NW8 ....3 H4
Worple Av ISLW TW7 ....124 B4
  WIM/MER SW19 ....146 B6
Worple Cl RYLN/HDSTN HA2 ....47 K7
Worple Rd ISLW TW7 ....124 B4
  RYNPK SW20 ....161 F1
  WIM/MER SW19 ....146 D6
Worple Road Ms WIM/MER SW19 ....146 D5
Worple St MORT/ESHN SW14 ....126 A2
Worple Wy RCHPK/HAM TW10 ....125 F4
  RYLN/HDSTN HA2 ....47 K7
Worship St SDTCH EC2A 13 H1
Worslade Rd TOOT SW17 ....147 H3
Worsley Bridge Rd SYD SE26 ....151 H4
Worsley Gv CLPT E5 ....74 C3
Worsley Rd WAN E11 ....76 C3
Worsopp Dr CLAP SW4 ....129 H4
Worthfield Cl HOR/WEW KT19 ....173 F6
Worth Gv WALW SE17 ....19 G8
Worthing Cl SRTFD E15 ....76 C7
Worthing Rd HEST TW5 ....102 E5
Worthington Cl MTCM CR4 ....163 G3
Worthington Rd SURB KT6 ....159 G6
Wortley Rd CROY/NA CRO 164 B6
  EHAM E6 ....77 H6
Worton Gdns ISLW TW7 ....123 J1
Worton Rd ISLW TW7 ....124 A2
Worton Wy ISLW TW7 ....123 J1
Wotton Rd CRICK NW2 ....70 A3
  DEPT SE8 ....112 C5
Wouldham Rd CAN/RD E16 ....94 D5
Wragby Rd WAN E11 * 76 C2
Wrampling Pl ED N9 ....30 C7
Wray Av CLAY IG5 ....60 A2
Wray Crs FSBYPK N4 ....72 E1
Wrayfield Rd CHEAM SM3 ....174 A2
Wray Rd BELMT SM2 ....174 D7
Wraysbury Cl HSLWW TW4 ....122 D4
Wrays Wy YEAD UB4 ....82 C4
Wrekin Rd WOOL/PLUM SE18 ....115 H6
Wren Av CRICK NW2 ....70 A3
  NWDGN UB2 ....102 E3
Wren Cl CAN/RD E16 ....94 D5
  ED N9 ....31 F7
Wren Crs BUSH WD23 ....22 C7
Wren Dr WDR/YW UB7 ....100 A1
Wren Gdns DAGW RM9 ....79 K4
  HCH RM12 ....63 H7
Wren La RSLP HA4 ....47 F5
Wren Ms LEW SE13 * 133 H3
Wren Rd CMBW SE5 ....110 E7
  DAGW RM9 ....79 K4
  SCUP DA14 ....155 J2
Wren's Av ASHF TW15 ....140 A4
Wren St FSBYW WC1X 5 M9
Wrentham Av WLSDN NW10 ....88 B1
Wrenthorpe Rd BMLY BR1 ....152 C7
Wrenwood Wy PIN HA5 ....47 F3
Wrexham Rd BOW E3 ....93 J1
Wricklemarsh Rd BKHTH/KID SE3 ....134 A1
Wrigglesworth St NWCR SE14 ....112 A6
Wright Cl LEW SE13 ....133 G3
Wright Rd HEST TW5 ....102 B6
Wrights Cl DAGE RM10 ....80 D3
Wrights Gn CLAP SW4 * 129 J3
Wright's La KENS W8 ....14 C3
Wrights Pl WLSDN NW10 * 68 E5
Wrights Rd SNWD SE25 ....165 F2
  BOW E3 ....93 H1
Wright's Rw WLGTN SM6 ....176 B3
Wrigley Cl CHING E4 ....44 B4
Wrotham Rd BAR EN5 ....26 C1
  CAMTN NW1 ....4 E3
  WEA W13 ....85 J7
  WELL DA16 ....116 D7
Wrottesley Rd WLSDN NW10 ....87 J1
  WOOL/PLUM SE18 ....115 H5
Wroughton Rd BTSEA SW11 ....128 E5
Wroughton Ter HDN NW4 ....51 K3
Wroxall Rd DAGW RM9 ....79 J5
Wroxham Gdns FBAR/BDGN N11 ....40 C7
Wroxham Rd THMD SE28 ....97 K6
Wroxton Rd PECK SE15 ....131 J1
Wrythe Gn CAR SM5 ....175 K2
Wrythe Green Rd CAR SM5 ....175 K2
Wrythe La CAR SM5 ....175 G2
Wulfstan St SHB W12 ....87 H5
Wyatt Cl BUSH WD23 ....22 E6
  FELT TW13 ....122 C7
  YEAD UB4 ....82 E4
Wyatt Dr BARN SW13 ....106 E5
Wyatt Park Rd BRXS/STRHM SW2 ....149 F1
Wyatt Rd DART DA1 ....138 C2
  FSTGT E7 ....76 E5
  HBRY N5 ....73 J2
Wyatt's La WALTH E17 ....58 A2
Wybert St CAMTN NW1 ....4 D9
Wyborne Wy WLSDN NW10 ....68 E6
Wyburn Av BAR EN5 ....26 D2
Wychcombe Studios HAMP NW3 * 71 K5
Wyche Gv SAND/SEL CR2 ....177 K6
Wych Elm Cl KUTN/CMB KT2 ....144 B6
Wycherley Cl BKHTH/KID SE3 ....113 J6
Wycherley Crs BAR EN5 ....27 F5
Wychwood Av EDGW HA8 ....35 K5
  THHTH CR7 ....164 C2
Wychwood Cl EDGW HA8 ....35 K5
  SUN TW16 ....140 E5
Wychwood End HGT N6 ....54 C6
Wychwood Gdns CLAY IG5 ....59 K3
Wychwood Wy NTHWD HA6 ....32 C6
Wycliffe Cl WELL DA16 ....116 A7
Wycliffe Rd BTSEA SW11 ....129 F1
  WIM/MER SW19 ....147 F5
Wyclif St FSBYE EC1V * 6 C8
Wycombe Gdns GLDGN NW11 ....70 D1
Wycombe Pl WAND/EARL SW18 ....128 B5
Wycombe Rd ALP/SUD HA0 ....68 C7
  GNTH/NBYPK IG2 ....59 K4
  TOTM N17 ....42 C7
Wycombe Sq KENS W8 ....8 A1
Wydell Cl MRDN SM4 ....161 F5
Wydenhurst Rd CROY/NA CRO 165 H6
Wydeville Manor Rd LEE/GVPK SE12 ....153 F3
Wye Cl RSLP HA4 ....46 A5
Wyemead Crs CHING E4 ....44 C1
Wye St BTSEA SW11 ....128 C2
Wyevale Cl PIN HA5 ....46 E2
Wyfold Rd FUL/PGN SW6 ....107 H6
Wyke Cl ISLW TW7 ....104 A5
Wyke Gdns HNWL W7 ....104 A2

Wykeham Av DAGW RM9 ....79 J5
Wykeham Cl WDR/YW UB7 ....100 D5
Wykeham Gn DAGW RM9 ....79 J5
Wykeham Hl WBLY HA9 ....50 B2
Wykeham Ri TRDG/WHET N20 ....26 C7
  KTN/HRWW/WS HA3 ....49 H3
Wykeham Rd HDN NW4 ....52 A4
  KTN/HRWW/WS HA3 ....49 H3
Wyke Rd BOW E3 ....75 J6
  RYNPK SW20 ....161 F1
Wylchin Cl PIN HA5 ....46 D3
Wyldes Cl GLDGN NW11 ....53 G7
Wyldfield Gdns ED N9 ....42 B1
Wyld Wy WBLY HA9 ....68 D5
Wyleu St FSTH SE23 ....132 B6
Wylie Rd NWDGN UB2 ....103 F2
Wyllen Cl WCHPL E1 ....92 E3
Wylo Dr BAR EN5 ....25 H5
Wymark Cl RAIN RM13 ....99 H1
Wymering Rd MV/WKIL W9 ....2 B8
Wymond St PUT/ROE SW15 ....127 F2
Wynan Rd POP/IOD E14 ....112 E4
Wynaud Ct WDGN N22 ....41 F5
Wyncham Av BFN/LL DA15 ....135 K7
Wynchgate KTN/HRWW/WS HA3 ....34 E1
  STHGT/OAK N14 ....28 E6
Wyncote Wy SAND/SEL CR2 ....179 F6
Wyncroft Cl BMLY BR1 ....168 E2
Wyndale Av CDALE/KGS NW9 ....50 B5
Wyndcliff Rd CHARL SE7 ....114 A5
Wyndcroft Cl ENC/FH EN2 ....29 H2
Wyndham Cl BELMT SM2 ....174 E6
  ORP BR6 ....169 H7
Wyndham Crs HSLWW TW4 ....122 E5
  KTTN NW5 ....72 A4
Wyndham Est CMBW SE5 ....110 D6
Wyndham Ms MBLAR W1H 9 L3
Wyndham Pl MBLAR W1H 9 L3
Wyndham Rd CMBW SE5 ....110 D6
  EBAR EN4 ....27 K7
  EHAM E6 ....77 H6
  KUTN/CMB KT2 ....144 B7
  WEA W13 ....104 C2
Wyndham St CAMTN NW1 ....9 L1
Wyndham Yd MBLAR W1H 9 L3
Wyndhurst Cl SAND/SEL CR2 ....177 H6
Wynell Rd FSTH SE23 ....151 F2
Wynford Pl BELV DA17 ....117 H5
Wynford Rd IS N1 ....5 L5
Wynford Wy ELTH/MOT SE9 ....153 K2
Wynlie Gdns PIN HA5 ....47 F1
Wynn Bridge Cl WFD IG8 * 45 H7
Wynndale Rd SWFD E18 ....45 F4
Wynne Rd BRXN/ST SW9 ....130 B1
Wynn's Av BFN/LL DA15 ....136 B4
Wynnstay Gdns KENS W8 ....14 B3
Wynter St BTSEA SW11 ....128 B3
Wynton Gdns SNWD SE25 ....165 F4
Wynton Pl ACT W3 ....86 D5
Wynyard Ter LBTH SE11 ....17 M7
Wynyatt St FSBYE EC1V 6 C7
Wyre Gv EDGW HA8 ....36 D2
  HYS/HAR UB3 ....101 K3
Wyresdale Crs GFD/PVL UB6 ....85 F2
Wyteleaf Cl RSLP HA4 ....46 A5
Wythburn Pl MBLAR W1H 9 L5
Wythenshawe Rd DAGE RM10 ....80 C2
Wythes Cl BMLY BR1 ....168 E1
Wythes Rd CAN/RD E16 ....95 J7
Wythfield Rd ELTH/MOT SE9 ....134 E5
Wyvenhoe Rd RYLN/HDSTN HA2 ....66 C2
Wyvern Cl DART DA1 ....139 F6
Wyvern Est NWMAL KT3 * 160 D2
Wyvil Rd VX/NE SW8 ....109 K6
Wyvis St POP/IOD E14 ....93 K4

Y

Yabsley St POP/IOD E14 ....94 A7
Yalding Rd BERM/RHTH SE16 ....111 H2
Yale Cl HSLWW TW4 ....122 E4
Yale Wy HCH RM12 ....81 J3
Yarborough Rd WIM/MER SW19 ....147 H7
Yardley Cl CHING E4 ....31 H7
Yardley La CHING E4 ....31 H4
Yardley St FSBYW WC1X 6 A8
Yarmouth Crs TOTM N17 ....56 D4
Yarmouth Pl MYFR/PICC W1J 10 C9
Yarnton Wy STHL/WRAY TW19 ....36 D7
  ERITHM DA18 ....117 F1
Yarrow Crs EHAM E6 ....95 J4
Yateley St WOOL/PLUM SE18 ....114 C2
Yeading Av RYLN/HDSTN HA2 ....65 J1
Yeading Fk YEAD UB4 ....83 G4
Yeading Gdns YEAD UB4 ....83 F4
Yeading La YEAD UB4 ....83 F5
Yeames Cl WEA W13 ....85 G5
Yeate St IS N1 ....7 G2
Yeatman Rd HGT N6 ....53 K5
Yeats Cl HNWL W7 ....85 F6
  LEW SE13 ....133 G1
  WLSDN NW10 ....69 G5
Ye Cnr OXHEY WD19 ....21 H5
Yeend Cl E/WMO/HCT KT8 ....157 F3
Yeldham Rd HMSMTH W6 ....107 G4
Yeldham Vls HMSMTH W6 * 107 G4
Yelverton Rd BTSEA SW11 ....128 C1
Yenston Cl MRDN SM4 ....161 K5
Yeoman Cl EHAM E6 ....96 B6
Yeoman Dr STHL/WRAY TW19 ....30 B7
Yeoman Rd NTHLT UB5 ....65 J6
Yeomans Acre RSLP HA4 ....46 E5
Yeoman's Rw CHEL SW3 ....15 K4
Yeoman St BERM/RHTH SE16 ....112 B3
Yeomans Wy PEND EN3 * 30 D1
Yeoman's Yd WCHPL E1 ....13 M6
Yeo St BOW E3 ....93 K4
Yeovilton Pl KUTN/CMB KT2 ....143 K4
Yerbury Rd ARCH N19 ....72 D2
Yester Dr CHST BR7 ....153 J6
Yester Pk CHST BR7 ....153 K6
Yester Rd CHST BR7 ....153 K6
Yew Cl BKHH IG9 ....45 H1
Yewdale Cl BMLY BR1 ....152 C5
Yewfield Rd WLSDN NW10 ....69 H5
Yew Gv CRICK NW2 ....70 B3
Yew Tree Cl LEW SE13 ....133 F2
  WCHMH N21 ....29 G6
Yew Tree Ct BORE WD6 * 23 K5
Yew Tree Gdns CHDH RM6 ....62 A4
  ROMW/RG RM7 ....63 F4
Yew Tree Rd BECK BR3 ....166 C3
  SHB W12 ....87 H6

Yew Tree Wk HSLWW TW4 ....122 E4
Yew Wk HRW HA1 ....48 E7
Yoakley Rd STNW/STAM N16 ....74 A1
Yoke Cl HOLWY N7 ....72 E5
Yolande Gdns ELTH/MOT SE9 ....134 D4
Yonge Pk HOLWY N7 ....73 G2
York Av BFN/LL DA15 ....154 E1
  HNWL W7 ....84 E7
  HYS/HAR UB3 ....82 A5
  MORT/ESHN SW14 ....125 K4
  STAN HA7 ....35 H7
York Br CAMTN NW1 ....4 A9
York Blds CHCR WC2N * 11 K7
York Cl CMBW SE5 * 130 D1
  EHAM E6 ....95 K5
  HNWL W7 ....84 E7
  MRDN SM4 ....162 A3
Yorke Ga WAT WD17 ....20 E1
York Ga CAMTN NW1 ....10 B3
  STHGT/OAK N14 ....28 E6
York Gv PECK SE15 ....111 K7
York Hl WNWD SE27 ....149 H2
York House Pl KENS W8 ....14 C1
Yorkland Av WELL DA16 ....136 A3
York Ms IL IG1 ....78 A1
  KTTN NW5 ....72 B4
York Pde BTFD TW8 * 104 E4
  CDALE/KGS NW9 * 51 J5
York Pl BTSEA SW11 ....128 B2
  IL IG1 ....78 A1
York Ri KTTN NW5 ....72 B2
  ORP BR6 ....169 H7
York Rd ACT W3 ....86 E5
  BAR EN5 ....27 G4
  BELMT SM2 ....174 E7
  BTFD TW8 ....104 E4
  BTSEA SW11 ....128 B3
  CHING E4 ....43 J4
  CROY/NA CRO 164 B6
  DART DA1 ....139 J6
  EA W5 ....104 D2
  FBAR/BDGN N11 ....40 D5
  FSTGT E7 ....76 E5
  HSLW TW3 ....123 G2
  IL IG1 ....78 A2
  KUTN/CMB KT2 ....144 B6
  LEY E10 ....76 A2
  NTHWD HA6 ....46 E1
  RAIN RM13 ....81 F6
  RCHPK/HAM TW10 ....125 G4
  STHWK SE1 ....17 M1
  TEDD TW11 ....142 E3
  TOTM N17 ....42 D1
  WALTH E17 ....57 F4
  WATW WD18 ....21 G4
  WCHMH N21 ....29 K6
  WIM/MER SW19 ....147 F6
Yorkshire Cl STNW/STAM N16 ....74 A2
Yorkshire Gdns UED N18 ....42 D4
Yorkshire Grey Yd GINN WC1R * 11 L3
Yorkshire Rd MTCM CR4 ....163 K4
  POP/IOD E14 ....93 G5
York Sq POP/IOD E14 ....93 G5
York St MBLAR W1H 9 L3
  MTCM CR4 ....163 F6
York Street Chambers MHST W1U * 9 M2
York Ter ERITH DA8 ....117 K7
York Ter East CAMTN NW1 ....10 B1
York Ter West CAMTN NW1 ....10 A1
Yorkton St BETH E2 ....92 C1
York Wy CHSGTN KT9 ....171 K6
  FELT TW13 ....141 K2
  HOLWY N7 ....72 D5
  KCROSS N1/C 5 K5
  TRDG/WHET N20 ....39 K2
York Way Ct IS N1 * 5 K4
York Way Est HOLWY N7 ....72 E5
Young Rd CAN/RD E16 ....95 G5
Youngs Rd GNTH/NBYPK IG2 ....60 D4
Young St KENS W8 ....14 C2
Yoxley Ap GNTH/NBYPK IG2 ....60 C5
Yoxley Dr GNTH/NBYPK IG2 ....60 C5
Yukon Rd BAL SW12 ....129 G6
Yunus Khan Cl WALTH E17 ....57 J4

Z

Zambezie Dr ED N9 ....42 E2
Zampa Rd BERM/RHTH SE16 ....111 K4
Zander Ct BETH E2 ....92 C2
Zangwill Rd BKHTH/KID SE3 ....114 C1
Zealand Av WDR/YW UB7 ....100 A6
Zealand Rd BOW E3 ....93 G1
Zennor Rd BAL SW12 ....129 H7
Zenoria St EDUL SE22 ....131 G3
Zermatt Rd THHTH CR7 ....164 D3
Zetland St POP/IOD E14 ....94 A4
Zion Pl THHTH CR7 ....164 E3
Zion Rd THHTH CR7 ....164 E3
Zoar St STHWK SE1 ....12 E8
Zoffany St ARCH N19 ....72 D1

02 Centre
HAMP NW3 ....71 G5
2 Willow Road (NT)
HAMP NW3 ....71 J3
30 St Mary Axe
HDTCH EC3A 13 K5
41 Hotel
BCVA SW1W 16 D3
7/7 Memorial
MYFR/PKLN W1K 10 A9
Aarotya Medical Centre
SEVS/STOTM N15 ....55 H3
Abbey Business Centre
VX/NE SW8 ....109 H7
Abbey Christian School for the
English Language
STJWD NW8 ....2 F6
The Abbey Clinic
BELV DA17 ....117 G4
Abbey College London
BAY/PAD W2 ....8 B5
Abbey Industrial Estate
ALP/SUD HA0 ....68 B7
MTCM CR4 ....162 A4
Abbey Lane Commercial Estate
SRTFD E15 ....94 B1
Abbey Medical Centre
STJWD NW8 ....2 D4
Abbey Mills
WIM/MER SW19 ....147 G7
Abbey Park Industrial Estate
BARK IG11 ....96 B1
Abbey Primary School
ABYW SE2 ....116 D2
MRDN SM4 ....161 K6
Abbey Road ⊖
SRTFD E15 ....94 B1
Abbey Road Health Centre
SRTFD E15 ....76 C7
Abbey Road Studios
STJWD NW8 ....2 F6
Abbey Sports Centre
BARK IG11 ....78 C7
Abbey Trading Estate
SYD SE26 ....151 G4
Abbey Wharf Industrial Estate
BARK IG11 ....96 D2
Abbey Wood ⇌
ABYW SE2 ....116 D2
Abbotsbury Primary School
MRDN SM4 ....161 K4
Abbs Cross School &
Arts College
HCH RM12 ....81 K2
ABC Cinema
PUT/ROE SW15 ....127 H2
Abercorn Place School
CAMTN NW1 ....9 K2
Abercorn School
MBLAR W1H 9 L3
STJWD NW8 ....2 F6
Aberdeen Wharf
WAP E1W 92 D7
Aberglen Industrial Estate
HYS/HAR UB3 ....101 G1
Abingdon House School
KENS W8 ....14 B3
Abney Park Cemetery
STNW/STAM N16 ....74 A1
Acacia Business Centre
WAN E11 ....76 C2
Academic College of London
WBLY HA9 ....67 K2
The Academy School
HAMP NW3 ....71 H3
Acland Burghley School
KTTN NW5 ....72 B3
Acorn Industrial Park
DART DA1 ....138 D4
Acorn Medical Centre
TWK TW1 ....124 B7
Acorns Independent College
STHL UB1 ....84 A7
Acre Road Health Clinic
KUTN/CMB KT2 ....144 B6
Acton Business Centre
WLSDN NW10 ....87 F3
Acton Central ⊖
ACT W3 ....87 F7
Acton Central Industrial Estate
ACT W3 ....86 D6
Acton Health Centre
ACT W3 ....86 E7
Acton High School
ACT W3 ....105 H1
Acton Hospital
ACT W3 ....105 H1
Acton Lane Medical Centre
CHSWK W4 ....105 K1
Acton Main Line ⇌
ACT W3 ....86 E5
Acton Park Industrial Estate
ACT W3 ....106 A1
Acton Superbowl
ACT W3 ....86 C4
Acton Swimming Baths
ACT W3 ....86 E7
Acton Town ⊖
ACT W3 ....105 H1
Acton & West London College
ACT W3 ....86 D7
Acumen (Anglo School)
NRWD SE19 ....150 A7
Adams Bridge Business Centre
WBLY HA9 ....68 D4
Adamsrill Primary School
SYD SE26 ....151 G2
Ad-Dean Primary School
IL IG1 ....78 C3
Addey & Stanhope School
NWCR SE14 ....112 C7
Addington Court Golf Club
CROY/NA CR0 ....179 H7
Addington Golf Club
CROY/NA CR0 ....179 H3
Addington Palace Golf Club
CROY/NA CR0 ....179 G5
Addington Village ⊖
CROY/NA CR0 ....179 J5
Addiscombe ⊖
CROY/NA CR0 ....165 H7
Addiscombe CC
CROY/NA CR0 ....178 C2
Addison Primary School
WKENS W14 ....107 G2
Adelphi Theatre
COVGDN WC2E 11 K7
Adler Industrial Estate
HYS/HAR UB3 ....101 G1
Admiral Hyson Industrial Estate
STHWK SE1 ....111 J3
Admiralty Arch
STJS SW1Y 11 H8

The Adult College of
Barking & Dagenham
BARK IG11 ....78 E5
The Aerodrome School
CROY/NA CR0 ....177 H4
Africa Centre
COVGDN WC2E 11 K6
Aga Khan University
CAN/RD E16 ....94 D4
RSQ WC1B 11 H3
Agnew's
CONDST W1S 10 E8
Agora Shopping Centre
PECK SE15 ....131 H1
AHA International
London Centre
BMSBY WC1N 11 M2
Ainslie Wood
Primary School
CHING E4 ....43 K4
Airbase Unity
Elementary School
RSLP HA4 ....64 A1
Airbus Coach Station
HTHAIR TW6 ....120 C2
Air Call Business Centre
CDALE/KGS NW9 ....51 F2
Airedale Physiotherapy Clinic
CHSWK W4 ....106 C4
Airlinks Golf Club
NWDGN UB2 ....102 B3
Air Links Industrial Estate
HEST TW5 ....102 B4
Airport Gate Business Centre
WDR/YW UB7 ....100 C6
Akiva School
FNCH N3 ....52 E1
Aksaray Sports Club
STNW/STAM N16 ....73 K3
Al-Azhar Primary School
WCHPL E1 ....92 C5
Albany Centre & Theatre
DEPT SE8 ....112 C6
Albany Clinic
BFN/LL DA15 ....155 G3
WIM/MER SW19 ....147 F6
Albany Park ⇌
SCUP DA14 ....155 K1
Albany Park Canoe &
Sailing Centre
KUTN/CMB KT2 ....143 K5
The Albany Theatre
WIM/MER SW19 ....146 C1
Albemarle Primary School
WIM/MER SW19 ....146 C1
Albert Memorial
SKENS SW7 ....15 G1
Albion College
RSQ WC1B 11 J3
Albion Health Centre
WCHPL E1 ....92 D4
Albion Primary School
BERM/RHTH SE16 ....111 K1
Albion Street Health Centre
BERM/RHTH SE16 ....111 K1
Albright Industrial Estate
RAIN RM13 ....99 H4
Alchemea College of
Audio Engineering
IS N1 ....6 D3
The Alchemy Gallery
CLKNW EC1R 6 A9
Aldenham Country Park
BORE WD6 ....23 H1
Aldenham Preparatory School
BORE WD6 ....23 H1
Alderbrook Primary School
BAL SW12 ....129 G6
Aldersbrook County
Secondary School
MNPK E12 ....59 G7
Aldersbrook Primary School
MNPK E12 ....59 F7
Alderwood Primary School
ELTH/MOT SE9 ....135 J5
Aldgate ⊖
TWRH EC3N 13 L5
Aldgate Bus Station
HDTCH EC3A 13 L4
Aldgate East ⊖
WCHPL E1 ....13 M4
Aldwych Theatre
HOL/ALD WC2B 11 L5
Alexander McLeod
Primary School
ABYW SE2 ....116 C4
Alexandra Avenue Clinic
RYLN/HDSTN HA2 ....65 K1
Alexandra Business Centre
PEND EN3 ....31 F3
Alexandra Infant School
KUTN/CMB KT2 ....144 C6
PGE/AN SE20 ....151 F6
Alexandra Junior School
HSLW TW3 ....123 G1
Alexandra Palace
WDGN N22 ....54 D2
Alexandra Palace Ice Rink
WDGN N22 ....54 D1
Alexandra Park School
FBAR/BDGN N11 ....40 C6
Alexandra Primary School
WDGN N22 ....55 F1
Alexandra School
RYLN/HDSTN HA2 ....65 K1
Al Falah Boys School
CLPT E5 ....74 D2
Al Falah Primary School
CLPT E5 ....74 D2
Alfred Salter Primary School
BERM/RHTH SE16 ....112 A1
Alfreds Way Industrial Estate
BARK IG11 ....79 G7
Al-Khair Primary &
Secondary School
CROY/NA CR0 ....164 E7
Allenby Primary School
STHL UB1 ....84 A5
Allen Edwards Primary School
CLAP SW4 ....109 K7
The All England Lawn Tennis &
Croquet Club
WIM/MER SW19 ....146 B2
Alleyns Junior School
EDUL SE22 ....131 F4
Allfarthing JMI School
WAND/EARL SW18 ....128 B5
All Saints
POP/IOD E14 ....94 A5
All Saints Benhilton CE Primary
SUT SM1 ....175 F2
All Saints Catholic School
BCTR RM8 ....62 C7

All Saints CE Primary School
BKHTH/KID SE3 ....133 H1
CAR SM5 ....176 A4
CRICK NW2 ....70 A4
FUL/PGN SW6 ....127 H1
PUT/ROE SW15 ....127 F1
TRDG/WHET N20 ....39 H1
WIM/MER SW19 ....147 G6
All Saints 1 & I School
NRWD SE19 ....150 A7
All Souls CE Primary School
GTPST W1W 10 E3
Allum Lane Cemetery
BORE WD6 ....24 A4
Allum Medical Centre
WAN E11 ....58 B6
Alma Primary School
BERM/RHTH SE16 ....111 H3
PEND EN3 ....31 H3
Almeida Theatre
IS N1 ....6 C2
Al-Noor Primary School
GDMY/SEVK IG3 ....61 H7
Alperton ⊖
ALP/SUD HA0 ....67 K7
Alperton Cemetery
ALP/SUD HA0 ....67 K7
Alperton Community School
ALP/SUD HA0 ....67 K6
Alperton Sports Ground
ALP/SUD HA0 ....85 K1
Alpha Business Centre
WALTH E17 ....57 H4
Alpha Preparatory School
HRW HA1 ....48 E4
Alpine Business Centre
EHAM E6 ....96 A4
Al-Risaala School
BAL SW12 ....129 G7
Al-Sadiq Boys & Al-Zahra
Girls Schools
KIL/WHAMP NW6 ....70 C7
Alscot Road Industrial Estate
STHWK SE1 ....19 M5
Altmore Infant School
EHAM E6 ....77 K6
The Alton School
PUT/ROE SW15 ....126 C6
Ambler Primary School
FSBYPK N4 ....73 H2
Ambleside Junior School
WOT/HER KT12 ....156 B7
AMC Business Centre
WLSDN NW10 ....86 D2
American
Intercontinental University
MHST W1U 10 B3
The American School in London
STJWD NW8 ....2 F5
AMF Bowling
LEW SE13 ....133 F2
Amida Golf
FELT TW13 ....142 A2
Ampere Way ⊖
CROY/NA CR0 ....164 A7
Ampthill Square
Medical Centre
CAMTN NW1 ....4 F6
Anchorage Point
Industrial Estate
CHARL SE7 ....114 B2
Anchor Bay Industrial Estate
ERITH DA8 ....118 C6
Anchor Retail Park
WCHPL E1 ....92 E3
The Anchor School
SUT SM1 ....175 F1
ANdAZ Hotel
LVPST EC2M 13 J3
Andover Medical Centre
HOLWY N7 ....73 F2
The Andrew Ewing
Primary School
HEST TW5 ....102 E6
Anerley ⇌
PGE/AN SE20 ....150 C7
Anerley School
NRWD SE19 ....150 C7
Angel ⊖
IS N1 ....6 C5
Angel Centre
DART DA1 ....139 H5
Angel Road ⇌
UED N18 ....42 E4
Angerstein Business Park
GNWCH SE10 ....113 K3
Anglian Industrial Estate
BARK IG11 ....97 F3
Animal Cemetery
REDBR IG4 ....59 H2
Annemount School
EFNCH N2 ....53 G5
Annunciation RC Infant School
EDGW HA8 ....37 F7
The Annunciation RC
Junior School
MLHL NW7 ....37 F5
Anson Primary School
CRICK NW2 ....70 B4
Apex Hotel
MON EC3R 13 K6
Apex Industrial Estate
WLSDN NW10 ....87 H3
Apex Primary School
IL IG1 ....60 A7
Apex Retail Park
FELT TW13 ....141 K2
Apollo Theatre
SOHO/CST W1F 11 G6
Apollo Victoria Theatre
PIM SW1V 16 E4
Apostolic Nuncio
WIM/MER SW19 ....146 A2
Applegarth Primary School
CROY/NA CR0 ....179 K5
Apsley House,
The Wellington Museum
KTBR SW1X 16 A1
Aquarius Business Park
CRICK NW2 ....51 J7
Aquarius Golf Club
EDUL SE22 ....131 K4
Aquatics Centre
OLYMPICPK E20 ....76 A6
Aragon Primary School
MRDN SM4 ....161 H6
Arcadia Shopping Centre
EA W5 ....85 K6
Arcadia University
BAY/PAD W2 ....8 C7
Archbishop Sumners CE
Primary School
LBTH SE11 ....18 B6

Archbishop Tenisons CE School
CROY/NA CR0 ....178 B2
Archbishop Tenison's School
VX/NE SW8 ....110 A5
Archdale Business Centre
RYLN/HDSTN HA2 ....66 C1
Archdeacon Cambridge's CE
Primary School
WHTN TW2 ....142 E1
Arches Business Centre
NWDGN UB2 ....102 E1
Arches Leisure Centre
GNWCH SE10 ....113 G5
Archgate Business Centre
NFNCH/WDSPK N12 ....39 G2
Architectural Association
School of Architecture
RSQ WC1B 11 G3
Archway ⊖
ARCH N19 ....72 C1
Archway Business Centre
ARCH N19 ....72 D2
Archway Leisure Centre
ARCH N19 ....72 C1
Arena ⊖
SNWD SE25 ....165 K4
Arena Estate
FSBYPK N4 ....55 H5
Argent Centre
Industrial Estate
HYS/HAR UB3 ....101 K4
Argyle Primary School
STPAN WC1H 5 K8
Ark Academy
WBLY HA9 ....68 C1
Ark Atwood Primary Academy
HOL/ALD WC2B 11 L4
Arkley Golf Club
BAR EN5 ....25 H4
Arklow Trading Estate
NWCR SE14 ....112 B5
Armourers & Braziers' Hall
LOTH EC2R 13 G3
Arndale Health Centre
WAND/EARL SW18 ....127 K5
Arnhem Wharf
Primary School
POP/IOD E14 ....112 C2
Arnold House School
STJWD NW8 ....3 D1
Arnos ⊖
FBAR/BDGN N11 ....40 C3
Arnos Pool
FBAR/BDGN N11 ....40 C3
Arrivals
HTHAIR TW6 ....120 C2
Arsenal ⊖
HBRY N5 ....73 G2
Arsenal FC (Emirates Stadium)
HOLWY N7 ....73 G3
Artsdepot
NFNCH/WDSPK N12 ....39 G4
The Arts Educational School
CHSWK W4 ....106 B3
Arts Theatre
LSQ/SEVD WC2H 11 H6
Ashbourne College
KENS W8 ....14 C1
Ashburnham Primary School
WBPTN SW10 ....108 C6
Ashby Mill
BRXS/STRHM SW2 ....129 K5
Ashby Mill School
CLAP SW4 ....129 K4
Ashcroft
Technology Academy
PUT/ROE SW15 ....127 J4
Ashfield Junior School
BUSH WD23 ....22 B6
Ashford Industrial Estate
ASHF TW15 ....140 A3
Ashford Sports Club
STWL/WRAY TW19 ....120 C7
Ashgrove College
WALTH E17 ....57 J2
Ashgrove School
BMLY BR1 ....168 A1
Ashgrove Trading Estate
BMLY BR1 ....152 B5
Ashleigh Commercial Estate
CHARL SE7 ....114 B3
Ashmead Primary School
BROCKY SE4 ....132 D1
Ashmole Academy
STHGT/OAK N14 ....28 C7
Ashmole Centre
STHGT/OAK N14 ....28 C7
Ashmole Primary School
VX/NE SW8 ....110 A5
Ashmount Primary School
ARCH N19 ....54 D6
Ashton House School
ISLW TW7 ....103 J1
Ashton Playing Fields Track
WFD IG8 ....45 J3
Aspen House School
LBTH SE11 ....110 C5
Aspen House Secondary &
Primary School
BRXS/STRHM SW2 ....129 K7
Asquith Court School
HPTN TW12 ....142 B7
KTN/HRWW/WS HA3 ....49 H5
Asquith School
PEND EN3 ....30 E3
Associated Newspapers Offices
BERM/RHTH SE16 ....112 A1
Assunah School
TOTM N17 ....56 B1
Aston Clinic
NWMAL KT3 ....160 B3
Aston House School
EA W5 ....85 K5
Asylum Medical Centre
CEND/HSY/T N8 ....55 C2
Athelney Primary School
CAT SE6 ....151 J2
Athelstan House School
HPTN TW12 ....142 A7
Athenaeum Hotel
MYFR/PICC W1J 10 C9
Athena Medical Centre
CLPT E5 ....74 E3
Atherton Leisure Centre
SRTFD E15 ....76 D5
Athletes Village
OLYMPICPK E20 ....76 A4
Athlone House Hospital
HGT N6 ....53 K7
Athlon Industrial Estate
ALP/SUD HA0 ....85 K1
Atkinson Morley Hospital
RYNPK SW20 ....145 K3

Atlantic House
(Richmond American
International University)
KENS W8 ....14 E3
Atlas Business Centre
CRICK NW2 ....69 K1
Atlas Transport Estate
BTSEA SW11 ....128 B1
Attlee Youth &
Community Centre
WCHPL E1 ....13 M3
Auriol Junior School
HOR/WEW KT19 ....173 H3
Australia House
HOL/ALD WC2B 11 M5
Avenue House Museum
FNCH N3 ....52 D1
Avenue House School
WEA W13 ....85 H5
Avenue Industrial Estate
CHING E4 ....43 H5
Avenue
Pre-Preparatory School
HGT N6 ....54 B6
Avenue Primary School
MNPK E12 ....77 J3
Avenue Road ⊖
BECK BR3 ....166 A1
Avery Hill Park
ELTH/MOT SE9 ....135 H5
Avondale Park Primary School
NTGHL W11 ....88 B6
Avon House School
WFD IG8 ....44 E3
Avon Trading Estate
WKENS W14 ....107 J3
Ayesha Community School
HDN NW4 ....51 J5
The Aylesham Centre
PECK SE15 ....111 H7
Aylward Academy
UED N18 ....41 K3
Aylward Primary School
STAN HA7 ....35 K4
Azhar Academy
FSTGT E7 ....76 E5
BAA Heathrow Visitor Centre
HTHAIR TW6 ....100 E7
Babington House School
CHST BR7 ....153 K5
BackCare Clinic
WPK KT4 ....160 D7
Bacon's College
BERM/RHTH SE16 ....93 G7
Baden Powell House
SKENS SW7 ....14 F5
Baglioni Hotel
KENS W8 ....14 E2
Bakers Hall
MON EC3R 13 K7
Baker Street ⊖
CAMTN NW1 ....9 M1
Balaam Leisure Centre
PLSTW E13 ....94 E3
Bales College
NKENS W10 ....88 B2
Balfour Business Centre
NWDGN UB2 ....102 C2
Balgowan Primary School
BECK BR3 ....166 B1
Balham ⊖
BAL SW12 ....129 G7
Balham Girls Preparatory
Secondary School
TOOT SW17 ....147 K2
Balham Health Centre
BAL SW12 ....148 B1
Balham Leisure Centre
TOOT SW17 ....148 A1
Balmoral Trading Estate
BARK IG11 ....97 F3
Baltic Exchange
HDTCH EC3A 13 K4
WFD IG8 ....44 E2
Bandon Hill Cemetery
WLGTN SM6 ....176 D4
Bandon Hill Primary School
WLGTN SM6 ....176 D5
Bangabandhu Primary School
BETH E2 ....92 E2
Bank ⊖
LOTH EC2R 13 G5
Bank of England Extension
CITYW EC2V 12 E5
Bank of England (& Museum)
LOTH EC2R 13 G5
Bankside Gallery
STHWK SE1 ....12 D7
Bankside Jetty
STHWK SE1 ....12 E7
Bankside Park Industrial Estate
BARK IG11 ....97 G2
Bannister Stadium
KTN/HRWW/WS HA3 ....34 C5
Bannockburn Primary School
WOOL/PLUM SE18 ....116 A3
The Banqueting
House, Whitehall
WHALL SW1A 11 J9
Barbara Speake Theatre School
ACT W3 ....87 G6
Barber Surgeons' Hall
BARB EC2Y 12 F3
Barbican ⊖
FARR EC1M 12 D2
Barbican Cinema
BARB EC2Y 12 E2
Barbican Exhibition Halls
BARB EC2Y 12 F2
The Barbican
BARB EC2Y 12 E2
Barbican Theatre
BARB EC2Y 12 E2
Barclay Primary School
LEY E10 ....58 B5
Barham Primary School
ALP/SUD HA0 ....67 J5
Baring Primary School
LEE/GVPK SE12 ....133 K6
Baring Road Medical Centre
BMLY BR1 ....152 E1
Barking ⇌⊖
BARK IG11 ....78 C6
Barking Abbey Comprehensive
School (Lower)
IL IG1 ....78 D4
Barking Abbey Comprehensive
School (Upper)
BARK IG11 ....79 F1
Barking Abbey Industrial Estate
BARK IG11 ....78 B7

Barking Abbey Leisure Centre
BARK IG11 .... 79 G5
Barking Abbey School
BARK IG11 .... 79 F5
Barking & Dagenham College
ROMW/RG RM7 .... 81 F1
Barking FC
BCTR RM8 .... 79 H4
Barking Hospital
BARK IG11 .... 79 F6
Barking Industrial Park
BARK IG11 .... 79 F7
Barking RUFC
DAGW RM9 .... 79 K7
Barkingside
BARK/HLT IG6 .... 60 D3
Barkingside Cemetery
BARK/HLT IG6 .... 60 D3
Barkingside FC
BARK/HLT IG6 .... 60 D3
Barlby Primary School
NKENS W10 .... 88 B3
Barley Lane Primary School
GDMY/SEVK IG3 .... 61 G6
Barnabas Medical Centre
NTHLT UB5 .... 66 C5
Barn Croft Primary School
WALTH E17 .... 57 G5
Barnehurst
BXLYHN DA7 .... 137 K1
Barnehurst Primary School
ERITH DA8 .... 117 K7
Barnehurst Public Golf Club
BXLYHN DA7 .... 138 A2
Barn Elms Athletics Track
BARN SW13 .... 126 E1
Barn Elms Sports Centre
BARN SW13 .... 107 F7
Barn Elms Water Sports Centre
PUT/ROE SW15 .... 127 F1
Barnes
BARN SW13 .... 126 D2
Barnes Bridge
BARN SW13 .... 126 B1
Barnes Hospital
MORT/ESHN SW14 .... 126 B2
Barnes Primary School
BARN SW13 .... 126 B2
Barnes Sports Club
BARN SW15 .... 106 C7
Barnet College
BAR EN5 .... 26 D3
CDALE/KGS NW9 .... 37 H7
EBAR EN4 .... 27 K7
FBAR/BDGN N11 .... 39 J2
NFNCH/WDSPK N12 .... 39 G4
Barnet Copthall Pool
HDN NW4 .... 37 K6
Barnet Copthall Stadium
HDN NW4 .... 38 A7
Barnet County Court
FNCH N3 .... 38 E7
Barnet FC (Underhill)
BAR EN5 .... 26 E4
Barnet General Hospital
BAR EN5 .... 26 B3
Barnet Health Centre
BAR EN5 .... 26 E4
Barnet Hospital Chest Clinic
BAR EN5 .... 26 B3
Barnet Magistrates Court
BAR EN5 .... 26 D3
Barnet Museum
BAR EN5 .... 26 C3
Barnet Trading Estate
BAR EN5 .... 26 D2
Barnfield Primary School
EDGW HA8 .... 36 E7
Barnhill Community High School
YEAD UB4 .... 83 F2
Barn Hotel
RSLP HA4 .... 64 C1
Barnsbury Complex
IS N1 .... 6 A1
Barnsbury School for Girls
IS N1 .... 73 G5
Barons Court
HMSMTH W6 .... 107 G4
Barons Court Theatre
WKENS W14 .... 107 H4
Barratt Industrial Park
BOW E3 .... 94 A3
Barrett Industrial Park
STHL UB1 .... 84 A7
Barrett Way Industrial Estate
RYLN/HDSTN HA2 .... 48 D2
Barrington Primary School
WELL DA16 .... 136 E1
Barrow Hedges Primary School
CAR SM5 .... 175 J6
Barrow Hill Junior School
STJWD NW8 .... 3 J6
Barton House Health Centre
STNW/STAM N16 .... 73 K2
Barwell Business Park
CHSGTN KT9 .... 171 K6
Basketball Arena
OLYMPICPK E20 .... 75 K4
Bassett House School
NKENS W10 .... 88 B5
Baston House School
HAYES BR2 .... 181 F1
Bath Factory Estate
HNHL SE24 .... 130 D5
Battersea Arts Centre (BAC)
BTSEA SW11 .... 128 C4
Battersea Business Centre
BTSEA SW11 .... 129 F2
Battersea Dogs' Home
VX/NE SW8 .... 109 G6
Battersea Park
BTSEA SW11 .... 109 G6
Battersea Park School
BTSEA SW11 .... 108 E7
Battersea Power Station (disused)
VX/NE SW8 .... 109 G5
Battersea Sports Centre
BTSEA SW11 .... 128 C2
Battersea Tutorial College
TOOT SW17 .... 148 A1
Bayswater
BAY/PAD W2 .... 8 C6
BBC Broadcasting House
REGST W1B 10 D3
BBC Media Village
SHB W12 .... 88 A6
BBC Studios
MV/WKIL W9 .... 2 C9
BBC Television Centre
SHB W12 .... 88 A6
BBC Worldwide
SHB W12 .... 88 A5

Beal High School
REDBR IG4 .... 59 J2
Beam Primary School
DAGE RM10 .... 98 E1
Beatrice Tate School
BETH E2 .... 92 D2
Beatrix Potter Primary School
WAND/EARL SW18 .... 128 B7
Beauclerc Infant School
SUN TW16 .... 156 B2
The Beaufort Hotel
CHEL SW3 .... 15 L4
Beaumont Primary School
LEY E10 .... 57 K6
Beaver College
BAY/PAD W2 .... 8 C7
The Beavers Community Primary School
HSLWW TW4 .... 122 B2
Beaverwood School for Girls
CHST BR7 .... 154 E5
Beckenham Business Centre
BECK BR3 .... 151 G5
Beckenham CC
BECK BR3 .... 151 K6
Beckenham Crematorium
BECK BR3 .... 165 K2
Beckenham Hill
CAT SE6 .... 152 A4
Beckenham Hospital
BECK BR3 .... 166 C1
Beckenham Junction
BECK BR3 .... 151 J7
Beckenham Leisure Centre
BECK BR3 .... 151 G7
Beckenham Road
BECK BR3 .... 151 F7
Beckenham RFC
BECK BR3 .... 166 B3
Beckenham School of Art
BECK BR3 .... 166 B4
Beckenham Theatre Centre
BECK BR3 .... 166 E1
Beckenham Town FC
BECK BR3 .... 166 D4
Becket Sports Centre
DART DA1 .... 139 F5
Beckford Primary School
KIL/WHAMP NW6 .... 70 D4
Beckmead School
BECK BR3 .... 166 D7
The Beck Theatre
HYS/HAR UB3 .... 82 D5
Beckton
EHAM E6 .... 96 A4
Beckton Park
EHAM E6 .... 95 K6
Beckton Ski Centre
EHAM E6 .... 96 A3
Beckton Triangle Retail Park
EHAM E6 .... 96 B2
Becontree
DAGW RM9 .... 79 J5
Becontree Day Hospital
BCTR RM8 .... 80 A1
Becontree Primary School
BCTR RM8 .... 79 H2
Bective House Clinic
PUT/ROE SW15 .... 127 J3
Beddington Infant School
WLGTN SM6 .... 176 C2
Beddington Lane
CROY/NA CR0 .... 163 H5
Beddington Medical Centre
CROY/NA CR0 .... 176 E3
Beddington Park Primary School
CROY/NA CR0 .... 176 D2
Beddington Trading Estate
CROY/NA CR0 .... 163 K7
Bedelsford School
KUT/HW KT1 .... 159 F2
Bedfont Cemetery
EBED/NFELT TW14 .... 121 F7
Bedfont Health Clinic
EBED/NFELT TW14 .... 121 H6
Bedfont Industrial Park
ASHF TW15 .... 140 B2
Bedfont Lakes Country Park
EBED/NFELT TW14 .... 140 A1
Bedfont Lakes Office Park
EBED/NFELT TW14 .... 121 F7
Bedfont Primary School
EBED/NFELT TW14 .... 121 H5
Bedford Hotel
RSQ WC1B 11 J2
Bedonwell Clinic
ABYW SE2 .... 117 F5
Bedonwell Medical Centre
BELV DA17 .... 117 G4
Bedonwell Primary School
BXLYHN DA7 .... 117 F5
Beecholme Primary School
MTCM CR4 .... 148 B7
Beechwood School
STRHM/NOR SW16 .... 148 E2
Beehive Preparatory School
REDBR IG4 .... 59 K3
The Beehive School
ARCH N19 .... 54 D6
Beis Chinuch Lebonos Girls School
FSBYPK N4 .... 55 J6
Beis Malka Girls School
STNW/STAM N16 .... 56 B7
Beis Rochel d'Satmar Girls School
STNW/STAM N16 .... 56 A6
Beis Trana Girls School
STNW/STAM N16 .... 56 C7
Beis Yaakov Primary School
CDALE/KGS NW9 .... 51 F2
Belgrave Walk
MTCM CR4 .... 162 C3
Bellamy's Wharf
BERM/RHTH SE16 .... 93 F7
Bellenden Primary School
PECK SE15 .... 131 H2
Bellenden Road Business Centre
PECK SE15 .... 131 G1
Bellenden Road Retail Park
PECK SE15 .... 111 G7
Bellerbys College
DEPT SE8 .... 112 E5
Belleville Primary School
BTSEA SW11 .... 128 E4
Belle Vue Cinema
WLSDN NW10 .... 69 K6
Bell Industrial Estate
CHSWK W4 .... 105 K3
Bellingham
CAT SE6 .... 151 K2

Bellingham Trading Estate
CAT SE6 .... 151 K2
Belmont Bowling Club
STRHM/NOR SW16 .... 148 E2
Belmont Infant School
TOTM N17 .... 55 J2
Belmont Mill Hill Preparatory School
MLHL NW7 .... 37 J2
Belmont Park School
LEY E10 .... 58 A5
Belmont Primary School
CHSWK W4 .... 106 A3
ERITH DA8 .... 117 H6
Belmont School
KTN/HRWW/WS HA3 .... 49 F1
Belmore Primary School
YEAD UB4 .... 83 F2
Belsize Park
HAMP NW3 .... 71 J4
Belvedere
BELV DA17 .... 117 J2
Belvedere Day Hospital
WLSDN NW10 .... 69 J7
Belvedere Industrial Estate
BELV DA17 .... 99 F7
Belvedere Link Business Park
ERITH DA8 .... 117 K2
Belvedere Primary School
BELV DA17 .... 117 J3
Belvue Business Centre
NTHLT UB5 .... 66 B6
Belvue School
NTHLT UB5 .... 66 A7
Benedict House Preparatory School
BFN/LL DA15 .... 155 F3
Benedict Primary School
MTCM CR4 .... 162 C2
Benjamin Franklin House
CHCR WC2N 11 J8
Ben Jonson Primary School
WCHPL E1 .... 93 G3
Bensham Manor School
THHTH CR7 .... 164 D4
Benson Primary School
CROY/NA CR0 .... 179 G2
The Bentall Centre
KUT/HW KT1 .... 158 E1
Benthal Primary School
STNW/STAM N16 .... 74 C2
The Bentley Hotel
SKENS SW7 .... 14 E5
Bentley Wood Girls School
STAN HA7 .... 35 K1
Bentworth Primary School
SHB W12 .... 87 K5
Ben Uri Gallery, The London Jewish Museum of Art
STJWD NW8 .... 2 D4
Beormund School
STHWK SE1 .... 19 G2
Beresford Square Outdoor Market
WOOL/PLUM SE18 .... 115 G3
Berger Primary School
HOM E9 .... 75 F5
The Berkeley Hotel
KTBR SW1X 16 A1
Berkeley Primary School
HEST TW5 .... 102 C5
Berlitz School of Languages
HHOL WC1V 11 M3
Bermondsey
BERM/RHTH SE16 .... 111 H2
Bermondsey Town Hall
STHWK SE1 .... 19 L4
Bermondsey Trading Estate
BERM/RHTH SE16 .... 111 K4
Berrylands
BRYLDS KT5 .... 159 J3
Berrymede Infant School
ACT W3 .... 105 J1
Berrymede Junior School
ACT W3 .... 105 J1
Bertram House School
TOOT SW17 .... 148 A1
Bessemer Grange J & I School
HNHL SE24 .... 130 E4
Bessemer Park Industrial Estate
BRXN/ST SW9 .... 130 C3
Best Western Bromley Court Hotel
BMLY BR1 .... 152 C5
Best Western Cumberland Hotel
HRW HA1 .... 49 F5
Best Western Lodge Hotel
PUT/ROE SW15 .... 127 J4
Best Western Mostyn Hotel
MBLAR W1H 9 M5
Best Western Phoenix Hotel
BAY/PAD W2 .... 8 C6
Best Western White House Hotel
WATW WD18 .... 20 E3
Beth Jacob Grammar School
HDN NW4 .... 52 B3
Bethlem Royal Hospital
BECK BR3 .... 166 D6
Bethnal Green
BETH E2 .... 92 E2
WCHPL E1 .... 92 D3
Bethnal Green Technology College
BETH E2 .... 7 M8
Beths Grammar School for Boys
BXLY DA5 .... 137 H5
The Betty Layward School
STNW/STAM N16 .... 73 K2
Beulah Infant School
THHTH CR7 .... 164 D1
Beverley School
NWMAL KT3 .... 160 D4
Beverley Trading Estate
MRDN SM4 .... 161 G6
Bevington Primary School
NKENS W10 .... 88 C4
Bexley
BXLY DA5 .... 137 H7
Bexley College
BELV DA17 .... 117 K3
Bexley CC
BXLY DA5 .... 137 H7
Bexley Grammar School
WELL DA16 .... 136 C3
Bexleyheath
BXLYHN DA7 .... 137 F1
Bexleyheath Cemetery
BXLYHN DA7 .... 137 G2
Bexleyheath Centre
BXLYHS DA6 .... 137 F3
Bexleyheath Golf Club
BXLYHS DA6 .... 137 F4

Bexleyheath Marriott Hotel
BXLYHS DA6 .... 137 J3
Bexleyheath School
BXLYHN DA7 .... 137 G2
Bexleyheath Superbowl
BXLYHS DA6 .... 137 G3
Bexley RFC
BXLY DA5 .... 137 H6
BFI
STHWK SE1 .... 11 M8
BFI London IMAX Cinema
STHWK SE1 .... 11 M9
Bickenhall College of Computing
CAMTN NW1 .... 9 K7
Bickerly School of Dance
STNW/STAM N16 .... 55 K6
Bickley
BMLY BR1 .... 168 C2
Bickley Park CC
BMLY BR1 .... 168 C1
Bickley Park Pre-Preparatory School
BMLY BR1 .... 168 D2
Bickley Park Preparatory School
BMLY BR1 .... 168 C2
Big Ben
WHALL SW1A 17 K2
Bigland Green Primary School
WCHPL E1 .... 92 D5
Billingsgate Fish Market
POP/IOD E14 .... 93 K7
Bingham Hotel
TWK TW1 .... 124 E5
Birchmere Business Park
THMD SE28 .... 116 B1
Bird College
SCUP DA14 .... 155 G2
Birkbeck
BECK BR3 .... 165 K1
Birkbeck College
GWRST WC1E 11 H1
RSQ WC1B 11 H3
Birkbeck Primary School
SCUP DA14 .... 155 H7
Birkenhall College of Computing
MBLAR W1H 9 M2
Bishop Challoner Catholic Collegiate School
WCHPL E1 .... 92 E6
Bishop Challoner Girls School
WCHPL E1 .... 92 C6
Bishop Challoner School
HAYES BR2 .... 167 G1
Bishop Douglass RC School
EFNCH N2 .... 53 G1
Bishop Gilpin Primary School
WIM/MER SW19 .... 146 D4
Bishop John Robinson CE Primary School
THMD SE28 .... 97 J7
Bishop Justus CE (Secondary) School
HAYES BR2 .... 168 D6
Bishop Perrin CE Primary School
WHTN TW2 .... 123 G6
Bishop Ramsey CE School
RSLP HA4 .... 46 D6
Bishopsgate Institute
LVPST EC2M 13 K3
Bishop Thomas Grant School
STRHM/NOR SW16 .... 149 F4
Bishop Winnington Ingram CE Primary School
RSLP HA4 .... 46 B6
Bittacy Business Centre
MLHL NW7 .... 38 C5
Blackburn Trading Estate
STWL/WRAY TW19 .... 120 C5
Blackfen Medical Centre
BFN/LL DA15 .... 136 A4
Blackfen School for Girls
BFN/LL DA15 .... 136 C5
Blackfriars
BLKFR EC4V 12 D5
Blackfriars Millennium Pier
EMB EC4Y 12 D6
Blackfriars Pier
BLKFR EC4V 12 D7
Blackheath
BKHTH/KID SE3 .... 133 J7
Blackheath Bluecoat School
BKHTH/KID SE3 .... 114 A6
Blackheath Business Estate
GNWCH SE10 .... 113 F7
The Blackheath Clinic
BKHTH/KID SE3 .... 133 K3
Blackheath High School GDST
BKHTH/KID SE3 .... 133 J1
Blackheath High Senior School
BKHTH/KID SE3 .... 113 K6
Blackheath Hospital
BKHTH/KID SE3 .... 133 J2
Blackheath Preparatory School
BKHTH/KID SE3 .... 113 K7
Blackheath RFC (The Rectory Field)
BKHTH/KID SE3 .... 114 A6
Blackhorse
CROY/NA CR0 .... 165 H6
Blackhorse Road
WALTH E17 .... 57 F3
Blackwall
POP/IOD E14 .... 94 A6
Blackwall Trading Estate
POP/IOD E14 .... 94 B4
Blair Peach Primary School
STHL UB1 .... 83 H7
Blake College
GTPST W1W 10 E2
Blanche Nevile School
HGT N6 .... 53 K5
MUSWH N10 .... 54 A2
Blenheim Business Centre
MTCM CR4 .... 147 K7
Blenheim Shopping Centre
PGE/AN SE20 .... 150 E6
Blessed Dominic RC Primary School
CDALE/KGS NW9 .... 51 G1
Blessed Sacrament RC Primary School
IS N1 .... 5 K4
Bloo School
ESH/CLAY KT10 .... 170 A4
Bloomfield Clinic Guys
STHWK SE1 .... 19 H1
Bloomsbury International
NOXST/BSQ WC1A 11 K3
Bloomsbury Theatre
GWRST WC1E 5 G9

Blossom House School
RYNPK SW20 .... 146 A6
Blossoms Inn Medical Centre
BLKFR EC4V 12 F6
Blue Gate Fields Infant School
WCHPL E1 .... 92 E6
The Blue School
ISLW TW7 .... 124 B2
Blyth's Wharf
POP/IOD E14 .... 93 G6
BMI Medical Centre
CAVSQ/HST W1G 10 B3
BMX Track
OLYMPICPK E20 .... 75 K4
Bnois Jerusalem Girls School
STNW/STAM N16 .... 55 K6
Bnos Beis Yaakov Primary School
CDALE/KGS NW9 .... 50 E4
The Bob Hope Theatre
ELTH/MOT SE9 .... 134 E5
Bobov Foundation School
STNW/STAM N16 .... 56 B6
The Bobov Foundation School for Girls
CLPT E5 .... 56 B6
Bodywise Natural Health Centre
BETH E2 .... 92 E2
Boleyn Cinema
EHAM E6 .... 95 H1
Bolingbroke Hospital
BTSEA SW11 .... 128 D4
Bolingbroke Primary School
BTSEA SW11 .... 108 C7
Bond First School
MTCM CR4 .... 162 E1
Bond Primary School
MTCM CR4 .... 162 E1
Bond Street
OXSTW W1C 10 B5
Bonner Primary School
BETH E2 .... 92 E2
Bonneville Primary School
CLAP SW4 .... 129 H5
Bonus Pastor Catholic College
BMLY BR1 .... 152 B3
Boomes Industrial Estate
RAIN RM13 .... 99 H3
Booster Cushion Theatre
WDGN N22 .... 55 F1
Borehamwood FC
BORE WD6 .... 24 D1
Borehamwood Industrial Park
BORE WD6 .... 25 C1
Borough
STHWK SE1 .... 18 F2
Borough Cemetery
HSLWW TW4 .... 123 F1
Borough Market
STHWK SE1 .... 13 G8
Borthwick Wharf
DEPT SE8 .... 112 D4
Boston Business Park
HNWL W7 .... 103 K2
Boston Manor
HNWL W7 .... 104 B3
Botwell House Catholic Primary School
HYS/HAR UB3 .... 101 J1
Boulevard 25 Retail Park
BORE WD6 .... 24 C2
Boundary Business Park
MTCM CR4 .... 162 C1
Bounds Green
FBAR/BDGN N11 .... 40 D6
Bounds Green Health Centre
FBAR/BDGN N11 .... 40 D6
Bounds Green Industrial Estate
FBAR/BDGN N11 .... 40 B5
Bounds Green Infant School
FBAR/BDGN N11 .... 40 D6
Bourne CP School
RSLP HA4 .... 65 G4
Bourne Hall Health Centre
EW KT17 .... 173 H5
Bournehall J & I School
BUSH WD23 .... 22 A4
Bourne Hall Museum
EW KT17 .... 173 H7
Bourne Road Industrial Park
DART DA1 .... 138 C4
Bourneside Sports Club
STHGT/OAK N14 .... 28 E7
Bousfield Primary School
ECT SW5 .... 14 E7
Boutcher CE Primary School
STHWK SE1 .... 19 L4
Bowater House
SKENS SW7 .... 15 L2
Bow Church
BOW E3 .... 93 J2
Bow County Court
SRTFD E15 .... 76 C5
Bowden House Clinic
HRW HA1 .... 66 E1
Bowes Park
WDGN N22 .... 40 E6
Bowes Primary School
FBAR/BDGN N11 .... 40 D4
Bowes Road Clinic
FBAR/BDGN N11 .... 40 C4
Bow Junior & Youth Centre
BOW E3 .... 93 H4
Bowman Trading Estate
CDALE/KGS NW9 .... 50 C2
Bow Road
BOW E3 .... 93 J2
Bow Secondary School
BOW E3 .... 93 J1
Bow Triangle Business Centre
BOW E3 .... 93 J3
Boxgrove Primary School
ABYW SE2 .... 116 D2
BPP Law School
HHOL WC1V 11 L3
Brackenbury Health Centre
HMSMTH W6 .... 106 E2
Brackenbury Primary School
HMSMTH W6 .... 106 E2
Brady Recreation Centre
WCHPL E1 .... 92 C4
Braincroft Primary School
CRICK NW2 .... 69 J2
Braintree Road Industrial Estate
RSLP HA4 .... 65 G3
Bramah's Tea & Coffee Museum
STHWK SE1 .... 12 F9
Brampton College
HDN NW4 .... 52 A3
Brampton Manor School
EHAM E6 .... 95 H4

Brampton Primary School *BXLYHN* DA7 ... 136 E1
EHAM E6 ... 95 J2
Brandlehow Primary School *PUT/ROE* SW15 ... 127 J3
Branollys Health Centre *PLSTW* E13 ... 94 E3
Breakspear Crematorium *RSLP* HA4 ... 46 A4
Breaside Preparatory School *BMLY* BR1 ... 153 G7
Brecknock Primary School *HOLWY* N7 ... 72 D5
Bredinghurst School *PECK* SE15 ... 131 K3
Brent Adult College *WLSDN* NW10 ... 69 F7
Brent Arts Council *CRICK* NW2 ... 69 J2
Brent Child & Family Clinic *WLSDN* NW10 ... 69 H4
Brent Cross ⊖ *GLDGN* NW11 ... 52 B6
Brent Cross Shopping Centre *HDN* NW4 ... 52 A6
Brentfield Medical Centre *WLSDN* NW10 ... 69 F5
Brentfield Primary School *WLSDN* NW10 ... 69 F5
Brentford ≷ *BTFD* TW8 ... 104 E5
Brentford Business Centre *BTFD* TW8 ... 104 D6
Brentford County Court *BTFD* TW8 ... 104 E6
Brentford FC (Griffin Park) *BTFD* TW8 ... 104 E5
Brentford Fountain Leisure Centre *BTFD* TW8 ... 105 G4
Brentford Health Centre *BTFD* TW8 ... 104 D5
Brentford School for Girls *BTFD* TW8 ... 104 E5
Brent Knoll School *FSTH* SE23 ... 151 F2
Brent Magistrates Court House *WLSDN* NW10 ... 69 G5
Brent Park Industrial Estate *NWDGN* UB2 ... 102 A2
Brentside First School *HNWL* W7 ... 84 E4
Brentside High School *HNWL* W7 ... 84 E3
Brentside Primary School *HNWL* W7 ... 84 E3
Brent Trading Estate *WLSDN* NW10 ... 69 G4
Brentwaters Business Park *BTFD* TW8 ... 104 D6
Brettenham Primary School *ED* N9 ... 42 C3
Brewers' Hall *CITYW* EC2V ... 12 F3
Brewery Industrial Estate *IS* N1 ... 6 E6
Brewery Mews Business Centre *ISLW* TW7 ... 124 A2
The Brewery *ROMW/RG* RM7 ... 63 G5
Brick Lane Music Hall *CAN/RD* E16 ... 95 H7
Brick Lane Music House *WCHPL* E1 ... 13 M1
Bricklayer Arms Industrial Estate *STHWK* SE1 ... 19 L6
The Bridewell Theatre *EMB* EC4Y ... 12 C5
The Bridge Academy *BETH* E2 ... 7 L4
The Bridge Business Centre *NWDGN* UB2 ... 103 F1
Bridge Lane Theatre *BTSEA* SW11 ... 108 D7
The Bridge Leisure Centre *SYD* SE26 ... 151 H4
Bridge Park Business & Leisure Centre *WLSDN* NW10 ... 68 D6
The Bridge School *ARCH* N19 ... 72 C1
HOLWY N7 ... 72 D5
Brigham Young University *BAY/PAD* W2 ... 8 C7
Bright Sparks Montessori School *WKENS* W14 ... 107 G1
Brigstock Medical Centre *THHTH* CR7 ... 164 C4
Brimsdown ≷ *PEND* EN3 ... 31 G1
Brimsdown Industrial Estate *PEND* EN3 ... 30 E1
Brimsdown Primary School *PEND* EN3 ... 31 F2
Brindishe Green School *LEW* SE13 ... 133 G5
Brindishe Lee School *LEE/GVPK* SE12 ... 133 J4
Britain & London Visitor Centre *STJS* SW1Y ... 11 G8
Britannia Business Centre *CRICK* NW2 ... 70 B3
Britannia College of Excellence *IS* N1 ... 7 H8
Britannia Leisure Centre *IS* N1 ... 7 H4
Britannia Sports Ground *WALTH* E17 ... 43 J6
Britannia Village Primary School *CAN/RD* E16 ... 95 F7
British Airways Museum *HTHAIR* TW6 ... 121 H3
The British American Drama Academy *CAMTN* NW1 ... 4 B4
British Cartoon Centre *BMSBY* WC1N ... 11 K1
British College of Osteopathy *HAMP* NW3 ... 71 G5
British Dental Association *CAVSO/HST* W1G ... 10 C3
The British Hernia Centre *HDN* NW4 ... 51 K4
British Library *CAMTN* NW1 ... 5 H7
British Library Newspaper Library *CDALE/KGS* NW9 ... 51 G2
British Medical Association *STPAN* WC1H ... 5 H9

British Museum *RSQ* WC1B ... 11 J3
British Telecom Tower *GTPST* W1W ... 10 E2
The BRIT School *SNWD* SE25 ... 164 E5
Brittons School Technology College *RAIN* RM13 ... 81 H6
Brixton ≷ ⊖ *BRXN/ST* SW9 ... 130 B3
Brixton Academy *BRXN/ST* SW9 ... 130 B2
Brixton Recreation Centre *BRXN/ST* SW9 ... 130 B2
Broadfields Primary School *EDGW* HA8 ... 36 C1
Broadgate *LVPST* EC2M ... 13 J3
Broadgate Ice Arena *LVPST* EC2M ... 13 J3
Broadhurst School *KIL/WHAMP* NW6 ... 2 E1
Broadmead Primary School *CROY/NA* CR0 ... 164 C6
Broadreach College *THMD* SE28 ... 116 A2
Broadwalk Shopping Centre *EDGW* HA8 ... 36 C5
Broadwater Farm Primary School *TOTM* N17 ... 55 K1
Broadwater Primary School *TOOT* SW17 ... 147 H3
Broadway Clinic *EDGW* HA8 ... 36 D7
Broadway Retail Park *CRICK* NW2 ... 70 B3
Broadway Shopping Centre *BXLYHS* DA6 ... 137 H3
HMSMTH W6 ... 107 F4
Broadway Squash & Fitness Centre *HMSMTH* W6 ... 107 G3
Brocklebank Health Centre *WAND/EARL* SW18 ... 128 A6
Brocklebank Industrial Estate *GNWCH* SE10 ... 113 K3
Brockley ⊖ *BROCKY* SE4 ... 132 C2
Brockley Cross Business Centre *BROCKY* SE4 ... 132 B2
Brockley Primary School *BROCKY* SE4 ... 132 C4
Brockwell Lido *HNHL* SE24 ... 130 C5
Bromet Primary School *OXHEY* WD19 ... 21 H6
Bromley by Bow ⊖ *BOW* E3 ... 93 K2
Bromley Cemetery *BMLY* BR1 ... 152 D6
Bromley Civic Centre *BMLY* BR1 ... 168 A1
Bromley College of Further & Higher Education *BMLY* BR1 ... 152 E7
HAYES BR2 ... 168 C5
Bromley County Court *BMLY* BR1 ... 152 E7
Bromley FC *HAYES* BR2 ... 168 A4
Bromley High School GDST *BMLY* BR1 ... 169 F3
Bromley Industrial Centre *BMLY* BR1 ... 168 C2
Bromley Mall Indoor Market *BMLY* BR1 ... 167 K1
Bromley North ≷ *BMLY* BR1 ... 152 E7
Bromley Road Infant School *BECK* BR3 ... 151 K7
Bromley Road Retail Park *CAT* SE6 ... 151 K1
Bromley Ski Centre *STMC/STPC* BR5 ... 155 K7
Bromley South ≷ *BMLY* BR1 ... 168 A2
Bromley Wendover Lawn Tennis Club *HAYES* BR2 ... 168 A3
Brompton Medical Centre *ECT* SW5 ... 14 D7
Brompton Oratory *SKENS* SW7 ... 15 J4
Bromyard Leisure Centre *ACT* W3 ... 87 G7
Brondesbury ⊖ *KIL/WHAMP* NW6 ... 70 D6
Brondesbury College for Boys *KIL/WHAMP* NW6 ... 70 B6
Brondesbury Park ⊖ *KIL/WHAMP* NW6 ... 70 C7
Brook Community Primary School *HACK* E8 ... 74 C4
Brooke Trading Estate *ROM* RM1 ... 63 H6
Brookfield House School *WFD* IG8 ... 44 C5
Brookfield Primary School *CHEAM* SM3 ... 161 H7
HGT N6 ... 72 B1
Brook House FC *YEAD* UB4 ... 82 D2
Brook Industrial Estate *YEAD* UB4 ... 83 H7
Brookland Junior School *GLDGN* NW11 ... 53 F3
Brooklands Primary School *BKHTH/KID* SE3 ... 133 K2
Brook Lane Business Centre *BTFD* TW8 ... 104 E4
Brookmarsh Trading Estate *DEPT* SE8 ... 112 E6
Brookmead Industrial Estate *CROY/NA* CR0 ... 163 H5
Brookside Primary School *YEAD* UB4 ... 83 G2
Broomfield House School *RCH/KEW* TW9 ... 105 J7
Broomfield School *FBAR/BDGN* N11 ... 40 D4
Broomsleigh Business Park *SYD* SE26 ... 151 H4
Broomwood Hall Lower School *BAL* SW12 ... 128 E5
STRHM/NOR SW16 ... 148 D2
Brownlow Medical Centre *FBAR/BDGN* N11 ... 40 E4
Brown's Hotel *MYFR/PICC* W1J ... 10 D7

Bruce Castle Museum *TOTM* N17 ... 42 A7
Bruce Grove ≷ *TOTM* N17 ... 56 B1
Bruce Grove Primary School *TOTM* N17 ... 56 B1
Brunei Gallery *STPAN* WC1H ... 11 J1
Brunel Engine House *BERM/RHTH* SE16 ... 111 K4
Brunel University *GLDGN* NW11 ... 52 B5
ISLW TW7 ... 103 K6
TWK TW1 ... 124 C3
Brunel University (Osterley Campus) Track *ISLW* TW7 ... 103 K6
Brunswick Health Centre *FBAR/BDGN* N11 ... 40 A1
Brunswick Housing & Shopping Centre *BMSBY* WC1N ... 5 K9
Brunswick Industrial Park *FBAR/BDGN* N11 ... 40 B3
Brunswick Medical Centre *BMSBY* WC1N ... 5 J9
Brunswick Park JMI School *STHGT/OAK* N14 ... 28 A7
Brunswick Park Primary School *CMBW* SE5 ... 110 E6
B Six Sixth Form College *CLPT* E5 ... 74 D2
BT Centre *STBT* EC1A ... 12 E4
Buckhurst Hill ⊖ *BKHH* IG9 ... 45 H1
Buckhurst Hill FC *BKHH* IG9 ... 45 J1
Buckingham College Preparatory School *PIN* HA5 ... 47 K6
Buckingham Palace *WHALL* SW1A ... 16 E2
Buckingham Primary School *HPTN* TW12 ... 141 K4
Buckingham Road Cemetery *IL* IG1 ... 78 D1
The Building Centre *GWRST* WC1E ... 11 G1
Building Crafts College *SRTFD* E15 ... 76 B1
Bullers Wood School *CHST* BR7 ... 153 K7
Bullsbridge Industrial Estate *NWDGN* UB2 ... 102 A3
The Bull Theatre *BAR* EN5 ... 26 D3
BUPA Roding Hospital *REDBR* IG4 ... 59 H2
Burbage School *IS* N1 ... 7 J5
Burdett Coutts CE Primary School *WEST* SW1P ... 17 G4
Burgess Business Park *CMBW* SE5 ... 110 E6
Burgess Park Tennis Centre *CMBW* SE5 ... 110 D5
Burlington College Independent Sixth Form *EDGW* HA8 ... 50 B2
Burlington Danes School *SHB* W12 ... 87 K5
Burlington Infant School *NWMAL* KT3 ... 160 C3
Burney Street Clinic *GNWCH* SE10 ... 113 F6
Burnham Trading Estate *DART* DA1 ... 139 G3
Burnhill Business Centre *BECK* BR3 ... 166 D1
Burnley Road Clinic *WLSDN* NW10 ... 69 J4
Burns Hotel *ECT* SW5 ... 14 C6
Burnt Ash Primary School *BMLY* BR1 ... 152 E4
Burnt Oak ⊖ *EDGW* HA8 ... 36 E7
Burnt Oak Junior School *BFN/LL* DA15 ... 136 B7
Burntwood School *TOOT* SW17 ... 147 H1
Bursted Wood Primary School *BXLYHN* DA7 ... 137 J3
Burwell Industrial Estate *LEY* E10 ... 57 G7
Bushey ≷ *OXHEY* WD19 ... 21 H5
Bushey Academy *BUSH* WD23 ... 21 K5
Bushey Golf & Country Club *BUSH* WD23 ... 22 A5
Bushey Grove Leisure Centre *BUSH* WD23 ... 21 K3
Bushey Hall Golf Club *BUSH* WD23 ... 21 J2
Bushey Hall Swimming Pool *BUSH* WD23 ... 21 K4
Bushey Health Centre *BUSH* WD23 ... 21 K5
Bushey Heath Primary School *BUSH* WD23 ... 22 D7
Bushey Jewish Cemetery *BUSH* WD23 ... 22 B2
Bushey Manor Junior School *BUSH* WD23 ... 21 K4
Bushey Meads School *BUSH* WD23 ... 22 C4
Bushey Museum & Art Gallery *BUSH* WD23 ... 22 A5
Bushey & Oxhey Infant School *BUSH* WD23 ... 21 J4
Bush Hill Park ≷ *EN* EN1 ... 30 B5
Bush Hill Park Golf Club *WCHMH* N21 ... 29 J4
Bush Hill Park Medical Centre *EN* EN1 ... 30 B5
Bush Hill Park Primary School *EN* EN1 ... 30 C4
Bush House (BBC) *HOL/ALD* WC2B ... 11 L5
Bush Industrial Estate *ARCH* N19 ... 72 C2
WLSDN NW10 ... 87 F3
The Business Academy Bexley *ERITHM* DA18 ... 117 F1
The Business Centre *CEND/HSY/T* N8 ... 54 E1
The Business Design Centre *IS* N1 ... 6 B4

Business Training & Solutions *CDALE/KGS* NW9 ... 37 H7
Bute House Preparatory School for Girls *HMSMTH* W6 ... 107 F3
Butlers Wharf *STHWK* SE1 ... 13 M9
Butler's Wharf Business Centre *STHWK* SE1 ... 19 M1
Butler's Wharf Pier *STHWK* SE1 ... 13 M9
Butterfly Sports Club *ELTH/MOT* SE9 ... 135 G5
Buxlow Preparatory School *WBLY* HA9 ... 68 A2
Buxton School *WAN* E11 ... 76 D2
Buzzard Creek Industrial Estate *BARK* IG11 ... 97 F4
Byam Shaw School of Art *ARCH* N19 ... 72 C1
Byfleet Industrial Estate *WATW* WD18 ... 20 A7
Bygrove Primary School *POP/IOD* E14 ... 93 K5
Byron Court Primary School *ALP/SUD* HA0 ... 67 J1
Cable Car *CAN/RD* E16 ... 94 D7
Cabot Place *POP/IOD* E14 ... 93 J7
Cadogan Hall *CHEL* SW3 ... 15 M5
The Cadogan Hotel *KTBR* SW1X ... 15 M4
Cadogan Pier *CHEL* SW3 ... 108 D5
Caledonian Market *STHWK* SE1 ... 19 K3
Caledonian Road ⊖ *HOLWY* N7 ... 72 E4
Caledonian Road & Barnsbury ⊖ *HOLWY* N7 ... 5 M1
Cally Pool *IS* N1 ... 5 L3
Calverton Primary School *CAN/RD* E16 ... 95 H5
Cambell Primary School *DAGW* RM9 ... 79 K6
Camberwell Business Centre *CMBW* SE5 ... 110 E6
Camberwell College of Arts *CMBW* SE5 ... 111 F7
Camberwell Leisure Centre *CMBW* SE5 ... 110 E7
Camberwell New Cemetery *PECK* SE15 ... 132 A5
Camberwell Trading Estate *CMBW* SE5 ... 130 C1
Cambodian Embassy *CRICK* NW2 ... 70 A6
Cambridge Heath ≷ *BETH* E2 ... 92 D1
Cambridge Heath Sixth Form *BETH* E2 ... 92 E2
Cambridge Park Bowling & Sports Club *TWK* TW1 ... 124 D5
Cambridge School *HMSMTH* W6 ... 106 E3
Cambridge Theatre *LSQ/SEVD* WC2H ... 11 J5
Camden Arts Centre *HAMP* NW3 ... 71 F4
Camden House Clinic *BKHTH/KID* SE3 ... 133 H1
Camden Junior School *CAR* SM5 ... 175 K3
Camden Market *CAMTN* NW1 ... 4 B2
Camden Mews Day Hospital *CAMTN* NW1 ... 4 F1
Camden People's Theatre *CAMTN* NW1 ... 4 E8
Camden Road ⊖ *CAMTN* NW1 ... 4 E1
Camden School for Girls *KTTN* NW5 ... 72 C5
Camden Theatre *CAMTN* NW1 ... 4 E5
Camden Town ⊖ *CAMTN* NW1 ... 4 D3
Camden Town Hall & St Pancras Library *CAMTN* NW1 ... 5 J7
Camelot Primary School *PECK* SE15 ... 111 J6
Cameron House School *CHEL* SW3 ... 15 H9
Camperdown House *WCHPL* E1 ... 13 M5
Campion House College *ISLW* TW7 ... 103 J6
Campsbourne School *CEND/HSY/T* N8 ... 54 E2
Camrose Primary School *EDGW* HA8 ... 36 B7
Canada House *STJS* SW1Y ... 11 H8
Canada House Business Centre *RSLP* HA4 ... 47 G7
Canada Place *POP/IOD* E14 ... 93 J7
Canada Square *POP/IOD* E14 ... 93 J7
Canada Water ⊖ *BERM/RHTH* SE16 ... 111 K2
Canada Water Retail Park *BERM/RHTH* SE16 ... 112 A2
Canada Wharf Museum *BERM/RHTH* SE16 ... 93 H7
Canal Cafe Theatre *BAY/PAD* W2 ... 8 D2
Canary Riverside *BERM/RHTH* SE16 ... 93 H7
Canary Wharf ⊖ *POP/IOD* E14 ... 93 J7
Canary Wharf Pier *POP/IOD* E14 ... 93 H7
Canberra Primary School *SHB* W12 ... 87 K6
Canbury 2000 Business Park *KUTN/CMB* KT2 ... 144 A7
Canbury Business Centre *KUTN/CMB* KT2 ... 144 A7
Canbury Medical Centre *KUTN/CMB* KT2 ... 144 B7
Canbury School *KUTN/CMB* KT2 ... 144 D5
Cann Hall Primary School *WAN* E11 ... 76 D2
The Canning School *ECT* SW5 ... 14 C5

KENS W8 ... 14 A3
Canning Town ⊖ *POP/IOD* E14 ... 94 C5
Cannizaro House Hotel *WIM/MER* SW19 ... 146 A5
Cannon Hill Clinic *STHGT/OAK* N14 ... 40 E2
Cannon Lane Junior School *PIN* HA5 ... 47 H5
Cannon Sports Club *CANST* EC4R ... 12 F6
Cannon Street ≷ ⊖ *CANST* EC4R ... 13 G7
Cannon Trading Estate *WBLY* HA9 ... 68 D3
Cannon Wharf Business Centre *DEPT* SE8 ... 112 B3
Canon Barnett Primary School *WCHPL* E1 ... 13 M4
Canonbury ≷ ⊖ *IS* N1 ... 73 J3
Canonbury Business Centre *IS* N1 ... 6 F3
Canonbury Primary School *IS* N1 ... 73 H4
Canon Palmer RC High School *IL* IG1 ... 60 E7
Canons High School *EDGW* HA8 ... 50 B1
The Canons Leisure Centre *MTCM* CR4 ... 162 E3
Canons Park ⊖ *EDGW* HA8 ... 36 A6
Canterbury Industrial Estate *NWCR* SE14 ... 112 A5
Cantium Retail Park *STHWK* SE1 ... 111 H5
Capital Business Centre *ALP/SUD* HA0 ... 85 K1
MTCM CR4 ... 162 E4
SAND/SEL CR2 ... 177 K5
Capital City Academy *WLSDN* NW10 ... 69 K7
The Capital Hotel *CHEL* SW3 ... 15 L2
Capital Industrial Estate *BELV* DA17 ... 98 E7
Capital Radio *LSQ/SEVD* WC2H ... 11 H7
Capital Wharf *WAP* E1W ... 92 C7
Capitol Industrial Park *CDALE/KGS* NW9 ... 50 E2
Caplan Estate *MTCM* CR4 ... 148 C7
Cardiff Road Industrial Estate *WATW* WD18 ... 21 F5
Cardinal Pole RC School *HOM* E9 ... 75 G5
Cardinal Pole RC School (Lower) *HOM* E9 ... 75 F6
Cardinal Road Infant School *FELT* TW13 ... 122 A7
The Cardinal Vaughan Memorial *WKENS* W14 ... 107 H1
Cardinal Wiseman RC School (Technology & Art College) *GFD/PVL* UB6 ... 84 C4
Cardwell Primary School *WOOL/PLUM* SE18 ... 114 E3
Carew Manor School *WLGTN* SM6 ... 176 D2
Carlisle Infant School *HPTN* TW12 ... 142 B5
Carlton House *STJS* SW1Y ... 11 G9
The Carlton Mitre Hotel *E/WMO/HCT* KT8 ... 157 K2
Carlton Primary School *KTTN* NW5 ... 72 A4
Carlton Vale Infant School *MV/WKIL* W9 ... 88 D2
Carlyle's House (NT) *CHEL* SW3 ... 108 D5
Carnwath Road Industrial Estate *FUL/PGN* SW6 ... 128 A2
Carpenders Park ⊖ *OXHEY* WD19 ... 33 H2
Carpenders Park Cemetery *OXHEY* WD19 ... 33 K3
Carpenters' Hall *OBST* EC2N ... 13 H3
Carpenters Primary School *SRTFD* E15 ... 76 A7
Carshalton ≷ *CAR* SM5 ... 175 J3
Carshalton AFC *SUT* SM1 ... 175 J2
Carshalton Beeches ≷ *CAR* SM5 ... 175 K5
Carshalton Boys Sports College *CAR* SM5 ... 175 H1
Carshalton College *CAR* SM5 ... 175 K2
Carshalton High School for Girls *CAR* SM5 ... 175 J2
Carshalton War Memorial Hospital *CAR* SM5 ... 175 K4
The Cartoon Museum *RSQ* WC1B ... 11 J3
Caryl Thomas Clinic *HRW* HA1 ... 48 E3
Cass Business School *STLK* EC1Y ... 13 G1
The Cassel Hospital *RCHPK/HAM* TW10 ... 143 K3
Cassidy Medical Centre *FUL/PGN* SW6 ... 107 K6
Castilion Primary School *THMD* SE28 ... 97 J5
Castle Bar Park ≷ *HNWL* W7 ... 85 F4
Castlebar School *HNWL* W7 ... 85 F4
Castlebar Special School *WEA* W13 ... 85 G4
Castlecombe Primary School *ELTH/MOT* SE9 ... 153 J4
Castle Hill Primary School *CROY/NA* CR0 ... 180 A5
Castle Industrial Estate *WALW* SE17 ... 18 E6
Casualty Plus Clinic *BTFD* TW8 ... 104 D4
Caterham High School *CLAY* IG5 ... 59 K1
Catford ≷ *CAT* SE6 ... 132 D6
Catford Bridge ≷ *CAT* SE6 ... 132 D6

Catford Cricket & Sports Club
CAT SE6 .... 132 E7
Catford Cyphers CC
CAT SE6 .... 151 H1
Catford Trading Estate
CAT SE6 .... 151 K1
Catford Wanderers Sports Club
CAT SE6 .... 152 A3
Cathall Leisure Centre
WAN E11 .... 76 B2
Cathedral School of St Saviour & St Mary Overy
STHWK SE1 .... 18 F1
Cator Park School for Girls
BECK BR3 .... 151 G6
Cavendish College
FITZ W1T 11 G2
Cavendish Hotel
STJS SW1Y 10 F8
Cavendish Primary School
CHSWK W4 .... 106 B6
Cavendish School
BERM/RHTH SE16 .... 111 K3
The Cavendish School
CAMTN NW1 .... 4 C3
Cavendish Special School
HNWL W7 .... 85 F5
Caxton Hall
STJSPK SW1H 17 G3
Caxton Trading Estate
HYS/HAR UB3 .... 101 H1
Cayley Primary School
WCHPL E1 .... 93 G4
Cecil Park Clinic
PIN HA5 .... 47 J3
Cecil Sharpe House
CAMTN NW1 .... 4 B3
The Cedar School
FSTGT E7 .... 77 G5
Cedars Manor School
KTN/HRWW/WS HA3 .... 34 C7
The Cedars Primary School
HEST TW5 .... 101 K6
Cedar Way Industrial Estate
CAMTN NW1 .... 5 G2
Cenotaph
WHALL SW1A 17 J1
Centaurs Business Centre
ISLW TW7 .... 104 B5
Centaurs RFC
ISLW TW7 .... 104 A5
Central Business Centre
WLSDN NW10 .... 69 G4
The Central College of London
WCHPL E1 .... 13 M3
Central Criminal Court
STP EC4M 12 C4
Centrale Shopping Centre
CROY/NA CR0 .... 177 J1
Central Foundation Boys School
SDTCH EC2A 7 H9
Central Foundation Girls School (Lower)
BOW E3 .... 93 G2
Central Foundation Girls School (Upper)
BOW E3 .... 93 H2
Central Hall
STJSPK SW1H 17 H2
Central Hendon Clinic
HDN NW4 .... 51 K3
Central London County Court
CAVSQ/HST W1G 10 C1
Central London Golf Club
TOOT SW17 .... 147 H1
Central London Markets
STBT EC1A 12 C3
Central Medical Centre
MRDN SM4 .... 162 B3
Central Middlesex Hospital
WLSDN NW10 .... 86 E2
Central Park Arena
DART DA1 .... 139 H7
Central Park Primary School
EHAM E6 .... 95 H1
Central Primary School
WAT WD17 .... 21 G3
Central St Martins College of Art & Design
RSQ WC1B 11 L3
Central School of Ballet
CLKNW EC1R 12 B1
Central School of Fashion
GTPST W1W 10 E3
Central School of Speech & Drama
HAMP NW3 .... 3 G1
Central Square Shopping Centre
WBLY HA9 .... 68 A5
Central YMCA
ELTH/MOT SE9 .... 153 H1
Centre Court Shopping Centre
WIM/MER SW19 .... 146 D5
The Centre Performing Arts College
CHARL SE7 .... 114 C2
Centre Point
LSO/SEVD WC2H 11 H4
Chadwell Heath ⇌
CHDH RM6 .... 61 K6
Chadwell Heath Academy
CHDH RM6 .... 61 H5
Chadwell Heath Industrial Park
BCTR RM8 .... 62 A7
Chadwell Heath Leisure Centre
CHDH RM6 .... 61 K5
Chadwell Infant & Primary School
CHDH RM6 .... 61 J6
Chaffinch Business Park
BECK BR3 .... 166 A2
Chailey Industrial Estate
HYS/HAR UB3 .... 101 K1
Chalcot School
CAMTN NW1 .... 4 C1
Chalgrove Primary School
FNCH N3 .... 52 C2
Chalk Farm ⊖
HAMP NW3 .... 4 A1
Chalkhill Primary School
WBLY HA9 .... 68 D2
The Chamberlain Hotel
TWRH EC3N 13 L6
Chambers Business Park
WDR/YW UB7 .... 100 D5
Chambers Wharf
BERM/RHTH SE16 .... 111 H1
Chancery Court Hotel
HHOL WC1V 11 L3
Chancery Lane ⊖
FSBYW WC1X 12 A3
Chandlers Field Primary School
E/WMO/HCT KT8 .... 157 F4

Chandos Business Centre
WLGTN SM6 .... 176 C5
Channelsea Business Centre
SRTFD E15 .... 94 B1
Channing School
HGT N6 .... 54 B7
Chapel End Infant School
WALTH E17 .... 57 K1
Chapel End Junior School
WALTH E17 .... 43 K7
Chapman Park Industrial Estate
WLSDN NW10 .... 69 H5
Charing Cross ⇌
CHCR WC2N 11 J8
Charing Cross Hospital
HMSMTH W6 .... 107 G5
Charing Cross Hotel
CHCR WC2N 11 J7
The Charles Dickens Museum
BMSBY WC1N 11 L1
Charles Dickens Primary School
STHWK SE1 .... 18 E2
Charles Edward Brooke School (Lower School)
CMBW SE5 .... 110 C7
Charles Edward Brooke School (Upper School)
BRXN/ST SW9 .... 110 C7
Charlotte Sharman Primary School
LBTH SE11 .... 18 C4
Charlton ⇌
CHARL SE7 .... 114 B4
Charlton Athletic FC (The Valley)
CHARL SE7 .... 114 B4
Charlton Cemetery
CHARL SE7 .... 114 D5
Charlton Health & Fitness Centre
CHARL SE7 .... 114 B4
Charlton House
CHARL SE7 .... 114 C5
Charlton Manor Junior School
CHARL SE7 .... 114 C6
Charlton RFC
ELTH/MOT SE9 .... 135 G6
Charlton School
CHARL SE7 .... 114 D5
Charrington Bowl
SURB KT6 .... 172 D1
Charrville Primary School
YEAD UB4 .... 82 C1
Charter Clinic
CHEL SW3 .... 15 L8
Charterhouse
FARR EC1M 12 D1
Charteris Road Sports Centre
HAMP NW3 .... 71 J4
KIL/WHAMP NW6 .... 70 D7
Charter Nightingale Hospital & Counselling Centre
CAMTN NW1 .... 9 K2
The Charter School
HNHL SE24 .... 130 E4
Chartwell Business Centre
BMLY BR1 .... 168 C2
Chase Bridge Primary School
WHTN TW2 .... 123 K5
Chase Lane Primary School
CHING E4 .... 43 H3
Chase Road Trading Estate
WLSDN NW10 .... 87 F3
Chase Side Primary School
ENC/FH EN2 .... 29 J1
Chaseville Clinic
WCHMH N21 .... 29 F5
Chater Infant School
WATW WD18 .... 20 E3
Chater Junior School
WATW WD18 .... 20 E3
Chatsworth Infant School
BFN/LL DA15 .... 136 B7
Chatsworth Primary School
HSLW TW3 .... 123 H3
Chaucer Clinic
NWDGN UB2 .... 103 J1
Cheam ⇌
BELMT SM2 .... 174 D6
Cheam Common J & I School
WPK KT4 .... 173 K1
Cheam Fields Primary School
CHEAM SM3 .... 174 C4
Cheam High School
CHEAM SM3 .... 174 C3
Cheam Leisure Centre
CHEAM SM3 .... 174 B3
Cheam Park Farm Junior School
CHEAM SM3 .... 174 C2
Cheam Sports Club
CHEAM SM3 .... 174 C6
Chelsea Bridge Business Centre
VX/NE SW8 .... 109 G6
Chelsea Centre & Theatre
WBPTN SW10 .... 108 B6
Chelsea Cinema
CHEL SW3 .... 15 K8
The Chelsea Club Leisure Centre
FUL/PGN SW6 .... 108 A5
Chelsea College of Art & Design
CHEL SW3 .... 15 J8
FUL/PGN SW6 .... 128 B1
SHB W12 .... 106 E1
WEST SW1P 17 H7
Chelsea FC (Stamford Bridge)
FUL/PGN SW6 .... 108 A6
Chelsea Fields Industrial Estate
WIM/MER SW19 .... 147 H7
Chelsea Group of Children
WBPTN SW10 .... 108 A6
Chelsea Independent College
FUL/PGN SW6 .... 108 A6
Chelsea Leisure Centre
CHEL SW3 .... 15 K8
Chelsea Old Town Hall
CHEL SW3 .... 15 K8
Chelsea Physic Garden
CHEL SW3 .... 15 L9
CHEL SW3 .... 108 E5
Chelsea & Westminster Hospital
WBPTN SW10 .... 108 B5
Chelsea Wharf
WBPTN SW10 .... 108 C6
Chennestone Community School
SUN TW16 .... 156 A1
Cherington House Health Centre
HNWL W7 .... 85 F7
Cherry Garden Pier
BERM/RHTH SE16 .... 111 J1
Cherry Garden School
BERM/RHTH SE16 .... 111 H3

Cherry Lane Primary School
WDR/YW UB7 .... 100 C3
Cherry Orchard Primary School
CHARL SE7 .... 114 B6
The Cherry Trees
BOW E3 .... 93 J2
Chesington Community College
CHSGTN KT9 .... 171 K6
Chessington CC
CHSGTN KT9 .... 171 J6
Chessington Golf Club
CHSGTN KT9 .... 171 K6
Chessington North ⇌
CHSGTN KT9 .... 172 A4
Chessington South ⇌
CHSGTN KT9 .... 171 K6
The Chesterfield Mayfair Hotel
MYFR/PICC W1J 10 C3
Chesterton Primary School
BTSEA SW11 .... 109 F7
Chestnut Grove School
BAL SW12 .... 129 F7
Chestnuts Primary School
SEVS/STOTM N15 .... 55 J4
Cheyne Centre
CHEL SW3 .... 108 C5
Chicken Shed Theatre
STHGT/OAK N14 .... 28 A4
Childeric Primary School
NWCR SE14 .... 112 B6
Childrens House Upper School
IS N1 .... 74 A4
Childs Hill Clinic
CRICK NW2 .... 70 D1
Childs Hill Primary School
CRICK NW2 .... 70 C2
Childs Welfare Clinic
BCTR RM8 .... 79 J4
Chiltonian Industrial Estate
LEE/GVPK SE12 .... 133 J5
Chimnocks Wharf
POP/IOD E14 .... 93 G6
Chingford Foundation School
CHING E4 .... 31 K7
Chingford Hall Primary School
CHING E4 .... 43 H5
Chingford Health Centre
CHING E4 .... 43 J3
Chingford Industrial Centre
CHING E4 .... 43 G4
Chingford Mount Cemetery
CHING E4 .... 43 K7
Chingford RFC
CHING E4 .... 31 J7
Chisenhale Primary School
BOW E3 .... 93 G1
Chislehurst ⇌
BMLY BR1 .... 169 F1
Chislehurst Caves
CHST BR7 .... 154 A7
Chislehurst Cemetery
CHST BR7 .... 154 E4
Chislehurst Golf Club
CHST BR7 .... 154 B6
Chislehurst Natural Health Centre
CHST BR7 .... 154 B5
Chislehurst & Sidcup Grammar School
BFN/LL DA15 .... 155 H1
Chiswick ⇌
CHSWK W4 .... 105 K6
Chiswick & Bedford Park Preparatory School
CHSWK W4 .... 106 B3
Chiswick Business Park
CHSWK W4 .... 105 J3
Chiswick Community School
CHSWK W4 .... 106 A6
Chiswick House
CHSWK W4 .... 106 A5
Chiswick Moran Hotel
CHSWK W4 .... 105 J4
Chiswick Park ⊖
CHSWK W4 .... 105 K3
Chrisp Street Health Centre
POP/IOD E14 .... 93 K5
Christ Church Bentinck CE Primary School
CAMTN NW1 .... 9 J2
Christ Church Brondesbury CE J & I School
KIL/WHAMP NW6 .... 70 D7
Christ Church CE Junior School
EA W5 .... 85 K6
Christ Church CE Primary School
BAR EN5 .... 26 B1
BRXN/ST SW9 .... 110 B7
BRYLDS KT5 .... 159 H5
BTSEA SW11 .... 128 D2
CHEL SW3 .... 15 K9
FSTH SE23 .... 151 F1
WOOL/PLUM SE18 .... 115 F7
Christchurch CE Primary School
HAMP NW3 .... 71 H2
WCHPL E1 .... 13 M3
Christ Church CE VA Primary School
ERITH DA8 .... 118 A5
Christchurch Industrial Centre
STHWK SE1 .... 12 C8
Christ Church New Malden CE Primary School
NWMAL KT3 .... 160 B2
Christchurch Primary School
IL IG1 .... 60 B7
Christ Church Primary School
NWMAL KT3 .... 160 A2
Christ Church School
CAMTN NW1 .... 4 D1
Christian Meeting Hall
BECK BR3 .... 151 J7
Christopher Hatton Primary School
FSBYW WC1X 12 A1
Christs College Finchley
FNCH N3 .... 53 F2
Christs College School
EFNCH N2 .... 53 F2
Christs School
RCHPK/HAM TW10 .... 125 G4
Christ the King RC Primary School
FSBYPK N4 .... 55 F7
Christ the King Sixth Form College
LEW SE13 .... 133 G2
Chrysalis Theatre
BAL SW12 .... 129 F7
Chrysanthemum Clinic
CHSWK W4 .... 105 K6

Chrysolyte Independent Christian School
STHWK SE1 .... 19 H3
Church Down Adult School
LEE/GVPK SE12 .... 152 E1
Church End Medical Centre
WLSDN NW10 .... 69 G5
Church Farm House Museum
HDN NW4 .... 51 K2
Church Farm Swimming Pool
EBAR EN4 .... 27 K7
Churchfield Primary School
ED N9 .... 30 B7
Churchfields J & I School
SWFD E18 .... 44 E7
Churchfields Primary School
BECK BR3 .... 166 A4
Church House
WEST SW1P 17 H3
Churchill Clinic
STHWK SE1 .... 18 B3
Churchill College
RYNPK SW20 .... 161 F1
Churchill Gardens Primary School
PIM SW1V 16 E8
Churchill Theatre
BMLY BR1 .... 167 K1
Churchill War Rooms
STJSPK SW1H 17 H1
Church Stairs
BERM/RHTH SE16 .... 111 J1
Church Street ⊖
CROY/NA CR0 .... 177 J1
Church Trading Estate
ERITH DA8 .... 118 D6
Cineworld
CHEL SW3 .... 15 H9
CRICK NW2 .... 51 K7
EA W5 .... 85 K6
EN EN1 .... 30 C3
FELT TW13 .... 141 F1
HMSMTH W6 .... 106 E3
SOHO/SHAV W1D 11 G7
WBPTN SW10 .... 14 F8
BXLYHS DA6 .... 137 J3
WDGN N22 .... 55 G1
Citigroup Tower
POP/IOD E14 .... 93 K7
The City Academy Hackney
HOM E9 .... 74 E4
City Banking College
STHWK SE1 .... 19 J1
City Business Centre
BERM/RHTH SE16 .... 111 K1
City Business College
FSBYE EC1V 6 D8
City Central Estate
FSBYE EC1V 6 E8
City College of Higher Education
IS N1 .... 7 H7
City & Guilds of London Art School
LBTH SE11 .... 18 B8
City Health Centre
FSBYE EC1V 7 G9
City & Islington College
FSBYE EC1V 6 F8
FSBYPK N4 .... 73 H1
HBRY N5 .... 73 G5
HOLWY N7 .... 72 E3
HOLWY N7 .... 73 F2
IS N1 .... 7 G3
City & Islington Sixth Form College
FSBYE EC1V 6 C6
City Literary College
HHOL WC1V 11 K4
City of London Academy
STHWK SE1 .... 111 H4
The City of London Academy Islington
IS N1 .... 6 E4
The City of London Academy
EDUL SE22 .... 131 H4
City of London Business College
SEVS/STOTM N15 .... 56 A4
SEVS/STOTM N15 .... 56 C4
City of London Cemetery
MNPK E12 .... 77 J1
City of London Club
OBST EC2N 13 J4
City of London College
WCHPL E1 .... 92 C5
City of London Crematorium
MNPK E12 .... 77 J2
City of London Magistrates Court
LOTH EC2R 13 G5
City of London School for Girls
BARB EC2Y 12 E2
City of London School Sports Ground
LEE/GVPK SE12 .... 153 G1
City of Westminster Cemetery
HNWL W7 .... 85 F7
City of Westminster College
BAY/PAD W2 .... 9 G2
MV/WKIL W9 .... 2 B8
City of Westminster Vehicle Pound
MYFR/PKLN W1K 9 M7
City Thameslink ⇌
FLST/FETLN EC4A 12 C4
City University
CLKNW EC1R 6 E6
IS N1 .... 6 E5
STBT EC1A 12 D4
WCHPL E1 .... 92 D4
City University Business School
BARB EC2Y 12 F2
Civic Medical Centre
HRW HA1 .... 48 E4
Civil Service Sports Ground
CHSWK W4 .... 106 B7
LEE/GVPK SE12 .... 134 B5
Clapham Common ⊖
CLAP SW4 .... 129 H3
Clapham Common Clinic
CLAP SW4 .... 129 H3
Clapham High Street ⇌
CLAP SW4 .... 129 J2
Clapham Junction ⇌
BTSEA SW11 .... 128 D2
Clapham Manor Primary School
CLAP SW4 .... 129 H2
Clapham Manor Street Public Baths
CLAP SW4 .... 129 J2
Clapham North ⊖
CLAP SW4 .... 129 J2

Clapham North Business Centre
CLAP SW4 .... 129 J2
Clapham Picture House
CLAP SW4 .... 129 H3
Clapham South ⊖
CLAP SW4 .... 129 G5
Clapton ⇌
CLPT E5 .... 74 D1
Clapton Girls Technology College
CLPT E5 .... 74 E3
Clara Grant Primary School
BOW E3 .... 93 J3
Clare House Primary School
BECK BR3 .... 167 F1
Claremont Clinic
FSTGT E7 .... 77 G4
Claremont Fan Court School
ESH/CLAY KT10 .... 170 B5
Claremont High School Academy Trust
KTN/HRWW/WS HA3 .... 50 A4
Claremont Landscape Garden (NT)
ESH/CLAY KT10 .... 170 A6
Claremont Primary School
CRICK NW2 .... 70 B1
Claremont Way Industrial Estate
CRICK NW2 .... 52 A7
Clarence House
WHALL SW1A 16 F1
Clarendon Special School
HPTN TW12 .... 142 B5
Claridge's Hotel
MYFR/PKLN W1K 10 C6
Claverings Industrial Estate
ED N9 .... 42 E1
Claygate ⇌
ESH/CLAY KT10 .... 170 D5
Claygate Primary School
ESH/CLAY KT10 .... 170 E6
Clayhall Clinic
CLAY IG5 .... 59 J2
Clayponds Hospital
BTFD TW8 .... 105 F3
Cleeve Park School
SCUP DA14 .... 155 J2
Clementine Churchill Hospital
HRW HA1 .... 66 E2
Cleopatra's Needle
CHCR WC2N 11 L8
Clerkenwell County Court
IS N1 .... 6 C5
Clerkenwell Heritage Centre
FARR EC1M 12 C1
Clerkenwell Parochial CE Primary School
IS N1 .... 6 A8
Cleveland Primary School
IL IG1 .... 78 B3
Cleves Primary School
EHAM E6 .... 77 H7
C & L Golf & Country Club
NTHLT UB5 .... 65 F6
Clifton Lodge School
EA W5 .... 85 J6
Clifton Primary School
NWDGN UB2 .... 102 D3
Clink Exhibition
STHWK SE1 .... 13 G8
Clissold Leisure Centre
STNW/STAM N16 .... 73 K2
Clissold Park Natural Health Centre
STNW/STAM N16 .... 74 A1
C & L Leisure Centre
RSLP HA4 .... 65 F6
Clock House ⇌
BECK BR3 .... 166 B1
Clockhouse Industrial Estate
EBED/NFELT TW14 .... 120 E7
Clock Mill
POP/IOD E14 .... 94 A2
Clock Museum
CITYW EC2V 12 F4
Cloisters Business Centre
VX/NE SW8 .... 109 G6
Clore Gallery
WEST SW1P 17 J6
Clore Tikva School
BARK/HLT IG6 .... 60 C7
Clothworkers' Hall
FENCHST EC3M 13 K6
Clouster's Green
WAP E1W 92 C7
Cobbold Estate
WLSDN NW10 .... 69 H5
Cobourg Primary School
CMBW SE5 .... 19 L9
Cochrane Theatre
GINN WC1R 11 L3
Cockfosters ⊖
EBAR EN4 .... 28 A3
Cockfosters Sports Ground
EBAR EN4 .... 27 K2
The Cockpit Theatre
STJWD NW8 .... 9 J1
Coldharbour Industrial Estate
CMBW SE5 .... 130 D1
Coldharbour Leisure Centre
ELTH/MOT SE9 .... 153 K1
Coldharbour Sports Ground
ELTH/MOT SE9 .... 154 A1
Colebrooke Primary School
IS N1 .... 6 C5
Colegrave School
SRTFD E15 .... 76 B4
Coleraine Park Primary School
TOTM N17 .... 42 D7
Coleridge Primary School
HGT N6 .... 54 D6
Colfes Pre-Preparatory School
LEE/GVPK SE12 .... 134 A5
Colfe's Preparatory School
LEE/GVPK SE12 .... 133 K5
Colindale ⊖
CDALE/KGS NW9 .... 51 G2
Colindale Business Park
CDALE/KGS NW9 .... 50 E2
Colindale Hospital
CDALE/KGS NW9 .... 51 G2
Colindale Primary School
CDALE/KGS NW9 .... 51 H3
Coliseum Theatre
CHCR WC2N 11 J7
College Fields Business Centre
WIM/MER SW19 .... 147 J3
College of Arms
BLKFR EC4V 12 C5
College of Central London
SDTCH EC2A 7 J9

College of Fuel Technology
HGT N6 .... 54 A5
College of Haringey, Enfield &
North East London
PEND EN3 .... 30 E2
SEVS/STOTM N15 .... 56 B3
The College of Law
FITZ W1T 11 G3
LINN WC2A 12 A4
College of North East London
CEND/HSY/T N8 .... 55 G3
WDGN N22 .... 40 G7
College of North West London
KIL/WHAMP NW6 .... 2 A3
WBLY HA9 .... 68 C2
WLSDN NW10 .... 69 H4
College of Organists
FLST/FETLN EC4A 12 B3
College of Osteopathy
BORE WD6 .... 24 D2
College Park School
BAY/PAD W2 .... 8 B5
Collier's Wood ⊖
WIM/MER SW19 .... 147 H6
Collingwood Business Centre
ARCH N19 .... 72 E2
Collingwood School
WLGTN SM6 .... 176 B4
Collins Method School
CRICK NW2 .... 70 A5
Collis Primary School
TEDD TW11 .... 143 H5
Colnbrook School
OXHEY WD19 .... 33 G1
Colne Bridge Retail Park
WAT WD17 .... 21 H4
Colne Valley Retail Park
WAT WD17 .... 21 H4
Colonnades Leisure Park
CROY/NA CR0 .... 177 G5
The Colonnades
Shopping Centre
BGVA SW1W 16 C5
Colours Sports Club
SUT SM1 .... 175 G4
Columbia Primary School
BETH E2 .... 7 M7
Colvestone Primary School
HACK E8 .... 74 B4
Colville Primary School
NTGHL W11 .... 88 D5
Colyers Lane Medical Centre
ERITH DA8 .... 118 A7
Comber Grove Primary School
CMBW SE5 .... 110 D6
Comedy Theatre
STJS SW1Y 11 G7
Comelle House Trading Estate
DEPT SE8 .... 112 B4
Comfort Hotel
ENC/FH EN2 .... 29 H1
Comfort Inn
HYS/HAR UB3 .... 101 H4
Commonwealth Institute
WKENS W14 .... 107 J2
Community Arts Centre
GNWCH SE10 .... 112 E6
Community Centre
(Island History Trust)
POP/IOD E14 .... 113 F3
Community College & School
GNWCH SE10 .... 113 F6
The Community College
HACK E8 .... 74 D7
Compass Theatre
HGDN/ICK UB10 .... 64 A2
Complementary
Health Centre
LEE/GVPK SE12 .... 133 H5
The Compton School
NFNCH/WDSPK N12 .... 39 J5
Compton Sports Centre
NFNCH/WDSPK N12 .... 39 J5
Concord Business Centre
ACT W3 .... 86 D4
Conduit House
GNWCH SE10 .... 113 G6
Coney Hill School
HAYES BR2 .... 180 D1
Conisborough College
CAT SE6 .... 152 B2
Connaught Business Centre
CDALE/KGS NW9 .... 51 H4
CROY/NA CR0 .... 177 F5
MTCM CR4 .... 162 E4
The Connaught Hotel
MYFR/PKLN W1K 10 B7
Connaught House School
BAY/PAD W2 .... 9 K5
Connaught School for Girls
WAN E11 .... 58 C7
Consort Clinic
PECK SE15 .... 131 J2
Consulate
General of Monaco
SKENS SW7 .... 15 G5
Consulate General of The
Republic of Guinea Bissau
KENS W8 .... 14 C3
Consulate of Burkina Faso
BTSEA SW11 .... 128 B2
Consulate of Chile
CAVSQ/HST W1G 10 C1
Consulate of Colombia
GTPST W1W 10 E4
Consulate of Eritrea
IS N1 .... 6 B5
Consulate of Guinea
MYFR/PKLN W1K 10 A7
Consulate of Panama
MYFR/PICC W1J 10 C9
The Continental Hotel
HSLW TW3 .... 123 F2
Convent of Jesus & Mary
Infant School
CRICK NW2 .... 70 A5
Convent of Jesus &
Mary Language College
WLSDN NW10 .... 69 H7
Convoy's Wharf
DEPT SE8 .... 112 C4
Conway Medical Centre
WOOL/PLUM SE18 .... 115 J4
Conway Primary School
WOOL/PLUM SE18 .... 115 K3
Coombe Girls School
NWMAL KT3 .... 160 A1
Coombe Hill Golf Club
KUTN/CMB KT2 .... 145 F6
Coombe Hill J & I School
NWMAL KT3 .... 145 F7
Coombe Lane ⊖
CROY/NA CR0 .... 178 E4

Coombe Wood Golf Club
KUTN/CMB KT2 .... 144 D6
Coopers' Hall
LVPST EC2M 13 K3
Coopers Lane Primary School
LEE/GVPK SE12 .... 152 E1
Coopers Technology College
CHST BR7 .... 154 C7
Copenhagen Primary School
IS N1 .... 5 K4
Copland Specialist
Science College
WBLY HA9 .... 68 B4
Coppermill Primary School
WALTH E17 .... 57 F4
Coppetts Wood Hospital
MUSWH N10 .... 39 K7
Coppetts Wood
Primary School
MUSWH N10 .... 40 A7
Copthall School
MLHL NW7 .... 37 K6
Copthorne Tara Hotel
KENS W8 .... 14 C3
Cordwainers College
HACK E8 .... 74 E6
Corinthian Casuals FC
SURB KT6 .... 172 C2
Coronet Cinema
NTGHL W11 .... 8 A8
SEVS/STOTM N15 .... 55 H2
Corpus Christi RC
Primary School
BRXS/STRHM SW2 .... 130 A4
Cosmopolitan College
IS N1 .... 5 L6
Coston Primary School
GFD/PVL UB6 .... 84 C2
Coteford Infant School
PIN HA5 .... 46 E4
County Council Offices
BUSH WD23 .... 22 D6
Courtauld Institute Gallery
TPL/STR WC2R 11 L6
Courtauld Institute of Art
TPL/STR WC2R 11 M6
Court Farm Industrial Estate
STWL/WRAY TW19 .... 120 C3
Courtfield Medical Centre
ECT SW5 .... 14 D6
Courtland JMI School
MLHL NW7 .... 37 J2
Covent Garden ⊖
COVGDN WC2E 11 J6
Covent Garden Flower Market
VX/NE SW8 .... 109 J3
Covent Garden Medical Centre
LSO/SEVD WC2H 11 J5
Crafts Council
IS N1 .... 6 B6
Crampton Primary School
WALW SE17 .... 18 D6
Cranbook College
IL IG1 .... 78 A1
Cranbrook Primary School
IL IG1 .... 59 K6
Crane Park Island
Nature Reserve
FELT TW13 .... 141 K1
Cranford Community College
HEST TW5 .... 102 A3
Cranford Infant School
HSLWW TW4 .... 121 K1
Cranford Junior School
HSLWW TW4 .... 122 A1
Cranford Park Junior School
HYS/HAR UB3 .... 101 J3
Cranford Park Primary School
HYS/HAR UB3 .... 101 J1
Cranleigh Gardens
Industrial Estate
STHL UB1 .... 83 K4
The Cranley Hotel
ECT SW5 .... 14 E7
Cranmer Primary School
MTCM CR4 .... 162 E3
The Craven Clinic
HMSMTH W6 .... 106 E3
Craven Park Health Centre
WLSDN NW10 .... 69 F7
Craven Park Medical Centre
WLSDN NW10 .... 69 F7
Crawford Primary School
CMBW SE5 .... 110 D7
Crayfields Business Park
STMC/STPC BR5 .... 155 J7
Crayford ≥
DART DA1 .... 138 B5
Crayford Commercial Centre
DART DA1 .... 138 B4
Crayford Industrial Estate
DART DA1 .... 138 C4
Crayford Leisure Centre &
Greyhound Stadium
DART DA1 .... 138 B5
Crayford Medical Centre
DART DA1 .... 138 C4
Crayside Industrial Estate
DART DA1 .... 138 C4
Creekmouth Industrial Estate
BARK IG11 .... 97 F3
Creek Road Health Centre
DEPT SE8 .... 112 D5
Creek Road Industrial Estate
DEPT SE8 .... 112 E5
The Crest Boys Academy
CRICK NW2 .... 69 H2
Crewe House
MYFR/PICC W1J 10 C8
Cricket Green School
MTCM CR4 .... 162 D2
Cricklefield Stadium
IL IG1 .... 78 E1
Cricklewood ≥
CRICK NW2 .... 70 B2
Cricklewood Trading Estate
CRICK NW2 .... 70 C2
Crispin Industrial Centre
UED N18 .... 42 E4
Criterion Theatre
MYFR/PICC W1J 10 F7
Crofton Leisure Centre
BROCKY SE4 .... 132 D5
Crofton Park ≥
BROCKY SE4 .... 132 C4
Croham Hurst Golf Club
SAND/SEL CR2 .... 178 B5
Cromer Road Primary School
BAR EN5 .... 27 F2
Cromwell Business Centre
BARK IG11 .... 96 E2
Cromwell Hospital
ECT SW5 .... 14 C5

Crook Log Primary School
BXLYHS DA6 .... 136 E3
Crook Log Sports Centre
WELL DA16 .... 136 E3
Crossharbour ⊖
POP/IOD E14 .... 112 E2
Crossways Sixth Form
BROCKY SE4 .... 132 B1
Crouch End Art School
CEND/HSY/T N8 .... 54 E4
Crouch End Health Centre
CEND/HSY/T N8 .... 54 E4
Crouch Hill ≥
FSBYPK N4 .... 55 F6
Crouch Hill Recreation Centre
CEND/HSY/T N8 .... 54 E6
Crowland Primary School
SEVS/STOTM N15 .... 56 C4
Crowlands Primary School
ROMW/RG RM7 .... 62 E5
Crown Close Business Centre
BOW E3 .... 75 J7
Crown Court at The Borough
STHWK SE1 .... 18 D1
Crowndale Health Centre
CAMTN NW1 .... 4 F5
Crowne Plaza
EA W5 .... 86 A2
WDR/YW UB7 .... 100 D3
Crowne Plaza Hotel
BETH E2 .... 7 L8
CAN/RD E16 .... 94 E6
EMB EC4Y 12 C6
SKENS SW7 .... 14 E5
Crownfield Primary School
ROMW/RG RM7 .... 62 C1
Crown Lane Clinic
STHGT/OAK N14 .... 28 C7
Crown Lane Primary School
WNWD SE27 .... 149 J3
Crown Moran Hotel
CRICK NW2 .... 70 B3
Crown Trading Centre
HYS/HAR UB3 .... 101 H1
Crown Woods School
ELTH/MOT SE9 .... 135 H4
Croydon Airport
Industrial Estate
CROY/NA CR0 .... 177 G6
Croydon Bowling Club
SAND/SEL CR2 .... 177 J4
Croydon Cemetery
CROY/NA CR0 .... 164 A4
Croydon Clocktower Cinema
CROY/NA CR0 .... 177 K2
Croydon College
CROY/NA CR0 .... 177 K2
Croydon Combined Courts
CROY/NA CR0 .... 177 K2
Croydon FC
SNWD SE25 .... 165 K4
Croydon Road
Industrial Estate
BECK BR3 .... 165 K3
Croydon Sports Arena
SNWD SE25 .... 165 K4
Crusader Industrial Estate
FSBYPK N4 .... 55 J5
Crystal Palace ≥ ⊖
PGE/AN SE20 .... 150 C5
Crystal Palace FC
(Selhurst Park)
SNWD SE25 .... 165 F3
Crystal Palace FC Soccer &
Sports Centre
BRXN/ST SW9 .... 130 A2
Crystal Palace Museum
NRWD SE19 .... 150 B5
Cuaco Sports Ground
BECK BR3 .... 151 J3
Cubitt Town Infant School
POP/IOD E14 .... 113 F2
Cuckoo Hall Academy
ED N9 .... 30 E6
Cuddington Cemetery
WPK KT4 .... 173 K1
Cuddington CP School
WPK KT4 .... 173 H2
Cuddington Croft
Primary School
BELMT SM2 .... 174 B7
Culloden Primary School
POP/IOD E14 .... 94 B5
Culvers House Primary School
MTCM CR4 .... 163 F7
Cumberland Business Park
WLSDN NW10 .... 86 D2
The Cumberland Hotel
FITZ W1H 11 G4
MBLAR W1H 9 M5
Cumberland Park
Industrial Estate
WAN E11 .... 87 J2
The Cumming Museum
WALW SE17 .... 18 E6
Cumnor House School
SAND/SEL CR2 .... 177 H7
Curwen Primary School
PLSTW E13 .... 94 E1
Curzon Mayfair Cinema
MYFR/PICC W1J 10 C9
Curzon Soho Cinema
SOHO/SHAV W1D 11 H6
Custom House
MON EC3R 13 J7
Custom House for ExCeL ⊖
CAN/RD E16 .... 95 H6
Custom House Hotel
CAN/RD E16 .... 95 K6
Cutlers' Hall
STP EC4M 12 D4
Cutty Sark
GNWCH SE10 .... 113 F5
Cutty Sark Clipper Ship
GNWCH SE10 .... 113 F5
Cygnet Clinic Beckton
EHAM E6 .... 96 B4
Cygnus Business Centre
WLSDN NW10 .... 69 H4
Cypress Infant School
SNWD SE25 .... 165 F1
Cypress Junior School
SNWD SE25 .... 165 F1
Cyprus ⊖
CAN/RD E16 .... 96 A6
Cyprus College of Art
WNWD SE27 .... 149 H1
Cyril Jackson Primary School
POP/IOD E14 .... 93 H6

Dagenham Chest Clinic
BCTR RM8 .... 80 B2
Dagenham Civic Centre
DAGE RM10 .... 80 D1
Dagenham Dock ≥
DAGW RM9 .... 98 B1
Dagenham East ⊖
DAGE RM10 .... 80 E5
Dagenham Heathway ⊖
DAGW RM9 .... 80 B5
Dagenham Park CE School
DAGE RM10 .... 80 D6
Dagenham & Redbridge FC
DAGE RM10 .... 80 C4
Dagenham Superbowl
DAGE RM10 .... 98 D2
Dagenham Swimming Pool
DAGE RM10 .... 80 C1
Daily Telegraph
Newspaper Offices
POP/IOD E14 .... 112 D2
Dairy Meadow
Primary School
NWDGN UB2 .... 102 E2
D'Albiac House
HTHAIR TW6 .... 120 C1
Dali Universe
STHWK SE1 .... 17 L1
Dallington School
FSBYE EC1V 6 D9
Dalmain Primary School
FSTH SE23 .... 132 B7
Dalston Junction ⊖
HACK E8 .... 74 B5
Dalston Kingsland ≥
IS N1 .... 74 A5
Damilola Taylor Centre
PECK SE15 .... 111 G6
Danegrove Primary School
EBAR EN4 .... 27 J5
Danetree School
HOR/WEW KT19 .... 172 E6
Danson House
BXLYHS DA6 .... 136 D3
Danson Primary School
WELL DA16 .... 136 C3
Danson Watersports Centre
BXLYHS DA6 .... 136 D4
Darell Primary School
RCH/KEW TW9 .... 125 H2
Darent Industrial Park
ERITH DA8 .... 119 G4
Dartford ≥
DART DA1 .... 139 H4
Dartford Adult
Education Centre
DART DA1 .... 139 F6
Dartford Bridge Community
Primary School
DART DA1 .... 139 J1
Dartford County Court
DART DA1 .... 139 H5
Dartford Grammar School
for Boys
DART DA1 .... 139 F5
Dartford Grammar School
for Girls
DART DA1 .... 139 F6
Dartford Magistrates Court
DART DA1 .... 139 G5
Dartford Museum & Library
DART DA1 .... 139 H6
Dartford
Natural Health Centre
DART DA1 .... 139 H6
Dartford Technology College
DART DA1 .... 139 F6
Dartford West Health Centre
DART DA1 .... 139 F5
Darwin Centre
SKENS SW7 .... 15 G4
Datapoint Business Centre
BOW E3 .... 94 B3
Date Valley School
MTCM CR4 .... 162 E2
Daubeney Primary School
CLPT E5 .... 75 G3
David Game College
KENS W8 .... 8 A8
David Ives (Erith) Stadium
ERITH DA8 .... 118 B5
David Livingstone
Primary School
THHTH CR7 .... 149 J7
David Lloyd Leisure
NFNCH/WDSPK N12 .... 39 H6
SKENS SW7 .... 14 D5
David Lloyd Sports Centre
EN EN1 .... 30 C1
David Lloyd Tennis Centre
SCUP DA14 .... 155 J4
Davidson Primary School
CROY/NA CR0 .... 165 G6
Davies Laing & Dick College
BAY/PAD W2 .... 8 C7
Davies Lane Primary School
WAN E11 .... 76 D1
Davies's College
STHWK SE1 .... 19 G1
Dawlish Primary School
LEY E10 .... 58 A7
Days Hotel
BETH E2 .... 92 D1
HSLW TW3 .... 123 G2
MLHL NW7 .... 36 E1
RSLP HA4 .... 65 G4
STHWK SE1 .... 18 A4
Days Hotel London
South Ruislip
RSLP HA4 .... 65 G3
Days Inn
BAY/PAD W2 .... 9 H5
PIM SW1V 16 F7
Days Lane Primary School
BFN/LL DA15 .... 136 A5
Dean College of London
HOLWY N7 .... 73 F2
Deanesfield Primary School
RSLP HA4 .... 65 H3
Deansbrook Infant School
MLHL NW7 .... 36 E5
Deansfield Primary School
ELTH/MOT SE9 .... 135 F2
De Bohun Primary School
STHGT/OAK N14 .... 28 B4
Delta Wharf
GNWCH SE10 .... 113 G1
Denmark Hill ≥ ⊖
CMBW SE5 .... 130 E2
Denmead School
HPTN TW12 .... 142 A6
Denver Industrial Estate
RAIN RM13 .... 99 H5

Department for Environment,
Food & Rural Affairs
CHCR WC2N 11 J3
Department for Transport
WEST SW1P 17 J7
Department of
Art & Design (London
Metropolitan University)
WCHPL E1 .... 13 M4
Department of Economics
(London Metropolitan
University)
TWRH EC3N 13 L5
Department of Education
STJSPK SW1H 17 H2
Department of Health
WHALL SW1A 17 J1
Department of Trade & Industry
STJSPK SW1H 17 H3
Deptford ≥
DEPT SE8 .... 112 D6
Deptford Bridge ⊖
DEPT SE8 .... 112 D7
Deptford Business Centre
NWCR SE14 .... 112 A4
Deptford Green School
NWCR SE14 .... 112 C6
Deptford Park Business Centre
DEPT SE8 .... 112 B4
Deptford Park Primary School
DEPT SE8 .... 112 B4
Deptford Trading Estate
DEPT SE8 .... 112 B4
Dersingham Primary School
MNPK E12 .... 77 K3
Derwentwater Primary School
ACT W3 .... 86 E1
Design Centre
FUL/PGN SW6 .... 108 A3
Design Museum
STHWK SE1 .... 13 M9
Deutsche Schule
RCHPK/HAM TW10 .... 124 E7
Devonshire Hospital
MHST W1U 10 B2
Devonshire House School
HAMP NW3 .... 71 G4
Devonshire Primary School
BELMT SM2 .... 175 G6
Devons Road ⊖
BOW E3 .... 93 K3
Diamond College
SOHO/SHAV W1D 11 H4
Diana Fountain
E/WMO/HCT KT8 .... 158 A1
Diana Princess of Wales
Memorial Fountain
BAY/PAD W2 .... 9 H9
Diane Matthews Clinic
ROMW/RG RM7 .... 63 J3
Dilloway Industrial Estate
NWDGN UB2 .... 102 D1
Discovery Business Park
BERM/RHTH SE16 .... 111 H2
Discovery Primary School
THMD SE28 .... 97 F7
Docklands Medical Centre
POP/IOD E14 .... 112 D3
Docklands Sailing &
Watersports Centre
POP/IOD E14 .... 112 D2
Dockwell's Industrial Estate
EBED/NFELT TW14 .... 122 A4
Dockyard Industrial Estate
WOOL/PLUM SE18 .... 114 D2
Dog Kennel Hill
Primary School
EDUL SE22 .... 131 F2
Dokal Industrial Estate
NWDGN UB2 .... 102 D1
Dollis Hill ⊖
WLSDN NW10 .... 69 J4
Dollis Infant School
MLHL NW7 .... 38 A6
The Dolphin Leisure Centre
ROM RM1 .... 63 H3
Dolphin School
BTSEA SW11 .... 128 D4
The Dominie
BTSEA SW11 .... 108 E7
Dominion Business Park
ED N9 .... 43 F1
Dominion Theatre
RSQ WC1B 11 H4
Donhead School
WIM/MER SW19 .... 146 B6
Donmar Warehouse Theatre
LSO/SEVD WC2H 11 J5
Donnington Primary School
WLSDN NW10 .... 69 K6
The Dorchester Hotel
MYFR/PKLN W1K 10 B8
Dorchester Primary School
WPK KT4 .... 161 F7
Dorma Trading Park
LEY E10 .... 57 F7
Dormers Wells High School
STHL UB1 .... 84 A5
Dormers Wells Junior School
STHL UB1 .... 84 B6
Dormers Wells Leisure Centre
STHL UB1 .... 84 B5
Dormers Wells Medical Centre
STHL UB1 .... 84 A5
Dorothy Barley Primary School
BCTR RM8 .... 79 H4
Dorset Road Infant School
ELTH/MOT SE9 .... 153 J1
Douglas Bader Foundation
PUT/ROE SW15 .... 126 D5
Dovers Corner
Industrial Estate
RAIN RM13 .... 99 H2
Downderry Primary School
BMLY BR1 .... 152 C3
Downe Manor Primary School
NTHLT UB5 .... 83 F2
Downham Health Centre
BMLY BR1 .... 152 C3
Downhills Primary School
TOTM N17 .... 55 K3
Downsell Primary School
SRTFD E15 .... 76 B3
Downshall Primary School
GDMY/SEVK IG2 .... 60 E6
Downsview Primary School
NRWD SE19 .... 149 J6
Downsview School
CLPT E5 .... 74 D3
Drama Centre London
KTTN NW5 .... 72 C4
Drapers Hall
LOTH EC2R 13 H4

The Draycott Hotel
  CHEL SW3 .... 15 M5
Drayton Green ⇌
  HNWL W7 .... 85 F6
Drayton Green Primary School
  WEA W13 .... 85 G6
Drayton Manor High School
  HNWL W7 .... 85 F6
Drayton Park ⇌
  HOLWY N7 .... 73 G4
Drayton Park Primary School
  HBRY N5 .... 73 G4
DRCA Business Centre
  BTSEA SW11 .... 109 F7
Drew Primary School
  CAN/RD E16 .... 95 J7
The Drill Hall
  GWRST WC1E 11 G2
The Drizen School
  EDGW HA8 .... 36 C6
Dr Johnson's House
  FLST/FETLN EC4A 12 B4
Dr Tripletts CE J & I School
  HYS/HAR UB3 .... 82 D5
Drury Way Industrial Estate
  WLSDN NW10 .... 69 F3
Duchess Theatre
  COVGDN WC2E 11 L6
Duff Miller College
  SKENS SW7 .... 14 F5
Duke of York Column
  STJS SW1Y 11 H9
Duke of York Theatre
  CHCR WC2N 11 J7
Dukes Hotel
  WHALL SW1A 10 E9
Dulverton Primary School
  ELTH/MOT SE9 .... 154 D1
Dulwich College
  DUL SE21 .... 131 F7
Dulwich College Pre-
  Preparatory School
  DUL SE21 .... 150 A2
Dulwich College Track
  DUL SE21 .... 150 A1
Dulwich Hamlet FC
  EDUL SE22 .... 131 F3
Dulwich Hamlet Junior School
  HNHL SE24 .... 130 E5
Dulwich Hospital
  EDUL SE22 .... 131 F3
Dulwich Leisure Centre
  EDUL SE22 .... 131 H3
Dulwich Medical Centre
  EDUL SE22 .... 131 H4
Dulwich Picture Gallery
  DUL SE21 .... 131 F6
Dulwich & Sydenham Hill
  Golf Club
  DUL SE21 .... 150 C1
Dulwich Village CE
  Infant School
  DUL SE21 .... 131 F5
Dunbar Wharf
  POP/IOD E14 .... 93 H6
Duncombe Primary School
  ARCH N19 .... 54 E7
Dundee Wharf
  POP/IOD E14 .... 93 H6
Dundonald Primary School
  WIM/MER SW19 .... 146 D6
Dundonald Road ⊖
  WIM/MER SW19 .... 146 D6
Dunraven Lower School
  STRHM/NOR SW16 .... 149 F2
Dunraven School Upper
  STRHM/NOR SW16 .... 149 F2
Durand Primary School
  BRXN/ST SW9 .... 110 A2
Durands Wharf
  BERM/RHTH SE16 .... 112 C1
Durdans Park Primary School
  STHL UB1 .... 83 K4
Durston House School
  EA W5 .... 85 K5
Dysart School
  KUTN/CMB KT2 .... 143 K3
  SURB KT6 .... 159 F6
Eaglesfield School
  WOOL/PLUM SE18 .... 115 F7
Eagle Trading Estate
  MTCM CR4 .... 162 C6
Ealdham Primary School
  ELTH/MOT SE9 .... 134 B3
Ealing Abbey
  EA W5 .... 85 J5
Ealing Abbey Scriptorium
  WEA W13 .... 85 J5
Ealing Broadway ⇌ ⊖
  EA W5 .... 85 K6
The Ealing Broadway Centre
  EA W5 .... 85 K6
Ealing Central Sports Ground
  GFD/PVL UB6 .... 85 G1
Ealing Civic Centre
  EA W5 .... 85 J6
Ealing College Upper School
  WEA W13 .... 85 H5
Ealing Common ⊖
  EA W5 .... 86 B7
Ealing Conservative
  Bowling Club
  EA W5 .... 85 J6
Ealing CC
  EA W5 .... 86 A5
Ealing Film Studios
  EA W5 .... 85 J7
Ealing Golf Club
  GFD/PVL UB6 .... 85 H2
Ealing Hammersmith &
  West London College
  WKENS W14 .... 107 G3
Ealing Hospital
  NWDGN UB2 .... 103 J1
Ealing Independent College
  EA W5 .... 85 J6
Ealing Northern Sports Centre
  GFD/PVL UB6 .... 66 D3
Ealing Park Health Centre
  EA W5 .... 104 C3
Ealing Road Trading Estate
  BTFD TW8 .... 104 E4
Ealing Snooker Club
  WEA W13 .... 85 H7
Ealing Sports Centre
  EA W5 .... 86 A4
Ealing & West London College
  EA W5 .... 85 J7
Eardley Primary School
  STRHM/NOR SW16 .... 148 C5
Earlham Primary School
  FSTGT E7 .... 76 D4
  WDGN N22 .... 41 F6

Earl's Court ⊖
  ECT SW5 .... 14 B7
Earl's Court Exhibition Centre
  ECT SW5 .... 14 A8
Earlsfield ⇌
  WAND/EARL SW18 .... 128 B7
Earlsfield Primary School
  WAND/EARL SW18 .... 147 G1
Earlsmead Primary School
  RYLN/HDSTN HA2 .... 65 K3
  SEVS/STOTM N15 .... 56 B3
Earth Galleries
  SKENS SW7 .... 15 H4
East Acton ⊖
  SHB W12 .... 87 H5
East Acton Primary School
  ACT W3 .... 87 G6
East Barking Centre
  BCTR RM8 .... 79 J4
East Barnet Health Centre
  EBAR EN4 .... 27 H4
East Barnet School
  EBAR EN4 .... 27 K5
East Beckton District Centre
  EHAM E6 .... 95 K5
Eastbrook
  Comprehensive School
  DAGE RM10 .... 80 E3
Eastbrook End Cemetery
  ROMW/RG RM7 .... 81 G2
Eastbrookend Country Park
  ROMW/RG RM7 .... 81 F3
Eastbury Comprehensive School
  BARK IG11 .... 79 F7
Eastbury Farm JMI School
  NTHWD HA6 .... 32 B3
Eastbury Primary School
  BARK IG11 .... 79 F6
Eastcote ⊖
  RSLP HA4 .... 47 G5
Eastcote CC
  PIN HA5 .... 47 F4
Eastcote Health Centre
  PIN HA5 .... 47 G6
Eastcote Industrial Estate
  RSLP HA4 .... 47 G6
Eastcote Lane Cemetery
  RYLN/HDSTN HA2 .... 66 B2
Eastcote Primary School
  WELL DA16 .... 135 J2
Eastcourt Independent School
  GDMY/SEVK IG3 .... 61 G7
East Croydon ⇌ ⊖
  CROY/NA CR0 .... 177 K1
East Dulwich ⇌
  EDUL SE22 .... 131 F3
East End Computing &
  Business College
  WCHPL E1 .... 92 D5
Eastern Business Park
  HTHAIR TW6 .... 121 J1
East Finchley ⊖
  EFNCH N2 .... 53 J3
East Finchley Cemetery
  EFNCH N2 .... 53 F2
East Finchley Medical Centre
  EFNCH N2 .... 53 J3
East Finchley School of English
  EFNCH N2 .... 53 J2
Eastgate Business Park
  LEY E10 .... 57 J7
East Greenwich Christ Church
  CE Primary School
  GNWCH SE10 .... 113 H3
East Ham ⊖
  EHAM E6 .... 77 J6
East Ham Industrial Estate
  EHAM E6 .... 95 H4
East Ham Jewish Cemetery
  EHAM E6 .... 95 J2
East Ham Leisure Centre
  EHAM E6 .... 77 K7
East Ham Memorial Hospital
  EHAM E6 .... 77 H6
East Ham Nature Reserve
  EHAM E6 .... 95 K3
East Hill Cemetery
  DART DA1 .... 139 K6
East India ⊖
  POP/IOD E14 .... 94 B6
Eastlea Community Centre
  CAN/RD E16 .... 94 D3
Eastlea Community School
  CAN/RD E16 .... 94 C3
East London Business College
  WAN E11 .... 58 C7
East London Cemetery
  PLSTW E13 .... 94 D2
East London Christian
  Choir School
  HACK E8 .... 7 L1
East London Crematorium
  SRTFD E15 .... 94 D2
East London RFC
  EHAM E6 .... 95 K4
East London RUFC
  SRTFD E15 .... 94 D1
Eastman Dental Hospital
  FSBYW WC1X 5 L9
East Molesey CC
  E/WMO/HCT KT8 .... 157 K7
East Putney ⊖
  PUT/ROE SW15 .... 127 H4
East Sheen Cemetery
  RCHPK/HAM TW10 .... 125 H4
East Sheen Primary School
  MORT/ESHN SW14 .... 126 B3
East Thamesmead
  Business Park
  ERITHM DA18 .... 117 G2
East Wickham Primary School
  WELL DA16 .... 116 A7
Eaton Manor RFC
  WAN E11 .... 59 G4
Eaton Square Pre-
  Preparatory School
  BGVA SW1W 16 C5
Eaton Square School
  PIM SW1V 16 E6
Ebrahim Community College
  WCHPL E1 .... 92 C4
Ecclesbourne Primary School
  THHTH CR7 .... 164 D4
Eden College
  STHWK SE1 .... 18 D3
Edenham High School
  CROY/NA CR0 .... 166 B6
Eden High School
  FUL/PGN SW6 .... 107 J7
Eden Medical Centre
  WKENS W14 .... 107 J3
Eden Park ⇌
  BECK BR3 .... 166 D4

Edenvale Child Health Clinic
  MTCM CR4 .... 148 A6
Eden Walk Shopping Centre
  KUT/HW KT1 .... 159 F1
Edes Business Park
  WLGTN SM6 .... 176 A1
Edgebury Primary School
  CHST BR7 .... 154 C3
Edge Business Centre
  CRICK NW2 .... 69 K1
Edgware ⊖
  EDGW HA8 .... 36 D5
Edgware Blood
  Transfusion Centre
  EDGW HA8 .... 36 D6
Edgwarebury Cemetery
  EDGW HA8 .... 36 C1
Edgware Clinic
  EDGW HA8 .... 36 C5
Edgware College
  KIL/WHAMP NW6 .... 71 G5
Edgware Community Hospital
  EDGW HA8 .... 36 D6
Edgware FC & Wealdstone FC
  EDGW HA8 .... 36 C5
Edgware Infant School
  EDGW HA8 .... 36 C5
Edgware Jewish Girls-
  Beis Chinuch
  EDGW HA8 .... 36 C5
Edgware Jewish Primary School
  EDGW HA8 .... 36 D5
Edgware Junior School
  EDGW HA8 .... 36 D5
Edgware Road ⊖
  BAY/PAD W2 .... 9 H3
Edinburgh Primary School
  WALTH E17 .... 57 H4
Edith Neville Primary School
  CAMTN NW1 .... 5 G6
Edmonton Cemetery
  WCHMH N21 .... 41 K1
Edmonton County Court
  UED N18 .... 42 C4
Edmonton County
  Lower School
  ED N9 .... 30 A7
Edmonton Green ⇌
  ED N9 .... 42 C1
Edmonton Green
  Shopping Centre
  ED N9 .... 42 D1
Edmonton Leisure Centre
  ED N9 .... 42 C2
Edmonton Upper School
  EN EN1 .... 30 B6
Edmund Waller Primary School
  NWCR SE14 .... 132 A1
Education Centre
  WOOL/PLUM SE18 .... 115 G4
Edward Betham CE
  Primary School
  GFD/PVL UB6 .... 84 D2
Edward Pauling School
  FELT TW13 .... 140 C1
Edward Wilson Primary School
  BAY/PAD W2 .... 8 C2
Edwin Lambert School
  EMPK RM11 .... 63 J5
Effra Road Retail Park
  BRXS/STRHM SW2 .... 130 B4
The Egerton House Hotel
  CHEL SW3 .... 15 K4
Eglinton Junior School
  WOOL/PLUM SE18 .... 115 F5
Eglinton Primary School
  WOOL/PLUM SE18 .... 115 F6
Elbourne Trading Estate
  BELV DA17 .... 117 J2
Eldenwall Industrial Estate
  BCTR RM8 .... 62 A7
Eldon Infant School
  ED N9 .... 30 D7
Eldon Junior School
  ED N9 .... 30 E7
Eleanor Palmer Primary School
  KTTN NW5 .... 72 C3
Eleanor Smith School
  CAN/RD E16 .... 95 G5
Eleanor Smith Special School &
  Primary Support Service
  PLSTW E13 .... 94 E1
Electrical Trades Union College
  ESH/CLAY KT10 .... 170 A3
Electric Cinema
  NTGHL W11 .... 88 D5
Elephant & Castle ⇌ ⊖
  STHWK SE1 .... 18 D4
Elephant & Castle
  Leisure Centre
  STHWK SE1 .... 18 D5
Elephant & Castle
  Shopping Centre
  STHWK SE1 .... 18 D4
Elers Clinic
  HYS/HAR UB3 .... 101 G3
Elfrida Primary School
  CAT SE6 .... 151 K3
Eliot Bank Primary School
  FSTH SE23 .... 150 D1
Elizabeth Garrett
  Anderson Hospital
  CAMTN NW1 .... 5 H8
Elizabeth Garrett Anderson
  Language College
  IS N1 .... 5 M5
Elizabeth Selby Infant School
  BETH E2 .... 92 C2
Elizabeth Trading Estate
  NWCR SE14 .... 112 A5
Ellen Wilkinson Primary School
  CAN/RD E16 .... 95 H4
Ellen Wilkinson School for Girls
  ACT W3 .... 86 B5
Ellern Mede School
  TRDG/WHET N20 .... 26 B7
Ellerslie Square
  Industrial Estate
  BRXS/STRHM SW2 .... 129 K3
Ellingham Primary School
  CHSGTN KT9 .... 171 K6
Elliott School
  PUT/ROE SW15 .... 127 F4
Elmbridge Leisure Centre
  WOT/HER KT12 .... 156 A4
Elm Court School
  WNWD SE27 .... 149 H1
Elmers End ⇌ ⊖
  BECK BR3 .... 166 A3
The Elmgreen School
  WNWD SE27 .... 149 H1
Elmgrove Junior School
  KTN/HRWW/WS HA3 .... 49 G3

Elmhurst Primary School
  FSTGT E7 .... 77 F6
Elmhurst School
  SAND/SEL CR2 .... 177 K4
Elm Lea Trading Estate
  TOTM N17 .... 42 C6
Elm Park ⊖
  HCH RM12 .... 81 J3
Elm Park Primary
  HCH RM12 .... 81 H4
The Elms Football & Tennis Club
  STAN HA7 .... 35 H4
Elmstead Woods ⇌
  CHST BR7 .... 153 J5
Elmwood J & I School
  CROY/NA CR0 .... 164 C6
Elm Wood Primary School
  DUL SE21 .... 149 K2
Elsdale Street Health Centre
  HOM E9 .... 74 E6
Elsley Primary School
  WBLY HA9 .... 68 B5
Elsley School
  BTSEA SW11 .... 129 F2
Elstree Aerodrome
  BORE WD6 .... 23 F2
Elstree & Borehamwood ⇌
  BORE WD6 .... 24 B3
Elstree Golf & Country Club
  BORE WD6 .... 23 K2
Elstree Studios
  BORE WD6 .... 24 C2
Elstree Way Clinic
  BORE WD6 .... 24 D1
Eltham ⇌
  ELTH/MOT SE9 .... 134 E3
Eltham Bus Station
  ELTH/MOT SE9 .... 134 E4
Eltham CE Primary School
  ELTH/MOT SE9 .... 134 E4
Eltham College Junior School
  ELTH/MOT SE9 .... 134 C7
Eltham College Senior School
  ELTH/MOT SE9 .... 153 H1
Eltham Crematorium
  ELTH/MOT SE9 .... 135 J3
The Eltham Foundation School
  ELTH/MOT SE9 .... 134 C5
Eltham Health Clinic
  ELTH/MOT SE9 .... 134 D4
Eltham Health & Fitness Centre
  ELTH/MOT SE9 .... 135 F5
Eltham Hill Technology College
  ELTH/MOT SE9 .... 134 D5
Eltham Palace
  ELTH/MOT SE9 .... 134 D6
Eltham Pools
  ELTH/MOT SE9 .... 134 D4
Eltham Warren Golf Club
  ELTH/MOT SE9 .... 135 G4
Elthorne Park High School
  HNWL W7 .... 104 A2
Elthorne Sports Centre
  HNWL W7 .... 104 A2
Elverson Road ⊖
  LEW SE13 .... 132 E1
Elystan Business Centre
  YEAD UB4 .... 83 G6
Emanuel School
  BTSEA SW11 .... 128 C3
Embankment ⊖
  CHCR WC2N 11 K8
Embankment Pier
  CHCR WC2N 11 L8
Embassy of Afghanistan
  SKENS SW7 .... 15 G2
Embassy of Albania
  BGVA SW1W 16 D4
Embassy of Algeria
  NTGHL W11 .... 88 C7
Embassy of Angola
  MYFR/PKLN W1K 10 A7
Embassy of Argentina
  MYFR/PKLN W1K 10 C6
Embassy of Armenia
  KENS W8 .... 14 C3
Embassy of Austria
  KTBR SW1X 16 A3
Embassy of Bahrain
  SKENS SW7 .... 14 E4
Embassy of Belarus
  KENS W8 .... 14 D2
Embassy of Belgium
  KTBR SW1X 16 B4
Embassy of Bolivia
  BGVA SW1W 16 B4
Embassy of Bosnia-Herzegovina
  CAVSQ/HST W1G 10 D4
Embassy of Brazil
  MYFR/PKLN W1K 10 A6
Embassy of Bulgaria
  SKENS SW7 .... 14 F3
Embassy of Cameroon
  NTGHL W11 .... 88 C7
Embassy of China
  CAVSQ/HST W1G 10 C2
Embassy of Costa Rica
  BAY/PAD W2 .... 8 F6
Embassy of Cote d'Ivoire
  KTBR SW1X 16 B3
Embassy of Croatia
  GTPST W1T 10 D1
Embassy of Cuba
  LSQ/SEVD WC2H 11 J4
Embassy of Democratic
  Republic of The Congo
  KTBR SW1X 15 M4
Embassy of Denmark
  KTBR SW1X 15 L3
Embassy of Dominican Republic
  BAY/PAD W2 .... 8 D5
Embassy of Ecuador
  KTBR SW1X 15 L3
Embassy of Egypt
  MYFR/PICC W1J 10 C8
Embassy of Estonia
  SKENS SW7 .... 14 F2
Embassy of Ethiopia
  SKENS SW7 .... 15 H2
Embassy of Finland
  KTBR SW1X 16 A3
Embassy of France
  KTBR SW1X 15 M1
Embassy of Gabon
  SKENS SW7 .... 14 F4
Embassy of Georgia
  KENS W8 .... 14 D1
Embassy of Germany
  KTBR SW1X 16 A3
Embassy of Ghana
  HGT N6 .... 54 B7
Embassy of Greece
  NTGHL W11 .... 88 D7

Embassy of Guatemala
  WBPTN SW10 .... 14 E9
Embassy of Honduras
  MBLAR W1H 9 L2
Embassy of Hungary
  KTBR SW1X 16 B4
Embassy of Iceland
  KTBR SW1X 16 A5
Embassy of Indonesia
  MYFR/PKLN W1K 10 B7
Embassy of Iran
  SKENS SW7 .... 15 H2
Embassy of Iraq
  SKENS SW7 .... 14 F3
Embassy of Ireland
  KTBR SW1X 16 C2
Embassy of Israel
  KENS W8 .... 14 D1
Embassy of Italy
  MYFR/PKLN W1K 10 B6
Embassy of Japan
  MYFR/PICC W1J 10 D9
Embassy of Jordan
  KENS W8 .... 14 A2
Embassy of Korea
  WESTW SW1E 16 F3
Embassy of Krygyzstan
  MBLAR W1H 9 L3
Embassy of Kuwait
  KTBR SW1X 15 M1
Embassy of Latvia
  CAMTN NW1 .... 10 A1
Embassy of Lebanon
  KENS W8 .... 8 C8
Embassy of Liberia
  BAY/PAD W2 .... 8 B6
Embassy of Lithuania
  MBLAR W1H 9 L3
Embassy of Luxembourg
  KTBR SW1X 16 A2
Embassy of Mexico
  MYFR/PICC W1J 10 C9
Embassy of Mongolia
  KENS W8 .... 14 D2
Embassy of Morocco
  SKENS SW7 .... 14 E5
Embassy of Mozambique
  FITZ W1T 10 E1
Embassy of Myanmar
  MYFR/PICC W1J 10 C8
Embassy of Nepal
  KENS W8 .... 8 C8
Embassy of Netherlands
  KTBR SW1X 14 F2
Embassy of Norway
  KTBR SW1X 16 B3
Embassy of Paraguay
  SKENS SW7 .... 14 D4
Embassy of Peru
  KTBR SW1X 15 M3
Embassy of Philippines
  KENS W8 .... 8 C8
Embassy of Poland
  CAVSQ/HST W1G 10 C2
Embassy of Portugal
  KTBR SW1X 16 A2
Embassy of Qatar
  MYFR/PKLN W1K 10 B9
Embassy of Romania
  KENS W8 .... 14 D3
Embassy of
  Russian Federation
  KENS W8 .... 8 C8
Embassy of Saudi Arabia
  MYFR/PICC W1J 10 C8
Embassy of Senegal
  CRICK NW2 .... 70 A6
Embassy of Slovak Republic
  KENS W8 .... 8 C8
Embassy of Slovenia
  MHST W1U 10 C4
Embassy of Spain
  KTBR SW1X 16 B3
Embassy of Sudan
  WHALL SW1A 10 E9
Embassy of Sweden
  MBLAR W1H 9 L3
Embassy of Switzerland
  MBLAR W1H 9 L2
Embassy of Syria
  KTBR SW1X 16 A2
Embassy of Thailand
  SKENS SW7 .... 14 F4
Embassy of The Holy See
  WIM/MER SW19 .... 146 D3
Embassy of The US
  MYFR/PKLN W1K 10 A6
Embassy of Tunisia
  SKENS SW7 .... 15 H2
Embassy of Turkey
  KTBR SW1X 16 B2
Embassy of Turkmenistan
  FITZ W1T 10 D7
Embassy of Ukraine
  NTGHL W11 .... 88 C7
Embassy of United
  Arab Emirates
  BAY/PAD W2 .... 15 H1
Embassy of Uruguay
  SKENS SW7 .... 15 K3
Embassy of Uzbekistan
  NTGHL W11 .... 88 D7
Embassy of Venezuela
  SKENS SW7 .... 15 H4
Embassy of Vietnam
  KENS W8 .... 14 D3
Embassy of Yemen
  SKENS SW7 .... 15 G5
Emberhurst School
  ESH/CLAY KT10 .... 157 J6
Ember Sports Club
  ESH/CLAY KT10 .... 157 H7
Embroidery World
  Business Centre
  WFD IG8 .... 59 H1
Emd Walthamstow Cinema
  WALTH E17 .... 57 J3
Emery Theatre
  POP/IOD E14 .... 93 K5
Emirates Air Line
  CAN/RD E16 .... 94 D7
Emmanuel CE Primary School
  KIL/WHAMP NW6 .... 70 E4
Empire Cinema
  LSQ/SEVD WC2H 11 H6
Endeavour Industrial Estate
  NWDGN UB2 .... 102 D3
Enfield Business Centre
  PEND EN3 .... 30 E1
Enfield CC
  EN EN1 .... 30 A3
Enfield Chase ⇌
  ENC/FH EN2 .... 29 J2

Enfield County School
ENC/FH EN2 .....29 K2
Enfield FC
ED N9 .....42 E1
Enfield Golf Club
ENC/FH EN2 .....29 H3
Enfield Grammar School Lower
EN EN1 .....29 K1
Enfield Grammar School Upper
ENC/FH EN2 .....29 K2
Enfield Town ≥
EN EN1 .....29 K3
English Martyrs RC
Primary School
WALW SE17 .....19 K6
WCHPL E1 .....13 M5
Ensham Secondary School
TOOT SW17 .....147 K4
Enterprise Business Park
POP/IOD E14 .....112 E1
Enterprise Industrial Estate
BERM/RHTH SE16 .....111 K4
Epsom & Ewell High School
HOR/WEW KT19 .....172 E5
Eric Liddell Sports Centre
ELTH/MOT SE9 .....153 H1
Eridge House
Preparatory School
FUL/PGN SW6 .....127 J1
Erith ≥
ERITH DA8 .....118 A4
Erith & District Hospital
ERITH DA8 .....118 A5
Erith Health Centre
ERITH DA8 .....118 B5
Erith Leisure Centre
ERITH DA8 .....118 B5
Erith Library & Museum
ERITH DA8 .....118 B4
Erith Playhouse
ERITH DA8 .....118 C4
Erith School
ERITH DA8 .....117 K6
Erith School Community
Sports Centre
ERITH DA8 .....117 K6
Erith Small Business Centre
ERITH DA8 .....118 C5
Ernest Bevin College
TOOT SW17 .....147 J2
Eros
MYFR/PICC W1J 11 G6
Esher ≥
ESH/CLAY KT10 .....170 D1
Esher CE High School
ESH/CLAY KT10 .....170 A2
Esher Church Primary School
ESH/CLAY KT10 .....170 C5
Esher College
THDIT KT7 .....157 K6
Essendine Primary School
KIL/WHAMP NW6 .....2 B8
Essex Primary School
MNPK E12 .....77 J5
Ethames Graduate School
POP/IOD E14 .....112 E1
Ethelburga GM School
BTSEA SW11 .....108 D7
Eton Manor
OLYMPICPK E20 .....75 K3
Euro Business Centre
SRTFD E15 .....76 D7
Euro Freightliner Terminal ≥
WLSDN NW10 .....87 G2
Eurolink Business Centre
BRXS/STRHM SW2 .....130 B3
Europa Trading Estate
ERITH DA8 .....118 A4
European Business Centre
CDALE/KGS NW9 .....51 F2
European Business
School London
CAMTN NW1 .....4 A9
European School of Economics
KTBR SW1X 16 B2
European Vocational College
HDTCH EC3A 13 K5
Euro Way School
CEND/HSY/T N8 .....55 G2
Euro Way School London
FSBYPK N4 .....55 H6
Euston ≥ ⊖ ⊖
CAMTN NW1 .....5 G8
Euston Centre University
of Westminster
CAMTN NW1 .....4 D9
Euston Square ⊖
CAMTN NW1 .....4 F9
Euston Tower
CAMTN NW1 .....4 E9
Evans Business Centre
CRICK NW2 .....69 J2
Eveline Day School
TOOT SW17 .....147 K1
Evelyn Grace Academy
BRXN/ST SW9 .....130 C3
Evendine College
SOHO/SHAV W1D 11 G4
Eversley Medical Centre
CROY/NA CR0 .....164 B5
Eversley Primary School
WCHMH N21 .....28 E4
Everyman Baker Street
MHST W1U 9 M2
Everyman Belsize Park
HAMP NW3 .....71 J4
Everyman Cinema
HAMP NW3 .....71 G3
Everyman Screen on the Green
IS N1 .....6 C4
Evolution House,
Kew Gardens
RCH/KEW TW9 .....125 F1
Ewell Athletics Track
HOR/WEW KT19 .....173 F5
Ewell Castle Junior School
EW KT17 .....173 J7
Ewell Castle School
EW KT17 .....173 J3
Ewell Grove Infant School
EW KT17 .....173 H7
Ewell West ≥
HOR/WEW KT19 .....173 G7
ExCeL London
CAN/RD E16 .....95 F6
Excellence Christian School
BETH E2 .....74 F1
Excelsior College
UED N18 .....42 C4
Exchange Square
SDTCH EC2A 13 J2
The Exchange
IL IG1 .....78 B1

Executive Medical &
Occupational Health Centre
CROY/NA CR0 .....177 K2
Exhibition Halls
WBLY HA9 .....68 C3
Express by Holiday Inn
CAN/RD E16 .....94 D5
CHING E4 .....43 J6
CROY/NA CR0 .....177 J1
FNCH N3 .....52 D3
FUL/PGN SW6 .....107 J5
GNTH/NBYPK IG2 .....60 C5
SDTCH EC2A 7 J8
STHWK SE1 .....12 D8
WAP E1W 93 F6
WIM/MER SW19 .....147 H6
The Eye Clinic
NOXST/BSQ WC1A 11 H4
Faculty of Engineering &
Science
(University of Westminster)
FITZ W1T 10 F2
Fairbrook Medical Centre
BORE WD6 .....24 D1
Faircharm Trading Estate
DEPT SE8 .....112 E6
IS N1 .....6 E1
The Faircross Complementary
Medical Centre
BARK IG11 .....78 E5
Fairfield Pool & Leisure Centre
DART DA1 .....139 H6
Fairfield Trade Park
KUT/HW KT1 .....159 G2
Fairholme Primary School
EBED/NFELT TW14 .....121 G7
Fairlawn Primary School
FSTH SE23 .....131 K6
Fairley House Junior School
STHWK SE1 .....17 L4
Fairley House School
PIM SW1V 17 G6
Fairview Industrial Centre
RAIN RM13 .....99 F5
Fairview Industrial Estate
HYS/HAR UB3 .....101 J1
Fairview Medical Centre
STRHM/NOR SW16 .....148 E7
Fairway Primary School
MLHL NW7 .....37 F1
Fairways Business Centre
LEY E10 .....75 J1
Falconbrook Primary School
BTSEA SW11 .....128 C1
Falcon Business Centre
BTSEA SW11 .....128 D3
Falconer Special School
BUSH WD23 .....21 K4
Falcon Park Industrial Estate
WLSDN NW10 .....69 G4
The Falcon Preparatory
School for Boys
RCH/KEW TW9 .....124 E4
The Falcons
Preparatory School
CHSWK W4 .....105 J5
The Falcons School for Girls
EA W5 .....86 B7
Falconwood ≥
ELTH/MOT SE9 .....135 J2
Falkner House School
SKENS SW7 .....14 F7
Family Records Centre
FSBYW WC1X 6 A8
Fanmakers' Hall
LVPST EC2M 13 J3
The Fan Museum
GNWCH SE10 .....113 F6
Faraday Building
BLKFR EC4V 12 D5
Faraday School
POP/IOD E14 .....94 C6
Farm Lane Trading Estate
FUL/PGN SW6 .....107 K5
Farnell House Medical Centre
HSLW TW3 .....103 G7
Farnham Green Primary School
GDMY/SEVK IG3 .....61 G2
Farringdon ≥ ⊖
FARR EC1M 12 B2
Farrington & Stratford
House School
CHST BR7 .....154 D6
Fashion Retail Academy
FITZ W1T 11 G4
Featherstone Industrial Estate
NWDGN UB2 .....102 D1
Featherstone Primary School
NWDGN UB2 .....102 C3
Featherstone Road Health Clinic
NWDGN UB2 .....102 D2
Federation of St Elpheges
RC School
WLGTN SM6 .....176 B5
Felnex Trading Estate
WLGTN SM6 .....176 A1
Feltham ≥
FELT TW13 .....122 A7
Feltham Airparcs
Leisure Centre
FELT TW13 .....141 H1
Feltham Athletics Arena
EBED/NFELT TW14 .....121 H6
Felthambrook Industrial Estate
FELT TW13 .....141 F2
Feltham Cemetery
FELT TW13 .....140 D2
Feltham Community College
FELT TW13 .....141 G1
Feltham Hill Infant School
FELT TW13 .....140 D3
Feltham Hill Junior School
FELT TW13 .....140 D2
Feltham & Hounslow
Borough FC
WLGTN SM6 .....176 D5
Feltham Superbowl
FELT TW13 .....141 F1
Fenchurch Street ≥
FENCHST EC3M 13 K6
Fenstanton J & I School
BRXS/STRHM SW2 .....130 B7
Fenton House (NT)
HAMP NW3 .....71 G2
Fern Hill Primary School
KUTN/CMB KT2 .....144 A5
Ferrier Industrial Estate
WAND/EARL SW18 .....128 A3
Ferry Island Retail Park
TOTM N17 .....56 B2
Ferry Lane Industrial Estate
RAIN RM13 .....99 J4
WALTH E17 .....56 K3

Ferry Lane Primary School
TOTM N17 .....56 D3
Festival Pier
STHWK SE1 .....11 M8
Field End J & I Schools
RSLP HA4 .....65 H1
Fielding Primary School
WEA W13 .....104 C2
Field Junior School
WATW WD18 .....21 G4
Fieldway ⊖
CROY/NA CR0 .....179 K6
Film House Cinema
RCH/KEW TW9 .....124 E4
Financial Times
STHWK SE1 .....12 F8
Financial Times
Newspaper Offices
POP/IOD E14 .....94 A5
Finchley Catholic High School
NFNCH/WDSPK N12 .....39 G2
Finchley Central ⊖
FNCH N3 .....38 E7
Finchley CC
FNCH N3 .....53 F1
Finchley Golf Club
MLHL NW7 .....38 D5
Finchley Industrial Centre
NFNCH/WDSPK N12 .....39 G3
Finchley Lawn Tennis Club
FNCH N3 .....38 D5
Finchley Lido Leisure Centre
NFNCH/WDSPK N12 .....39 H6
Finchley Memorial Hospital
NFNCH/WDSPK N12 .....39 G6
Finchley Road ⊖
KIL/WHAMP NW6 .....71 G5
Finchley Road & Frognal ⊖
KIL/WHAMP NW6 .....71 F4
Finchley Youth Theatre
EFNCH N2 .....53 J2
Finsbury Circus Medical Centre
LVPST EC2M 13 H3
Finsbury Health Centre
CLKNW EC1R 6 A9
Finsbury Leisure Centre
FSBYE EC1V 6 F8
Finsbury Park ≥ ⊖
FSBYPK N4 .....73 G1
Finsbury Park Track
FSBYPK N4 .....55 H6
Finton House School
TOOT SW17 .....147 K1
Fircroft Primary School
TOOT SW17 .....147 K1
Fire Brigade HQ
STHWK SE1 .....17 L5
Fire Brigade Museum
STHWK SE1 .....18 C1
Firepower Royal
Artillery Museum
WOOL/PLUM SE18 .....115 G2
Firs Farm Primary School
PLMGR N13 .....41 K2
Fisher Athletic FC
BERM/RHTH SE16 .....93 F7
Fisher Industrial Estate
WATW WD18 .....21 G4
Fishmonger's Hall
CANST EC4R 13 G7
Fitness Unlimited
Leisure Centre
BOW E3 .....93 J1
Fitzrovia Medical Centre
FITZ W1T 10 E1
Fitzroy Nuffield Hospital
MBLAR W1H 9 L4
Five Bridges
LBTH SE11 .....17 M8
Five Elms Primary School
DAGW RM9 .....80 B2
Five Ways Business Centre
FELT TW13 .....141 F2
Flamstead House Museum
GNWCH SE10 .....113 G6
Flaxman Sports Centre
CMBW SE5 .....130 D1
Fleecefield Primary School
ED N9 .....42 C3
Fleet Primary School
HAMP NW3 .....71 K4
Fleetway Business Park
GFD/PVL UB6 .....85 H1
Fleming Lab Museum
BAY/PAD W2 .....9 H4
Flora Gardens Primary School
HMSMTH W6 .....106 E3
Flutters Leisure Centre
FUL/PGN SW6 .....107 K6
Follys End
Christian High School
SNWD SE25 .....165 F5
Follys End Christian School
SAND/SEL CR2 .....178 A3
The Foot Clinic
WIM/MER SW19 .....146 C5
The Ford College
CONDST W1S 10 D5
Fordgate Business Park
BELV DA17 .....117 K1
Ford Industrial Park
DAGW RM9 .....98 D2
Fordview Industrial Estate
RAIN RM13 .....99 F2
Foreign &
Commonwealth Office
WHALL SW1A 17 H1
Foreland Medical Centre
NTGHL W11 .....88 C6
Forest Business Park
LEY E10 .....57 F6
Forestdale Primary School
CROY/NA CR0 .....179 G7
Foresters Primary School
WLGTN SM6 .....176 D5
Forest Gate ⊖
FSTGT E7 .....76 E4
Forest Gate Community School
FSTGT E7 .....76 E4
Forest Hill ≥ ⊖
FSTH SE23 .....150 E1
Forest Hill Business Centre
FSTH SE23 .....150 E1
Forest Hill Industrial Estate
FSTH SE23 .....150 E1
Forest Hill Pools
SYD SE26 .....150 E1
Forest Hill School
FSTH SE23 .....151 F2
Forest House Business Centre
WAN E11 .....58 D6
Forest Pathway College
WALTH E17 .....57 K3

Forest Road Medical Centre
WALTH E17 .....57 H2
Forest Trading Estate
WALTH E17 .....57 F2
Forge Close Clinic
HAYES BR2 .....167 K7
Forge Lane Primary School
FELT TW13 .....141 J5
The Former Health Centre
CHARL SE7 .....114 C3
Forster Park Primary School
CAT SE6 .....152 C2
Fortis Green Health Clinic
EFNCH N2 .....54 A2
Fortismere School
EFNCH N2 .....53 K1
Fortune Theatre
HOL/ALD WC2B 11 K5
The Forum
HDLW HA8 .....36 C5
Fossdene Primary School
CHARL SE7 .....114 A4
Foster's Primary School
WELL DA16 .....136 D2
Foulds School
BAR EN5 .....26 B2
The Foundling Museum
BMSBY WC1N 5 K9
The Fountain Studios
WBLY HA9 .....68 C2
Fountayne Business Centre
SEVS/STOTM N15 .....56 C3
Fountayne Road
Health Centre
STNW/STAM N16 .....74 C1
Four Seasons Hotel
BERM/RHTH SE16 .....93 H7
MYFR/PKLN W1K 16 C1
Foxfield Primary School
WOOL/PLUM SE18 .....115 H4
Fox Primary School
KENS W8 .....8 A9
Frances Bardsley School
for Girls
ROM RM1 .....63 J5
Franciscan Primary School
TOOT SW17 .....148 A3
Francis Holland School
BCVA SW1W 16 B6
CAMTN NW1 .....9 L1
Frank Barnes Primary School
STJWD NW8 .....3 H2
Franklin Industrial Estate
PGE/AN SE20 .....150 E7
Frederick Bremer
Secondary School
WALTH E17 .....58 A1
Frederick Hugh House
CHEL SW3 .....15 J9
Freehold Industrial Centre
HSLWW TW4 .....122 B4
Free Trade Wharf
WAP E1W 93 F6
The French Institute
SKENS SW7 .....15 G5
Fresh Wharf Estate
BARK IG11 .....78 B7
Freuchen Medical Centre
WLSDN NW10 .....87 H1
Freud Museum
HAMP NW3 .....71 H5
Friars Primary
Foundation School
STHWK SE1 .....18 C1
Friends House
CAMTN NW1 .....5 G8
Friern Barnet School
FBAR/BDGN N11 .....39 K4
Friern Bridge Retail Park
FBAR/BDGN N11 .....40 B5
Frithwood Primary School
NTHWD HA6 .....32 D5
Fromondes Industrial Estate
HBRY N5 .....73 J3
HYS/HAR UB3 .....101 H1
WLSDN NW10 .....86 E2
Fryent Country Park
KTN/HRWW/WS HA3 .....50 C6
Fryent Medical Centre
CDALE/KGS NW9 .....50 E6
Fryent Primary School
CDALE/KGS NW9 .....50 E6
Fulham Broadway ⊖
FUL/PGN SW6 .....107 K6
Fulham Cemetery
FUL/PGN SW6 .....107 G6
Fulham & Chelsea College
FUL/PGN SW6 .....127 H1
Fulham Clinic
HMSMTH W6 .....107 H5
Fulham Cross Girls School
FUL/PGN SW6 .....107 G6
Fulham FC (Craven Cottage)
PUT/ROE SW15 .....107 F7
Fulham Medical Centre
FUL/PGN SW6 .....108 A6
Fulham Palace
FUL/PGN SW6 .....127 G1
Fulham Pools
FUL/PGN SW6 .....107 J5
Fulham Preparatory School
WKENS W14 .....107 H5
Fulham
Pre-Preparatory School
FUL/PGN SW6 .....127 H1
Fulham Primary School
FUL/PGN SW6 .....107 K5
Fuller Smith & Turner
Sports Club
CHSWK W4 .....106 B7
Fullwell Cross Health Centre
BARK/HLT IG6 .....60 C1
Fullwell Cross Swimming
Pool & Recreation Centre
BARK/HLT IG6 .....60 C1
Fullwood Primary School
BARK/HLT IG6 .....60 C3
Fulwell ≥
WHTN TW2 .....142 D3
Fulwell Golf Club
HPTN TW12 .....142 D3
Furness Primary School
WLSDN NW10 .....87 J1
Furzedown Primary School
TOOT SW17 .....148 B5
Furze Infant School
CHDH RM6 .....62 A5
Future Business College
CONDST W1S 10 D5
Gaflac Sports Ground Pavilion
SUN TW16 .....140 E7
Gainsborough Clinic
PLMGR N13 .....41 F3

Gainsborough Primary School
HOM E9 .....75 H5
SRTFD E15 .....94 C2
Galliard Primary School
ED N9 .....30 C5
Gallions Mount
Primary School
WOOL/PLUM SE18 .....116 A4
Gallions Primary School
EHAM E6 .....96 B5
Gallions Reach ⊖
EHAM E6 .....96 B6
Gallions Reach Shopping Park
EHAM E6 .....96 B4
Gants Hill ⊖
GNTH/NBYPK IG2 .....60 A5
Gants Hill Medical Centre
GNTH/NBYPK IG2 .....60 A5
Gardener Industrial Estate
SYD SE26 .....151 G3
Garden House School
BGVA SW1W 16 A7
The Garden Museum
STHWK SE1 .....17 K4
Garden Primary School
MTCM CR4 .....163 J2
Garden Suburb Infant School
GLDGN NW11 .....52 D4
Garfield Primary School
FBAR/BDGN N11 .....40 B4
WIM/MER SW19 .....147 G5
Garratt Park Secondary
Special School
WAND/EARL SW18 .....147 G2
Garrick Industrial Centre
CDALE/KGS NW9 .....51 H4
Garrick Theatre
LSQ/SEVD WC2H 11 J7
Garth Primary School
MRDN SM4 .....162 C4
The Garth Road
Industrial Centre
MRDN SM4 .....161 F6
Gascoigne Primary School
BARK IG11 .....78 C7
Gate Cinema
KENS W8 .....8 A7
Gatehouse School
BETH E2 .....93 J1
The Gatehouse Theatre
HGT N6 .....54 A6
The Gate Theatre
NTGHL W11 .....8 A8
Gateway Business Centre
SYD SE26 .....151 G3
Gateway Industrial Estate
WLSDN NW10 .....87 H2
Gateway Primary School
STJWD NW8 .....3 H9
Gateway Retail Park
EHAM E6 .....96 B3
Gatton School
TOOT SW17 .....147 J3
Gayhurst Primary School
HACK E8 .....74 C6
Gazelda Industrial Estate
WAT WD17 .....21 G4
Gearies Infant School
GNTH/NBYPK IG2 .....60 A4
Gearies Junior School
GNTH/NBYPK IG2 .....60 B4
Geffrye Museum
BETH E2 .....7 K6
Gem Hampshire School
SKENS SW7 .....15 J2
Gemini Business Estate
NWCR SE14 .....112 A4
General Medical Clinics
WCHPL E1 .....13 L2
Genesis Cinema
WCHPL E1 .....92 E3
The Geoffrey Lloyd
Foulkes Clinic
IL IG1 .....78 A1
Geoffrey Whitworth Theatre
DART DA1 .....138 D3
George Eliot Community
Primary School
STJWD NW8 .....2 F3
George Greens School
POP/IOD E14 .....113 F4
George Mitchell Primary School
LEY E10 .....57 K7
George Spicer Primary School
EN EN1 .....30 B2
George Street ⊖
CROY/NA CR0 .....177 J1
George Tomlinson
Primary School
WAN E11 .....58 C7
Germal College
FSBYPK N4 .....55 G2
Getters Talmud Torah School
SEVS/STOTM N15 .....55 K5
Gibbs Green Special School
WKENS W14 .....107 J3
Gibson Business Centre
TOTM N17 .....42 B5
Gidea Park ≥
GPK RM2 .....63 K3
Gidea Park College
GPK RM2 .....63 J2
Gidea Park Primary School
GPK RM2 .....63 H3
Gidea Park Tennis Club
GPK RM2 .....63 J2
The Gielgud Theatre
SOHO/CST W1F 11 G6
Giffin Business Centre
DEPT SE8 .....112 D6
Gifford Primary School
NTHLT UB5 .....83 K1
Gilbert Collection
TPL/STR WC2R 11 M6
Gilbert Scott Primary School
SAND/SEL CR2 .....179 G6
Gillespie Primary School
HBRY N5 .....73 H2
Gipsy Hill ≥
NRWD SE19 .....150 A4
Girdlers' Hall
CITYW EC2V 12 F3
Glade Primary School
CLAY IG5 .....45 K7
The Glades Shopping Centre
BMLY BR1 .....167 K1
Gladstone Medical Centre
CRICK NW2 .....69 H3
Gladstone Park Primary School
WLSDN NW10 .....69 H4
Glaziers/Scientific Instrument
Makers Hall
STHWK SE1 .....13 G8

Glebe Primary School
HGDN/ICK UB10 .... 64 B3
KTN/HRWW/WS HA3 ...... 49 K3
Glebe School
WWKM BR4 .... 167 G7
Gleen Lecky Health Centre
PUT/ROE SW15 .... 127 C3
Glenbrook Primary School
CLAP SW4 .... 129 J5
Glencairn Sports Club
FBAR/BDGN N11 .... 40 C6
Glenham College
IL IG1 .... 78 B1
Glenlyn Medical Centre
E/WMO/HCT KT8 .... 157 H4
Glenthorne High Specialist
Arts College
CHEAM SM3 .... 161 K7
Globe Academy Lower School
STHWK SE1 .... 19 G4
Globe Primary School
BETH E2 .... 92 E2
Globe Wharf
BERM/RHTH SE16 .... 93 H1
Gloucester House
HAMP NW3 .... 71 H4
Gloucester Primary School
PECK SE15 .... 111 F6
Gloucester Road ⊖
SKENS SW7 .... 14 C5
Godolphin & Latymer School
HMSMTH W6 .... 106 E3
Godwin Junior School
FSTGT E7 .... 77 F3
Godwin Primary School
DAGW RM9 .... 80 A6
Goethe Institute
SKENS SW7 .... 15 H3
Golborne Medical Centre
NKENS W10 .... 88 D3
Goldbeaters Primary School
EDGW HA8 .... 37 F7
Golden Hinde Educational Trust
STHWK SE1 .... 13 G7
Golden Lane Campus
STLK EC1Y 12 F1
Golders Green ⊖
GLDGN NW11 .... 52 E6
Golders Green Crematorium
GLDGN NW11 .... 52 E6
Golders Green Health Centre
GLDGN NW11 .... 53 F7
Golders Hill Health Centre
GLDGN NW11 .... 53 G5
Golders Hill School
GLDGN NW11 .... 52 E6
Goldhawk Industrial Estate
SHB W12 .... 106 E2
Goldhawk Road ⊖
SHB W12 .... 107 F1
Goldsmiths Hall
STBT EC1A 12 E4
Goldsmiths University
of London
BROCKY SE4 .... 132 C2
DEPT SE8 .... 112 D5
LEW SE13 .... 133 H3
NWCR SE14 .... 112 B7
Gonville Academy
THHTH CR7 .... 164 A4
Goodge St ⊖
FITZ W1T 10 F1
Goodinge Health Centre
HOLWY N7 .... 72 E5
Goodmayes ⊖
GDMY/SEVK IG3 .... 61 G7
Goodmayes Retail Park
GDMY/SEVK IG3 .... 61 H6
Goodrich J & I School
EDUL SE22 .... 131 H5
Good Shepherd RC
Primary School
BMLY BR1 .... 152 D3
CROY/NA CR0 .... 179 K6
The Good Shepherd RC Primary
SHB W12 .... 106 C1
Goodwyn School
MLHL NW7 .... 37 J4
Goose Green Primary School
EDUL SE22 .... 131 G3
Goose Green Trading Estate
EDUL SE22 .... 131 H3
Gordonbrook Primary School
BROCKY SE4 .... 132 D4
Gordon Hospital
WEST SW1P 17 G6
Gordon House Health Centre
WEA W13 .... 85 H7
Gordon Infant School
IL IG1 .... 78 D2
Gordon Primary School
ELTH/MOT SE9 .... 134 E3
Goresbrook Leisure Centre
DAGW RM9 .... 79 K7
Goresbrook Sports Centre
DAGW RM9 .... 79 K7
The Goring Hotel
BGVA SW1W 16 A5
Gorringe Park Primary School
MTCM CR4 .... 148 A7
Gosai Cinema
WEA W13 .... 85 H7
Gosbury Hill Health Centre
CHSGTN KT9 .... 172 A3
Gosford Primary School
REDBR IG4 .... 59 K4
Gospel Oak ⊖
KTTN NW5 .... 72 A3
Gospel Oak Primary School
HAMP NW3 .... 72 A3
Gove Farm Retail Park
CHDH RM6 .... 61 J6
Government Offices
WHALL SW1A 11 J8
Gower House School
CDALE/KGS NW9 .... 68 E1
The Gower School
IS N1 .... 5 M6
Grace Business Centre
MTCM CR4 .... 162 E5
Grace Theatre at
The Latchmere
BTSEA SW11 .... 128 E1
Graduate School
of Management
TOTM N17 .... 42 B7
Grafton Primary School
BCTR RM8 .... 80 A1
HOLWY N7 .... 72 E2
Grahame Park Health Centre
CDALE/KGS NW9 .... 37 G7
Grahame Park J & I School
CDALE/KGS NW9 .... 37 G7

Granard Business Centre
MLHL NW7 .... 37 C5
Granard Primary School
PUT/ROE SW15 .... 126 E5
Granby Sports Club
CHST BR7 .... 153 J4
Grand Avenue Primary School
BRYLDS KT5 .... 159 K5
Grande Vitesse Industrial Centre
STHWK SE1 .... 12 D9
Grand Union Industrial Estate
WLSDN NW10 .... 86 D1
The Grange City Hotel
TWRH EC3N 13 L6
Grange J & I School
RYLN/HDSTN HA2 .... 48 B7
The Grange Museum
CRICK NW2 .... 69 H3
Grange Park ⊖
WCHMH N21 .... 29 H4
Grange Park Clinic
YEAD UB4 .... 82 D3
Grange Park Junior School
YEAD UB4 .... 82 D3
Grange Park
Preparatory School
WCHMH N21 .... 29 H5
Grange Park Primary School
WCHMH N21 .... 29 G3
Grange Primary School
CAN/RD E16 .... 94 D3
EA W5 .... 104 E1
STHWK SE1 .... 19 J4
Grange Whitehall Hotel
RSQ WC1B 11 J3
Grangewood
Independent School
FSTGT E7 .... 77 H6
Grangewood School
PIN HA5 .... 46 E4
Granton Primary School
STRHM/NOR SW16 .... 148 C6
Granville Road Industrial Estate
CRICK NW2 .... 70 D1
Grasmere Primary School
STNW/STAM N16 .... 73 K3
Grasshoppers RFC
ISLW TW7 .... 104 A5
Grassroots School
HPTN TW12 .... 142 A7
Grasvenor Avenue
Infant School
BAR EN5 .... 26 E5
Gravel Hill ⊖
CROY/NA CR0 .... 179 G6
Gravel Hill Primary School
BXLYHS DA6 .... 137 J4
Graveney School
TOOT SW17 .... 148 B5
Graves Yard Industrial Estate
WELL DA16 .... 136 B1
Grays Farm Primary School
STMC/STPC BR5 .... 155 H7
Grazebrook Primary School
STNW/STAM N16 .... 74 A1
Great Cambridge
Industrial Estate
EN EN1 .... 30 D4
Great Chapel Street
Medical Centre
SOHO/SHAV W1D 11 G4
Greater London Authority
Headquarters (City Hall)
STHWK SE1 .... 13 K9
Greatham Road
Industrial Estate
BUSH WD23 .... 21 J3
Great Jubilee Wharf
WAP E1W 92 E7
Great Ormond Street
Hospital for Children
BMSBY WC1N 11 K1
Great Portland Street ⊖
GTPST W1W 10 D1
Great Scotland Yard
WHALL SW1A 11 J8
Great Western Industrial Park
NWDGN UB2 .... 103 G1
Great West London College
GFD/PVL UB6 .... 66 D7
Great West Trading Estate
BTFD TW8 .... 104 C5
Greek School of London
ACT W3 .... 86 D6
Greenacres Primary School
ELTH/MOT SE9 .... 154 A1
The Green CE Primary School
TOTM N17 .... 56 B2
Green Dragon Primary School
BTFD TW8 .... 105 F4
Greenfield Medical Centre
CRICK NW2 .... 70 C2
Greenfields Junior School
SHB W12 .... 87 H6
Greenfields Primary School
OXHEY WD19 .... 33 G4
Greenfields Special School
MUSWH N10 .... 39 K7
Greenford ⊖
GFD/PVL UB6 .... 66 D7
Greenford Avenue
Medical Centre
HNWL W7 .... 84 E4
Greenford Green Clinic
GFD/PVL UB6 .... 66 E4
Greenford High School
STHL UB1 .... 84 A2
Greenford Industrial Estate
GFD/PVL UB6 .... 66 B7
Greenford Park Cemetery
GFD/PVL UB6 .... 84 B4
Greenford Road Medical Centre
GFD/PVL UB6 .... 84 D1
Greenford Sports Centre
STHL UB1 .... 84 A2
Greengate Medical Centre
PLSTW E13 .... 95 F2
Greengrove College
STHGT/OAK N14 .... 40 E1
Greenheath Business Centre
BETH E2 .... 92 D2
Greenhill College
HRW HA1 .... 49 F4
Greenhill Park Medical Centre
WLSDN NW10 .... 69 G7
Greenland Pier
BERM/RHTH SE16 .... 112 C2
Green Lane Business Park
ELTH/MOT SE9 .... 154 A1
Green Lane Primary School
WPK KT4 .... 160 E6
Greenleaf Primary School
WALTH E17 .... 57 H2

Greenmead Primary School
PUT/ROE SW15 .... 126 E4
Green Park ⊖
MYFR/PICC W1J 10 E8
The Green School
ISLW TW7 .... 104 B6
Greenshaw High School
SUT SM1 .... 175 G1
Greenshields Industrial Estate
CAN/RD E16 .... 94 E7
Greenside Primary School
SHB W12 .... 106 D1
Greenslade Primary School
WOOL/PLUM SE18 .... 115 J5
Greenvale School
FSTH SE23 .... 151 G2
Greenwich ⇌
GNWCH SE10 .... 112 E6
Greenwich Centre Business Park
DEPT SE8 .... 112 E6
Greenwich Cinema
GNWCH SE10 .... 113 F6
Greenwich Community College
WOOL/PLUM SE18 .... 115 G3
WOOL/PLUM SE18 .... 115 J5
Greenwich Industrial Estate
CHARL SE7 .... 114 A3
GNWCH SE10 .... 112 E6
Greenwich Natural
Health Centre
GNWCH SE10 .... 113 F6
Greenwich Odeon Cinema
GNWCH SE10 .... 113 J3
Greenwich Park
GNWCH SE10 .... 113 J3
Greenwich Pier
GNWCH SE10 .... 113 F4
Greenwich School
of Management
GNWCH SE10 .... 113 G6
Greenwich Steiner School
BKHTH/KID SE3 .... 113 K5
Greenwich Theatre & Art Gallery
GNWCH SE10 .... 113 G6
Greenwood Primary School
NTHLT UB5 .... 66 C4
Greenwood Theatre
STHWK SE1 .... 19 H1
Green Wrythe Primary School
CAR SM5 .... 162 C5
Gresham Way Industrial Estate
WIM/MER SW19 .... 147 F2
Grey Coat Hospital CE School
for Girls
WEST SW1P 17 G4
Grey Coat Hospital St Michaels
WEST SW1P 17 G6
Grey Court School
RCHPK/HAM TW10 .... 143 K2
Griffen Manor School
WOOL/PLUM SE18 .... 115 K7
Grimsdell Mill Hill Pre-
Preparatory School
MLHL NW7 .... 37 K4
Grims Dyke Golf Club
PIN HA5 .... 34 A4
Grim's Dyke Hotel
KTN/HRWW/WS HA3 .... 34 C3
Grimsdyke School
PIN HA5 .... 33 K5
Grinling Gibbons
Primary School
DEPT SE8 .... 112 C5
Grist Memorial Sports Club
E/WMO/HCT KT8 .... 157 K4
Grocers' Hall
CITYW EC2V 13 G5
The Grosvenor Hotel
BGVA SW1W 16 D4
Grosvenor House Hotel
MYFR/PKLN W1K 10 A7
Grove Health Centre
KENS W8 .... 8 B8
The Grove Health Centre
SHB W12 .... 106 E1
Grove House (Froebel College)
PUT/ROE SW15 .... 126 C5
Grove House Primary School for
Deaf Children
WNWD SE27 .... 149 H1
Grovelands Priory Hospital
STHGT/OAK N14 .... 28 E7
Grovelands School
WOT/HER KT12 .... 156 A5
Grove Medical Centre
DEPT SE8 .... 112 B3
The Grove Medical Centre
ARCH N19 .... 72 D1
Grove Park ⇌
BMLY BR1 .... 152 E2
Grove Park Cemetery
LEE/GVPK SE12 .... 153 H3
Grove Park Industrial Estate
CDALE/KGS NW9 .... 51 F3
Grove Park Primary School
CHSWK W4 .... 105 K5
Grove Primary School
CHDH RM6 .... 61 H4
Grove Road Primary School
HSLW TW3 .... 123 F3
The Groves Medical Centre
NWMAL KT3 .... 160 B2
Grove Village Medical Centre
EBED/NFELT TW14 .... 121 H7
Guardian Angels RC
Primary School
BOW E3 .... 93 G3
Guardian Newspapers
POP/IOD E14 .... 112 E1
Guards' Chapel & Museum
STJSPK SW1H 16 F2
Gumley House Convent School
ISLW TW7 .... 124 B2
Gunnersbury ⊖ ⇌
CHSWK W4 .... 105 J4
Gunnersbury Catholic School
BTFD TW8 .... 104 D4
Gunnersbury Cemetery
BTFD TW8 .... 105 H3
Gunnersbury Park Museum
ACT W3 .... 105 H2
Gurnell Leisure Centre
WEA W13 .... 85 F2
Guru Nanak Medical Centre
STHL UB1 .... 83 H7
Guru Nanak Sikh Academy
YEAD UB4 .... 83 G7
Guy's Hospital
STHWK SE1 .... 13 H9
Guys Kings & Thomas
Medical School (Kings
College London)
STHWK SE1 .... 12 E8

Gwyn Jones Primary School
HARH RM3 .... 58 B6
GX Superbowl
EHAM E6 .... 96 A4
Gypsy Moth IV
CNWCH SE10 .... 113 F5
Haberdashers Askes
Crayford Academy
DART DA1 .... 138 D3
Haberdashers Askes
Hatcham College
NWCR SE14 .... 132 A1
Haberdashers Askes
Knights Academy
BMLY BR1 .... 152 E3
Haberdashers Askes
Hatcham College
FSTH SE23 .... 151 G2
The Haberdashers
Askes School
BORE WD6 .... 23 H2
Haberdashers' Hall
STBT EC1A 12 C3
Haberdashers RUFC
BORE WD6 .... 24 B1
Hackbridge ⇌
WLGTN SM6 .... 176 B1
Hackbridge Primary School
WLGTN SM6 .... 163 F7
Hackney Business Centre
HACK E8 .... 74 D5
Hackney Central ⊖
HACK E8 .... 74 D5
Hackney City Farm
BETH E2 .... 92 C1
Hackney Community College
IS N1 .... 7 J6
Hackney Downs ⇌
HACK E8 .... 74 C4
Hackney Empire Variety Theatre
HACK E8 .... 74 D5
Hackney Free & Parochial
CE School
HOM E9 .... 74 E5
Hackney Marshes Centre
HOM E9 .... 75 J3
The Hackney Museum
HACK E8 .... 74 D5
Hackney Wick ⇌
HOM E9 .... 75 J5
The Haelan Clinic
CEND/HSY/T N8 .... 54 E5
Haggerston ⊖
HACK E8 .... 7 L2
Haggerston School
BETH E2 .... 7 M5
Haggerston Swimming Pool
BETH E2 .... 7 M4
Hague Primary School
BETH E2 .... 92 D3
Hailey Road Business Park
ERITHM DA18 .... 117 H1
Haimo Primary School
ELTH/MOT SE9 .... 134 C4
Hakim Qureshi Clinic
NWDGN UB2 .... 102 D2
The Hale Clinic
CAMTN NW1 .... 10 D1
Half Moon Theatre
WCHPL E1 .... 93 F3
The Halkin Hotel
KTBR SW1X 16 B2
Halley Primary School
POP/IOD E14 .... 93 G4
Hallfield Clinic
BAY/PAD W2 .... 8 E5
Hallfield Primary School
BAY/PAD W2 .... 8 E5
Hallmark Trading Estate
WBLY HA9 .... 68 C3
Hall Place & Gardens
BXLY DA5 .... 137 K5
The Hall Pre-Preparatory School
NTHWD HA6 .... 32 B7
Halls Business Centre
HYS/HAR UB3 .... 101 K2
The Hall School
HAMP NW3 .... 71 H5
Hall Grove Wimbledon
RYNPK SW20 .... 146 B7
Hall School Wimbledon
Junior Department
PUT/ROE SW15 .... 145 J2
Hallsville Primary School
CAN/RD E16 .... 94 E5
Halstow Primary School
GNWCH SE10 .... 113 J4
Hambledon Clinic
CMBW SE5 .... 130 E2
Hambrough Primary School
STHL UB1 .... 83 J7
Hamer Indoor Market
BOW E3 .... 93 H1
Ham Health Clinic
RCHPK/HAM TW10 .... 143 J2
Ham House & Garden (NT)
RCHPK/HAM TW10 .... 124 D7
Hamilton Road Industrial Estate
WNWD SE27 .... 149 K3
Ham Lands Nature Reserve
RCHPK/HAM TW10 .... 143 H3
Hamlet International
Industrial Estate
ERITH DA8 .... 118 A4
Hammersmith ⊖
HMSMTH W6 .... 107 F3
Hammersmith Apollo
HMSMTH W6 .... 107 F4
Hammersmith Cemetery
HMSMTH W6 .... 107 G4
Hammersmith Hospital
SHB W12 .... 87 J4
Hammersmith Industrial Estate
HMSMTH W6 .... 107 F5
Hammersmith New Cemetery
RCH/KEW TW9 .... 125 J1
Hammersmith Physio & Sports
Injury Clinic
HMSMTH W6 .... 107 F3
Hammersmith & West
London College
WKENS W14 .... 107 H3
Hampden Gurney School
MBLAR W1H 9 K4
Hampstead ⊖
HAMP NW3 .... 71 G3
Hampstead Cemetery
CRICK NW2 .... 70 D3
Hampstead College of Fine Arts
HAMP NW3 .... 71 J5
Hampstead CC
KIL/WHAMP NW6 .... 71 F5
Hampstead Golf Club
GLDGN NW11 .... 53 G6

Hampstead Heath ⊖
HAMP NW3 .... 71 J3
Hampstead Medical Centre
HAMP NW3 .... 71 G3
Hampstead Parochial CE School
HAMP NW3 .... 71 G3
Hampstead School
CRICK NW2 .... 70 C3
The Hampstead School of Art
HAMP NW3 .... 70 E3
Hampstead School of English
KIL/WHAMP NW6 .... 70 E3
Hampstead Theatre
HAMP NW3 .... 3 G1
Hampton ⇌
HPTN TW12 .... 142 A7
Hampton Academy
HPTN TW12 .... 142 A4
Hampton Cemetery
HPTN TW12 .... 142 A6
Hampton Court ⇌
E/WMO/HCT KT8 .... 157 K3
Hampton Court House School
E/WMO/HCT KT8 .... 157 K1
Hampton Court Palace
E/WMO/HCT KT8 .... 158 A2
Hampton Court Palace Golf Club
SURB KT6 .... 158 D4
Hampton Farm Industrial Estate
FELT TW13 .... 141 J2
Hampton FC
HPTN TW12 .... 142 B7
Hampton Hill Junior School
HPTN TW12 .... 142 C4
Hampton Infant School
HPTN TW12 .... 141 K6
Hampton Junior School
HPTN TW12 .... 142 A7
The Hampton Medical Centre
HPTN TW12 .... 142 A6
Hampton Open Air Pool
HPTN TW12 .... 142 C6
Hampton Road Industrial Park
CROY/NA CR0 .... 164 D5
Hampton School
HPTN TW12 .... 142 A4
Hampton Wick ⇌
KUT/HW KT1 .... 143 K5
Hampton Wick Infant School
TEDD TW11 .... 143 J6
Handball Arena
OLYMPICPK E20 .... 75 J5
Handel's House
MYFR/PKLN W1K 10 C5
Handsworth Health Clinic
CHING E4 .... 44 B5
Hanger Lane ⊖
EA W5 .... 86 B2
Hanover Primary School
IS N1 .... 6 D5
Hanover Trading Estate
HOLWY N7 .... 72 E4
Hanover West Industrial Estate
WLSDN NW10 .... 86 E2
Hanwell ⇌
HNWL W7 .... 84 E6
Hanworth Trading Estate
FELT TW13 .... 141 J2
Harbinger Primary School
POP/IOD E14 .... 112 D3
Harenc School
SCUP DA14 .... 155 J4
Hargrave Park Primary School
ARCH N19 .... 72 C1
Haringey Arts Council
ED N9 .... 42 C1
Haringey Community
Health Centre
SEVS/STOTM N15 .... 56 A3
Haringey Magistrates Court
HGT N6 .... 54 A5
Haringey Sixth Form Centre
TOTM N17 .... 42 B6
Harkness Industrial Estate
BORE WD6 .... 24 C1
The Harlequin Shopping Centre
WAT WD17 .... 21 G3
Harlequins RFC & Harlequins RL
(The Stoop)
WHTN TW2 .... 123 K6
Harlesden ⊖ ⇌
WLSDN NW10 .... 87 F1
Harlesden Primary School
WLSDN NW10 .... 87 G1
Harley Medical Centre
CAVSQ/HST W1G 10 D4
The Harley Medical Centre
CANST EC4R 12 F6
Harley Street Clinic
CAVSQ/HST W1G 10 C3
The Harley Street Clinic
CAVSQ/HST W1G 10 C2
Harlington Community School
HYS/HAR UB3 .... 101 G3
Harlyn Primary School
PIN HA5 .... 47 F2
The Harold Macmillan
Medical Centre
HRW HA1 .... 48 D3
Harp Business Centre
CRICK NW2 .... 69 J1
Harringay ⇌
FSBYPK N4 .... 55 G5
Harringay Green Lanes ⇌
FSBYPK N4 .... 55 H5
Harrington Hall Hotel
SKENS SW7 .... 14 E6
Harrington Hill Primary School
CLPT E5 .... 56 D7
Harrington Road ⇌
SNWD SE25 .... 165 K2
Harris Academy at Peckham
PECK SE15 .... 111 G7
Harris Academy Bermondsey
STHWK SE1 .... 19 M5
Harris Academy Falconwood
WELL DA16 .... 135 J4
Harris Academy Merton
STRHM/NOR SW16 .... 163 J2
Harris Academy South Norwood
SNWD SE25 .... 165 G3
Harris Boys Academy
East Dulwich
EDUL SE22 .... 131 J4
Harris City Academy
Crystal Palace
NRWD SE19 .... 150 B7
Harris Girls Academy
EDUL SE22 .... 131 K4
Harrodian School
BARN SW13 .... 106 C6
Harrods Store
CHEL SW3 .... 15 L3

Harrovian Business Village HRW HA5 ...48 D6
Harrow Arts Centre PIN HA5 ...34 A6
Harrow Borough FC RYLN/HDSTN HA2 ...66 A3
Harrow Cemetery HRW HA1 ...48 D5
Harrow College HRW HA1 ...48 E6
  KTN/HRWW/WS HA3 ...34 E5
Harrow CC HRW HA1 ...66 E3
Harrow Crown Courts HRW HA1 ...48 D2
Harrow Driving Cycling & Road Safety Centre KTN/HRWW/WS HA3 ...49 G3
Harrow Heritage Museum RYLN/HDSTN HA2 ...48 C2
Harrow High School HRW HA1 ...49 G5
Harrow Leisure Centre KTN/HRWW/WS HA3 ...49 F2
Harrow Magistrates Court HRW HA1 ...49 F3
Harrow-on-the-Hill ≠ ⊖ HRW HA1 ...48 E5
Harrow RFC STAN HA7 ...35 H2
Harrow Road Health Centre BAY/PAD W2 ...8 B2
Harrow School RYLN/HDSTN HA2 ...66 E1
Harrow Town CC RYLN/HDSTN HA2 ...48 A7
Harrow Weald Cemetery KTN/HRWW/WS HA3 ...34 E5
Harrow & Wealdstone ≠ ⊖ HRW HA1 ...48 E3
Harry Gosling Primary School WCHPL E1 ...92 C5
Hartley Primary School EHAM E6 ...77 J7
Hartsbourne Primary School BUSH WD23 ...34 D1
Hartspring Industrial Park BUSH WD23 ...22 A1
Hartspring Sports Centre BUSH WD23 ...22 A1
Harvington School EA W5 ...85 J5
Haseltine Primary School SYD SE26 ...151 H3
Haslemere Business Centre EN EN1 ...30 D3
Haslemere Industrial Estate EBED/NFELT TW14 ...121 K4
  WAND/EARL SW18 ...147 F1
Haslemere Primary School MTCM CR4 ...162 C1
Hasmonean High School Boys Site HDN NW4 ...52 B3
Hasmonean High School Girls Site MLHL NW7 ...37 J7
Hasmonean Primary School HDN NW4 ...52 B4
Haste Hill Golf Club NTHWD HA6 ...46 C1
Hastings Clinic BRXS/STRHM SW2 ...130 A4
Hastingwood Trading Estate UED N18 ...43 G5
Hatcham Mews Business Centre NWCR SE14 ...112 A6
Hatch End PIN HA5 ...34 A6
Hatch End High School KTN/HRWW/WS HA3 ...34 B6
Hatch End Swimming Pool PIN HA5 ...34 A6
Hatfield Primary School MRDN SM4 ...161 H5
Hatton Cross ⊖ HTHAIR TW6 ...121 J3
Hatton School WFD IG8 ...59 H2
Havelock Primary School NWDGN UB2 ...102 E2
Haven Green Clinic EA W5 ...85 K5
Havering College of Further & Higher Education EMPK RM11 ...63 K6
Havering Magistrates Court ROM RM1 ...63 G3
Haverstock School HAMP NW3 ...4 A1
Hawes Down Clinic WWKM BR4 ...180 B1
Hawes Down Primary School WWKM BR4 ...167 G7
The Hawker Centre KUTN/CMB KT2 ...143 K4
Hawkesdown House School KENS W8 ...8 B9
Hawkins Clinic PUT/ROE SW15 ...127 G3
  RYNPK SW20 ...145 H7
Hawksmoor Primary School THMD SE28 ...97 H6
Hawley Infant School CAMTN NW1 ...4 D2
Haydon School PIN HA5 ...46 E2
Haydons Road ≠ WIM/MER SW19 ...147 G4
Hayes ≠ HAYES BR2 ...167 J7
Hayes Bridge Middle School STHL UB1 ...102 D1
Hayes Bridge Retail Park YEAD UB4 ...83 G6
Hayes CC HYS/HAR UB3 ...82 D5
Hayes FC HYS/HAR UB3 ...82 D6
Hayes Grove Priory Hospital HAYES BR2 ...180 E1
Hayes & Harlington ≠ HYS/HAR UB3 ...101 J2
The Hayes Manor School HYS/HAR UB3 ...82 B5
Hayes Park J & I School YEAD UB4 ...82 D3
Hayes Pool HYS/HAR UB3 ...82 D7
Hayes Primary School HAYES BR2 ...168 A7

Hayes School HAYES BR2 ...181 F1
Hayes Social & Sports Club HYS/HAR UB3 ...82 B6
Hayes Stadium Sports Centre HYS/HAR UB3 ...82 B5
Hay Lane School CDALE/KGS NW9 ...50 E3
Haymerle School PECK SE15 ...111 H5
Hays Galleria STHWK SE1 ...13 J8
Hayward Gallery STHWK SE1 ...11 M9
Hazelbury Junior School ED N9 ...42 A2
Hazeldene Medical Centre WBLY HA9 ...68 D3
Hazelwood Schools PLMGR N13 ...41 J3
Headstart Montessori School TOOT SW17 ...147 G1
Headstone Lane ⊖ RYLN/HDSTN HA2 ...34 B7
Health & Vitality Osteopathic Clinic HOR/WEW KT19 ...173 H6
Healy Medical Centre CLPT E5 ...56 D7
The Heart Hospital CAVSQ/HST W1G ...10 B3
Heartlands High School WDGN N22 ...55 F1
The Heart of Greenwich Development GNWCH SE10 ...113 J4
Heathbrook Primary School VX/NE SW8 ...129 H1
Heath Business Centre HSLW TW3 ...123 H3
Heathcote School CHING E4 ...44 C1
The Heatherley School of Fine Art FUL/PGN SW6 ...108 B5
Heathfield College HAYES BR2 ...181 G5
Heathfield House School CHSWK W4 ...105 K4
Heathfield Primary School WHTN TW2 ...123 F7
Heathfield School PIN HA5 ...47 H6
Heath House Preparatory School BKHTH/KID SE3 ...133 J1
Heathland School RYLN/HDSTN HA2 ...66 A2
The Heathland School HSLWW TW4 ...122 E6
Heathmere Primary School PUT/ROE SW15 ...126 D3
Heathrow Airport Central Bus & Coach Station HTHAIR TW6 ...120 D2
Heathrow Airport Terminal 4 HTHAIR TW6 ...120 E4
Heathrow Airport (Terminals 1, 2, 3) HTHAIR TW6 ...120 C3
Heathrow Air Traffic Control Tower HTHAIR TW6 ...120 D1
Heathrow International Trading Estate HSLWW TW4 ...122 A2
Heathrow Medical Centre HYS/HAR UB3 ...101 G4
Heathrow Primary School WDR/YW UB7 ...100 C5
Heathrow Terminal 4 ≠ ⊖ HTHAIR TW6 ...120 E4
Heathrow Terminals 1 & 3 ≠ ⊖ HTHAIR TW6 ...120 E1
Heathrow Viewing Area HTHAIR TW6 ...120 D2
Heathrow World Cargo Centre HTHAIR TW6 ...120 C4
Heathside Preparatory School HAMP NW3 ...71 G3
Heathside Preparatory School (Upper) HAMP NW3 ...71 G3
Heathway Industrial Estate DAGE RM10 ...80 D3
Heathway Medical Centre DAGW RM9 ...80 B3
Heavers Farm Primary School SNWD SE25 ...165 G4
Heber Primary School EDUL SE22 ...131 G5
Heckford Street Business Centre WAP E1W ...93 F6
Hedges & Butler Estate SRTFD E15 ...94 A1
Hedgewood School YEAD UB4 ...82 C2
Helena Road Clinic WLSDN NW10 ...69 K3
Heliport Industrial Estate BTSEA SW11 ...128 C1
Helston Court Business Centre WIM/MER SW19 ...145 K4
Henderson Hospital BELMT SM2 ...174 E7
Hendon ⊖ HDN NW4 ...51 J5
Hendon Cemetery MLHL NW7 ...38 B7
Hendon Central ⊖ HDN NW4 ...51 K4
Hendon Crematorium MLHL NW7 ...38 B6
Hendon FC CRICK NW2 ...70 B1
Hendon Golf Club MLHL NW7 ...38 A6
Hendon Hall Hotel HDN NW4 ...52 A2
Hendon Preparatory School HDN NW4 ...52 B2
Hendon School HDN NW4 ...52 B4
Hendon Secretarial College HDN NW4 ...51 K4
Hendon Youth Sports Centre CRICK NW2 ...52 B6
Henrietta Barnett School GLDGN NW11 ...53 F4
Henry Cavendish Primary School BAL SW12 ...129 H7

Henry Compton School FUL/PGN SW6 ...107 G7
Henry Fawcett Primary School LBTH SE11 ...18 A9
Henry Green Primary School BCTR RM8 ...61 K7
Henwick Primary School ELTH/MOT SE9 ...134 C2
Herbert Morrison Primary School VX/NE SW8 ...109 K6
Hereward House School HAMP NW3 ...71 J5
Her Majestys' Theatre STJS SW1Y ...11 H8
Hermitage Primary School WAP E1W ...92 C7
Herne Hill ≠ HNHL SE24 ...130 C4
Herne Hill School HNHL SE24 ...130 D4
Herne Hill Stadium (Cycle Centre) HNHL SE24 ...130 E5
Heron Industrial Estate SRTFD E15 ...93 K1
Heron Quays ⊖ POP/IOD E14 ...93 J7
Heronsgate Primary School THMD SE28 ...115 J2
Heron Trading Estate ACT W3 ...86 D4
Hertswood School BORE WD6 ...24 E1
Heston Community School HEST TW5 ...103 F6
Heston Community Sports Hall HEST TW5 ...103 F6
Heston Industrial Mall HEST TW5 ...103 F5
Heston Infant School HEST TW5 ...103 F6
Heston Junior School HEST TW5 ...103 F6
Heston Park CC HEST TW5 ...102 E5
Heston Swimming Baths HEST TW5 ...102 E5
Heythrop College KENS W8 ...14 C3
Higgs Industrial Estate HNHL SE24 ...130 C2
Highams Lodge Business Centre WALTH E17 ...57 F2
Highams Park ≠ CHING E4 ...44 A5
Highams Park Primary School CHING E4 ...44 B5
High Barnet ⊖ BAR EN5 ...26 E3
Highbury Corner Magistrates Court HOLWY N7 ...73 G5
Highbury Fields School HBRY N5 ...73 H3
Highbury Grove School HBRY N5 ...73 J4
Highbury & Islington ≠ ⊖ IS N1 ...73 G5
Highbury Park Clinic HBRY N5 ...73 H2
Highbury Pool HBRY N5 ...73 H5
Highbury Quadrant Primary School HBRY N5 ...73 J3
Highbury Square Development HBRY N5 ...73 H2
High Commission of Angola MHST W1U ...9 M3
High Commission of Antigua & Barbuda MHST W1U ...10 A4
High Commission of Bahamas MYFR/PICC W1J ...10 B8
High Commission of Bangladesh SKENS SW7 ...14 F3
High Commission of Barbados FITZ W1T ...11 G4
High Commission of Belize CAVSQ/HST W1G ...10 D4
High Commission of Botswana OXSTW W1C ...10 C5
High Commission of Brunei KTBR SW1X ...16 A3
High Commission of Canada MYFR/PKLN W1K ...10 B6
High Commission of Cyprus MYFR/PKLN W1K ...10 A6
High Commission of Dominica ECT SW5 ...14 D6
High Commission of Fiji SKENS SW7 ...14 E2
High Commission of Guyana BAY/PAD W2 ...8 C7
High Commission of Jamaica SKENS SW7 ...15 G2
High Commission of Kenya CAVSQ/HST W1G ...10 C2
High Commission of Lesotho KTBR SW1X ...16 A3
High Commission of Malawi MYFR/PKLN W1K ...10 C6
High Commission of Malaysia KTBR SW1X ...16 B2
High Commission of Maldives MHST W1U ...10 A2
High Commission of Malta CONDST W1S ...10 F7
High Commission of Mauritius SKENS SW7 ...14 F4
High Commission of Namibia CAVSQ/HST W1G ...10 D3
High Commission of New Zealand STJS SW1Y ...11 G8
High Commission of Nigeria CHCR WC2N ...11 J8
  EMB EC4Y ...12 B5
High Commission of Pakistan KTBR SW1X ...15 M3
High Commission of Papua New Guinea STJS SW1Y ...10 F8
High Commission of St Vincent & The Grenadines KENS W8 ...14 D2
High Commission of Seychelles MHST W1U ...9 M2
High Commission of Sierra Leone REGST W1B ...10 E4

High Commission of Singapore KTBR SW1X ...15 M2
  KTBR SW1X ...16 A1
High Commission of South Africa CHCR WC2N ...11 J8
High Commission of Sri Lanka BAY/PAD W2 ...9 H6
High Commission of Swaziland WESTW SW1E ...16 E3
High Commission of The Gambia KENS W8 ...14 D2
High Commission of Tonga MBLAR W1H ...9 K3
High Commission of Trinidad & Tobago KTBR SW1X ...16 A3
High Commission of Uganda CHCR WC2N ...11 H8
High Commission of Zambia KENS W8 ...14 E2
High Commission of Zimbabwe CHCR WC2N ...11 J7
High Cross Centre SEVS/STOTM N15 ...56 C3
Highfield Infant School HAYES BR2 ...167 J3
Highfield Junior School HAYES BR2 ...167 H3
Highfield Primary School WCHMH N21 ...29 H7
Highfield School WAND/EARL SW18 ...128 D6
Highgate ⊖ HGT N6 ...54 B5
Highgate Cemetery HGT N6 ...54 A7
Highgate Golf Club EFNCH N2 ...53 J5
Highgate Junior School HGT N6 ...53 K6
Highgate Private Hospital HGT N6 ...53 K5
Highgate School HGT N6 ...53 K6
Highgate Wood School MUSWH N10 ...54 C4
Highgrove Pool RSLP HA4 ...46 E6
Highlands J & I School IL IG1 ...59 K7
Highlands Primary School IL IG1 ...59 J7
Highshore School PECK SE15 ...111 G7
High Street Kensington ⊖ KENS W8 ...14 C2
High View Primary School BTSEA SW11 ...128 C3
Highview Primary School WLGTN SM6 ...176 E4
The Highway Trading Centre WAP E1W ...93 F6
Hillbrook Primary School TOOT SW17 ...147 K3
Hillcroft College SURB KT6 ...159 F5
Hillcross Primary School MRDN SM4 ...161 J3
Hill House International Junior School KTBR SW1X ...15 M4
Hill House School CHEL SW3 ...15 K9
  CHEL SW3 ...15 L4
Hill Mead Infant School BRXN/ST SW9 ...130 C3
Hillmead Primary School BRXN/ST SW9 ...130 C3
Hills Grove Primary School WELL DA16 ...116 D6
Hillside Infant School NTHWD HA6 ...32 E6
Hillyfield Primary School WALTH E17 ...57 G2
Hilly Fields Medical Centre BROCKY SE4 ...132 D4
Hilton Docklands Pier BERM/RHTH SE16 ...93 H7
The Hiltongrove Business Centre WALTH E17 ...57 J3
Hinchley Wood ≠ ESH/CLAY KT10 ...171 F2
Hinchley Wood Primary School ESH/CLAY KT10 ...171 G1
Hinchley Wood School & Sixth Form Centre ESH/CLAY KT10 ...171 G1
Hinley Clinic LBTH SE11 ...18 B6
Hispaniola WHALL SW1A ...11 K9
Hitherfield Primary School STRHM/NOR SW16 ...149 G1
Hither Green ≠ LEW SE13 ...133 H5
Hither Green Cemetery CAT SE6 ...152 D1
HM Customs & Excise HTHAIR TW6 ...100 E7
HM Prison BRXS/STRHM SW2 ...129 K5
  HOLWY N7 ...72 E3
  SHB W12 ...87 J5
  THMD SE28 ...115 K2
  WAND/EARL SW18 ...128 C6
HMS Belfast STHWK SE1 ...13 K8
HMS President EMB EC4Y ...12 B6
HM Young Offenders Institution FELT TW13 ...140 B2
Hobbayne First & Middle School HNWL W7 ...85 F5
Hobbayne Primary School HNWL W7 ...84 E5
Hockey Centre OLYMPICPK E20 ...75 J4
Hogarth Business Park CHSWK W4 ...106 B5
Hogarth Industrial Estate WLSDN NW10 ...87 J3
Hogarth's House CHSWK W4 ...106 A5
Holbeach Primary School CAT SE6 ...132 D6
Holborn ⊖ HHOL WC1V ...11 K4
Holborn College WOOL/PLUM SE18 ...114 C3

Holborn College Independent School HMSMTH W6 ...107 F4
Holborn Medical Centre BMSBY WC1N ...11 L1
Holborn Town Hall HHOL WC1V ...11 K4
Holiday Inn BMSBY WC1N ...11 J1
  BORE WD6 ...25 G2
  BTFD TW8 ...104 D6
  BXLY DA5 ...137 J3
  CAMTN NW1 ...4 C2
  CHSGTN KT9 ...171 J7
  CRICK NW2 ...52 A3
  FSBYW WC1X ...5 M8
  GTPST W1W ...10 D1
  HYS/HAR UB3 ...101 G7
  MYFR/PICC W1J ...10 D7
  SKENS SW7 ...14 C5
  SURB KT6 ...158 C5
  SUT SM1 ...175 F4
  WDR/YW UB7 ...100 C4
  WDR/YW UB7 ...100 D3
Holiday Inn Express ACT W3 ...87 F4
  HMSMTH W6 ...106 C3
  PIM SW1V ...16 F7
  WAND/EARL SW18 ...128 A3
  WAT WD17 ...21 F1
Holland House WKENS W14 ...107 J1
Holland House School EDGW HA8 ...36 C3
Holland Park ⊖ NTGHL W11 ...88 D3
Holland Park Pre-Preparatory School WKENS W14 ...107 J1
Holland Park School KENS W8 ...107 J1
Holland Park Theatre WKENS W14 ...107 J1
Holland Street Clinic KENS W8 ...14 C3
Hollickwood JMI School MUSWH N10 ...40 B6
Holloway Road ⊖ HOLWY N7 ...73 H4
Holloway School HOLWY N7 ...72 E4
Hollydale Primary School PECK SE15 ...131 K1
The Hollyfield School SURB KT6 ...159 F4
Holly House Private Hospital BKHH IG9 ...45 F1
Hollymount Primary School RYNPK SW20 ...146 A7
Holly Park JMI School FBAR/BDGN N11 ...40 A4
Holly Park Montessori School FSBYPK N4 ...54 E4
Hollywood Bowl BERM/RHTH SE16 ...112 A2
The Holme CAMTN NW1 ...3 M8
The Holmewood School London NFNCH/WDSPK N12 ...39 F3
Holmleigh Primary School STNW/STAM N16 ...56 B7
Holocaust Memorial Garden KTBR SW1X ...15 M1
The Holy Cross Catholic Girls School NWMAL KT3 ...160 A3
Holy Cross Preparatory School KUTN/CMB KT2 ...144 C3
Holy Cross Primary School FUL/PGN SW6 ...107 K7
Holy Cross RC Primary School CAT SE6 ...133 F7
Holy Family RC Primary School BKHTH/KID SE3 ...134 A3
  POP/IOD E14 ...93 J3
Holy Family Technology College WALTH E17 ...57 K3
  WALTH E17 ...58 A2
Holy Ghost RC Primary School BAL SW12 ...128 E6
Holy Trinity CE Junior School WLGTN SM6 ...176 C3
Holy Trinity CE Primary School BRXS/STRHM SW2 ...130 A6
  DART DA1 ...139 F4
  EFNCH N2 ...53 H2
  KIL/WHAMP NW6 ...71 G5
  KTBR SW1X ...16 A5
  NTHWD HA6 ...32 A5
  RCHPK/HAM TW10 ...125 H5
  SYD SE26 ...150 E1
Holy Trinity College BMLY BR1 ...153 G7
Holy Trinity in St Silas CAMTN NW1 ...4 C1
Holy Trinity Lamorbey CE Primary School BFN/LL DA15 ...136 B7
Holy Trinity Primary School HACK E8 ...74 B5
  WIM/MER SW19 ...146 B5
Holy Trinity School CHEL SW3 ...15 M5
Holywell School WATW WD18 ...20 D5
Homefield Preparatory School SUT SM1 ...174 E4
Home Office WEST SW1P ...17 H4
Homerton ⊖ HOM E9 ...75 F5
Homerton University Hospital HOM E9 ...75 F4
Homoeopathic Health Centre PLSTW E13 ...94 E3
The Homoeopathic Health Centre MLHL NW7 ...37 H4
Honeypot Business Centre STAN HA7 ...36 B7
Honeypot Lane Centre STAN HA7 ...35 K7
Honeypot Medical Centre STAN HA7 ...50 A1
Honeywell Primary School BTSEA SW11 ...128 E5
Honor Oak Crematorium FSTH SE23 ...132 A4
Honor Oak Gallery FSTH SE23 ...132 A5
Honor Oak Health Centre BROCKY SE4 ...132 B3

Honor Oak Park ≥ ⊖
FSTH SE23....132 A5
Honourable Artillery Company HQ
STLK EC1Y....13 G1
Hook Lane Primary School
WELL DA16....136 B2
Hook Rise South Industrial Park
CHSGTN KT9....172 B3
Hopewell School
BARK IG11....78 D5
Horizon Business Centre
ED N9....43 F1
Horizon Industrial Estate
PECK SE15....111 H5
Horizon School
STNW/STAM N16....74 A3
The Horniman Museum & Gardens
FSTH SE23....131 J7
Horniman Primary School
FSTH SE23....131 J7
Horn Park Primary School
LEE/GVPK SE12....134 A6
Hornsby House School
BAL SW12....129 F7
Hornsey ≥
CEND/HSY/T N8....55 F3
Hornsey Central Hospital
CEND/HSY/T N8....54 C4
Hornsey Coroners Court & Public Mortuary
CEND/HSY/T N8....54 E3
Hornsey Rise Health Centre
ARCH N19....54 D6
Hornsey Secondary School for Girls
CEND/HSY/T N8....55 F4
Horn Stairs
BERM/RHTH SE16....93 H7
Horseferry Road Magistrates Court
WEST SW1P....17 H1
Horse Guards Parade
WHALL SW1A....11 H9
Horsenden Hill Golf Club
GFD/PVL UB6....67 H5
Horsenden Primary School
GFD/PVL UB6....66 E5
Horton Country Park
HOR/WEW KT19....172 C7
Horton Park Golf & Country Club
HOR/WEW KT19....172 E6
Hortus Cemetery
NWDGN UB2....102 E1
Hospital of St John & St Elizabeth
STJWD NW8....3 G6
Hotel Indigo
BAY/PAD W2....9 H5
Hotel Russell
RSQ WC1B....11 J1
Hotel Verta
BTSEA SW11....128 C1
Hotham Primary School
PUT/ROE SW15....127 G3
Hotspur Industrial Estate
TOTM N17....42 D5
Houndsfield Primary School
ED N9....30 C6
Hounslow ≥
HSLW TW3....123 H3
Hounslow Business Park
HSLW TW3....123 F3
Hounslow CC
HSLW TW3....122 E1
Hounslow Cemetery
HSLWW TW4....122 E6
Hounslow Central ⊖
HSLW TW3....123 C1
Hounslow East ⊖
HSLW TW3....123 H1
Hounslow Heath Infant School
HSLWW TW4....122 D2
Hounslow Heath Junior School
HSLWW TW4....122 D2
Hounslow Manor School
HSLW TW3....123 G2
Hounslow Manor Sports Hall
HSLW TW3....123 G2
Hounslow Town Primary School
HSLW TW3....123 H2
Hounslow West ⊖
HSLWW TW4....122 D1
The Household Cavalry Museum
WHALL SW1A....11 J9
House Mill
POP/IOD E14....94 A2
House of Detention
CLKNW EC1R....6 B9
House of St Barnabus
SOHO/SHAV W1D....11 G5
Houses of Parliament
WHALL SW1A....17 K2
Houston Business Park
YEAD UB4....83 G7
Howard Primary School
SAND/SEL CR2....177 J3
Howbury Centre
ERITH DA8....118 D6
Howland Quay
BERM/RHTH SE16....112 A2
Hoxton ≥
BETH E2....7 L6
Hoxton Hall Community Theatre
IS N1....7 J5
HQS Wellington (Master Mariners)
TPL/STR WC2R....12 A7
HSBC Sports Club
BECK BR3....151 G5
HSBC Tower
POP/IOD E14....93 K7
Hubbinet Industrial Estate
ROMW/RG RM7....62 E2
Hugh Myddelton Primary School
CLKNW EC1R....6 B8
The Humana Wellington Hospital
STJWD NW8....3 H7
Humber Trading Estate
CRICK NW2....69 K1
Hunterian Museum
LINN WC2A....11 M4
Hunters Hall Primary School
DAGE RM10....80 D4
Hunter Street Health Centre
STPAN WC1H....5 J9
Huntsman Sports Club
BKHTH/KID SE3....133 K3

Hurlingham Business Park
FUL/PGN SW6....127 K2
Hurlingham & Chelsea Secondary School
FUL/PGN SW6....127 K2
Hurlingham House
FUL/PGN SW6....127 K2
Hurlingham Private School
PUT/ROE SW15....127 J3
Huron University
RSQ WC1B....11 J2
Hurricane Trading Centre
CDALE/KGS NW9....37 H7
Hurstmere School
BFN/LL DA15....136 C7
Hurst Park Primary School
E/WMO/HCT KT8....157 F2
Hurst Primary School
BXLY DA5....136 E7
Hyatt Carlton Tower Hotel
KTBR SW1X....15 M4
Hyatt Regency-The Churchill
MBLAR W1H....9 M4
The Hyde Industrial Estate
CDALE/KGS NW9....51 H4
Hyde Park
BAY/PAD W2....9 L9
Hyde Park Corner ⊖
KTBR SW1X....16 A1
The Hyde School
CDALE/KGS NW9....51 H4
Hyland House School
WALTH E17....58 B1
Hylands Primary School
EMPK RM11....63 J5
Hyleford Leavers Unit School
BARK/HLT IG6....60 D1
Hythe Road Industrial Estate
WLSDN NW10....87 J3
Ian Mikardo High School
BOW E3....93 K2
POP/IOD E14....93 K6
Ibis Hotel
BARK IG11....78 B7
BORE WD6....24 E1
CAMTN NW1....4 F8
CAN/RD E16....94 E6
FUL/PGN SW6....14 A9
GNWCH SE10....113 F5
HYS/HAR UB3....101 H7
POP/IOD E14....94 A6
SRTFD E15....76 C5
WBLY HA9....68 C4
WCHPL E1....13 M4
Ibstock Place School
PUT/ROE SW15....126 B5
ICA Cinema
STJS SW1Y....11 H8
ICC London
CAN/RD E16....95 G6
Ickburgh School
CLPT E5....74 D2
Ickenham ⊖
HGDN/ICK UB10....64 A3
Ickenham Clinic
HGDN/ICK UB10....64 A2
Icon College of Technology & Management
WCHPL E1....92 C5
Ihlara Sport FC
HBRY N5....73 J3
Ilderton Primary School
PECK SE15....111 K5
Ilford ≥
IL IG1....78 A2
Ilford County High School
BARK/HLT IG6....60 C1
Ilford Golf Club
IL IG1....59 K7
Ilford Jewish Primary School
BARK/HLT IG6....60 D2
Ilford Medical Centre
IL IG1....78 B2
Ilford Preparatory School
GDMY/SEVK IG3....61 F7
Ilford Retail Park
IL IG1....78 C1
Ilford Swimming Pool
IL IG1....78 D1
Ilford Ursuline High School
IL IG1....78 A1
Ilford Ursuline Preparatory School
IL IG1....78 B1
Iman Zakaria Academy
FSTGT E7....77 F4
Imber Court Trading Estate
E/WMO/HCT KT8....157 J5
Immanuel CE Primary School
STRHM/NOR SW16....148 E5
Immanuel College
BUSH WD23....22 E6
Imperial College
PUT/ROE SW15....127 G1
SKENS SW7....15 G3
SKENS SW7....15 G8
Imperial College Athletic Ground
HYS/HAR UB3....101 F5
Imperial College of London
SKENS SW7....15 G2
Imperial College of Science
FUL/PGN SW6....14 A9
Imperial College of Science & Technology
SKENS SW7....15 H2
Imperial College of Science Technology & Medicine
SKENS SW7....14 F3
Imperial College School of Medicine
PIM SW1V....17 G6
Imperial War Museum
STHWK SE1....18 B4
Imperial War Museum Annexe
LBTH SE11....18 B4
Imperial Wharf ≥ ⊖
FUL/PGN SW6....108 B7
Inchbald School of Design
BGVA SW1W....16 A5
India House
HOL/ALD WC2B....11 L6
The Infirmary Royal Hospital
CHEL SW3....16 A8
Inner London Sessions House (Crown Court)
STHWK SE1....18 E3
Innholders Hall
CANST EC4R....13 G6
Innkeeper's Lodge
BORE WD6....24 E1
CHEAM SM3....161 K7

NTHLT UB5....66 A5
SAND/SEL CR2....177 J7
Inns of Court & Chancery
TPL/STR WC2R....12 A5
Inns of Court Law School
GINN WC1R....11 M2
Insight Independent School
WEA W13....85 H6
Institute for Arts & Therapy in Education
IS N1....6 D3
The Institute Hampstead Garden Suburb
EFNCH N2....53 J3
Institute of Cancer Research
ECT SW5....14 F7
Institute of Education University of London
RSQ WC1B....11 H1
Institute of European Studies
RSQ WC1B....11 K2
Instituto Espanol Canada Blanch
NKENS W10....88 C4
International Broadcast Centre
OLYMPICPK E20....75 J4
International Business Park
SRTFD E15....76 B7
International Community School Primary
BAY/PAD W2....9 J4
International Community School Primary
CAMTN NW1....10 A1
International Medical Centre
ECT SW5....14 B6
International School of Business Studies
PIN HA5....48 A6
International School of London
ACT W3....105 H3
International Trading Estate
NWDGN UB2....102 A2
International University
BUSH WD23....21 K3
Invicta Industrial Estate
SRTFD E15....94 A2
Invicta Primary School
BKHTH/KID SE3....113 K5
Invicta Sports Club
DART DA1....139 G4
Inwood Business Centre
HSLW TW3....123 G3
Ironmonger Row Baths
FSBYE EC1V....6 E3
Ironmongers Hall
STBT EC1A....12 E3
Islamia Girls School
KIL/WHAMP NW6....70 C7
Islamic College for Advanced Studies
WLSDN NW10....69 K6
The Islamic Grammar School
WAND/EARL SW18....127 J6
Islamic Shaksiyah Foundation School
WALTH E17....57 G4
Island Clinic
POP/IOD E14....113 F1
Island Gardens ⊖
POP/IOD E14....113 F3
Isleworth ≥
ISLW TW7....124 A1
Isleworth Cemetery
ISLW TW7....124 B1
Isleworth Recreation Centre
ISLW TW7....124 A3
Isleworth Crown Court
ISLW TW7....103 K7
Isleworth & Syon School for Boys
ISLW TW7....103 K6
Isleworth Town Primary School
ISLW TW7....124 A1
Islington Arts & Media School
FSBYPK N4....55 F7
Islington Business Centre
IS N1....6 F3
Islington Crematorium
MUSWH N10....39 K7
Islington Green Medical Centre
IS N1....6 C3
Islington Tennis Centre
HOLWY N7....72 E5
Islington Town Hall
IS N1....6 C1
Ismaili Centre
SKENS SW7....15 H5
Italia Conti Academy of Theatre Arts
BRXN/ST SW9....129 K2
FARR EC1M....12 E1
Italian Hospital
PIM SW1V....16 E5
Ivybridge Primary School
TWK TW1....124 A5
Ivybridge Retail Park
TWK TW1....124 A4
Ivydale Primary School
PECK SE15....132 A3
Jack & Jill School
HPTN TW12....142 A5
Jack Taylor School
STJWD NW8....2 E3
Jack Tizard School
FUL/PGN SW6....107 G7
SHB W12....88 A6
Jacques Prevert School
HMSMTH W6....107 G3
James Allens Preparatory Girls School
HNHL SE24....130 E4
James Dixon Primary School
PGE/AN SE20....150 C7
Jamestown Mental Health Centre
HAMP NW3....3 L1
James Wolfe Primary School
GNWCH SE10....112 E6
Jamiah Madaniyah Primary School
FSTGT E7....77 H5
Jamiatul Ummah School
WCHPL E1....92 D5
Janet Adegoke Leisure Centre
SHB W12....87 J6
The Japanese School
ACT W3....86 C6
Japan Green Medical Centre
ACT W3....86 D7
Jenner Health Centre
FSTH SE23....132 B7

Jenny Hammond Primary School
WAN E11....76 C3
Jermyn Street Theatre
MYFR/PICC W1J....10 F7
Jessop Primary School
HNHL SE24....130 C3
Jewel Tower
WEST SW1P....17 J3
Jewish Cemetery
GLDGN NW11....52 E5
Jewish Community Theatre
HNHL SE24....130 E2
Jewish Free School
KTN/HRWW/WS HA3....50 C5
KTTN NW10....72 D5
The Jewish Museum
CAMTN NW1....4 C4
FNCH N3....53 F1
Johanna Primary School
STHWK SE1....18 A2
John Ball Primary School
BKHTH/KID SE3....133 H1
John Betts Primary School
HMSMTH W6....106 D2
John Burns Primary School
BTSEA SW11....129 F1
John Chilton School
NTHLT UB5....65 J6
John Dixon Clinic
BERM/RHTH SE16....111 J2
John Donne Primary School
PECK SE15....111 J7
John F Kennedy School
CAN/RD E16....95 H4
John F Kennedy Special School
SRTFD E15....76 C7
John Keble Anglican Church Primary School
WLSDN NW10....87 H1
The John Loughborough School
TOTM N17....56 B1
John Lyon School
RYLN/HDSTN HA2....48 D7
John Nightingale School
E/WMO/HCT KT8....156 E2
John Orwell Sports Centre
WAP E1W....92 C7
John Paul II RC School
WIM/MER SW19....127 G6
John Perryn Primary School
ACT W3....87 G5
John Perry Primary School
DAGE RM10....81 F5
John Roan School
BKHTH/KID SE3....113 H6
John Ruskin College
SAND/SEL CR2....179 G6
John Ruskin Primary School
WALW SE17....18 E9
John Scott Health Centre
FSBYPK N4....55 J7
John Scurr Primary School
WCHPL E1....92 E3
John Smith House
WALW SE17....18 E6
Johnsons Industrial Estate
HYS/HAR UB3....101 K2
John Stainer Primary School
BROCKY SE4....132 B2
The Jo Richardson Community School
DAGW RM9....79 K7
Joseph Clarke Special School
CHING E4....44 B3
Joseph Hood Primary School
RYNPK SW20....161 H1
Jubilee Country Park
BMLY BR1....169 G3
Jubilee Market
COVGDN WC2E....11 L6
Jubilee Primary School
BRXS/STRHM SW2....130 B5
THMD SE28....97 J6
Jubilee Sports Ground
CHING E4....44 B3
Julians Primary School
STRHM/NOR SW16....149 G3
Jumeirah Carlton Tower Hotel
KTBR SW1X....15 M3
Jumeirah Lowndes Hotel
KTBR SW1X....15 M3
Juno Way Industrial Estate
NWCR SE14....112 A5
Jurys Inn Chelsea
FUL/PGN SW6....108 C7
Jurys Inn Hotel
HTHAIR TW6....121 J2
JVC Business Park
CRICK NW2....51 J2
Kaizen Primary School
PLSTW E13....95 G2
Kangley Business Centre
SYD SE26....151 H4
Katella Trading Estate
BARK IG11....96 C2
Katherine Road Medical Centre
FSTGT E7....77 G3
Keats House
HAMP NW3....71 H3
Keble Preparatory School
WCHMH N21....29 G6
Keen Students Supplementary School
WCHPL E1....92 C4
Keir Hardie Primary School
CAN/RD E16....94 E4
Keith Davis Cue Sports Club
DAGW RM9....79 K6
Kelmscott Community Centre
WALTH E17....57 H5
Kelmscott Leisure Centre
WALTH E17....57 H5
Kelmscott School
WALTH E17....57 H5
Kelsey Park Sports College
BECK BR3....166 D2
Kelvin Industrial Estate
GFD/PVL UB6....66 B7
Kemnal Technology College
STMC/STPC BR5....155 H6
Kempton Park ≥
SUN TW16....141 F6
Kempton Park Racecourse
SUN TW16....141 F6
Ken Barrington Centre
LBTH SE11....110 A5
Kender Primary School
NWCR SE14....111 K7
Kenilworth Primary School
BORE WD6....25 F2
Kenmont Primary School
WLSDN NW10....87 J2

Kenmore Park Infant School
KTN/HRWW/WS HA3....49 K2
Kenneth More Theatre
IL IG1....78 C2
Kennington ⊖
LBTH SE11....18 C7
Kensal Green ⊖
WLSDN NW10....88 A2
Kensal Green Cemetery
WLSDN NW10....87 K2
Kensal Rise ⊖
WLSDN NW10....88 A1
Kensal Rise Primary School
KIL/WHAMP NW6....88 B1
Kensington & Chelsea College
NKENS W10....88 C3
Kensington & Chelsea Town Hall
KENS W8....14 C2
Kensington Avenue Primary School
THHTH CR7....149 G7
Kensington Business Centre
SKENS SW7....15 K3
Kensington & Chelsea College
CHEL SW3....15 H9
KENS W8....14 A1
NTGHL W11....107 J1
WBPTN SW10....108 B6
The Kensington Clinic
KENS W8....14 C4
Kensington College of Business
HOL/ALD WC2B....11 L4
Kensington House Hotel
KENS W8....14 E2
Kensington Leisure Centre
NTGHL W11....88 B6
Kensington Market
KENS W8....14 C2
Kensington (Olympia) ≥ ⊖
WKENS W14....107 H2
Kensington Palace State Apartments & Royal Ceremonial Dress Collection
KENS W8....8 D9
Kensington Park School
REGST W1B....10 D2
Kensington Preparatory School
FUL/PGN SW6....107 J7
Kensington Primary School
MNPK E12....77 K5
Kensington School of Business
HCIRC EC1N....12 B7
Kensington Wharf
WBPTN SW10....108 C6
Kensit Memorial College
FNCH N3....52 C1
Kent House ≥
BECK BR3....151 C7
Kentish Town ≥ ⊖
KTTN NW5....72 C4
Kentish Town CE Primary School
KTTN NW5....72 C4
Kentish Town Health Centre
KTTN NW5....72 C5
Kentish Town Industrial Estate
KTTN NW5....72 B4
Kentish Town Sports Centre
KTTN NW5....72 A5
Kentish Town West ⊖
KTTN NW5....72 B5
Kenton ⊖
KTN/HRWW/WS HA3....49 H5
Kenton CC
KTN/HRWW/WS HA3....49 J3
Kenton Clinic
KTN/HRWW/WS HA3....50 A4
Kent Park Industrial Estate
PECK SE15....111 J5
Kenwood House
HAMP NW3....53 J7
Kenyngton Manor Primary School
SUN TW16....140 E4
The Kerem School
EFNCH N2....53 H4
Keston CE Primary School
HAYES BR2....181 H4
Kestrel House School
CEND/HSY/T N8....54 E1
Kew Bridge ≥
BTFD TW8....105 G4
Kew Bridge Steam Museum
BTFD TW8....105 G4
Kew College
RCH/KEW TW9....105 H6
Kew Gardens ≥ ⊖
RCH/KEW TW9....105 H7
Kew Palace
RCH/KEW TW9....105 F6
Kew Retail Park
RCH/KEW TW9....105 J7
Kew Riverside Primary School
RCH/KEW TW9....125 J1
Keyplan & Roxburghe College
FITZ W1T....10 F1
Keyworth Primary School
WALW SE17....18 C8
Khalsa College London
HRW HA1....49 F6
Khalsa VA Primary School
NWDGN UB2....103 F3
Kidbrooke ≥
BKHTH/KID SE3....134 B2
Kidbrooke Park Primary School
BKHTH/KID SE3....134 B1
Kidbrooke School
BKHTH/KID SE3....134 C1
Kilburn ⊖
CRICK NW2....70 C4
Kilburn High Road ⊖
KIL/WHAMP NW6....2 B2
Kilburn Park ⊖
KIL/WHAMP NW6....2 B5
Kilburn Park Junior School
KIL/WHAMP NW6....2 C6
KIL/WHAMP NW6....88 D2
Killick Street Medical Centre
IS N1....5 L5
Kilmorie Primary School
FSTH SE23....151 G1
Kimberley Industrial Estate
WALTH E17....43 H6
Kimpton Industrial Estate
CHEAM SM3....174 D3
Kinetic Business Centre
BORE WD6....24 B2
King Alfred School
GLDGN NW11....53 F7
King Athelstan Primary School
KUT/HW KT1....159 G2
King Edwards Road Clinic
RSLP HA4....46 B7

King Edward VII Hospital
for Officers
MHST W1U..........10 B2
King Fahad Academy
ACT W3..........87 G6
King Fahad Academy
(Girls Upper School)
EA W5..........104 D3
The Kingfisher Medical Centre
DEPT SE8..........112 C5
The Kingfisher Sports Centre
KUT/HW KT1..........159 F1
King George Hospital
GNTH/NBYPK IG2..........61 G4
King George V ⊖
CAN/RD E16..........96 A7
King George VI Youth Hostel
KENS W8..........107 J1
Kingham Industrial Estate
WLSDN NW10..........87 F2
King Henry's Drive ⊖
CROY/NA CR0..........179 K7
King Henry VIII Mound
RCHPK/HAM TW10..........125 F7
King & Queen Wharf
BERM/RHTH SE16..........93 F6
Kings Avenue Medical Centre
STHL UB1..........84 C5
Kings Avenue School
CLAP SW4..........129 K4
Kingsbury ⊖
CDALE/KGS NW9..........50 C4
Kingsbury Green
Primary School
CDALE/KGS NW9..........50 D4
Kingsbury High School
CDALE/KGS NW9..........50 E3
Kingsbury High Upper School
CDALE/KGS NW9..........50 D3
Kingsbury Hospital
CDALE/KGS NW9..........50 C3
Kingsbury Trading Estate
CDALE/KGS NW9..........50 E5
Kings College
(Hampstead Campus)
HAMP NW3..........70 E2
King's College Hospital
CMBW SE5..........130 D2
Kings College London
CMBW SE5..........130 E1
HOL/ALD WC2B..........11 K5
STHWK SE1..........12 C8
STHWK SE1..........12 F9
WEST SW1P..........16 F5
Kings College London
- Humanities
TPL/STR WC2R..........11 L6
Kings College London - Law
TPL/STR WC2R..........11 M6
Kings College London
(Waterloo Campus)
STHWK SE1..........12 A9
Kings College School
WIM/MER SW19..........146 A5
Kings College School of
Medicine & Dentistry
DUL SE21..........130 E5
Kings College Sports Ground
RSLP HA4..........46 C5
King's Cross ≢ ⊖
KCROSS N1C..........5 J6
King's Cross St Pancras ⊖
CAMTN NW1..........5 J7
Kingsdale School
DUL SE21..........150 A2
Kings Estate
HCH RM12..........81 J3
Kingsford Community School
PLSTW E13..........95 G5
Kingsgate Business Centre
KUTN/CMB KT2..........144 A7
Kingsgate Primary School
KIL/WHAMP NW6..........2 A1
Kings Hall Leisure Centre
CLPT E5..........74 E2
Kings Head Theatre
IS N1..........6 C3
Kings House School
RCHPK/HAM TW10..........125 G4
Kingsland College of
Business Studies
SRTFD E15..........94 B1
Kingsland Health Centre
IS N1..........7 K1
Kingsland Shopping Centre
HACK E8..........74 B5
Kings Langley College
of Management
NWCR SE14..........112 B6
The Kingsley Hotel
NOXST/BSQ WC1A..........11 J3
Kingsley Primary School
CROY/NA CR0..........164 A7
Kings Mall Shopping Centre
HMSMTH W6..........107 F3
Kingsmeadow
Athletics Centre
KUT/HW KT1..........159 H2
Kingsmead Primary School
CLPT E5..........75 G3
Kingsmead School
EN1 N1..........30 C2
Kings Oak Primary School
NWMAL KT3..........159 J2
King Solomon Academy
CAMTN NW1..........9 J2
King Solomon High School
BARK/HLT IG6..........60 D1
Kings Place
IS N1..........5 K5
Kings Private Clinic
GDMY/SEVK IG3..........61 F7
MHST W1U..........10 A2
Kings School of English
BECK BR3..........166 C1
Kings Stairs
BERM/RHTH SE16..........111 J1
Kingston ≢
KUTN/CMB KT2..........144 A7
Kingston Business Centre
CHSGTN KT9..........172 A3
Kingston Cemetery
KUT/HW KT1..........159 G2
Kingston College
KUT/HW KT1..........159 F2
Kingston College Theatre
KUT/HW KT1..........158 E2
Kingston Crematorium
KUT/HW KT1..........159 H2
Kingston Crown Court
KUT/HW KT1..........158 E2
Kingston Grammar School
KUT/HW KT1..........159 G1

Kingston Hospital
KUTN/CMB KT2..........144 C7
Kingstonian FC
NWMAL KT3..........159 J2
Kingston University
KUT/HW KT1..........159 F3
KUT/HW KT1..........159 F3
KUTN/CMB KT2..........145 F4
KUTN/CMB KT2..........145 F6
PUT/ROE SW15..........145 H1
King Street College
HMSMTH W6..........107 F3
Kingsway Business Park
HPTN TW12..........141 K7
Kingsway College
CAMTN NW1..........4 E9
KTTN NW5..........72 B5
STPAN WC1H..........5 L4
Kingswood Primary School
WNWD SE27..........149 K3
Kisharon School
GLDGN NW11..........52 D5
Kisimul School
SURB KT6..........171 J1
K+K Hotel George
ECT SW5..........14 B6
KLC School of Design
WBPTN SW10..........108 B7
Knightsbridge ⊖
CHEL SW3..........15 K3
Knightsbridge Barracks
SKENS SW7..........15 K2
Knightsbridge Medical Centre
KTBR SW1X..........15 M3
Knightsbridge School
KTBR SW1X..........15 L4
Knollmead Primary School
BRYLDS KT5..........172 E1
Knowledge Point School
HOLWY N7..........73 F5
KP Estate
RAIN RM13..........99 G6
Krishna-Avanti
Primary School
EDGW HA8..........36 A3
Kubrick Business Estate
FSTGT E7..........77 F3
K West Hotel
SHB W12..........107 G1
Laban Centre for
Movement & Dance
DEPT SE8..........112 E6
Laburnum Health Centre
DAGE RM10..........80 C1
Ladbroke Grove ⊖
NKENS W10..........88 C5
Lady Bankes Junior School
RSLP HA4..........64 E1
The Lady Eleanor Holles School
HPTN TW12..........142 B4
Lady Margaret
Primary School
STHL UB1..........83 K4
Lady Margaret School
FUL/PGN SW6..........107 K7
Ladywell ≢
LEW SE13..........132 E4
Ladywell Arena
LEW SE13..........132 E5
Ladywell Cemetery
BROCKY SE4..........132 C4
Ladywell Leisure Centre
LEW SE13..........133 F4
Laings Sports Ground
BAR EN5..........25 G3
Lake Business Centre
TOTM N17..........42 C5
Laker Industrial Estate
BECK BR3..........151 H4
Lambeth Academy
CLAP SW4..........129 H4
Lambeth Cemetery
TOOT SW17..........147 G4
Lambeth College
CLAP SW4..........129 H4
STHWK SE1..........13 K9
STRHM/NOR SW16..........148 E1
VX/NE SW8..........109 J7
Lambeth County Court
LBTH SE11..........18 B7
Lambeth Crematorium
TOOT SW17..........147 G3
Lambeth Hospital
BRXN/ST SW9..........129 K2
Lambeth North ⊖
STHWK SE1..........18 A3
Lambeth Palace
STHWK SE1..........17 L4
Lambs Court
POP/IOD E14..........93 G4
Lammas School
LEY E10..........57 H7
Lamont Business Centre
CROY/NA CR0..........163 K6
Lamorbey Swimming Centre
BFN/LL DA15..........155 G1
Lampton School
HSLW TW3..........103 F7
The Lanark Medical Centre
MV/WKIL W9..........2 D7
Lancaster Gate ⊖
BAY/PAD W2..........9 G6
Lancaster Hotel
BAY/PAD W2..........9 G6
Lancaster House
WHALL SW1A..........16 E1
Lancasterian Primary School
TOTM N17..........42 A7
Lancaster Road
Industrial Estate
EBAR EN4..........27 H4
Lancelot Medical Centre
ALP/SUD HA0..........67 K4
The Landmark Hotel
CAMTN NW1..........9 L2
The Lanesborough Hotel
KTBR SW1X..........16 A1
Lanford Obesity Clinic
ED N9..........30 D6
Langbourne Primary School
DUL SE21..........150 A2
Langdon Down Centre
TEDD TW11..........143 J6
Langdon Park ⊖
POP/IOD E14..........93 K4
Langdon Park School
POP/IOD E14..........93 K5
Langdon School
EHAM E6..........96 B1
Langford Primary School
FUL/PGN SW6..........128 A1
The Langham Hotel
REGST W1B..........10 D3

Langhedge Lane
Industrial Estate
UED N18..........42 B5
Langley Park Girls School &
Sports Centre
BECK BR3..........166 C3
Langley Park Golf Club
BECK BR3..........167 G5
Langley Park School for Boys
BECK BR3..........166 C3
Langthorne Health Centre
WAN E11..........76 B2
Langthorne Hospital
WAN E11..........76 B3
Lansbury Lawrence
Primary School
POP/IOD E14..........93 K5
Lansdowne College
BAY/PAD W2..........8 C7
Lansdowne School
BRXN/ST SW9..........130 A2
Lantern of Knowledge Boys
LEY E10..........76 A1
La Retraite RC Girls School
BAL SW12..........129 H6
Lark Hall Primary School
CLAP SW4..........129 J1
Larkshall Business Centre
CHING E4..........44 B1
Larkswood Primary School
CHING E4..........43 K3
Larmenier & Sacred Catholic
Primary School
HMSMTH W6..........107 G3
La Sainte Union Catholic
Secondary School
HGT N6..........72 A2
La Sainte Union Convent School
KTTN NW5..........72 B2
La Salette RC Primary School
RAIN RM13..........99 J2
Latchmere Leisure Centre
BTSEA SW11..........128 E1
Latchmere Primary School
KUTN/CMB KT2..........144 B5
Lathom Junior School
EHAM E6..........77 J6
Latimer Road ⊖
NTGHL W11..........88 B6
Latymer All Saints CE
Primary School
ED N9..........42 B1
The Latymer
Preparatory School
HMSMTH W6..........106 D4
The Latymer School
ED N9..........42 A1
Latymer Upper School
HMSMTH W6..........106 D3
Launcelot Primary School
BMLY BR1..........152 E3
Laurance Haines
Primary School
WATW WD18..........20 E5
Laurel Clinic
EA W5..........104 D3
Laurel Lane Primary
WDR/YW UB7..........100 A3
Lauriston Primary School
HOM E9..........75 F7
Lawdale Junior School
BETH E2..........92 C2
Lawrence Trading Estate
GNWCH SE10..........113 H3
Lawrence University
SKENS SW7..........14 F6
Lawrence Wharf
BERM/RHTH SE16..........93 H7
Laycock Primary School
IS N1..........73 G5
Lazards Sports Club
SUN TW16..........141 F7
Leadenhall Market
BANK EC3V..........13 J5
Lea Park Trading Estate
LEY E10..........57 H6
Leaside Business Centre
PEND EN3..........31 H1
Leathermarket Gardens
STHWK SE1..........19 J2
Leathersellers Sports Ground
LEE/GVPK SE12..........134 B6
Leathers Hall
HDTCH EC3A..........13 J4
Lea Valley Primary School
TOTM N17..........42 C6
Lea Valley Trading Estate
UED N18..........42 E3
UED N18..........43 F5
Lebanon Road ⊖
CROY/NA CR0..........178 A1
L'Ecole de Battersea
BTSEA SW11..........108 C7
L'Ecole des Petits
FUL/PGN SW6..........128 A1
Lee ≢
LEE/GVPK SE12..........133 K5
Lee Manor Primary School
LEW SE13..........133 H5
Leeside Court
BERM/RHTH SE16..........93 F7
Leeside Trading Estate
TOTM N17..........42 E6
Lee Valley Camping &
Caravan Park
ED N9..........31 G7
Lee Valley Campsite
CHING E4..........31 K1
Lee Valley Ice Centre
LEY E10..........75 F7
Lee Valley Leisure Complex,
Athletics Centre & Golf Club
ED N9..........31 G6
Lee Valley Watersports Centre
CHING E4..........43 G5
Leicester Square ⊖
LSO/SEVD WC2H..........11 H6
Leigh Close Industrial Estate
NWMAL KT3..........160 A3
Leigh Technology Academy
DART DA1..........139 K7
Leighton House Museum
WKENS W14..........107 J2
Le Meridien Hotel
REGST W1B..........10 F7
Lena Gardens Primary School
HMSMTH W6..........107 F2
Leopold Primary School
WLSDN NW10..........69 H6
Leopold Street Clinic
BOW E3..........93 H4
Lesnes Abbey
BELV DA17..........116 E3

Lessness Heath Primary School
BELV DA17..........117 H4
The Levin Hotel
KTBR SW1X..........15 L3
Lewin Mead Community
Mental Health Centre
STRHM/NOR SW16..........148 D5
Lewis Clinic
CAR SM5..........176 A3
Lewisham ≢ ⊖
DEPT SE8..........132 E1
Lewisham Bridge
Primary School
LEW SE13..........132 E2
Lewisham Business Centre
NWCR SE14..........112 A5
Lewisham Centre
LEW SE13..........133 F3
Lewisham College
BROCKY SE4..........132 D1
Lewisham Crematorium
CAT SE6..........152 D1
Lewisham Lions Centre
BERM/RHTH SE16..........111 K4
Lexi Cinema
WLSDN NW10..........70 A7
The Leys Primary School
DAGE RM10..........80 E6
Leyton ⊖
LEY E10..........76 A2
Leyton Business Centre
LEY E10..........75 H1
Leyton FC
LEY E10..........57 H7
Leyton Industrial Village
LEY E10..........57 F6
Leyton Leisure Centre
LEY E10..........57 K6
Leyton Midland Road ⊖
LEY E10..........58 A7
Leyton Mills Retail Park
LEY E10..........76 A2
Leyton Orient FC
(Matchroom Stadium)
LEY E10..........75 K2
Leyton Sixth Form College
LEY E10..........58 B5
Leytonstone ⊖
WAN E11..........58 C7
Leytonstone Business &
Enterprise Specialist School
WAN E11..........58 C5
Leytonstone High Road ⊖
WAN E11..........76 C1
Leyton Youth Sports Ground
LEY E10..........57 K7
The Liberty City Clinic
SDTCH EC2A..........7 J9
Liberty II Centre
ROM RM1..........63 G3
Liberty Middle School
MTCM CR4..........162 D1
The Liberty
ROM RM1..........63 G4
Library & Community Centre
BTSEA SW11..........128 C2
The Lighthouse Group
(TLG) Centre
STHWK SE11..........110 B5
L'ile Aux Enfants
KTTN NW5..........72 A4
Lilian Baylis School
VX/NE SW8..........17 L9
Lilian Baylis
Technology School
VX/NE SW8..........17 L9
Lilian Baylis School
LBTH SE11..........17 M6
Lillian Baylis Theatre
CLKNW EC1R..........6 C7
Lillian Bishop School of English
SKENS SW7..........15 G5
Limehouse ≢ ⊖
WCHPL E1..........93 G5
Limehouse Hole Stairs
BERM/RHTH SE16..........93 H7
Lime Trees Park Golf Club
NTHLT UB5..........65 G7
Lincoln Road Clinic
EN EN1..........30 C4
Lincoln's Inn
LINN WC2A..........11 M4
Linden Bridge School
WPK KT4..........173 G2
Linden Lodge School
WIM/MER SW19..........127 H7
Lindon Bennett School
FELT TW13..........141 H4
Linford Christie Stadium
SHB W12..........87 H2
The Link Day Primary School
CROY/NA CR0..........176 E3
The Link Secondary School
CROY/NA CR0..........177 F3
Links Primary School
TOOT SW17..........148 A5
Linley House School
BRYLDS KT5..........159 G5
Linley Sambourne House
KENS W8..........14 A2
WKENS W14..........107 J1
Linnet House Clinic
STJWD NW8..........3 J6
Linton Mead Primary School
THMD SE28..........97 H6
Lionel Road Primary School
BTFD TW8..........105 F3
Lion House School
PUT/ROE SW15..........127 G3
Lismarrine Industrial Park
BORE WD6..........23 H5
Lisson Grove Health Centre
STJWD NW8..........3 J9
Lister Community School
PLSTW E13..........95 F1
The Lister Hospital
BGVA SW1W..........16 C8
Lister House Clinic
CAVSQ/HST W1G..........10 C4
Little Danson Welfare Clinic
WELL DA16..........136 B3
Little Davids School
CROY/NA CR0..........179 K5
Little Hands Theatre
HDN NW4..........52 A3
Little Heath School
CHDH RM6..........61 H3
Little Ilford School
MNPK E12..........77 K4
Little Reddings Primary School
BUSH WD23..........22 B4
Little St Helens School
NTHWD HA6..........32 C5

Little Venice Medical Centre
MV/WKIL W9..........8 F1
Little Wandsworth School
TOOT SW17..........148 A1
Liverpool Street ≢ ⊖
LVPST EC2M..........13 J2
Livesey Museum for Children
PECK SE15..........111 J5
Livingstone Hospital
DART DA1..........139 J4
Livingstone Primary School
EBAR EN4..........27 H2
The Livity School
BRXS/STRHM SW2..........129 K4
Lloyd Park ⊖
CROY/NA CR0..........178 B3
Lloyd Park Centre
WALTH E17..........57 J1
Lloyd's of London
HDTCH EC3A..........13 J5
Lloyds Register CC
DUL SE21..........130 E7
Lloyd Williamson School
NKENS W10..........88 C4
Locks View Court
POP/IOD E14..........93 G6
Lockwood Industrial Park
TOTM N17..........56 D2
Lombard Business Centre
BTSEA SW11..........128 C1
Lombard Business Park
CROY/NA CR0..........164 A6
WAND/EARL SW18..........128 C3
WIM/MER SW19..........162 B1
Lombard Trading Estate
CHARL SE7..........114 A3
Lombardy Retail Park
HYS/HAR UB3..........83 F6
London 2012 Games Venues:
Aquatics Centre
OLYMPICPK E20..........76 A6
Basketball Arena
OLYMPICPK E20..........75 K4
BMX Track
OLYMPICPK E20..........75 K4
Earl's Court
ECT SW5..........14 A8
Eton Manor
OLYMPICPK E20..........75 K3
ExCeL
CAN/RD E16..........95 F6
Greenwich Park
GNWCH SE10..........113 G5
Hampton Court Palace
E/WMO/HCT KT8..........158 A2
Handball Arena
OLYMPICPK E20..........75 J5
Hockey Centre
OLYMPICPK E20..........75 J4
Horse Guards Parade
WHALL SW1A..........11 H9
Hyde Park
BAY/PAD W2..........9 L9
Lord's Cricket Ground
STJWD NW8..........3 H7
The Mall
WHALL SW1A..........16 F1
North Greenwich Arena
POP/IOD E14..........94 C5
Olympic Stadium
OLYMPICPK E20..........75 K6
Royal Artillery Barracks
WOOL/PLUM SE18..........114 C5
Velodrome
OLYMPICPK E20..........75 K4
Water Polo Arena
OLYMPICPK E20..........75 K6
Wembley Arena
WBLY HA9..........68 C3
Wembley Stadium
WBLY HA9..........68 C3
Wimbledon
WIM/MER SW19..........146 C2
London Academy
EDGW HA8..........36 B3
London Academy of
Music & Dramatic Art
KENS W8..........14 A5
London Allergy Clinic
CAVSQ/HST W1G..........10 C3
London Ambassador College
WCHPL E1..........92 C4
London Bridge ≢ ⊖
STHWK SE1..........13 H9
London Bridge City Pier
STHWK SE1..........13 J8
London Bridge Hospital
STHWK SE1..........13 H8
London Bridge Hotel
STHWK SE1..........13 G9
London Bridge Sports Centre
CANST EC4R..........13 G7
London Brookes College
HDN NW4..........51 K3
London Business School
CAMTN NW1..........3 L9
London Butterfly House
BTFD TW8..........104 D7
The London Canal Museum
IS N1..........5 K5
London Capital College
CAMTN NW1..........4 D3
The London Centre for
Children with Cerebral Palsy
MLSWH N10..........54 D7
London Centre of
Contemporary Music
STHWK SE1..........12 F9
London Chest Hospital
BETH E2..........92 E1
London Chinese Dance School
CAN/RD E16..........94 B4
REGST W1B..........10 D2
London Christian
Learning Centre
MNPK E12..........77 H3
London Christian School
STHWK SE1..........19 G2
London City Airport
CAN/RD E16..........95 H7
London City Airport ⊖
CAN/RD E16..........95 J7
London City College (English
Language Institute) & Schiller
International University
STHWK SE1..........11 M9
London City Mission
STHWK SE1..........19 K1
The London Clinic
CAVSQ/HST W1G..........10 A1
London College of Business &
Computer Studies
CLAP SW4..........129 J3

London College of Business
& Computing
BETH E2 ....92 D1
London College
of Communication
LBTH SE11 ....18 D3
London College of Fashion
CAVSO/HST W1G 10 D4
MHST W1U 10 B4
SDTCH EC2A 7 K9
London College of
Further Education
LBTH SE11 ....18 C6
London College of
Higher Education
CLAP SW4 ....129 G2
London College of International
Business Studies
HHOL WC1V 11 K3
London Commodity Exchange
WAP E1W 13 M7
London Contemporary
Dance School
PLSTW E13 ....94 D2
London Contemporary Dance
School at The Place
STPAN WC1H 5 H8
London Cornish RFC
PUT/ROE SW15 ....145 H2
The London Dungeon
STHWK SE1 ....13 H9
London Electronics College
ECT SW5 ....14 C7
London Esthetique
POP/IOD E14 ....94 C5
London Eye
STHWK SE1 ....17 L1
London Eye Clinic
CAVSO/HST W1G 10 C3
London Eye Millennium Pier
STHWK SE1 ....17 L1
London Fields ⇌
HACK E8 ....74 D6
London Fields Lido
HACK E8 ....74 D6
London Fields Primary School
HACK E8 ....74 D7
London Film Academy
FUL/PGN SW6 ....107 K6
London Film School
LSO/SEVD WC2H 11 J5
London Financial
Training College
FSBYPK N4 ....55 H4
London Foot Hospital
FITZ W1T 10 E1
London Gender Clinic
HDN NW4 ....51 K5
London Group Business Park
CRICK NW2 ....51 H7
London Heart Clinic
CAVSO/HST W1G 10 C3
The London Industrial Estate
EHAM E6 ....96 A4
London Industrial Park
EHAM E6 ....96 B4
London International College
POP/IOD E14 ....94 C5
SOHO/SHAV W1D 10 F4
London Irish RFC
SUN TW16 ....140 E7
The London Irish Youth Theatre
HGT N6 ....54 B7
London Islamic School
WCHPL E1 ....92 D5
London Jewish Girls High School
HDN NW4 ....52 A4
London Ladies & Girls FC
CAT SE6 ....151 K4
London Lane Clinic
BMLY BR1 ....152 D6
London Lighthouse
NTGHL W11 ....88 C5
London Living Theatre
SYD SE26 ....151 F3
The London Make-Up Academy
UED N18 ....42 D4
London Marriott Hotel
HAMP NW3 ....3 H2
MYFR/PKLN W1K 10 B6
OXSTW W1C 9 M6
STHWK SE1 ....17 L1
WHTN TW2 ....123 K5
London Marriott West India
Quay Hotel
POP/IOD E14 ....93 J6
London Metrocity College
BOW E3 ....93 J2
London Metropolitan University
HBRY N5 ....73 J4
HOLWY N7 ....73 F3
LVPST EC2M 13 H3
WCHPL E1 ....13 L4
WCHPL E1 ....92 C5
London Natural Therapy School
POP/IOD E14 ....94 C6
SOHO/CST W1F 10 F6
London Nautical School
STHWK SE1 ....12 B8
London Open College
FSBYE EC1V 6 D7
London Oratory School
FUL/PGN SW6 ....107 K6
London Road Medical Centre
CROY/NA CR0 ....164 B5
London School of Business
& Finance
HCIRC EC1N 12 A3
London School of Economics
CLKNW EC1R 6 B8
HHOL WC1V 11 J4
STHWK SE1 ....12 E8
London School of Economics &
Political Science
HOL/ALD WC2B 11 L5
London School of Hygiene &
Tropical Medicine
GWRST WC1E 11 H2
London School of
Jewish Studies
HDN NW4 ....52 B3
London School of Theology
NTHWD HA6 ....32 B5
London Scottish Golf Club
WIM/MER SW19 ....145 K2
London Silver Vaults
LINN WC2A 12 A3
London Soccerdome
GNWCH SE10 ....113 J1
London South Bank University
STHWK SE1 ....18 D3
London Stock Exchange
STBT EC1A 12 D4

The London Television Centre
STHWK SE1 ....12 A8
London Tourist Board &
Convention Centre
BCVA SW1E 16 C3
London Toy & Model Museum
BAY/PAD W2 ....8 F6
London Transport Bus Depot
BXLYHN DA7 ....137 J2
London Transport Museum
HOL/ALD WC2B 11 K6
London Underwriting Centre
MON EC3R 13 J6
London Wall
BARB EC2Y 12 E3
London Weather Centre
HCIRC EC1N 12 A2
The London Welbeck Hospital
CAVSO/HST W1G 10 B3
London Welsh FC
RCH/KEW TW9 ....125 F2
London West Crematorium
WLSDN NW10 ....87 K3
Lonesome Primary School
MTCM CR4 ....163 G1
Long Ditton Cemetery
SURB KT6 ....171 J1
Long Ditton County
Infant School
SURB KT6 ....158 D7
Long Ditton St Marys CE
Junior School
THDIT KT7 ....158 C7
Longfield J & I School
RYLN/HDSTN HA2 ....48 A5
Longford Community School
EBED/NFELT TW14 ....121 J6
Longford Industrial Estate
HPTN TW12 ....142 B5
Longlands Primary School
BFN/LL DA15 ....154 E2
Long Lane AFC
BKHTH/KID SE3 ....134 B1
Longshaw Primary School
CHING E4 ....44 B2
Longwood School
BUSH WD23 ....21 J3
Lord Chancellors Department
WEST SW1P 17 H4
Lord Lister Health Centre
FSTGT E7 ....76 E3
Lord's Cricket Ground
STJWD NW8 ....3 H7
Lordship Lane Clinic
TOTM N17 ....56 A1
Lordship Lane
Primary School
WDGN N22 ....41 J7
Lord's Tour & MCC Museum
STJWD NW8 ....3 G8
Lorimar Business Centre
RAIN RM13 ....99 C5
Loughborough Junction ⇌
CMBW SE5 ....130 C1
Loughborough
Primary School
CMBW SE5 ....130 C1
Lovelace Primary School
CHSGTN KT9 ....171 J4
Lovell's Wharf
GNWCH SE10 ....113 G4
Lower Clapton Health Centre
CLPT E5 ....74 E4
Lower Place Business Centre
WLSDN NW10 ....86 E1
Lower Sydenham ⇌
SYD SE26 ....151 H4
Lower Sydenham
Industrial Estate
SYD SE26 ....151 H4
Lowfield Medical Centre
DART DA1 ....139 H6
Low Hall Sports Ground
LEY E10 ....57 F5
Lowther Primary School
BARN SW13 ....106 D5
Loxford School of
Science & Technology
IL IG1 ....78 D4
LSE Sports Club
NWMAL KT3 ....160 A5
Lubavitch Boys Primary School
CLPT E5 ....56 B6
Lubavitch House School
(Senior Girls)
STNW/STAM N16 ....56 A6
Lucas Vale Primary School
DEPT SE8 ....112 D7
Lutomer House Business Centre
POP/IOD E14 ....93 K7
Lux Cinema
IS N1 ....7 J8
Lycee Francais
SKENS SW7 ....15 G5
Lycee Francais
Charles de Gaulle
BTSEA SW11 ....129 G3
Lyceum Independent School
SDTCH EC2A 13 J1
The Lyceum Theatre
COVGDN WC2E 11 L6
Lyndean Industrial Estate
ABYW SE2 ....116 D2
Lyndhurst House
Preparatory School
HAMP NW3 ....71 H4
Lyndhurst Primary School
CMBW SE5 ....130 E1
Lyon Business Park
BARK IG11 ....96 E1
Lyon Park Infant School
ALP/SUD HA0 ....68 B6
Lyonsdown School
BAR EN5 ....27 G4
Lyric Theatre
SOHO/SHAV W1D 11 G6
Lyric Theatre Hammersmith
HMSMTH W6 ....107 F3
Mabwin Supplementary School
ED N9 ....42 D1
Macaulay CE Primary School
CLAP SW4 ....129 G2
Madame Tussauds
CAMTN NW1 ....10 A1
Madeira Grove Clinic
WFD IG8 ....45 F4
Madison Bowl
NTHWD HA6 ....32 C6
Madni Girls School
WCHPL E1 ....92 D5
Madrasah-E-Darue Qirat
Majidiah School
WCHPL E1 ....92 D6

Mahatma Gandhi
Industrial Estate
BRXN/ST SW9 ....130 C2
Maida Vale ⊖
MV/WKIL W9 ....2 D8
Maida Vale Medical Centre
MV/WKIL W9 ....2 C8
Malcolm Primary School
PGE/AN SE20 ....150 E6
The Malden Centre
NWMAL KT3 ....160 C3
Malden Golf Club
NWMAL KT3 ....160 B1
Malden Manor ⇌
NWMAL KT3 ....160 B6
Malden Manor Primary School
NWMAL KT3 ....160 B6
Malden Parochial
Primary School
WPK KT4 ....160 B7
Malden Road Baths
CHEAM SM3 ....174 B3
Malham Road Industrial Estate
FSTH SE23 ....132 A7
The Mall Bexleyheath
BXLYHS DA6 ....137 H3
Mall Galleries
STJS SW1Y 11 H8
The Mall School
WHTN TW2 ....142 D2
The Mall
WHALL SW1A 16 F1
Malmaison Charterhouse
Square Hotel
FARR EC1M 12 D2
Malmesbury Primary School
BOW E3 ....93 H2
MRDN SM4 ....162 B6
Malorees Junior School
KIL/WHAMP NW6 ....70 B6
Malvern Way Infant School
RKW/CH/CXG WD3 ....20 A4
Mandarin Oriental Hotel
KTBR SW1X 15 M1
The Mandeville Hotel
MHST W1U 10 B4
Mandeville Primary School
CLPT E5 ....75 G2
Mandeville Special School
NTHLT UB5 ....65 K5
Manford Industrial Estate
ERITH DA8 ....118 E5
Manor Brook Medical Centre
BKHTH/KID SE3 ....134 A1
Manor Drive Health Centre
WPK KT4 ....160 C7
Manorfield Primary School
POP/IOD E14 ....93 K4
Manor House ⊖
FSBYPK N4 ....55 J7
Manor Infant School
BARK IG11 ....79 F5
Manor Park ⇌
MNPK E12 ....77 H3
Manor Park Cemetery
FSTGT E7 ....77 H3
Manor Park Crematorium
FSTGT E7 ....77 G3
Manor Park Methodist School
MNPK E12 ....77 J3
Manor Park Primary School
SUT SM1 ....175 G4
Manor Place Industrial Estate
BORE WD6 ....24 E2
Manor Primary School
SRTFD E15 ....94 C1
Manorside Primary School
FNCH N3 ....39 F7
Manor Special School
WLSDN NW10 ....88 B1
Manor Way Business Centre
RAIN RM13 ....99 F4
Mansfield Infant College
IL IG1 ....78 A1
Mansion House ⊖
STP EC4M 12 F5
Mapledown School
CRICK NW2 ....52 B6
Maple Grove Business Centre
HSLWW TW4 ....122 B3
Maple House Independant
Montessori School
THHTH CR7 ....164 D2
Maple Industrial Estate
FELT TW13 ....140 E1
Maples Business Centre
IS N1 ....6 D3
Maple Walk School
WLSDN NW10 ....69 H7
Marble Arch ⊖
OXSTW W1C 9 M5
Marble Hill House
TWK TW1 ....124 D6
Maria Fidelis
Convent School
CAMTN NW1 ....4 F8
Maria Montessori
Childrens House
HAMP NW3 ....71 H4
Mariner Business Centre
CROY/NA CR0 ....177 F4
Marion Richardson
Primary School
WCHPL E1 ....93 F5
Marion Vian Primary School
BECK BR3 ....166 A4
Maritime Greenwich College
DEPT SE8 ....112 D6
Maritime Industrial Estate
CHARL SE7 ....114 A3
Maritime Museum
GNWCH SE10 ....113 H3
Marjorie McClure School
CHST BR7 ....154 C7
The Marjory Kinnon School
EBED/NFELT TW14 ....121 J4
Market Trading Estate
NWDGN UB2 ....102 A3
Marks Gate Clinic
CHDH RM6 ....62 A2
Marks Gate Junior School
CHDH RM6 ....62 A2
Marlborough College of
Business & Technology
FSTGT E7 ....76 E2
Marlborough CC
DUL SE21 ....131 H7
Marlborough Day Hospital
STJWD NW8 ....2 D1
Marlborough House
STJS SW1Y 10 F9

Marlborough Primary School
CHEL SW3 ....15 K6
HRW HA1 ....48 E3
ISLW TW7 ....104 B7
Marlborough School
BFN/LL DA15 ....136 B7
Marlborough Trading Estate
RCH/KEW TW9 ....105 J7
Marlowe Business Centre
NWCR SE14 ....112 B6
Marner Primary School
BOW E3 ....93 K3
Marriott Hotel
ECT SW5 ....14 C5
HYS/HAR UB3 ....101 G6
KIL/WHAMP NW6 ....2 C5
MBLAR W1H 9 K4
Marshalls Park School
ROM RM1 ....63 G5
Marsh Gate Business Centre
SRTFD E15 ....94 A1
Marshgate Primary School
RCHPK/HAM TW10 ....125 G4
Marsh Green School
DAGW RM9 ....98 C1
Martan College
HOL/ALD WC2B 11 K4
Martinbridge Industrial Estate
EN EN1 ....30 D5
Martindale Industrial Estate
EN EN1 ....30 A4
Martin Primary School
EFNCH N2 ....53 J3
Marvels Lane Primary School
LEE/GVPK SE12 ....153 G3
Maryland ⇌
SRTFD E15 ....76 C4
Maryland Industrial Estate
SRTFD E15 ....76 C4
Maryland Primary School
SRTFD E15 ....76 C4
Marylebone ⇌ ⊖
CAMTN NW1 ....9 K1
Marylebone Health Centre
CAMTN NW1 ....10 B1
Marylebone Magistrates Court
CAMTN NW1 ....9 K2
Marymount
International School
KUTN/CMB KT2 ....144 E6
Mary Wallace Theatre
TWK TW1 ....124 B7
Maswell Park Health Centre
HSLW TW3 ....123 H4
Mathilda Marks Kennedy
Primary School
MLHL NW7 ....37 F4
Matrix Business Centre
DART DA1 ....139 H4
Maudlin's Green
WAP E1W 13 M8
The Maudsley Hospital
CMBW SE5 ....130 E1
Maughan Library (Kings College)
LINN WC2A 12 A4
Mawbrey Brough Health Centre
VX/NE SW8 ....109 K6
The Mawney School
ROMW/RG RM7 ....63 H4
Mayday University Hospital
THHTH CR7 ....164 C5
Mayesbrook Park Arena
BARK IG11 ....79 G4
Mayespark Primary School
GDMY/SEVK IG3 ....79 G2
Mayfield Primary School
HNWL W7 ....84 D5
Mayfield School
BCTR RM8 ....61 J7
PIN HA5 ....47 J2
Mayflower Primary School
POP/IOD E14 ....93 J3
Mayplace Primary School
BXLYHN DA7 ....138 A3
Maytime School
IL IG1 ....78 A2
Mayville Junior &
Primary School
WAN E11 ....76 C2
Maze Hill ⇌
GNWCH SE10 ....113 H5
McKay Trading Estate
NKENS W10 ....88 C3
McMillan Clinic
HYS/HAR UB3 ....82 A4
MDO Majidiah School
WCHPL E1 ....92 D6
The Mead Infant School
WPK KT4 ....173 H2
Meadlands Primary School
RCHPK/HAM TW10 ....143 J3
Meadowgate School
BROCKY SE4 ....132 A2
Meadowside Leisure Centre
BKHTH/KID SE3 ....134 B3
The Meadow Special School
STMC/STPC BR5 ....155 G6
Meadow Wood School
BUSH WD23 ....22 C4
Mead Road Infant School
CHST BR7 ....154 C5
Medical Centres
CROY/NA CR0 ....179 G1
The Medical Centre
WAND/EARL SW18 ....128 A5
WAT WD17 ....21 F1
Medical Express Clinic
CAVSO/HST W1G 10 C2
Mednurs Clinic
STNW/STAM N16 ....55 K6
Megabowl
KUTN/CMB KT2 ....159 F1
Melcombe Primary School
HMSMTH W6 ....107 H4
Melia White House Hotel
CAMTN NW1 ....4 D9
Mellish Industrial Estate
WOOL/PLUM SE18 ....114 C2
Mellow Lane School
HGDN/ICK UB10 ....82 A3
Melrose Special School
MTCM CR4 ....162 D4
Memorial Hospital
WOOL/PLUM SE18 ....135 F1
Menorah Grammar School
EDGW HA8 ....36 E6
GLDGN NW11 ....52 C6
Menorah High School for Girls
CRICK NW2 ....69 H2
Menorah Primary School
GLDGN NW11 ....52 C6
MERC Education
WOOL/PLUM SE18 ....115 G2

Mercers' Hall
LOTH EC2R 13 G5
The Merchant Taylors Hall
BANK EC3V 13 H5
Merchant Taylors School
NTHWD HA6 ....20 C7
Mercure London City
Bankside Hotel
STHWK SE1 ....12 E9
Meridian Clinic
BRXN/ST SW9 ....130 A2
Meridian Locality Mental
Health Centre
CHARL SE7 ....114 B5
Meridian Primary School
GNWCH SE10 ....113 G4
Meridian Sports Club
CHARL SE7 ....114 D6
Meridian Trading Estate
CHARL SE7 ....114 A3
Merlin Primary School
BMLY BR1 ....152 E2
Merlin School
PUT/ROE SW15 ....127 G4
Mermaid Theatre
BLKFR EC4V 12 D6
Merrielands Retail Park
DAGW RM9 ....80 B7
Merry Hill Infant School
BUSH WD23 ....22 B6
Merryhills Clinic
ENC/FH EN2 ....29 F2
Merryhills Primary School
ENC/FH EN2 ....29 F3
Merton Abbey Primary School
WIM/MER SW19 ....147 F7
Merton Adult College
RYNPK SW20 ....161 H2
Merton College
MRDN SM4 ....161 J5
Merton Court
Preparatory School
SCUP DA14 ....155 J3
Merton Industrial Park
WIM/MER SW19 ....147 G7
Merton Park ⊖
WIM/MER SW19 ....146 E7
Merton Park Primary School
WIM/MER SW19 ....161 J1
Merton Road Industrial Estate
WAND/EARL SW18 ....127 K6
The Method Studio
FSBYW WC1X 11 L2
Metro Business Centre
SYD SE26 ....151 H5
The Metro Golf Centre
HDN NW4 ....38 A7
Metro Industrial Centre
ISLW TW7 ....123 K1
Metropolis Centre
BORE WD6 ....24 C2
Metropolitan Business Centre
HACK E8 ....7 K2
Metropolitan Hospital
STHWK SE1 ....18 B3
Metropolitan London Hotel
MYFR/PKLN W1K 10 C9
Metropolitan Police Bushey
Sports Ground
BUSH WD23 ....22 A2
Metropolitan Police FC
E/WMO/HCT KT8 ....157 J5
Metropolitan Police Hayes
Sports Club
HAYES BR2 ....180 D1
Metropolitan Police
(Hendon) Track
CDALE/KGS NW9 ....51 K4
Metropolitan Police Training
School, Hendon
CDALE/KGS NW9 ....51 K4
Metropolitan Tabernacle
STHWK SE1 ....18 D5
Metro Trading Centre
WBLY HA9 ....68 D3
Michael Faraday Primary School
WALW SE17 ....19 H4
Michael Manley
Industrial Estate
VX/NE SW8 ....109 H4
Michael Sobell Sinai School
KTN/HRWW/WS HA3 ....50 C5
The Michael Tippett School
LBTH SE11 ....18 B6
Midas Business Centre
DAGE RM10 ....80 C3
Midas Industrial Estate
DAGE RM10 ....80 C3
Middle Park Primary School
ELTH/MOT SE9 ....134 C6
Middle Row Primary School
NKENS W10 ....88 C3
Middlesex Business Centre
NWDGN UB2 ....103 F1
Middlesex CCC (Lord's
Cricket Ground)
STJWD NW8 ....3 H7
Middlesex Hospital
Medical School
FITZ W1T 10 F2
Middlesex Hospital
Nurses Home
GTPST W1W 10 E2
Middlesex Hospital School
of Physiotherapy
FITZ W1T 10 F2
Middlesex Hospital
Sports Ground
CHST BR7 ....155 F4
Middlesex School of
Complementary Medicine
STAN HA7 ....36 A7
Middlesex University
ARCH N19 ....54 C7
GLDGN NW11 ....53 F7
PEND EN3 ....31 F4
WDGN N22 ....54 E1
Middlesex University (Cat
Hill Campus)
EBAR EN4 ....28 A5
Middlesex University
(Enfield Campus)
PEND EN3 ....30 D4
Middlesex University
(Hendon Campus)
HDN NW4 ....51 K3
Middlesex University (Trent
Park Campus)
EBAR EN4 ....28 C1
Midfield Primary School
STMC/STPC BR5 ....155 H4
Midway Mission Hospital
BETH E2 ....7 L8

Milbourne Lodge School
ESH/CLAY KT10......................170 D5
Mile End ⊖
BOW E3......................93 H3
Mile End & Bow Business Centre
WCHPL E1......................92 D4
Mile End Hospital
WCHPL E1......................93 F2
Mile End Stadium
POP/IOD E14......................93 H4
Milehams Industrial Estate
PUR RM19......................119 K2
Miles Coverdale Primary School
SHB W12......................107 F1
Milestone Hotel
KENS W8......................14 D2
Military Barracks
WOOL/PLUM SE18......................115 F4
Millbank Millennium Pier
WEST SW1P......................17 J6
Millbank Primary School
WEST SW1P......................17 H6
Millbank Tower
WEST SW1P......................17 J6
Millennium Arena
BTSEA SW11......................109 F6
Millennium Bailey's Hotel
SKENS SW7......................14 E5
Millennium Balloon
STHWK SE1......................13 K9
Millennium & Copthorne Hotels
at Chelsea FC
FUL/PGN SW6......................108 A6
Millennium Dance 2000
Theatre School
HAMP NW3......................71 J4
Millennium Gloucester Hotel
ECT SW5......................14 D6
Millennium Harbour
POP/IOD E14......................112 C1
Millennium Hotel
KTBR SW1X......................15 M2
Millennium Hotel
London Mayfair
MYFR/PKLN W1K......................10 B7
Millennium Primary School
GNWCH SE10......................113 J2
Millennium Quay
DEPT SE8......................112 E5
Millennium Wharf
POP/IOD E14......................113 G2
Mill Farm Business Park
HSLWW TW4......................122 D6
Millfields Primary School
CLPT E5......................74 E3
Millfield Theatre
UED N18......................41 K3
Mill Green Business Park
MTCM CR4......................162 E6
Mill Hill Broadway ⇌
MLHL NW7......................37 G5
Mill Hill Cemetery
MLHL NW7......................38 A5
Mill Hill County High School
EBAR EN4......................27 K4
MLHL NW7......................37 G1
The Mill Hill CC
MLHL NW7......................38 A2
Mill Hill East ⊖
MLHL NW7......................38 B6
Mill Hill Golf Club
MLHL NW7......................37 G1
Mill Hill Industrial Estate
MLHL NW7......................37 H5
Mill Hill School
MLHL NW7......................37 K3
Mill Lane Medical Centre
KIL/WHAMP NW6......................70 E4
Mill Lane Trading Estate
CROY/NA CR0......................177 F2
Mill River Trading Estate
PEND EN3......................31 G3
Millside Industrial Estate
DART DA1......................139 G3
Mill Street Clinic
STHWK SE1......................19 M1
Mill Trading Estate
WLSDN NW10......................86 D1
The Mill Trading Estate
WLSDN NW10......................86 E2
Millwall FC (The New Den)
BERM/RHTH SE16......................111 K4
Milmead Industrial Centre
TOTM N17......................56 D1
Milton Natural Health Centre
HGT N6......................54 C6
Minet Clinic
HYS/HAR UB3......................82 E7
Minet J & I Schools
HYS/HAR UB3......................83 F7
Ministry of Defence
WHALL SW1A......................11 J9
Mint Business Park
CAN/RD E16......................94 E4
Mint Hotel
WEST SW1P......................17 J5
Mirravale Trading Estate
CHDH RM6......................62 A6
Mission Grove Primary School
WALTH E17......................57 H4
Mitcham ⊖
MTCM CR4......................162 D3
Mitcham CC
MTCM CR4......................162 D3
Mitcham Eastfields ⇌
MTCM CR4......................163 F1
Mitcham Golf Club
MTCM CR4......................163 F4
Mitcham Industrial Estate
MTCM CR4......................148 A7
Mitcham Junction ⇌ ⊖
MTCM CR4......................163 F4
Mitcham Vale High School
STRHM/NOR SW16......................163 H1
Mitchell Brook Primary School
WLSDN NW10......................69 F5
Mitre Bridge Industrial Park
NKENS W10......................87 K3
Mitre House Hotel
BAY/PAD W2......................9 G3
Moatbridge School
ELTH/MOT SE9......................134 C5
The Moat Club
FUL/PGN SW6......................127 H1
Moberly Sports &
Education Centre
WLSDN NW10......................88 B2
Molesey Cemetery
E/WMO/HCT KT8......................157 F2
Molesey Hospital
E/WMO/HCT KT8......................157 F4
Mollison Drive Health Centre
WLGTN SM6......................176 E6

Monega Primary School
MNPK E12......................77 H4
Monkfrith Primary School
EBAR EN4......................28 A6
Monks Hill Sports Centre
SAND/SEL CR2......................179 F6
Monksmead School
BORE WD6......................24 D4
Monks Orchard Primary School
CROY/NA CR0......................166 A6
The Montague on The
Gardens Hotel
RSQ WC1B......................11 J2
Montbelle Primary School
ELTH/MOT SE9......................154 A3
The Montcalm Hotel
MBLAR W1H......................9 M5
Monteagle Primary School
DAGW RM9......................79 H7
Montem Primary School
HOLWY N7......................73 F2
Montpelier Primary School
EA W5......................85 K4
Monument ⊖
MANHO EC4N......................13 H6
The Monument
CANST EC4R......................13 H6
Moore Place Golf Club
ESH/CLAY KT10......................170 A4
Moorfields Eye Hospital
FSBYE EC1V......................7 G8
Moorgate ⇌ ⊖
BARB EC2Y......................13 G3
Moor Lane Junior School
CHSGTN KT9......................172 B4
Moor Park ⊖
NTHWD HA6......................32 B2
Moor Park Industrial Estate
WATW WD18......................20 A6
Mora Primary School
CRICK NW2......................70 A3
Morasha Jewish Primary School
FNCH N3......................39 F5
Morden ⊖
WIM/MER SW19......................162 A2
Morden Cemetery
MRDN SM4......................161 F5
Morden College Homes
BKHTH/KID SE3......................133 K1
Morden First School
MRDN SM4......................161 K4
Morden Hall Medical Centre
WIM/MER SW19......................162 A2
Morden Hall Park (NT)
MRDN SM4......................162 B3
Morden Mount Primary School
LEW SE13......................132 E1
Morden Park Pool
MRDN SM4......................161 J4
Morden Road ⇌
WIM/MER SW19......................162 A1
Morden Road Clinic
WIM/MER SW19......................162 A2
Morden South ⇌
MRDN SM4......................161 K4
Moreland Primary School
FSBYE EC1V......................6 C1
Moriah Jewish Day School
PIN HA5......................47 J7
Morley College
STHWK SE1......................18 B3
Morningside Primary School
HOM E9......................74 E5
Mornington Crescent ⊖
CAMTN NW1......................4 C5
Mornington Sports &
Fitness Centre
CAMTN NW1......................4 D3
Morpeth School
BETH E2......................92 E2
Mortimer Road Clinic
WLSDN NW10......................88 A2
Mortimer School
STRHM/NOR SW16......................148 D1
Mortlake ⇌
MORT/ESHN SW14......................125 K2
Mortlake Cemetery
MORT/ESHN SW14......................126 B1
Mortlake Crematorium
RCH/KEW TW9......................125 J1
Moselle School
TOTM N17......................56 A1
Moselle Special School
TOTM N17......................55 K1
Mosiah Foundation
Supplementary School
STNW/STAM N16......................56 A7
Mossbourne
Community Academy
HACK E8......................74 C3
Mossford Green Primary School
BARK/HLT IG6......................60 C1
The Mother & Baby Clinic
HOM E9......................74 E5
Motspur Park ⇌
NWMAL KT3......................160 E4
Mottingham ⇌
ELTH/MOT SE9......................134 E7
Mottingham Community
Health Clinic
ELTH/MOT SE9......................153 J3
Mottingham Primary School
ELTH/MOT SE9......................153 K2
Mount Carmel RC
Primary School
EA W5......................104 D2
Mount Carmel RC Technical
College for Girls
ARCH N19......................54 D7
Mount Medical Centre
FELT TW13......................141 J1
Mount School
MLHL NW7......................37 K4
Mount Stewart Infant School
KTN/HRWW/WS HA3......................49 K5
The Moviuem of London
STHWK SE1......................17 L1
Mowlem Primary School
BETH E2......................92 E1
Mowlem Trading Estate
TOTM N17......................42 E6
MPR Eurotots School
KIL/WHAMP NW6......................70 B6
MS Business Centre
PIN HA5......................47 H2
MSP Business Centre
WBLY HA9......................68 C3
Mudchute ⊖
POP/IOD E14......................112 E3
Mudchute City Farm
POP/IOD E14......................113 F3
Mudlands Estate
RAIN RM13......................99 G2

Mulberry Business Centre
BERM/RHTH SE16......................112 A1
Mulberry House School
CRICK NW2......................70 C4
Mulberry Primary School
TOTM N17......................56 B1
Mulberry School for Girls
WCHPL E1......................92 D5
Mulgrave Primary School
WOOL/PLUM SE18......................115 F3
Munroe Centre
STHWK SE1......................19 H1
Murky Puddle Theatre
NWMAL KT3......................160 C3
Muschamp Primary School
CAR SM5......................175 J4
Museum of Brands, Packaging
& Advertising
NTGHL W11......................88 D3
Museum of Domestic Design
& Architecture
EBAR EN4......................27 K4
Museum of Fulham Palace
FUL/PGN SW6......................127 G1
Museum of London
BARB EC2Y......................12 E3
Museum of
London Archaeology
IS N1......................6 C4
Museum of London Docklands
POP/IOD E14......................93 J6
Museum of Richmond
TWK TW1......................124 E4
Museum of The Artillery in
The Rotunda
CHARL SE7......................114 D4
Museum of The Order of
St John
FARR EC1M......................12 D1
Musical Museum
BTFD TW8......................105 F5
Mustard School
IS N1......................7 K5
Muswell Hill Bowling Club
MUSWH N10......................54 A2
Muswell Hill Golf Club
MUSWH N10......................40 B7
Muswell Hill Primary School
MUSWH N10......................54 B2
Myatt Garden Primary School
BROCKY SE4......................132 C1
Myatts Field Clinic
BRXN/ST SW9......................110 C7
N1 Shopping Centre
IS N1......................6 B5
Nagi Business Centre
ALP/SUD HA0......................85 K1
Nags Head Shopping Centre
HOLWY N7......................72 E2
Naima Jewish
Preparatory School
KIL/WHAMP NW6......................2 C5
Nancy Reuben
Primary School
HDN NW4......................52 B3
Nash College of
Further Education
WWKM BR4......................180 C2
The National Archives
RCH/KEW TW9......................105 H6
National Army Museum
CHEL SW3......................15 M7
National Gallery
LSQ/SEVD WC2H......................11 H7
National Hospital for
Neurology & Neurosurgery
RSQ WC1B......................11 J1
National Maritime Museum
GNWCH SE10......................113 G5
National Physical Laboratory
TEDD TW11......................142 E5
National Portrait Gallery
LSQ/SEVD WC2H......................11 H7
National Sports Centre
NRWD SE19......................150 C5
National Temperance Hospital
CAMTN NW1......................4 E7
National Tennis Centre
PUT/ROE SW15......................126 B4
National Youth Theatre
Great Britain
HOLWY N7......................72 E2
The Natural History Museum
SKENS SW7......................15 M4
Natural Therapy Clinic
TOOT SW17......................148 A3
Natwest Sports Club
BECK BR3......................151 H5
Neasden ⊖
WLSDN NW10......................69 G4
Negus Sixth Form Centre
WOOL/PLUM SE18......................115 J3
Nelson Dock Museum
BERM/RHTH SE16......................93 H7
Nelson Hospital
RYNPK SW20......................161 J1
Nelson Primary School
EHAM E6......................96 A1
WHTN TW2......................123 G5
Nelson's Column
STJS SW1Y......................11 H8
Nelson Trading Estate
WIM/MER SW19......................147 F3
Neo Clinic
PIM SW1V......................16 E5
The New Ambassadors Theatre
LSQ/SEVD WC2H......................11 H5
New Atlas Wharf
POP/IOD E14......................112 C2
The New Aylesbury
Medical Centre
WALW SE17......................19 H7
New Barnet ⇌
BAR EN5......................27 G4
New Beckenham ⇌
BECK BR3......................151 G6
New Brentford Cemetery
HSLW TW3......................122 A1
Newbridge School
CHDH RM6......................61 H4
IL IG1......................78 E3
Newbury Park ⊖
GNTH/NBYPK IG2......................60 D5
Newbury Park Health Centre
GNTH/NBYPK IG2......................60 D5
The New Business Centre
WLSDN NW10......................87 H2
New Caledonian Wharf
BERM/RHTH SE16......................112 C2
New Chiswick Pool
CHSWK W4......................106 B6
New City Primary School
PLSTW E13......................95 G2

New Connaught Rooms
HOL/ALD WC2B......................11 K5
New Covent Garden Market
VX/NE SW8......................109 J6
New Crane Wharf
WAP E1W......................92 E7
New Cross ⇌
NWCR SE14......................112 C6
New Cross Gate ⇌ ⊖
NWCR SE14......................112 B6
New Cross Sports Arena
NWCR SE14......................112 B6
New Eltham ⇌
ELTH/MOT SE9......................135 G7
New End Primary School
HAMP NW3......................71 G3
New End Theatre
HAMP NW3......................71 G2
New England Industrial Estate
BARK IG11......................96 C1
Newfield Primary School
WLSDN NW10......................69 H6
Newham College of
Further Education
EHAM E6......................95 K1
SRTFD E15......................76 C6
Newham General Hospital
PLSTW E13......................95 G3
Newham Leisure Centre
PLSTW E13......................95 G4
Newham Medical Centre
PLSTW E13......................95 G1
Newham Sixth Form College
PLSTW E13......................95 G4
Newham Training &
Education Centre
SRTFD E15......................76 C5
New Hope Christian School
EDUL SE22......................131 G3
New Horizons Computer
Learning Centre
FSBYE EC1V......................7 G8
Newington Court
Business Centre
STHWK SE1......................18 E4
Newington Green
Primary School
STNW/STAM N16......................74 A4
Newington Industrial Estate
WALW SE17......................18 D6
New Kings Primary School
FUL/PGN SW6......................127 J1
Newland House School
TWK TW1......................143 F3
New London Theatre
LSQ/SEVD WC2H......................11 K4
New Malden ⇌
NWMAL KT3......................160 B2
Newman Catholic College
WLSDN NW10......................69 J7
Newnham Junior School
RSLP HA4......................47 G2
New North Community School
IS N1......................7 G1
Newport School
LEY E10......................76 A1
New River College
ARCH N19......................72 D1
New River Sports Centre
WDGN N22......................41 H6
New River Village
CEND/HSY/T N8......................55 F2
New Rush Hall School
IL IG1......................78 C1
New School
FUL/PGN SW6......................107 J7
New Scotland Yard
WEST SW1H......................17 G3
News International
WAP E1W......................92 D6
New Southgate ⇌
FBAR/BDGN N11......................40 A4
New Southgate Cemetery
FBAR/BDGN N11......................40 B2
New Southgate
Crematorium
FBAR/BDGN N11......................40 B2
New Southgate
Industrial Estate
FBAR/BDGN N11......................40 C4
New Southgate Pain Clinic &
Medical Centre
FBAR/BDGN N11......................40 C4
New Spitalfields Market
LEY E10......................75 J3
Newton Farm J & I School
RYLN/HDSTN HA2......................65 K1
Newton Industrial Estate
CHDH RM6......................61 K3
Newton Medical Centre
BAY/PAD W2......................8 C4
Newton Preparatory School
VX/NE SW8......................109 G6
Newtons Primary School
RAIN RM13......................99 F1
New Victoria Hospital
KUTN/CMB KT2......................145 G7
New Woodlands School
BMLY BR1......................152 C3
Nightingale Academy
ED N9......................30 E6
Nightingale Clinic
PLSTW E13......................95 G1
Nightingale Primary School
CLPT E5......................74 C2
SWFD E18......................59 G3
WDGN N22......................41 F7
WOOL/PLUM SE18......................115 G5
Nightingale School
TOOT SW17......................147 J1
No1 Poultry
MANHO EC4N......................12 F5
Noel Coward Theatre
CHCR WC2N......................11 J6
Noel Park Primary School
WDGN N22......................55 H1
Nonsuch High School for Girls
CHEAM SM3......................174 B6
Nonsuch Primary School
EW KT17......................173 K4
Noor Ul Islam Primary School
LEY E10......................76 A1
Norbiton ⇌
KUTN/CMB KT2......................144 C7
Norbury ⇌
STRHM/NOR SW16......................149 F7
Norbury Complementary
Therapy Clinic
STRHM/NOR SW16......................149 F7
Norbury First & Middle School
HRW HA1......................48 E4

Norbury Health Centre
STRHM/NOR SW16......................164 A1
Norbury Manor Business &
Enterprise College for Girls
STRHM/NOR SW16......................149 G7
Norbury Manor Primary School
STRHM/NOR SW16......................148 E7
Norbury Trading Estate
STRHM/NOR SW16......................164 A1
Norfolk House School
MUSWH N10......................54 B1
Norland Place School
NTGHL W11......................88 C7
Norlington School
LEY E10......................58 B7
Normanby College
CMBW SE5......................130 D1
Normand Croft
Community School
WKENS W14......................107 J5
Normandy Primary School
BXLYHN DA7......................118 A7
Norman Park Athletics Track
HAYES BR2......................168 A5
Norman Shaw Building
(MP's Offices)
WHALL SW1A......................17 J1
North Acton ⊖
WLSDN NW10......................87 F3
North Acton Business Park
ACT W3......................87 F5
North Beckton Primary School
EHAM E6......................95 K3
North Bridge House
Junior School
HAMP NW3......................71 G3
North Bridge House
Preparatory School
CAMTN NW1......................4 C4
North Bridge House School
HAMP NW3......................71 H5
Northbury Primary School
BARK IG11......................78 B5
North Clinic
BMLY BR1......................152 E7
Northcote Lodge School
BTSEA SW11......................128 E5
North Croydon Medical Centre
THHTH CR7......................164 C5
North Dulwich ⇌
HNHL SE24......................130 E4
North Ealing ⊖
ACT W3......................86 B5
North Ealing Primary School
WEA W13......................85 H3
North East Surrey Crematorium
NWMAL KT3......................161 F5
North End Trading Estate
ERITH DA8......................118 B6
North Feltham Trading Estate
EBED/NFELT TW14......................122 A3
Northfields ⊖
WEA W13......................104 D2
Northfields Industrial Estate
ALP/SUD HA0......................68 C7
Northfields Prospect
Business Centre
PUT/ROE SW15......................127 J3
Northgate Business Centre
EN EN1......................30 D2
Northgate Clinic
CDALE/KGS NW9......................51 G5
Northgate Industrial Park
CRW RM5......................62 B1
North Greenwich ⊖
GNWCH SE10......................113 H1
North Greenwich Arena
POP/IOD E14......................94 C7
North Greenwich Pier
POP/IOD E14......................94 D7
North Harringay Primary School
CEND/HSY/T N8......................55 G3
North Harrow ⊖
RYLN/HDSTN HA2......................48 A4
North Havering College of
Adult Education
ROM RM1......................63 G3
North Kensington
Video-Drama Project
NKENS W10......................88 C5
North London College
SEVS/STOTM N15......................56 B2
North London
Collegiate School
EDGW HA8......................36 A5
The North London Hospice
NFNCH/WDSPK N12......................39 F2
North London
International School
FBAR/BDGN N11......................39 K4
NFNCH/WDSPK N12......................39 F4
North London International
School (Diploma Centre)
NFNCH/WDSPK N12......................39 J4
North London International
School (Lower School)
NFNCH/WDSPK N12......................39 F2
North London Nuffield Hospital
ENC/FH EN2......................29 G1
North London School
of Physiotherapy
ARCH N19......................54 C7
North London Tutorial College
HDN NW4......................52 A5
North Middlesex Golf Club
NFNCH/WDSPK N12......................39 H2
North Middlesex Hospital
UED N18......................42 A4
North Millfields
NTHLT UB5......................66 A6
Northolt Aerodrome
RSLP HA4......................64 E5
Northolt High School
NTHLT UB5......................65 K5
Northolt Park ⇌
RYLN/HDSTN HA2......................66 B3
Northolt Road Clinic
RYLN/HDSTN HA2......................66 C5
Northolt Swimarama
NTHLT UB5......................66 A5
North Pole Depot
WLSDN NW10......................87 H3
North Primary School
STHL UB1......................83 K6
North Sheen ⇌
RCH/KEW TW9......................125 H3
Northside Primary School
NFNCH/WDSPK N12......................39 G4
The North Street Health Centre
CLAP SW4......................129 H2

Northumberland Heath
  Medical Centre
  ERITH DA8 .... 118 A6
Northumberland
  Heath Primary
  ERITH DA8 .... 117 J6
Northumberland Park ⇌
  TOTM N17 .... 42 D7
Northumberland Park
  Community School
  TOTM N17 .... 42 C6
Northumberland Park
  Industrial Estate
  TOTM N17 .... 42 D5
Northview Primary School
  WLSDN NW10 .... 69 G3
Northway School
  MLHL NW7 .... 37 F1
North Wembley ⊖ ⊖
  ALP/SUD HA0 .... 67 K2
North West London Jewish
  Day School
  CRICK NW2 .... 70 C6
North West London
  Medical Centre
  MV/WKIL W9 .... 2 E6
North Westminster Community
  Secondary School
  MV/WKIL W9 .... 2 B9
Northwick Park ⊖
  KTN/HRWW/WS HA3 .... 49 H6
Northwick Park Hospital &
  Clinical Research Centre
  HRW HA1 .... 49 H6
Northwold Primary School
  CLPT E5 .... 74 C1
Northwood ⊖
  NTHWD HA6 .... 32 C6
Northwood Cemetery
  NTHWD HA6 .... 46 D1
Northwood College
  NTHWD HA6 .... 32 B6
Northwood FC
  NTHWD HA6 .... 46 D1
Northwood Golf Club
  NTHWD HA6 .... 32 B6
Northwood Hills ⊖
  NTHWD HA6 .... 46 E1
Northwood & Pinner
  Community Hospital
  NTHWD HA6 .... 32 E7
Northwood Preparatory School
  RKW/CH/CXG WD3 .... 32 A1
Northwood Primary School
  ERITH DA18 .... 117 F2
Northwood School
  NTHWD HA6 .... 33 F7
Northwood Sports Centre
  NTHWD HA6 .... 33 F7
Norwegian/British Monument
  BAY/PAD W2 .... 9 J8
The Norwegian School
  WIM/MER SW19 .... 146 A6
Norwood Green Infant School
  NWDGN UB2 .... 102 D4
Norwood Green Junior School
  NWDGN UB2 .... 102 D4
Norwood Heights
  Shopping Centre
  NRWD SE19 .... 150 A5
Norwood Junction ⇌ ⊖
  SNWD SE25 .... 165 H3
Norwood School
  NRWD SE19 .... 149 J4
Notre Dame RC Girls School
  STHWK SE1 .... 18 C3
Notre Dame RC Primary School
  WOOL/PLUM SE18 .... 115 G5
Notre Dame University
  LSQ/SEVD WC2H 11 H7
Notting Hill & Ealing
  High School
  WEA W13 .... 85 H4
Notting Hill Gate ⊖
  NTGHL W11 .... 8 A8
Novello Theatre
  HOL/ALD WC2B 11 L6
Novotel
  BAY/PAD W2 .... 8 E3
  CAMTN NW1 .... 5 H7
  CAN/RD E16 .... 95 F6
  GNWCH SE10 .... 112 C6
  STHWK SE1 .... 17 L5
  WDR/YW UB7 .... 100 D3
Novotel London West
  HMSMTH W6 .... 107 G4
Nower Hill High School
  PIN HA5 .... 48 A3
NTGB Sports Ground
  EHAM E6 .... 78 A5
Number 10 Bowling
  ROM RM1 .... 63 G4
Nunhead ⇌
  PECK SE15 .... 131 K2
Nutrilife Clinic
  MHST W1U 10 A2
The O₂
  POP/IOD E14 .... 94 B7
Oakdale Infant School
  SWFD E18 .... 59 F1
Oakdale Junior School
  SWFD E18 .... 59 G1
Oakfield Preparatory School
  DUL SE21 .... 149 K1
Oakfield Road Industrial Estate
  PGE/AN SE20 .... 150 D6
Oak Heights
  Independent School
  HSLW TW3 .... 123 G2
Oak Hill Health Centre
  SURB KT6 .... 159 F5
Oak Hill Theological College
  STHGT/OAK N14 .... 28 A5
Oakington Manor School
  WBLY HA9 .... 68 D4
Oakland CP School
  EBAR EN4 .... 27 K5
Oaklands College
  BORE WD6 .... 24 E1
Oaklands Primary School
  HNWL W7 .... 104 A1
Oaklands School
  ISLW TW7 .... 123 J2
Oaklands Secondary School
  BETH E2 .... 92 C2
Oak Lane Cemetery
  TWK TW1 .... 124 B6
Oak Lane Medical Centre
  TWK TW1 .... 124 C6
Oak Lee Montessori School
  PIN HA5 .... 47 H2
Oakleigh Park ⇌
  TRDG/WHET N20 .... 27 H6

Oakleigh School
  TRDG/WHET N20 .... 39 J2
Oak Lodge JMI School
  WWKM BR4 .... 166 E6
Oak Lodge Medical Centre
  EDGW HA8 .... 36 D6
Oak Lodge School
  BAL SW12 .... 128 E6
  EFNCH N2 .... 53 L2
Oaks Park High School
  GNTH/NBYPK IG2 .... 60 E4
Oakthorpe Primary School
  UED N18 .... 41 J4
Oak Tree Medical Centre
  GDMY/SEVK IG3 .... 78 A4
Oakwood ⊖
  STHGT/OAK N14 .... 28 C3
Oakwood Business Park
  WLSDN NW10 .... 87 F2
Oakwood Medical Centre
  STHGT/OAK N14 .... 28 C4
Oakwood School
  BXLYHN DA7 .... 138 A3
Oasis Academy Shirley Park
  CROY/NA CR0 .... 165 J5
Oasis Sports Centre
  LSQ/SEVD WC2H 11 J4
Odeon Cinema
  BAR EN5 .... 26 E4
  BAY/PAD W2 .... 9 L5
  BECK BR3 .... 166 D1
  BERM/RHTH SE16 .... 112 A1
  CAMTN NW1 .... 4 D3
  ED N9 .... 31 F6
  ELTH/MOT SE9 .... 134 D3
  ESH/CLAY KT10 .... 170 A4
  FITZ W1T 11 G3
  HAMP NW3 .... 3 G1
  HAYES BR2 .... 167 K1
  HOLWY N7 .... 72 E2
  KENS W8 .... 14 A4
  KUT/HW KT1 .... 159 F1
  MUSWH N10 .... 54 A5
  RCH/KEW TW9 .... 124 E4
  ROM RM1 .... 63 H4
  STJS SW1Y 11 G7
  STRHM/NOR SW16 .... 148 E2
  SWFD E18 .... 58 E1
  WIM/MER SW19 .... 146 B6
Odeon Covent Garden Cinema
  LSQ/SEVD WC2H 11 H5
Odeon
  Wardour Street Cinema
  SOHO/SHAV W1D 11 G6
Odessa Infant School
  FSTGT E7 .... 76 E4
Odyssey Business Park
  RSLP HA4 .... 65 F4
Old Abbotstonians RFC
  YEAD UB4 .... 82 B1
Old Actonians Sports Club
  EA W5 .... 105 G1
Old Admiralty
  STJS SW1Y 11 H9
Old Bancroftians FC
  BKHH IG9 .... 45 H3
Old Barnes Cemetery
  BARN SW13 .... 126 E1
Old Beckenhamian RFC
  WWKM BR4 .... 180 B2
Old Bellgate Wharf
  POP/IOD E14 .... 112 C2
Old Bexley Business Park
  BXLY DA5 .... 137 J6
Old Bexley CE Primary School
  BXLY DA5 .... 137 G7
Old Brockleians Sports Ground
  LEE/GVPK SE12 .... 134 B5
Old Bromlians CC
  HAYES BR2 .... 168 A4
Old Cemetery
  EDUL SE22 .... 131 J5
Old Colfeian Sports Club
  LEE/GVPK SE12 .... 133 K4
Old Curiosity Shop
  LINN WC2A 11 L4
Old Elthamians Sports Club
  CHST BR7 .... 154 E5
Oldfield House Special School
  HPTN TW12 .... 141 K7
Oldfield Primary School
  GFD/PVL UB6 .... 84 D1
Oldfields Trading Estate
  SUT SM1 .... 174 E2
Old Ford Primary School
  BOW E3 .... 93 H1
Oldhill Medical Centre
  STNW/STAM N16 .... 56 B7
Old Jamaica Business Estate
  BERM/RHTH SE16 .... 19 M3
Old Lyonian Sports Ground
  RYLN/HDSTN HA2 .... 48 C4
Old Millhillians Sports Ground
  RYLN/HDSTN HA2 .... 34 A7
Old Oak Primary School
  SHB W12 .... 87 H5
Old Operating Theatre &
  Herb Garret Museum
  STHWK SE1 .... 13 G9
Old Owens Sports Ground
  TRDG/WHET N20 .... 27 H7
Old Palace Primary School
  BOW E3 .... 93 K2
Old Palace School
  CROY/NA CR0 .... 177 H2
Old Palace School of
  John Whitgift Junior Site
  SAND/SEL CR2 .... 178 B5
Old Royal Naval College
  GNWCH SE10 .... 113 G4
Old
  Observatory Greenwich
  GNWCH SE10 .... 113 G6
Old Spitalfields Market Hall
  WCHPL E1 .... 13 L2
Old Street ⇌ ⊖
  FSBYE EC1V 7 G8
Old Sun Wharf
  POP/IOD E14 .... 93 G6
Old Tiffinians Sports Ground
  E/WMO/HCT KT8 .... 157 K4
Old Treasury
  WHALL SW1A 17 J1
Old Vicarage School
  RCHPK/HAM TW10 .... 125 F5
Old Vic Theatre
  STHWK SE1 .... 18 B1
Old War Office
  WHALL SW1A 11 J9
Old Wilsonians Sports Club
  WWKM BR4 .... 167 H7
Olga Primary School
  BOW E3 .... 93 G1

Oliver Business Park
  WLSDN NW10 .... 86 E1
Oliver Goldsmith Primary School
  CDALE/KGS NW9 .... 51 F4
  CMBW SE5 .... 111 G7
Oliver House
  Preparatory School
  CLAP SW4 .... 129 G5
Olympia
  WKENS W14 .... 107 H2
Olympia Industrial Estate
  WDGN N22 .... 55 F1
Olympic Industrial Estate
  WBLY HA9 .... 68 D3
Olympic Park
  OLYMPICPK E20 .... 75 J6
Olympic Retail Park
  WBLY HA9 .... 68 C3
Olympic Stadium
  OLYMPICPK E20 .... 75 K6
Olympic Trading Estate
  WBLY HA9 .... 68 D3
One Aldwych Hotel
  COVGDN WC2E 11 L6
One New Change
  CITYW EC2V 12 E5
The One Stanley
  Medical Centre
  ALP/SUD HA0 .... 68 A6
On Sai Clinic
  ECT SW5 .... 14 C6
The Open University
  FSBYW WC1X 5 L7
  HAMP NW3 .... 3 H3
Ophabeom Theatre
  WLSDN NW10 .... 87 K1
Optimax Laser Eye Clinic
  MV/WKIL W9 .... 8 B1
Orange Tree Theatre
  RCH/KEW TW9 .... 125 F3
Oratory RC Primary School
  CHEL SW3 .... 15 J7
The Orbit Tower
  OLYMPICPK E20 .... 75 K6
Orchard Business Centre
  BECK BR3 .... 151 H4
The Orchard Health Centre
  BARK IG11 .... 96 C1
Orchard Hill College
  WLGTN SM6 .... 176 B5
Orchard House School
  CHSWK W4 .... 106 A3
Orchard J & I School
  HOM E9 .... 74 E6
The Orchard Junior School
  HSLWW TW4 .... 123 F3
Orchard Primary School
  SCUP DA14 .... 155 H4
The Orchard School
  BRXS/STRHM SW2 .... 130 A4
  E/WMO/HCT KT8 .... 157 J4
Orchard Shopping Centre
  DART DA1 .... 139 H5
The Orchard Theatre
  DART DA1 .... 139 H5
Orchard Way Primary School
  CROY/NA CR0 .... 166 B6
Oriel Primary School
  FELT TW13 .... 141 J2
Orient Industrial Park
  LEY E10 .... 75 J1
Orion Business Centre
  NWCR SE14 .... 112 A4
The Orion Primary School
  CDALE/KGS NW9 .... 37 G7
Orleans House Gallery
  TWK TW1 .... 124 C7
Orleans Infant School
  TWK TW1 .... 124 C7
Orley Farm School
  HRW HA1 .... 66 D2
Osidge JMI School
  STHGT/OAK N14 .... 28 C7
Osier Industrial Estate
  WAND/EARL SW18 .... 127 K3
Osmani Primary School
  WCHPL E1 .... 92 C4
Osterley ⊖
  ISLW TW7 .... 103 J5
Osterley Park & House (NT)
  ISLW TW7 .... 103 H5
Osterley RFC
  NWDGN UB2 .... 103 G3
Our Lady Immaculate RC
  Primary School
  BRYLDS KT5 .... 159 J7
Our Lady of Dolours RC
  Primary School
  BAY/PAD W2 .... 8 C2
Our Lady of Grace RC
  Junior School
  CRICK NW2 .... 69 K2
Our Lady of Grace RC
  Primary School
  CHARL SE7 .... 114 A5
Our Lady of Lourdes RC Primary
  FBAR/BDGN N11 .... 40 B4
  NFNCH/WDSPK N12 .... 39 G6
Our Lady of Lourdes RC
  Primary School
  WAN E11 .... 58 D5
  WLSDN NW10 .... 68 E7
Our Lady of Muswell RC Primary
  MUSWH N10 .... 54 A1
Our Lady of The Rosary RC
  Primary School
  ELTH/MOT SE9 .... 135 K5
Our Lady of The Sacred
  Heart School
  HOLWY N7 .... 73 F4
Our Lady of The Visitation RC
  Combined Primary School
  GFD/PVL UB6 .... 84 C3
Our Lady of Victories RC
  Primary School
  PUT/ROE SW15 .... 127 G3
  SKENS SW7 .... 14 F6
Our Lady Queen of Heaven RC
  Primary School
  PUT/ROE SW15 .... 127 G6
Our Lady RC Primary School
  CAMTN NW1 .... 4 F3
  POP/IOD E14 .... 93 H5
Our Lady & St Georges Catholic
  Primary School
  WALTH E17 .... 57 K2
  WALTH E17 .... 57 K3
Our Lady & St Johns RC
  Primary School
  BTFD TW8 .... 104 D4
Our Lady & St Joseph
  Primary School
  IS N1 .... 74 A4

Our Lady & St Philip Neri RC
  Infant School
  FSTH SE23 .... 151 F2
Our Lady & St Philip Neri RC
  Primary School
  SYD SE26 .... 151 G3
Our Ladys Catholic
  Primary School
  DART DA1 .... 139 G5
Our Ladys Convent High School
  CLPT E5 .... 56 D7
Oval ⊖
  LBTH SE11 .... 110 B5
Oval Business Centre
  LBTH SE11 .... 17 M8
Oval House Theatre
  LBTH SE11 .... 110 B5
Oval Primary School
  CROY/NA CR0 .... 165 F7
Overton Grange School
  BELMT SM2 .... 175 F7
Oxford Circus ⊖
  REGST W1B 10 D4
Oxford Gardens Primary School
  NKENS W10 .... 88 B5
Oxford House College
  SOHO/SHAV W1D 11 G4
Oxhey Park Golf Centre
  OXHEY WD19 .... 21 H7
Oxhey Wood Primary School
  OXHEY WD19 .... 33 G3
Oxo Tower Wharf
  STHWK SE1 .... 12 B7
Paddington ⇌ ⊖
  BAY/PAD W2 .... 9 G4
Paddington Academy
  MV/WKIL W9 .... 8 B1
Paddington Bowling &
  Sports Club
  MV/WKIL W9 .... 2 C9
Paddington
  Community Hospital
  MV/WKIL W9 .... 8 A2
Paddington Green
  Primary School
  BAY/PAD W2 .... 9 G1
Paddington Recreation Ground
  Athletics Track
  KIL/WHAMP NW6 .... 2 D1
Paddington Recreation
  Ground Pavilion
  MV/WKIL W9 .... 2 C7
Paddock Primary School
  BTSEA SW11 .... 129 F3
Paddock School
  PUT/ROE SW15 .... 126 C3
Paines Lane Cemetery
  PIN HA5 .... 47 J2
Pain Relief Clinic
  HDN NW4 .... 51 K5
Paint Pots Montessori School
  WBPTN SW10 .... 108 B5
Pakeman Primary School
  HOLWY N7 .... 73 F2
Palace Gardens
  Shopping Centre
  ENC/FH EN2 .... 29 K2
Palace of Westminster
  WHALL SW1A 17 K2
Palace Theatre
  SOHO/SHAV W1D 11 H6
  WAT WD17 .... 21 F2
Palladium Theatre
  SOHO/CST W1F 10 E5
Palmers Green ⇌
  PLMGR N13 .... 41 F3
Palmers Green High School
  WCHMH N21 .... 41 G1
Palmerston Business Centre
  SUT SM1 .... 175 G4
Palm House, Kew Gardens
  RCH/KEW TW9 .... 105 G2
Panorama Pier
  STHWK SE1 .... 12 E7
Paradise Swimming Pools
  MLHL NW7 .... 37 G4
Paragon Christian Academy
  CLPT E5 .... 75 F3
Paray House School
  FUL/PGN SW6 .... 127 J1
Parayhouse School
  WBPTN SW10 .... 108 B6
Parchmore Medical Centre
  THHTH CR7 .... 164 D2
Pardes House & Beis
  Yaakov School
  FNCH N3 .... 52 D1
Parent Infant Clinic
  HAMP NW3 .... 71 G4
Parish CE Primary School
  BMLY BR1 .... 152 E6
Park Avenue Clinic
  WAT WD17 .... 20 E1
Park Business Centre
  KIL/WHAMP NW6 .... 2 A8
Parkfield Industrial Estate
  BTSEA SW11 .... 129 F1
Parkfield JMI School
  HDN NW4 .... 51 K6
Parkgate House School
  CLAP SW4 .... 129 F3
Park Hall Trading Estate
  WNWD SE27 .... 149 J2
Park High School
  STAN HA7 .... 49 K1
Park Hill Junior School
  CROY/NA CR0 .... 177 K2
Parkhill Primary School
  CLAY IG5 .... 59 K2
Park Hill School
  KUTN/CMB KT2 .... 144 C6
Park House Medical Centre
  KIL/WHAMP NW6 .... 88 C1
Park House RFC
  HAYES BR2 .... 181 G1
Park Inn
  WAT WD17 .... 21 F1
  WDR/YW UB7 .... 100 D3
Parklands Primary School
  ROM RM1 .... 63 F2
Park Lane Business Centre
  WBLY HA9 .... 68 A3
Park Medical Centre
  BERM/RHTH SE16 .... 112 C4
Park Mews Small
  Business Centre
  HNHL SE24 .... 130 D5
Park Plaza Hotel
  PIM SW1V 16 E5
  STHWK SE1 .... 17 L6
  STHWK SE1 .... 17 M1
Park Primary School
  SRTFD E15 .... 76 D7

Park Road Clinic
  CEND/HSY/T N8 .... 54 D4
Park Road Swimming Centre
  CEND/HSY/T N8 .... 54 D4
Park Royal ⊖
  EA W5 .... 86 C3
Park Royal Business Centre
  WLSDN NW10 .... 87 F3
Park School for Girls
  IL IG1 .... 78 A1
Parkside Business Estate
  DEPT SE8 .... 112 C5
Parkside Clinic
  NTGHL W11 .... 88 C5
Parkside Health
  NTGHL W11 .... 88 C5
Parkside Hospital
  WIM/MER SW19 .... 146 B2
Park View School
  SEVS/STOTM N15 .... 55 J3
Park Walk Primary School
  WBPTN SW10 .... 108 C5
Parkway Primary School
  ERITH DA18 .... 117 F2
Parkway Trading Estate
  HEST TW5 .... 102 B5
Parkwood Primary School
  FSBYPK N4 .... 73 H1
Parliament Hill Fields
  Athletics Track
  HAMP NW3 .... 71 K3
Parliament Hill Lido
  HAMP NW3 .... 72 A3
Parliament Hill School
  KTTN NW5 .... 72 A3
Parmiter Industrial Centre
  BETH E2 .... 92 D1
Parnells Sports Ground
  KTN/HRWW/WS HA3 .... 50 B5
Parsloes Primary School
  DAGW RM9 .... 80 B5
Parsons Green ⊖
  FUL/PGN SW6 .... 107 K7
Parsons Green Health Clinic
  FUL/PGN SW6 .... 107 K7
Pascals College
  BECK BR3 .... 166 D1
Passport Language Schools
  BMLY BR1 .... 153 F7
Pastoria Hotel
  LSQ/SEVD WC2H 11 H7
Patent Office
  FLST/FETLN EC4A 12 A3
The Patrick Doody Clinic &
  Health Centre
  WIM/MER SW19 .... 146 E6
Pattinson Clinic
  RCH/KEW TW9 .... 124 E4
The Paul Robeson Theatre
  HSLW TW3 .... 123 G2
Pavilion Barclays Sports Ground
  EA W5 .... 86 A4
The Pavilion Leisure Centre
  BMLY BR1 .... 167 K1
Pavilion Restaurant
  RCH/KEW TW9 .... 125 F1
Paxton Primary School
  NRWD SE19 .... 150 B5
PCMS London
  SRTFD E15 .... 94 B3
PDSA Hospital
  REDBR IG4 .... 59 H2
Peace Pagoda
  CHEL SW3 .... 108 E6
Peacock Estate
  TOTM N17 .... 42 B5
Peacock Industrial Estate
  TOTM N17 .... 42 B6
The Peacock Theatre
  HOL/ALD WC2B 11 L5
Peall Road Industrial Estate
  CROY/NA CR0 .... 164 A5
Pearswood Primary School
  ERITH DA8 .... 118 C7
Peckham Park Primary School
  PECK SE15 .... 111 H6
The Peckham Pulse Health &
  Leisure Centre
  PECK SE15 .... 111 H7
Peckham Rye ⇌
  PECK SE15 .... 131 H1
Pelham Primary School
  BXLYHN DA7 .... 137 H2
  WIM/MER SW19 .... 146 E6
Pembridge Hall Preparatory
  School for Girls
  BAY/PAD W2 .... 8 B6
Pendragon School
  BMLY BR1 .... 152 E2
Penge East ⇌
  SYD SE26 .... 150 E5
Penge West ⇌ ⊖
  PGE/AN SE20 .... 150 D6
Pentavia Retail Park
  MLHL NW7 .... 37 H6
Penwortham Primary School
  STRHM/NOR SW16 .... 148 B5
Percival David Foundation of
  Chinese Art
  STPAN WC1H 5 H9
Perivale ⊖
  GFD/PVL UB6 .... 85 G1
Perivale Industrial Park
  GFD/PVL UB6 .... 67 G7
  GFD/PVL UB6 .... 85 G1
Perivale New Business Centre
  GFD/PVL UB6 .... 85 J1
Perivale Park Athletics Track
  GFD/PVL UB6 .... 84 E2
Perivale Park Golf Course
  GFD/PVL UB6 .... 84 E2
Perrin Road Clinic
  ALP/SUD HA0 .... 67 H3
Perrymount Primary School
  FSTH SE23 .... 151 F1
The Petchy Academy
  HACK E8 .... 74 B4
Peterborough & St Margarets
  High School
  STAN HA7 .... 34 E2
Peter Hills School
  BERM/RHTH SE16 .... 93 F7
Peter James Business Centre
  HYS/HAR UB3 .... 101 K1
Peterley Business Centre
  BETH E2 .... 92 D1
Peter Pan Statue
  BAY/PAD W2 .... 9 G8
The Petersham Hotel
  RCHPK/HAM TW10 .... 125 F6
Petrie Museum of
  Egyptian Archaeology
  FITZ W1T 10 F1

Petts Hill Primary School
NTHLT UB5 .... 66 B4

Petts Wood ⇌
STMC/STPC BR5 .... 169 H4

Pewterers' Hall
CITYW EC2V 12 F3

Pheasantry Welcome Centre
TEDD TW11 .... 143 F7

Phipps Bridge ⇌
WIM/MER SW19 .... 162 B2

Phoenix Academy
ED N9 .... 30 D7

Phoenix Business Centre
POP/IOD E14 .... 93 J4

Phoenix Cinema
EFNCH N2 .... 53 J3

Phoenix College
MRDN SM4 .... 162 A4

Phoenix High School
SHB W12 .... 87 J6

Phoenix Industrial Estate
HRW HA1 .... 49 F3

Phoenix Leisure Centre
CAT SE6 .... 132 E6

Phoenix Primary School
STHWK SE1 .... 111 H4

Phoenix School
HAMP NW3 .... 71 H5

Phoenix Secondary &
Primary School
BOW E3 .... 93 H2

Phoenix Theatre
LSQ/SEVD WC2H 11 H5

Phoenix Trading Estate
GFD/PVL UB6 .... 67 J7

Physical Energy Statue
BAY/PAD W2 .... 9 G9

Piccadilly Circus ⊖
MYFR/PICC W1J 11 G7

Piccadilly Theatre
SOHO/SHAV W1D 11 G6

Pickford Lane Medical Centre
BXLYHN DA7 .... 117 F7

Pickhurst Infant School
WWKM BR4 .... 167 H5

Pickhurst Junior School
WWKM BR4 .... 167 H5

Picture House Cinema
SRTFD E15 .... 76 B5

Pilgrims Way J & I School
PECK SE15 .... 111 K5

Pilot Industrial Centre
WLSDN NW10 .... 87 G3

Pilton Estate
CROY/NA CR0 .... 177 H1

Pimlico ⊖
PIM SW1V 17 G7

Pimlico Academy
PIM SW1V 16 F8

Pinkwell Primary School
HYS/HAR UB3 .... 101 F3

Pinnacles
Cricket & Squash Club
SUT SM1 .... 174 E5

Pinner ⊖
PIN HA5 .... 47 J3

Pinner Hill Golf Club
PIN HA5 .... 33 F5

Pinner Medical Centre
PIN HA5 .... 47 J3

Pinner New Cemetery
PIN HA5 .... 48 A2

Pinner Park Infant School
PIN HA5 .... 48 B2

Pinner Park Junior School
PIN HA5 .... 48 B2

Pinner View Medical Centre
RYLN/HDSTN HA2 .... 48 B2

Pinner View Medical Centre
HRW HA1 .... 48 C4

Pinner Wood School
PIN HA5 .... 33 G7

Pioneers Industrial Park
CROY/NA CR0 .... 163 K7

Pitshanger Manor Museum
EA W5 .... 85 J7

Plaisterers Hall
STBT EC1A 12 E3

Plaistow ⇌
SRTFD E15 .... 94 D1

Plaistow Hospital
PLSTW E13 .... 95 F1

Plaistow
Jamia Islamia School
PLSTW E13 .... 95 F2

Plaistow Primary School
PLSTW E13 .... 77 G7
PLSTW E13 .... 95 F1

Plantation House
Medical Centre
LOTH EC2R 13 H4

Plashet Jewish Cemetery
MNPK E12 .... 77 H5

Plashet Road Medical Centre
FSTGT E7 .... 77 F6

Plashet School
EHAM E6 .... 77 J6

Players Theatre
CHCR WC2N 11 K8

Playgolf Northwick Park
HRW HA1 .... 49 G7

The Playhouse
CHCR WC2N 11 K8

Plaza Business Centre
PEND EN3 .... 31 H1

Plaza on the River Hotel
STHWK SE1 .... 17 L6

Pleasance Theatre
HOLWY N7 .... 72 E5

Plumcroft Primary School
WOOL/PLUM SE18 .... 115 H5

Plumstead ⇌
WOOL/PLUM SE18 .... 115 J3

Plumstead Cemetery
ABYW SE2 .... 116 C6

Plumstead Leisure Centre
WOOL/PLUM SE18 .... 116 A4

Plumstead Manor School
WOOL/PLUM SE18 .... 115 J4

The Pointer School
BKHTH/KID SE3 .... 113 K7

Police Cadet School
WAN E11 .... 58 E7

The Polish Institute &
Sikorski Museum
SKENS SW7 .... 15 H2

Polish War Memorial
RSLP HA4 .... 65 F5

Polka Theatre for Children
WIM/MER SW19 .... 147 F5

Ponders End ⇌
PEND EN3 .... 31 G4

Ponders End
Industrial Estate
PEND EN3 .... 31 H3

Pontoon Dock ⊖
CAN/RD E16 .... 95 G7

Pooles Park Primary School
FSBYPK N4 .... 73 F1

Pools on the Park
RCH/KEW TW9 .... 124 E3

Pope John Primary School
SHB W12 .... 87 K6

Pop In Business Centre
WBLY HA9 .... 68 D4

Poplar ⇌
POP/IOD E14 .... 93 K6

Poplar Business Park
POP/IOD E14 .... 112 D1

Poplar Coroners Court
POP/IOD E14 .... 93 K6

Poplar Primary School
WIM/MER SW19 .... 161 K2

Pop Up Theatre
CLKNW EC1R 6 B6

Porchester Leisure Centre
BAY/PAD W2 .... 8 C4

Portcullis House
WHALL SW1A 17 K2

Portico City Learning Centre
CLPT E5 .... 74 E3

The Portland Hospital
REGST W1B 10 D1

Portland House Medical Centre
GFD/PVL UB6 .... 84 B3

Portland Medical Centre
SNWD SE25 .... 165 J4

Portland Place School
REGST W1B 10 D2

The Portman Clinic
HAMP NW3 .... 71 H5

Portobello Market
NKENS W10 .... 88 C4

Portobello Medical Centre
NTGHL W11 .... 88 C5

Portway Primary School
SRTFD E15 .... 76 E7

The Pountney Clinic
HSLW TW3 .... 123 F2

Powergate Business Park
WLSDN NW10 .... 87 F2

Power Industrial Estate
ERITH DA8 .... 118 C7

Premier Cinema
PECK SE15 .... 131 H1

Premier Inn
BARK IG11 .... 78 B7

Prendergast Hilly Fields College
BROCKY SE4 .... 132 D3

Prendergast Ladywell
Fields College
BROCKY SE4 .... 132 D5

Preston Manor School
WBLY HA9 .... 68 B1

Preston Medical Centre
WBLY HA9 .... 68 A2

Preston Park Primary School
WBLY HA9 .... 49 K7

Preston Road ⊖
WBLY HA9 .... 50 A7

Priestmead Primary School
KTN/HRWW/WS HA3 .... 49 H2

Primrose Hill School
CAMTN NW1 .... 4 B3

Primrose Montessori School
HBRY N5 .... 73 J2

Prince Charles Cinema
LSQ/SEVD WC2H 11 H6

Prince Edward Theatre
SOHO/SHAV W1D 11 G5

Prince of Wales Theatre
STJS SW1Y 11 G7

Prince Regent ⊖
CAN/RD E16 .... 95 G6

Princes College
NOXST/BSQ WC1A 11 J4

Princes Court Business Centre
WAP E1W 92 D6

Princes Park Stadium
DART DA1 .... 139 K7

Princes Plain Primary School
HAYES BR2 .... 168 D4

Princess Avenue School
MUSWH N10 .... 54 B2

Princess Frederica CE J &
I School
WLSDN NW10 .... 87 K1

Princess Grace Hospital
MHST W1U 10 A1

Princess Louise Hospital
NKENS W10 .... 88 A4

Princess May Primary School
STNW/STAM N16 .... 74 A4

Princess of Wales Conservatory
RCH/KEW TW9 .... 105 G6

The Princess Royal
Distribution Centre
WLSDN NW10 .... 68 D7

Priory CE Primary School
WIM/MER SW19 .... 147 F4

Priory Retail Park
WIM/MER SW19 .... 147 H6

Priory Shopping Centre
DART DA1 .... 139 G5

Priory Special School
SNWD SE25 .... 165 G3

Privy Council
STJS SW1Y 11 G9

Privy Council Office
WHALL SW1A 11 J9

Progress Business Park
CROY/NA CR0 .... 177 F1

Promised Land Academy
PLSTW E13 .... 94 E3

Pronto Trading Estate
YEAD UB4 .... 82 C4

Prospect House School
PUT/ROE SW15 .... 127 G6

Proud Gallery
CHCR WC2N 11 J7

Provident Industrial Estate
HYS/HAR UB3 .... 101 K1

PS Tattershall Castle
WHALL SW1A 11 K9

Pudding Mill Lane ⊖
SRTFD E15 .... 75 K7

Pumphouse
Educational Museum
BERM/RHTH SE16 .... 93 G7

Pump House Theatre
WATW WD18 .... 21 G4

Pump Lane Industrial Estate
HYS/HAR UB3 .... 102 A1

The Purcell School
BUSH WD23 .... 22 A1
HRW HA1 .... 66 D2

Purdy Hicks Gallery
STHWK SE1 .... 12 C8

Purfleet ⇌
PUR RM19 .... 119 K4

Purfleet Industrial Park
SOCK/AV RM15 .... 119 J1

Purfleet Primary School
PUR RM19 .... 119 K3

Purley Oaks ⇌
SAND/SEL CR2 .... 177 K7

Purley Oaks Primary School
SAND/SEL CR2 .... 177 K6

Pursuit Centre
WAP E1W 92 E6

Putney ⇌
PUT/ROE SW15 .... 127 G3

Putney Animal Hospital
PUT/ROE SW15 .... 127 G3

Putney Arts Theatre
PUT/ROE SW15 .... 127 G3

Putney Bridge ⊖
FUL/PGN SW6 .... 127 J2

Putney Exchange
Shopping Centre
PUT/ROE SW15 .... 127 G3

Putney High School
PUT/ROE SW15 .... 127 G4

Putney Leisure Centre
PUT/ROE SW15 .... 127 F3

Putney Lower
Common Cemetery
BARN SW13 .... 126 E1

Putneymead Medical Centre
PUT/ROE SW15 .... 127 G3

Putney Park School
PUT/ROE SW15 .... 126 E3

Putney School of Art & Design
PUT/ROE SW15 .... 127 H3

Putney Town Social &
Bowls Club
PUT/ROE SW15 .... 127 F1

Putney Vale Cemetery
PUT/ROE SW15 .... 145 J1

Putney Vale Crematorium
PUT/ROE SW15 .... 145 J1

Pylon Trading Estate
CAN/RD E16 .... 94 B3

Quadrant Business Park
KIL/WHAMP NW6 .... 70 C7

Quality Hotel
WBLY HA9 .... 68 C3

Quebec Industrial Estate
BERM/RHTH SE16 .... 112 B1

Queen Charlotte's &
Chelsea Hospital
SHB W12 .... 87 K5

Queen Charlotte's Cottage,
Kew Gardens
RCH/KEW TW9 .... 124 E1

Queen Elizabeth College
KENS W8 .... 14 A1

Queen Elizabeth
Conference Centre
WEST SW1P 17 H2

Queen Elizabeth Hall
STHWK SE1 .... 11 L8

Queen Elizabeth Hospital
WOOL/PLUM SE18 .... 114 E5

Queen Elizabeth II School
MV/WKIL W9 .... 88 D3

Queen Elizabeth Leisure Centre
BAR EN5 .... 26 C3

Queen Elizabeths Boys School
BAR EN5 .... 26 B2

Queen Elizabeths Girls School
BAR EN5 .... 26 D3

Queen Elizabeth Stadium
EN EN1 .... 30 B1

Queenhithe Stairs
BLKFR EC4V 12 E7

Queen Mary College
WCHPL E1 .... 93 F3

Queen Marys Hospital
SCUP DA14 .... 155 G4

Queen Mary's Hospital
HAMP NW3 .... 71 G2

Queen Mary's Hospital
for Children
SUT SM1 .... 162 B7

Queen Mary's
University Hospital
PUT/ROE SW15 .... 126 D3

Queen Mary's & Westfield College
SWFD E18 .... 44 E7

Queen Mother Sports Centre
PIM SW1V 16 E5

Queensbridge Primary School
HACK E8 .... 7 M2

Queensbridge Sports Centre
HACK E8 .... 7 M1

Queen's Building
HTHAIR TW6 .... 120 E2

Queensbury ⊖
STAN HA7 .... 50 B2

Queens Business &
Secretarial College
SKENS SW7 .... 15 G5

The Queens CE Primary School
RCH/KEW TW9 .... 105 G6

Queen's Club
WKENS W14 .... 107 H4

Queens College London
CAVSO/HST W1G 10 C3

Queens College
Preparatory School
CAVSO/HST W1G 10 C3

The Queen's Gallery
BGVA SW1W 16 D2

Queens Gate School
SKENS SW7 .... 15 G5

Queens Hospital
ROMW/RG RM7 .... 63 G6

The Queens House
GNWCH SE10 .... 113 G5

Queens Ice Rink & Bowl
BAY/PAD W2 .... 8 D7

Queensland College London -
London Campus
ACT W3 .... 86 D7

Queens Manor Primary School
FUL/PGN SW6 .... 107 F6

Queensmead School
RSLP HA4 .... 65 H3

Queensmead Sports Centre
RSLP HA4 .... 65 H4

Queens Medical Centre
RCHPK/HAM TW10 .... 125 G4

Queensmill School
FUL/PGN SW6 .... 127 K1

Queens Park ⇌
KIL/WHAMP NW6 .... 88 D1

Queens Park Community School
WLSDN NW10 .... 70 A7

Queens Park Health Centre
NKENS W10 .... 88 C2

Queens Park Primary School
NKENS W10 .... 88 C2

Queens Park Rangers FC
(Loftus Road Stadium)
SHB W12 .... 87 K7

Queen's Road Cemetery
CROY/NA CR0 .... 164 D5

Queen's Road Peckham ⇌ ⊖
PECK SE15 .... 111 J7

Queens School
BUSH WD23 .... 21 K2

Queens Theatre
SOHO/SHAV W1D 11 G6

Queenstown Road Battersea ⇌
VX/NE SW8 .... 109 G7

Queensway ⊖
BAY/PAD W2 .... 8 D7

Queensway Business Centre
PEND EN3 .... 30 E3

Queenswell Infant School
TRDG/WHET N20 .... 39 H1

Queen Victoria Memorial
WHALL SW1A 16 E2

The Quest Academy
SAND/SEL CR2 .... 179 F6

Quest Business Training
SKENS SW7 .... 14 D6

The Questors Theatre
EA W5 .... 85 J6

Quintin Kynaston School
STJWD NW8 .... 2 F4

Quwwat UL Islam Girl's School
FSTGT E7 .... 76 E5

Radcliffe College
SOHO/SHAV W1D 11 H5

Radisson Edwardian Hotel
POP/IOD E14 .... 94 A6

Radisson Blu Hotel
MBLAR W1H 9 M4

Radisson Edwardian
Berkshire Hotel
OXSTW W1C 10 C5

Radisson Edwardian
Grafton Hotel
CAMTN NW1 .... 4 E9

Radisson Edwardian Hotel
HYS/HAR UB3 .... 101 F6
RSQ WC1B 11 H3

Radisson Edwardian
Marlborough Hotel
NOXST/BSQ WC1A 11 H4

Radisson Edwardian
Mayfair Hotel
MYFR/PICC W1J 10 D7

Radisson Edwardian
Mountbatten Hotel
LSQ/SEVD WC2H 11 J5

Radisson Edwardian
Vanderbilt Hotel
SKENS SW7 .... 14 F5

Radnor House
TWK TW1 .... 143 G1

RAF West Ruislip (University
of Maryland)
HGDN/ICK UB10 .... 64 A1

Raglan Infant School
EN EN1 .... 30 A5

Raglan Junior School
EN EN1 .... 30 A6

Raglan Primary School
HAYES BR2 .... 168 B3

Railton Road Clinic
HNHL SE24 .... 130 C4

Rainbow Clinic
BAY/PAD W2 .... 9 H1

Rainbow Industrial Estate
RYNPK SW20 .... 160 E1

Rainbow Montessori School
KIL/WHAMP NW6 .... 2 C2

Rainbow Quay
BERM/RHTH SE16 .... 112 B2

Rainbow School for
Autistic Children
WAND/EARL SW18 .... 147 G1

Raines Foundation School
BETH E2 .... 92 D2

Rainham ⇌
RAIN RM13 .... 99 H3

Rainham Hall (NT)
RAIN RM13 .... 99 J3

Rainham Marshes RSPB Reserve
RAIN RM13 .... 99 K6

Rainham Trading Estate
RAIN RM13 .... 99 G2

Rainham Village Primary School
RAIN RM13 .... 99 H3

Ramac Industrial Estate
CHARL SE7 .... 113 K4

Ramada Encore Hotel
ACT W3 .... 87 F4

Ramada Hotel
BAY/PAD W2 .... 8 D7

Ramada Hotel & Suites
CAN/RD E16 .... 95 H6

Ramada London Heathrow
HEST TW5 .... 101 K7

Rambert School of Ballet &
Contemporary Dance
TWK TW1 .... 124 C4

Randal Cremer Primary School
BETH E2 .... 7 L5

Ranelagh Gardens (site of
Chelsea Flower Show)
BGVA SW1W 16 B8

Ranelagh Primary School
SRTFD E15 .... 94 C1

Rangefield Primary School
BMLY BR1 .... 152 C4

Ransomes Dock Business Centre
BTSEA SW11 .... 108 D6

The Rathbone Education Centre
CAN/RD E16 .... 94 D4

Rathfern Primary School
FSTH SE23 .... 132 C7

Ravenor Primary School
GFD/PVL UB6 .... 84 A2

Ravensbourne ⇌
GNWCH SE10 .... 94 C7

Ravensbourne ⇌
BECK BR3 .... 152 A6

The Ravensbourne School
HAYES BR2 .... 168 A3

Ravenscourt Park ⊖
HMSMTH W6 .... 106 D3

Ravenscourt Park
Preparatory School
HMSMTH W6 .... 106 D3

Ravenscroft Medical Centre
GLDGN NW11 .... 52 D6

Ravenscroft Primary School
CAN/RD E16 .... 94 E3

Ravenscroft School
TRDG/WHET N20 .... 26 D6

Ravenside Retail Park
UED N18 .... 43 F5

Ravens Lawn Tennis Club
NFNCH/WDSPK N12 .... 39 H3

Ravenstone
Preparatory School
SKENS SW7 .... 14 F4

Ravenstone Primary School
BAL SW12 .... 129 F7

Ravenswood Industrial Estate
WALTH E17 .... 58 A3

Ravens Wood School
HAYES BR2 .... 181 H2

Rayat London College
HEST TW5 .... 102 E6

Ray Lodge Primary School
WFD IG8 .... 45 H5

Rayners Lane ⊖
RYLN/HDSTN HA2 .... 47 K7

Raynes Park ⇌
RYNPK SW20 .... 161 F1

Raynes Park High School
RYNPK SW20 .... 160 E2

Raynes Park Sports Ground
RYNPK SW20 .... 160 D1

Raynes Park Vale FC
RYNPK SW20 .... 161 G4

Raynham Primary School
UED N18 .... 42 C4

RCA Sculpture School
BTSEA SW11 .... 108 D6

Reay Primary School
BRXN/ST SW9 .... 110 B6

Records Office
CLKNW EC1R 6 B9

Rectory Business Centre
SCUP DA14 .... 155 H3

Rectory Road ⇌
STNW/STAM N16 .... 74 C2

Red Balloon Learner Centre
HRW HA1 .... 49 F6

Redbridge ⊖
REDBR IG4 .... 59 H5

Redbridge College
CHDH RM6 .... 61 H4

Redbridge Drama Centre
SWFD E18 .... 44 E7

Redbridge Museum
IL IG1 .... 78 B2

Redbridge Primary School
REDBR IG4 .... 59 J4

Redburn Industrial Estate
PEND EN3 .... 31 F5

Redcliffe School
WBPTN SW10 .... 14 E9

Reddiford School
PIN HA5 .... 47 J3

Redford Lodge
Psychiatric Hospital
ED N9 .... 42 C1

Red Gates School
CROY/NA CR0 .... 177 G4

Redhill Primary School
CHST BR7 .... 154 B5

Red House (NT)
BXLYHS DA6 .... 137 F3

Redlands Primary School
WCHPL E1 .... 92 E4

Red Lion Business Park
SURB KT6 .... 172 B1

Rediff Primary School
BERM/RHTH SE16 .... 112 B1

Red Rose Trading Estate
EBAR EN4 .... 27 H4

Reeves Corner ⊖
CROY/NA CR0 .... 177 H1

Regal International College
ALP/SUD HA0 .... 68 A4

Regent Business Centre
HYS/HAR UB3 .... 102 A1

Regent Clinic
CAVSO/HST W1G 10 C3

Regent College London
PIN HA5 .... 47 K6

Regent's Park ⊖
CAMTN NW1 .... 10 C1

Regent's Park Barracks
CAMTN NW1 .... 4 C6

Regent's Park Clinic
CAMTN NW1 .... 3 L9

Regent's Park Medical Centre
CAMTN NW1 .... 4 A6

Regent's Park Open Air Theatre
CAMTN NW1 .... 4 A8

Regent's Park Track
STJWD NW8 .... 3 L5

Regina Coeli RC Primary School
SAND/SEL CR2 .... 177 H6

Renaissance Hotel
HTHAIR TW6 .... 100 E7

Renoir Cinema
BMSBY WC1N 5 K9

Renwick Industrial Estate
BARK IG11 .... 97 H1

Rewards Centre
HSLW TW3 .... 123 F2

Reynard Mills Trading Estate
BTFD TW8 .... 104 D3

Reynolds Sports Centre
ACT W3 .... 105 H1

Rhodes Avenue Primary School
WDGN N22 .... 40 C7

Rhodes Farm Clinic
MLHL NW7 .... 38 A3

Rhyl Primary School
KTTN NW5 .... 72 A5

RIBA Library Drawings &
Manuscript Collection
MBLAR W1H 9 M4

Ricards Lodge High School
WIM/MER SW19 .... 146 D3

Richard Alibon Primary School
DAGE RM10 .... 80 C4

Richard Atkins Primary School
BRXS/STRHM SW2 .... 129 K6

Richard Cloudesley School
STLK EC1Y 12 E1

Richard Cobden
Primary School
CAMTN NW1 .... 4 F4

Richdales Institute
ALP/SUD HA0 .... 67 K7

Rich Industrial Estate
PECK SE15 .... 111 J5
STHWK SE1 .... 19 K4

Richmond ⇌ ⊖
RCH/KEW TW9 .... 125 F3

Richmond Adult &
Community College
RCH/KEW TW9 .... 124 E3

Richmond American
International University
KENS W8 .... 14 C2

Richmond American
International University
in London
RCHPK/HAM TW10 .... 125 F5
The Richmond Clinic
RCH/KEW TW9 .... 125 G3
Richmond Community College
TWK TW1 .... 124 A7
Richmond FC
RCH/KEW TW9 .... 124 E3
The Richmond Gate Hotel
RCHPK/HAM TW10 .... 125 F6
The Richmond Golf Club
RCHPK/HAM TW10 .... 144 A1
The Richmond Green
Medical Centre
RCH/KEW TW9 .... 124 E4
The Richmond Hill Hotel
RCHPK/HAM TW10 .... 125 F6
Richmond House School
HPTN TW12 .... 141 K4
Richmond Magistrates Court
RCH/KEW TW9 .... 124 E3
Richmond Park Academy
MORT/ESHN SW14 .... 126 B3
Richmond Park Golf Club
PUT/ROE SW15 .... 126 B6
Richmond Park National
Nature Reserve
RCHPK/HAM TW10 .... 145 G1
Richmond Road
Medical Centre
KUTN/CMB KT2 .... 144 A6
Richmond Theatre
RCH/KEW TW9 .... 124 E4
Richmond upon Thames College
WHTN TW2 .... 123 K6
Ridge House Clinic
WCHMH N21 .... 29 K6
Ridgeway Primary School
SAND/SEL CR2 .... 178 A3
Rio Cinema
HACK E8 .... 74 B4
Ripley Arts Centre
BMLY BR1 .... 153 H7
Ripple Primary School
BARK IG11 .... 78 E7
Rippleside Cemetery
BARK IG11 .... 79 G7
Risley Avenue Primary School
TOTM N17 .... 42 A7
The Ritz Hotel
WHALL SW1A 10 E8
Ritzy Cinema
BRXN/ST SW9 .... 130 B3
River Brent Business Park
HNWL W7 .... 103 K2
River Gardens Business Centre
EBED/NFELT TW14 .... 122 A3
River House Montessori School
POP/IOD E14 .... 93 J4
Riverley Primary School
LEY E10 .... 57 J7
River Mole Business Park
ESH/CLAY KT10 .... 157 F7
River Place Health Centre
IS N1 .... 6 E2
River Road Business Park
BARK IG11 .... 96 E2
Riversdale Primary School
WAND/EARL SW18 .... 127 K4
Riverside Business Centre
WAND/EARL SW18 .... 128 A7
Riverside Business Park
WIM/MER SW19 .... 147 G7
Riverside Community
Health Care
WKENS W14 .... 107 H1
Riverside Golf Club
THMD SE28 .... 98 A5
Riverside Industrial Estate
BARK IG11 .... 97 G2
DART DA1 .... 139 H4
Riverside Primary School
BERM/RHTH SE16 .... 111 H1
Riverside Quarter
WAND/EARL SW18 .... 127 K3
Riverside Studios Cinema
HMSMTH W6 .... 107 F4
Riverside Wandle Trading Estate
MTCM CR4 .... 162 E6
Riverston School
LEE/GVPK SE12 .... 133 K4
Riverview CE Primary School
HOR/WEW KT19 .... 172 K3
The RJ Mitchell Primary School
HCH RM12 .... 81 K5
RNLI Lifeboat Station
TWRH EC3N 13 K8
Roan Industrial Estate
MTCM CR4 .... 147 J7
Robert Blair Primary School
HOLWY N7 .... 72 K1
Robert Browning
Primary School
WALW SE17 .... 18 F7
Robert Clack School
BCTR RM8 .... 80 B1
Robin Hood Infant School
SUT SM1 .... 174 K4
Robin Hood Junior School
SUT SM1 .... 175 F4
Robin Hood Lane Health Centre
SUT SM1 .... 174 K4
Robin Hood Primary School
KUTN/CMB KT2 .... 145 F4
Robinsfield Infant School
STJWD NW8 .... 3 H3
The Roche School
WAND/EARL SW18 .... 127 K4
Rockliffe Manor
Primary School
WOOL/PLUM SE18 .... 116 A5
Rockmount Primary School
NRWD SE19 .... 149 J5
Rockware Business Centre
GFD/PVL UB6 .... 66 D1
Roding Lane Cemetery
WFD IG8 .... 45 J7
Roding Primary School
BCTR RM8 .... 79 J3
WFD IG8 .... 45 J6
Roding Valley ⊖
BKHH IG9 .... 45 H3
Roe Green Junior School
CDALE/KGS NW9 .... 50 D3
Roehampton Church School
PUT/ROE SW15 .... 126 E6
The Roehampton
Priory Hospital
PUT/ROE SW15 .... 126 C3
Roehampton Recreation Centre
PUT/ROE SW15 .... 126 C6

Roehampton University
(Digby Stuart College)
PUT/ROE SW15 .... 126 C4
Roehampton University
(Froebel College)
PUT/ROE SW15 .... 126 C5
Roehampton University
(Southlands College)
PUT/ROE SW15 .... 126 C4
Roehampton University
(Whitelands College)
PUT/ROE SW15 .... 126 C6
Roger Ascham Primary School
WALTH E17 .... 43 H7
Roger Bannister Sports Ground
KTN/HRWW/WS HA3 .... 34 C5
Rokeby School
KUTN/CMB KT2 .... 144 E6
SRTFD E15 .... 76 B6
Rokesly Junior School
CEND/HSY/T N8 .... 54 E4
Roman Bath
TPL/STR WC2R 11 M6
Roman Industrial Estate
CROY/NA CR0 .... 165 F6
Roman Road Primary School
EHAM E6 .... 95 H3
Romford ⇄
ROM RM1 .... 63 G5
Romford Cemetery
ROMW/RG RM7 .... 62 E6
Romford Clinic
ROM RM1 .... 63 H3
Romford County Court
ROM RM1 .... 63 H3
Romford Golf Club
GPK RM2 .... 63 J2
Romford Ice Arena
ROMW/RG RM7 .... 63 G6
Romford IT Learning Centre
ROM RM1 .... 63 G4
Romford Shopping Hall
ROM RM1 .... 63 G3
Ronald Rose Primary School
PUT/ROE SW15 .... 127 G6
Rood Lane Medical Centre
FENCHST EC3M 13 J6
Rooks Heath College Business
& Enterprise
RYLN/HDSTN HA2 .... 66 A2
Roosevelt Memorial
MYFR/PKLN W1K 10 B6
Ropery Business Park
CHARL SE7 .... 114 B3
Rosary Priory High School
BUSH WD23 .... 22 E5
Rosary RC Infant School
HEST TW5 .... 102 E5
Rosary RC Primary School
HAMP NW3 .... 71 J4
Rosebery Industrial Park
TOTM N17 .... 56 D1
Rose Bruford College
BFN/LL DA15 .... 136 C7
Rosedale College
HYS/HAR UB3 .... 82 B5
Roselands Clinic
MNPK KT3 .... 159 K3
Rosemary Works School
IS N1 .... 7 H3
Rose McAndrew Clinic
BRXN/ST SW9 .... 130 A1
Rosemead Preparatory School
DUL SE21 .... 149 J1
Rosendale Primary School
DUL SE21 .... 130 D6
Rose of Kingston
(Kingston Theatre)
KUT/HW KT1 .... 158 E1
Rose Theatre Exhibition
STHWK SE1 .... 12 E8
Rosetta Primary School
CAN/RD E16 .... 95 F4
Rosewood Medical Centre
HCH RM12 .... 81 K4
Rosh Pinah Primary School
EDGW HA8 .... 36 D1
Rosslyn Park RFC
PUT/ROE SW15 .... 126 C3
Rotherfield Primary School
IS N1 .... 6 F3
Rotherhithe ⊖
BERM/RHTH SE16 .... 111 K1
Rotherhithe Civic Centre
BERM/RHTH SE16 .... 111 K1
Rotherhithe Primary School
BERM/RHTH SE16 .... 111 K3
The Rotunda
KUT/HW KT1 .... 159 F1
The Roundhouse Theatre
CAMTN NW1 .... 4 A1
Roundshaw J & I School
WLGTN SM6 .... 176 E6
Rowan Preparatory School
ESH/CLAY KT10 .... 171 F6
Rowans School
RYNPK SW20 .... 145 J6
Rowley Industrial Park
ACT W3 .... 105 J2
Roxbourne Junior School
RYLN/HDSTN HA2 .... 65 H1
Roxbourne Medical Centre
RYLN/HDSTN HA2 .... 66 B1
Roxeth Mead School
RYLN/HDSTN HA2 .... 66 D1
Roxeth Primary School
RYLN/HDSTN HA2 .... 66 D1
Roxwell Trading Park
LEY E10 .... 57 G6
Royal Academy of Arts
MYFR/PICC W1J 10 E7
Royal Academy of Dramatic Art
GWRST WC1E 11 G2
Royal Academy of Music
CAMTN NW1 .... 10 B1
Royal Air Force
Museum London
CDALE/KGS NW9 .... 51 J1
Royal Albert ⊖
CAN/RD E16 .... 95 J6
Royal Albert Hall
SKENS SW7 .... 15 G2
Royal Arsenal
WOOL/PLUM SE18 .... 115 G2
Royal Artillery Barracks
WOOL/PLUM SE18 .... 114 E5
The Royal Ballet School
(White Lodge)
RCHPK/HAM TW10 .... 126 A7
Royal Ballet Upper School
COVGDN WC2E 11 K5
Royal Blackheath Golf Club
ELTH/MOT SE9 .... 134 E6

Royal Botanic Gardens, Kew
BTFD TW8 .... 105 F6
Royal Botanic Gardens
Kew School
RCH/KEW TW9 .... 105 G6
Royal Brompton Hospital
CHEL SW3 .... 15 J7
Royal College of Anaesthetists
RSO WC1B 11 J2
Royal College of Art
SKENS SW7 .... 14 F2
SKENS SW7 .... 14 F4
Royal College of Music
SHB W12 .... 106 D2
SKENS SW7 .... 15 G3
Royal College of Nursing
CAMTN NW1 .... 4 F9
IS N1 .... 6 C4
Royal College of Obstetricians
& Gynaecologists
CAMTN NW1 .... 3 L9
Royal College
of Ophthalmologists
CAMTN NW1 .... 10 A1
Royal College of
Paediatrics & Child Health
GTPST W1W 10 D2
The Royal College of Pathology
STJS SW1Y 11 G9
Royal College of Physicians
CAMTN NW1 .... 4 C9
Royal College of Surgeons
LINN WC2A 11 M4
Royal College of
Veterinary Surgeons
WEST SW1P 17 J5
Royal Courts of Justice
LINN WC2A 11 M5
Royal Court Theatre
BGVA SW1W 16 A6
Royal Court Young
Peoples Theatre
NKENS W10 .... 88 C4
The Royal Docks
Community School
CAN/RD E16 .... 95 G5
Royal Docks Medical Centre
EHAM E6 .... 96 A5
Royal Exchange
BANK EC3V 13 H5
Royal Festival Hall
STHWK SE1 .... 11 L9
Royal Free Hospital School
of Medicine
HAMP NW3 .... 71 J4
Royal Garden Hotel
KENS W8 .... 14 D1
Royal Geographical Society
SKENS SW7 .... 15 G2
The Royal Horseguards Hotel
WHALL SW1A 11 K9
Royal Horticultural Society
New Hall
WEST SW1P 17 J5
Royal Horticultural Society
Old Hall
WEST SW1P 17 G5
Royal Hospital
RCH/KEW TW9 .... 125 F2
Royal Hospital Chelsea
CHEL SW3 .... 16 A9
Royal Hospital for
Neuro-disability
PUT/ROE SW15 .... 127 H5
Royal Hospital & Home
PUT/ROE SW15 .... 126 E6
Royal Hospital Museum
CHEL SW3 .... 16 A8
Royal Institute of
British Architects
REGST W1B 10 D2
Royal Institution's
Faraday Museum
CONDST W1S 10 E7
The Royal London Estate
TOTM N17 .... 42 D6
Royal London
Homeopathic Hospital
BMSBY WC1N 11 K2
Royal Marsden Hospital
CHEL SW3 .... 15 H7
The Royal Mews
BGVA SW1W 16 D3
Royal Mid-Surrey Golf Club
RCH/KEW TW9 .... 124 E2
Royal Military School of Music
WHTN TW2 .... 123 J5
Royal Mint Court
TWRH EC3N 13 M7
Royal National
Orthopaedic Hospital
GTPST W1W 10 D1
STAN HA7 .... 23 H7
Royal National Theatre
STHWK SE1 .... 12 A8
Royal National
Throat Nose & Ear Hospital
FSBYW WC1X 5 L7
Royal Oak ⊖
BAY/PAD W2 .... 8 D3
Royal Opera House
COVGDN WC2E 11 K5
The Royal School
HAMP NW3 .... 71 H4
Royal Society of Arts
CHCR WC2N 11 K7
Royal Society of Medicine
CAVSQ/HST W1G 10 C4
The Royal Trafalgar Hotel
LSQ/SEVD WC2H 11 H7
Royal Veterinary College
CAMTN NW1 .... 5 G4
Royal Victoria ⊖
CAN/RD E16 .... 94 E6
Royal Victoria Docks
Watersports Centre
CAN/RD E16 .... 94 E6
Royal Wimbledon Golf Club
WIM/MER SW19 .... 145 K4
Royston Primary School
PGE/AN SE20 .... 151 F7
RSPCA Animal Hospital
FSBYPK N4 .... 73 F1
Rudolph Steiner Hall
CAMTN NW1 .... 3 L9
Rufus Business Centre
WIM/MER SW19 .... 147 F1
Ruislip ⊖
RSLP HA4 .... 64 C1
Ruislip Gardens ⊖
RSLP HA4 .... 64 E3
Ruislip Gardens Primary School
RSLP HA4 .... 64 C3

Ruislip Golf Club
HGDN/ICK UB10 .... 64 A1
Ruislip High School
RSLP HA4 .... 64 E2
Ruislip Manor ⊖
RSLP HA4 .... 46 E7
Ruislip Manor FC
RSLP HA4 .... 64 D1
Ruislip RFC
RSLP HA4 .... 64 C1
Ruislip Woods
National Nature Reserve
NTHWD HA6 .... 46 A2
RSLP HA4 .... 46 C4
Rushcroft School
CHING E4 .... 43 K6
Rushey Green Primary School
CAT SE6 .... 132 E7
Rush Green Primary School
ROMW/RG RM7 .... 63 F7
Rushmore Primary School
CLPT E5 .... 74 E3
Ruskin House School
HNHL SE24 .... 130 D4
The Russell School
RCHPK/HAM TW10 .... 124 C7
Russell Square ⊖
STPAN WC1H 11 J1
Rutlish School
RYNPK SW20 .... 161 J1
Ruxley Corner
Industrial Estate
SCUP DA14 .... 155 K5
Ruxley Park Golf Centre
STMC/STPC BR5 .... 155 K7
Ryefield Primary School
HGDN/ICK UB10 .... 64 B7
Ryelands Primary School
SNWD SE25 .... 165 J4
Rye Oak Primary School
PECK SE15 .... 131 J2
Saatchi Gallery
CHEL SW3 .... 15 M7
Sacred Heart Catholic
Primary School
PUT/ROE SW15 .... 126 D4
Sacred Heart High School
HMSMTH W6 .... 107 F3
Sacred Heart Language College
KTN/HRWW/WS HA3 .... 48 E1
Sacred Heart RC Infant School
BTSEA SW11 .... 128 D1
Sacred Heart RC JMI School
TRDG/WHET N20 .... 39 J1
Sacred Heart RC Primary School
NWMAL KT3 .... 160 D3
OXHEY WD19 .... 21 K5
RSLP HA4 .... 64 C1
TEDD TW11 .... 143 H6
Sacred Heart RC School
CMBW SE5 .... 110 D7
Sacred Heart School
HOLWY N7 .... 73 F4
Saddlers Hall
CITYW EC2V 12 F4
Sadler's Wells Theatre
CLKNW EC1R 6 B7
SAE Institute
HOLWY N7 .... 72 E4
Safari Cinema
CROY/NA CR0 .... 164 C7
Safari Cinema & Bingo
HRW HA1 .... 49 F4
Saffron Green Primary School
BORE WD6 .... 25 F3
Sai Medical Centre
POP/IOD E14 .... 94 A6
St Agathas RC Primary School
KUTN/CMB KT2 .... 144 B5
St Agnes RC Primary School
BOW E3 .... 93 J2
CRICK NW2 .... 70 C2
St Aidans Primary School
FSBYPK N4 .... 55 G6
St Aidans RC Primary School
IL IG1 .... 60 D7
St Albans CE Primary School
HCIRC EC1N 12 A2
St Albans Health Clinic
HGT N6 .... 72 A2
St Albans RC Aided
Primary School
E/WMO/HCT KT8 .... 157 K4
St Albans RC Church &
School Presbytery
HCH RM12 .... 81 J4
St Albans RC JMI School
HCH RM12 .... 81 K6
St Albans Road Infant School
DART DA1 .... 139 J5
St Alfege with St Peter CE
Primary School
GNWCH SE10 .... 113 F5
St Aloysius RC College
HGT N6 .... 54 C7
St Aloysius RC Infant School
CAMTN NW1 .... 5 G7
St Aloysius RC Junior School
CAMTN NW1 .... 4 F6
St Andrew & St Francis CE
JMI School
CRICK NW2 .... 69 J5
St Andrews CE High School
CROY/NA CR0 .... 177 H2
St Andrews CE JMI School
TRDG/WHET N20 .... 38 D1
St Andrews CE Primary School
EN EN1 .... 29 K1
STHGT/OAK N14 .... 28 C6
St Andrews Greek School
CAMTN NW1 .... 72 B5
St Andrews Primary School
BRXN/ST SW9 .... 130 A1
IS N1 .... 5 M3
St Andrews & St Marks CE
Junior School
SURB KT6 .... 158 E4
St Andrews School
RYLN/HDSTN HA2 .... 48 B4
WLSDN NW10 .... 69 K6
St Angela's & St Bonaventures
Sixth Form Centre
FSTGT E7 .... 77 F5
St Angela's Ursuline School
FSTGT E7 .... 77 F5
St Annes Catholic High School
for Girls
ENC/FH EN2 .... 30 A3
PLMGR N13 .... 41 J2
St Annes CE Primary School
WAND/EARL SW18 .... 128 A4
St Annes RC Primary School
VX/NE SW8 .... 17 L9

St Anne's Special School
MRDN SM4 .... 161 K4
St Anne's Trading Estate
POP/IOD E14 .... 93 H5
St Annes CE Primary School
SEVS/STOTM N15 .... 55 K4
St Ann's General Hospital
FSBYPK N4 .... 55 J4
St Anns School
HNWL W7 .... 84 E7
St Ann's Shopping Centre
HRW HA1 .... 48 E5
St Anselms RC Primary School
DART DA1 .... 139 J4
HRW HA1 .... 48 E6
NWDGN UB2 .... 102 F2
St Anslems RC Primary School
TOOT SW17 .... 148 A1
St Anthonys Hospital
WPK KT4 .... 161 G7
St Anthonys RC Primary School
EDUL SE22 .... 131 H5
PGE/AN SE20 .... 150 D7
WATW WD18 .... 20 C4
St Anthony's School
(Junior House)
HAMP NW3 .... 71 H4
St Anthony's School
(Senior House)
HAMP NW3 .... 71 G4
St Antonys RC Primary School
FSTGT E7 .... 76 E6
WFD IG8 .... 44 E3
St Aubyns School
WFD IG8 .... 44 D6
St Augustines CE High School
KIL/WHAMP NW6 .... 2 B6
St Augustines Primary School
BELV DA17 .... 117 G2
KIL/WHAMP NW6 .... 2 B5
St Augustines Priory School
EA W5 .... 86 A4
St Augustines RC
Infant School
GNTH/NBYPK IG2 .... 60 B4
St Augustines RC
Primary School
CAT SE6 .... 151 K4
GNTH/NBYPK IG2 .... 60 B4
WKENS W14 .... 107 H5
St Barnabas CE Primary School
BGVA SW1W 16 B7
St Barnabas & St Philip's CE
Primary School
KENS W8 .... 14 A4
St Bartholomews CE
Primary School
SYD SE26 .... 150 E3
St Bartholomews Hospital
STBT EC1A 12 D3
St Bartholomews
Medical School
FARR EC1M 12 D1
St Bartholomews & Royal
London School of Medicine
FARR EC1M 12 E2
St Bartholomew's the Great
STBT EC1A 12 D3
St Bartholomews & The Royal
London Hospital
WCHPL E1 .... 92 D4
St Barts Hospital Sports Ground
CHST BR7 .... 154 D5
St Bedes RC Infant School
BAL SW12 .... 129 J7
St Bedes RC Primary School
CHDH RM6 .... 61 J4
St Benedicts Junior School
EA W5 .... 85 J4
St Benedicts School
EA W5 .... 85 K4
St Bernadette Catholic
Junior School
BAL SW12 .... 129 H6
St Bernadettes RC First &
Middle School
KTN/HRWW/WS HA3 .... 50 A3
St Bonaventures School
FSTGT E7 .... 76 E6
St Boniface RC Primary School
TOOT SW17 .... 147 K4
St Catherines RC Girls School
BXLYHS DA6 .... 137 J4
St Catherines RC J & I School
WDR/YW UB7 .... 100 A3
St Catherines RC Primary School
BAR EN5 .... 26 D3
St Catherines School
TWK TW1 .... 143 F1
St Cecilias CE School
WAND/EARL SW18 .... 127 J6
St Cecilias RC Primary School
WPK KT4 .... 174 B1
St Chads RC Primary School
SNWD SE25 .... 165 J4
St Charles Hospital
NKENS W10 .... 88 B4
St Charles Primary School
NKENS W10 .... 88 B4
St Christinas RC
Preparatory School
STJWD NW8 .... 3 K5
St Christophers School
BECK BR3 .... 167 F2
HAMP NW3 .... 71 H4
WBLY HA9 .... 68 B2
St Clare Business Park
HPTN TW12 .... 142 C5
St Clement Danes CE
Primary School
HOL/ALD WC2B 11 L5
St Clement & St James CE
Primary School
NTGHL W11 .... 88 C7
St Clements Hospital
BOW E3 .... 93 H2
St Clements Primary School
EW KT17 .... 173 H7
St Columbas RC Boys School
BXLYHS DA6 .... 137 J4
St Cuthbert with St Matthias CE
Primary School
ECT SW5 .... 14 B7
St Cyprians Greek Orthodox
Primary School
THHTH CR7 .... 164 D1
St Davids College
WWKM BR4 .... 166 E6
St Davids Health Centre
STWL/WRAY TW19 .... 120 A6
St Dominics RC Primary School
HAMP NW3 .... 71 K4
HOM E9 .... 75 G5

St Dominics Sixth Form College
  HRW HA1 .... 66 E1
St Dunstans CE Primary School
  CHEAM SM3 .... 174 C5
St Dunstans College
  CAT SE6 .... 132 C7
St Ebba's Hospital
  HOR/WEW KT19 .... 172 E7
St Edmunds RC Primary School
  ED N9 .... 30 D7
  POP/IOD E14 .... 112 D3
  WHTN TW2 .... 123 G6
St Edwards CE
  Comprehensive School
  CHDH RM6 .... 62 C5
St Edwards CE Primary School
  ROM RM1 .... 63 F3
St Edwards RC JMI School
  STJWD NW8 .... 9 J1
St Elizabeths RC
  Primary School
  BETH E2 .... 92 E1
  RCHPK/HAM TW10 .... 125 C5
St Eugene de Mazenod RC
  Primary School
  KIL/WHAMP NW6 .... 2 B2
St Faiths CE Primary School
  WAND/EARL SW18 .... 128 A4
St Fidelis Catholic
  Primary School
  ERITH DA8 .... 117 K5
St Francesca Cabrini
  Primary School
  FSTH SE23 .... 131 K5
St Francis de Sales RC
  J & I School
  TOTM N17 .... 42 B6
St Francis of Assisi
  Primary School
  NKENS W10 .... 88 B6
St Francis RC Primary School
  PECK SE15 .... 111 H5
  SRTFD E15 .... 76 C4
St Francis Xavier College
  BAL SW12 .... 129 C5
St Gabriels CE Primary School
  PIM SW1V 16 E8
St George's Cathedral
  STHWK SE1 .... 18 B3
St Georges CE Primary School
  BMLY BR1 .... 168 B1
  CMBW SE5 .... 111 K4
  VX/NE SW8 .... 109 H6
St Georges College
  HOLWY N7 .... 73 G2
St Georges Elizabethan Theatre
  HOLWY N7 .... 72 D3
St Georges Hanover Square CE
  Primary School
  MYFR/PKLN W1K 10 B7
St Georges Hospital
  TOOT SW17 .... 147 J4
St Georges Industrial Estate
  KUTN/CMB KT2 .... 143 K4
  PLMGR N13 .... 41 H6
St Georges Medical Centre
  HDN NW4 .... 51 K2
St Georges RC Primary School
  ENC/FH EN2 .... 29 K1
  HRW HA1 .... 67 F2
St Georges RC School
  MV/WKIL W9 .... 2 D6
St Georges Shopping Centre
  & Cinema
  HRW HA1 .... 48 D5
St Georges University
  of London
  TOOT SW17 .... 147 H4
St George the Martyr CE
  Primary School
  BMSBY WC1N 11 L1
St George Wharf
  VX/NE SW8 .... 17 J9
St Gildas RC Junior School
  CEND/HSY/T N8 .... 54 E6
St Giles College London Central
  RSQ WC1B 11 K2
St Giles School
  SAND/SEL CR2 .... 177 H5
St Gregorys High School
  KTN/HRWW/WS HA3 .... 49 K4
St Gregorys RC Primary School
  EA W5 .... 85 J3
St Helens Catholic Infant School
  WALTH E17 .... 58 A4
St Helens RC Primary School
  BRXN/ST SW9 .... 130 B2
  CAN/RD E16 .... 94 D3
St Helens School
  NTHWD HA6 .... 32 C5
St Helier ≋
  MRDN SM4 .... 161 K5
St Helier Hospital
  CAR SM5 .... 162 B7
St Hildas School
  BUSH WD23 .... 22 B6
St Ignatius RC Primary School
  SEVS/STOTM N15 .... 56 A5
  SUN TW16 .... 140 E7
St James CE J & I School
  BERM/RHTH SE16 .... 111 H2
St James CE Primary School
  MUSWH N10 .... 54 A3
  PEND EN3 .... 30 E1
St James CE Junior School
  FSTGT E7 .... 76 D4
St James Hatcham CE School
  NWCR SE14 .... 112 B7
St James Independent School
  for Girls
  NTGHL W11 .... 8 A6
St James Junior School
  WKENS W14 .... 107 H3
St James Medical Centre
  CROY/NA CR0 .... 164 C6
St James RC Primary School
  HAYES BR2 .... 169 G4
  WHTN TW2 .... 142 E2
St James & St Michaels CE
  Primary School
  BAY/PAD W2 .... 8 E6
St James Senior Girls School
  WKENS W14 .... 107 H3
St James's Health Centre
  WALTH E17 .... 57 G4
St James's Hotel & Club
  WHALL SW1A 10 E8
St James's Palace
  WHALL SW1A 10 F9
St James's Park ⊖
  STJSPK SW1H 17 G3
St James Street ≋
  WALTH E17 .... 57 G4

St James the Great RC
  Primary School
  PECK SE15 .... 111 G7
  THHTH CR7 .... 164 C5
St Joachims RC
  Primary School
  CAN/RD E16 .... 95 G5
St Joan of Arc RC
  Primary School
  HBRY N5 .... 73 H3
St John Fisher RC
  Primary School
  ERITHM DA18 .... 117 F2
  GFD/PVL UB6 .... 85 J2
  PIN HA5 .... 48 A3
  RYNPK SW20 .... 161 F4
St John of Jerusalem CE
  Primary School
  HOM E9 .... 74 E6
St Johns ⊖
  DEPT SE8 .... 132 D1
St Johns Ambulance Station
  WEA W13 .... 85 H7
St Johns & St James CE School
  UED N18 .... 42 B4
St Johns Angell Town CE
  Primary School
  BRXN/ST SW9 .... 130 B1
St Johns CE Primary School
  BETH E2 .... 92 E1
  CROY/NA CR0 .... 179 F2
  FBAR/BDGN N11 .... 39 K3
  KUT/HW KT1 .... 159 F2
  PGE/AN SE20 .... 150 E6
  TRDG/WHET N20 .... 39 G1
St Johns CE School
  CDALE/KGS NW9 .... 51 G4
St John's CE Walham Green
  Primary School
  FUL/PGN SW6 .... 107 H7
St Johns Church of
  England School
  STAN HA7 .... 35 G3
St John's Concert Hall
  WEST SW1P 17 J4
St Johns Highbury Vale CE
  Primary School
  HBRY N5 .... 73 H3
St John's Hospital Day Centre
  BTSEA SW11 .... 128 C3
St John's Lodge
  CAMTN NW1 .... 4 A7
St Johns Primary School
  WEA W13 .... 85 G6
St Johns RC Primary School
  BERM/RHTH SE16 .... 112 B1
St Johns & St Clements CE
  J & I School
  PECK SE15 .... 131 H2
St Johns School
  NTHWD HA6 .... 33 F5
St Johns Upper Holloway CE
  Primary School
  ARCH N19 .... 72 C1
St Johns Walworth CE
  Primary School
  WALW SE17 .... 18 E6
St Johns Way Medical Centre
  ARCH N19 .... 54 D7
St John's Wood ⊖
  STJWD NW8 .... 3 G5
St Johns Wood
  Pre-Preparatory School
  STJWD NW8 .... 3 J7
St John the Baptist CE
  Junior School
  KUT/HW KT1 .... 143 K6
St John the Baptist CE
  Primary School
  BMLY BR1 .... 152 A3
St John the Baptist VA CE
  Primary School
  IS N1 .... 7 J6
St John the Divine CE
  Primary School
  CMBW SE5 .... 110 C6
St John the Evangelist RC
  Primary School
  IS N1 .... 6 C5
St John Vianney RC
  Primary School
  SEVS/STOTM N15 .... 55 J1
St Joseph's Annexe
  ABYW SE2 .... 116 D5
St Josephs Catholic
  Infant School
  LEY E10 .... 57 H7
St Josephs Catholic
  Junior School
  CMBW SE5 .... 110 D6
St Josephs Catholic
  Primary School
  BMLY BR1 .... 153 G6
  DAGW RM9 .... 80 B7
  KUT/HW KT1 .... 159 G1
St Josephs College
  STRHM/NOR SW16 .... 149 H5
St Josephs Convent School
  WAN E11 .... 58 C5
St Josephs Primary School
  WAND/EARL SW18 .... 127 K4
St Joseph's RC College
  MLHL NW7 .... 37 J3
St Josephs RC First &
  Middle School
  KTN/HRWW/WS HA3 .... 49 G1
St Josephs RC Infant School
  NRWD SE19 .... 149 K5
St Josephs RC J & I School
  HDN NW4 .... 51 K3
  WBLY HA9 .... 68 B4
St Josephs RC Junior School
  LEY E10 .... 57 J7
  NRWD SE19 .... 149 J5
St Josephs RC
  Primary School
  ARCH N19 .... 54 D7
  BARK IG11 .... 78 C7
  BERM/RHTH SE16 .... 111 K2
  CHEL SW3 .... 15 L6
  DART DA1 .... 138 D6
  DEPT SE8 .... 112 D6
  GNWCH SE10 .... 113 H4
  HNWL W7 .... 84 E7
  HOL/ALD WC2B 11 K4
  MV/WKIL W9 .... 2 E8
  STHWK SE1 .... 18 F1
  STHWK SE1 .... 111 H1
  WLSDN NW10 .... 69 G6
St Judes CE Primary School
  HNHL SE24 .... 130 C3
  STHWK SE1 .... 18 C4

St Judes & St Pauls CE
  Primary School
  IS N1 .... 74 A4
St Katharine Pier
  WAP E1W 13 M8
St Katherine
  TPL/STR WC2R 11 M7
St Lawrence Business Centre
  FELT TW13 .... 141 F1
St Lawrence Catholic School
  FELT TW13 .... 141 F1
St Lawrence Junior School
  E/WMO/HCT KT8 .... 157 J2
St Lawrence University
  BMSBY WC1N 11 M1
St Leonards CE Primary School
  STRHM/NOR SW16 .... 148 D4
St Leonards Hospital
  IS N1 .... 7 K5
St Luke's Catholic
  Sixth Form College
  SCUP DA14 .... 155 F4
St Lukes Cemetery
  HAYES BR2 .... 168 E5
St Lukes CE Primary School
  CAN/RD E16 .... 94 D5
  FSBYE EC1V 6 F8
  KUTN/CMB KT2 .... 144 B7
  MV/WKIL W9 .... 88 D1
  POP/IOD E14 .... 113 G3
  WNWD SE27 .... 149 J4
St Luke's Health Centre
  CAN/RD E16 .... 94 D5
St Lukes Hospital for The Clergy
  FITZ W1T 10 E1
St Lukes School
  THHTH CR7 .... 164 B3
St Lukes Woodside Hospital
  MUSWH N10 .... 54 A3
St Margaret Clitherow RC
  Primary School
  THMD SE28 .... 97 H7
St Margaret Lee CE
  Primary School
  LEW SE13 .... 133 H1
St Margaret's ≋
  TWK TW1 .... 124 C5
St Margarets Business Centre
  TWK TW1 .... 124 B6
St Margarets CE Primary School
  WOOL/PLUM SE18 .... 115 H5
St Margarets Clitherow RC
  Primary School
  WBLY HA9 .... 68 E2
St Margarets Primary School
  BARK IG11 .... 78 B7
St Margarets School
  BUSH WD23 .... 22 A6
  HAMP NW3 .... 71 F3
St Marks Catholic School
  HSLW TW3 .... 122 E2
St Marks CE Academy
  MTCM CR4 .... 163 G1
St Marks CE Primary School
  ARCH N19 .... 72 E1
  HAYES BR2 .... 167 K2
  LBTH SE11 .... 17 M9
  SNWD SE25 .... 165 H3
St Marks Industrial Estate
  CAN/RD E16 .... 95 H7
St Marks Primary School
  HNWL W7 .... 103 K1
  MTCM CR4 .... 162 E1
St Martin-in-the-Fields
  CHCR WC2N 11 J7
St Martin in the Fields
  High School
  BRXS/STRHM SW2 .... 130 C7
St Martin of Porres
  Primary School
  FBAR/BDGN N11 .... 40 C5
St Martins Hospital
  MYFR/PKLN W1K 10 A6
St Martins Medical Centre
  RSLP HA4 .... 46 C6
St Martins School
  MLHL NW7 .... 37 G4
St Martins School of Art
  SOHO/SHAV W1D 11 H5
St Martins Theatre
  LSO/SEVD WC2H 11 H6
St Mary Abbots CE
  Primary School
  KENS W8 .... 14 C2
St Mary Abbots Church Hall
  KENS W8 .... 14 C1
St Mary & St Pancras CE
  Primary School
  CAMTN NW1 .... 5 G6
The St Marylebone CE School
  MHST W1U 10 B2
St Marylebone Crematorium
  FNCH N3 .... 53 F2
St Mary Magdalene Academy
  HOLWY N7 .... 73 G5
St Mary Magdalene CE
  Primary School
  MV/WKIL W9 .... 8 A1
  WOOL/PLUM SE18 .... 114 E3
St Mary Magdalen RC
  Junior School
  CRICK NW2 .... 69 K5
St Mary Magdalens Catholic
  Primary School
  MORT/ESHN SW14 .... 126 A2
St Mary of The Angels RC
  Primary School
  NTGHL W11 .... 8 A4
St Marys Abbey
  MLHL NW7 .... 37 J2
St Mary & St Michael
  Primary School
  WCHPL E1 .... 92 E5
St Mary & St Peters CE
  Primary School
  TEDD TW11 .... 142 E4
St Marys Bryanston Square CE
  Primary School
  MBLAR W1H 9 K2
St Marys Catholic
  Primary School
  HCH RM12 .... 63 J7
St Marys CE High School
  HDN NW4 .... 51 K2
St Marys CE Infant School
  CEND/HSY/T N8 .... 55 F3
St Marys CE Junior School
  CEND/HSY/T N8 .... 54 E3
  STWL/WRAY TW19 .... 120 B5
St Mary's Cemetery
  BTSEA SW11 .... 128 D4
St Marys CE Primary School
  CHSGTN KT9 .... 172 A5

EBAR EN4 .... 27 J5
  FNCH N3 .... 38 D7
  IS N1 .... 6 D2
  LEW SE13 .... 132 E4
  STNW/STAM N16 .... 73 K1
  TWK TW1 .... 124 B6
  WALTH E17 .... 57 K3
  WLSDN NW10 .... 69 G3
St Mary's CE Primary School
  PUT/ROE SW15 .... 127 G2
St Marys CE School
  HDN NW4 .... 51 K2
St Marys College
  TWK TW1 .... 143 F2
St Marys Greek Cathedral
  WDGN N22 .... 41 F7
St Marys High School
  CROY/NA CR0 .... 164 D7
St Marys Hospital
  BAY/PAD W2 .... 9 H4
St Marys Hospital
  Medical School
  BAY/PAD W2 .... 9 H4
St Marys Infant School
  CAR SM5 .... 175 J3
St Marys Kilburn Primary School
  KIL/WHAMP NW6 .... 2 B3
St Marys Magdalens Catholic
  Primary School
  BROCKY SE4 .... 132 B3
St Marys Primary School
  WKENS W14 .... 107 G2
St Marys RC Infant School
  CAR SM5 .... 175 K4
St Marys RC J & I School
  CROY/NA CR0 .... 164 E7
St Marys RC Junior School
  FSBYPK N4 .... 55 K4
St Marys RC Primary School
  BECK BR3 .... 152 A6
  CLAP SW4 .... 129 H4
  ELTH/MOT SE9 .... 135 F4
  ISLW TW7 .... 124 B2
  KIL/WHAMP NW6 .... 2 A5
  NKENS W10 .... 88 C3
  PEND EN3 .... 31 F3
  VX/NE SW8 .... 109 G7
  WIM/MER SW19 .... 146 E6
St Mary's RC Primary School
  CHSWK W4 .... 106 B4
St Marys & St Johns CE
  Primary School
  HDN NW4 .... 51 K4
St Marys School
  CEND/HSY/T N8 .... 55 F4
  HAMP NW3 .... 71 G4
St Mary's Western
  Eye Hospital
  MBLAR W1H 9 L2
St Matthew Academy
  LEW SE13 .... 133 G2
St Matthews CE Primary School
  PEND EN3 .... 30 E4
  RYNPK SW20 .... 145 J7
  SURB KT6 .... 159 F6
St Matthias CE Primary School
  BETH E2 .... 7 M9
  STNW/STAM N16 .... 74 A4
St Meryl JMI School
  OXHEY WD19 .... 33 J2
St Michael & All Angels
  CE Academy
  CMBW SE5 .... 110 C6
St Michael at Bowes CE
  Junior School
  PLMGR N13 .... 41 G5
St Michaels & St Martins RC
  Primary School
  HSLWW TW4 .... 122 E2
St Michaels Catholic College
  BERM/RHTH SE16 .... 111 H1
St Michaels Catholic
  Grammar School
  NFNCH/WDSPK N12 .... 39 F4
St Michaels CE Primary School
  CAMTN NW1 .... 4 E3
  HGT N6 .... 54 A6
  WAND/EARL SW18 .... 127 K3
  WDGN N22 .... 41 F7
  WELL DA16 .... 116 D7
St Michaels Sydenham CE
  Primary School
  SYD SE26 .... 151 G3
The St Michael Steiner School
  WAND/EARL SW18 .... 127 K4
St Monicas RC Primary School
  STHGT/OAK N14 .... 40 E2
St Monica's RC Primary School
  IS N1 .... 7 J7
St Nicholas Centre
  SUT SM1 .... 175 F4
St Nicholas Preparatory School
  SKENS SW7 .... 15 H2
St Nicholas School
  BORE WD6 .... 24 A5
  CDALE/KGS NW9 .... 68 E1
  CHST BR7 .... 154 C6
St Olaves Preparatory School
  ELTH/MOT SE9 .... 154 B1
St Pancras Hospital
  CAMTN NW1 .... 5 G4
St Pancras International ≋ ⊖
  KCROSS N1C 5 J6
St Pancras International
  Youth Hostel
  CAMTN NW1 .... 5 H7
St Pancras & Islington Cemetery
  EFNCH N2 .... 39 J7
St Pancras Renaissance Hotel
  CAMTN NW1 .... 5 H7
St Patricks Church School
  STHWK SE1 .... 12 A9
St Patricks Infant School
  WAP E1W 92 D7
St Patricks International School
  SOHO/SHAV W1D 10 F4
St Patricks Primary School
  KTTN NW5 .... 72 B5
St Patricks RC Primary School
  WALTH E17 .... 57 G3
  WOOL/PLUM SE18 .... 115 J3
St Paulinus CE Primary School
  DART DA1 .... 138 B3
St Paul's ⊖
  STP EC4M 12 E4
St Pauls & All Hallows
  Junior School
  TOTM N17 .... 42 C6
St Pauls & All Hallows CE
  Infant School
  TOTM N17 .... 42 C6

St Paul's Cathedral
  STP EC4M 12 E4
St Pauls Catholic College
  SUN TW16 .... 140 E7
St Pauls CE Primary School
  BTFD TW8 .... 104 E5
  CHSGTN KT9 .... 172 A3
  FBAR/BDGN N11 .... 40 A1
  HAMP NW3 .... 3 K2
  MLHL NW7 .... 37 K3
  WALW SE17 .... 18 D8
  WCHMH N21 .... 29 H6
St Pauls CE Junior School
  KUTN/CMB KT2 .... 144 C6
St Pauls Girls School
  HMSMTH W6 .... 107 G3
St Paul's Primary School
  HMSMTH W6 .... 107 F4
St Pauls RC Primary School
  THDIT KT7 .... 157 K6
  WDGN N22 .... 55 F7
St Pauls RC School
  ABYW SE2 .... 116 E5
St Pauls Road Medical Centre
  IS N1 .... 73 K5
St Pauls School
  BARN SW13 .... 106 E4
St Pauls Steiner School
  IS N1 .... 73 K5
St Pauls Trust School
  BOW E3 .... 93 J4
St Pauls with St Lukes CE
  Primary School
  BOW E3 .... 93 J4
St Pauls with St Michaels CE
  Primary School
  HACK E8 .... 74 C7
St Peter Chanel RC
  Primary School
  SCUP DA14 .... 155 F4
St Peter In Chains RC
  Infant School
  CEND/HSY/T N8 .... 54 E5
St Peters Catholic
  Primary School
  ROM RM1 .... 63 F2
St Peters CE Primary School
  HMSMTH W6 .... 106 D4
  MV/WKIL W9 .... 8 A1
  WALW SE17 .... 19 G8
  WAP E1W 92 E7
St Peter's Church
  KTBR SW1X 16 C3
St Peters Eaton Square CE
  Primary School
  BGVA SW1W 16 C4
St Peter's Hospital
  COVGDN WC2E 11 K6
St Peters Primary School
  SAND/SEL CR2 .... 177 K5
St Peters RC Primary School
  DAGW RM9 .... 80 B7
  WOOL/PLUM SE18 .... 115 G4
St Peter & St Paul RC
  Primary School
  MTCM CR4 .... 162 E3
  STMC/STPC BR5 .... 169 K1
St Peter & St Pauls
  Primary School
  FSBYE EC1V 6 C9
St Philips School
  CHSGTN KT9 .... 171 K5
  SKENS SW7 .... 14 F6
St Phillips Infant School
  SYD SE26 .... 150 D3
St Philomenas Catholic
  High School
  CAR SM5 .... 175 J4
St Quintins Health Centre
  NKENS W10 .... 88 A4
St Raphaels Hospice
  WPK KT4 .... 174 B1
St Raphaels RC Primary School
  NTHLT UB5 .... 83 F1
St Raphaels Way Medical Centre
  WLSDN NW10 .... 68 E4
St Richards with St Andrews CE
  Primary School
  RCHPK/HAM TW10 .... 143 H2
St Robert Southwell RC
  Primary School
  CDALE/KGS NW9 .... 50 E5
St Saviour & St Olaves School
  STHWK SE1 .... 19 H4
St Saviours CE Primary School
  CMBW SE5 .... 130 D2
  MV/WKIL W9 .... 8 C2
  POP/IOD E14 .... 93 K4
St Saviour's CE Primary School
  WALTH E17 .... 57 H6
St Saviours CE Infant School
  EA W5 .... 85 K7
St Saviours RC Primary School
  LEW SE13 .... 133 F3
St Scholasticas RC
  Primary School
  CLPT E5 .... 74 C2
St Stephens CE Junior School
  TWK TW1 .... 124 B5
St Stephens CE Primary School
  BAY/PAD W2 .... 8 B3
  DEPT SE8 .... 132 C1
  SHB W12 .... 87 K7
St Stephens CE School
  VX/NE SW8 .... 109 K6
St Stephens RC
  Primary School
  WELL DA16 .... 136 D1
St Stephens School &
  Childrens Centre
  EHAM E6 .... 77 G6
St Swithun Wells Catholic
  Primary School
  RSLP HA4 .... 65 G2
The St Teresa Catholic
  Primary School
  BCTR RM8 .... 79 J3
St Teresa RC First &
  Middle School
  KTN/HRWW/WS HA3 .... 34 C7
St Teresa's Catholic
  Primary School
  KTN/HRWW/WS HA3 .... 34 B7
St Teresa's RC Primary School
  NTHLT UB5 ....
St Theresas RC Primary School
  FNCH N3 .... 53 K1
St Thomas a' Becket RC
  Primary School
  ABYW SE2 .... 116 B2
St Thomas Becket RC
  Primary School
  SNWD SE25 .... 165 H5

St Thomas CE Primary School
NKENS W10 .... 88 C3
St Thomas Childrens
Day Hospital
LBTH SE11 .... 17 M7
St Thomas' Hospital
STHWK SE1 .... 17 L3
St Thomas More
Language College
CHEL SW3 .... 15 L6
St Thomas More RC
Primary School
BXLYHN DA7 .... 137 G1
ELTH/MOT SE9 .... 134 D2
St Thomas More RC School
ELTH/MOT SE9 .... 135 F5
WDGN N22 .... 41 G6
St Thomas of Canterbury
Catholic Primary School
FUL/PGN SW6 .... 107 J6
MTCM CR4 .... 163 F2
St Thomas the Apostle College
PECK SE15 .... 111 K7
St Ursulas Convent School
GNWCH SE10 .... 113 G6
St Vincent De Paul RC
Primary School
WEST SW1P 16 E4
St Vincents Catholic
Primary School
ELTH/MOT SE9 .... 153 J3
St Vincents Hospital
PIN HA5 .... 46 C2
St Vincents RC Primary School
BCTR RM8 .... 79 J1
MLHL NW7 .... 37 K3
St Vincent's RC Primary School
MHST W1U 10 A3
St Walter & St John
Sports Ground
TOOT SW17 .... 128 D7
St William of York
Primary School
FSTH SE23 .... 132 B7
St Winefrides Catholic
Primary School
MNPK E12 .... 77 K4
St Winifreds Catholic
Junior School
LEE/GVPK SE12 .... 133 J5
St Winifreds RC Infant School
LEW SE13 .... 133 H4
Salcombe Preparatory
Lower School
STHGT/OAK N14 .... 28 D6
Salcombe Preparatory
School (Infants)
STHGT/OAK N14 .... 28 B5
Salcombe Preparatory
School (Juniors)
STHGT/OAK N14 .... 28 B6
Salesian College
BTSEA SW11 .... 108 D7
Salisbury Primary School
MNPK E12 .... 77 H4
Salisbury School
ED N9 .... 30 E7
Salters' Hall
BARB EC2Y 12 F3
Salusbury Primary School
KIL/WHAMP NW6 .... 70 C7
Salvatorian College
KTN/HRWW/WS HA3 .... 48 D1
Samuel Jones Industrial Estate
PECK SE15 .... 111 F6
Samuel Rhodes School
IS N1 .... 6 A3
Sanderstead ⇌
SAND/SEL CR2 .... 177 K7
Sanderstead Junior School
SAND/SEL CR2 .... 177 K7
Sandgate Trading Estate
BERM/RHTH SE16 .... 111 J4
Sandhurst Primary School
CAT SE6 .... 133 H6
Sandilands ⊖
CROY/NA CR0 .... 178 B1
Sandown Grandstand &
Exhibition Centre
ESH/CLAY KT10 .... 170 B2
Sandown Industrial Park
ESH/CLAY KT10 .... 170 A1
Sandown Park Racecourse
ESH/CLAY KT10 .... 170 B2
Sandown Sports Club &
Dry Ski Slope
ESH/CLAY KT10 .... 170 B2
Sandringham Primary School
FSTGT E7 .... 77 G5
Sandy Lodge Golf Club
NTHWD HA6 .... 32 B1
Sapcote Trading Centre
WLSDN NW10 .... 69 H4
Sarah Bonnell School
SRTFD E15 .... 76 C5
Sarum Hall School
HAMP NW3 .... 3 K1
Satmer Trust School
STNW/STAM N16 .... 74 C1
Savoy Pier
TPL/STR WC2R 11 L7
The Savoy
TPL/STR WC2R 11 K7
Savoy Theatre
TPL/STR WC2R 11 L7
Saxon Business Centre
WIM/MER SW19 .... 162 B1
Sayer Clinic
CROY/NA CR0 .... 177 F3
Sayer Clinics
MBLAR W1H 9 M5
Scargill Infant School
RAIN RM13 .... 81 J6
Scargill Junior School
RAIN RM13 .... 81 J5
Scarsdale Place
Medical Centre
KENS W8 .... 14 C3
Schomberg House
STJS SW1Y 10 F9
School of English
GLDGN NW11 .... 52 E1
School of Oriental &
African Studies
GWRST WC1E 11 H1
The School of Pharmacy
BMSBY WC1N 5 K9
The School of St David &
St Katharine
CEND/HSY/T N8 .... 54 E3
The School of
the Islamic Republic
KIL/WHAMP NW6 .... 2 A6

Science Museum
SKENS SW7 .... 15 H4
Science Museum IMAX Cinema
SKENS SW7 .... 15 G4
The Science Museum Library
SKENS SW7 .... 15 G3
Scotts Park Primary School
BMLY BR1 .... 153 G7
Sealife London Aquarium
WHALL SW1A 17 L2
Sebright Primary School
BETH E2 .... 92 C1
Secombe Centre
SUT SM1 .... 175 F5
Sedgehill School
CAT SE6 .... 151 K4
Sedgewick Centre
WCHPL E1 .... 13 M4
Selborne Primary School
GFD/PVL UB6 .... 85 F1
Selhurst ⇌
SNWD SE25 .... 165 H4
The Selhurst Medical Centre
SNWD SE25 .... 165 H5
Sellincourt School
TOOT SW17 .... 147 J5
Selsdon Primary School
SAND/SEL CR2 .... 178 E7
Selsdon Road Industrial Estate
SAND/SEL CR2 .... 177 K6
Selwyn Primary School
CHING E4 .... 44 A6
PLSTW E13 .... 76 E7
Sergeant Industrial Estate
WAND/EARL SW18 .... 128 A5
Serpentine Gallery
BAY/PAD W2 .... 9 H9
Serpentine Lido & Cafe
SKENS SW7 .... 15 J1
Servite RC Primary School
WBPTN SW10 .... 14 E9
Seven Islands Leisure Centre
BERM/RHTH SE16 .... 111 K2
Seven Kings ⇌
GDMY/SEVK IG3 .... 60 E7
Seven Kings Health Centre
GDMY/SEVK IG3 .... 60 E7
Seven Kings High School
GNTH/NBYPK IG2 .... 60 D6
Seven Mills Primary School
POP/IOD E14 .... 112 D1
Seven Sisters ⇌ ⊖
SEVS/STOTM N15 .... 56 A4
Seven Sisters Primary School
SEVS/STOTM N15 .... 55 M4
Seymour Gardens
Medical Centre
IL IG1 .... 59 K7
Seymour Leisure Centre
MBLAR W1H 9 L3
Shaare Zedek Medical Centre
GLDGN NW11 .... 52 D5
Shacklewell Primary School
HACK E8 .... 74 B3
Shadwell ⇌
WCHPL E1 .... 92 D5
Shadwell Dock Stairs
WAP E1W 93 H6
Shaftesbury Hospital
LSO/SEVD WC2H 11 J5
Shaftesbury Medical Centre
RYLN/HDSTN HA2 .... 48 C7
Shaftesbury Park
Primary School
BTSEA SW11 .... 129 F2
Shaftesbury Primary School
FSTGT E7 .... 77 G4
Shaftesbury Theatre
LSO/SEVD WC2H 11 J4
Shahjalal Medical Centre
WCHPL E1 .... 92 C5
Shakespeare Business Centre
BRXN/ST SW9 .... 130 C1
Shakespeare's Globe Exhibition
& Theatre Tour
STHWK SE1 .... 12 E8
The Shamrock Sports Club
ACT W3 .... 86 C1
Shannon Corner Retail Park
NWMAL KT3 .... 160 D3
Shapla Primary School
WCHPL E1 .... 92 C6
Sharp Sports Centre
EDGW HA8 .... 36 C5
Sheen Lane Health Centre
MORT/ESHN SW14 .... 125 J2
Sheen Lawn Tennis &
Squash Club
MORT/ESHN SW14 .... 125 K4
Sheen Mount Primary School
RCHPK/HAM TW10 .... 125 J4
Sheen Sports Centre
MORT/ESHN SW14 .... 126 B3
Shell Centre
STHWK SE1 .... 11 M9
Shelley School
CLAP SW4 .... 129 K2
Shenstone School
DART DA1 .... 138 A7
Shepherd's Bush ⇌ ⊖ ⊖
SHB W12 .... 107 K1
Shepherd's Bush CC
ACT W3 .... 87 G6
Shepherd's Bush Empire
SHB W12 .... 107 F1
Shepherd's Bush Market ⊖
SHB W12 .... 88 A7
Sheraton Business Centre
GFD/PVL UB6 .... 85 J1
Sheraton Park Tower Hotel
KTBR SW1X 15 M1
Sheraton Skyline Hotel
HYS/HAR UB3 .... 101 G6
Sheringdale Primary School
WAND/EARL SW18 .... 127 J7
Sheringham Junior School
MNPK E12 .... 77 K3
Sherington Primary School
CHARL SE7 .... 114 B3
Sherlock Holmes Hotel
MHST W1U 9 M2
Sherlock Holmes Museum
CAMTN NW1 .... 9 M1
Sherwood Park Primary School
BFN/LL DA15 .... 136 C5
Sherwood Park School
WLGTN SM6 .... 176 D2
Sherwood School
MTCM CR4 .... 163 H3
Shirley Clinic
CROY/NA CR0 .... 165 K7
Shirley High School
CROY/NA CR0 .... 179 F7

Shirley Oaks Hospital
CROY/NA CR0 .... 165 K6
Shirley Park Golf Club
CROY/NA CR0 .... 178 D1
Shirley Wanderers RFC
WWKM BR4 .... 180 A3
Shirley Windmill
CROY/NA CR0 .... 178 E2
Shooters Hill Golf Club
WOOL/PLUM SE18 .... 115 H7
Shooters Hill Post 16 Campus
WOOL/PLUM SE18 .... 115 F6
Shooting Star House
(Childrens Hospice)
HPTN TW12 .... 141 K5
Shopping City
WDGN N22 .... 55 F1
The Shopping Hall
EHAM E6 .... 77 J7
Shopping Mall
SWFD E18 .... 58 E1
Shore Business Centre
HOM E9 .... 74 E6
Shoreditch
Comprehensive School
IS N1 .... 7 K6
Shoreditch County Court
STLK EC1Y 7 H9
Shoreditch High Street ⊖
WCHPL E1 .... 13 L1
Shortlands ⇌
HAYES BR2 .... 167 H1
Shotfield Health Clinic
WLGTN SM6 .... 176 B5
Showcase Cinema
WDGN N22 .... 55 G1
Showcase Newham Cinema
BARK IG11 .... 96 C2
Shrewsbury House School
SURB KT6 .... 171 K1
Shrewsbury Lodge School
ESH/CLAY KT10 .... 170 C4
Shrewsbury Road Health Centre
FSTGT E7 .... 77 H6
Sidcup ⇌
BFN/LL DA15 .... 155 H1
Sidcup Cemetery
BXLY DA5 .... 155 K1
Sidcup Golf Club
BFN/LL DA15 .... 155 J3
Sidcup Health Centre
SCUP DA14 .... 155 G2
Sidcup Sports Club
SCUP DA14 .... 155 F3
Sidney Russell School
DAGW RM9 .... 80 A3
Silicon Business Centre
GFD/PVL UB6 .... 85 J1
Silverdale Industrial Estate
HYS/HAR UB3 .... 101 K1
Silver Industrial Estate
TOTM N17 .... 56 B1
Silver Street ⇌
UED N18 .... 42 B3
Silver Street Medical Centre
UED N18 .... 42 A3
Silver Wing Industrial Estate
CROY/NA CR0 .... 177 F5
Simon Marks Jewish
Primary School
STNW/STAM N16 .... 56 B7
Singlegate Primary School
WIM/MER SW19 .... 147 H6
Sion College
EMB EC4Y 12 B6
Sion Manning RC Girls School
NKENS W10 .... 88 B4
Sir Francis Drake
Primary School
DEPT SE8 .... 112 B4
Sir George Monoux College
WALTH E17 .... 57 K1
Sir James Altham
Swimming Pool
OXHEY WD19 .... 33 J4
Sir James Barrie School
VX/NE SW8 .... 109 H7
Sir John Cass Foundation &
Redcoat CE Secondary School
WCHPL E1 .... 93 F4
Sir John Heron Primary School
MNPK E12 .... 77 K3
Sir John Lillie Primary School
HMSMTH W6 .... 107 H5
Sir John Soane's Museum
LINN WC2A 11 L4
Sir Thomas Abney
Primary School
STNW/STAM N16 .... 55 K6
Sir Thomas Lipton
Memorial Hospital
STHGT/OAK N14 .... 28 B6
Sir William Burrough
Primary School
POP/IOD E14 .... 93 G5
Six Bridges Trading Estate
STHWK SE1 .... 111 H4
Skillion Business Park
BARK IG11 .... 97 F2
Skinners Academy Hackney
STNW/STAM N16 .... 56 A6
Slade Green ⇌
ERITH DA8 .... 118 D7
Slade Green FC
ERITH DA8 .... 118 E7
Slade Green Primary School
ERITH DA8 .... 118 D6
Slade School of Fine Art
STPAN WC1H 5 H8
Sleaford Industrial Estate
VX/NE SW8 .... 109 H6
Sloane Hospital
BECK BR3 .... 152 B7
Sloane Square ⊖
BGVA SW1W 16 A6
Smallberry Green
Primary School
ISLW TW7 .... 124 B1
Smallwood Primary School
TOOT SW17 .... 147 H3
SMA Medical Centre
LEY E10 .... 57 K6
Smithy Street School
WCHPL E1 .... 92 E4
Snaresbrook ⊖
WAN E11 .... 58 E4
Snaresbrook College
Preparatory School
SWFD E18 .... 58 E1
Snaresbrook Crown Court
WAN E11 .... 58 D4
Snaresbrook Primary School
SWFD E18 .... 58 E3

Snowflake School for Children
with Autism
ECT SW5 .... 14 A6
Snowsfields Primary School
STHWK SE1 .... 19 J1
Sobell Leisure Centre
HOLWY N7 .... 73 F2
Sobell Medical Centre
HOLWY N7 .... 73 G3
Sofitel Hotel
STJS SW1Y 11 G8
Soho Parish CE Primary School
SOHO/CST W1F 11 G6
Solent Road Health Centre
KIL/WHAMP NW6 .... 70 E5
Somerset House
COVGDN WC2E 11 L6
Somers Town Community
Sports Centre
CAMTN NW1 .... 4 F6
Sorsby Health Centre
CLPT E5 .... 75 F3
South Acton ⊖
ACT W3 .... 105 K2
Southall ⇌
STHL UB1 .... 102 E1
Southall & West London College
STHL UB1 .... 102 D1
South Bank Business Centre
VX/NE SW8 .... 109 J7
Southbank International
School Hampstead
HAMP NW3 .... 71 G5
Southbank International
School Kensington
NTGHL W11 .... 88 D6
Southbank International
School Westminster
BAY/PAD W2 .... 8 B7
South Bank University
STHWK SE1 .... 18 C3
South Bermondsey ⇌
BERM/RHTH SE16 .... 111 K4
Southborough High School
SURB KT6 .... 172 A2
Southborough Primary School
HAYES BR2 .... 169 F4
Southbury ⇌
EN EN1 .... 30 D3
Southbury Primary School
PEND EN3 .... 30 D3
South Camden
Community School
CAMTN NW1 .... 4 F5
South Chelsea College
BRXN/ST SW9 .... 130 A3
South Croydon ⇌
SAND/SEL CR2 .... 177 K4
South Croydon Medical Centre
SAND/SEL CR2 .... 177 J6
South Croydon Sports Club
CROY/NA CR0 .... 178 A4
South Ealing ⊖
EA W5 .... 104 E2
South Ealing Cemetery
EA W5 .... 104 E3
South Eastern University
HOLWY N7 .... 73 F2
Southern Road Primary School
PLSTW E13 .... 95 F1
Southern Spectator
Transport Mall
SRTFD E15 .... 76 A7
Southfield First & Middle School
CHSWK W4 .... 106 B1
Southfield Medical Centre
CHSWK W4 .... 106 A1
Southfields ⊖
WAND/EARL SW18 .... 127 J7
The Southfields Clinic
WAND/EARL SW18 .... 127 K5
Southfields Community College
WAND/EARL SW18 .... 127 K7
Southgate ⊖
STHGT/OAK N14 .... 28 D7
Southgate Cemetery
STHGT/OAK N14 .... 40 C1
Southgate College
STHGT/OAK N14 .... 40 C1
Southgate Compton CC
EBAR EN4 .... 27 K3
Southgate Leisure Centre
STHGT/OAK N14 .... 28 D6
Southgate Road Medical Centre
IS N1 .... 7 H1
Southgate School
EBAR EN4 .... 28 B4
South Greenford ⇌
GFD/PVL UB6 .... 84 E2
South Grove Primary School
WALTH E17 .... 57 G5
South Hampstead ⊖
KIL/WHAMP NW6 .... 2 F2
South Hampstead CC
CRICK NW2 .... 70 A6
South Hampstead
High School
HAMP NW3 .... 71 G3
South Harringay
Junior School
FSBYPK N4 .... 55 H4
South Harrow ⊖
RYLN/HDSTN HA2 .... 66 C2
South Herts Golf Club
TRDG/WHET N20 .... 26 E7
South Kensington ⊖
SKENS SW7 .... 15 H5
South Kenton ⊖
ALP/SUD HA0 .... 49 J7
Southlake Primary School
ABYW SE2 .... 116 E1
South Lewisham Health Centre
CAT SE6 .... 152 A3
South London Crematorium
MTCM CR4 .... 163 H1
South London Gallery
CMBW SE5 .... 111 F7
The South London
Natural Health Centre
CLAP SW4 .... 129 H3
South London Tamil School
CROY/NA CR0 .... 164 D6
South London Theatre
WNWD SE27 .... 149 J2
Southmead Primary School
WIM/MER SW19 .... 127 H7
South Merton ⇌
RYNPK SW20 .... 161 J2
South Norwood Country Park
SNWD SE25 .... 165 K3
South Norwood Hill
Medical Centre
SNWD SE25 .... 165 F1

South Norwood Medical Centre
SNWD SE25 .... 165 F3
South Norwood Pools &
Fitness Centre
SNWD SE25 .... 165 H4
South Norwood Primary School
SNWD SE25 .... 165 H4
South Park Business Centre
IL IG1 .... 78 E1
South Park Hotel
SAND/SEL CR2 .... 178 A3
South Park Primary School
GDMY/SEVK IG3 .... 78 E2
South Quay ⊖
POP/IOD E14 .... 112 E1
South Quay Plaza
POP/IOD E14 .... 112 E1
South Rise Primary School
WOOL/PLUM SE18 .... 115 J4
South Ruislip ⇌ ⊖
RSLP HA4 .... 65 G3
Southside Industrial Estate
VX/NE SW8 .... 109 H6
Southside Shopping Centre
WAND/EARL SW18 .... 128 A5
South Thames College
MRDN SM4 .... 161 J4
PUT/ROE SW15 .... 126 C5
PUT/ROE SW15 .... 127 G4
TOOT SW17 .... 147 J4
WAND/EARL SW18 .... 128 A4
South Tottenham ⇌
SEVS/STOTM N15 .... 56 B4
Southville Infant School
EBED/NFELT TW14 .... 121 J7
Southwark ⊖
STHWK SE1 .... 12 C9
Southwark Bridge Stairs
BLKFR EC4V 12 E7
Southwark Cathedral
STHWK SE1 .... 13 G8
Southwark College
BERM/RHTH SE16 .... 111 J2
CMBW SE5 .... 111 F6
STHWK SE1 .... 18 B1
STHWK SE1 .... 19 K3
Southwark Coroners Court
STHWK SE1 .... 19 G1
Southwark Crown Court
STHWK SE1 .... 13 J8
Southwark Park Primary School
BERM/RHTH SE16 .... 111 J2
Southwark Park Sports Centre
BERM/RHTH SE16 .... 111 K3
Southwark Rose Hotel
STHWK SE1 .... 12 F9
Southwark Sports Ground
DUL SE21 .... 131 G7
South West
Middlesex Crematorium
FELT TW13 .... 122 D7
South Wimbledon ⊖
WIM/MER SW19 .... 147 F6
Southwold Primary School
CLPT E5 .... 74 E1
South Woodford ⊖
SWFD E18 .... 58 E1
South Woodford Health Centre
SWFD E18 .... 44 E7
Southwood Hospital
HGT N6 .... 54 A6
Southwood Primary School
DAGW RM9 .... 80 A3
Sovereign Business Centre
PEND EN5 .... 31 H2
The Space Arts Centre Cinema
DEPT SE8 .... 112 C3
Sparrow Farm Infant School
EBED/NFELT TW14 .... 122 B6
Sparrow Farm Junior School
EBED/NFELT TW14 .... 122 B6
Spa School
STHWK SE1 .... 111 H3
Speakers Corner
BAY/PAD W2 .... 9 M6
The Speech & Language
Hearing Centre
CAMTN NW1 .... 5 H8
Speedway Industrial Estate
HYS/HAR UB3 .... 101 G1
Speke's Monument
BAY/PAD W2 .... 8 F8
Spelthorne Clinic
ASHF TW15 .... 140 B5
Spelthorne Infant School
ASHF TW15 .... 140 B6
Spelthorne Sports Club
ASHF TW15 .... 140 B6
Spencer House
WHALL SW1A 10 E9
The Spires Shopping Centre
BAR EN5 .... 26 C2
Spitalfields Community Farm
WCHPL E1 .... 92 C3
Spitalfields Health Centre
WCHPL E1 .... 13 M3
Spitfire Business Park
CROY/NA CR0 .... 177 G5
Splashworld Swimming Centre
BXLYHS DA6 .... 136 D3
Springfield Christian School
CAT SE6 .... 151 H2
Springfield Community
Primary School
SEVS/STOTM N15 .... 56 C5
Springfield Hospital
TOOT SW17 .... 147 J2
Springfield Primary School
SUN TW16 .... 140 C7
VX/NE SW8 .... 109 J6
Spring Grove Primary School
ISLW TW7 .... 123 J1
Springhallow School
HNWL W7 .... 85 E5
Spring Park Primary School
CROY/NA CR0 .... 179 J2
Springwell Infant School
HEST TW5 .... 102 D6
Springwell Junior School
HEST TW5 .... 102 D6
Spurgeons College
SNWD SE25 .... 165 F1
Squirrels Heath Infant School
GPK RM2 .... 63 K4
Squirrels Heath Junior School
GPK RM2 .... 63 K4
Squirrels Trading Estate
HYS/HAR UB3 .... 101 J2
SS Peter & Pauls Catholic
Primary School
IL IG1 .... 78 D2
St Johns Health Centre
TWK TW1 .... 124 B6

The Stables Gallery & Art Centre
CRICK NW2 .... 69 J3
Stadium Business Centre
WBLY HA9 .... 68 D2
Stadium Industrial Estate
WBLY HA9 .... 68 D4
Stadium Retail Park
WBLY HA9 .... 68 C2
Stafford Cross Business Park
CROY/NA CR0 .... 177 F4
The Stafford London Hotel
WHALL SW1A 10 D9
Stag Lane J & I School
EDGW HA8 .... 50 C1
Stag Lane Medical Centre
CDALE/KGS NW9 .... 50 E2
Staines RFC
FELT TW13 .... 140 E4
Stamford Brook ⊖
CHSWK W4 .... 106 C3
Stamford Clinic
HMSMTH W6 .... 106 D2
Stamford Hill ⇌
SEVS/STOTM N15 .... 56 A5
Stamford Hill Primary School
SEVS/STOTM N15 .... 55 K5
Stanburn First School
STAN HA7 .... 35 J6
Stanburn Junior School
STAN HA7 .... 35 J6
Standard Industrial Estate
CAN/RD E16 .... 114 C1
Stanford Primary School
STRHM/NOR SW16 .... 148 D7
Stanhope Primary School
GFD/PVL UB6 .... 84 C3
Stanley Park High School
CAR SM5 .... 176 A5
Stanley Park Primary School
CAR SM5 .... 175 K6
Stanley Primary School
TEDD TW11 .... 142 E3
Stanmore ⊖
STAN HA7 .... 35 K3
Stanmore College
STAN HA7 .... 35 H5
Stanmore Golf Club
STAN HA7 .... 35 H6
Stanmore Medical Centre
STAN HA7 .... 35 G5
Stanton Square
Industrial Estate
SYD SE26 .... 151 H3
Stanwell Fields CE School
STWL/WRAY TW19 .... 120 B6
Staple Inn Buildings
HHOL WC1V 12 A3
Staples Corner Business Park
CRICK NW2 .... 51 J7
Star Business Centre
RAIN RM13 .... 99 F4
Starksfield Primary School
ED N9 .... 30 A7
Star Lane
CAN/RD E16 .... 94 C3
Star Primary School
CAN/RD E16 .... 94 C3
Stationers Hall
STP EC4M 12 D5
Stationery Office
HOL/ALD WC2B 11 L4
Stebon Primary School
POP/IOD E14 .... 93 H4
Stephen Hawking Primary
Special School
POP/IOD E14 .... 93 G5
Stepney Day Hospital
WCHPL E1 .... 92 E5
Stepney Green ⊖
WCHPL E1 .... 93 F3
Stepney Greencoat CE
Primary School
POP/IOD E14 .... 93 H5
Stepney Green Maths &
Computing College
WCHPL E1 .... 93 F4
Sterling Industrial Estate
DAGE RM10 .... 80 D3
Sterling Way Clinic
UED N18 .... 42 B4
Stewart Fleming
Primary School
PGE/AN SE20 .... 165 K2
Stewart Headlam
Primary School
WCHPL E1 .... 92 D3
Stillness Primary School
FSTH SE23 .... 132 B5
Stirling Industrial Centre
BORE WD6 .... 25 F4
Stirling Retail Park
BORE WD6 .... 25 F5
Stirling Way
Industrial Estates
CROY/NA CR0 .... 163 K6
Stockley Park
Business Centre
STKPK UB11 .... 82 A7
Stockley Park Golf Club
STKPK UB11 .... 82 A6
Stockwell ⊖
CLAP SW4 .... 129 K1
Stockwell Park School
BRXN/ST SW9 .... 110 A7
Stockwell Primary School
BRXN/ST SW9 .... 130 A2
Stoke Newington ⇌
STNW/STAM N16 .... 74 B1
Stoke Newington School &
Sixth Form
STNW/STAM N16 .... 73 K2
Stonebridge Park ⊖ ⊖
ALP/SUD HA0 .... 68 C6
The Stonebridge Primary
School (London Welsh School)
WLSDN NW10 .... 68 E7
Stonebridge Shopping Centre
WLSDN NW10 .... 69 F7
Stonehill Business Centre
UED N18 .... 43 F5
Stonehill Business Park
UED N18 .... 43 F4
Stone Lake Retail Park
CHARL SE7 .... 114 B3
Stoneleigh ⇌
HOR/WEW KT19 .... 173 H4
Stoneleigh First School
EW KT17 .... 173 K3
Stonedown Park
Primary School
WALTH E17 .... 57 G3
Strand on the Green J & I School
CHSWK W4 .... 105 H5

Strand Palace Hotel
COVGDN WC2E 11 K6
Stratford College
SRTFD E15 .... 76 C6
Stratford High Street ⇌
SRTFD E15 .... 76 B7
Stratford International ⇌ ⊖
OLYMPICPK E20 .... 76 A5
Stratford Magistrates Court
SRTFD E15 .... 76 B6
Stratford ⇌ ⊖ ⊖
OLYMPICPK E20 .... 76 A5
Stratford School
FSTGT E7 .... 76 E6
Stratford Shopping Centre
SRTFD E15 .... 76 B6
Strathmore School
RCHPK/HAM TW10 .... 124 E7
Strawberry Fields School
NTGHL W11 .... 8 B5
Strawberry Hill ⇌
WHTN TW2 .... 142 E2
Strawberry Hill Golf Club
WHTN TW2 .... 142 E2
Streatham ⇌
STRHM/NOR SW16 .... 148 D4
Streatham Cemetery
TOOT SW17 .... 147 J2
Streatham & Clapham
High School
STRHM/NOR SW16 .... 148 C2
BRXS/STRHM SW2 .... 130 A4
Streatham Common ⇌
STRHM/NOR SW16 .... 148 D5
Streatham & Croydon RFC
THHTH CR7 .... 164 B4
Streatham Hill ⇌
STRHM/NOR SW16 .... 148 B1
Streatham Ice Rink
STRHM/NOR SW16 .... 148 E4
Streatham Leisure Centre
STRHM/NOR SW16 .... 148 E1
Streatham Modern School
STRHM/NOR SW16 .... 148 E5
Streatham Park Cemetery
MTCM CR4 .... 163 H1
Streatham Swimming Pool
STRHM/NOR SW16 .... 148 E4
Streatham Vale Sports Club
STRHM/NOR SW16 .... 148 C6
Streatham Wells
Primary School
BRXS/STRHM SW2 .... 149 F1
Stroud Green Primary School
FSBYPK N4 .... 55 G7
The Study Preparatory School
WIM/MER SW19 .... 146 B4
The Study School
NWMAL KT3 .... 160 B4
Sudbourne Primary School
BRXS/STRHM SW2 .... 130 A4
Sudbury Court Sports Club
ALP/SUD HA0 .... 67 J2
Sudbury Golf Club
GFD/PVL UB6 .... 67 J5
Sudbury & Harrow Road ⇌
ALP/SUD HA0 .... 67 H4
Sudbury Hill ⊖
HRW HA1 .... 66 E3
Sudbury Primary School
ALP/SUD HA0 .... 67 H3
Sudbury Town ⊖
GFD/PVL UB6 .... 67 H5
Suffolks Primary School
EN EN1 .... 30 D1
Sulivan Primary School
FUL/PGN SW6 .... 127 K1
Summerside JMI School
NFNCH/WDSPK N12 .... 39 H5
Summerswood Primary School
BORE WD6 .... 24 D3
Summit Business Park
SUN TW16 .... 140 E6
Sunbury ⇌
SUN TW16 .... 140 E7
Sunbury Business Centre
SUN TW16 .... 140 C7
Sunbury Court
SUN TW16 .... 156 C1
Sunbury Leisure Centre
SUN TW16 .... 140 D7
Sunbury Manor School
SUN TW16 .... 140 D7
Sundridge Park ⇌
BMLY BR1 .... 153 F6
Sundridge Park Golf Club
BMLY BR1 .... 153 G5
Sun Life Trading Estate
EBED/NFELT TW14 .... 121 K2
Sunnyfields Primary School
HDN NW4 .... 51 K2
Sunnyhill Primary School
STRHM/NOR SW16 .... 149 F3
Sunrise School
TOTM N17 .... 42 C5
Sunshine House School
NTHWD HA6 .... 32 B5
Surbiton ⇌
SURB KT6 .... 159 F5
Surbiton Assembly Rooms
SURB KT6 .... 159 F5
Surbiton Business Centre
SURB KT6 .... 158 E5
Surbiton Cemetery
KUT/HW KT1 .... 159 H3
Surbiton Golf Club
CHSGTN KT9 .... 171 H3
Surbiton High School
KUT/HW KT1 .... 159 F3
Surbiton Hospital
SURB KT6 .... 159 F5
Surbiton
Natural Health Centre
SURB KT6 .... 159 F5
Surrey County CC (The Oval)
LBTH SE11 .... 17 M9
Surrey Docks Farm
BERM/RHTH SE16 .... 112 C1
Surrey Docks Health Centre
BERM/RHTH SE16 .... 112 B1
Surrey Docks
Watersports Centre
BERM/RHTH SE16 .... 112 B2
Surrey Quays ⊖
BERM/RHTH SE16 .... 112 A3
Surrey Quays Leisure Park
BERM/RHTH SE16 .... 112 A2
Surrey Quays Shopping Centre
BERM/RHTH SE16 .... 112 A2
Surrey Square Primary School
WALW SE17 .... 19 J7
Susi Earnshaw Theatre School
BAR EN5 .... 26 D2

Sussex Hotel
OXSTW W1C 10 A5
Sussex House School
KTBR SW1X 15 L5
Sutcliffe Park Athletics Track
LEE/GVPK SE12 .... 134 A4
Sutton ⇌
SUT SM1 .... 175 G5
Sutton Alternative
Health Centre
SUT SM1 .... 175 F4
Sutton Arena
CAR SM5 .... 162 C6
Sutton Bowling Club
BELMT SM2 .... 174 E7
Sutton Cemetery
CHEAM SM3 .... 174 D1
Sutton Civic Centre
SUT SM1 .... 175 F4
Sutton College of Learning
for Adults
SUT SM1 .... 175 F4
Sutton Common ⇌
SUT SM1 .... 174 E1
Sutton Grammar School
SUT SM1 .... 175 G4
Sutton High Junior School
SUT SM1 .... 175 F5
Sutton High School for
Girls GDST
SUT SM1 .... 174 E5
Sutton House
HACK E8 .... 74 E4
Suttons Business Park
RAIN RM13 .... 99 F2
Sutton Superbowl
SUT SM1 .... 175 F4
Sutton United FC
SUT SM1 .... 174 E3
Sutton West Centre
SUT SM1 .... 174 E4
Swaffield Primary School
WAND/EARL SW18 .... 128 B5
Swaminarayan School
WLSDN NW10 .... 69 F5
Swan Business Centre
CHSWK W4 .... 106 A3
Swan Business Park
DART DA1 .... 139 G3
Swan Lane Pier
CANST EC4R 13 G7
Swanlea School
WCHPL E1 .... 92 D3
Swansmere School
WOT/HER KT12 .... 156 B7
Swedish School
BARN SW13 .... 106 D5
Swiss Cottage ⊖
KIL/WHAMP NW6 .... 3 G1
Swiss Cottage Leisure Centre
HAMP NW3 .... 3 H2
Swiss Cottage School
STJWD NW8 .... 3 G1
Sybil Elgar School
EA W5 .... 86 A3
The Sybil Elgar School
NWDGN UB2 .... 102 E2
Sybourn Infant School
LEY E10 .... 57 H6
The Sybourn Junior School
WALTH E17 .... 57 H6
Sybourn Primary School
WALTH E17 .... 57 H6
Sydenham ⇌
SYD SE26 .... 150 E4
Sydenham Girls School
SYD SE26 .... 150 D2
Sydenham High School
SYD SE26 .... 150 D3
Sydenham High School
Sports Ground
CAT SE6 .... 151 J4
Sydenham High
Senior School
SYD SE26 .... 150 D4
Sydenham Hill ⇌
DUL SE21 .... 150 A2
The Sydney Russell School
DAGW RM9 .... 79 K4
Syon House
BTFD TW8 .... 104 D7
Syon Lane ⇌
ISLW TW7 .... 104 B6
Syon Park
BTFD TW8 .... 124 D1
Syracuse University
NTGHL W11 .... 88 D6
Tabard Theatre
CHSWK W4 .... 106 B3
Tabernacle School
NTGHL W11 .... 88 B7
Taberner House
CROY/NA CR0 .... 177 J2
TA Centre
EDGW HA8 .... 36 D6
HRW HA1 .... 49 F4
NFNCH/WDSPK N12 .... 39 H7
Tait Road Industrial Estate
CROY/NA CR0 .... 165 G2
Taj Suites & Residences Hotel
WESTW SW1E 16 C1
Talmud Torah Machzikei
Hadass School
STNW/STAM N16 .... 56 C6
Tamian Industrial Estate
HSLWW TW4 .... 122 B3
Tandem Centre
WIM/MER SW19 .... 147 H7
Tashbar of Edgware
Primary School
EDGW HA8 .... 36 C3
Tate Britain
WEST SW1P 17 J6
Tate Modern
STHWK SE1 .... 12 D8
Tavistock Clinic
HAMP NW3 .... 71 H5
TAVR Centre
KUT/HW KT1 .... 158 E3
Tavy Clinic
ABYW SE2 .... 116 D1
Tawhid Boys School
STNW/STAM N16 .... 74 B1
Tayyibah Girls School
STNW/STAM N16 .... 56 C7
Teddington ⇌
TEDD TW11 .... 143 G5
Teddington Business Park
TEDD TW11 .... 143 F4
Teddington Cemetery
TEDD TW11 .... 142 E3
Teddington Clinic
TEDD TW11 .... 142 E5

Teddington Memorial Hospital
TEDD TW11 .... 142 E5
Teddington Pool &
Fitness Centre
TEDD TW11 .... 143 G4
Teddington School
TEDD TW11 .... 143 K5
The Teddington Theatre Club
E/WMO/HCT KT8 .... 157 J4
Telferscot Primary School
BAL SW12 .... 129 H7
Temperate House, Kew Gardens
RCH/KEW TW9 .... 125 G1
Temple Hill Primary School
DART DA1 .... 139 K4
Temple of Bacchus
CMBW SE5 .... 130 D1
Temple of Mithras
MANHO EC4N 13 G5
Tenby Road Clinic
EDGW HA8 .... 50 B1
Tenterden Sports Ground
KTN/HRWW/WS HA3 .... 50 A6
Terence McMillan Stadium
PLSTW E13 .... 95 G3
Tetherdown Primary School
MUSWH N10 .... 54 A3
Thames Barrier
CAN/RD E16 .... 114 C1
Thames Barrier Information &
Learning Centre
CHARL SE7 .... 114 C2
Thames Christian College
BTSEA SW11 .... 128 C2
Thames College of Technology
WOOL/PLUM SE18 .... 115 F7
Thames Ditton ⇌
THDIT KT7 .... 157 G4
Thames Ditton & Esher
Golf Club
ESH/CLAY KT10 .... 170 D1
Thames Ditton Infant School
THDIT KT7 .... 158 A5
Thames Ditton Junior School
THDIT KT7 .... 158 A6
Thames Gateway Park
DAGW RM9 .... 98 B2
Thames House
WEST SW1P 17 J5
Thameside Industrial Estate
CAN/RD E16 .... 95 H7
Thames Magistrates Court
BOW E3 .... 93 J2
Thamesmead Leisure Centre
THMD SE28 .... 97 H6
Thamesmead Shopping Centre
THMD SE28 .... 97 G6
Thamesview Business Centre
RAIN RM13 .... 99 G4
Thames View Clinic
BARK IG11 .... 97 F1
Thames View J & I School
BARK IG11 .... 97 G1
Thames Water Tower
NTGHL W11 .... 107 G1
Theatre de l'Ange Fou
International School of
Corporeal Mime
ARCH N19 .... 54 E7
Theatre for Mankind
FSBYPK N4 .... 55 F7
Theatre Museum Library
& Archive
COVGDN WC2E 11 K6
Theatre of The Dispossessed
WIM/MER SW19 .... 127 G7
Theatre Royal
HOL/ALD WC2B 11 K5
SRTFD E15 .... 76 B5
Theatre Royal Haymarket
STJS SW1Y 11 H7
Theodore McLeary
Primary School
EDUL SE22 .... 131 G3
Therapia Lane ⊖
CROY/NA CR0 .... 163 K6
Therapia Trading Estate
CROY/NA CR0 .... 163 J6
Thistlebrook Industrial Estate
ABYW SE2 .... 116 D2
Thistle Hotel
BAY/PAD W2 .... 8 E7
CAMTN NW1 .... 4 F8
FITZ W1T 10 F4
FSBYE EC1V 6 E8
WESTW SW1E 16 D4
Thistle Marble Arch Hotel
MBLAR W1H 9 M5
Thistle Piccadilly Hotel
SOHO/SHAV W1D 11 H7
Thomas Arnold Primary School
DAGW RM9 .... 80 B6
Thomas Buxton Infant School
WCHPL E1 .... 92 C3
Thomas Fairchild
Primary School
IS N1 .... 7 G5
Thomas Francis Academy
BRXN/ST SW9 .... 130 C3
Thomas Gamuel
Primary School
WALTH E17 .... 57 J5
Thomas Jones Primary School
NTGHL W11 .... 88 C5
Thomas London Independent
Day School
KENS W8 .... 14 D3
Thomas Road Industrial Estate
POP/IOD E14 .... 93 J4
Thomas's Clapham
Primary School
BTSEA SW11 .... 128 E4
Thomas's Fulham
FUL/PGN SW6 .... 128 A2
Thomas's London Day Schools
KENS W8 .... 14 E3
Thomas's Preparatory School
BTSEA SW11 .... 108 C7
Thomas Tallis School
BKHTH/KID SE3 .... 134 A2
Thornhill Primary School
IS N1 .... 6 A1
Thornton Heath ⇌
THHTH CR7 .... 164 D3
Thornton Heath Health Centre
THHTH CR7 .... 164 D3
Thornton Heath Pools &
Fitness Centre
THHTH CR7 .... 164 D3
Thornton Road Industrial Estate
CROY/NA CR0 .... 163 K5
Thorntree Primary School
CHARL SE7 .... 114 C4

Thorpe Hall Primary School
WALTH E17 .... 44 A7
Three Bridges Business Centre
NWDGN UB2 .... 103 H1
Three Bridges Primary School
NWDGN UB2 .... 103 G2
Three Mills Heritage Centre
BOW E3 .... 94 A2
Thurston Industrial Estate
LEW SE13 .... 132 E2
Tidemill Primary School
DEPT SE8 .... 112 D6
Tideway Industrial Estate
VX/NE SW8 .... 109 H5
Tiffin Girls School
KUTN/CMB KT2 .... 144 A5
Tiffin School & Sports Centre
KUTN/CMB KT2 .... 159 G1
Tiller Centre (Swimming Baths)
POP/IOD E14 .... 112 D2
Tiller Leisure Centre
POP/IOD E14 .... 112 D2
Timbercroft Primary School
WOOL/PLUM SE18 .... 115 K6
Timbers Clinic
KTN/HRWW/WS HA3 .... 34 D5
Timebridge Youth &
Community Centre
CROY/NA CR0 .... 179 K4
Times Square Shopping Centre
SUT SM1 .... 175 F4
Tiverton Primary School
SEVS/STOTM N15 .... 55 K5
Tobacco Dock
WAP E1W 92 D6
Tokyngton Community Centre
WBLY HA9 .... 68 D4
Toldos School
STNW/STAM N16 .... 55 K7
Tollgate
DUL SE21 .... 150 A1
Tollgate Primary School
PLSTW E13 .... 95 G3
Tolworth ⇌
BRYLDS KT5 .... 172 D1
Tolworth CP School
SURB KT6 .... 159 G7
Tolworth Girls School
SURB KT6 .... 172 B2
Tolworth Recreation Centre
SURB KT6 .... 172 B2
Tooting ⊖
TOOT SW17 .... 147 K5
Tooting Bec ⊖
TOOT SW17 .... 148 A2
Tooting Bec Athletics Track
TOOT SW17 .... 148 B3
Tooting Broadway ⊖
TOOT SW17 .... 147 J4
Tooting Leisure Centre
TOOT SW17 .... 147 H3
Tooting & Mitcham United FC
MTCM CR4 .... 148 A7
Torah Temimah Primary School
CRICK NW2 .... 69 K3
Torah Vodaas
GLDGN NW11 .... 70 D1
Torat Emet Primary School
HDN NW4 .... 52 B4
Torriano Junior School
KTTN NW5 .... 72 C4
Torridon Primary School
CAT SE6 .... 152 B1
Torrington Clinic
NFNCH/WDSPK N12 .... 39 G4
Torrington Park Health Centre
NFNCH/WDSPK N12 .... 39 G3
Total Health Clinic
SHB W12 .... 106 E1
Tottenham Cemetery
TOTM N17 .... 42 A6
Tottenham Court Road ⊖
SOHO/SHAV W1D 11 G4
Tottenham Green
Leisure Centre
SEVS/STOTM N15 .... 56 A3
Tottenham Hale ⊖
TOTM N17 .... 56 D2
Tottenham Hale Retail Park
SEVS/STOTM N15 .... 56 C3
Tottenham Hotspur FC
(White Hart Lane)
TOTM N17 .... 42 B6
Tottenham Park Cemetery
ED N9 .... 42 D2
Tottenham Sports Centre
TOTM N17 .... 42 B7
Totteridge CC
TRDG/WHET N20 .... 38 E1
Totteridge & Whetstone ⊖
TRDG/WHET N20 .... 39 F1
Tower 42
OBST EC2N 13 J4
The Tower Bridge Exhibition
STHWK SE1 .... 13 L9
Tower Bridge Primary School
STHWK SE1 .... 19 L1
Tower Bridge Wharf
WAP E1W 92 C7
Tower Gateway ⊖
TWRH EC3N 13 L6
Tower Hamlets College
POP/IOD E14 .... 93 K6
WCHPL E1 .... 92 E4
Tower Hill ⊖
TWRH EC3N 13 L7
The Tower Hotel
WAP E1W 13 M8
Tower House School
MORT/ESHN SW14 .... 125 K3
Tower Industrial Estate
SNWD SE25 .... 165 H3
Tower Medical Centre
WCHPL E1 .... 92 C5
Tower Millennium Pier
TWRH EC3N 13 K8
Tower of London
TWRH EC3N 13 L7
Tower Retail Park
DART DA1 .... 138 C4
Towers Business Park
WBLY HA9 .... 68 D3
Tower Stairs
MON EC3R 13 J7
Town Farm Primary School
STWL/WRAY TW19 .... 120 A6
Townley Grammar School
for Girls
BXLYHS DA6 .... 137 G5
Townmead Business Centre
FUL/PGN SW6 .... 128 A2
Townsend Industrial Estate
WLSDN NW10 .... 68 G7

Townsend Primary School
  WALW WC1A 19 H5
Toynbee Hall & Curtain Theatre
  WCHPL E1 .... 13 L3
Trade Union Congress
  NOXST/BSQ WC1A 11 H4
Trafalgar Business Centre
  BARK IG11 .... 97 F3
Trafalgar Infant School
  WHTN TW2 .... 123 J7
Trafalgar Junior School
  WHTN TW2 .... 142 D1
Trafalgar Square
  STJS SW1Y 11 H8
Trafalgar Trading Estate
  PEND EN3 .... 31 H3
Tramshed Theatre
  WOOL/PLUM SE18 .... 115 G3
Trans Atlantic College
  BETH E2 .... 7 K5
Transport for London
  Lost Property Office
  CAMTN NW1 .... 9 M1
Transport House
  WEST SW1P 17 J4
Travelodge
  CAN/RD E16 .... 95 H7
  FELT TW13 .... 121 K7
  FSBYW WC1X 5 M8
  HEST TW5 .... 102 B5
  IL IG1 .... 78 B2
  SUN TW16 .... 140 E6
  SURB KT6 .... 159 J7
Treasury
  WHALL SW1A 17 J2
The Treaty Centre
  HSLW TW3 .... 123 G2
Treehouse School
  MUSWH N10 .... 54 A3
The Treehouse School
  BMSBY WC1N 5 L9
Trent CE Primary School
  EBAR EN4 .... 27 K3
Trent Country Park
  EBAR EN4 .... 28 A1
Trent Park Cemetery
  EBAR EN4 .... 28 A2
Trent Park Golf Club
  STHGT/OAK N14 .... 28 C3
Trevor Roberts School
  HAMP NW3 .... 3 H1
Tricycle Theatre
  KIL/WHAMP NW6 .... 70 D6
Trident Business Centre
  TOOT SW17 .... 147 K4
Trinity Business Centre
  BERM/RHTH SE16 .... 112 C1
Trinity Catholic High School
  WFD IG8 .... 44 E3
Trinity College Centre
  PECK SE15 .... 111 F6
Trinity College of Music
  CNWCH SE10 .... 113 F5
  MHST W1U 10 B3
Trinity Hospital
  GNWCH SE10 .... 113 G4
Trinity House
  TWRH EC3N 13 K6
Trinity RC High School Upper
  WFD IG8 .... 44 E3
Trinity St Marys
  Primary School
  BAL SW12 .... 129 F7
Trinity School
  DAGE RM10 .... 80 C2
  LEE/GVPK SE12 .... 133 H4
Trinity School Belvedere
  BELV DA17 .... 117 K3
Trinity Trading Estate
  HYS/HAR UB3 .... 101 K2
Tripcock Point
  Development Site
  THMD SE28 .... 97 F2
Triumph Trading Estate
  TOTM N17 .... 42 C5
Trocadero
  SOHO/SHAV W1D 11 G7
Trojan Business Centre
  WLSDN NW10 .... 69 H5
Troy Industrial Estate
  HRW HA1 .... 49 F4
True Buddha School
  IS N1 .... 5 L4
TS Queen Mary
  TPL/STR WC2R 11 L7
Tudor Enterprise Park
  KTN/HRWW/WS HA3 .... 48 D2
Tudor Lodge Health Centre
  WIM/MER SW19 .... 127 J6
Tudor Lodge Hotel
  PIN HA5 .... 47 F5
Tudor Primary School
  FNCH N3 .... 39 G2
  STHL UB1 .... 83 J6
Tufnell Park ⊖
  KTTN NW5 .... 72 B3
Tufnell Park Primary School
  HOLWY N7 .... 72 D3
Uplands Business Park
  WALTH E17 .... 57 F1
Tuke School
  PECK SE15 .... 111 J7
Tulse Hill ⊜
  WNWD SE27 .... 149 H1
Tunnel Avenue Trading Estate
  GNWCH SE10 .... 113 G1
Turney School
  DUL SE21 .... 130 D6
Turnham Green ⊖
  CHSWK W4 .... 106 B3
Turnham Primary School
  BROCKY SE4 .... 132 B3
Turnpike Lane ⊖
  SEVS/STOTM N15 .... 55 H2
Turtle Key Arts Centre
  FUL/PGN SW6 .... 107 K5
Tweeddale Primary School
  CAR SM5 .... 162 C6
Twenty Nevern Square Hotel
  ECT SW5 .... 14 B6
Twickenham ⇌
  TWK TW1 .... 124 B6
Twickenham Academy
  WHTN TW2 .... 142 B1
Twickenham Cemetery
  WHTN TW2 .... 123 G7
Twickenham Park Health Centre
  TWK TW1 .... 124 D5
Twickenham
  Preparatory School
  HPTN TW12 .... 142 B7
Twickenham Stadium
  ISLW TW7 .... 123 K5
Twickenham Trading Estate
  TWK TW1 .... 124 A5

Two Bridges Business Park
  SAND/SEL CR2 .... 177 K5
Twyford CE High School
  ACT W3 .... 86 C7
Twyford Sports Centre
  ACT W3 .... 86 D7
Tyburn Infant School
  STJWD NW8 .... 3 H9
Tynemouth Road Health Centre
  SEVS/STOTM N15 .... 56 B3
The Type Museum
  BRXN/ST SW9 .... 110 A7
Tyssen Primary School
  STNW/STAM N16 .... 56 C7
UCI Cinema
  BAY/PAD W2 .... 8 D5
  SUT SM1 .... 175 F4
UCI Empire Cinema
  LSQ/SEVD WC2H 11 H7
UK Passport Office
  PIM SW1V 16 D5
Underhill Infant School
  BAR EN5 .... 26 C4
Unicorn Primary School
  BECK BR3 .... 166 E4
Unicorn School
  RCH/KEW TW9 .... 105 G7
Unicorn Theatre
  STHWK SE1 .... 19 K1
United Medical &
  Dental Schools
  STHWK SE1 .... 17 L3
Unity Trading Estate
  WFD IG8 .... 59 H2
University Church of Christ
  the King
  STPAN WC1H 11 G1
University College Hospital
  CAMTN NW1 .... 4 F9
  HAMP NW3 .... 71 H5
University College London
  FITZ W1T 10 F2
  STPAN WC1H 5 G9
University College London,
  Astor College
  FITZ W1T 10 F2
University College London C/O
  The Chorley Institute
  GWRST WC1E 11 G1
University College London
  Medical School
  FITZ W1T 10 E2
University College London
  Obstetrics Hospital
  GWRST WC1E 10 F1
University College School
  HAMP NW3 .... 71 G4
University Hospital Lewisham
  LEW SE13 .... 132 E4
University of California
  WHALL SW1A 10 E9
University of East London
  BARK IG11 .... 79 G3
  CAN/RD E16 .... 96 A6
  PLSTW E13 .... 95 F2
  SRTFD E15 .... 76 B7
  SRTFD E15 .... 94 D1
University of Greenwich
  GNWCH SE10 .... 113 G4
  WOOL/PLUM SE18 .... 115 F2
University of Greenwich
  (Mansion Site)
  ELTH/MOT SE9 .... 135 H5
University of Greenwich
  (Southwood Site)
  ELTH/MOT SE9 .... 135 H6
University of Greenwich
  Sports Ground
  ELTH/MOT SE9 .... 134 D3
  ELTH/MOT SE9 .... 135 H6
University of London
  BAY/PAD W2 .... 9 C5
  BMSBY WC1N 11 K1
  CLKNW EC1R 6 B9
  GWRST WC1E 11 H2
  MBLAR W1H 9 K4
  STHWK SE1 .... 13 G9
  STPAN WC1H 5 H9
University of London
  Athletics Ground
  NWMAL KT3 .... 160 D4
University of West London
  EA W5 .... 85 J6
  EA W5 .... 85 J7
University of Westminster
  CAMTN NW1 .... 4 E9
  CAVSQ/HST W1G 10 D3
  CHSWK W4 .... 105 K7
  GTPST W1W 10 D3
  HRW HA1 .... 49 G6
University of Westminster
  - Environment
  MHST W1U 10 A2
Uphall Primary School
  IL IG1 .... 78 B4
Upland Primary School
  BXLYHN DA7 .... 137 G2
Uplands Business Park
  WALTH E17 .... 57 F1
Upney ⊖
  BARK IG11 .... 79 F6
Upper Holloway ⊖
  ARCH N19 .... 72 D1
Upper Montagu Street Clinic
  CAMTN NW1 .... 9 L2
Upper Tooting Independent
  High School
  TOOT SW17 .... 147 J1
Upton Cross Primary School
  PLSTW E13 .... 77 F7
Upton Day Hospital
  BXLYHS DA6 .... 137 F3
Upton Lane Medical Centre
  FSTGT E7 .... 77 F5
Upton Park ⊖
  PLSTW E13 .... 77 G7
Upton Primary School
  BXLY DA5 .... 137 F4
Upton Road School
  BXLYHS DA6 .... 137 H3
The Urdang Academy
  FSBYW WC1X 6 A8
  LSQ/SEVD WC2H 11 J5
Ursuline High School
  RYNPK SW20 .... 146 B6
Ursuline Preparatory School
  RYNPK SW20 .... 146 B6
Uxbridge College
  HYS/HAR UB3 .... 82 E6
Uxbridge County Court
  HYS/HAR UB3 .... 82 C4
Uxendon Manor JMI School
  KTN/HRWW/WS HA3 .... 50 A3

Vale Farm Sports Centre
  ALP/SUD HA0 .... 67 H3
Vale Industrial Estate
  WATW WD18 .... 20 A7
The Vale Medical Centre
  FSTH SE23 .... 151 G1
Valence House Museum
  & Library
  BCTR RM8 .... 79 K1
Valence Primary School
  BCTR RM8 .... 79 K1
Valentine High School
  GNTH/NBYPK IG2 .... 60 A5
Valentines High Lower School
  GNTH/NBYPK IG2 .... 60 B4
Vale Park Industrial
  ACT W3 .... 106 B1
The Vale School
  SKENS SW7 .... 14 A1
Valley Link Business centre
  PEND EN3 .... 31 G5
Valley Link Business Estate
  PEND EN3 .... 31 G5
Valley Primary School
  HAYES BR2 .... 167 J1
Valmar Trading Estate
  CMBW SE5 .... 110 D7
V & A Museum of Childhood
  BETH E2 .... 92 E2
Vanbrugh Theatre
  GWRST WC1E 11 G1
Vaudeville Theatre
  COVGDN WC2E 11 K6
Vaughan Primary School
  RYLN/HDSTN HA2 .... 48 C5
Vauxhall ⊖ ⇌
  VX/NE SW8 .... 17 K8
Vauxhall Primary School
  LBTH SE11 .... 17 L7
Velodrome
  OLYMPICPK E20 .... 75 K4
Vernon House Special School
  WLSDN NW10 .... 68 E4
Vestry Hall
  MTCM CR4 .... 162 E2
Vestry House Museum
  WALTH E17 .... 57 K3
Vicarage Fields Health Clinic
  BARK IG11 .... 78 C6
The Vicarage Field
  Shopping Centre
  BARK IG11 .... 78 C6
Vicarage Primary School
  EHAM E6 .... 95 K2
Vicarage Road Cemetery
  WATW WD18 .... 20 E3
Vicars Green Primary School
  GFD/PVL UB6 .... 85 J1
V I Components Industrial Park
  ERITH DA8 .... 118 B4
Victoria ⇌ ⊖
  PIM SW1V 16 D5
Victoria & Albert Museum
  SKENS SW7 .... 15 H4
Victoria Business Centre
  WELL DA16 .... 136 B1
Victoria Bus Station
  PIM SW1V 16 D4
Victoria Chiropractic Clinic
  SKENS SW7 .... 15 L2
Victoria Coach Station
  BGVA SW1W 16 C6
Victoria Hall
  FNCH N3 .... 38 D7
Victoria Industrial Estate
  ACT W3 .... 87 G4
Victoria Industrial Park
  DART DA1 .... 139 G4
Victoria Junior School
  FELT TW13 .... 122 A7
Victoria Medical Centre
  PIM SW1V 16 F6
Victoria Palace Theatre
  BGVA SW1W 16 D4
Victoria Park Industrial Centre
  HOM E9 .... 75 H6
Victoria Place Shopping Centre
  BGVA SW1W 16 D5
Victoria Rail/Air Terminal
  PIM SW1V 16 D5
Victoria Retail Park
  RSLP HA4 .... 65 H4
Victoria Wharf
  POP/IOD E14 .... 93 G6
Victoria Wharf Industrial Estate
  DEPT SE8 .... 112 B4
Victor Seymour Infant School
  CAR SM5 .... 175 K2
Victory Business Centre
  ISLW TW7 .... 124 A3
Victory Day School
  THHTH CR7 .... 164 D3
Victory Primary School
  WALW SE17 .... 18 F5
Viking Business Centre
  ROMW/RG RM7 .... 62 E6
Viking Primary School
  NTHLT UB5 .... 83 H2
Village Infant School
  DAGE RM10 .... 80 C6
Village Operations Support Area
  SRTFD E15 .... 76 A3
The Village School
  CDALE/KGS NW9 .... 50 E3
Villiers High School
  STHL UB1 .... 84 A7
The Vine Clinic
  KUTN/CMB KT2 .... 144 A5
Vine Medical Centre
  E/WMO/HCT KT8 .... 157 F2
The Vines School
  BTSEA SW11 .... 129 F3
The Vineyard Primary School
  RCHPK/HAM TW10 .... 125 F4
Vinopolis, City of Wine
  STHWK SE1 .... 12 F8
Vinters' Hall
  BLKFR EC4V 12 F6
VIP Trading Estate
  CHARL SE7 .... 114 B3
Virginia Primary School
  BETH E2 .... 7 L8
Virgo Fidelis Convent Schools
  NRWD SE19 .... 149 J5
Visage School of Hair & Beauty
  ELTH/MOT SE9 .... 135 F5
Vision College of Technology
  HOM E9 .... 75 J5
Vita et Pax School
  STHGT/OAK N14 .... 28 B4
Vittoria Primary School
  IS N1 .... 6 A4

Voyager Business Estate
  BERM/RHTH SE16 .... 111 H2
Vue Cinema
  ACT W3 .... 86 C3
  CROY/NA CR0 .... 177 F1
  DAGW RM9 .... 80 A7
  FUL/PGN SW6 .... 107 K6
  HAMP NW3 .... 71 G5
  HRW HA1 .... 48 E5
  LSO/SEVD WC2H 11 H6
  NFNCH/WDSPK N12 .... 39 H6
  ROMW/RG RM7 .... 63 G4
  SHB W12 .... 107 G1
Vulcan Business Centre
  CROY/NA CR0 .... 180 C7
Waddon ⇌
  CROY/NA CR0 .... 177 G5
Waddon Clinic
  CROY/NA CR0 .... 177 G4
Waddon Marsh ⊖
  CROY/NA CR0 .... 177 G1
Wadham Lodge Sports Centre
  WALTH E17 .... 43 K7
Wadsworth Business Centre
  GFD/PVL UB6 .... 85 J1
The Waldegrave Clinic
  TEDD TW11 .... 143 F4
Waldegrave Girls School
  WHTN TW2 .... 142 D1
Waldo Industrial Estate
  BMLY BR1 .... 168 B2
Waldorf School of SW London
  BAL SW12 .... 148 C1
Waldron Health Centre
  & Surgery
  NWCR SE14 .... 112 C1
Walker Primary School
  STHGT/OAK N14 .... 40 D1
The Wallace Centre
  DEPT SE8 .... 112 E5
The Wallace Collection
  MHST W1U 10 A4
Wallbrook Business Centre
  HSLWW TW4 .... 122 A2
Wall Hotel
  LOTH EC2R 13 G7
Wallington ⇌
  WLGTN SM6 .... 176 B5
Wallington County
  Grammar School
  WLGTN SM6 .... 176 B2
Wallington High School for Girls
  WLGTN SM6 .... 176 B7
Walmer Road Clinic
  NTGHL W11 .... 88 C5
Walm Lane Clinic
  CRICK NW2 .... 70 A4
Walnut Tree Walk
  Primary School
  LBTH SE11 .... 18 A5
Waltham Forest College
  WALTH E17 .... 56 E2
  WALTH E17 .... 57 K5
Waltham Forest
  Magistrates Court
  WALTH E17 .... 57 K2
Waltham Forest Pool & Track
  WALTH E17 .... 57 K1
Waltham Forest Theatre
  WALTH E17 .... 57 H2
Walthamstow Academy
  WALTH E17 .... 43 H7
Walthamstow
  Business Centre
  WALTH E17 .... 58 A1
Walthamstow Central ⇌ ⊖
  WALTH E17 .... 57 J4
Walthamstow Marsh
  Nature Reserve
  CLPT E5 .... 56 D6
Walthamstow Queens Road ⊖
  WALTH E17 .... 57 J4
Walthamstow School for Girls
  WALTH E17 .... 57 K3
Walton Business Centre
  WOT/HER KT12 .... 156 A3
Walton Casuals FC
  WOT/HER KT12 .... 156 A5
Walton Swimming Pool
  WOT/HER KT12 .... 156 A7
Walworth Lower
  Secondary School
  WALW SE17 .... 19 H7
Walworth Town Hall
  WALW SE17 .... 18 E6
Wandle Park
  CROY/NA CR0 .... 177 G1
Wandle Recreation Centre
  WAND/EARL SW18 .... 128 A5
Wandle Trading Estate
  MTCM CR4 .... 162 E6
Wandle Valley School Sutton
  Parent Partnership
  CAR SM5 .... 162 D6
Wandsworth Adult College
  BTSEA SW11 .... 109 F7
  TOOT SW17 .... 147 J1
Wandsworth Cemetery
  WAND/EARL SW18 .... 128 B7
Wandsworth Common ⇌
  TOOT SW17 .... 128 D6
Wandsworth County Court
  PUT/ROE SW15 .... 127 H4
Wandsworth Road ⇌ ⊖
  VX/NE SW8 .... 129 H1
Wandsworth Town ⇌
  WAND/EARL SW18 .... 128 A3
Wandsworth Trading Estate
  WAND/EARL SW18 .... 128 A6
Wanstead ⊖
  WAN E11 .... 59 F5
Wanstead CC
  WAN E11 .... 59 F6
Wanstead CE Primary School
  WAN E11 .... 58 E4
Wanstead Golf Club
  WAN E11 .... 59 G6
Wanstead High School
  WAN E11 .... 59 G5
Wanstead Hospital
  WAN E11 .... 59 F3
Wanstead Leisure Centre
  WAN E11 .... 59 G5
Wanstead Park ⊜
  FSTGT E7 .... 77 J3
Wapping ⊖
  WAP E1W 92 C7
Wapping Wharf
  WAP E1W 92 E7
War Memorial Sports Ground
  SUT SM1 .... 175 J3
Warnford Industrial Estate
  HYS/HAR UB3 .... 101 H1

Warren Comprehensive School
  CHDH RM6 .... 62 B4
Warren Dell Primary School
  OXHEY WD19 .... 33 G2
Warrender School
  RSLP HA4 .... 46 D6
Warren Junior School
  CHDH RM6 .... 62 B4
The Warren Medical Centre
  YEAD UB4 .... 83 F5
Warren Sports Centre
  CHDH RM6 .... 62 B4
Warren Street ⊖
  CAMTN NW1 .... 4 E9
Warwick Avenue ⊖
  MV/WKIL W9 .... 8 E1
Warwick Dubbing Theatre
  SOHO/CST W1F 11 G5
Warwick Estate
  BAY/PAD W2 .... 8 D3
Warwick Leadlay Gallery
  GNWCH SE10 .... 113 F5
Warwick School for Boys
  WALTH E17 .... 58 A3
The Washington Mayfair Hotel
  MYFR/PICC W1J 10 D8
Waterfields Retail Park
  WAT WD17 .... 21 H3
Waterfront Leisure Centre
  WOOL/PLUM SE18 .... 115 F2
Watergate School
  CAT SE6 .... 151 K4
  LEW SE13 .... 132 E3
Waterloo ⇌ ⊖
  STHWK SE1 .... 18 A1
Waterloo East ⇌
  STHWK SE1 .... 12 B9
Waterloo Health Centre
  STHWK SE1 .... 18 A2
Watermans Arts, Cinema &
  Theatre Centre
  BTFD TW8 .... 105 F5
The Watermans Hall
  MON EC3R 13 J7
Watermeads High School
  MRDN SM4 .... 162 C5
Watermill Business Centre
  PEND EN3 .... 31 H1
Water Polo Arena
  OLYMPICPK E20 .... 75 K6
Water Rats Theatre
  STPAN WC1H 5 K7
Waterside Business Centre
  ISLW TW7 .... 124 C3
Waterside Primary School
  WOOL/PLUM SE18 .... 115 J4
The Waterside Trading Centre
  HNWL W7 .... 103 K2
Watersports Centre
  STNW/STAM N16 .... 55 J7
Watford ⇌
  WATW WD18 .... 20 D3
Watford Arches Retail Park
  WAT WD17 .... 21 G4
Watford Business Centre
  WAT WD17 .... 21 F2
Watford County Court
  WAT WD17 .... 21 F1
Watford FC & Saracens RFC
  (Vicarage Road Stadium)
  WATW WD18 .... 21 F4
Watford Field School (Infant)
  WATW WD18 .... 21 G4
Watford General Hospital
  WATW WD18 .... 21 F4
Watford Grammar School
  for Boys
  WATW WD18 .... 20 D3
Watford Grammar School
  for Girls
  WATW WD18 .... 21 G4
Watford High Street ⊜
  WATW WD18 .... 21 G3
Watford Junction ⇌ ⊖
  WAT WD17 .... 21 G1
Watford Museum
  WATW WD18 .... 21 G4
Watling Boys' Club
  EDGW HA8 .... 36 C6
Watling Clinic
  EDGW HA8 .... 37 F6
Watling Medical Centre
  EDGW HA8 .... 36 E7
Wavelengths Leisure Pool
  & Library
  DEPT SE8 .... 112 D5
Waverley Industrial Estate
  HRW HA1 .... 48 D2
Waverley Lower
  Secondary School
  EDUL SE22 .... 131 J4
Waverley School
  PEND EN3 .... 30 E3
Waxchandlers' Hall
  CITYW EC2V 12 F4
Weald Junior School
  KTN/HRWW/WS HA3 .... 35 F5
Wealdstone Cemetery
  KTN/HRWW/WS HA3 .... 49 G3
Webber Douglas Academy of
  Dramatic Art
  SKENS SW7 .... 14 F7
Webster Graduate
  Studies Center
  CAMTN NW1 .... 3 M9
Welbeck Clinic
  CRICK NW2 .... 70 E2
Welbourne Primary School
  SEVS/STOTM N15 .... 56 C3
Welfare Clinic
  HGT N6 .... 54 A5
Wellcome Institute
  CAMTN NW1 .... 5 G9
Welldon Park Junior School
  RYLN/HDSTN HA2 .... 66 C3
Wellesley Road ⊜
  CROY/NA CR0 .... 177 J1
Well Grove School
  TRDG/WHET N20 .... 27 H7
Welling ⇌
  WELL DA16 .... 136 B1
The Welling Clinic
  WELL DA16 .... 136 B1
Welling Medical Centre
  WELL DA16 .... 136 A3
Welling School Academy
  WELL DA16 .... 116 C7
Wellington Arch
  MYFR/PICC W1J 16 B1
Wellington Barracks
  WESTW SW1E 16 F2
Wellington Primary School
  BOW E3 .... 93 J2

CHING E4 .... 43 K1
HSLW TW3 .... 122 E1
Welling United FC
WELL DA16 .... 136 D2
Wells Primary School
WFD IG8 .... 45 F3
Wembley Arena
WBLY HA9 .... 68 C3
Wembley Central ⇌ ⊖
WBLY HA9 .... 68 A4
Wembley Commercial Centre
WBLY HA9 .... 67 K1
Wembley Conference Centre
WBLY HA9 .... 68 B3
Wembley FC
ALP/SUD HA0 .... 67 H3
Wembley High Technology College
ALP/SUD HA0 .... 67 J2
Wembley Hospital
ALP/SUD HA0 .... 67 K5
Wembley Park ⊖
WBLY HA9 .... 68 C2
Wembley Park Business Centre
WBLY HA9 .... 68 D2
Wembley Primary School
WBLY HA9 .... 68 A2
Wembley Stadium
WBLY HA9 .... 68 C3
Wembley Stadium ⇌
WBLY HA9 .... 68 C4
Wembley Stadium Industrial Estate
WBLY HA9 .... 68 C2
Wendell Park Primary School
SHB W12 .... 106 C1
Wentworth Tutorial College
GLDGN NW11 .... 52 B5
The Wernher Collection at Ranger's House
CNWCH SE10 .... 113 G7
Wesley's Chapel, House & Museum of Methodism
STLK EC1Y 7 C9
Wessex Gardens Primary School
GLDGN NW11 .... 52 C7
West 12 Shopping & Leisure Centre
SHB W12 .... 107 G1
West Acton ⊖
ACT W3 .... 86 C5
West Acton Primary School
ACT W3 .... 86 D5
West Beckton Health Centre
CAN/RD E16 .... 95 G4
Westbourne Green Sports Complex
BAY/PAD W2 .... 8 B3
Westbourne Park ⊖
NKENS W10 .... 88 D4
Westbourne Primary School
SUT SM1 .... 174 E2
Westbridge College
BTSEA SW11 .... 108 D7
West Brompton ⇌ ⊖ ⊖
ECT SW5 .... 14 B8
Westbrooke School
WELL DA16 .... 136 E2
The Westbury Hotel
CONDST W1S 10 D6
Westbury Medical Centre
WDGN N22 .... 55 J1
Westcombe Park ⇌
BKHTH/KID SE3 .... 113 K4
Westcroft Leisure Centre
CAR SM5 .... 176 A3
West Croydon ⇌
CROY/NA CR0 .... 164 D7
West Drayton Cemetery
WDR/YW UB7 .... 100 B2
West Drayton Primary School
WDR/YW UB7 .... 100 B1
West Dulwich ⇌
DUL SE21 .... 130 E7
West Ealing ⇌
WEA W13 .... 85 H6
West Ealing Business Centre
WEA W13 .... 85 G6
Western Avenue Business Park
ACT W3 .... 86 D3
Western International Market
NWDGN UB2 .... 102 A3
Western Trading Estate
WLSDN NW10 .... 86 E3
West Ewell Infant School
HOR/WEW KT19 .... 173 F4
Westferry ⊖
POP/IOD E14 .... 93 H6
Westfield Community Technology College
WATW WD18 .... 20 D4
Westfield London
SHB W12 .... 88 A7
Westfields Primary School
BARN SW13 .... 126 C1
Westfield Stratford City
OLYMPICPK E20 .... 76 A5
West Finchley ⊖
FNCH N3 .... 39 F5
Westgate Business Centre
NKENS W10 .... 88 C3
Westgate Primary School
DART DA1 .... 139 G6
West Green Primary School
SEVS/STOTM N15 .... 55 J3
West Ham ⇌ ⊖ ⊖
SRTFD E15 .... 94 C2
West Ham Church Primary School
SRTFD E15 .... 76 D7
West Ham Lane Clinic
SRTFD E15 .... 76 C7
West Hampstead ⇌ ⊖
KIL/WHAMP NW6 .... 70 E5
West Hampstead ⊖
KIL/WHAMP NW6 .... 71 F5
West Hampstead Clinic
KIL/WHAMP NW6 .... 2 B1
West Hampstead Thameslink ⇌
KIL/WHAMP NW6 .... 70 E5
West Ham United FC (Upton Park)
PLSTW E13 .... 95 H1
West Harrow ⊖
HRW HA1 .... 48 C5
West Hatch High School
WFD IG8 .... 45 K4
West Hendon Clinic
CDALE/KGS NW9 .... 51 H5
West Herts Business Centre
BORE WD6 .... 24 D2

West Herts College (Watford Campus)
WAT WD17 .... 20 E1
West Herts Golf Club
RKW/CH/CXG WD3 .... 20 B2
West Hill Primary School
DART DA1 .... 139 F5
WAND/EARL SW18 .... 127 K4
West India Pier
POP/IOD E14 .... 112 C1
West India Quay ⊖
POP/IOD E14 .... 93 J6
West India Shopping Centre
POP/IOD E14 .... 93 J7
West Kensington ⊖
WKENS W14 .... 107 J4
Westland Heliport
BTSEA SW11 .... 128 C2
West Lea School
ED N9 .... 42 A2
West Lodge Preparatory School
BFN/LL DA15 .... 155 F2
West Lodge Primary School
PIN HA5 .... 47 H3
West London Academy
NTHLT UB5 .... 65 H7
West London College
OXSTW W1C 10 A5
West London County Court
WKENS W14 .... 107 H3
West London Magistrates Court
HMSMTH W6 .... 107 G4
West London Tamil School
WLSDN NW10 .... 87 H1
West Mead Clinic
RSLP HA4 .... 65 G2
West Middlesex Golf Club
STHL UB1 .... 84 C6
West Middlesex University Hospital
ISLW TW7 .... 124 B1
Westminster ⊖
WHALL SW1A 17 K2
Westminster Abbey
WEST SW1P 17 J3
Westminster Abbey Choir School
WEST SW1P 17 H3
Westminster Academy
BAY/PAD W2 .... 8 B3
Westminster Bridge Park Plaza Hotel
STHWK SE1 .... 17 L2
Westminster Business Square
LBTH SE11 .... 17 L8
Westminster Cathedral
WESTW SW1E 16 E4
Westminster Cathedral Choir School
WEST SW1P 16 F4
Westminster Cathedral RC Primary School
PIM SW1V 17 H7
Westminster City Hall
WESTW SW1E 16 F4
Westminster City School
WESTW SW1E 16 F3
Westminster Industrial Estate
WOOL/PLUM SE18 .... 114 C2
Westminster Kingsway College
CAMTN NW1 .... 4 E8
WEST SW1P 16 F5
Westminster Natural Health Centre
PIM SW1V 16 E6
Westminster Pier
WHALL SW1A 17 K2
Westminster School
WEST SW1P 17 J4
Westminster Theatre
WESTW SW1E 16 E3
Westminster Under School
WEST SW1P 17 G6
Westmoor Community Clinic
PUT/ROE SW15 .... 126 D6
West Norwood ⇌
WNWD SE27 .... 149 H3
West Norwood Clinic
WNWD SE27 .... 149 J1
West Norwood Crematorium
WNWD SE27 .... 149 J2
West One Shopping Centre
MYFR/PKLN W1K 10 B5
Weston Green School
THDIT KT7 .... 157 K7
Weston Park Clinic
CEND/HSY/T N8 .... 54 E4
Weston Park Primary School
CEND/HSY/T N8 .... 55 F4
Westpoint Trading Estate
ACT W3 .... 86 D4
West Ramp Coach Park
HTHAIR TW6 .... 100 D7
West Ruislip ⇌ ⊖
RSLP HA4 .... 64 A1
West Silvertown ⊖
CAN/RD E16 .... 94 E7
West Sutton ⇌
SUT SM1 .... 174 E3
West Thames College
ISLW TW7 .... 103 K7
West Thamesmead Business Park
THMD SE28 .... 116 A2
West Thornton Primary School
CROY/NA CR0 .... 164 A6
West Twyford Primary School
WLSDN NW10 .... 86 C1
Westway Business Centre
BAY/PAD W2 .... 8 C3
Westway Sports Centre
NKENS W10 .... 88 B5
West Wickham ⇌
WWKM BR4 .... 167 F6
West Wickham Swimming Baths
WWKM BR4 .... 167 F7
West Wimbledon Primary School
RYNPK SW20 .... 160 E2
Westwood Language College
NRWD SE19 .... 149 J6
Westwood Primary School
WELL DA16 .... 135 K3
Wetherby Preparatory School
BAY/PAD W2 .... 8 B6
Whaddon House Clinic
CMBW SE5 .... 131 F2
Whipps Cross Hospital
LEY E10 .... 58 B5
Whitchurch First School
STAN HA7 .... 35 H7

Whitchurch Junior School
STAN HA7 .... 35 K6
Whitechapel ⊖
WCHPL E1 .... 92 D1
Whitechapel Art Gallery
WCHPL E1 .... 13 M4
Whitechapel Sports Centre
WCHPL E1 .... 92 C4
White City ⊖
SHB W12 .... 88 A6
Whitefield School
CRICK NW2 .... 52 B6
Whitefield School & Leisure Centre
WALTH E17 .... 44 B7
Whitefriars Community School
KTN/HRWW/WS HA3 .... 48 E1
Whitefriars Trading Estate
KTN/HRWW/WS HA3 .... 48 D1
Whitehall Theatre
WHALL SW1A 11 H8
White Hart Lane ⇌
TOTM N17 .... 42 B6
Whiteheath Junior School
RSLP HA4 .... 46 A5
Whitehorse Manor Primary School
THHTH CR7 .... 164 E4
The White House Preparatory School
BAL SW12 .... 129 J7
Whiteleys Shopping Centre
BAY/PAD W2 .... 8 C5
Whiterose Trading Estate
EBAR EN4 .... 27 J6
Whitgift Almshouses
CROY/NA CR0 .... 177 J1
Whitgift School
SAND/SEL CR2 .... 177 J4
Whitgift Shopping Centre
CROY/NA CR0 .... 177 J1
Whitings Hill Primary School
BAR EN5 .... 26 A4
Whitmore High School
RYLN/HDSTN HA2 .... 48 C7
Whitmore Primary School
IS N1 .... 7 H5
Whittingham Community Primary School
WALTH E17 .... 43 J2
Whittington Hospital
ARCH N19 .... 72 B1
Whitton ⇌
WHTN TW2 .... 123 H6
Whitton Health Centre
WHTN TW2 .... 123 H7
Whitton Health Clinic
WHTN TW2 .... 123 G7
Whitton Sports & Fitness Centre
WHTN TW2 .... 142 B1
Whybridge Infant School
RAIN RM13 .... 81 J7
Whybridge Junior School
RAIN RM13 .... 81 H7
Wickham Theatre
WWKM BR4 .... 180 B2
Wide Way Health Clinic
MTCM CR4 .... 163 J2
Widmore Centre
BMLY BR1 .... 168 A3
Wigmore Hall
CAVSQ/HST W1G 10 C3
Wigram House (University of Westminster)
WEST SW1P 17 G4
Wilberforce Primary School
NKENS W10 .... 88 C2
Wilbury Primary School
UED N18 .... 41 K4
Willesden Centre for Health & Care
WLSDN NW10 .... 69 J6
Willesden County Court
WLSDN NW10 .... 87 G1
Willesden Green ⊖
CRICK NW2 .... 70 A5
Willesden Junction ⇌ ⊖
WLSDN NW10 .... 87 H1
Willesden Medical Centre
CRICK NW2 .... 69 K5
Willesden New Cemetery
WLSDN NW10 .... 69 H6
Willesden Sports Centre
WLSDN NW10 .... 69 K7
Willesden Sports Stadium
WLSDN NW10 .... 69 K7
William Bellamy J & I School
DAGE RM10 .... 80 C1
William Booth College
CMBW SE5 .... 130 E2
William Byrd School
HYS/HAR UB3 .... 101 F5
William Ellis School
KTTN NW5 .... 72 A2
William Ellis Sports Ground
EDGW HA8 .... 36 C3
William Ford CE Junior School
DAGE RM10 .... 80 C6
William Hogarth School
CHSWK W4 .... 106 B5
William Morris Academy
HMSMTH W6 .... 107 J4
William Morris Gallery
WALTH E17 .... 57 J2
William Morris Primary School
MTCM CR4 .... 163 J2
William Morris School
WALTH E17 .... 43 G7
William Patten Primary School
STNW/STAM N16 .... 74 B1
William Torbitt J & I School
CNTH/NBYPK IG2 .... 60 E4
William Tyndale Primary School
IS N1 .... 6 D1
Willington School
WIM/MER SW19 .... 146 D5
Willow Brook Primary School
LEY E10 .... 57 J7
Willow Business Centre
MTCM CR4 .... 162 E4
Willow Business Park
SYD SE26 .... 150 E2
Willowfield Humanities College
WALTH E17 .... 57 F2
Willowfield School
WALTH E17 .... 57 G2
The Willows Clinic
CHST BR7 .... 154 A3
The Willows School
YEAD UB4 .... 83 H3
Willow Tree Primary School
NTHLT UB5 .... 65 J5

Wilson's School
WLGTN SM6 .... 176 E5
Wimbledon ⇌
WIM/MER SW19 .... 146 C2
Wimbledon ⊖ ⊖
WIM/MER SW19 .... 146 D5
Wimbledon Chase ⇌
RYNPK SW20 .... 161 H1
Wimbledon Chase Primary School
RYNPK SW20 .... 146 C7
Wimbledon College
WIM/MER SW19 .... 146 B6
Wimbledon Common Golf Club
WIM/MER SW19 .... 145 K4
Wimbledon Common Pre-Preparatory School
WIM/MER SW19 .... 146 B6
Wimbledon (Gap Road) Cemetery
WIM/MER SW19 .... 147 F3
Wimbledon High School
WIM/MER SW19 .... 146 C5
Wimbledon House School
WIM/MER SW19 .... 146 D7
Wimbledon Lawn Tennis Museum
WIM/MER SW19 .... 146 C2
Wimbledon Magistrates Court
WIM/MER SW19 .... 146 E5
Wimbledon Park ⊖
WIM/MER SW19 .... 146 E2
Wimbledon Park Athletics Track
WIM/MER SW19 .... 146 D1
Wimbledon Park Golf Club
WIM/MER SW19 .... 146 D2
Wimbledon Park Primary School
WIM/MER SW19 .... 146 E2
Wimbledon Recreation Centre
WIM/MER SW19 .... 147 F5
Wimbledon RFC
RYNPK SW20 .... 145 H6
Wimbledon School of Art
WIM/MER SW19 .... 146 C7
WIM/MER SW19 .... 146 E6
Wimbledon Squash & Badminton Club
WIM/MER SW19 .... 146 C6
Wimbledon Stadium
WIM/MER SW19 .... 147 F3
Wimbledon Stadium Business Centre
WIM/MER SW19 .... 147 F2
Wimbledon Theatre
WIM/MER SW19 .... 146 E6
Wimbledon Windmill
WIM/MER SW19 .... 146 A2
Winchcombe Business Centre
PECK SE15 .... 111 F5
Winchester Hill ⇌
WCHMH N21 .... 29 H6
Winchmore Hill Clinic
WCHMH N21 .... 29 H7
Winchmore Hill CC
WCHMH N21 .... 29 J7
Winchmore School
WCHMH N21 .... 41 J1
Windmill Business Centre
NWDGN UB2 .... 84 C7
Windmill Trading Estate
MTCM CR4 .... 163 H4
SUN TW16 .... 140 B7
Windrush Primary School
THMD SE28 .... 97 H7
Winfield House
CAMTN NW1 .... 3 K7
Wingate & Finchley FC
NFNCH/WDSPK N12 .... 39 H6
Wingate Trading Estate
TOTM N17 .... 42 B6
Wingfield Primary School
BKHTH/KID SE3 .... 133 K2
Winns Primary School
WALTH E17 .... 57 H1
Winsor Primary School
EHAM E6 .... 96 A5
Winston Churchill's Britain at War Experience
STHWK SE1 .... 13 H9
Winston House Preparatory School
SWFD E18 .... 44 E7
Winston Way Primary School
IL IG1 .... 78 A2
Winterbourne Infant School
THHTH CR7 .... 164 B3
Winton Primary School
IS N1 .... 5 L6
Wisdom School
SEVS/STOTM N15 .... 55 K3
Witley Industrial Estate
NWDGN UB2 .... 102 E3
Wolf Fields Primary School
NWDGN UB2 .... 102 E3
Wolfson Hillel Primary School
STHGT/OAK N14 .... 28 D5
Wolfson Medical Centre
RYNPK SW20 .... 145 J6
Wolsey Business Park
WATW WD18 .... 20 B6
Wolsey Junior School
CROY/NA CR0 .... 180 B6
The Women's Library
WCHPL E1 .... 13 L4
The Woodberry Clinic
MUSWH N10 .... 54 B2
Woodberry Down Centre
FSBYPK N4 .... 55 J7
Woodberry Down Community Primary School
FSBYPK N4 .... 55 J6
Woodbridge High School
WFD IG8 .... 45 F6
Woodcroft Primary School
EDGW HA8 .... 37 F6
Wood End J & I Schools
GFD/PVL UB6 .... 66 D4
Wood End Park Junior School
UX/CGN UB8 .... 82 A6
Woodfield School
CDALE/KGS NW9 .... 51 G7
Woodford ⊖
WFD IG8 .... 45 F5
Woodford County High School for Girls
WFD IG8 .... 44 D5
Woodford Golf Club
WFD IG8 .... 44 D4

Woodford Green Preparatory School
WFD IG8 .... 44 E5
Woodford Green Primary School
WFD IG8 .... 44 D4
Woodford Trading Estate
WFD IG8 .... 59 G1
Woodgrange Infant School
FSTGT E7 .... 77 F3
Woodgrange Park ⇌
FSTGT E7 .... 77 H4
Woodgrange Park Cemetery
MNPK E12 .... 77 H4
Wood Green ⊖
WDGN N22 .... 55 G1
Wood Green Crown Court
WDGN N22 .... 41 G7
Wood Green Health Centre
WDGN N22 .... 41 F7
Wood Green Old Boys FC
WDGN N22 .... 41 G6
Woodhall School
OXHEY WD19 .... 33 J3
Woodhill Primary School
CHARL SE7 .... 114 D3
Woodhouse College
NFNCH/WDSPK N12 .... 39 H5
Woodlands First & Middle School
KTN/HRWW/WS HA3 .... 34 C6
Woodlands J & I School
IL IG1 .... 78 D3
Woodlands Medical Centre
LEW SE13 .... 133 G5
Wood Lane ⊖
SHB W12 .... 88 A6
Wood Lane Medical Centre
RSLP HA4 .... 46 C7
Wood Lane School
FUL/PGN SW6 .... 108 B7
Wood Lane Sports Centre
BCTR RM8 .... 62 D7
Woodmansterne Primary School
STRHM/NOR SW16 .... 148 D7
Woodridge Primary School
NFNCH/WDSPK N12 .... 38 E2
Woodside ⊖
SNWD SE25 .... 165 J5
Woodside Childrens Centre & Infant School
CROY/NA CR0 .... 165 H6
Woodside Health Centre
SNWD SE25 .... 165 J4
Woodside High School
WDGN N22 .... 41 H6
Woodside Park ⊖
NFNCH/WDSPK N12 .... 38 E3
NFNCH/WDSPK N12 .... 39 F3
Woodside Park Golf Club
NFNCH/WDSPK N12 .... 38 E3
Woodside Primary School
WALTH E17 .... 58 A2
Woodside School
BELV DA17 .... 117 J3
Wood Street ⇌
WALTH E17 .... 58 B3
Wood Wharf
POP/IOD E14 .... 93 K7
Wood Wharf Business Park
POP/IOD E14 .... 113 F1
Woolmore Primary School
POP/IOD E14 .... 94 A3
Woolwich Arsenal ⇌ ⊖
WOOL/PLUM SE18 .... 115 G3
Woolwich Cemetery
WOOL/PLUM SE18 .... 116 A6
Woolwich County Court
WOOL/PLUM SE18 .... 115 F2
Woolwich Crown Court
THMD SE28 .... 115 K1
Woolwich Dockyard ⇌
WOOL/PLUM SE18 .... 114 E3
Woolwich Polytechnic School
THMD SE28 .... 97 G7
Worcester Park ⇌
WPK KT4 .... 160 D7
World Business Centre Heathrow
HTHAIR TW6 .... 101 F7
World Rugby Museum & Twickenham Stadium Tours
WHTN TW2 .... 123 K5
Worlds End Place
WBPTN SW10 .... 108 B6
World Spiritual University
WLSDN NW10 .... 69 J6
World University Service
STLK EC1Y 13 G1
Wormholt Park Primary School
SHB W12 .... 87 J6
Worple Primary School
ISLW TW7 .... 124 B3
Worsley Bridge Junior School
BECK BR3 .... 151 H6
Worton Hall Industrial Estate
ISLW TW7 .... 123 K3
Wren Academy
NFNCH/WDSPK N12 .... 39 H4
Wrencote House
CROY/NA CR0 .... 177 J2
WWT London Wetland Centre
BARN SW13 .... 106 E7
Wyborne Primary School
ELTH/MOT SE9 .... 135 G2
Wyke Green Golf Club
ISLW TW7 .... 104 A5
Wykeham Primary School
HCH RM12 .... 63 J7
WLSDN NW10 .... 69 F2
Wyndham Grand London Hotel
WBPTN SW10 .... 108 B7
Wyndhams Theatre
CHCR WC2N 11 H6
Wyvil Primary School
VX/NE SW8 .... 109 K6
Yale University Press
HAMP NW3 .... 71 J3
Yardley Primary School
CHING E4 .... 31 K5
Yavneh College
BORE WD6 .... 24 D3
Yeading FC
YEAD UB4 .... 83 G2
Yeading Junior School
YEAD UB4 .... 83 G4
Yeading Medical Centre
NTHLT UB5 .... 83 G2
Yeading Primary School
YEAD UB4 .... 83 G4
Yerbury Primary School
ARCH N19 .... 72 D2

River bus map

Map of scheduled River Bus services

River Bus

- Putney Pier to Blackfriars Pier
  Operates Monday-Friday peak hours only
  Service operated by Thames River Taxi
- Embankment Pier to Woolwich Arsenal Pier
  Daily
  Service operated by Thames Clippers
- Canary Wharf Pier to Hilton Docklands Pier
  Daily
  Service operated by City Cruises
- Woolwich Free Ferry
  Daily (except evenings)
  Service operated by Serco for Transport for London

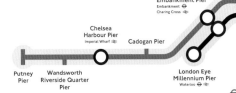

This map is a guide to services provided by the River Bus operators along the Thames on weekdays, but does not guarantee direct services between the piers shown. Some services/piers are not served outside of peak commuter hours. Please refer to tfl.gov.uk/rivers for full timetable information of scheduled River Bus services.

© Transport for London

Reg. user No. 11/1894/P

Acknowledgements

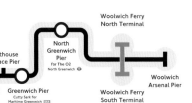

Schools address data provided by Education Direct

Petrol station information supplied by Johnsons

Post office data provided by Post Office Limited and who accept no reponsibility for any data inaccuracies. Data accurate as of 12 July 2011

Garden centre information provided by:

Garden Centre Association 🌳 Britains best garden centres

Wyevale Garden Centres 🌳

The boundary of the London Congestion Charging Zone and Low Emission Zone supplied by 💠 Transport for London

The statement on the front cover of this atlas is sourced, selected and quoted from a reader comment and feedback form received in 2004

AA Travel Guides
The world at your fingertips

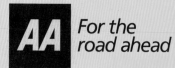